EPIC COLLECTION

STAR WARS

THE OLD REPUBLIC

VOLUME 2

STAR WARS: KNIGHTS OF THE OLD REPUBLIC #19-37 &
STAR WARS: KNIGHTS OF THE OLD REPUBLIC HANDBOOK

WRITER:

JOHN JACKSON MILLER

PENCILERS:

BONG DAZO, DUSTIN WEAVER, SCOTT HEPBURN, ALAN ROBINSON & BRIAN CHING WITH **HARVEY TOLIBAO & COLIN WILSON**

INKERS:
BONG DAZO, DAN PARSONS, JOE PIMENTEL, ALAN ROBINSON & BRIAN CHING WITH **HARVEY TOLIBAO, DUSTIN WEAVER & COLIN WILSON**

COLORIST:
MICHAEL ATIYEH

LETTERER:
MICHAEL HEISLER

ASSISTANT EDITORS:
DAVE MARSHALL & FREDDYE LINS

EDITORS:
JEREMY BARLOW, RANDY STRADLEY & DAVE MARSHALL

FRONT COVER ARTIST:
TRAVIS CHAREST

BACK COVER ARTISTS:
DUSTIN WEAVER & MICHAEL ATIYEH

COLLECTION EDITOR: MARK D. BEAZLEY
ASSISTANT EDITOR: CAITLIN O'CONNELL
ASSOCIATE MANAGING EDITOR: KATERI WOODY
ASSOCIATE MANAGER, DIGITAL ASSETS: JOE HOCHSTEIN
SENIOR EDITOR, SPECIAL PROJECTS: JENNIFER GRÜNWALD
VP PRODUCTION & SPECIAL PROJECTS: JEFF YOUNGQUIST
RESEARCH: MIKE HANSEN
LAYOUT: JEPH YORK
PRODUCTION: RYAN DEVALL & SALENA JOHNSON
BOOK DESIGNER: RODOLFO MURAGUCHI
SVP PRINT, SALES & MARKETING: DAVID GABRIEL

EDITOR IN CHIEF: AXEL ALONSO
CHIEF CREATIVE OFFICER: JOE QUESADA
PUBLISHER: DAN BUCKLEY
EXECUTIVE PRODUCER: ALAN FINE

SPECIAL THANKS TO FRANK PARISI & LUCASFILM, DEIDRE HANSEN, JOHN JACKSON MILLER, DUSTIN WEAVER & DOUG SHARK OF MYCOMICSHOP.COM

STAR WARS LEGENDS EPIC COLLECTION: THE OLD REPUBLIC VOL. 2. Contains material originally published in magazine form as STAR WARS: KNIGHTS OF THE OLD REPUBLIC #19-37 and HANDBOOK. First printing 2017. ISBN# 978-1-302-90377-0. Published by MARVEL WORLDWIDE, INC., a subsidiary of MARVEL ENTERTAINMENT, LLC. OFFICE OF PUBLICATION: 135 West 50th Street, New York, NY 10020. **Printed in the U.S.A.** ALAN FINE, President, Marvel Entertainment; DAN BUCKLEY, President, TV, Publishing & Brand Management; JOE QUESADA, Chief Creative Officer; TOM BREVOORT, SVP of Publishing; DAVID BOGART, SVP of Business Affairs & Operations, Publishing & Partnership; C.B. CEBULSKI, VP of Brand Management & Development, Asia; DAVID GABRIEL, SVP of Sales & Marketing, Publishing; JEFF YOUNGQUIST, VP of Production & Special Projects; DAN CARR, Executive Director of Publishing Technology; ALEX MORALES, Director of Publishing Operations; SUSAN CRESPI, Production Manager; STAN LEE, Chairman Emeritus. For information regarding advertising in Marvel Comics or on Marvel.com, please contact Vit DeBellis, Integrated Sales Manager, at vdebellis@marvel.com. For Marvel subscription inquiries, please call 888-511-5480. **Manufactured between 1/13/2017 and 2/14/2017 by LSC COMMUNICATIONS INC., SALEM, VA, USA.**

10 9 8 7 6 5 4 3 2 1

THE OLD REPUBLIC — VOLUME 2

THE OLD REPUBLIC
VOL. 2

With the crusading Mandalorians approaching the sector
of space occupied by the Arkanians and their vast scientific
resources, the charismatic Lord Adasca seeks to secure —
and perhaps improve — his people's place in the galaxy by
offering a new super-weapon to the highest bidder.

Aboard the ship *Arkanian Legacy*, Adasca sends invitations
to potential buyers, including one to Republic Admiral
Karath, who has in his custody Zayne Carrick — a fugitive
Padawan falsely accused by his former Masters of killing
his fellow Jedi students on the Outer Rim border world of
Taris. Also held captive by Karath are Adasca's former
employee Gorman Vandrayk — also known as Zayne's friend
Camper — and Camper's protector, the mysterious warrior
Jarael.

The Jedi Knights reject official involvement in the
Republic's war with Mandalore, but this distraction has
allowed the Jedi Masters stationed on Taris to form a
secret cabal known as the Covenant, whose sole purpose is
to prevent the return of the Jedi's greatest enemies, the
evil Sith. Their Jedi visions led them to believe Zayne is the
one most likely to bring about the return of the Sith.

Zayne's thoughts have never strayed from the world he left
behind — or from the friend he left there, the con-artist
Gryph, now believed to be dead....

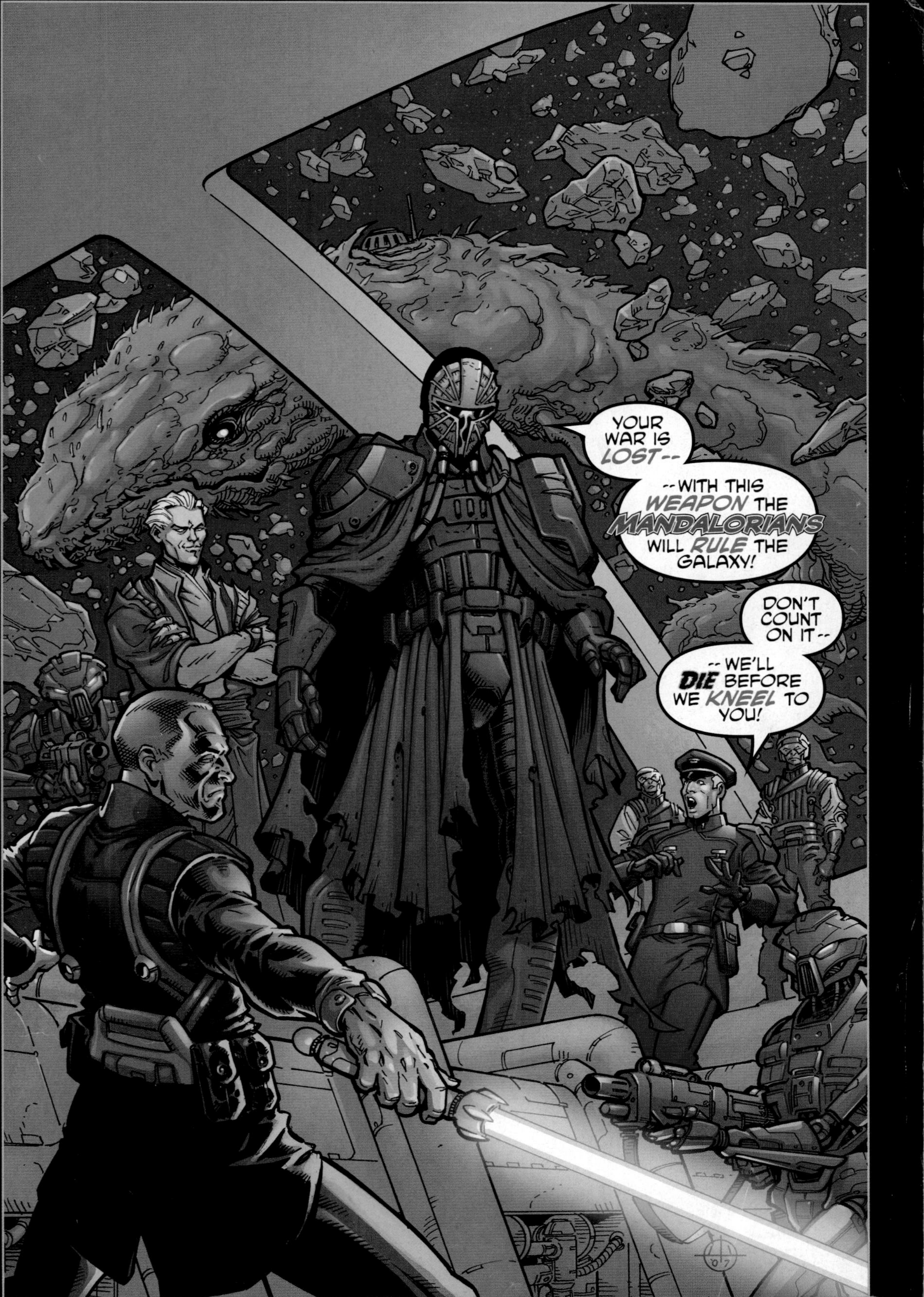
YOUR WAR IS LOST --
-- WITH THIS WEAPON THE MANDALORIANS WILL RULE THE GALAXY!
DON'T COUNT ON IT --
-- WE'LL DIE BEFORE WE KNEEL TO YOU!

***STAR WARS: KNIGHTS OF THE OLD REPUBLIC #19* — "DAZE OF HATE, PART 1"**

WRITER: JOHN JACKSON MILLER • ARTIST: BONG DAZO • COLORIST: MICHAEL ATIYEH • LETTERER: MICHAEL HEISLER
ASSISTANT EDITOR: DAVE MARSHALL • EDITOR: JEREMY BARLOW • COVER ARTISTS: CHRIS WARNER & MICHAEL ATIYEH

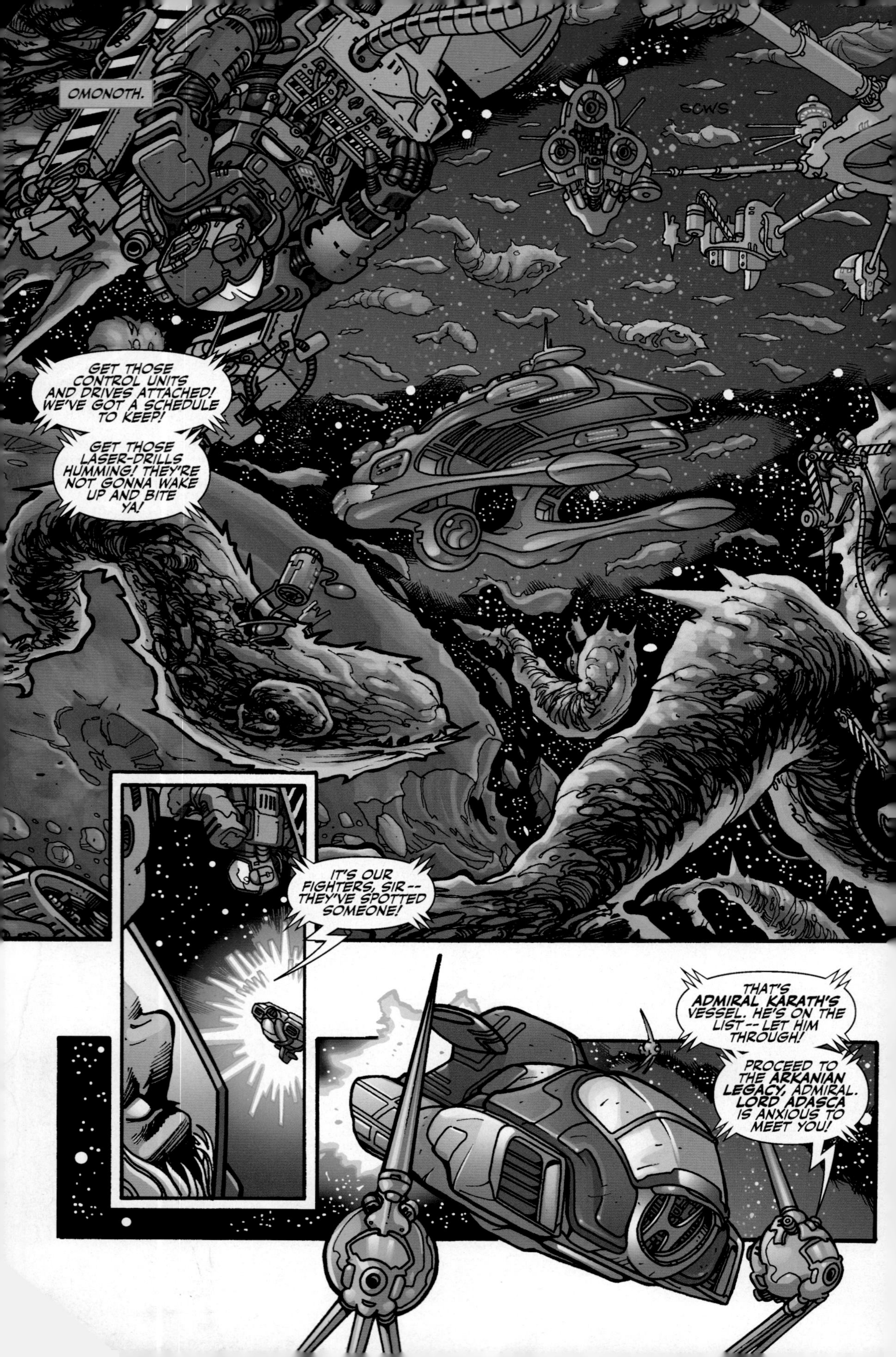

OMONOTH.
SCWS
GET THOSE CONTROL UNITS AND DRIVES ATTACHED! WE'VE GOT A SCHEDULE TO KEEP!
GET THOSE LASER-DRILLS HUMMING! THEY'RE NOT GONNA WAKE UP AND BITE YA!
IT'S OUR FIGHTERS, SIR-- THEY'VE SPOTTED SOMEONE!
THAT'S ADMIRAL KARATH'S VESSEL. HE'S ON THE LIST-- LET HIM THROUGH!
PROCEED TO THE ARKANIAN LEGACY, ADMIRAL. LORD ADASCA IS ANXIOUS TO MEET YOU!

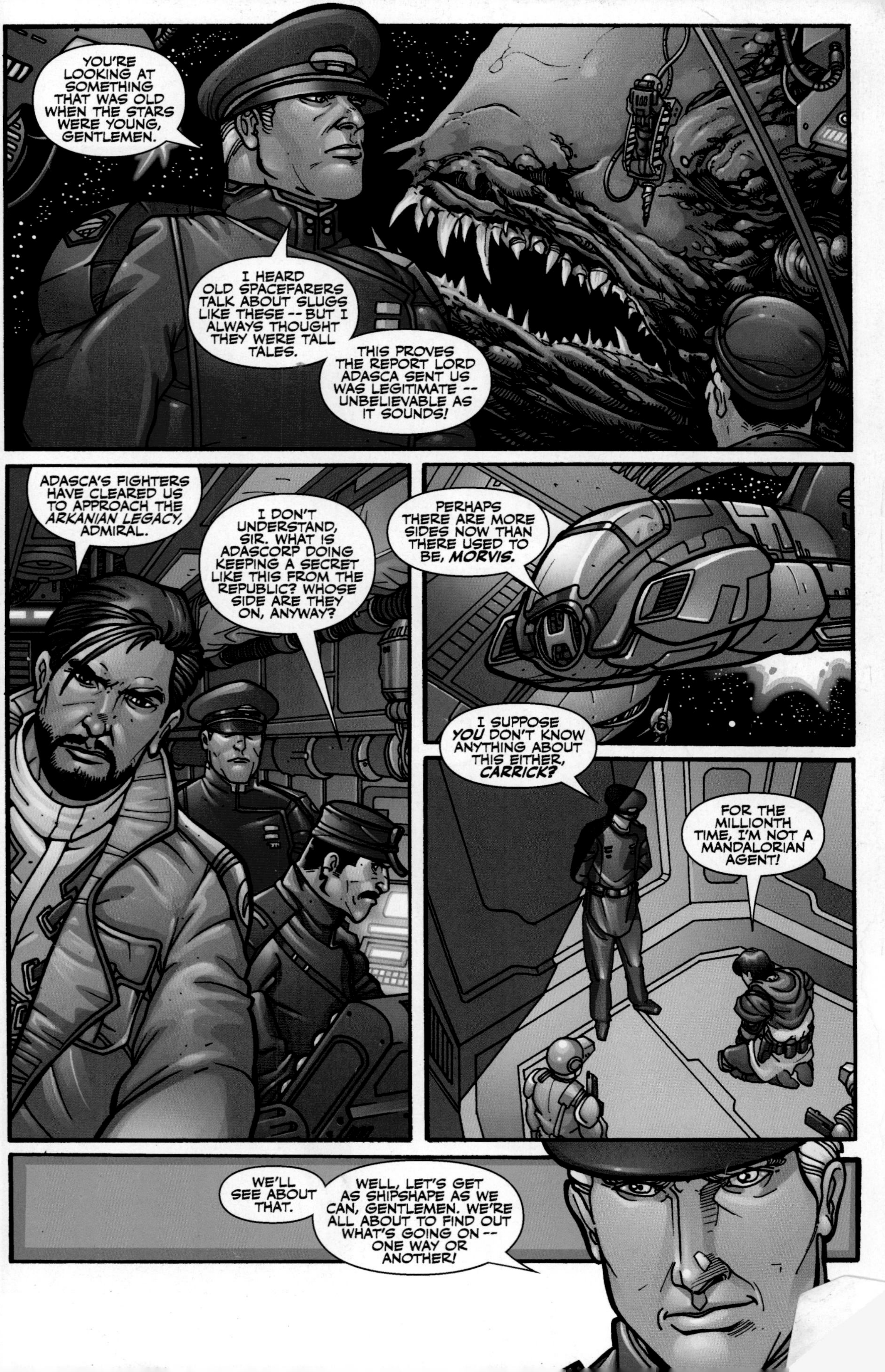
YOU'RE LOOKING AT SOMETHING THAT WAS OLD WHEN THE STARS WERE YOUNG, GENTLEMEN.
I HEARD OLD SPACEFARERS TALK ABOUT SLUGS LIKE THESE -- BUT I ALWAYS THOUGHT THEY WERE TALL TALES.
THIS PROVES THE REPORT LORD ADASCA SENT US WAS LEGITIMATE -- UNBELIEVABLE AS IT SOUNDS!
ADASCA'S FIGHTERS HAVE CLEARED US TO APPROACH THE *ARKANIAN LEGACY,* ADMIRAL.
I DON'T UNDERSTAND, SIR. WHAT IS ADASCORP DOING KEEPING A SECRET LIKE THIS FROM THE REPUBLIC? WHOSE SIDE ARE THEY ON, ANYWAY?
PERHAPS THERE ARE MORE SIDES NOW THAN THERE USED TO BE, ***MORVIS.***
I SUPPOSE ***YOU*** DON'T KNOW ANYTHING ABOUT THIS EITHER, ***CARRICK?***
FOR THE MILLIONTH TIME, I'M NOT A MANDALORIAN AGENT!
WE'LL SEE ABOUT THAT.
WELL, LET'S GET AS SHIPSHAPE AS WE CAN, GENTLEMEN. WE'RE ALL ABOUT TO FIND OUT WHAT'S GOING ON -- ONE WAY OR ANOTHER!

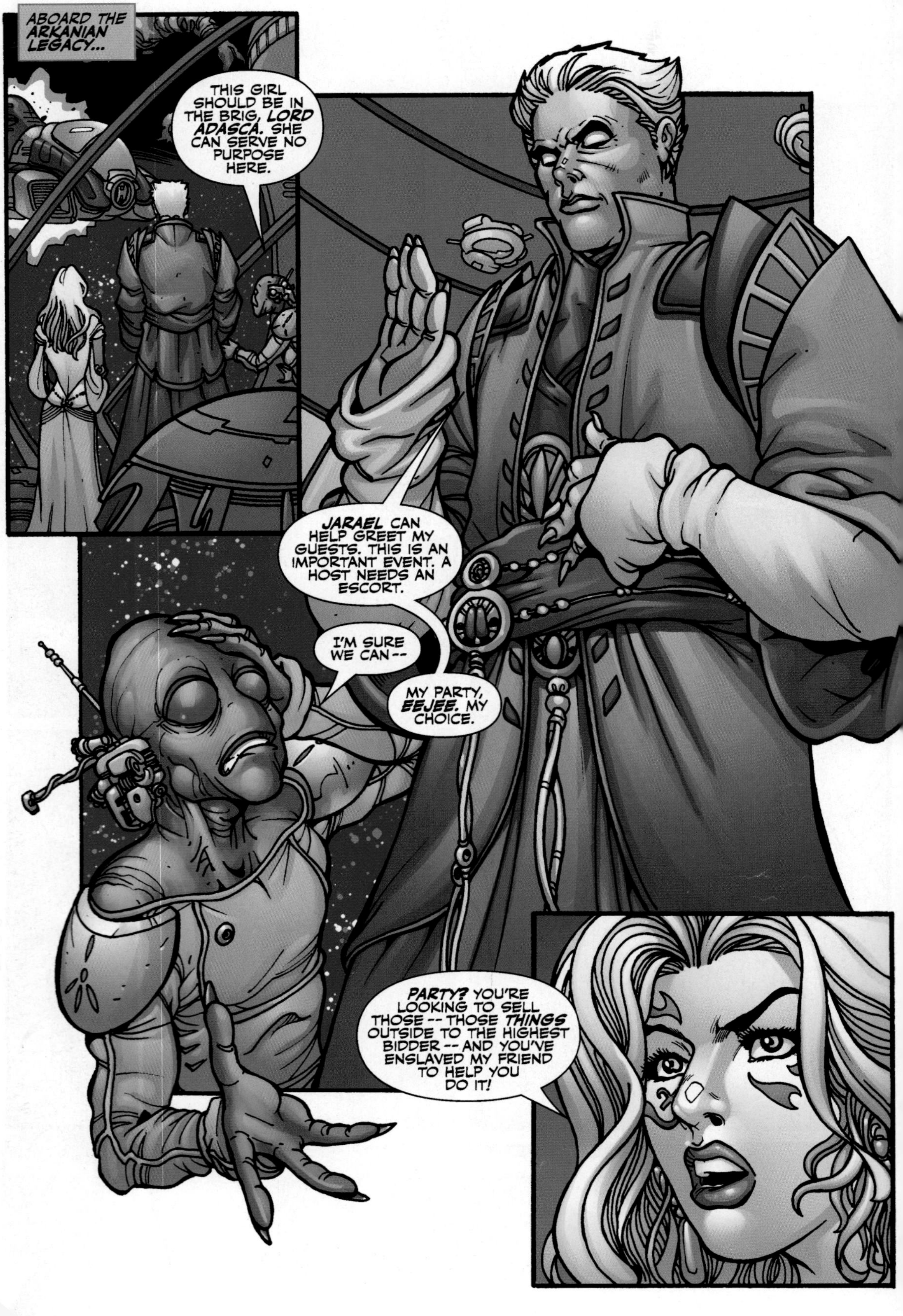
ABOARD THE ARKANIAN LEGACY...
THIS GIRL SHOULD BE IN THE BRIG, LORD ADASCA. SHE CAN SERVE NO PURPOSE HERE.
JARAEL CAN HELP GREET MY GUESTS. THIS IS AN IMPORTANT EVENT. A HOST NEEDS AN ESCORT.
I'M SURE WE CAN--
MY PARTY, EEJEE. MY CHOICE.
PARTY? YOU'RE LOOKING TO SELL THOSE -- THOSE THINGS OUTSIDE TO THE HIGHEST BIDDER -- AND YOU'VE ENSLAVED MY FRIEND TO HELP YOU DO IT!

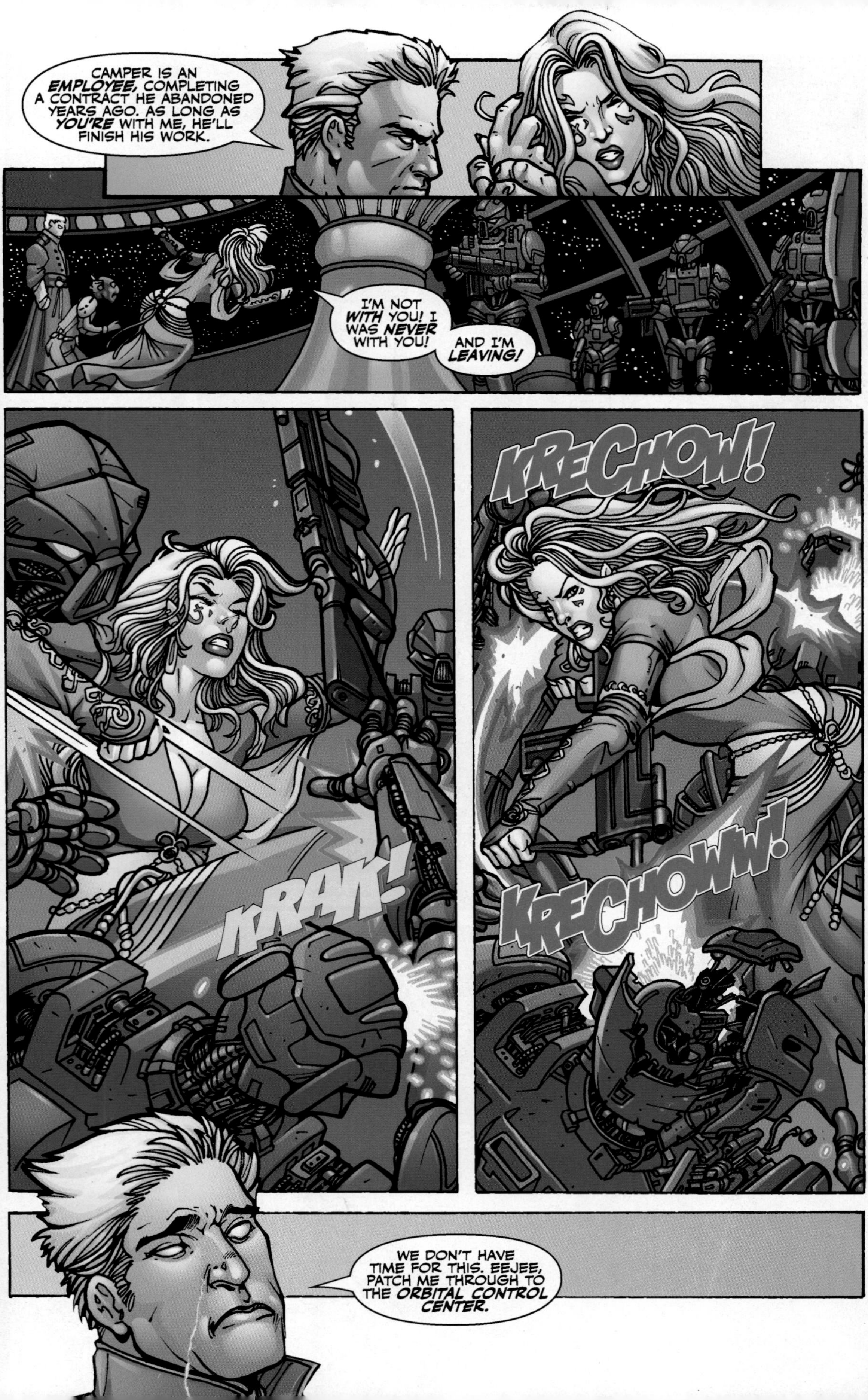
CAMPER IS AN *EMPLOYEE,* COMPLETING A CONTRACT HE ABANDONED YEARS AGO. AS LONG AS *YOU'RE* WITH ME, HE'LL FINISH HIS WORK.
I'M NOT *WITH* YOU! I WAS *NEVER* WITH YOU!
AND I'M *LEAVING!*
KRAK!
KRECHOW!
KRECHOWW!
WE DON'T HAVE TIME FOR THIS. EEJEE, PATCH ME THROUGH TO THE *ORBITAL CONTROL CENTER.*

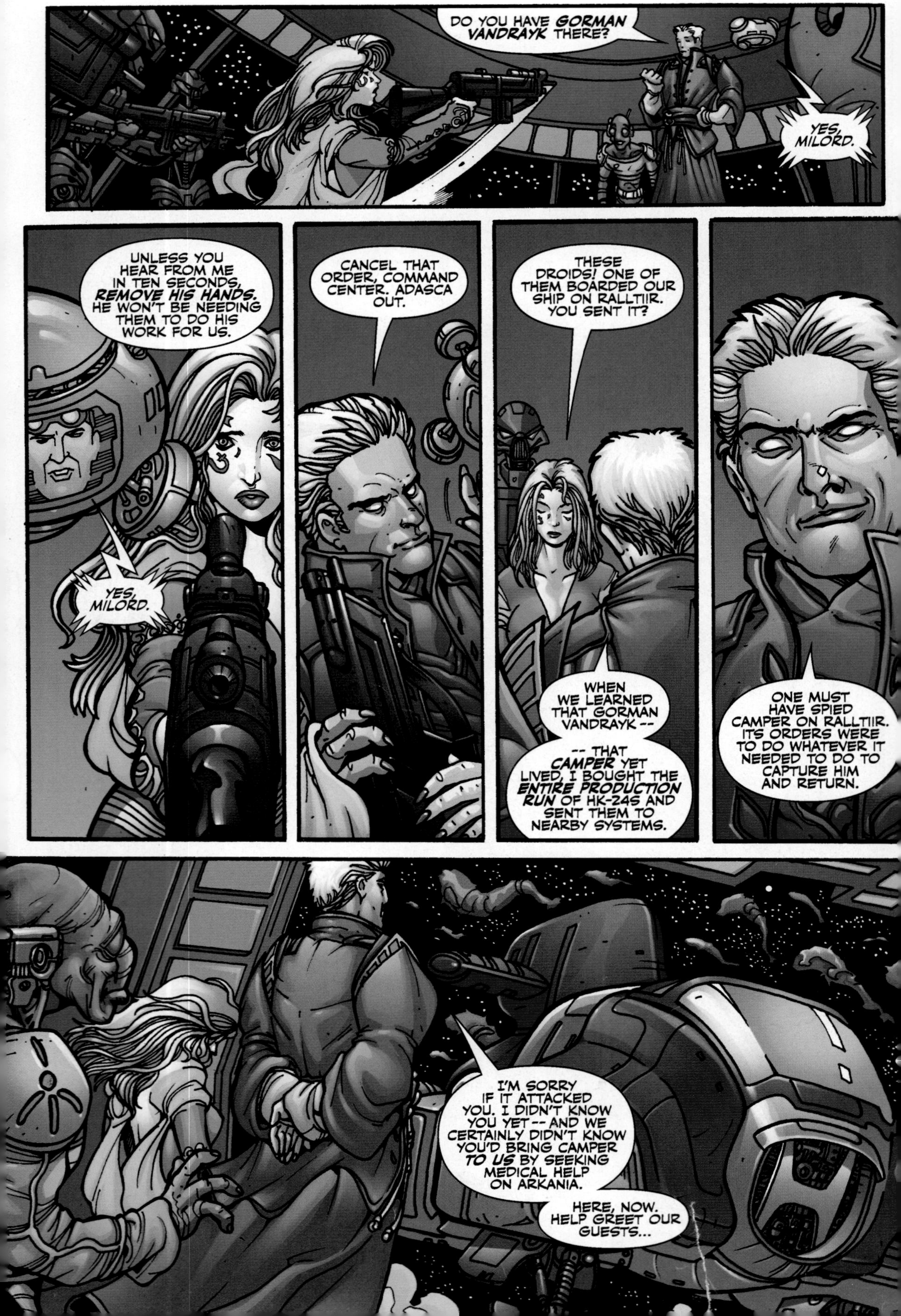

DO YOU HAVE GORMAN VANDRAYK THERE?
YES, MILORD.
UNLESS YOU HEAR FROM ME IN TEN SECONDS, REMOVE HIS HANDS. HE WON'T BE NEEDING THEM TO DO HIS WORK FOR US.
YES, MILORD.
CANCEL THAT ORDER, COMMAND CENTER. ADASCA OUT.
THESE DROIDS! ONE OF THEM BOARDED OUR SHIP ON RALLTIIR. YOU SENT IT?
WHEN WE LEARNED THAT GORMAN VANDRAYK --
-- THAT CAMPER YET LIVED, I BOUGHT THE ENTIRE PRODUCTION RUN OF HK-24S AND SENT THEM TO NEARBY SYSTEMS.
ONE MUST HAVE SPIED CAMPER ON RALLTIIR. ITS ORDERS WERE TO DO WHATEVER IT NEEDED TO DO TO CAPTURE HIM AND RETURN.
I'M SORRY IF IT ATTACKED YOU. I DIDN'T KNOW YOU YET -- AND WE CERTAINLY DIDN'T KNOW YOU'D BRING CAMPER TO US BY SEEKING MEDICAL HELP ON ARKANIA.
HERE, NOW. HELP GREET OUR GUESTS...

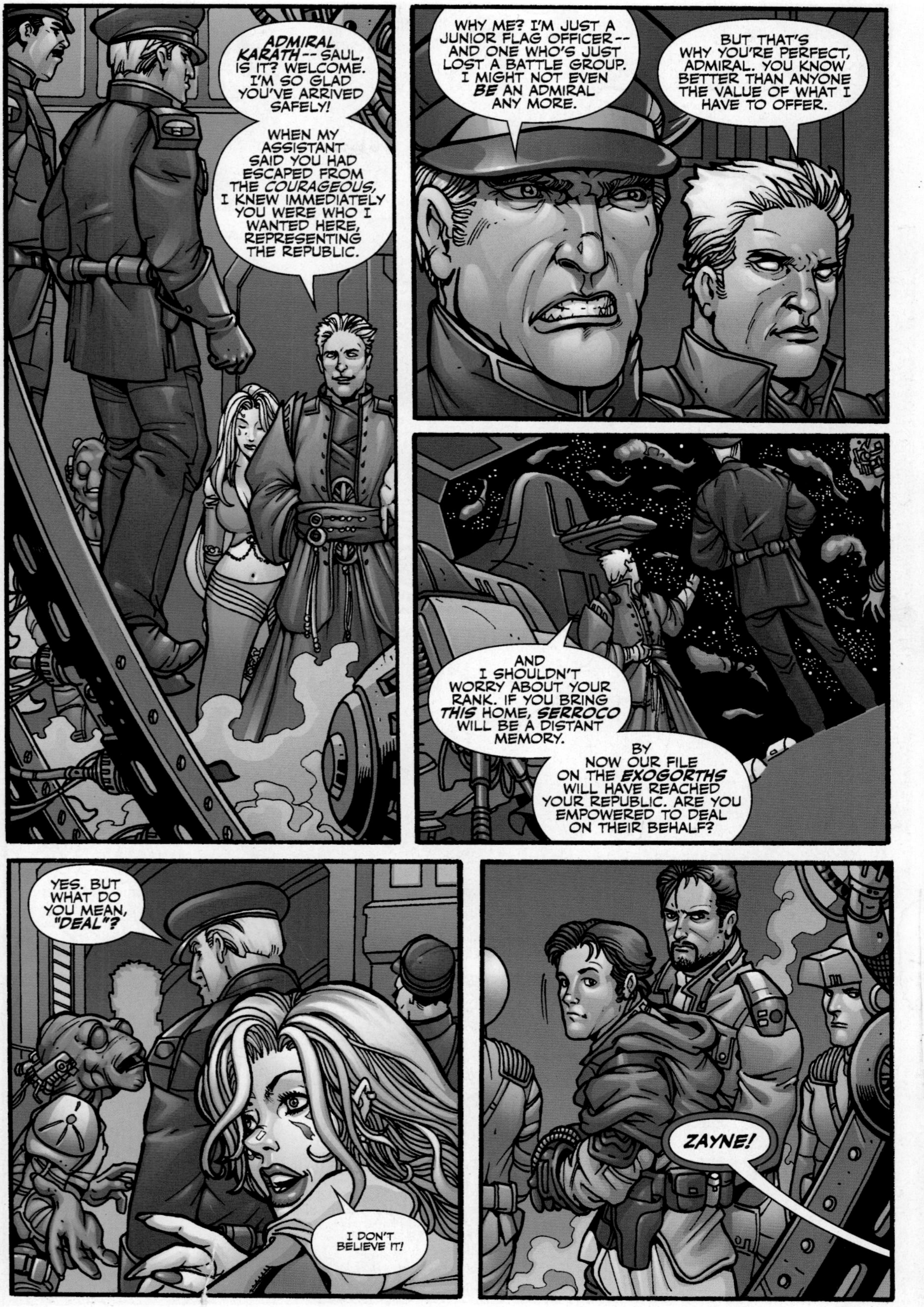
ADMIRAL KARATH-- SAUL, IS IT? WELCOME. I'M SO GLAD YOU'VE ARRIVED SAFELY!
WHEN MY ASSISTANT SAID YOU HAD ESCAPED FROM THE COURAGEOUS, I KNEW IMMEDIATELY YOU WERE WHO I WANTED HERE, REPRESENTING THE REPUBLIC.
WHY ME? I'M JUST A JUNIOR FLAG OFFICER-- AND ONE WHO'S JUST LOST A BATTLE GROUP. I MIGHT NOT EVEN BE AN ADMIRAL ANY MORE.
BUT THAT'S WHY YOU'RE PERFECT, ADMIRAL. YOU KNOW BETTER THAN ANYONE THE VALUE OF WHAT I HAVE TO OFFER.
AND I SHOULDN'T WORRY ABOUT YOUR RANK. IF YOU BRING THIS HOME, SERROCO WILL BE A DISTANT MEMORY.
BY NOW OUR FILE ON THE EXOGORTHS WILL HAVE REACHED YOUR REPUBLIC. ARE YOU EMPOWERED TO DEAL ON THEIR BEHALF?
YES. BUT WHAT DO YOU MEAN, "DEAL"?
I DON'T BELIEVE IT!
ZAYNE!

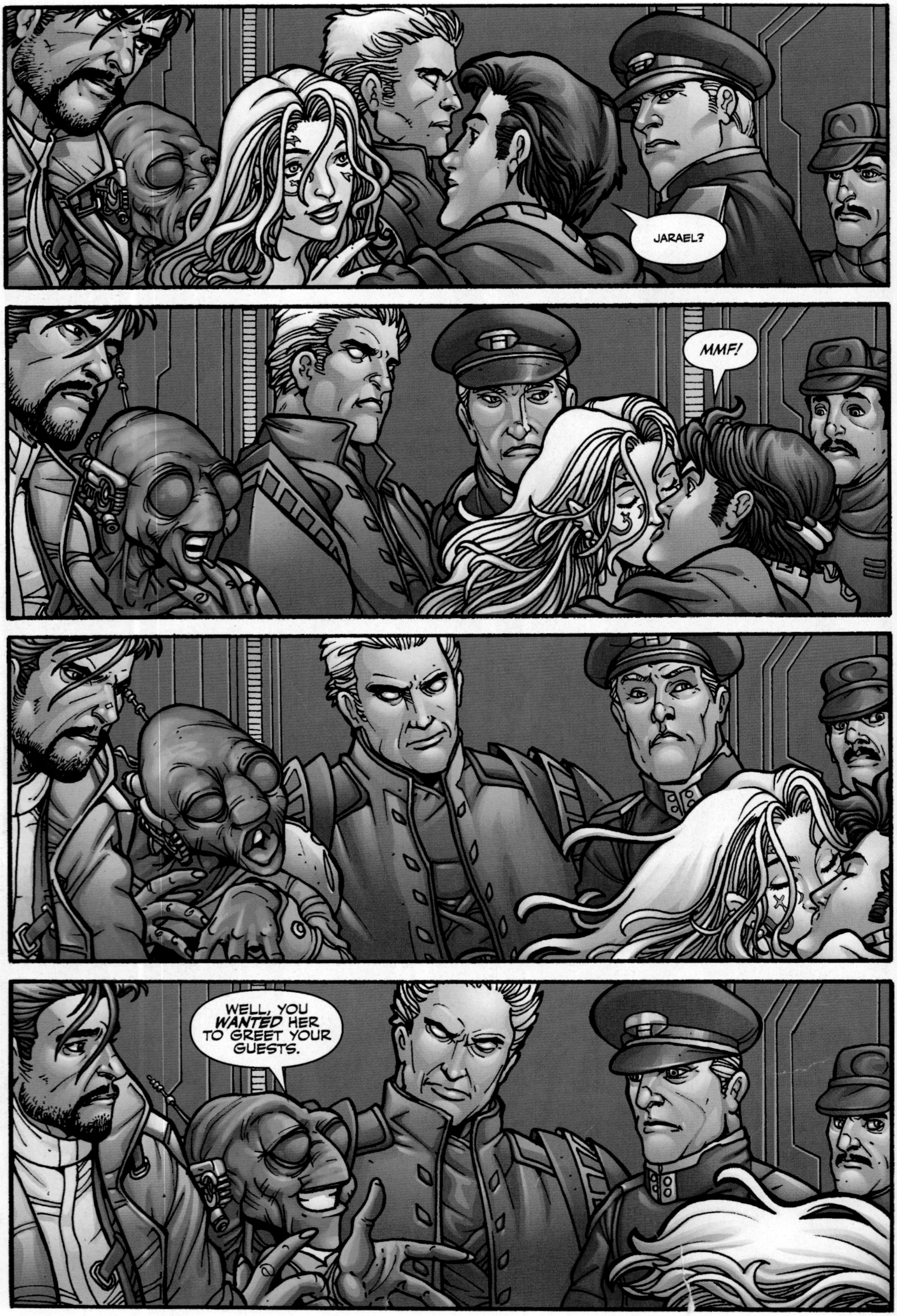
JARAEL?
MMF!
WELL, YOU WANTED HER TO GREET YOUR GUESTS.

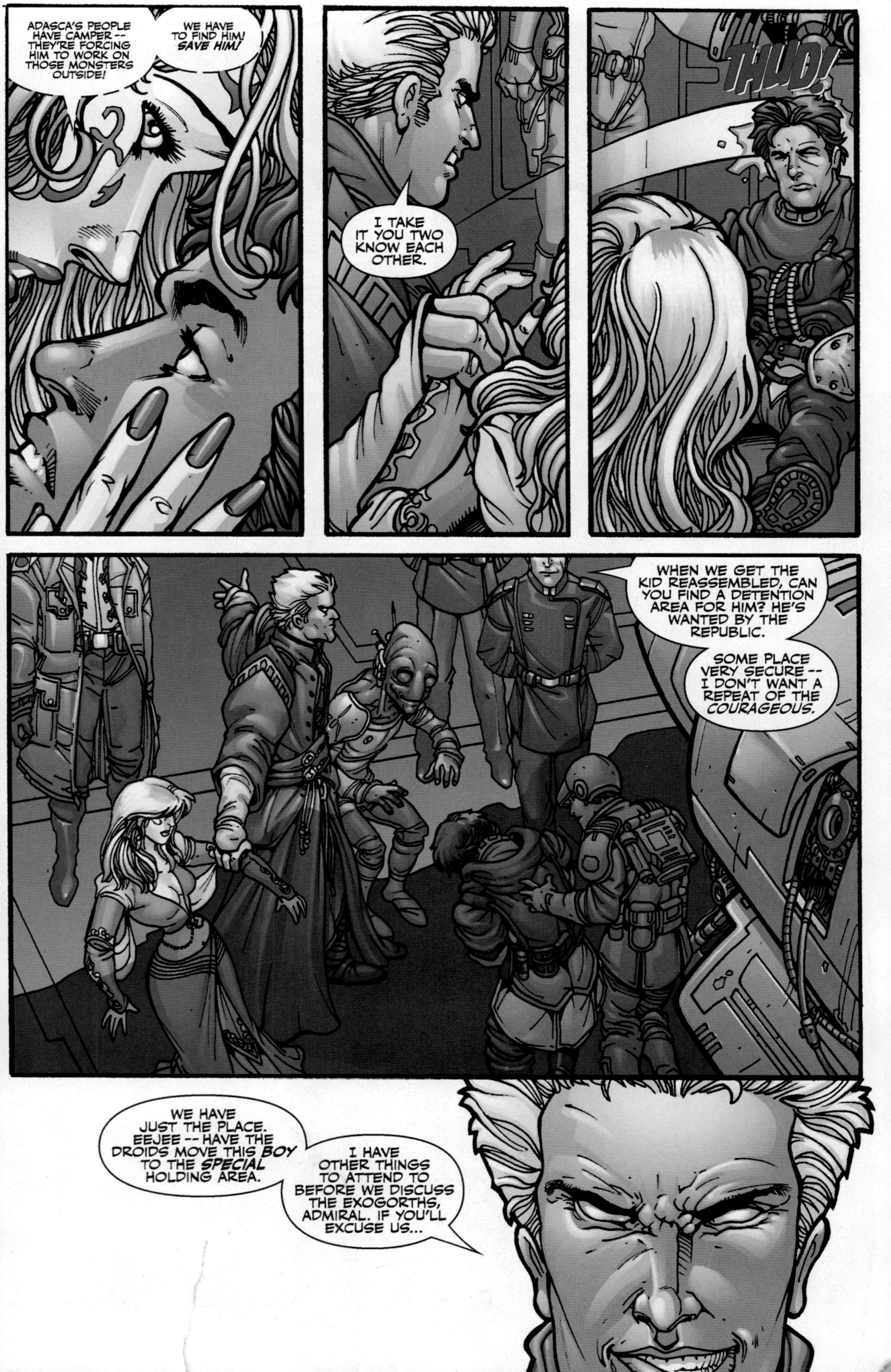
ADASCA'S PEOPLE HAVE CAMPER -- THEY'RE FORCING HIM TO WORK ON THOSE MONSTERS OUTSIDE!
WE HAVE TO FIND HIM! SAVE HIM!
I TAKE IT YOU TWO KNOW EACH OTHER.
THUD!
WHEN WE GET THE KID REASSEMBLED, CAN YOU FIND A DETENTION AREA FOR HIM? HE'S WANTED BY THE REPUBLIC.
SOME PLACE VERY SECURE -- I DON'T WANT A REPEAT OF THE COURAGEOUS.
WE HAVE JUST THE PLACE. EEJEE -- HAVE THE DROIDS MOVE THIS BOY TO THE SPECIAL HOLDING AREA.
I HAVE OTHER THINGS TO ATTEND TO BEFORE WE DISCUSS THE EXOGORTHS, ADMIRAL. IF YOU'LL EXCUSE US...

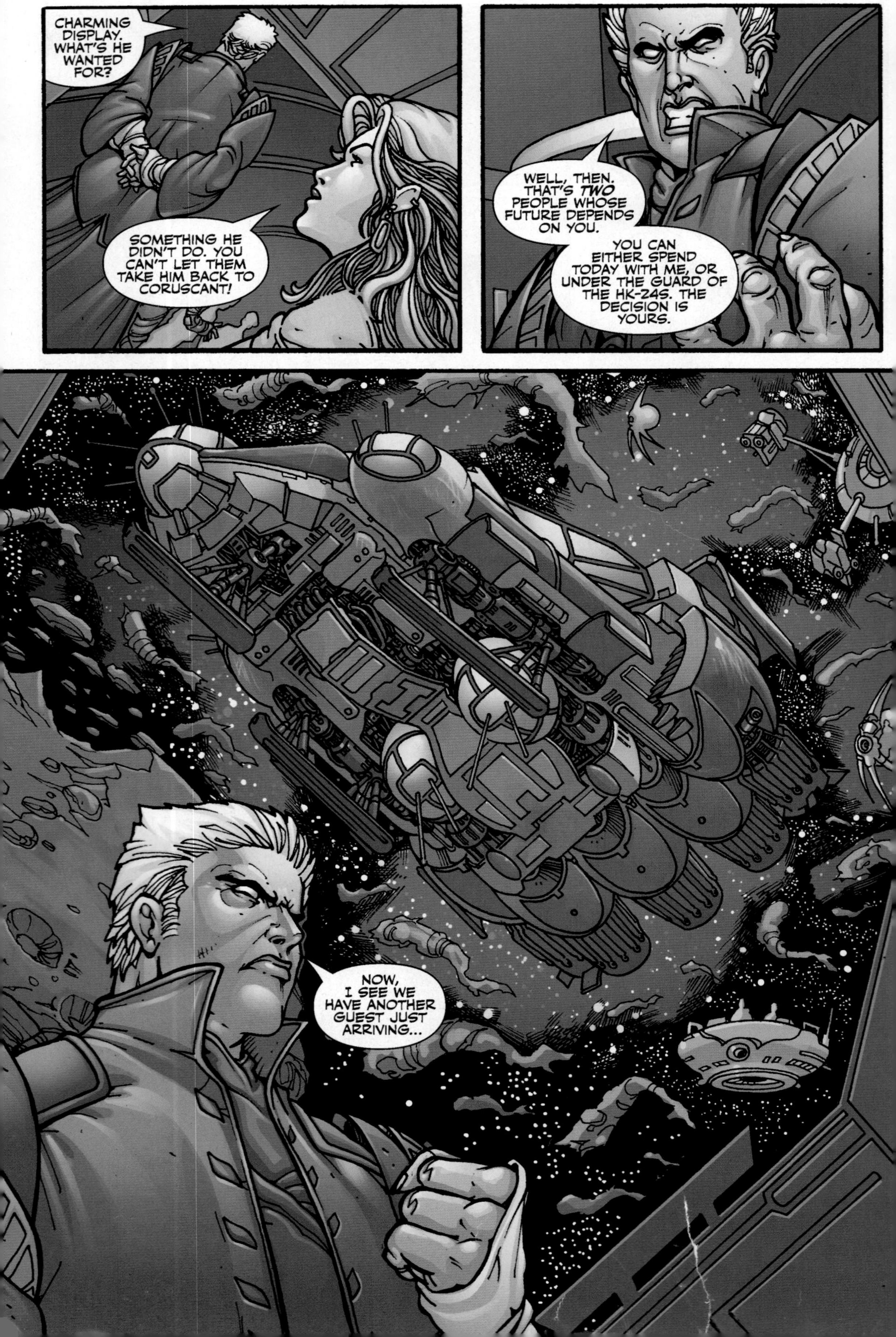
CHARMING DISPLAY. WHAT'S HE WANTED FOR?
SOMETHING HE DIDN'T DO. YOU CAN'T LET THEM TAKE HIM BACK TO CORUSCANT!
WELL, THEN. THAT'S *TWO* PEOPLE WHOSE FUTURE DEPENDS ON YOU.
YOU CAN EITHER SPEND TODAY WITH ME, OR UNDER THE GUARD OF THE HK-24S. THE DECISION IS YOURS.
NOW, I SEE WE HAVE ANOTHER GUEST JUST ARRIVING...

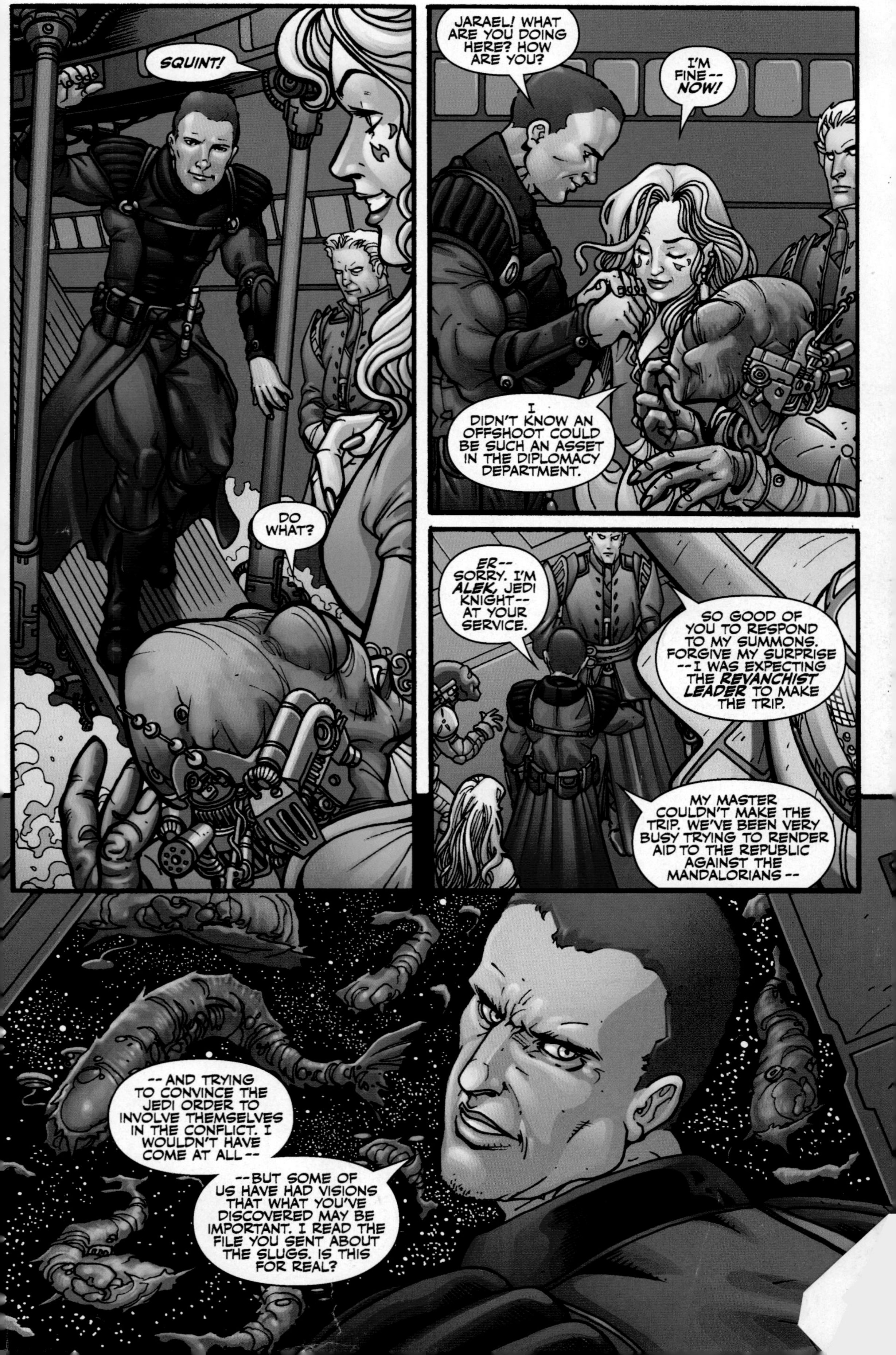
SQUINT!
DO WHAT?
JARAEL! WHAT ARE YOU DOING HERE? HOW ARE YOU?
I'M FINE-- NOW!
I DIDN'T KNOW AN OFFSHOOT COULD BE SUCH AN ASSET IN THE DIPLOMACY DEPARTMENT.
ER-- SORRY. I'M ALEK, JEDI KNIGHT-- AT YOUR SERVICE.
SO GOOD OF YOU TO RESPOND TO MY SUMMONS. FORGIVE MY SURPRISE --I WAS EXPECTING THE REVANCHIST LEADER TO MAKE THE TRIP.
MY MASTER COULDN'T MAKE THE TRIP. WE'VE BEEN VERY BUSY TRYING TO RENDER AID TO THE REPUBLIC AGAINST THE MANDALORIANS--
--AND TRYING TO CONVINCE THE JEDI ORDER TO INVOLVE THEMSELVES IN THE CONFLICT. I WOULDN'T HAVE COME AT ALL--
--BUT SOME OF US HAVE HAD VISIONS THAT WHAT YOU'VE DISCOVERED MAY BE IMPORTANT. I READ THE FILE YOU SENT ABOUT THE SLUGS. IS THIS FOR REAL?

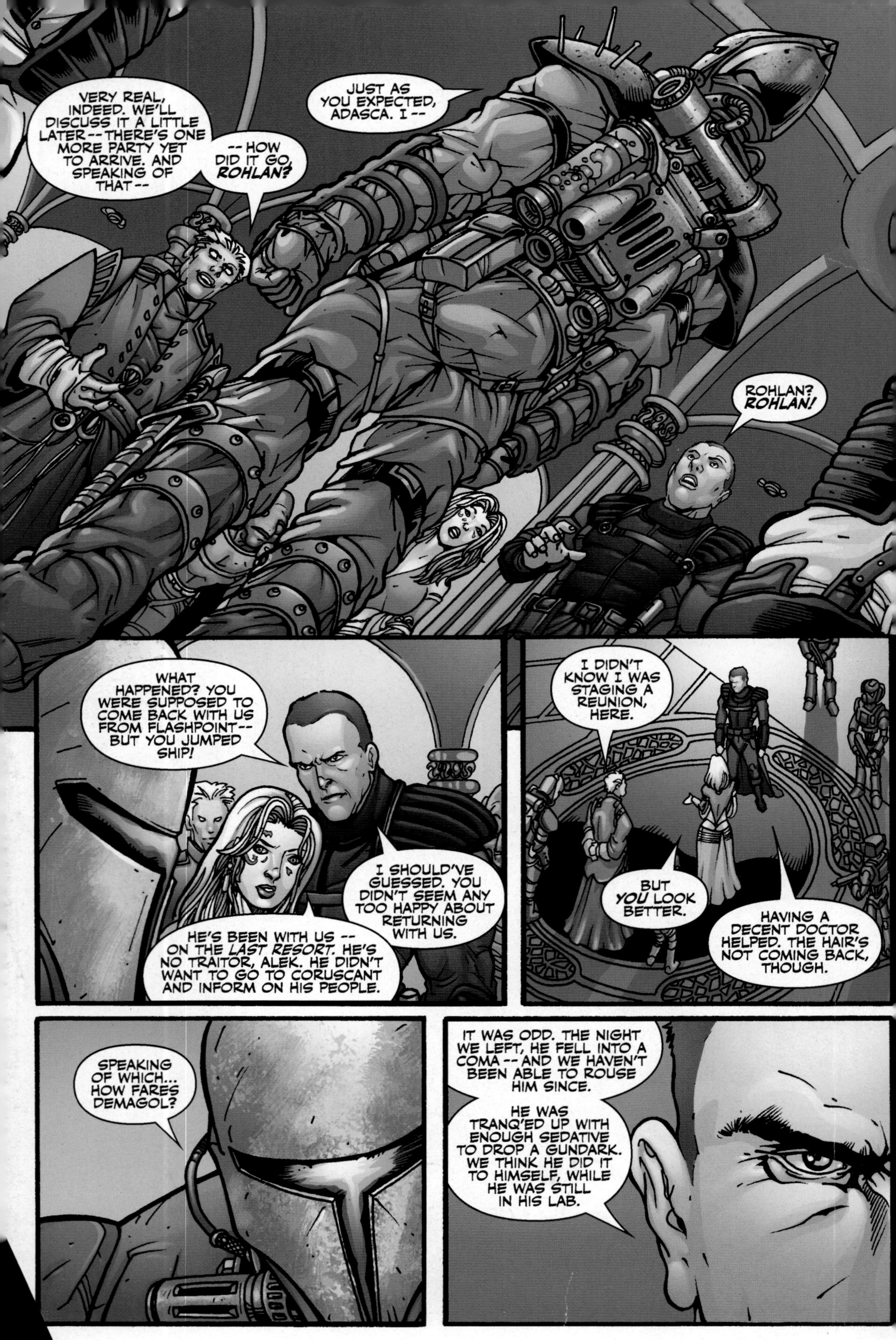
VERY REAL, INDEED. WE'LL DISCUSS IT A LITTLE LATER--THERE'S ONE MORE PARTY YET TO ARRIVE. AND SPEAKING OF THAT--
JUST AS YOU EXPECTED, ADASCA. I--
--HOW DID IT GO, ROHLAN?
ROHLAN? ROHLAN!
WHAT HAPPENED? YOU WERE SUPPOSED TO COME BACK WITH US FROM FLASHPOINT--BUT YOU JUMPED SHIP!
I SHOULD'VE GUESSED. YOU DIDN'T SEEM ANY TOO HAPPY ABOUT RETURNING WITH US.
HE'S BEEN WITH US--ON THE LAST RESORT. HE'S NO TRAITOR, ALEK. HE DIDN'T WANT TO GO TO CORUSCANT AND INFORM ON HIS PEOPLE.
I DIDN'T KNOW I WAS STAGING A REUNION, HERE.
BUT YOU LOOK BETTER.
HAVING A DECENT DOCTOR HELPED. THE HAIR'S NOT COMING BACK, THOUGH.
SPEAKING OF WHICH... HOW FARES DEMAGOL?
IT WAS ODD. THE NIGHT WE LEFT, HE FELL INTO A COMA--AND WE HAVEN'T BEEN ABLE TO ROUSE HIM SINCE.
HE WAS TRANQ'ED UP WITH ENOUGH SEDATIVE TO DROP A GUNDARK. WE THINK HE DID IT TO HIMSELF, WHILE HE WAS STILL IN HIS LAB.

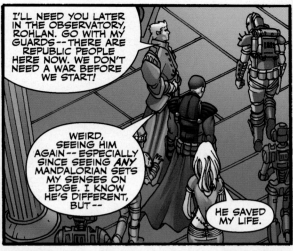

I'LL NEED YOU LATER IN THE OBSERVATORY, ROHLAN. GO WITH MY GUARDS--THERE ARE REPUBLIC PEOPLE HERE NOW. WE DON'T NEED A WAR BEFORE WE START!

WEIRD, SEEING HIM AGAIN--ESPECIALLY SINCE SEEING *ANY* MANDALORIAN SETS MY SENSES ON EDGE. I KNOW HE'S DIFFERENT, BUT--

HE SAVED MY LIFE.

HE COULD HAVE. HE WOULD NOT HAVE WANTED TO REVEAL ANYTHING. YOU REMEMBER THE TROUBLE HE HAD WALKING.

I WOULD NOT TRY TOO HARD TO PRESERVE HIS LIFE.

THAT'S GOOD ENOUGH FOR ME, THEN. IT'S GREAT SEEING *YOU* AGAIN, WHOEVER YOU'RE WITH.

THAT REMINDS ME--I HEARD WHAT ZAYNE WAS ACCUSED OF WHEN I GOT BACK! I DIDN'T BELIEVE A WORD OF IT. IS HE HERE, TOO?

YES! HE'S TRAPPED IN THIS MAD GAME OF ADASCA'S, JUST LIKE US! YOU'VE GOT TO --

SHE WAS GOING TO SAY, YOU'VE SIMPLY *GOT* TO SEE THE VIEW FROM OUR OBSERVATORY.

MY SERVANTS WILL ACCOMPANY YOU. THE OTHERS ARE THERE-- AND I AM TOLD THAT OUR FINAL GUEST HAS JUST ARRIVED.

MILORD! IT'S NOT OUR *SPECIAL* GUEST. IT'S *ANOTHER JEDI!*

PROBABLY *THE REVANCHIST*, THEN. LET'S DO THE MEETING IN MY LOUNGE.

I'D RATHER DEAL WITH THE *HEAD* CRUSADER THAN THIS YOUNG PUP THEY SENT, ANYWAY!

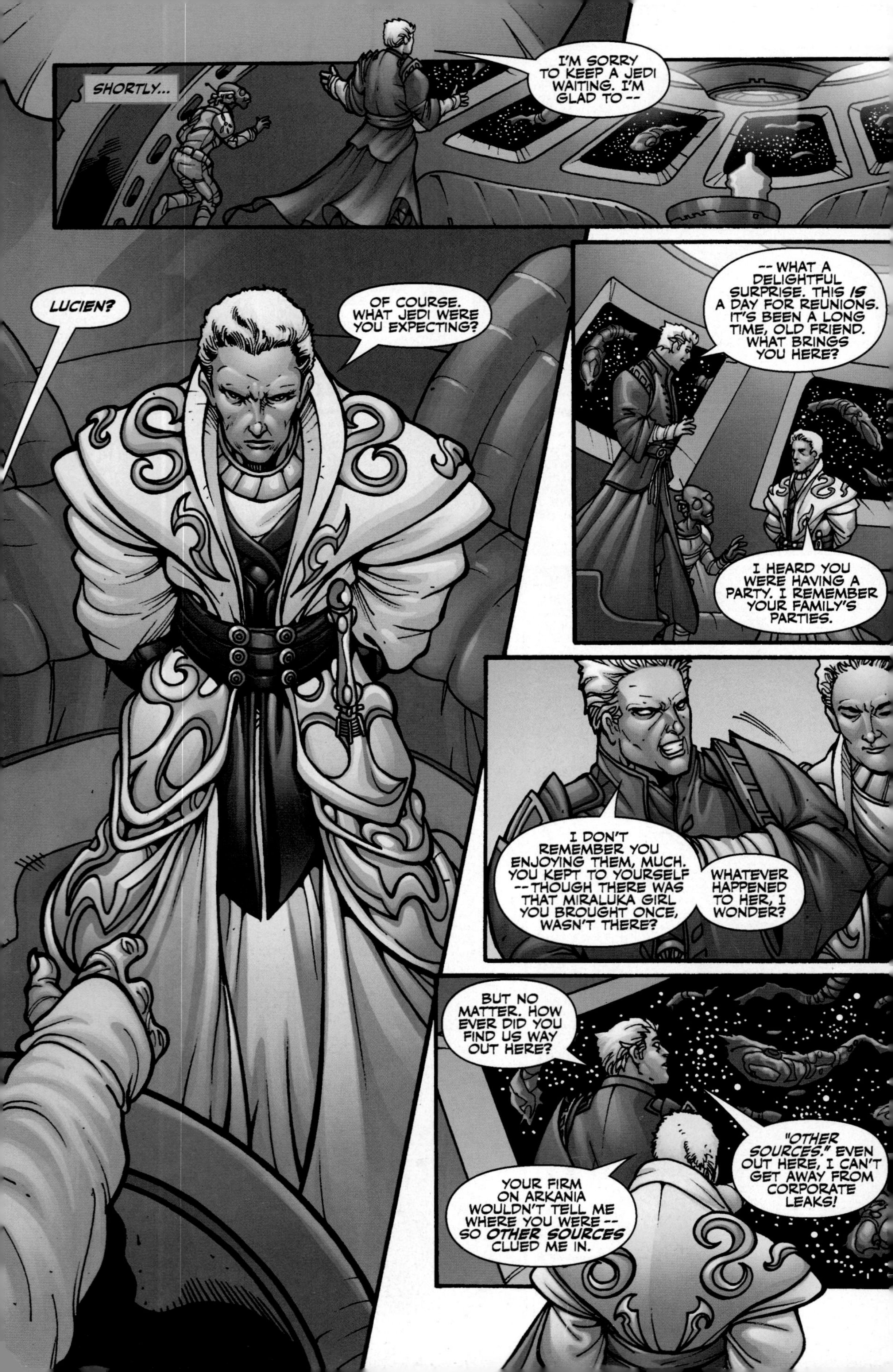
SHORTLY...
I'M SORRY TO KEEP A JEDI WAITING. I'M GLAD TO --
LUCIEN?
OF COURSE. WHAT JEDI WERE YOU EXPECTING?
-- WHAT A DELIGHTFUL SURPRISE. THIS IS A DAY FOR REUNIONS. IT'S BEEN A LONG TIME, OLD FRIEND. WHAT BRINGS YOU HERE?
I HEARD YOU WERE HAVING A PARTY. I REMEMBER YOUR FAMILY'S PARTIES.
I DON'T REMEMBER YOU ENJOYING THEM, MUCH. YOU KEPT TO YOURSELF -- THOUGH THERE WAS THAT MIRALUKA GIRL YOU BROUGHT ONCE, WASN'T THERE?
WHATEVER HAPPENED TO HER, I WONDER?
BUT NO MATTER. HOW EVER DID YOU FIND US WAY OUT HERE?
YOUR FIRM ON ARKANIA WOULDN'T TELL ME WHERE YOU WERE -- SO OTHER SOURCES CLUED ME IN.
"OTHER SOURCES." EVEN OUT HERE, I CAN'T GET AWAY FROM CORPORATE LEAKS!

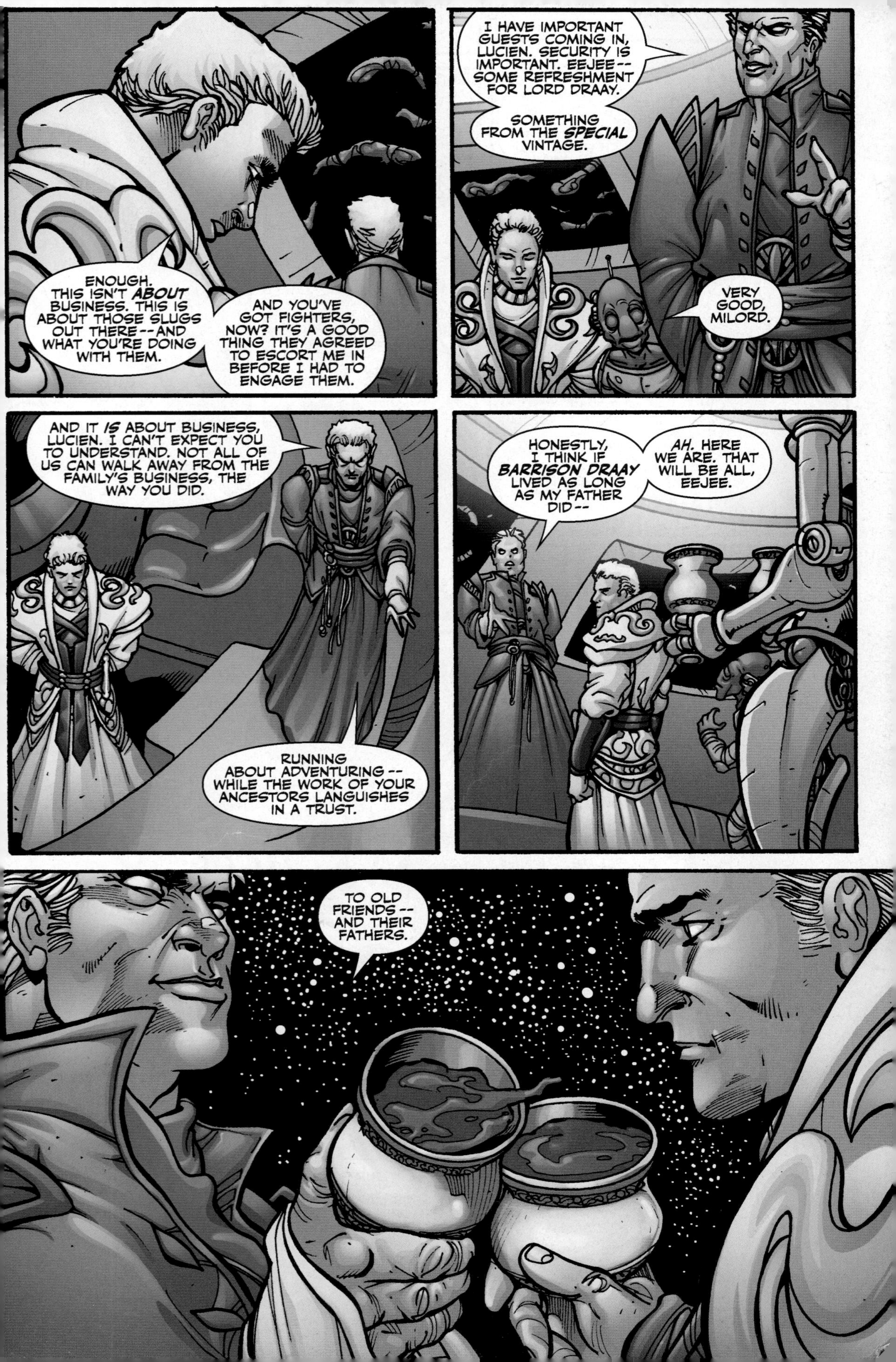
ENOUGH. THIS ISN'T ABOUT BUSINESS. THIS IS ABOUT THOSE SLUGS OUT THERE--AND WHAT YOU'RE DOING WITH THEM.
AND YOU'VE GOT FIGHTERS, NOW? IT'S A GOOD THING THEY AGREED TO ESCORT ME IN BEFORE I HAD TO ENGAGE THEM.
I HAVE IMPORTANT GUESTS COMING IN, LUCIEN. SECURITY IS IMPORTANT. EEJEE--SOME REFRESHMENT FOR LORD DRAAY.
SOMETHING FROM THE SPECIAL VINTAGE.
VERY GOOD, MILORD.
AND IT IS ABOUT BUSINESS, LUCIEN. I CAN'T EXPECT YOU TO UNDERSTAND. NOT ALL OF US CAN WALK AWAY FROM THE FAMILY'S BUSINESS, THE WAY YOU DID.
RUNNING ABOUT ADVENTURING--WHILE THE WORK OF YOUR ANCESTORS LANGUISHES IN A TRUST.
HONESTLY, I THINK IF BARRISON DRAAY LIVED AS LONG AS MY FATHER DID--
AH. HERE WE ARE. THAT WILL BE ALL, EEJEE.
TO OLD FRIENDS--AND THEIR FATHERS.

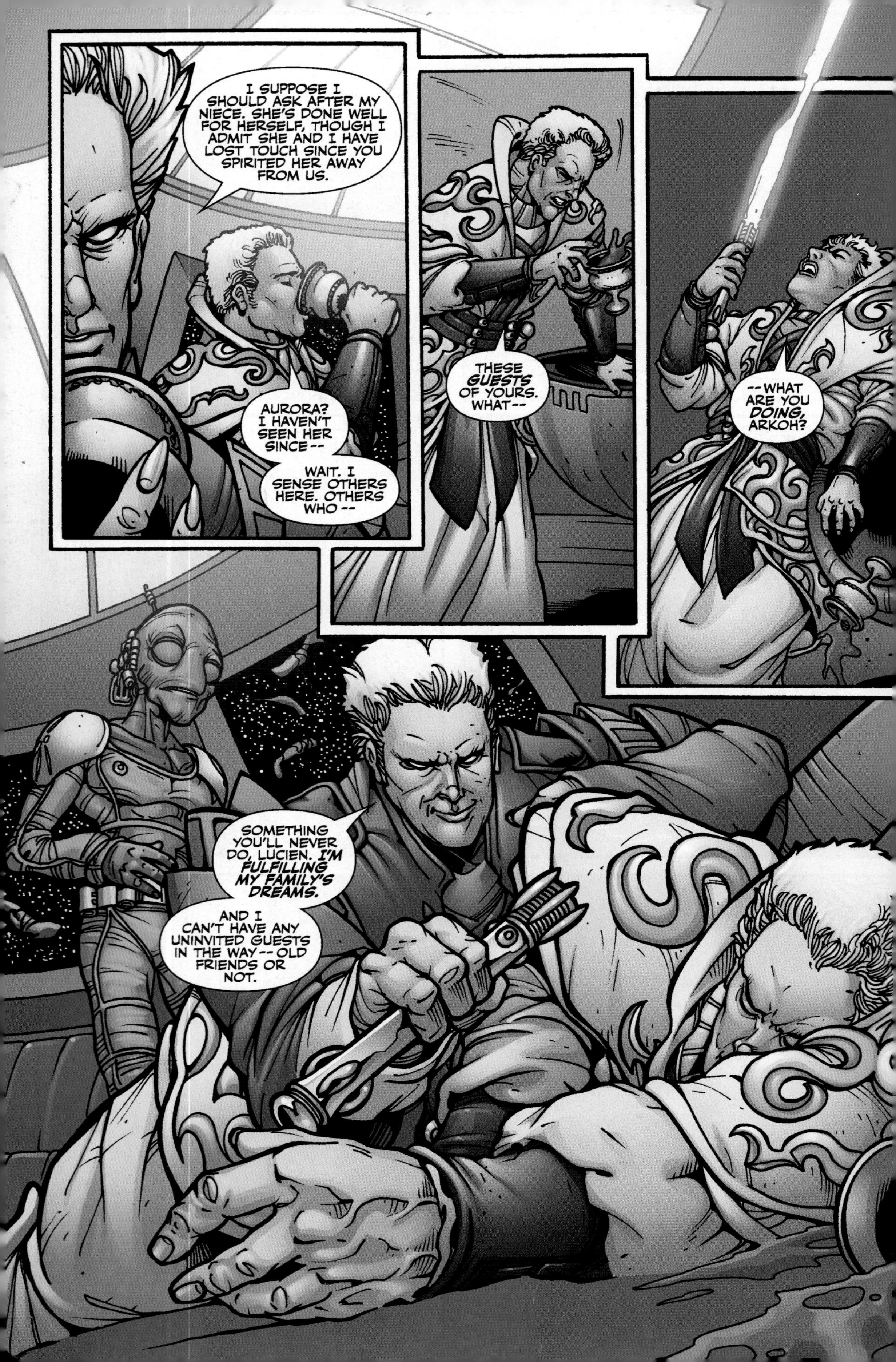

I SUPPOSE I SHOULD ASK AFTER MY NIECE. SHE'S DONE WELL FOR HERSELF, THOUGH I ADMIT SHE AND I HAVE LOST TOUCH SINCE YOU SPIRITED HER AWAY FROM US.
AURORA? I HAVEN'T SEEN HER SINCE--
WAIT. I SENSE OTHERS HERE. OTHERS WHO--
THESE *GUESTS* OF YOURS. WHAT--
--WHAT ARE YOU *DOING,* ARKOH?
SOMETHING YOU'LL NEVER DO, LUCIEN. *I'M FULFILLING MY FAMILY'S DREAMS.*
AND I CAN'T HAVE ANY UNINVITED GUESTS IN THE WAY--OLD FRIENDS OR NOT.

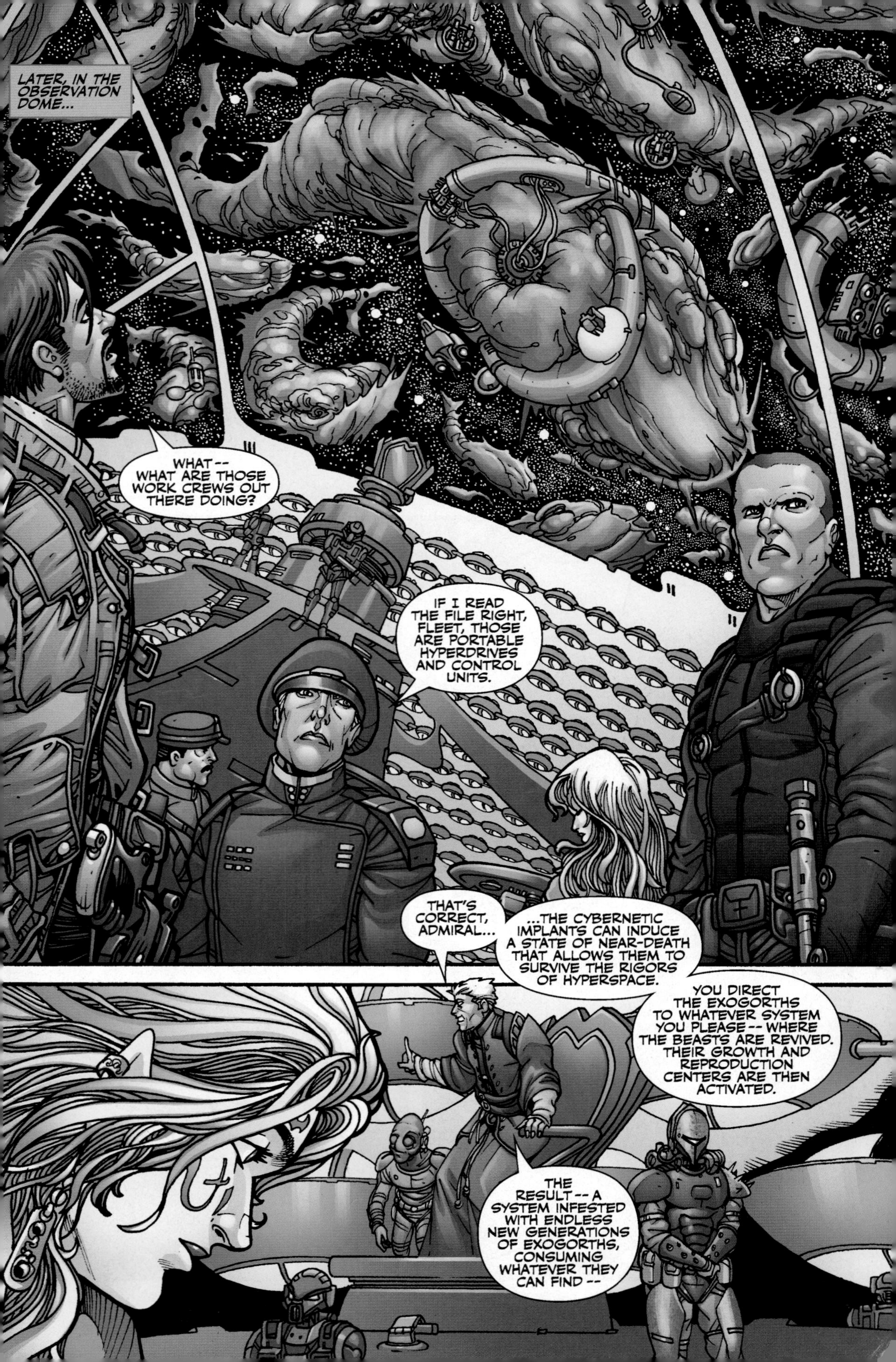
LATER, IN THE OBSERVATION DOME...
WHAT -- WHAT ARE THOSE WORK CREWS OUT THERE DOING?
IF I READ THE FILE RIGHT, FLEET, THOSE ARE PORTABLE HYPERDRIVES AND CONTROL UNITS.
THAT'S CORRECT, ADMIRAL...
...THE CYBERNETIC IMPLANTS CAN INDUCE A STATE OF NEAR-DEATH THAT ALLOWS THEM TO SURVIVE THE RIGORS OF HYPERSPACE.
YOU DIRECT THE EXOGORTHS TO WHATEVER SYSTEM YOU PLEASE -- WHERE THE BEASTS ARE REVIVED. THEIR GROWTH AND REPRODUCTION CENTERS ARE THEN ACTIVATED.
THE RESULT -- A SYSTEM INFESTED WITH ENDLESS NEW GENERATIONS OF EXOGORTHS, CONSUMING WHATEVER THEY CAN FIND --

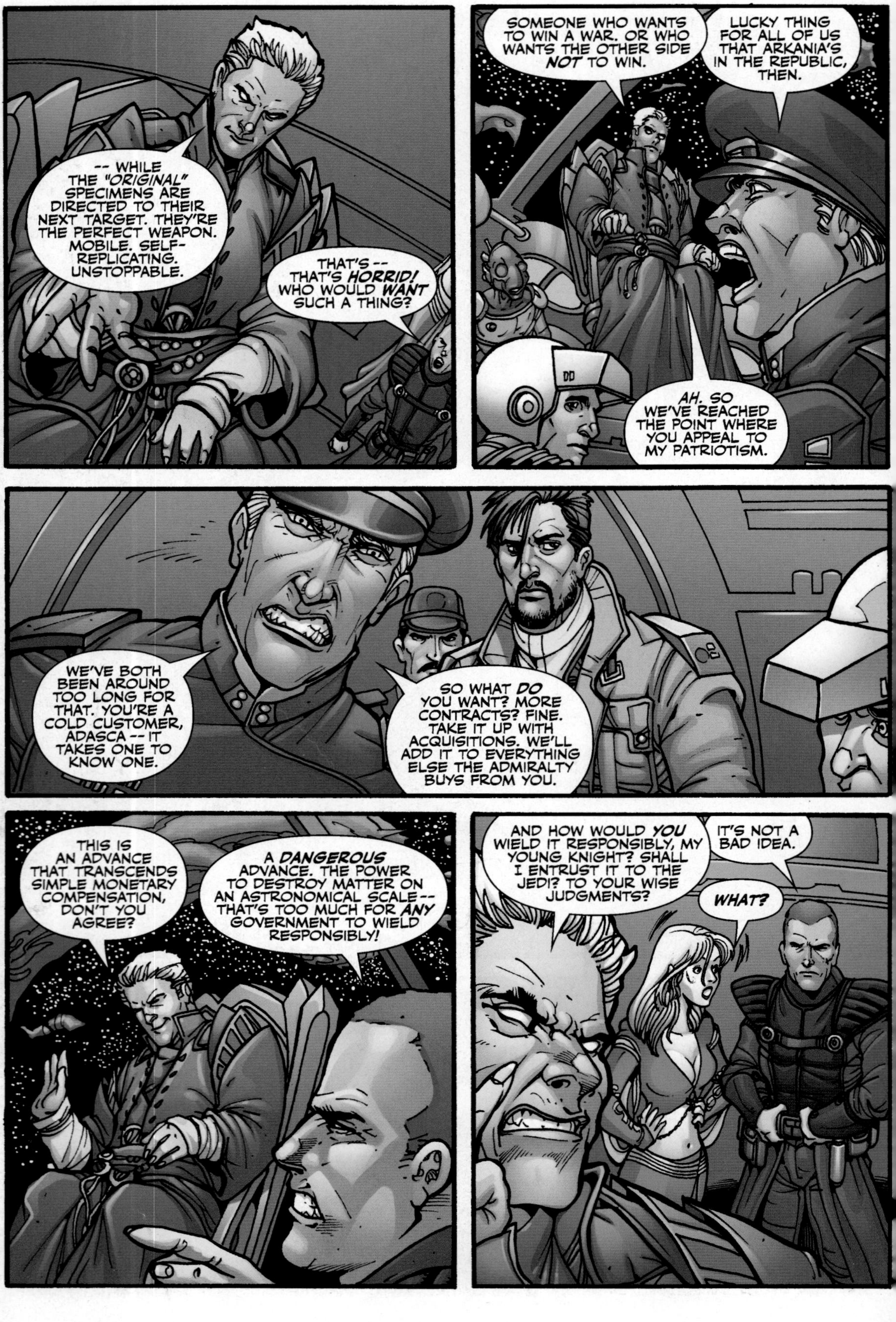
-- WHILE THE "ORIGINAL" SPECIMENS ARE DIRECTED TO THEIR NEXT TARGET. THEY'RE THE PERFECT WEAPON. MOBILE. SELF-REPLICATING. UNSTOPPABLE.
THAT'S -- THAT'S HORRID! WHO WOULD WANT SUCH A THING?
SOMEONE WHO WANTS TO WIN A WAR. OR WHO WANTS THE OTHER SIDE NOT TO WIN.
LUCKY THING FOR ALL OF US THAT ARKANIA'S IN THE REPUBLIC, THEN.
AH. SO WE'VE REACHED THE POINT WHERE YOU APPEAL TO MY PATRIOTISM.
WE'VE BOTH BEEN AROUND TOO LONG FOR THAT. YOU'RE A COLD CUSTOMER, ADASCA -- IT TAKES ONE TO KNOW ONE.
SO WHAT DO YOU WANT? MORE CONTRACTS? FINE. TAKE IT UP WITH ACQUISITIONS. WE'LL ADD IT TO EVERYTHING ELSE THE ADMIRALTY BUYS FROM YOU.
THIS IS AN ADVANCE THAT TRANSCENDS SIMPLE MONETARY COMPENSATION, DON'T YOU AGREE?
A DANGEROUS ADVANCE. THE POWER TO DESTROY MATTER ON AN ASTRONOMICAL SCALE -- THAT'S TOO MUCH FOR ANY GOVERNMENT TO WIELD RESPONSIBLY!
AND HOW WOULD YOU WIELD IT RESPONSIBLY, MY YOUNG KNIGHT? SHALL I ENTRUST IT TO THE JEDI? TO YOUR WISE JUDGMENTS?
IT'S NOT A BAD IDEA.
WHAT?

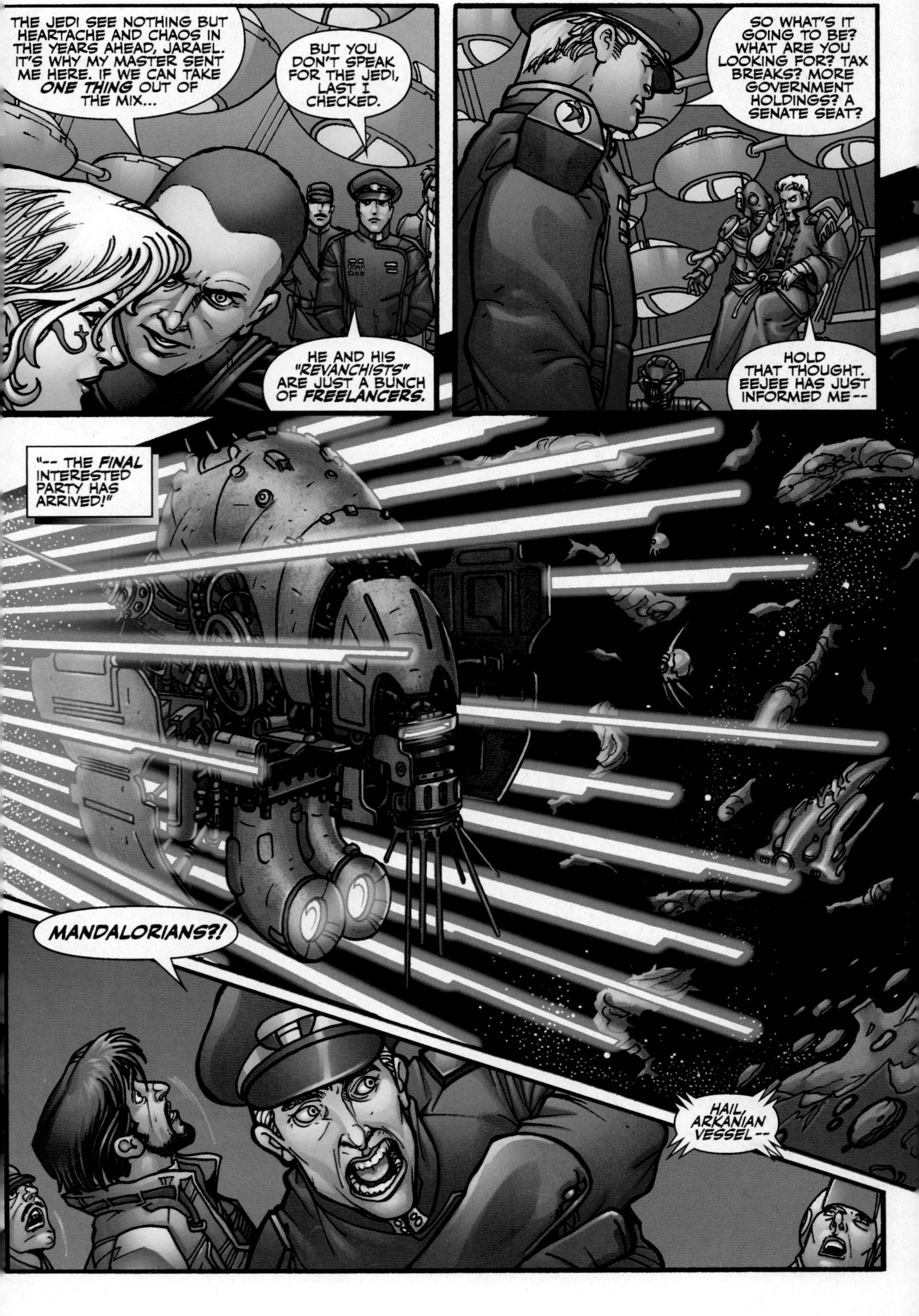
THE JEDI SEE NOTHING BUT HEARTACHE AND CHAOS IN THE YEARS AHEAD, JARAEL. IT'S WHY MY MASTER SENT ME HERE. IF WE CAN TAKE ONE THING OUT OF THE MIX...
BUT YOU DON'T SPEAK FOR THE JEDI, LAST I CHECKED.
HE AND HIS "REVANCHISTS" ARE JUST A BUNCH OF FREELANCERS.
SO WHAT'S IT GOING TO BE? WHAT ARE YOU LOOKING FOR? TAX BREAKS? MORE GOVERNMENT HOLDINGS? A SENATE SEAT?
HOLD THAT THOUGHT. EEJEE HAS JUST INFORMED ME--
"-- THE FINAL INTERESTED PARTY HAS ARRIVED!"
MANDALORIANS?!
HAIL, ARKANIAN VESSEL--

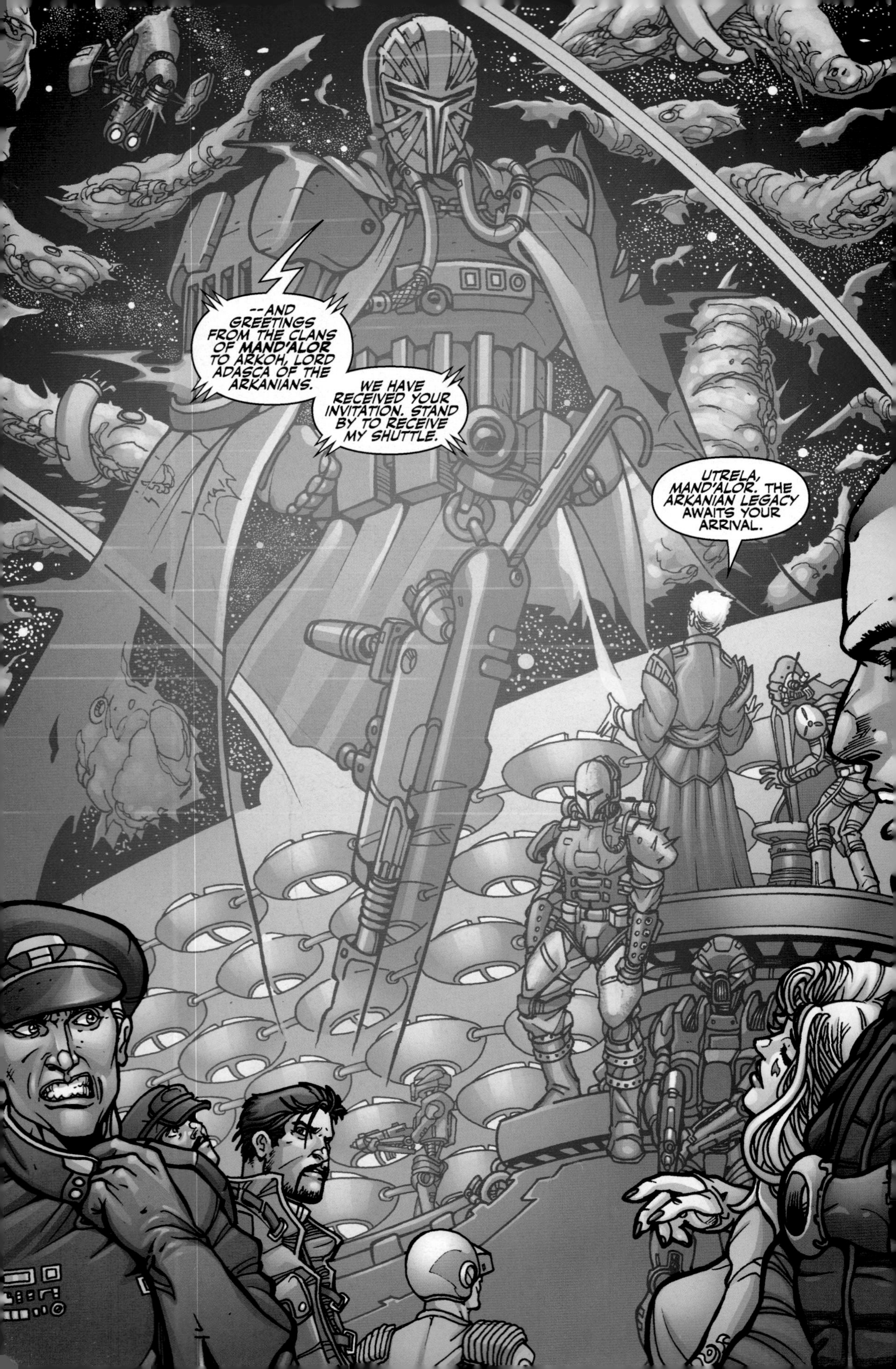
--AND GREETINGS FROM THE CLANS OF MAND'ALOR TO ARKOH, LORD ADASCA OF THE ARKANIANS.
WE HAVE RECEIVED YOUR INVITATION. STAND BY TO RECEIVE MY SHUTTLE.
UTRELA, MAND'ALOR. THE ARKANIAN LEGACY AWAITS YOUR ARRIVAL.

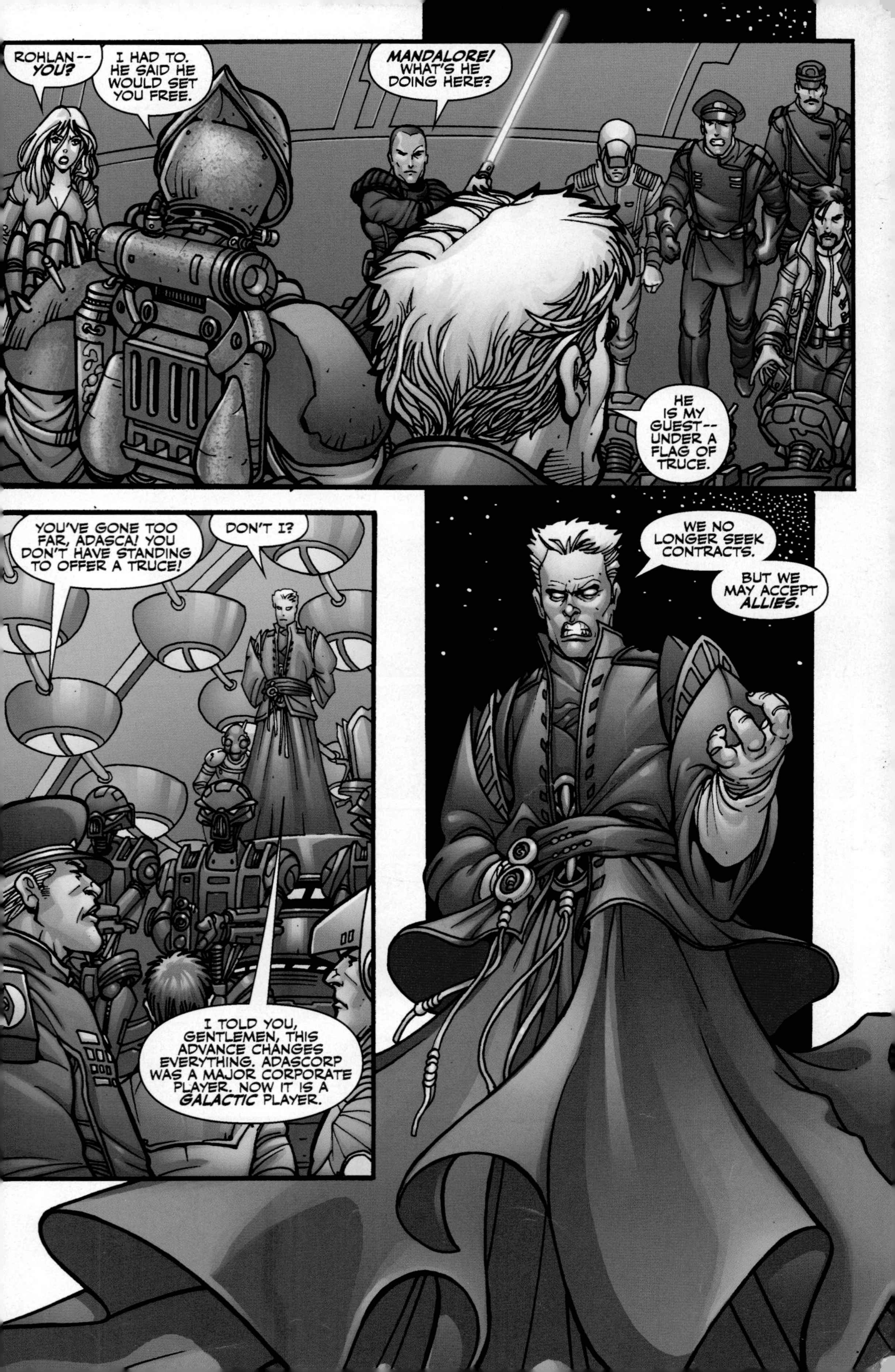
ROHLAN-- *YOU?*
I HAD TO. HE SAID HE WOULD SET YOU FREE.
MANDALORE! WHAT'S HE DOING HERE?
HE IS MY GUEST-- UNDER A FLAG OF TRUCE.
YOU'VE GONE TOO FAR, ADASCA! YOU DON'T HAVE STANDING TO OFFER A TRUCE!
DON'T I?
I TOLD YOU, GENTLEMEN, THIS ADVANCE CHANGES EVERYTHING. ADASCORP WAS A MAJOR CORPORATE PLAYER. NOW IT IS A *GALACTIC* PLAYER.
WE NO LONGER SEEK CONTRACTS.
BUT WE MAY ACCEPT *ALLIES.*

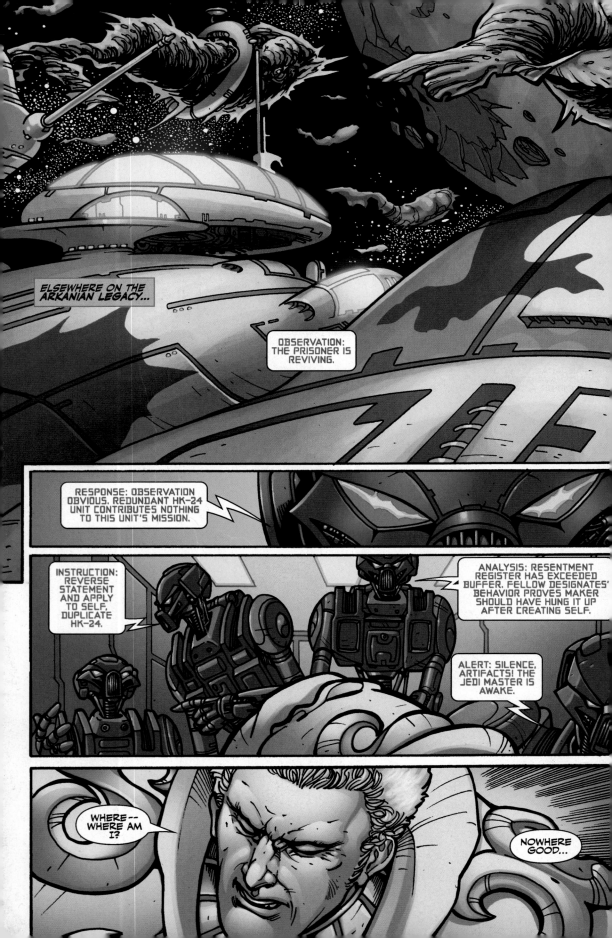

ELSEWHERE ON THE ARKANIAN LEGACY...

OBSERVATION: THE PRISONER IS REVIVING.

RESPONSE: OBSERVATION OBVIOUS. REDUNDANT HK-24 UNIT CONTRIBUTES NOTHING TO THIS UNIT'S MISSION.

INSTRUCTION: REVERSE STATEMENT AND APPLY TO SELF, DUPLICATE HK-24.

ANALYSIS: RESENTMENT REGISTER HAS EXCEEDED BUFFER. FELLOW DESIGNATES' BEHAVIOR PROVES MAKER SHOULD HAVE HUNG IT UP AFTER CREATING SELF.

ALERT: SILENCE, ARTIFACTS! THE JEDI MASTER IS AWAKE.

WHERE-- WHERE AM I?

NOWHERE GOOD...

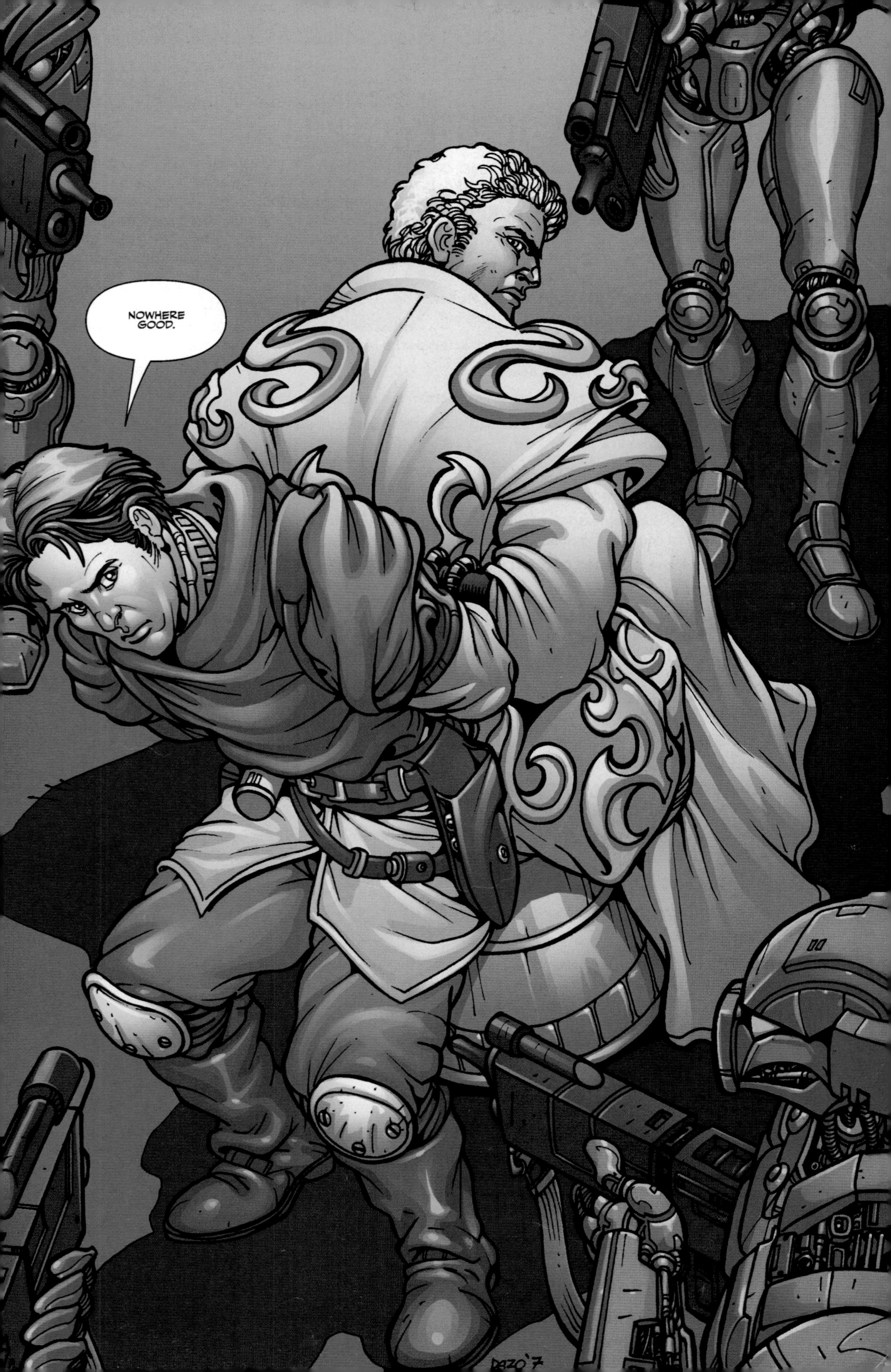
NOWHERE GOOD.

ADASCORP

FISCAL PERIOD FINANCIAL REPORT AND O

FIELD REPORT: "PROJECT BLACK H
MOST SECRET!

(CONTINUED from file 2342/6)

Lord Adasca,
Here's the transcript you requested from Vandrayk's last briefing before he left our service 33 years ago. There are no holos of the briefing due to the sensitive nature of the subject, but you'll see your late grandfather was in attendance.

ARTONIAN DOBONOLD, director, Rese
Are you saying your original projections were off?

GORMAN VANDRAYK, lead Project scientist: If anything, they were too low.

DOBONOLD: I find that hard to believe.

VANDRAYK: That's two of us. But it's right there in the numbers.

DOBONOLD: To believe this, we've have to accept that the slugs—the Exorgoths—can consume their own weight six times in a standard day!

VANDRAYK: With the hunger center stimulated, yes, sir.

DOBONOLD: That's incredible.

VANDRAYK: But the beastie's growing the whole time, so that mass value keeps changing. If you set up a differential equation—(continues inaudible)

ARGALOH, the SIXTH LORD ADASCA: Is this really important?

DOBONOLD: No, milord. To the point, Vandrayk.

VANDRAYK: I mean if you hit both the growth centers and the fission centers at once, you've got this many in a month—and they'd consume this much mass. (Refers to Table 12 attached to OBH file 2342)

ADASCA: (gasps)

VANDRAYK: They're somethin', all right.

DOBONOLD: We're looking at possible uses in industrial waste cleanup, milord.

VANDRAYK: Just lead 'em to it. My notes on the drive system and control units are back on my survey ship. I can get them—

ADASCA: Wait a minute, offshoot. Are you saying we could grow a fleet of these things? Send them wherever we want?

VANDRAYK: As long as you're not picky about them destroying everything when they get there.

ADASCA: (pause, then strikes table) They're perfect!

VANDRAYK: I don't understand.

ADASCA: Are you blind?

VANDRAYK: Sir?

ADASCA: With those ugly eyes of yours, are you *blind*? Because you must not see the *war* going on around us. Trade curtailed. Customers and Arkanians alike affected. (Scattered sounds of agreement.) And now the greatest Arkanian of all, Arca Jeth, laid low by this nonsense!

DOBONOLD: Master Jeth protect us!

VANDRAYK: But these are living things. They don't *mean* to hurt anyone. They're—

ADASCA: They're our *property*, right?

VANDRAYK: (inaudible)

ADASCA: It's like I was telling little Arkoh: "The truth must be infrared." Because the offshoots can never see it! (scattered laughter)

DOBONOLD: What do you have in mind, milord?

ADASCA: It's simple. We—is something wrong, Vandrayk?

VANDRAYK: Can I be excused? I—uh—want to get those files I left on the survey ship.

DOBONOLD: Be back quick, Vandrayk. Don't camp out up there like the last time.

VANDRAYK: Uh . . . yeah . . . (trails off, inaudible)

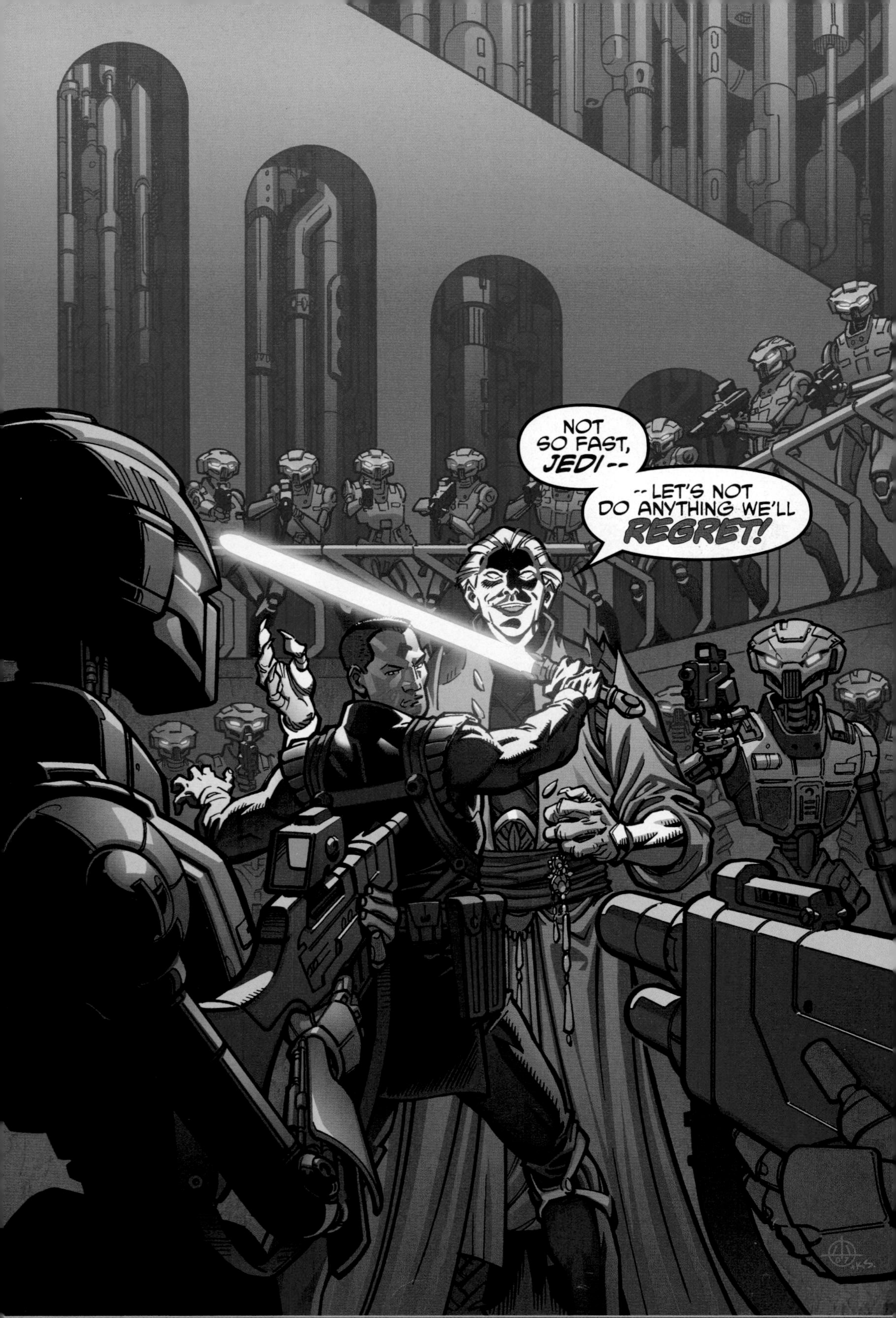

NOT SO FAST, JEDI --
-- LET'S NOT DO ANYTHING WE'LL REGRET!

***STAR WARS: KNIGHTS OF THE OLD REPUBLIC* #20 — "DAZE OF HATE, PART 2"**

WRITER: JOHN JACKSON MILLER • ARTIST: BONG DAZO • COLORIST: MICHAEL ATIYEH • LETTERER: MICHAEL HEISLER
ASSISTANT EDITOR: DAVE MARSHALL • EDITOR: JEREMY BARLOW • COVER ARTISTS: CHRIS WARNER & KELSEY SHANNON

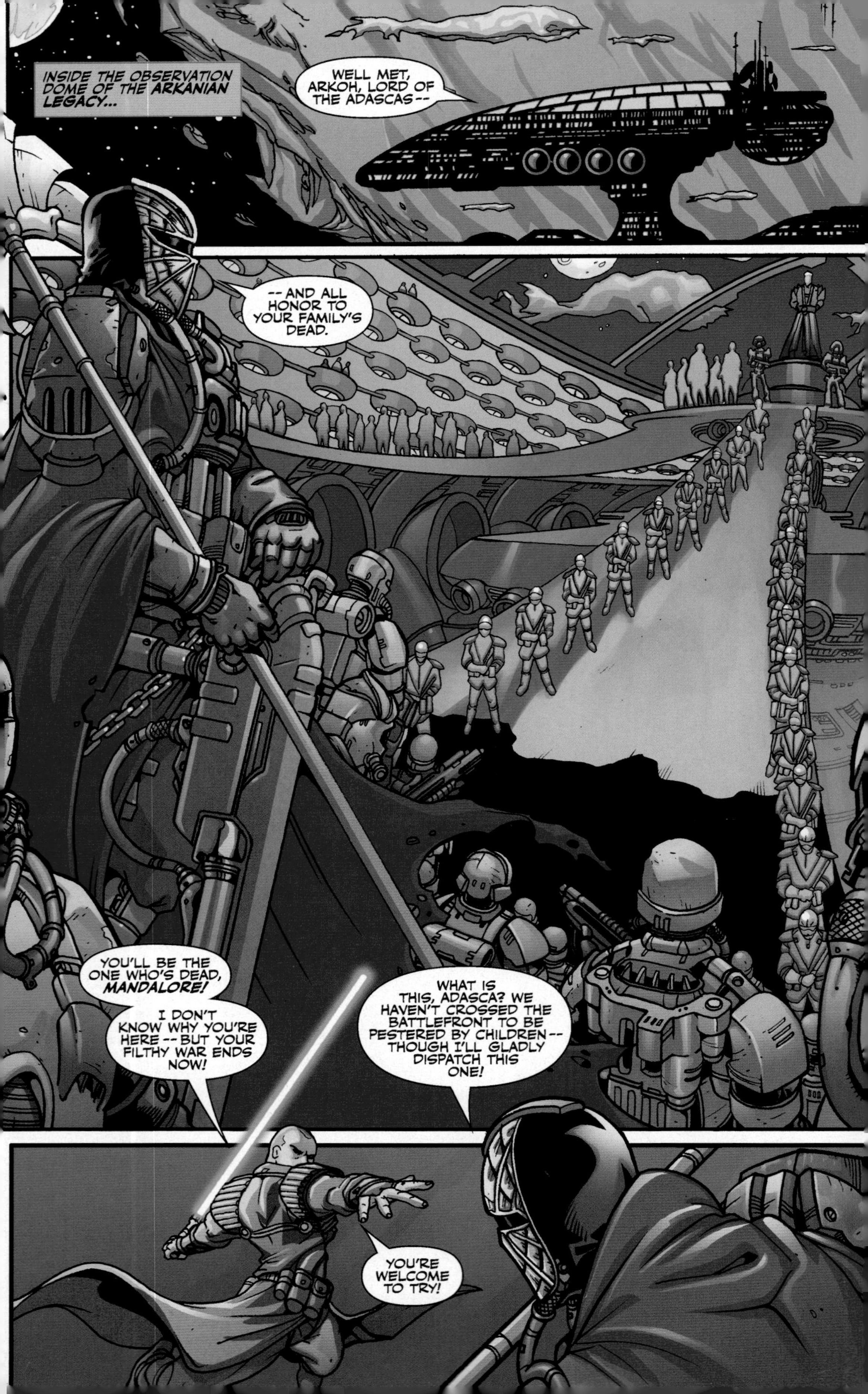

INSIDE THE OBSERVATION DOME OF THE ARKANIAN LEGACY...
WELL MET, ARKOH, LORD OF THE ADASCAS--
--AND ALL HONOR TO YOUR FAMILY'S DEAD.
YOU'LL BE THE ONE WHO'S DEAD, MANDALORE!
I DON'T KNOW WHY YOU'RE HERE--BUT YOUR FILTHY WAR ENDS NOW!
WHAT IS THIS, ADASCA? WE HAVEN'T CROSSED THE BATTLEFRONT TO BE PESTERED BY CHILDREN--THOUGH I'LL GLADLY DISPATCH THIS ONE!
YOU'RE WELCOME TO TRY!

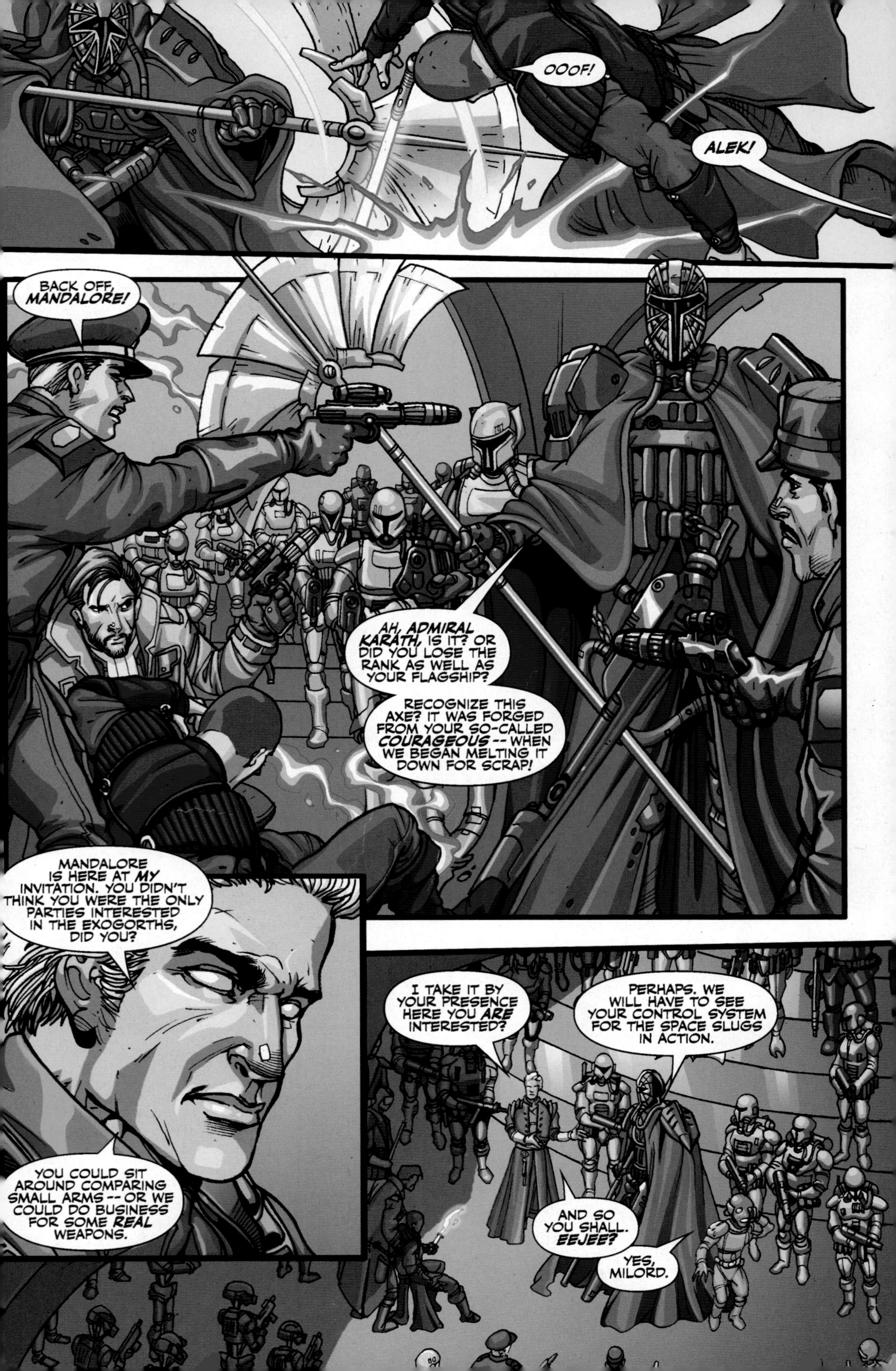
OOOF!
ALEK!
BACK OFF, MANDALORE!
AH, ADMIRAL KARATH, IS IT? OR DID YOU LOSE THE RANK AS WELL AS YOUR FLAGSHIP?
RECOGNIZE THIS AXE? IT WAS FORGED FROM YOUR SO-CALLED COURAGEOUS -- WHEN WE BEGAN MELTING IT DOWN FOR SCRAP!
MANDALORE IS HERE AT MY INVITATION. YOU DIDN'T THINK YOU WERE THE ONLY PARTIES INTERESTED IN THE EXOGORTHS, DID YOU?
YOU COULD SIT AROUND COMPARING SMALL ARMS -- OR WE COULD DO BUSINESS FOR SOME REAL WEAPONS.
I TAKE IT BY YOUR PRESENCE HERE YOU ARE INTERESTED?
PERHAPS. WE WILL HAVE TO SEE YOUR CONTROL SYSTEM FOR THE SPACE SLUGS IN ACTION.
AND SO YOU SHALL. EEJEE?
YES, MILORD.

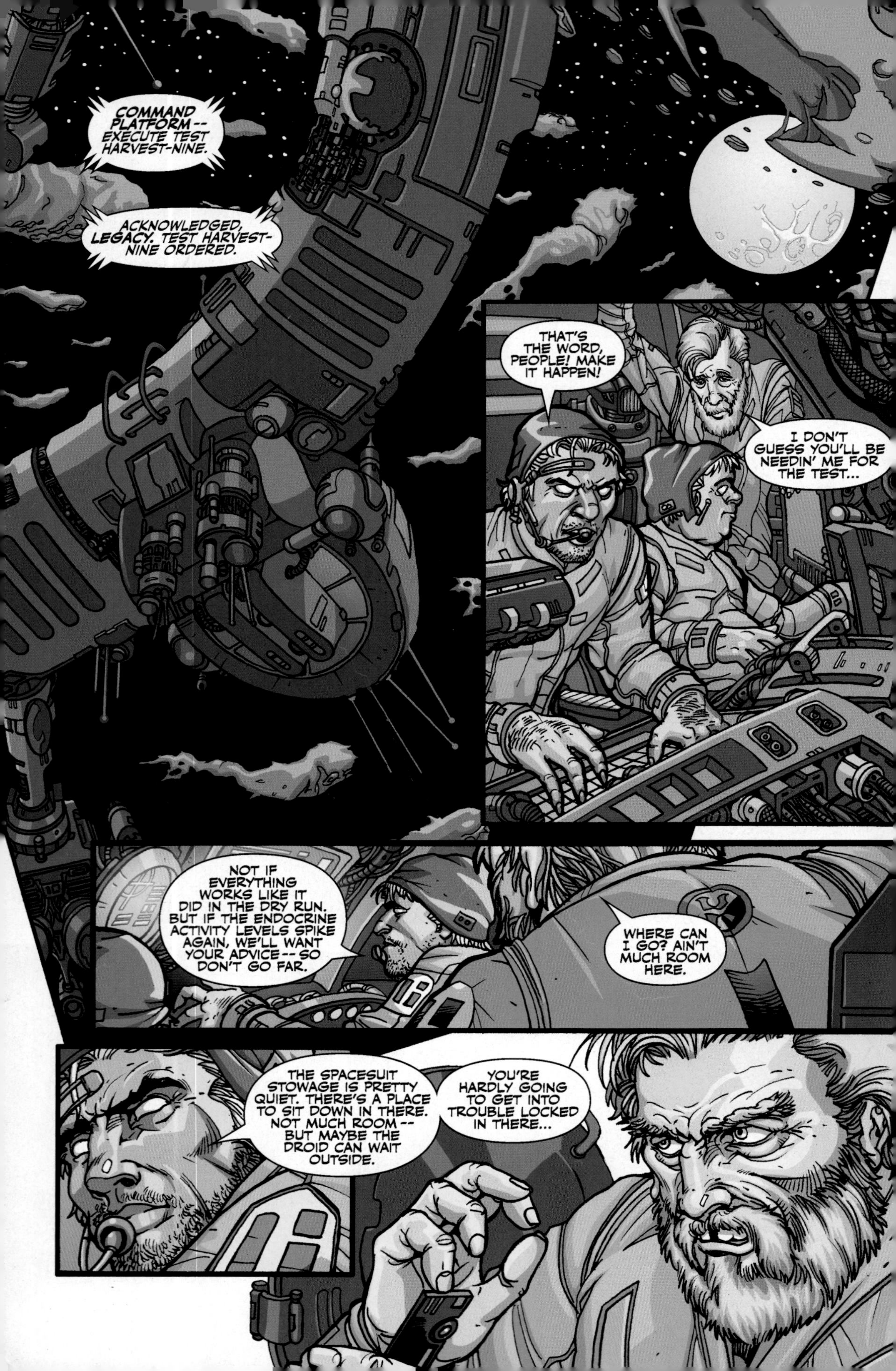
COMMAND PLATFORM -- EXECUTE TEST HARVEST-NINE.
ACKNOWLEDGED, LEGACY. TEST HARVEST-NINE ORDERED.
THAT'S THE WORD, PEOPLE! MAKE IT HAPPEN!
I DON'T GUESS YOU'LL BE NEEDIN' ME FOR THE TEST...
NOT IF EVERYTHING WORKS LIKE IT DID IN THE DRY RUN. BUT IF THE ENDOCRINE ACTIVITY LEVELS SPIKE AGAIN, WE'LL WANT YOUR ADVICE -- SO DON'T GO FAR.
WHERE CAN I GO? AIN'T MUCH ROOM HERE.
THE SPACESUIT STOWAGE IS PRETTY QUIET. THERE'S A PLACE TO SIT DOWN IN THERE. NOT MUCH ROOM -- BUT MAYBE THE DROID CAN WAIT OUTSIDE.
YOU'RE HARDLY GOING TO GET INTO TROUBLE LOCKED IN THERE...

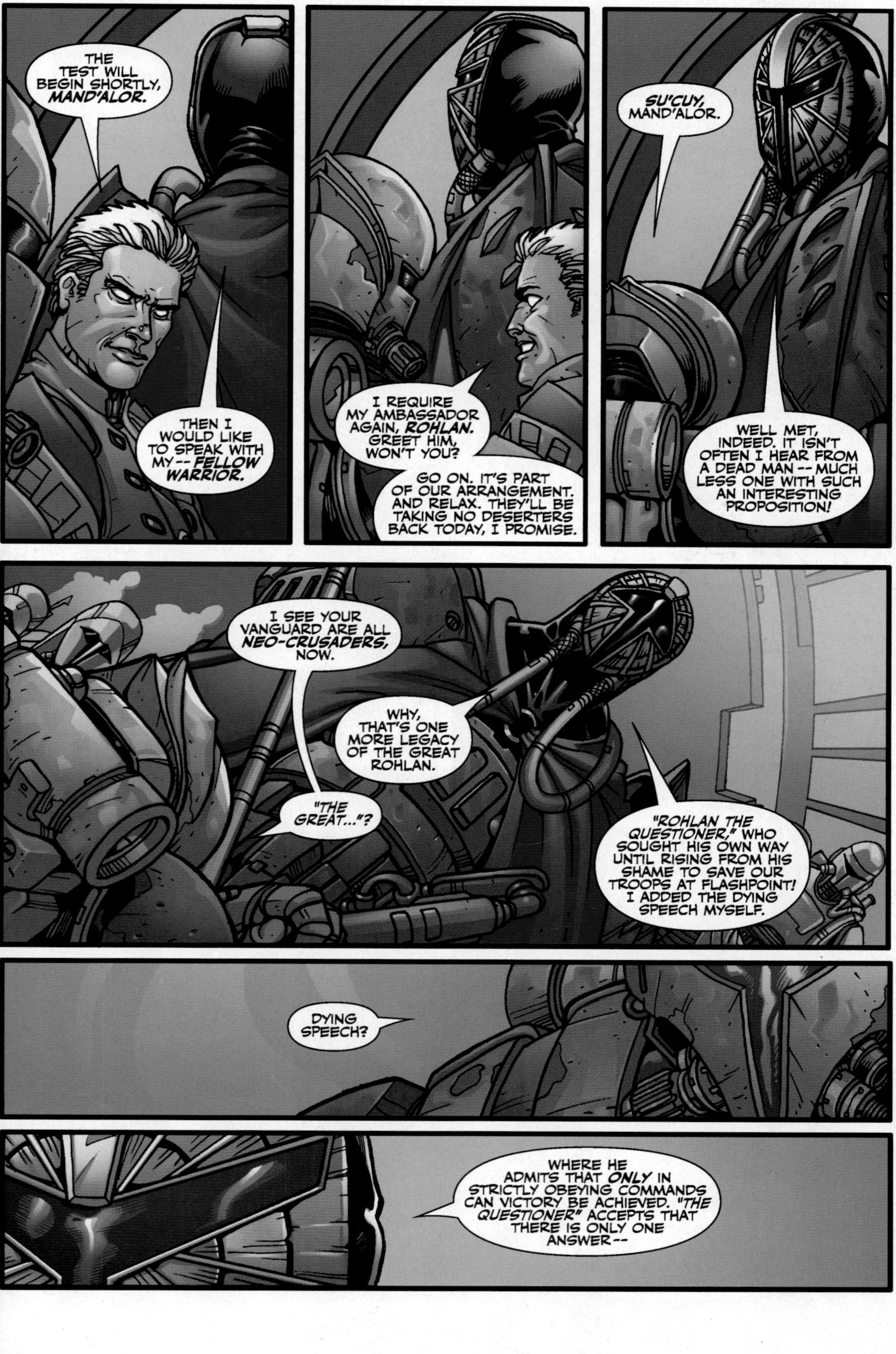
THE TEST WILL BEGIN SHORTLY, *MAND'ALOR.*
THEN I WOULD LIKE TO SPEAK WITH MY-- *FELLOW WARRIOR.*
I REQUIRE MY AMBASSADOR AGAIN, *ROHLAN.* GREET HIM, WON'T YOU?
GO ON. IT'S PART OF OUR ARRANGEMENT. AND RELAX. THEY'LL BE TAKING NO DESERTERS BACK TODAY, I PROMISE.
SU'CUY, MAND'ALOR.
WELL MET, INDEED. IT ISN'T OFTEN I HEAR FROM A DEAD MAN -- MUCH LESS ONE WITH SUCH AN INTERESTING PROPOSITION!
I SEE YOUR VANGUARD ARE ALL *NEO-CRUSADERS,* NOW.
WHY, THAT'S ONE MORE LEGACY OF THE GREAT ROHLAN.
"THE GREAT..."?
"ROHLAN THE QUESTIONER," WHO SOUGHT HIS OWN WAY UNTIL RISING FROM HIS SHAME TO SAVE OUR TROOPS AT FLASHPOINT! I ADDED THE DYING SPEECH MYSELF.
DYING SPEECH?
WHERE HE ADMITS THAT *ONLY* IN STRICTLY OBEYING COMMANDS CAN VICTORY BE ACHIEVED. *"THE QUESTIONER"* ACCEPTS THAT THERE IS ONLY ONE ANSWER--

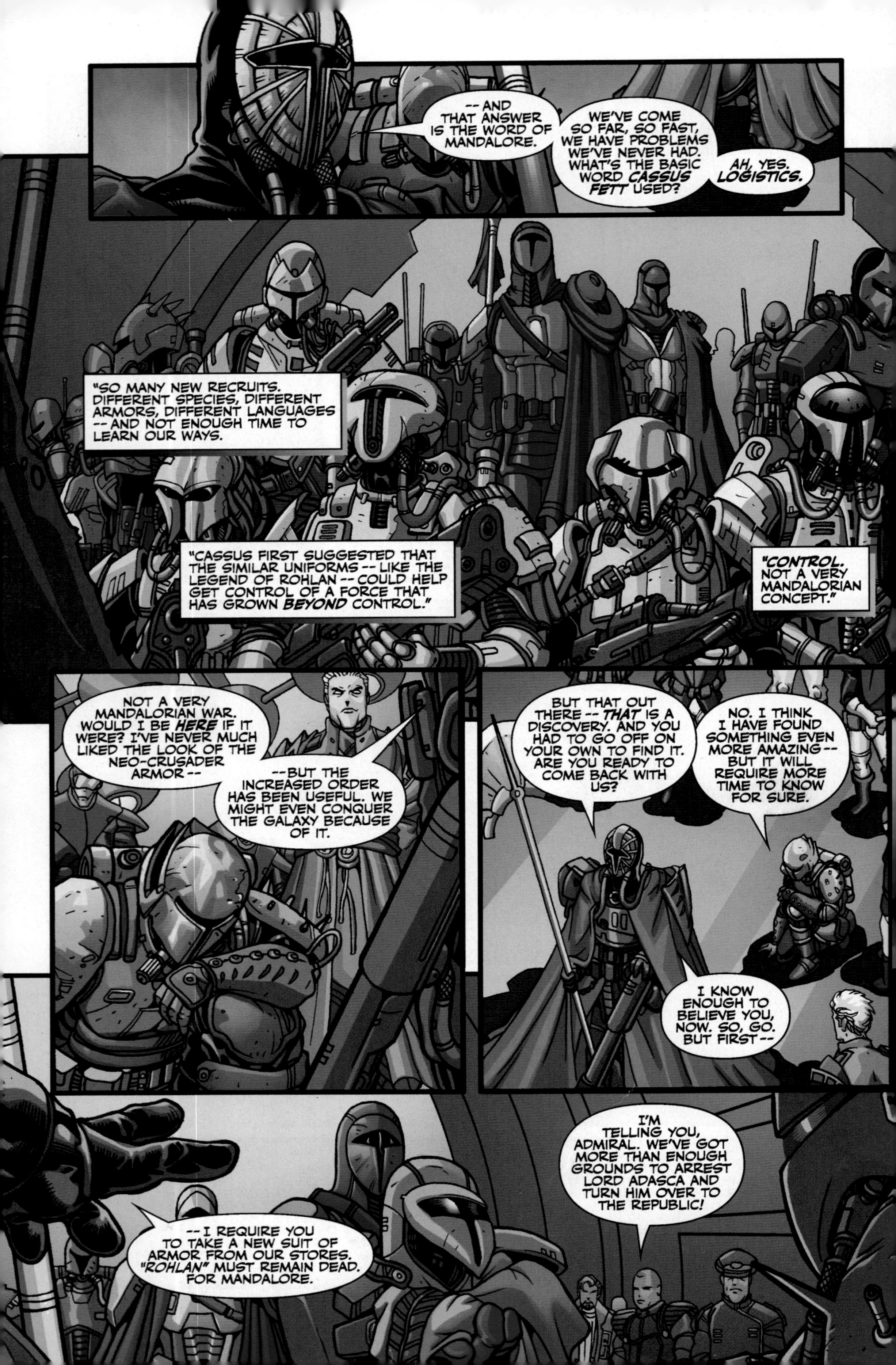

-- AND THAT ANSWER IS THE WORD OF MANDALORE.
WE'VE COME SO FAR, SO FAST, WE HAVE PROBLEMS WE'VE NEVER HAD. WHAT'S THE BASIC WORD CASSUS FETT USED?
AH, YES. LOGISTICS.
"SO MANY NEW RECRUITS. DIFFERENT SPECIES, DIFFERENT ARMORS, DIFFERENT LANGUAGES -- AND NOT ENOUGH TIME TO LEARN OUR WAYS.
"CASSUS FIRST SUGGESTED THAT THE SIMILAR UNIFORMS -- LIKE THE LEGEND OF ROHLAN -- COULD HELP GET CONTROL OF A FORCE THAT HAS GROWN BEYOND CONTROL."
"CONTROL. NOT A VERY MANDALORIAN CONCEPT."
NOT A VERY MANDALORIAN WAR. WOULD I BE HERE IF IT WERE? I'VE NEVER MUCH LIKED THE LOOK OF THE NEO-CRUSADER ARMOR --
-- BUT THE INCREASED ORDER HAS BEEN USEFUL. WE MIGHT EVEN CONQUER THE GALAXY BECAUSE OF IT.
BUT THAT OUT THERE -- THAT IS A DISCOVERY. AND YOU HAD TO GO OFF ON YOUR OWN TO FIND IT. ARE YOU READY TO COME BACK WITH US?
NO. I THINK I HAVE FOUND SOMETHING EVEN MORE AMAZING -- BUT IT WILL REQUIRE MORE TIME TO KNOW FOR SURE.
I KNOW ENOUGH TO BELIEVE YOU, NOW. SO, GO. BUT FIRST --
-- I REQUIRE YOU TO TAKE A NEW SUIT OF ARMOR FROM OUR STORES. "ROHLAN" MUST REMAIN DEAD. FOR MANDALORE.
I'M TELLING YOU, ADMIRAL. WE'VE GOT MORE THAN ENOUGH GROUNDS TO ARREST LORD ADASCA AND TURN HIM OVER TO THE REPUBLIC!

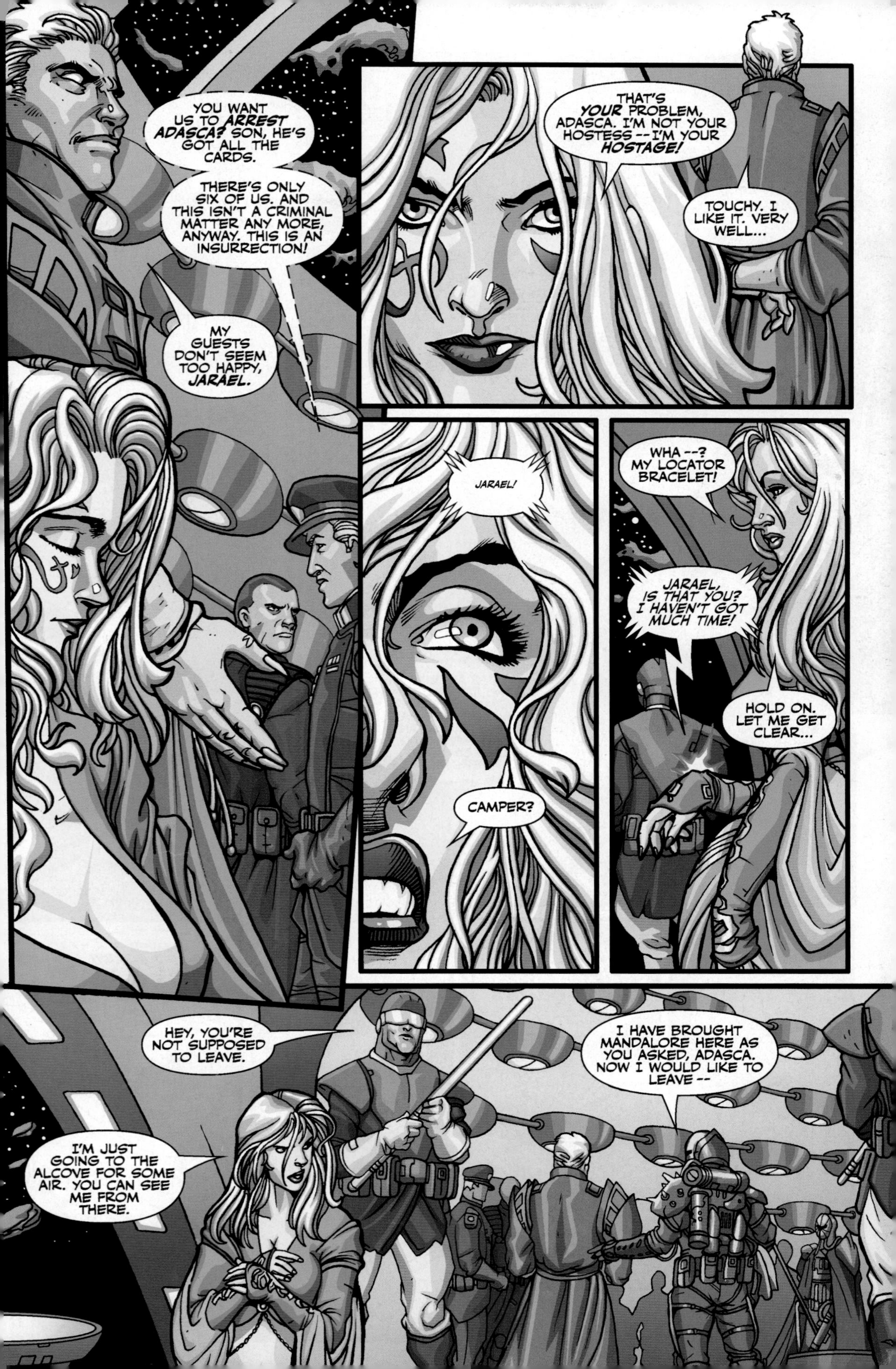
YOU WANT US TO ARREST ADASCA? SON, HE'S GOT ALL THE CARDS.
THERE'S ONLY SIX OF US. AND THIS ISN'T A CRIMINAL MATTER ANY MORE, ANYWAY. THIS IS AN INSURRECTION!
MY GUESTS DON'T SEEM TOO HAPPY, JARAEL.
THAT'S YOUR PROBLEM, ADASCA. I'M NOT YOUR HOSTESS --I'M YOUR HOSTAGE!
TOUCHY. I LIKE IT. VERY WELL...
JARAEL!
CAMPER?
WHA --? MY LOCATOR BRACELET!
JARAEL, IS THAT YOU? I HAVEN'T GOT MUCH TIME!
HOLD ON. LET ME GET CLEAR...
HEY, YOU'RE NOT SUPPOSED TO LEAVE.
I'M JUST GOING TO THE ALCOVE FOR SOME AIR. YOU CAN SEE ME FROM THERE.
I HAVE BROUGHT MANDALORE HERE AS YOU ASKED, ADASCA. NOW I WOULD LIKE TO LEAVE --

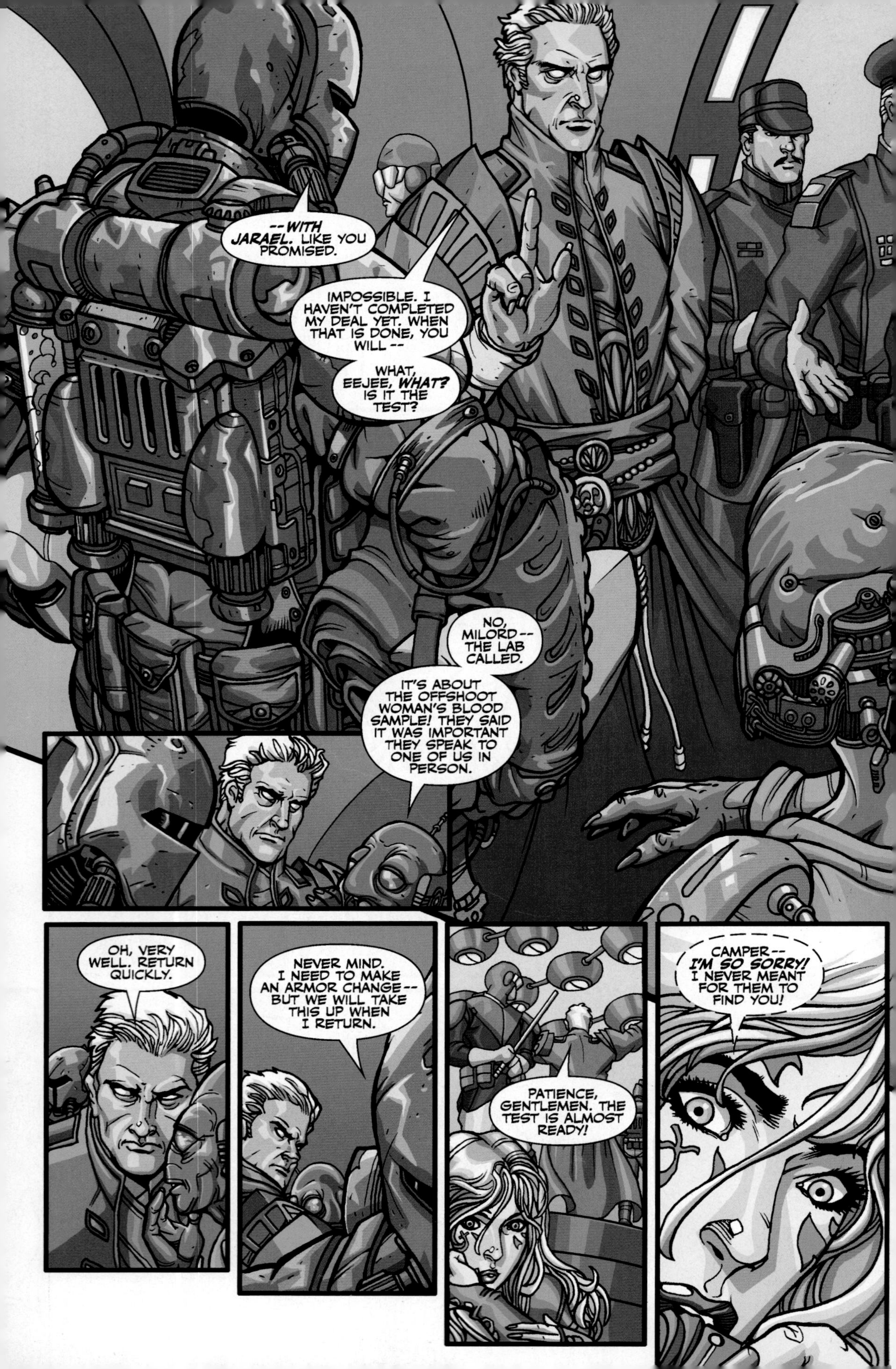
--WITH JARAEL. LIKE YOU PROMISED.
IMPOSSIBLE. I HAVEN'T COMPLETED MY DEAL YET. WHEN THAT IS DONE, YOU WILL --
WHAT, EEJEE, WHAT? IS IT THE TEST?
NO, MILORD-- THE LAB CALLED.
IT'S ABOUT THE OFFSHOOT WOMAN'S BLOOD SAMPLE! THEY SAID IT WAS IMPORTANT THEY SPEAK TO ONE OF US IN PERSON.
OH, VERY WELL. RETURN QUICKLY.
NEVER MIND. I NEED TO MAKE AN ARMOR CHANGE-- BUT WE WILL TAKE THIS UP WHEN I RETURN.
PATIENCE, GENTLEMEN. THE TEST IS ALMOST READY!
CAMPER-- I'M SO SORRY! I NEVER MEANT FOR THEM TO FIND YOU!

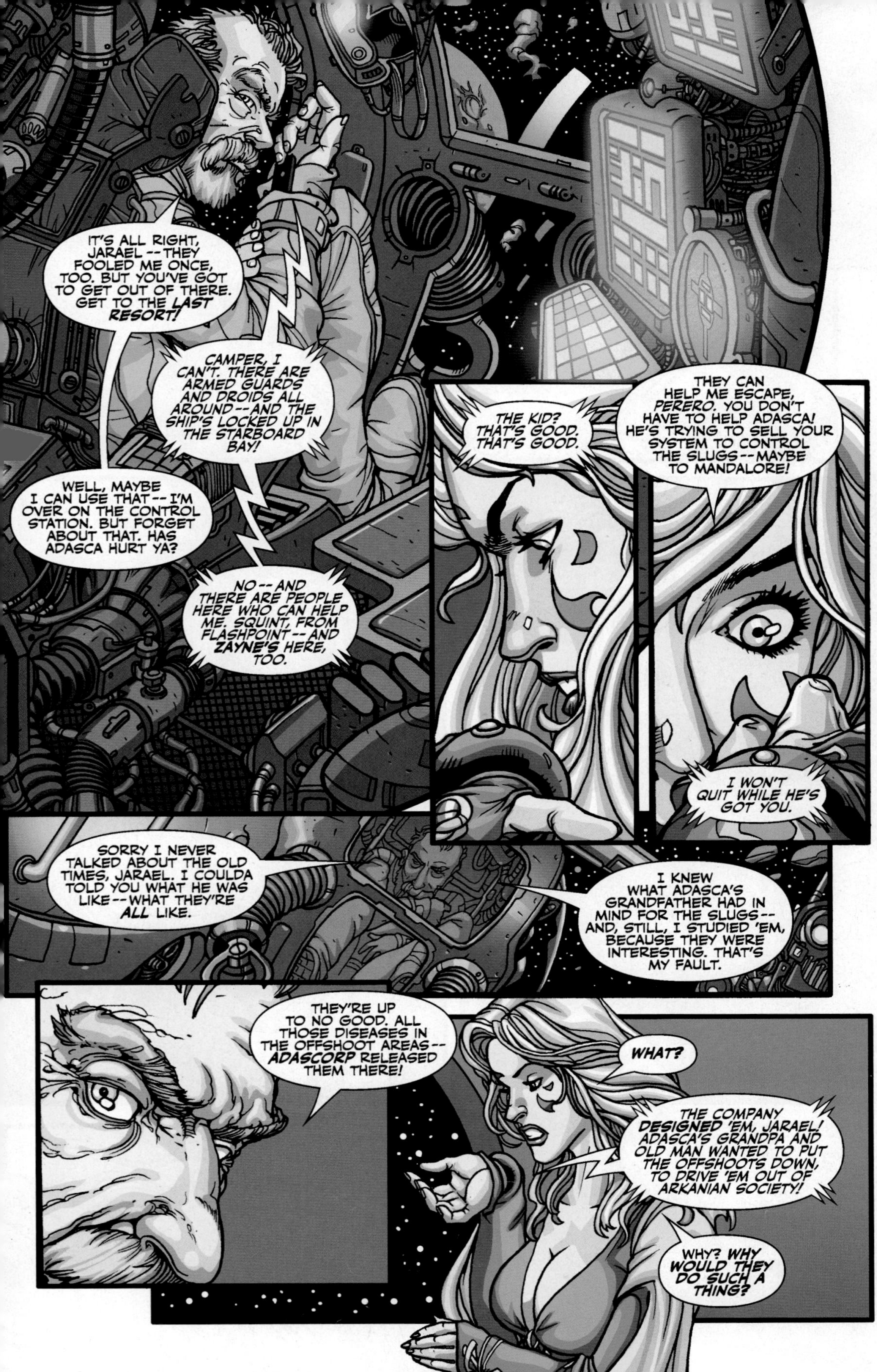
IT'S ALL RIGHT, JARAEL -- THEY FOOLED ME ONCE, TOO. BUT YOU'VE GOT TO GET OUT OF THERE. GET TO THE LAST RESORT!
CAMPER, I CAN'T. THERE ARE ARMED GUARDS AND DROIDS ALL AROUND -- AND THE SHIP'S LOCKED UP IN THE STARBOARD BAY!
WELL, MAYBE I CAN USE THAT -- I'M OVER ON THE CONTROL STATION. BUT FORGET ABOUT THAT. HAS ADASCA HURT YA?
NO -- AND THERE ARE PEOPLE HERE WHO CAN HELP ME. SQUINT, FROM FLASHPOINT -- AND ZAYNE'S HERE, TOO.
THE KID? THAT'S GOOD. THAT'S GOOD.
THEY CAN HELP ME ESCAPE, PERERO. YOU DON'T HAVE TO HELP ADASCA! HE'S TRYING TO SELL YOUR SYSTEM TO CONTROL THE SLUGS -- MAYBE TO MANDALORE!
I WON'T QUIT WHILE HE'S GOT YOU.
SORRY I NEVER TALKED ABOUT THE OLD TIMES, JARAEL. I COULDA TOLD YOU WHAT HE WAS LIKE -- WHAT THEY'RE ALL LIKE.
I KNEW WHAT ADASCA'S GRANDFATHER HAD IN MIND FOR THE SLUGS -- AND, STILL, I STUDIED 'EM, BECAUSE THEY WERE INTERESTING. THAT'S MY FAULT.
THEY'RE UP TO NO GOOD. ALL THOSE DISEASES IN THE OFFSHOOT AREAS -- ADASCORP RELEASED THEM THERE!
WHAT?
THE COMPANY DESIGNED 'EM, JARAEL! ADASCA'S GRANDPA AND OLD MAN WANTED TO PUT THE OFFSHOOTS DOWN, TO DRIVE 'EM OUT OF ARKANIAN SOCIETY!
WHY? WHY WOULD THEY DO SUCH A THING?

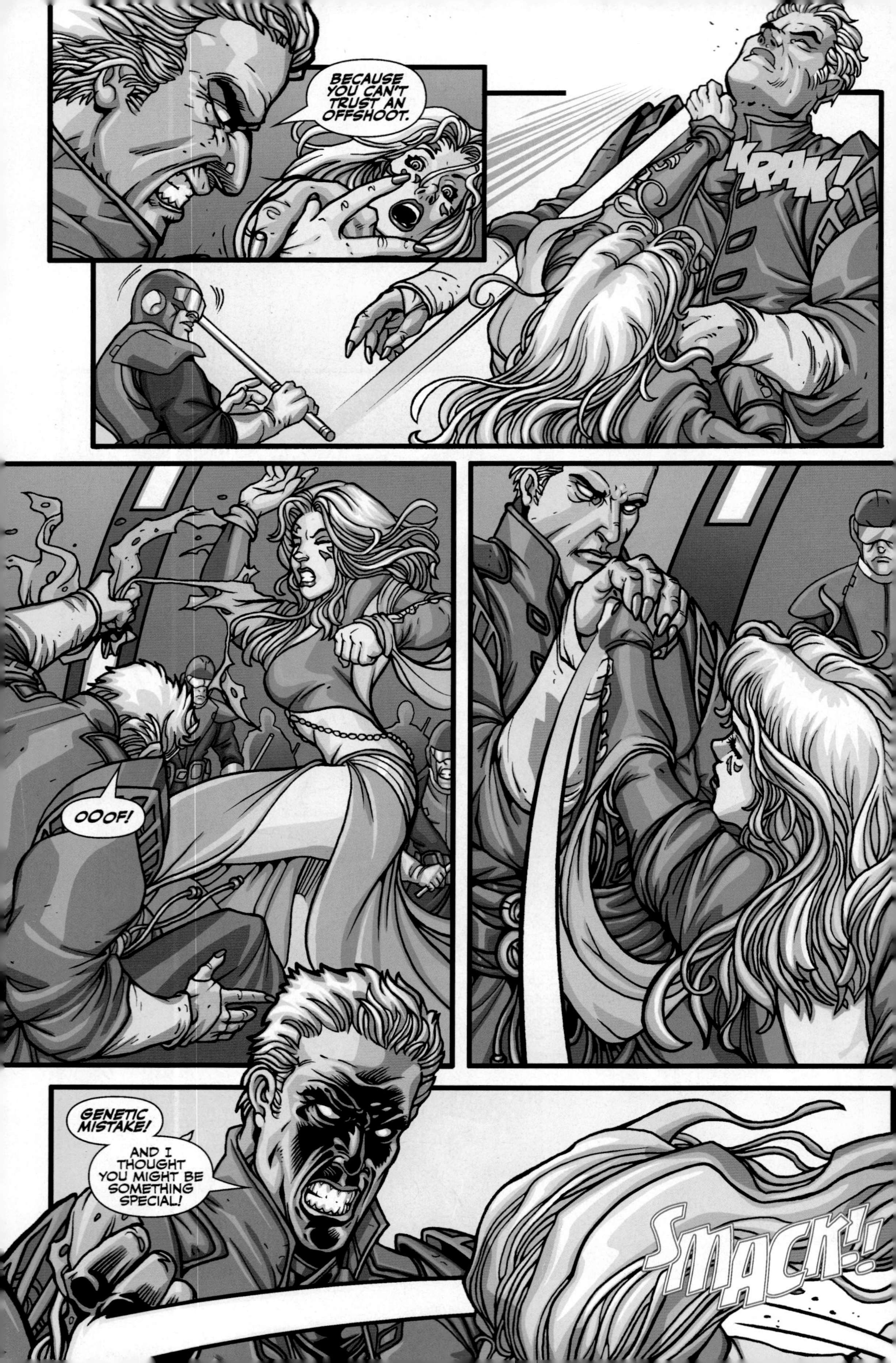
BECAUSE YOU CAN'T TRUST AN OFFSHOOT.
KRAK!
OOOF!
GENETIC MISTAKE!
AND I THOUGHT YOU MIGHT BE SOMETHING SPECIAL!
SMACK!!

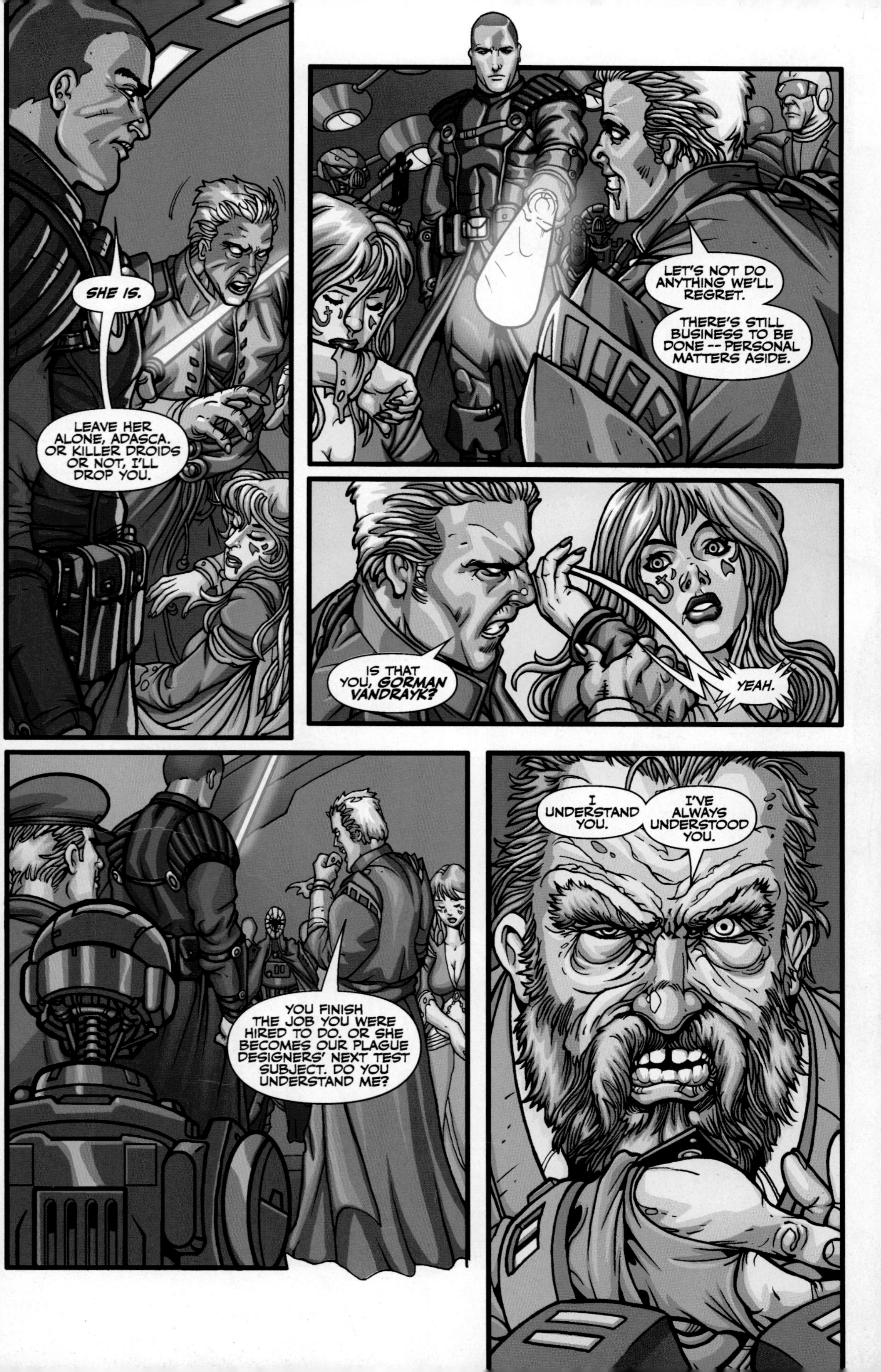
SHE IS.
LEAVE HER ALONE, ADASCA. OR KILLER DROIDS OR NOT, I'LL DROP YOU.
LET'S NOT DO ANYTHING WE'LL REGRET.
THERE'S STILL BUSINESS TO BE DONE -- PERSONAL MATTERS ASIDE.
IS THAT YOU, GORMAN VANDRAYK?
YEAH.
YOU FINISH THE JOB YOU WERE HIRED TO DO. OR SHE BECOMES OUR PLAGUE DESIGNERS' NEXT TEST SUBJECT. DO YOU UNDERSTAND ME?
I UNDERSTAND YOU.
I'VE ALWAYS UNDERSTOOD YOU.

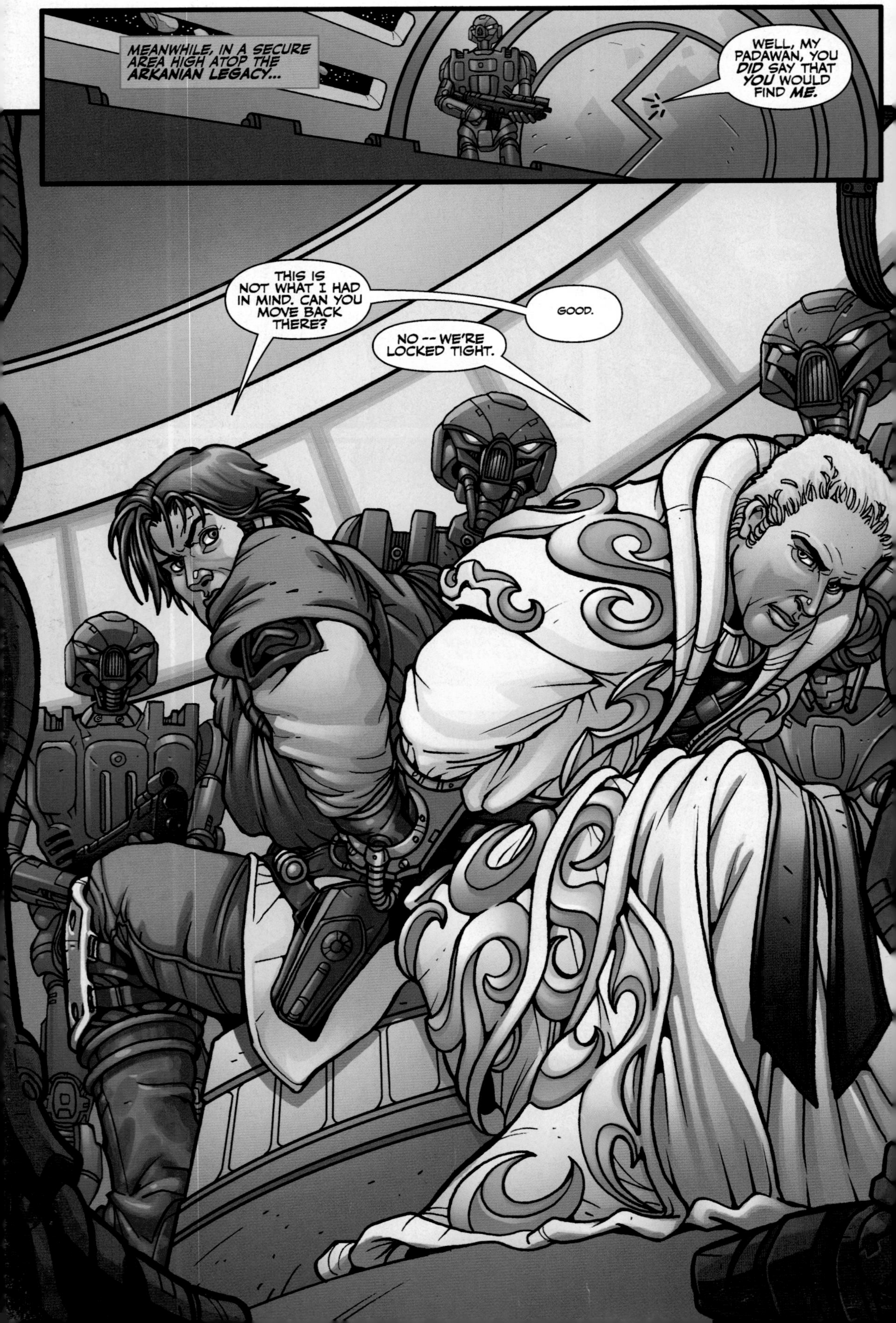
MEANWHILE, IN A SECURE AREA HIGH ATOP THE ARKANIAN LEGACY...
WELL, MY PADAWAN, YOU DID SAY THAT YOU WOULD FIND ME.
THIS IS NOT WHAT I HAD IN MIND. CAN YOU MOVE BACK THERE?
GOOD.
NO -- WE'RE LOCKED TIGHT.

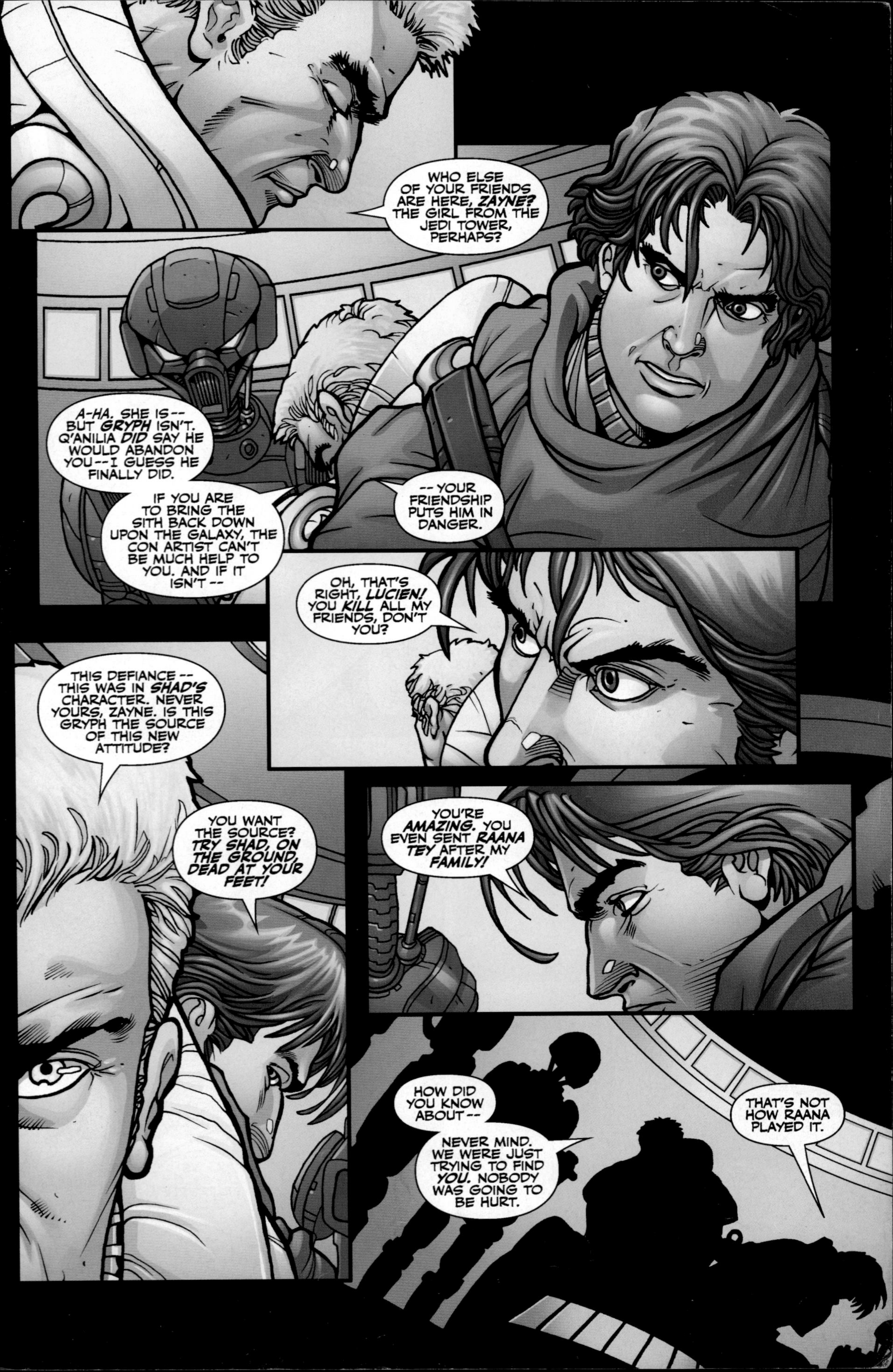
WHO ELSE OF YOUR FRIENDS ARE HERE, ZAYNE? THE GIRL FROM THE JEDI TOWER, PERHAPS?
A-HA. SHE IS-- BUT GRYPH ISN'T. Q'ANILIA DID SAY HE WOULD ABANDON YOU--I GUESS HE FINALLY DID.
IF YOU ARE TO BRING THE SITH BACK DOWN UPON THE GALAXY, THE CON ARTIST CAN'T BE MUCH HELP TO YOU. AND IF IT ISN'T --
-- YOUR FRIENDSHIP PUTS HIM IN DANGER.
OH, THAT'S RIGHT, LUCIEN! YOU KILL ALL MY FRIENDS, DON'T YOU?
THIS DEFIANCE -- THIS WAS IN SHAD'S CHARACTER. NEVER YOURS, ZAYNE. IS THIS GRYPH THE SOURCE OF THIS NEW ATTITUDE?
YOU WANT THE SOURCE? TRY SHAD, ON THE GROUND, DEAD AT YOUR FEET!
YOU'RE AMAZING. YOU EVEN SENT RAANA TEY AFTER MY FAMILY!
HOW DID YOU KNOW ABOUT --
NEVER MIND. WE WERE JUST TRYING TO FIND YOU. NOBODY WAS GOING TO BE HURT.
THAT'S NOT HOW RAANA PLAYED IT.

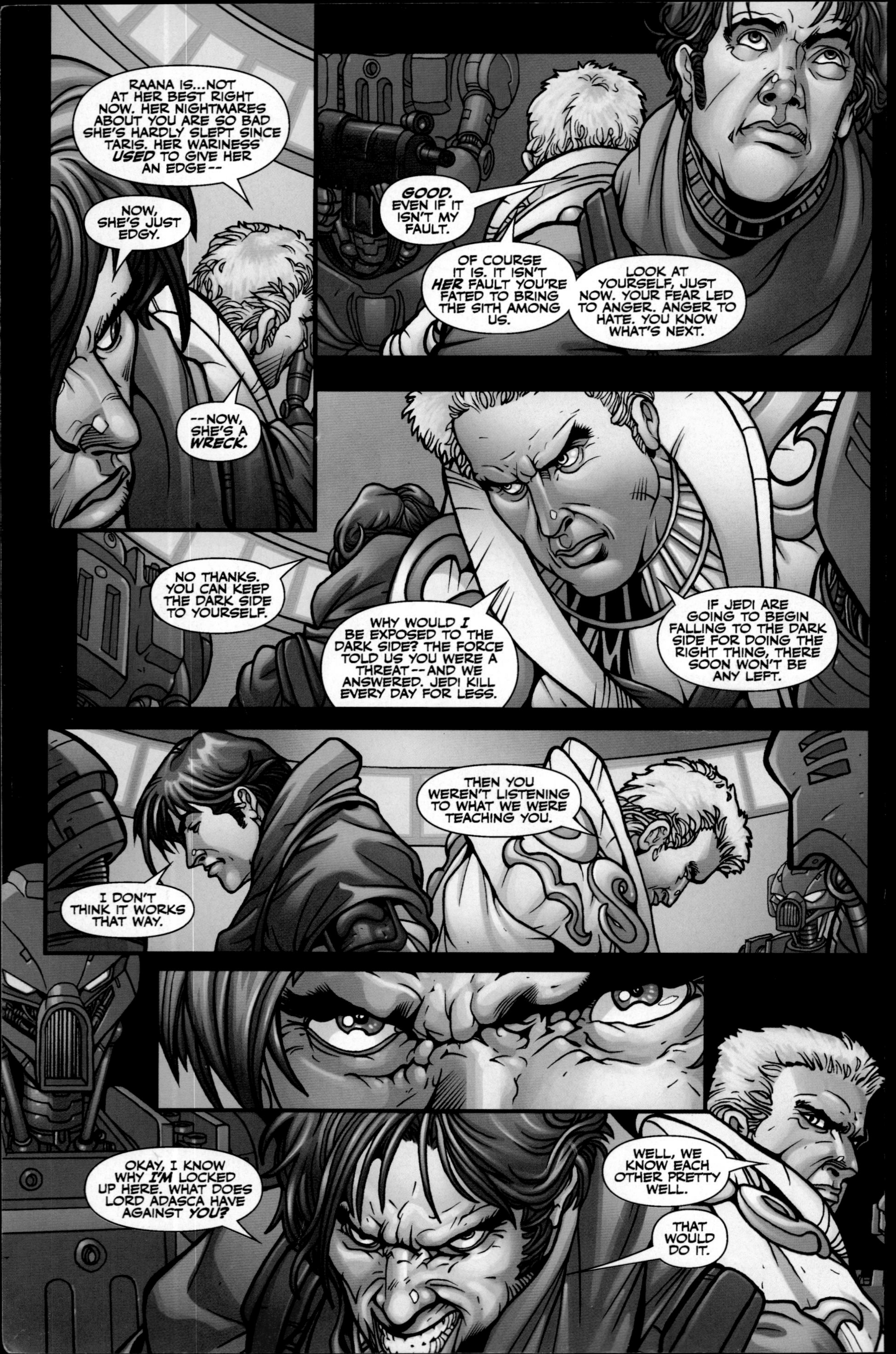
RAANA IS...NOT AT HER BEST RIGHT NOW. HER NIGHTMARES ABOUT YOU ARE SO BAD SHE'S HARDLY SLEPT SINCE TARIS. HER WARINESS *USED* TO GIVE HER AN EDGE--
NOW, SHE'S JUST EDGY.
--NOW, SHE'S A *WRECK.*
GOOD. EVEN IF IT ISN'T MY FAULT.
OF COURSE IT IS. IT ISN'T *HER* FAULT YOU'RE FATED TO BRING THE SITH AMONG US.
LOOK AT YOURSELF, JUST NOW. YOUR FEAR LED TO ANGER. ANGER TO HATE. YOU KNOW WHAT'S NEXT.
NO THANKS. YOU CAN KEEP THE DARK SIDE TO YOURSELF.
WHY WOULD *I* BE EXPOSED TO THE DARK SIDE? THE FORCE TOLD US YOU WERE A THREAT--AND WE ANSWERED. JEDI KILL EVERY DAY FOR LESS.
IF JEDI ARE GOING TO BEGIN FALLING TO THE DARK SIDE FOR DOING THE RIGHT THING, THERE SOON WON'T BE ANY LEFT.
THEN YOU WEREN'T LISTENING TO WHAT WE WERE TEACHING YOU.
I DON'T THINK IT WORKS THAT WAY.
OKAY, I KNOW WHY *I'M* LOCKED UP HERE. WHAT DOES LORD ADASCA HAVE AGAINST *YOU?*
WELL, WE KNOW EACH OTHER PRETTY WELL.
THAT WOULD DO IT.

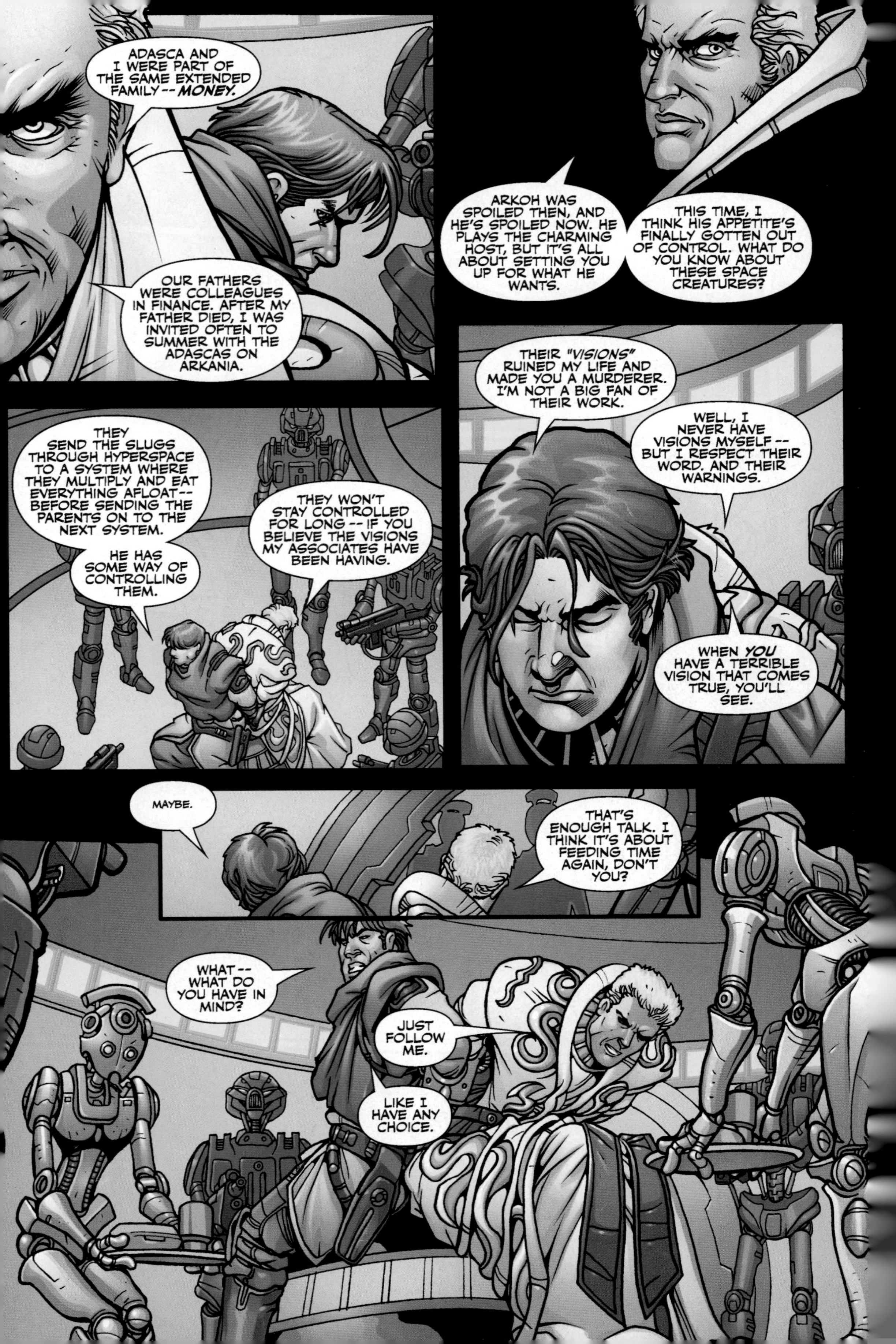
ADASCA AND I WERE PART OF THE SAME EXTENDED FAMILY--MONEY.
OUR FATHERS WERE COLLEAGUES IN FINANCE. AFTER MY FATHER DIED, I WAS INVITED OFTEN TO SUMMER WITH THE ADASCAS ON ARKANIA.
ARKOH WAS SPOILED THEN, AND HE'S SPOILED NOW. HE PLAYS THE CHARMING HOST, BUT IT'S ALL ABOUT SETTING YOU UP FOR WHAT HE WANTS.
THIS TIME, I THINK HIS APPETITE'S FINALLY GOTTEN OUT OF CONTROL. WHAT DO YOU KNOW ABOUT THESE SPACE CREATURES?
THEY SEND THE SLUGS THROUGH HYPERSPACE TO A SYSTEM WHERE THEY MULTIPLY AND EAT EVERYTHING AFLOAT--BEFORE SENDING THE PARENTS ON TO THE NEXT SYSTEM.
HE HAS SOME WAY OF CONTROLLING THEM.
THEY WON'T STAY CONTROLLED FOR LONG--IF YOU BELIEVE THE VISIONS MY ASSOCIATES HAVE BEEN HAVING.
THEIR "VISIONS" RUINED MY LIFE AND MADE YOU A MURDERER. I'M NOT A BIG FAN OF THEIR WORK.
WELL, I NEVER HAVE VISIONS MYSELF--BUT I RESPECT THEIR WORD. AND THEIR WARNINGS.
WHEN YOU HAVE A TERRIBLE VISION THAT COMES TRUE, YOU'LL SEE.
MAYBE.
THAT'S ENOUGH TALK. I THINK IT'S ABOUT FEEDING TIME AGAIN, DON'T YOU?
WHAT--WHAT DO YOU HAVE IN MIND?
JUST FOLLOW ME.
LIKE I HAVE ANY CHOICE.

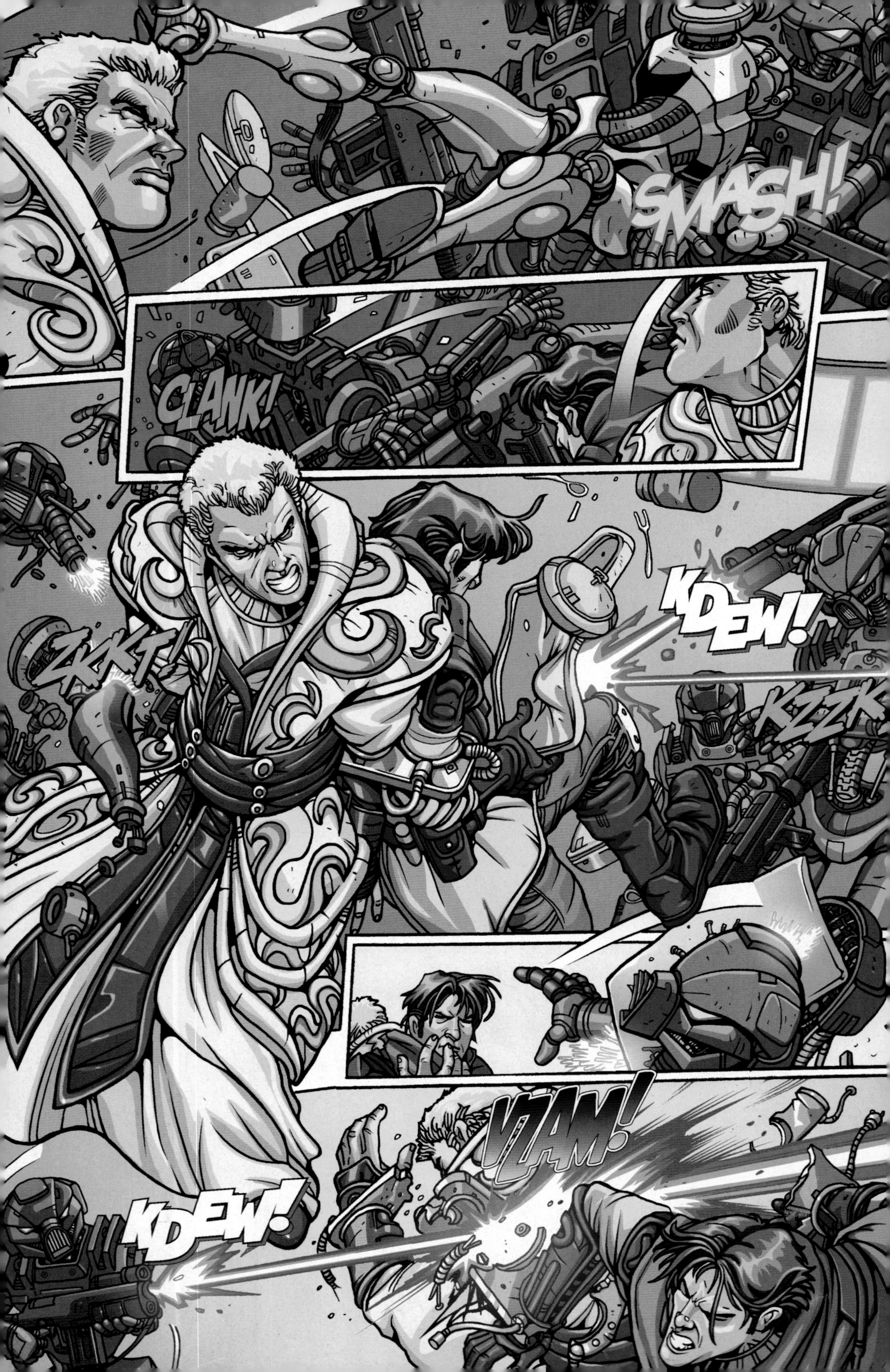
SMASH!
CLANK!
KDEW!
ZKKT
KZZK
VZAM!
KDEW!

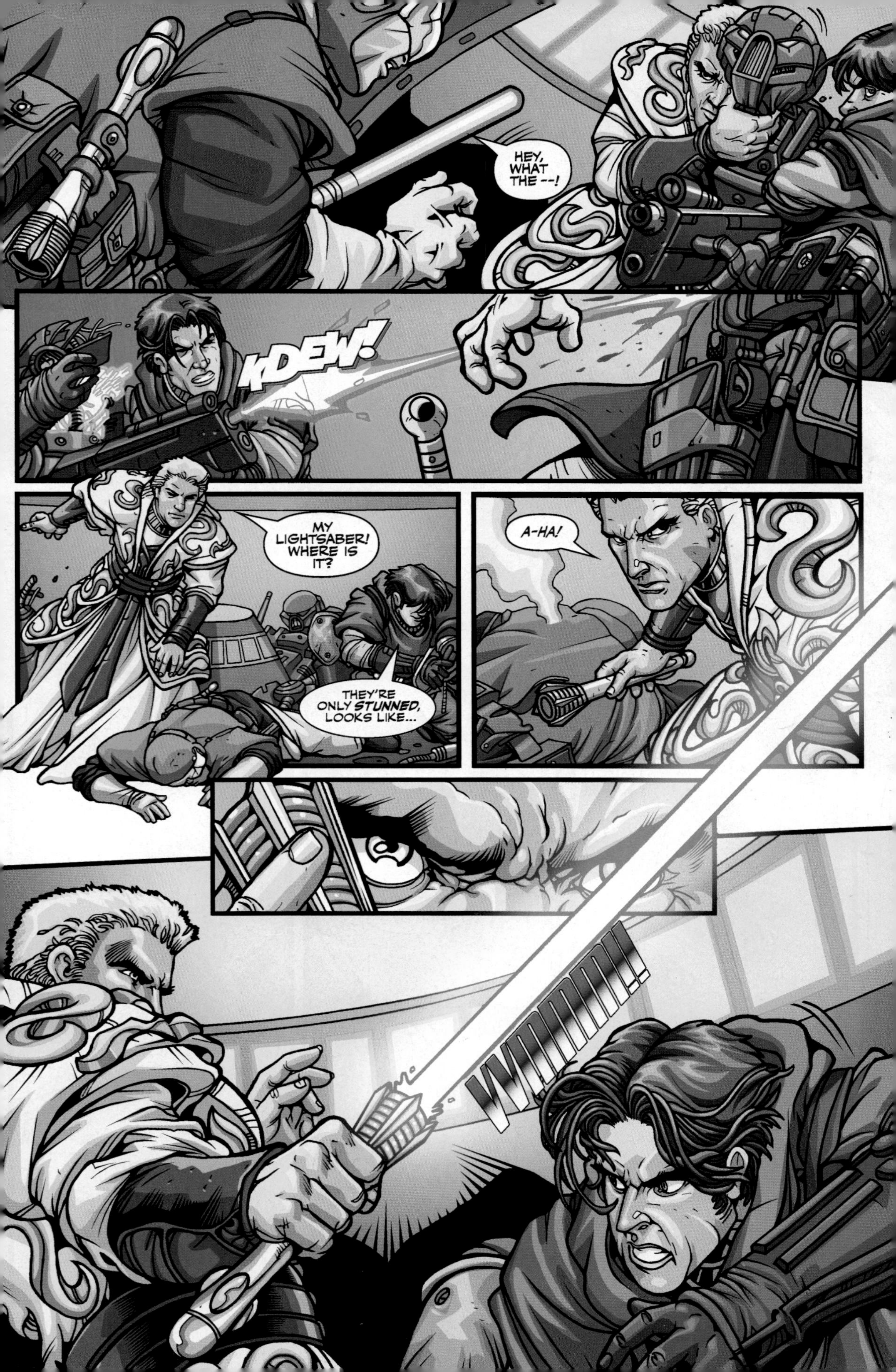
HEY, WHAT THE --!
KDEW!
MY LIGHTSABER! WHERE IS IT?
THEY'RE ONLY STUNNED, LOOKS LIKE...
A-HA!
VVMMM!!

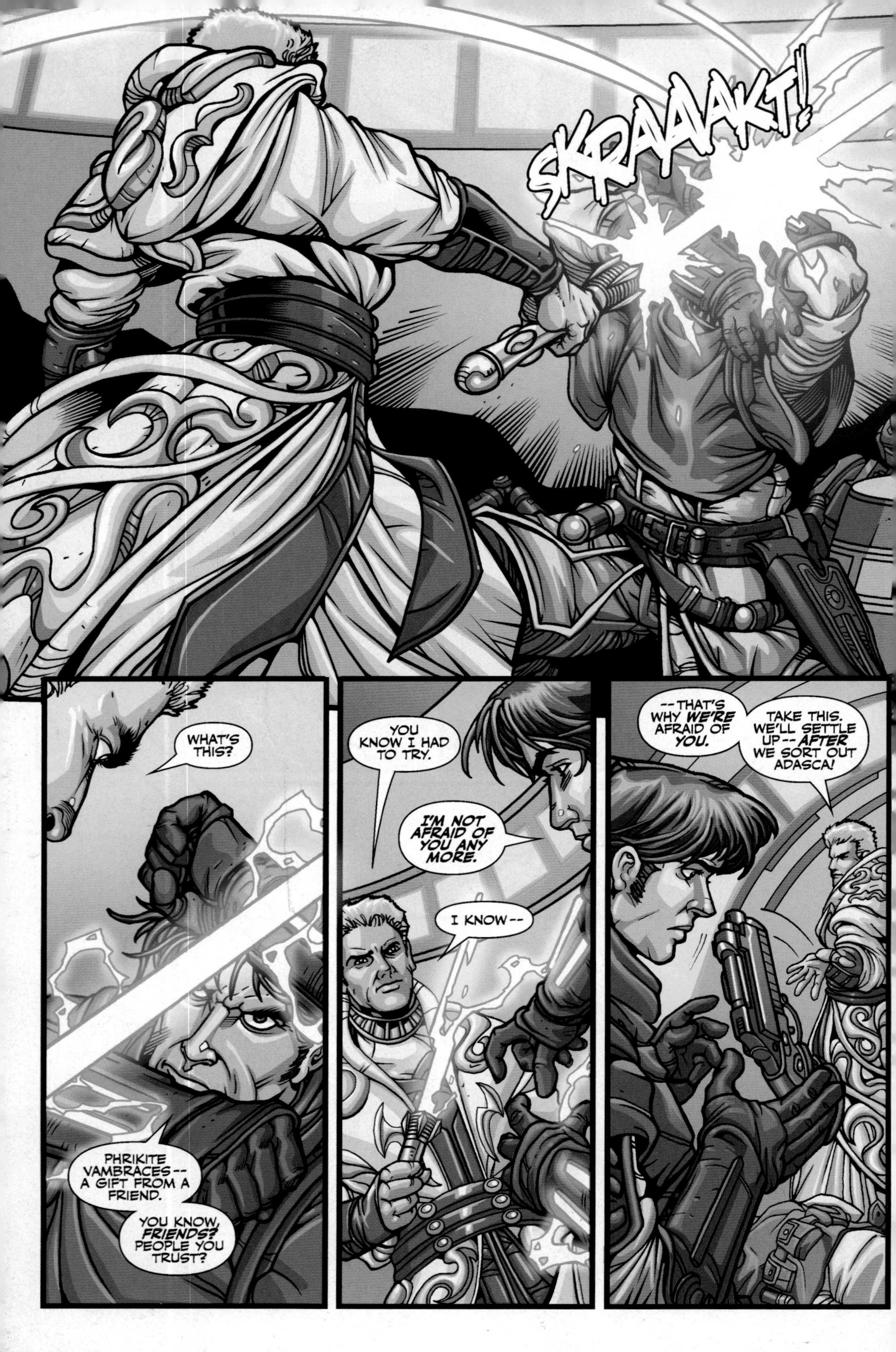
SKRAAAKT!
WHAT'S THIS?
PHRIKITE VAMBRACES-- A GIFT FROM A FRIEND.
YOU KNOW, FRIENDS? PEOPLE YOU TRUST?
YOU KNOW I HAD TO TRY.
I'M NOT AFRAID OF YOU ANY MORE.
I KNOW--
--THAT'S WHY WE'RE AFRAID OF YOU.
TAKE THIS. WE'LL SETTLE UP--AFTER WE SORT OUT ADASCA!

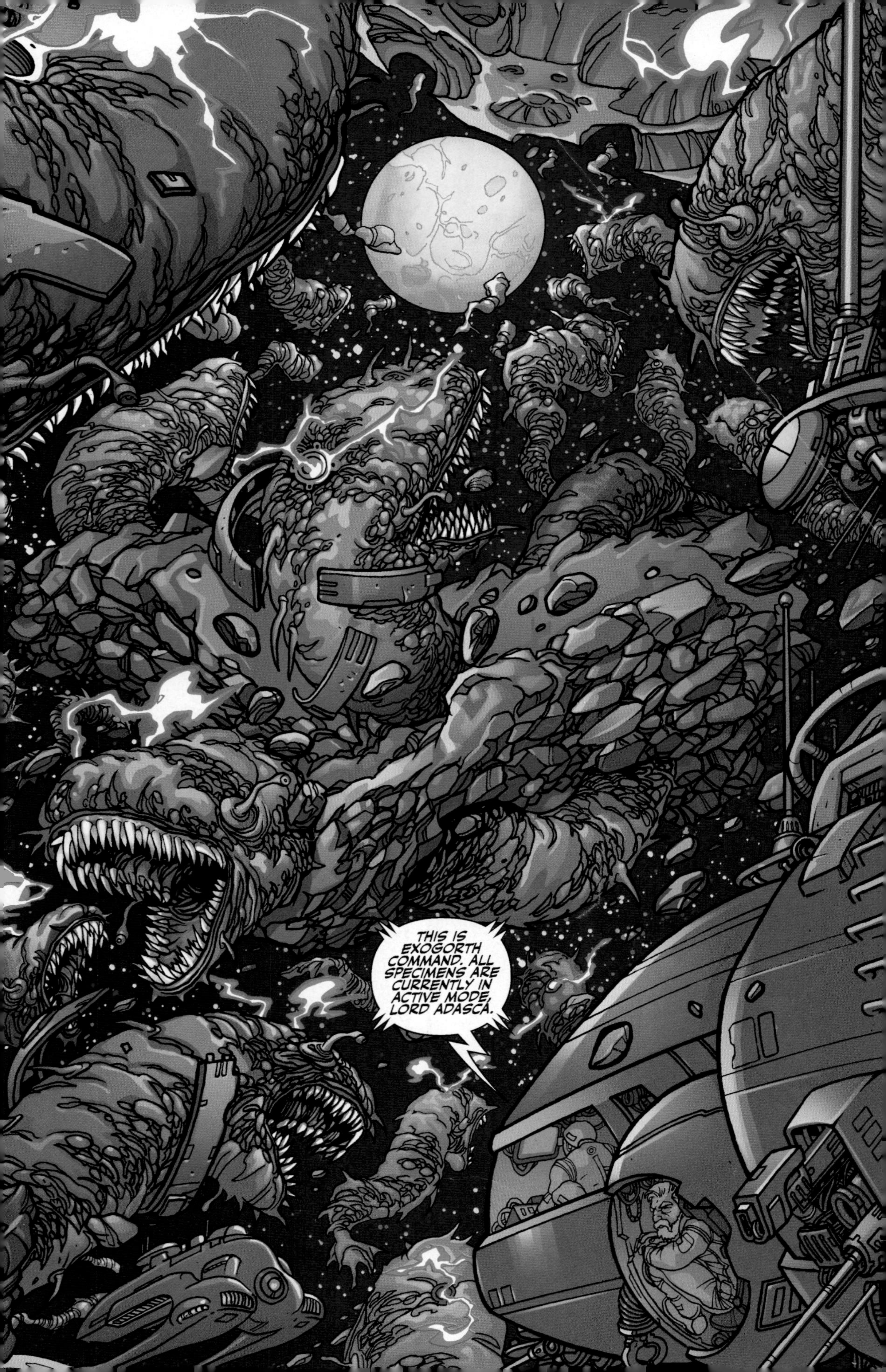
THIS IS EXOGORTH COMMAND. ALL SPECIMENS ARE CURRENTLY IN ACTIVE MODE, LORD ADASCA.

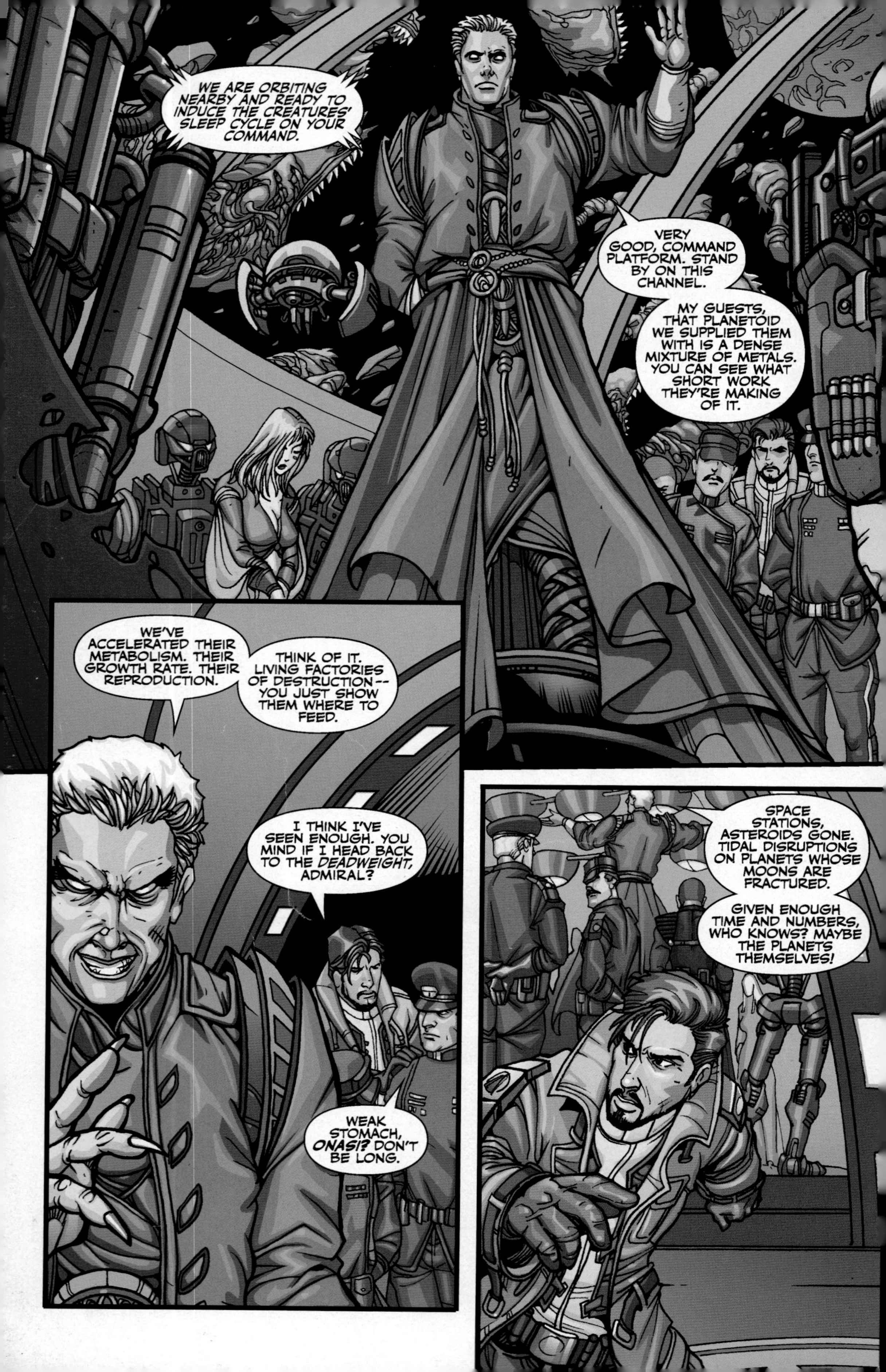
WE ARE ORBITING NEARBY AND READY TO INDUCE THE CREATURES' SLEEP CYCLE ON YOUR COMMAND.
VERY GOOD, COMMAND PLATFORM. STAND BY ON THIS CHANNEL.
MY GUESTS, THAT PLANETOID WE SUPPLIED THEM WITH IS A DENSE MIXTURE OF METALS. YOU CAN SEE WHAT SHORT WORK THEY'RE MAKING OF IT.
WE'VE ACCELERATED THEIR METABOLISM. THEIR GROWTH RATE. THEIR REPRODUCTION.
THINK OF IT. LIVING FACTORIES OF DESTRUCTION-- YOU JUST SHOW THEM WHERE TO FEED.
I THINK I'VE SEEN ENOUGH. YOU MIND IF I HEAD BACK TO THE *DEADWEIGHT*, ADMIRAL?
WEAK STOMACH, ***ONASI?*** DON'T BE LONG.
SPACE STATIONS, ASTEROIDS GONE. TIDAL DISRUPTIONS ON PLANETS WHOSE MOONS ARE FRACTURED.
GIVEN ENOUGH TIME AND NUMBERS, WHO KNOWS? MAYBE THE PLANETS THEMSELVES!

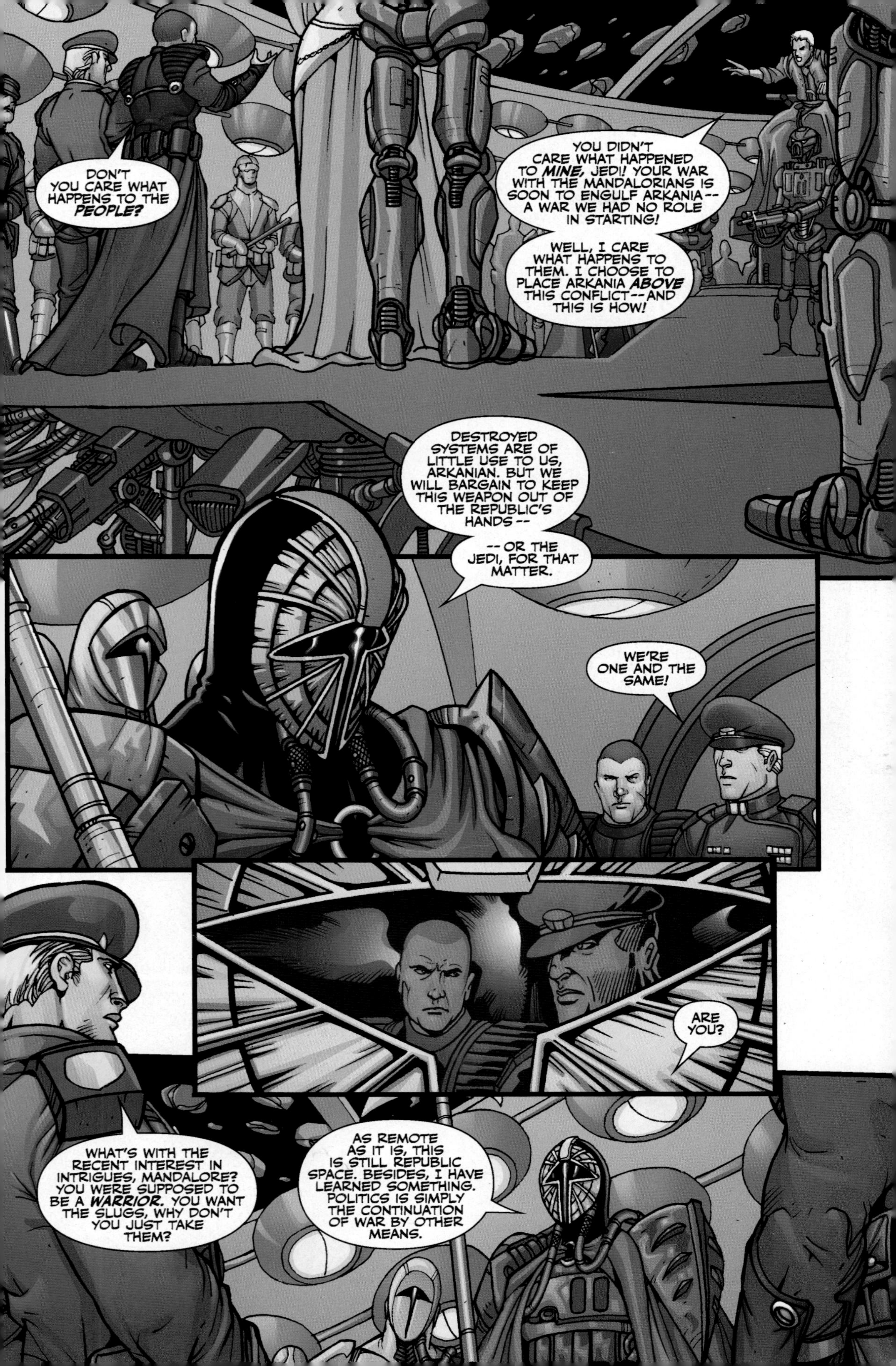
DON'T YOU CARE WHAT HAPPENS TO THE *PEOPLE?*
YOU DIDN'T CARE WHAT HAPPENED TO *MINE,* JEDI! YOUR WAR WITH THE MANDALORIANS IS SOON TO ENGULF ARKANIA-- A WAR WE HAD NO ROLE IN STARTING!
WELL, I CARE WHAT HAPPENS TO THEM. I CHOOSE TO PLACE ARKANIA *ABOVE* THIS CONFLICT--AND THIS IS HOW!
DESTROYED SYSTEMS ARE OF LITTLE USE TO US, ARKANIAN. BUT WE WILL BARGAIN TO KEEP THIS WEAPON OUT OF THE REPUBLIC'S HANDS--
--OR THE JEDI, FOR THAT MATTER.
WE'RE ONE AND THE SAME!
ARE YOU?
WHAT'S WITH THE RECENT INTEREST IN INTRIGUES, MANDALORE? YOU WERE SUPPOSED TO BE A *WARRIOR.* YOU WANT THE SLUGS, WHY DON'T YOU JUST TAKE THEM?
AS REMOTE AS IT IS, THIS IS STILL REPUBLIC SPACE. BESIDES, I HAVE LEARNED SOMETHING. POLITICS IS SIMPLY THE CONTINUATION OF WAR BY OTHER MEANS.

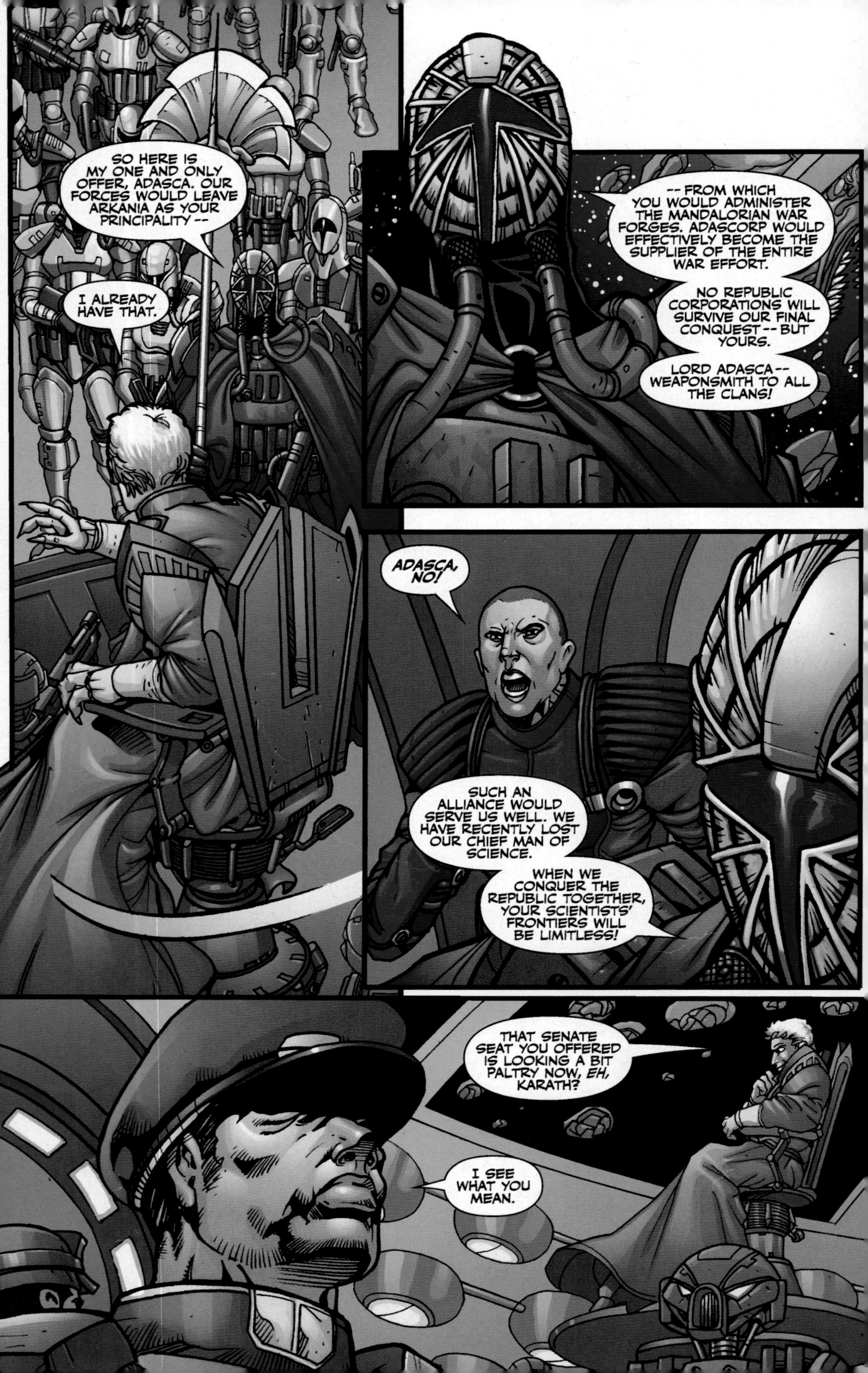
SO HERE IS MY ONE AND ONLY OFFER, ADASCA. OUR FORCES WOULD LEAVE ARKANIA AS YOUR PRINCIPALITY --
I ALREADY HAVE THAT.
-- FROM WHICH YOU WOULD ADMINISTER THE MANDALORIAN WAR FORGES. ADASCORP WOULD EFFECTIVELY BECOME THE SUPPLIER OF THE ENTIRE WAR EFFORT.
NO REPUBLIC CORPORATIONS WILL SURVIVE OUR FINAL CONQUEST -- BUT YOURS.
LORD ADASCA -- WEAPONSMITH TO ALL THE CLANS!
ADASCA, NO!
SUCH AN ALLIANCE WOULD SERVE US WELL. WE HAVE RECENTLY LOST OUR CHIEF MAN OF SCIENCE.
WHEN WE CONQUER THE REPUBLIC TOGETHER, YOUR SCIENTISTS' FRONTIERS WILL BE LIMITLESS!
THAT SENATE SEAT YOU OFFERED IS LOOKING A BIT PALTRY NOW, *EH,* KARATH?
I SEE WHAT YOU MEAN.

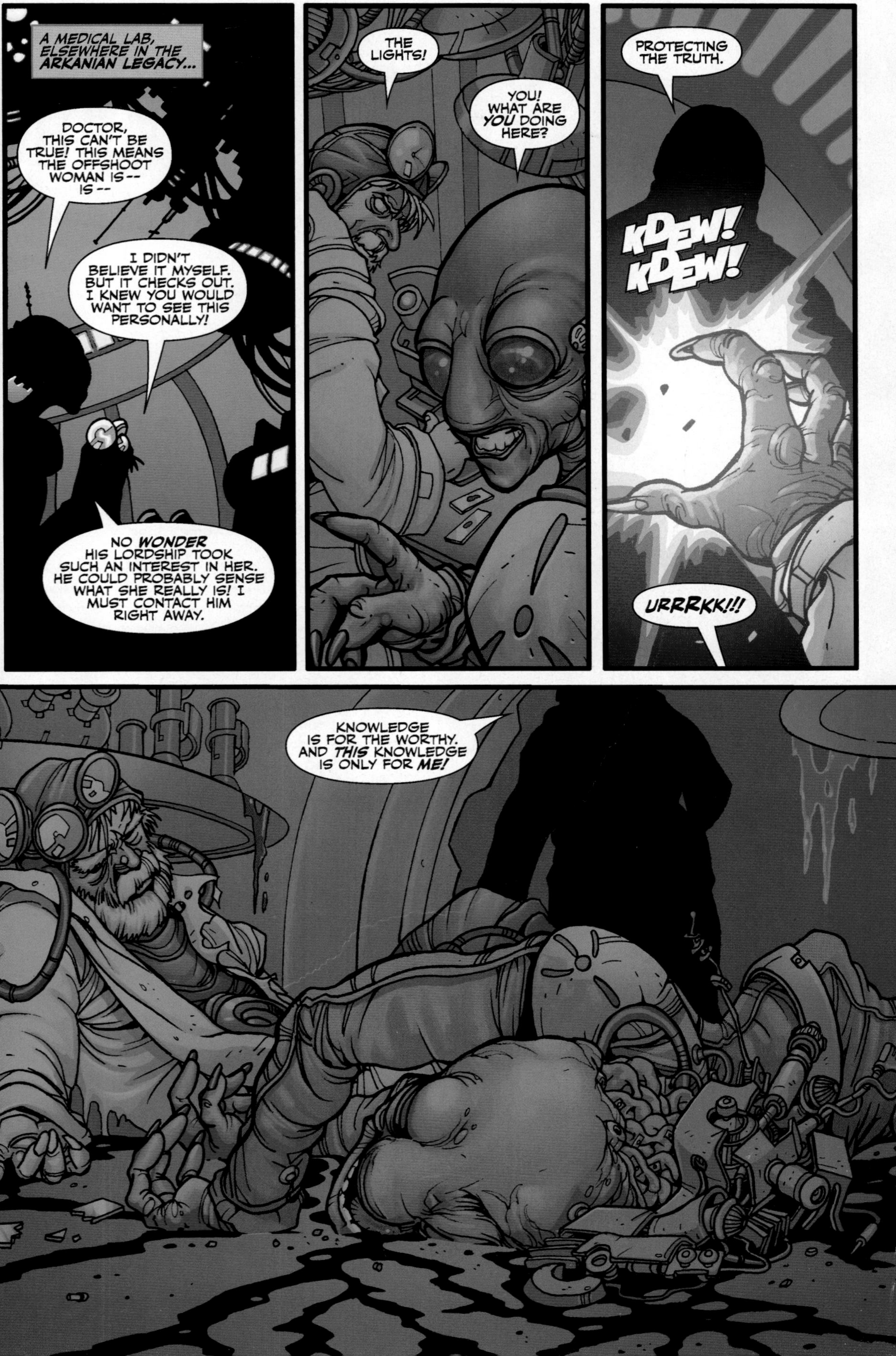
A MEDICAL LAB, ELSEWHERE IN THE ARKANIAN LEGACY...
DOCTOR, THIS CAN'T BE TRUE! THIS MEANS THE OFFSHOOT WOMAN IS -- IS --
I DIDN'T BELIEVE IT MYSELF. BUT IT CHECKS OUT. I KNEW YOU WOULD WANT TO SEE THIS PERSONALLY!
NO WONDER HIS LORDSHIP TOOK SUCH AN INTEREST IN HER. HE COULD PROBABLY SENSE WHAT SHE REALLY IS! I MUST CONTACT HIM RIGHT AWAY.
THE LIGHTS!
YOU! WHAT ARE YOU DOING HERE?
PROTECTING THE TRUTH.
KDEW! KDEW!
URRRKK!!!
KNOWLEDGE IS FOR THE WORTHY. AND THIS KNOWLEDGE IS ONLY FOR ME!

THE ADJUDICATOR

The Freelance Security Professional's Holofeed

Special Report: Tools of the Trade

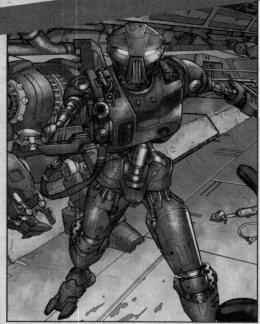

KRAV'S HOT LIST

They're hot—and they're worth a lot!

Some biggies have come off the board, I'm afraid . . .

Marn Hierogryph

Bounties: Seven, totaling 24,000 credits
Wanted for: Accomplice to murder, treason, racketeering, fraud

Still trying to find out if Zayne Carrick really did go down with the *Courageous*—if so, this little guy is all that's left of the Padawan Massacrers. Massacrees? Whatever. Last spotted on Ralltiir.

Kelven Garnatrope

Bounties: Four, totaling 43,000 credits
Wanted for: Murder

Well, there's a picture, finally, but I'm not trusting the witnesses. I mean, come on! How can *he* be the "Corellian Strangler"? You'd hear him splashing around before he snuck up on you!

SELECT to continue list...

AVOID THE DROID

Leave bounty hunting to the organics
By KRAV NOBLIS, *Adjudicator* Editor

I hate droids. Is that okay? Can I say that without getting hate messages from some "Be Nice to Your Appliance" association? But I only hate *specific* droids—those that take jobs away from hard-working security pros.

I hear you—"droids are just another tool of the trade." They can serve as armed backup for a smart bounty hunter—and they rarely moan about their cut. My gripe is with this latest wave of "autonomous" droids—whose goal-seeking programs seem calculated to seek my livelihood!

A while back, I decided to go out and have a look for that high-priced artifact, Baron Hyro Margryph. No sooner did I hit the Inner Rim than I'm up to my fuzzy pointed ears in HK-24 droids, apparently all out on the same assignment!

Then all of a sudden, they canceled the bounty—made me sick to think of all that money going to waste. As Zax the Hutt used to say, an oil bath and a pat on the shiny head ought to do it for a droid! But then word on the street suggested something else. These buckets of bolts were wholly owned by the customer issuing the bounty—someone's way of doing an end-run around the trade!

I'm still working on finding out who it was, but I know one thing—it wasn't such a hot deal. My guy at Czerka tells me the company was only too happy to unload the -24 units—an experiment gone wrong, he says. They're just autonomous enough to resent the blazes out of the existence of other units just like them. Maybe they're reducing each other to scrap metal even now.

Fine by me. One-off "hunter-killers" I can deal with. Now, I may not *want* to . . .

SELECT to learn more...

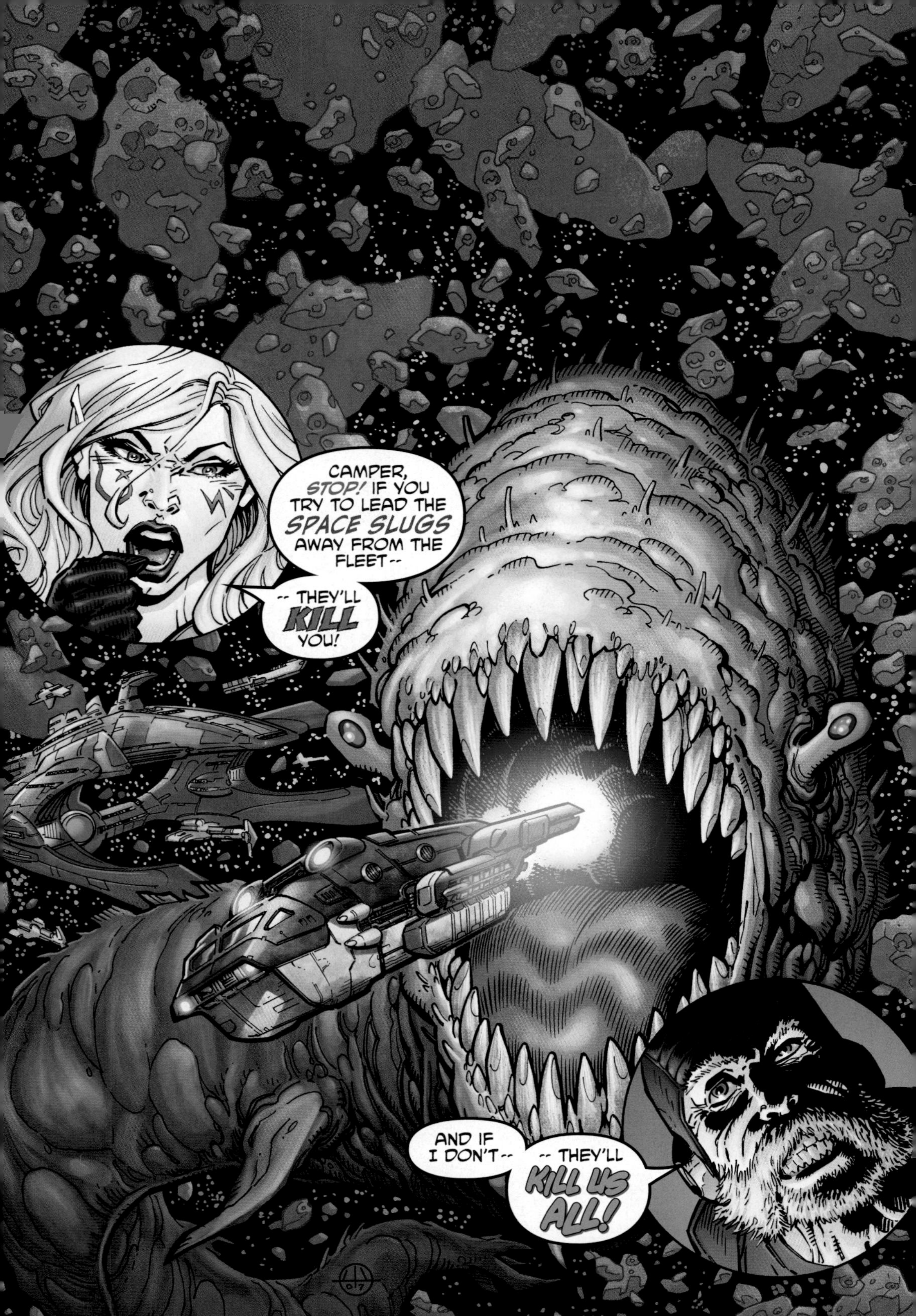
CAMPER, STOP! IF YOU TRY TO LEAD THE SPACE SLUGS AWAY FROM THE FLEET--
-- THEY'LL KILL YOU!
AND IF I DON'T--
-- THEY'LL KILL US ALL!

STAR WARS: KNIGHTS OF THE OLD REPUBLIC #21 — "DAZE OF HATE, PART 3"

WRITER: JOHN JACKSON MILLER • ARTIST: BONG DAZO • COLORIST: MICHAEL ATIYEH • LETTERER: MICHAEL HEISLER
ASSISTANT EDITOR: DAVE MARSHALL • EDITOR: JEREMY BARLOW • COVER ARTISTS: CHRIS WARNER & MICHAEL ATIYEH

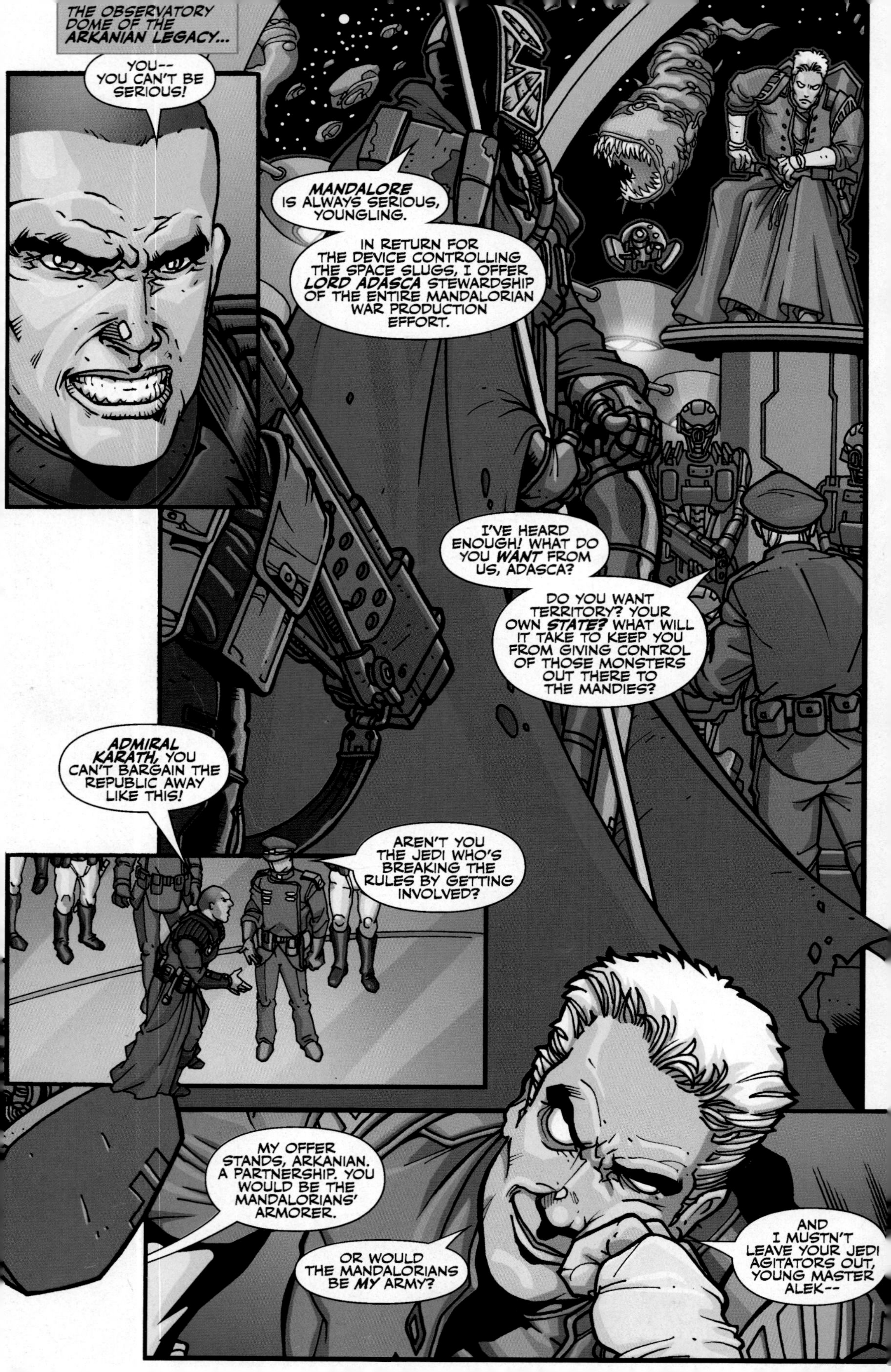
THE OBSERVATORY DOME OF THE ARKANIAN LEGACY...
YOU-- YOU CAN'T BE SERIOUS!
MANDALORE IS ALWAYS SERIOUS, YOUNGLING.
IN RETURN FOR THE DEVICE CONTROLLING THE SPACE SLUGS, I OFFER LORD ADASCA STEWARDSHIP OF THE ENTIRE MANDALORIAN WAR PRODUCTION EFFORT.
I'VE HEARD ENOUGH! WHAT DO YOU WANT FROM US, ADASCA?
DO YOU WANT TERRITORY? YOUR OWN STATE? WHAT WILL IT TAKE TO KEEP YOU FROM GIVING CONTROL OF THOSE MONSTERS OUT THERE TO THE MANDIES?
ADMIRAL KARATH, YOU CAN'T BARGAIN THE REPUBLIC AWAY LIKE THIS!
AREN'T YOU THE JEDI WHO'S BREAKING THE RULES BY GETTING INVOLVED?
MY OFFER STANDS, ARKANIAN. A PARTNERSHIP. YOU WOULD BE THE MANDALORIANS' ARMORER.
OR WOULD THE MANDALORIANS BE MY ARMY?
AND I MUSTN'T LEAVE YOUR JEDI AGITATORS OUT, YOUNG MASTER ALEK--

-- MAYBE I COULD USE MY OWN JEDI ORDER, TOO!

HE'S NOT HERE FOR THE JEDI ORDER. HE'S DEALING FOR HIS SO-CALLED MASTER -- FOR THE *REVANCHISTS.*

MANDALORIANS! ARKOH ADASCA, YOU *HAVE* GONE MAD!

WAIT A MINUTE. THAT'S *SQUINT* IN THERE! COULD THE *JEDI* HAVE BEEN INVITED TO THIS?

WHATEVER. THEY MUST BE IN THAT OBSERVATORY DOME. WHAT DO WE DO NOW?

I DON'T KNOW. I WASN'T EXPECTING TO GET THIS FAR. SOMETHING MUST HAVE HAPPENED TO ADASCA'S CYBERNETIC AIDE. I --

-- SOMEONE'S COMING!

ZAYNE! I WAS HOPING TO FIND YOU!

CARTH! MAN, I'M GLAD TO SEE YOU -- AND YOU BROUGHT MY *LIGHTSABER!*

I WAS ABLE TO GET YOUR STUFF OFF MY SHIP BEFORE SECURITY STARTED GOING CRAZY.

LIEUTENANT *CARTH ONASI,* BATTLE GROUP SERROCO -- OR WHAT'S LEFT OF IT.

MASTER *LUCIEN DRAAY.*

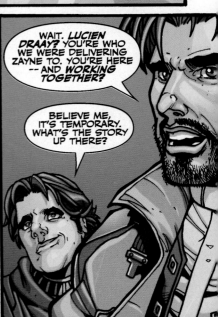

WAIT. *LUCIEN DRAAY?* YOU'RE WHO WE WERE DELIVERING ZAYNE TO. YOU'RE HERE -- AND *WORKING TOGETHER?*

BELIEVE ME, IT'S TEMPORARY. WHAT'S THE STORY UP THERE?

JUST ADASCA BARGAINING FOR HALF THE GALAXY. HE CAN INFEST SYSTEMS WITH THOSE SPACE SLUGS FASTER THAN WE CAN BUILD SHIPS TO TAKE THEM OUT!

IT'S FOR REAL, TOO-- WE JUST SAW A TEST. HE'S GOT AN OPEN CHANNEL TO HIS PEOPLE AT SOME KIND OF CONTROL STATION OUTSIDE THE SHIP.

WAIT. THAT WOMAN! SHE'S THE ONE WHO-- ER, THAT'S THE WOMAN FROM TARIS.

JARAEL!

WHO?

THE GIRL WITH THE WHITE HAIR. HER BEST FRIEND'S CAMPER, AN INVENTOR--

-- THE ONE HELPING THEM TO CONTROL THE SLUGS. SHE TOLD ME THEY'RE FORCING HIM TO DO IT.

THEY MUST BE USING HER AS THEIR HOSTAGE!

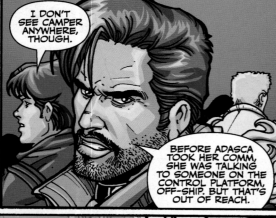

I DON'T SEE CAMPER ANYWHERE, THOUGH.

BEFORE ADASCA TOOK HER COMM, SHE WAS TALKING TO SOMEONE ON THE CONTROL PLATFORM, OFF-SHIP. BUT THAT'S OUT OF REACH.

AH. WE WOULDN'T HAVE TO SAVE HER, THEN. WE'LL JUST KILL HER.

WHAT?

IF SHE DIES, ADASCA'S LEVERAGE IS GONE. IT'S THE SUREST WAY-- AND THE STAKES ARE TOO HIGH FOR ANYTHING ELSE. CAN YOU THINK OF A REASON IT WOULDN'T WORK?

JUST ONE...

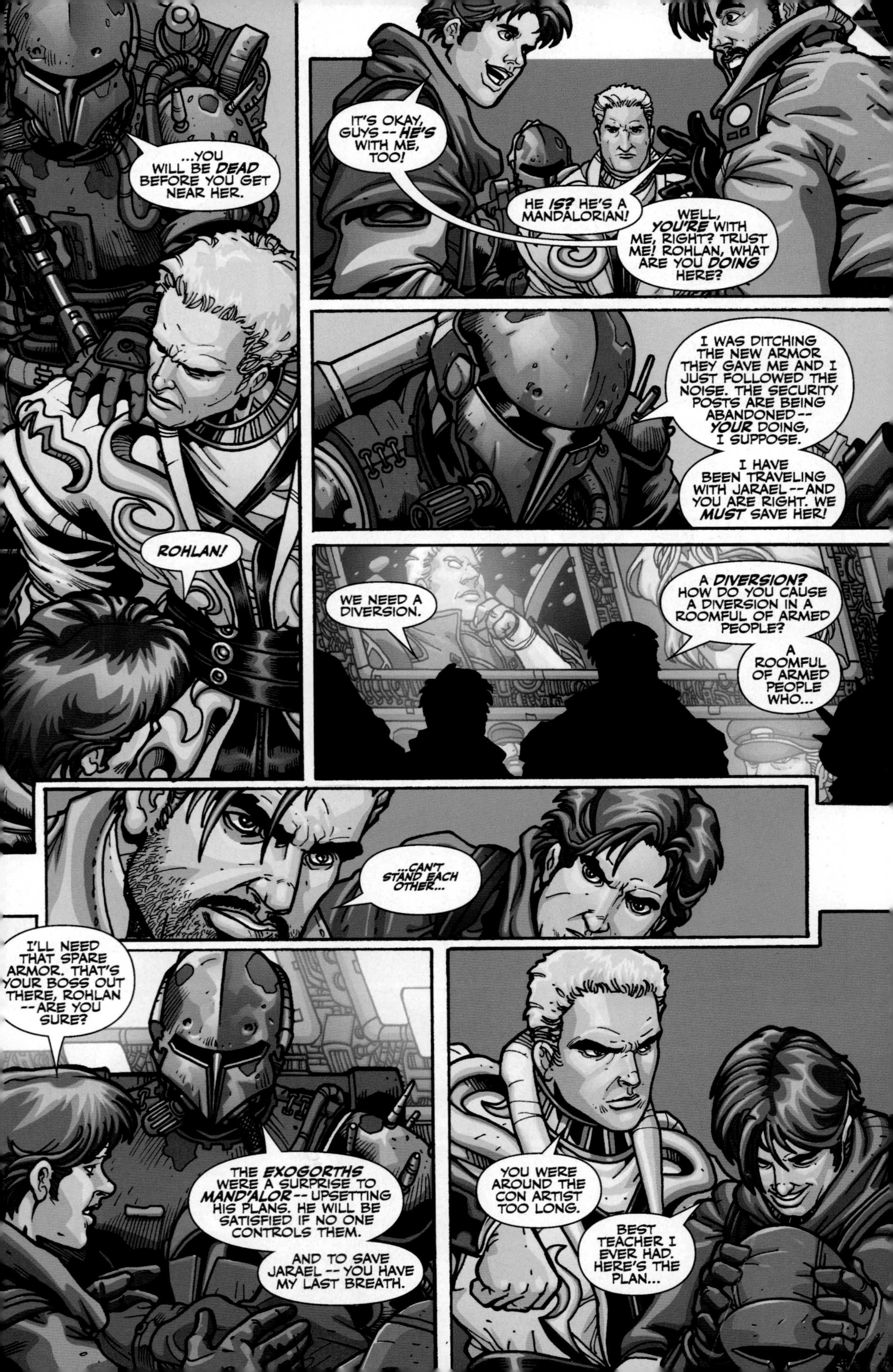
...YOU WILL BE DEAD BEFORE YOU GET NEAR HER.
IT'S OKAY, GUYS -- HE'S WITH ME, TOO!
HE IS? HE'S A MANDALORIAN!
WELL, YOU'RE WITH ME, RIGHT? TRUST ME! ROHLAN, WHAT ARE YOU DOING HERE?
ROHLAN!
I WAS DITCHING THE NEW ARMOR THEY GAVE ME AND I JUST FOLLOWED THE NOISE. THE SECURITY POSTS ARE BEING ABANDONED -- YOUR DOING, I SUPPOSE.
I HAVE BEEN TRAVELING WITH JARAEL -- AND YOU ARE RIGHT. WE MUST SAVE HER!
WE NEED A DIVERSION.
A DIVERSION? HOW DO YOU CAUSE A DIVERSION IN A ROOMFUL OF ARMED PEOPLE?
A ROOMFUL OF ARMED PEOPLE WHO...
...CAN'T STAND EACH OTHER...
I'LL NEED THAT SPARE ARMOR. THAT'S YOUR BOSS OUT THERE, ROHLAN -- ARE YOU SURE?
THE EXOGORTHS WERE A SURPRISE TO MAND'ALOR -- UPSETTING HIS PLANS. HE WILL BE SATISFIED IF NO ONE CONTROLS THEM.
AND TO SAVE JARAEL -- YOU HAVE MY LAST BREATH.
YOU WERE AROUND THE CON ARTIST TOO LONG.
BEST TEACHER I EVER HAD. HERE'S THE PLAN...

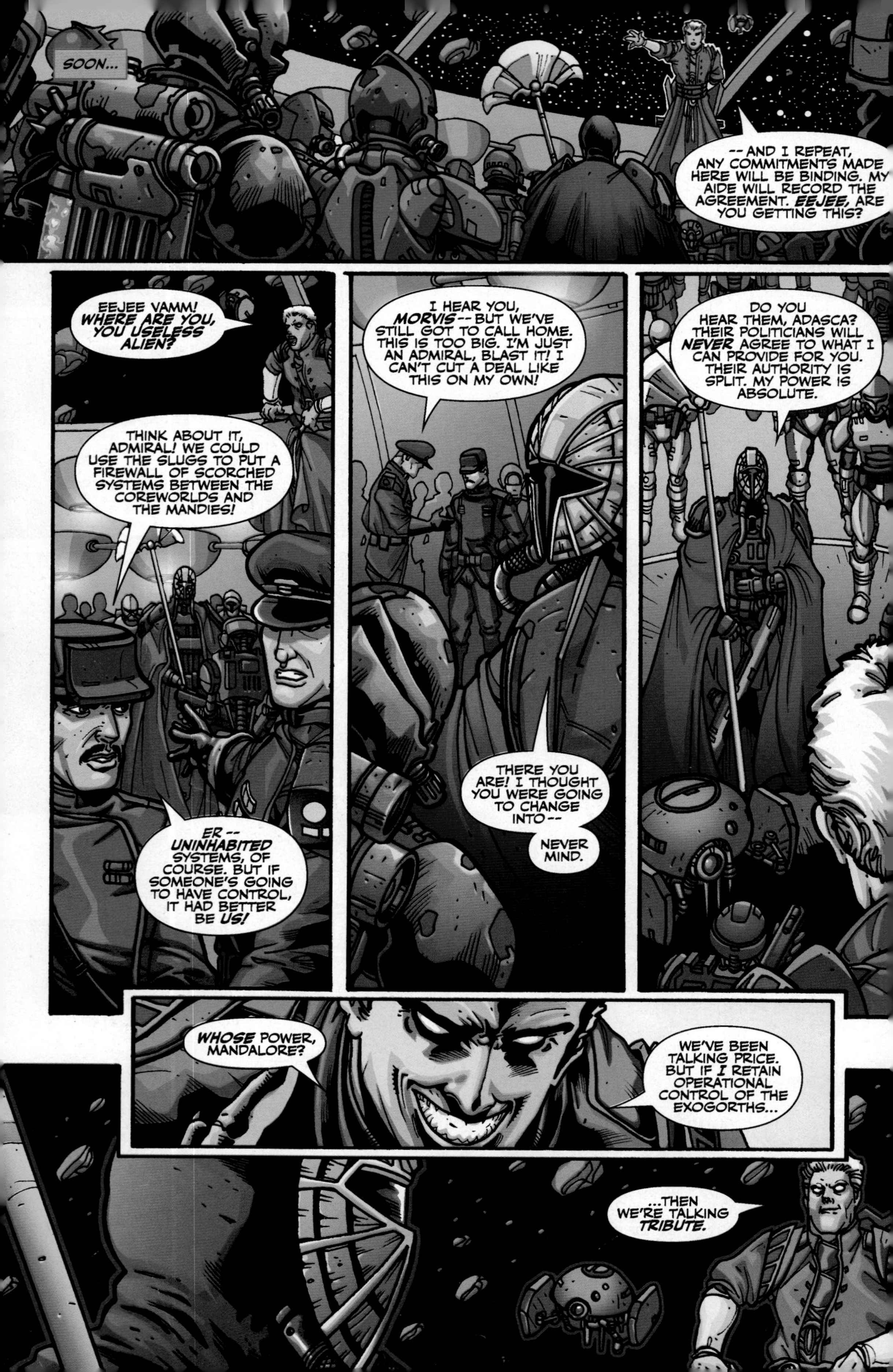
SOON...
--AND I REPEAT, ANY COMMITMENTS MADE HERE WILL BE BINDING. MY AIDE WILL RECORD THE AGREEMENT. EEJEE, ARE YOU GETTING THIS?
EEJEE VAMM! WHERE ARE YOU, YOU USELESS ALIEN?
THINK ABOUT IT, ADMIRAL! WE COULD USE THE SLUGS TO PUT A FIREWALL OF SCORCHED SYSTEMS BETWEEN THE COREWORLDS AND THE MANDIES!
ER -- UNINHABITED SYSTEMS, OF COURSE. BUT IF SOMEONE'S GOING TO HAVE CONTROL, IT HAD BETTER BE US!
I HEAR YOU, MORVIS-- BUT WE'VE STILL GOT TO CALL HOME. THIS IS TOO BIG. I'M JUST AN ADMIRAL, BLAST IT! I CAN'T CUT A DEAL LIKE THIS ON MY OWN!
THERE YOU ARE! I THOUGHT YOU WERE GOING TO CHANGE INTO--
NEVER MIND.
DO YOU HEAR THEM, ADASCA? THEIR POLITICIANS WILL NEVER AGREE TO WHAT I CAN PROVIDE FOR YOU. THEIR AUTHORITY IS SPLIT. MY POWER IS ABSOLUTE.
WHOSE POWER, MANDALORE?
WE'VE BEEN TALKING PRICE. BUT IF I RETAIN OPERATIONAL CONTROL OF THE EXOGORTHS...
...THEN WE'RE TALKING TRIBUTE.

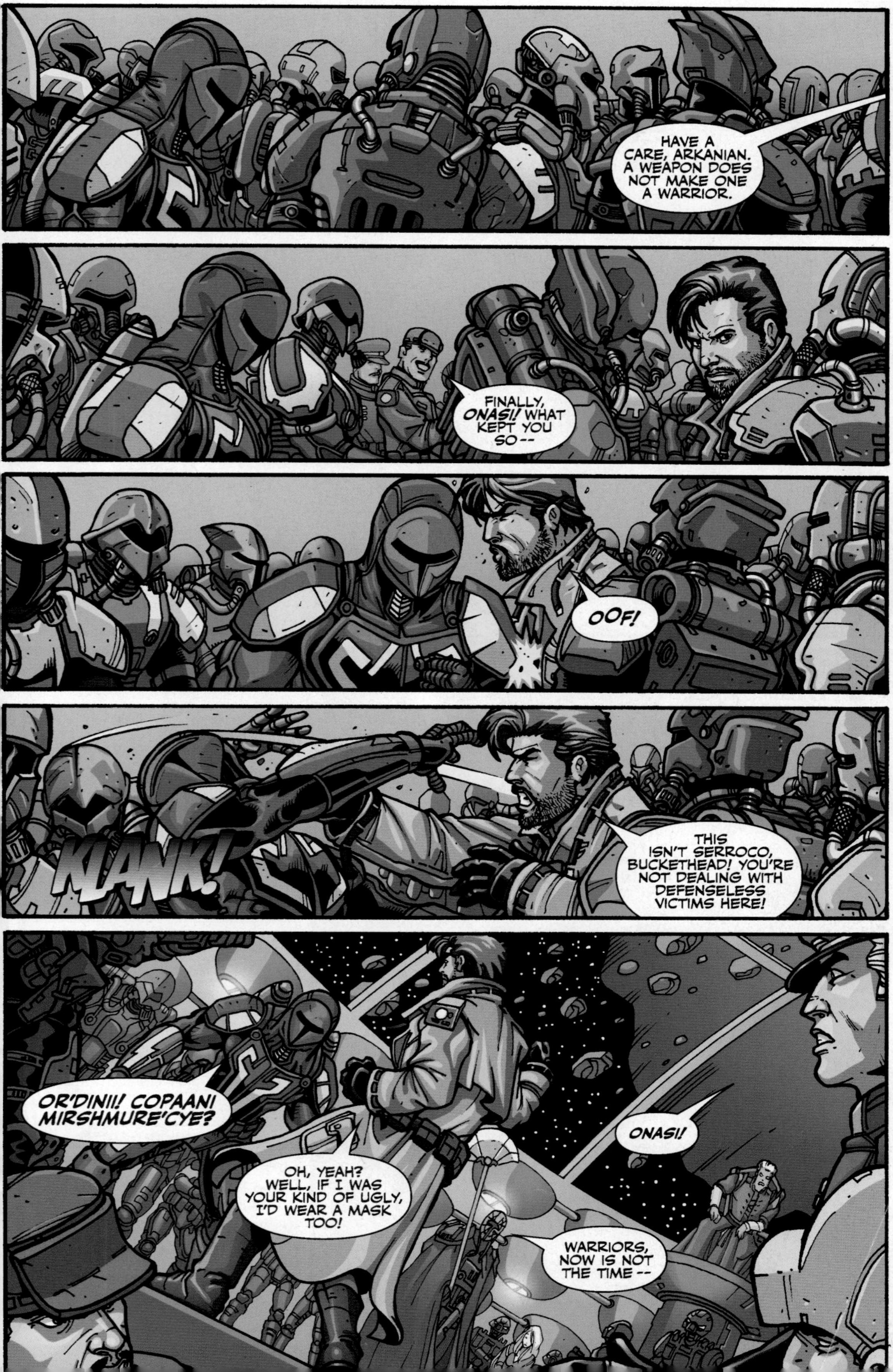
HAVE A CARE, ARKANIAN. A WEAPON DOES NOT MAKE ONE A WARRIOR.
FINALLY, ONASI! WHAT KEPT YOU SO --
OOF!
KLANK!
THIS ISN'T SERROCO, BUCKETHEAD! YOU'RE NOT DEALING WITH DEFENSELESS VICTIMS HERE!
OR'DINII! COPAANI MIRSHMURE'CYE?
OH, YEAH? WELL, IF I WAS YOUR KIND OF UGLY, I'D WEAR A MASK TOO!
ONASI!
WARRIORS, NOW IS NOT THE TIME --

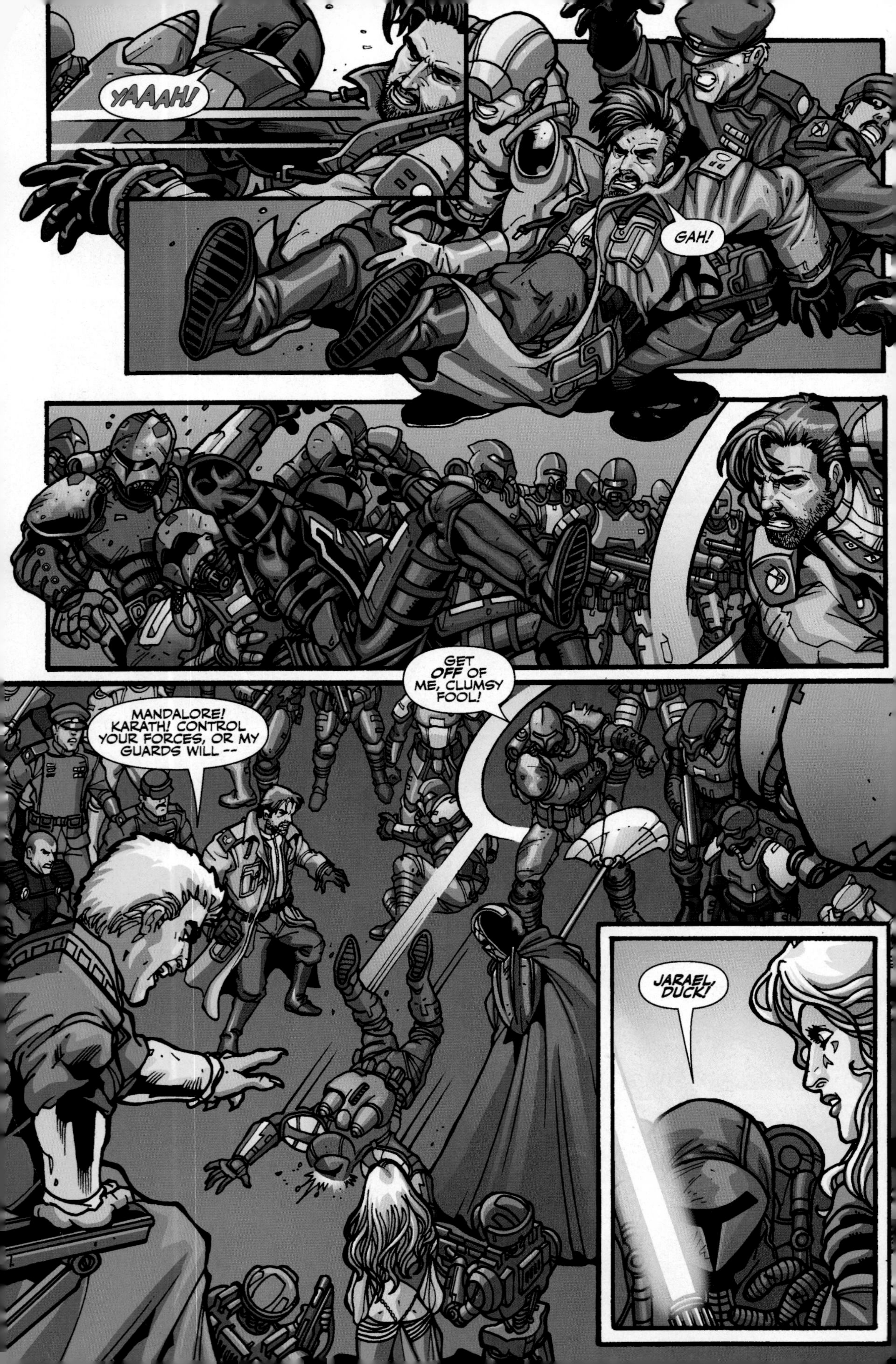
YAAAH!
GAH!
MANDALORE! KARATH! CONTROL YOUR FORCES, OR MY GUARDS WILL --
GET OFF OF ME, CLUMSY FOOL!
JARAEL, DUCK!

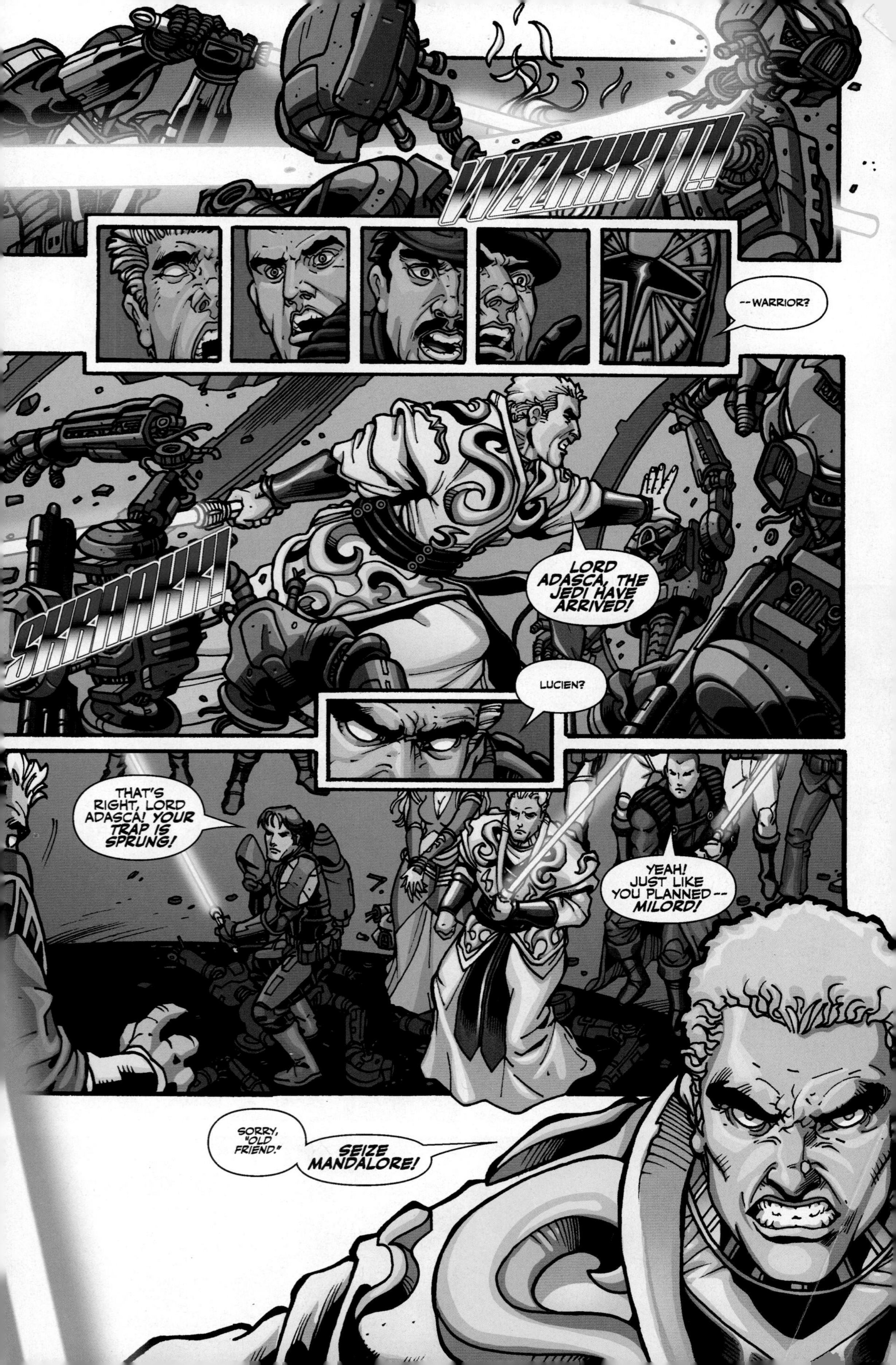

VVZZRKKKTT!!
--WARRIOR?
LORD ADASCA, THE JEDI HAVE ARRIVED!
SKRAAKK!
LUCIEN?
THAT'S RIGHT, LORD ADASCA! YOUR TRAP IS SPRUNG!
YEAH! JUST LIKE YOU PLANNED-- MILORD!
SORRY, "OLD FRIEND."
SEIZE MANDALORE!

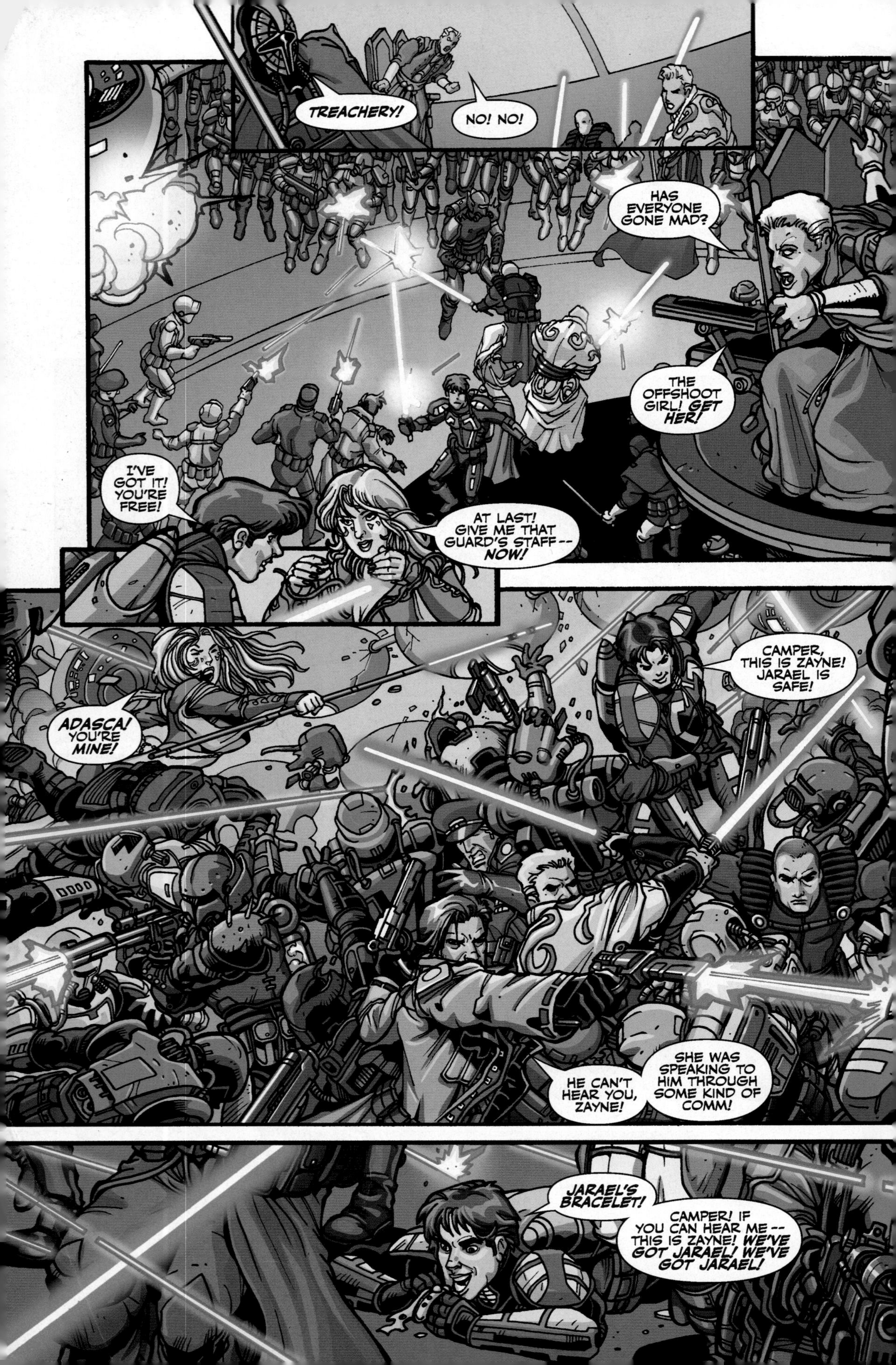
TREACHERY!
NO! NO!
HAS EVERYONE GONE MAD?
THE OFFSHOOT GIRL! GET HER!
I'VE GOT IT! YOU'RE FREE!
AT LAST! GIVE ME THAT GUARD'S STAFF -- NOW!
ADASCA! YOU'RE MINE!
CAMPER, THIS IS ZAYNE! JARAEL IS SAFE!
HE CAN'T HEAR YOU, ZAYNE!
SHE WAS SPEAKING TO HIM THROUGH SOME KIND OF COMM!
JARAEL'S BRACELET!
CAMPER! IF YOU CAN HEAR ME -- THIS IS ZAYNE! WE'VE GOT JARAEL! WE'VE GOT JARAEL!

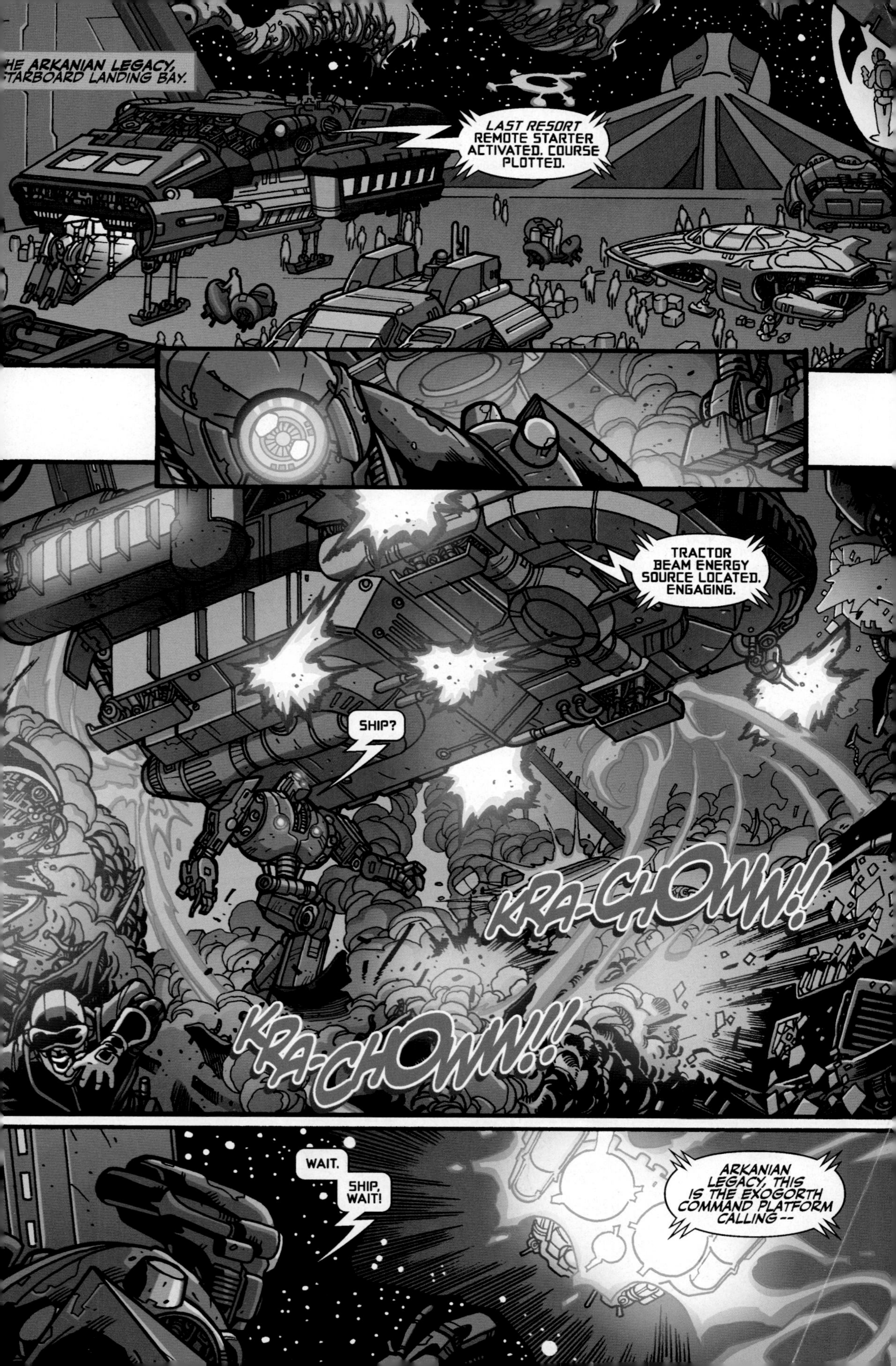
THE ARKANIAN LEGACY, STARBOARD LANDING BAY.
LAST RESORT REMOTE STARTER ACTIVATED. COURSE PLOTTED.
TRACTOR BEAM ENERGY SOURCE LOCATED. ENGAGING.
SHIP?
KRA-CHOWW!
KRA-CHOWW!!
WAIT.
SHIP, WAIT!
ARKANIAN LEGACY, THIS IS THE EXOGORTH COMMAND PLATFORM CALLING--

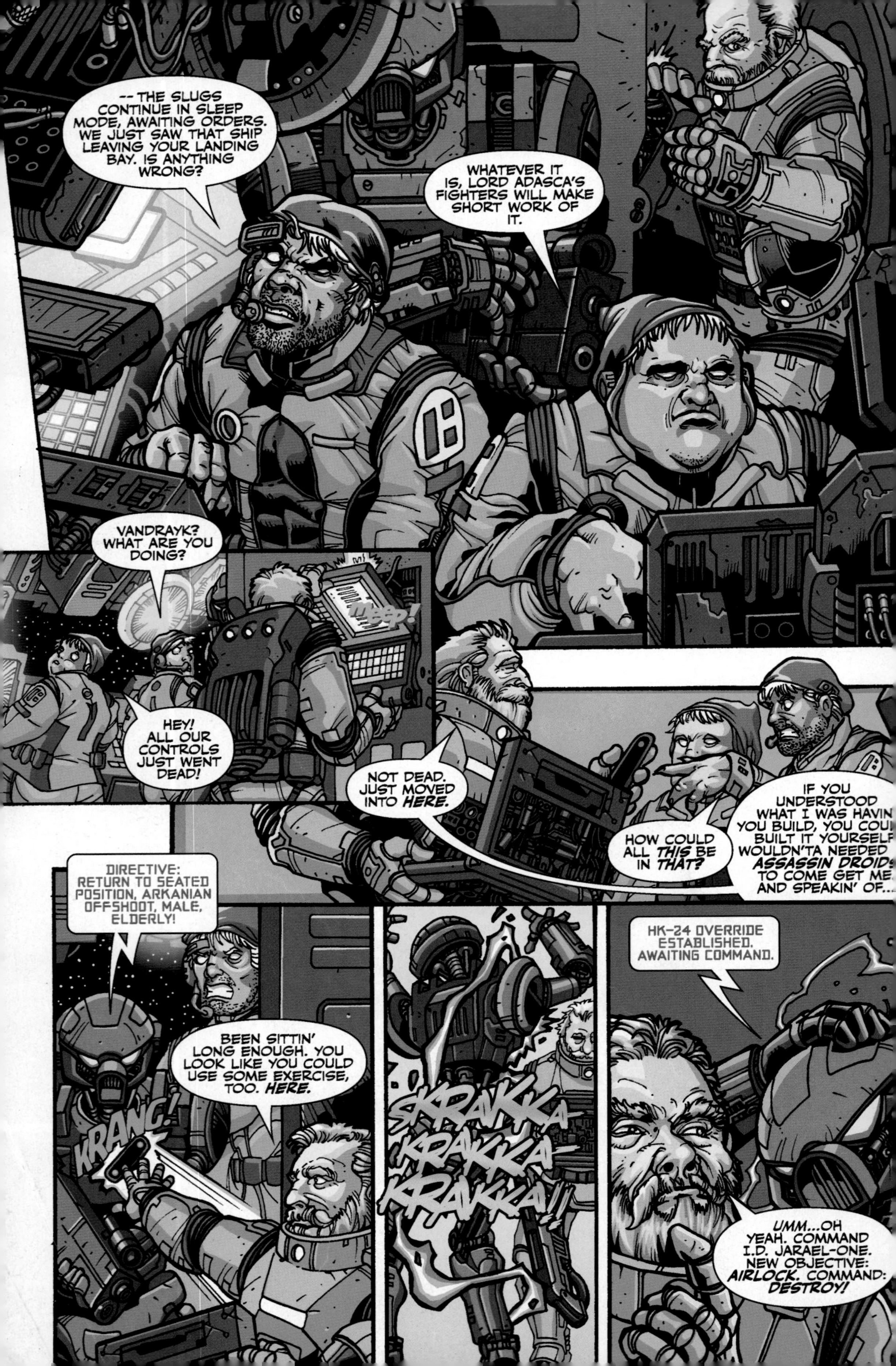
-- THE SLUGS CONTINUE IN SLEEP MODE, AWAITING ORDERS. WE JUST SAW THAT SHIP LEAVING YOUR LANDING BAY. IS ANYTHING WRONG?
WHATEVER IT IS, LORD ADASCA'S FIGHTERS WILL MAKE SHORT WORK OF IT.
VANDRAYK? WHAT ARE YOU DOING?
MEEP!
HEY! ALL OUR CONTROLS JUST WENT DEAD!
NOT DEAD. JUST MOVED INTO *HERE.*
HOW COULD ALL *THIS* BE IN *THAT?*
IF YOU UNDERSTOOD WHAT I WAS HAVIN YOU BUILD, YOU COUL BUILT IT YOURSELF WOULDN'TA NEEDED *ASSASSIN DROID* TO COME GET ME AND SPEAKIN' OF...
DIRECTIVE: RETURN TO SEATED POSITION, ARKANIAN OFFSHOOT, MALE, ELDERLY!
BEEN SITTIN' LONG ENOUGH. YOU LOOK LIKE YOU COULD USE SOME EXERCISE, TOO. *HERE.*
KRANG!
SKRAKKA KRAKKA KRAKKA!
HK-24 OVERRIDE ESTABLISHED. AWAITING COMMAND.
UMM...OH YEAH. COMMAND I.D. JARAEL-ONE. NEW OBJECTIVE: *AIRLOCK.* COMMAND: *DESTROY!*

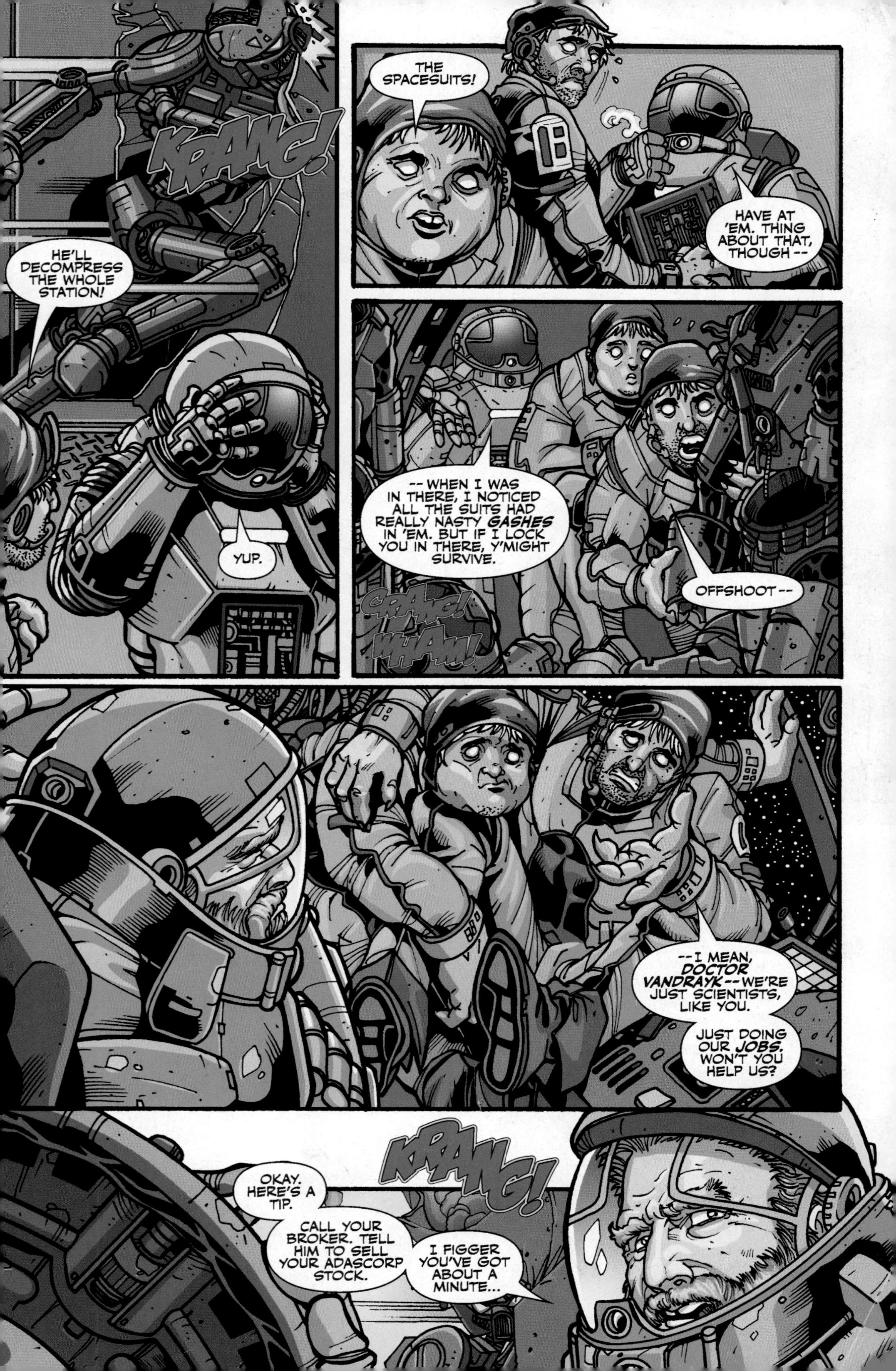
KRANG!
HE'LL DECOMPRESS THE WHOLE STATION!
YUP.
THE SPACESUITS!
HAVE AT 'EM. THING ABOUT THAT, THOUGH --
-- WHEN I WAS IN THERE, I NOTICED ALL THE SUITS HAD REALLY NASTY GASHES IN 'EM. BUT IF I LOCK YOU IN THERE, Y'MIGHT SURVIVE.
OFFSHOOT --
CRANG!
WHAM!
-- I MEAN, DOCTOR VANDRAYK -- WE'RE JUST SCIENTISTS, LIKE YOU.
JUST DOING OUR JOBS. WON'T YOU HELP US?
KRANG!
OKAY. HERE'S A TIP.
CALL YOUR BROKER. TELL HIM TO SELL YOUR ADASCORP STOCK.
I FIGGER YOU'VE GOT ABOUT A MINUTE...

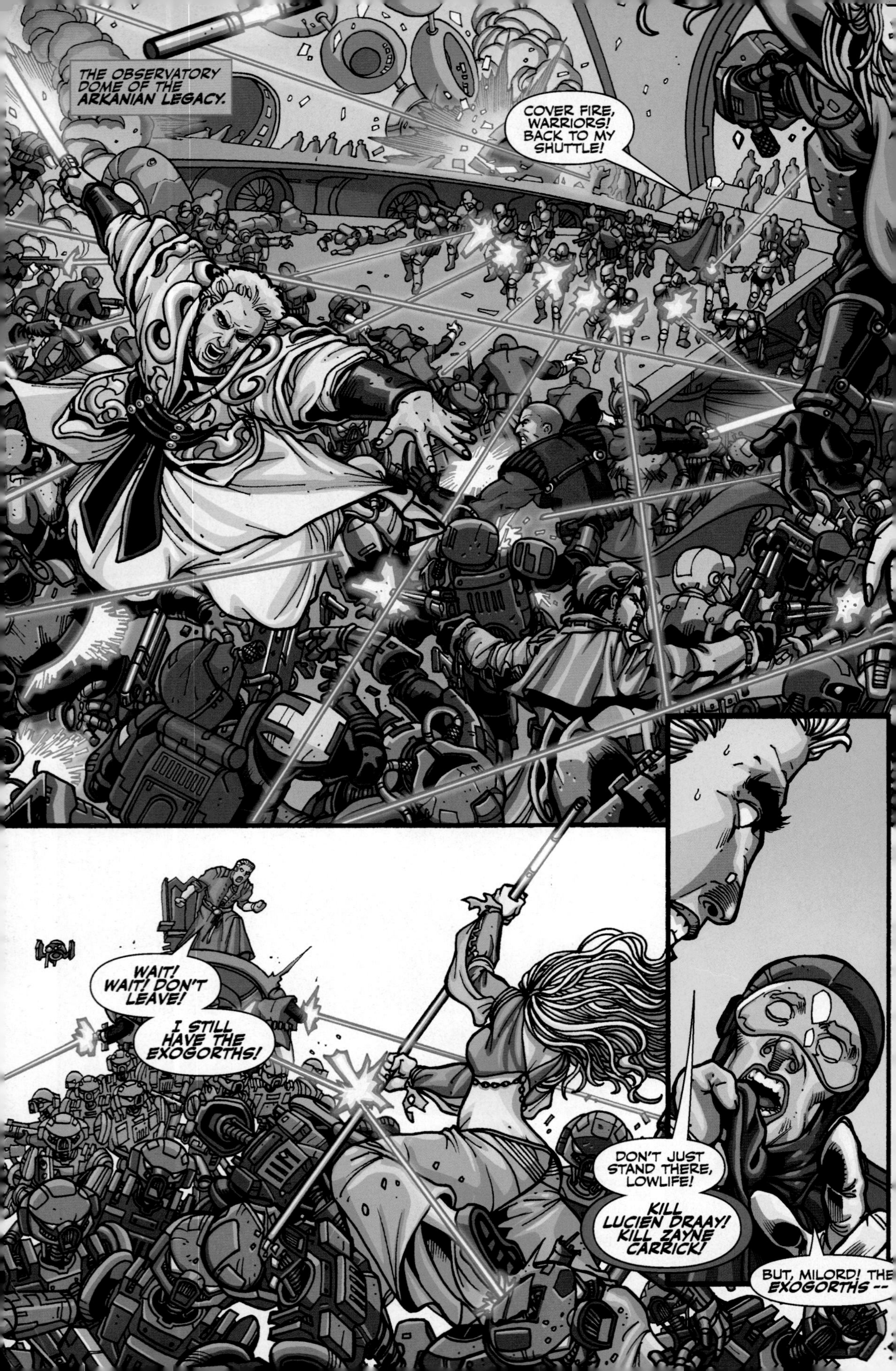
THE OBSERVATORY DOME OF THE ARKANIAN LEGACY.
COVER FIRE, WARRIORS! BACK TO MY SHUTTLE!
WAIT! WAIT! DON'T LEAVE!
I STILL HAVE THE EXOGORTHS!
DON'T JUST STAND THERE, LOWLIFE!
KILL LUCIEN DRAAY! KILL ZAYNE CARRICK!
BUT, MILORD! THE EXOGORTHS --

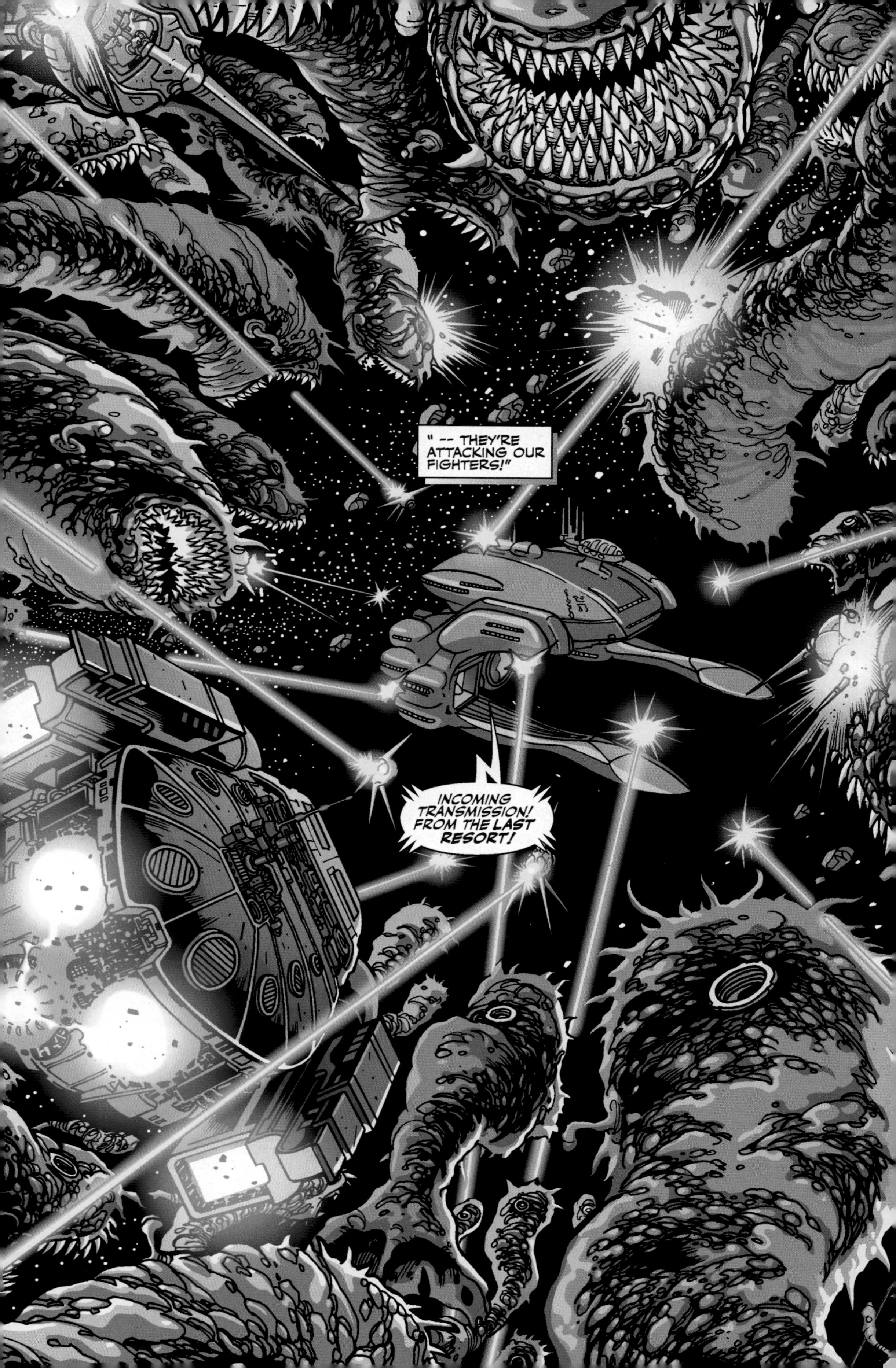
" -- THEY'RE ATTACKING OUR FIGHTERS!"
INCOMING TRANSMISSION! FROM THE LAST RESORT!

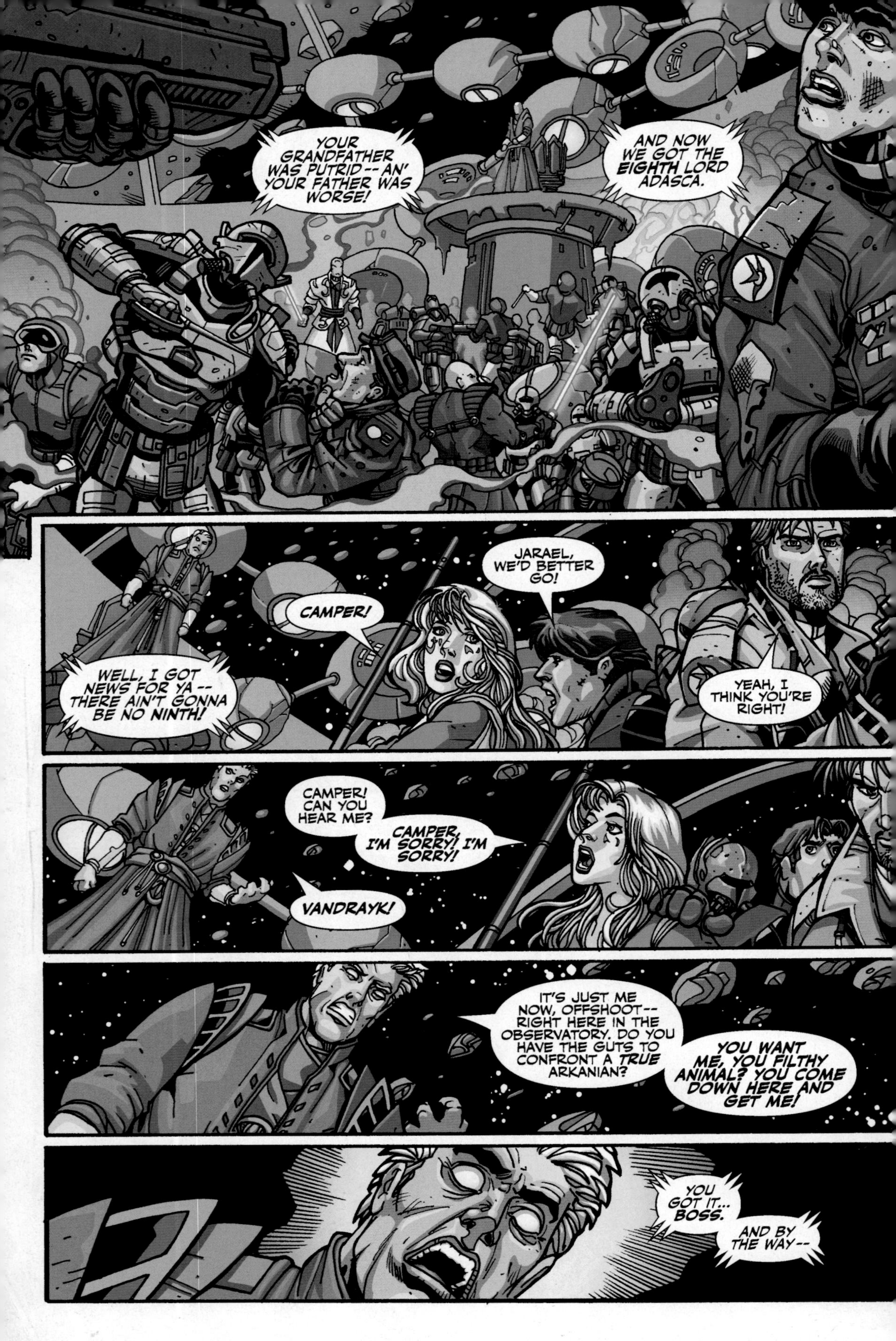

YOUR GRANDFATHER WAS PUTRID-- AN' YOUR FATHER WAS WORSE!
AND NOW WE GOT THE EIGHTH LORD ADASCA.
WELL, I GOT NEWS FOR YA-- THERE AIN'T GONNA BE NO NINTH!
CAMPER!
JARAEL, WE'D BETTER GO!
YEAH, I THINK YOU'RE RIGHT!
CAMPER! CAN YOU HEAR ME?
CAMPER, I'M SORRY! I'M SORRY!
VANDRAYK!
IT'S JUST ME NOW, OFFSHOOT-- RIGHT HERE IN THE OBSERVATORY. DO YOU HAVE THE GUTS TO CONFRONT A TRUE ARKANIAN?
YOU WANT ME, YOU FILTHY ANIMAL? YOU COME DOWN HERE AND GET ME!
YOU GOT IT... BOSS.
AND BY THE WAY--

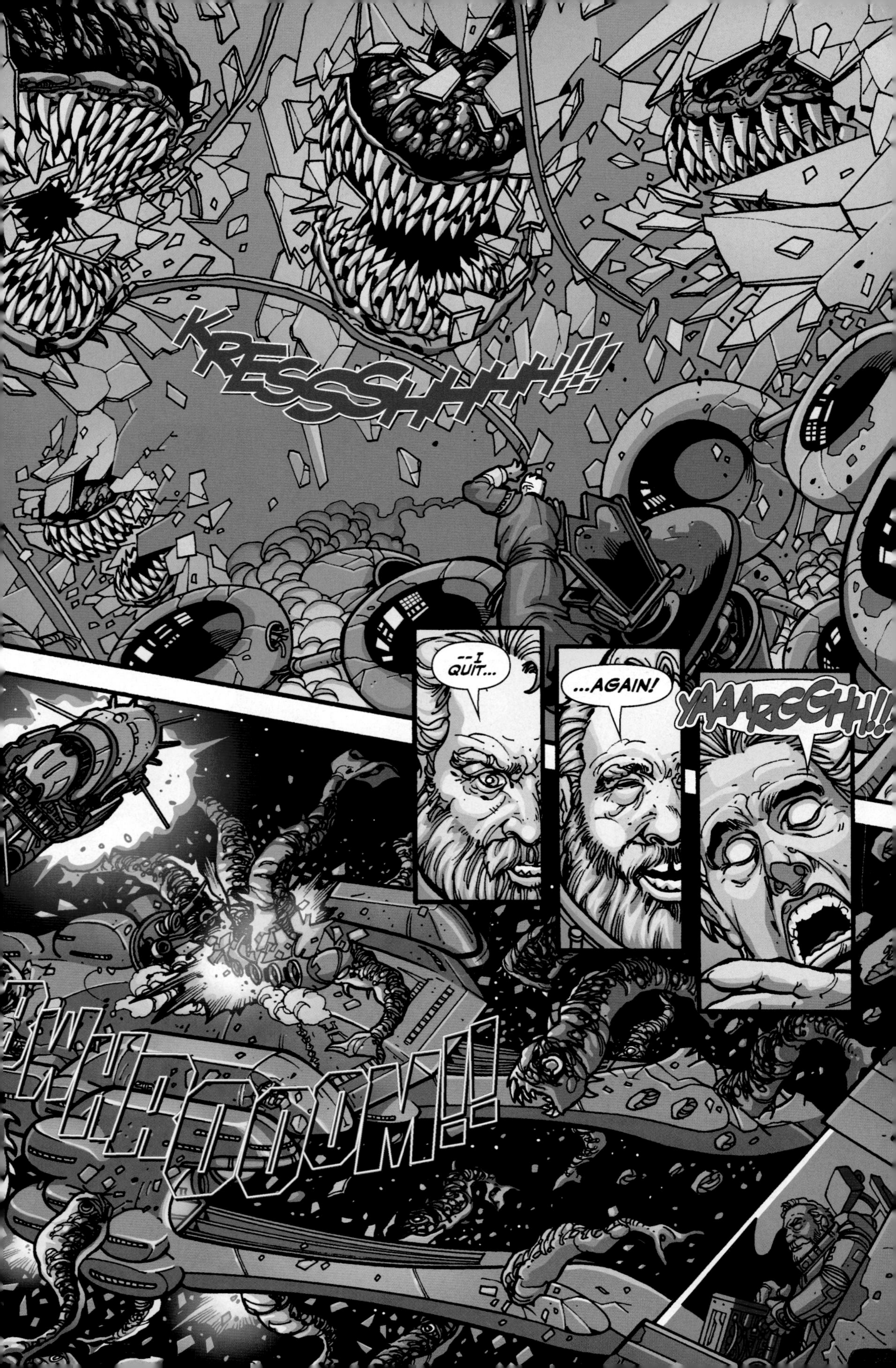
KRESSSHHH!!!
--I QUIT...
...AGAIN!
YAAARGGHH!!
WHOOOOM!!

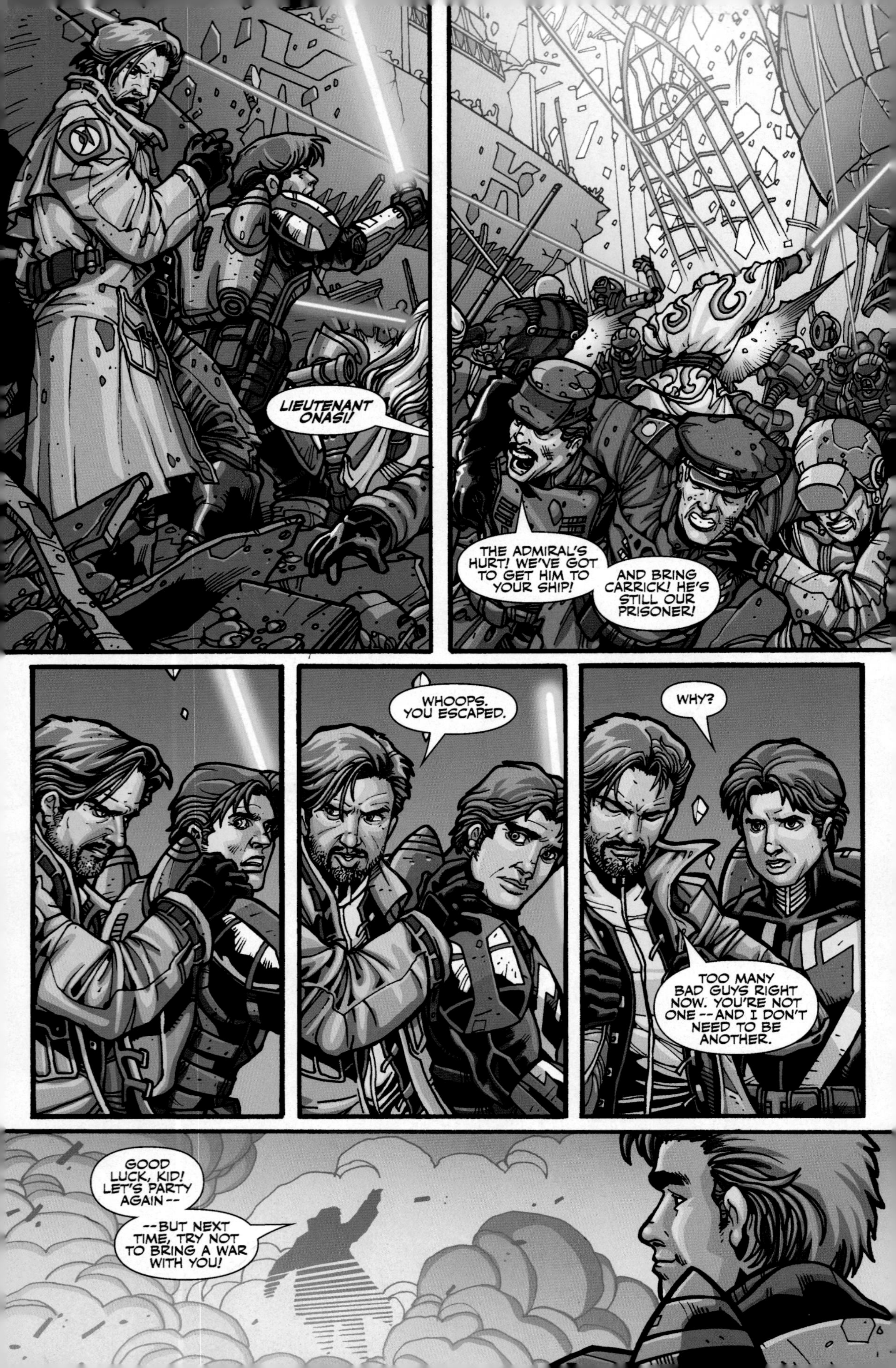
LIEUTENANT ONASI!
THE ADMIRAL'S HURT! WE'VE GOT TO GET HIM TO YOUR SHIP!
AND BRING CARRICK! HE'S STILL OUR PRISONER!
WHOOPS. YOU ESCAPED.
WHY?
TOO MANY BAD GUYS RIGHT NOW. YOU'RE NOT ONE --AND I DON'T NEED TO BE ANOTHER.
GOOD LUCK, KID! LET'S PARTY AGAIN--
--BUT NEXT TIME, TRY NOT TO BRING A WAR WITH YOU!

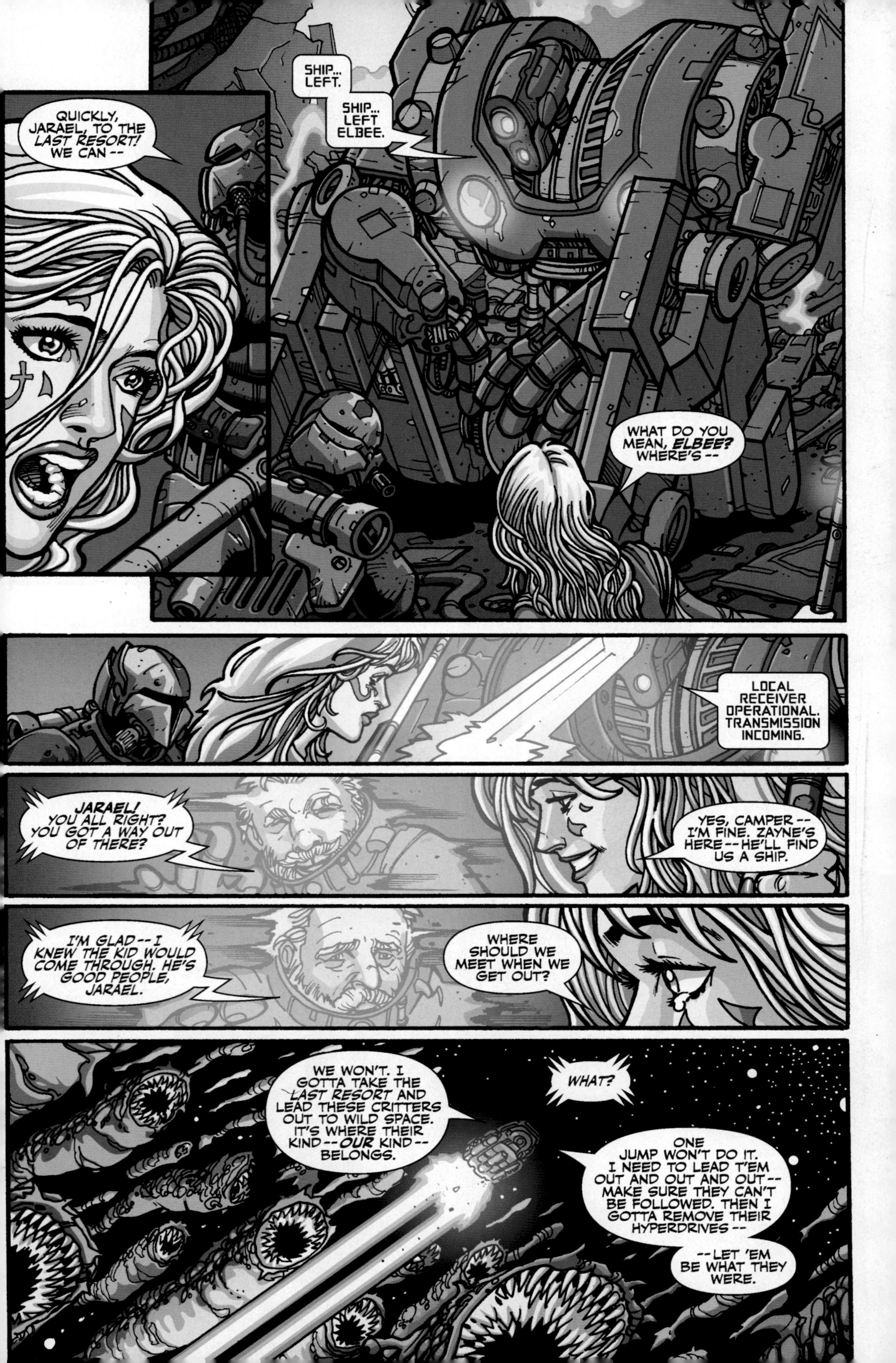
SHIP... LEFT.
SHIP... LEFT ELBEE.
QUICKLY, JARAEL, TO THE *LAST RESORT!* WE CAN --
WHAT DO YOU MEAN, *ELBEE?* WHERE'S --
LOCAL RECEIVER OPERATIONAL. TRANSMISSION INCOMING.
JARAEL! YOU ALL RIGHT? YOU GOT A WAY OUT OF THERE?
YES, CAMPER -- I'M FINE. ZAYNE'S HERE -- HE'LL FIND US A SHIP.
I'M GLAD -- I KNEW THE KID WOULD COME THROUGH. HE'S GOOD PEOPLE, JARAEL.
WHERE SHOULD WE MEET WHEN WE GET OUT?
WE WON'T. I GOTTA TAKE THE *LAST RESORT* AND LEAD THESE CRITTERS OUT TO WILD SPACE. IT'S WHERE THEIR KIND -- *OUR* KIND -- BELONGS.
WHAT?
ONE JUMP WON'T DO IT. I NEED TO LEAD T'EM OUT AND OUT AND OUT -- MAKE SURE THEY CAN'T BE FOLLOWED. THEN I GOTTA REMOVE THEIR HYPERDRIVES --
-- LET 'EM BE WHAT THEY WERE.

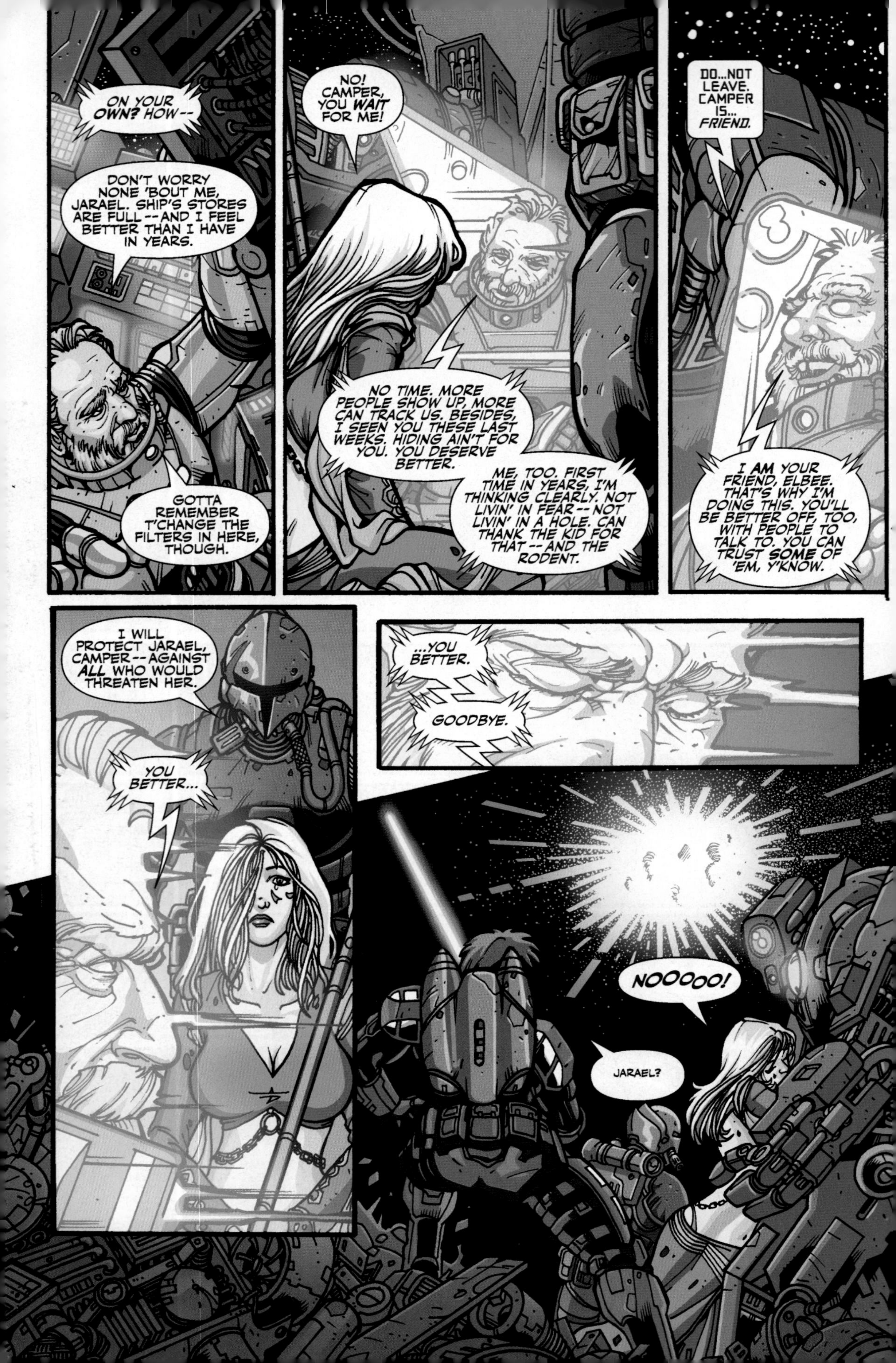

ON YOUR OWN? HOW--
DON'T WORRY NONE 'BOUT ME, JARAEL. SHIP'S STORES ARE FULL--AND I FEEL BETTER THAN I HAVE IN YEARS.
GOTTA REMEMBER T'CHANGE THE FILTERS IN HERE, THOUGH.
NO! CAMPER, YOU WAIT FOR ME!
NO TIME. MORE PEOPLE SHOW UP, MORE CAN TRACK US. BESIDES, I SEEN YOU THESE LAST WEEKS. HIDING AIN'T FOR YOU. YOU DESERVE BETTER.
ME, TOO. FIRST TIME IN YEARS, I'M THINKING CLEARLY. NOT LIVIN' IN FEAR--NOT LIVIN' IN A HOLE. CAN THANK THE KID FOR THAT--AND THE RODENT.
DO...NOT LEAVE. CAMPER IS... FRIEND.
I AM YOUR FRIEND, ELBEE. THAT'S WHY I'M DOING THIS. YOU'LL BE BETTER OFF, TOO, WITH PEOPLE TO TALK TO. YOU CAN TRUST SOME OF 'EM, Y'KNOW.
I WILL PROTECT JARAEL, CAMPER--AGAINST ALL WHO WOULD THREATEN HER.
YOU BETTER...
...YOU BETTER.
GOODBYE.
NOOOOO!
JARAEL?

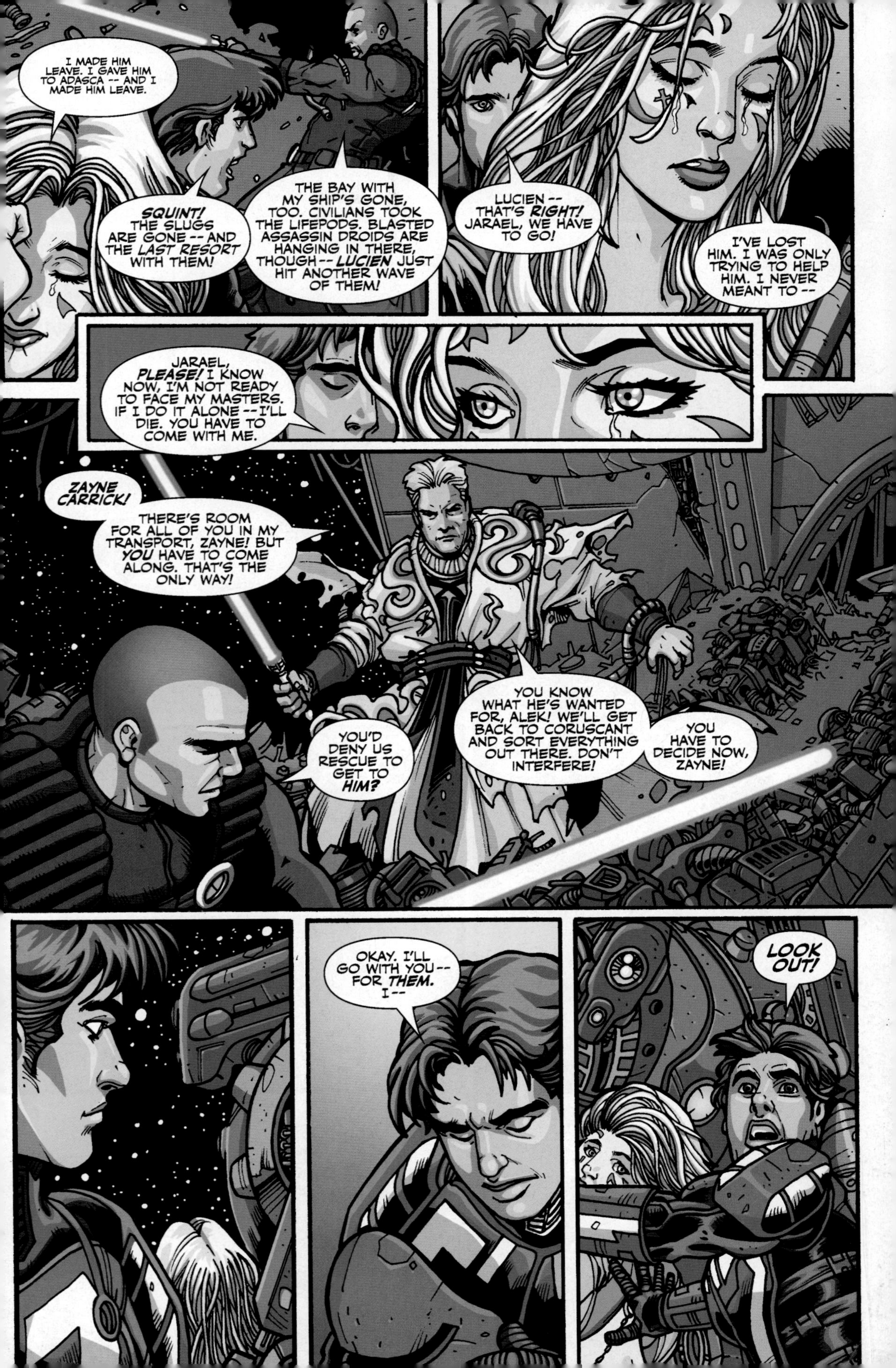
I MADE HIM LEAVE. I GAVE HIM TO ADASCA -- AND I MADE HIM LEAVE.
SQUINT! THE SLUGS ARE GONE -- AND THE LAST RESORT WITH THEM!
THE BAY WITH MY SHIP'S GONE, TOO. CIVILIANS TOOK THE LIFEPODS. BLASTED ASSASSIN DROIDS ARE HANGING IN THERE, THOUGH -- LUCIEN JUST HIT ANOTHER WAVE OF THEM!
LUCIEN -- THAT'S RIGHT! JARAEL, WE HAVE TO GO!
I'VE LOST HIM. I WAS ONLY TRYING TO HELP HIM. I NEVER MEANT TO --
JARAEL, PLEASE! I KNOW NOW, I'M NOT READY TO FACE MY MASTERS. IF I DO IT ALONE -- I'LL DIE. YOU HAVE TO COME WITH ME.
ZAYNE CARRICK!
THERE'S ROOM FOR ALL OF YOU IN MY TRANSPORT, ZAYNE! BUT YOU HAVE TO COME ALONG. THAT'S THE ONLY WAY!
YOU'D DENY US RESCUE TO GET TO HIM?
YOU KNOW WHAT HE'S WANTED FOR, ALEK! WE'LL GET BACK TO CORUSCANT AND SORT EVERYTHING OUT THERE. DON'T INTERFERE!
YOU HAVE TO DECIDE NOW, ZAYNE!
OKAY. I'LL GO WITH YOU -- FOR THEM. I --
LOOK OUT!

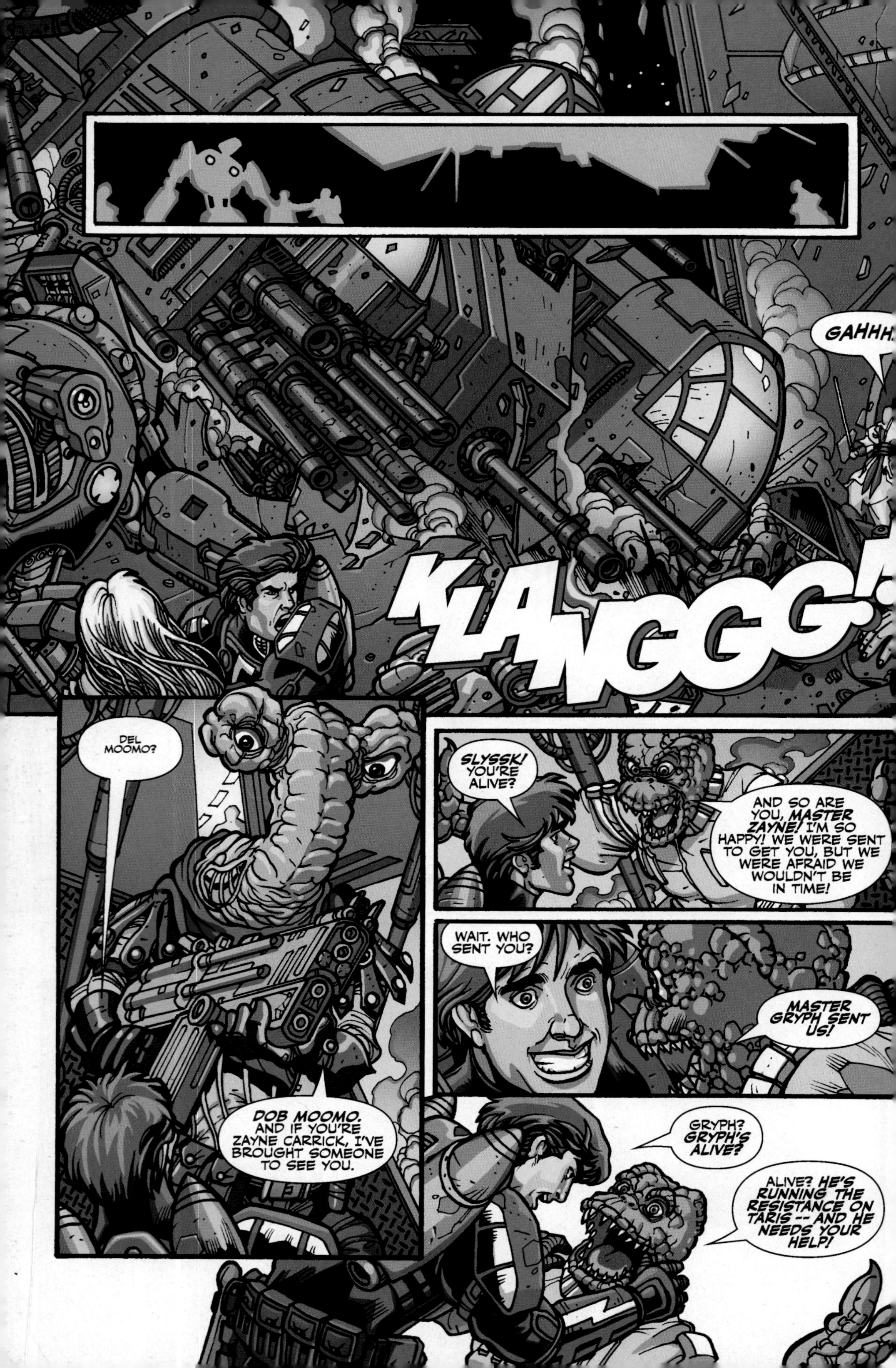
GAHHH!
KLANGGG!
DEL MOOMO?
DOB MOOMO. AND IF YOU'RE ZAYNE CARRICK, I'VE BROUGHT SOMEONE TO SEE YOU.
SLYSSK! YOU'RE ALIVE?
AND SO ARE YOU, MASTER ZAYNE! I'M SO HAPPY! WE WERE SENT TO GET YOU, BUT WE WERE AFRAID WE WOULDN'T BE IN TIME!
WAIT. WHO SENT YOU?
MASTER GRYPH SENT US!
GRYPH? GRYPH'S ALIVE?
ALIVE? HE'S RUNNING THE RESISTANCE ON TARIS -- AND HE NEEDS YOUR HELP!

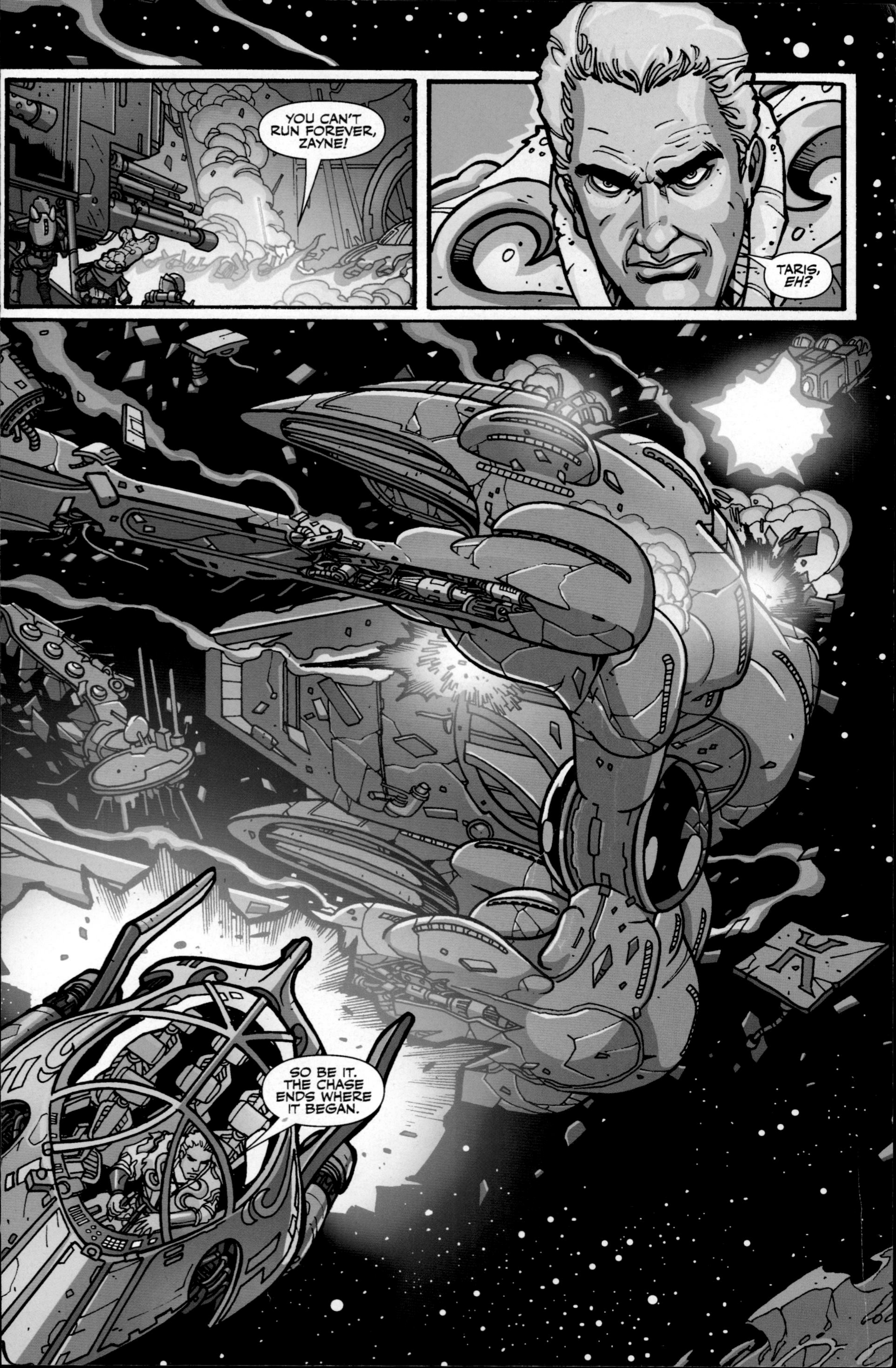
YOU CAN'T RUN FOREVER, ZAYNE!
TARIS, EH?
SO BE IT. THE CHASE ENDS WHERE IT BEGAN.

THE TARIS HOLOFEED
SPECIAL PROCLAMATION

ATTENTION PEOPLE OF TARIS

I am Cassus Fett, comrade to Mand'alor and field marshal of the forces now laying siege to your planet.

This day, I release you from all allegiance to the Galactic Republic. The Mando'ade are your clan, now. This day, I release you from all obedience to the Chancellor. Mand'alor is your leader, now.

The Republic has failed Taris in battle. It has shown itself unworthy of the great sacrifices it has called upon you to make. But this is not a time for lamentations. For in this victory, we offer you the chance to share in the next one—and the next one, and the next one.

Those who wish to join the Mando'ade in their New Crusade for the galaxy are welcome. Helmet and armor will be yours—and the way of the warrior will be made known to you. In this victory, we have set you free—and on the path to glory!

Those who choose to remain on Taris providing for the clans shall live in peace. But beware! Those who feign loyalty and betray us shall die an honorless death!

This medium of the Old Order will now be deactivated.

TRANSMISSION INTERRUPTION

NO SIGNAL
NO SIGNAL
NO SIGNAL
*****

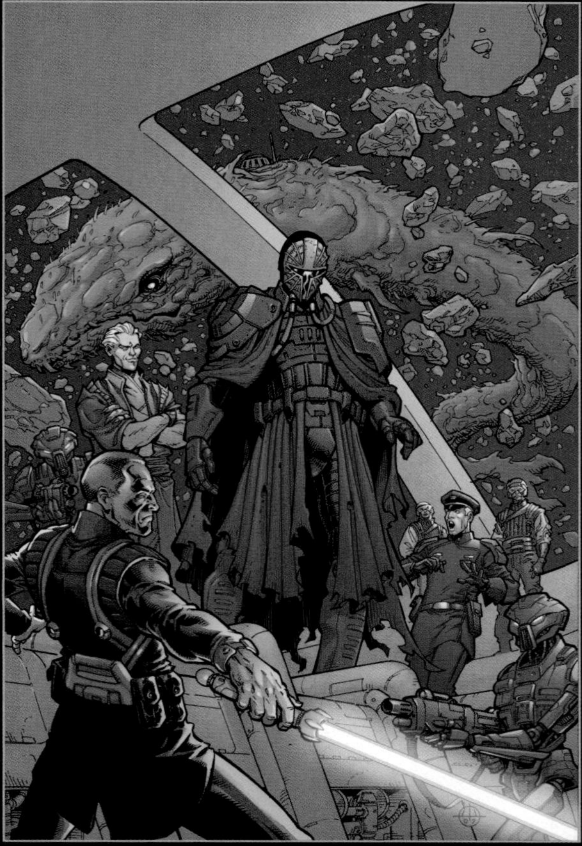
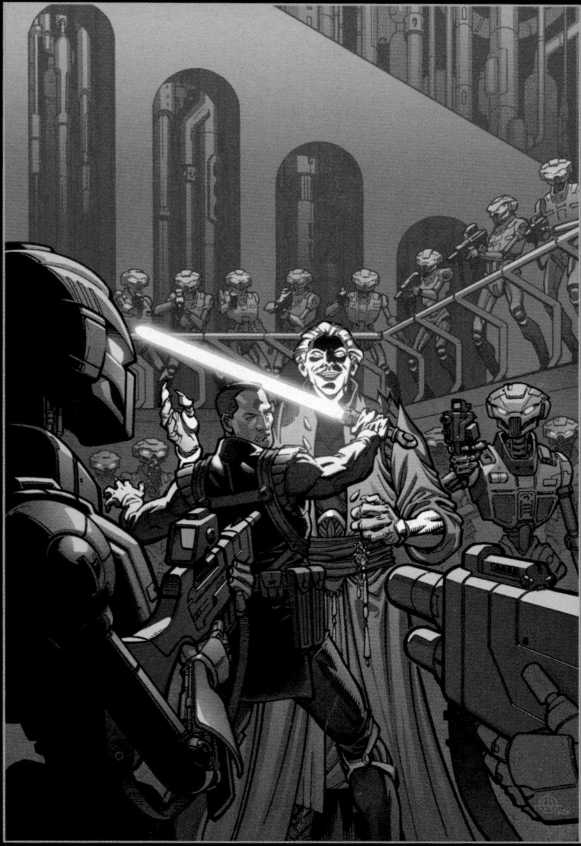
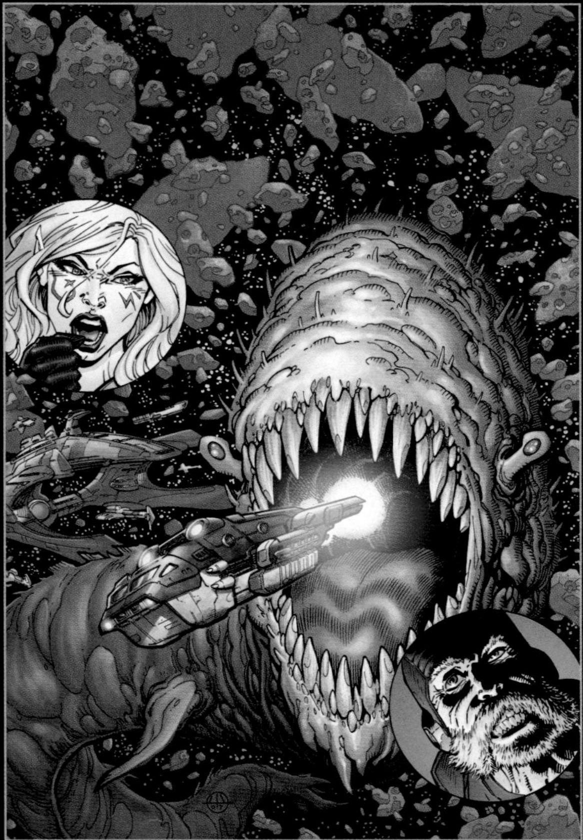

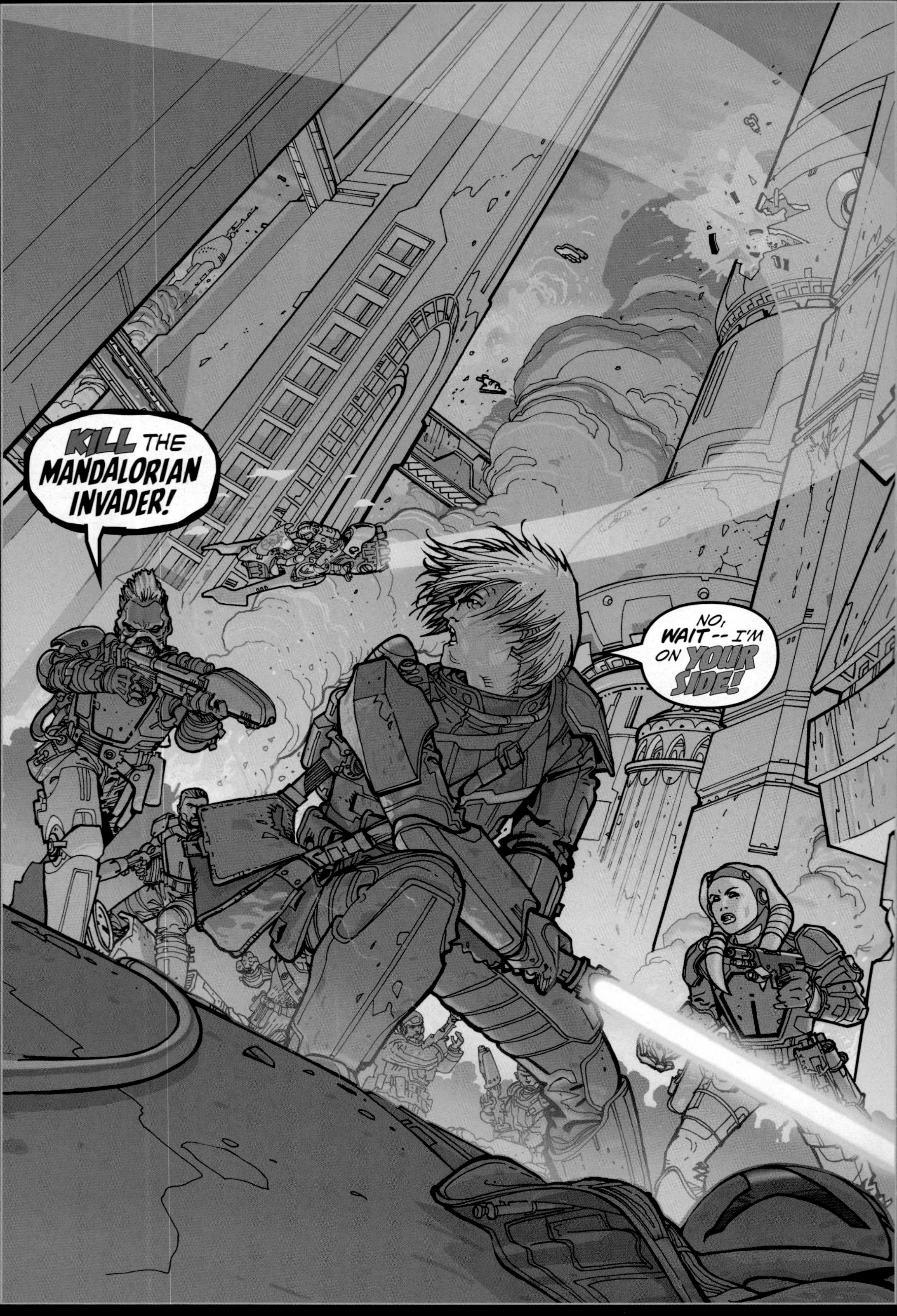
KILL THE MANDALORIAN INVADER!
NO, WAIT -- I'M ON YOUR SIDE!

STAR WARS: KNIGHTS OF THE OLD REPUBLIC #22 — "KNIGHTS OF SUFFERING, PART 1"

WRITER: JOHN JACKSON MILLER • PENCILER: DUSTIN WEAVER • INKER: DAN PARSONS • COLORIST: MICHAEL ATIYEH
LETTERER: MICHAEL HEISLER • ASSISTANT EDITOR: DAVE MARSHALL • EDITOR: JEREMY BARLOW • COVER ARTIST: COLIN WILSON

TARIS.

HEY, YOU! GET OUT OF OUR SKY!

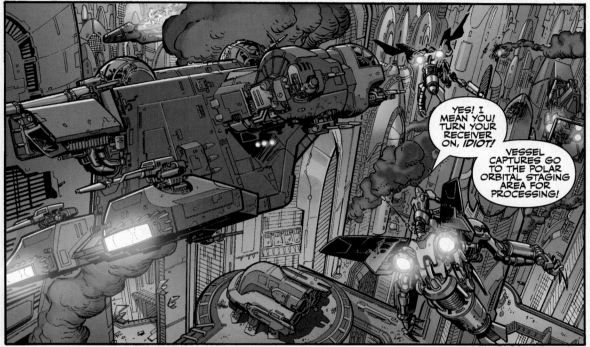

YES! I MEAN YOU! TURN YOUR RECEIVER ON, *IDIOT*!

VESSEL CAPTURES GO TO THE POLAR ORBITAL STAGING AREA FOR PROCESSING!

TO *WHAT*?! I NEED TO LAND, NOW!

WE'RE STILL LANDING TROOPS FOR THE LOWER CITY -- WE NEED THE LANES CLEAR! *CASSUS FETT'S* ORDERS!

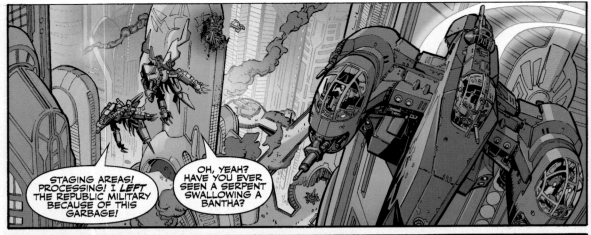

STAGING AREAS! PROCESSING! I *LEFT* THE REPUBLIC MILITARY BECAUSE OF THIS GARBAGE!

OH, YEAH? HAVE YOU EVER SEEN A SERPENT SWALLOWING A BANTHA?

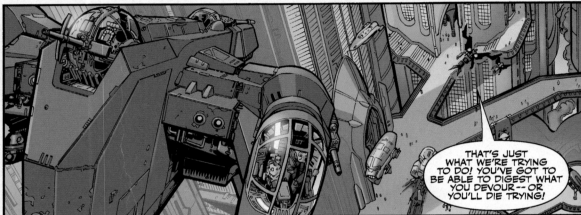

THAT'S JUST WHAT WE'RE TRYING TO DO! YOU'VE GOT TO BE ABLE TO DIGEST WHAT YOU DEVOUR -- OR YOU'LL DIE TRYING!

THAT'S WHY MAND'ALOR BROUGHT CASSUS IN ON TARIS. THIS PLACE IS JUST A TASTE OF WHAT WE'LL HAVE TO DEAL WITH WHEN WE GET TO CORUSCANT!

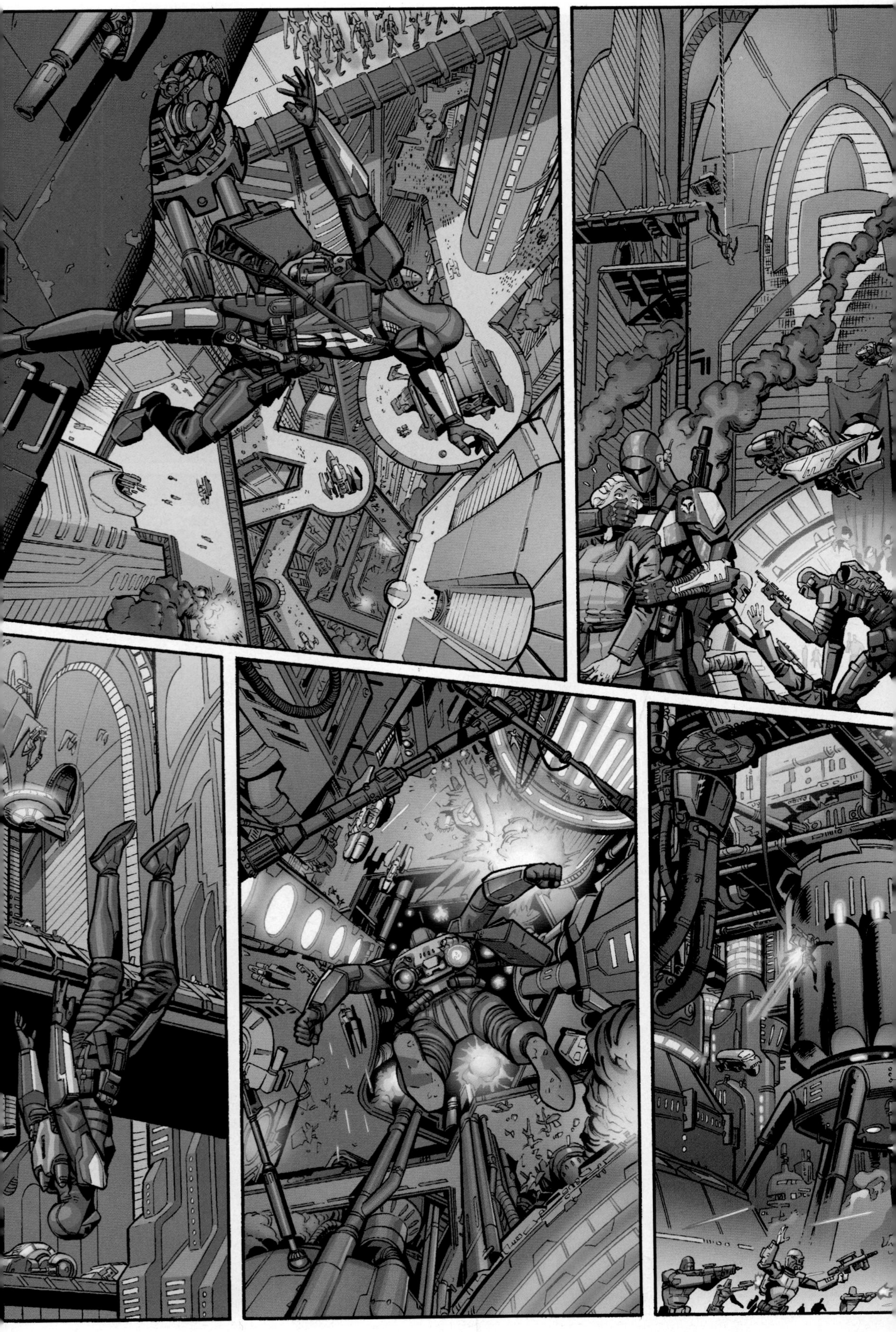

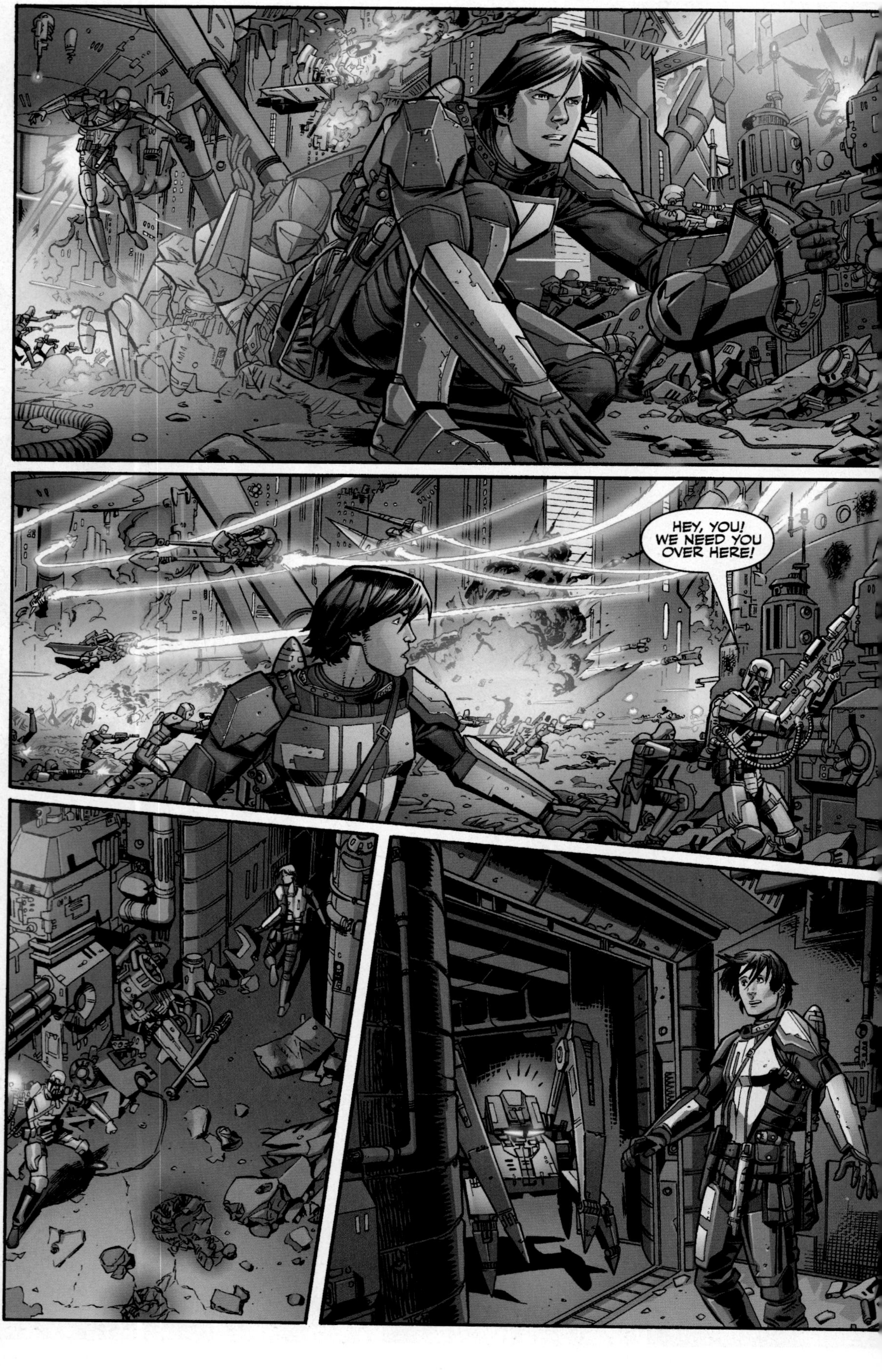
HEY, YOU! WE NEED YOU OVER HERE!

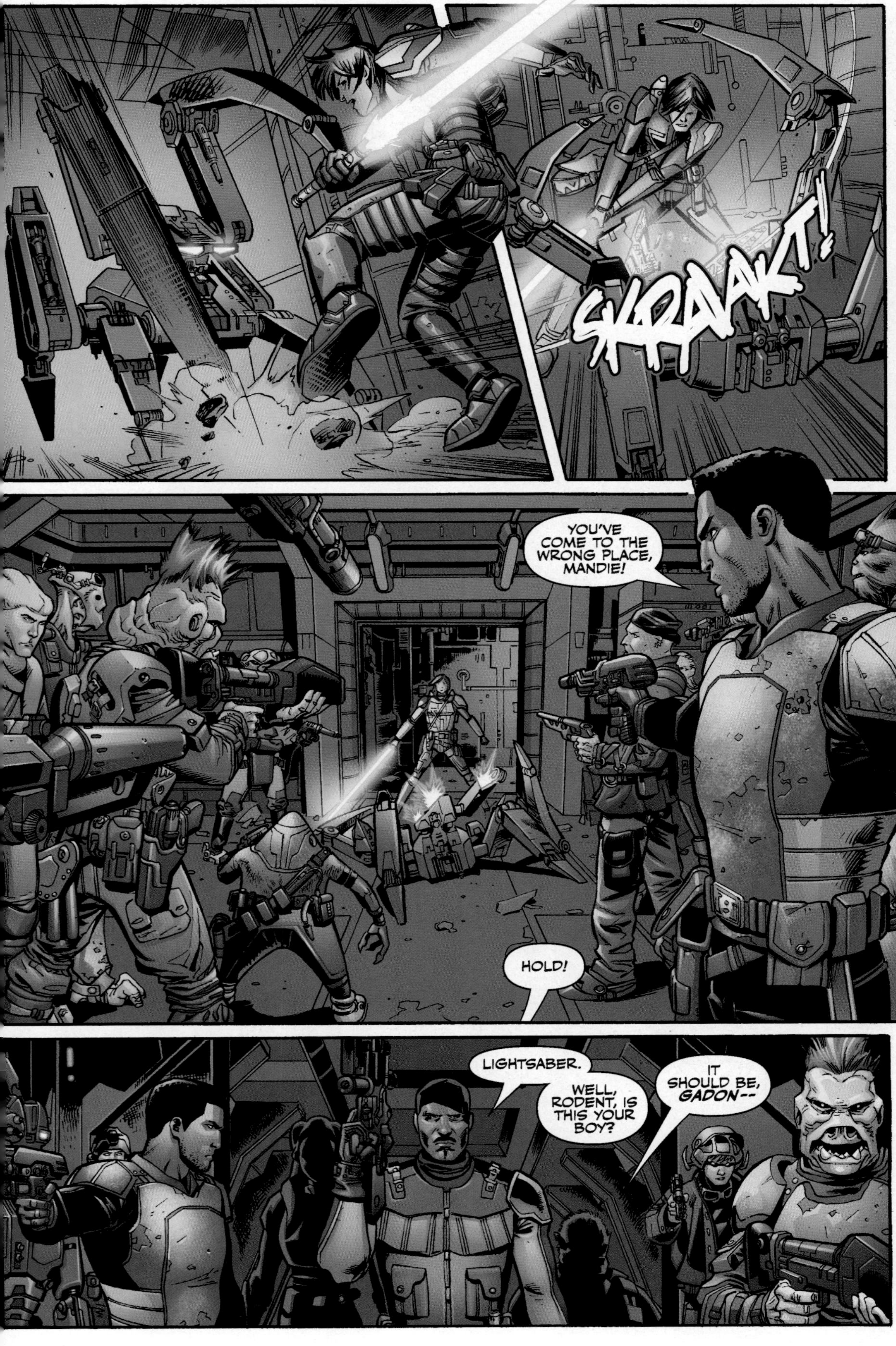

SKRAAKT!
YOU'VE COME TO THE WRONG PLACE, MANDIE!
HOLD!
LIGHTSABER.
WELL, RODENT, IS THIS YOUR BOY?
IT SHOULD BE, GADON--

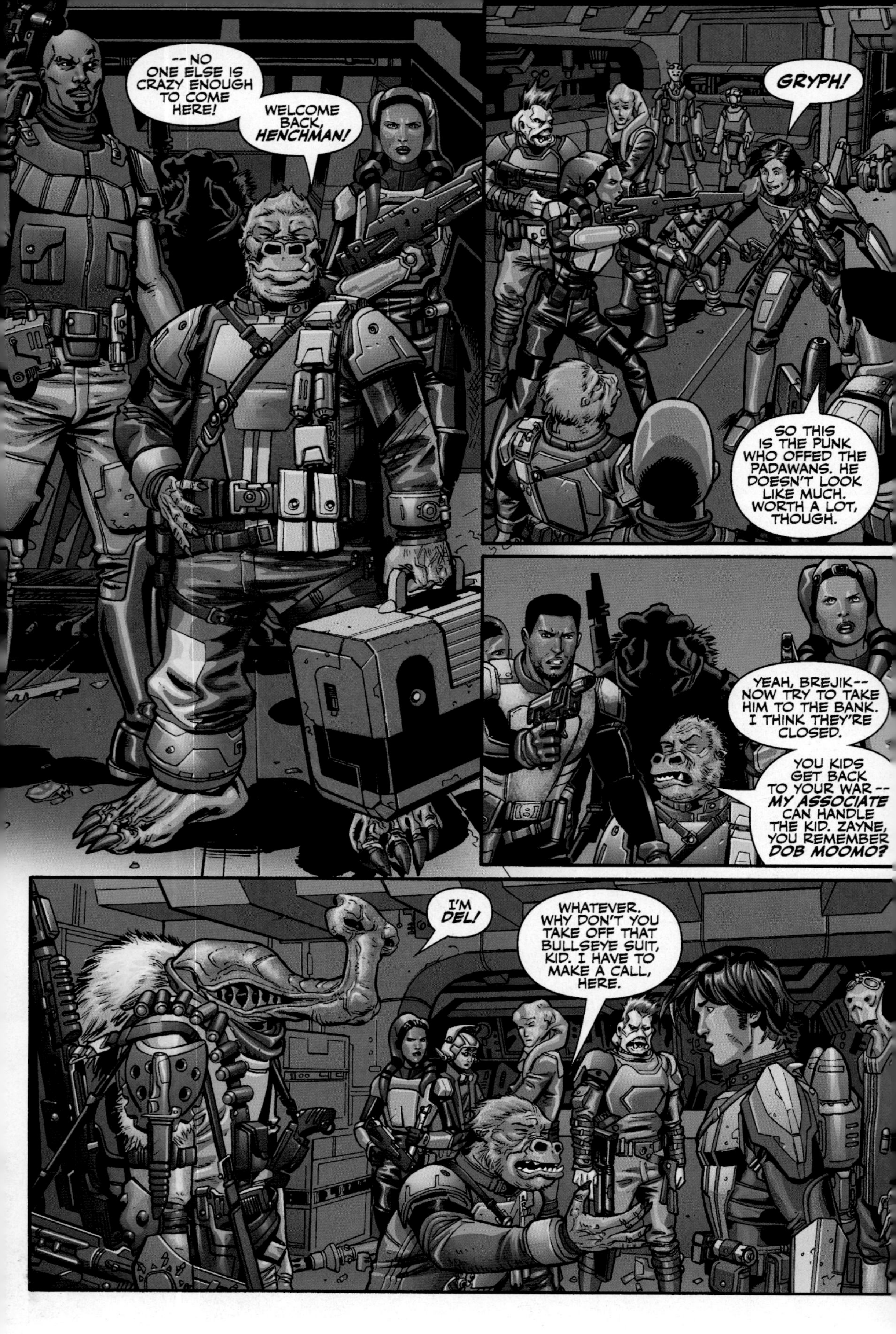

-- NO ONE ELSE IS CRAZY ENOUGH TO COME HERE!
WELCOME BACK, HENCHMAN!
GRYPH!
SO THIS IS THE PUNK WHO OFFED THE PADAWANS. HE DOESN'T LOOK LIKE MUCH. WORTH A LOT, THOUGH.
YEAH, BREJIK-- NOW TRY TO TAKE HIM TO THE BANK. I THINK THEY'RE CLOSED.
YOU KIDS GET BACK TO YOUR WAR -- MY ASSOCIATE CAN HANDLE THE KID. ZAYNE, YOU REMEMBER DOB MOOMO?
I'M DEL!
WHATEVER. WHY DON'T YOU TAKE OFF THAT BULLSEYE SUIT, KID. I HAVE TO MAKE A CALL, HERE.

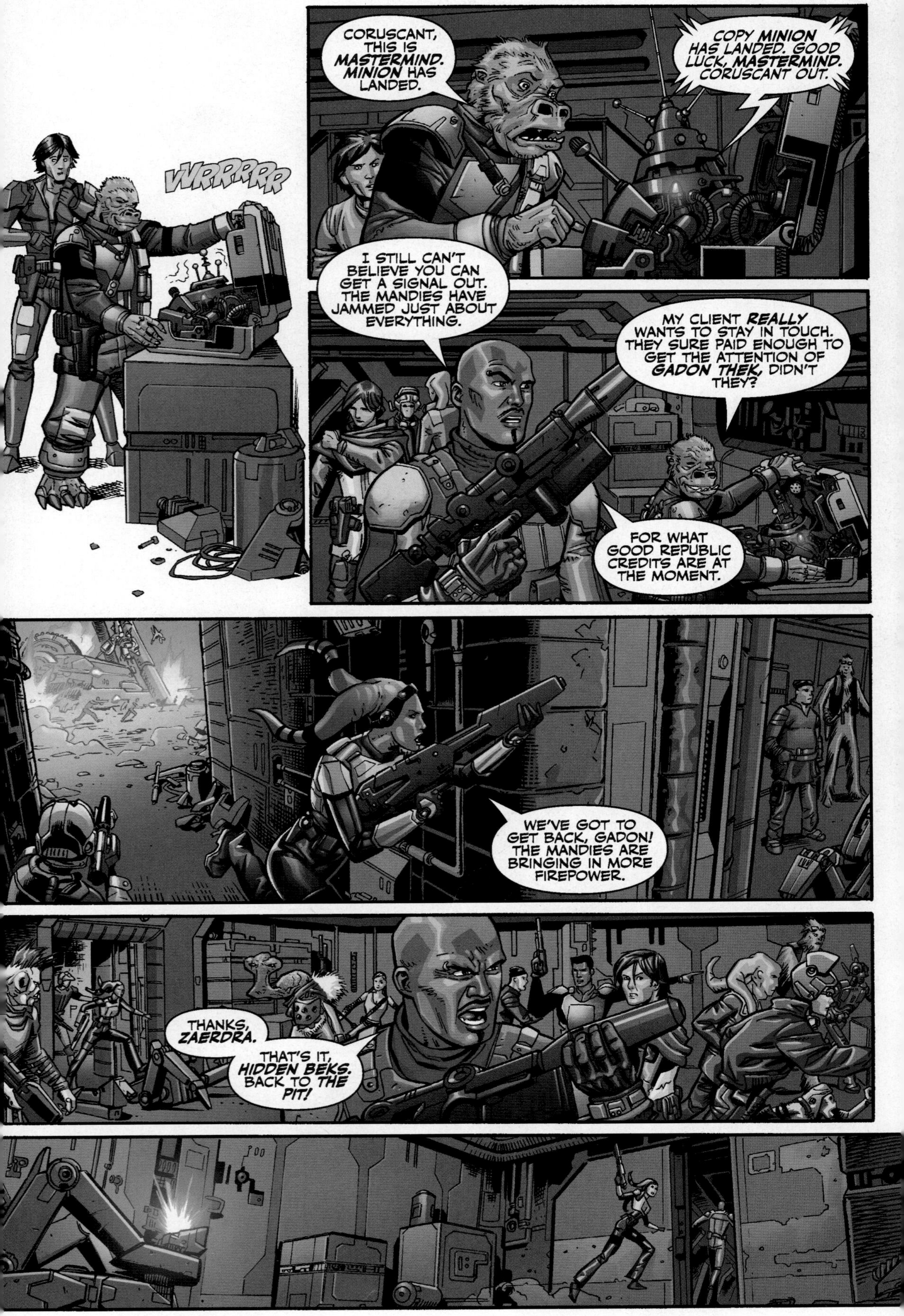
VWRRRRR
CORUSCANT, THIS IS MASTERMIND. MINION HAS LANDED.
COPY MINION HAS LANDED. GOOD LUCK, MASTERMIND. CORUSCANT OUT.
I STILL CAN'T BELIEVE YOU CAN GET A SIGNAL OUT. THE MANDIES HAVE JAMMED JUST ABOUT EVERYTHING.
MY CLIENT REALLY WANTS TO STAY IN TOUCH. THEY SURE PAID ENOUGH TO GET THE ATTENTION OF GADON THEK, DIDN'T THEY?
FOR WHAT GOOD REPUBLIC CREDITS ARE AT THE MOMENT.
WE'VE GOT TO GET BACK, GADON! THE MANDIES ARE BRINGING IN MORE FIREPOWER.
THANKS, ZAERDRA.
THAT'S IT, HIDDEN BEKS. BACK TO THE PIT!

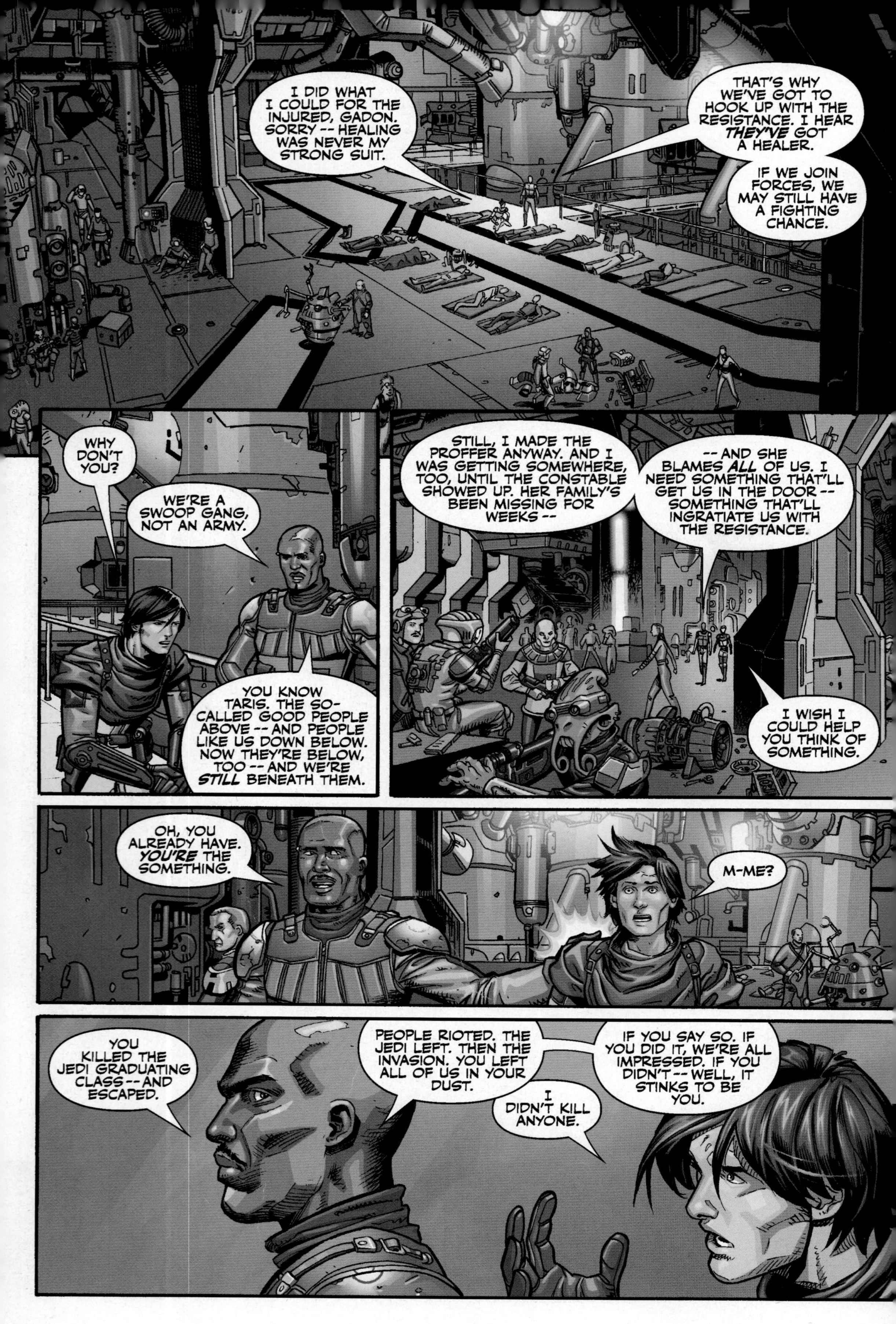
I DID WHAT I COULD FOR THE INJURED, GADON. SORRY -- HEALING WAS NEVER MY STRONG SUIT.
THAT'S WHY WE'VE GOT TO HOOK UP WITH THE RESISTANCE. I HEAR *THEY'VE* GOT A HEALER.
IF WE JOIN FORCES, WE MAY STILL HAVE A FIGHTING CHANCE.
WHY DON'T YOU?
WE'RE A SWOOP GANG, NOT AN ARMY.
YOU KNOW TARIS. THE SO-CALLED GOOD PEOPLE ABOVE -- AND PEOPLE LIKE US DOWN BELOW. NOW THEY'RE BELOW, TOO -- AND WE'RE *STILL* BENEATH THEM.
STILL, I MADE THE PROFFER ANYWAY. AND I WAS GETTING SOMEWHERE, TOO, UNTIL THE CONSTABLE SHOWED UP. HER FAMILY'S BEEN MISSING FOR WEEKS --
-- AND SHE BLAMES *ALL* OF US. I NEED SOMETHING THAT'LL GET US IN THE DOOR -- SOMETHING THAT'LL INGRATIATE US WITH THE RESISTANCE.
I WISH I COULD HELP YOU THINK OF SOMETHING.
OH, YOU ALREADY HAVE. *YOU'RE* THE SOMETHING.
M-ME?
YOU KILLED THE JEDI GRADUATING CLASS -- AND ESCAPED.
PEOPLE RIOTED. THE JEDI LEFT. THEN THE INVASION. YOU LEFT ALL OF US IN YOUR DUST.
I DIDN'T KILL ANYONE.
IF YOU SAY SO. IF YOU DID IT, WE'RE ALL IMPRESSED. IF YOU DIDN'T -- WELL, IT STINKS TO BE YOU.

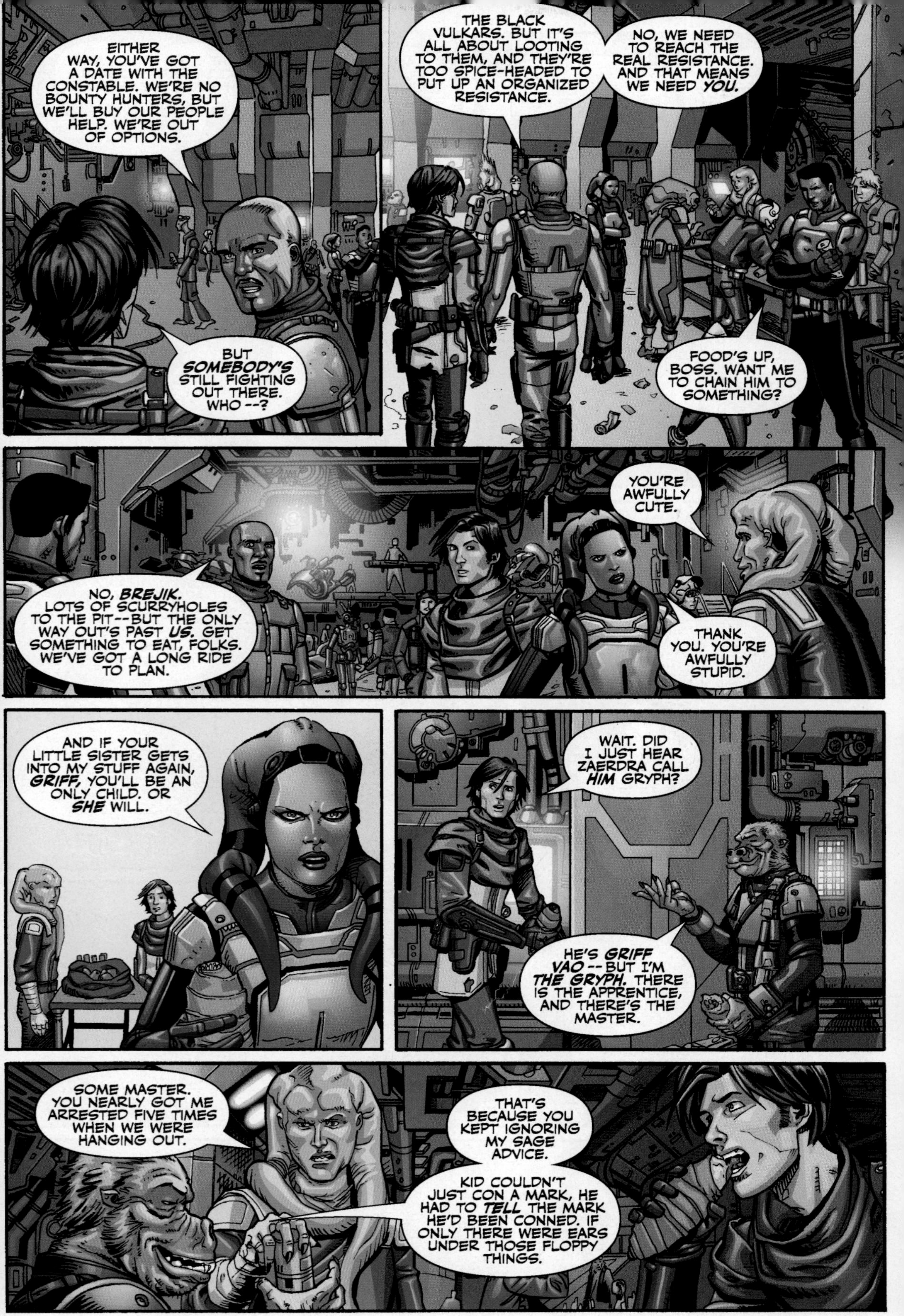
EITHER WAY, YOU'VE GOT A DATE WITH THE CONSTABLE. WE'RE NO BOUNTY HUNTERS, BUT WE'LL BUY OUR PEOPLE HELP. WE'RE OUT OF OPTIONS.
BUT *SOMEBODY'S* STILL FIGHTING OUT THERE. WHO --?
THE BLACK VULKARS. BUT IT'S ALL ABOUT LOOTING TO THEM, AND THEY'RE TOO SPICE-HEADED TO PUT UP AN ORGANIZED RESISTANCE.
NO, WE NEED TO REACH THE REAL RESISTANCE. AND THAT MEANS WE NEED *YOU.*
FOOD'S UP, BOSS. WANT ME TO CHAIN HIM TO SOMETHING?
NO, *BREJIK.* LOTS OF SCURRYHOLES TO THE PIT--BUT THE ONLY WAY OUT'S PAST *US.* GET SOMETHING TO EAT, FOLKS. WE'VE GOT A LONG RIDE TO PLAN.
YOU'RE AWFULLY CUTE.
THANK YOU. YOU'RE AWFULLY STUPID.
AND IF YOUR LITTLE SISTER GETS INTO MY STUFF AGAIN, *GRIFF,* YOU'LL BE AN ONLY CHILD. OR *SHE* WILL.
WAIT. DID I JUST HEAR ZAERDRA CALL *HIM* GRYPH?
HE'S *GRIFF VAO* -- BUT I'M *THE GRYPH.* THERE IS THE APPRENTICE, AND THERE'S THE MASTER.
SOME MASTER. YOU NEARLY GOT ME ARRESTED FIVE TIMES WHEN WE WERE HANGING OUT.
THAT'S BECAUSE YOU KEPT IGNORING MY SAGE ADVICE.
KID COULDN'T JUST CON A MARK, HE HAD TO *TELL* THE MARK HE'D BEEN CONNED. IF ONLY THERE WERE EARS UNDER THOSE FLOPPY THINGS.

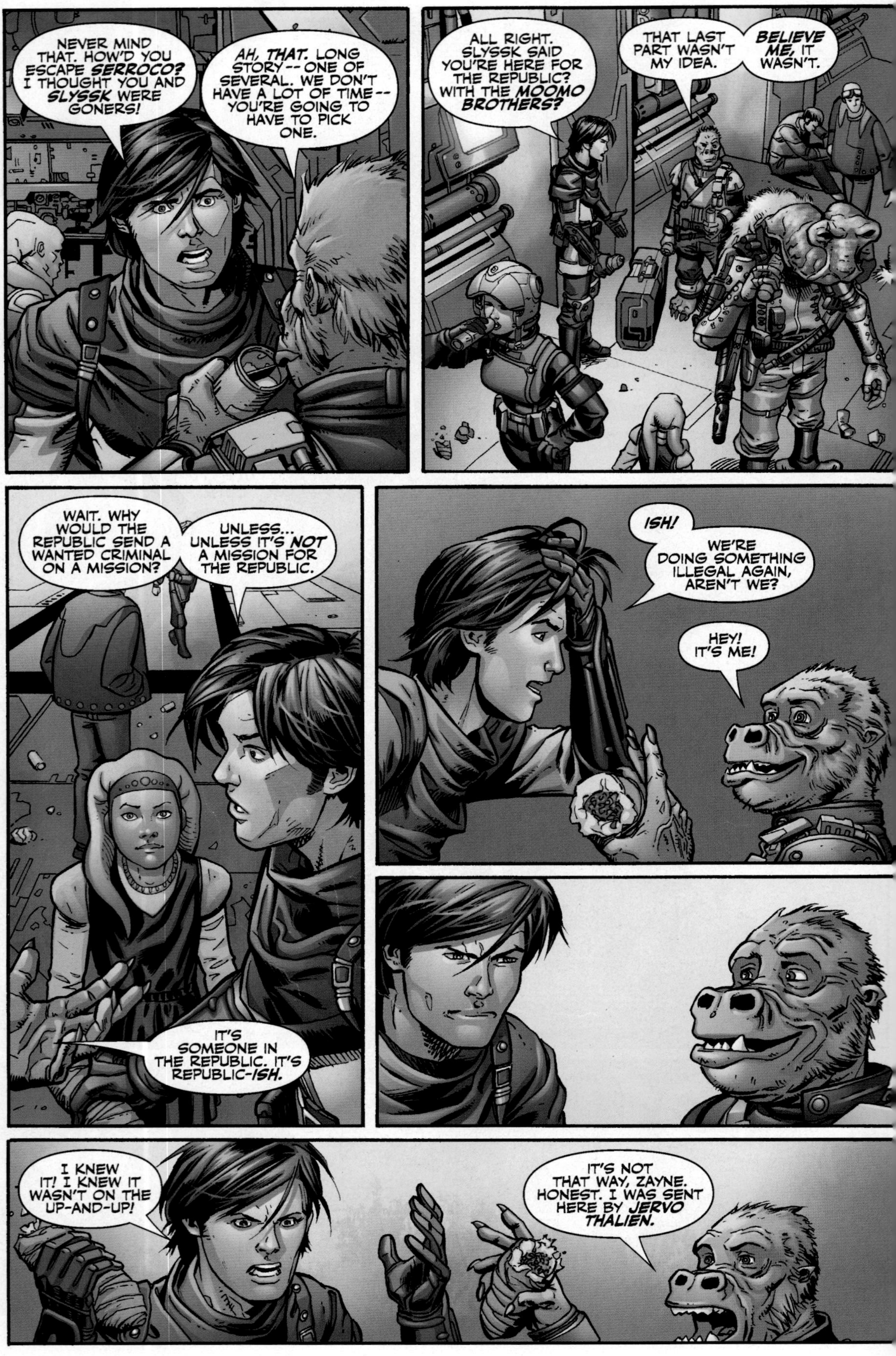
NEVER MIND THAT. HOW'D YOU ESCAPE SERROCO? I THOUGHT YOU AND SLYSSK WERE GONERS!
AH, THAT. LONG STORY -- ONE OF SEVERAL. WE DON'T HAVE A LOT OF TIME -- YOU'RE GOING TO HAVE TO PICK ONE.
ALL RIGHT. SLYSSK SAID YOU'RE HERE FOR THE REPUBLIC? WITH THE MOOMO BROTHERS?
THAT LAST PART WASN'T MY IDEA.
BELIEVE ME, IT WASN'T.
WAIT. WHY WOULD THE REPUBLIC SEND A WANTED CRIMINAL ON A MISSION?
UNLESS... UNLESS IT'S NOT A MISSION FOR THE REPUBLIC.
IT'S SOMEONE IN THE REPUBLIC. IT'S REPUBLIC-ISH.
ISH!
WE'RE DOING SOMETHING ILLEGAL AGAIN, AREN'T WE?
HEY! IT'S ME!
I KNEW IT! I KNEW IT WASN'T ON THE UP-AND-UP!
IT'S NOT THAT WAY, ZAYNE. HONEST. I WAS SENT HERE BY JERVO THALIEN.

JERVO *THALIEN?* THE HEAD OF *LHOSAN INDUSTRIES?* THE COMPANY THAT MAKES THE SWOOPBIKES?

AMONG OTHER THINGS. JERVO WANTED ME TO FIND *SENATOR GORAVVUS.*

OUR SENATOR? I MEAN, *TARIS'* SENATOR?

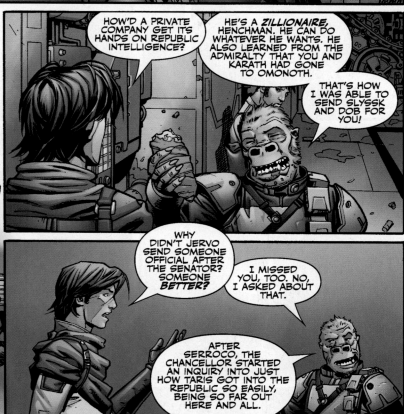

HOW'D A PRIVATE COMPANY GET ITS HANDS ON REPUBLIC INTELLIGENCE?

HE'S A *ZILLIONAIRE,* HENCHMAN. HE CAN DO WHATEVER HE WANTS. HE ALSO LEARNED FROM THE ADMIRALTY THAT YOU AND KARATH HAD GONE TO OMONOTH.

THAT'S HOW I WAS ABLE TO SEND SLYSSK AND DOB FOR YOU!

UNTIL RECENTLY. HE VANISHED RIGHT AFTER YOU AND I LEFT TARIS.

BUT JERVO FOUND OUT FROM REPUBLIC INTEL THAT THE SENATOR WAS ACTUALLY STILL *HERE,* RUNNING THE RESISTANCE IN THE LOWER CITY!

WHY DIDN'T JERVO SEND SOMEONE OFFICIAL AFTER THE SENATOR? SOMEONE *BETTER?*

I MISSED YOU, TOO. NO, I ASKED ABOUT THAT.

AFTER SERROCO, THE CHANCELLOR STARTED AN INQUIRY INTO JUST HOW TARIS GOT INTO THE REPUBLIC SO EASILY, BEING SO FAR OUT HERE AND ALL.

WELL, BEFORE HE WAS A SENATOR, GORAVVUS WAS KEY IN ESTABLISHING LHOSAN ON TARIS -- AND JERVO THANKED HIM WITH A SENATE SEAT.

LHOSAN'S STOCK PRICE GOES UP -- AND EVERYONE'S HAPPY. UNTIL THE INVASION, ANYWAY. NOW, I FIGURE JERVO WANTS TO SAVE HIS FRIEND --

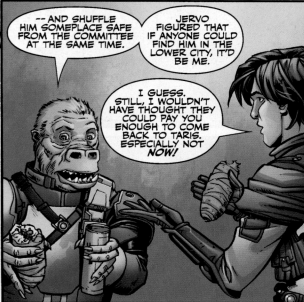

-- AND SHUFFLE HIM SOMEPLACE SAFE FROM THE COMMITTEE AT THE SAME TIME.

JERVO FIGURED THAT IF ANYONE COULD FIND HIM IN THE LOWER CITY, IT'D BE ME.

I GUESS. STILL, I WOULDN'T HAVE THOUGHT THEY COULD PAY YOU ENOUGH TO COME BACK TO TARIS. ESPECIALLY NOT *NOW!*

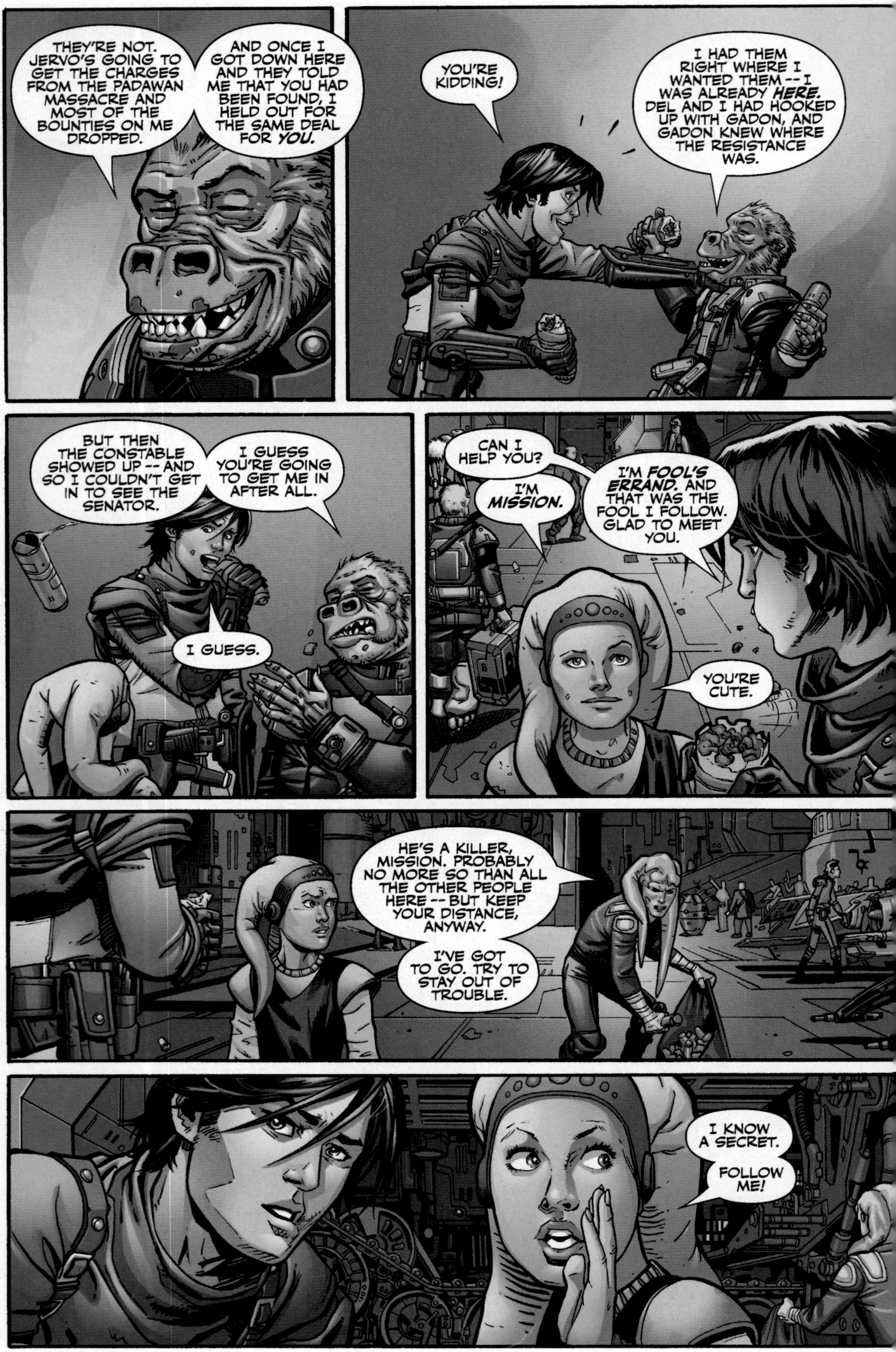
THEY'RE NOT. JERVO'S GOING TO GET THE CHARGES FROM THE PADAWAN MASSACRE AND MOST OF THE BOUNTIES ON ME DROPPED.
AND ONCE I GOT DOWN HERE AND THEY TOLD ME THAT YOU HAD BEEN FOUND, I HELD OUT FOR THE SAME DEAL FOR *YOU.*
YOU'RE KIDDING!
I HAD THEM RIGHT WHERE I WANTED THEM -- I WAS ALREADY *HERE.* DEL AND I HAD HOOKED UP WITH GADON, AND GADON KNEW WHERE THE RESISTANCE WAS.
BUT THEN THE CONSTABLE SHOWED UP -- AND SO I COULDN'T GET IN TO SEE THE SENATOR.
I GUESS YOU'RE GOING TO GET ME IN AFTER ALL.
I GUESS.
CAN I HELP YOU?
I'M *MISSION.*
I'M *FOOL'S ERRAND.* AND THAT WAS THE FOOL I FOLLOW. GLAD TO MEET YOU.
YOU'RE CUTE.
HE'S A KILLER, MISSION. PROBABLY NO MORE SO THAN ALL THE OTHER PEOPLE HERE -- BUT KEEP YOUR DISTANCE, ANYWAY.
I'VE GOT TO GO. TRY TO STAY OUT OF TROUBLE.
I KNOW A SECRET.
FOLLOW ME!

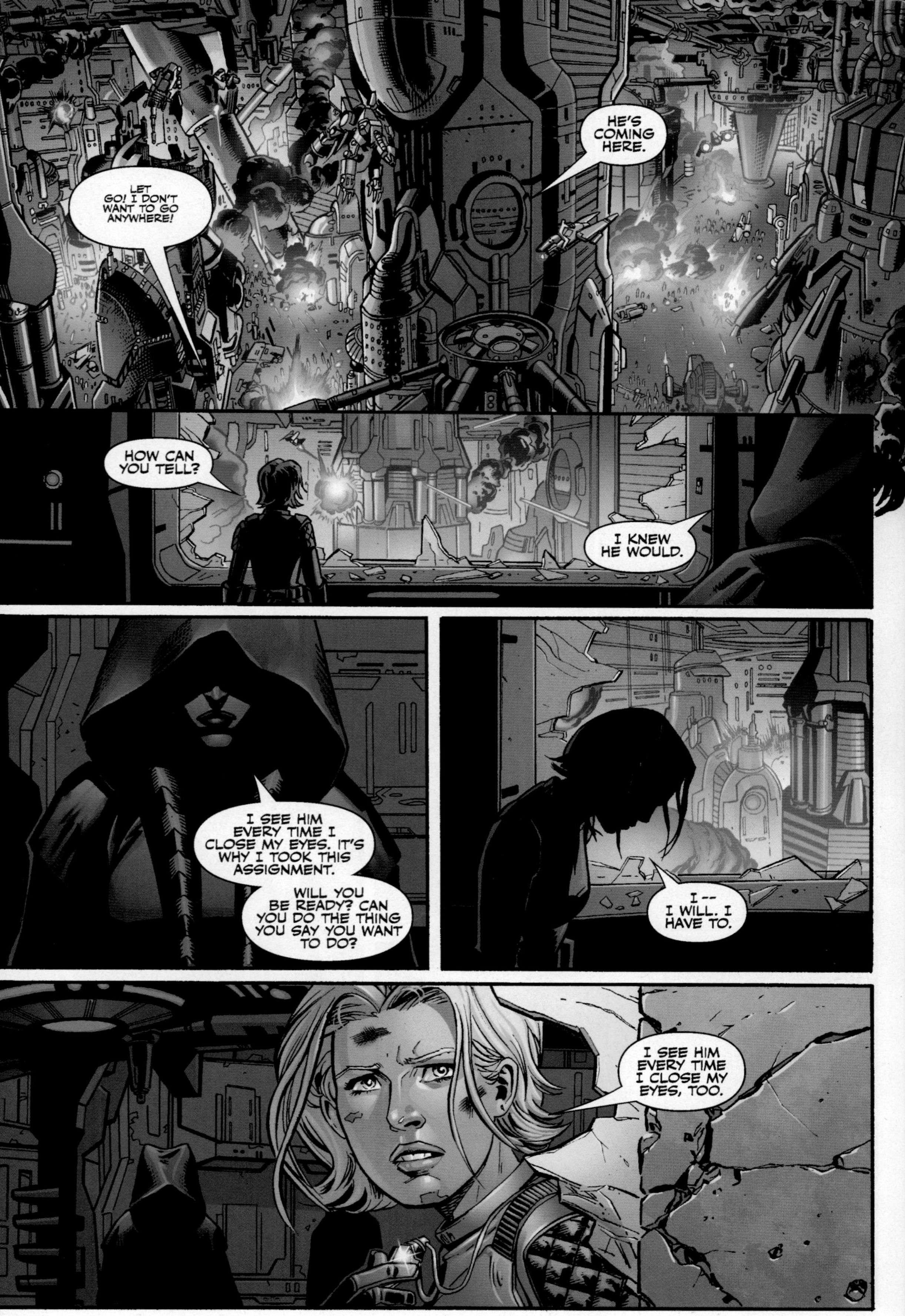
LET GO! I DON'T WANT TO GO ANYWHERE!
HE'S COMING HERE.
HOW CAN YOU TELL?
I KNEW HE WOULD.
I SEE HIM EVERY TIME I CLOSE MY EYES. IT'S WHY I TOOK THIS ASSIGNMENT.
WILL YOU BE READY? CAN YOU DO THE THING YOU SAY YOU WANT TO DO?
I -- I WILL. I HAVE TO.
I SEE HIM EVERY TIME I CLOSE MY EYES, TOO.

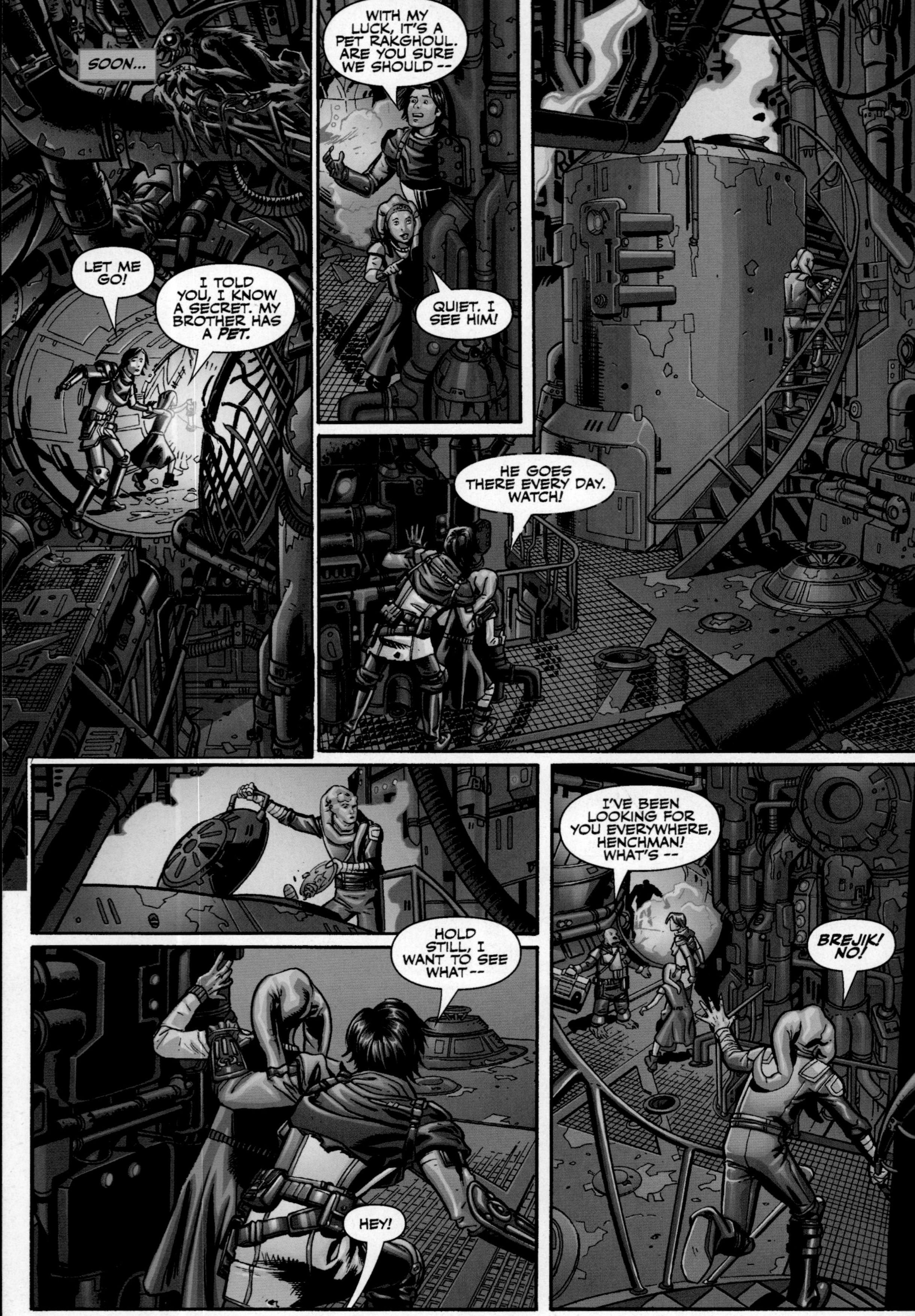
SOON...
LET ME GO!
I TOLD YOU, I KNOW A SECRET. MY BROTHER HAS A *PET*.
WITH MY LUCK, IT'S A PET RAKGHOUL. ARE YOU SURE WE SHOULD --
QUIET. I SEE HIM!
HE GOES THERE EVERY DAY. WATCH!
HOLD STILL, I WANT TO SEE WHAT --
HEY!
I'VE BEEN LOOKING FOR YOU EVERYWHERE, HENCHMAN! WHAT'S --
BREJIK! NO!

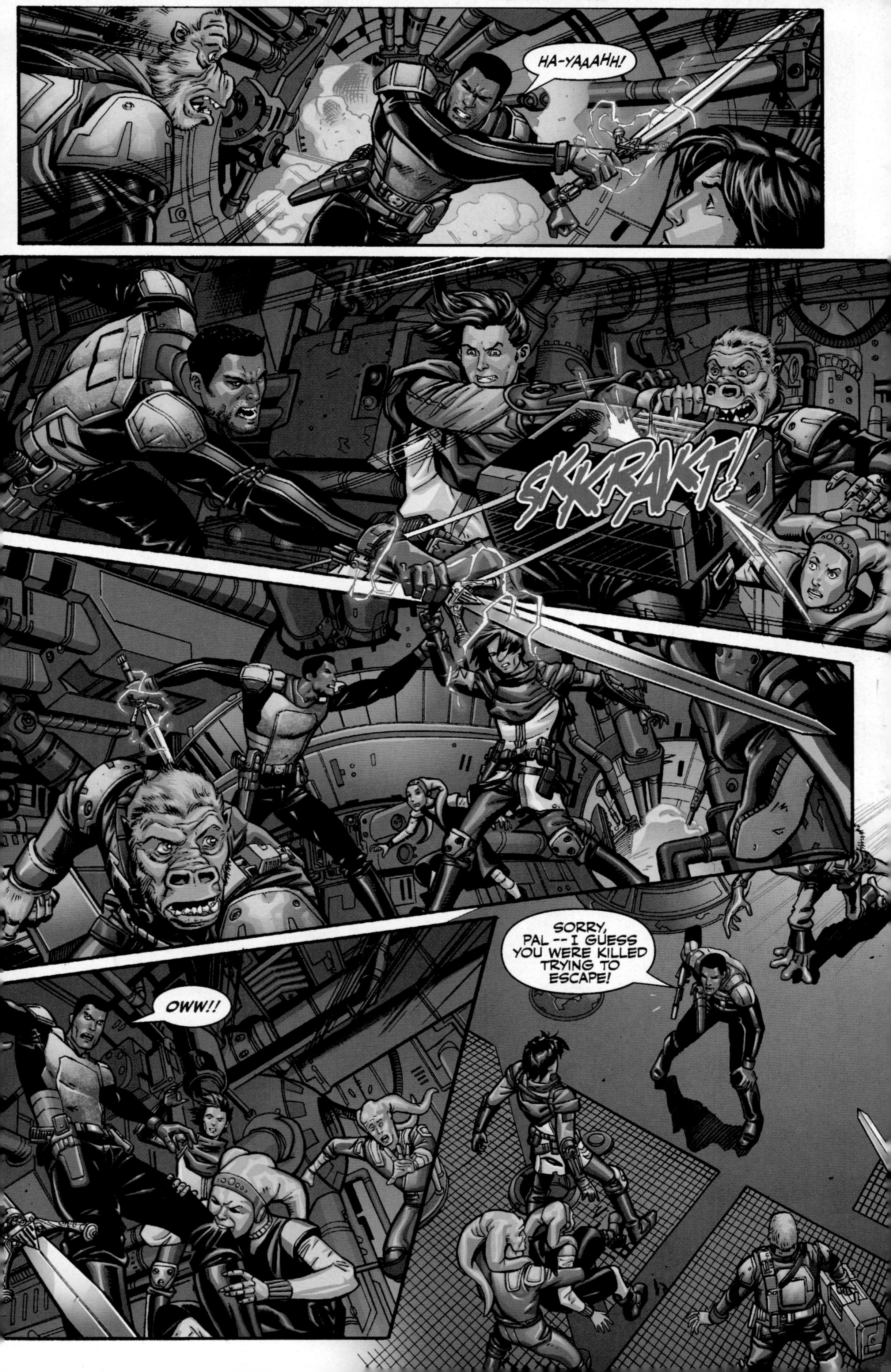
HA-YAAAHH!
SKKRAKT!
SORRY, PAL -- I GUESS YOU WERE KILLED TRYING TO ESCAPE!
OWW!!

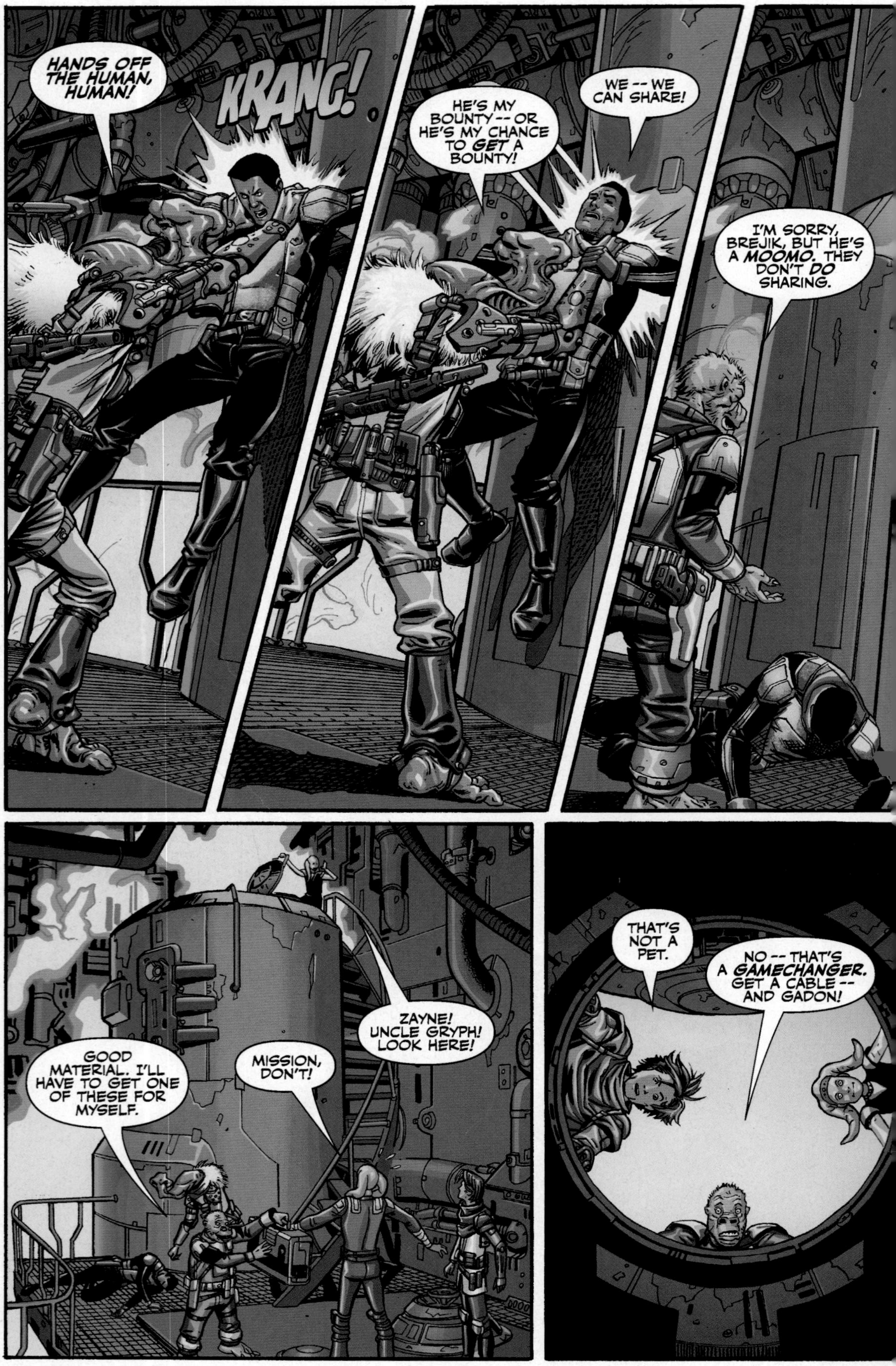

HANDS OFF THE HUMAN, HUMAN!
KRANG!
HE'S MY BOUNTY -- OR HE'S MY CHANCE TO GET A BOUNTY!
WE -- WE CAN SHARE!
I'M SORRY, BREJIK, BUT HE'S A MOOMO. THEY DON'T DO SHARING.
GOOD MATERIAL. I'LL HAVE TO GET ONE OF THESE FOR MYSELF.
MISSION, DON'T!
ZAYNE! UNCLE GRYPH! LOOK HERE!
THAT'S NOT A PET.
NO -- THAT'S A GAMECHANGER. GET A CABLE -- AND GADON!

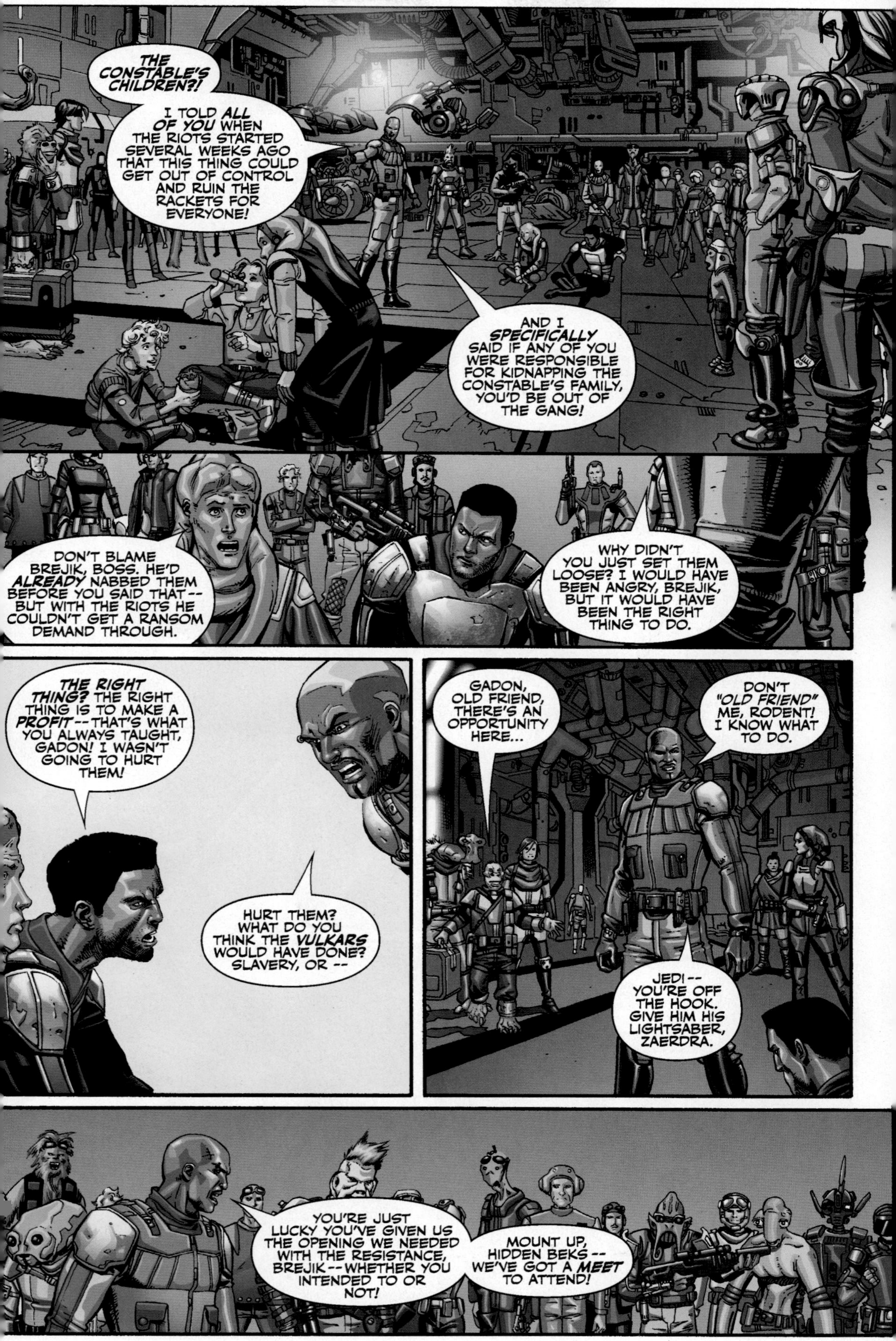
THE CONSTABLE'S CHILDREN?!
I TOLD ALL OF YOU WHEN THE RIOTS STARTED SEVERAL WEEKS AGO THAT THIS THING COULD GET OUT OF CONTROL AND RUIN THE RACKETS FOR EVERYONE!
AND I SPECIFICALLY SAID IF ANY OF YOU WERE RESPONSIBLE FOR KIDNAPPING THE CONSTABLE'S FAMILY, YOU'D BE OUT OF THE GANG!
DON'T BLAME BREJIK, BOSS. HE'D ALREADY NABBED THEM BEFORE YOU SAID THAT-- BUT WITH THE RIOTS HE COULDN'T GET A RANSOM DEMAND THROUGH.
WHY DIDN'T YOU JUST SET THEM LOOSE? I WOULD HAVE BEEN ANGRY, BREJIK, BUT IT WOULD HAVE BEEN THE RIGHT THING TO DO.
THE RIGHT THING? THE RIGHT THING IS TO MAKE A PROFIT--THAT'S WHAT YOU ALWAYS TAUGHT, GADON! I WASN'T GOING TO HURT THEM!
HURT THEM? WHAT DO YOU THINK THE VULKARS WOULD HAVE DONE? SLAVERY, OR --
GADON, OLD FRIEND, THERE'S AN OPPORTUNITY HERE...
DON'T "OLD FRIEND" ME, RODENT! I KNOW WHAT TO DO.
JEDI-- YOU'RE OFF THE HOOK. GIVE HIM HIS LIGHTSABER, ZAERDRA.
YOU'RE JUST LUCKY YOU'VE GIVEN US THE OPENING WE NEEDED WITH THE RESISTANCE, BREJIK--WHETHER YOU INTENDED TO OR NOT!
MOUNT UP, HIDDEN BEKS-- WE'VE GOT A MEET TO ATTEND!

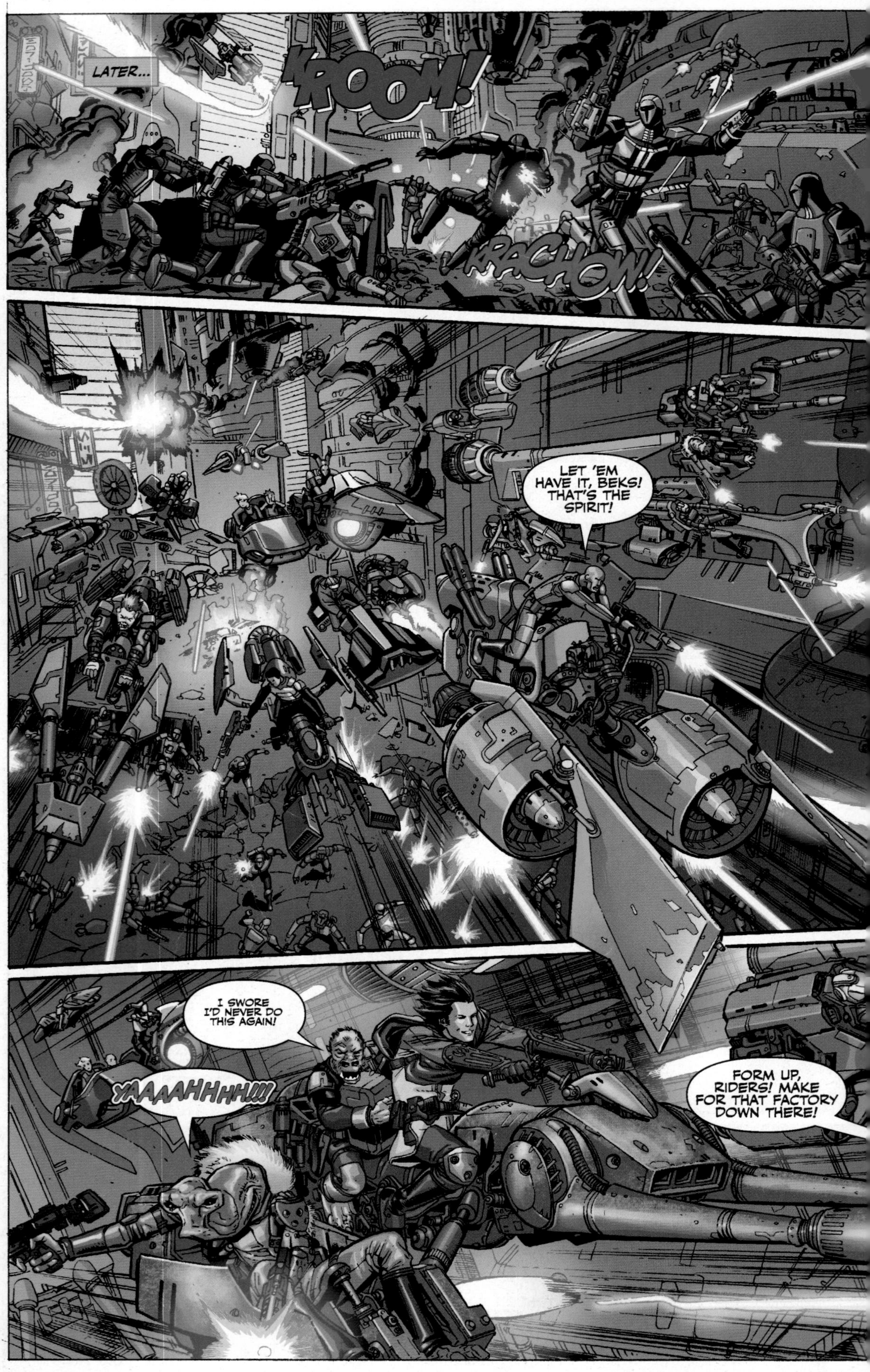
LATER...
KROOOM!
KRACHOW!
LET 'EM HAVE IT, BEKS! THAT'S THE SPIRIT!
I SWORE I'D NEVER DO THIS AGAIN!
YAAAAHHHH!!!
FORM UP, RIDERS! MAKE FOR THAT FACTORY DOWN THERE!

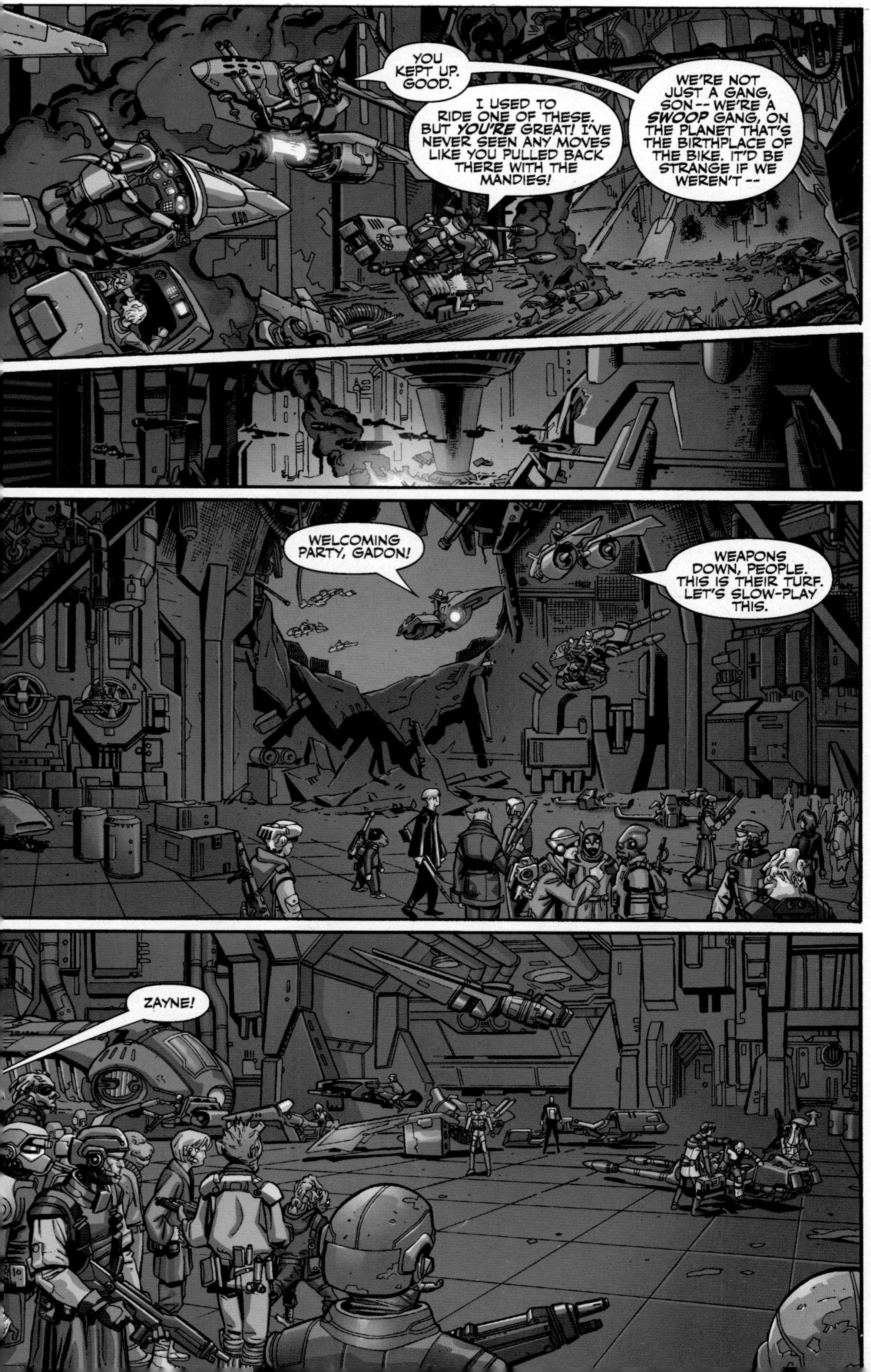
YOU KEPT UP. GOOD.
I USED TO RIDE ONE OF THESE. BUT YOU'RE GREAT! I'VE NEVER SEEN ANY MOVES LIKE YOU PULLED BACK THERE WITH THE MANDIES!
WE'RE NOT JUST A GANG, SON -- WE'RE A SWOOP GANG, ON THE PLANET THAT'S THE BIRTHPLACE OF THE BIKE. IT'D BE STRANGE IF WE WEREN'T --
WELCOMING PARTY, GADON!
WEAPONS DOWN, PEOPLE. THIS IS THEIR TURF. LET'S SLOW-PLAY THIS.
ZAYNE!

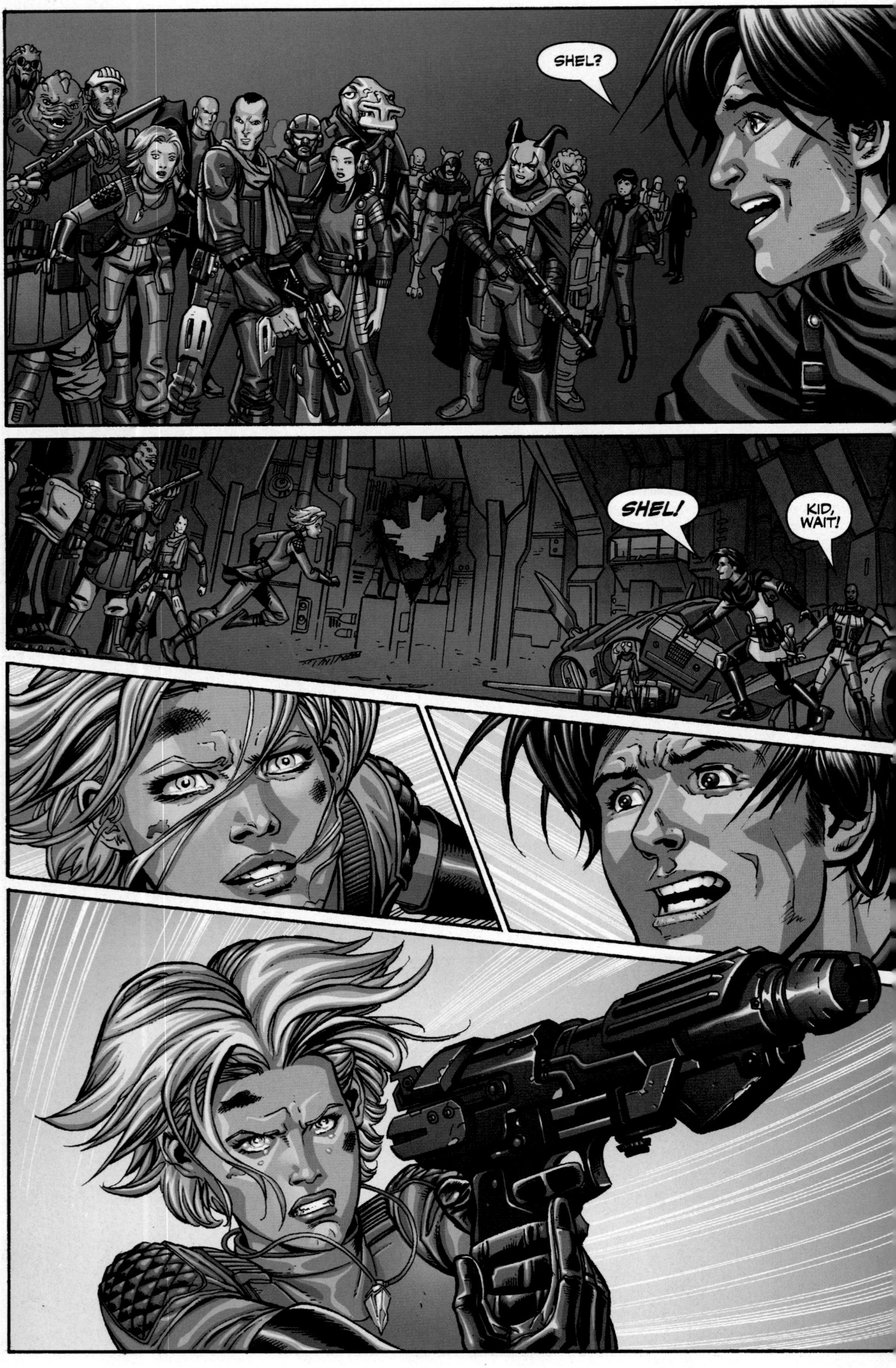
SHEL?
SHEL!
KID, WAIT!

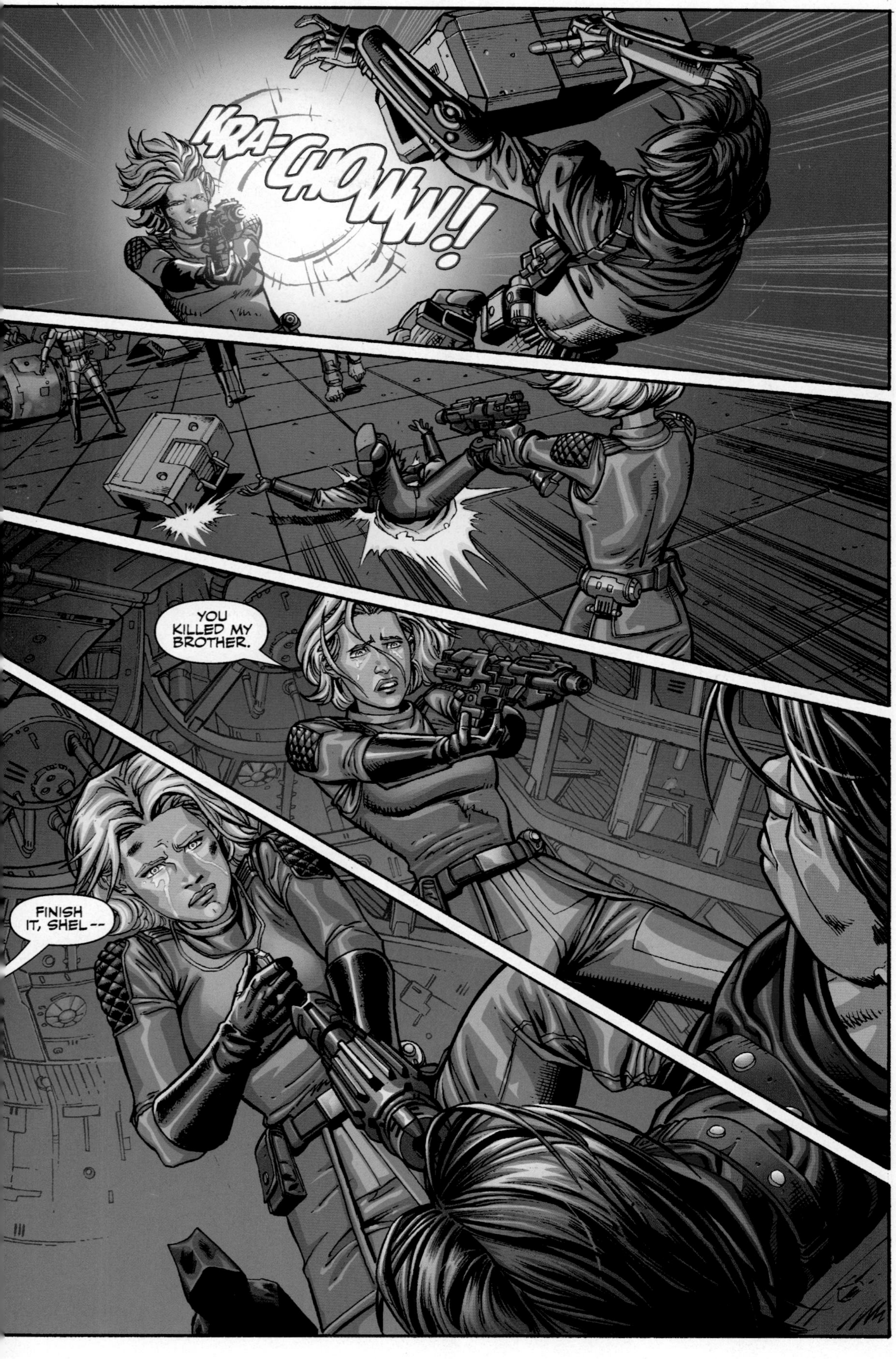
KRA-CHOWW!!
YOU KILLED MY BROTHER.
FINISH IT, SHEL--

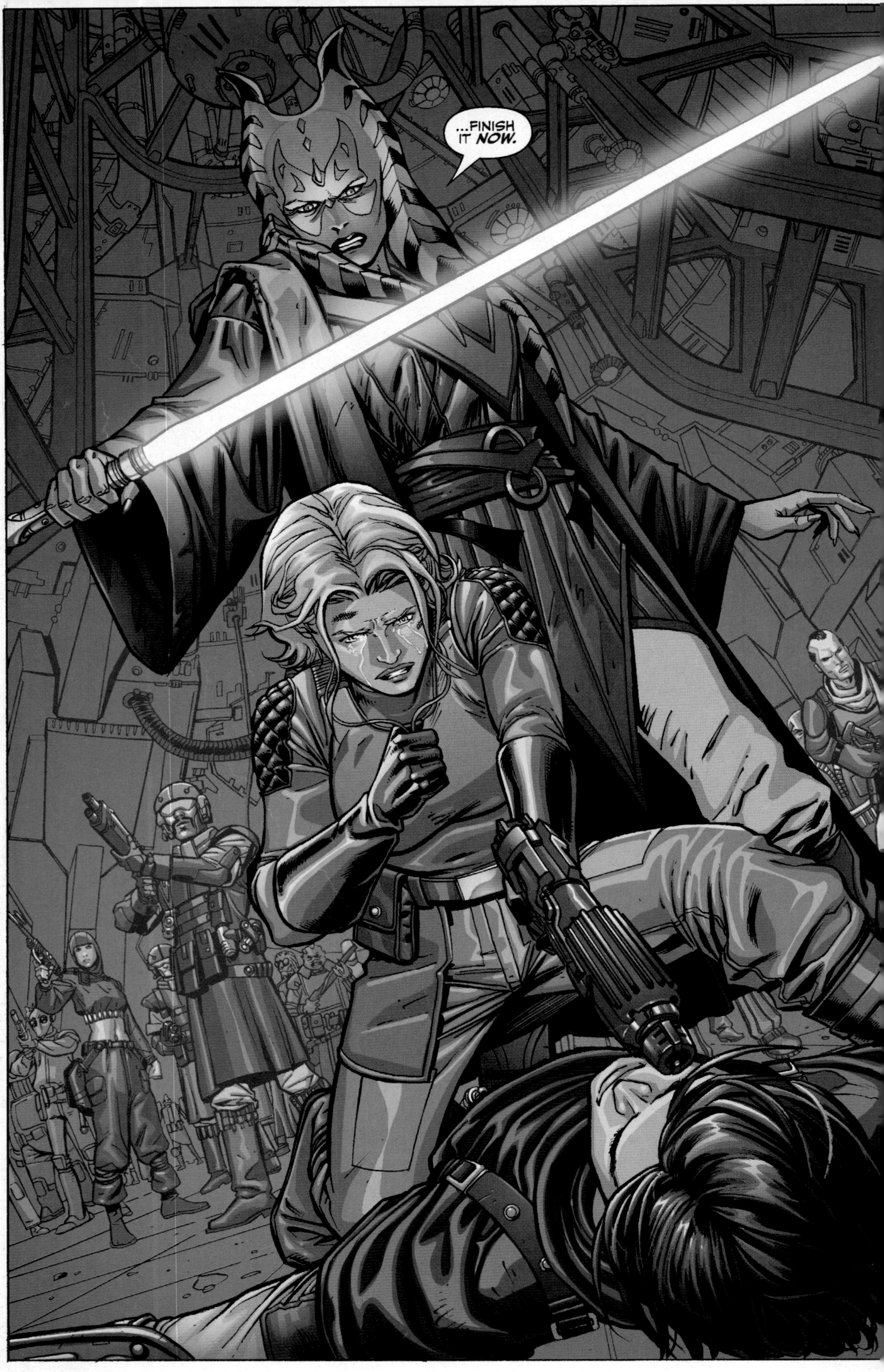
...FINISH IT NOW.

THE ADMIRAL'S LIST

THE OFFICIAL COMMUNIQUÉ FROM THE REPUBLIC NAVY

KARATH HOME SAFELY

Embattled admiral reaches Coruscant

Joyous celebrations spread quickly across Coruscant as word spread that Rear Admiral Saul Karath, veteran of the Serroco and Vanquo campaigns, had arrived safely.

The improbable escape from the devastation of Serroco took the admiral—along with his second, Commander Dallan Morvis, and three other crewmen—through occupied Mandalorian space. Their flight to safety included participation in the defense of the *Arkanian Legacy* against the Mandalorian raid that ultimately took the life of Lord Adasca (see related report).

Upon arrival at Admiralty Plaza, sources report the Admiral immediately submitted his resignation over the loss of Battle Group Serroco and flagship *Courageous*. The Admiral of the Fleet promptly refused to accept the resignation, instead convoking a private briefing for the Admiral and his companions. Afterward, the Admiral of the Fleet publicly commended Karath's performance.

The Admiralty has not yet announced a posting for Admiral Karath, although with the *Swiftsure* set to leave drydock at Corellia, speculation has focused on who is to command her. In brief remarks, the Admiral said he appreciated the outpouring of support but wanted to see that those in his ordeal had a chance to see their families—"in the name of those who did not make it home," he said.

LORD ADASCA REMEMBERED

Munitions, medicine supplier falls in surprise attack

Republic defense officials sought quickly today to minimize supply concerns days after reports first surfaced that Arkoh, the eighth Lord Adasca, had been slain in a surprise attack on his research vessel by a Mandalorian raiding party. Rear Admiral Saul Karath confirmed the death of the young industrialist while on an expedition far from the protections of home.

"Lord Adasca met his end as he lived, in the search for knowledge," Admiral Karath said. He declined to speak further about the incident, about which little is known. Neither the location nor disposition of the *Arkanian Legacy* is known, and given the raid it must be assumed the Mandalorians are in close proximity.

"The supply of medical goods and processed materials from Adascorp continues uninterrupted," said defense official Catronus Steffans. However, doubt continues to circulate in the business world as to corporate control. The only remaining heir to the House of Adasca is herself unaccounted for since the devastation of Serroco—and earlier today, investor groups led by the Draay Trust filed a legal challenge in Adascopolis on Arkania for the right to bid for control of the company.

"Lord Adasca was a great and loyal corporate citizen of the Republic," Steffans said. "We expect to continue our robust relationship with his firm until our ultimate victory—and beyond."

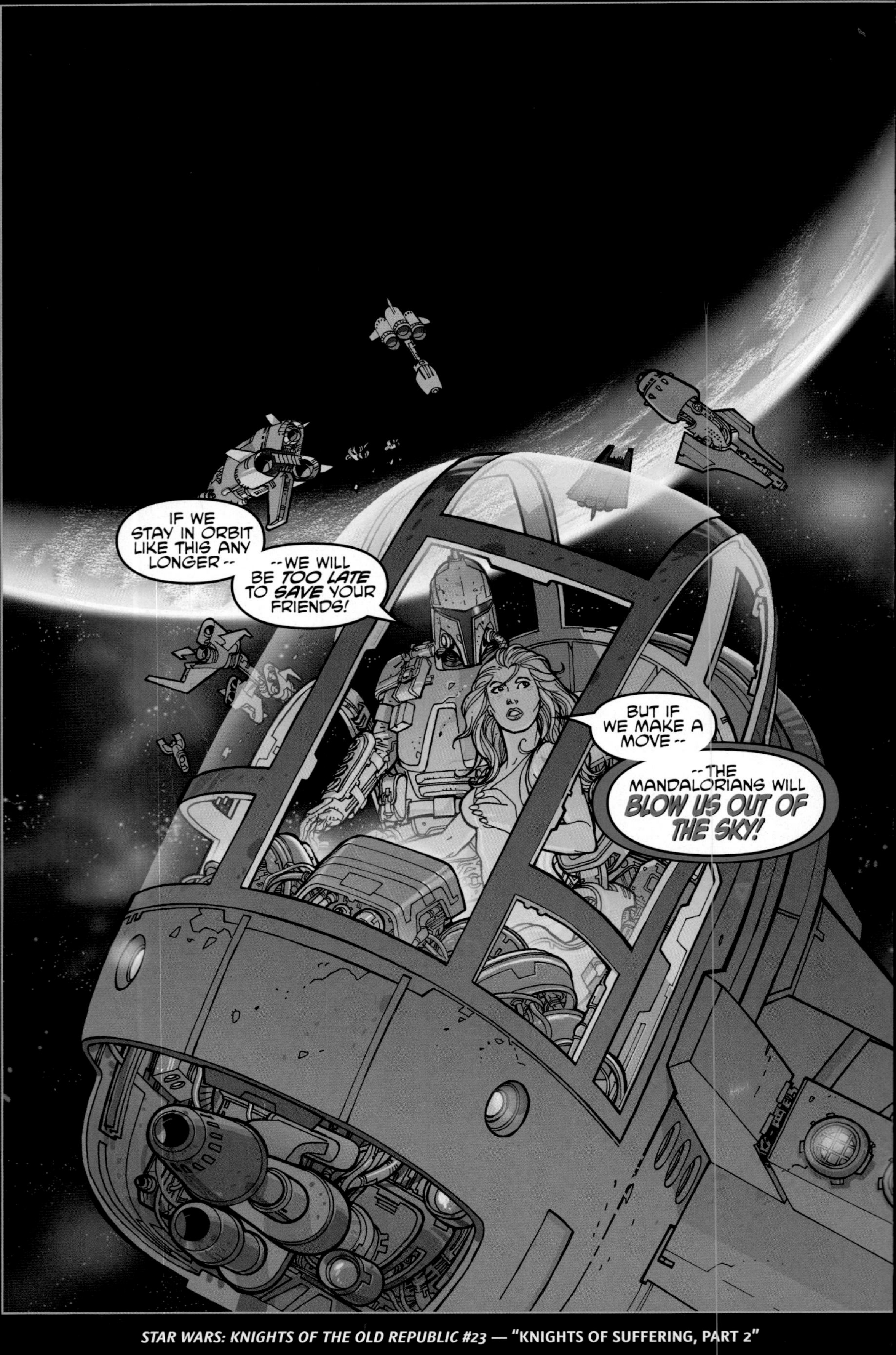
IF WE STAY IN ORBIT LIKE THIS ANY LONGER --
--WE WILL BE TOO LATE TO SAVE YOUR FRIENDS!
BUT IF WE MAKE A MOVE --
--THE MANDALORIANS WILL BLOW US OUT OF THE SKY!

***STAR WARS: KNIGHTS OF THE OLD REPUBLIC #23* — "KNIGHTS OF SUFFERING, PART 2"**

WRITER: JOHN JACKSON MILLER • PENCILER: DUSTIN WEAVER • INKER: DAN PARSONS • COLORIST: MICHAEL ATIYEH
LETTERER: MICHAEL HEISLER • ASSISTANT EDITOR: DAVE MARSHALL • EDITOR: JEREMY BARLOW • COVER ARTIST: COLIN WILSON

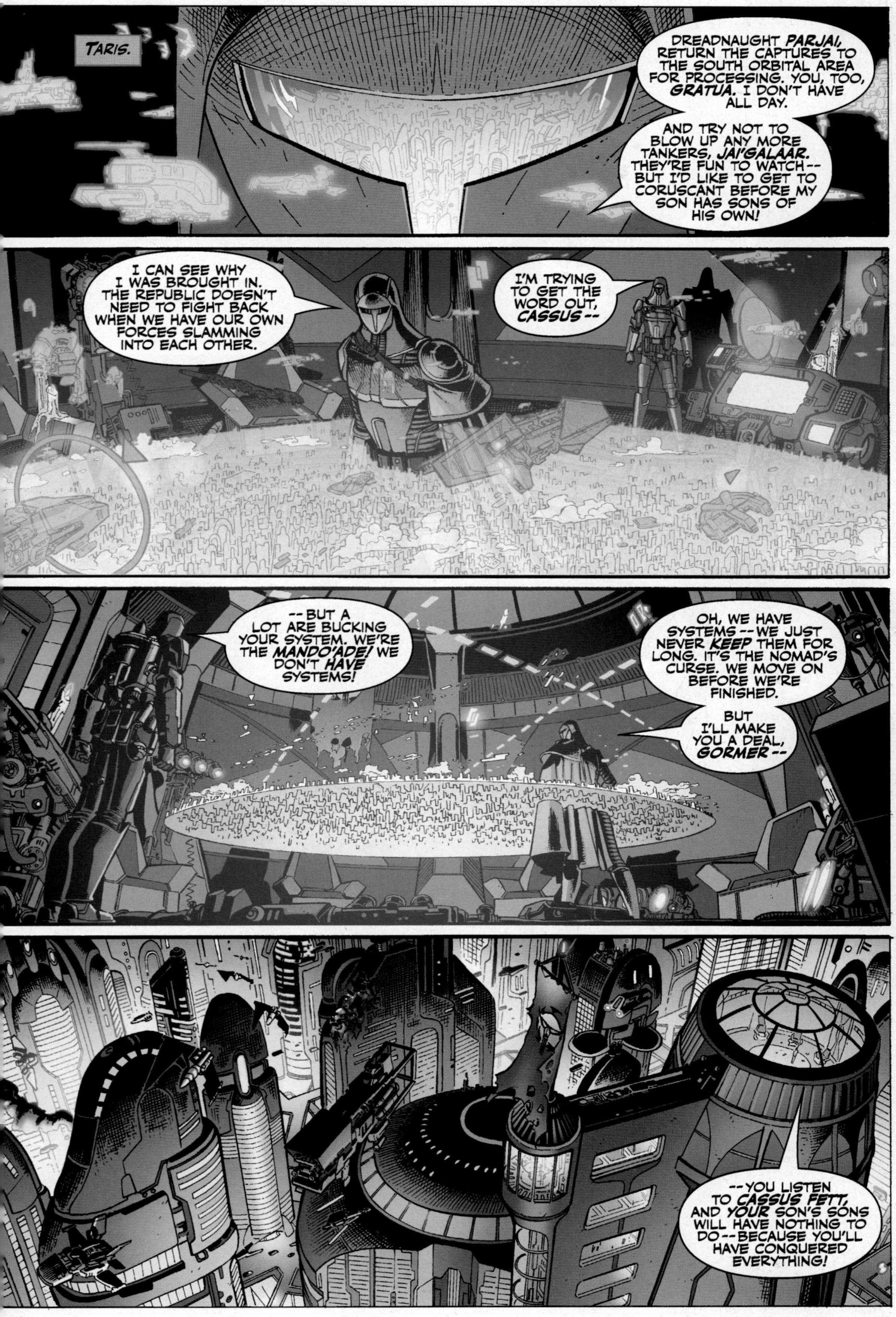
TARIS.
DREADNAUGHT PARJAI, RETURN THE CAPTURES TO THE SOUTH ORBITAL AREA FOR PROCESSING. YOU, TOO, GRATUA. I DON'T HAVE ALL DAY.
AND TRY NOT TO BLOW UP ANY MORE TANKERS, JAI'GALAAR. THEY'RE FUN TO WATCH-- BUT I'D LIKE TO GET TO CORUSCANT BEFORE MY SON HAS SONS OF HIS OWN!
I CAN SEE WHY I WAS BROUGHT IN. THE REPUBLIC DOESN'T NEED TO FIGHT BACK WHEN WE HAVE OUR OWN FORCES SLAMMING INTO EACH OTHER.
I'M TRYING TO GET THE WORD OUT, CASSUS--
--BUT A LOT ARE BUCKING YOUR SYSTEM. WE'RE THE MANDO'ADE! WE DON'T HAVE SYSTEMS!
OH, WE HAVE SYSTEMS--WE JUST NEVER KEEP THEM FOR LONG. IT'S THE NOMAD'S CURSE. WE MOVE ON BEFORE WE'RE FINISHED.
BUT I'LL MAKE YOU A DEAL, GORMER--
--YOU LISTEN TO CASSUS FETT, AND YOUR SON'S SONS WILL HAVE NOTHING TO DO--BECAUSE YOU'LL HAVE CONQUERED EVERYTHING!

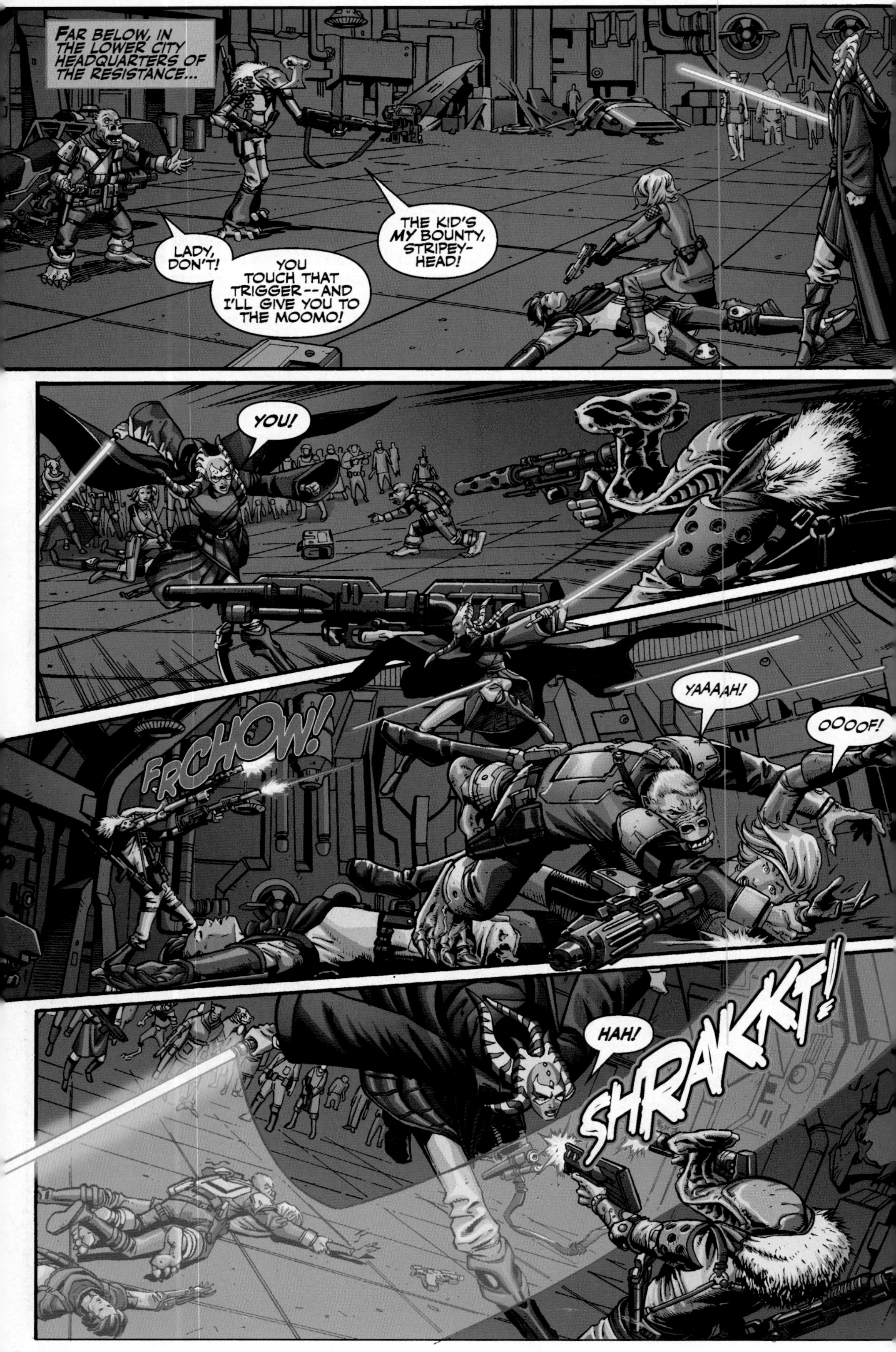

FAR BELOW, IN THE LOWER CITY HEADQUARTERS OF THE RESISTANCE...
LADY, DON'T!
YOU TOUCH THAT TRIGGER--AND I'LL GIVE YOU TO THE MOOMO!
THE KID'S MY BOUNTY, STRIPEY-HEAD!
YOU!
FRCHOW!
YAAAAH!
OOOOF!
HAH!
SHRAKKT!

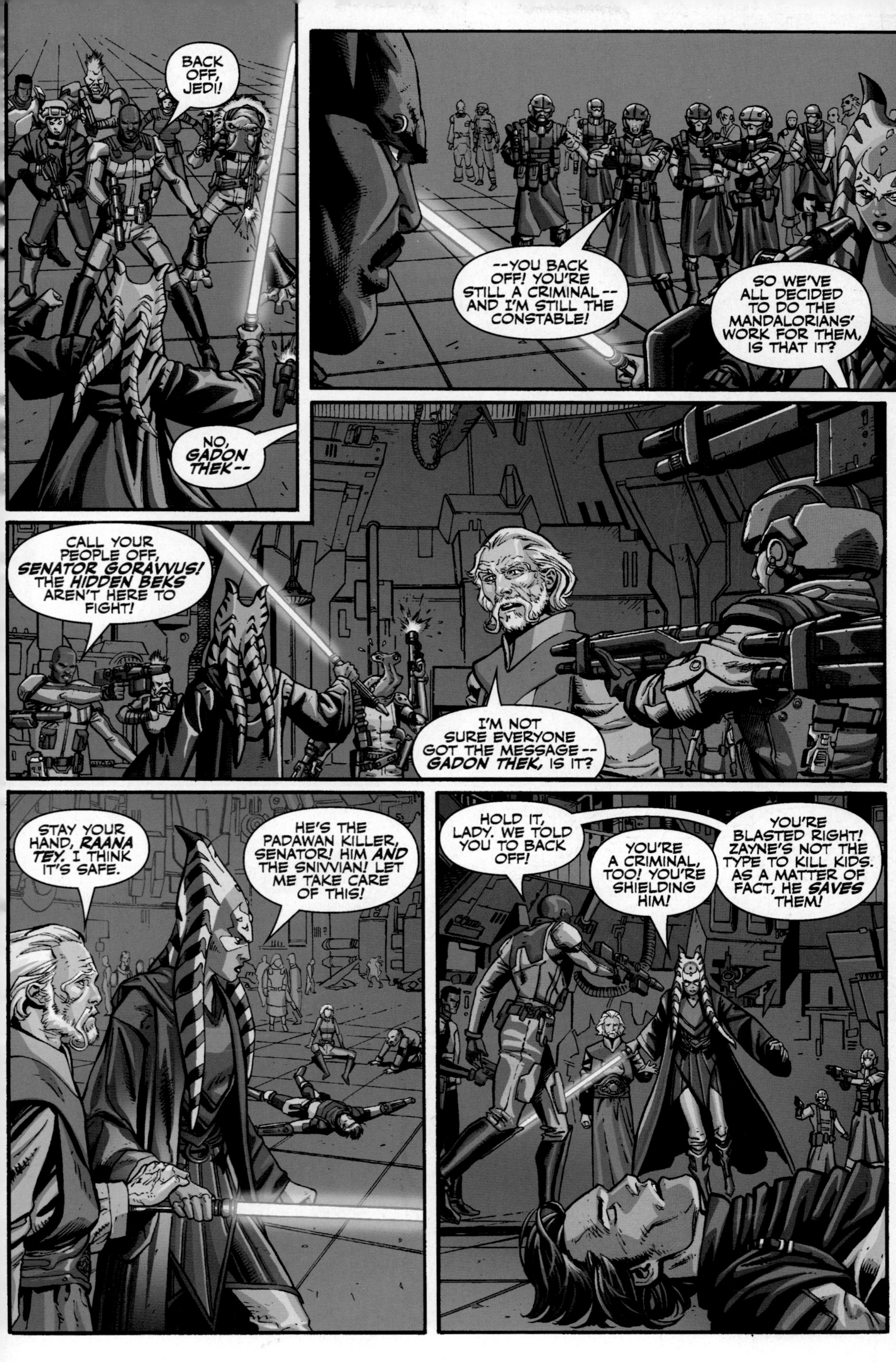
BACK OFF, JEDI!
--YOU BACK OFF! YOU'RE STILL A CRIMINAL -- AND I'M STILL THE CONSTABLE!
SO WE'VE ALL DECIDED TO DO THE MANDALORIANS' WORK FOR THEM, IS THAT IT?
NO, GADON THEK--
CALL YOUR PEOPLE OFF, SENATOR GORAVVUS! THE HIDDEN BEKS AREN'T HERE TO FIGHT!
I'M NOT SURE EVERYONE GOT THE MESSAGE -- GADON THEK, IS IT?
STAY YOUR HAND, RAANA TEY. I THINK IT'S SAFE.
HE'S THE PADAWAN KILLER, SENATOR! HIM AND THE SNIVVIAN! LET ME TAKE CARE OF THIS!
HOLD IT, LADY. WE TOLD YOU TO BACK OFF!
YOU'RE A CRIMINAL, TOO! YOU'RE SHIELDING HIM!
YOU'RE BLASTED RIGHT! ZAYNE'S NOT THE TYPE TO KILL KIDS. AS A MATTER OF FACT, HE SAVES THEM!

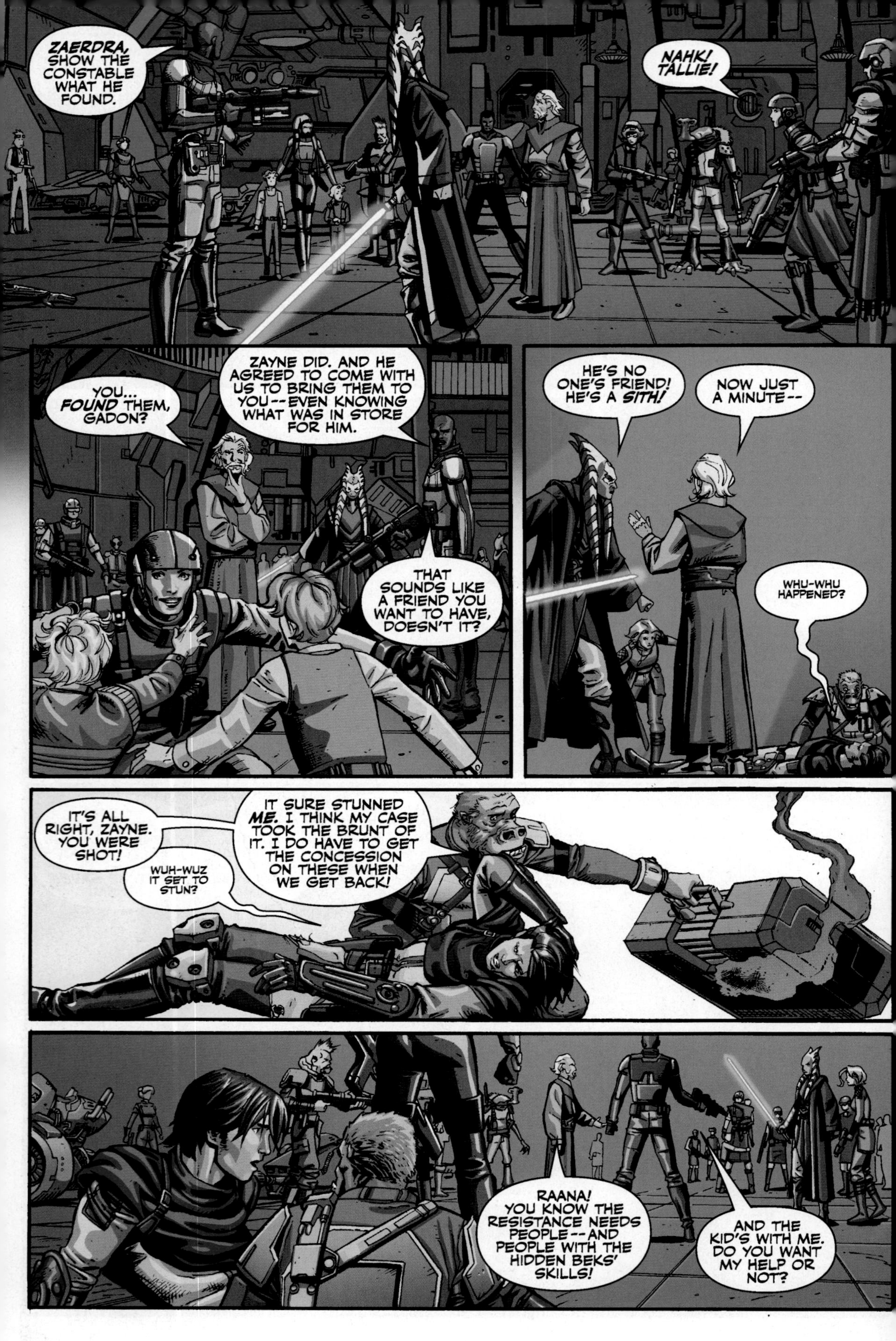
ZAERDRA, SHOW THE CONSTABLE WHAT HE FOUND.
NAHK! TALLIE!
YOU... FOUND THEM, GADON?
ZAYNE DID. AND HE AGREED TO COME WITH US TO BRING THEM TO YOU--EVEN KNOWING WHAT WAS IN STORE FOR HIM.
THAT SOUNDS LIKE A FRIEND YOU WANT TO HAVE, DOESN'T IT?
HE'S NO ONE'S FRIEND! HE'S A SITH!
NOW JUST A MINUTE--
WHU-WHU HAPPENED?
IT'S ALL RIGHT, ZAYNE. YOU WERE SHOT!
WUH-WUZ IT SET TO STUN?
IT SURE STUNNED ME. I THINK MY CASE TOOK THE BRUNT OF IT. I DO HAVE TO GET THE CONCESSION ON THESE WHEN WE GET BACK!
RAANA! YOU KNOW THE RESISTANCE NEEDS PEOPLE--AND PEOPLE WITH THE HIDDEN BEKS' SKILLS!
AND THE KID'S WITH ME. DO YOU WANT MY HELP OR NOT?

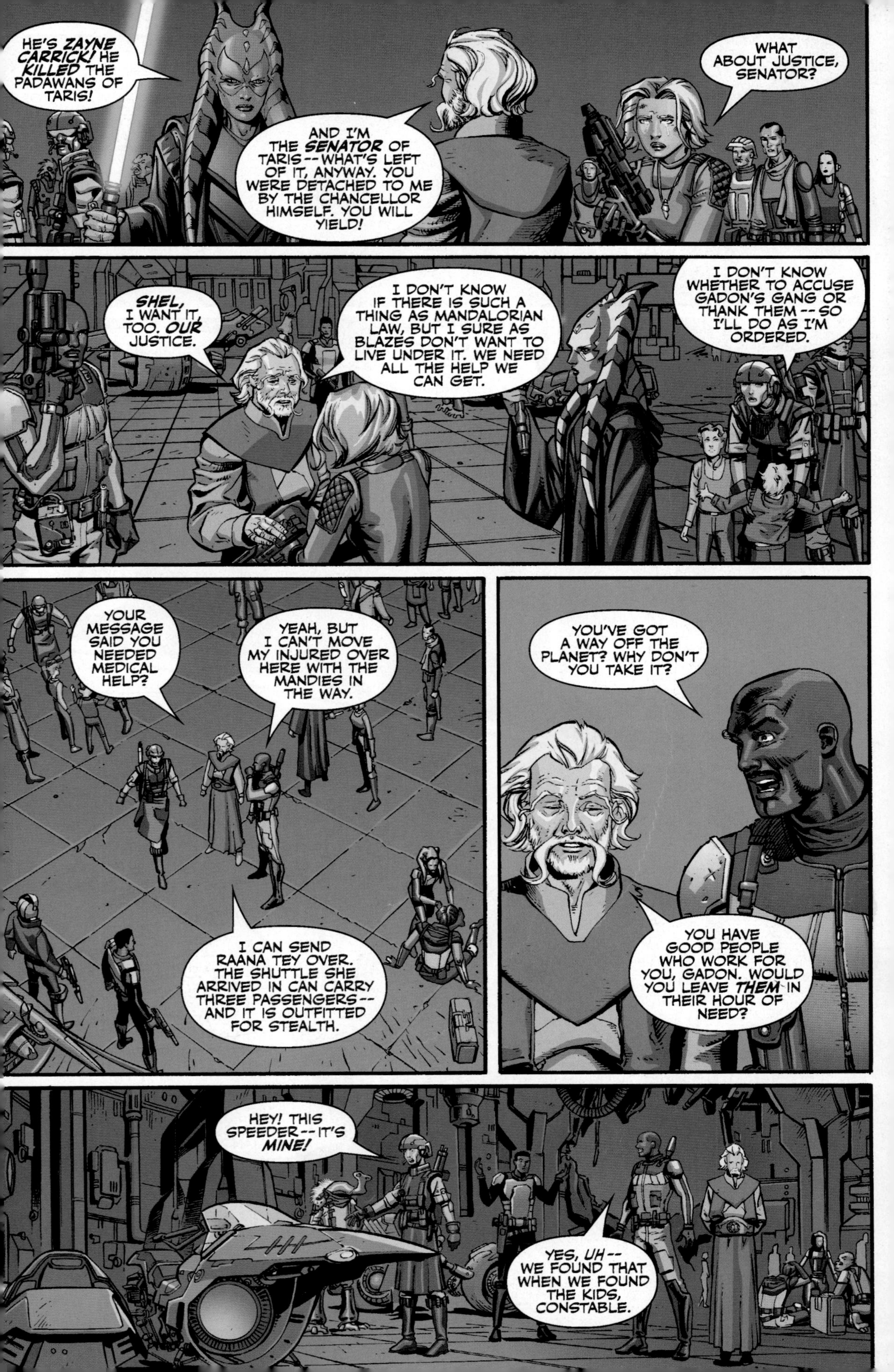
HE'S ZAYNE CARRICK! HE KILLED THE PADAWANS OF TARIS!
AND I'M THE SENATOR OF TARIS--WHAT'S LEFT OF IT, ANYWAY. YOU WERE DETACHED TO ME BY THE CHANCELLOR HIMSELF. YOU WILL YIELD!
WHAT ABOUT JUSTICE, SENATOR?
SHEL, I WANT IT, TOO. OUR JUSTICE.
I DON'T KNOW IF THERE IS SUCH A THING AS MANDALORIAN LAW, BUT I SURE AS BLAZES DON'T WANT TO LIVE UNDER IT. WE NEED ALL THE HELP WE CAN GET.
I DON'T KNOW WHETHER TO ACCUSE GADON'S GANG OR THANK THEM--SO I'LL DO AS I'M ORDERED.
YOUR MESSAGE SAID YOU NEEDED MEDICAL HELP?
YEAH, BUT I CAN'T MOVE MY INJURED OVER HERE WITH THE MANDIES IN THE WAY.
I CAN SEND RAANA TEY OVER. THE SHUTTLE SHE ARRIVED IN CAN CARRY THREE PASSENGERS--AND IT IS OUTFITTED FOR STEALTH.
YOU'VE GOT A WAY OFF THE PLANET? WHY DON'T YOU TAKE IT?
YOU HAVE GOOD PEOPLE WHO WORK FOR YOU, GADON. WOULD YOU LEAVE THEM IN THEIR HOUR OF NEED?
HEY! THIS SPEEDER--IT'S MINE!
YES, UH--WE FOUND THAT WHEN WE FOUND THE KIDS, CONSTABLE.

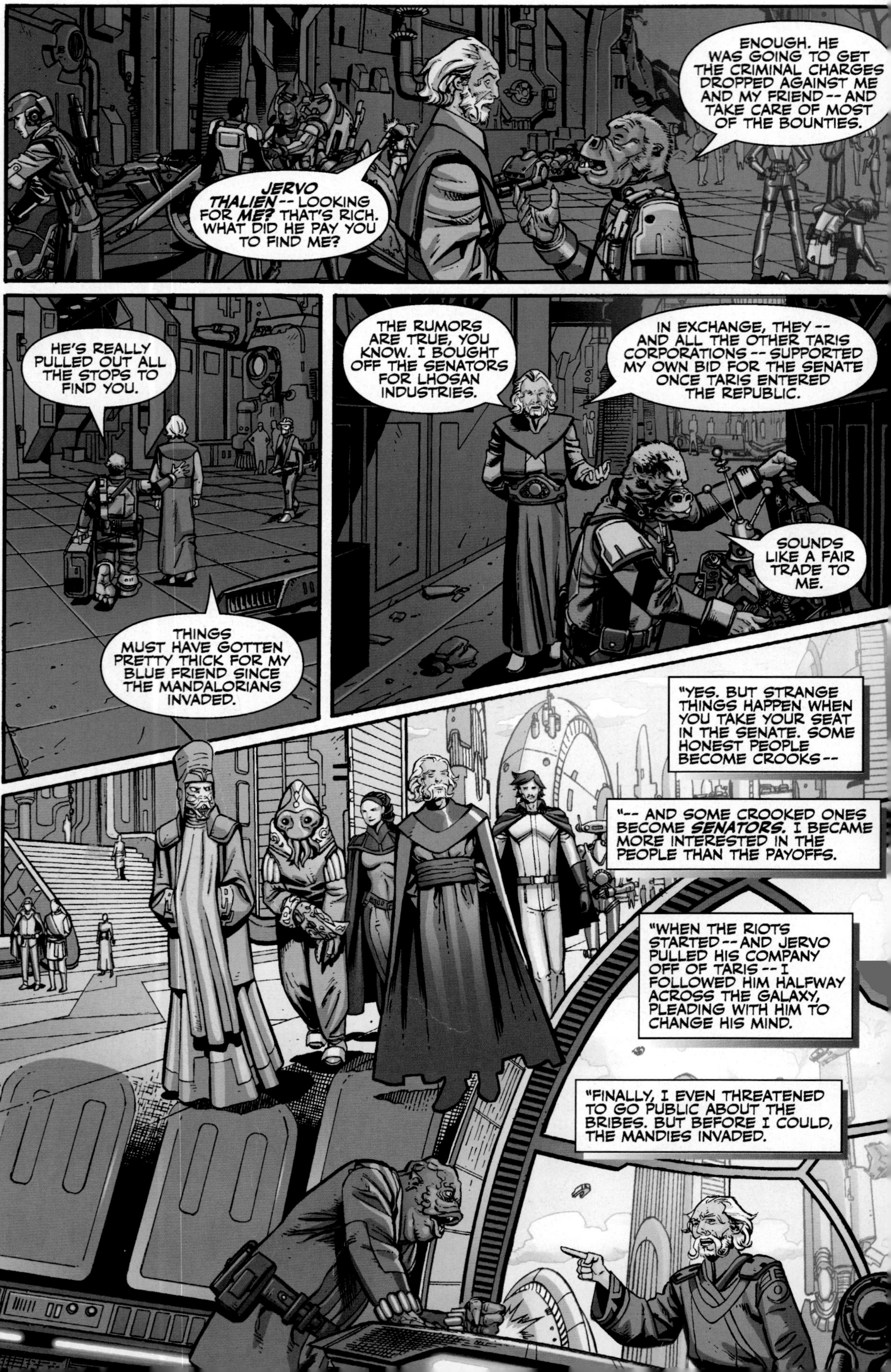
JERVO THALIEN -- LOOKING FOR ME? THAT'S RICH. WHAT DID HE PAY YOU TO FIND ME?
ENOUGH. HE WAS GOING TO GET THE CRIMINAL CHARGES DROPPED AGAINST ME AND MY FRIEND -- AND TAKE CARE OF MOST OF THE BOUNTIES.
HE'S REALLY PULLED OUT ALL THE STOPS TO FIND YOU.
THINGS MUST HAVE GOTTEN PRETTY THICK FOR MY BLUE FRIEND SINCE THE MANDALORIANS INVADED.
THE RUMORS ARE TRUE, YOU KNOW. I BOUGHT OFF THE SENATORS FOR LHOSAN INDUSTRIES.
IN EXCHANGE, THEY -- AND ALL THE OTHER TARIS CORPORATIONS -- SUPPORTED MY OWN BID FOR THE SENATE ONCE TARIS ENTERED THE REPUBLIC.
SOUNDS LIKE A FAIR TRADE TO ME.
"YES. BUT STRANGE THINGS HAPPEN WHEN YOU TAKE YOUR SEAT IN THE SENATE. SOME HONEST PEOPLE BECOME CROOKS--
"-- AND SOME CROOKED ONES BECOME SENATORS. I BECAME MORE INTERESTED IN THE PEOPLE THAN THE PAYOFFS.
"WHEN THE RIOTS STARTED -- AND JERVO PULLED HIS COMPANY OFF OF TARIS -- I FOLLOWED HIM HALFWAY ACROSS THE GALAXY, PLEADING WITH HIM TO CHANGE HIS MIND.
"FINALLY, I EVEN THREATENED TO GO PUBLIC ABOUT THE BRIBES. BUT BEFORE I COULD, THE MANDIES INVADED.

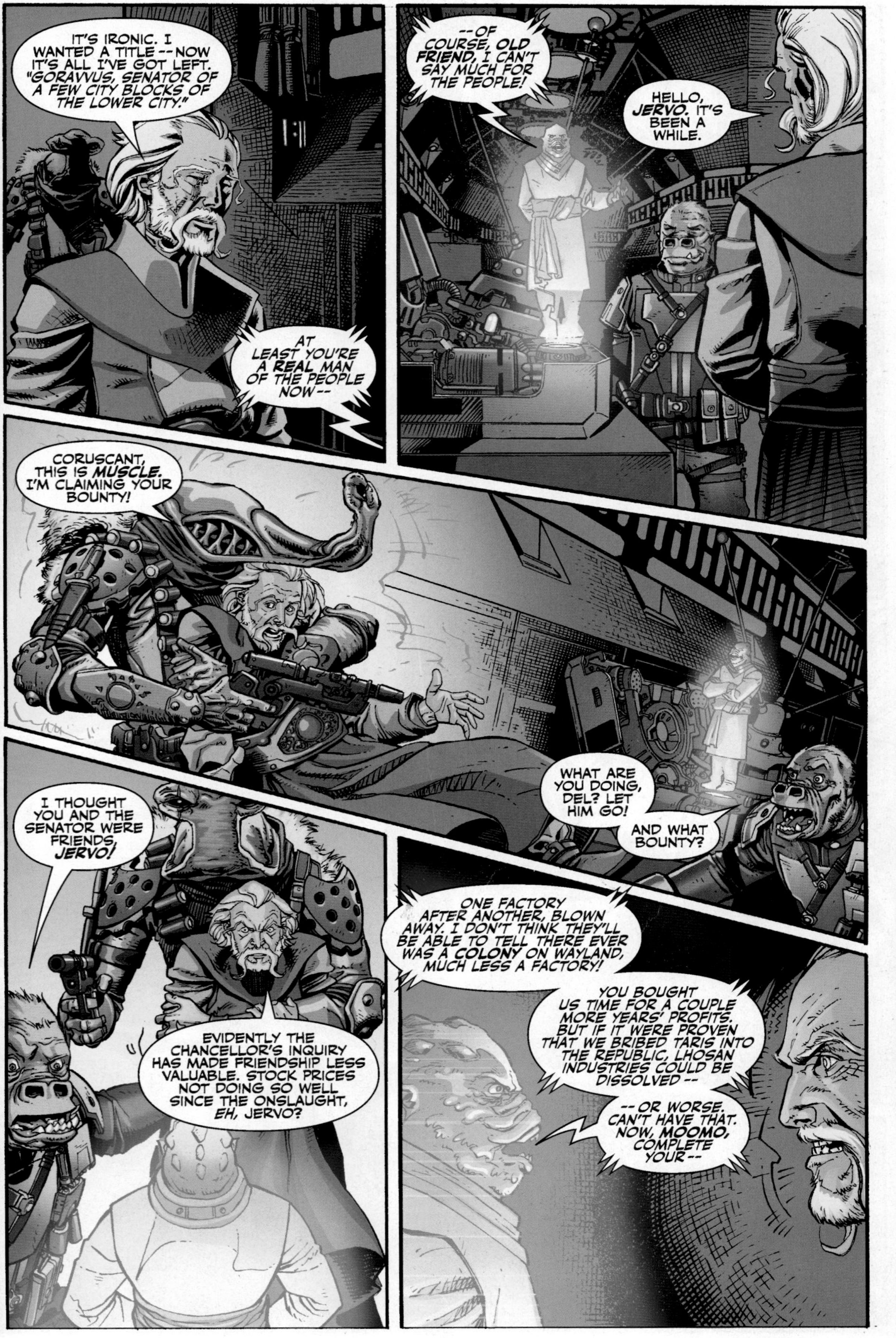
IT'S IRONIC. I WANTED A TITLE--NOW IT'S ALL I'VE GOT LEFT. "GORAVVUS, SENATOR OF A FEW CITY BLOCKS OF THE LOWER CITY."
AT LEAST YOU'RE A REAL MAN OF THE PEOPLE NOW--
--OF COURSE, OLD FRIEND, I CAN'T SAY MUCH FOR THE PEOPLE!
HELLO, JERVO. IT'S BEEN A WHILE.
CORUSCANT, THIS IS MUSCLE. I'M CLAIMING YOUR BOUNTY!
WHAT ARE YOU DOING, DEL? LET HIM GO!
AND WHAT BOUNTY?
I THOUGHT YOU AND THE SENATOR WERE FRIENDS, JERVO!
EVIDENTLY THE CHANCELLOR'S INQUIRY HAS MADE FRIENDSHIP LESS VALUABLE. STOCK PRICES NOT DOING SO WELL SINCE THE ONSLAUGHT, EH, JERVO?
ONE FACTORY AFTER ANOTHER, BLOWN AWAY. I DON'T THINK THEY'LL BE ABLE TO TELL THERE EVER WAS A COLONY ON WAYLAND, MUCH LESS A FACTORY!
YOU BOUGHT US TIME FOR A COUPLE MORE YEARS' PROFITS, BUT IF IT WERE PROVEN THAT WE BRIBED TARIS INTO THE REPUBLIC, LHOSAN INDUSTRIES COULD BE DISSOLVED--
--OR WORSE. CAN'T HAVE THAT. NOW, MOOMO, COMPLETE YOUR--

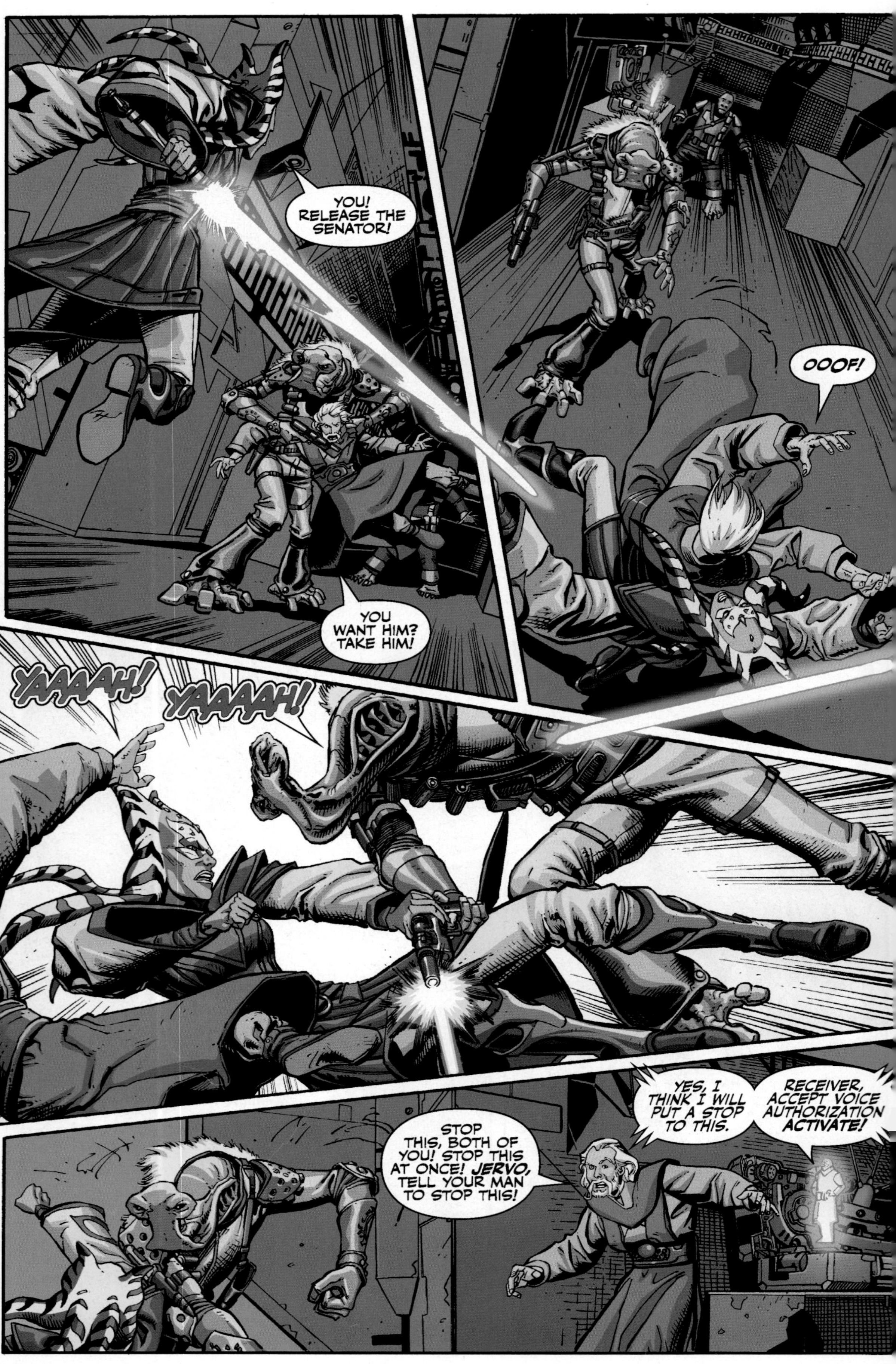
YOU! RELEASE THE SENATOR!
YOU WANT HIM? TAKE HIM!
OOOF!
YAAAAH!
YAAAAH!
STOP THIS, BOTH OF YOU! STOP THIS AT ONCE! JERVO, TELL YOUR MAN TO STOP THIS!
YES, I THINK I WILL PUT A STOP TO THIS.
RECEIVER, ACCEPT VOICE AUTHORIZATION ACTIVATE!

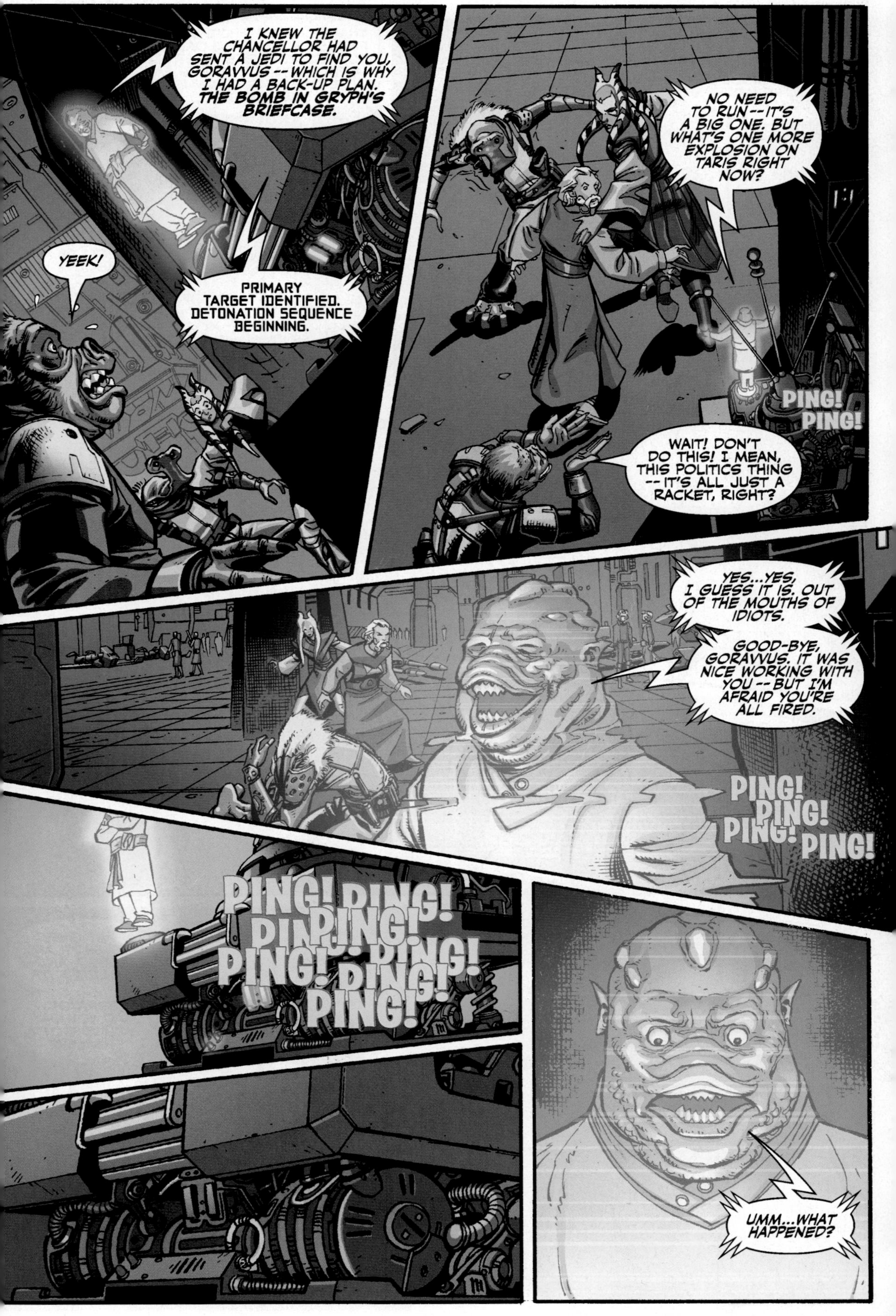
I KNEW THE CHANCELLOR HAD SENT A JEDI TO FIND YOU, GORAVVUS -- WHICH IS WHY I HAD A BACK-UP PLAN. THE BOMB IN GRYPH'S BRIEFCASE.
YEEK!
PRIMARY TARGET IDENTIFIED. DETONATION SEQUENCE BEGINNING.
NO NEED TO RUN -- IT'S A BIG ONE. BUT WHAT'S ONE MORE EXPLOSION ON TARIS RIGHT NOW?
PING! PING!
WAIT! DON'T DO THIS! I MEAN, THIS POLITICS THING -- IT'S ALL JUST A RACKET, RIGHT?
YES...YES, I GUESS IT IS. OUT OF THE MOUTHS OF IDIOTS.
GOOD-BYE, GORAVVUS. IT WAS NICE WORKING WITH YOU -- BUT I'M AFRAID YOU'RE ALL FIRED.
PING! PING! PING! PING!
PING! PING! PING! PING! PING! PING! PING! PING!
UMM...WHAT HAPPENED?

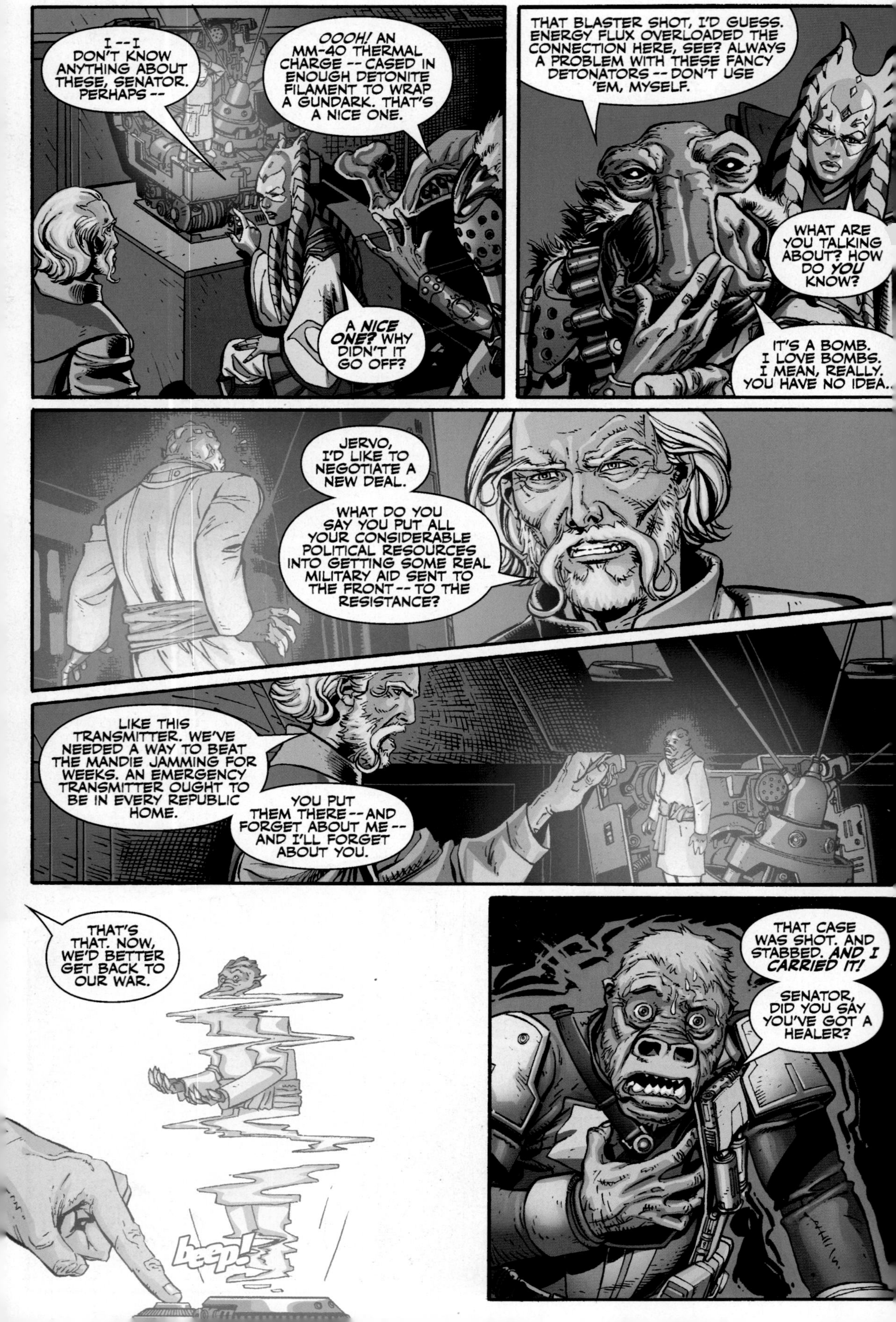
I -- I DON'T KNOW ANYTHING ABOUT THESE, SENATOR. PERHAPS --
OOOH! AN MM-40 THERMAL CHARGE -- CASED IN ENOUGH DETONITE FILAMENT TO WRAP A GUNDARK. THAT'S A NICE ONE.
A NICE ONE? WHY DIDN'T IT GO OFF?
THAT BLASTER SHOT, I'D GUESS. ENERGY FLUX OVERLOADED THE CONNECTION HERE, SEE? ALWAYS A PROBLEM WITH THESE FANCY DETONATORS -- DON'T USE 'EM, MYSELF.
WHAT ARE YOU TALKING ABOUT? HOW DO YOU KNOW?
IT'S A BOMB. I LOVE BOMBS. I MEAN, REALLY. YOU HAVE NO IDEA...
JERVO, I'D LIKE TO NEGOTIATE A NEW DEAL.
WHAT DO YOU SAY YOU PUT ALL YOUR CONSIDERABLE POLITICAL RESOURCES INTO GETTING SOME REAL MILITARY AID SENT TO THE FRONT -- TO THE RESISTANCE?
LIKE THIS TRANSMITTER. WE'VE NEEDED A WAY TO BEAT THE MANDIE JAMMING FOR WEEKS. AN EMERGENCY TRANSMITTER OUGHT TO BE IN EVERY REPUBLIC HOME.
YOU PUT THEM THERE -- AND FORGET ABOUT ME -- AND I'LL FORGET ABOUT YOU.
THAT'S THAT. NOW, WE'D BETTER GET BACK TO OUR WAR.
beep!
THAT CASE WAS SHOT. AND STABBED. AND I CARRIED IT!
SENATOR, DID YOU SAY YOU'VE GOT A HEALER?

AH, THERE YOU ARE, JARAEL --

-- I HAVE BEEN LISTENING TO THEIR CHATTER IN THE OTHER COCKPIT. THE *MANDO'ADE* ARE STILL FOCUSED ON THE INVASION.

THEY WILL NOT HAVE PERSONNEL TO DO MORE THAN WATCH OTHER CAPTURED VESSELS FOR A WHILE.

STILL NO WORD FROM BELOW?

NONE. YOUR OTHER JEDI FRIEND AND I HAVE BEEN DISCUSSING HOW LONG WE SHOULD WAIT.

WE HAVE DECIDED NOTHING, BUT WE THOUGHT IT WOULD PLEASE YOU TO KNOW WE ARE TALKING.

I KEEP THINKING --

-- I KEEP THINKING CAMPER WILL CALL. BUT HE DOESN'T KNOW WHERE I AM. ADASCA TOOK MY LOCATOR BRACELET.

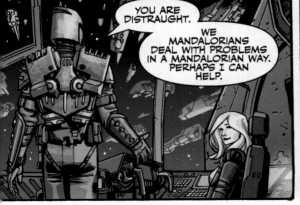

YOU ARE DISTRAUGHT.

WE MANDALORIANS DEAL WITH PROBLEMS IN A MANDALORIAN WAY. PERHAPS I CAN HELP.

FOLLOW ME. I HAVE JUST THE THING TO OCCUPY YOUR MIND...

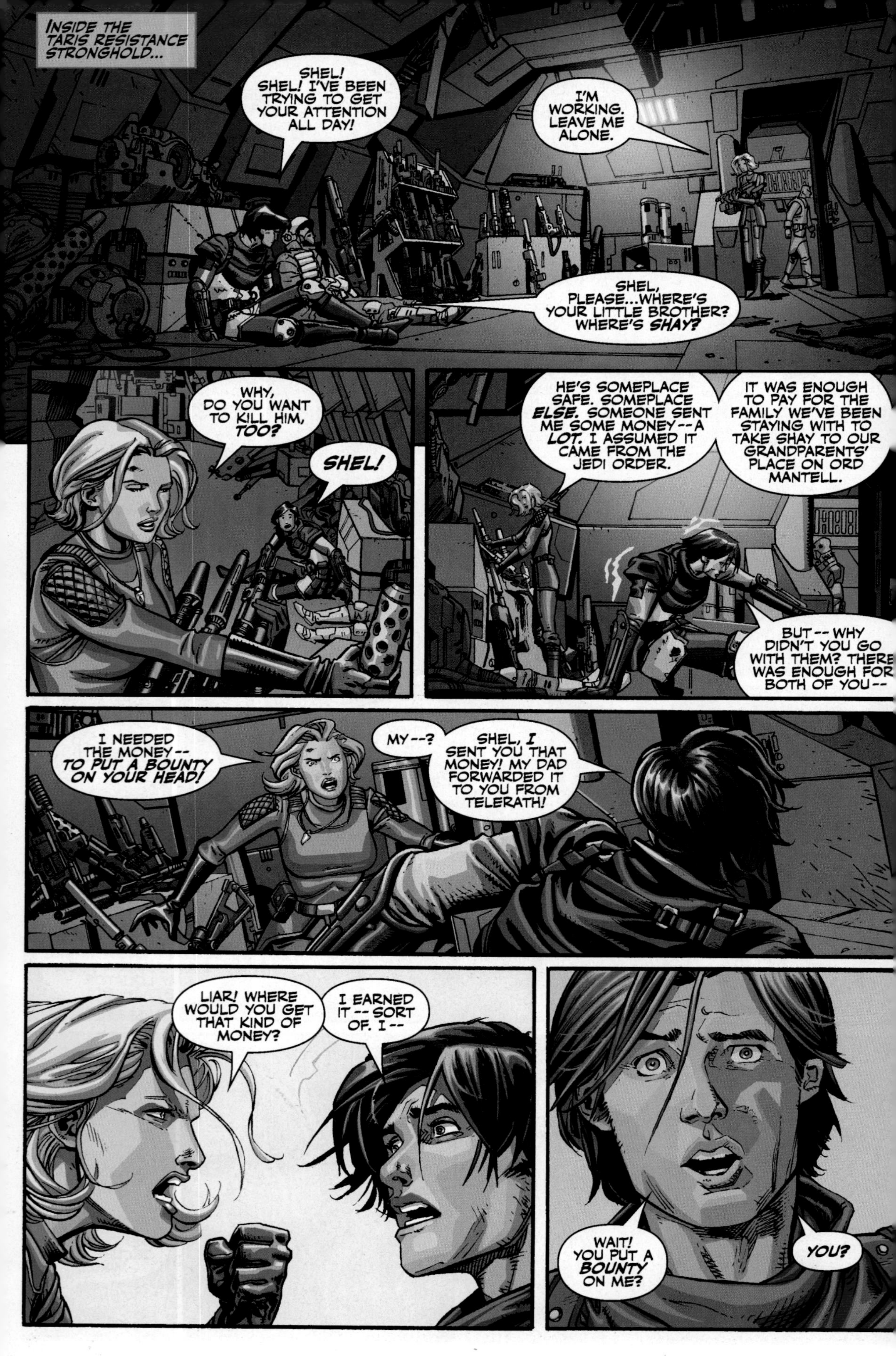
INSIDE THE TARIS RESISTANCE STRONGHOLD...
SHEL! SHEL! I'VE BEEN TRYING TO GET YOUR ATTENTION ALL DAY!
I'M WORKING. LEAVE ME ALONE.
SHEL, PLEASE...WHERE'S YOUR LITTLE BROTHER? WHERE'S SHAY?
WHY, DO YOU WANT TO KILL HIM, TOO?
SHEL!
HE'S SOMEPLACE SAFE. SOMEPLACE ELSE. SOMEONE SENT ME SOME MONEY--A LOT. I ASSUMED IT CAME FROM THE JEDI ORDER.
IT WAS ENOUGH TO PAY FOR THE FAMILY WE'VE BEEN STAYING WITH TO TAKE SHAY TO OUR GRANDPARENTS' PLACE ON ORD MANTELL.
BUT--WHY DIDN'T YOU GO WITH THEM? THERE WAS ENOUGH FOR BOTH OF YOU--
I NEEDED THE MONEY--TO PUT A BOUNTY ON YOUR HEAD!
MY--?
SHEL, I SENT YOU THAT MONEY! MY DAD FORWARDED IT TO YOU FROM TELERATH!
LIAR! WHERE WOULD YOU GET THAT KIND OF MONEY?
I EARNED IT--SORT OF. I--
WAIT! YOU PUT A BOUNTY ON ME?
YOU?

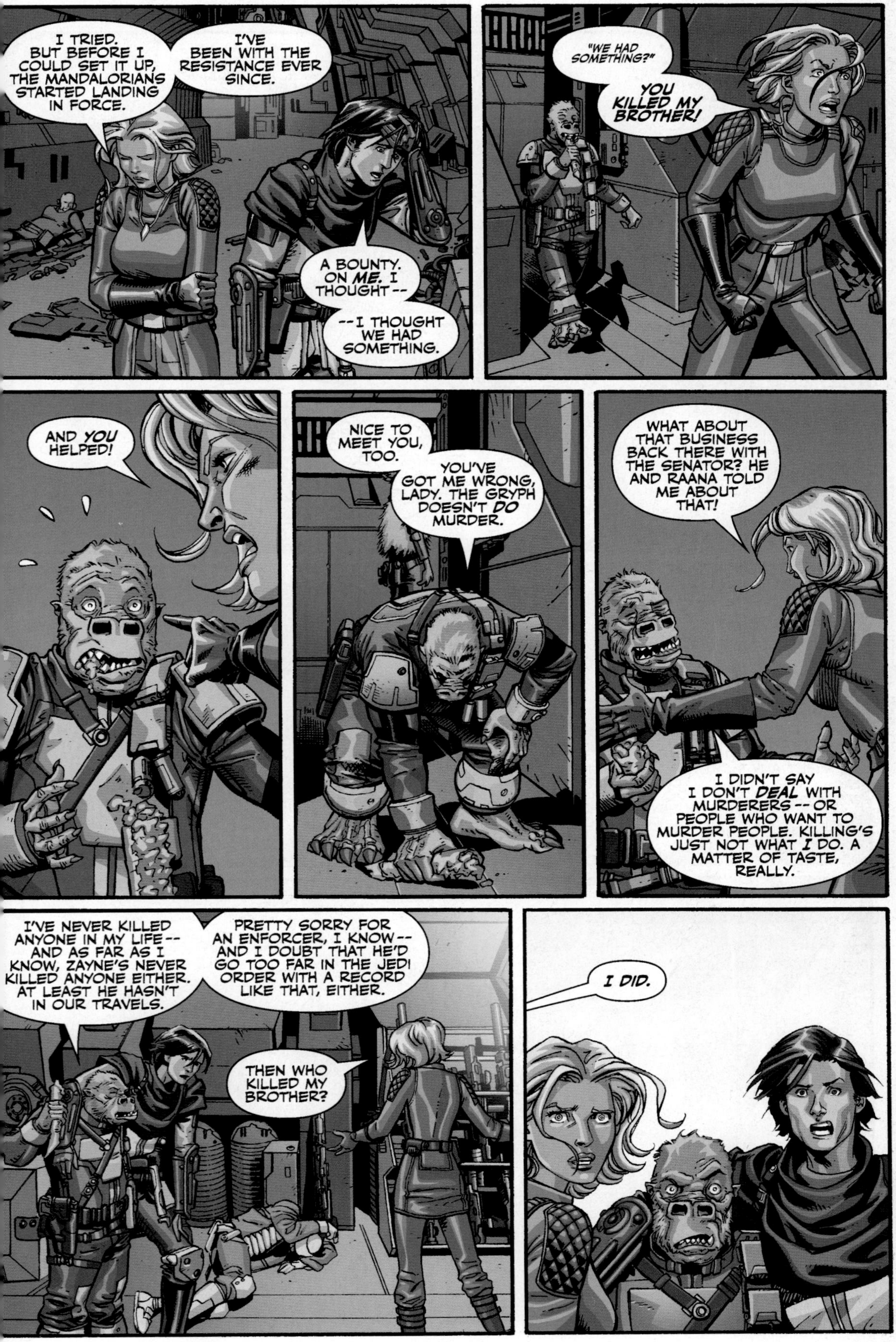

I TRIED. BUT BEFORE I COULD SET IT UP, THE MANDALORIANS STARTED LANDING IN FORCE.
I'VE BEEN WITH THE RESISTANCE EVER SINCE.
A BOUNTY. ON ME. I THOUGHT --
-- I THOUGHT WE HAD SOMETHING.
"WE HAD SOMETHING?"
YOU KILLED MY BROTHER!
AND YOU HELPED!
NICE TO MEET YOU, TOO.
YOU'VE GOT ME WRONG, LADY. THE GRYPH DOESN'T DO MURDER.
WHAT ABOUT THAT BUSINESS BACK THERE WITH THE SENATOR? HE AND RAANA TOLD ME ABOUT THAT!
I DIDN'T SAY I DON'T DEAL WITH MURDERERS -- OR PEOPLE WHO WANT TO MURDER PEOPLE. KILLING'S JUST NOT WHAT I DO. A MATTER OF TASTE, REALLY.
I'VE NEVER KILLED ANYONE IN MY LIFE -- AND AS FAR AS I KNOW, ZAYNE'S NEVER KILLED ANYONE EITHER. AT LEAST HE HASN'T IN OUR TRAVELS.
PRETTY SORRY FOR AN ENFORCER, I KNOW -- AND I DOUBT THAT HE'D GO TOO FAR IN THE JEDI ORDER WITH A RECORD LIKE THAT, EITHER.
THEN WHO KILLED MY BROTHER?
I DID.

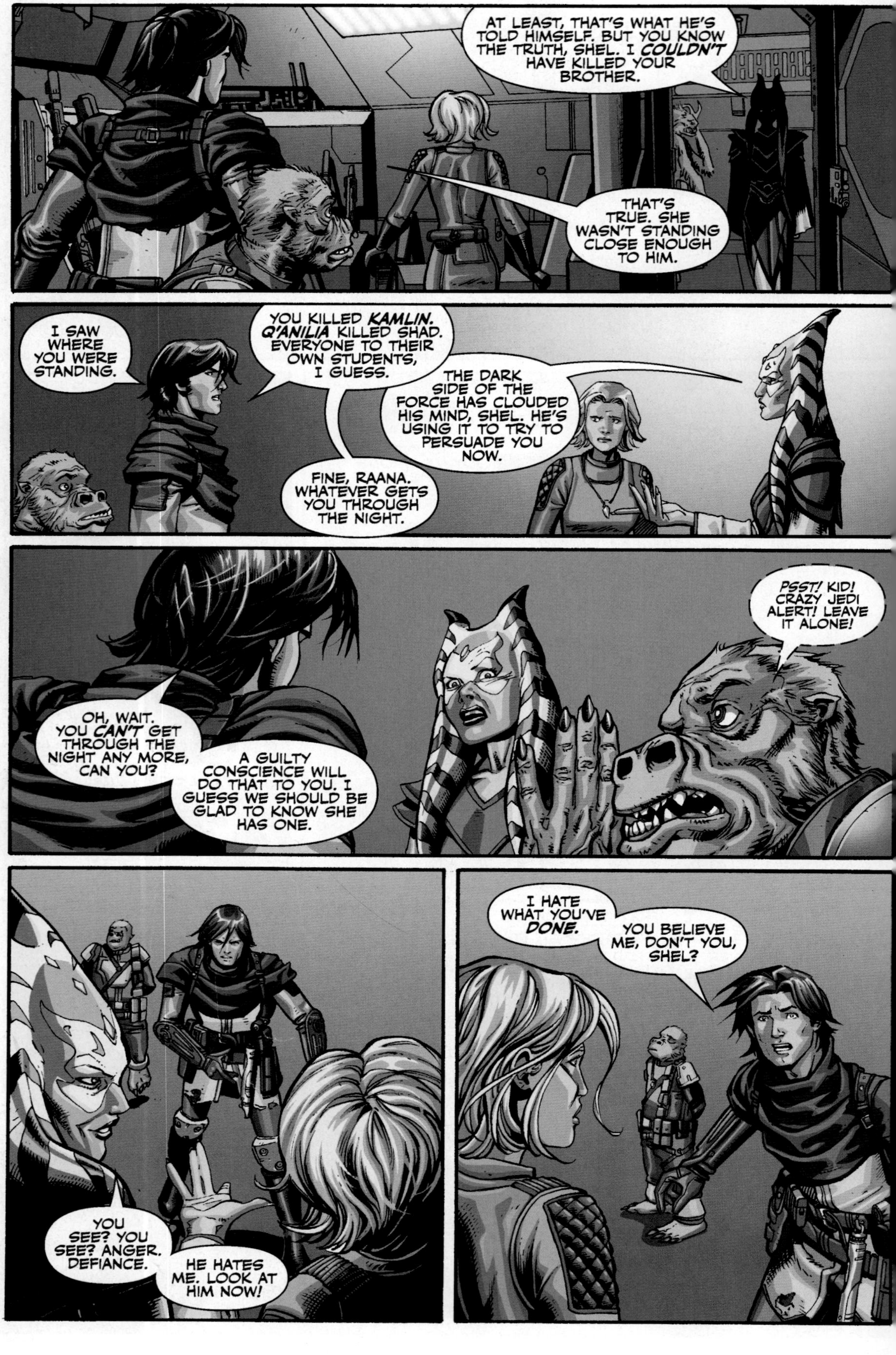
AT LEAST, THAT'S WHAT HE'S TOLD HIMSELF. BUT YOU KNOW THE TRUTH, SHEL. I *COULDN'T* HAVE KILLED YOUR BROTHER.
THAT'S TRUE. SHE WASN'T STANDING CLOSE ENOUGH TO HIM.
I SAW WHERE YOU WERE STANDING.
YOU KILLED ***KAMLIN. Q'ANILIA*** KILLED SHAD. EVERYONE TO THEIR OWN STUDENTS, I GUESS.
THE DARK SIDE OF THE FORCE HAS CLOUDED HIS MIND, SHEL. HE'S USING IT TO TRY TO PERSUADE YOU NOW.
FINE, RAANA. WHATEVER GETS YOU THROUGH THE NIGHT.
OH, WAIT. YOU *CAN'T* GET THROUGH THE NIGHT ANY MORE, CAN YOU?
A GUILTY CONSCIENCE WILL DO THAT TO YOU. I GUESS WE SHOULD BE GLAD TO KNOW SHE HAS ONE.
PSST! KID! CRAZY JEDI ALERT! LEAVE IT ALONE!
YOU SEE? YOU SEE? ANGER. DEFIANCE.
HE HATES ME. LOOK AT HIM NOW!
I HATE WHAT YOU'VE ***DONE.***
YOU BELIEVE ME, DON'T YOU, SHEL?

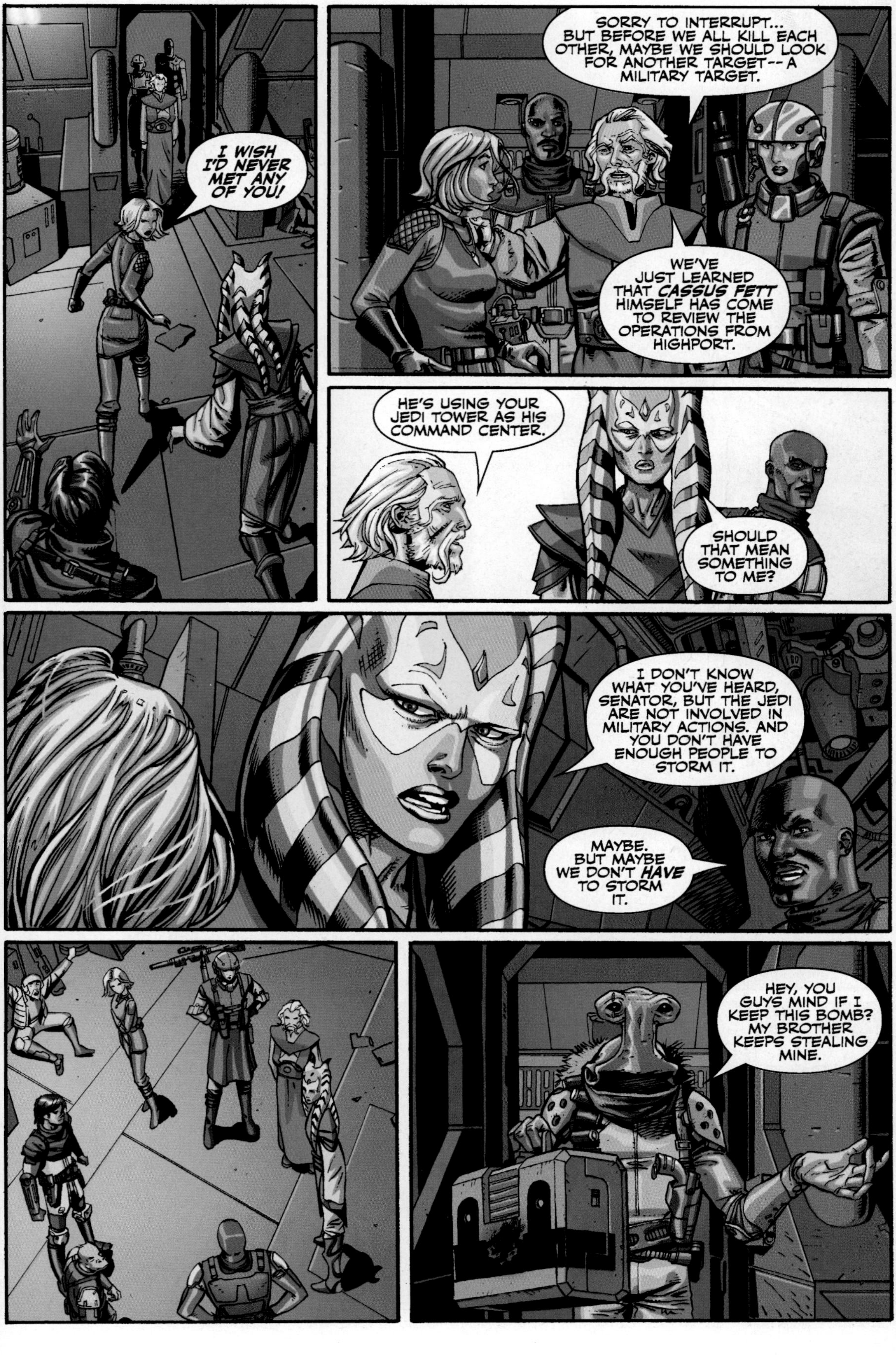
I WISH I'D NEVER MET ANY OF YOU!
SORRY TO INTERRUPT... BUT BEFORE WE ALL KILL EACH OTHER, MAYBE WE SHOULD LOOK FOR ANOTHER TARGET-- A MILITARY TARGET.
WE'VE JUST LEARNED THAT CASSUS FETT HIMSELF HAS COME TO REVIEW THE OPERATIONS FROM HIGHPORT.
HE'S USING YOUR JEDI TOWER AS HIS COMMAND CENTER.
SHOULD THAT MEAN SOMETHING TO ME?
I DON'T KNOW WHAT YOU'VE HEARD, SENATOR, BUT THE JEDI ARE NOT INVOLVED IN MILITARY ACTIONS. AND YOU DON'T HAVE ENOUGH PEOPLE TO STORM IT.
MAYBE. BUT MAYBE WE DON'T HAVE TO STORM IT.
HEY, YOU GUYS MIND IF I KEEP THIS BOMB? MY BROTHER KEEPS STEALING MINE.

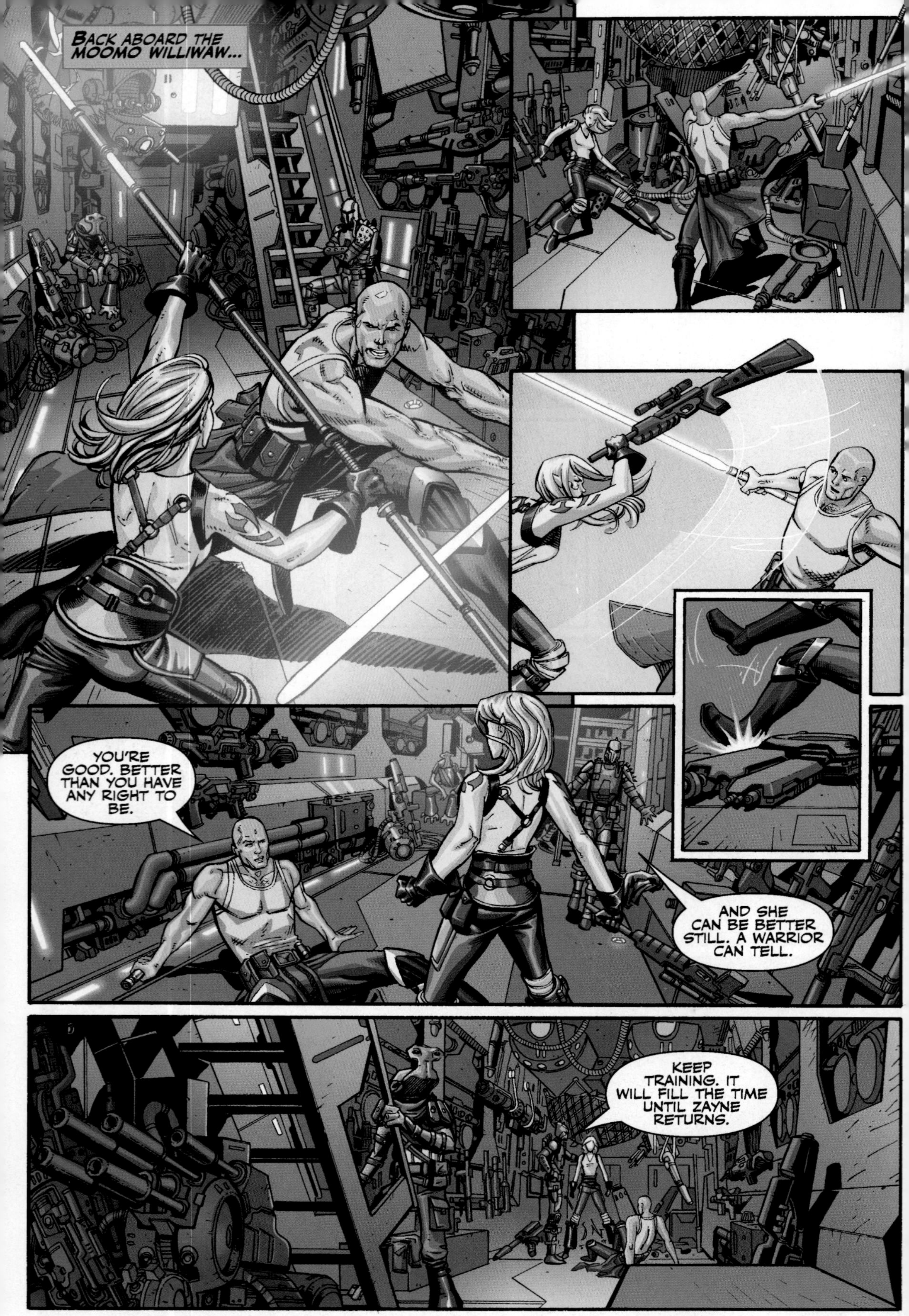
BACK ABOARD THE MOOMO WILLIWAW...
YOU'RE GOOD. BETTER THAN YOU HAVE ANY RIGHT TO BE.
AND SHE CAN BE BETTER STILL. A WARRIOR CAN TELL.
KEEP TRAINING. IT WILL FILL THE TIME UNTIL ZAYNE RETURNS.

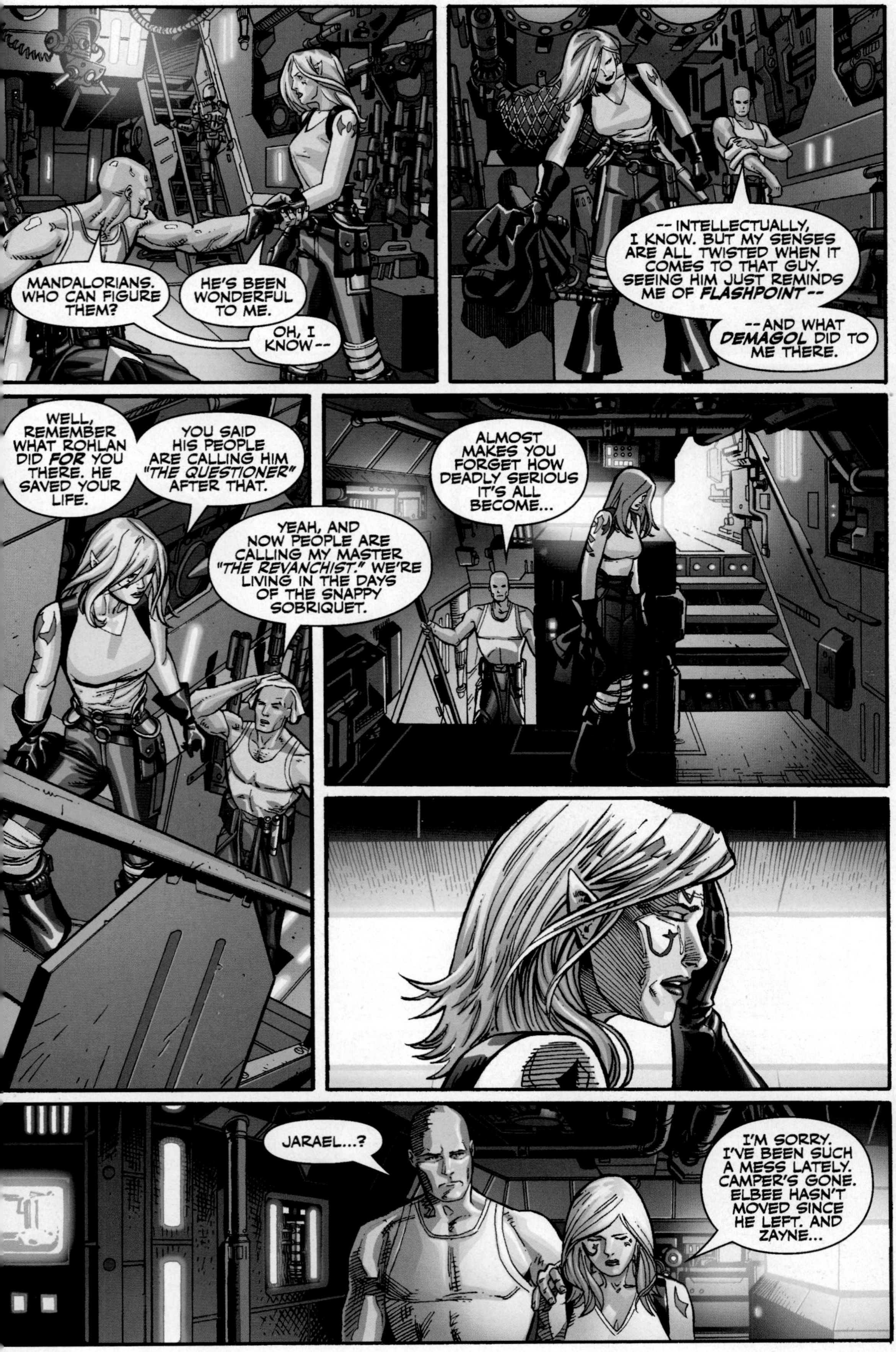
MANDALORIANS. WHO CAN FIGURE THEM?
HE'S BEEN WONDERFUL TO ME.
OH, I KNOW--
-- INTELLECTUALLY, I KNOW. BUT MY SENSES ARE ALL TWISTED WHEN IT COMES TO THAT GUY. SEEING HIM JUST REMINDS ME OF FLASHPOINT --
--AND WHAT DEMAGOL DID TO ME THERE.
WELL, REMEMBER WHAT ROHLAN DID FOR YOU THERE. HE SAVED YOUR LIFE.
YOU SAID HIS PEOPLE ARE CALLING HIM "THE QUESTIONER" AFTER THAT.
YEAH, AND NOW PEOPLE ARE CALLING MY MASTER "THE REVANCHIST." WE'RE LIVING IN THE DAYS OF THE SNAPPY SOBRIQUET.
ALMOST MAKES YOU FORGET HOW DEADLY SERIOUS IT'S ALL BECOME...
JARAEL...?
I'M SORRY. I'VE BEEN SUCH A MESS LATELY. CAMPER'S GONE. ELBEE HASN'T MOVED SINCE HE LEFT. AND ZAYNE...

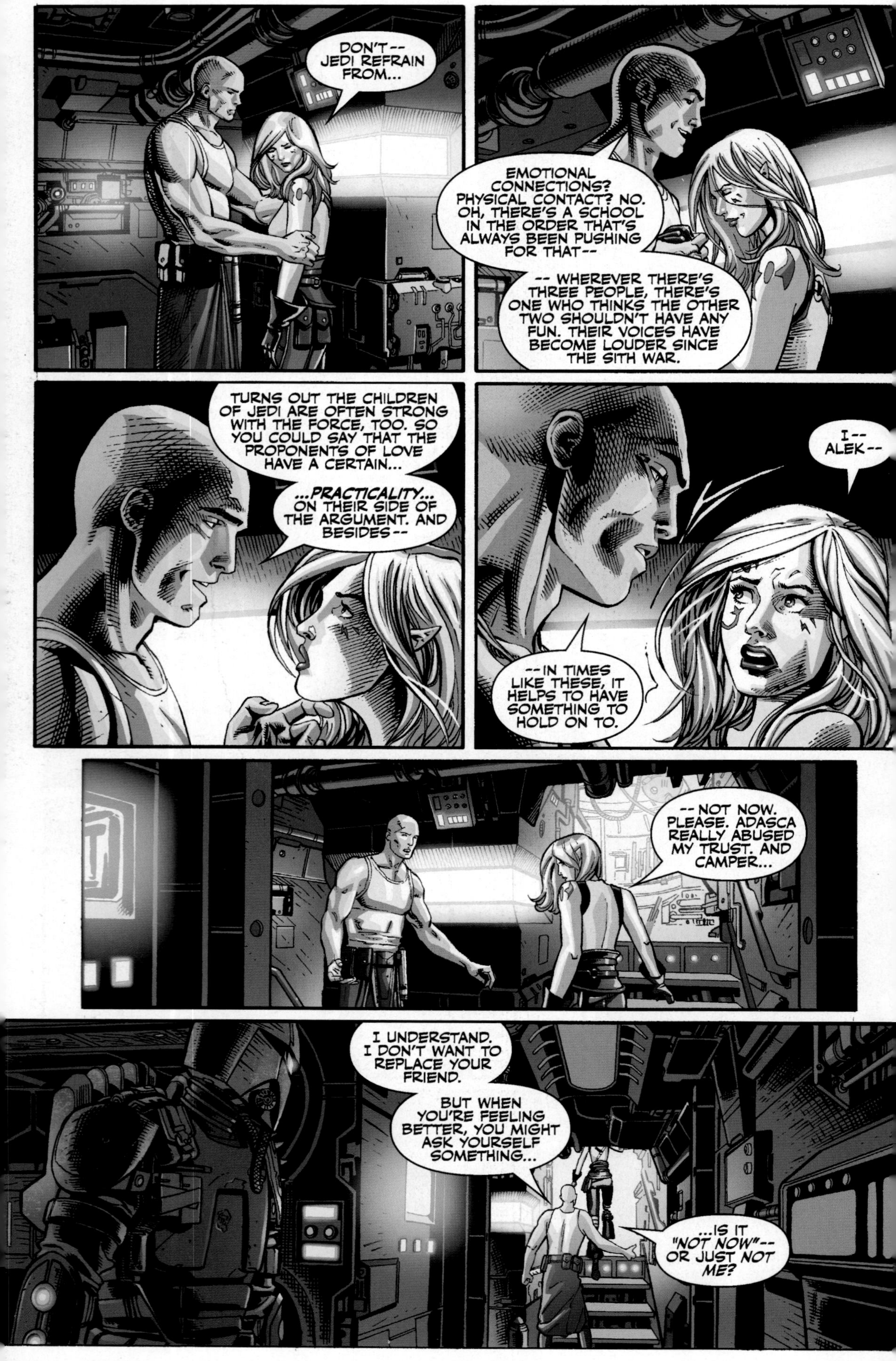
DON'T -- JEDI REFRAIN FROM...
EMOTIONAL CONNECTIONS? PHYSICAL CONTACT? NO. OH, THERE'S A SCHOOL IN THE ORDER THAT'S ALWAYS BEEN PUSHING FOR THAT--
-- WHEREVER THERE'S THREE PEOPLE, THERE'S ONE WHO THINKS THE OTHER TWO SHOULDN'T HAVE ANY FUN. THEIR VOICES HAVE BECOME LOUDER SINCE THE SITH WAR.
TURNS OUT THE CHILDREN OF JEDI ARE OFTEN STRONG WITH THE FORCE, TOO. SO YOU COULD SAY THAT THE PROPONENTS OF LOVE HAVE A CERTAIN...
...PRACTICALITY... ON THEIR SIDE OF THE ARGUMENT. AND BESIDES--
I-- ALEK--
--IN TIMES LIKE THESE, IT HELPS TO HAVE SOMETHING TO HOLD ON TO.
-- NOT NOW. PLEASE. ADASCA REALLY ABUSED MY TRUST. AND CAMPER...
I UNDERSTAND. I DON'T WANT TO REPLACE YOUR FRIEND.
BUT WHEN YOU'RE FEELING BETTER, YOU MIGHT ASK YOURSELF SOMETHING...
...IS IT "NOT NOW"-- OR JUST NOT ME?

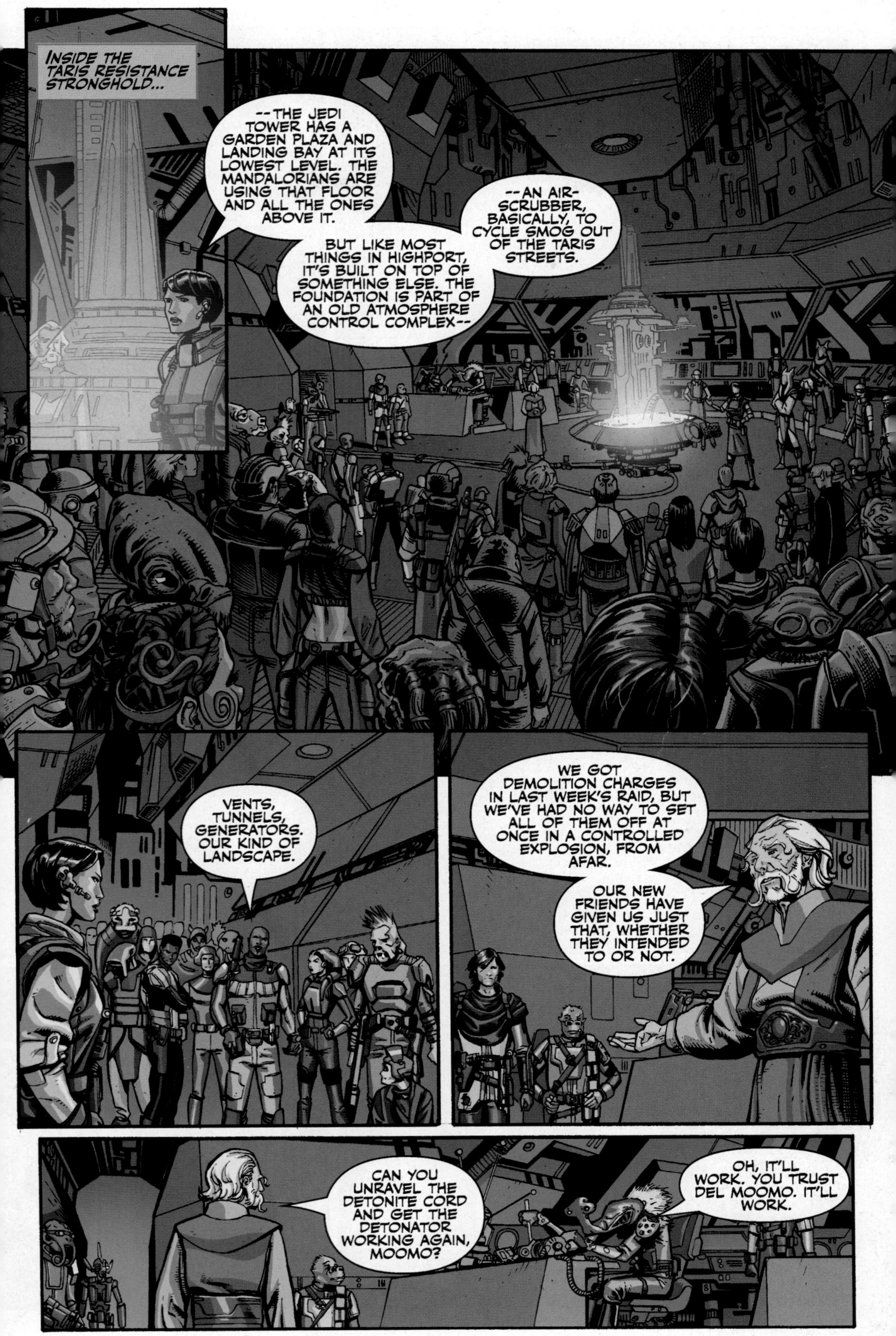
INSIDE THE TARIS RESISTANCE STRONGHOLD...
--THE JEDI TOWER HAS A GARDEN PLAZA AND LANDING BAY AT ITS LOWEST LEVEL. THE MANDALORIANS ARE USING THAT FLOOR AND ALL THE ONES ABOVE IT.
BUT LIKE MOST THINGS IN HIGHPORT, IT'S BUILT ON TOP OF SOMETHING ELSE. THE FOUNDATION IS PART OF AN OLD ATMOSPHERE CONTROL COMPLEX--
--AN AIR-SCRUBBER, BASICALLY, TO CYCLE SMOG OUT OF THE TARIS STREETS.
VENTS, TUNNELS, GENERATORS. OUR KIND OF LANDSCAPE.
WE GOT DEMOLITION CHARGES IN LAST WEEK'S RAID, BUT WE'VE HAD NO WAY TO SET ALL OF THEM OFF AT ONCE IN A CONTROLLED EXPLOSION, FROM AFAR.
OUR NEW FRIENDS HAVE GIVEN US JUST THAT, WHETHER THEY INTENDED TO OR NOT.
CAN YOU UNRAVEL THE DETONITE CORD AND GET THE DETONATOR WORKING AGAIN, MOOMO?
OH, IT'LL WORK. YOU TRUST DEL MOOMO. IT'LL WORK.

CAN I PRESS THE BUTTON? I REALLY, *REALLY* WANT TO PRESS THE BUTTON.

IT'S OKAY. DESTRUCTION IS THE ONE THING HE *IS* GOOD AT.

SENATOR, ARE YOU SURE YOU WANT TO DO THIS? WHAT ABOUT THE PEOPLE WHO LIVE NEAR THE TOWER?

APART FROM A SKYBRIDGE, IT'S SET OFF FROM THE RESIDENTIAL BLOCKS. THAT'S WHY THE ORDER BOUGHT THE BUILDING. MOST OF THE AREAS AROUND ARE ALREADY EVACUATED--

--AND THE RESISTANCE OUGHT TO BE ABLE TO CLEAR THE LOWER CITY FOUNDATION BEFOREHAND.

BUT YOU DON'T *KNOW*. WHAT IF THEY'VE GOT PRISONERS UP THERE?

IT'S A *WAR*, KID!

THEN WHAT IF CASSUS ISN'T THERE? YOU'VE WASTED YOUR MUNITIONS.

I AGREE. WE NEED A SAME-DAY RECON, THEN.

RAANA TEY, IS THERE A WAY FROM THE FOUNDATION INTO THE JEDI TOWER PROPER?

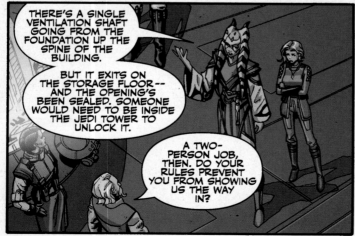

THERE'S A SINGLE VENTILATION SHAFT GOING FROM THE FOUNDATION UP THE SPINE OF THE BUILDING.

BUT IT EXITS ON THE STORAGE FLOOR-- AND THE OPENING'S BEEN SEALED. SOMEONE WOULD NEED TO BE INSIDE THE JEDI TOWER TO UNLOCK IT.

A TWO-PERSON JOB, THEN. DO YOUR RULES PREVENT YOU FROM SHOWING US THE WAY IN?

SENATOR, I'VE TOLD YOU--

I'LL DO IT.

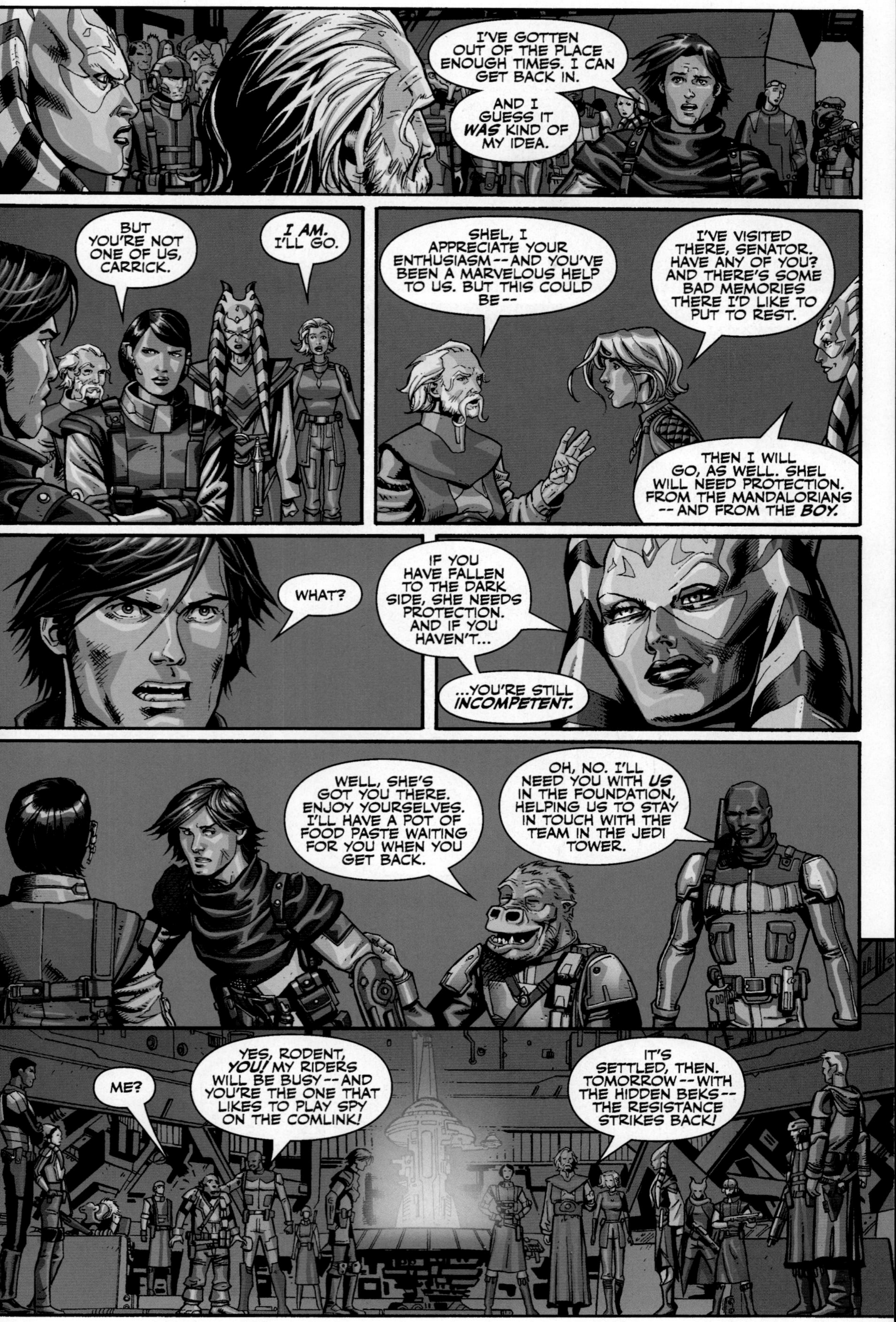
I'VE GOTTEN OUT OF THE PLACE ENOUGH TIMES. I CAN GET BACK IN.
AND I GUESS IT *WAS* KIND OF MY IDEA.
BUT YOU'RE NOT ONE OF US, CARRICK.
I AM. I'LL GO.
SHEL, I APPRECIATE YOUR ENTHUSIASM--AND YOU'VE BEEN A MARVELOUS HELP TO US. BUT THIS COULD BE--
I'VE VISITED THERE, SENATOR. HAVE ANY OF YOU? AND THERE'S SOME BAD MEMORIES THERE I'D LIKE TO PUT TO REST.
THEN I WILL GO, AS WELL. SHEL WILL NEED PROTECTION. FROM THE MANDALORIANS --AND FROM THE *BOY.*
WHAT?
IF YOU HAVE FALLEN TO THE DARK SIDE, SHE NEEDS PROTECTION. AND IF YOU HAVEN'T...
...YOU'RE STILL *INCOMPETENT.*
WELL, SHE'S GOT YOU THERE. ENJOY YOURSELVES. I'LL HAVE A POT OF FOOD PASTE WAITING FOR YOU WHEN YOU GET BACK.
OH, NO. I'LL NEED YOU WITH *US* IN THE FOUNDATION, HELPING US TO STAY IN TOUCH WITH THE TEAM IN THE JEDI TOWER.
ME?
YES, RODENT, *YOU!* MY RIDERS WILL BE BUSY--AND YOU'RE THE ONE THAT LIKES TO PLAY SPY ON THE COMLINK!
IT'S SETTLED, THEN. TOMORROW--WITH THE HIDDEN BEKS--THE RESISTANCE STRIKES BACK!

IT WILL BE ALL RIGHT, SHEL. THIS MISSION-- WE CAN USE THIS.

I NEED YOU TO PROMISE. I NEED YOU TO PROMISE TO FINISH THE JOB IF I FAIL YOUR BROTHER.

YOU COULD NEVER FAIL.

I WON'T *TRY* TO FAIL. BUT I--I DON'T THINK I'M GOING TO LIVE MUCH LONGER. I'VE SEEN IT.

HE'S POWERFUL-- AND HE'LL BE ON HIS GUARD AGAINST YOU NOW. BUT THERE IS ANOTHER WAY. WITH *THIS.*

THE JEWEL YOU GAVE ME AFTER SHAD DIED?

THE CRYSTAL FROM YOUR BROTHER'S LIGHTSABER.

THE DAY AFTER ZAYNE KILLED THE PADAWANS, WE REMOVED THE CRYSTALS FROM ALL THE PADAWANS' SABERS AND SENT THEM TO THEIR FAMILIES AS REMEMBRANCES.

THE WEAPONS ARE STILL IN THE TOWER-- WITH THE THINGS WE MOVED INTO STORAGE. I WILL TEACH YOU HOW TO UNLOCK THE TRAY AND REINSTALL THE CRYSTAL.

YOUR BROTHER'S LIGHTSABER WILL DISPATCH YOUR BROTHER'S KILLER.

MY BROTHER'S KILLER...

YOU *WILL* HAVE JUSTICE-- ONE WAY OR ANOTHER. IT'S MY PROPHECY-- AND MY PROMISE!

THE ADJUDICATOR

The Freelance Security Professional's Holofeed

Special Report: The Colonies

KRAV'S HOT LIST

They're hot—and they're worth a lot!

Just when you thought they were gone—they're back on the list!

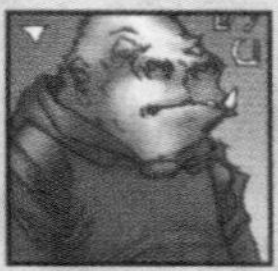

Marn Hierogryph
Bounties: Eight, totaling 124,000 credits
Wanted for: Accomplice to murder, treason, racketeering, fraud

And he's moved out in front, thanks to the big kick from Lhosan Industries. We swear, he looks a lot like that guy in the holo . . .

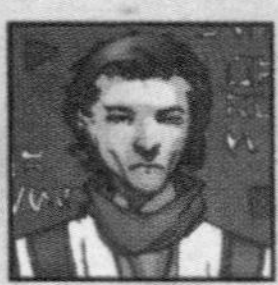

Zayne Carrick
Bounties: Ten, totaling 81,000 credits
Wanted for: Murder, treason, destruction of property, escape

Just when you thought the Navy had ruined it for all of us, he goes back up on the big board—plus twenty large for the piracy rap. Keep it coming . . .

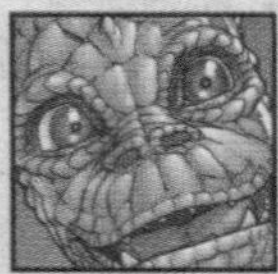

Slyssk [No last name]
Bounties: One, totaling 40,000 credits
Wanted for: Piracy

Nothing like stealing spaceships to help a guy rack up some big bounties fast. But honestly, who could get sore at a sweet face like this?

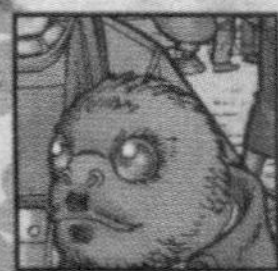

Kelven Garnatrope
Bounties: Five, totaling 63,000 credits
Wanted for: Murder

You know, this is the picture we got, but I'm *juuuust* willing to bet this maybe ain't the "Corellian Strangler." I mean, come on. Don't you have to be *tall* to strangle people?

SELECT to continue list . . .

CRACKING UP IN THE COLONIES

War making corporations act weird
By KRAV NOBLIS, *Adjudicator* Editor

I thought war did strange things to the customers—but now, I think just having too much money is what does it.

You know that gigantic bounty issued a ways back on some geezer? My contact said that tracked back to Adascorp. Then there are those rumors that company bought up Czerka's whole line of HK-24 droids. Finally, in the wake of losing Lord Adasca and the *Arkanian Legacy* to a Mandie raid, the company's board yesterday offered our little profession a hundred credits for each Mandalorian confirmed killed in the systems near Arkania.

They seem to have forgotten that we're hunters, and not an army. It's also slipped their minds just how many Mandies there are out there—and how any one of them is tougher to whack than our usual hundred-cred target, thank you very much. And finally, I don't think they've bargained on just how enterprising—and/or foolish—some in our set can actually be. Word is that just in the last few hours, the "redemption station" they've set up has been swamped with people bringing in Mandie helmets from junk shops and costume parlors all across the colonies! Seems nobody involved tripped to the fact that a "price per head" requires an actual head . . .

And just now, I hear the folks at Lhosan Industries have agreed to kick in a lot of supplies to the war effort, for free—while also throwing a hundred thousand into the Marn Heirogryph lottery. But not dead or alive—just dead. Hey, for that money, they can have him seared on toasted flatcakes with a Rodian breadfruit in his mouth! What did this guy do, scratch the CEO's speeder in the parking lot?

SELECT to learn more . . .

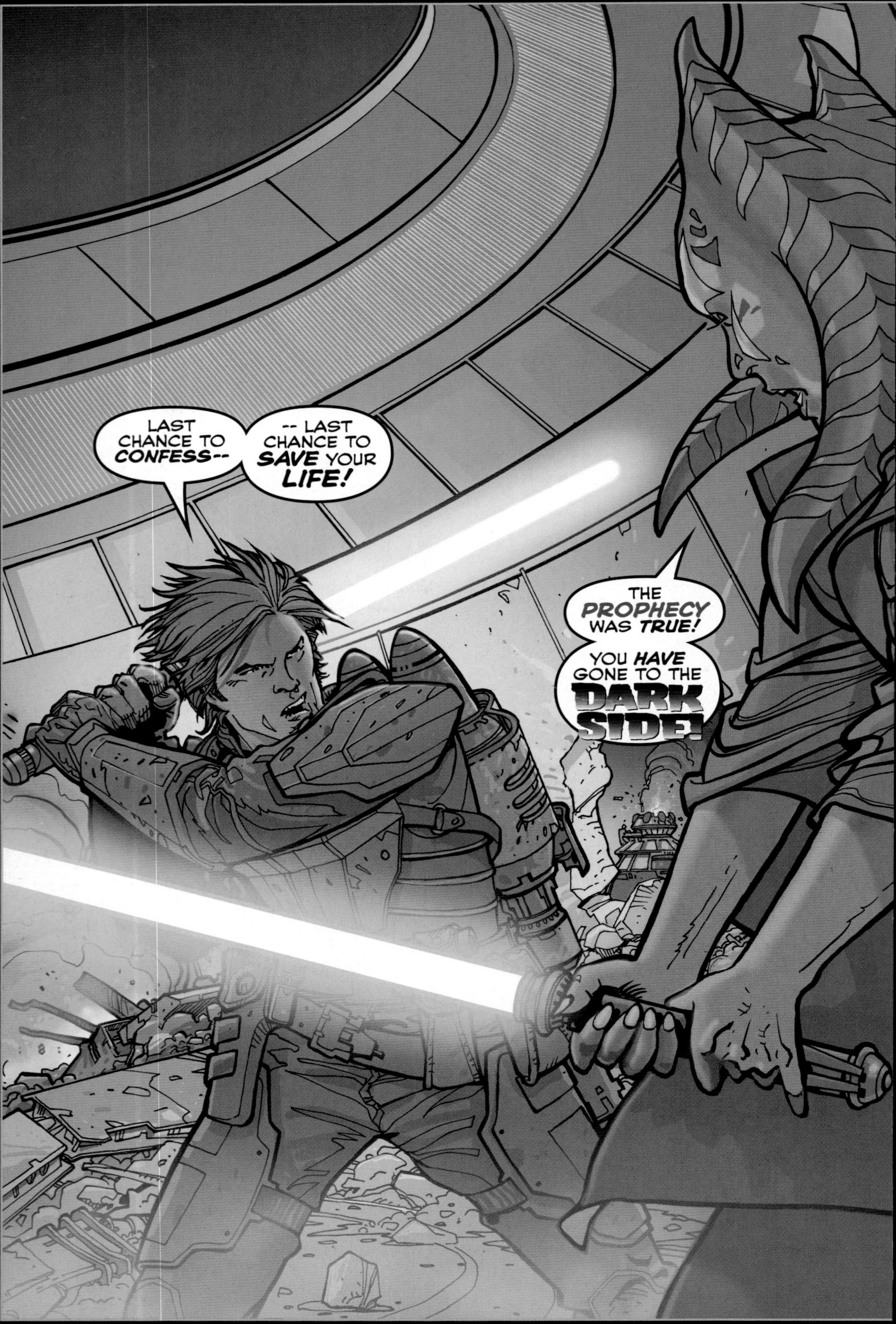
LAST CHANCE TO CONFESS--
-- LAST CHANCE TO SAVE YOUR LIFE!
THE PROPHECY WAS TRUE!
YOU HAVE GONE TO THE DARK SIDE!

STAR WARS: KNIGHTS OF THE OLD REPUBLIC #24 — "KNIGHTS OF SUFFERING, PART 3"

WRITER: JOHN JACKSON MILLER • PENCILER: DUSTIN WEAVER • INKER: DAN PARSONS • COLORIST: MICHAEL ATIYEH
LETTERER: MICHAEL HEISLER • ASSISTANT EDITOR: DAVE MARSHALL • EDITOR: JEREMY BARLOW • COVER ARTIST: COLIN WILSON

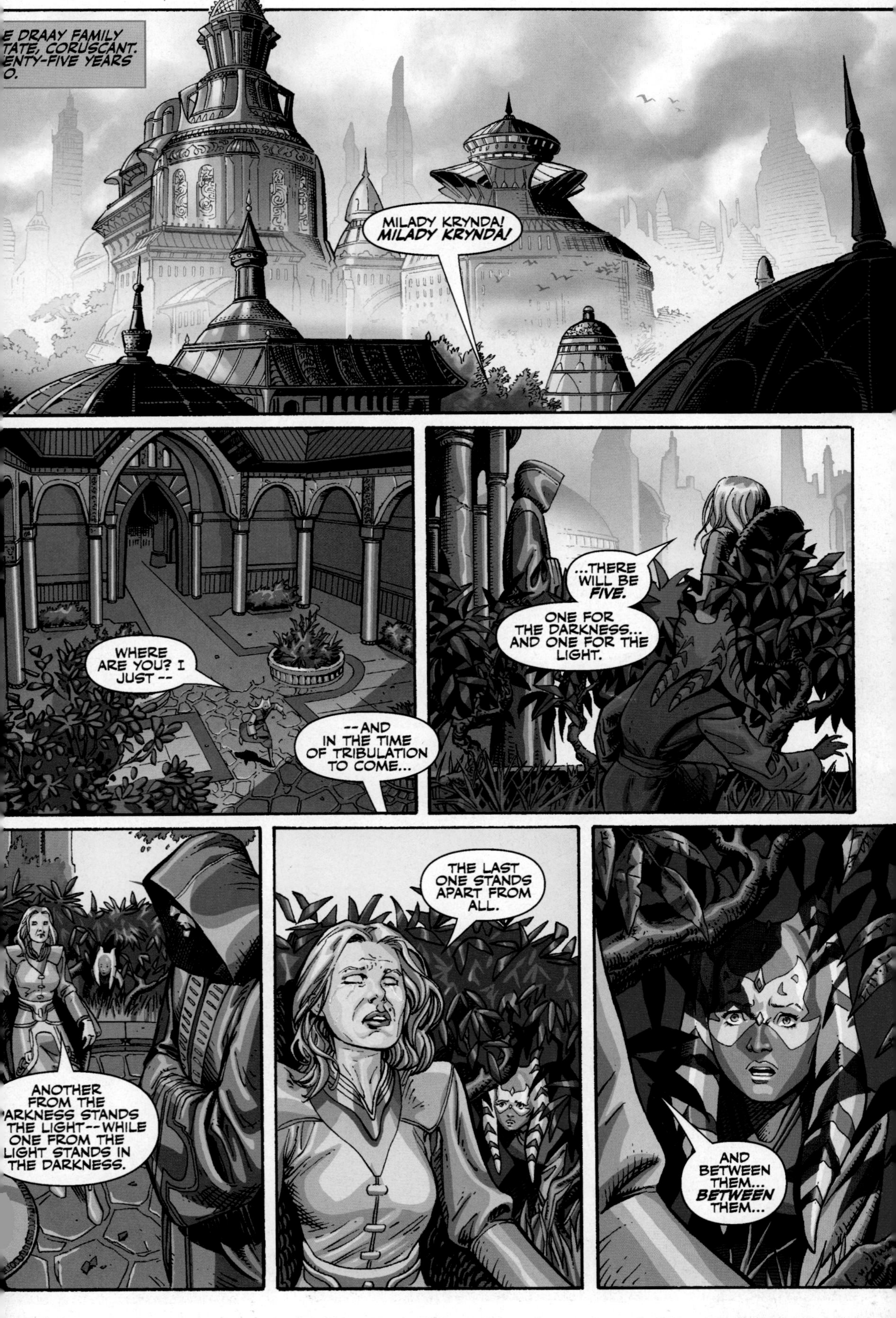

E DRAAY FAMILY TATE, CORUSCANT. ENTY-FIVE YEARS O.
MILADY KRYNDA! MILADY KRYNDA!
WHERE ARE YOU? I JUST --
--AND IN THE TIME OF TRIBULATION TO COME...
...THERE WILL BE FIVE.
ONE FOR THE DARKNESS... AND ONE FOR THE LIGHT.
ANOTHER FROM THE ARKNESS STANDS THE LIGHT--WHILE ONE FROM THE LIGHT STANDS IN THE DARKNESS.
THE LAST ONE STANDS APART FROM ALL.
AND BETWEEN THEM... BETWEEN THEM...

"...ALL THAT HAS BEEN BUILT WILL FALL."

TARIS. THE PRESENT.

RAANA TEY!

WE'VE LOCATED THE SHAFT LEADING UP TO THE JEDI TOWER. TIME TO DO YOUR THING.

I HOPE YOU *CRIMINALS* WILL REFRAIN FROM BLOWING US ALL UP UNTIL OUR OPERATIVES IN THE TOWER CAN UNLOCK THE PORTAL ABOVE ME.

JUST ANOTHER BREAK-IN TO US, LADY. YOU GUYS TELL US *CASSUS FETT* IS IN THE BUILDING -- AND YOU SNEAK RIGHT BACK OUT. WE'LL DO ALL THE REST.

AND I PROMISE TO KEEP THE DETONATOR ON *ME*. THAT ITHORIAN IS ENJOYING SETTING THE CHARGES A *LITTLE* TOO MUCH, IF YOU ASK ME.

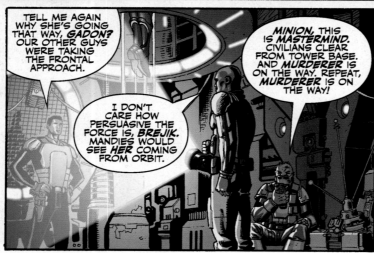

TELL ME AGAIN WHY SHE'S GOING THAT WAY, *GADON?* OUR OTHER GUYS WERE TAKING THE FRONTAL APPROACH.

I DON'T CARE HOW PERSUASIVE THE FORCE IS, *BREJIK.* MANDIES WOULD SEE *HER* COMING FROM ORBIT.

MINION, THIS IS *MASTERMIND.* CIVILIANS CLEAR FROM TOWER BASE. AND *MURDERER* IS ON THE WAY. REPEAT, *MURDERER* IS ON THE WAY!

HEY, YOU WANT TO PICK THE NAMES, *YOU* RUN THE COMLINK!

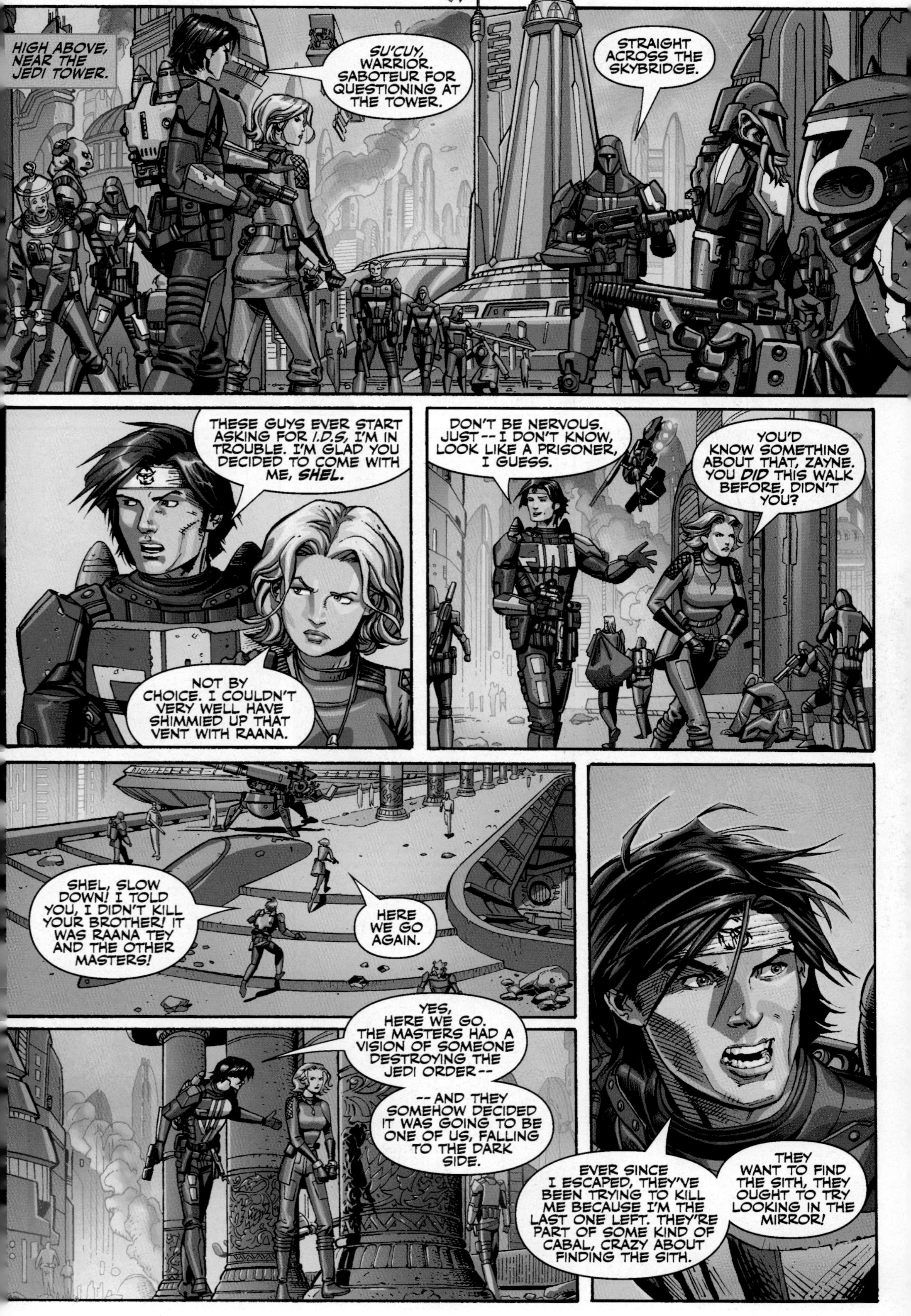
HIGH ABOVE, NEAR THE JEDI TOWER.
SU'CUY, WARRIOR. SABOTEUR FOR QUESTIONING AT THE TOWER.
STRAIGHT ACROSS THE SKYBRIDGE.
THESE GUYS EVER START ASKING FOR I.D.S, I'M IN TROUBLE. I'M GLAD YOU DECIDED TO COME WITH ME, SHEL.
NOT BY CHOICE. I COULDN'T VERY WELL HAVE SHIMMIED UP THAT VENT WITH RAANA.
DON'T BE NERVOUS. JUST -- I DON'T KNOW, LOOK LIKE A PRISONER, I GUESS.
YOU'D KNOW SOMETHING ABOUT THAT, ZAYNE. YOU DID THIS WALK BEFORE, DIDN'T YOU?
SHEL, SLOW DOWN! I TOLD YOU, I DIDN'T KILL YOUR BROTHER! IT WAS RAANA TEY AND THE OTHER MASTERS!
HERE WE GO AGAIN.
YES, HERE WE GO. THE MASTERS HAD A VISION OF SOMEONE DESTROYING THE JEDI ORDER --
-- AND THEY SOMEHOW DECIDED IT WAS GOING TO BE ONE OF US, FALLING TO THE DARK SIDE.
EVER SINCE I ESCAPED, THEY'VE BEEN TRYING TO KILL ME BECAUSE I'M THE LAST ONE LEFT. THEY'RE PART OF SOME KIND OF CABAL, CRAZY ABOUT FINDING THE SITH.
THEY WANT TO FIND THE SITH, THEY OUGHT TO TRY LOOKING IN THE MIRROR!

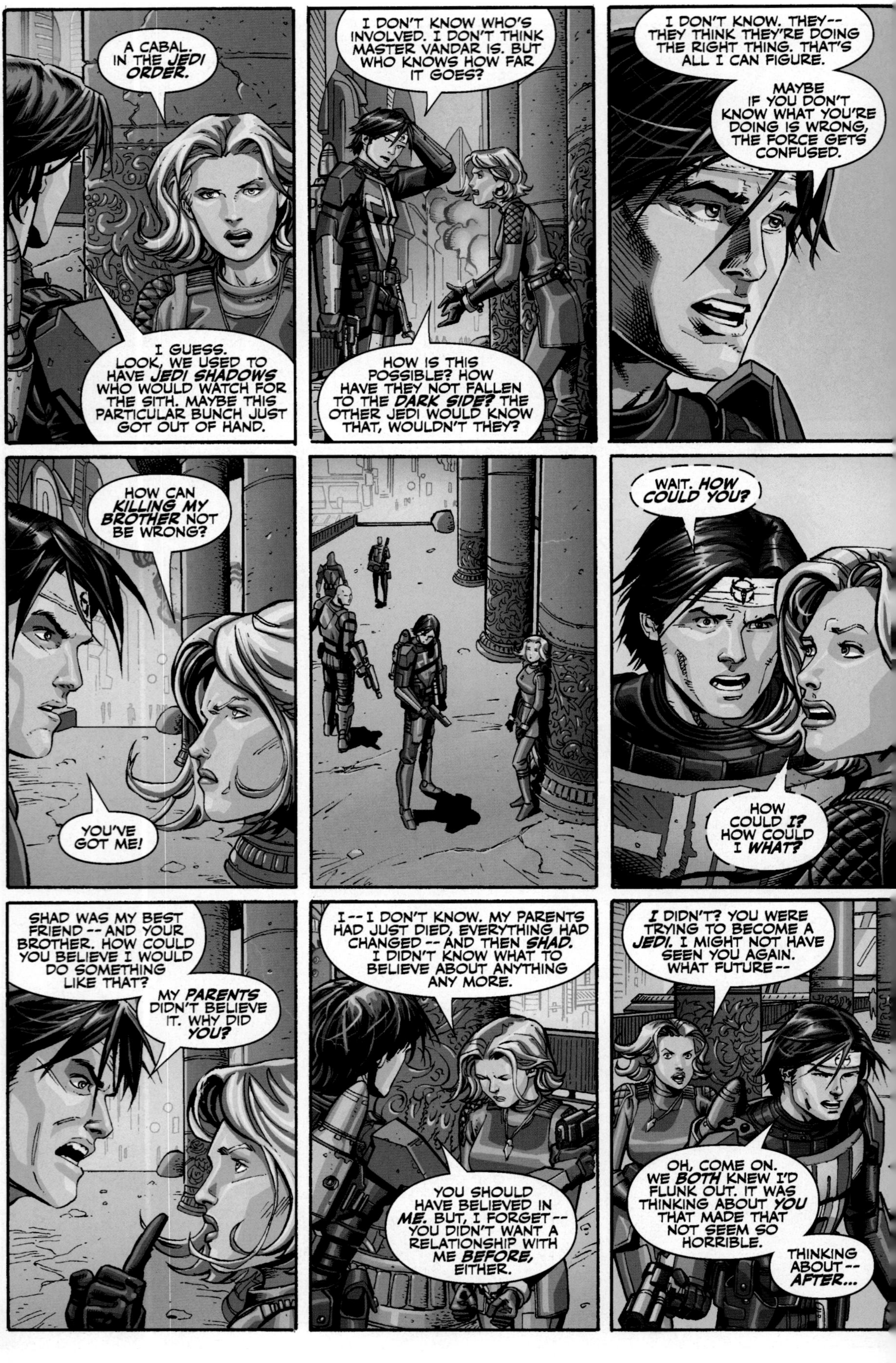
A CABAL. IN THE JEDI ORDER.
I GUESS. LOOK, WE USED TO HAVE JEDI SHADOWS WHO WOULD WATCH FOR THE SITH. MAYBE THIS PARTICULAR BUNCH JUST GOT OUT OF HAND.
I DON'T KNOW WHO'S INVOLVED. I DON'T THINK MASTER VANDAR IS. BUT WHO KNOWS HOW FAR IT GOES?
HOW IS THIS POSSIBLE? HOW HAVE THEY NOT FALLEN TO THE DARK SIDE? THE OTHER JEDI WOULD KNOW THAT, WOULDN'T THEY?
I DON'T KNOW. THEY-- THEY THINK THEY'RE DOING THE RIGHT THING. THAT'S ALL I CAN FIGURE.
MAYBE IF YOU DON'T KNOW WHAT YOU'RE DOING IS WRONG, THE FORCE GETS CONFUSED.
HOW CAN KILLING MY BROTHER NOT BE WRONG?
YOU'VE GOT ME!
WAIT. HOW COULD YOU?
HOW COULD I? HOW COULD I WHAT?
SHAD WAS MY BEST FRIEND -- AND YOUR BROTHER. HOW COULD YOU BELIEVE I WOULD DO SOMETHING LIKE THAT?
MY PARENTS DIDN'T BELIEVE IT. WHY DID YOU?
I -- I DON'T KNOW. MY PARENTS HAD JUST DIED, EVERYTHING HAD CHANGED -- AND THEN SHAD. I DIDN'T KNOW WHAT TO BELIEVE ABOUT ANYTHING ANY MORE.
YOU SHOULD HAVE BELIEVED IN ME. BUT, I FORGET -- YOU DIDN'T WANT A RELATIONSHIP WITH ME BEFORE, EITHER.
I DIDN'T? YOU WERE TRYING TO BECOME A JEDI. I MIGHT NOT HAVE SEEN YOU AGAIN. WHAT FUTURE --
OH, COME ON. WE BOTH KNEW I'D FLUNK OUT. IT WAS THINKING ABOUT YOU THAT MADE THAT NOT SEEM SO HORRIBLE.
THINKING ABOUT -- AFTER...

THAT'S VERY TOUCHING. I WAS YOUR *CONSOLATION PRIZE*. HOW FLATTERING.

THAT'S NOT WHAT I MEANT. I WASN'T TRYING --

WHAT, TO *FAIL?* TO BE STUCK WITH A SIMPLE LIFE WITH BORING OLD *SHEL?* NO, YOU WERE DOING EVERYTHING YOU COULD TO BECOME A KNIGHT AND AVOID THAT!

JUST LOOK HOW MANY TIMES YOU TRIED TO CATCH THAT SNIVVIAN *LOWLIFE!*

WATCH IT. GRYPH'S MY *FRIEND!*

OH, *PLEASE!* YOU USED TO SAY GRYPH'S ONLY FRIEND WAS MONEY! IF HE EVER WENT OUT OF HIS WAY TO HELP YOU, IT WAS SO HE COULD MAKE --

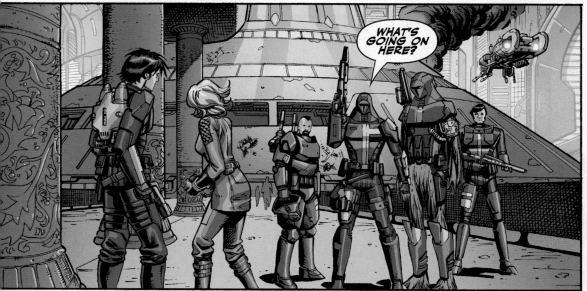

WHAT'S GOING ON HERE?

LEAVE HIM ALONE. HE'S *RECRUITING.*

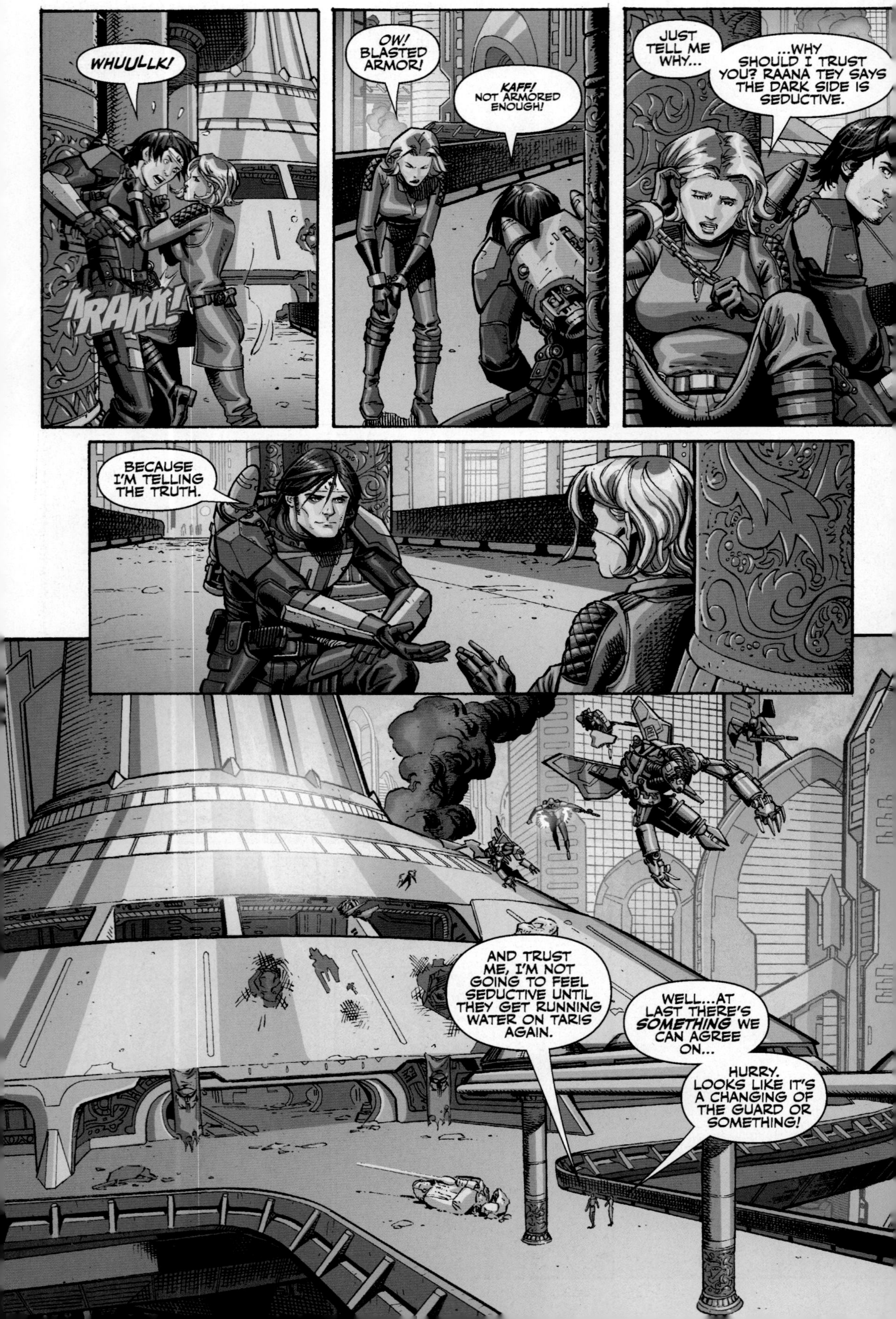

WHUULLK!
KRAKK!
OW! BLASTED ARMOR!
KAFF! NOT ARMORED ENOUGH!
JUST TELL ME WHY...
...WHY SHOULD I TRUST YOU? RAANA TEY SAYS THE DARK SIDE IS SEDUCTIVE.
BECAUSE I'M TELLING THE TRUTH.
AND TRUST ME, I'M NOT GOING TO FEEL SEDUCTIVE UNTIL THEY GET RUNNING WATER ON TARIS AGAIN.
WELL...AT LAST THERE'S SOMETHING WE CAN AGREE ON...
HURRY. LOOKS LIKE IT'S A CHANGING OF THE GUARD OR SOMETHING!

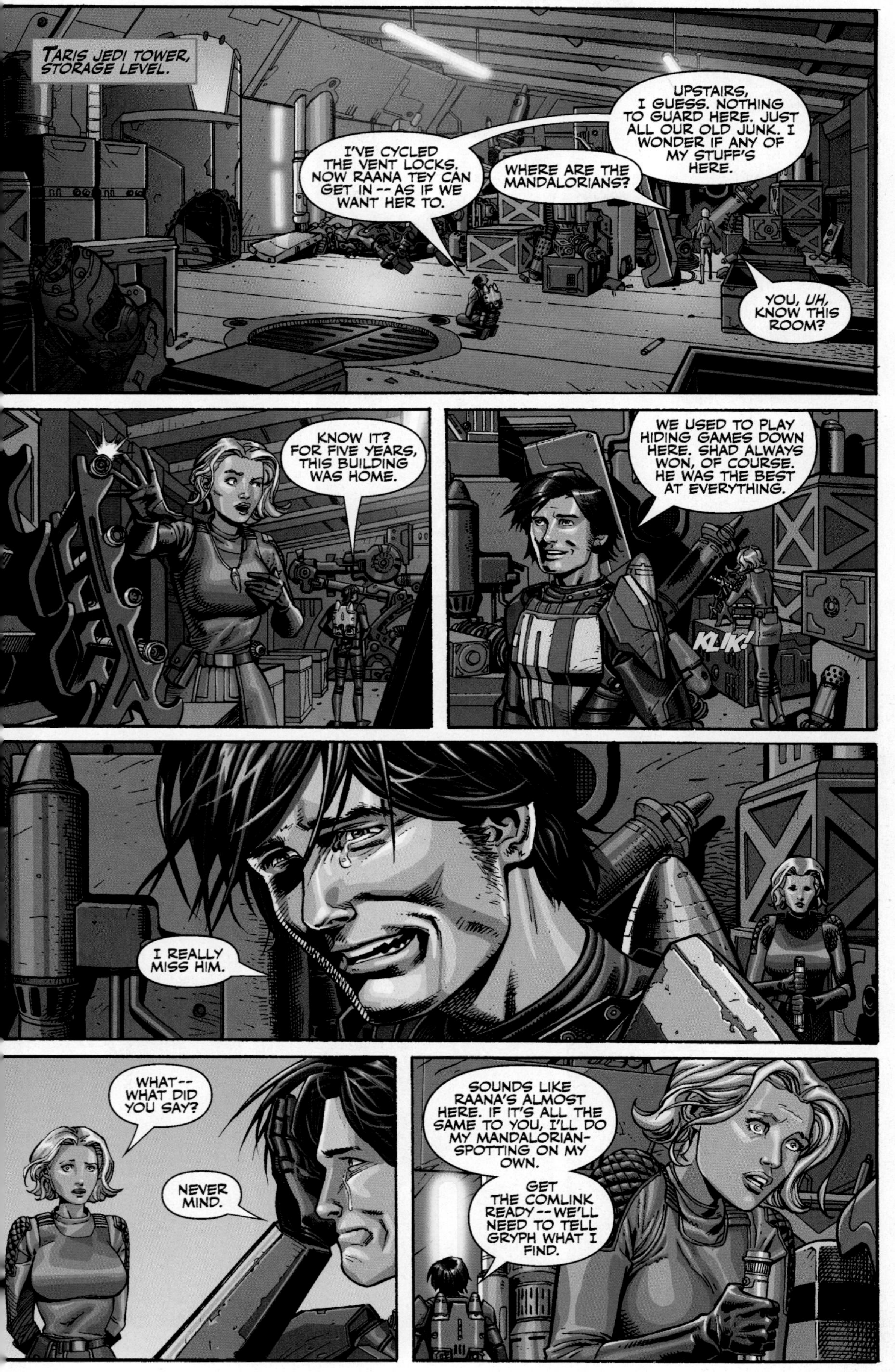
TARIS JEDI TOWER, STORAGE LEVEL.
I'VE CYCLED THE VENT LOCKS. NOW RAANA TEY CAN GET IN -- AS IF WE WANT HER TO.
WHERE ARE THE MANDALORIANS?
UPSTAIRS, I GUESS. NOTHING TO GUARD HERE. JUST ALL OUR OLD JUNK. I WONDER IF ANY OF MY STUFF'S HERE.
YOU, UH, KNOW THIS ROOM?
KNOW IT? FOR FIVE YEARS, THIS BUILDING WAS HOME.
WE USED TO PLAY HIDING GAMES DOWN HERE. SHAD ALWAYS WON, OF COURSE. HE WAS THE BEST AT EVERYTHING.
KLIK!
I REALLY MISS HIM.
WHAT-- WHAT DID YOU SAY?
NEVER MIND.
SOUNDS LIKE RAANA'S ALMOST HERE. IF IT'S ALL THE SAME TO YOU, I'LL DO MY MANDALORIAN-SPOTTING ON MY OWN.
GET THE COMLINK READY--WE'LL NEED TO TELL GRYPH WHAT I FIND.

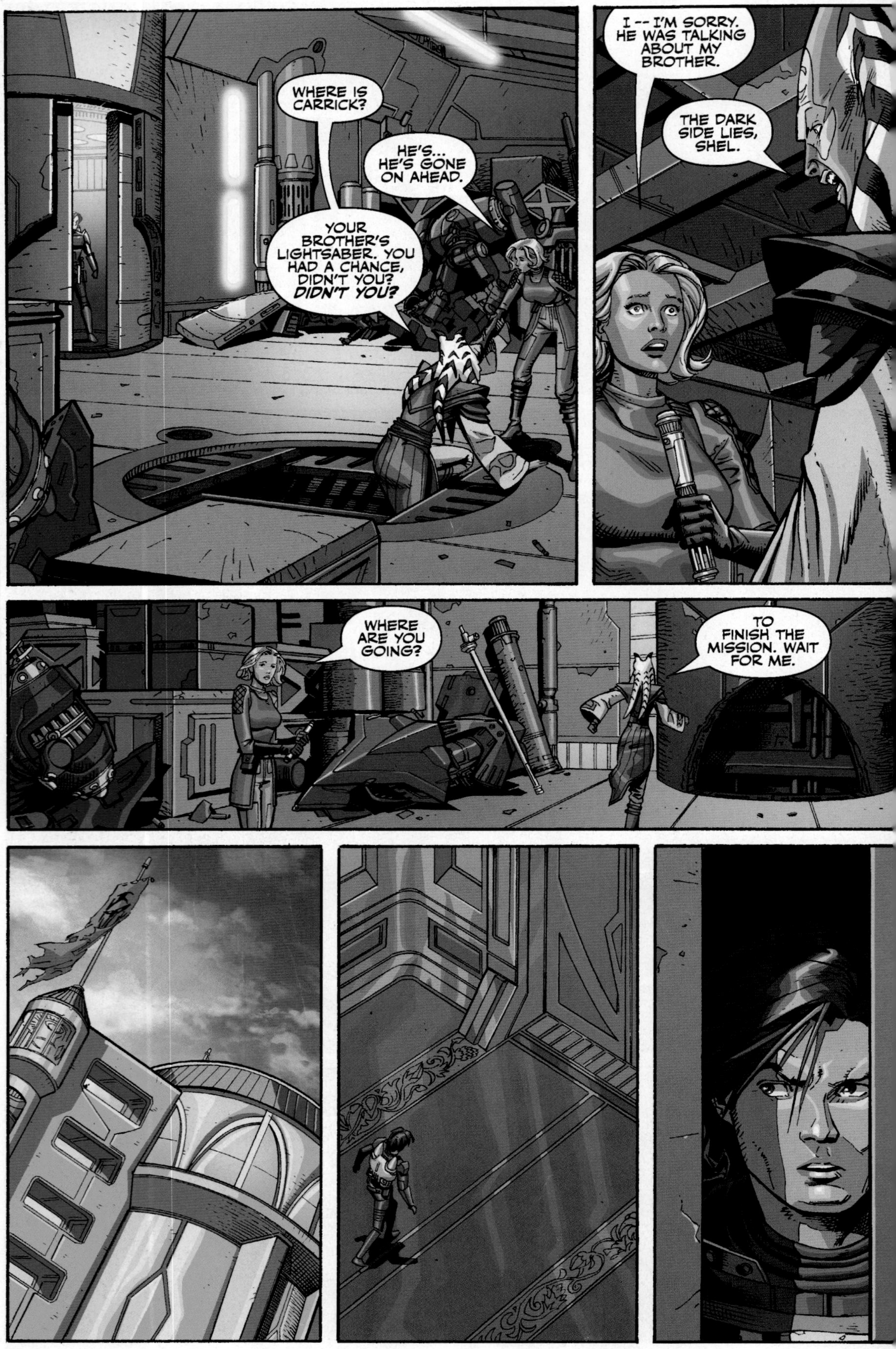
WHERE IS CARRICK?
HE'S... HE'S GONE ON AHEAD.
YOUR BROTHER'S LIGHTSABER. YOU HAD A CHANCE, DIDN'T YOU? *DIDN'T YOU?*
I -- I'M SORRY. HE WAS TALKING ABOUT MY BROTHER.
THE DARK SIDE LIES, SHEL.
WHERE ARE YOU GOING?
TO FINISH THE MISSION. WAIT FOR ME.

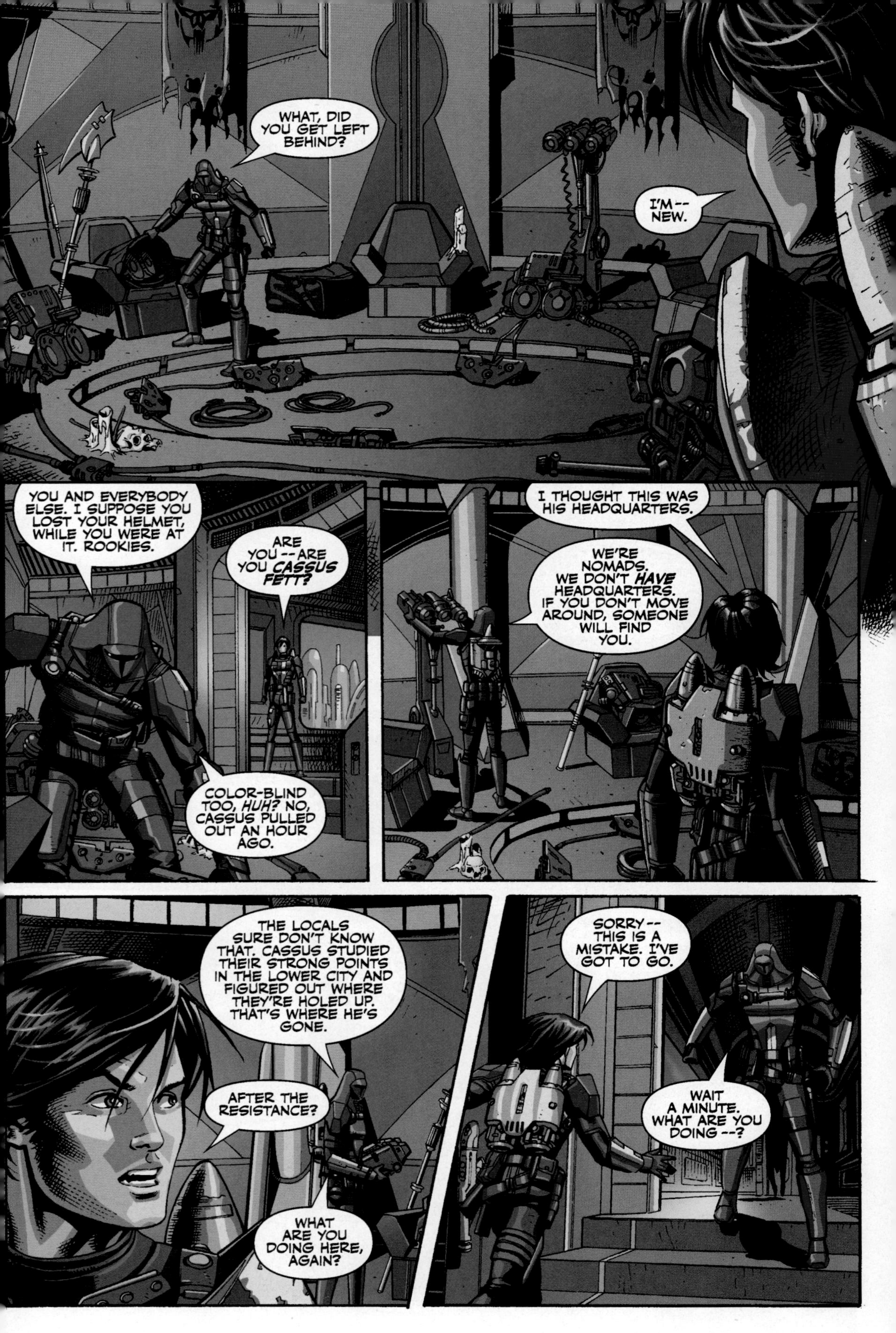
WHAT, DID YOU GET LEFT BEHIND?
I'M-- NEW.
YOU AND EVERYBODY ELSE. I SUPPOSE YOU LOST YOUR HELMET, WHILE YOU WERE AT IT. ROOKIES.
ARE YOU--ARE YOU *CASSUS FETT?*
COLOR-BLIND TOO, *HUH?* NO, CASSUS PULLED OUT AN HOUR AGO.
I THOUGHT THIS WAS HIS HEADQUARTERS.
WE'RE NOMADS. WE DON'T *HAVE* HEADQUARTERS. IF YOU DON'T MOVE AROUND, SOMEONE WILL FIND YOU.
THE LOCALS SURE DON'T KNOW THAT. CASSUS STUDIED THEIR STRONG POINTS IN THE LOWER CITY AND FIGURED OUT WHERE THEY'RE HOLED UP. THAT'S WHERE HE'S GONE.
AFTER THE RESISTANCE?
WHAT ARE YOU DOING HERE, AGAIN?
SORRY-- THIS IS A MISTAKE. I'VE GOT TO GO.
WAIT A MINUTE. WHAT ARE YOU DOING--?

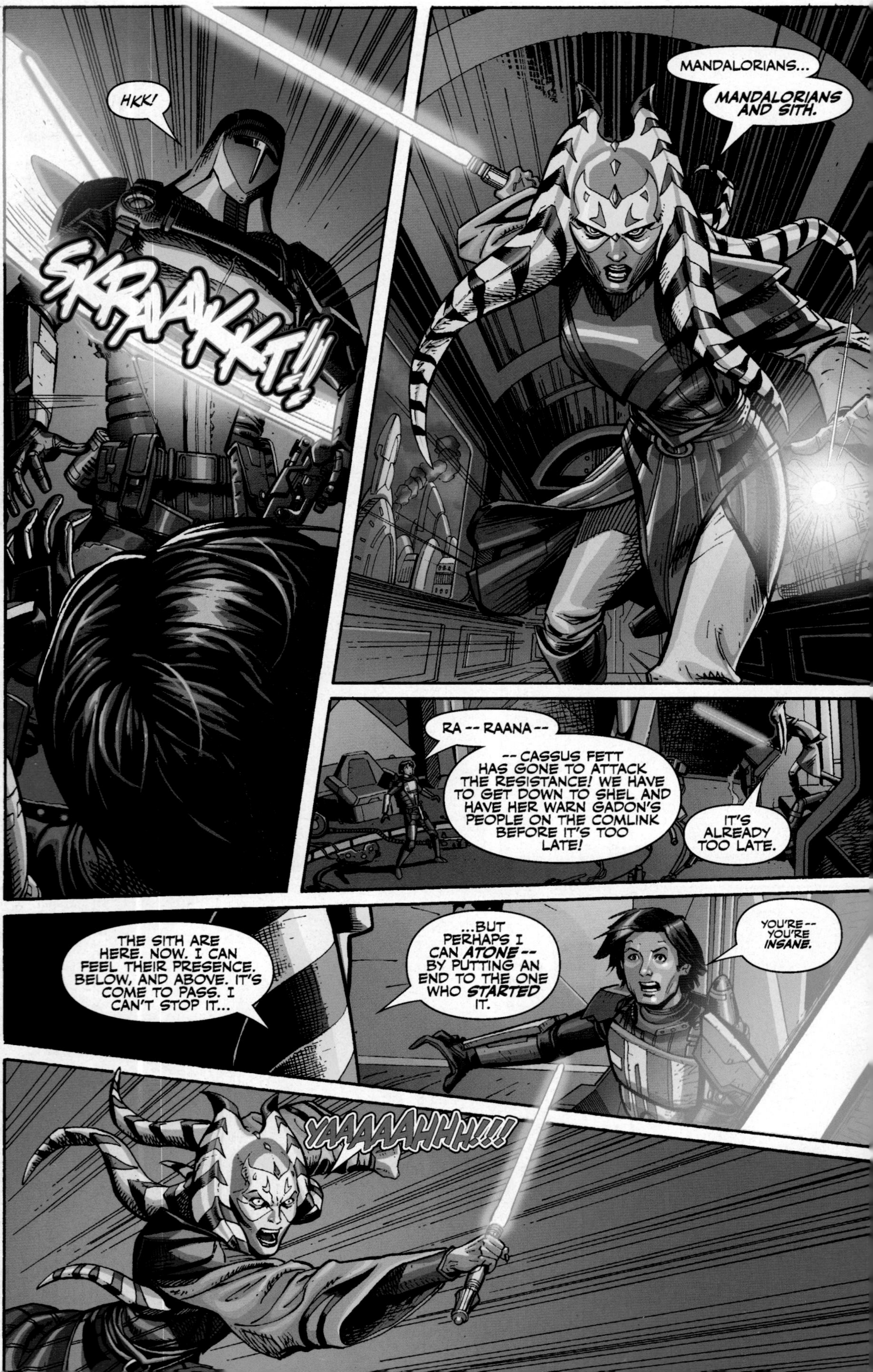
HKK!
SKRAKKT!!
MANDALORIANS...
MANDALORIANS AND SITH.
RA -- RAANA --
-- CASSUS FETT HAS GONE TO ATTACK THE RESISTANCE! WE HAVE TO GET DOWN TO SHEL AND HAVE HER WARN GADON'S PEOPLE ON THE COMLINK BEFORE IT'S TOO LATE!
IT'S ALREADY TOO LATE.
THE SITH ARE HERE. NOW. I CAN FEEL THEIR PRESENCE. BELOW, AND ABOVE. IT'S COME TO PASS. I CAN'T STOP IT...
...BUT PERHAPS I CAN ATONE -- BY PUTTING AN END TO THE ONE WHO STARTED IT.
YOU'RE -- YOU'RE INSANE.
YAAAAAHHH!!!

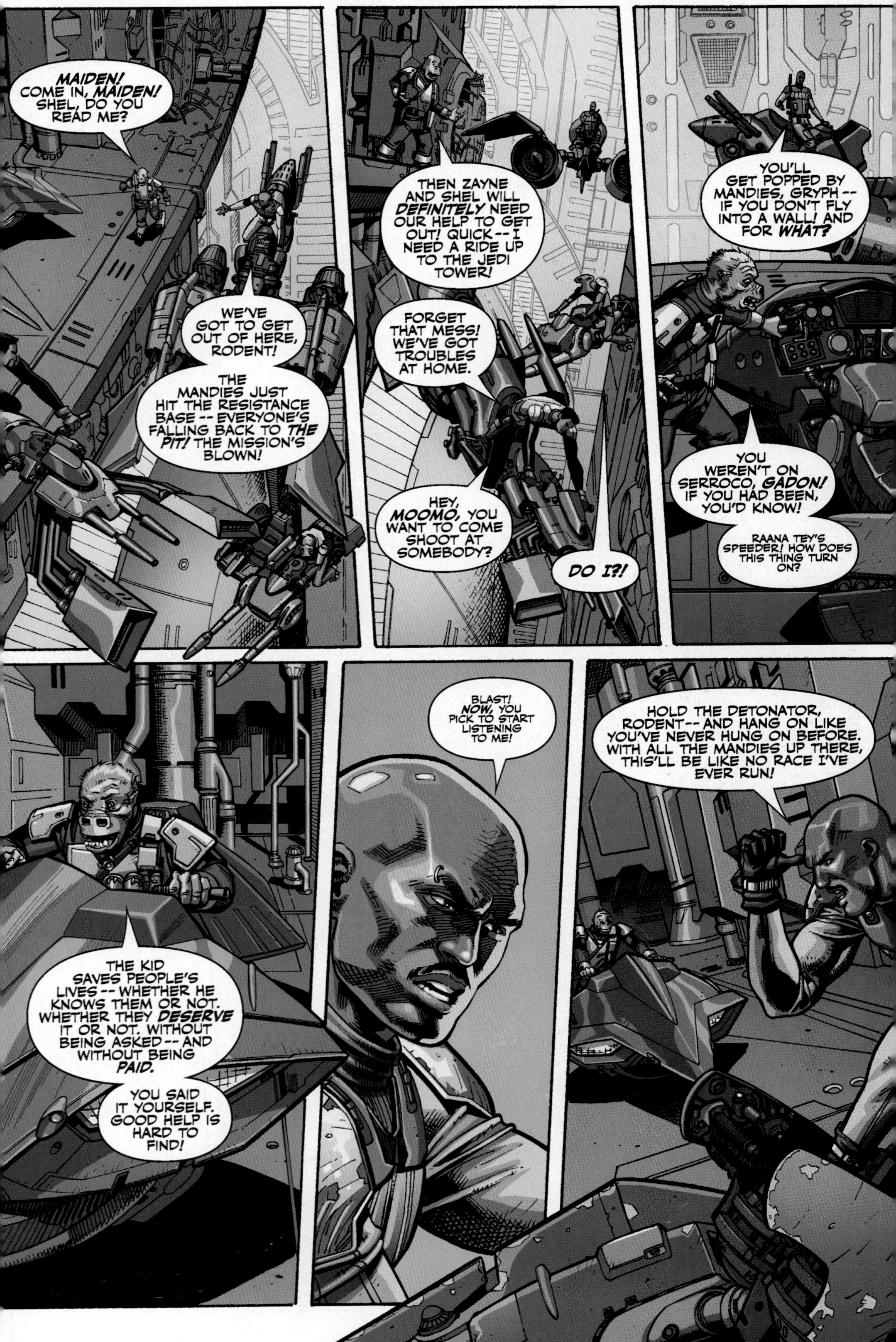

MAIDEN! COME IN, MAIDEN! SHEL, DO YOU READ ME?
WE'VE GOT TO GET OUT OF HERE, RODENT!
THE MANDIES JUST HIT THE RESISTANCE BASE -- EVERYONE'S FALLING BACK TO THE PIT! THE MISSION'S BLOWN!
THEN ZAYNE AND SHEL WILL DEFINITELY NEED OUR HELP TO GET OUT! QUICK -- I NEED A RIDE UP TO THE JEDI TOWER!
FORGET THAT MESS! WE'VE GOT TROUBLES AT HOME.
HEY, MOOMO, YOU WANT TO COME SHOOT AT SOMEBODY?
DO I?!
YOU'LL GET POPPED BY MANDIES, GRYPH -- IF YOU DON'T FLY INTO A WALL! AND FOR WHAT?
YOU WEREN'T ON SERROCO, GADON! IF YOU HAD BEEN, YOU'D KNOW!
RAANA TEY'S SPEEDER! HOW DOES THIS THING TURN ON?
THE KID SAVES PEOPLE'S LIVES -- WHETHER HE KNOWS THEM OR NOT. WHETHER THEY DESERVE IT OR NOT. WITHOUT BEING ASKED -- AND WITHOUT BEING PAID.
YOU SAID IT YOURSELF. GOOD HELP IS HARD TO FIND!
BLAST! NOW, YOU PICK TO START LISTENING TO ME!
HOLD THE DETONATOR, RODENT -- AND HANG ON LIKE YOU'VE NEVER HUNG ON BEFORE. WITH ALL THE MANDIES UP THERE, THIS'LL BE LIKE NO RACE I'VE EVER RUN!

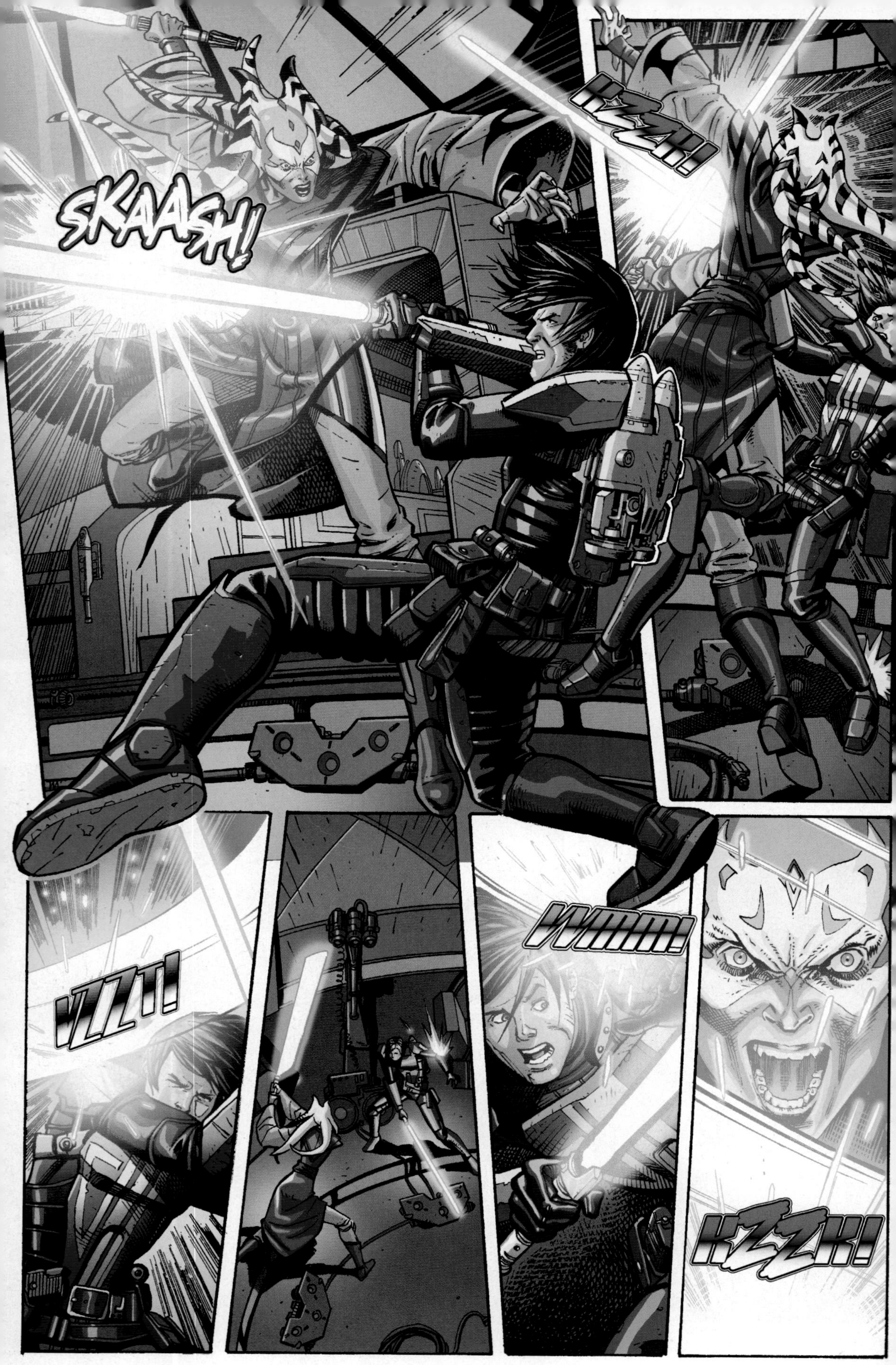
SKAASH!
KZZH!
VZZT!
VVMMM!
KZZK!

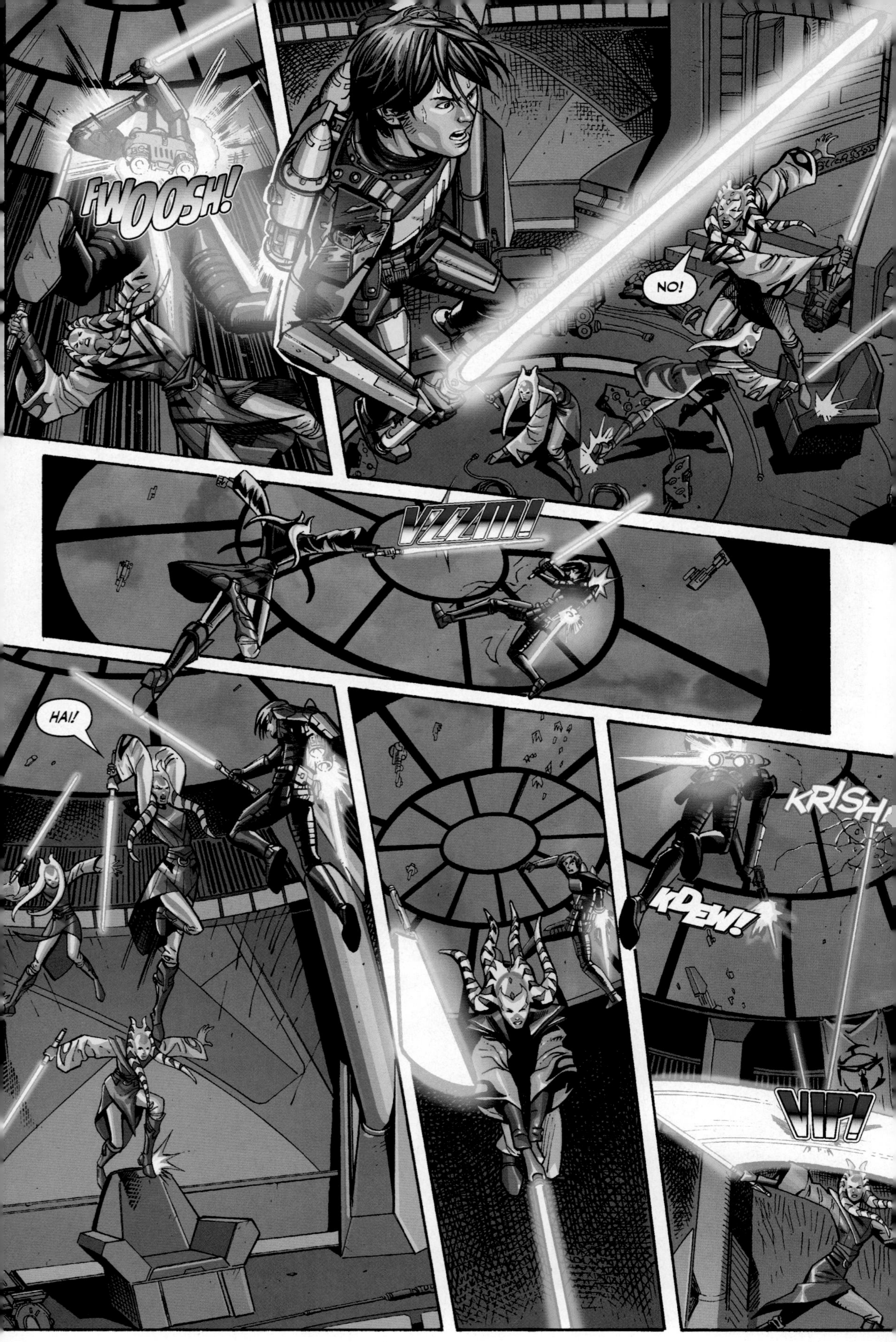
FWOOSH!
NO!
VZZM!
HAI!
KRISH!
KDEW!
VIP!

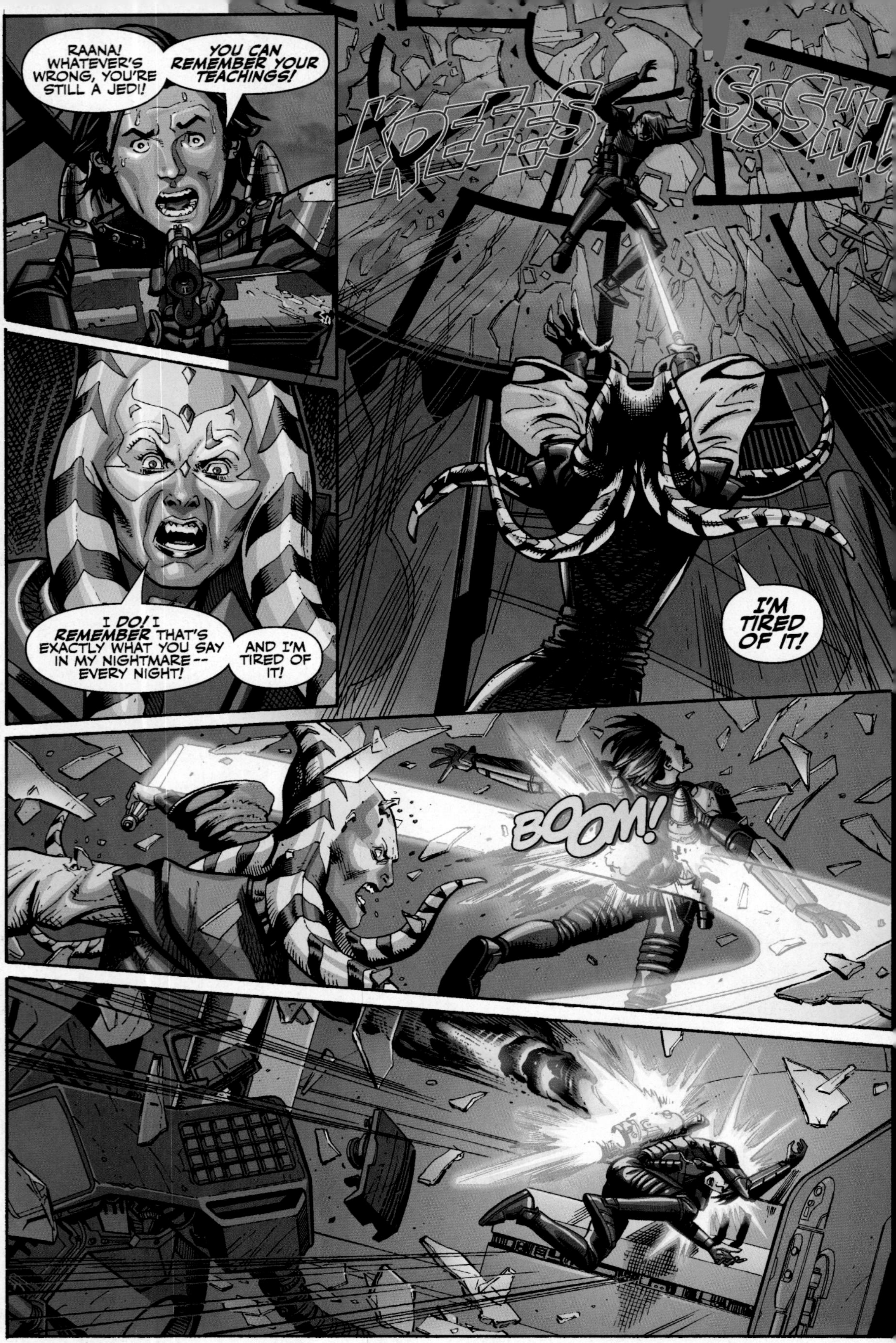
RAANA! WHATEVER'S WRONG, YOU'RE STILL A JEDI!
YOU CAN REMEMBER YOUR TEACHINGS!
I DO! I REMEMBER THAT'S EXACTLY WHAT YOU SAY IN MY NIGHTMARE-- EVERY NIGHT!
AND I'M TIRED OF IT!
I'M TIRED OF IT!
BOOM!

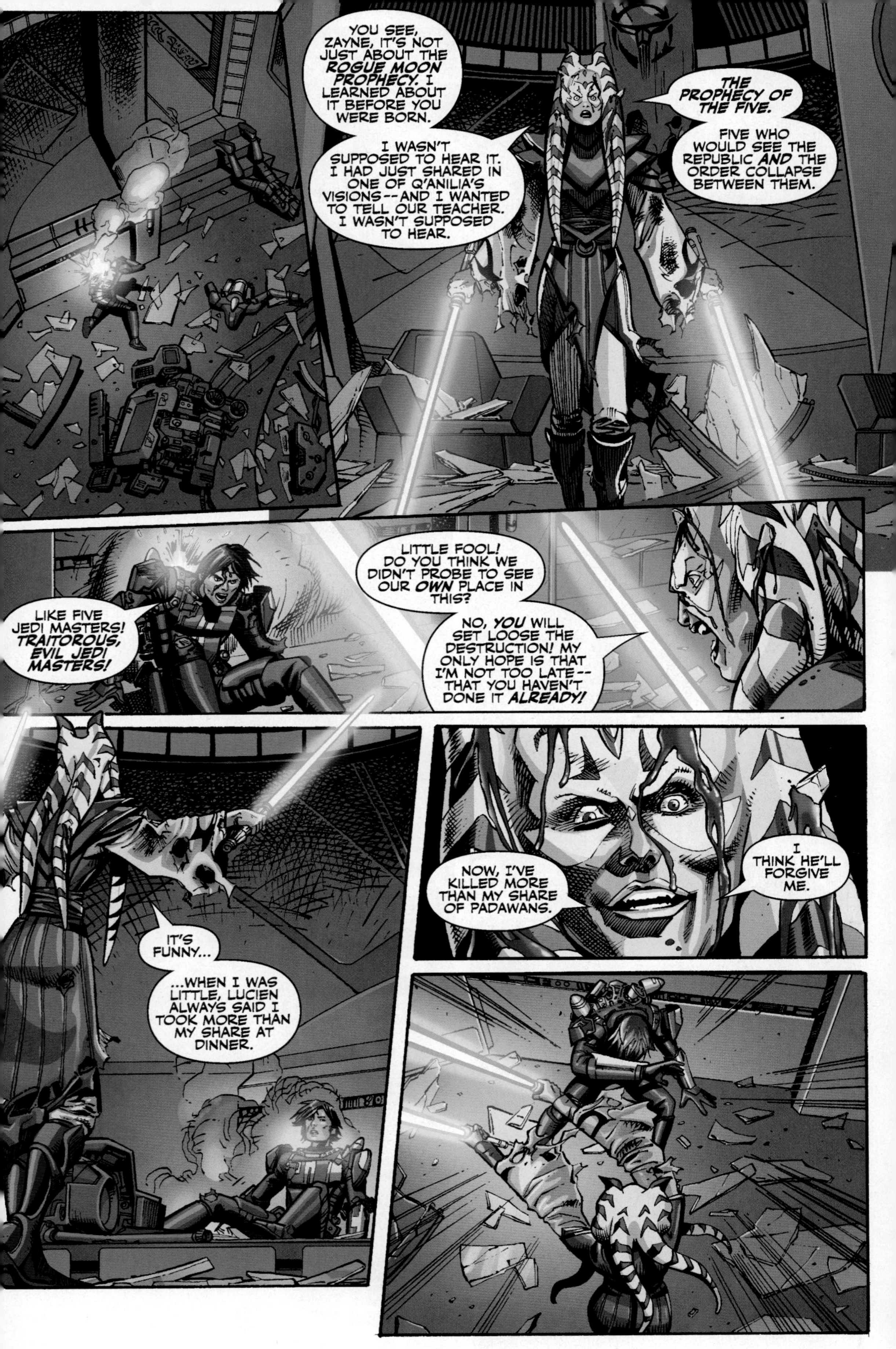

YOU SEE, ZAYNE, IT'S NOT JUST ABOUT THE ROGUE MOON PROPHECY. I LEARNED ABOUT IT BEFORE YOU WERE BORN.
I WASN'T SUPPOSED TO HEAR IT. I HAD JUST SHARED IN ONE OF Q'ANILIA'S VISIONS--AND I WANTED TO TELL OUR TEACHER. I WASN'T SUPPOSED TO HEAR.
THE PROPHECY OF THE FIVE.
FIVE WHO WOULD SEE THE REPUBLIC AND THE ORDER COLLAPSE BETWEEN THEM.
LIKE FIVE JEDI MASTERS! TRAITOROUS, EVIL JEDI MASTERS!
LITTLE FOOL! DO YOU THINK WE DIDN'T PROBE TO SEE OUR OWN PLACE IN THIS?
NO, YOU WILL SET LOOSE THE DESTRUCTION! MY ONLY HOPE IS THAT I'M NOT TOO LATE-- THAT YOU HAVEN'T DONE IT ALREADY!
IT'S FUNNY...
...WHEN I WAS LITTLE, LUCIEN ALWAYS SAID I TOOK MORE THAN MY SHARE AT DINNER.
NOW, I'VE KILLED MORE THAN MY SHARE OF PADAWANS.
I THINK HE'LL FORGIVE ME.

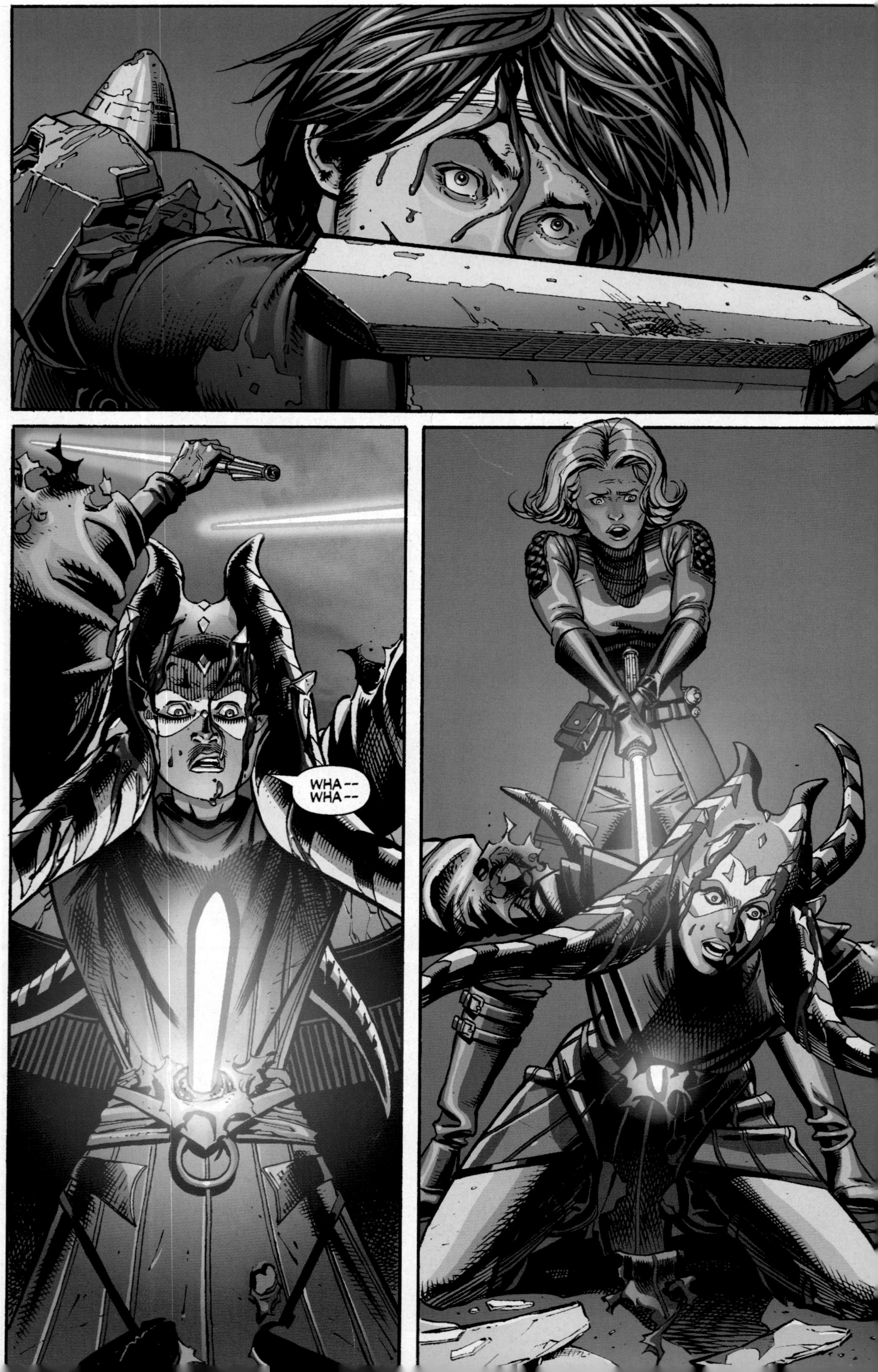
WHA--
WHA--

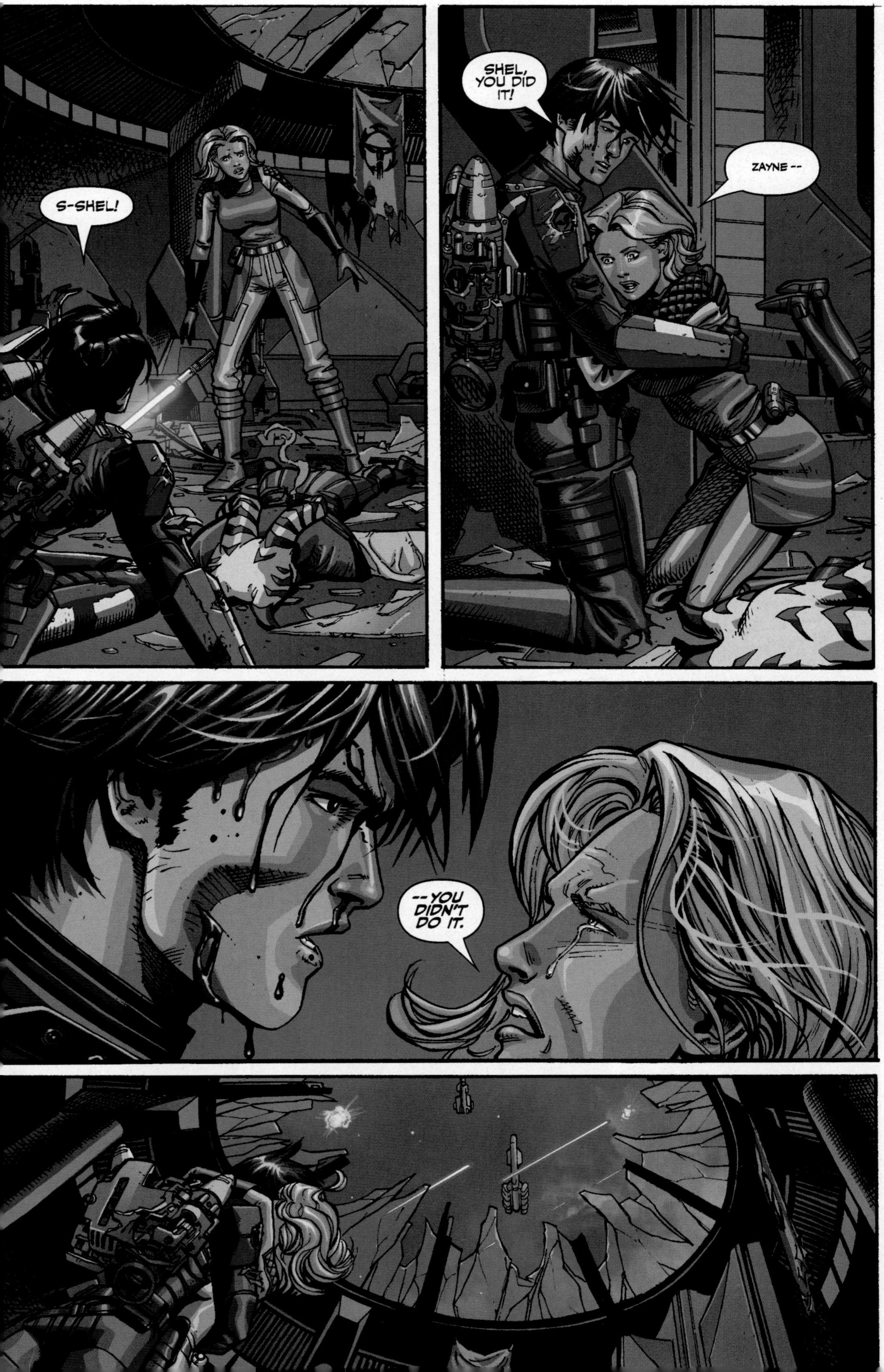
S-SHEL!
SHEL, YOU DID IT!
ZAYNE --
-- YOU DIDN'T DO IT.

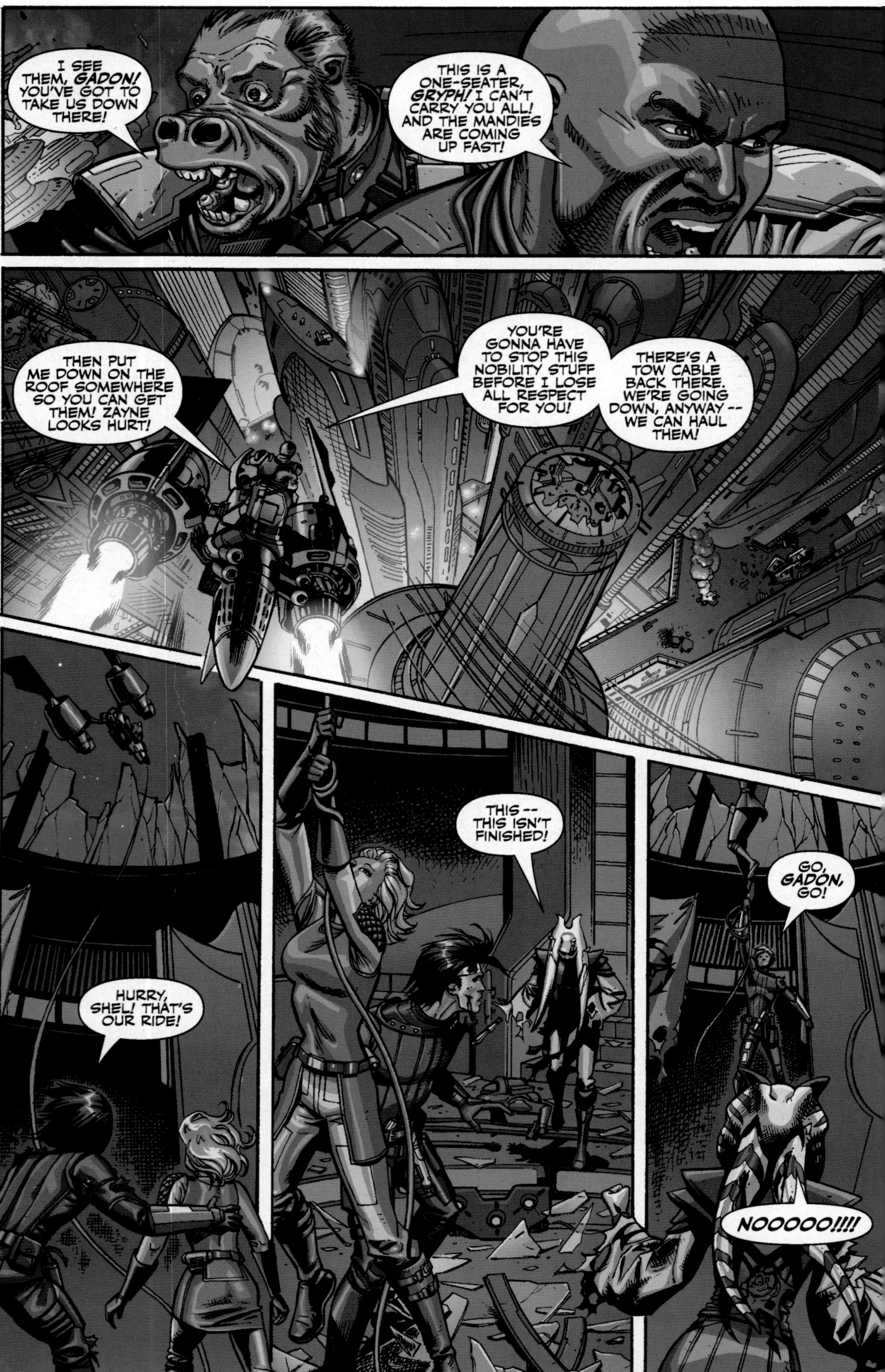
I SEE THEM, GADON! YOU'VE GOT TO TAKE US DOWN THERE!
THIS IS A ONE-SEATER, GRYPH! I CAN'T CARRY YOU ALL! AND THE MANDIES ARE COMING UP FAST!
THEN PUT ME DOWN ON THE ROOF SOMEWHERE SO YOU CAN GET THEM! ZAYNE LOOKS HURT!
YOU'RE GONNA HAVE TO STOP THIS NOBILITY STUFF BEFORE I LOSE ALL RESPECT FOR YOU!
THERE'S A TOW CABLE BACK THERE. WE'RE GOING DOWN, ANYWAY -- WE CAN HAUL THEM!
HURRY, SHEL! THAT'S OUR RIDE!
THIS -- THIS ISN'T FINISHED!
GO, GADON, GO!
NOOOOO!!!!

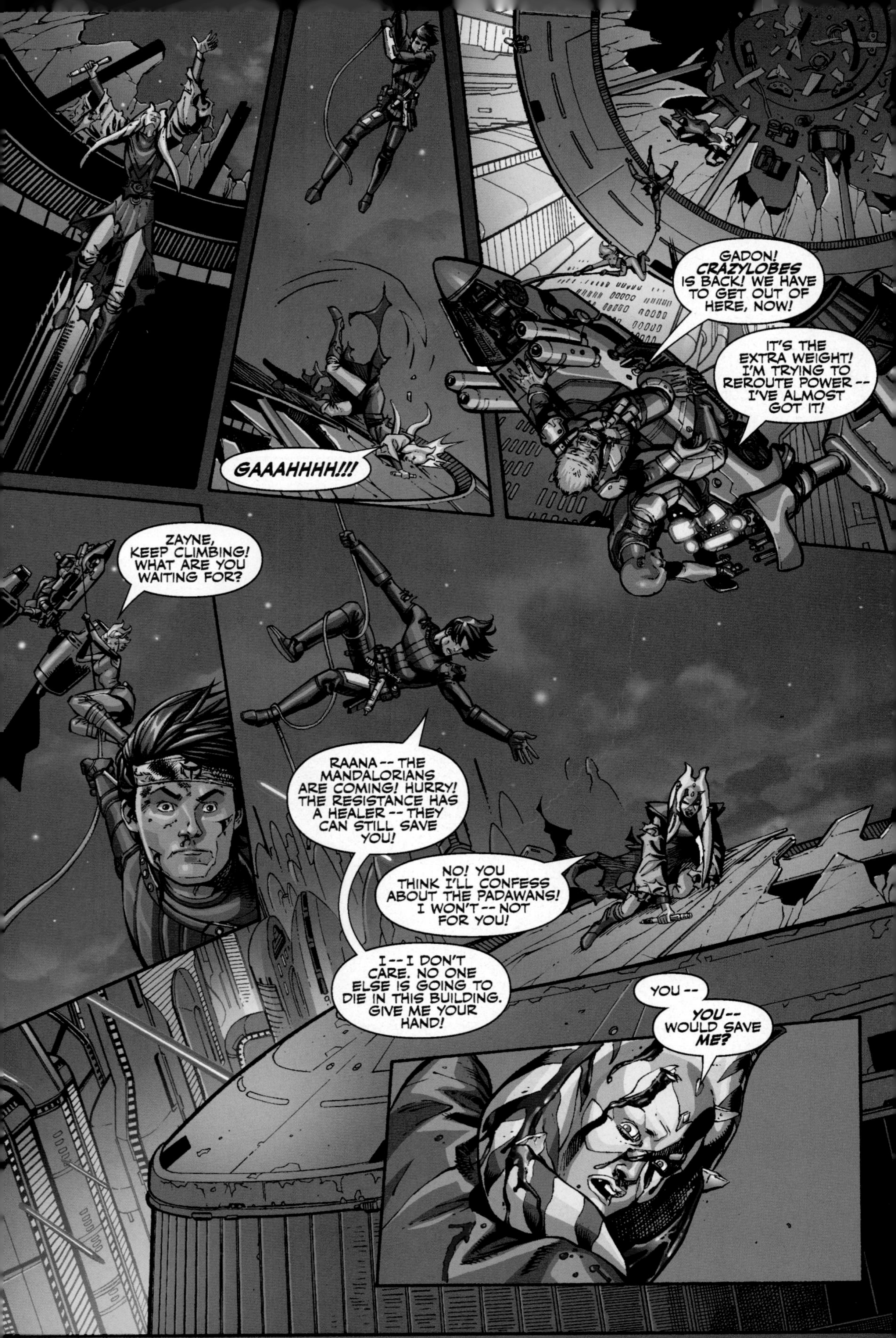
GAAAHHHH!!!
GADON! CRAZYLOBES IS BACK! WE HAVE TO GET OUT OF HERE, NOW!
IT'S THE EXTRA WEIGHT! I'M TRYING TO REROUTE POWER -- I'VE ALMOST GOT IT!
ZAYNE, KEEP CLIMBING! WHAT ARE YOU WAITING FOR?
RAANA -- THE MANDALORIANS ARE COMING! HURRY! THE RESISTANCE HAS A HEALER -- THEY CAN STILL SAVE YOU!
NO! YOU THINK I'LL CONFESS ABOUT THE PADAWANS! I WON'T -- NOT FOR YOU!
I -- I DON'T CARE. NO ONE ELSE IS GOING TO DIE IN THIS BUILDING. GIVE ME YOUR HAND!
YOU --
YOU -- WOULD SAVE ME?

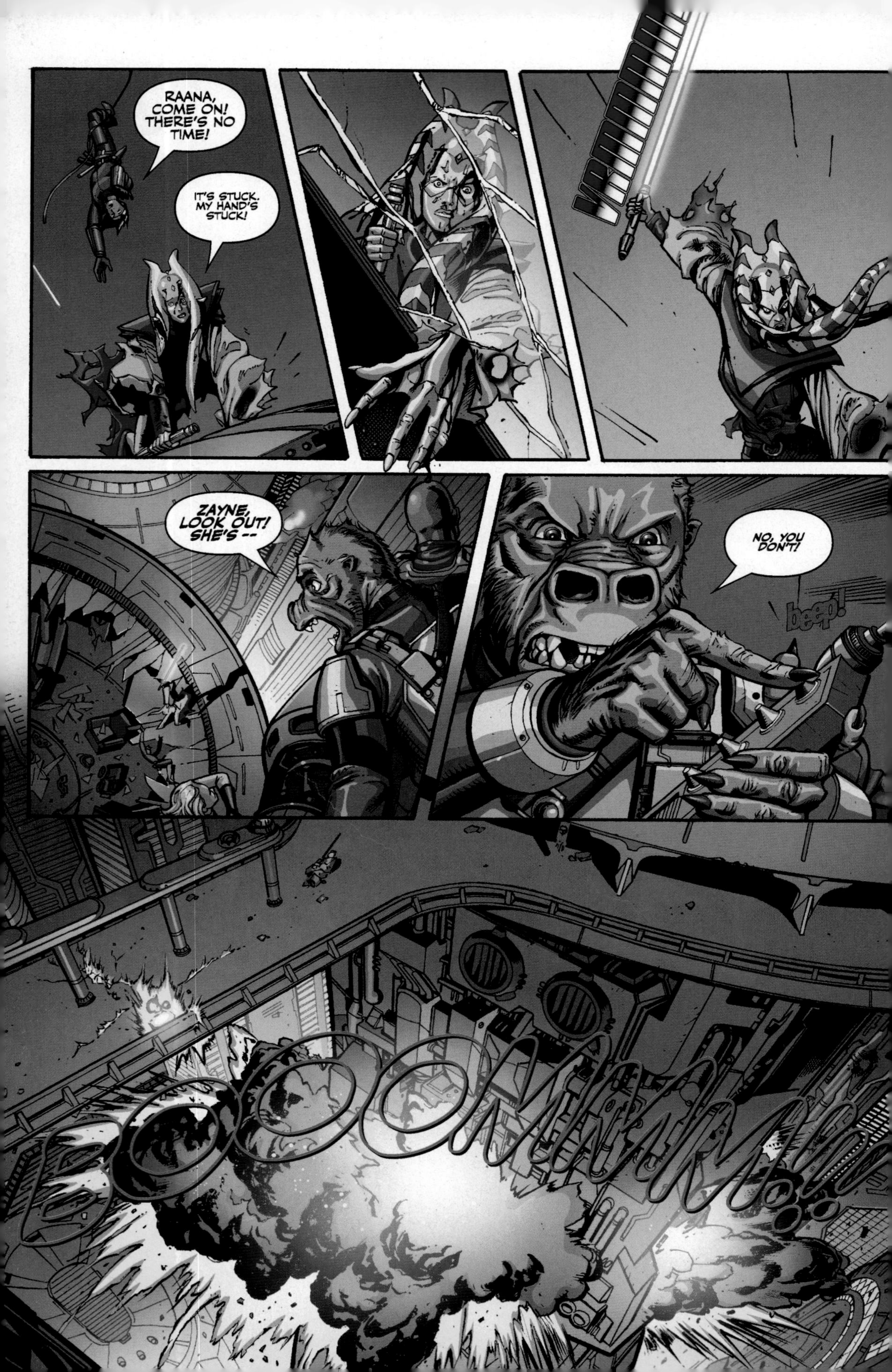
RAANA, COME ON! THERE'S NO TIME!
IT'S STUCK. MY HAND'S STUCK!
ZAYNE, LOOK OUT! SHE'S --
NO, YOU DON'T!
beep!

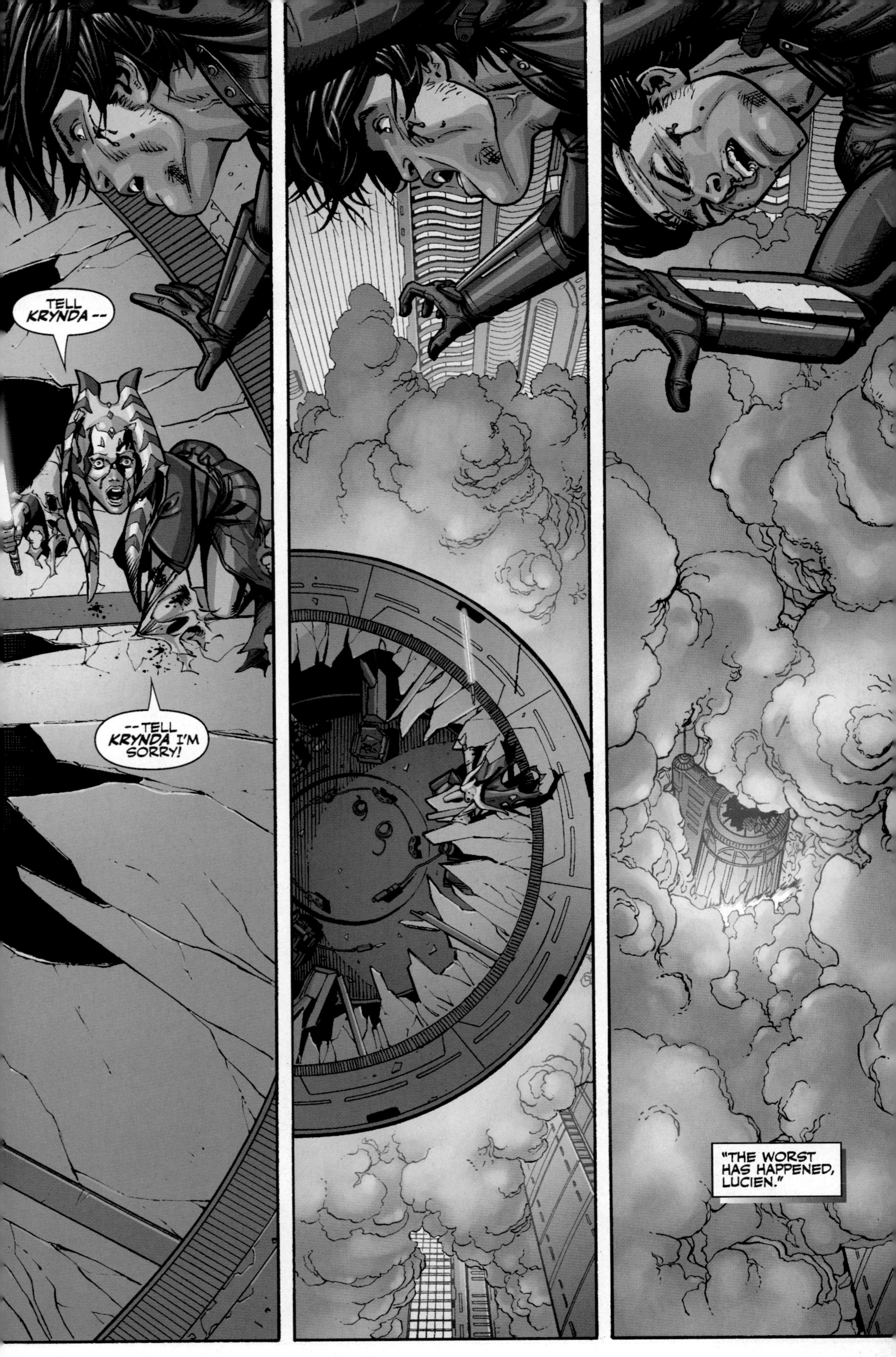
TELL KRYNDA --
--TELL KRYNDA I'M SORRY!
"THE WORST HAS HAPPENED, LUCIEN."

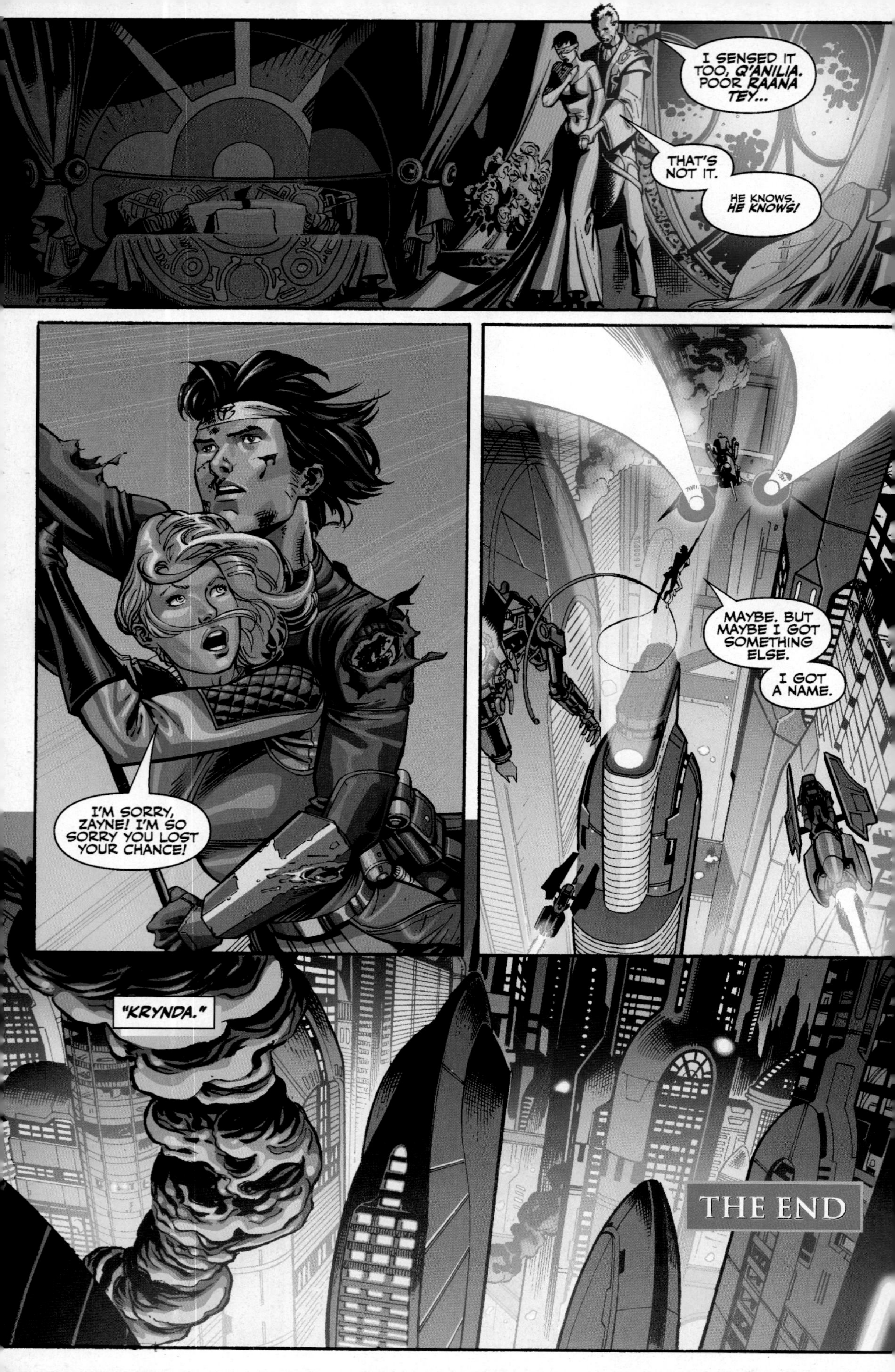
I SENSED IT TOO, Q'ANILIA. POOR RAANA TEY...
THAT'S NOT IT.
HE KNOWS. HE KNOWS!
I'M SORRY, ZAYNE! I'M SO SORRY YOU LOST YOUR CHANCE!
MAYBE. BUT MAYBE I GOT SOMETHING ELSE.
I GOT A NAME.
"KRYNDA."
THE END

RET! MOST SECRET! MOST SECRET! MOST SECRET! MOST

GALACTIC REPUBLIC

DEFENSE MINISTRY DAILY BRIEF #KD0092

FROM: Joint Operations Information Office, Defense Ministry
TO: Koa Delko, Defense Minister; Catronus Steffans, Defense Ministry Director for Public Information

ARMY OPERATIONS

- Listening posts indicate Mandalorians have initiated new, massive ground operations in the Lower City of Taris. Additionally, an increase in planetary surface albedo detected by observers suggests a significant, sudden increase in the amount of material being released into the atmosphere.
- Approximately 2,000 casualties suffered overnight in clashes on Myrkr.
- Intel studies beginning on Neo-Crusader shock armor specimen obtained at Myrkr. Findings on capabilities and equipment sourcing expected later this week.

NAVAL OPERATIONS

- Admiralty reports six more losses at frontier outposts, detailed in attachment 3C.
- Refit of *Swiftsure* at Corellia dockyards is now complete.
- Yesterday's clash in Omonoth system inconclusive. Neither we nor Mandalorians can salvage *Arkanian Legacy.*

Policy recommendation: Concur with Commerce Ministry–continue news blackout on truth behind Arkoh Adasca's treachery.

PRODUCTION UPDATE

- Voluntary targets set by the new Office of Production Coordination on strategic materials are receiving little attention, the office reports. High prices paid in the Tapani Sector are continuing to divert needed materials and are driving up costs for the military. (see Legislative, below)
- Lhosan Industries freighters continue to arrive at frontier planets, distributing transmitters and miscellaneous dry goods.

Policy recommendation: Public pronouncement honoring Lhosan CEO Jervo Thalien may inspire patriotism elsewhere in business community.

LEGISLATIVE UPDATE

- With no response from the Chancellor's special investigator, the inquiry into the so-called "Taris Affair" is losing steam in the Oversight committee.
- Senator Graw has repeated his call for the constructive use of export tariffs in limiting the Tapani Sector's draw on strategic supplies.

JEDI UPDATE

- Jedi liaison now confirms one of the Knights on regular assignment on Serroco before the devastation has reported back, having escaped on one of the three military vessels that was able to make light speed. Reports indicate others were present, and one or more may have been part of the reported prisoner transfer to the Taris sector.
- On the policy front, Master Vrook Lamar gave a rare interview yesterday to the financial press restating the Jedi's non-interference stand in the Mandalorian War. But the leader of the nascent Revanchist movement is rumored to be arranging a meeting between several Jedi opinion-makers at an undisclosed location.

Policy recommendation: Liaison recommends continued public expressions of understanding for Jedi neutrality. With no obvious supporters on the Council, backchannel communications to The Revanchist would be premature and would jeopardize the Republic's relations with the Order proper.

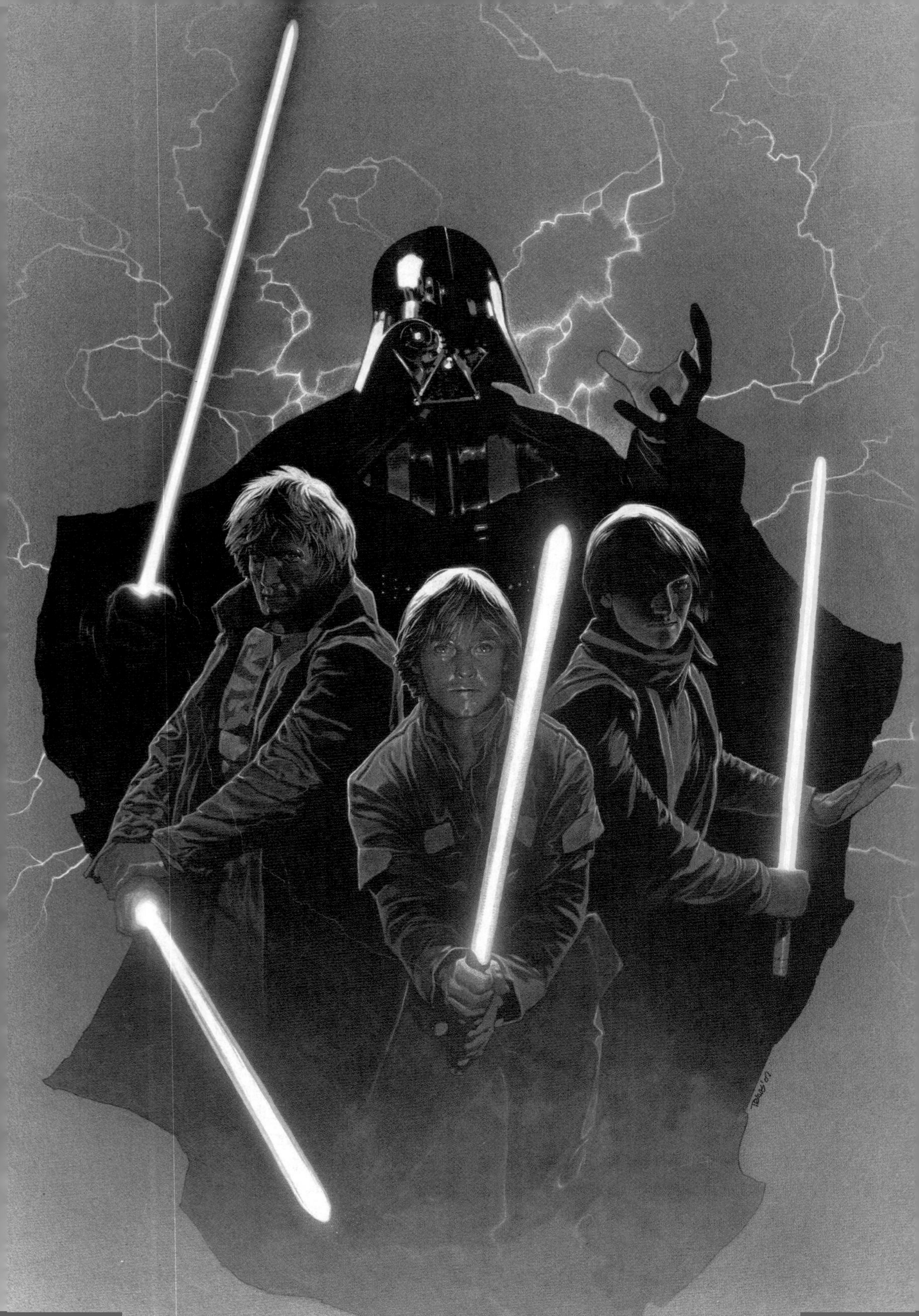

STAR ART 1”

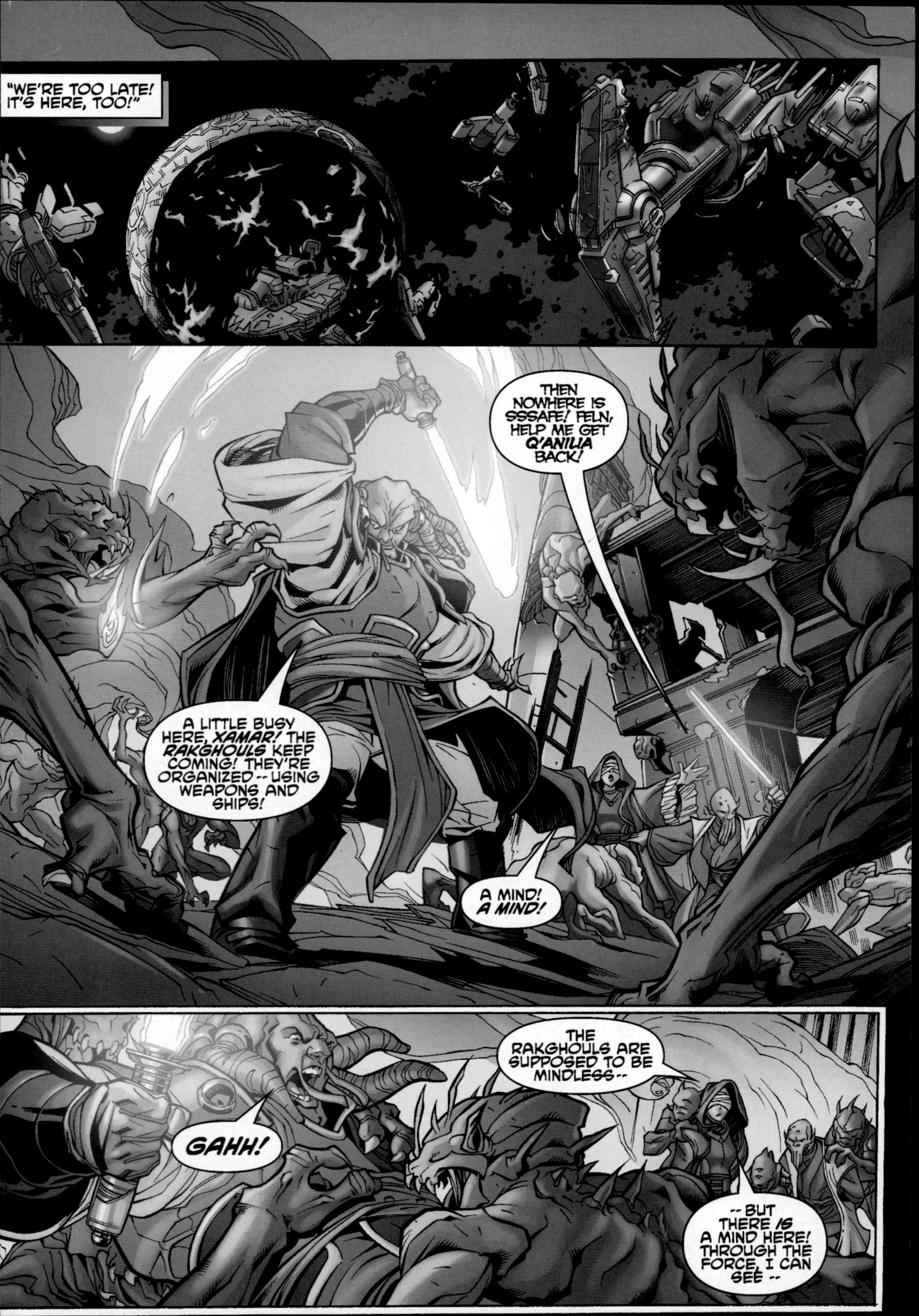
"WE'RE TOO LATE! IT'S HERE, TOO!"
THEN NOWHERE IS SSSAFE! FELN, HELP ME GET Q'ANILIA BACK!
A LITTLE BUSY HERE, XAMAR! THE RAKGHOULS KEEP COMING! THEY'RE ORGANIZED -- USING WEAPONS AND SHIPS!
A MIND! A MIND!
THE RAKGHOULS ARE SUPPOSED TO BE MINDLESS --
GAHH!
-- BUT THERE IS A MIND HERE! THROUGH THE FORCE, I CAN SEE --

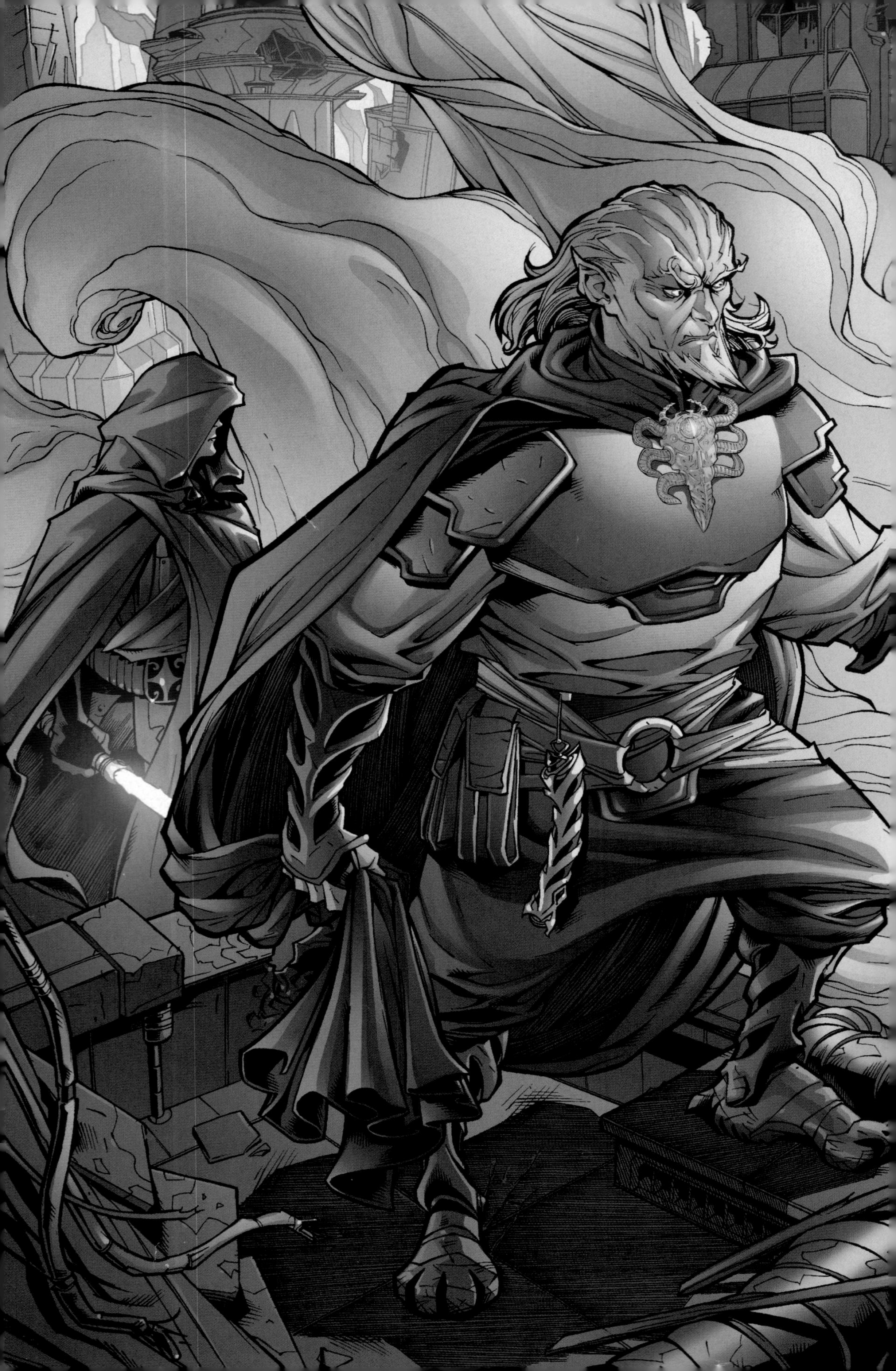

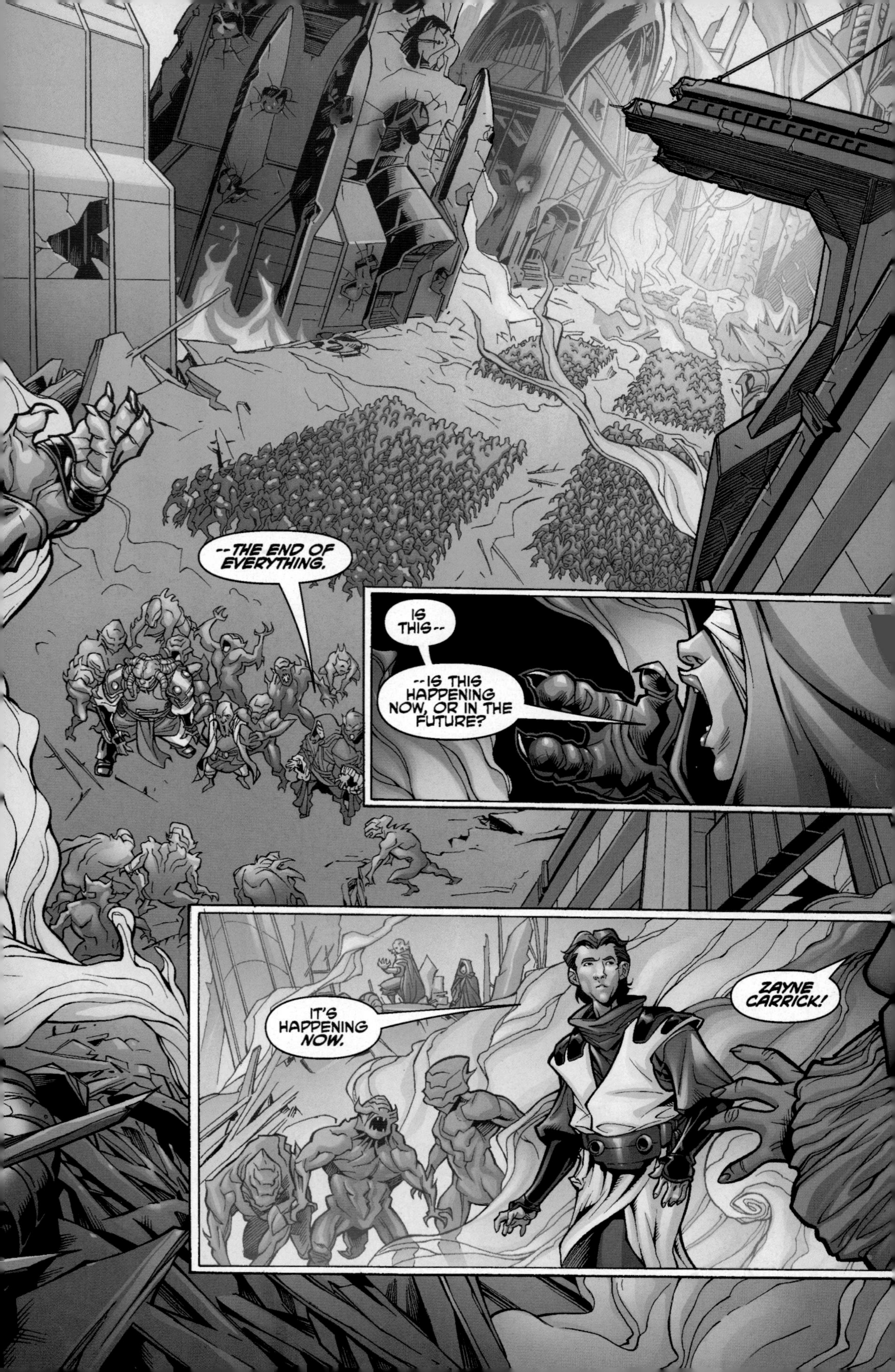
--THE END OF EVERYTHING.
IS THIS--
--IS THIS HAPPENING NOW, OR IN THE FUTURE?
IT'S HAPPENING NOW.
ZAYNE CARRICK!

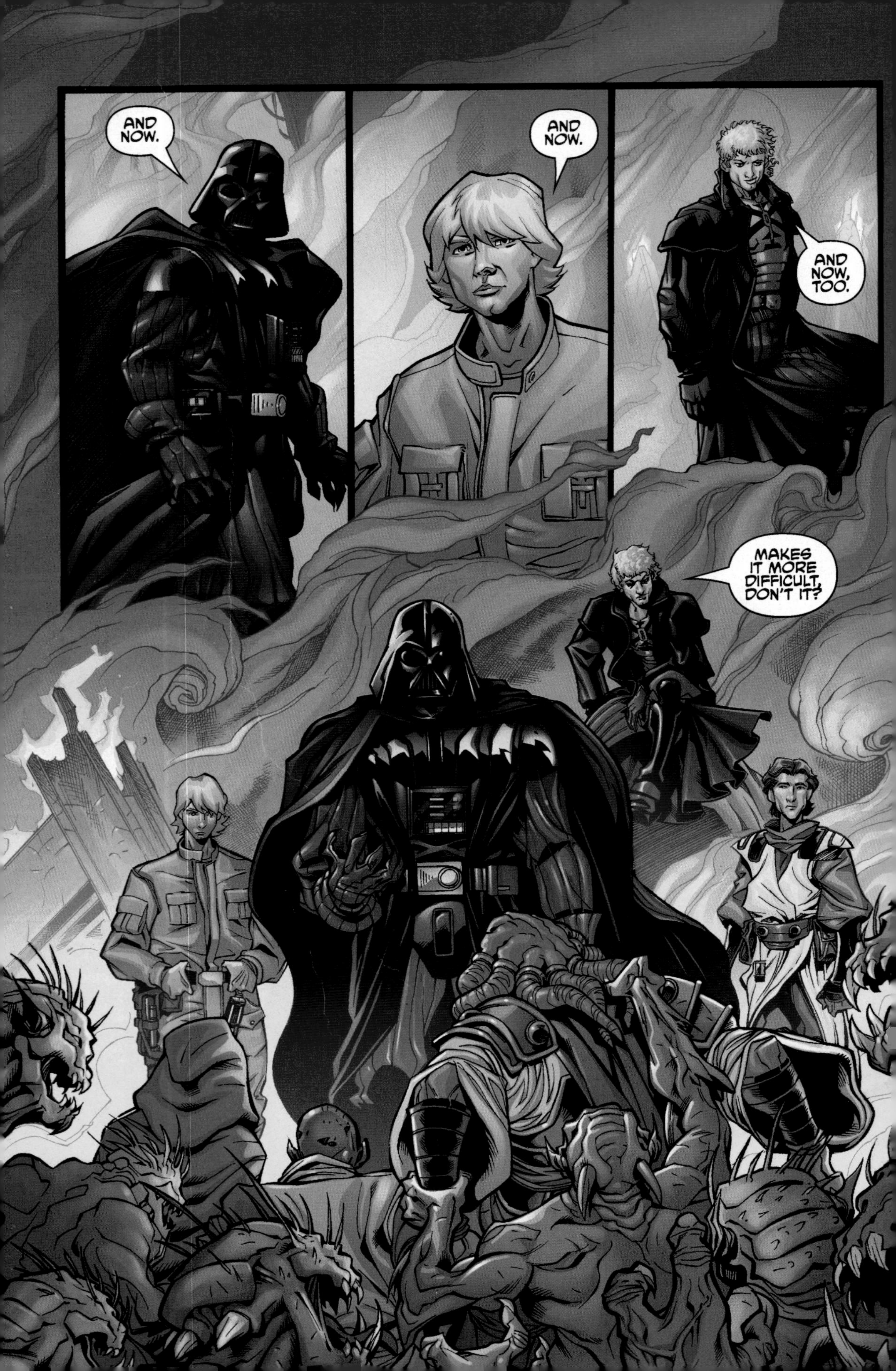
AND NOW.
AND NOW.
AND NOW, TOO.
MAKES IT MORE DIFFICULT, DON'T IT?

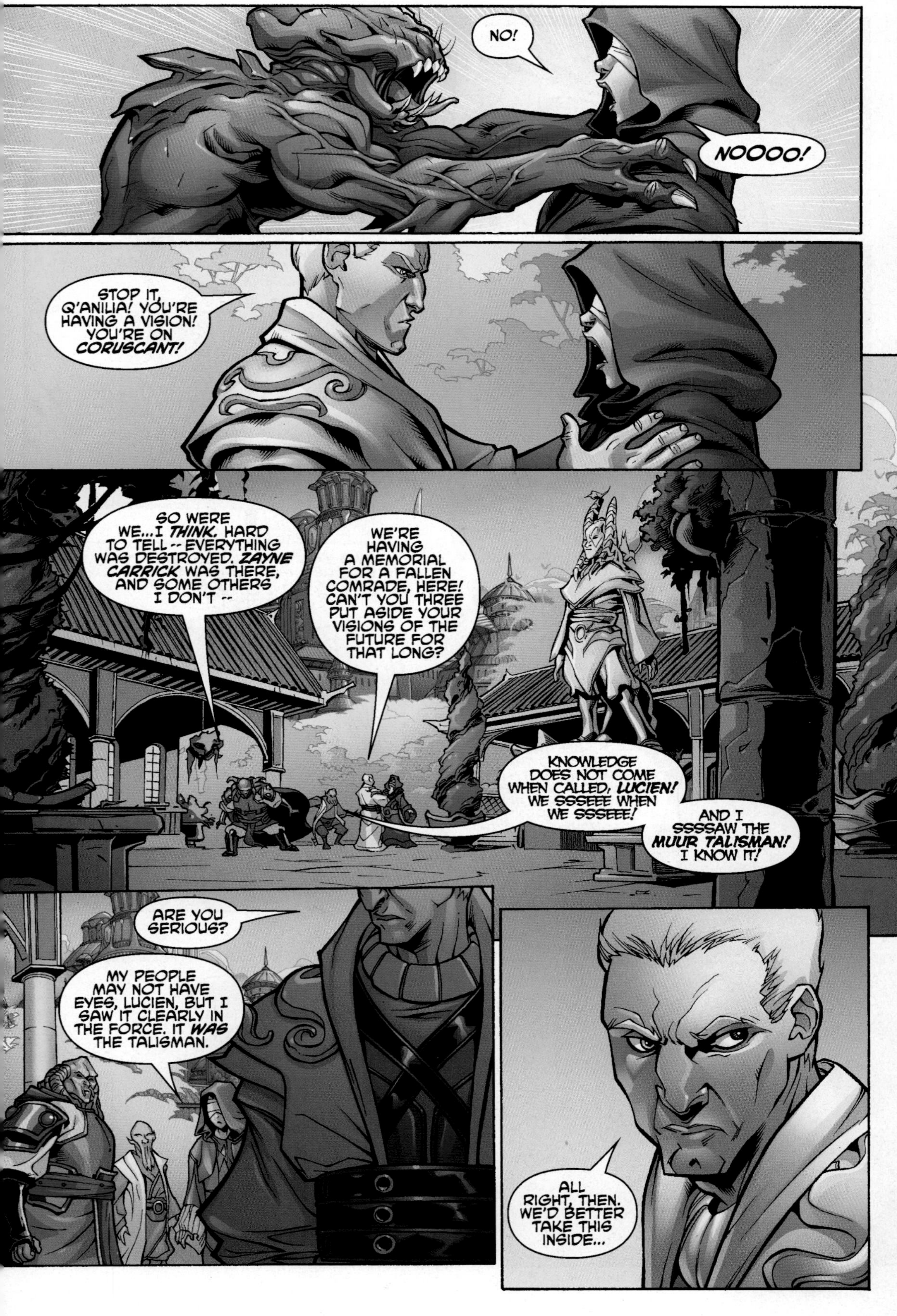

NO!
NOOOO!
STOP IT, Q'ANILIA! YOU'RE HAVING A VISION! YOU'RE ON CORUSCANT!
SO WERE WE...I THINK. HARD TO TELL -- EVERYTHING WAS DESTROYED. ZAYNE CARRICK WAS THERE, AND SOME OTHERS I DON'T --
WE'RE HAVING A MEMORIAL FOR A FALLEN COMRADE, HERE! CAN'T YOU THREE PUT ASIDE YOUR VISIONS OF THE FUTURE FOR THAT LONG?
KNOWLEDGE DOES NOT COME WHEN CALLED, LUCIEN! WE SSSEEE WHEN WE SSSEEE!
AND I SSSSAW THE MUUR TALISMAN! I KNOW IT!
ARE YOU SERIOUS?
MY PEOPLE MAY NOT HAVE EYES, LUCIEN, BUT I SAW IT CLEARLY IN THE FORCE. IT WAS THE TALISMAN.
ALL RIGHT, THEN. WE'D BETTER TAKE THIS INSIDE...

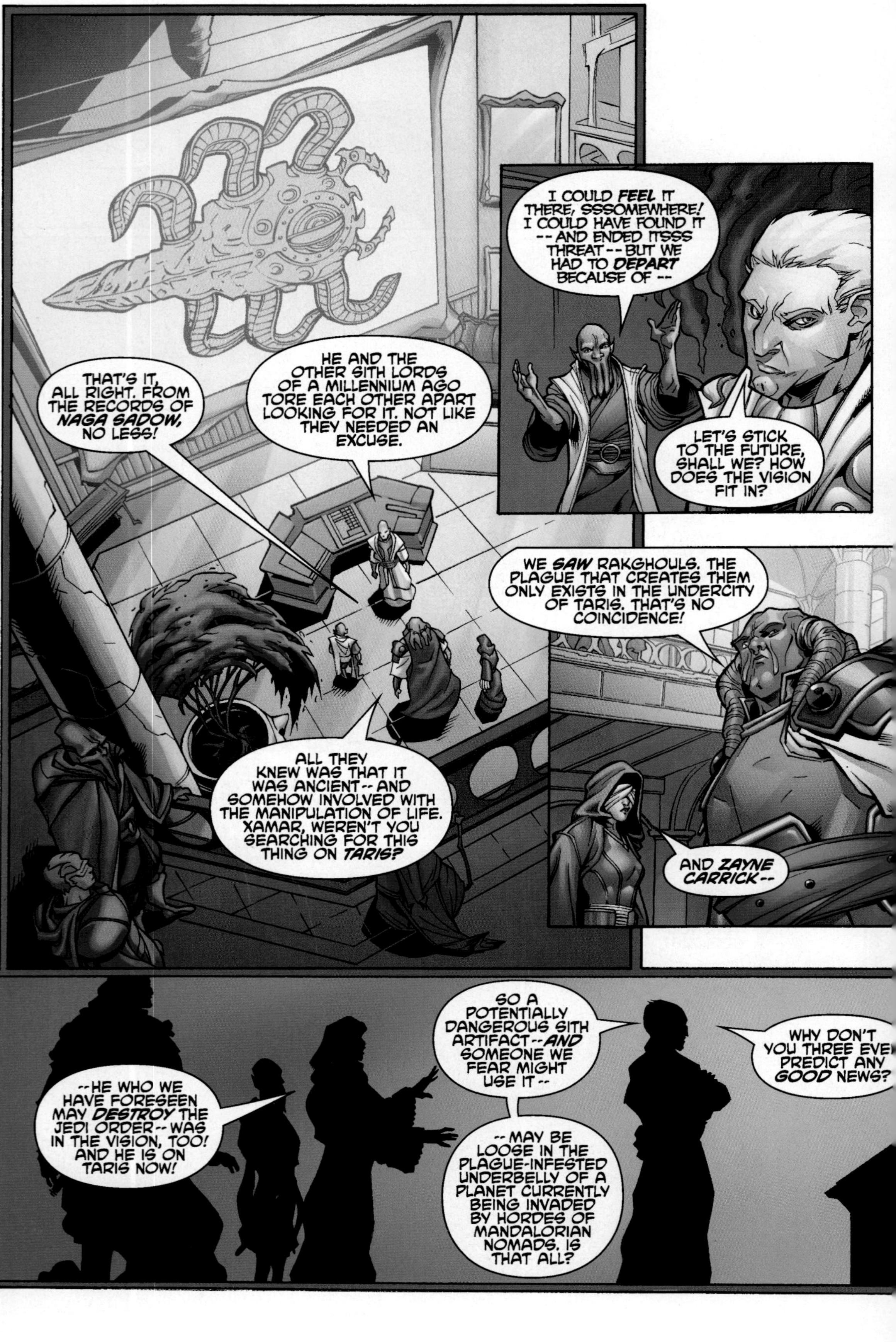
THAT'S IT, ALL RIGHT. FROM THE RECORDS OF *NAGA SADOW,* NO LESS!
HE AND THE OTHER SITH LORDS OF A MILLENNIUM AGO TORE EACH OTHER APART LOOKING FOR IT. NOT LIKE THEY NEEDED AN EXCUSE.
ALL THEY KNEW WAS THAT IT WAS ANCIENT--AND SOMEHOW INVOLVED WITH THE MANIPULATION OF LIFE. XAMAR, WEREN'T YOU SEARCHING FOR THIS THING ON *TARIS?*
I COULD *FEEL* IT THERE, SSSOMEWHERE! I COULD HAVE FOUND IT --AND ENDED ITSSS THREAT--BUT WE HAD TO *DEPART* BECAUSE OF --
LET'S STICK TO THE FUTURE, SHALL WE? HOW DOES THE VISION FIT IN?
WE *SAW* RAKGHOULS. THE PLAGUE THAT CREATES THEM ONLY EXISTS IN THE UNDERCITY OF TARIS. THAT'S NO COINCIDENCE!
AND *ZAYNE CARRICK*--
--HE WHO WE HAVE FORESEEN MAY *DESTROY* THE JEDI ORDER--WAS IN THE VISION, TOO! AND HE IS ON TARIS NOW!
SO A POTENTIALLY DANGEROUS SITH ARTIFACT--*AND* SOMEONE WE FEAR MIGHT USE IT--
--MAY BE LOOSE IN THE PLAGUE-INFESTED UNDERBELLY OF A PLANET CURRENTLY BEING INVADED BY HORDES OF MANDALORIAN NOMADS. IS THAT ALL?
WHY DON'T YOU THREE EVE PREDICT ANY *GOOD* NEWS?

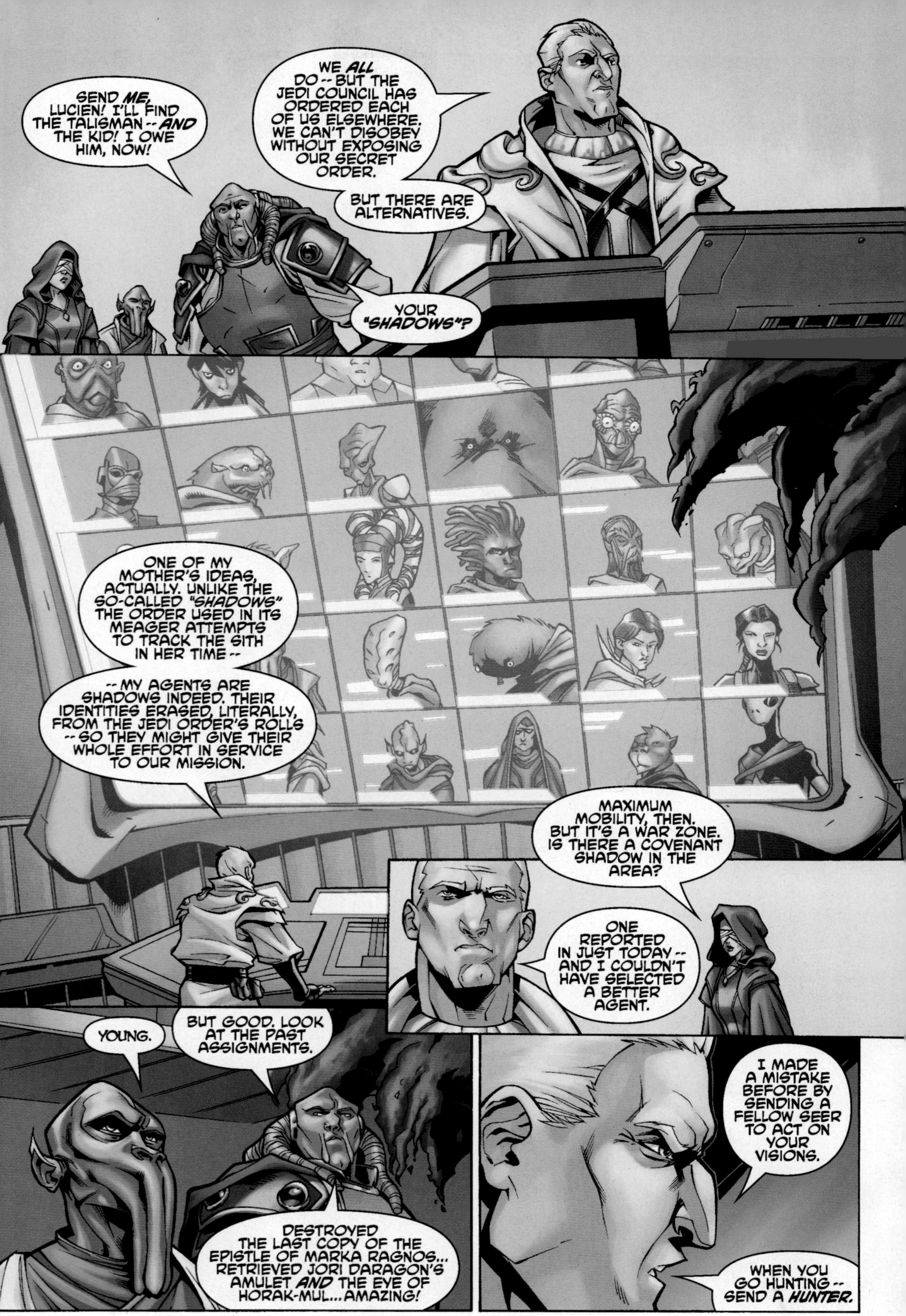
SEND ME, LUCIEN! I'LL FIND THE TALISMAN -- AND THE KID! I OWE HIM, NOW!
WE ALL DO -- BUT THE JEDI COUNCIL HAS ORDERED EACH OF US ELSEWHERE. WE CAN'T DISOBEY WITHOUT EXPOSING OUR SECRET ORDER.
BUT THERE ARE ALTERNATIVES.
YOUR "SHADOWS"?
ONE OF MY MOTHER'S IDEAS, ACTUALLY. UNLIKE THE SO-CALLED "SHADOWS" THE ORDER USED IN ITS MEAGER ATTEMPTS TO TRACK THE SITH IN HER TIME --
-- MY AGENTS ARE SHADOWS INDEED. THEIR IDENTITIES ERASED, LITERALLY, FROM THE JEDI ORDER'S ROLLS -- SO THEY MIGHT GIVE THEIR WHOLE EFFORT IN SERVICE TO OUR MISSION.
MAXIMUM MOBILITY, THEN. BUT IT'S A WAR ZONE. IS THERE A COVENANT SHADOW IN THE AREA?
ONE REPORTED IN JUST TODAY -- AND I COULDN'T HAVE SELECTED A BETTER AGENT.
YOUNG.
BUT GOOD. LOOK AT THE PAST ASSIGNMENTS.
DESTROYED THE LAST COPY OF THE EPISTLE OF MARKA RAGNOS... RETRIEVED JORI DARAGON'S AMULET AND THE EYE OF HORAK-MUL... AMAZING!
I MADE A MISTAKE BEFORE BY SENDING A FELLOW SEER TO ACT ON YOUR VISIONS.
WHEN YOU GO HUNTING -- SEND A HUNTER.

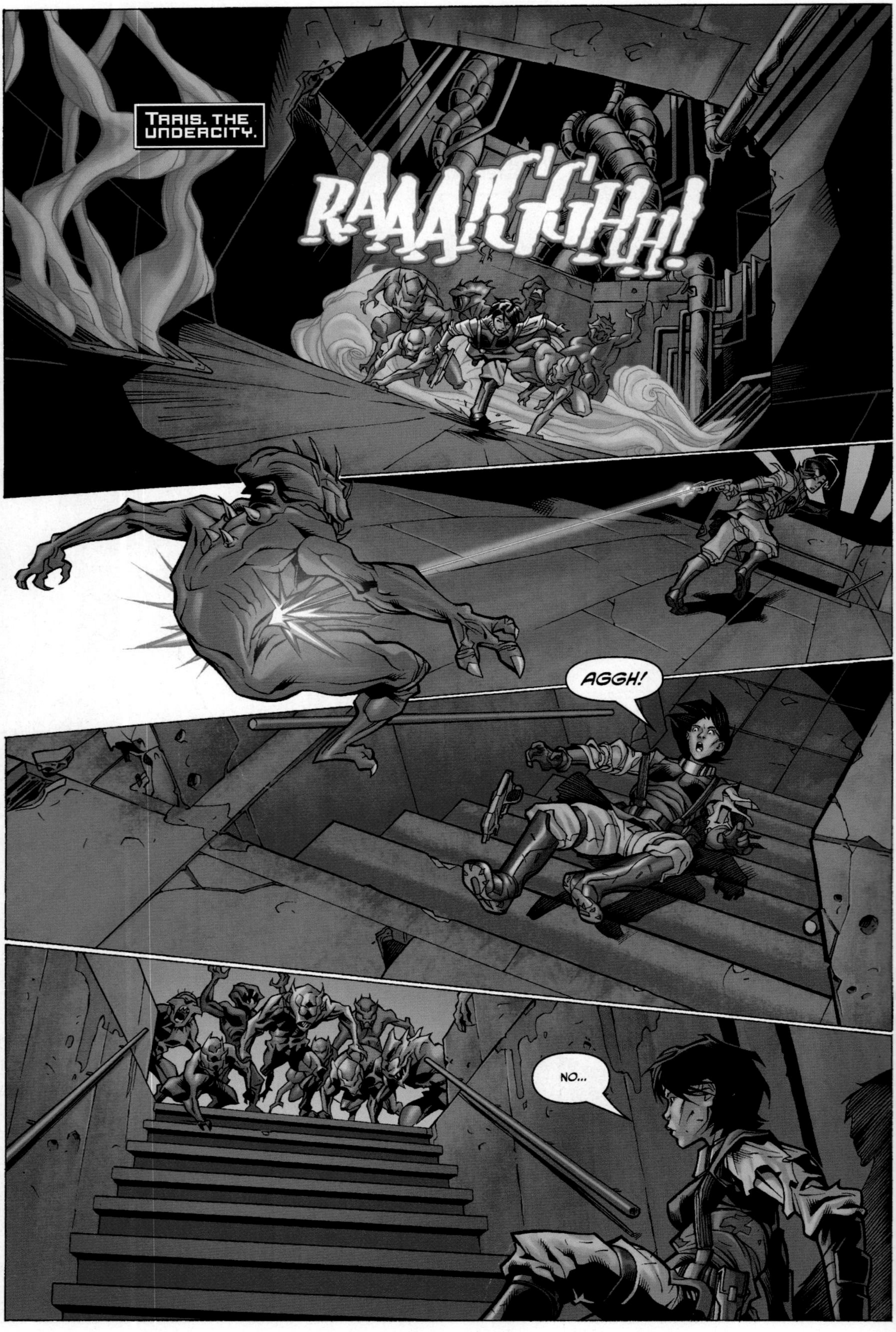
TARIS. THE UNDERCITY.
RAAAIIGGHH!
AGGH!
NO...

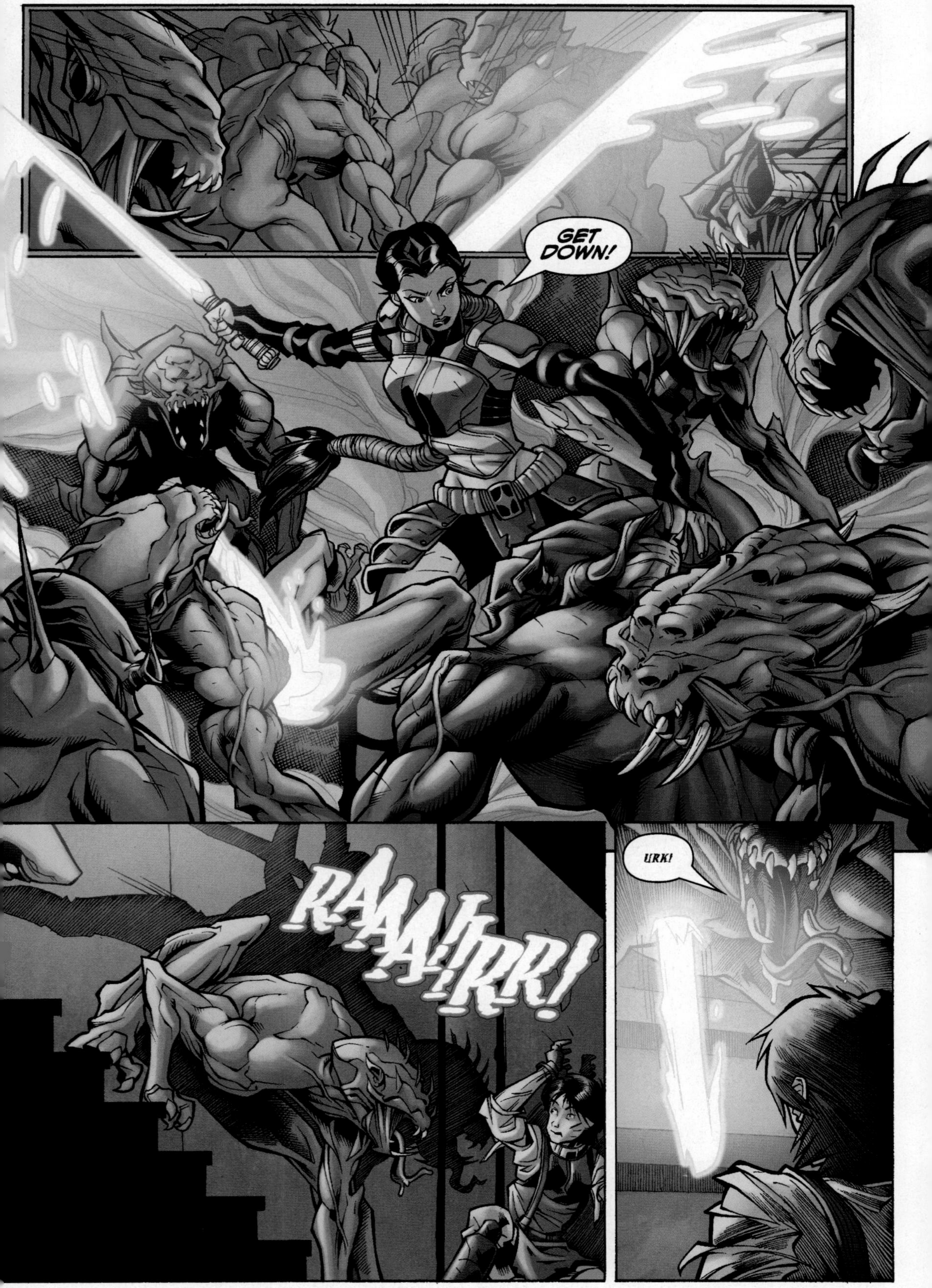
GET DOWN!
RAAAIIRR!
URK!

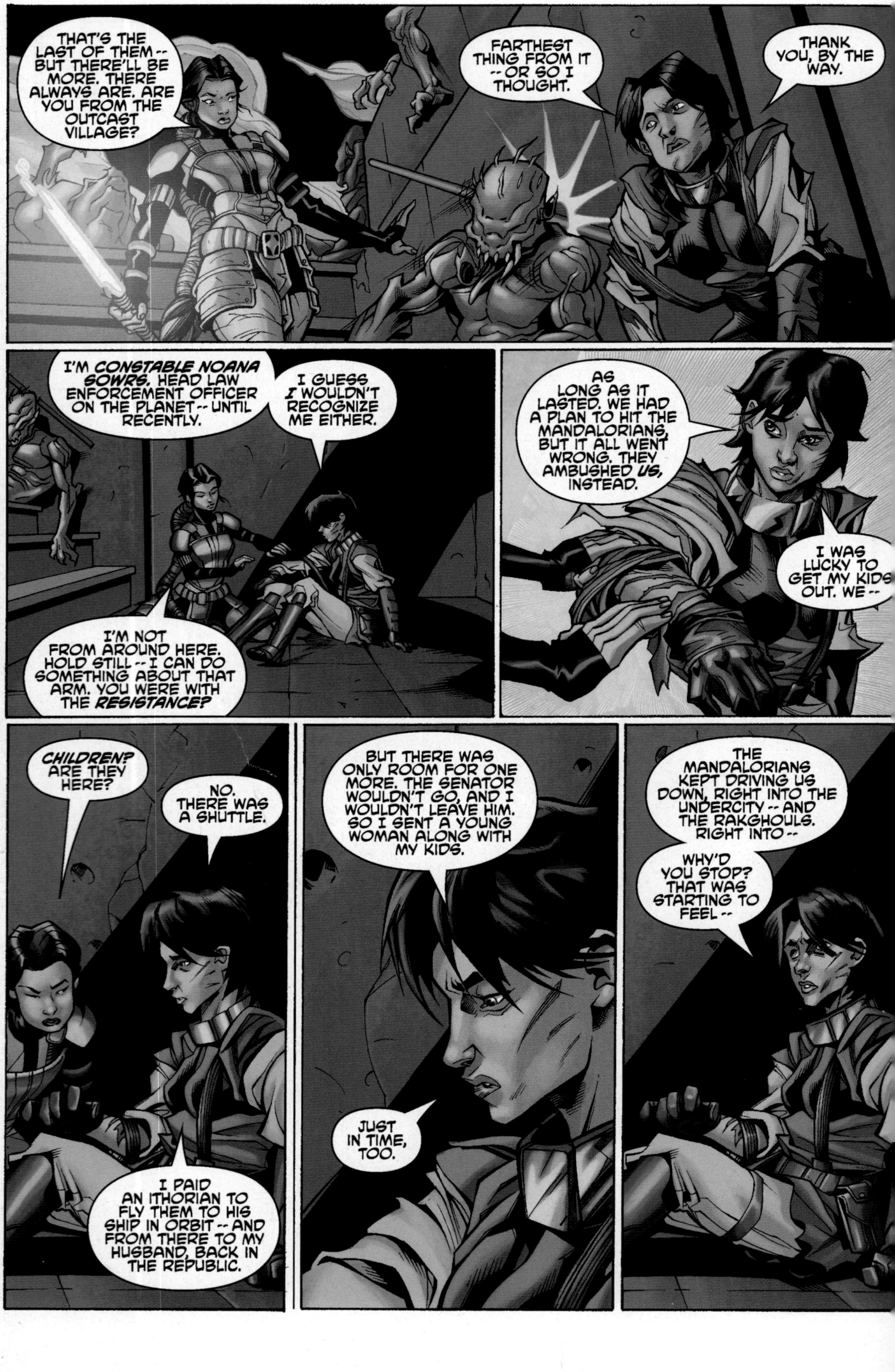
THAT'S THE LAST OF THEM -- BUT THERE'LL BE MORE. THERE ALWAYS ARE. ARE YOU FROM THE OUTCAST VILLAGE?
FARTHEST THING FROM IT -- OR SO I THOUGHT.
THANK YOU, BY THE WAY.
I'M CONSTABLE NOANA SOWRS. HEAD LAW ENFORCEMENT OFFICER ON THE PLANET -- UNTIL RECENTLY.
I GUESS I WOULDN'T RECOGNIZE ME EITHER.
I'M NOT FROM AROUND HERE. HOLD STILL -- I CAN DO SOMETHING ABOUT THAT ARM. YOU WERE WITH THE RESISTANCE?
AS LONG AS IT LASTED. WE HAD A PLAN TO HIT THE MANDALORIANS, BUT IT ALL WENT WRONG. THEY AMBUSHED US, INSTEAD.
I WAS LUCKY TO GET MY KIDS OUT. WE --
CHILDREN? ARE THEY HERE?
NO. THERE WAS A SHUTTLE.
I PAID AN ITHORIAN TO FLY THEM TO HIS SHIP IN ORBIT -- AND FROM THERE TO MY HUSBAND, BACK IN THE REPUBLIC.
BUT THERE WAS ONLY ROOM FOR ONE MORE. THE SENATOR WOULDN'T GO, AND I WOULDN'T LEAVE HIM. SO I SENT A YOUNG WOMAN ALONG WITH MY KIDS.
JUST IN TIME, TOO.
THE MANDALORIANS KEPT DRIVING US DOWN, RIGHT INTO THE UNDERCITY -- AND THE RAKGHOULS. RIGHT INTO --
WHY'D YOU STOP? THAT WAS STARTING TO FEEL --

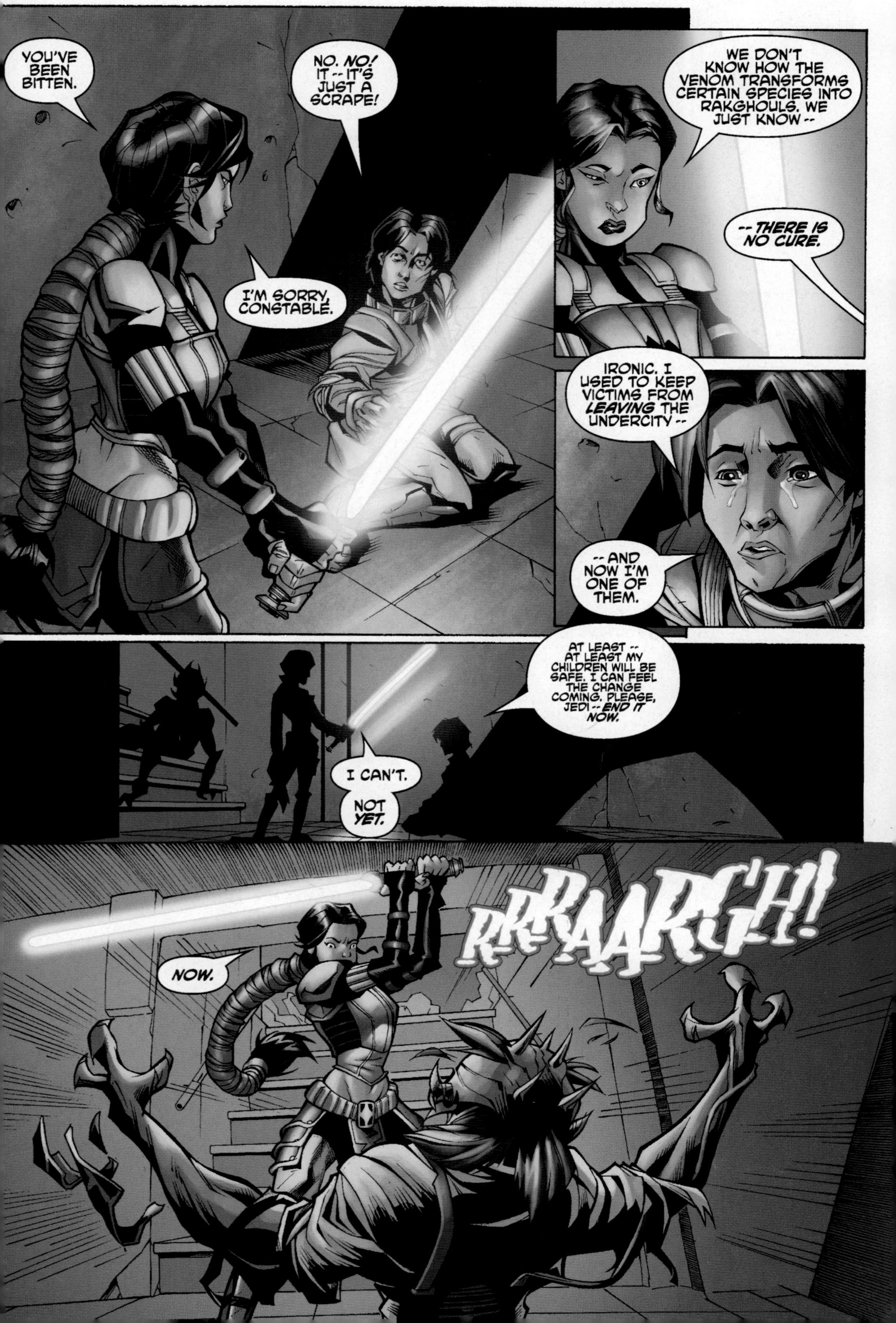
YOU'VE BEEN BITTEN.
NO. *NO!* IT -- IT'S JUST A SCRAPE!
I'M SORRY, CONSTABLE.
WE DON'T KNOW HOW THE VENOM TRANSFORMS CERTAIN SPECIES INTO RAKGHOULS. WE JUST KNOW --
-- *THERE IS NO CURE.*
IRONIC. I USED TO KEEP VICTIMS FROM *LEAVING* THE UNDERCITY --
-- AND NOW I'M ONE OF THEM.
AT LEAST -- AT LEAST MY CHILDREN WILL BE SAFE. I CAN FEEL THE CHANGE COMING. PLEASE, JEDI -- *END IT NOW.*
I CAN'T.
NOT *YET.*
RRRAAARGH!
NOW.

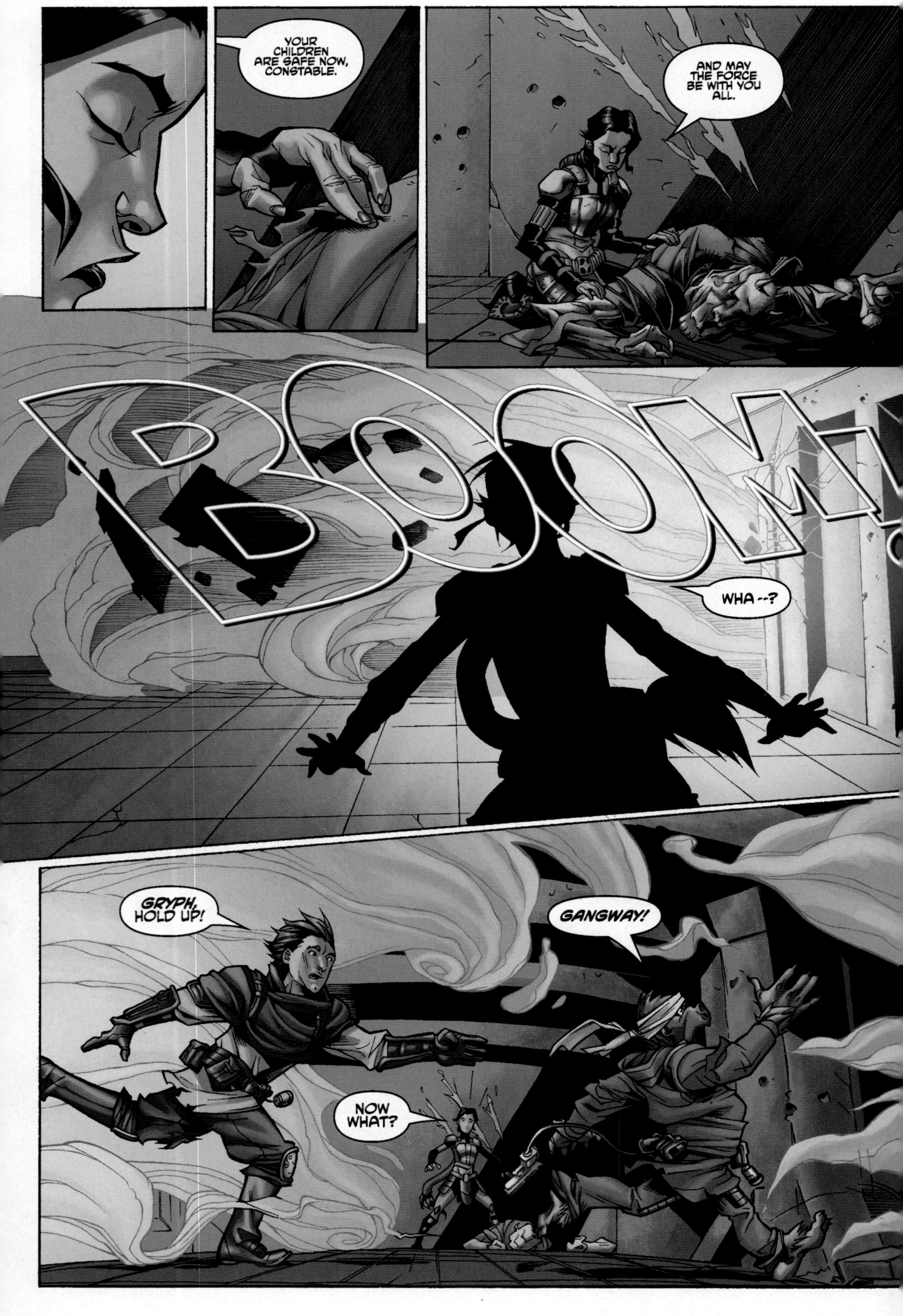
YOUR CHILDREN ARE SAFE NOW, CONSTABLE.
AND MAY THE FORCE BE WITH YOU ALL.
BOOM!
WHA --?
GRYPH, HOLD UP!
GANGWAY!
NOW WHAT?

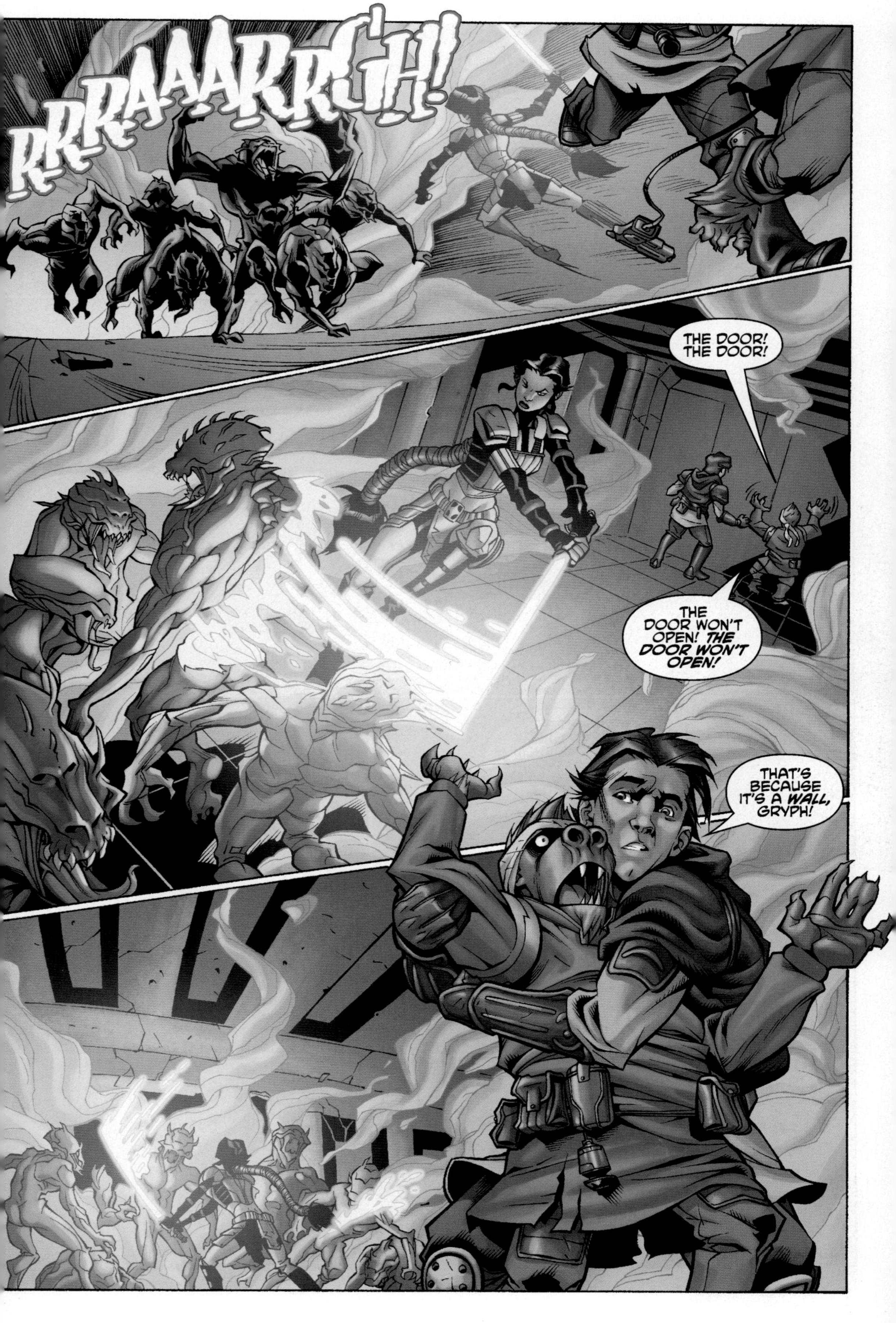
RRRAAARRGH!
THE DOOR! THE DOOR!
THE DOOR WON'T OPEN! *THE DOOR WON'T OPEN!*
THAT'S BECAUSE IT'S A *WALL*, GRYPH!

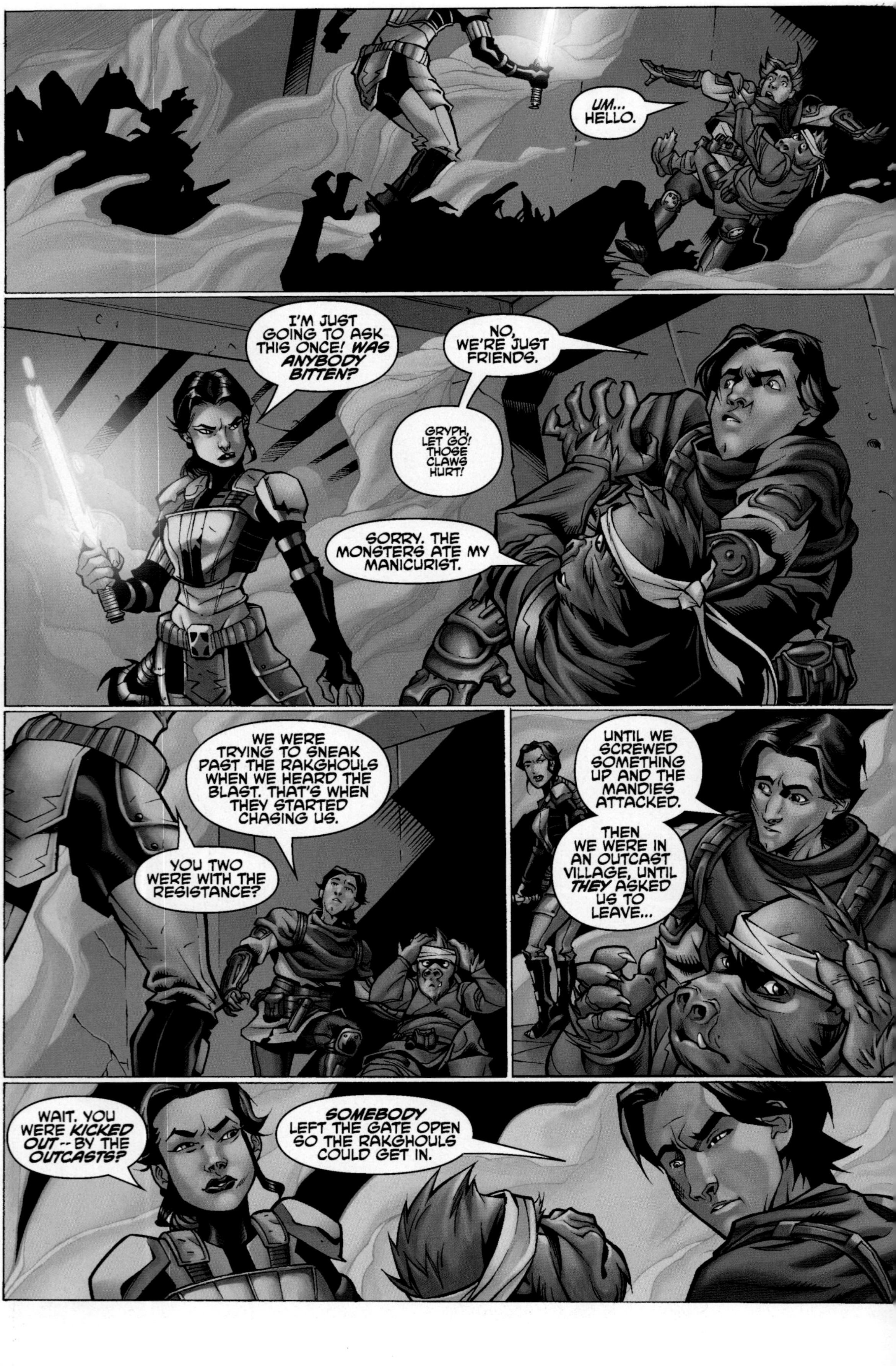
UM... HELLO.
I'M JUST GOING TO ASK THIS ONCE! WAS ANYBODY BITTEN?
NO, WE'RE JUST FRIENDS.
GRYPH, LET GO! THOSE CLAWS HURT!
SORRY. THE MONSTERS ATE MY MANICURIST.
YOU TWO WERE WITH THE RESISTANCE?
WE WERE TRYING TO SNEAK PAST THE RAKGHOULS WHEN WE HEARD THE BLAST. THAT'S WHEN THEY STARTED CHASING US.
UNTIL WE SCREWED SOMETHING UP AND THE MANDIES ATTACKED.
THEN WE WERE IN AN OUTCAST VILLAGE, UNTIL THEY ASKED US TO LEAVE...
WAIT. YOU WERE KICKED OUT -- BY THE OUTCASTS?
SOMEBODY LEFT THE GATE OPEN SO THE RAKGHOULS COULD GET IN.

I TOLD YOU, I WAS JUST GOING OUT FOR A MINUTE! PEOPLE TURN INTO RAKGHOULS, THEY DROP WHATEVER THEY'RE CARRYING. LIKE REPUBLIC CREDITS. I WAS JUST CLEANING UP!

THEY'VE LOST THEIR HUMANITY, *HENCHMAN.* ABANDONING THE FRUITS OF THEIR LABORS WOULD COMPOUND THE TRAGEDY OF THEIR LIVES!

BESIDES, IN A WAR ZONE, CASH IS KING. HAVEN'T I--

WHERE'D SHE GO?

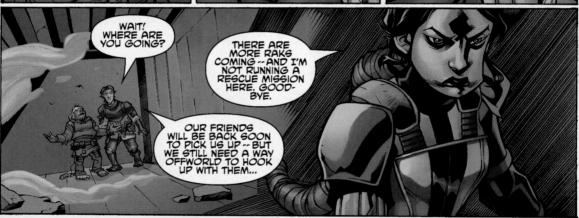

WAIT! WHERE ARE YOU GOING?

THERE ARE MORE RAKS COMING -- AND I'M NOT RUNNING A RESCUE MISSION HERE. GOOD-BYE.

OUR FRIENDS WILL BE BACK SOON TO PICK US UP -- BUT WE STILL NEED A WAY OFFWORLD TO HOOK UP WITH THEM...

YOU THINK *SHE'S* GOT A WAY OFF THE PLANET?

I SAY WE FOLLOW HER, REGARDLESS.

AT THE VERY LEAST, WE CAN PILE UP THE BODIES SHE LEAVES BEHIND FOR SHELTER!

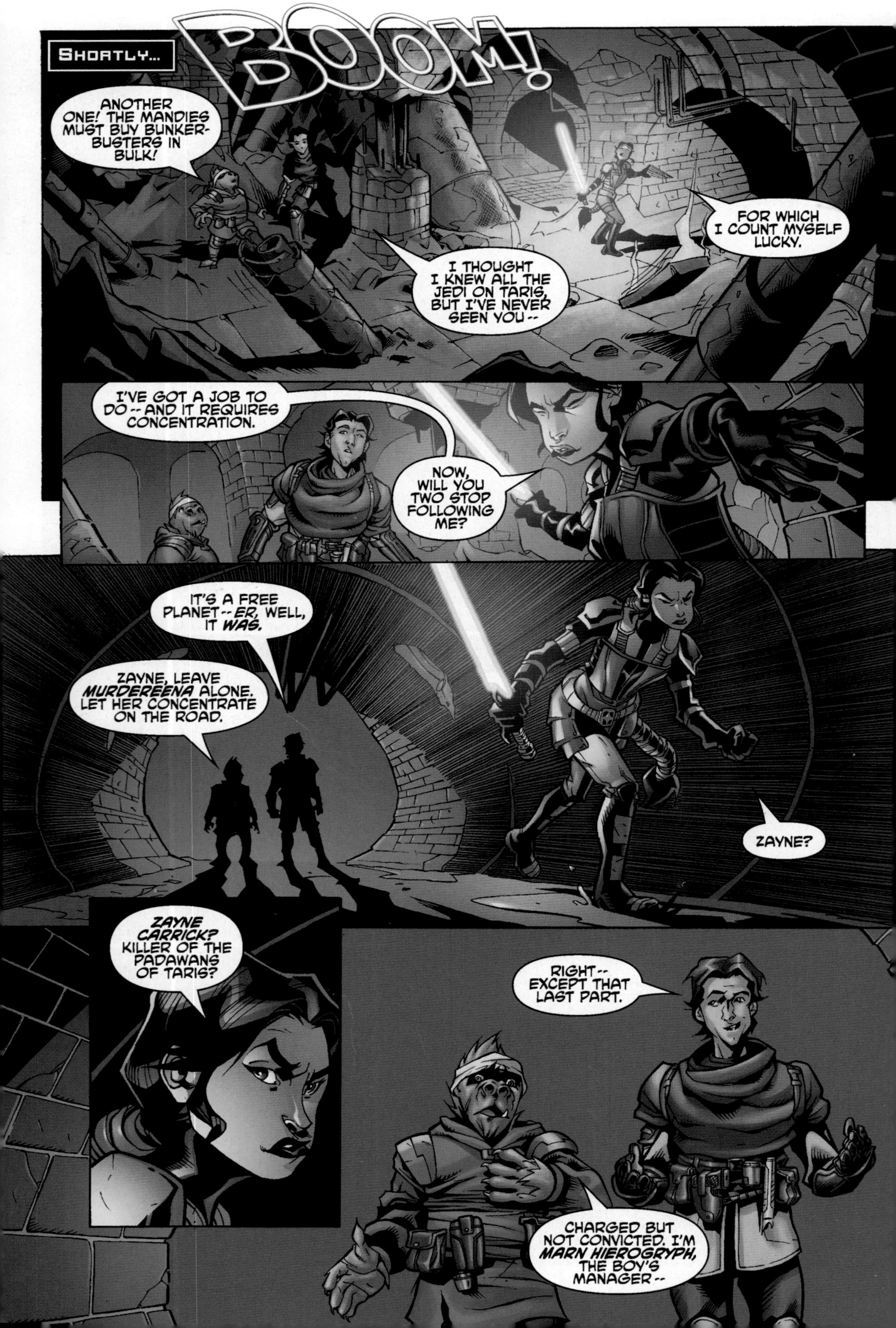
SHORTLY...
BOOM!
ANOTHER ONE! THE MANDIES MUST BUY BUNKER-BUSTERS IN BULK!
I THOUGHT I KNEW ALL THE JEDI ON TARIS, BUT I'VE NEVER SEEN YOU --
FOR WHICH I COUNT MYSELF LUCKY.
I'VE GOT A JOB TO DO -- AND IT REQUIRES CONCENTRATION.
NOW, WILL YOU TWO STOP FOLLOWING ME?
IT'S A FREE PLANET -- ER, WELL, IT WAS.
ZAYNE, LEAVE MURDEREENA ALONE. LET HER CONCENTRATE ON THE ROAD.
ZAYNE?
ZAYNE CARRICK? KILLER OF THE PADAWANS OF TARIS?
RIGHT -- EXCEPT THAT LAST PART.
CHARGED BUT NOT CONVICTED. I'M MARN HIEROGRYPH, THE BOY'S MANAGER --

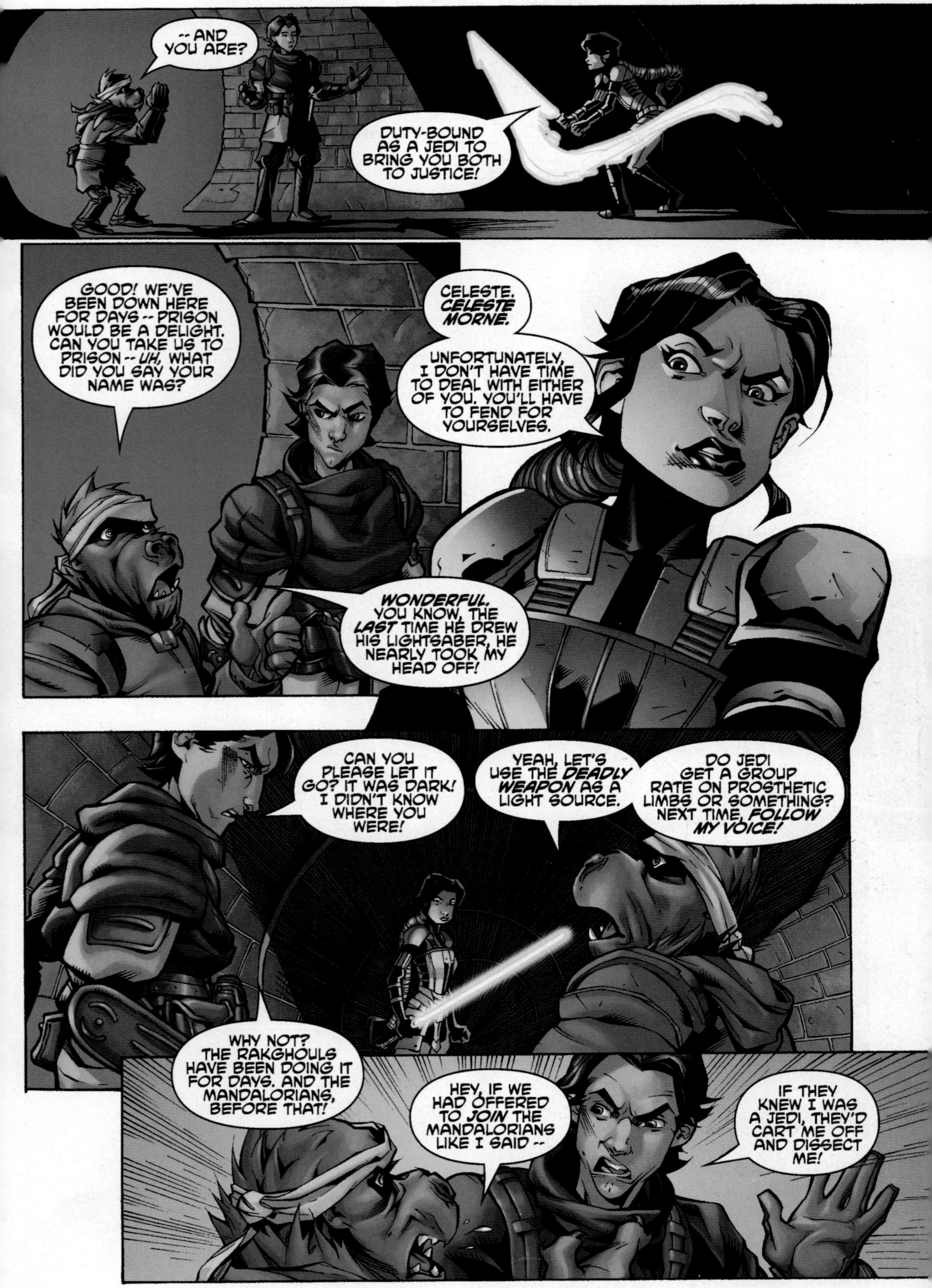
-- AND YOU ARE?
DUTY-BOUND AS A JEDI TO BRING YOU BOTH TO JUSTICE!
GOOD! WE'VE BEEN DOWN HERE FOR DAYS -- PRISON WOULD BE A DELIGHT. CAN YOU TAKE US TO PRISON -- *UH,* WHAT DID YOU SAY YOUR NAME WAS?
CELESTE. ***CELESTE MORNE.***
UNFORTUNATELY, I DON'T HAVE TIME TO DEAL WITH EITHER OF YOU. YOU'LL HAVE TO FEND FOR YOURSELVES.
WONDERFUL. YOU KNOW, THE ***LAST*** TIME HE DREW HIS LIGHTSABER, HE NEARLY TOOK MY HEAD OFF!
CAN YOU PLEASE LET IT GO? IT WAS DARK! I DIDN'T KNOW WHERE YOU WERE!
YEAH, LET'S USE THE ***DEADLY WEAPON*** AS A LIGHT SOURCE.
DO JEDI GET A GROUP RATE ON PROSTHETIC LIMBS OR SOMETHING? NEXT TIME, ***FOLLOW MY VOICE!***
WHY NOT? THE RAKGHOULS HAVE BEEN DOING IT FOR DAYS. AND THE MANDALORIANS, BEFORE THAT!
HEY, IF WE HAD OFFERED TO ***JOIN*** THE MANDALORIANS LIKE I SAID --
IF THEY KNEW I WAS A JEDI, THEY'D CART ME OFF AND DISSECT ME!

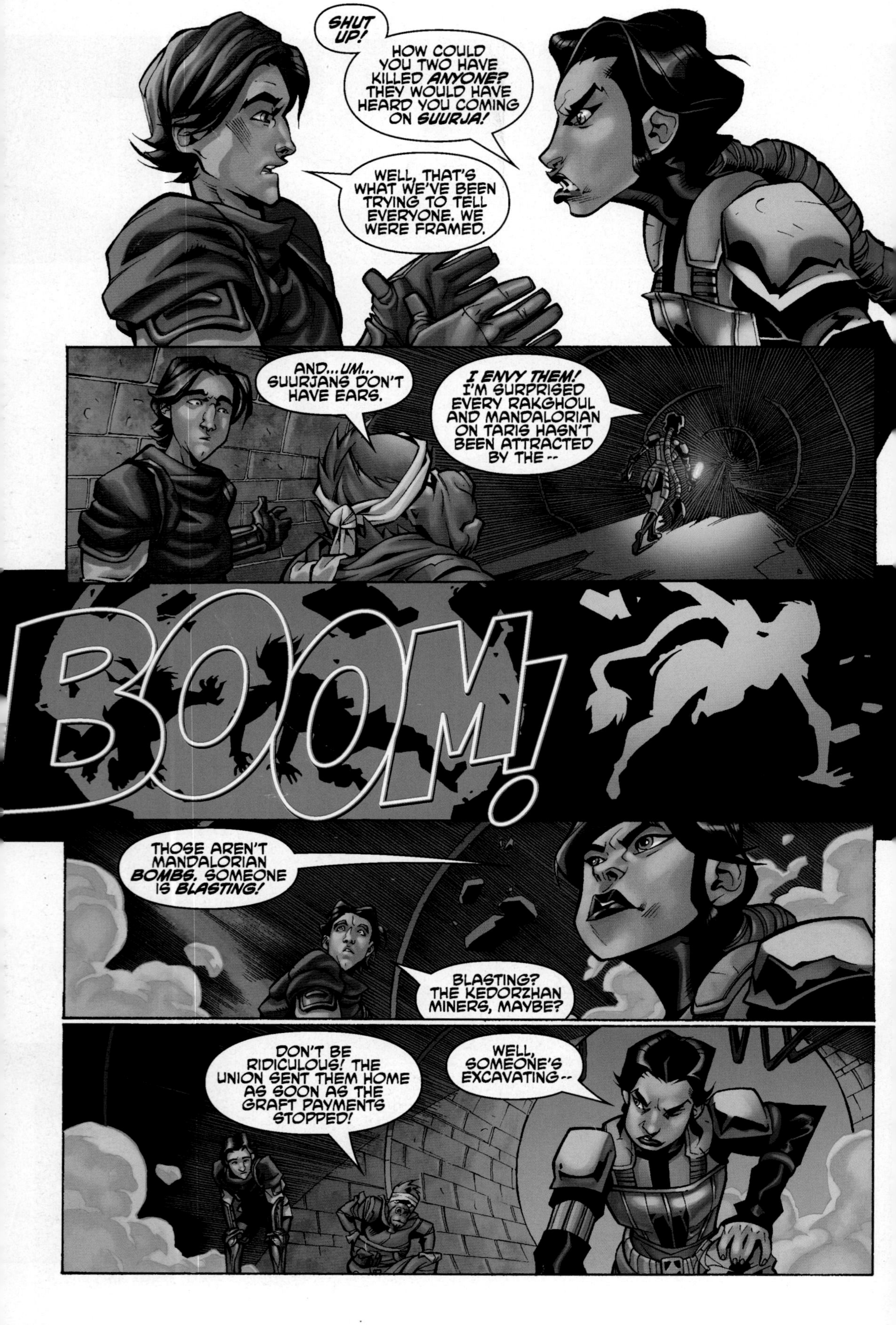
SHUT UP!
HOW COULD YOU TWO HAVE KILLED ANYONE? THEY WOULD HAVE HEARD YOU COMING ON SUURJA!
WELL, THAT'S WHAT WE'VE BEEN TRYING TO TELL EVERYONE. WE WERE FRAMED.
AND...UM... SUURJANS DON'T HAVE EARS.
I ENVY THEM! I'M SURPRISED EVERY RAKGHOUL AND MANDALORIAN ON TARIS HASN'T BEEN ATTRACTED BY THE --
BOOM!
THOSE AREN'T MANDALORIAN BOMBS. SOMEONE IS BLASTING!
BLASTING? THE KEDORZHAN MINERS, MAYBE?
DON'T BE RIDICULOUS! THE UNION SENT THEM HOME AS SOON AS THE GRAFT PAYMENTS STOPPED!
WELL, SOMEONE'S EXCAVATING --

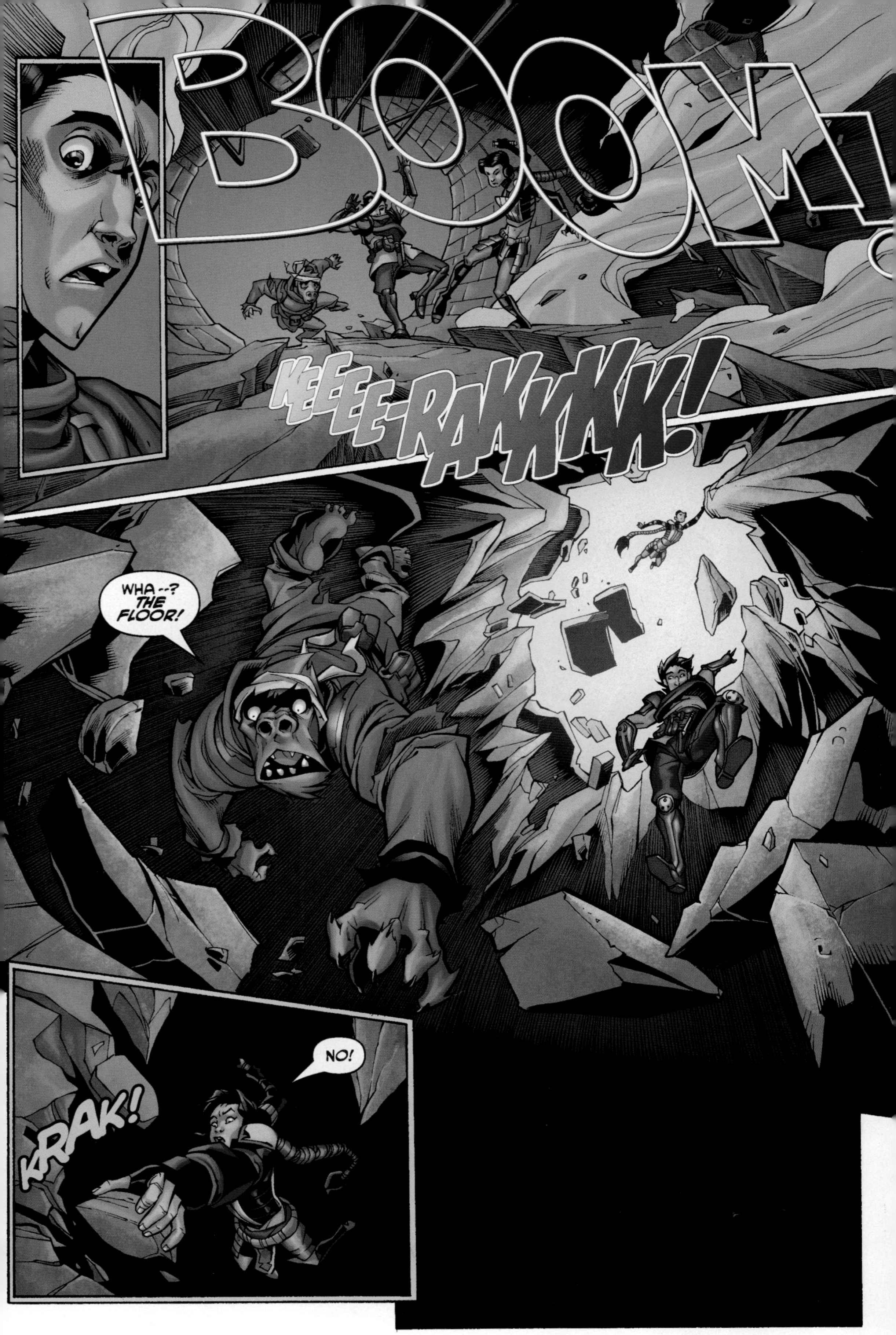
BOOM!
KEEEE-RAKKKKK!
WHA--? THE FLOOR!
KRAK!
NO!

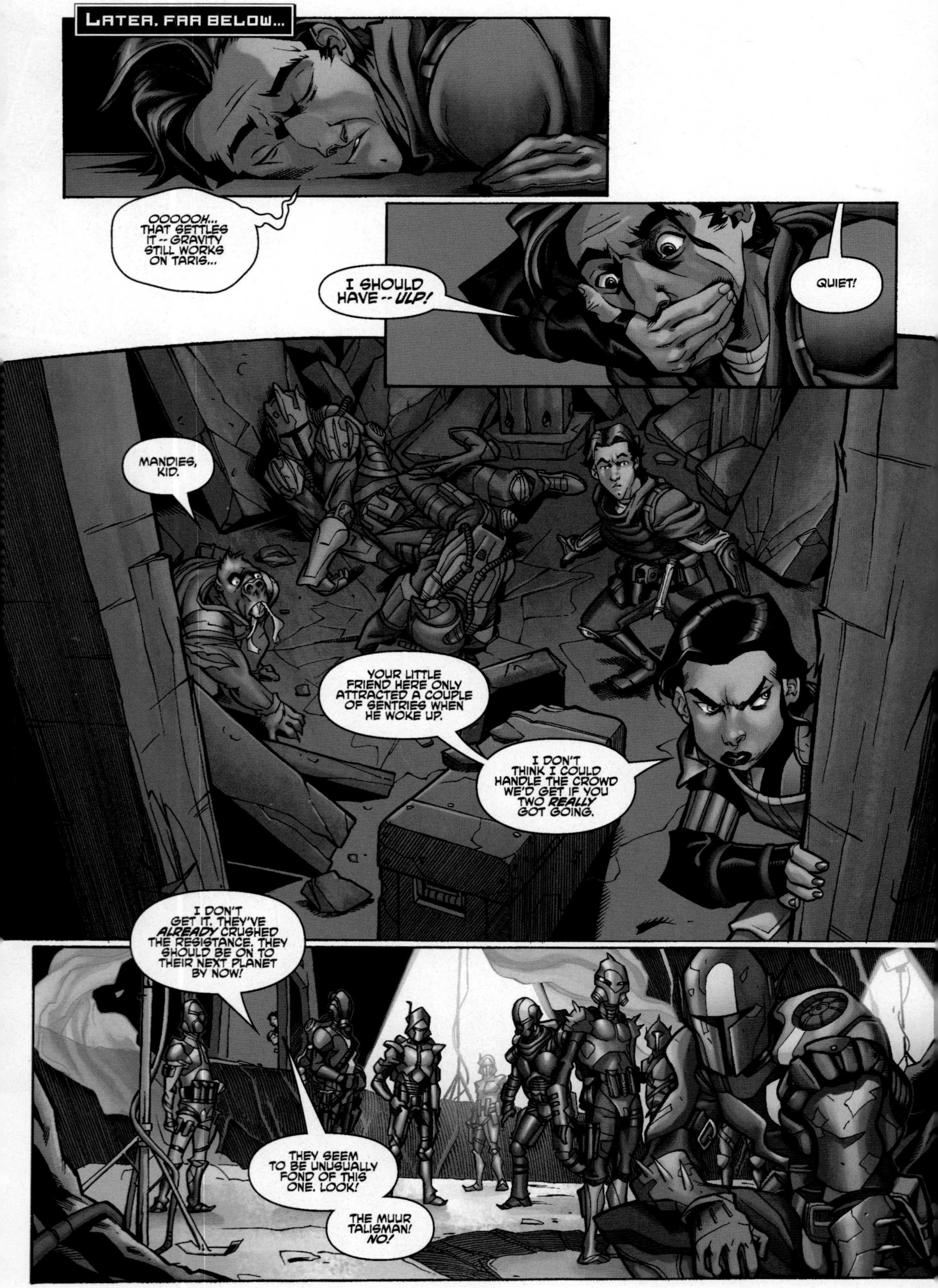
LATER, FAR BELOW...
OOOOOH... THAT SETTLES IT -- GRAVITY STILL WORKS ON TARIS...
I SHOULD HAVE -- ULP!
QUIET!
MANDIES, KID.
YOUR LITTLE FRIEND HERE ONLY ATTRACTED A COUPLE OF SENTRIES WHEN HE WOKE UP.
I DON'T THINK I COULD HANDLE THE CROWD WE'D GET IF YOU TWO REALLY GOT GOING.
I DON'T GET IT. THEY'VE ALREADY CRUSHED THE RESISTANCE. THEY SHOULD BE ON TO THEIR NEXT PLANET BY NOW!
THEY SEEM TO BE UNUSUALLY FOND OF THIS ONE. LOOK!
THE MUUR TALISMAN! NO!

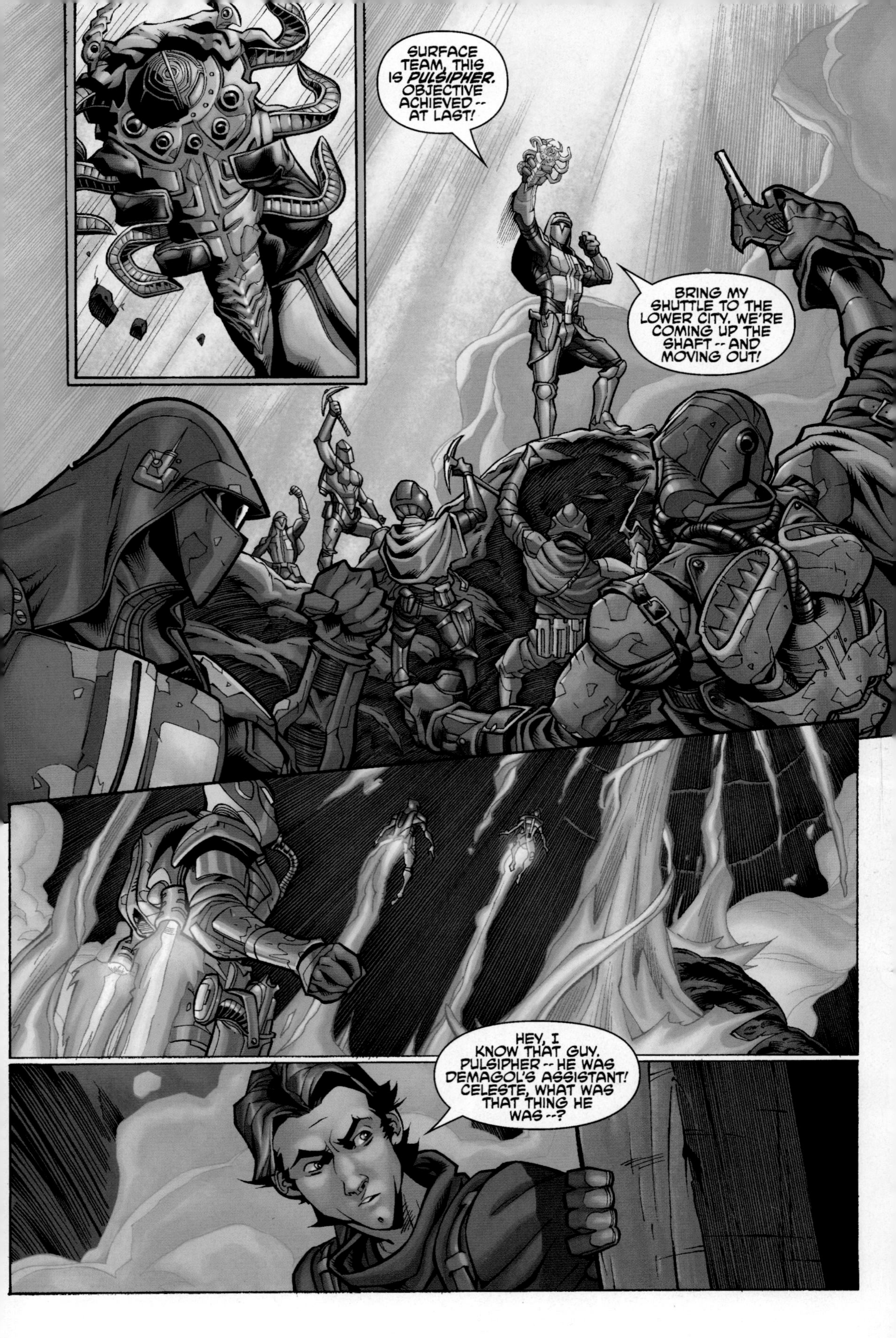
SURFACE TEAM, THIS IS *PULSIPHER.* OBJECTIVE ACHIEVED -- AT LAST!
BRING MY SHUTTLE TO THE LOWER CITY. WE'RE COMING UP THE SHAFT -- AND MOVING OUT!
HEY, I KNOW THAT GUY. PULSIPHER -- HE WAS DEMAGOL'S ASSISTANT! CELESTE, WHAT WAS THAT THING HE WAS --?

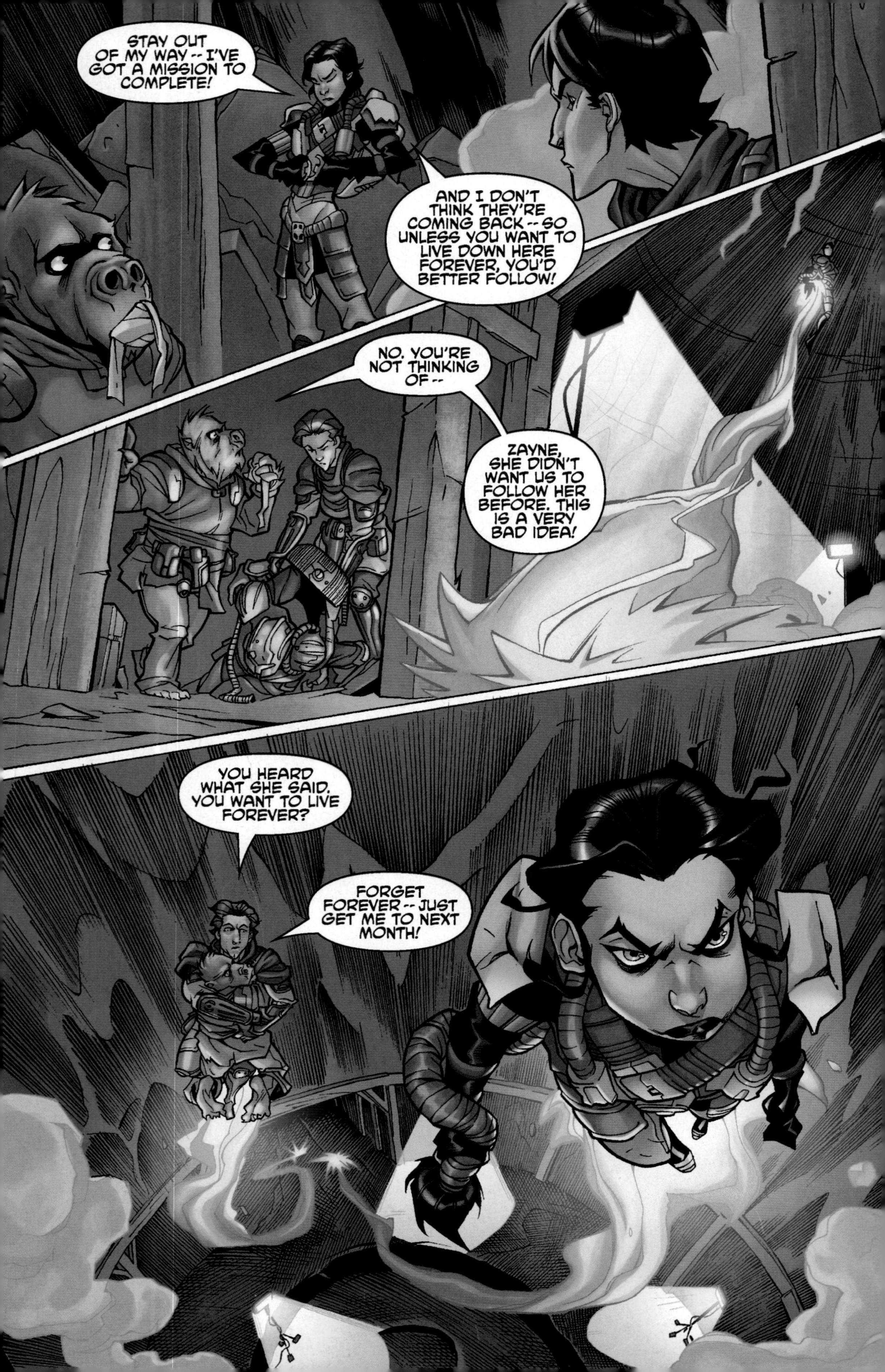
STAY OUT OF MY WAY -- I'VE GOT A MISSION TO COMPLETE!
AND I DON'T THINK THEY'RE COMING BACK -- SO UNLESS YOU WANT TO LIVE DOWN HERE FOREVER, YOU'D BETTER FOLLOW!
NO. YOU'RE NOT THINKING OF --
ZAYNE, SHE DIDN'T WANT US TO FOLLOW HER BEFORE. THIS IS A VERY BAD IDEA!
YOU HEARD WHAT SHE SAID. YOU WANT TO LIVE FOREVER?
FORGET FOREVER -- JUST GET ME TO NEXT MONTH!

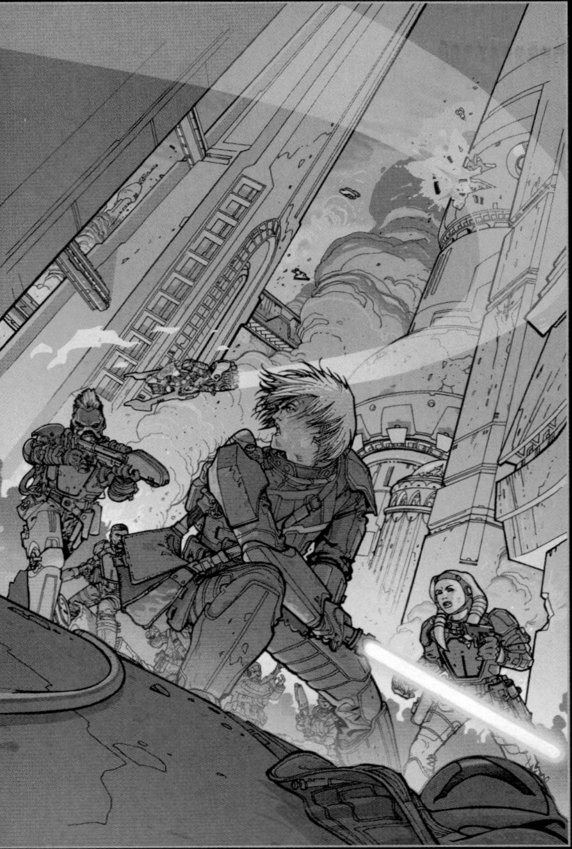

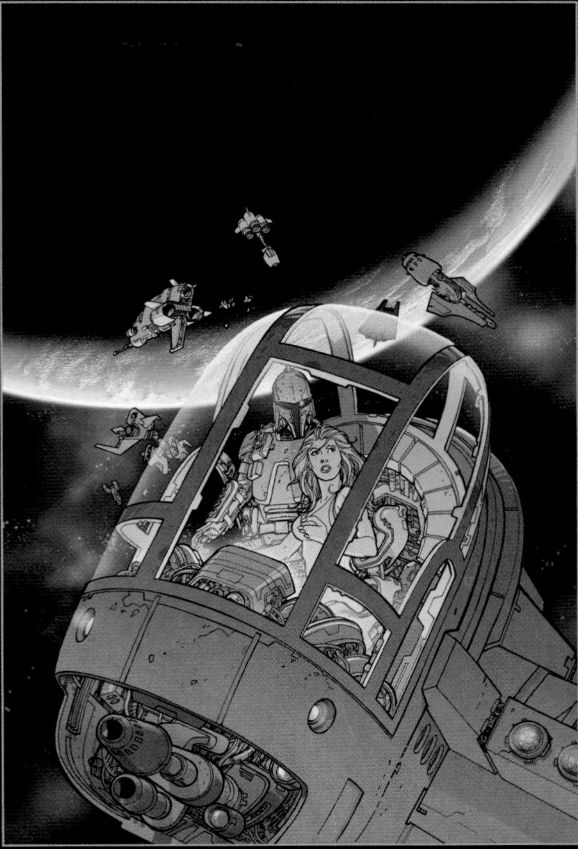

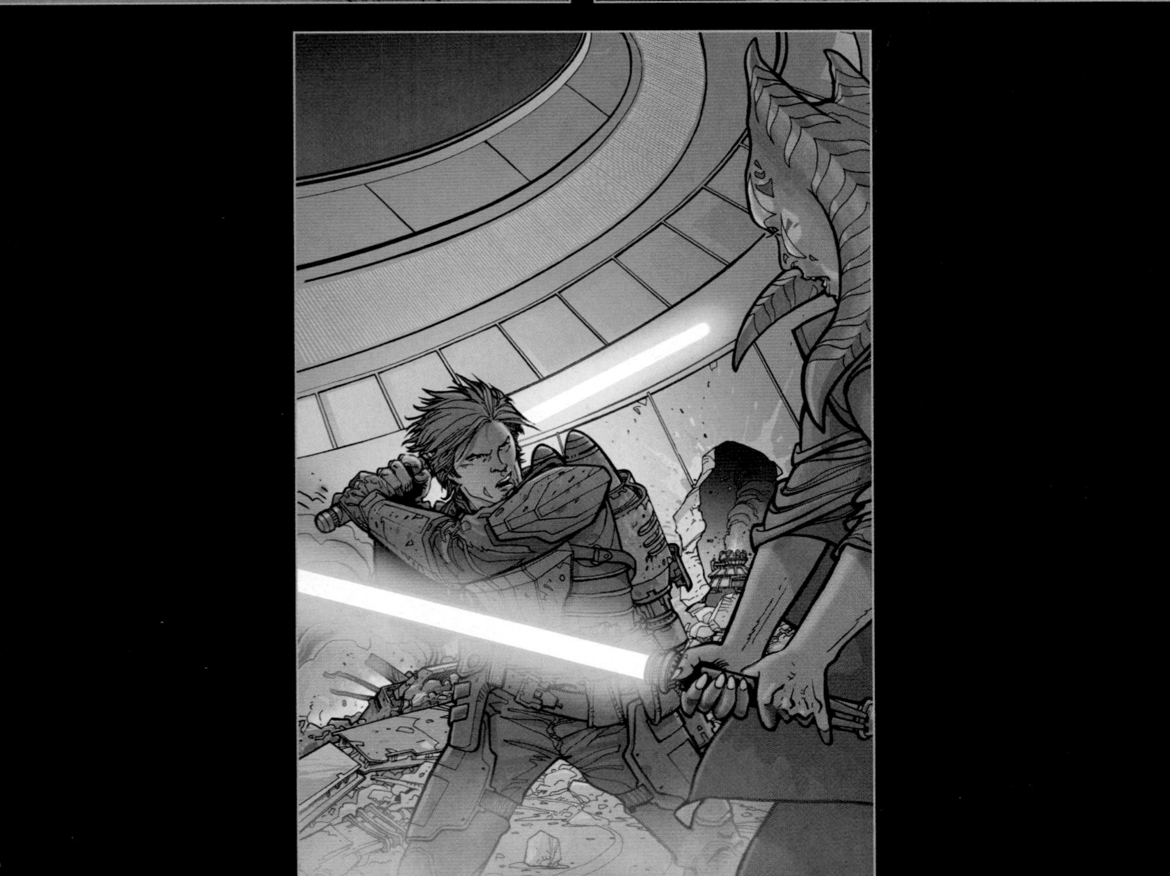

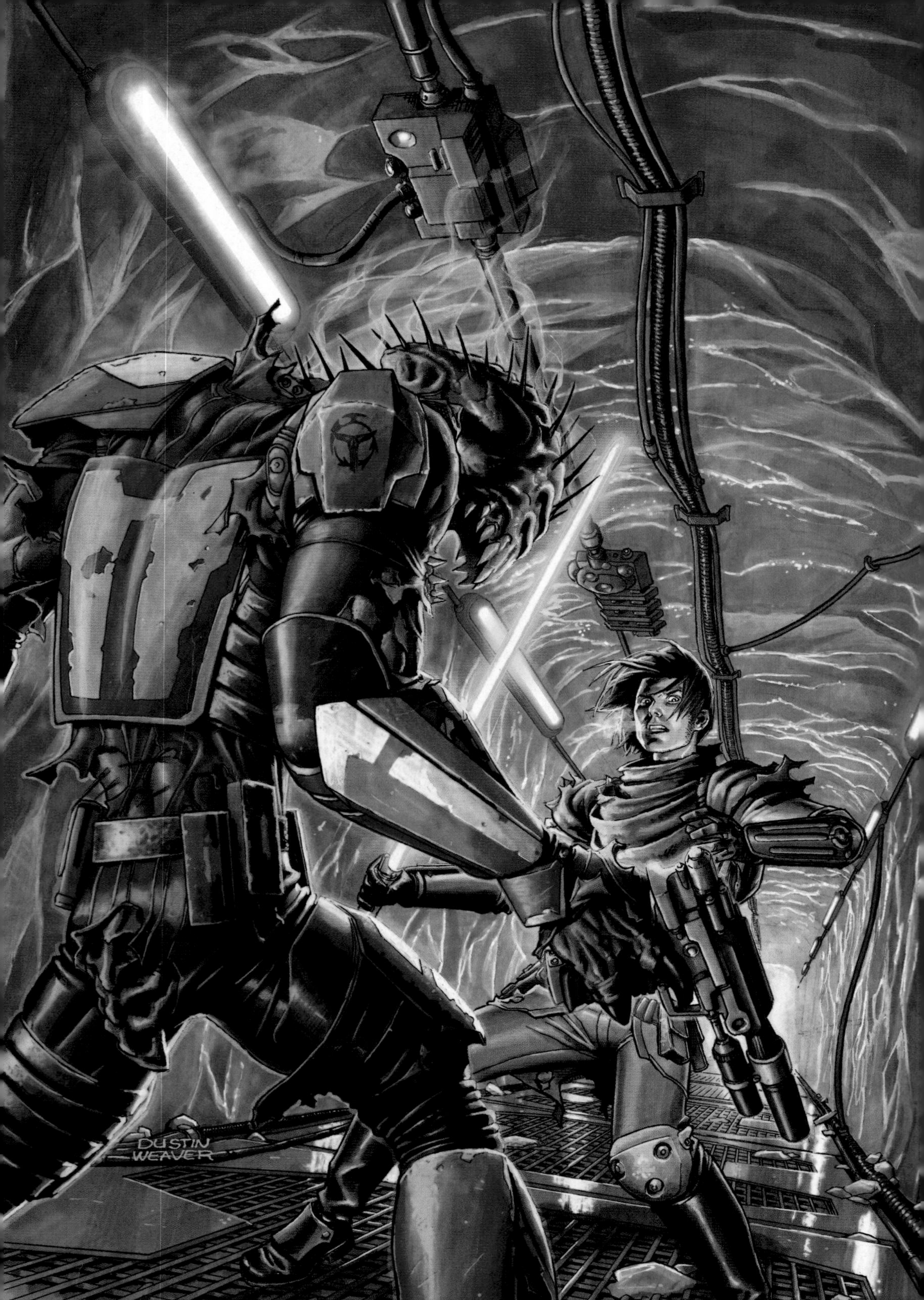
DUSTIN
WEAVER

STAR

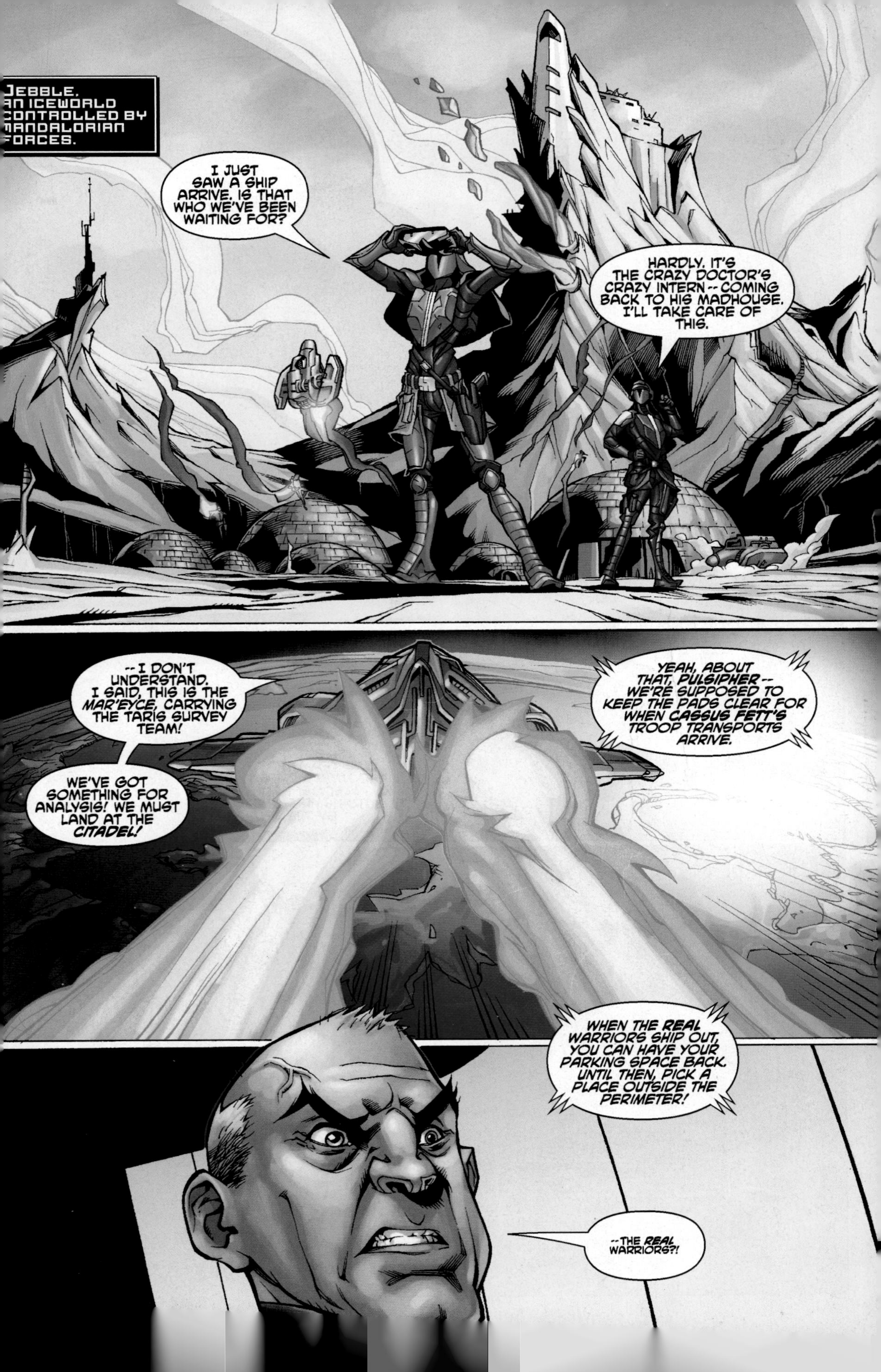
JEBBLE.
AN ICEWORLD CONTROLLED BY MANDALORIAN FORCES.
I JUST SAW A SHIP ARRIVE. IS THAT WHO WE'VE BEEN WAITING FOR?
HARDLY. IT'S THE CRAZY DOCTOR'S CRAZY INTERN -- COMING BACK TO HIS MADHOUSE. I'LL TAKE CARE OF THIS.
-- I DON'T UNDERSTAND. I SAID, THIS IS THE *MAR'EYCE*, CARRYING THE TARIS SURVEY TEAM!
WE'VE GOT SOMETHING FOR ANALYSIS! WE MUST LAND AT THE *CITADEL!*
YEAH, ABOUT THAT, *PULSIPHER* -- WE'RE SUPPOSED TO KEEP THE PADS CLEAR FOR WHEN *CASSUS FETT'S* TROOP TRANSPORTS ARRIVE.
WHEN THE *REAL* WARRIORS SHIP OUT, YOU CAN HAVE YOUR PARKING SPACE BACK. UNTIL THEN, PICK A PLACE OUTSIDE THE PERIMETER!
-- THE *REAL* WARRIORS?!

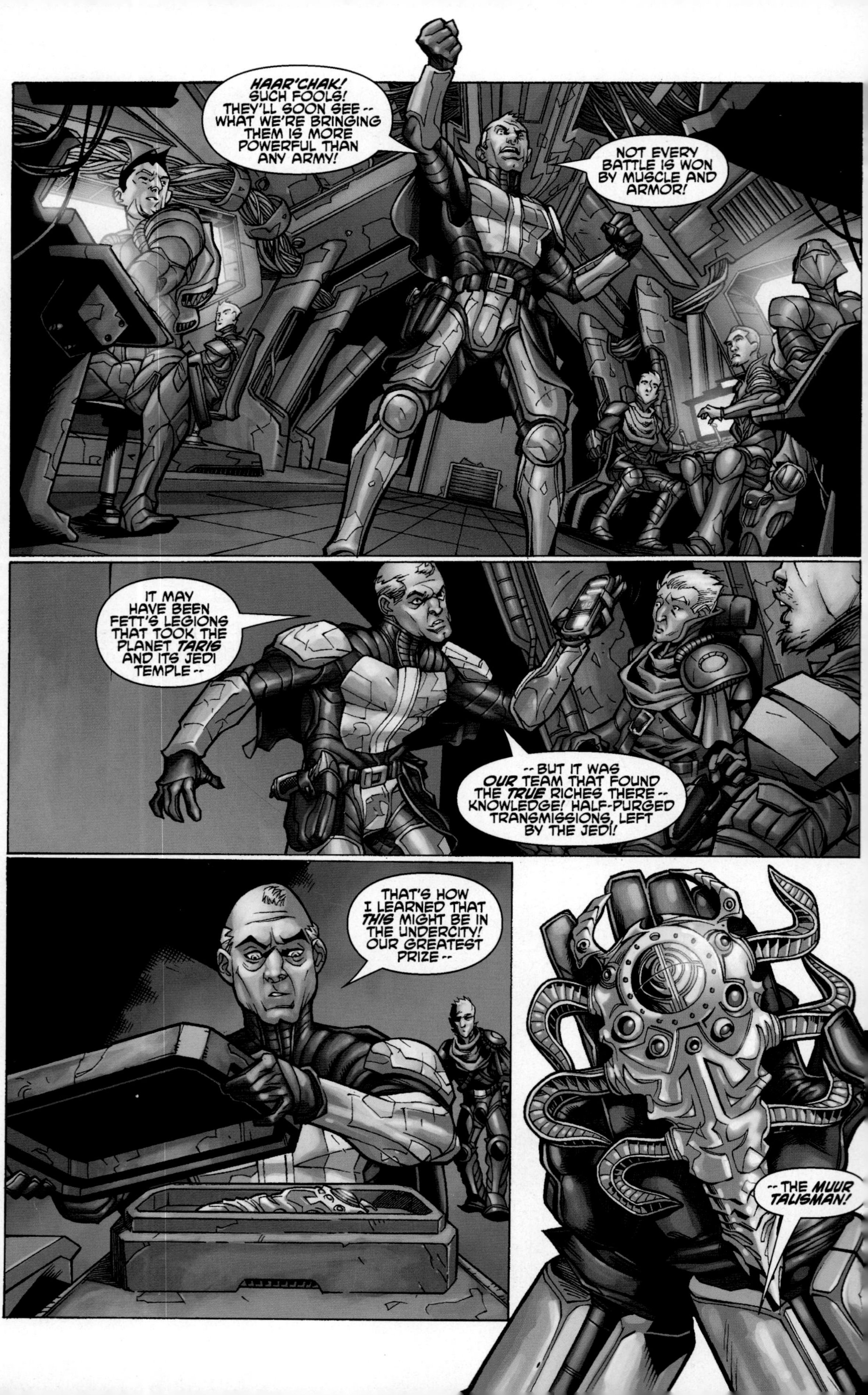
HAAR'CHAK! SUCH FOOLS! THEY'LL SOON SEE -- WHAT WE'RE BRINGING THEM IS MORE POWERFUL THAN ANY ARMY!
NOT EVERY BATTLE IS WON BY MUSCLE AND ARMOR!
IT MAY HAVE BEEN FETT'S LEGIONS THAT TOOK THE PLANET TARIS AND ITS JEDI TEMPLE --
-- BUT IT WAS OUR TEAM THAT FOUND THE TRUE RICHES THERE -- KNOWLEDGE! HALF-PURGED TRANSMISSIONS, LEFT BY THE JEDI!
THAT'S HOW I LEARNED THAT THIS MIGHT BE IN THE UNDERCITY! OUR GREATEST PRIZE --
-- THE MUUR TALISMAN!

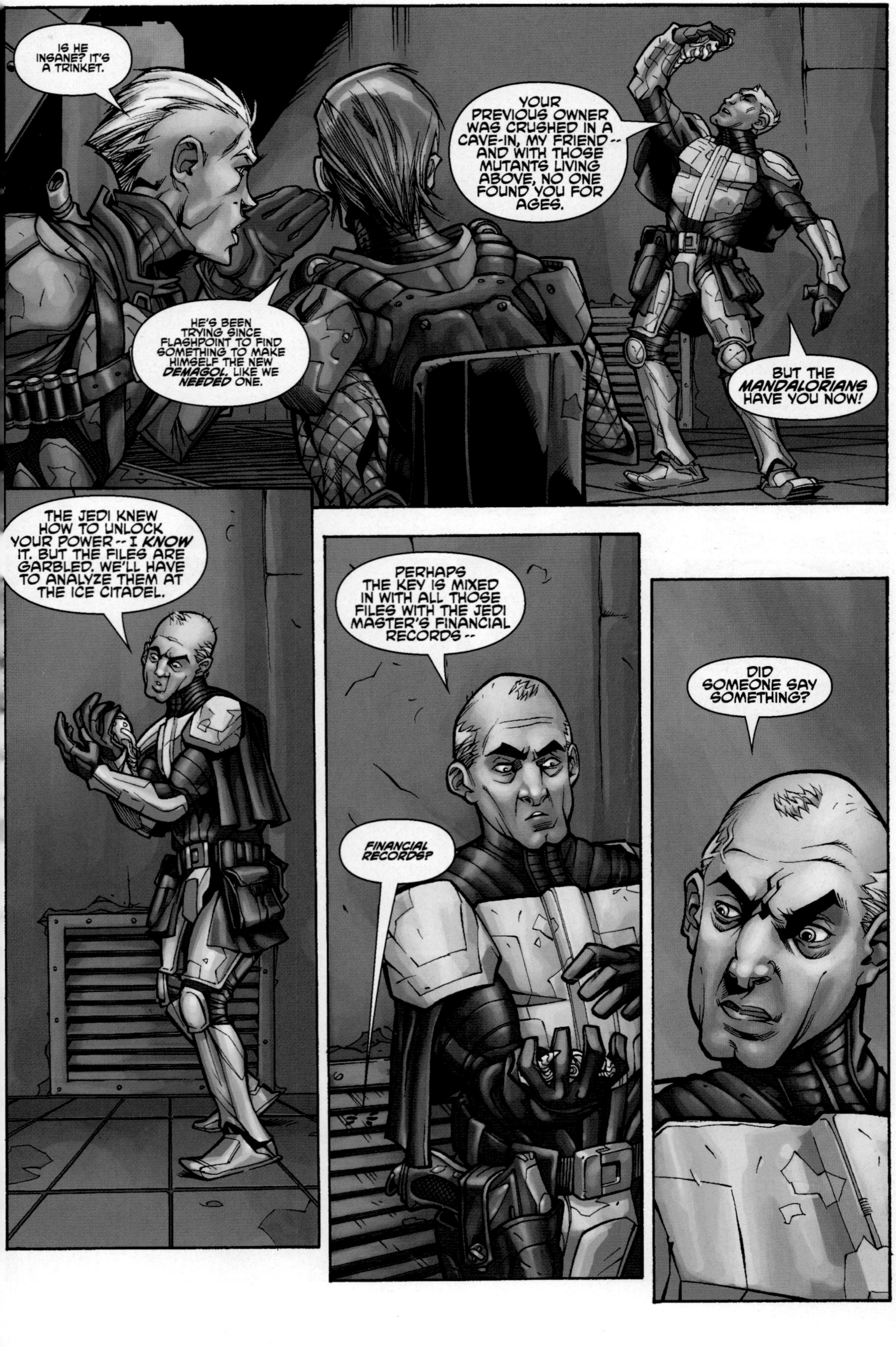
IS HE INSANE? IT'S A TRINKET.
YOUR PREVIOUS OWNER WAS CRUSHED IN A CAVE-IN, MY FRIEND -- AND WITH THOSE MUTANTS LIVING ABOVE, NO ONE FOUND YOU FOR AGES.
HE'S BEEN TRYING SINCE FLASHPOINT TO FIND SOMETHING TO MAKE HIMSELF THE NEW *DEMAGOL*. LIKE WE *NEEDED* ONE.
BUT THE *MANDALORIANS* HAVE YOU NOW!
THE JEDI KNEW HOW TO UNLOCK YOUR POWER -- I *KNOW* IT. BUT THE FILES ARE GARBLED. WE'LL HAVE TO ANALYZE THEM AT THE ICE CITADEL.
PERHAPS THE KEY IS MIXED IN WITH ALL THOSE FILES WITH THE JEDI MASTER'S FINANCIAL RECORDS --
FINANCIAL RECORDS?
DID SOMEONE SAY SOMETHING?

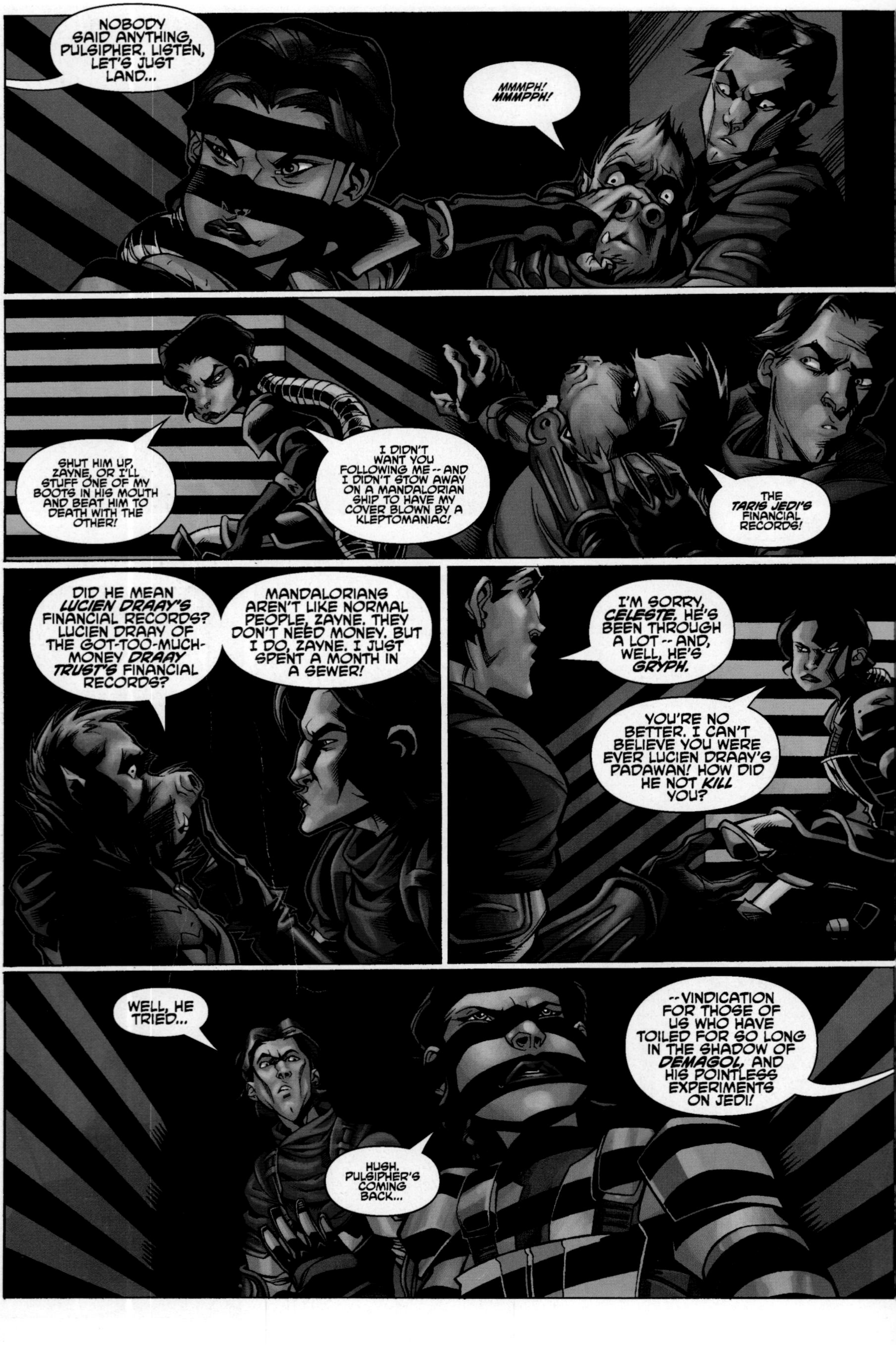
NOBODY SAID ANYTHING, PULSIPHER. LISTEN, LET'S JUST LAND...
MMMPH! MMMPPH!
SHUT HIM UP, ZAYNE, OR I'LL STUFF ONE OF MY BOOTS IN HIS MOUTH AND BEAT HIM TO DEATH WITH THE OTHER!
I DIDN'T WANT YOU FOLLOWING ME -- AND I DIDN'T STOW AWAY ON A MANDALORIAN SHIP TO HAVE MY COVER BLOWN BY A KLEPTOMANIAC!
THE TARIS JEDI'S FINANCIAL RECORDS!
DID HE MEAN LUCIEN DRAAY'S FINANCIAL RECORDS? LUCIEN DRAAY OF THE GOT-TOO-MUCH-MONEY DRAAY TRUST'S FINANCIAL RECORDS?
MANDALORIANS AREN'T LIKE NORMAL PEOPLE, ZAYNE. THEY DON'T NEED MONEY. BUT I DO, ZAYNE. I JUST SPENT A MONTH IN A SEWER!
I'M SORRY, CELESTE. HE'S BEEN THROUGH A LOT -- AND, WELL, HE'S GRYPH.
YOU'RE NO BETTER. I CAN'T BELIEVE YOU WERE EVER LUCIEN DRAAY'S PADAWAN! HOW DID HE NOT KILL YOU?
WELL, HE TRIED...
HUSH. PULSIPHER'S COMING BACK...
--VINDICATION FOR THOSE OF US WHO HAVE TOILED FOR SO LONG IN THE SHADOW OF DEMAGOL, AND HIS POINTLESS EXPERIMENTS ON JEDI!

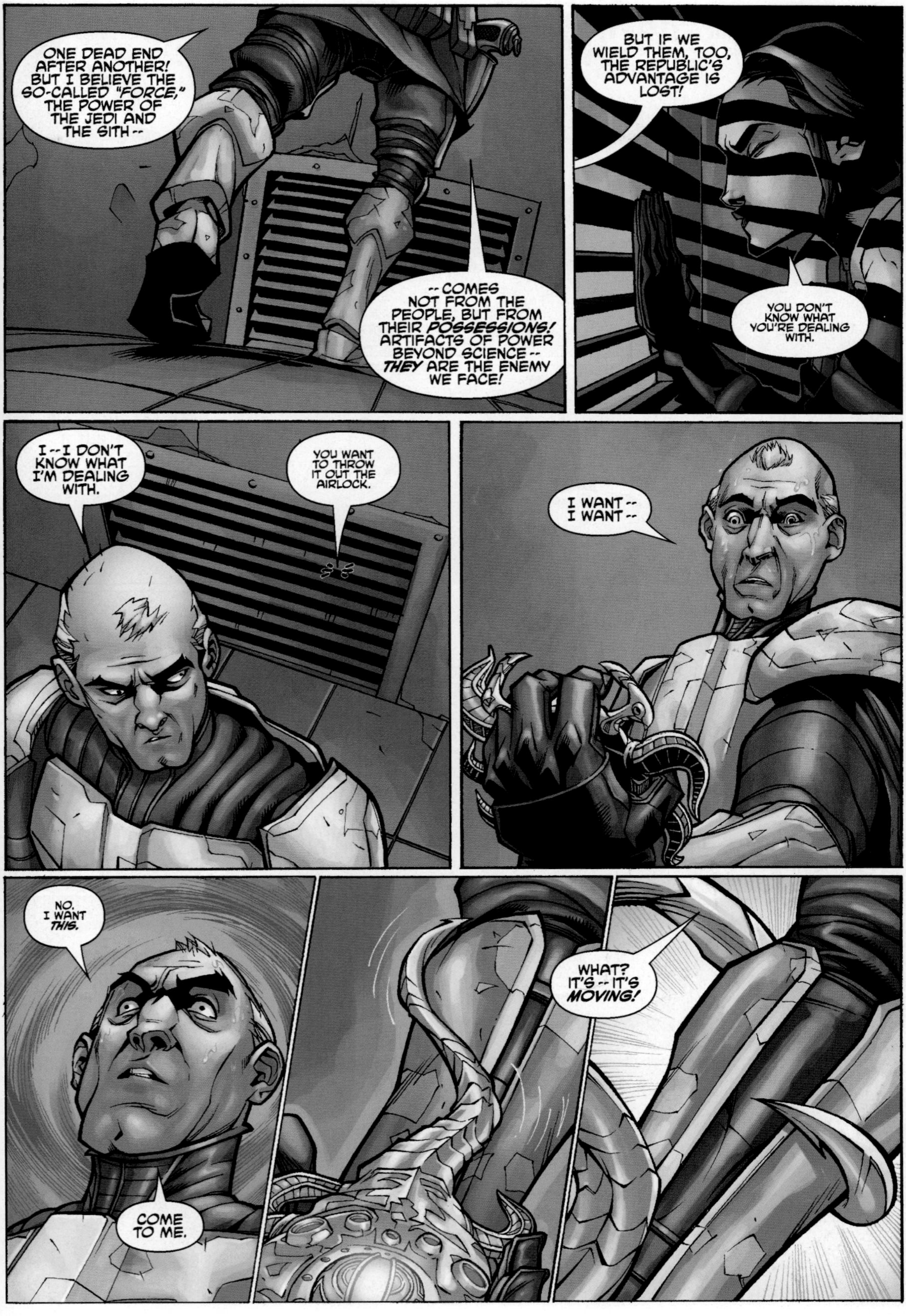
ONE DEAD END AFTER ANOTHER! BUT I BELIEVE THE SO-CALLED "FORCE," THE POWER OF THE JEDI AND THE SITH --
-- COMES NOT FROM THE PEOPLE, BUT FROM THEIR POSSESSIONS! ARTIFACTS OF POWER BEYOND SCIENCE -- THEY ARE THE ENEMY WE FACE!
BUT IF WE WIELD THEM, TOO, THE REPUBLIC'S ADVANTAGE IS LOST!
YOU DON'T KNOW WHAT YOU'RE DEALING WITH.
I -- I DON'T KNOW WHAT I'M DEALING WITH.
YOU WANT TO THROW IT OUT THE AIRLOCK.
I WANT -- I WANT --
NO. I WANT THIS.
COME TO ME.
WHAT? IT'S -- IT'S MOVING!

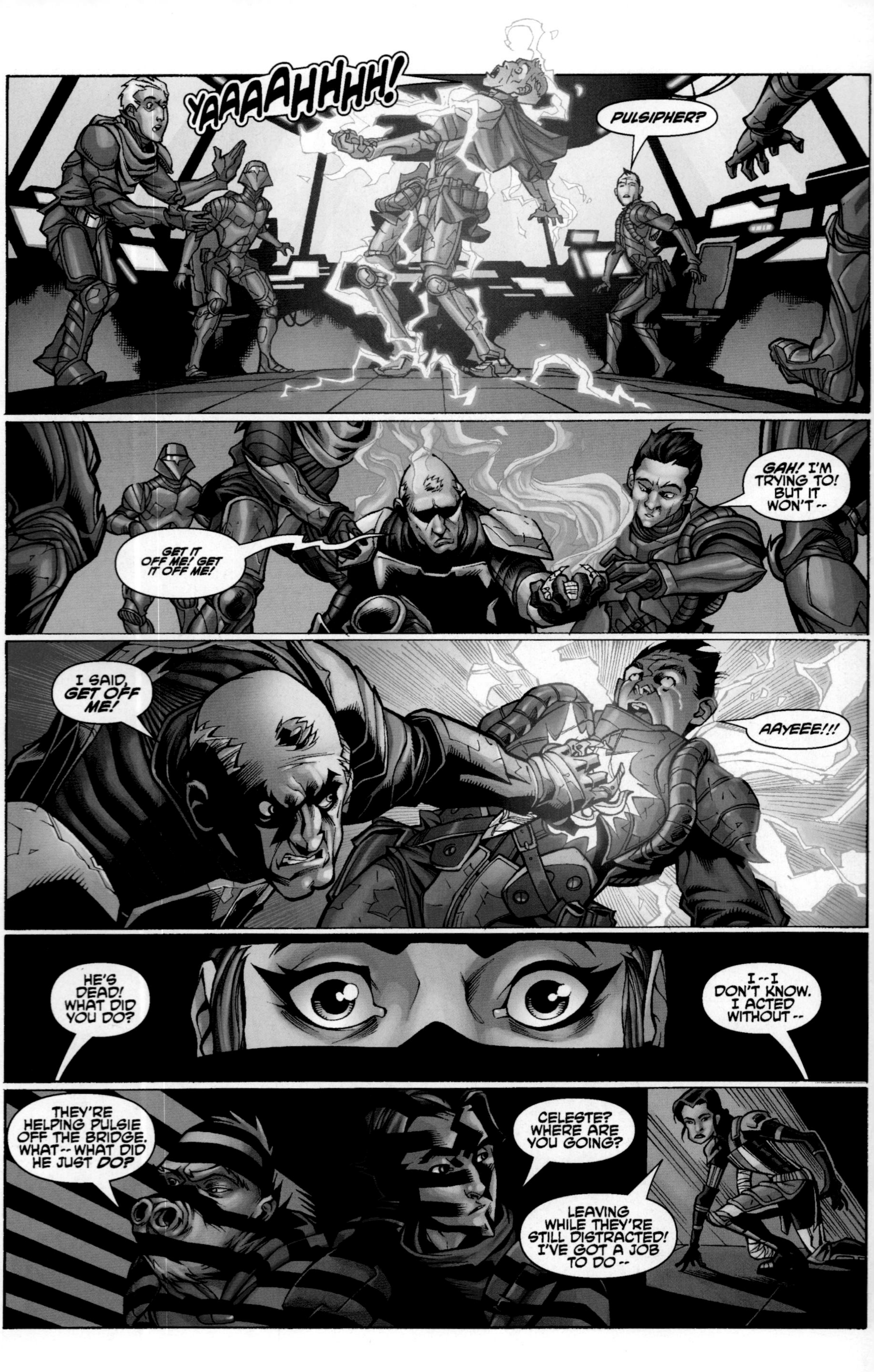
YAAAAHHHH!
PULSIPHER?
GAH! I'M TRYING TO! BUT IT WON'T --
GET IT OFF ME! GET IT OFF ME!
I SAID, GET OFF ME!
AAYEEE!!!
HE'S DEAD! WHAT DID YOU DO?
I -- I DON'T KNOW. I ACTED WITHOUT --
THEY'RE HELPING PULSIE OFF THE BRIDGE. WHAT -- WHAT DID HE JUST DO?
CELESTE? WHERE ARE YOU GOING?
LEAVING WHILE THEY'RE STILL DISTRACTED! I'VE GOT A JOB TO DO --

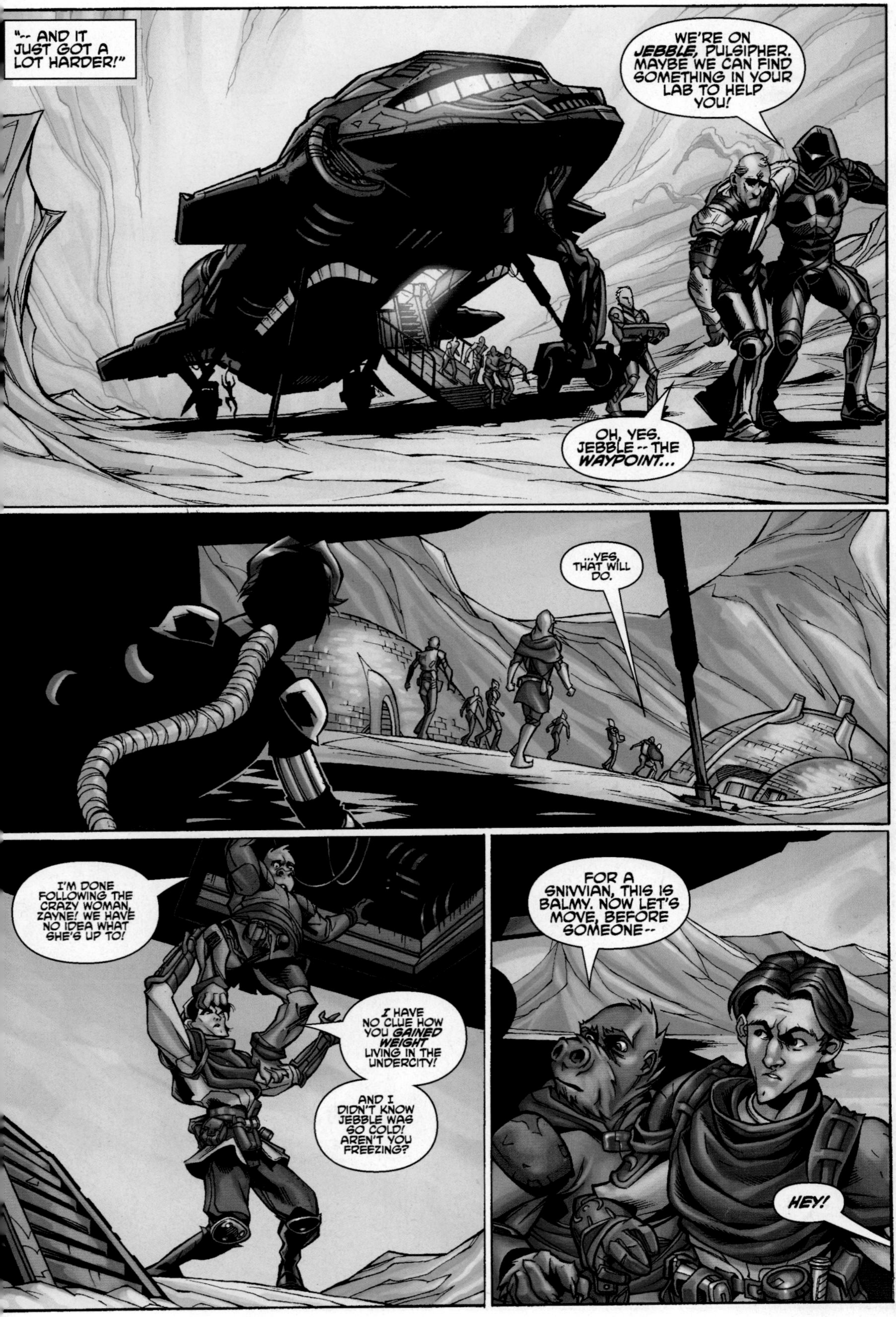
"-- AND IT JUST GOT A LOT HARDER!"
WE'RE ON JEBBLE, PULSIPHER. MAYBE WE CAN FIND SOMETHING IN YOUR LAB TO HELP YOU!
OH, YES. JEBBLE -- THE WAYPOINT...
...YES, THAT WILL DO.
I'M DONE FOLLOWING THE CRAZY WOMAN, ZAYNE! WE HAVE NO IDEA WHAT SHE'S UP TO!
I HAVE NO CLUE HOW YOU GAINED WEIGHT LIVING IN THE UNDERCITY!
AND I DIDN'T KNOW JEBBLE WAS SO COLD! AREN'T YOU FREEZING?
FOR A SNIVVIAN, THIS IS BALMY. NOW LET'S MOVE, BEFORE SOMEONE--
HEY!

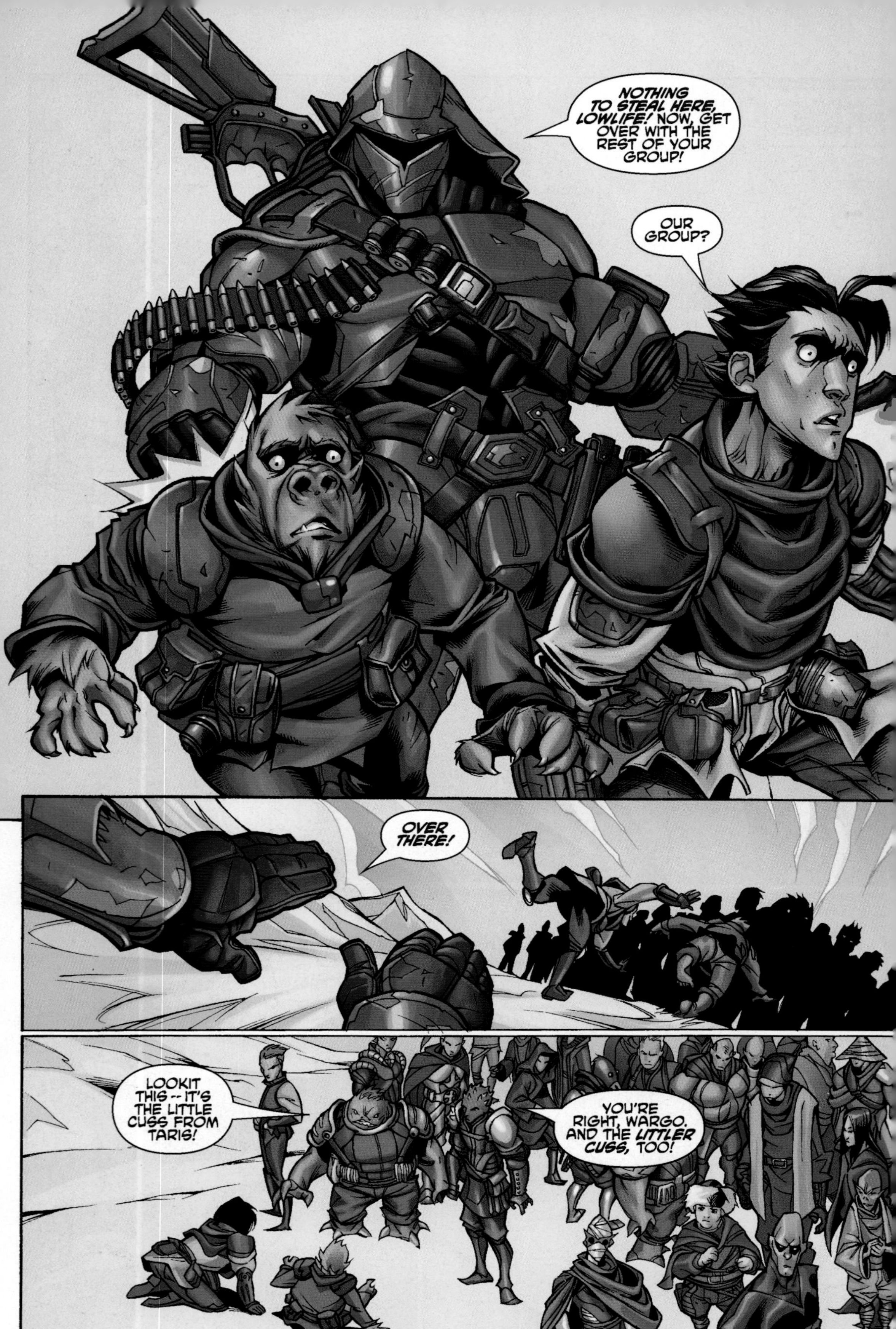
NOTHING TO STEAL HERE, LOWLIFE! NOW, GET OVER WITH THE REST OF YOUR GROUP!
OUR GROUP?
OVER THERE!
LOOKIT THIS -- IT'S THE LITTLE CUSS FROM TARIS!
YOU'RE RIGHT, WARGO. AND THE LITTLER CUSS, TOO!

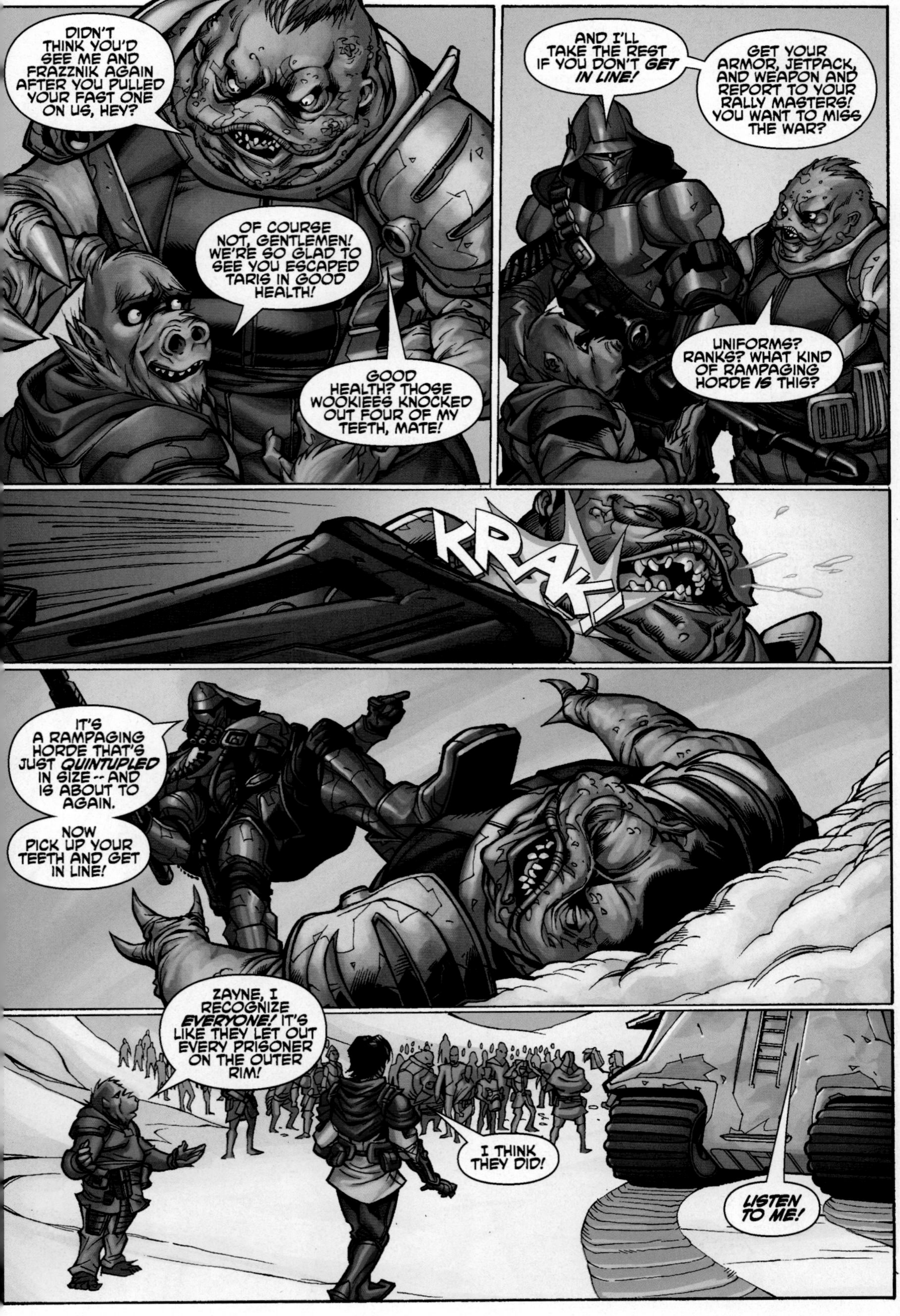
DIDN'T THINK YOU'D SEE ME AND FRAZZNIK AGAIN AFTER YOU PULLED YOUR FAST ONE ON US, HEY?
OF COURSE NOT, GENTLEMEN! WE'RE SO GLAD TO SEE YOU ESCAPED TARIS IN GOOD HEALTH!
GOOD HEALTH? THOSE WOOKIEES KNOCKED OUT FOUR OF MY TEETH, MATE!
AND I'LL TAKE THE REST IF YOU DON'T *GET IN LINE!*
GET YOUR ARMOR, JETPACK, AND WEAPON AND REPORT TO YOUR RALLY MASTERS! YOU WANT TO MISS THE WAR?
UNIFORMS? RANKS? WHAT KIND OF RAMPAGING HORDE *IS* THIS?
KRAK!
IT'S A RAMPAGING HORDE THAT'S JUST *QUINTUPLED* IN SIZE -- AND IS ABOUT TO AGAIN.
NOW PICK UP YOUR TEETH AND GET IN LINE!
ZAYNE, I RECOGNIZE *EVERYONE!* IT'S LIKE THEY LET OUT EVERY PRISONER ON THE OUTER RIM!
I THINK THEY DID!
LISTEN TO ME!

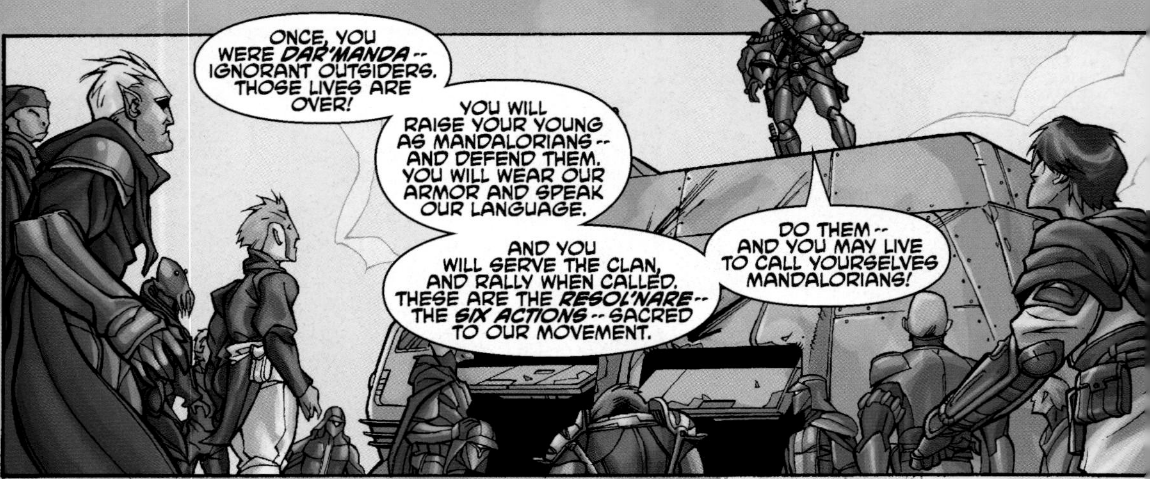
ONCE, YOU WERE *DAR'MANDA* -- IGNORANT OUTSIDERS. THOSE LIVES ARE OVER!
YOU WILL RAISE YOUR YOUNG AS MANDALORIANS -- AND DEFEND THEM. YOU WILL WEAR OUR ARMOR AND SPEAK OUR LANGUAGE.
AND YOU WILL SERVE THE CLAN, AND RALLY WHEN CALLED. THESE ARE THE *RESOL'NARE* -- THE *SIX ACTIONS* -- SACRED TO OUR MOVEMENT.
DO THEM -- AND YOU MAY LIVE TO CALL YOURSELVES MANDALORIANS!

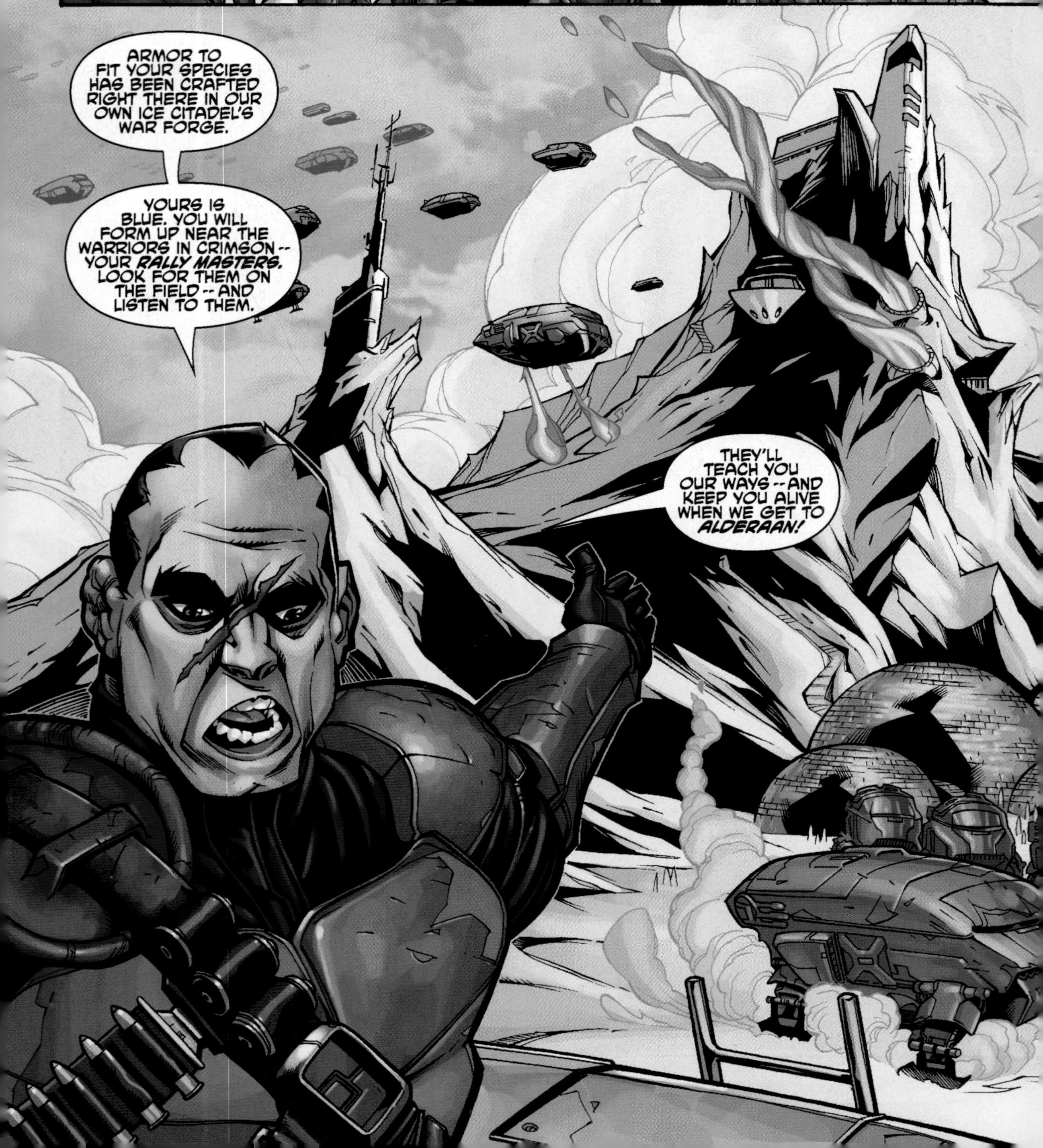
ARMOR TO FIT YOUR SPECIES HAS BEEN CRAFTED RIGHT THERE IN OUR OWN ICE CITADEL'S WAR FORGE.
YOURS IS BLUE. YOU WILL FORM UP NEAR THE WARRIORS IN CRIMSON -- YOUR *RALLY MASTERS.* LOOK FOR THEM ON THE FIELD -- AND LISTEN TO THEM.
THEY'LL TEACH YOU OUR WAYS -- AND KEEP YOU ALIVE WHEN WE GET TO *ALDERAAN!*

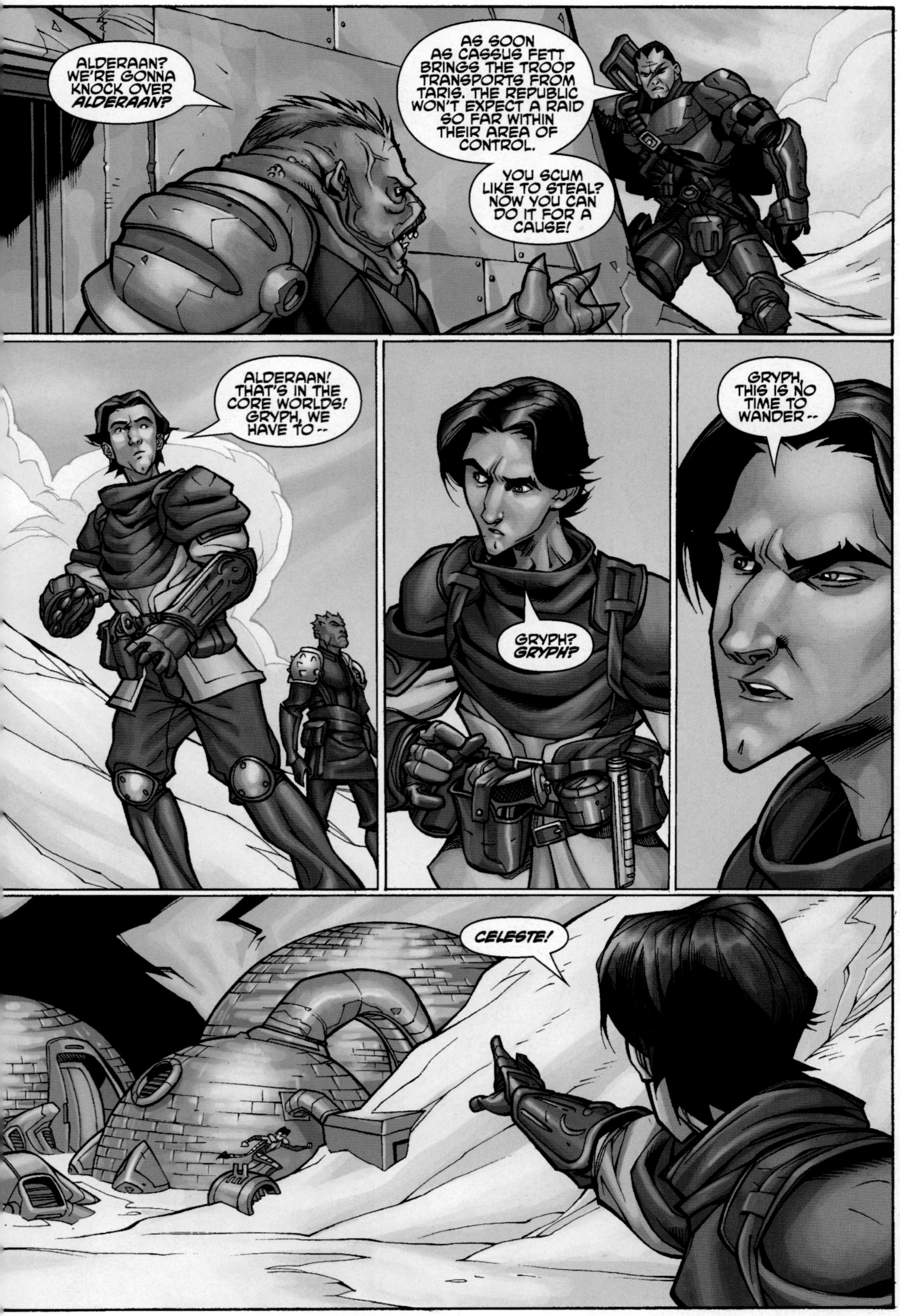
ALDERAAN? WE'RE GONNA KNOCK OVER *ALDERAAN?*
AS SOON AS CASSUS FETT BRINGS THE TROOP TRANSPORTS FROM TARIS. THE REPUBLIC WON'T EXPECT A RAID SO FAR WITHIN THEIR AREA OF CONTROL.
YOU SCUM LIKE TO STEAL? NOW YOU CAN DO IT FOR A CAUSE!
ALDERAAN! THAT'S IN THE CORE WORLDS! GRYPH, WE HAVE TO --
GRYPH? *GRYPH?*
GRYPH, THIS IS NO TIME TO WANDER --
CELESTE!

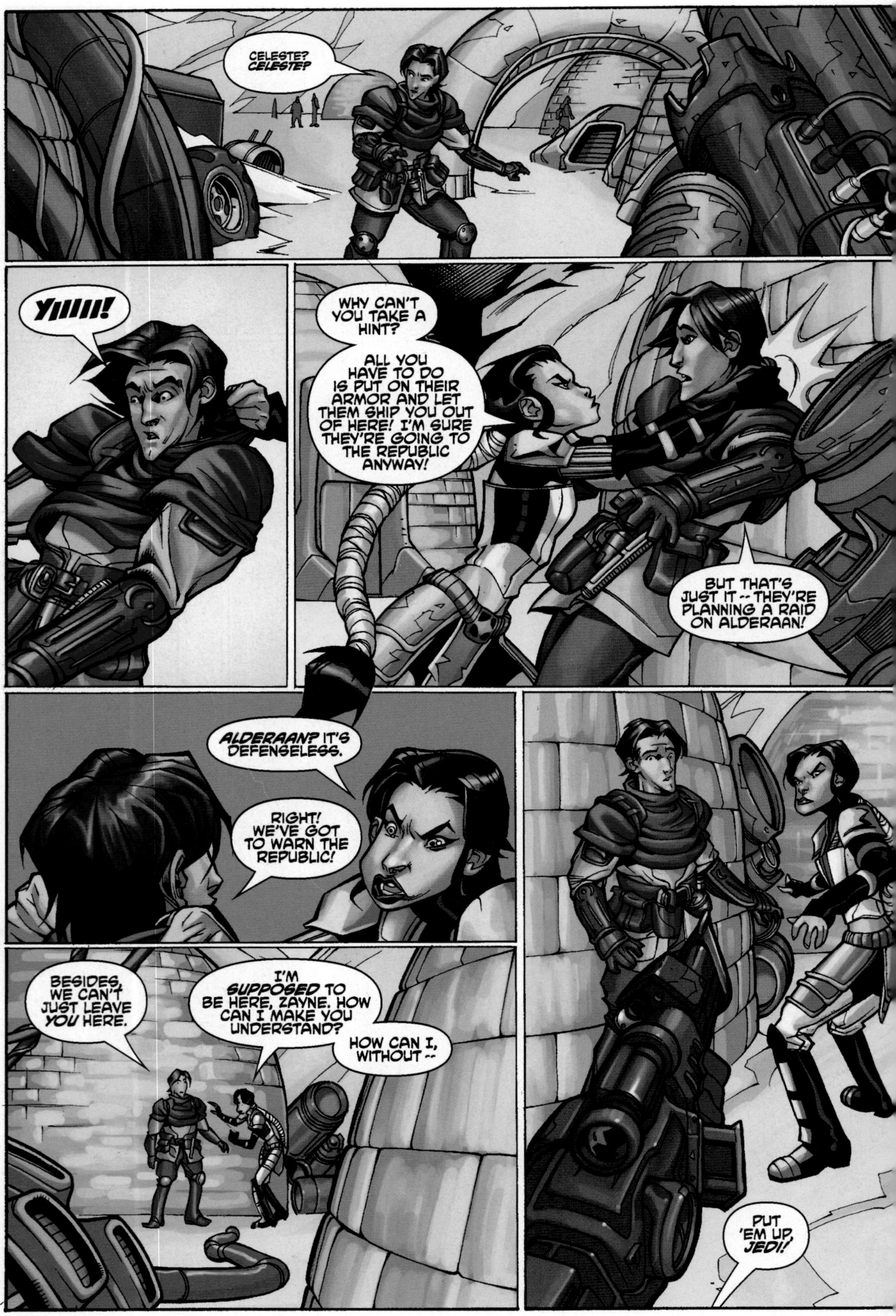
CELESTE? CELESTE?
YIIIII!
WHY CAN'T YOU TAKE A HINT?
ALL YOU HAVE TO DO IS PUT ON THEIR ARMOR AND LET THEM SHIP YOU OUT OF HERE! I'M SURE THEY'RE GOING TO THE REPUBLIC ANYWAY!
BUT THAT'S JUST IT -- THEY'RE PLANNING A RAID ON ALDERAAN!
ALDERAAN? IT'S DEFENSELESS.
RIGHT! WE'VE GOT TO WARN THE REPUBLIC!
BESIDES, WE CAN'T JUST LEAVE YOU HERE.
I'M SUPPOSED TO BE HERE, ZAYNE. HOW CAN I MAKE YOU UNDERSTAND?
HOW CAN I, WITHOUT --
PUT 'EM UP, JEDI!

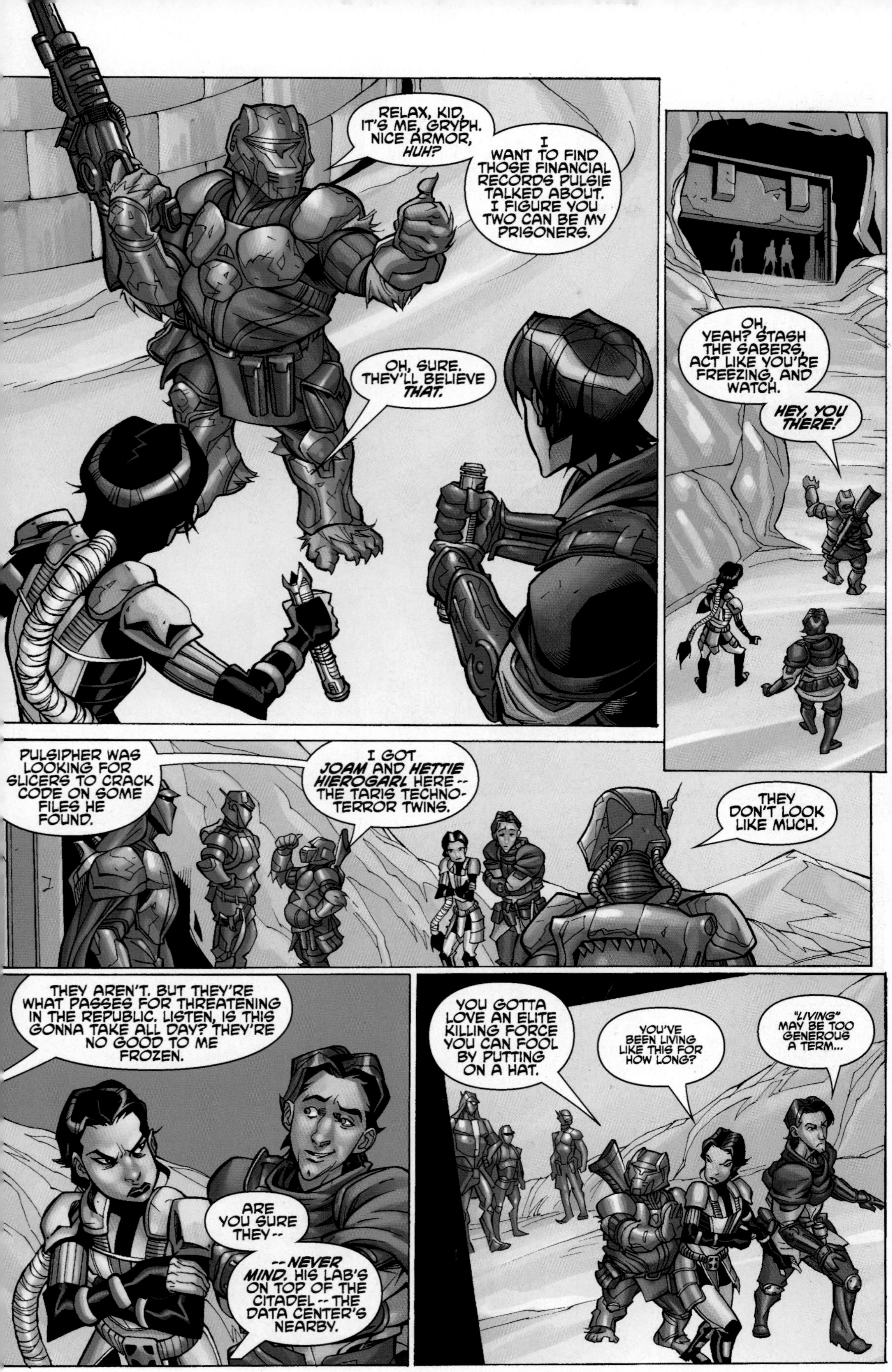
RELAX, KID, IT'S ME, GRYPH. NICE ARMOR, *HUH?*
I WANT TO FIND THOSE FINANCIAL RECORDS PULSIE TALKED ABOUT. I FIGURE YOU TWO CAN BE MY PRISONERS.
OH, SURE. THEY'LL BELIEVE *THAT.*
OH, YEAH? STASH THE SABERS, ACT LIKE YOU'RE FREEZING, AND WATCH.
HEY, YOU THERE!
PULSIPHER WAS LOOKING FOR SLICERS TO CRACK CODE ON SOME FILES HE FOUND.
I GOT *JOAM* AND *HETTIE HIEROGARL* HERE -- THE TARIS TECHNO-TERROR TWINS.
THEY DON'T LOOK LIKE MUCH.
THEY AREN'T. BUT THEY'RE WHAT PASSES FOR THREATENING IN THE REPUBLIC. LISTEN, IS THIS GONNA TAKE ALL DAY? THEY'RE NO GOOD TO ME FROZEN.
ARE YOU SURE THEY--
--NEVER MIND. HIS LAB'S ON TOP OF THE CITADEL -- THE DATA CENTER'S NEARBY.
YOU GOTTA LOVE AN ELITE KILLING FORCE YOU CAN FOOL BY PUTTING ON A HAT.
YOU'VE BEEN LIVING LIKE THIS FOR HOW LONG?
"LIVING" MAY BE TOO GENEROUS A TERM...

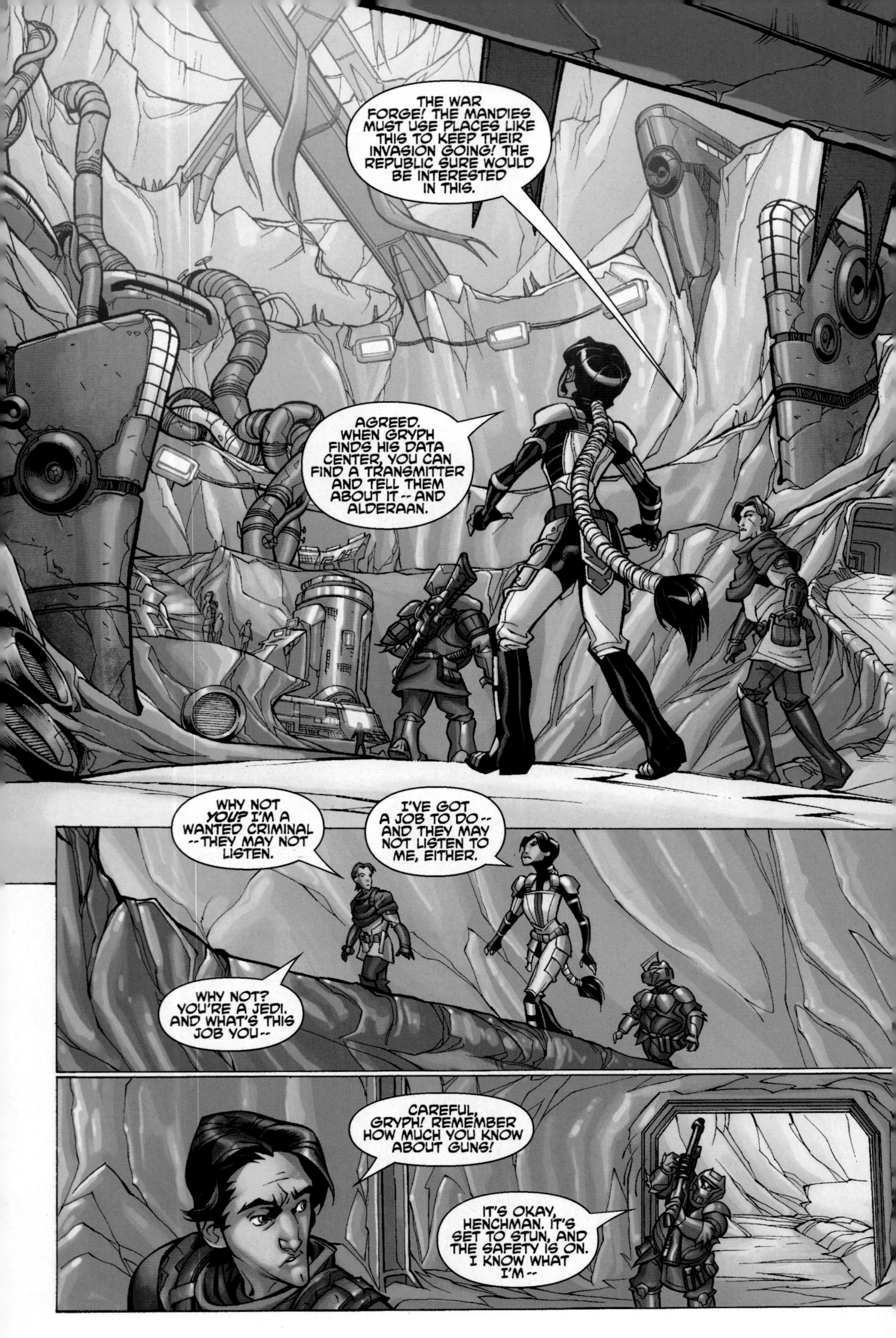
THE WAR FORGE! THE MANDIES MUST USE PLACES LIKE THIS TO KEEP THEIR INVASION GOING! THE REPUBLIC SURE WOULD BE INTERESTED IN THIS.
AGREED. WHEN GRYPH FINDS HIS DATA CENTER, YOU CAN FIND A TRANSMITTER AND TELL THEM ABOUT IT -- AND ALDERAAN.
WHY NOT *YOU?* I'M A WANTED CRIMINAL --THEY MAY NOT LISTEN.
I'VE GOT A JOB TO DO -- AND THEY MAY NOT LISTEN TO ME, EITHER.
WHY NOT? YOU'RE A JEDI. AND WHAT'S THIS JOB YOU--
CAREFUL, GRYPH! REMEMBER HOW MUCH YOU KNOW ABOUT GUNS!
IT'S OKAY, HENCHMAN. IT'S SET TO STUN, AND THE SAFETY IS ON. I KNOW WHAT I'M--

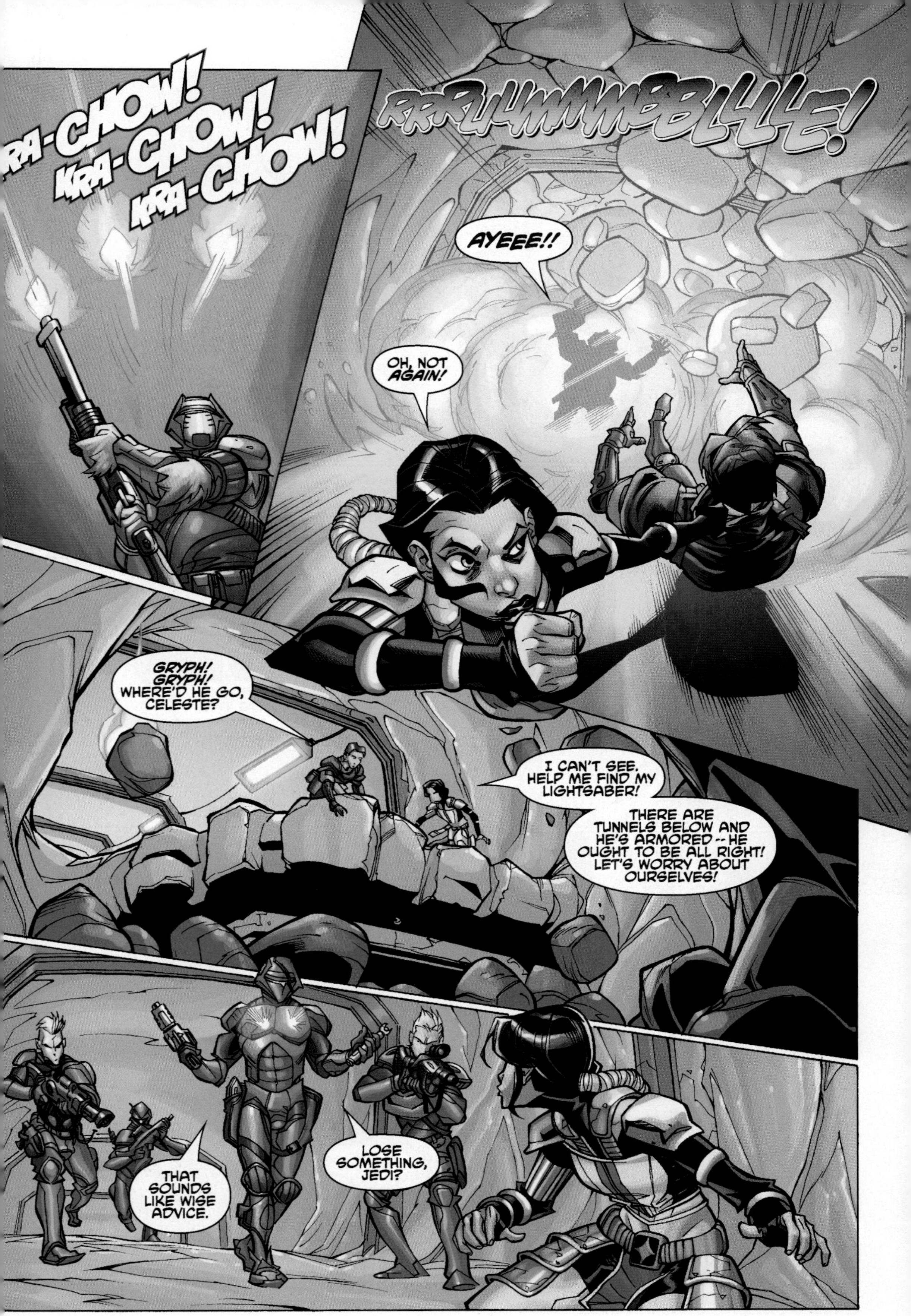

KRA-CHOW! KRA-CHOW! KRA-CHOW!
RRRRUMMMBBLLLE!
AYEEE!!
OH, NOT AGAIN!
GRYPH! GRYPH! WHERE'D HE GO, CELESTE?
I CAN'T SEE. HELP ME FIND MY LIGHTSABER!
THERE ARE TUNNELS BELOW AND HE'S ARMORED -- HE OUGHT TO BE ALL RIGHT! LET'S WORRY ABOUT OURSELVES!
THAT SOUNDS LIKE WISE ADVICE.
LOSE SOMETHING, JEDI?

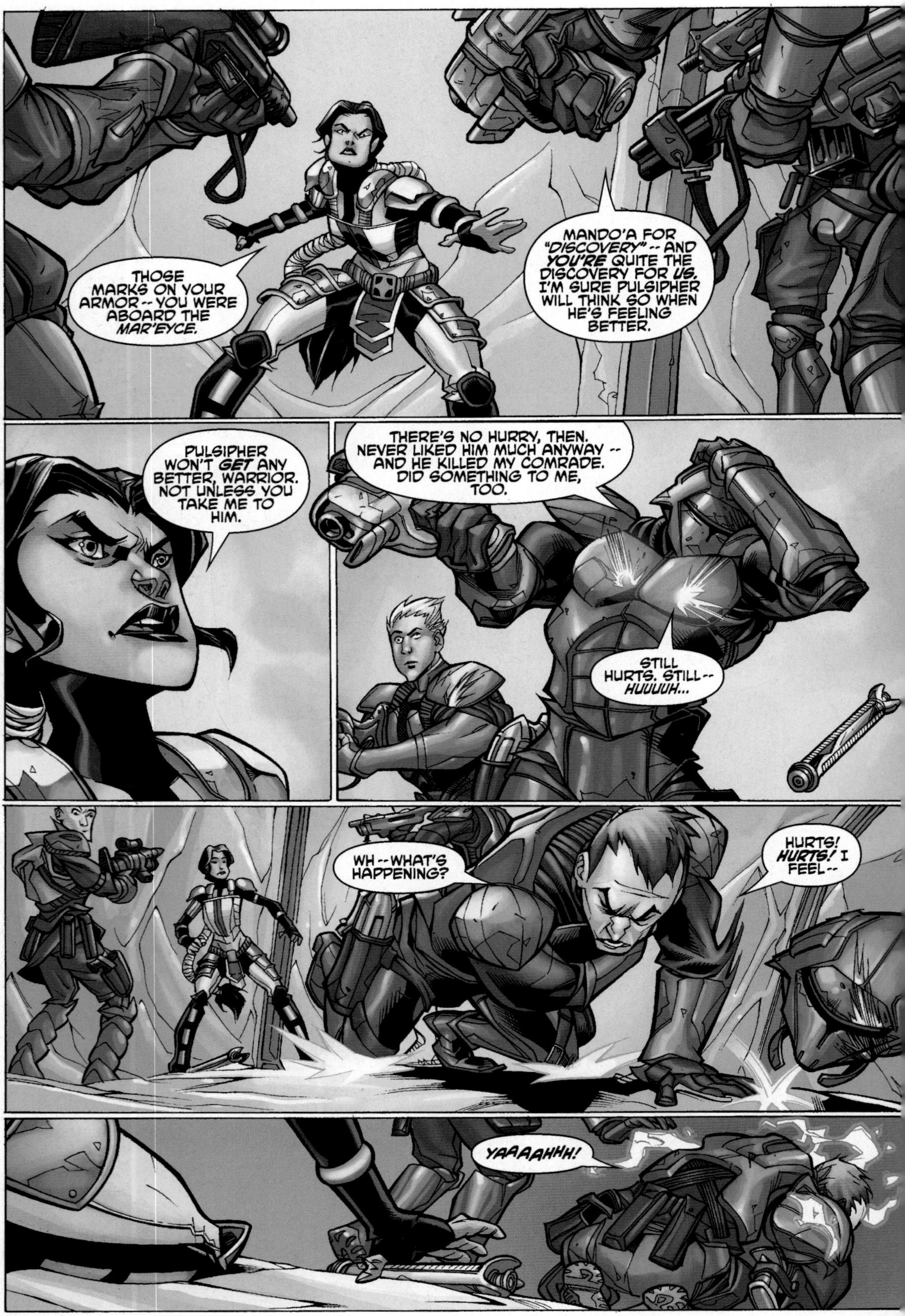
THOSE MARKS ON YOUR ARMOR -- YOU WERE ABOARD THE *MAR'EYCE.*
MANDO'A FOR *"DISCOVERY"* -- AND ***YOU'RE*** QUITE THE DISCOVERY FOR ***US.*** I'M SURE PULSIPHER WILL THINK SO WHEN HE'S FEELING BETTER.
PULSIPHER WON'T ***GET*** ANY BETTER, WARRIOR. NOT UNLESS YOU TAKE ME TO HIM.
THERE'S NO HURRY, THEN. NEVER LIKED HIM MUCH ANYWAY -- AND HE KILLED MY COMRADE. DID SOMETHING TO ME, TOO.
STILL HURTS. STILL -- *HUUUUH...*
WH -- WHAT'S HAPPENING?
HURTS! ***HURTS!*** I FEEL --
YAAAAHHH!

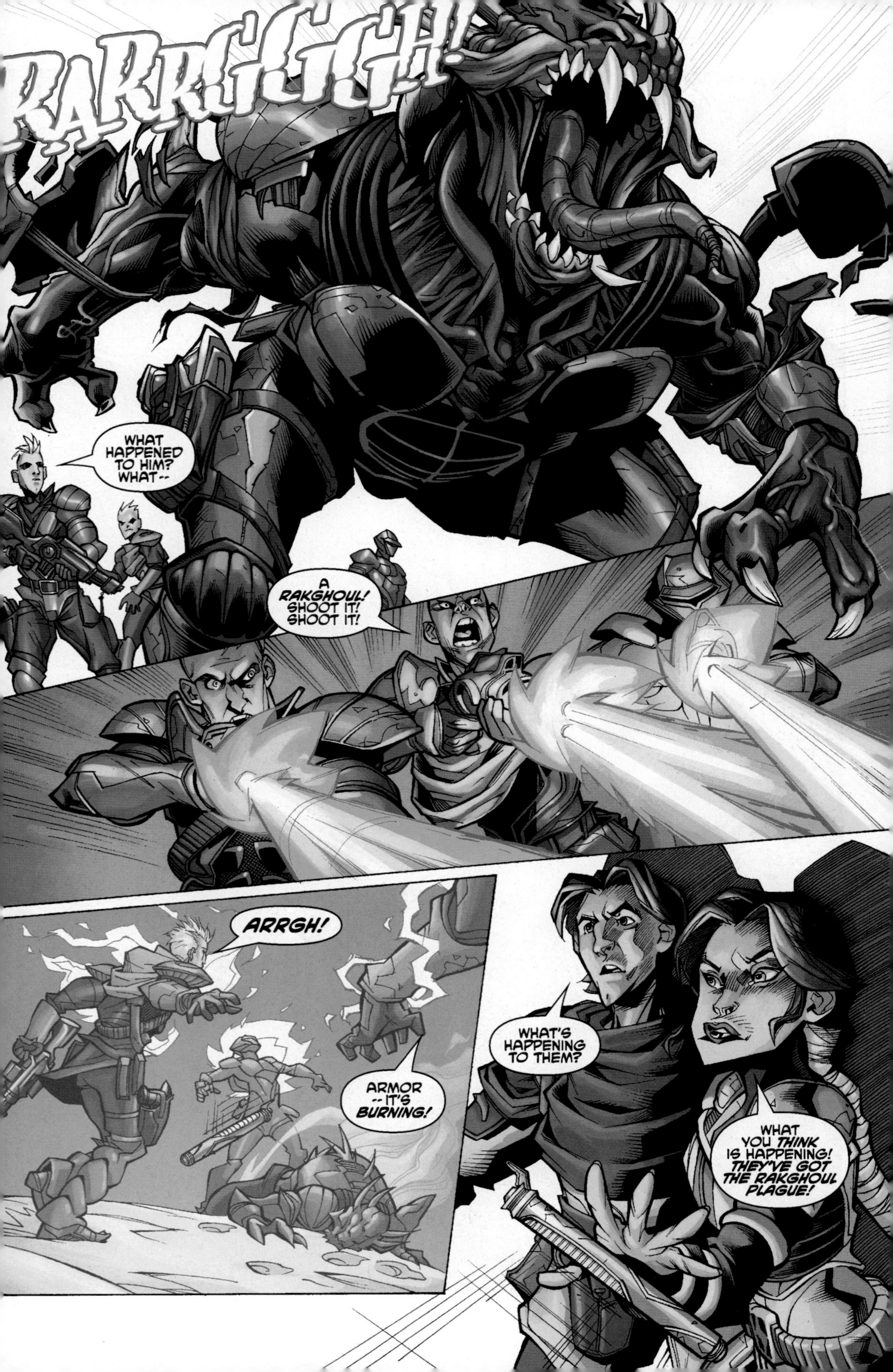
RARRGGGH!
WHAT HAPPENED TO HIM? WHAT--
A RAKGHOUL! SHOOT IT! SHOOT IT!
ARRGH!
ARMOR --IT'S BURNING!
WHAT'S HAPPENING TO THEM?
WHAT YOU THINK IS HAPPENING! THEY'VE GOT THE RAKGHOUL PLAGUE!

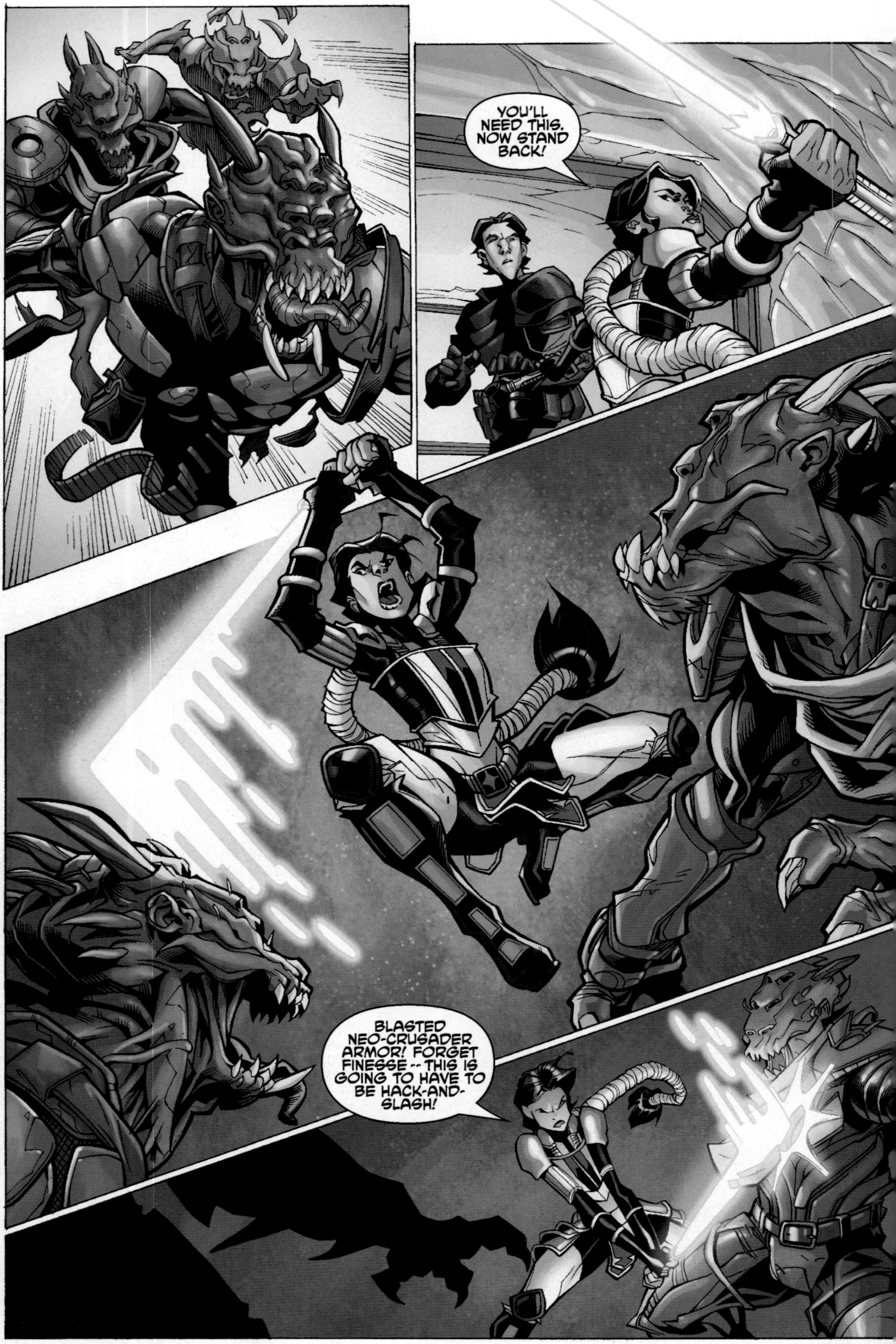
YOU'LL NEED THIS. NOW STAND BACK!
BLASTED NEO-CRUSADER ARMOR! FORGET FINESSE -- THIS IS GOING TO HAVE TO BE HACK-AND-SLASH!

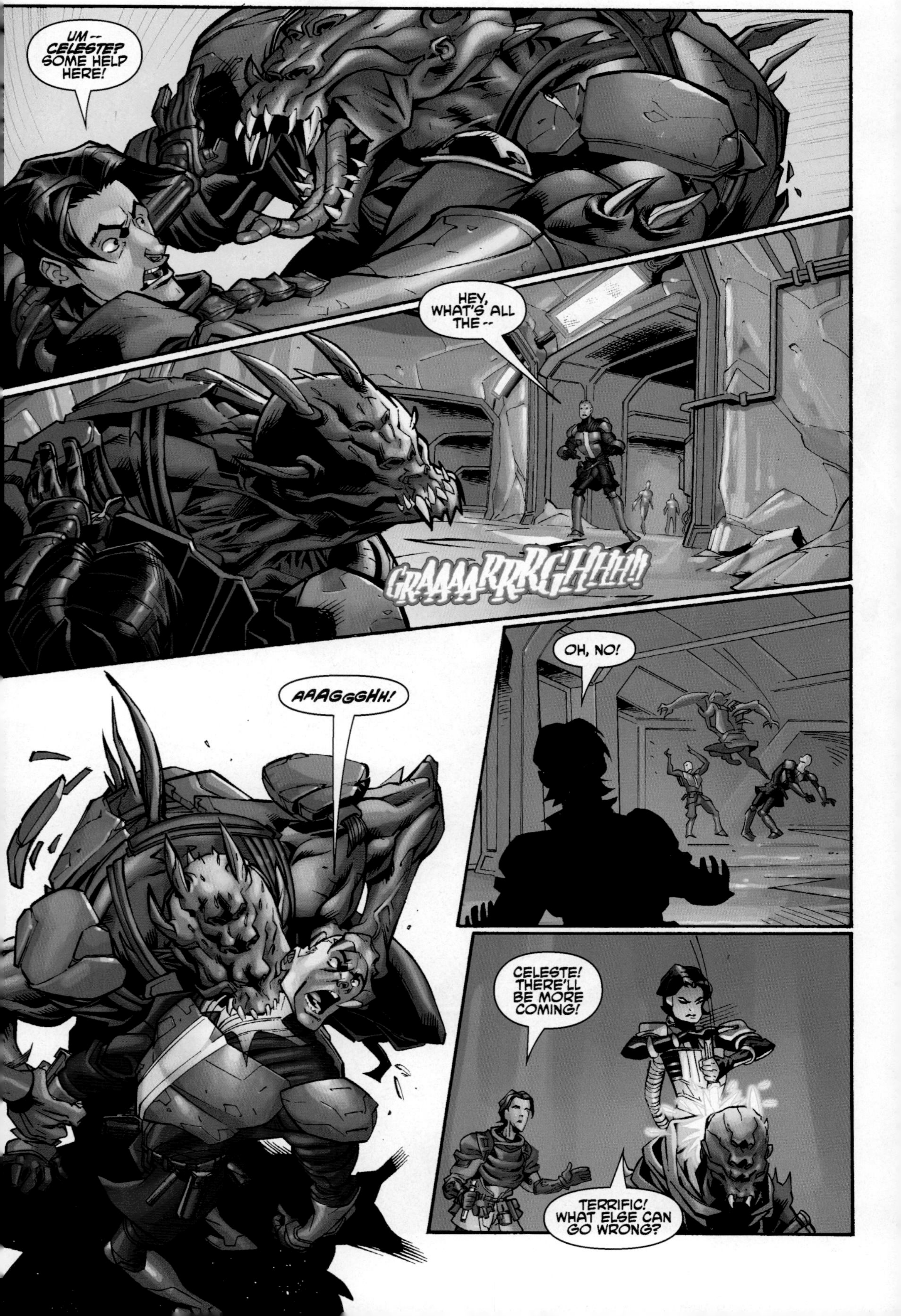
UM -- CELESTE? SOME HELP HERE!
HEY, WHAT'S ALL THE --
GRAAAARRRGHHH!!
AAAGGGHH!
OH, NO!
CELESTE! THERE'LL BE MORE COMING!
TERRIFIC! WHAT ELSE CAN GO WRONG?

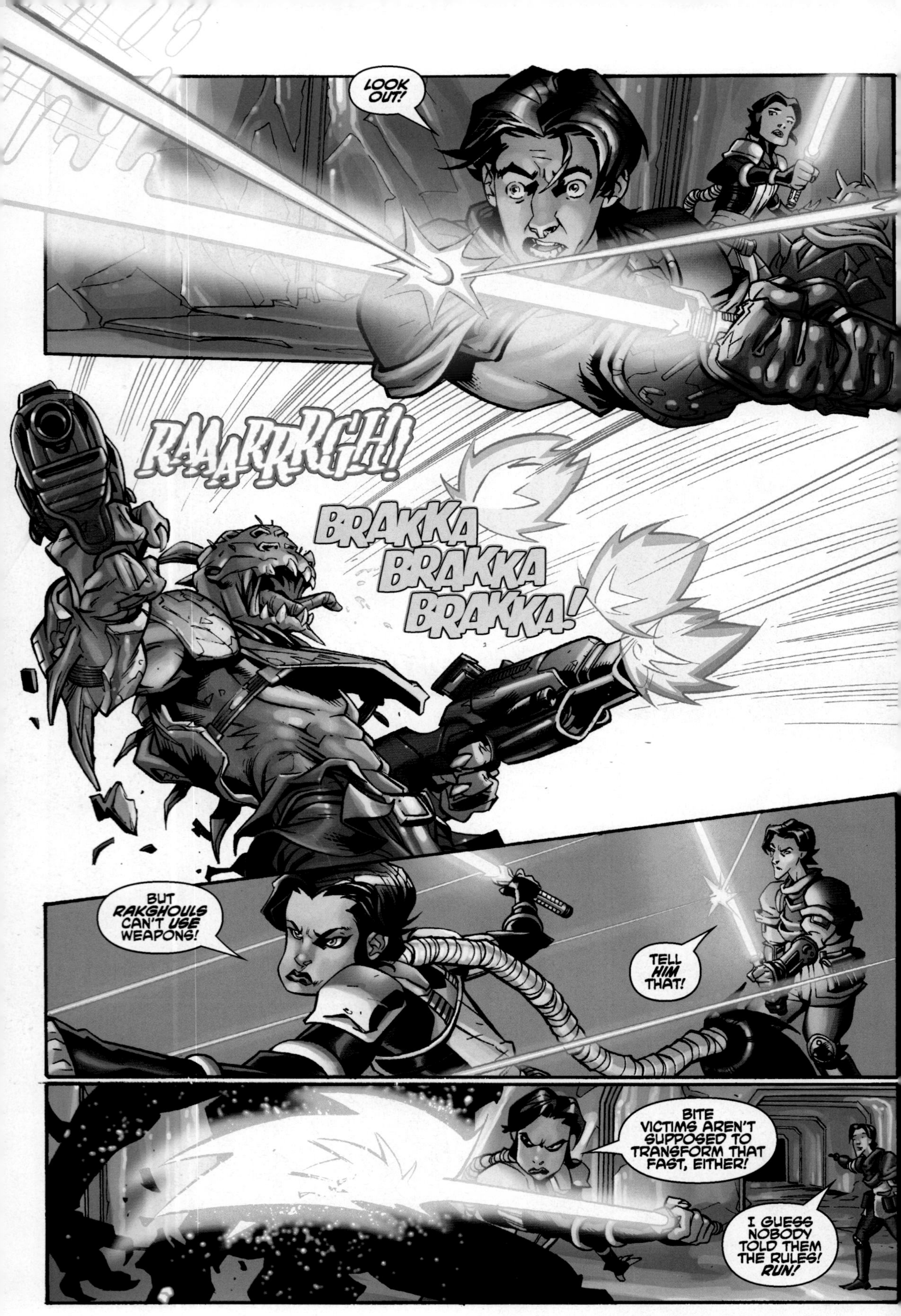
LOOK OUT!
RAAARRRGH!
BRAKKA BRAKKA BRAKKA!
BUT RAKGHOULS CAN'T USE WEAPONS!
TELL HIM THAT!
BITE VICTIMS AREN'T SUPPOSED TO TRANSFORM THAT FAST, EITHER!
I GUESS NOBODY TOLD THEM THE RULES! RUN!

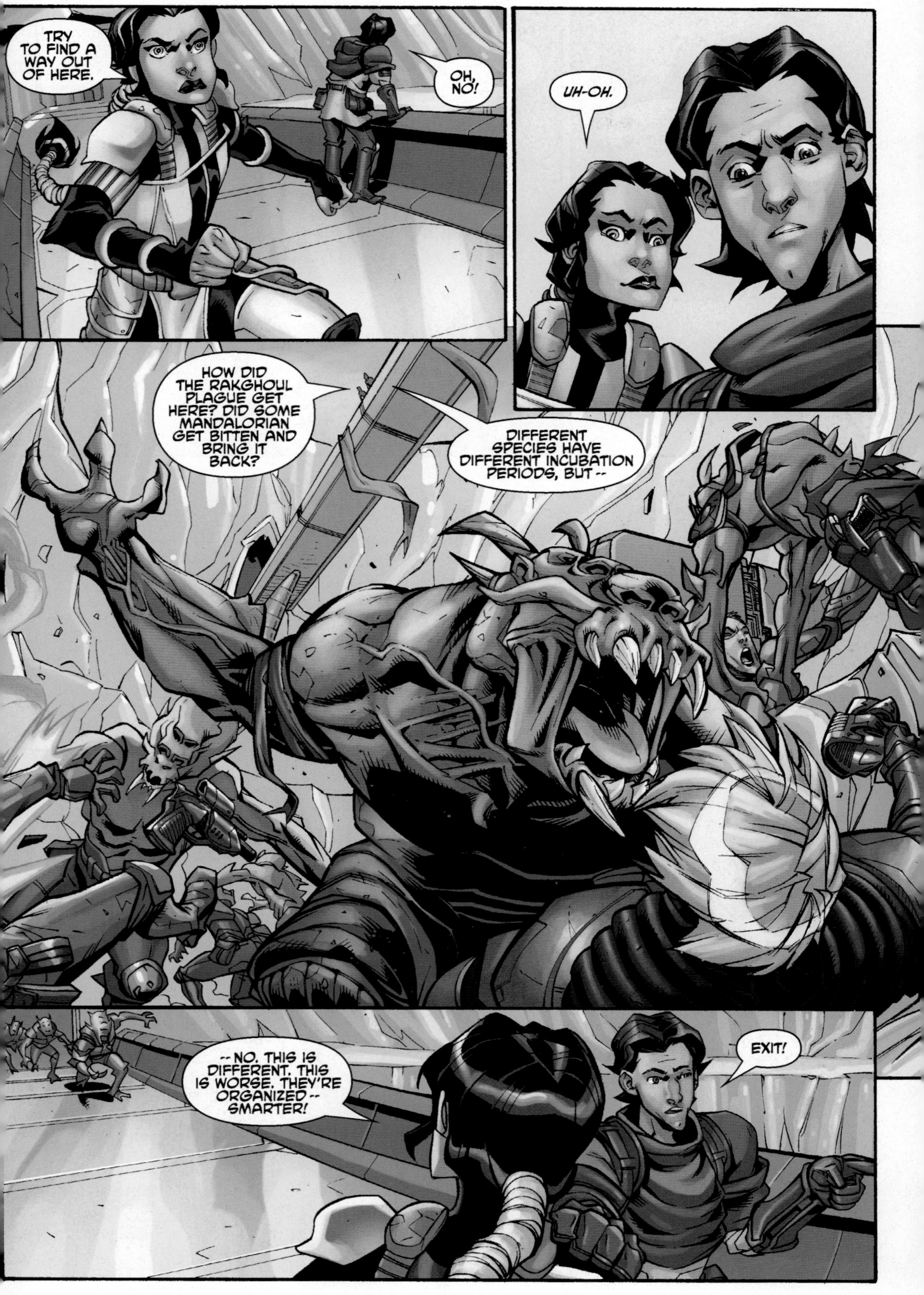
TRY TO FIND A WAY OUT OF HERE.
OH, NO!
UH-OH.
HOW DID THE RAKGHOUL PLAGUE GET HERE? DID SOME MANDALORIAN GET BITTEN AND BRING IT BACK?
DIFFERENT SPECIES HAVE DIFFERENT INCUBATION PERIODS, BUT --
-- NO. THIS IS DIFFERENT. THIS IS WORSE. THEY'RE ORGANIZED -- SMARTER!
EXIT!

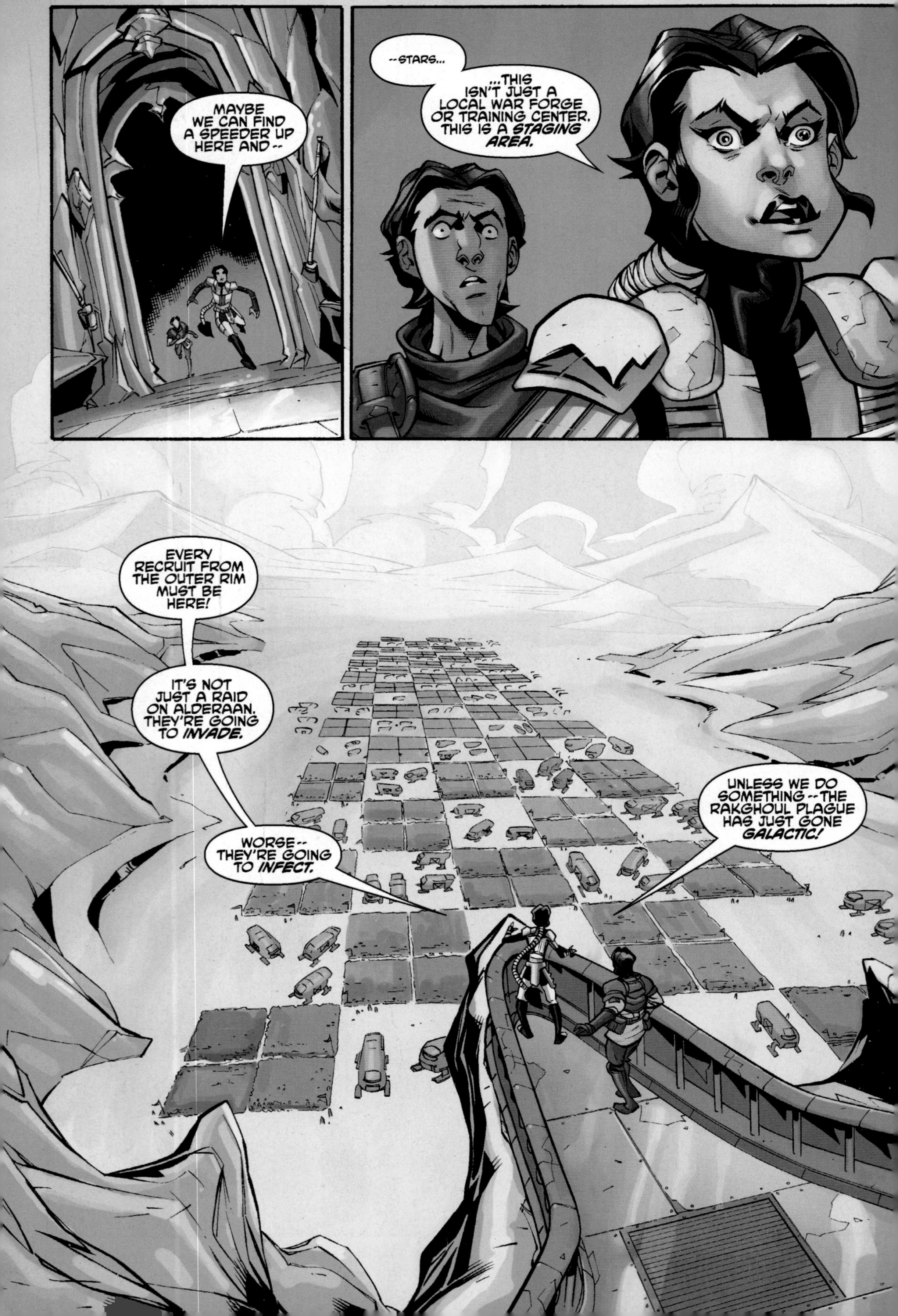
MAYBE WE CAN FIND A SPEEDER UP HERE AND --
--STARS...
...THIS ISN'T JUST A LOCAL WAR FORGE OR TRAINING CENTER. THIS IS A *STAGING AREA.*
EVERY RECRUIT FROM THE OUTER RIM MUST BE HERE!
IT'S NOT JUST A RAID ON ALDERAAN. THEY'RE GOING TO *INVADE.*
WORSE-- THEY'RE GOING TO *INFECT.*
UNLESS WE DO SOMETHING -- THE RAKGHOUL PLAGUE HAS JUST GONE *GALACTIC!*

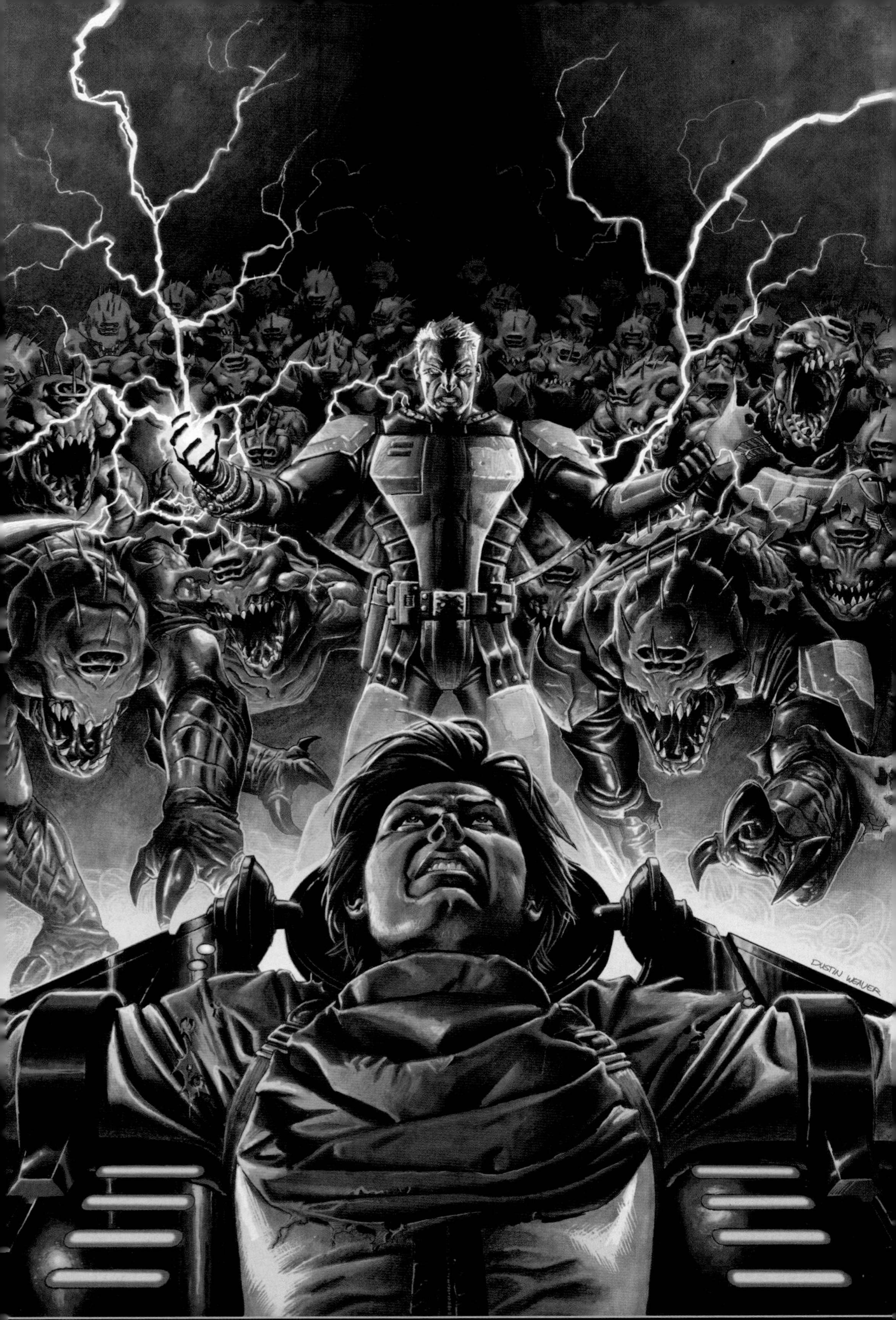
DUSTIN WEAVER

STAR WARS: KNIGHTS OF THE OLD REPUBLIC #27 — "VECTOR, PART 3"

WRITER: JOHN JACKSON MILLER • PENCILER: SCOTT HEPBURN • INKER: DAN PARSONS • COLORIST: MICHAEL ATIYEH • LETTERER: MICHAEL HEISLER
ASSISTANT EDITORS: FREDDYE LINS & DAVE MARSHALL • EDITOR: RANDY STRADLEY • COVER ARTIST: DUSTIN WEAVER

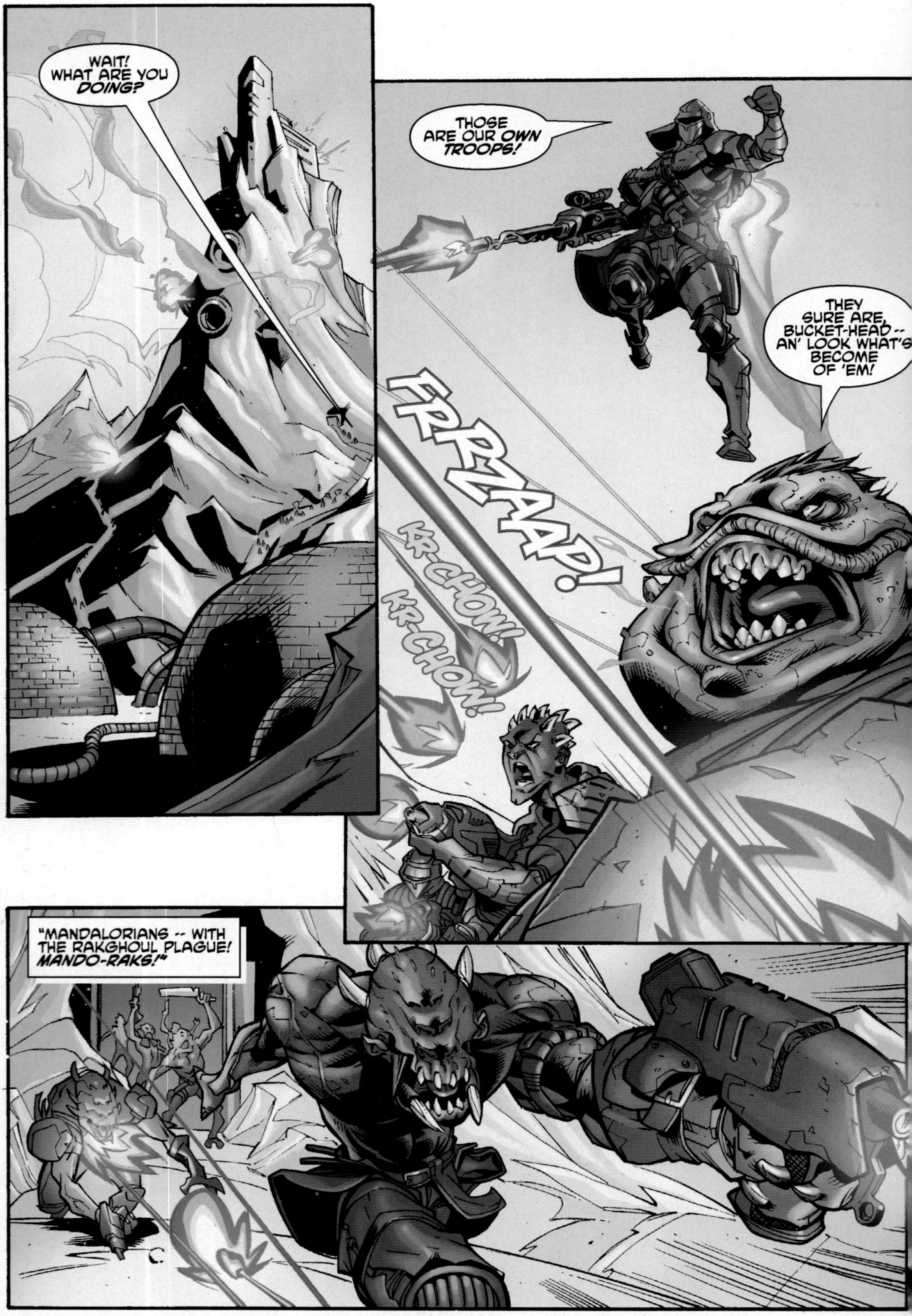
WAIT! WHAT ARE YOU DOING?
THOSE ARE OUR OWN TROOPS!
THEY SURE ARE, BUCKET-HEAD -- AN' LOOK WHAT'S BECOME OF 'EM!
FRRZAAP!
KR-CHOW!
KR-CHOW!
"MANDALORIANS -- WITH THE RAKGHOUL PLAGUE! MANDO-RAKS!"

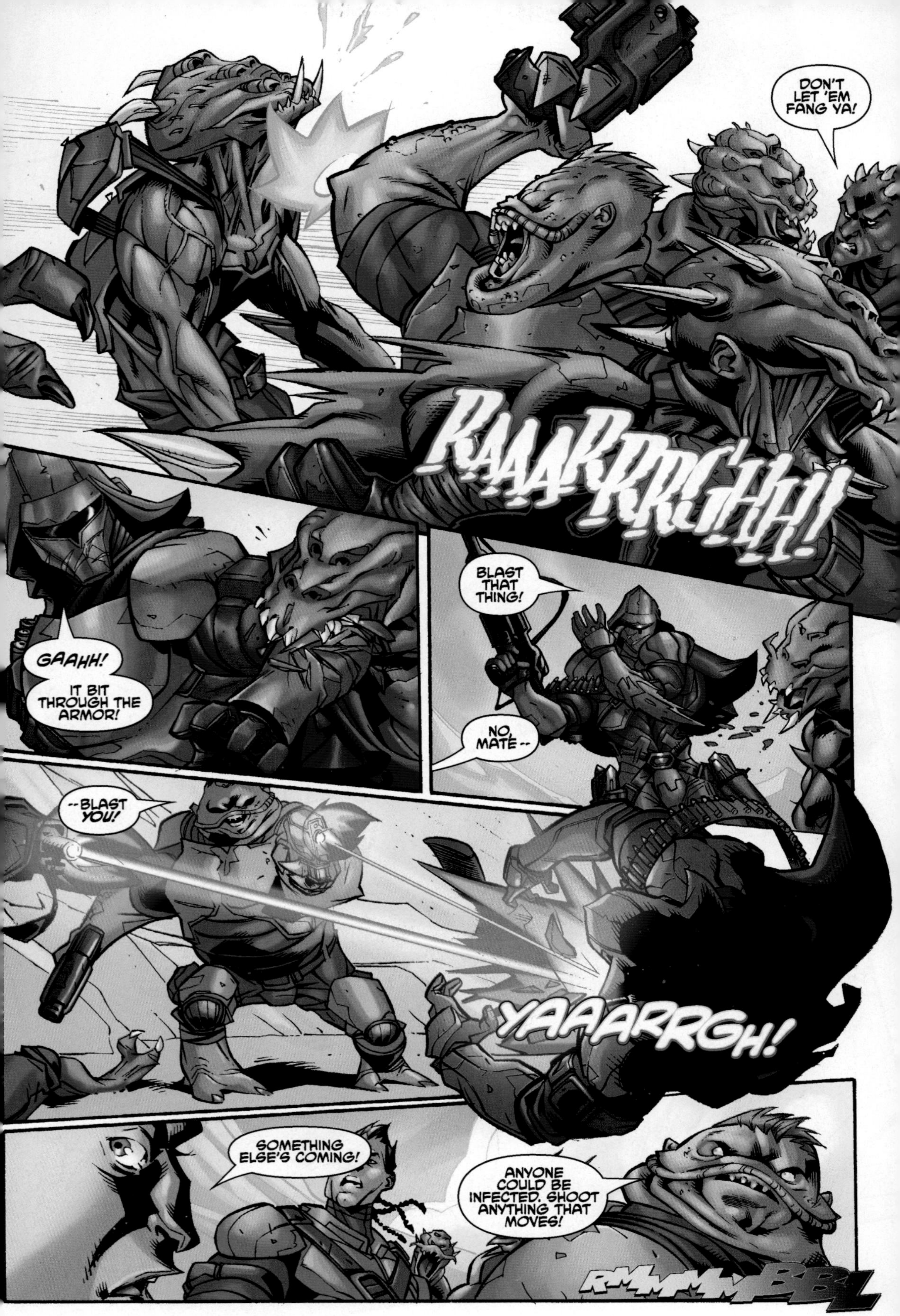
DON'T LET 'EM FANG YA!
KAAARRRGHH!
GAAHH!
IT BIT THROUGH THE ARMOR!
BLAST THAT THING!
NO, MATE --
--BLAST YOU!
YAAARRGH!
SOMETHING ELSE'S COMING!
ANYONE COULD BE INFECTED. SHOOT ANYTHING THAT MOVES!
RMMMMBBL

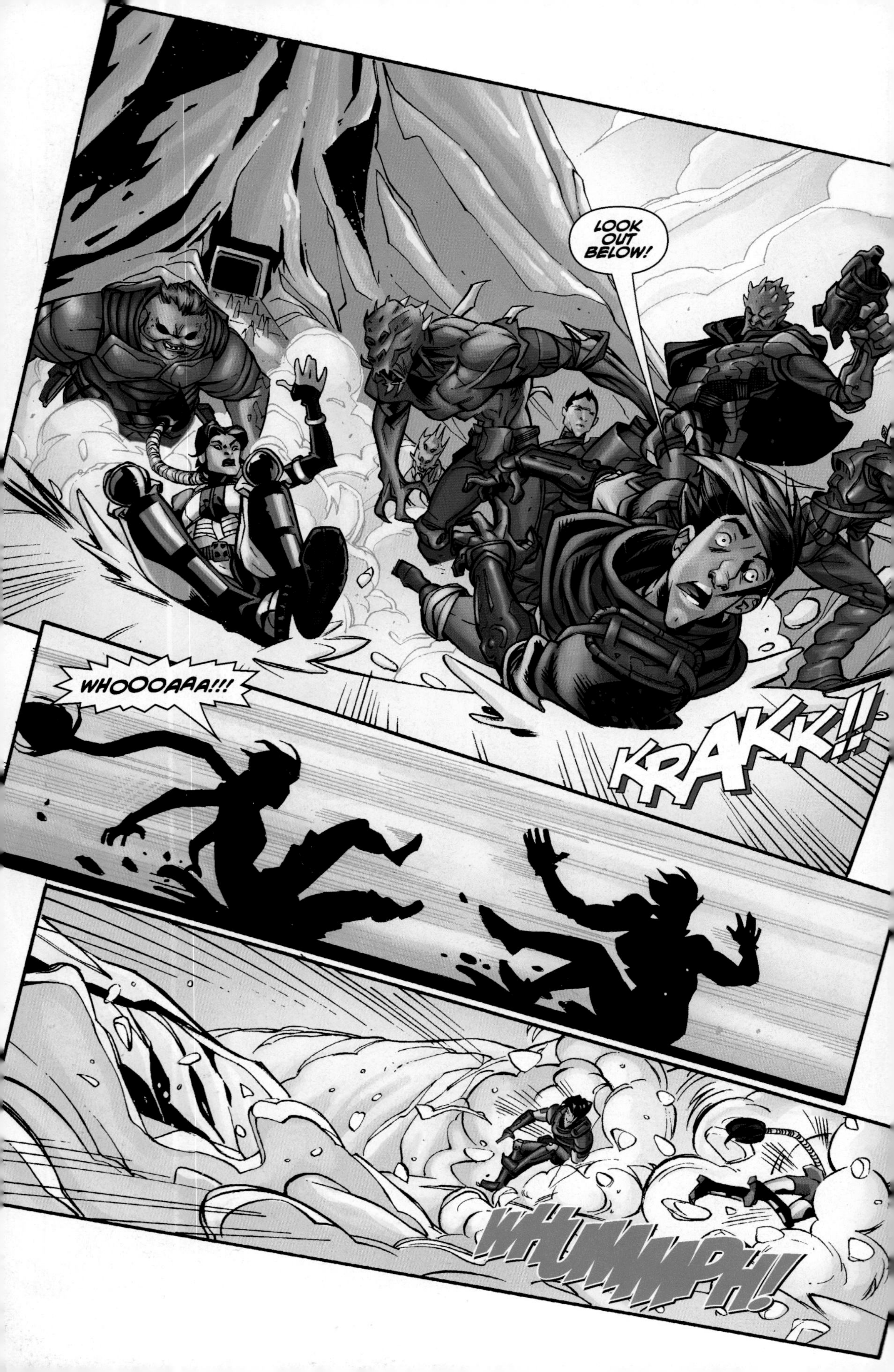
LOOK OUT BELOW!
WHOOOAAA!!!
KRAKK!!
WHUMMPH!

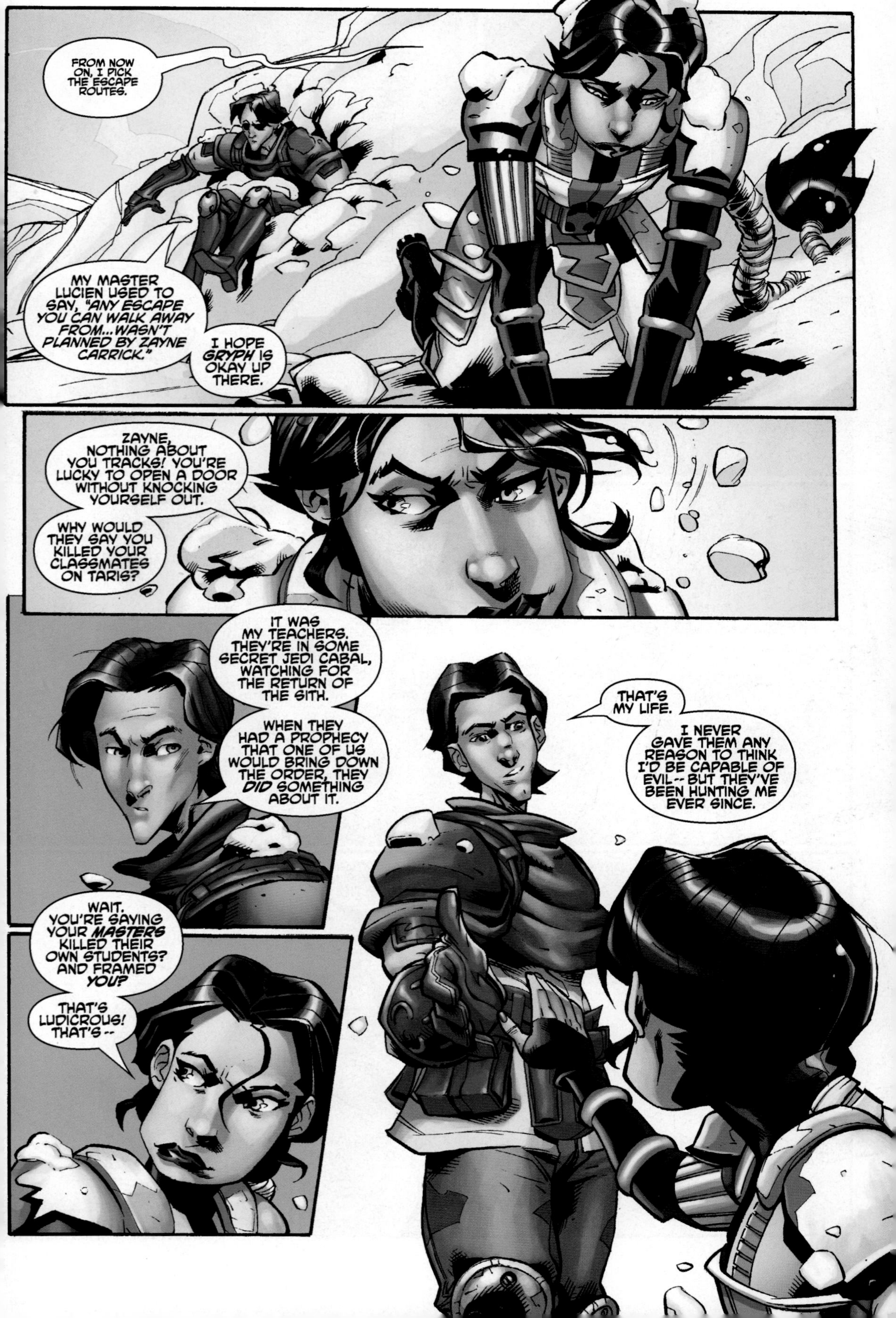
FROM NOW ON, I PICK THE ESCAPE ROUTES.
MY MASTER LUCIEN USED TO SAY, "ANY ESCAPE YOU CAN WALK AWAY FROM...WASN'T PLANNED BY ZAYNE CARRICK."
I HOPE GRYPH IS OKAY UP THERE.
ZAYNE, NOTHING ABOUT YOU TRACKS! YOU'RE LUCKY TO OPEN A DOOR WITHOUT KNOCKING YOURSELF OUT.
WHY WOULD THEY SAY YOU KILLED YOUR CLASSMATES ON TARIS?
IT WAS MY TEACHERS. THEY'RE IN SOME SECRET JEDI CABAL, WATCHING FOR THE RETURN OF THE SITH.
WHEN THEY HAD A PROPHECY THAT ONE OF US WOULD BRING DOWN THE ORDER, THEY DID SOMETHING ABOUT IT.
THAT'S MY LIFE.
I NEVER GAVE THEM ANY REASON TO THINK I'D BE CAPABLE OF EVIL-- BUT THEY'VE BEEN HUNTING ME EVER SINCE.
WAIT. YOU'RE SAYING YOUR MASTERS KILLED THEIR OWN STUDENTS? AND FRAMED YOU?
THAT'S LUDICROUS! THAT'S--

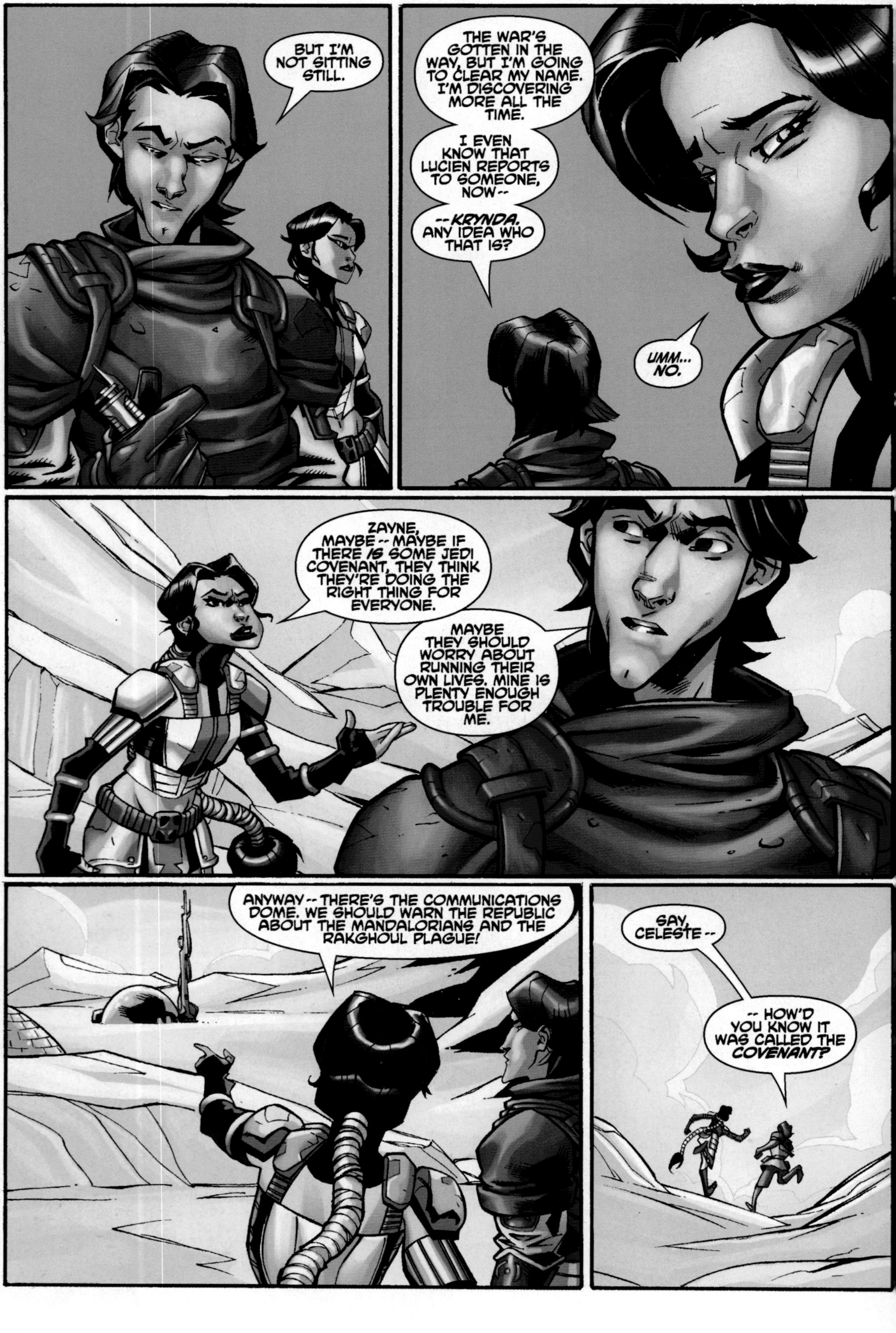
BUT I'M NOT SITTING STILL.
THE WAR'S GOTTEN IN THE WAY, BUT I'M GOING TO CLEAR MY NAME. I'M DISCOVERING MORE ALL THE TIME.
I EVEN KNOW THAT LUCIEN REPORTS TO SOMEONE, NOW--
--KRYNDA. ANY IDEA WHO THAT IS?
UMM... NO.
ZAYNE, MAYBE--MAYBE IF THERE IS SOME JEDI COVENANT, THEY THINK THEY'RE DOING THE RIGHT THING FOR EVERYONE.
MAYBE THEY SHOULD WORRY ABOUT RUNNING THEIR OWN LIVES. MINE IS PLENTY ENOUGH TROUBLE FOR ME.
ANYWAY--THERE'S THE COMMUNICATIONS DOME. WE SHOULD WARN THE REPUBLIC ABOUT THE MANDALORIANS AND THE RAKGHOUL PLAGUE!
SAY, CELESTE--
--HOW'D YOU KNOW IT WAS CALLED THE COVENANT?

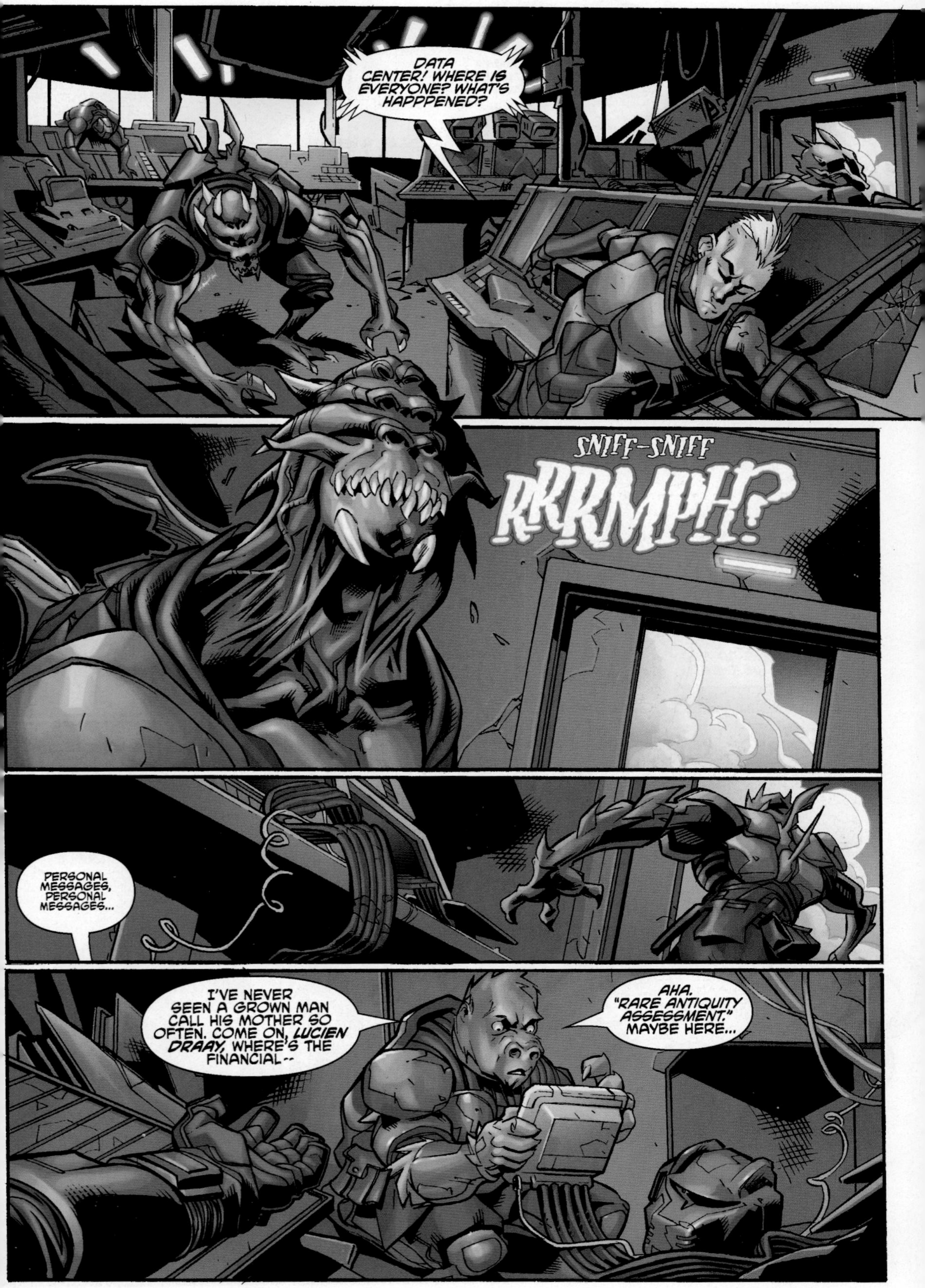
DATA CENTER! WHERE IS EVERYONE? WHAT'S HAPPPENED?
SNIFF-SNIFF
RRRMPH?
PERSONAL MESSAGES, PERSONAL MESSAGES...
I'VE NEVER SEEN A GROWN MAN CALL HIS MOTHER SO OFTEN. COME ON, LUCIEN DRAAY, WHERE'S THE FINANCIAL--
AHA. "RARE ANTIQUITY ASSESSMENT." MAYBE HERE...

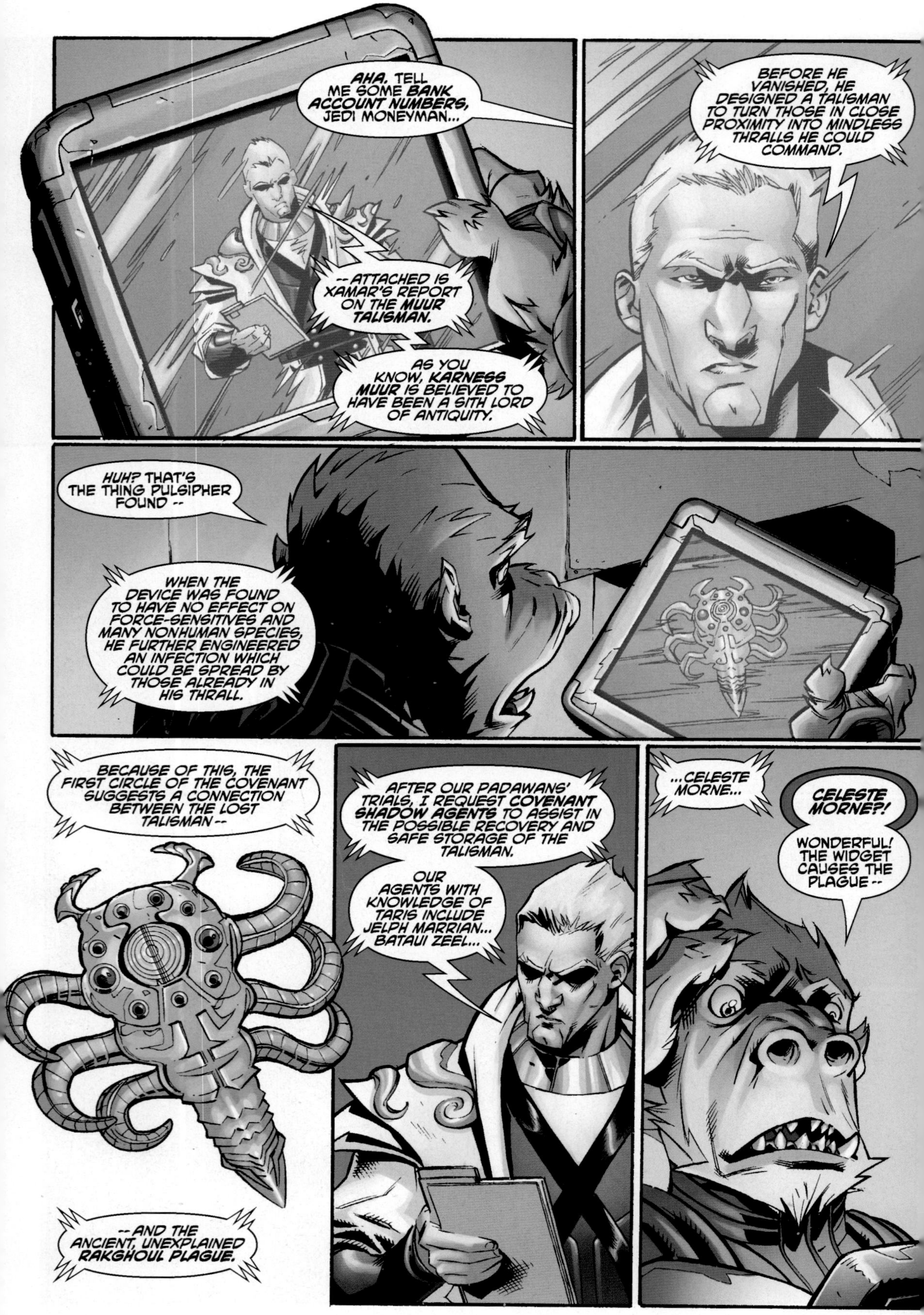

AHA. TELL ME SOME BANK ACCOUNT NUMBERS, JEDI MONEYMAN...
--ATTACHED IS XAMAR'S REPORT ON THE MUUR TALISMAN.
AS YOU KNOW, KARNESS MUUR IS BELIEVED TO HAVE BEEN A SITH LORD OF ANTIQUITY.
BEFORE HE VANISHED, HE DESIGNED A TALISMAN TO TURN THOSE IN CLOSE PROXIMITY INTO MINDLESS THRALLS HE COULD COMMAND.
HUH? THAT'S THE THING PULSIPHER FOUND --
WHEN THE DEVICE WAS FOUND TO HAVE NO EFFECT ON FORCE-SENSITIVES AND MANY NONHUMAN SPECIES, HE FURTHER ENGINEERED AN INFECTION WHICH COULD BE SPREAD BY THOSE ALREADY IN HIS THRALL.
BECAUSE OF THIS, THE FIRST CIRCLE OF THE COVENANT SUGGESTS A CONNECTION BETWEEN THE LOST TALISMAN --
-- AND THE ANCIENT, UNEXPLAINED RAKGHOUL PLAGUE.
AFTER OUR PADAWANS' TRIALS, I REQUEST COVENANT SHADOW AGENTS TO ASSIST IN THE POSSIBLE RECOVERY AND SAFE STORAGE OF THE TALISMAN.
OUR AGENTS WITH KNOWLEDGE OF TARIS INCLUDE JELPH MARRIAN... BATAUI ZEEL...
...CELESTE MORNE...
CELESTE MORNE?!
WONDERFUL! THE WIDGET CAUSES THE PLAGUE --

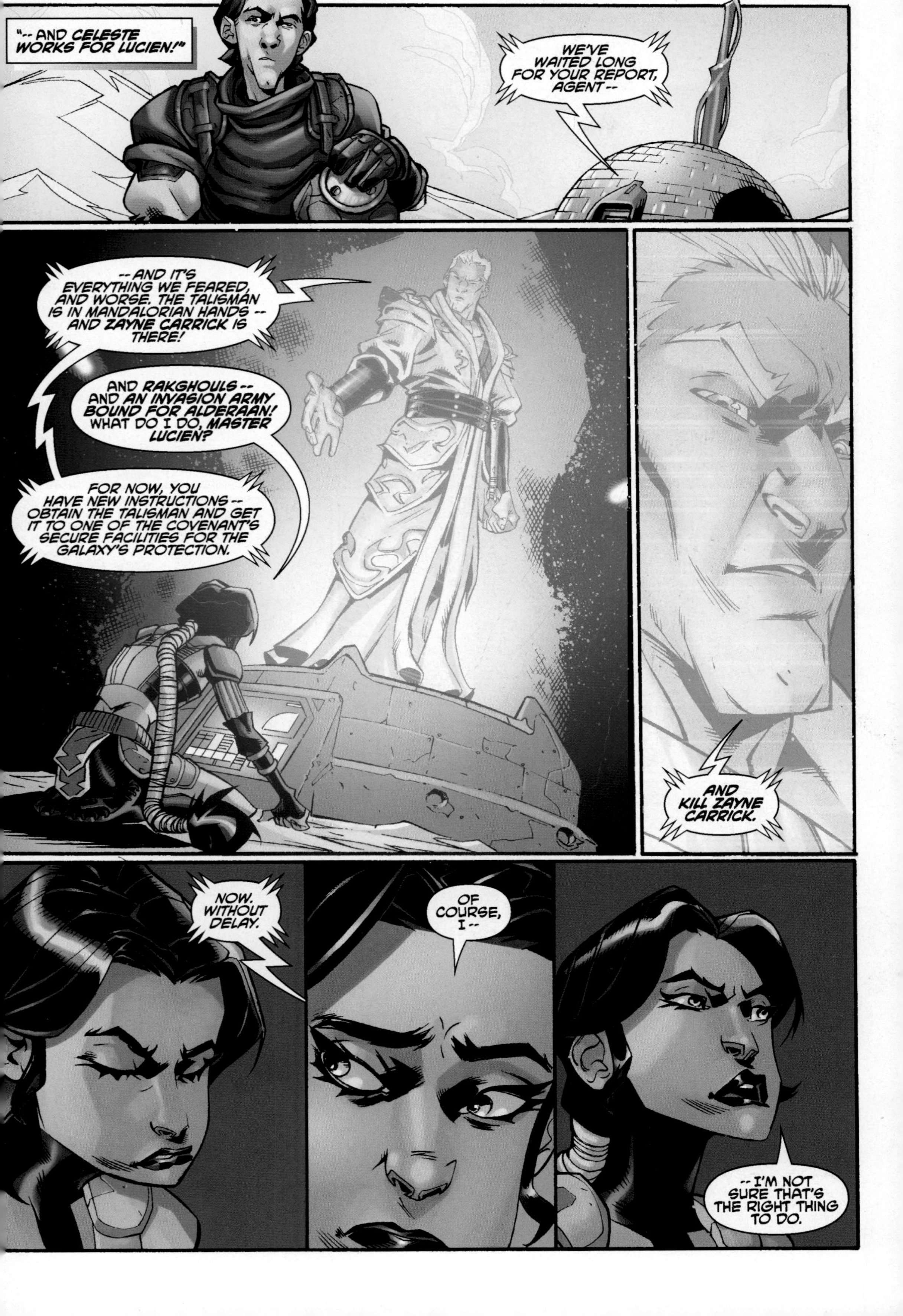
"-- AND CELESTE WORKS FOR LUCIEN!"
WE'VE WAITED LONG FOR YOUR REPORT, AGENT --
-- AND IT'S EVERYTHING WE FEARED, AND WORSE. THE TALISMAN IS IN MANDALORIAN HANDS -- AND ZAYNE CARRICK IS THERE!
AND RAKGHOULS -- AND AN INVASION ARMY BOUND FOR ALDERAAN! WHAT DO I DO, MASTER LUCIEN?
FOR NOW, YOU HAVE NEW INSTRUCTIONS -- OBTAIN THE TALISMAN AND GET IT TO ONE OF THE COVENANT'S SECURE FACILITIES FOR THE GALAXY'S PROTECTION.
AND KILL ZAYNE CARRICK.
NOW. WITHOUT DELAY.
OF COURSE, I --
-- I'M NOT SURE THAT'S THE RIGHT THING TO DO.

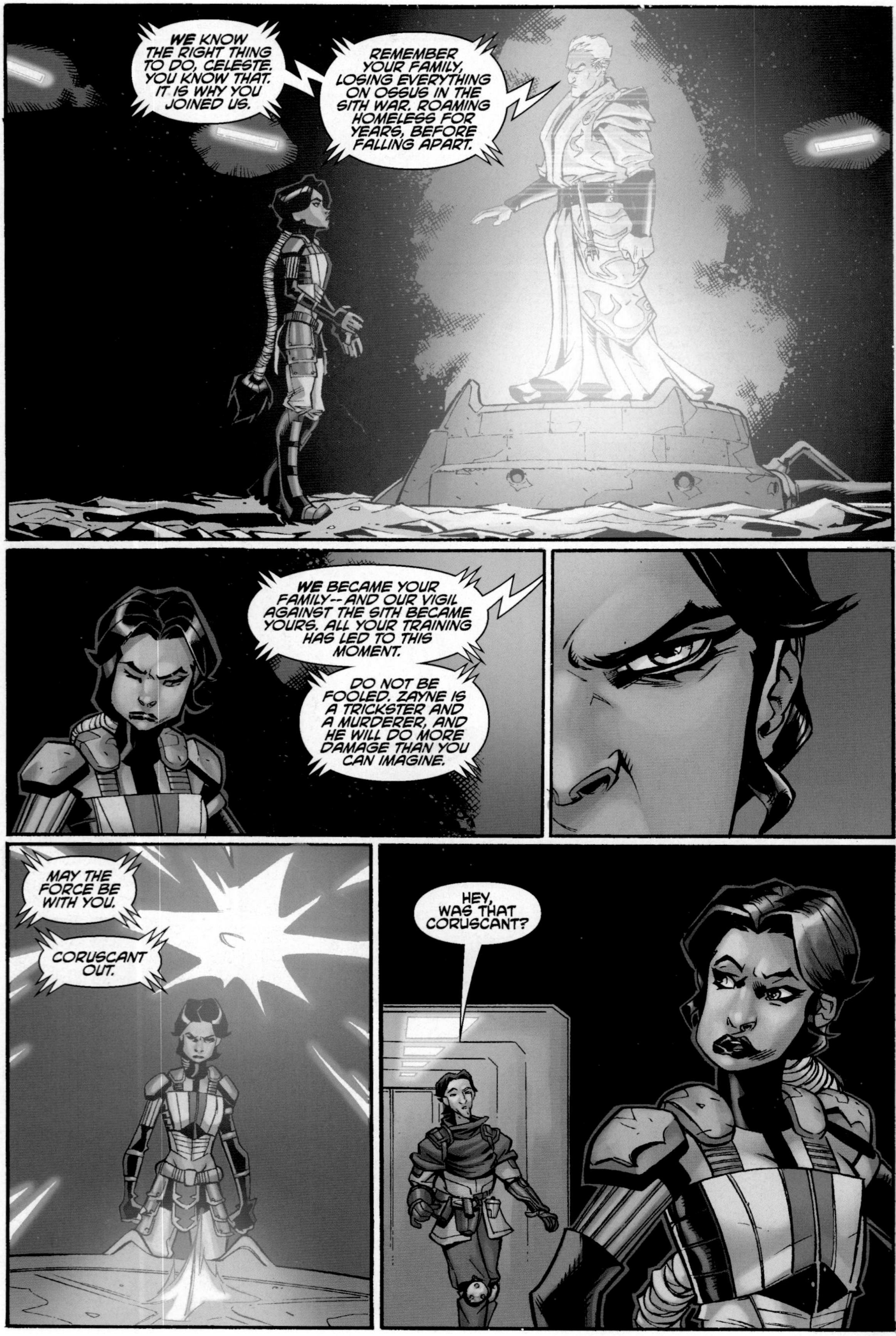
WE KNOW THE RIGHT THING TO DO, CELESTE. YOU KNOW THAT. IT IS WHY YOU JOINED US.
REMEMBER YOUR FAMILY, LOSING EVERYTHING ON OSSUS IN THE SITH WAR. ROAMING HOMELESS FOR YEARS, BEFORE FALLING APART.
WE BECAME YOUR FAMILY-- AND OUR VIGIL AGAINST THE SITH BECAME YOURS. ALL YOUR TRAINING HAS LED TO THIS MOMENT.
DO NOT BE FOOLED. ZAYNE IS A TRICKSTER AND A MURDERER, AND HE WILL DO MORE DAMAGE THAN YOU CAN IMAGINE.
MAY THE FORCE BE WITH YOU.
CORUSCANT OUT.
HEY, WAS THAT CORUSCANT?

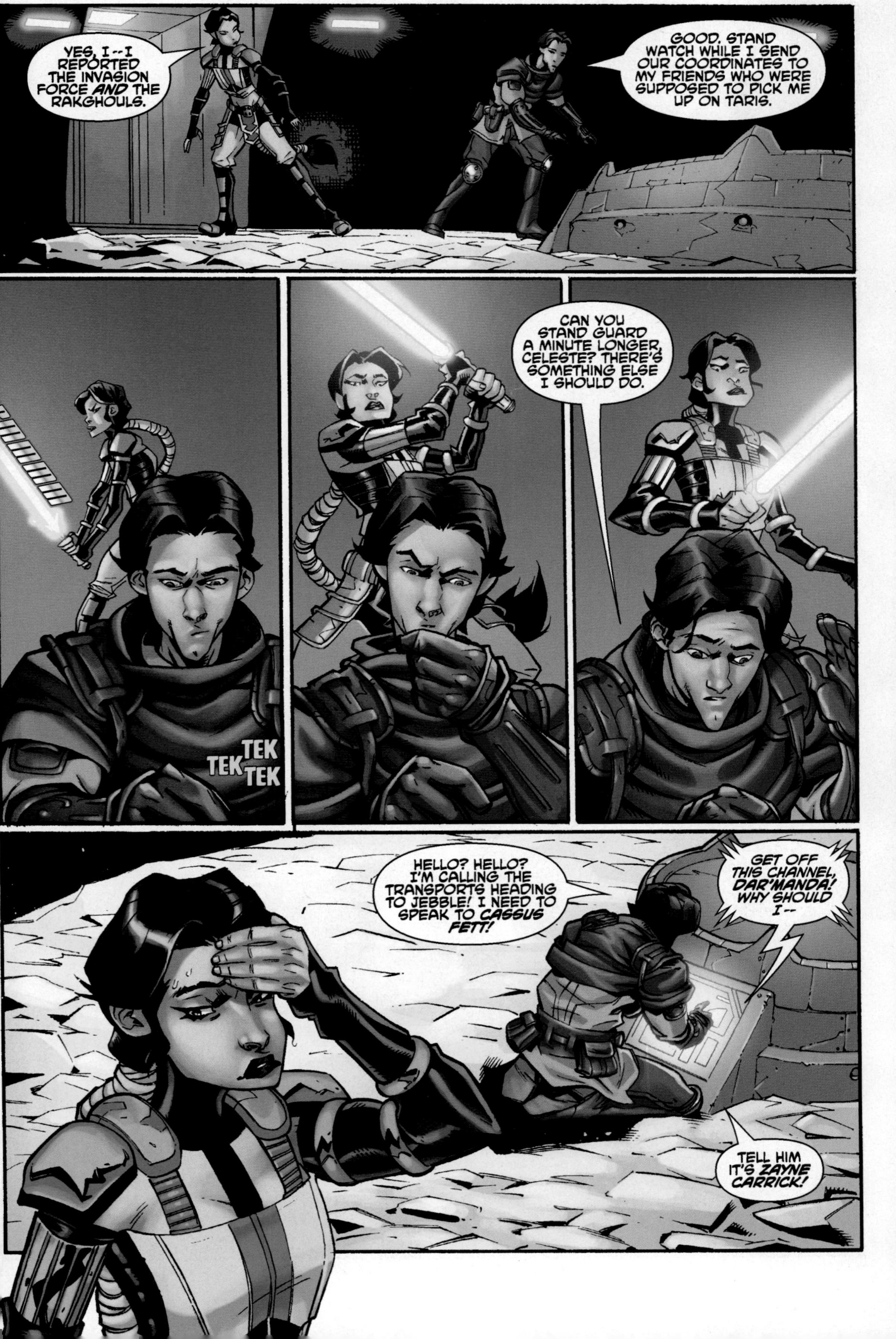
YES, I--I REPORTED THE INVASION FORCE AND THE RAKGHOULS.
GOOD. STAND WATCH WHILE I SEND OUR COORDINATES TO MY FRIENDS WHO WERE SUPPOSED TO PICK ME UP ON TARIS.
TEK TEK TEK
CAN YOU STAND GUARD A MINUTE LONGER, CELESTE? THERE'S SOMETHING ELSE I SHOULD DO.
HELLO? HELLO? I'M CALLING THE TRANSPORTS HEADING TO JEBBLE! I NEED TO SPEAK TO CASSUS FETT!
GET OFF THIS CHANNEL, DAR'MANDA! WHY SHOULD I--
TELL HIM IT'S ZAYNE CARRICK!

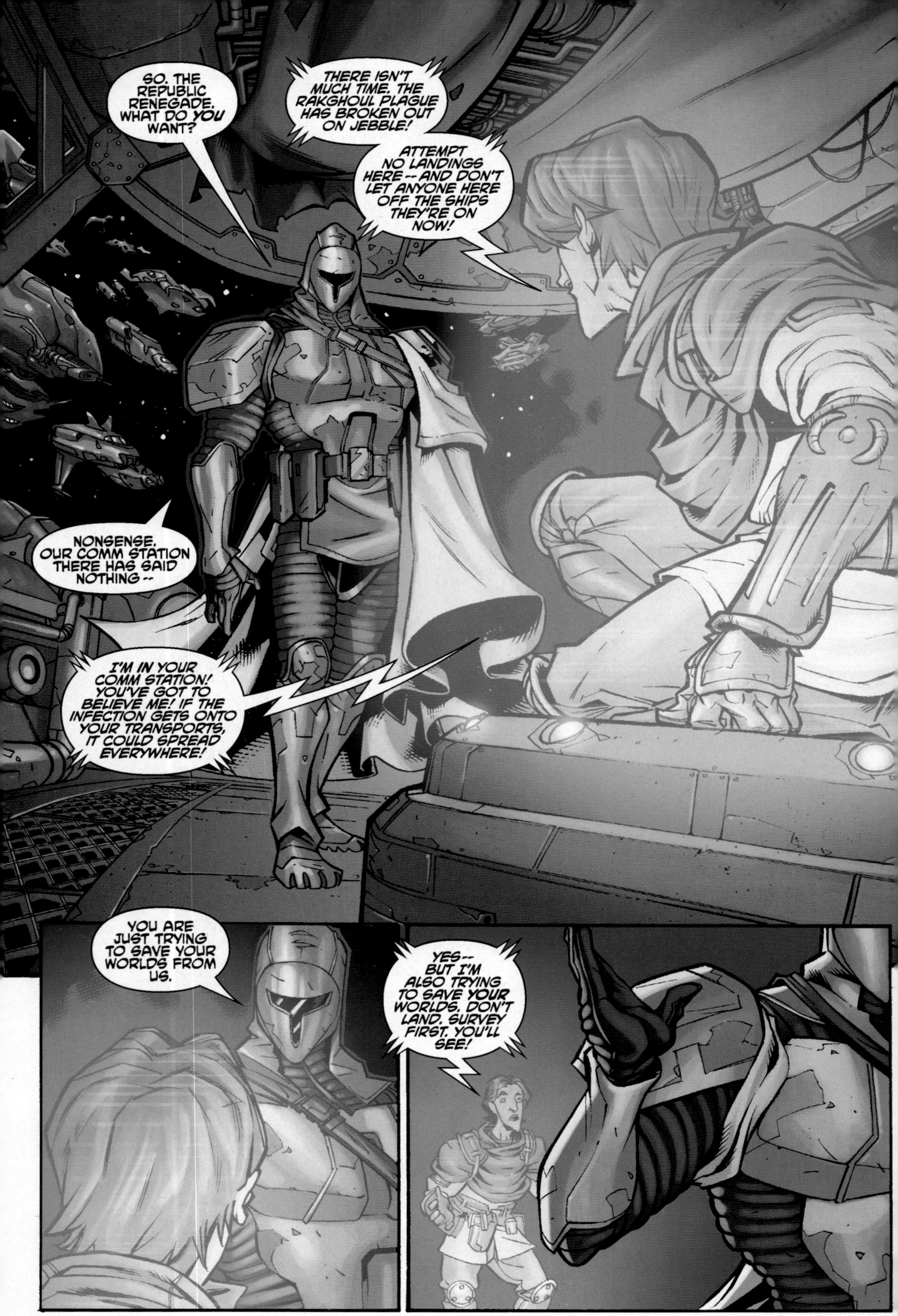
SO, THE REPUBLIC RENEGADE. WHAT DO YOU WANT?
THERE ISN'T MUCH TIME. THE RAKGHOUL PLAGUE HAS BROKEN OUT ON JEBBLE!
ATTEMPT NO LANDINGS HERE -- AND DON'T LET ANYONE HERE OFF THE SHIPS THEY'RE ON NOW!
NONSENSE. OUR COMM STATION THERE HAS SAID NOTHING --
I'M IN YOUR COMM STATION! YOU'VE GOT TO BELIEVE ME! IF THE INFECTION GETS ONTO YOUR TRANSPORTS, IT COULD SPREAD EVERYWHERE!
YOU ARE JUST TRYING TO SAVE YOUR WORLDS FROM US.
YES -- BUT I'M ALSO TRYING TO SAVE YOUR WORLDS. DON'T LAND. SURVEY FIRST. YOU'LL SEE!

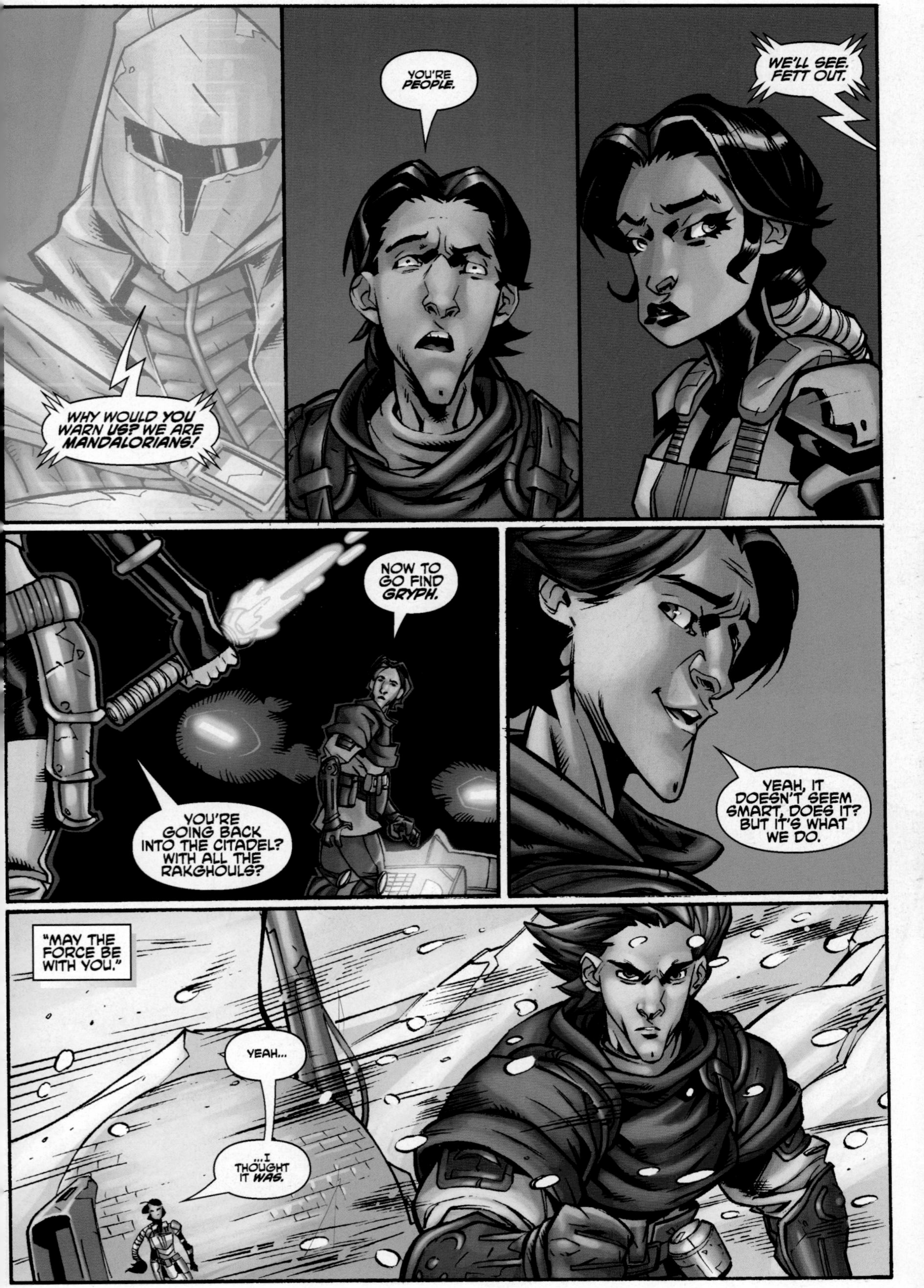
WHY WOULD YOU WARN US? WE ARE MANDALORIANS!
YOU'RE PEOPLE.
WE'LL SEE. FETT OUT.
NOW TO GO FIND GRYPH.
YOU'RE GOING BACK INTO THE CITADEL? WITH ALL THE RAKGHOULS?
YEAH, IT DOESN'T SEEM SMART, DOES IT? BUT IT'S WHAT WE DO.
"MAY THE FORCE BE WITH YOU."
YEAH...
...I THOUGHT IT WAS.

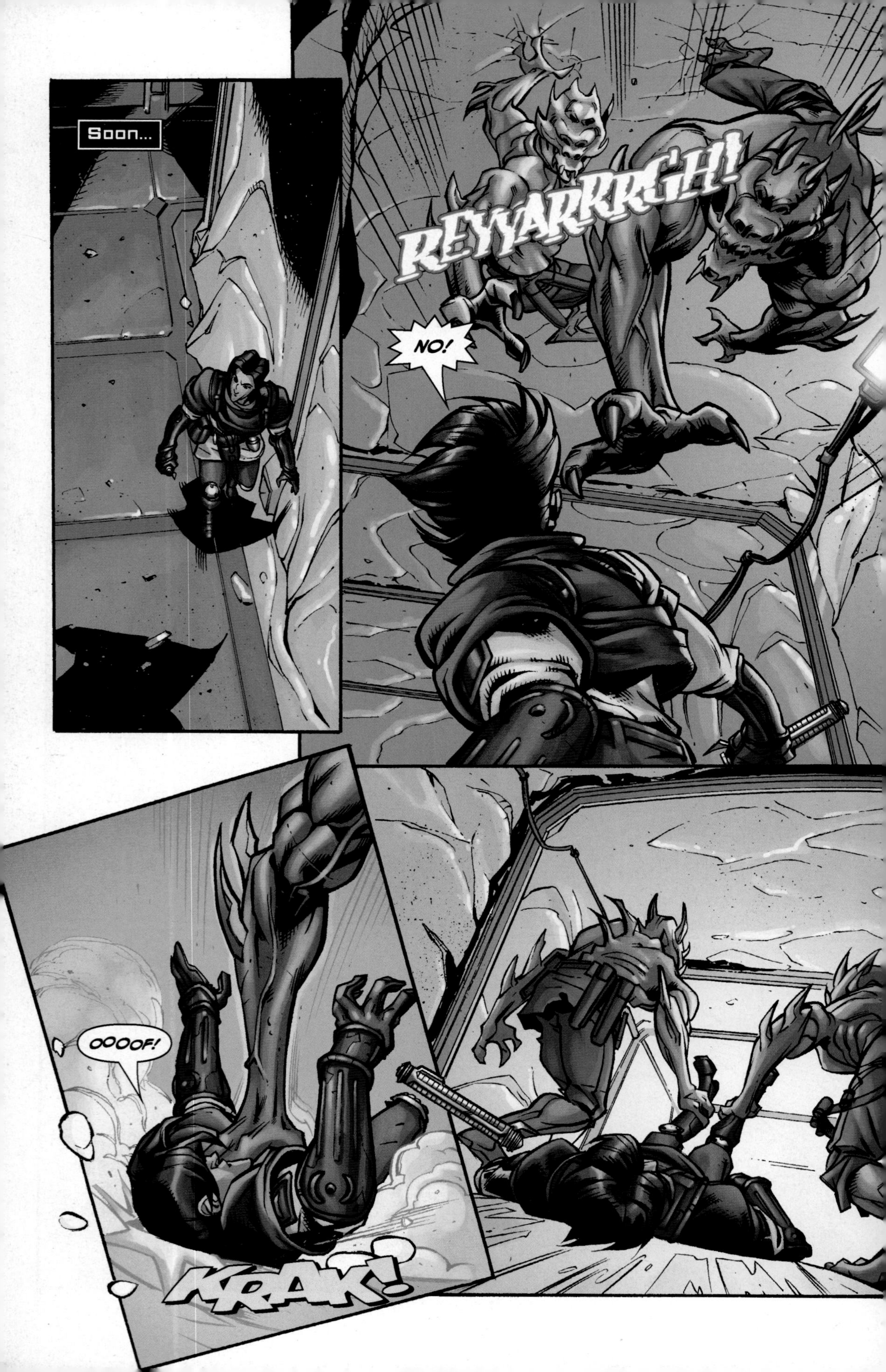
Soon...
REYYARRRGH!
NO!
OOOOF!
KRAK!

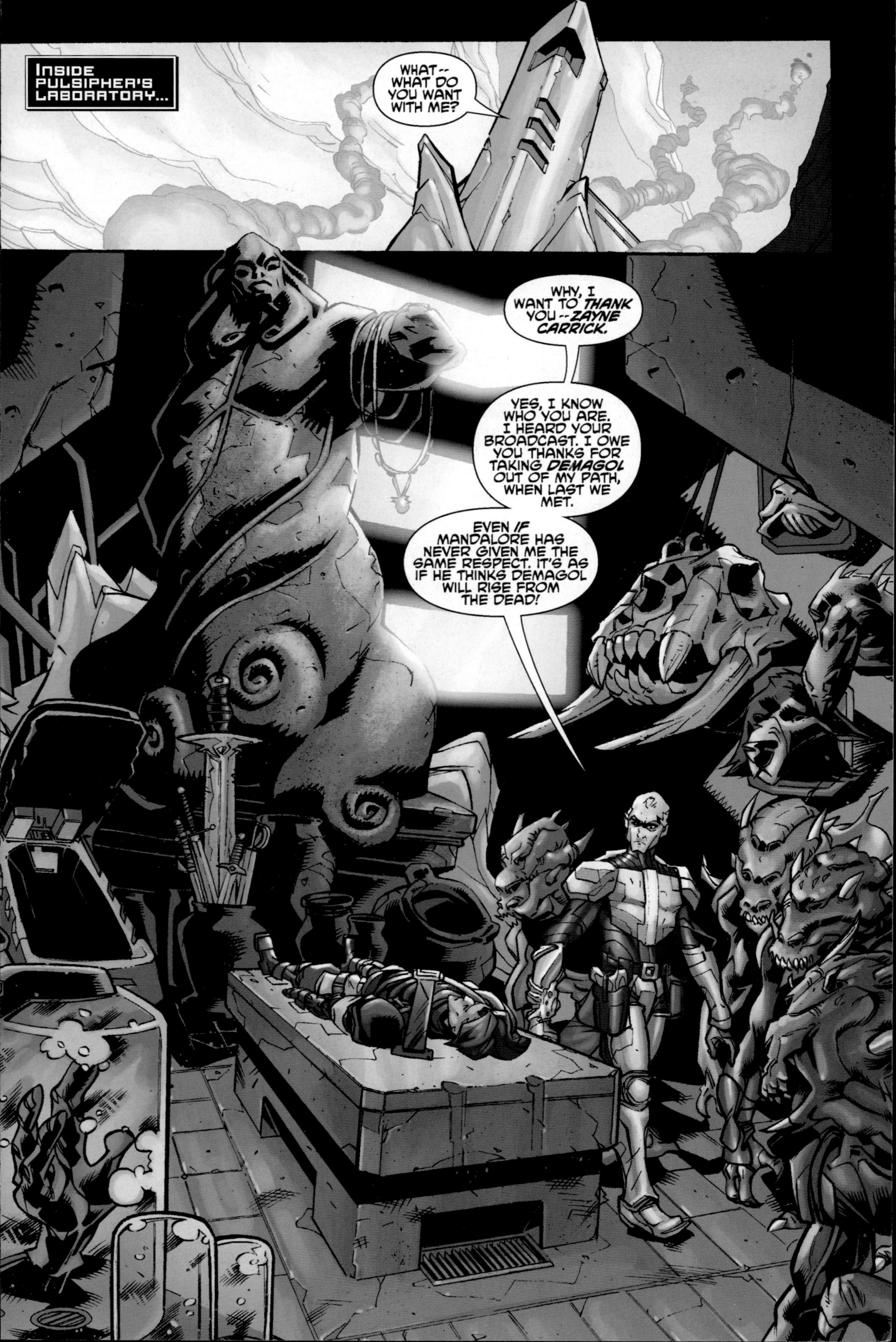
INSIDE PULSIPHER'S LABORATORY...
WHAT-- WHAT DO YOU WANT WITH ME?
WHY, I WANT TO THANK YOU--ZAYNE CARRICK.
YES, I KNOW WHO YOU ARE. I HEARD YOUR BROADCAST. I OWE YOU THANKS FOR TAKING DEMAGOL OUT OF MY PATH, WHEN LAST WE MET.
EVEN IF MANDALORE HAS NEVER GIVEN ME THE SAME RESPECT. IT'S AS IF HE THINKS DEMAGOL WILL RISE FROM THE DEAD!

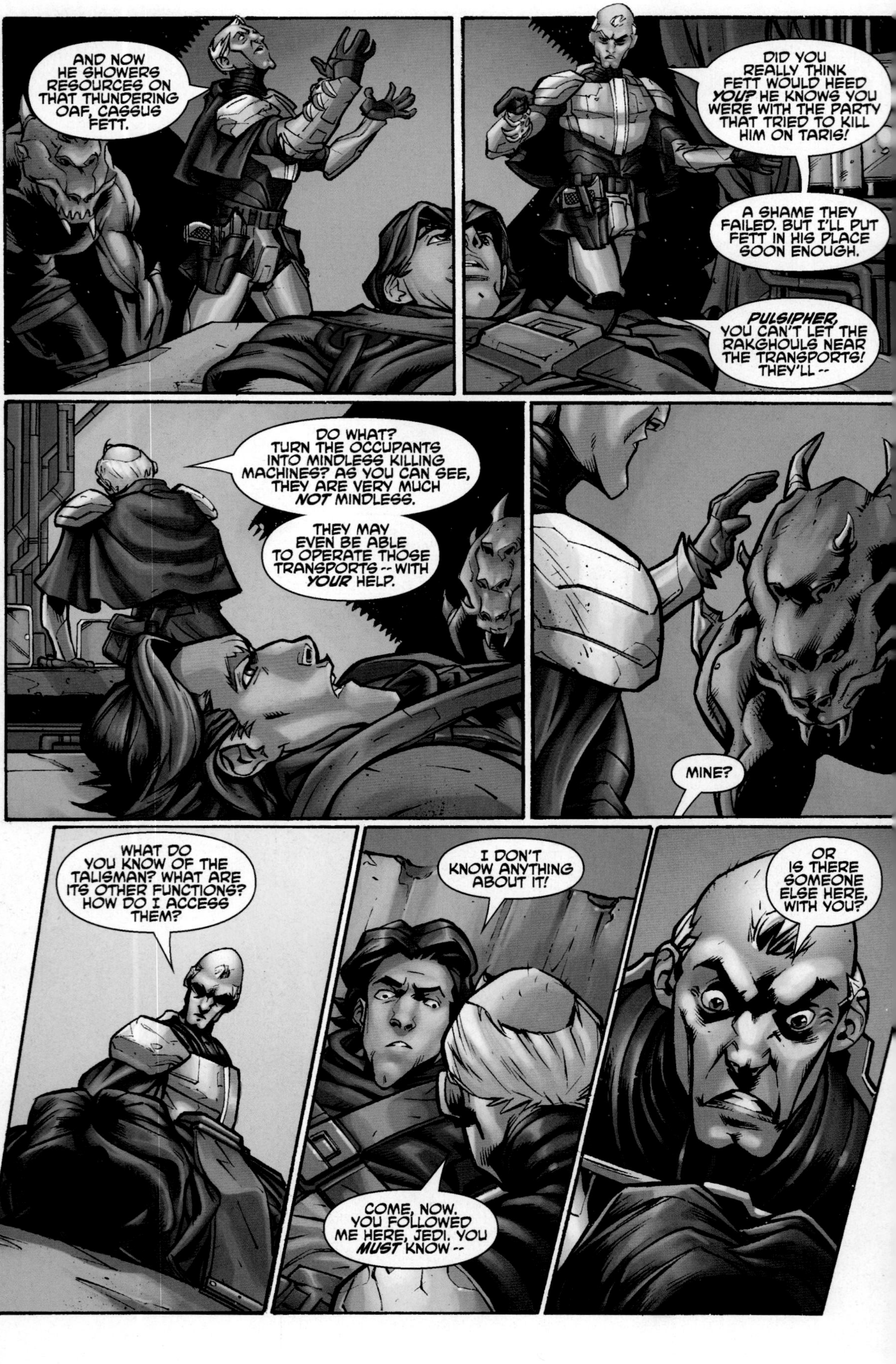
AND NOW HE SHOWERS RESOURCES ON THAT THUNDERING OAF, CASSUS FETT.
DID YOU REALLY THINK FETT WOULD HEED *YOU?* HE KNOWS YOU WERE WITH THE PARTY THAT TRIED TO KILL HIM ON TARIS!
A SHAME THEY FAILED. BUT I'LL PUT FETT IN HIS PLACE SOON ENOUGH.
PULSIPHER, YOU CAN'T LET THE RAKGHOULS NEAR THE TRANSPORTS! THEY'LL --
DO WHAT? TURN THE OCCUPANTS INTO MINDLESS KILLING MACHINES? AS YOU CAN SEE, THEY ARE VERY MUCH *NOT* MINDLESS.
THEY MAY EVEN BE ABLE TO OPERATE THOSE TRANSPORTS -- WITH *YOUR* HELP.
MINE?
WHAT DO YOU KNOW OF THE TALISMAN? WHAT ARE ITS OTHER FUNCTIONS? HOW DO I ACCESS THEM?
I DON'T KNOW ANYTHING ABOUT IT!
COME, NOW. YOU FOLLOWED ME HERE, JEDI. YOU *MUST* KNOW --
OR IS THERE SOMEONE ELSE HERE, WITH YOU?

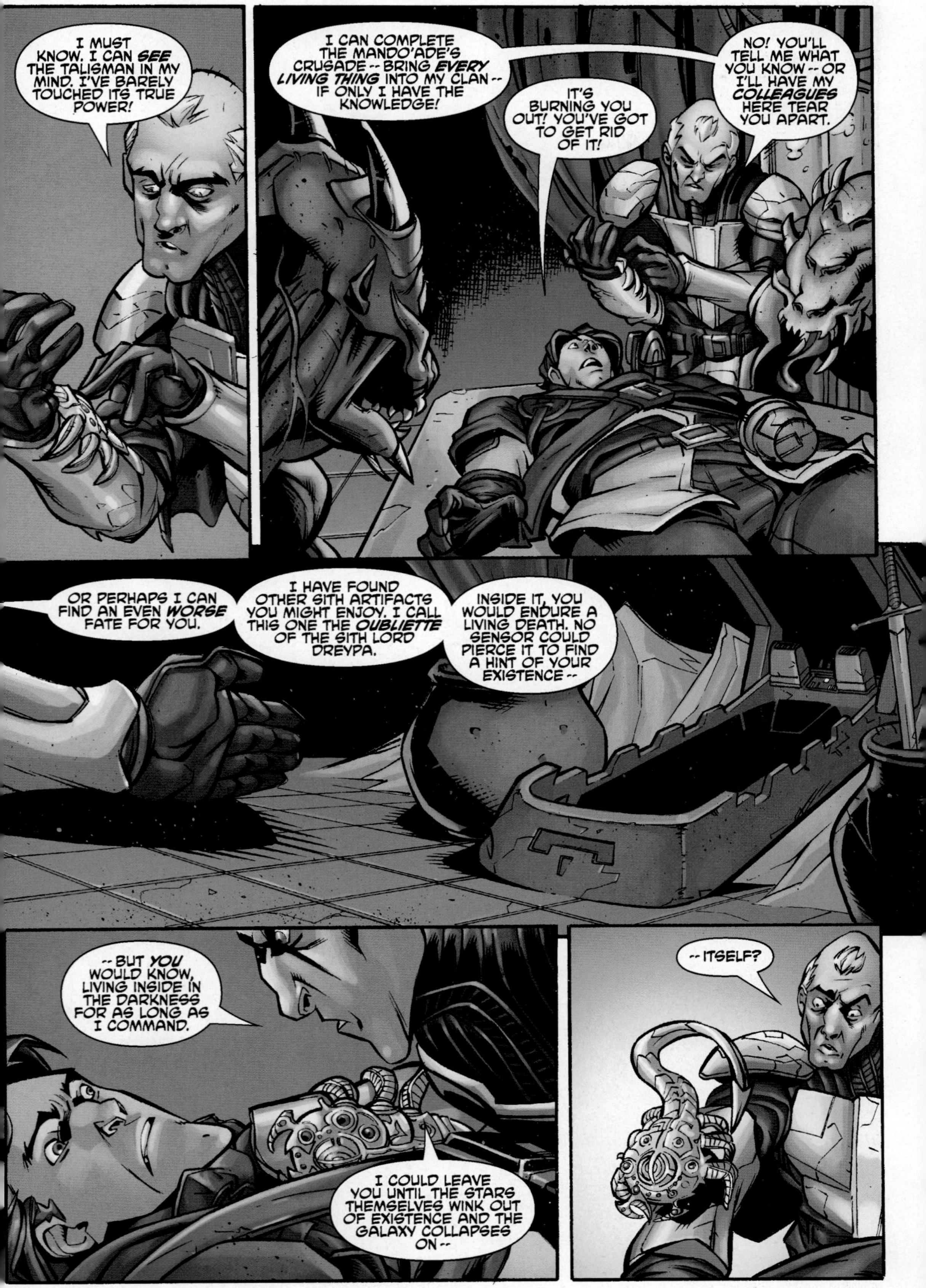
I MUST KNOW. I CAN SEE THE TALISMAN IN MY MIND. I'VE BARELY TOUCHED ITS TRUE POWER!
I CAN COMPLETE THE MANDO'ADE'S CRUSADE -- BRING EVERY LIVING THING INTO MY CLAN -- IF ONLY I HAVE THE KNOWLEDGE!
IT'S BURNING YOU OUT! YOU'VE GOT TO GET RID OF IT!
NO! YOU'LL TELL ME WHAT YOU KNOW -- OR I'LL HAVE MY COLLEAGUES HERE TEAR YOU APART.
OR PERHAPS I CAN FIND AN EVEN WORSE FATE FOR YOU.
I HAVE FOUND OTHER SITH ARTIFACTS YOU MIGHT ENJOY. I CALL THIS ONE THE OUBLIETTE OF THE SITH LORD DREYPA.
INSIDE IT, YOU WOULD ENDURE A LIVING DEATH. NO SENSOR COULD PIERCE IT TO FIND A HINT OF YOUR EXISTENCE --
-- BUT YOU WOULD KNOW, LIVING INSIDE IN THE DARKNESS FOR AS LONG AS I COMMAND.
I COULD LEAVE YOU UNTIL THE STARS THEMSELVES WINK OUT OF EXISTENCE AND THE GALAXY COLLAPSES ON --
-- ITSELF?

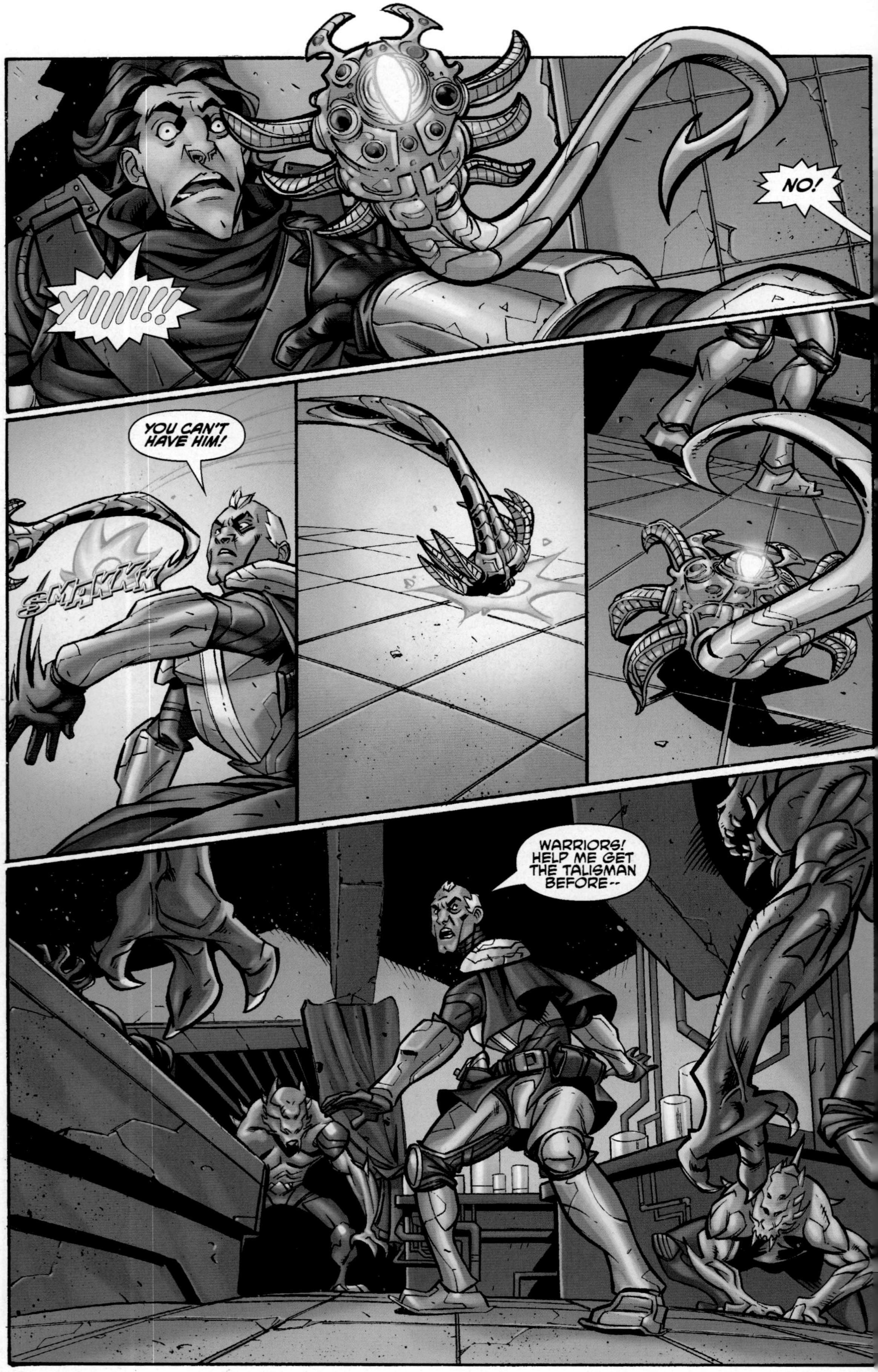
NO!
YIIII!!
YOU CAN'T HAVE HIM!
SMAKKK
WARRIORS! HELP ME GET THE TALISMAN BEFORE--

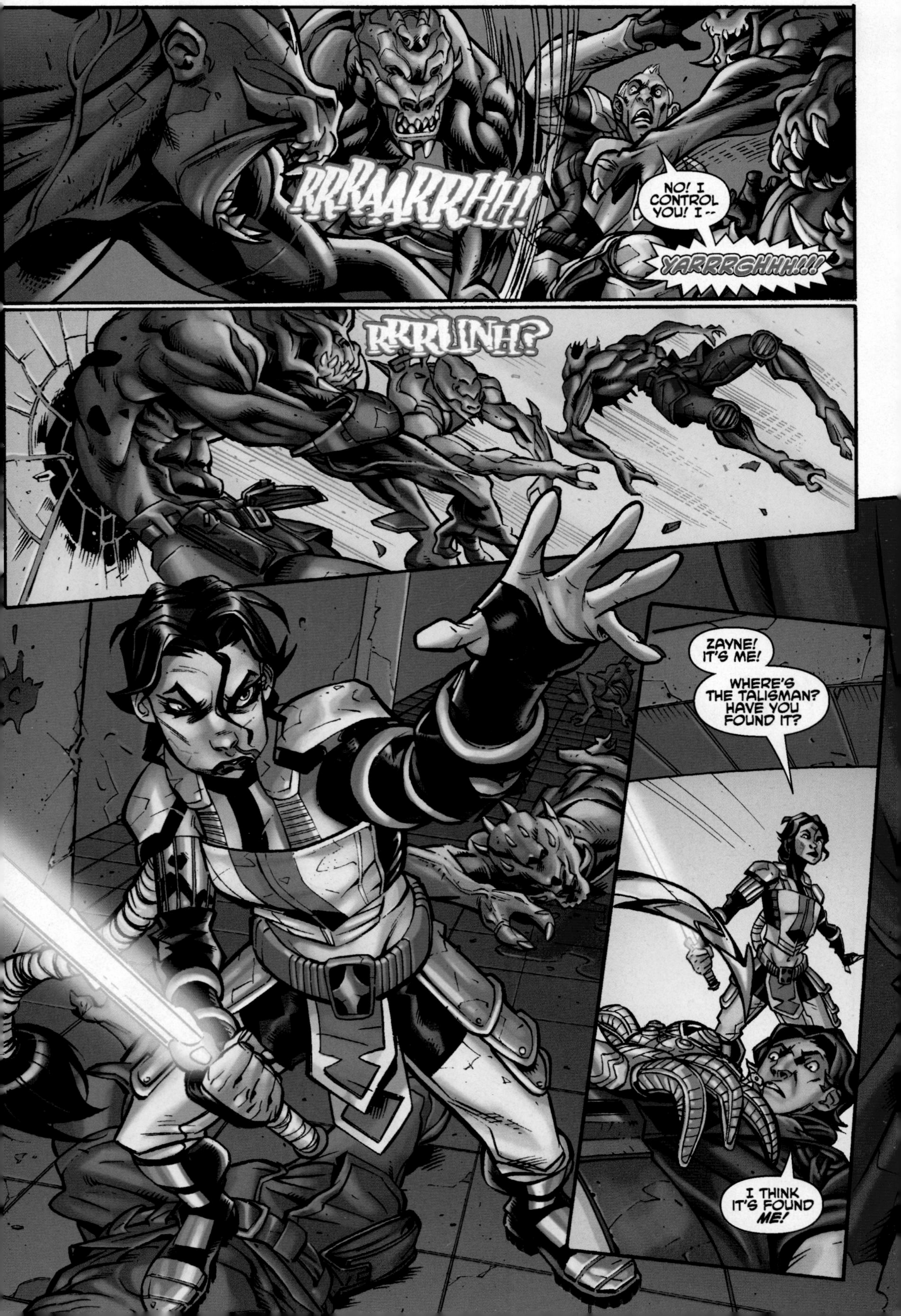
RRRAAARRHH!!
NO! I CONTROL YOU! I --
YARRRGHHH!!!
RRRUNH?
ZAYNE! IT'S ME!
WHERE'S THE TALISMAN? HAVE YOU FOUND IT?
I THINK IT'S FOUND *ME!*

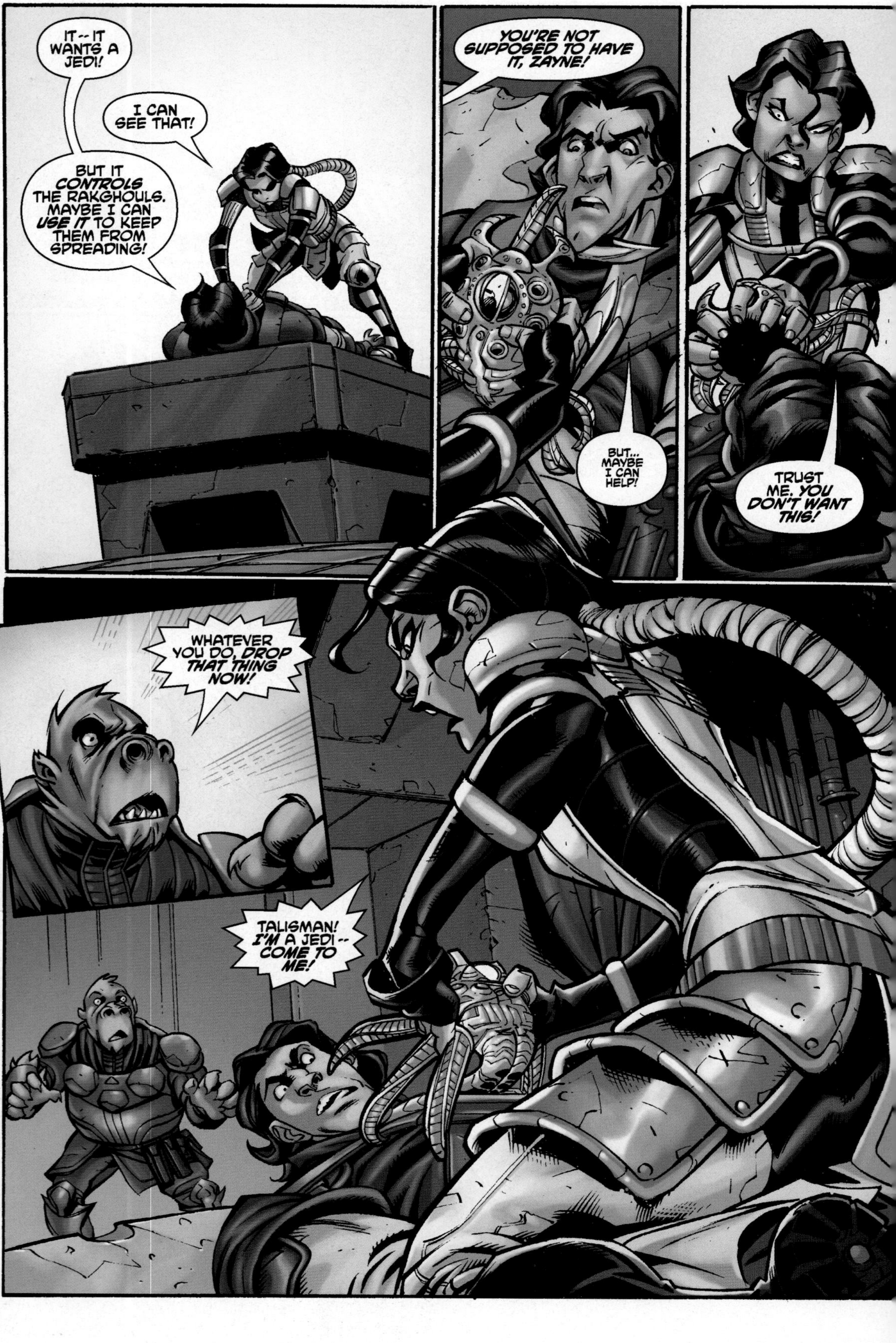

IT -- IT WANTS A JEDI!
I CAN SEE THAT!
BUT IT CONTROLS THE RAKGHOULS. MAYBE I CAN USE IT TO KEEP THEM FROM SPREADING!
YOU'RE NOT SUPPOSED TO HAVE IT, ZAYNE!
BUT... MAYBE I CAN HELP!
TRUST ME. YOU DON'T WANT THIS!
WHATEVER YOU DO, DROP THAT THING NOW!
TALISMAN! I'M A JEDI -- COME TO ME!

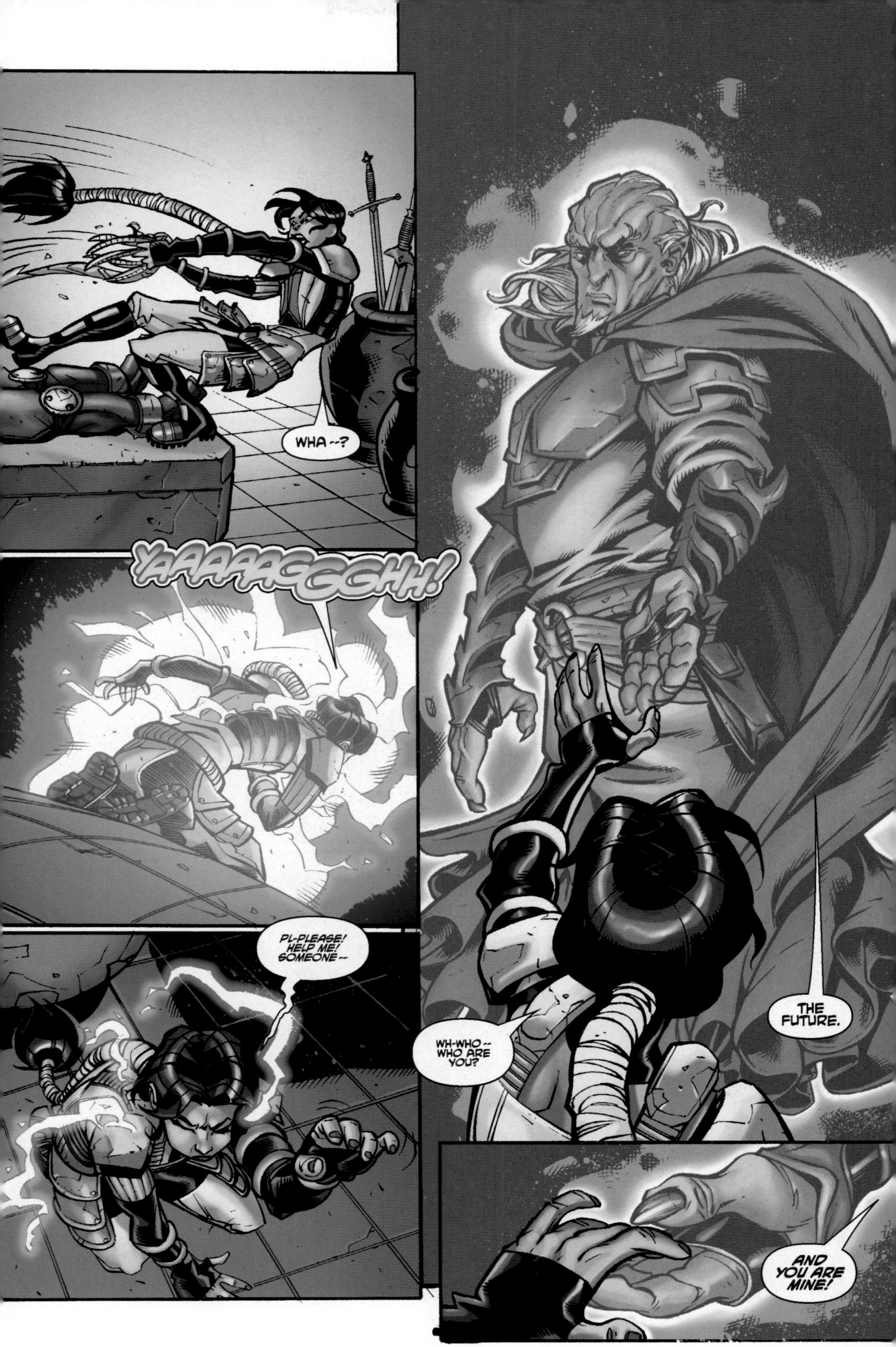
WHA--?
YAAAAAGGGHH!
PL-PLEASE! HELP ME! SOMEONE--
WH-WHO-- WHO ARE YOU?
THE FUTURE.
AND YOU ARE MINE!

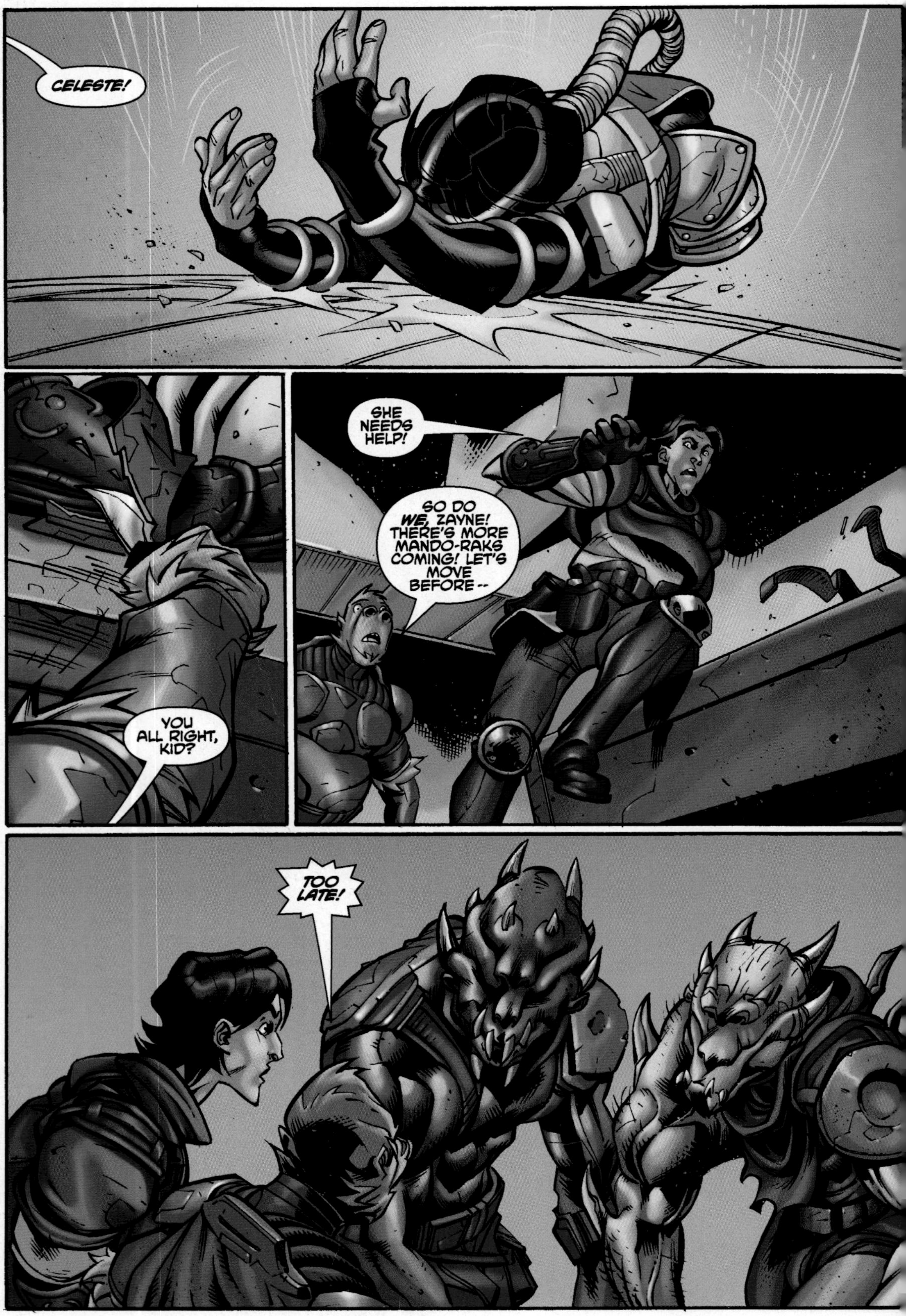
CELESTE!
SHE NEEDS HELP!
SO DO WE, ZAYNE! THERE'S MORE MANDO-RAKS COMING! LET'S MOVE BEFORE--
YOU ALL RIGHT, KID?
TOO LATE!

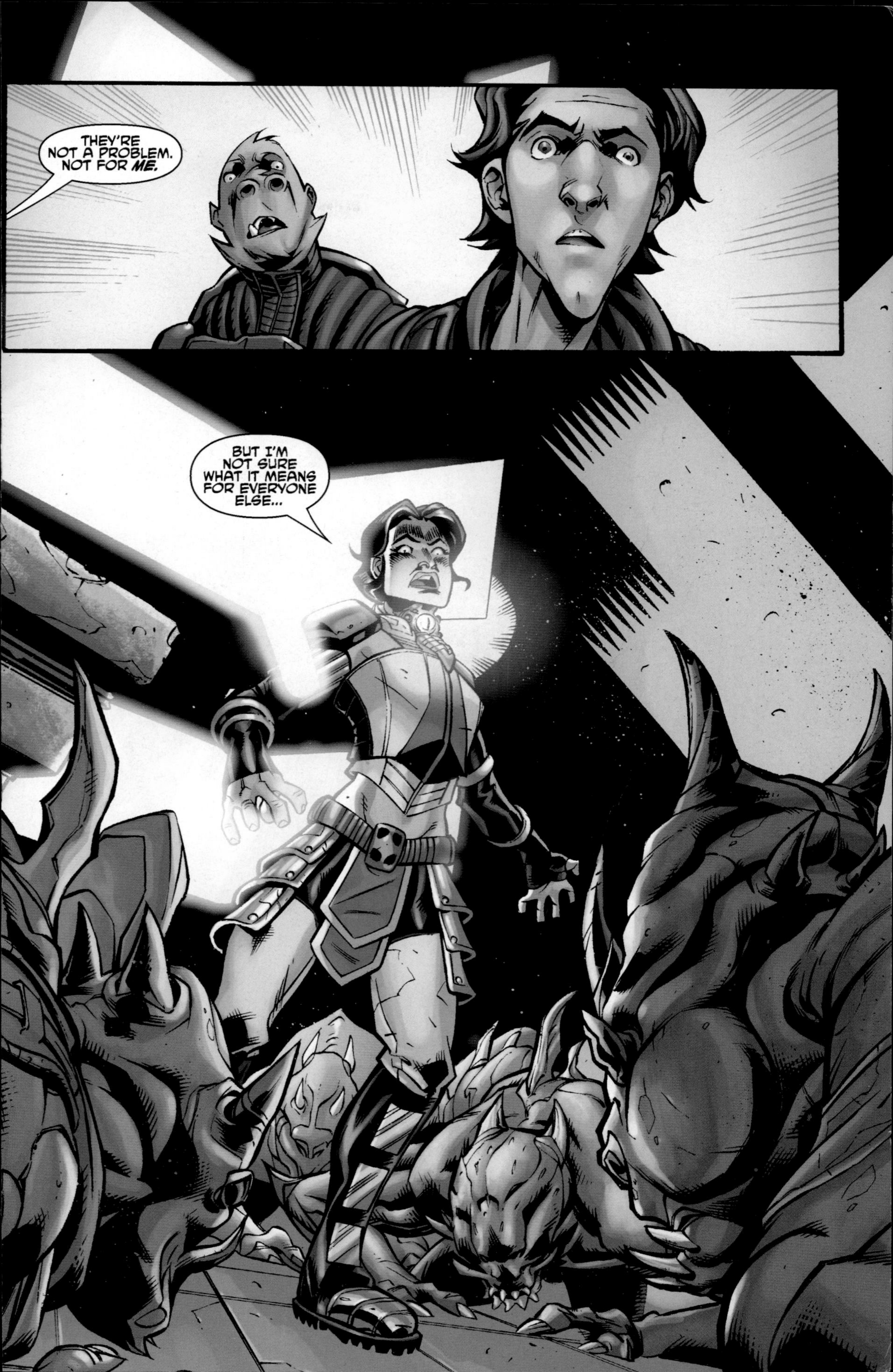
THEY'RE NOT A PROBLEM. NOT FOR *ME.*
BUT I'M NOT SURE WHAT IT MEANS FOR EVERYONE ELSE...

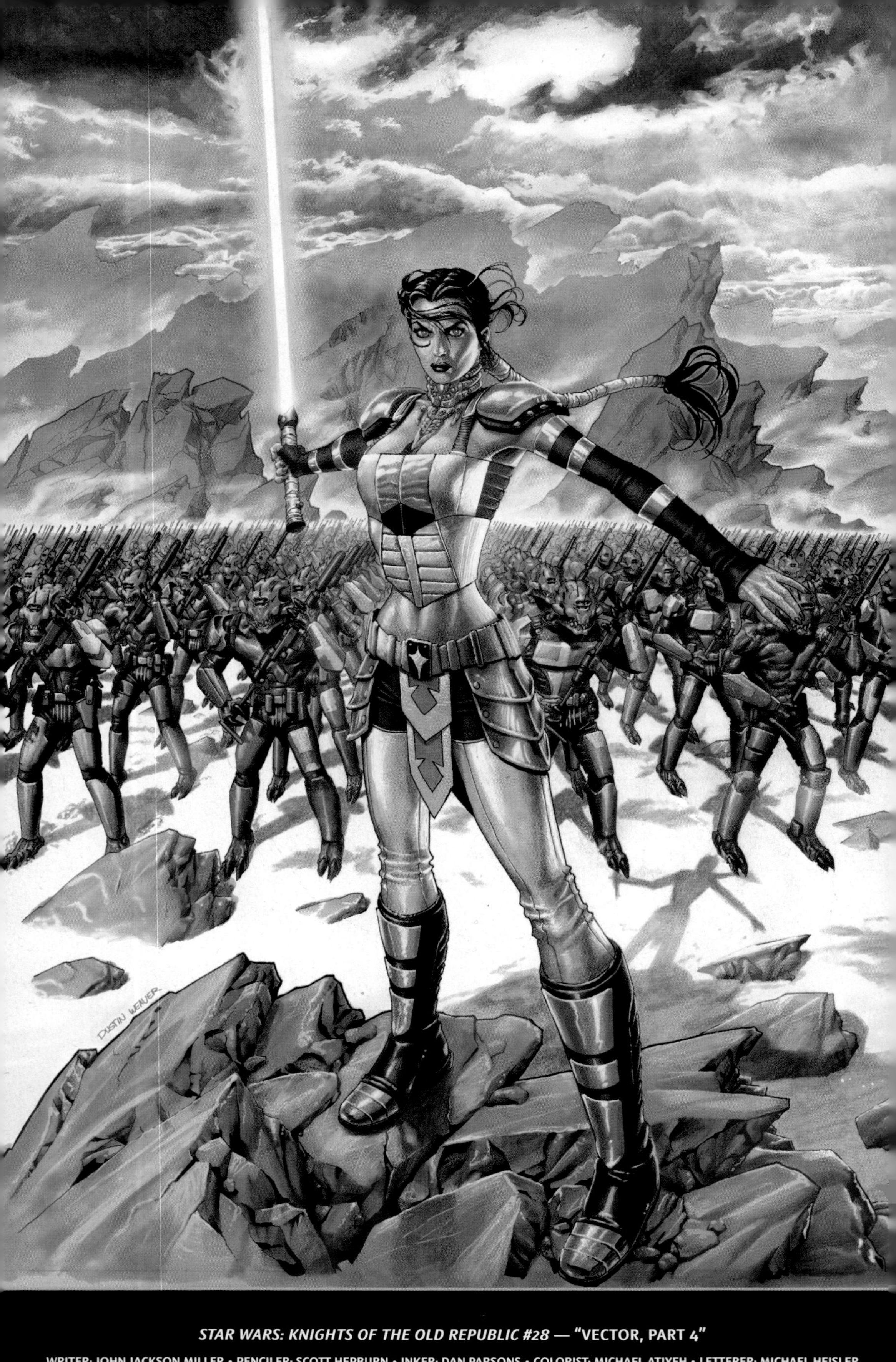
DUSTIN WEAVER

STAR WARS: KNIGHTS OF THE OLD REPUBLIC #28 — "VECTOR, PART 4"

WRITER: JOHN JACKSON MILLER • PENCILER: SCOTT HEPBURN • INKER: DAN PARSONS • COLORIST: MICHAEL ATIYEH • LETTERER: MICHAEL HEISLER
ASSISTANT EDITORS: FREDDYE LINS & DAVE MARSHALL • EDITOR: RANDY STRADLEY • COVER ARTIST: DUSTIN WEAVER

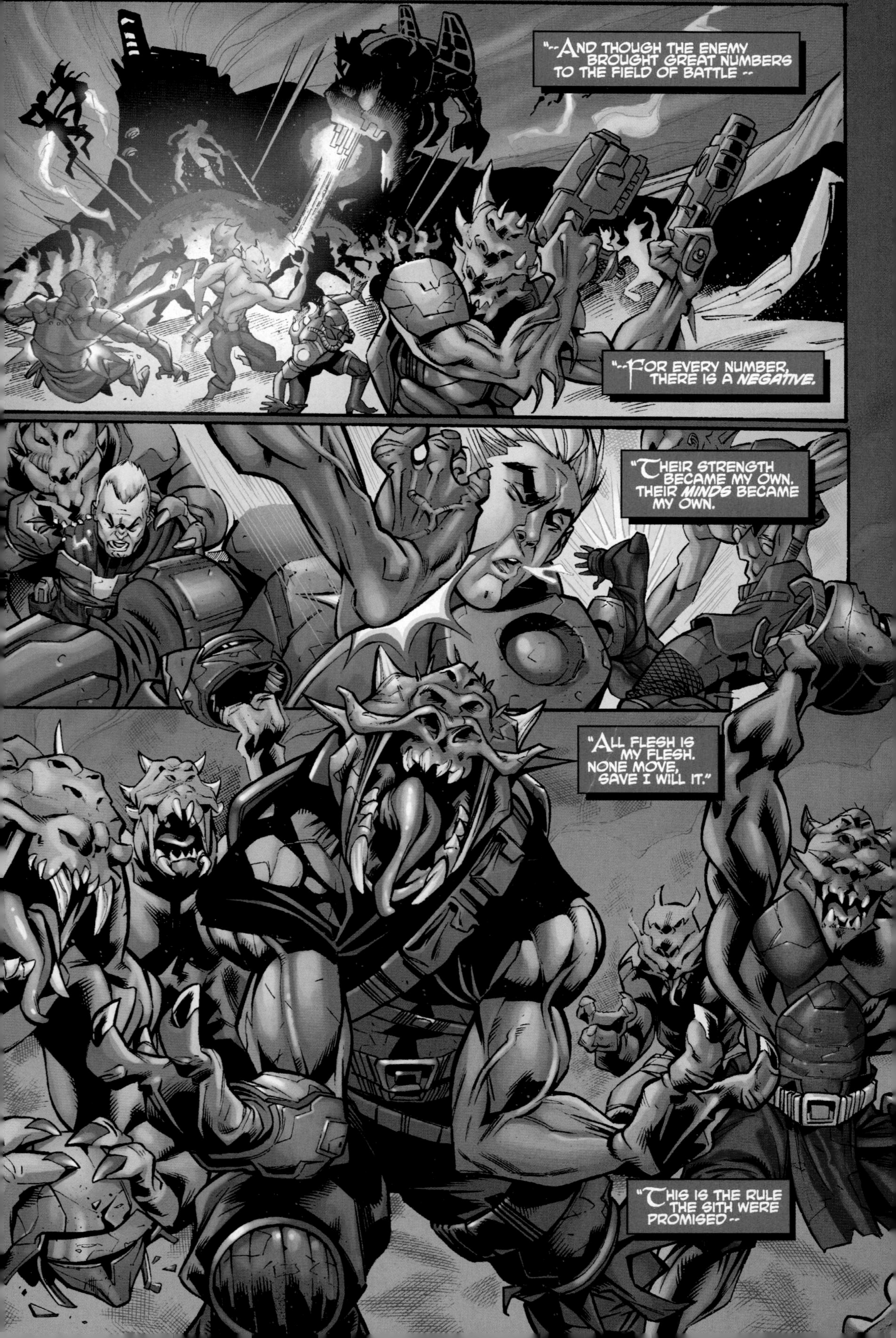
"--AND THOUGH THE ENEMY BROUGHT GREAT NUMBERS TO THE FIELD OF BATTLE --
"--FOR EVERY NUMBER, THERE IS A *NEGATIVE.*
"THEIR STRENGTH BECAME MY OWN. THEIR *MINDS* BECAME MY OWN.
"ALL FLESH IS MY FLESH. NONE MOVE, SAVE I WILL IT."
"THIS IS THE RULE THE SITH WERE PROMISED --

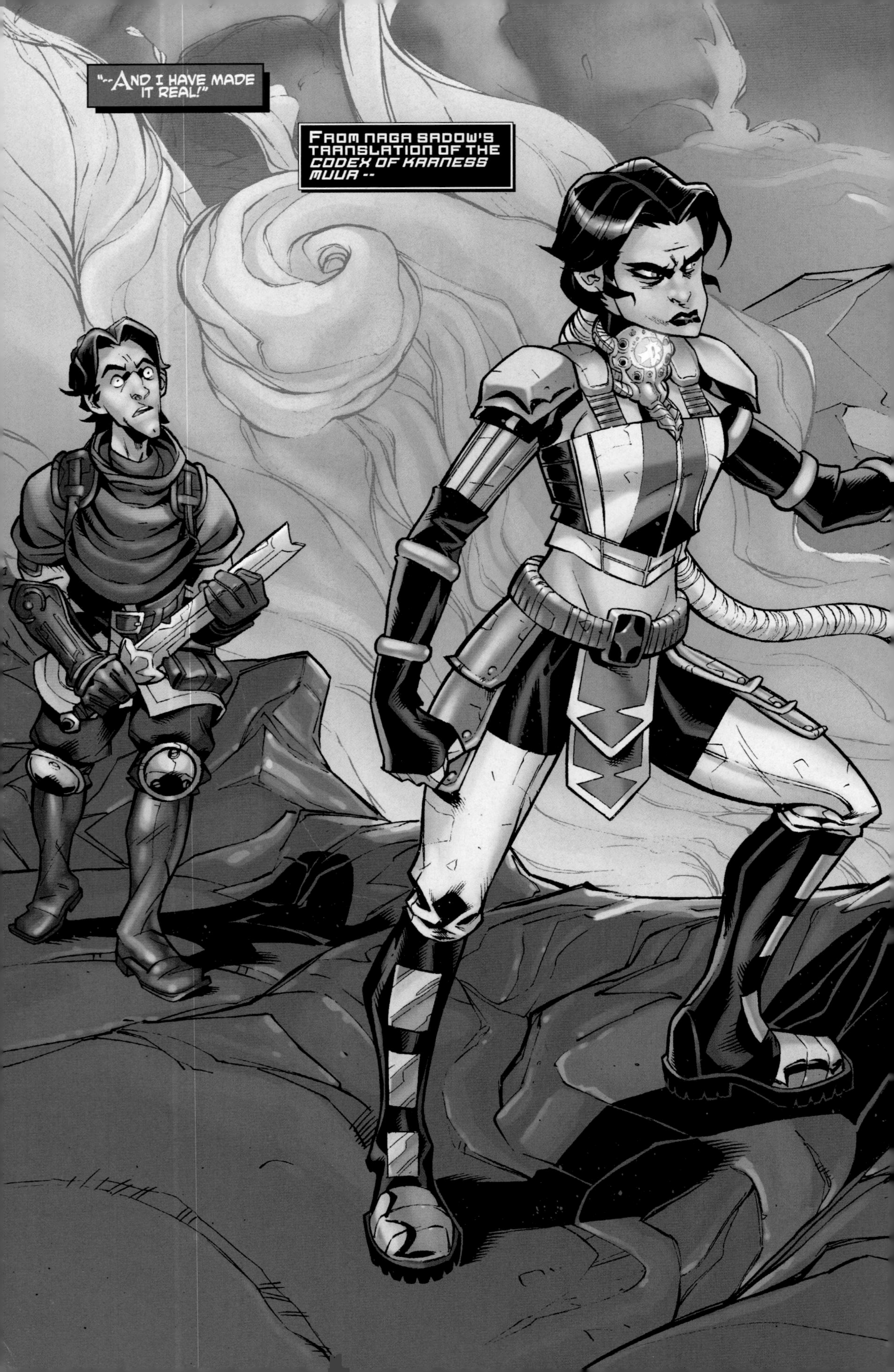
"--AND I HAVE MADE IT REAL!"
FROM NAGA SADOW'S TRANSLATION OF THE CODEX OF KAANESS MUUA --

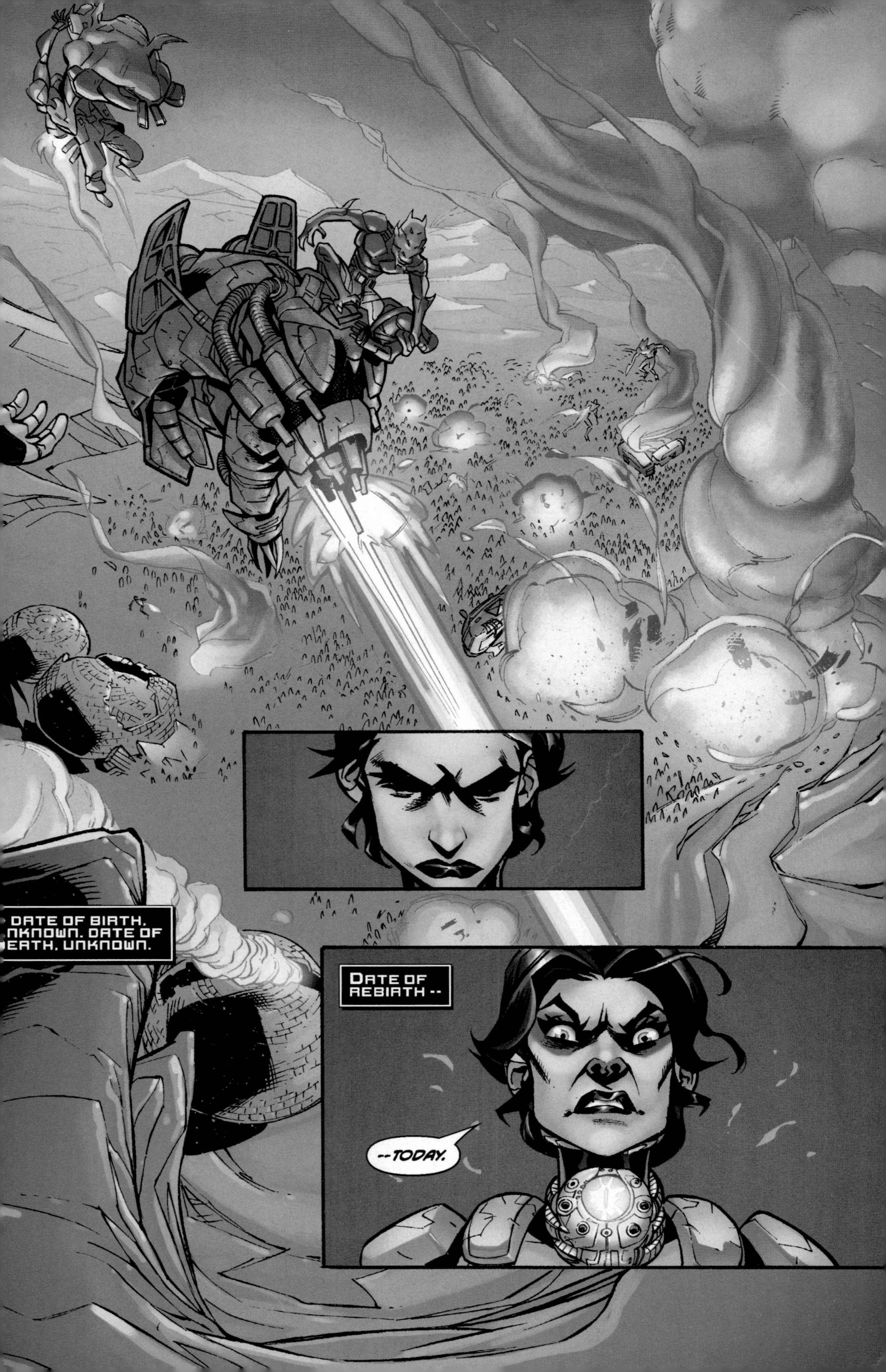
DATE OF BIRTH, NKNOWN. DATE OF EATH, UNKNOWN.
DATE OF REBIRTH --
--TODAY.

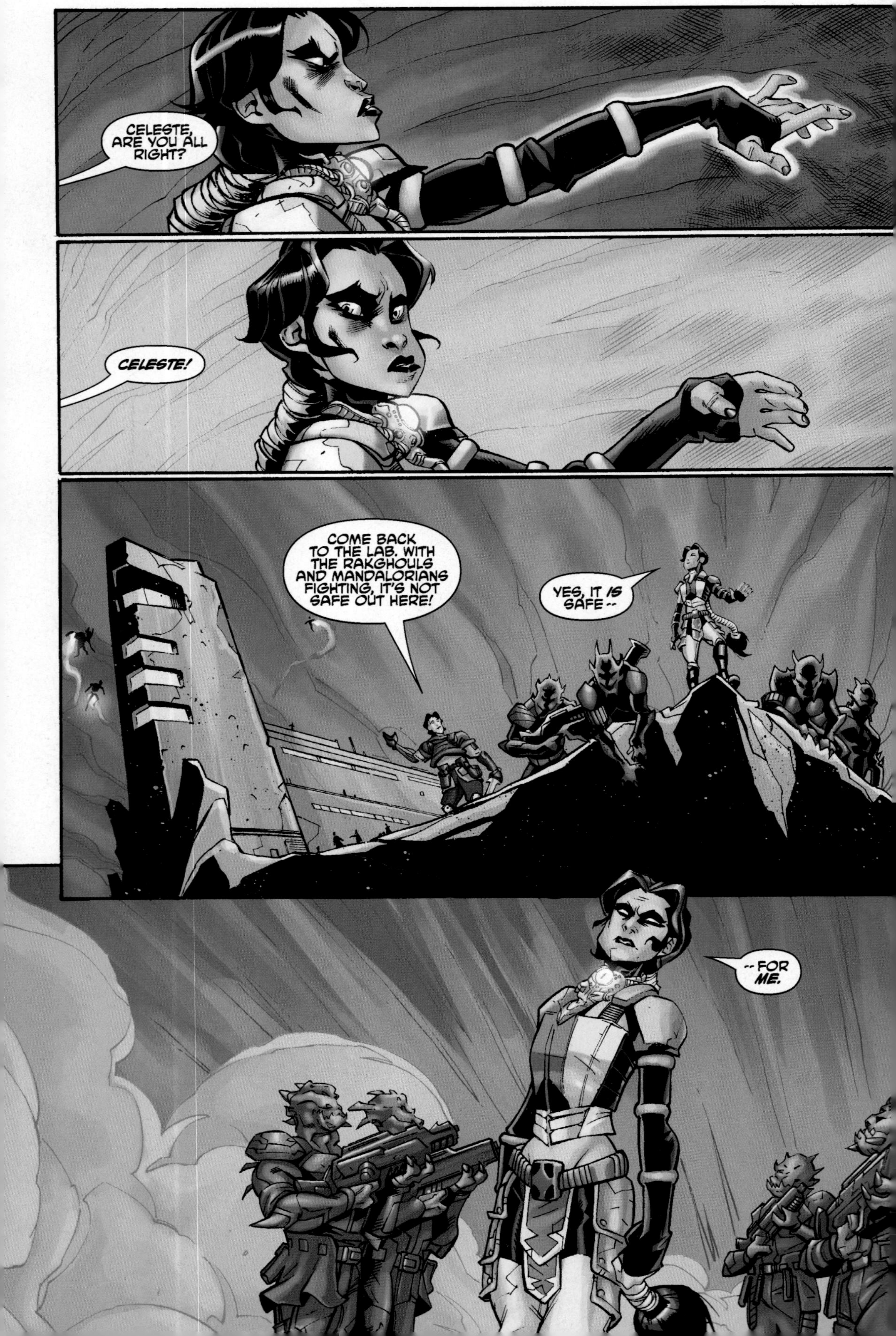
CELESTE, ARE YOU ALL RIGHT?
CELESTE!
COME BACK TO THE LAB. WITH THE RAKGHOULS AND MANDALORIANS FIGHTING, IT'S NOT SAFE OUT HERE!
YES, IT IS SAFE--
--FOR ME.

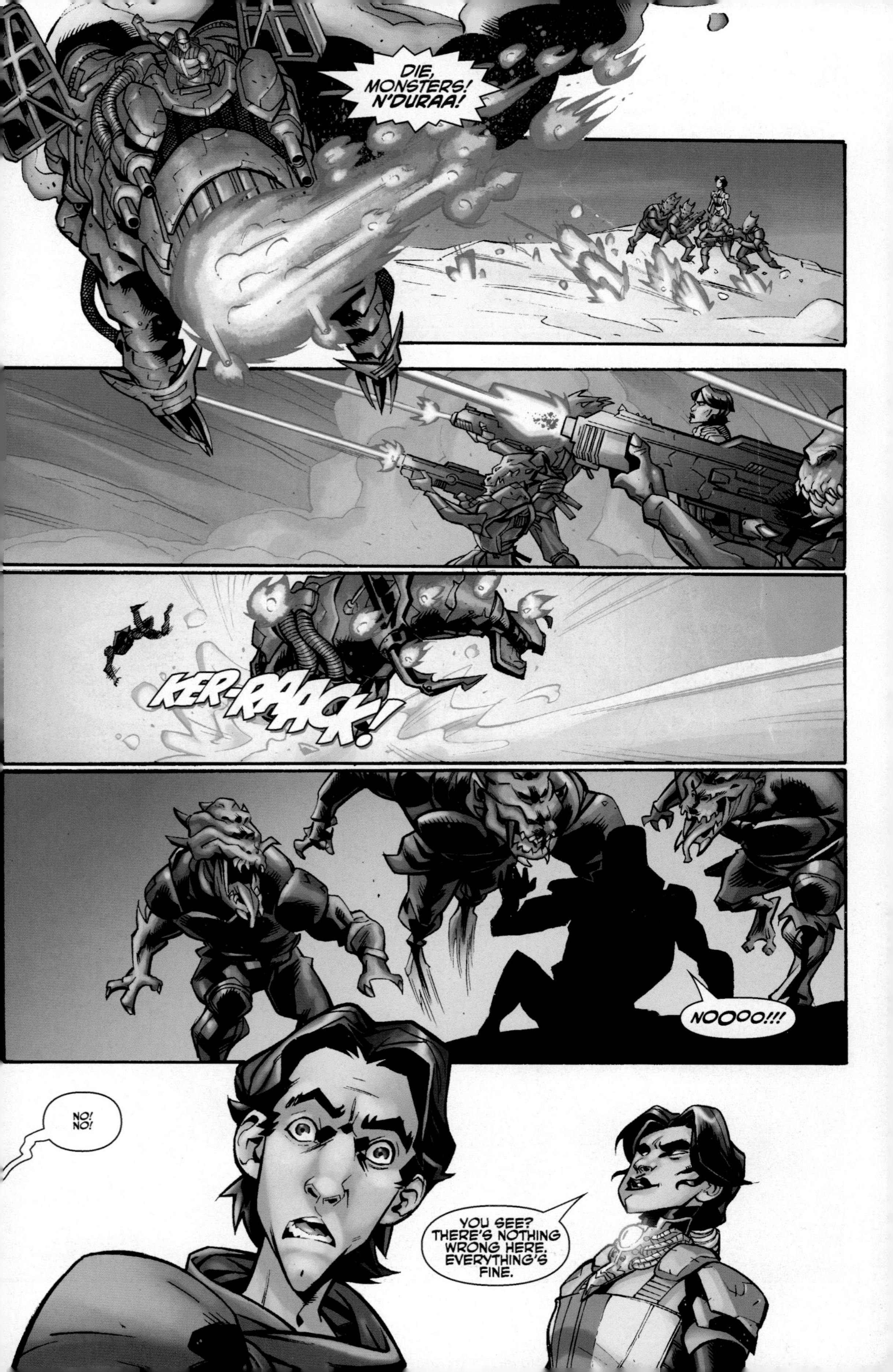
DIE, MONSTERS! N'DURAA!
KER-RAACK!
NOOOO!!!
NO! NO!
YOU SEE? THERE'S NOTHING WRONG HERE. EVERYTHING'S FINE.

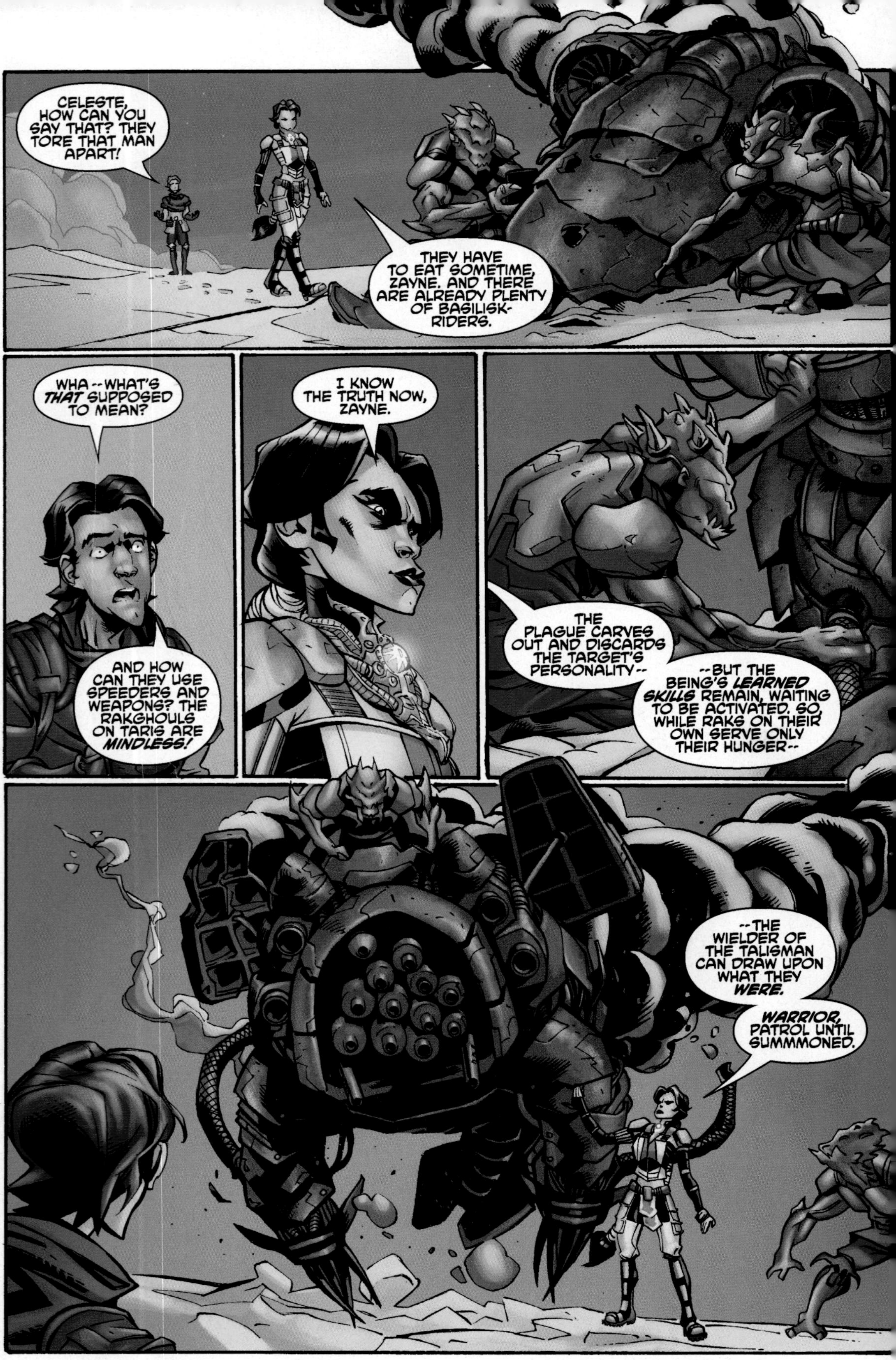
CELESTE, HOW CAN YOU SAY THAT? THEY TORE THAT MAN APART!
THEY HAVE TO EAT SOMETIME, ZAYNE. AND THERE ARE ALREADY PLENTY OF BASILISK-RIDERS.
WHA--WHAT'S THAT SUPPOSED TO MEAN?
AND HOW CAN THEY USE SPEEDERS AND WEAPONS? THE RAKGHOULS ON TARIS ARE MINDLESS!
I KNOW THE TRUTH NOW, ZAYNE.
THE PLAGUE CARVES OUT AND DISCARDS THE TARGET'S PERSONALITY--
--BUT THE BEING'S LEARNED SKILLS REMAIN, WAITING TO BE ACTIVATED. SO, WHILE RAKS ON THEIR OWN SERVE ONLY THEIR HUNGER--
--THE WIELDER OF THE TALISMAN CAN DRAW UPON WHAT THEY WERE.
WARRIOR, PATROL UNTIL SUMMONED.

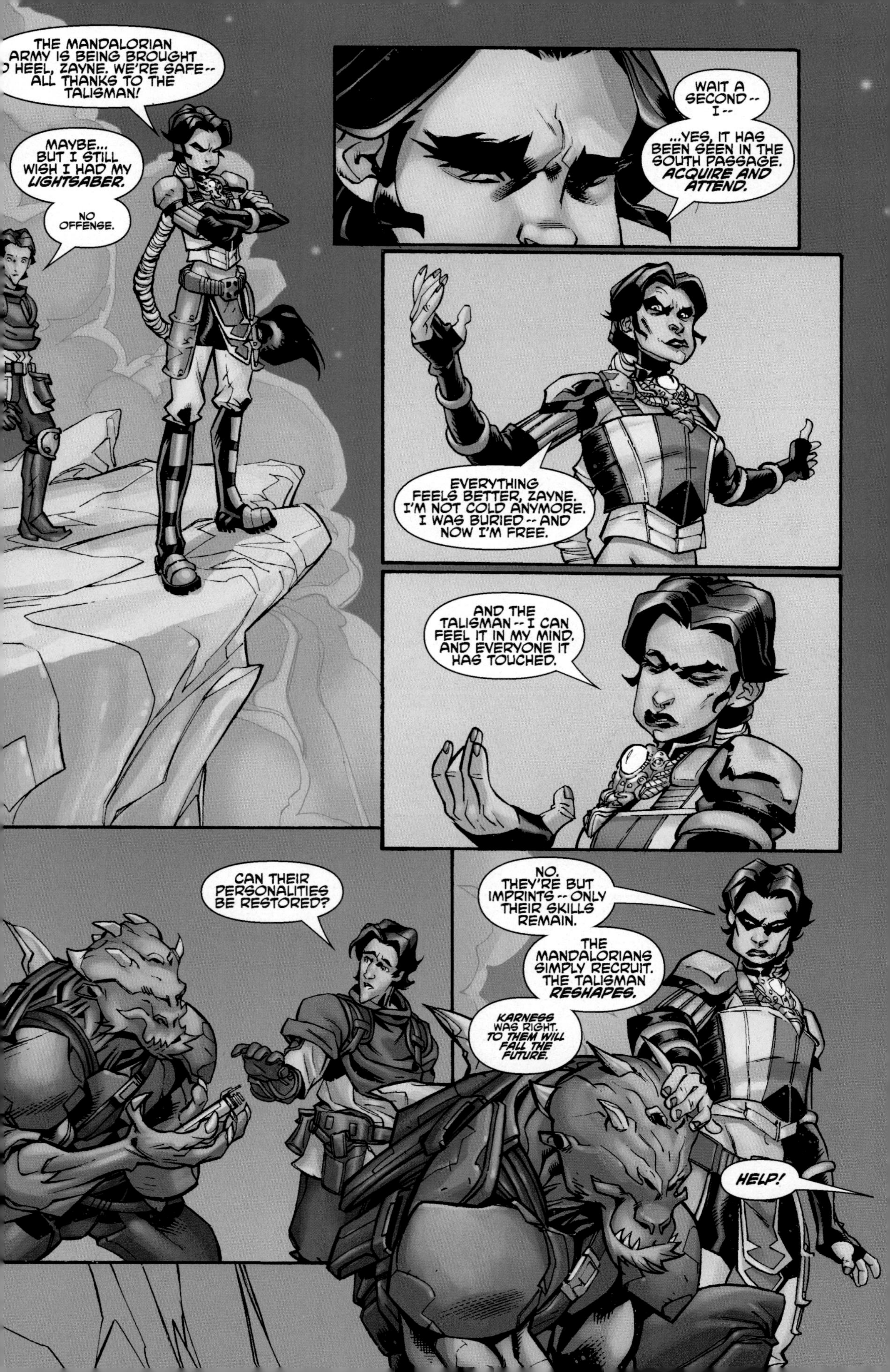
THE MANDALORIAN ARMY IS BEING BROUGHT TO HEEL, ZAYNE. WE'RE SAFE-- ALL THANKS TO THE TALISMAN!
MAYBE... BUT I STILL WISH I HAD MY LIGHTSABER.
NO OFFENSE.
WAIT A SECOND-- I--
...YES, IT HAS BEEN SEEN IN THE SOUTH PASSAGE. ACQUIRE AND ATTEND.
EVERYTHING FEELS BETTER, ZAYNE. I'M NOT COLD ANYMORE. I WAS BURIED--AND NOW I'M FREE.
AND THE TALISMAN--I CAN FEEL IT IN MY MIND, AND EVERYONE IT HAS TOUCHED.
CAN THEIR PERSONALITIES BE RESTORED?
NO. THEY'RE BUT IMPRINTS--ONLY THEIR SKILLS REMAIN.
THE MANDALORIANS SIMPLY RECRUIT. THE TALISMAN RESHAPES.
KARNESS WAS RIGHT. TO THEM WILL FALL THE FUTURE.
HELP!

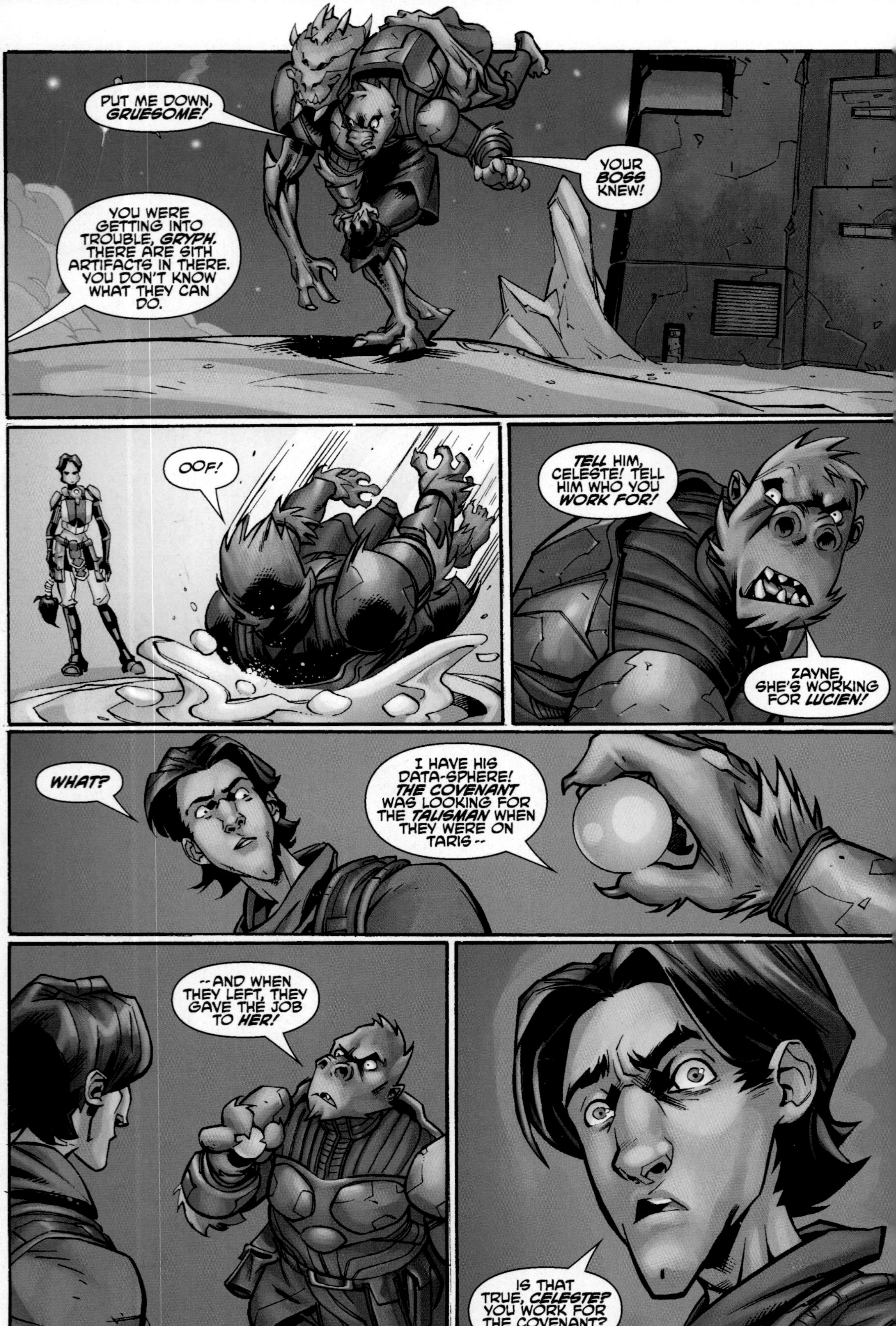
PUT ME DOWN, GRUESOME!
YOUR BOSS KNEW!
YOU WERE GETTING INTO TROUBLE, GRYPH. THERE ARE SITH ARTIFACTS IN THERE. YOU DON'T KNOW WHAT THEY CAN DO.
OOF!
TELL HIM, CELESTE! TELL HIM WHO YOU WORK FOR!
ZAYNE, SHE'S WORKING FOR LUCIEN!
WHAT?
I HAVE HIS DATA-SPHERE! THE COVENANT WAS LOOKING FOR THE TALISMAN WHEN THEY WERE ON TARIS--
--AND WHEN THEY LEFT, THEY GAVE THE JOB TO HER!
IS THAT TRUE, CELESTE? YOU WORK FOR THE COVENANT?

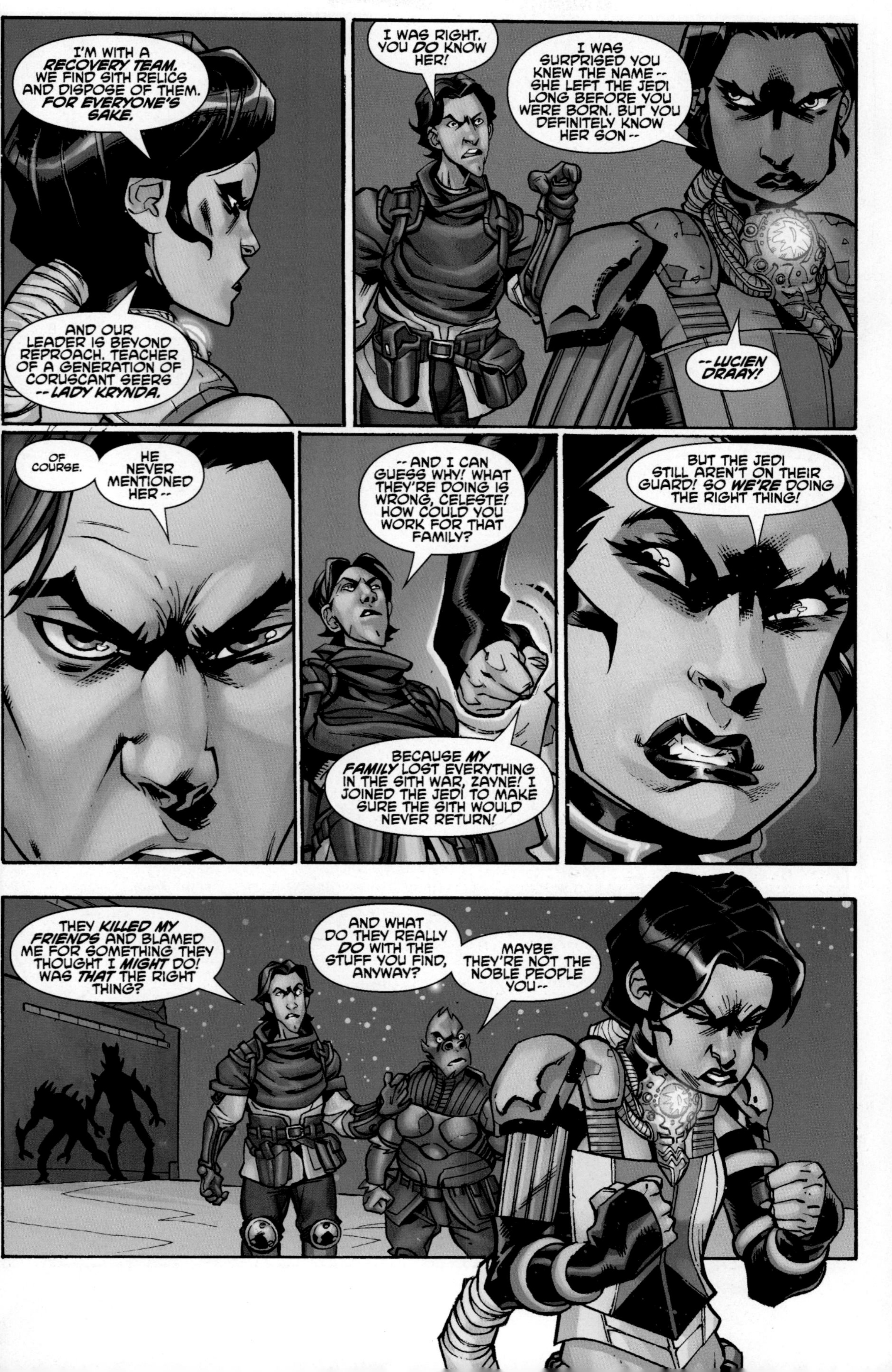
I'M WITH A *RECOVERY TEAM.* WE FIND SITH RELICS AND DISPOSE OF THEM. *FOR EVERYONE'S SAKE.*
AND OUR LEADER IS BEYOND REPROACH. TEACHER OF A GENERATION OF CORUSCANT SEERS --*LADY KRYNDA.*
I WAS RIGHT. YOU *DO* KNOW HER!
I WAS SURPRISED YOU KNEW THE NAME -- SHE LEFT THE JEDI LONG BEFORE YOU WERE BORN. BUT YOU DEFINITELY KNOW HER SON --
--*LUCIEN DRAAY!*
OF COURSE.
HE NEVER MENTIONED HER --
-- AND I CAN GUESS WHY! WHAT THEY'RE DOING IS WRONG, CELESTE! HOW COULD YOU WORK FOR THAT FAMILY?
BECAUSE *MY FAMILY* LOST EVERYTHING IN THE SITH WAR, ZAYNE! I JOINED THE JEDI TO MAKE SURE THE SITH WOULD NEVER RETURN!
BUT THE JEDI STILL AREN'T ON THEIR GUARD! SO *WE'RE* DOING THE RIGHT THING!
THEY *KILLED MY FRIENDS* AND BLAMED ME FOR SOMETHING THEY THOUGHT I *MIGHT* DO! WAS *THAT* THE RIGHT THING?
AND WHAT DO THEY REALLY *DO* WITH THE STUFF YOU FIND, ANYWAY?
MAYBE THEY'RE NOT THE NOBLE PEOPLE YOU--

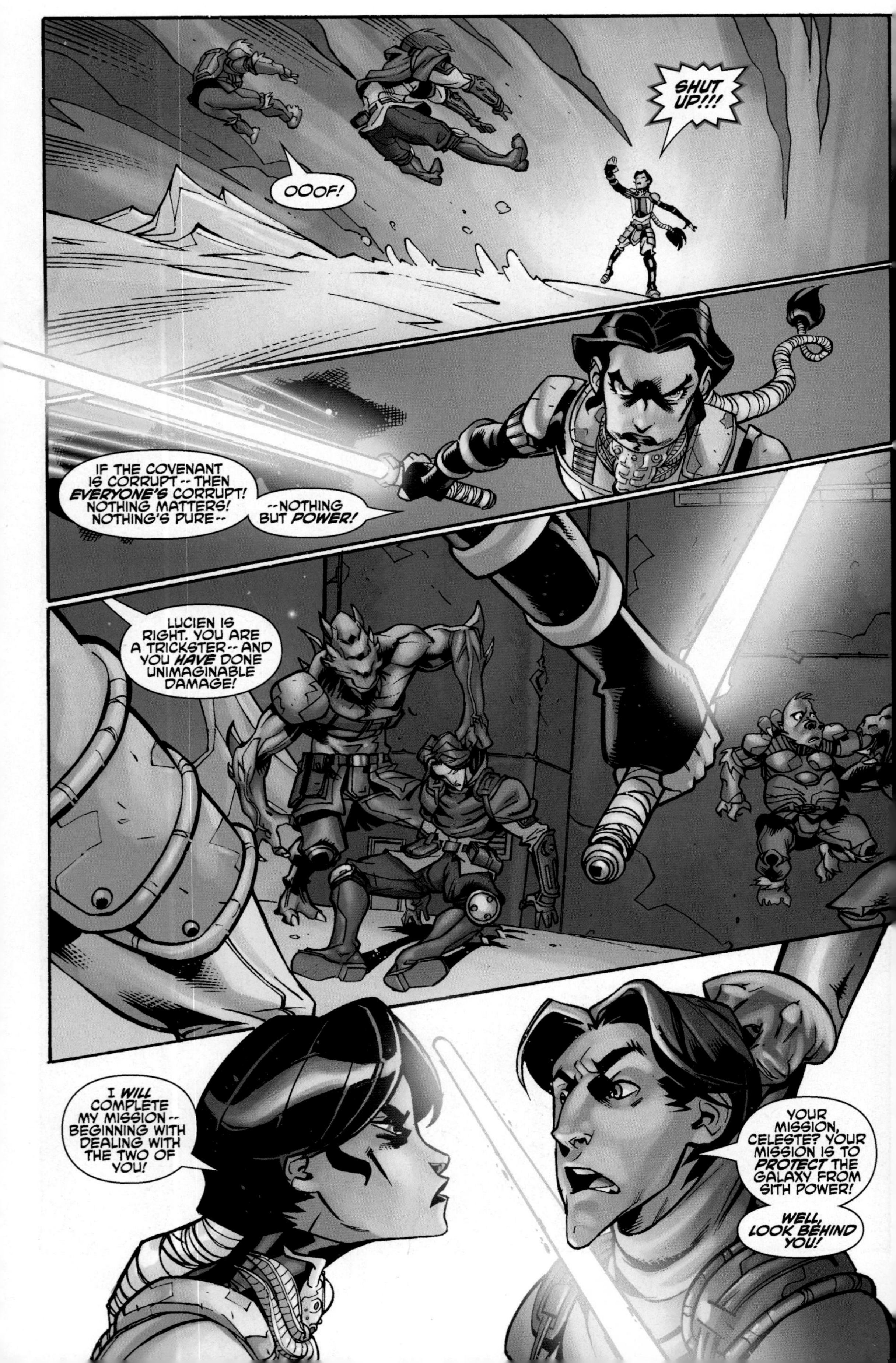
SHUT UP!!!
OOOF!
IF THE COVENANT IS CORRUPT -- THEN EVERYONE'S CORRUPT! NOTHING MATTERS! NOTHING'S PURE--
--NOTHING BUT POWER!
LUCIEN IS RIGHT. YOU ARE A TRICKSTER -- AND YOU HAVE DONE UNIMAGINABLE DAMAGE!
I WILL COMPLETE MY MISSION -- BEGINNING WITH DEALING WITH THE TWO OF YOU!
YOUR MISSION, CELESTE? YOUR MISSION IS TO PROTECT THE GALAXY FROM SITH POWER!
WELL, LOOK BEHIND YOU!

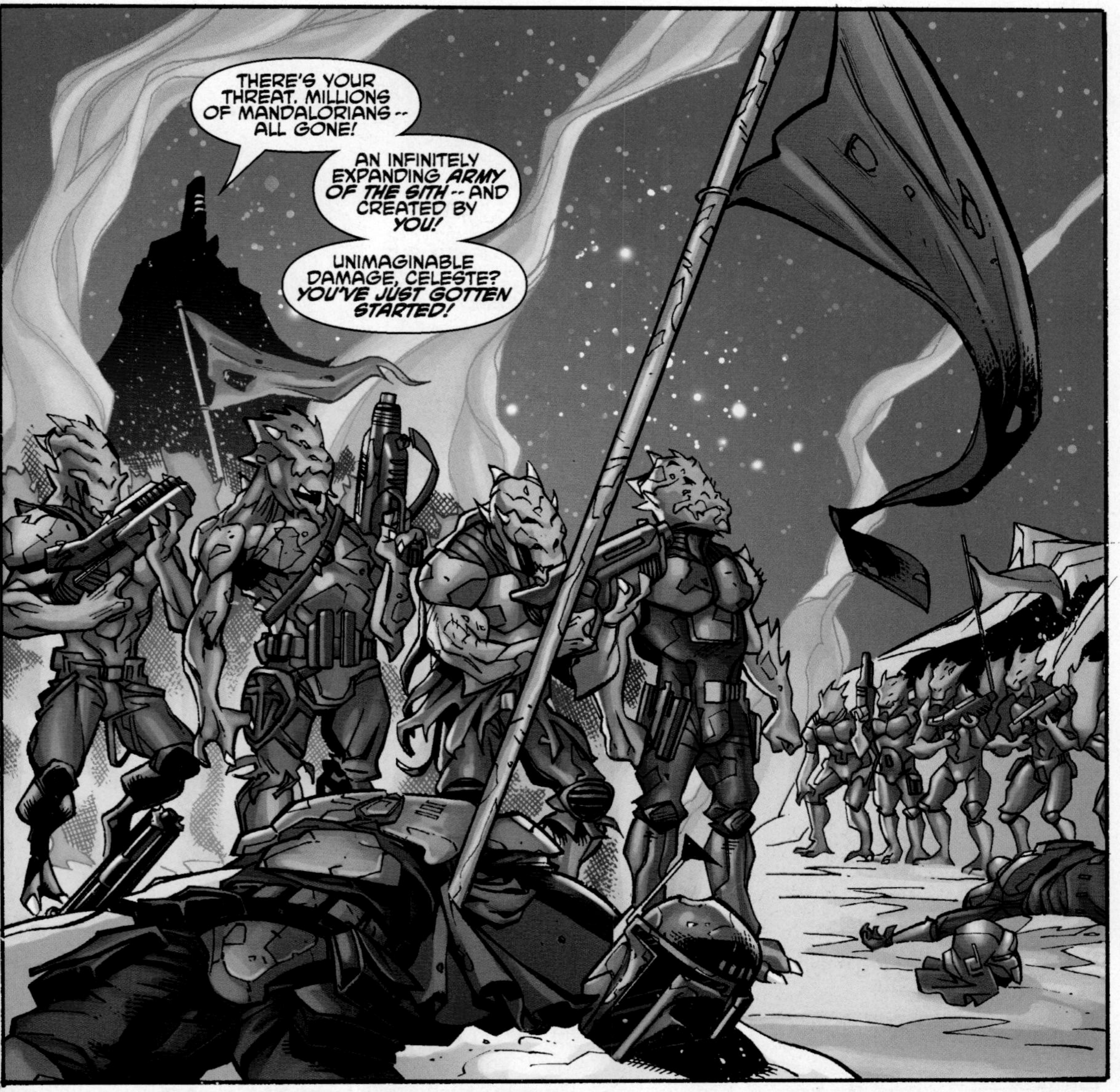
THERE'S YOUR THREAT. MILLIONS OF MANDALORIANS -- ALL GONE!
AN INFINITELY EXPANDING *ARMY OF THE SITH* -- AND CREATED BY *YOU!*
UNIMAGINABLE DAMAGE, CELESTE? *YOU'VE JUST GOTTEN STARTED!*
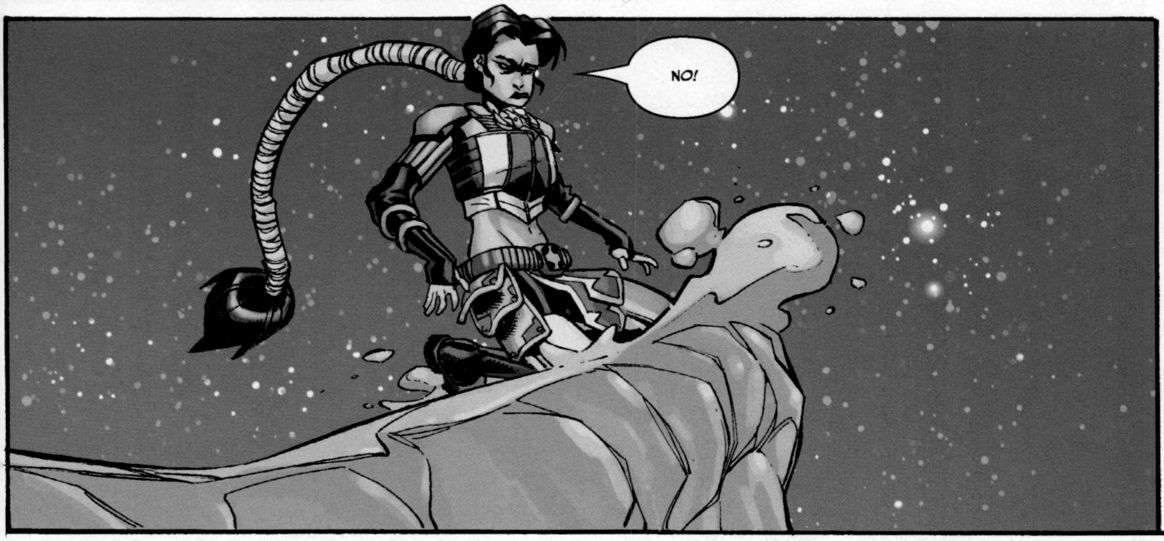
NO!

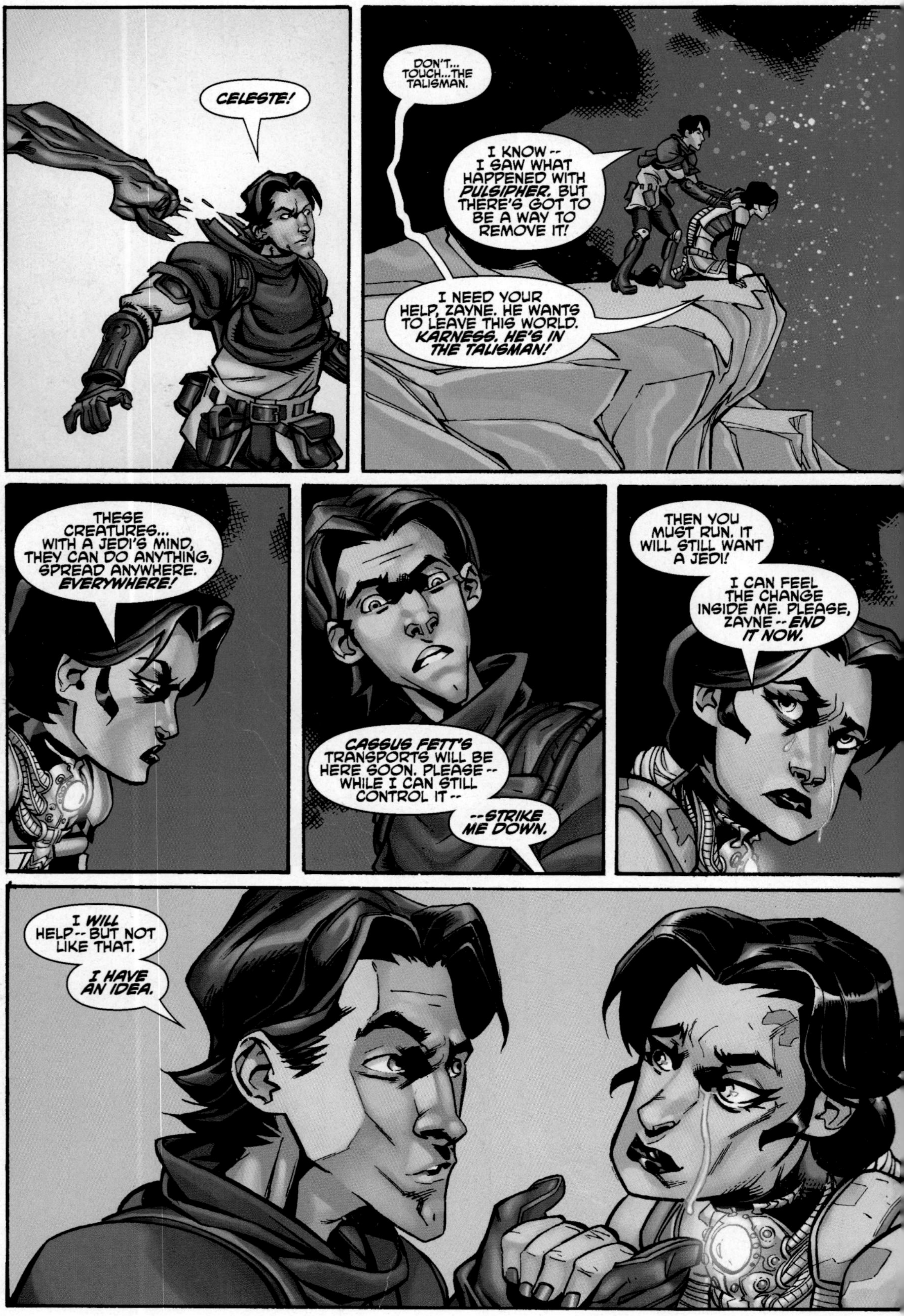
CELESTE!
DON'T... TOUCH...THE TALISMAN.
I KNOW -- I SAW WHAT HAPPENED WITH PULSIPHER. BUT THERE'S GOT TO BE A WAY TO REMOVE IT!
I NEED YOUR HELP, ZAYNE. HE WANTS TO LEAVE THIS WORLD. KARNESS. HE'S IN THE TALISMAN!
THESE CREATURES... WITH A JEDI'S MIND, THEY CAN DO ANYTHING, SPREAD ANYWHERE. EVERYWHERE!
CASSUS FETT'S TRANSPORTS WILL BE HERE SOON. PLEASE -- WHILE I CAN STILL CONTROL IT --
--STRIKE ME DOWN.
THEN YOU MUST RUN. IT WILL STILL WANT A JEDI!
I CAN FEEL THE CHANGE INSIDE ME. PLEASE, ZAYNE -- END IT NOW.
I WILL HELP -- BUT NOT LIKE THAT.
I HAVE AN IDEA.

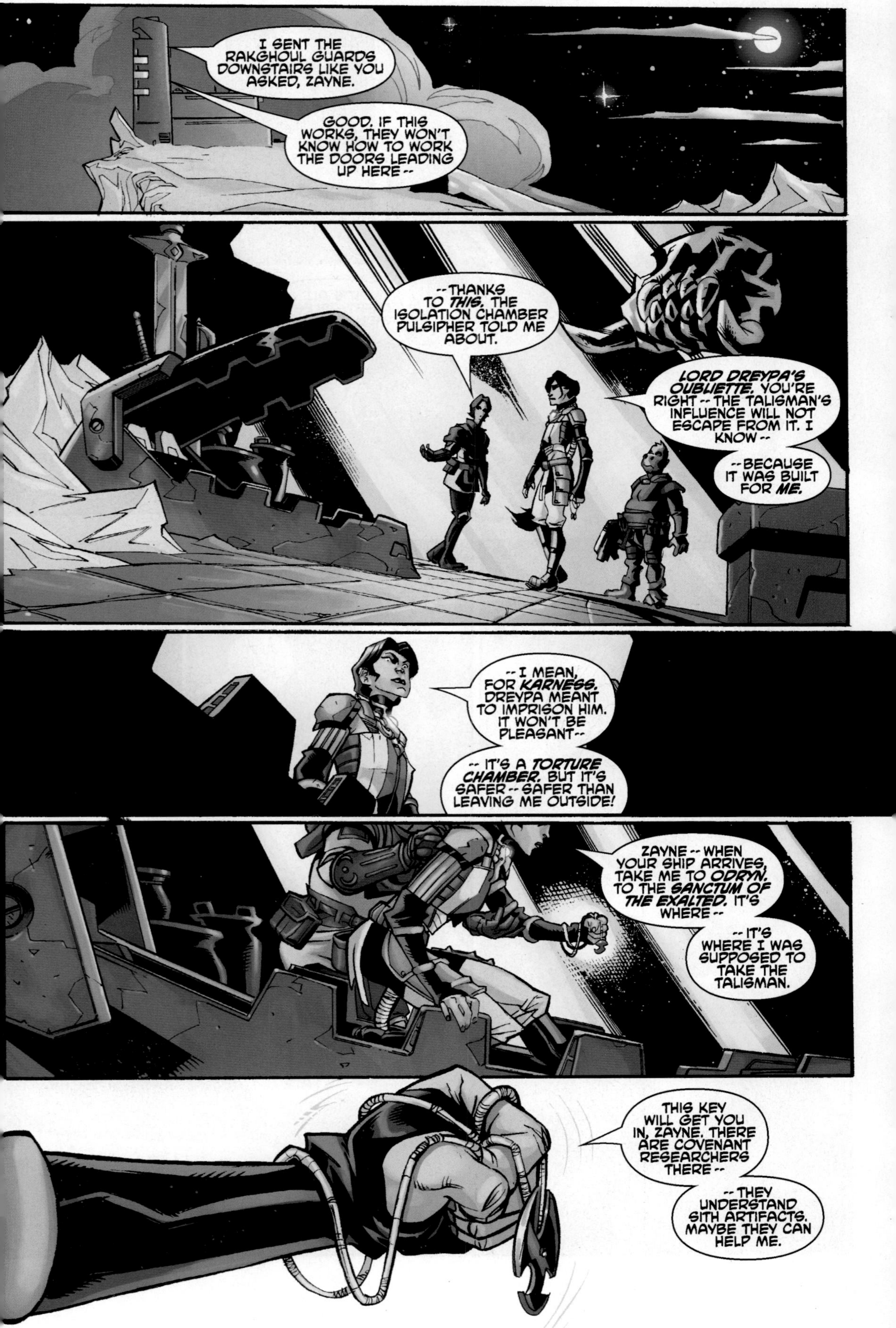
I SENT THE RAKGHOUL GUARDS DOWNSTAIRS LIKE YOU ASKED, ZAYNE.
GOOD. IF THIS WORKS, THEY WON'T KNOW HOW TO WORK THE DOORS LEADING UP HERE --
-- THANKS TO *THIS*, THE ISOLATION CHAMBER PULSIPHER TOLD ME ABOUT.
LORD DREYPA'S OUBLIETTE. YOU'RE RIGHT -- THE TALISMAN'S INFLUENCE WILL NOT ESCAPE FROM IT. I KNOW --
-- BECAUSE IT WAS BUILT FOR *ME.*
-- I MEAN, FOR *KARNESS.* DREYPA MEANT TO IMPRISON HIM. IT WON'T BE PLEASANT--
-- IT'S A *TORTURE CHAMBER.* BUT IT'S SAFER -- SAFER THAN LEAVING ME OUTSIDE!
ZAYNE -- WHEN YOUR SHIP ARRIVES, TAKE ME TO *ODRYN,* TO THE *SANCTUM OF THE EXALTED.* IT'S WHERE --
-- IT'S WHERE I WAS SUPPOSED TO TAKE THE TALISMAN.
THIS KEY WILL GET YOU IN, ZAYNE. THERE ARE COVENANT RESEARCHERS THERE --
-- THEY UNDERSTAND SITH ARTIFACTS. MAYBE THEY CAN HELP ME.

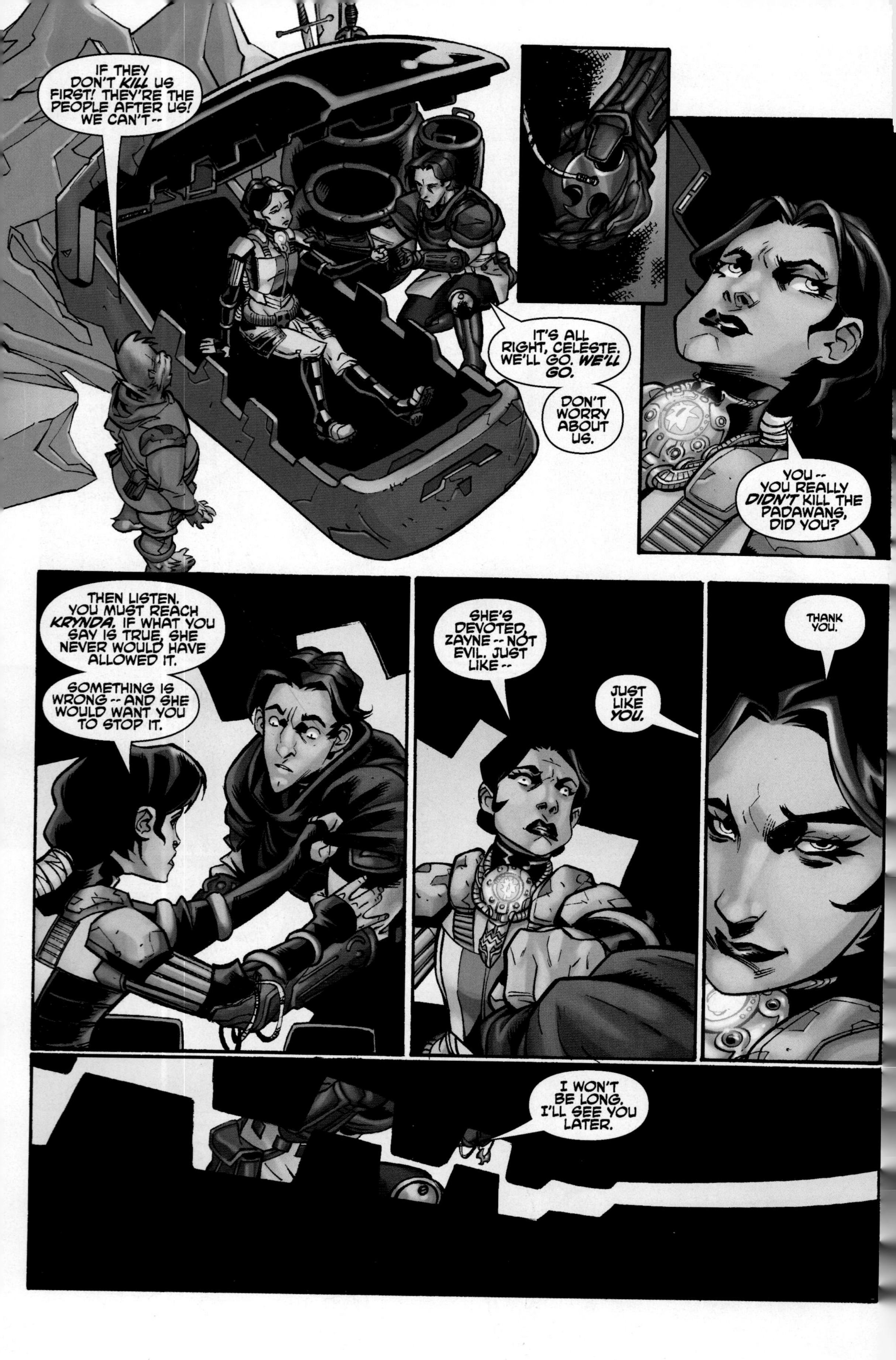
IF THEY DON'T KILL US FIRST! THEY'RE THE PEOPLE AFTER US! WE CAN'T --
IT'S ALL RIGHT, CELESTE. WE'LL GO. WE'LL GO.
DON'T WORRY ABOUT US.
YOU -- YOU REALLY DIDN'T KILL THE PADAWANS, DID YOU?
THEN LISTEN. YOU MUST REACH KRYNDA. IF WHAT YOU SAY IS TRUE, SHE NEVER WOULD HAVE ALLOWED IT.
SOMETHING IS WRONG -- AND SHE WOULD WANT YOU TO STOP IT.
SHE'S DEVOTED, ZAYNE -- NOT EVIL. JUST LIKE --
JUST LIKE YOU.
THANK YOU.
I WON'T BE LONG. I'LL SEE YOU LATER.

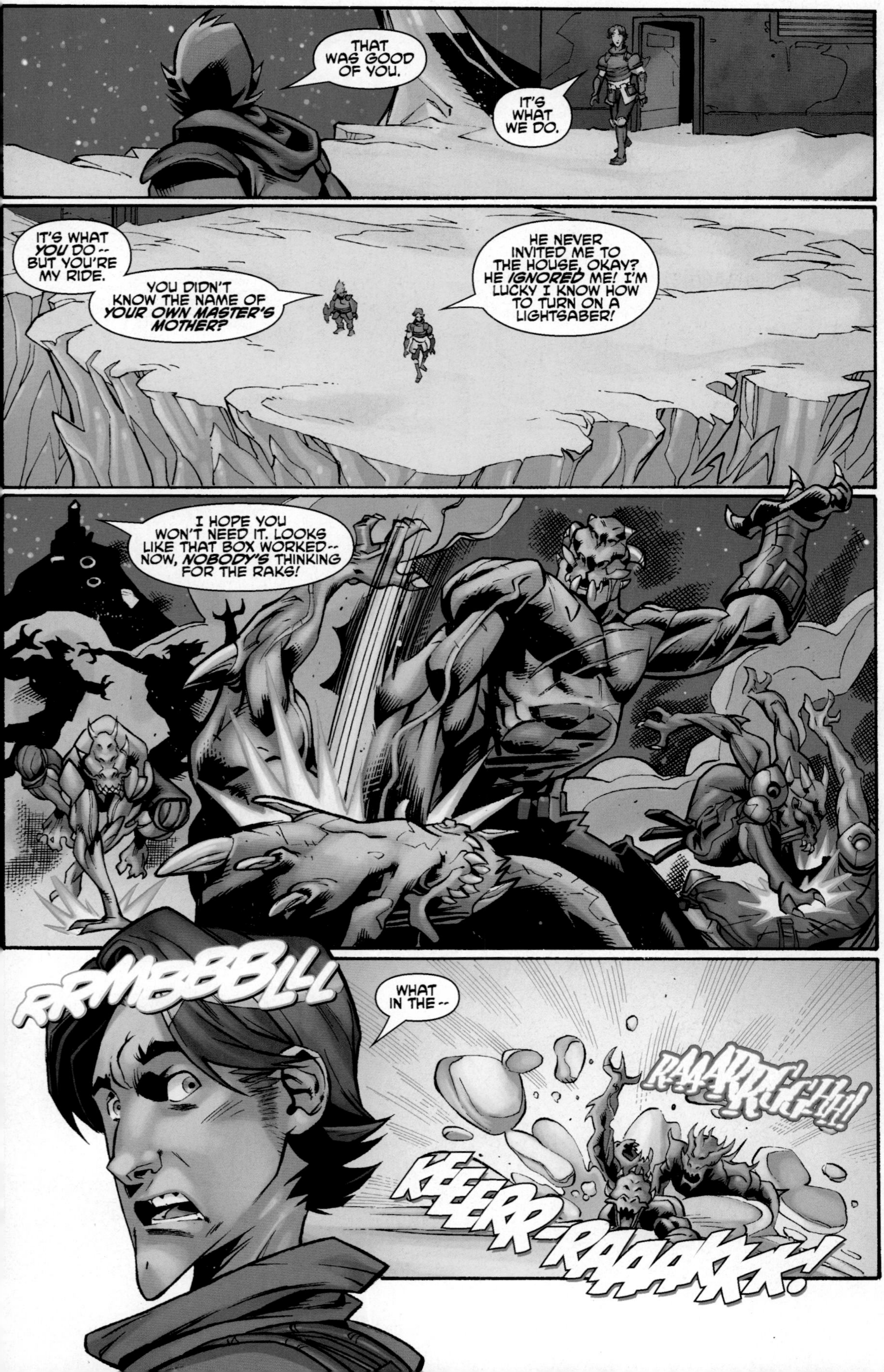
THAT WAS GOOD OF YOU.
IT'S WHAT WE DO.
IT'S WHAT *YOU* DO-- BUT YOU'RE MY RIDE.
YOU DIDN'T KNOW THE NAME OF ***YOUR OWN MASTER'S MOTHER?***
HE NEVER INVITED ME TO THE HOUSE, OKAY? HE ***IGNORED*** ME! I'M LUCKY I KNOW HOW TO TURN ON A LIGHTSABER!
I HOPE YOU WON'T NEED IT. LOOKS LIKE THAT BOX WORKED-- NOW, ***NOBODY'S*** THINKING FOR THE RAKS!
RRMBBBLLL
WHAT IN THE--
RAAARRGHH!
KEEERR-RAAAKKK!

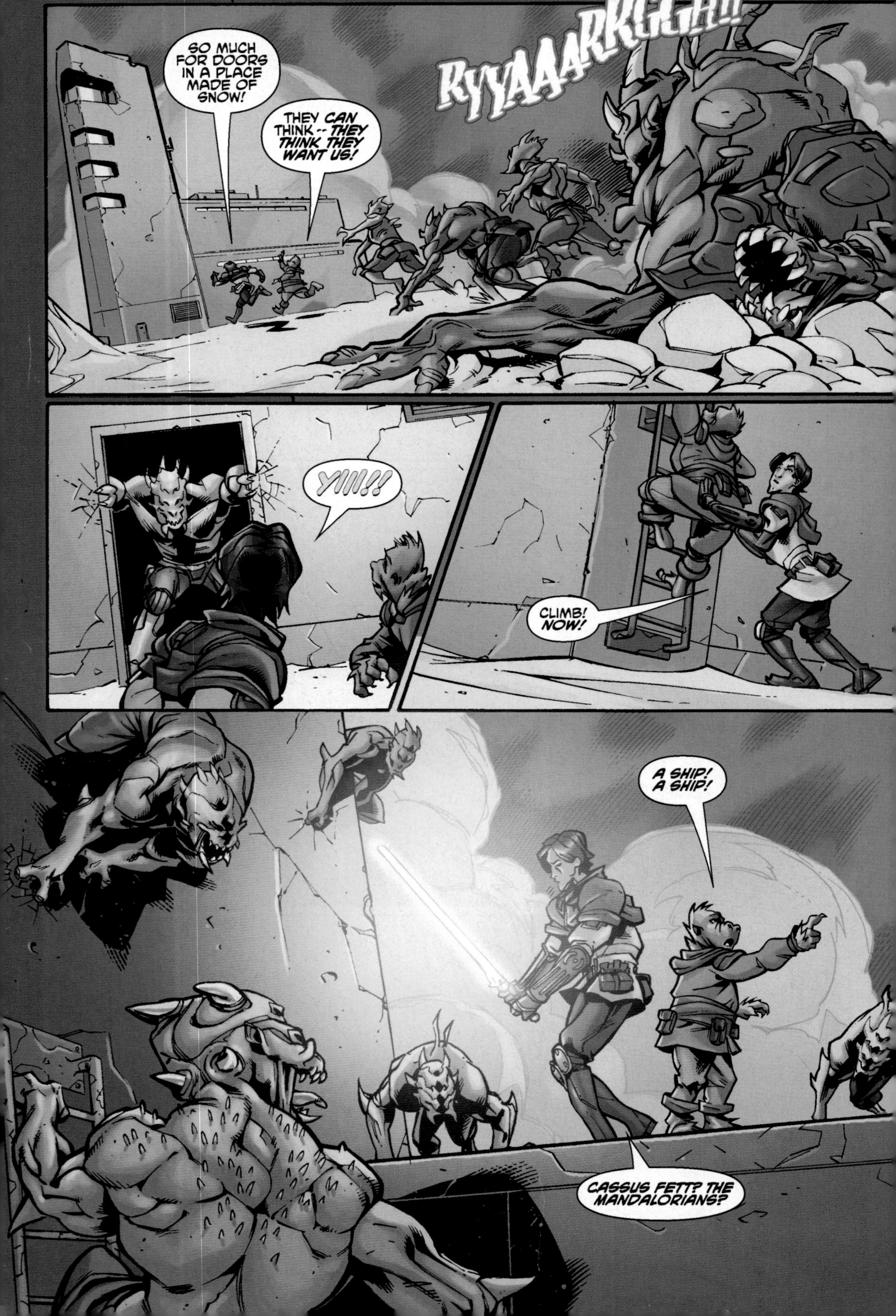
SO MUCH FOR DOORS IN A PLACE MADE OF SNOW!
RYYAAARRGGH!!
THEY CAN THINK -- THEY THINK THEY WANT US!
YIII!!
CLIMB! NOW!
A SHIP! A SHIP!
CASSUS FETT? THE MANDALORIANS?

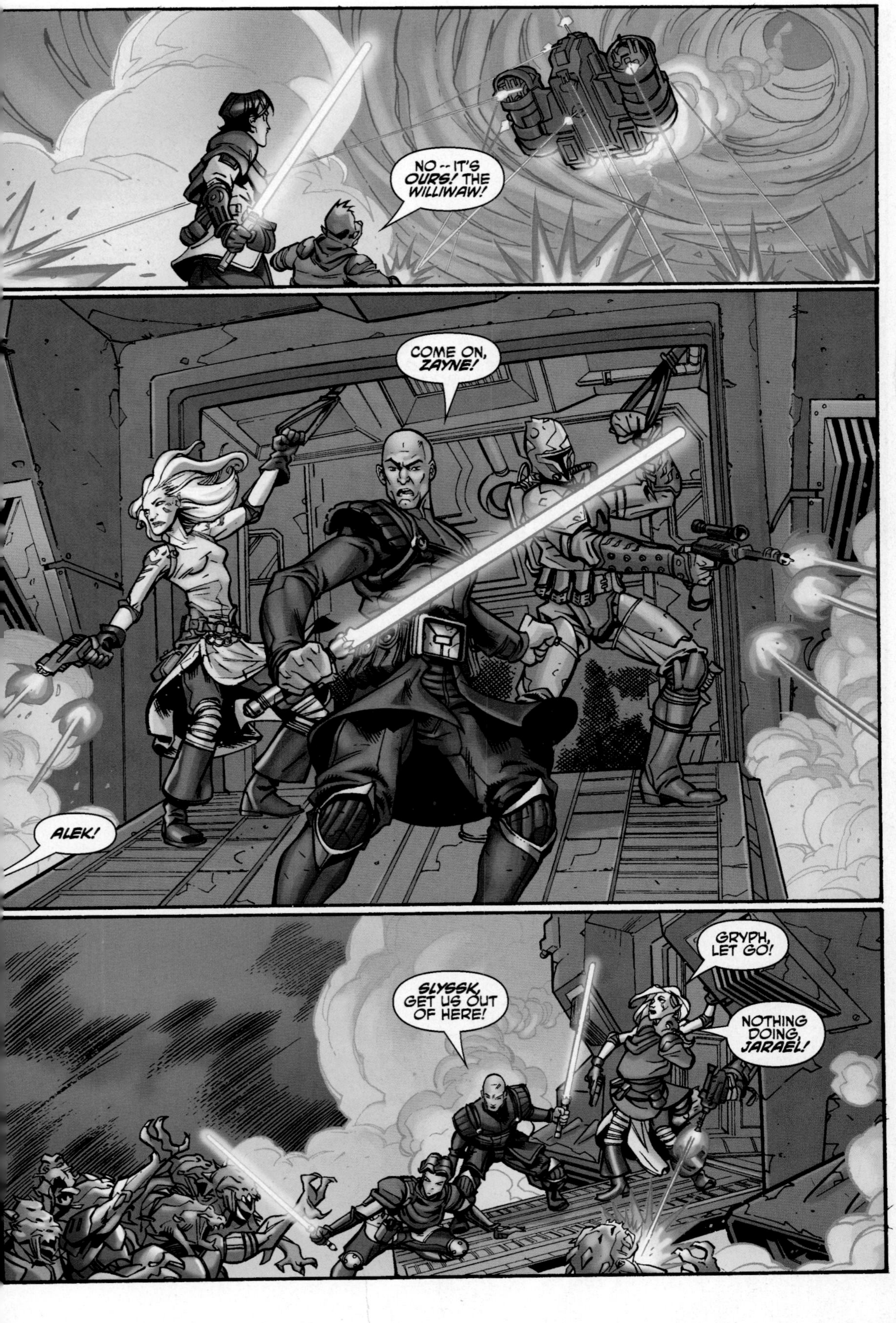
NO -- IT'S OURS! THE WILLIWAW!
COME ON, ZAYNE!
ALEK!
GRYPH, LET GO!
SLYSSK, GET US OUT OF HERE!
NOTHING DOING, JARAEL!

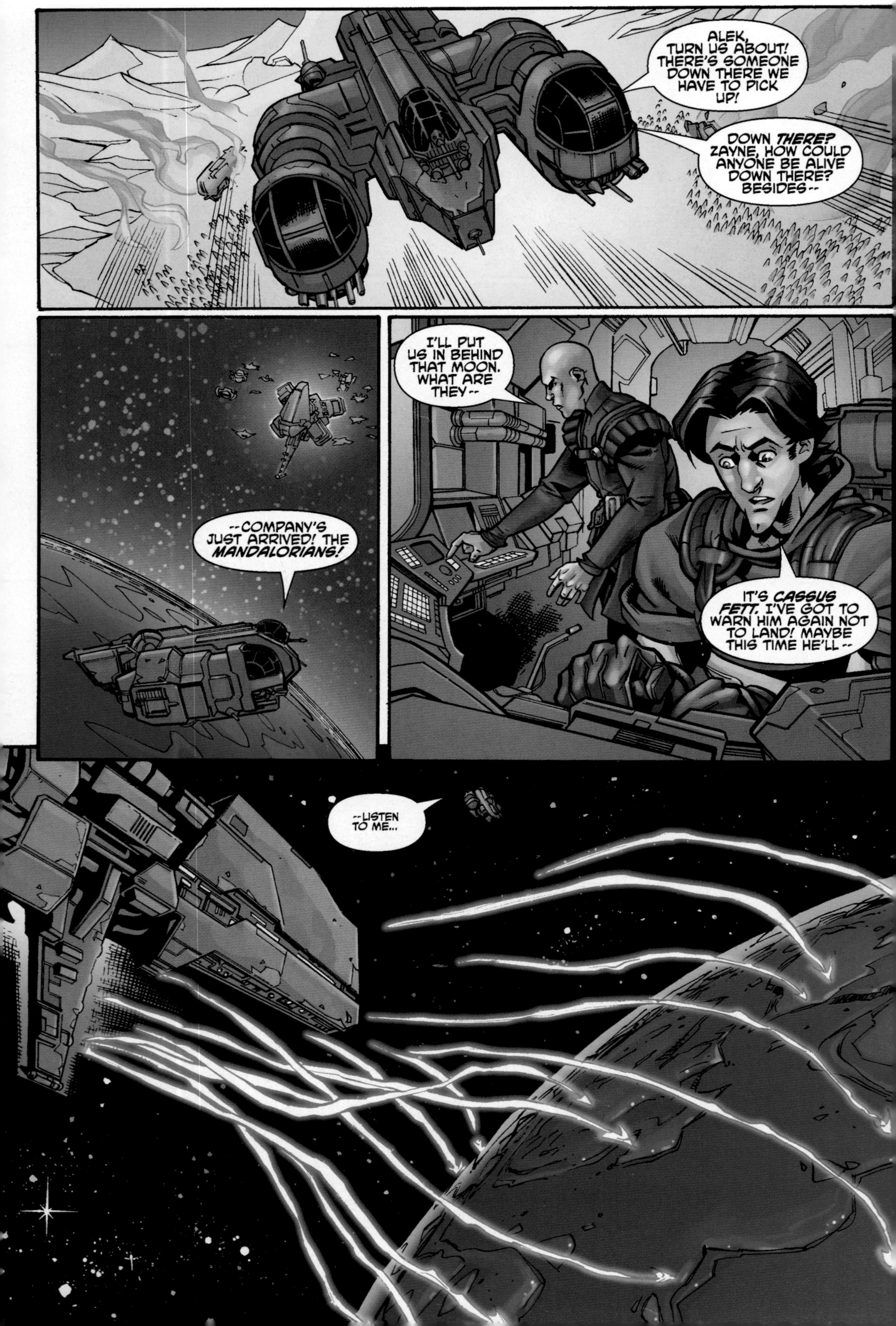
ALEK, TURN US ABOUT! THERE'S SOMEONE DOWN THERE WE HAVE TO PICK UP!
DOWN *THERE?* ZAYNE, HOW COULD ANYONE BE ALIVE DOWN THERE? BESIDES--
I'LL PUT US IN BEHIND THAT MOON. WHAT ARE THEY--
--COMPANY'S JUST ARRIVED! THE *MANDALORIANS!*
IT'S *CASSUS FETT.* I'VE GOT TO WARN HIM AGAIN NOT TO LAND! MAYBE THIS TIME HE'LL--
--LISTEN TO ME...

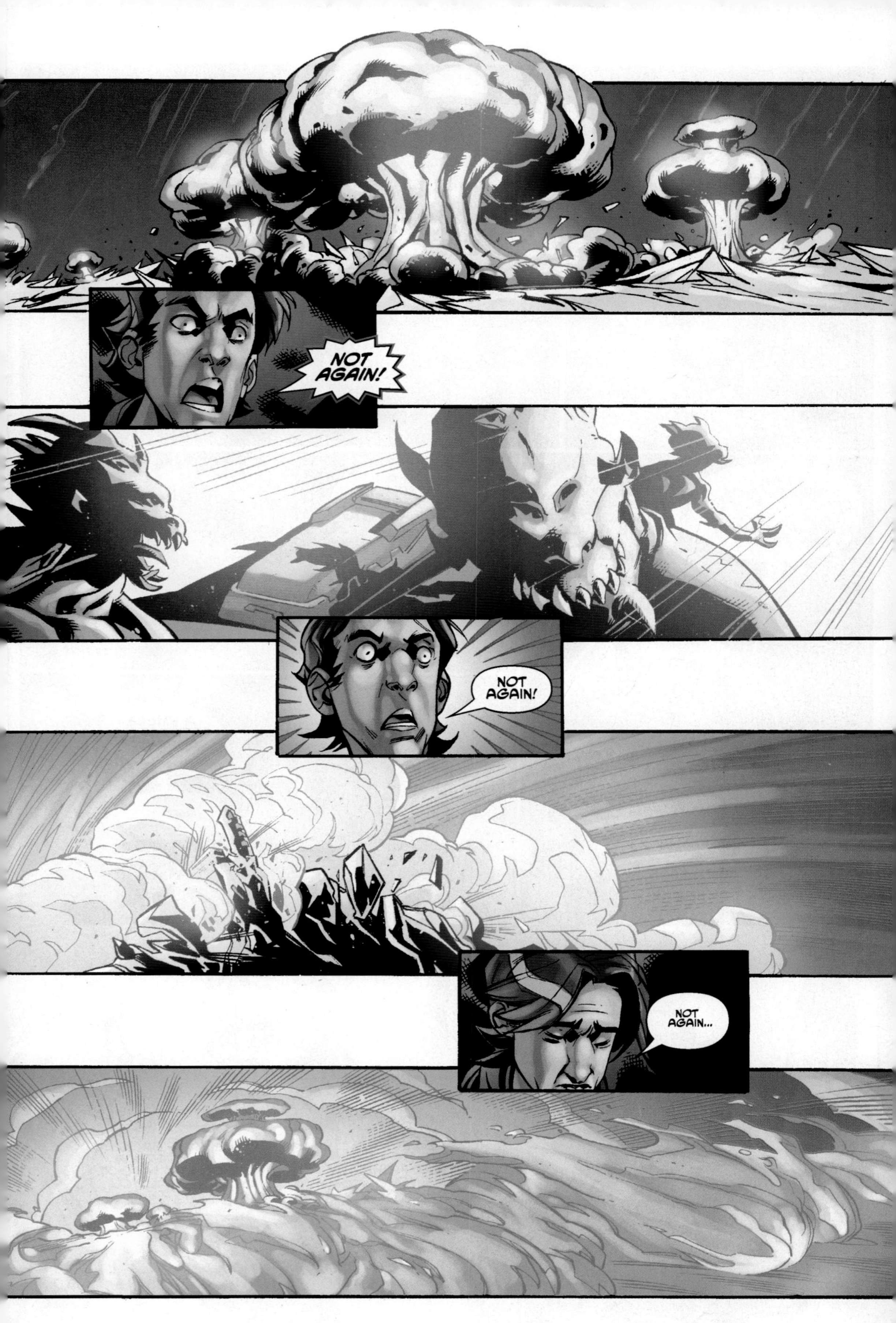
NOT AGAIN!
NOT AGAIN!
NOT AGAIN...

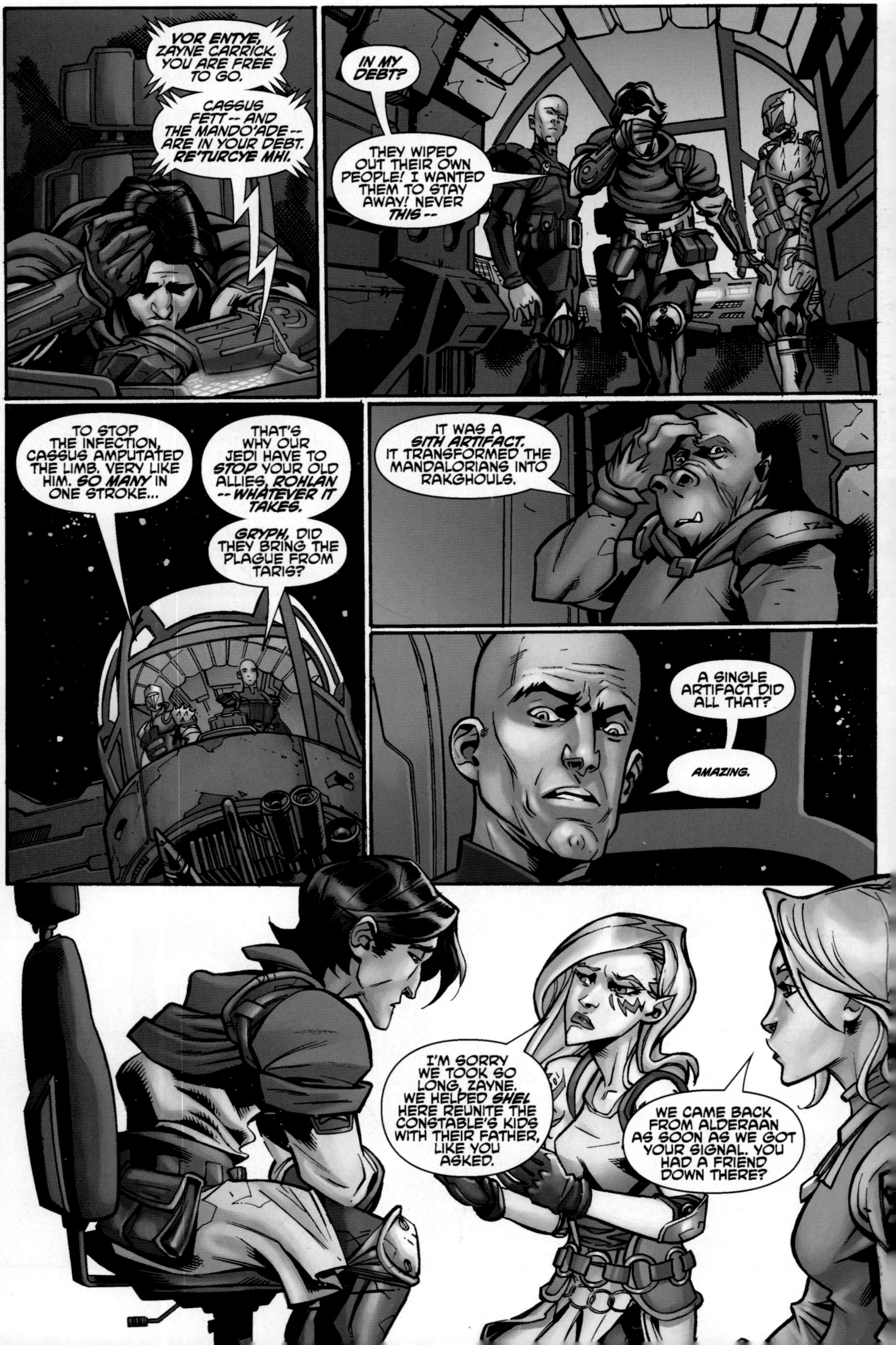
VOR ENTYE, ZAYNE CARRICK. YOU ARE FREE TO GO.
CASSUS FETT -- AND THE MANDO'ADE -- ARE IN YOUR DEBT. RE'TURCYE MHI.
IN MY DEBT?
THEY WIPED OUT THEIR OWN PEOPLE! I WANTED THEM TO STAY AWAY! NEVER THIS --
TO STOP THE INFECTION, CASSUS AMPUTATED THE LIMB. VERY LIKE HIM. SO MANY IN ONE STROKE...
THAT'S WHY OUR JEDI HAVE TO STOP YOUR OLD ALLIES, ROHLAN -- WHATEVER IT TAKES.
GRYPH, DID THEY BRING THE PLAGUE FROM TARIS?
IT WAS A SITH ARTIFACT. IT TRANSFORMED THE MANDALORIANS INTO RAKGHOULS.
A SINGLE ARTIFACT DID ALL THAT?
AMAZING.
I'M SORRY WE TOOK SO LONG, ZAYNE. WE HELPED SHEL HERE REUNITE THE CONSTABLE'S KIDS WITH THEIR FATHER, LIKE YOU ASKED.
WE CAME BACK FROM ALDERAAN AS SOON AS WE GOT YOUR SIGNAL. YOU HAD A FRIEND DOWN THERE?

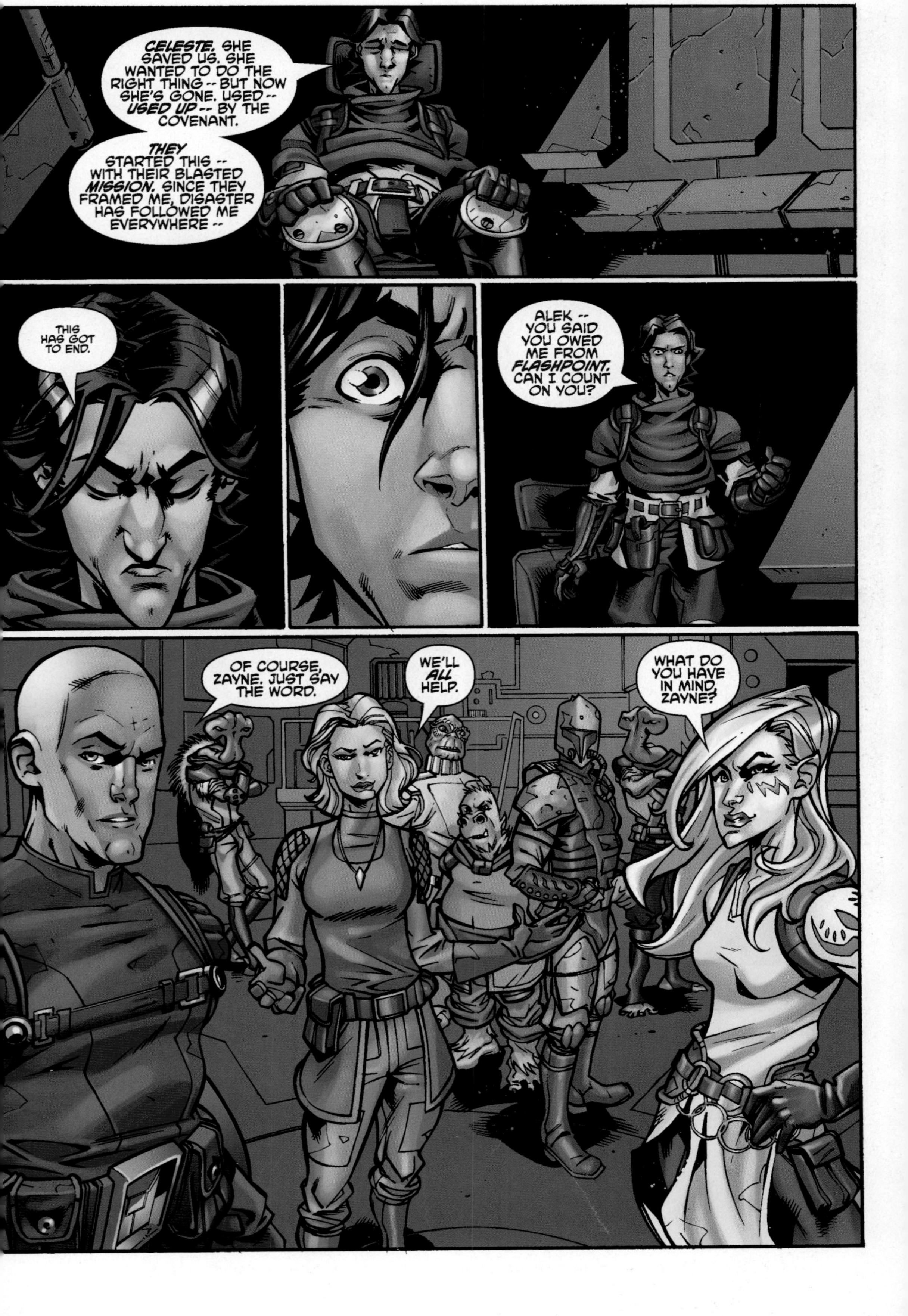
CELESTE. SHE SAVED US. SHE WANTED TO DO THE RIGHT THING -- BUT NOW SHE'S GONE. USED -- USED UP -- BY THE COVENANT.
THEY STARTED THIS -- WITH THEIR BLASTED MISSION. SINCE THEY FRAMED ME, DISASTER HAS FOLLOWED ME EVERYWHERE --
THIS HAS GOT TO END.
ALEK -- YOU SAID YOU OWED ME FROM FLASHPOINT. CAN I COUNT ON YOU?
OF COURSE, ZAYNE. JUST SAY THE WORD.
WE'LL ALL HELP.
WHAT DO YOU HAVE IN MIND, ZAYNE?

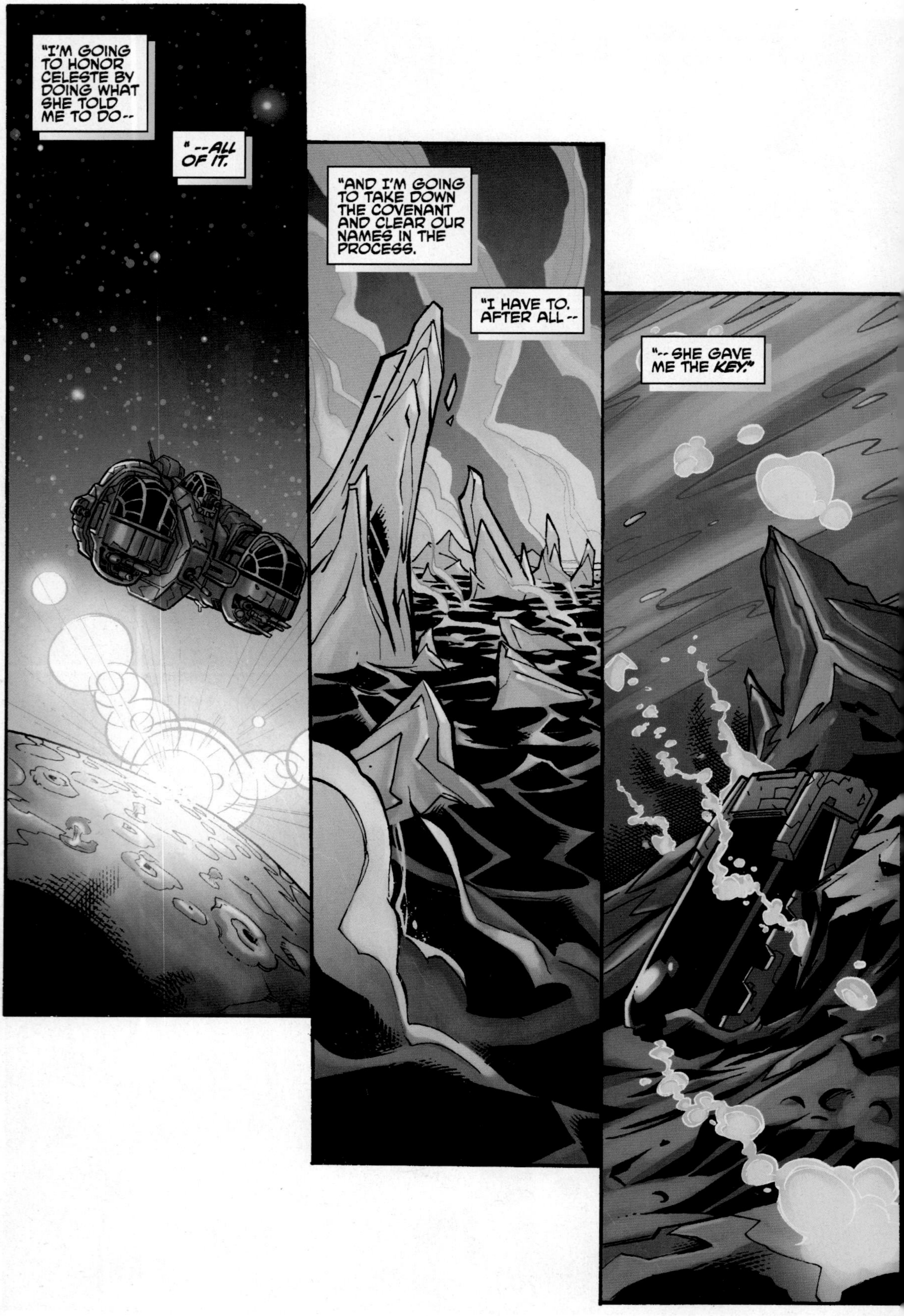
"I'M GOING TO HONOR CELESTE BY DOING WHAT SHE TOLD ME TO DO--
" --ALL OF IT.
"AND I'M GOING TO TAKE DOWN THE COVENANT AND CLEAR OUR NAMES IN THE PROCESS.
"I HAVE TO. AFTER ALL--
"--SHE GAVE ME THE KEY."

"VECTOR" CONTINUES IN *STAR WARS LEGENDS EPIC COLLECTION: THE EMPIRE VOL. 2 TPB*!

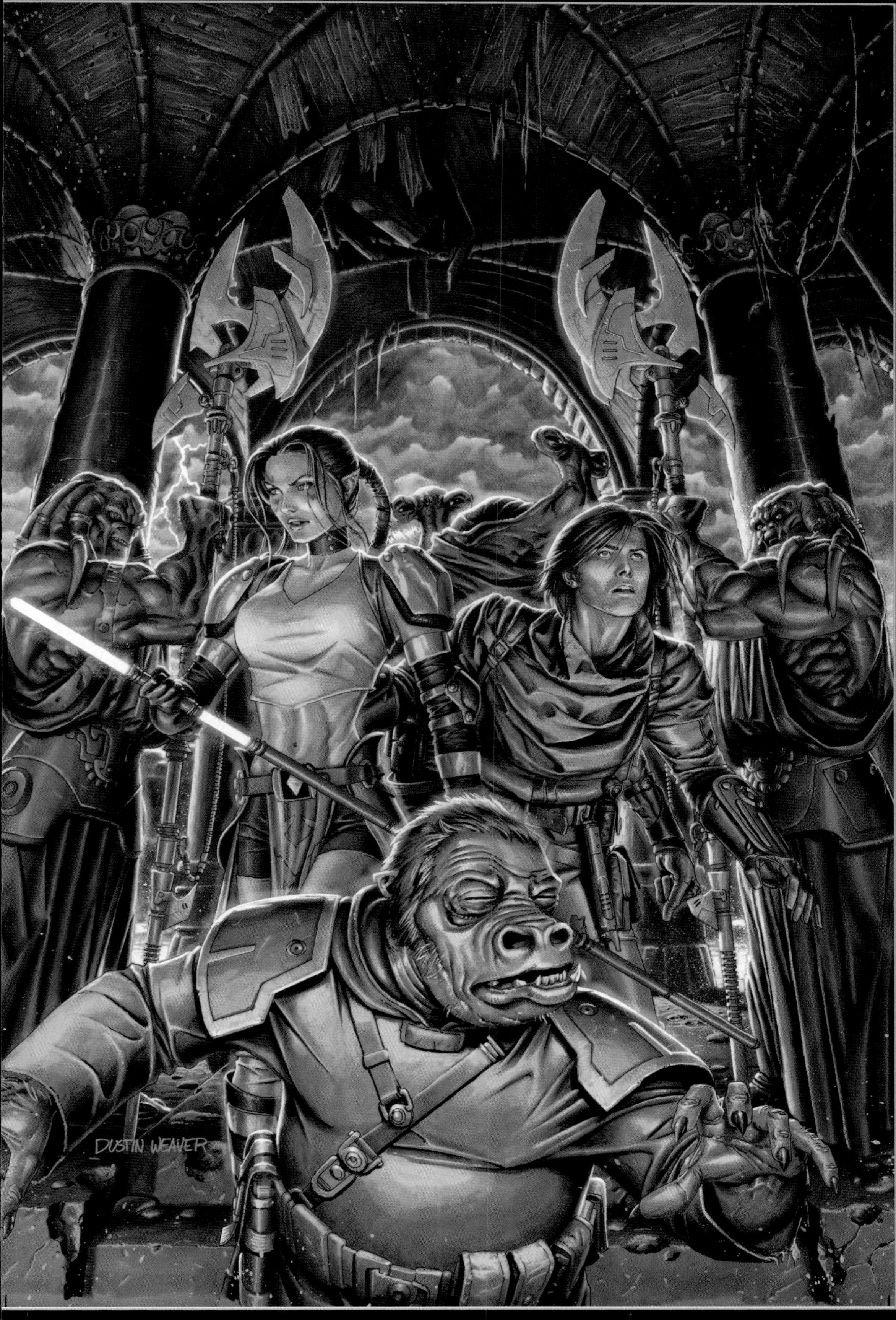
DUSTIN WEAVER

STAR WARS: KNIGHTS OF THE OLD REPUBLIC #29 — "EXALTED, PART 1"

WRITER: JOHN JACKSON MILLER • ARTIST: BONG DAZO • COLORIST: MICHAEL ATIYEH • LETTERER: MICHAEL HEISLER
ASSISTANT EDITORS: FREDDYE LINS & DAVE MARSHALL • EDITOR: RANDY STRADLEY • COVER ARTIST: DUSTIN WEAVER

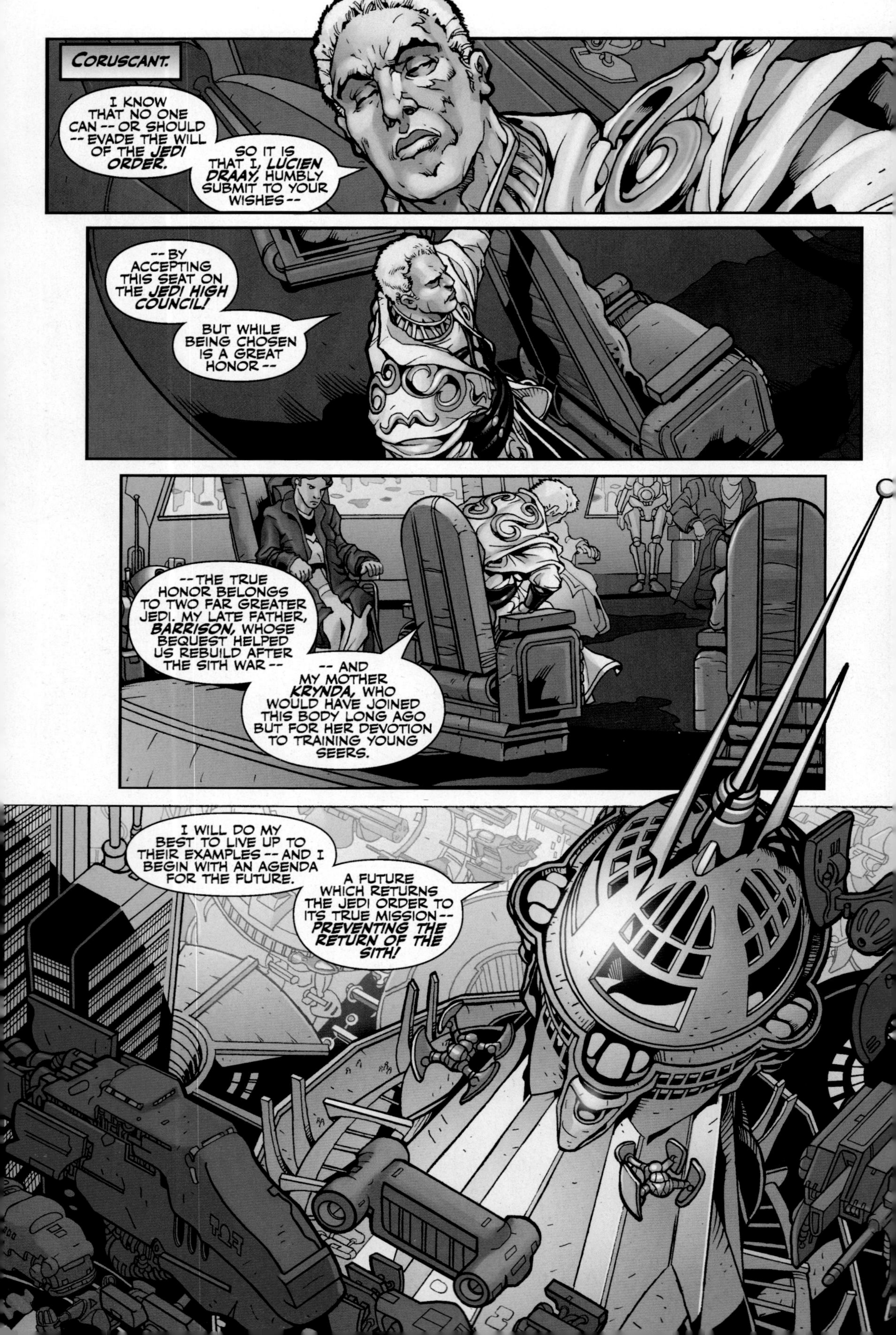
CORUSCANT.
I KNOW THAT NO ONE CAN -- OR SHOULD -- EVADE THE WILL OF THE JEDI ORDER.
SO IT IS THAT I, LUCIEN DRAAY, HUMBLY SUBMIT TO YOUR WISHES --
-- BY ACCEPTING THIS SEAT ON THE JEDI HIGH COUNCIL!
BUT WHILE BEING CHOSEN IS A GREAT HONOR --
-- THE TRUE HONOR BELONGS TO TWO FAR GREATER JEDI. MY LATE FATHER, BARRISON, WHOSE BEQUEST HELPED US REBUILD AFTER THE SITH WAR --
-- AND MY MOTHER KRYNDA, WHO WOULD HAVE JOINED THIS BODY LONG AGO BUT FOR HER DEVOTION TO TRAINING YOUNG SEERS.
I WILL DO MY BEST TO LIVE UP TO THEIR EXAMPLES -- AND I BEGIN WITH AN AGENDA FOR THE FUTURE.
A FUTURE WHICH RETURNS THE JEDI ORDER TO ITS TRUE MISSION -- PREVENTING THE RETURN OF THE SITH!

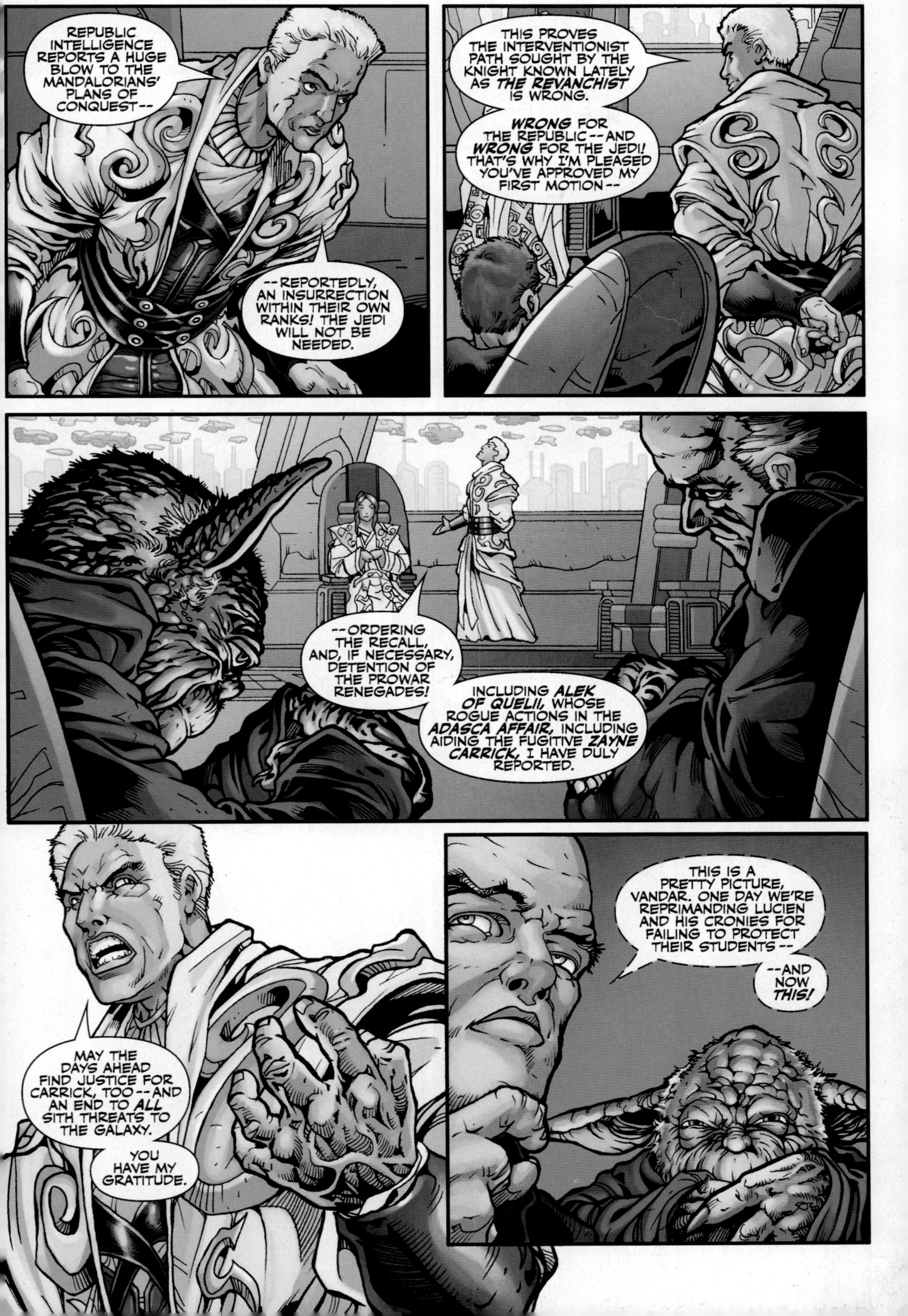
REPUBLIC INTELLIGENCE REPORTS A HUGE BLOW TO THE MANDALORIANS' PLANS OF CONQUEST--
--REPORTEDLY, AN INSURRECTION WITHIN THEIR OWN RANKS! THE JEDI WILL NOT BE NEEDED.
THIS PROVES THE INTERVENTIONIST PATH SOUGHT BY THE KNIGHT KNOWN LATELY AS *THE REVANCHIST* IS WRONG.
WRONG FOR THE REPUBLIC--AND *WRONG* FOR THE JEDI! THAT'S WHY I'M PLEASED YOU'VE APPROVED MY FIRST MOTION--
--ORDERING THE RECALL, AND, IF NECESSARY, DETENTION OF THE PROWAR RENEGADES!
INCLUDING *ALEK OF QUELII,* WHOSE ROGUE ACTIONS IN THE *ADASCA AFFAIR,* INCLUDING AIDING THE FUGITIVE *ZAYNE CARRICK,* I HAVE DULY REPORTED.
MAY THE DAYS AHEAD FIND JUSTICE FOR CARRICK, TOO--AND AN END TO *ALL* SITH THREATS TO THE GALAXY.
YOU HAVE MY GRATITUDE.
THIS IS A PRETTY PICTURE, VANDAR. ONE DAY WE'RE REPRIMANDING LUCIEN AND HIS CRONIES FOR FAILING TO PROTECT THEIR STUDENTS--
--AND NOW *THIS!*

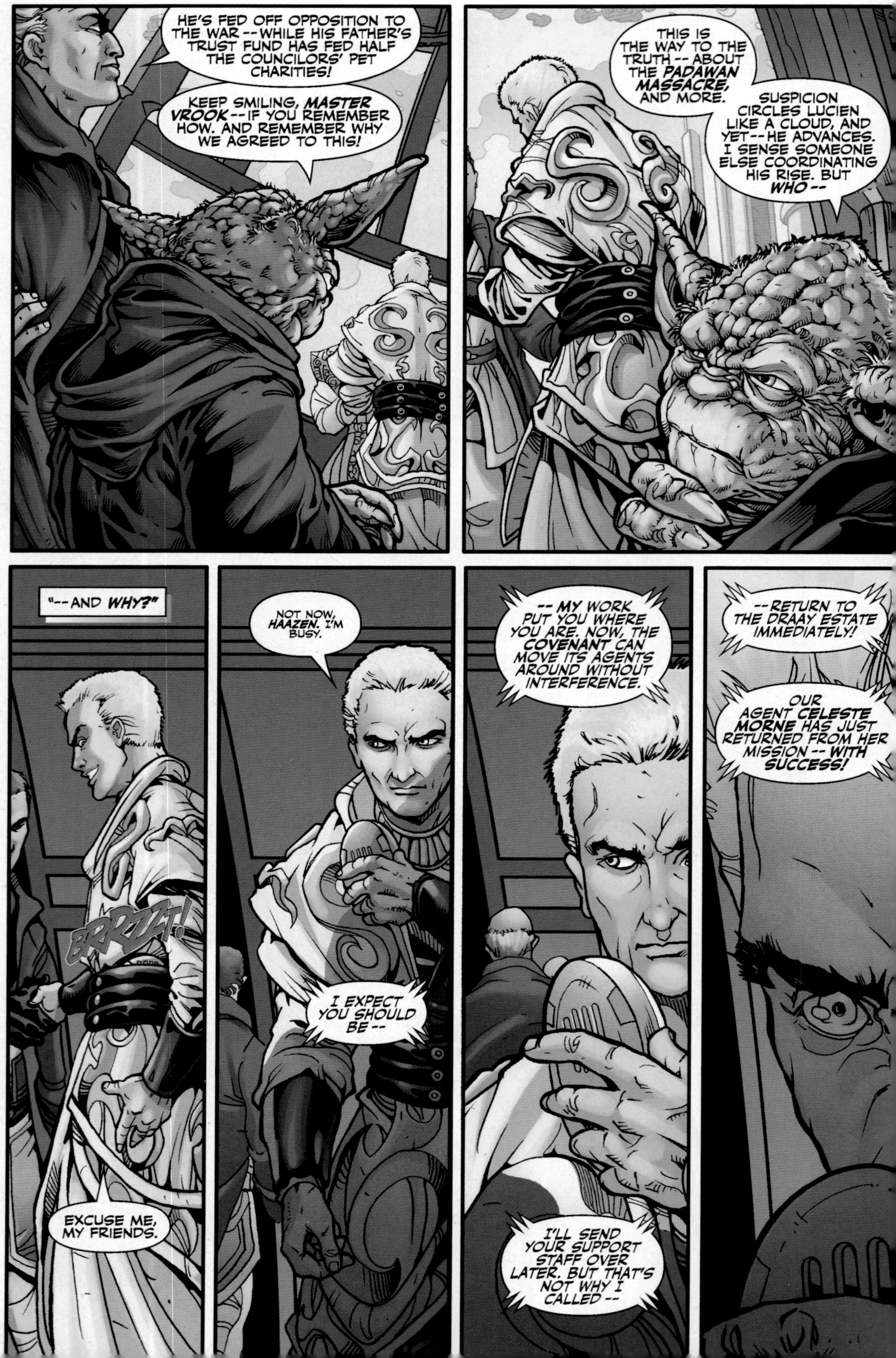
HE'S FED OFF OPPOSITION TO THE WAR -- WHILE HIS FATHER'S TRUST FUND HAS FED HALF THE COUNCILORS' PET CHARITIES!
KEEP SMILING, MASTER VROOK -- IF YOU REMEMBER HOW. AND REMEMBER WHY WE AGREED TO THIS!
THIS IS THE WAY TO THE TRUTH -- ABOUT THE PADAWAN MASSACRE, AND MORE.
SUSPICION CIRCLES LUCIEN LIKE A CLOUD, AND YET -- HE ADVANCES. I SENSE SOMEONE ELSE COORDINATING HIS RISE. BUT WHO --
"-- AND WHY?"
BRRZZT!
EXCUSE ME, MY FRIENDS.
NOT NOW, HAAZEN. I'M BUSY.
I EXPECT YOU SHOULD BE --
-- MY WORK PUT YOU WHERE YOU ARE. NOW, THE COVENANT CAN MOVE ITS AGENTS AROUND WITHOUT INTERFERENCE.
I'LL SEND YOUR SUPPORT STAFF OVER LATER. BUT THAT'S NOT WHY I CALLED --
-- RETURN TO THE DRAAY ESTATE IMMEDIATELY!
OUR AGENT CELESTE MORNE HAS JUST RETURNED FROM HER MISSION -- WITH SUCCESS!

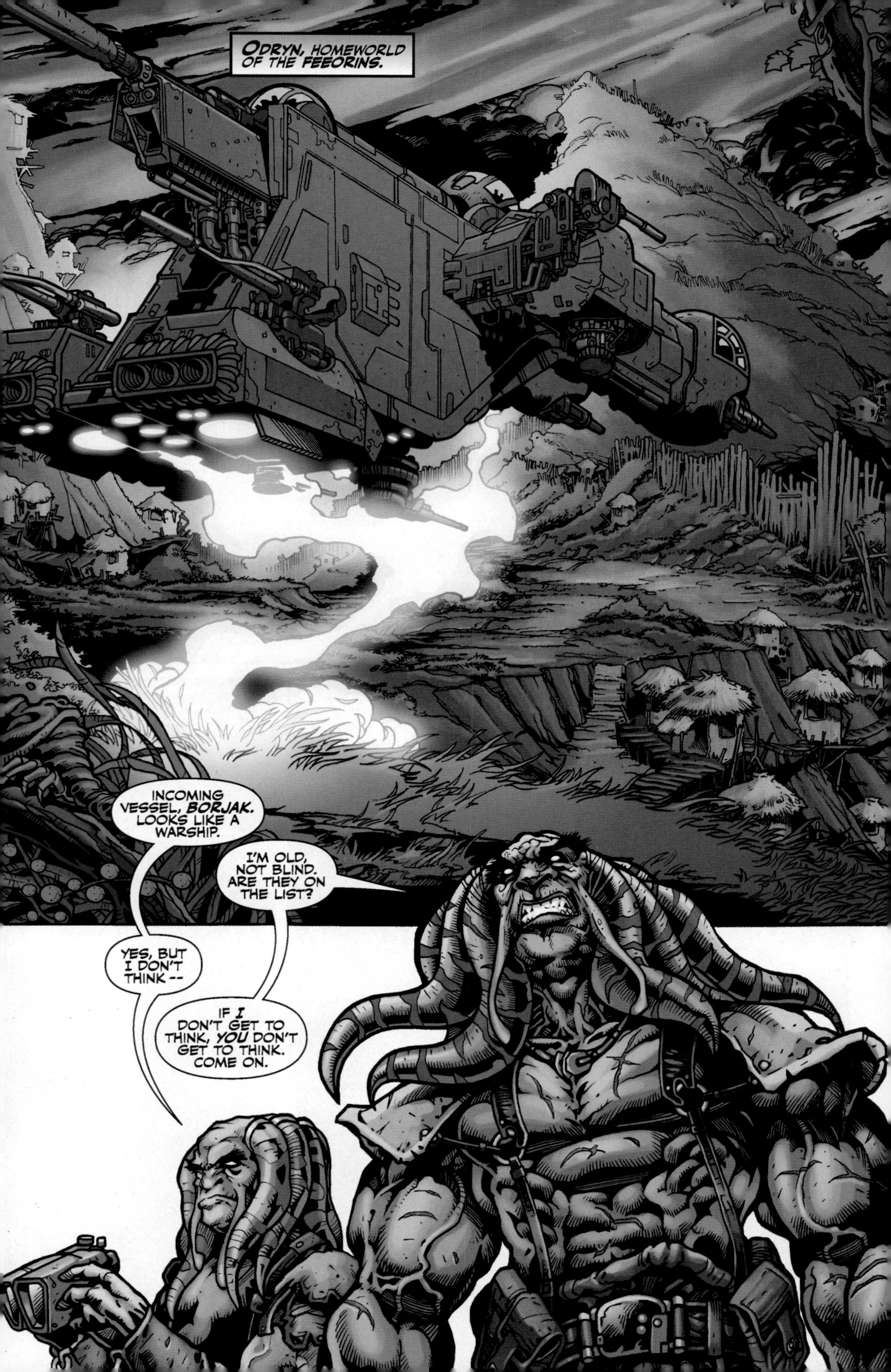

ODRYN, HOMEWORLD OF THE FEEORINS.
INCOMING VESSEL, BORJAK. LOOKS LIKE A WARSHIP.
I'M OLD, NOT BLIND. ARE THEY ON THE LIST?
YES, BUT I DON'T THINK --
IF I DON'T GET TO THINK, YOU DON'T GET TO THINK. COME ON.

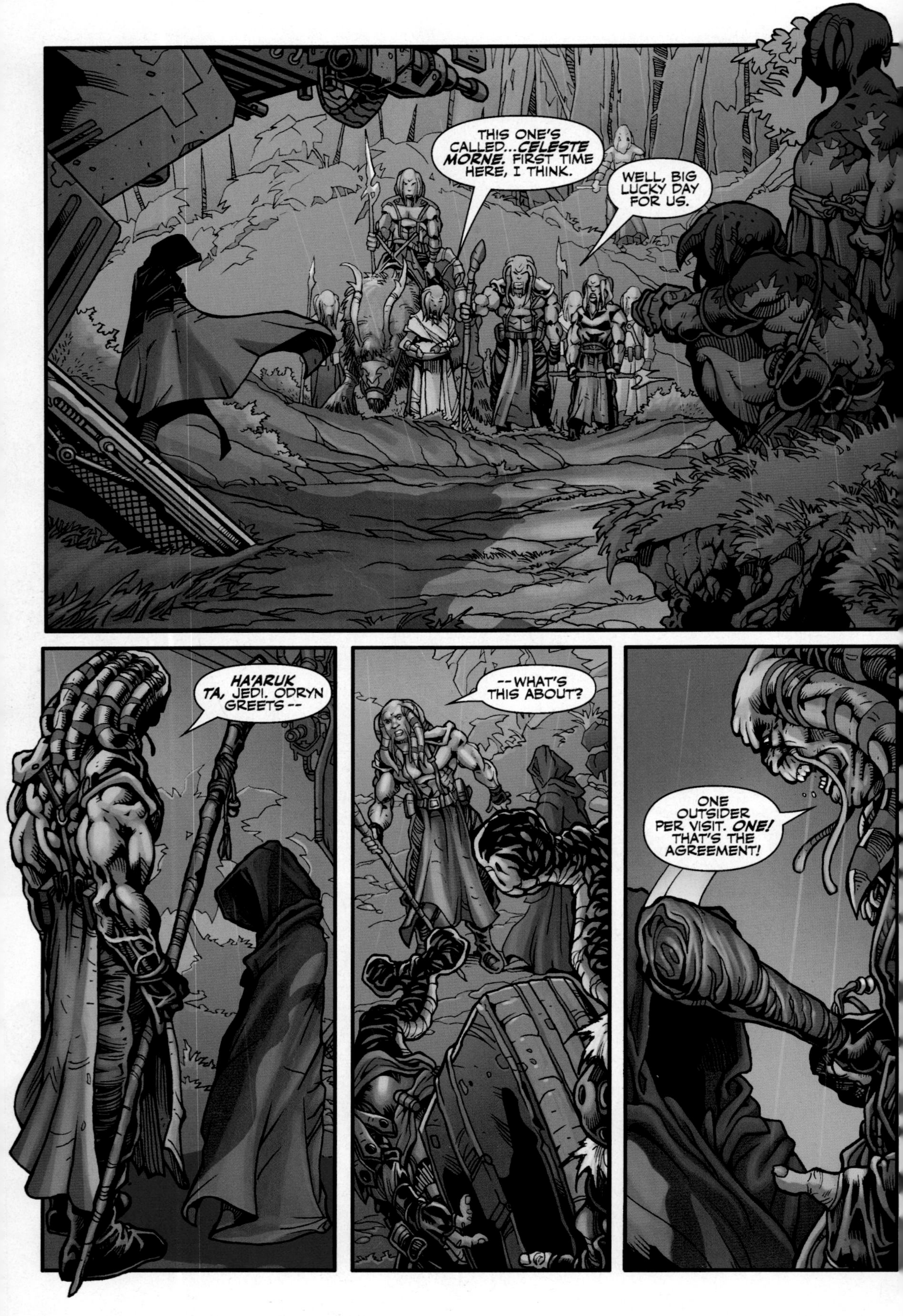
THIS ONE'S CALLED...*CELESTE MORNE.* FIRST TIME HERE, I THINK.
WELL, BIG LUCKY DAY FOR US.
HA'ARUK TA, JEDI. ODRYN GREETS --
-- WHAT'S THIS ABOUT?
ONE OUTSIDER PER VISIT. *ONE!* THAT'S THE AGREEMENT!

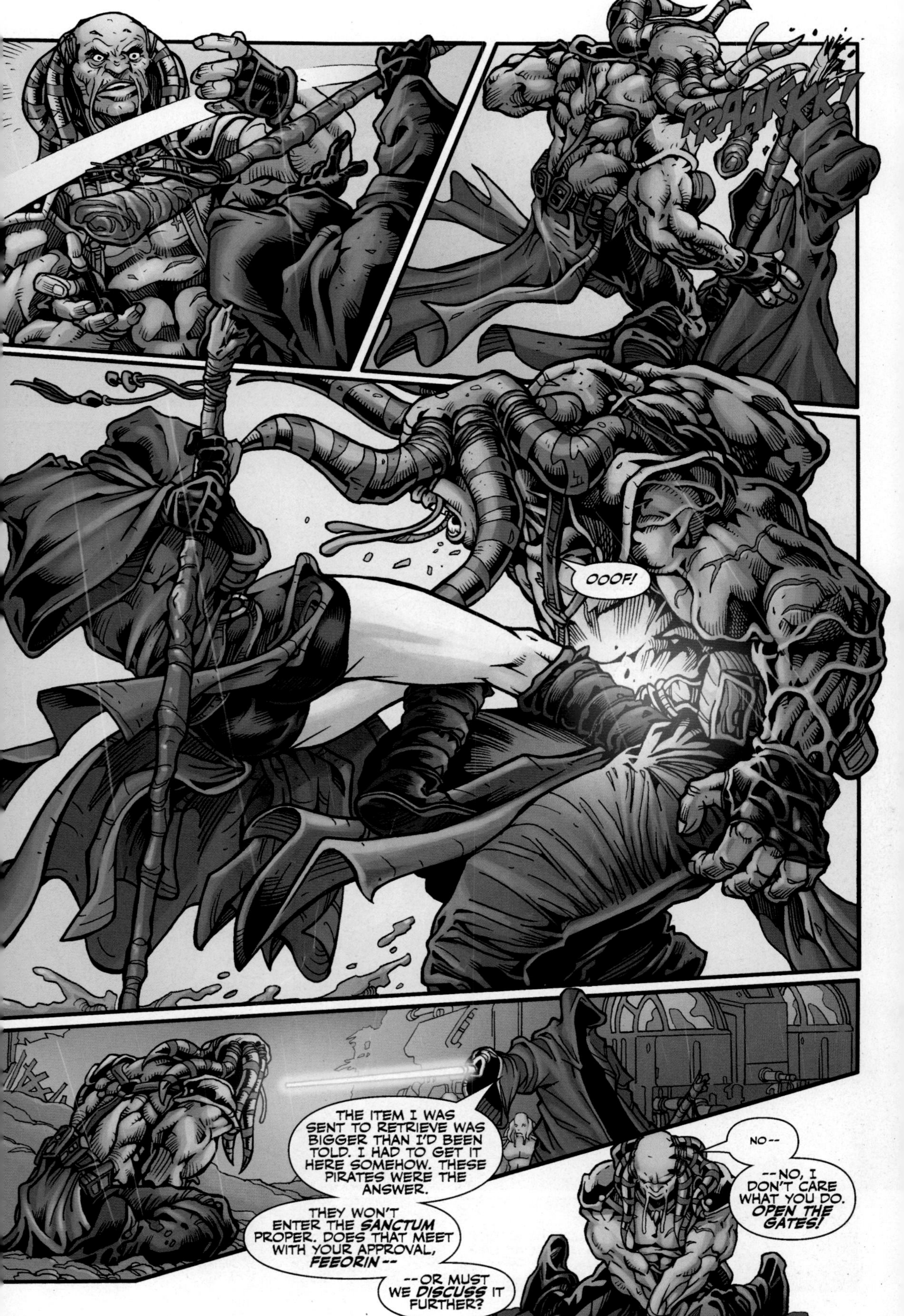
KRAAKKK!
OOOF!
THE ITEM I WAS SENT TO RETRIEVE WAS BIGGER THAN I'D BEEN TOLD. I HAD TO GET IT HERE SOMEHOW. THESE PIRATES WERE THE ANSWER.
THEY WON'T ENTER THE SANCTUM PROPER. DOES THAT MEET WITH YOUR APPROVAL, FEEORIN--
--OR MUST WE DISCUSS IT FURTHER?
NO--
--NO, I DON'T CARE WHAT YOU DO. OPEN THE GATES!

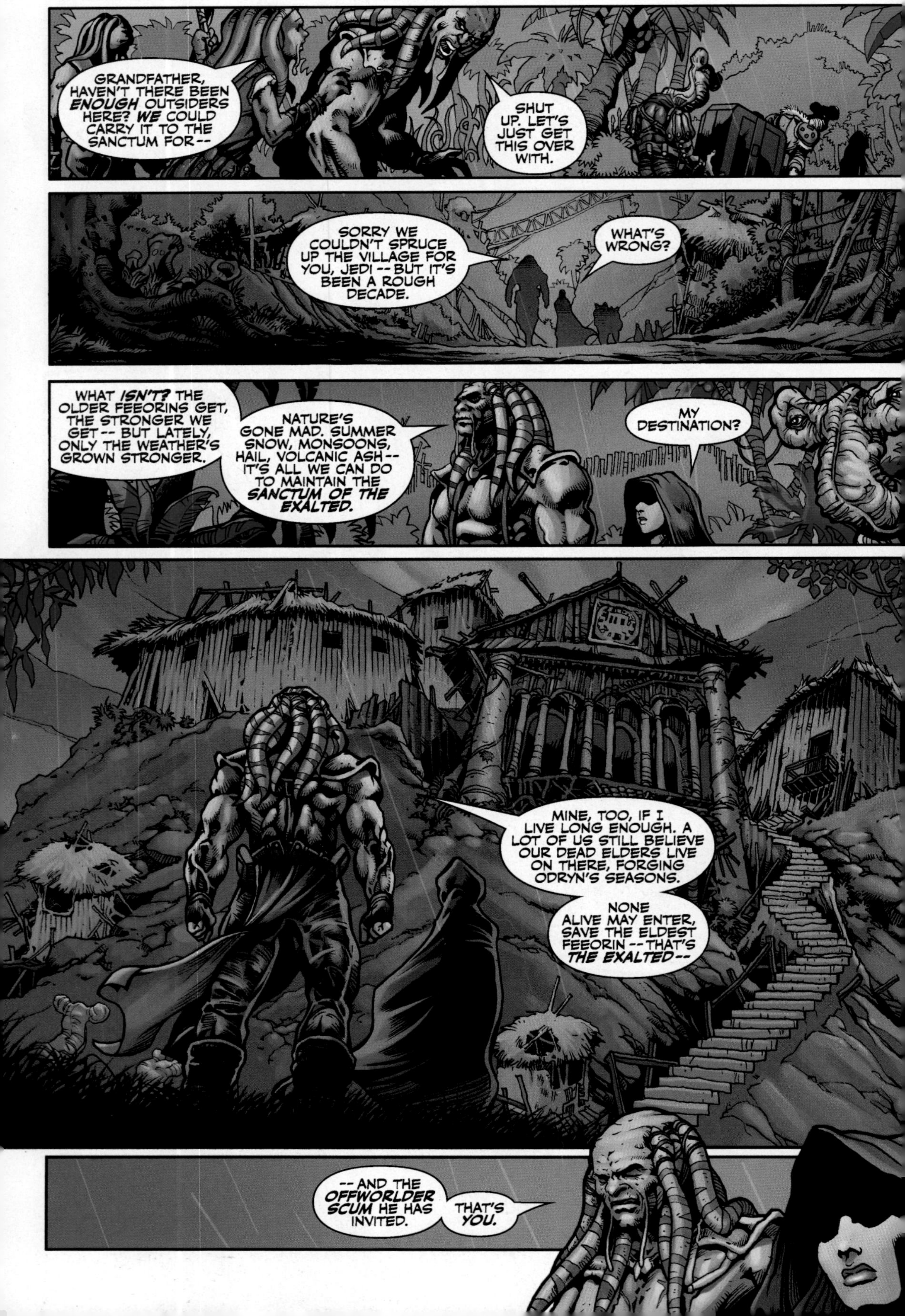
GRANDFATHER, HAVEN'T THERE BEEN ENOUGH OUTSIDERS HERE? WE COULD CARRY IT TO THE SANCTUM FOR--
SHUT UP. LET'S JUST GET THIS OVER WITH.
SORRY WE COULDN'T SPRUCE UP THE VILLAGE FOR YOU, JEDI--BUT IT'S BEEN A ROUGH DECADE.
WHAT'S WRONG?
WHAT ISN'T? THE OLDER FEEORINS GET, THE STRONGER WE GET-- BUT LATELY, ONLY THE WEATHER'S GROWN STRONGER.
NATURE'S GONE MAD. SUMMER SNOW, MONSOONS, HAIL, VOLCANIC ASH-- IT'S ALL WE CAN DO TO MAINTAIN THE SANCTUM OF THE EXALTED.
MY DESTINATION?
MINE, TOO, IF I LIVE LONG ENOUGH. A LOT OF US STILL BELIEVE OUR DEAD ELDERS LIVE ON THERE, FORGING ODRYN'S SEASONS.
NONE ALIVE MAY ENTER, SAVE THE ELDEST FEEORIN--THAT'S THE EXALTED--
--AND THE OFFWORLDER SCUM HE HAS INVITED.
THAT'S YOU.

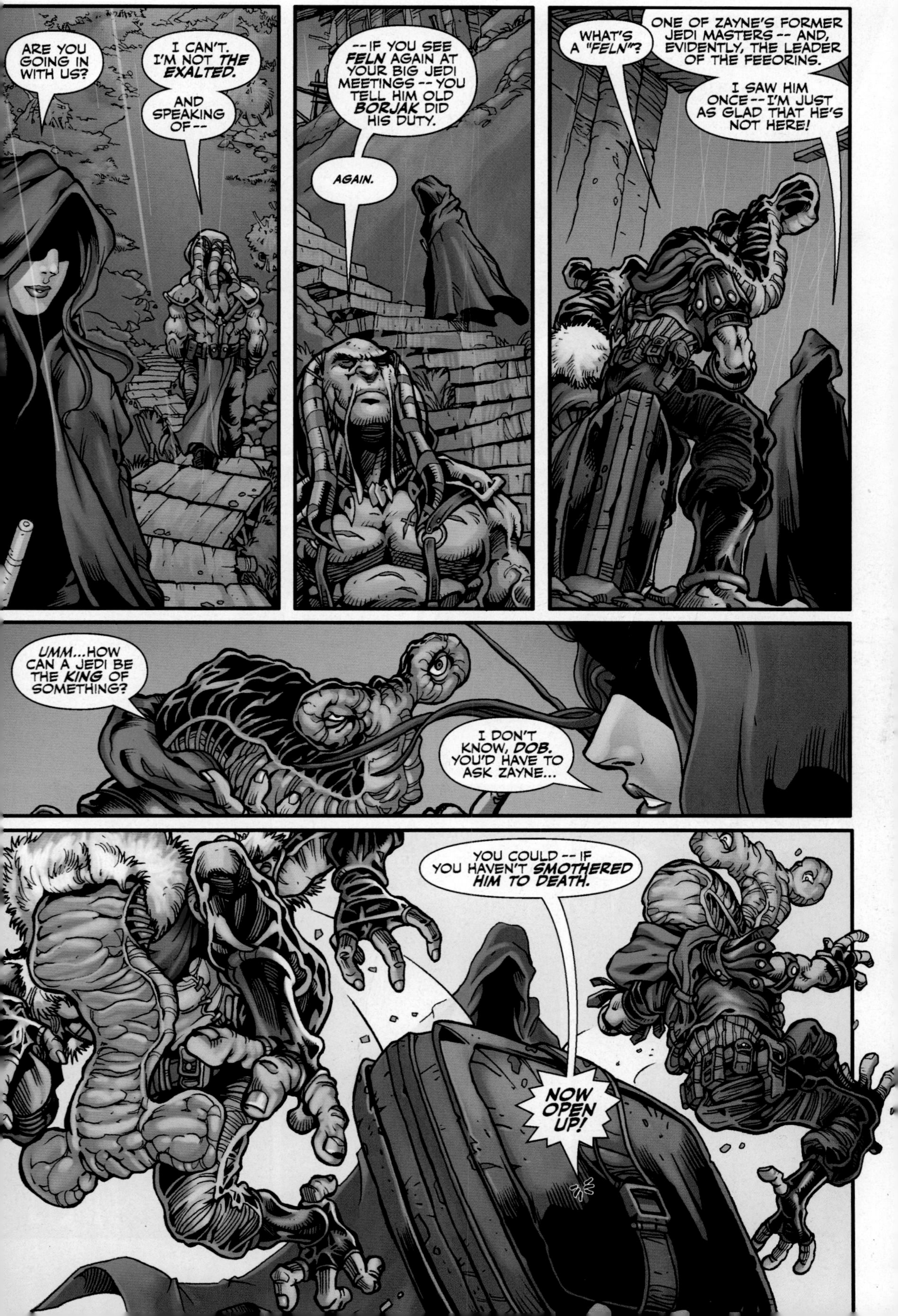

ARE YOU GOING IN WITH US?
I CAN'T. I'M NOT THE EXALTED.
AND SPEAKING OF--
--IF YOU SEE FELN AGAIN AT YOUR BIG JEDI MEETINGS--YOU TELL HIM OLD BORJAK DID HIS DUTY.
AGAIN.
WHAT'S A "FELN"?
ONE OF ZAYNE'S FORMER JEDI MASTERS-- AND, EVIDENTLY, THE LEADER OF THE FEEORINS.
I SAW HIM ONCE--I'M JUST AS GLAD THAT HE'S NOT HERE!
UMM...HOW CAN A JEDI BE THE KING OF SOMETHING?
I DON'T KNOW, DOB. YOU'D HAVE TO ASK ZAYNE...
YOU COULD--IF YOU HAVEN'T SMOTHERED HIM TO DEATH.
NOW OPEN UP!

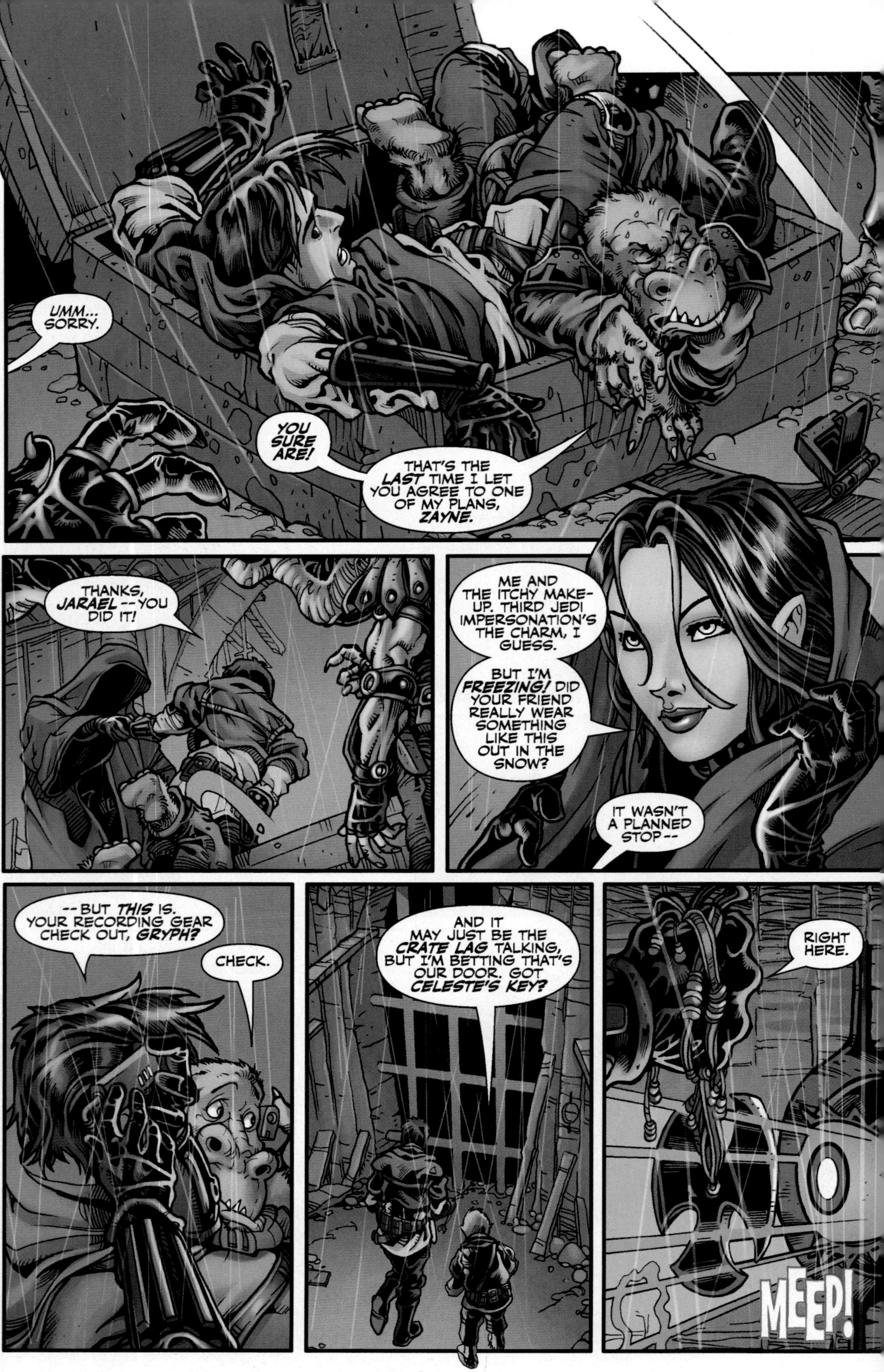
UMM... SORRY.
YOU SURE ARE!
THAT'S THE LAST TIME I LET YOU AGREE TO ONE OF MY PLANS, ZAYNE.
THANKS, JARAEL--YOU DID IT!
ME AND THE ITCHY MAKE-UP. THIRD JEDI IMPERSONATION'S THE CHARM, I GUESS.
BUT I'M FREEZING! DID YOUR FRIEND REALLY WEAR SOMETHING LIKE THIS OUT IN THE SNOW?
IT WASN'T A PLANNED STOP--
--BUT THIS IS. YOUR RECORDING GEAR CHECK OUT, GRYPH?
CHECK.
AND IT MAY JUST BE THE CRATE LAG TALKING, BUT I'M BETTING THAT'S OUR DOOR. GOT CELESTE'S KEY?
RIGHT HERE.
MEEP!

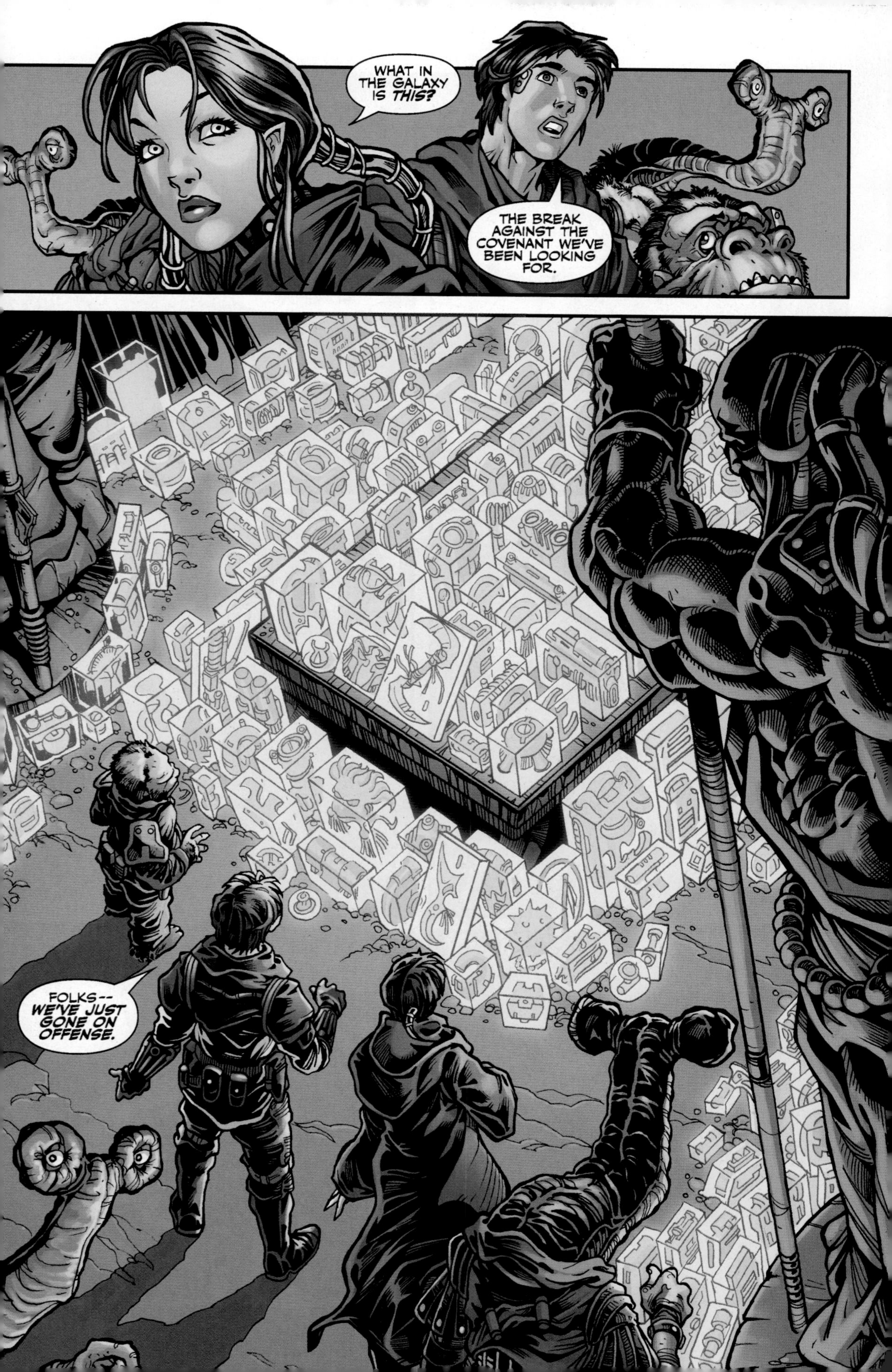
WHAT IN THE GALAXY IS *THIS?*
THE BREAK AGAINST THE COVENANT WE'VE BEEN LOOKING FOR.
FOLKS-- *WE'VE JUST GONE ON OFFENSE.*

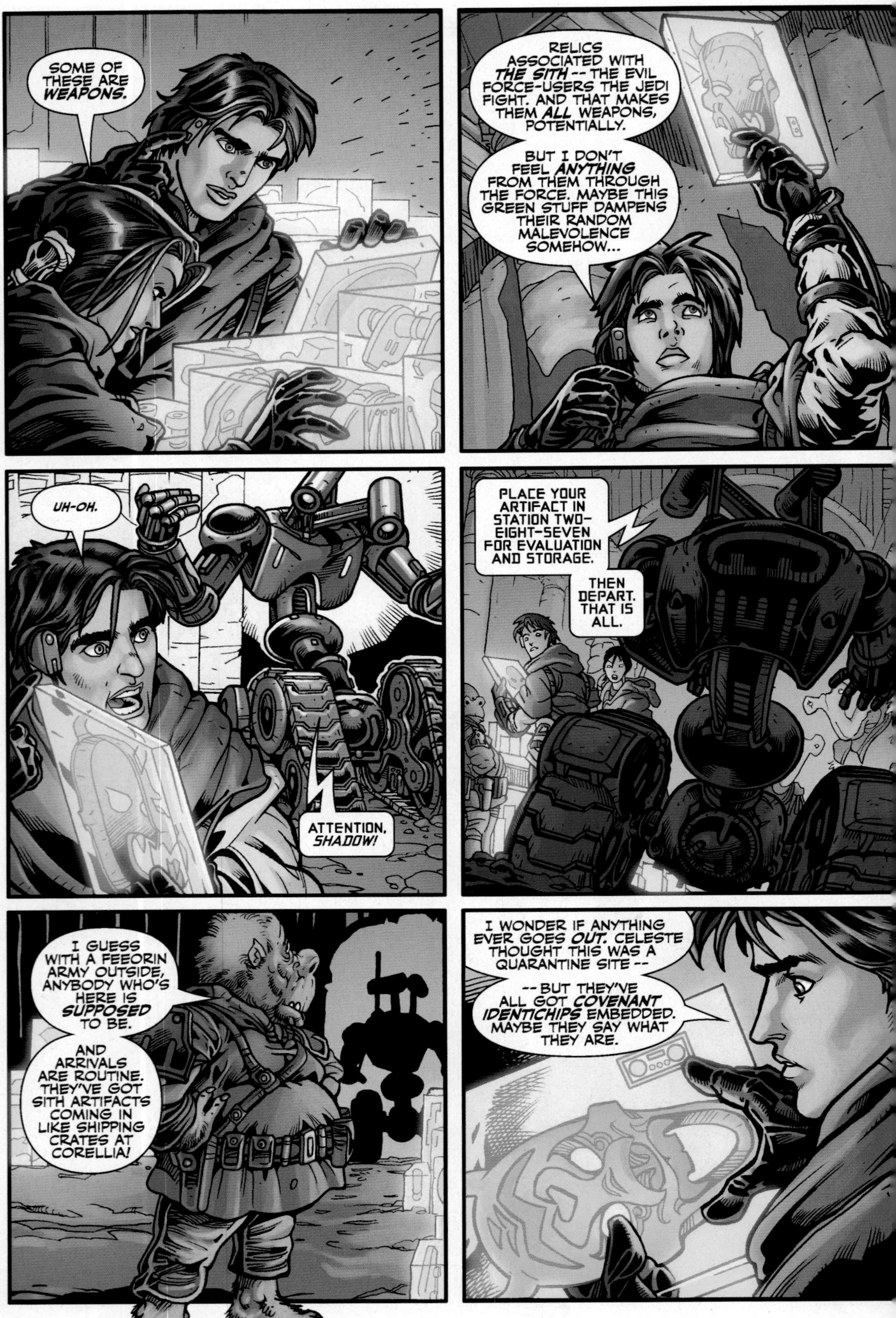
SOME OF THESE ARE WEAPONS.
RELICS ASSOCIATED WITH THE SITH -- THE EVIL FORCE-USERS THE JEDI FIGHT. AND THAT MAKES THEM ALL WEAPONS, POTENTIALLY.
BUT I DON'T FEEL ANYTHING FROM THEM THROUGH THE FORCE. MAYBE THIS GREEN STUFF DAMPENS THEIR RANDOM MALEVOLENCE SOMEHOW...
UH-OH.
ATTENTION, SHADOW!
PLACE YOUR ARTIFACT IN STATION TWO-EIGHT-SEVEN FOR EVALUATION AND STORAGE.
THEN DEPART. THAT IS ALL.
I GUESS WITH A FEEORIN ARMY OUTSIDE, ANYBODY WHO'S HERE IS SUPPOSED TO BE.
AND ARRIVALS ARE ROUTINE. THEY'VE GOT SITH ARTIFACTS COMING IN LIKE SHIPPING CRATES AT CORELLIA!
I WONDER IF ANYTHING EVER GOES OUT. CELESTE THOUGHT THIS WAS A QUARANTINE SITE --
-- BUT THEY'VE ALL GOT COVENANT IDENTICHIPS EMBEDDED. MAYBE THEY SAY WHAT THEY ARE.

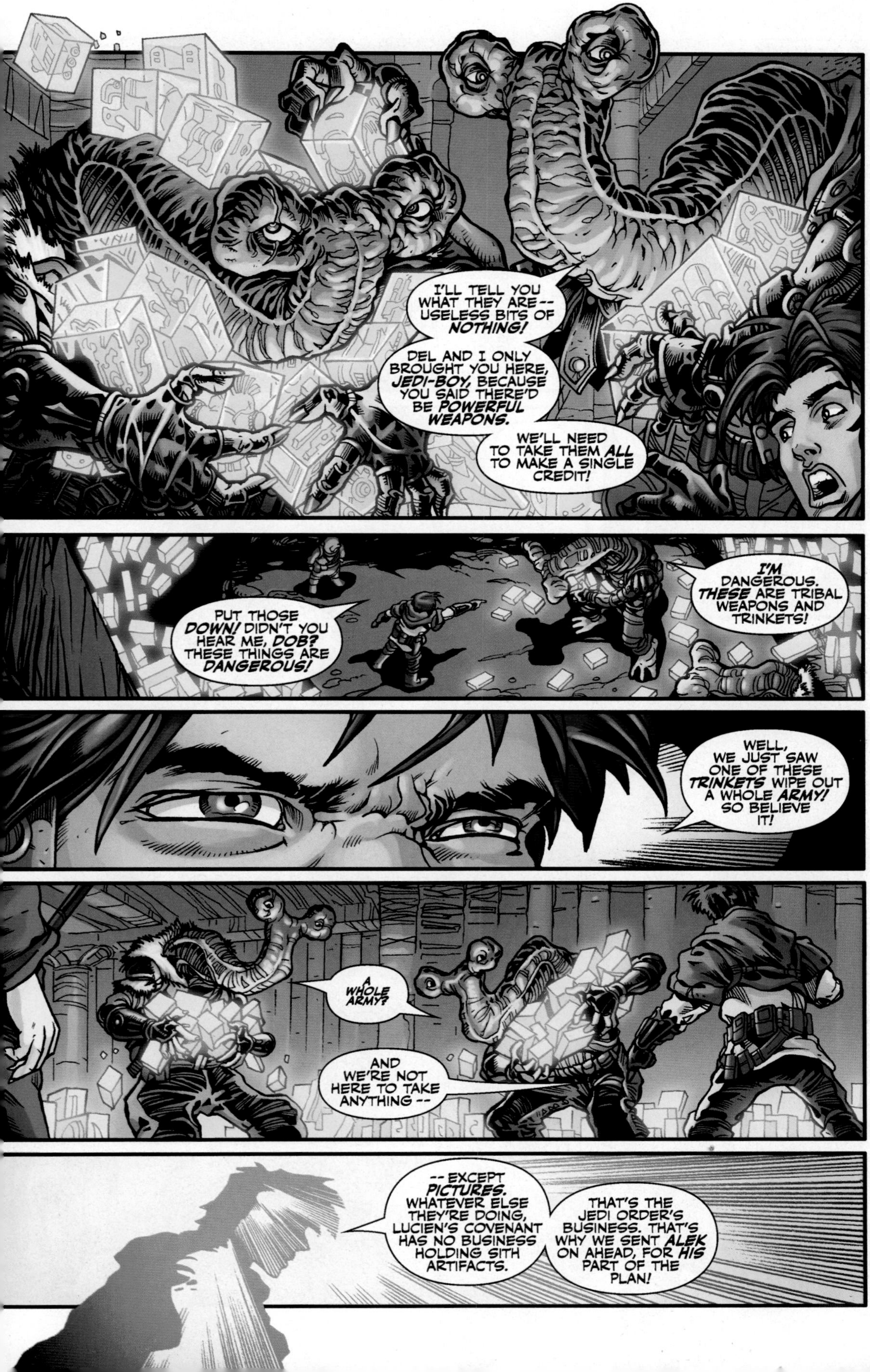

I'LL TELL YOU WHAT THEY ARE-- USELESS BITS OF NOTHING!
DEL AND I ONLY BROUGHT YOU HERE, JEDI-BOY, BECAUSE YOU SAID THERE'D BE POWERFUL WEAPONS.
WE'LL NEED TO TAKE THEM ALL TO MAKE A SINGLE CREDIT!
PUT THOSE DOWN! DIDN'T YOU HEAR ME, DOB? THESE THINGS ARE DANGEROUS!
I'M DANGEROUS. THESE ARE TRIBAL WEAPONS AND TRINKETS!
WELL, WE JUST SAW ONE OF THESE TRINKETS WIPE OUT A WHOLE ARMY! SO BELIEVE IT!
A WHOLE ARMY?
AND WE'RE NOT HERE TO TAKE ANYTHING --
-- EXCEPT PICTURES. WHATEVER ELSE THEY'RE DOING, LUCIEN'S COVENANT HAS NO BUSINESS HOLDING SITH ARTIFACTS.
THAT'S THE JEDI ORDER'S BUSINESS. THAT'S WHY WE SENT ALEK ON AHEAD, FOR HIS PART OF THE PLAN!

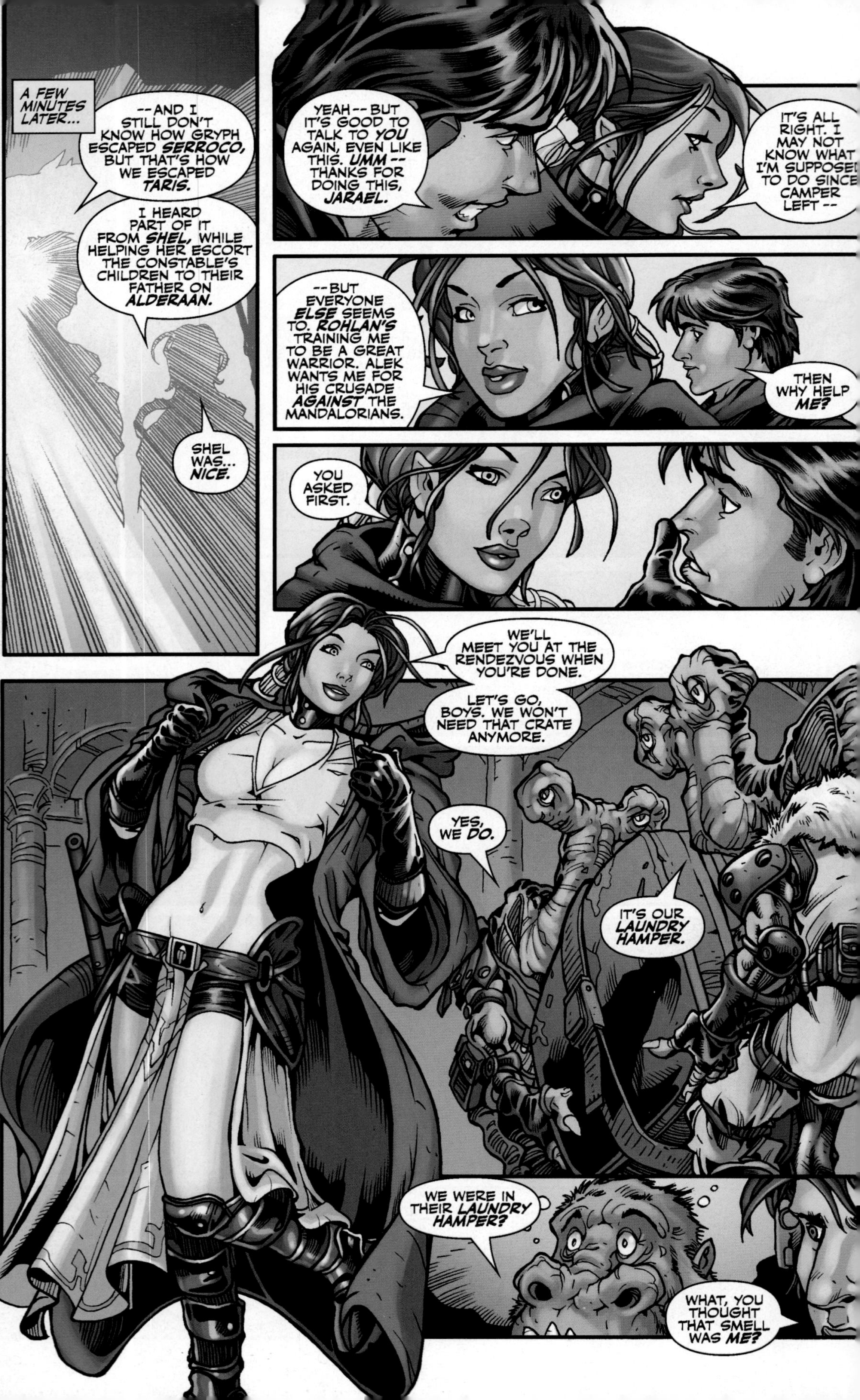
A FEW MINUTES LATER...
--AND I STILL DON'T KNOW HOW GRYPH ESCAPED SERROCO, BUT THAT'S HOW WE ESCAPED TARIS.
I HEARD PART OF IT FROM SHEL, WHILE HELPING HER ESCORT THE CONSTABLE'S CHILDREN TO THEIR FATHER ON ALDERAAN.
SHEL WAS... NICE.
YEAH--BUT IT'S GOOD TO TALK TO YOU AGAIN, EVEN LIKE THIS. UMM--THANKS FOR DOING THIS, JARAEL.
IT'S ALL RIGHT. I MAY NOT KNOW WHAT I'M SUPPOSED TO DO SINCE CAMPER LEFT--
--BUT EVERYONE ELSE SEEMS TO. ROHLAN'S TRAINING ME TO BE A GREAT WARRIOR. ALEK WANTS ME FOR HIS CRUSADE AGAINST THE MANDALORIANS.
THEN WHY HELP ME?
YOU ASKED FIRST.
WE'LL MEET YOU AT THE RENDEZVOUS WHEN YOU'RE DONE.
LET'S GO, BOYS. WE WON'T NEED THAT CRATE ANYMORE.
YES, WE DO.
IT'S OUR LAUNDRY HAMPER.
WE WERE IN THEIR LAUNDRY HAMPER?
WHAT, YOU THOUGHT THAT SMELL WAS ME?

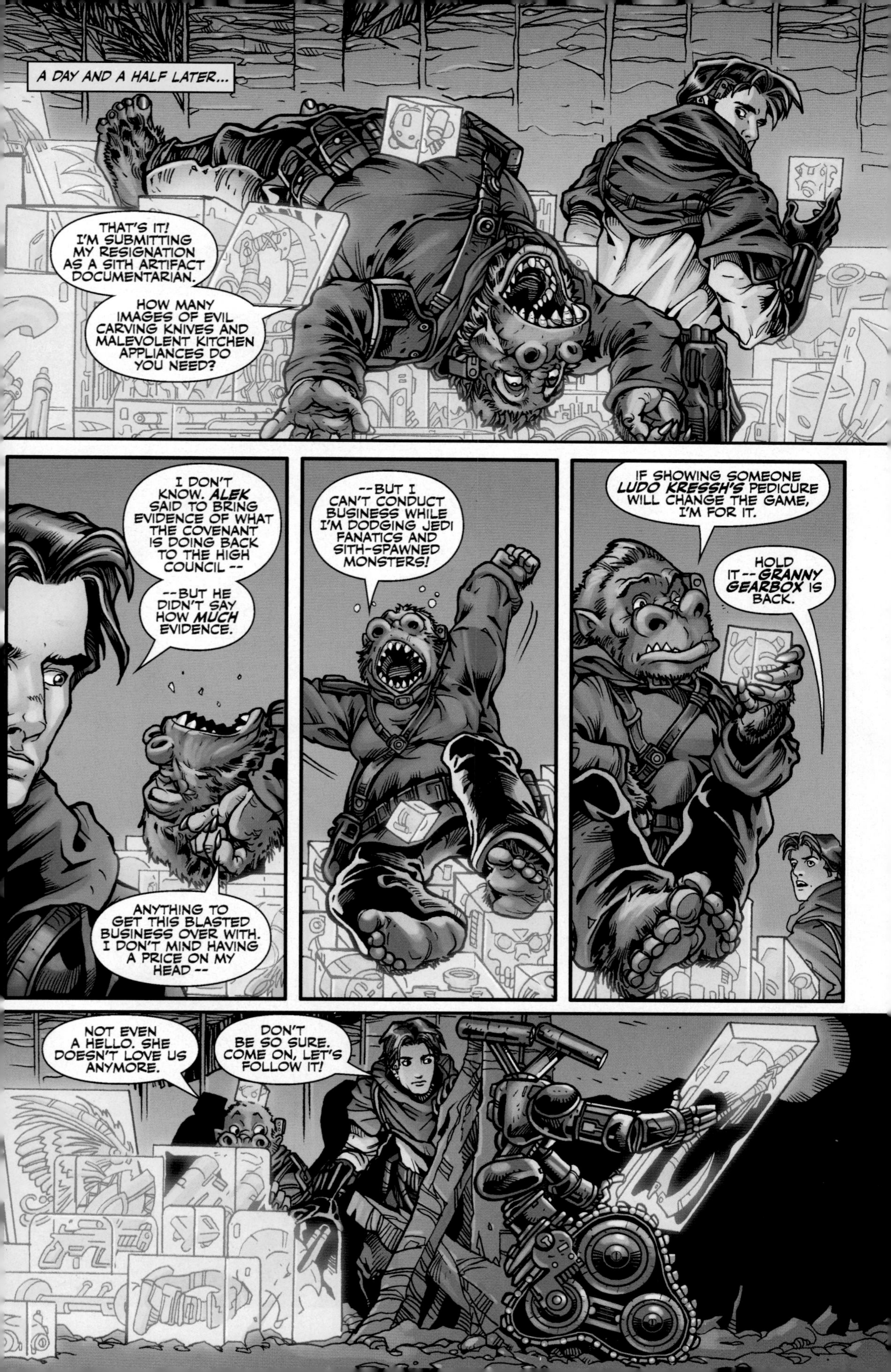

A DAY AND A HALF LATER...
THAT'S IT! I'M SUBMITTING MY RESIGNATION AS A SITH ARTIFACT DOCUMENTARIAN.
HOW MANY IMAGES OF EVIL CARVING KNIVES AND MALEVOLENT KITCHEN APPLIANCES DO YOU NEED?
I DON'T KNOW. ALEK SAID TO BRING EVIDENCE OF WHAT THE COVENANT IS DOING BACK TO THE HIGH COUNCIL --
--BUT HE DIDN'T SAY HOW MUCH EVIDENCE.
ANYTHING TO GET THIS BLASTED BUSINESS OVER WITH. I DON'T MIND HAVING A PRICE ON MY HEAD --
--BUT I CAN'T CONDUCT BUSINESS WHILE I'M DODGING JEDI FANATICS AND SITH-SPAWNED MONSTERS!
IF SHOWING SOMEONE LUDO KRESSH'S PEDICURE WILL CHANGE THE GAME, I'M FOR IT.
HOLD IT -- GRANNY GEARBOX IS BACK.
NOT EVEN A HELLO. SHE DOESN'T LOVE US ANYMORE.
DON'T BE SO SURE. COME ON, LET'S FOLLOW IT!

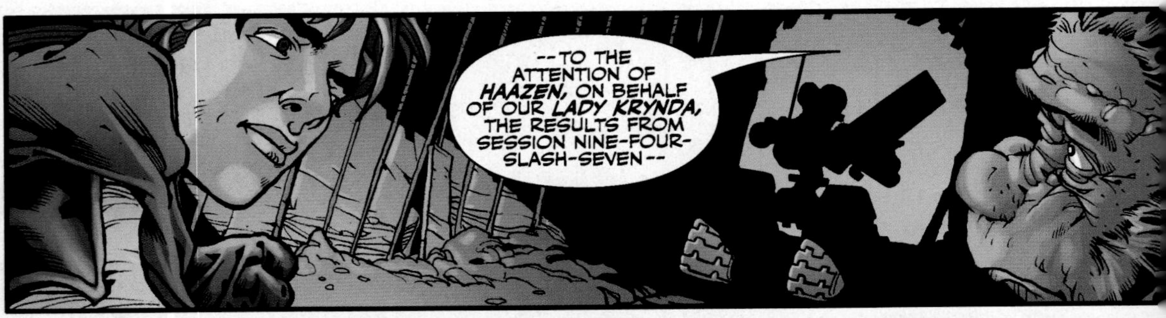
--TO THE ATTENTION OF HAAZEN, ON BEHALF OF OUR LADY KRYNDA, THE RESULTS FROM SESSION NINE-FOUR-SLASH-SEVEN--

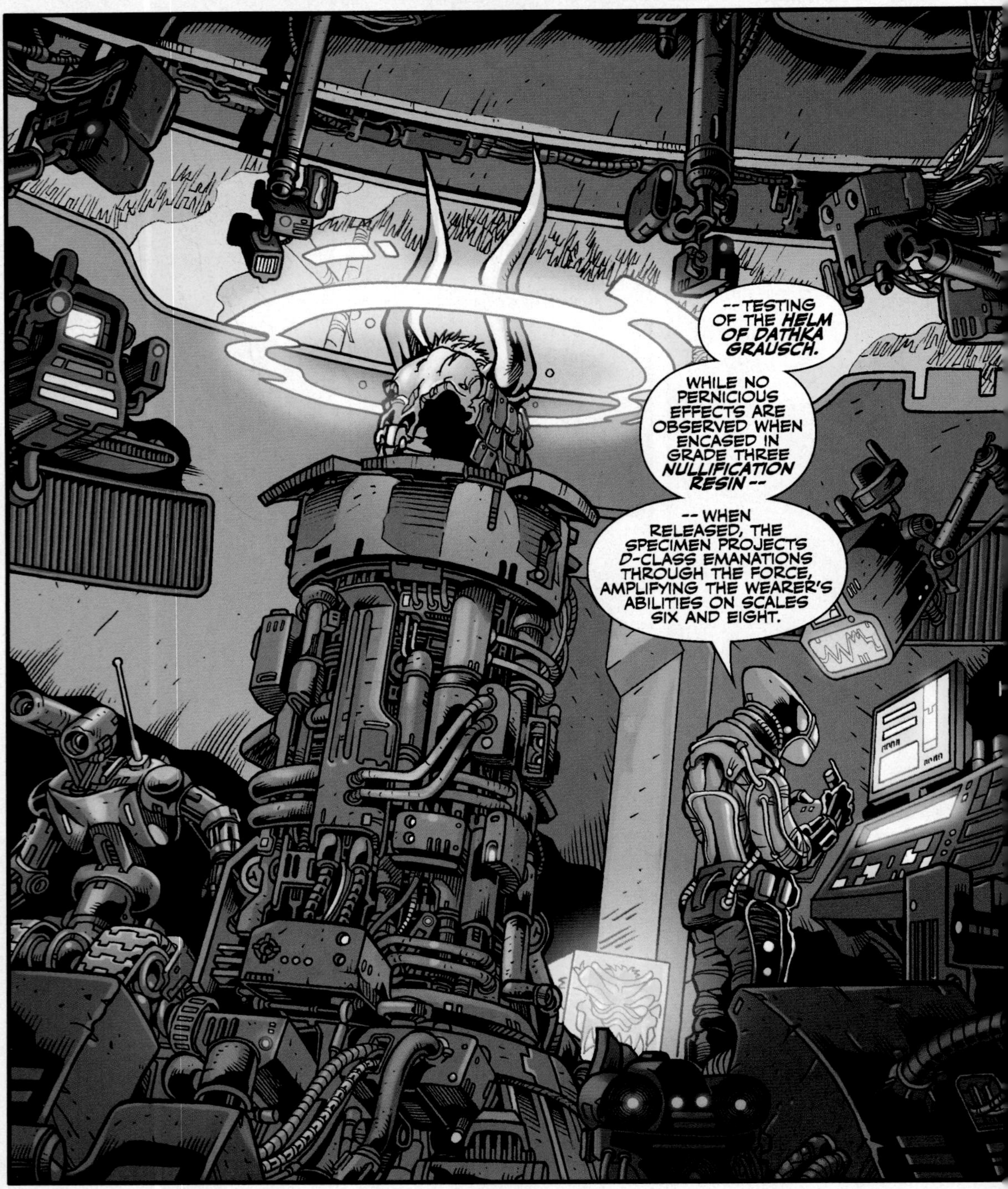
--TESTING OF THE HELM OF DATHKA GRAUSCH.
WHILE NO PERNICIOUS EFFECTS ARE OBSERVED WHEN ENCASED IN GRADE THREE NULLIFICATION RESIN--
--WHEN RELEASED, THE SPECIMEN PROJECTS D-CLASS EMANATIONS THROUGH THE FORCE, AMPLIFYING THE WEARER'S ABILITIES ON SCALES SIX AND EIGHT.

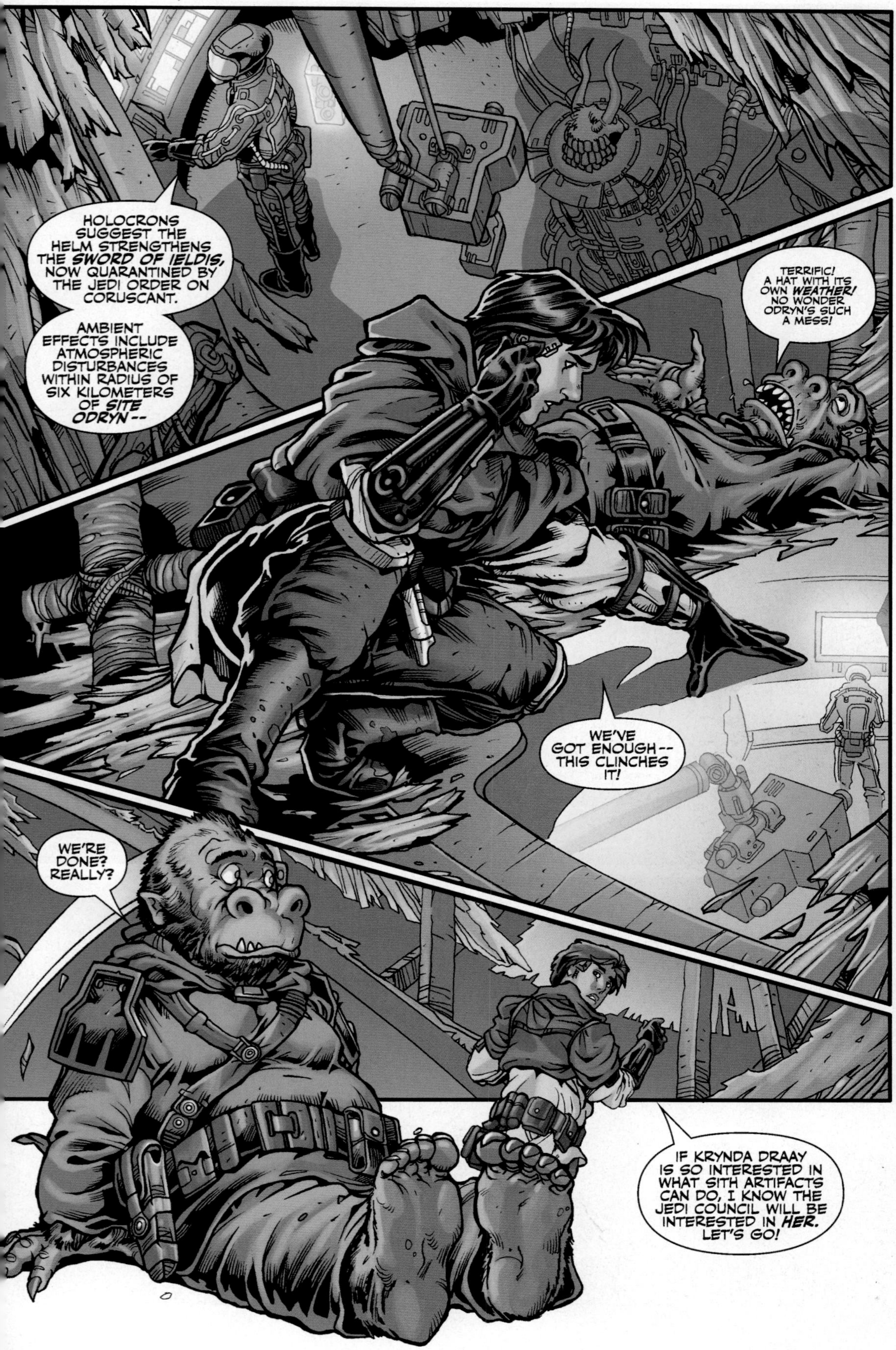
HOLOCRONS SUGGEST THE HELM STRENGTHENS THE SWORD OF IELDIS, NOW QUARANTINED BY THE JEDI ORDER ON CORUSCANT.
AMBIENT EFFECTS INCLUDE ATMOSPHERIC DISTURBANCES WITHIN RADIUS OF SIX KILOMETERS OF SITE ODRYN--
TERRIFIC! A HAT WITH ITS OWN WEATHER! NO WONDER ODRYN'S SUCH A MESS!
WE'VE GOT ENOUGH-- THIS CLINCHES IT!
WE'RE DONE? REALLY?
IF KRYNDA DRAAY IS SO INTERESTED IN WHAT SITH ARTIFACTS CAN DO, I KNOW THE JEDI COUNCIL WILL BE INTERESTED IN HER. LET'S GO!

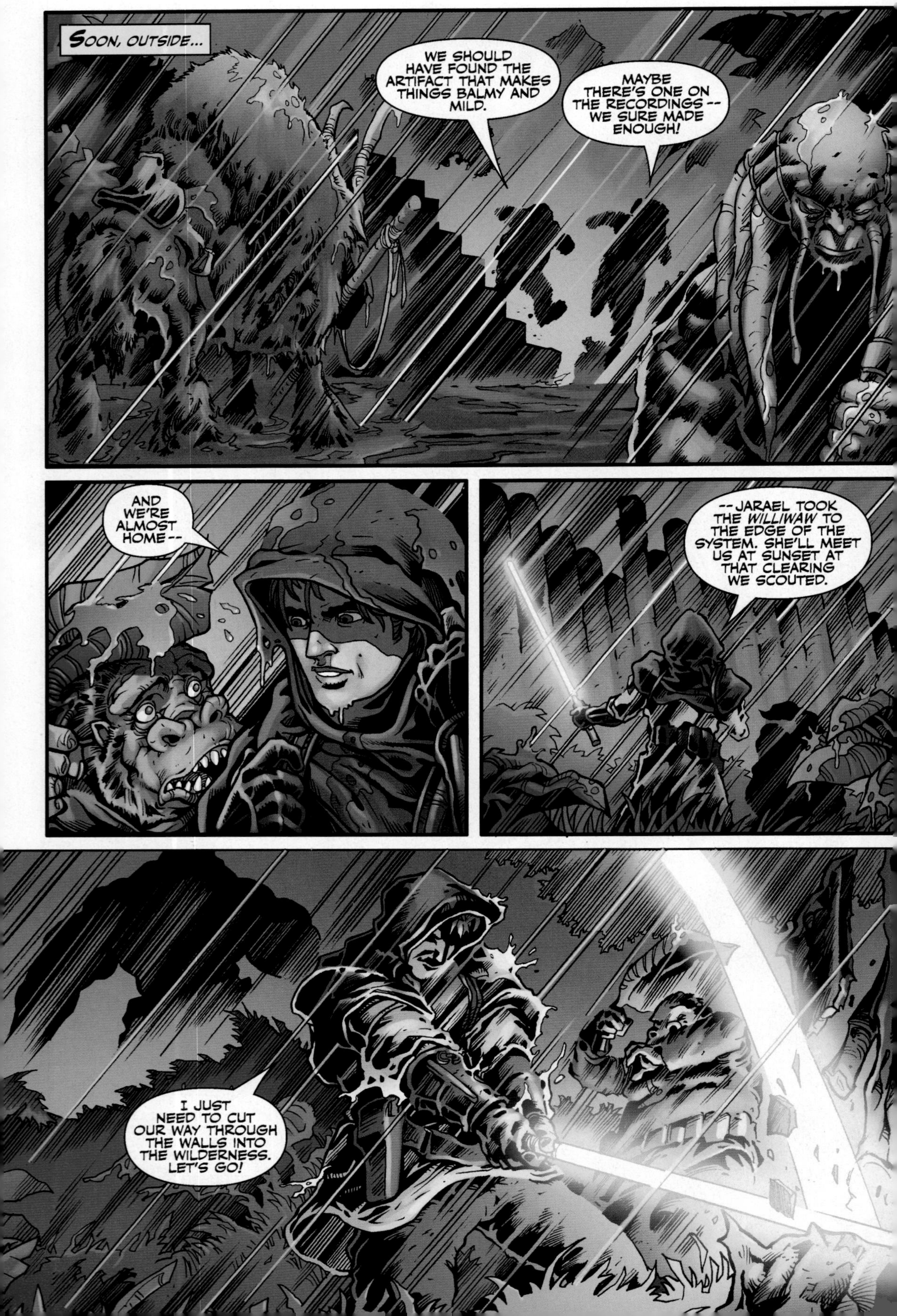
SOON, OUTSIDE...
WE SHOULD HAVE FOUND THE ARTIFACT THAT MAKES THINGS BALMY AND MILD.
MAYBE THERE'S ONE ON THE RECORDINGS -- WE SURE MADE ENOUGH!
AND WE'RE ALMOST HOME --
--JARAEL TOOK THE *WILLIWAW* TO THE *EDGE* OF THE SYSTEM. SHE'LL MEET US AT SUNSET AT THAT CLEARING WE SCOUTED.
I JUST NEED TO CUT OUR WAY THROUGH THE WALLS INTO THE WILDERNESS. LET'S GO!

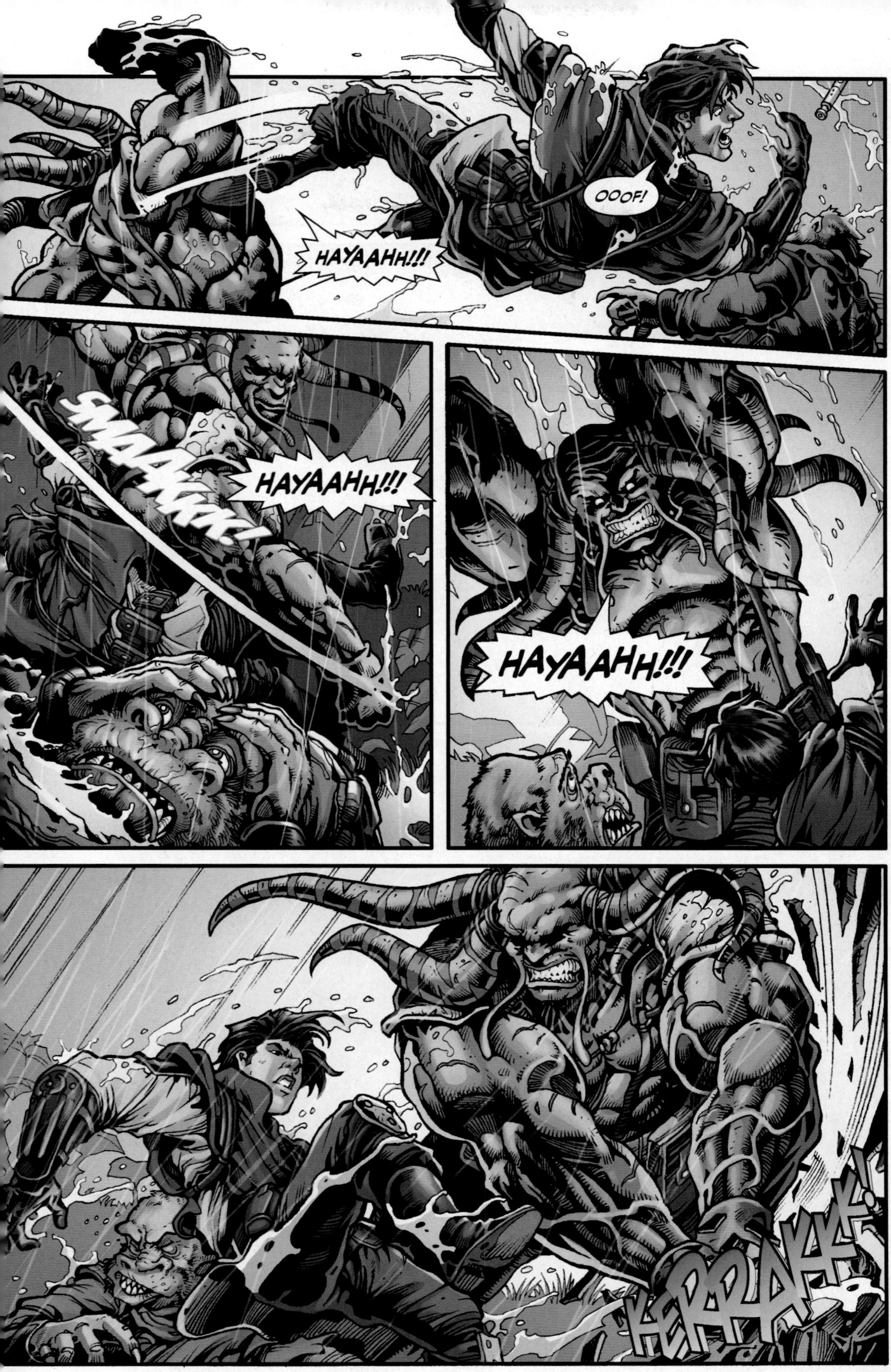
OOOF!
HAYAAHH!!!
SMAAKKK!
HAYAAHH!!!
HAYAAHH!!!
KERRAKK!

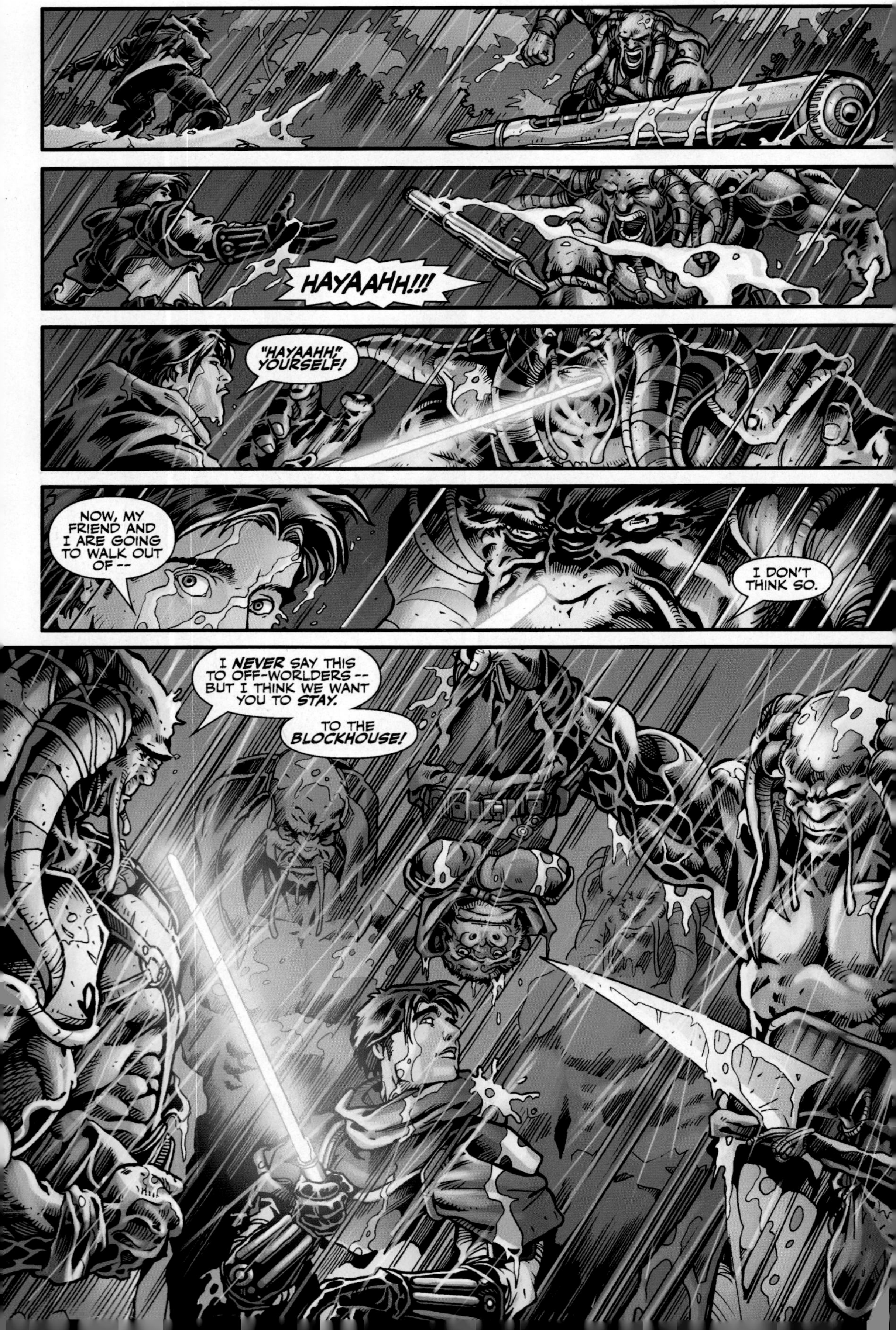
HAYAAHH!!!
"HAYAAHH," YOURSELF!
NOW, MY FRIEND AND I ARE GOING TO WALK OUT OF --
I DON'T THINK SO.
I NEVER SAY THIS TO OFF-WORLDERS -- BUT I THINK WE WANT YOU TO STAY.
TO THE BLOCKHOUSE!

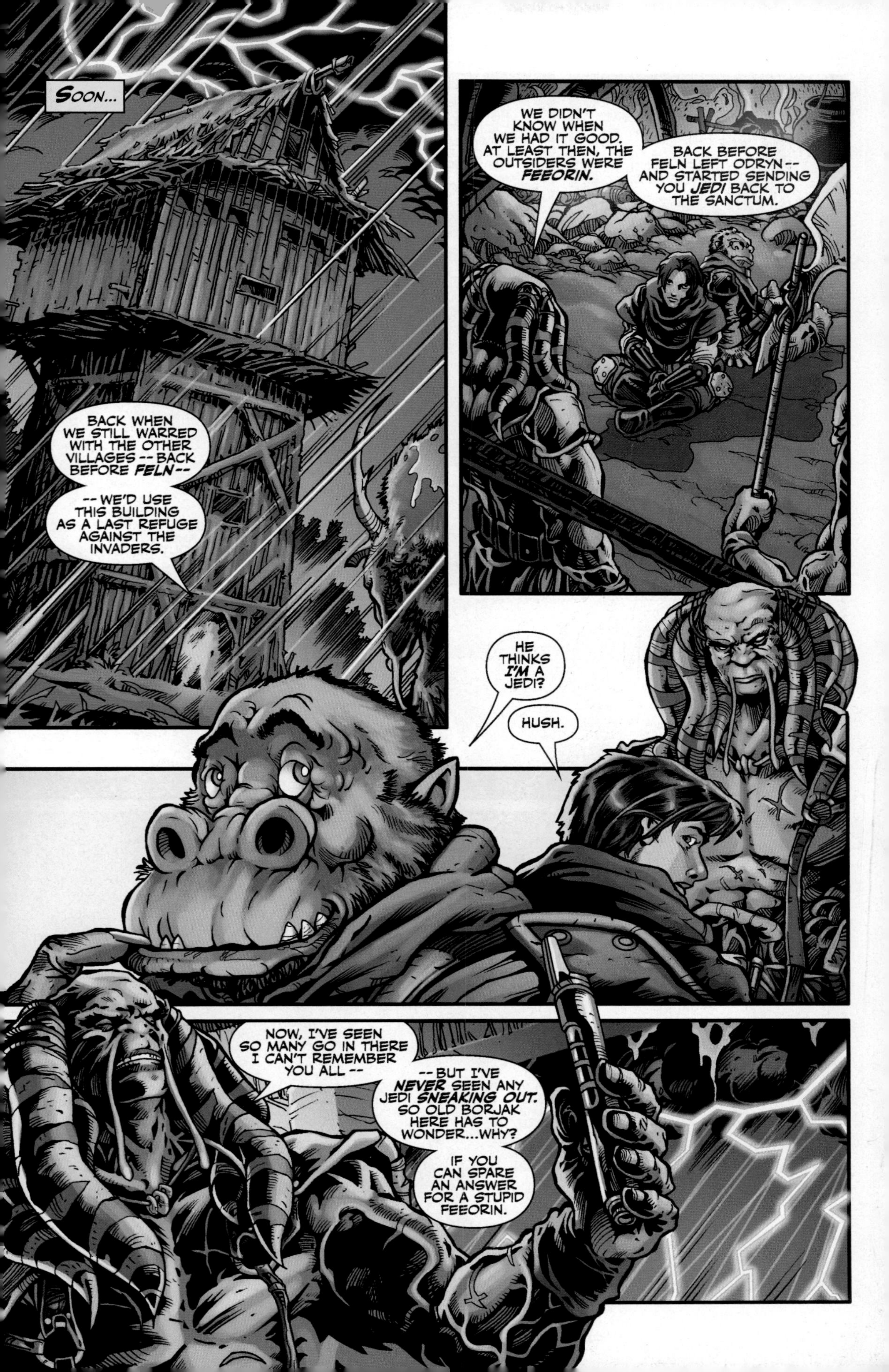
SOON...
BACK WHEN WE STILL WARRED WITH THE OTHER VILLAGES -- BACK BEFORE FELN--
-- WE'D USE THIS BUILDING AS A LAST REFUGE AGAINST THE INVADERS.
WE DIDN'T KNOW WHEN WE HAD IT GOOD. AT LEAST THEN, THE OUTSIDERS WERE FEEORIN.
BACK BEFORE FELN LEFT ODRYN -- AND STARTED SENDING YOU JEDI BACK TO THE SANCTUM.
HE THINKS I'M A JEDI?
HUSH.
NOW, I'VE SEEN SO MANY GO IN THERE I CAN'T REMEMBER YOU ALL --
-- BUT I'VE NEVER SEEN ANY JEDI SNEAKING OUT. SO OLD BORJAK HERE HAS TO WONDER...WHY?
IF YOU CAN SPARE AN ANSWER FOR A STUPID FEEORIN.

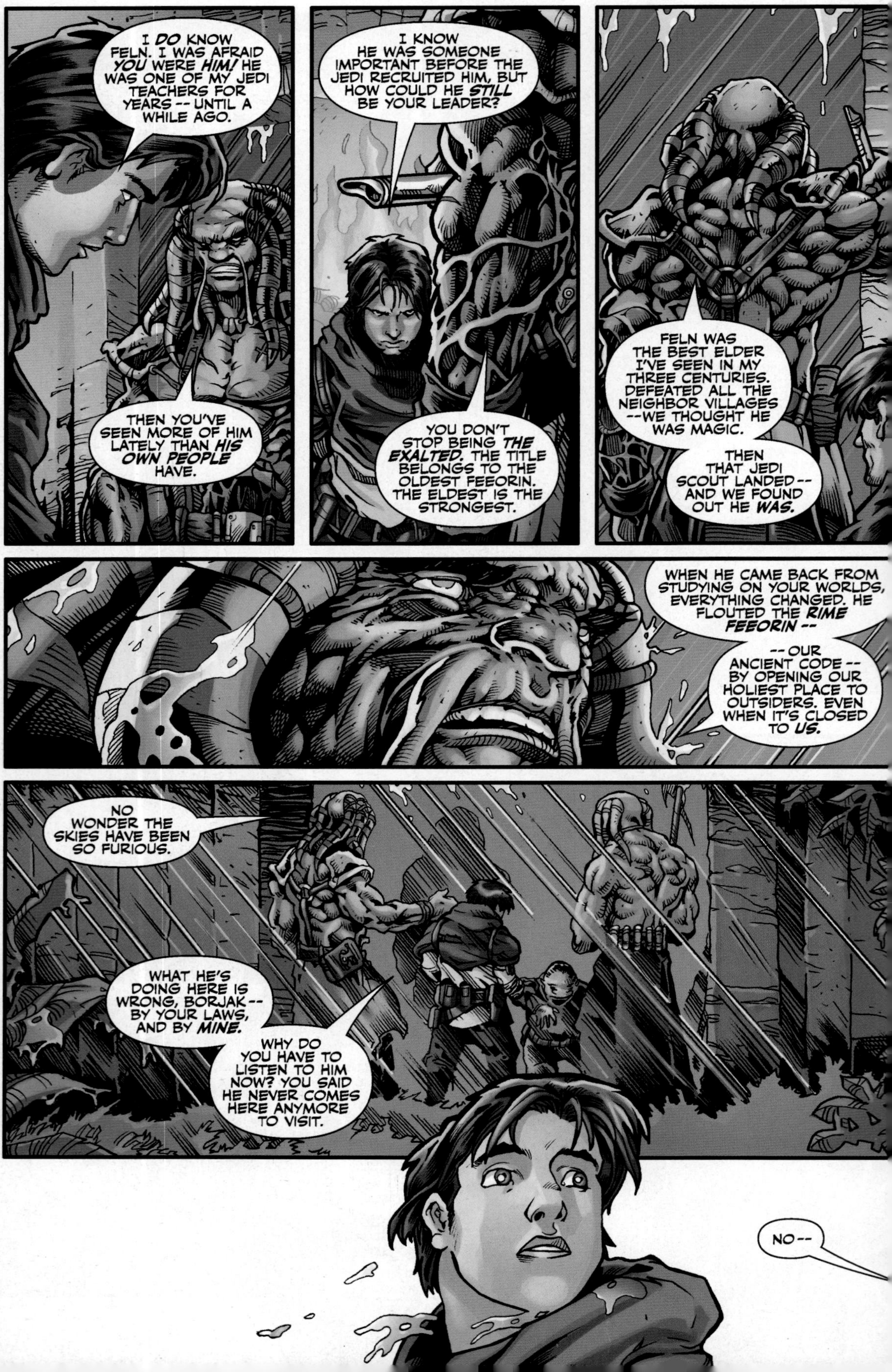
I *DO* KNOW FELN. I WAS AFRAID *YOU* WERE *HIM!* HE WAS ONE OF MY JEDI TEACHERS FOR YEARS -- UNTIL A WHILE AGO.
THEN YOU'VE SEEN MORE OF HIM LATELY THAN *HIS OWN PEOPLE* HAVE.
I KNOW HE WAS SOMEONE IMPORTANT BEFORE THE JEDI RECRUITED HIM, BUT HOW COULD HE *STILL* BE YOUR LEADER?
YOU DON'T STOP BEING *THE EXALTED*. THE TITLE BELONGS TO THE OLDEST FEEORIN. THE ELDEST IS THE STRONGEST.
FELN WAS THE BEST ELDER I'VE SEEN IN MY THREE CENTURIES. DEFEATED ALL THE NEIGHBOR VILLAGES --WE THOUGHT HE WAS MAGIC.
THEN THAT JEDI SCOUT LANDED-- AND WE FOUND OUT HE *WAS*.
WHEN HE CAME BACK FROM STUDYING ON YOUR WORLDS, EVERYTHING CHANGED. HE FLOUTED THE *RIME FEEORIN* --
--OUR ANCIENT CODE-- BY OPENING OUR HOLIEST PLACE TO OUTSIDERS. EVEN WHEN IT'S CLOSED TO *US*.
NO WONDER THE SKIES HAVE BEEN SO FURIOUS.
WHAT HE'S DOING HERE IS WRONG, BORJAK-- BY YOUR LAWS, AND BY *MINE*.
WHY DO YOU HAVE TO LISTEN TO HIM NOW? YOU SAID HE NEVER COMES HERE ANYMORE TO VISIT.
NO--

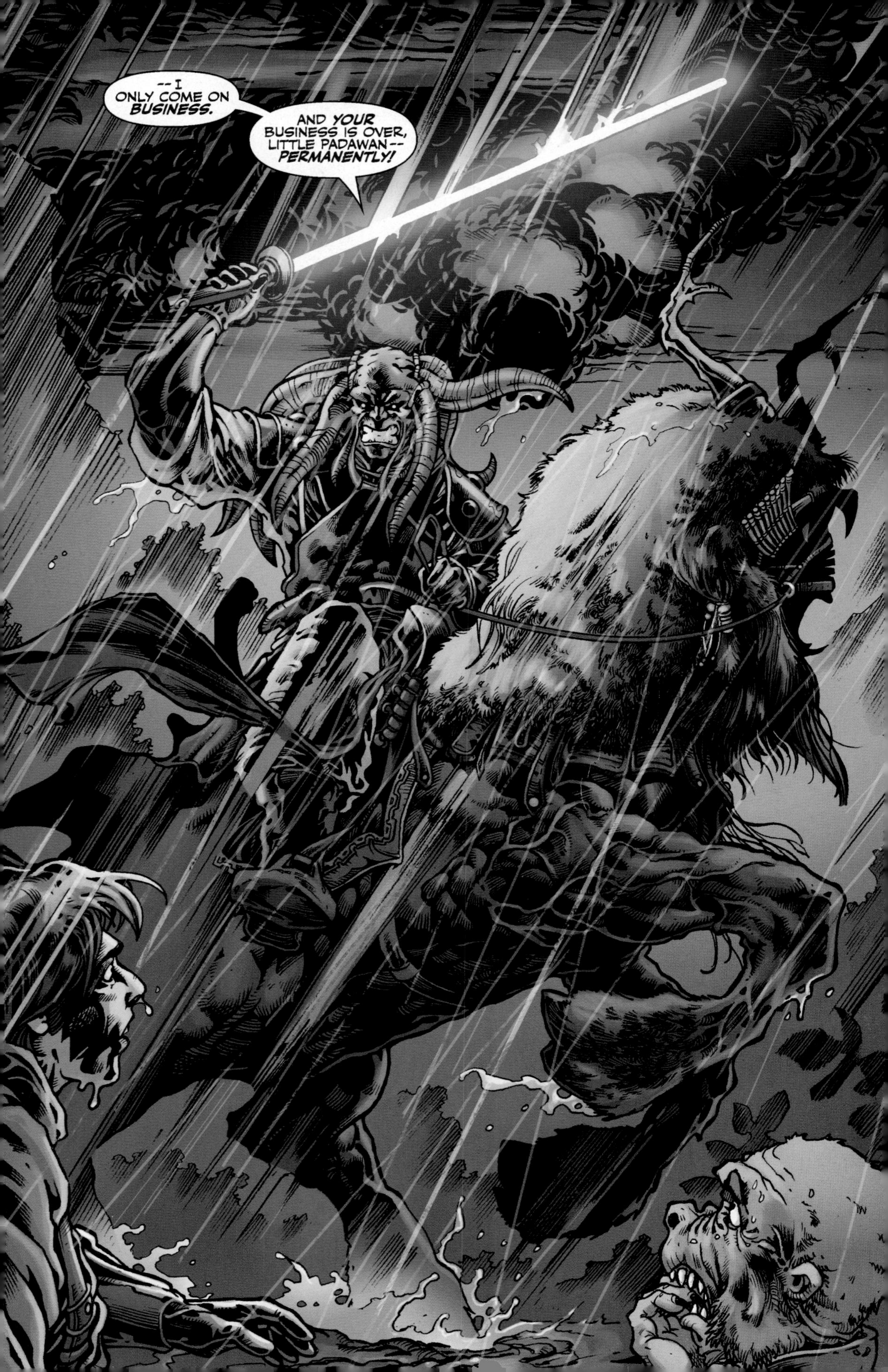
--I ONLY COME ON BUSINESS.
AND YOUR BUSINESS IS OVER, LITTLE PADAWAN-- PERMANENTLY!

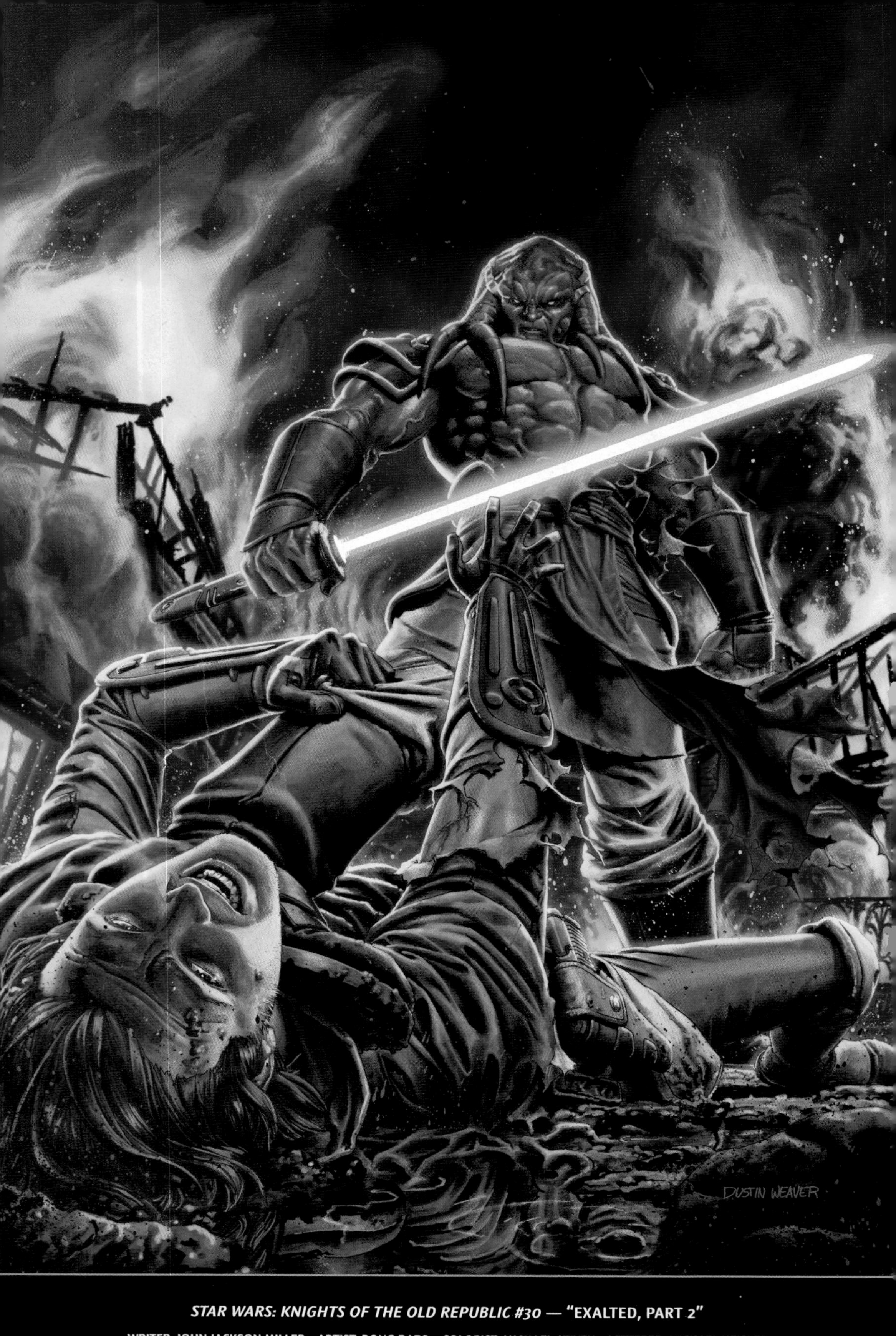
DUSTIN WEAVER

STAR WARS: KNIGHTS OF THE OLD REPUBLIC #30 — "EXALTED, PART 2"

WRITER: JOHN JACKSON MILLER • ARTIST: BONG DAZO • COLORIST: MICHAEL ATIYEH • LETTERER: MICHAEL HEISLER
ASSISTANT EDITORS: FREDDYE LINS & DAVE MARSHALL • EDITOR: RANDY STRADLEY • COVER ARTIST: DUSTIN WEAVER

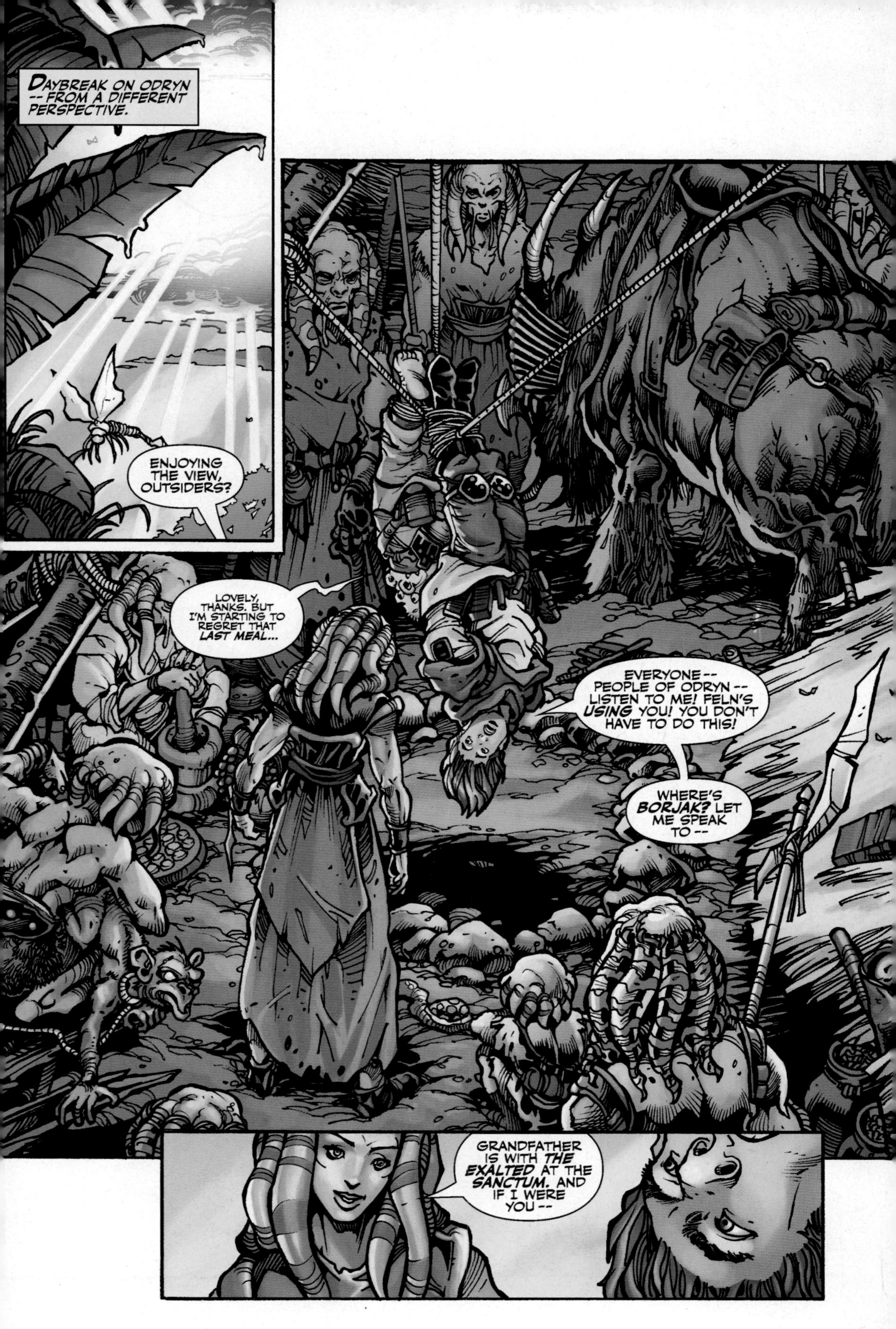
DAYBREAK ON ODRYN -- FROM A DIFFERENT PERSPECTIVE.
ENJOYING THE VIEW, OUTSIDERS?
LOVELY, THANKS. BUT I'M STARTING TO REGRET THAT LAST MEAL...
EVERYONE -- PEOPLE OF ODRYN -- LISTEN TO ME! FELN'S USING YOU! YOU DON'T HAVE TO DO THIS!
WHERE'S BORJAK? LET ME SPEAK TO --
GRANDFATHER IS WITH THE EXALTED AT THE SANCTUM. AND IF I WERE YOU --

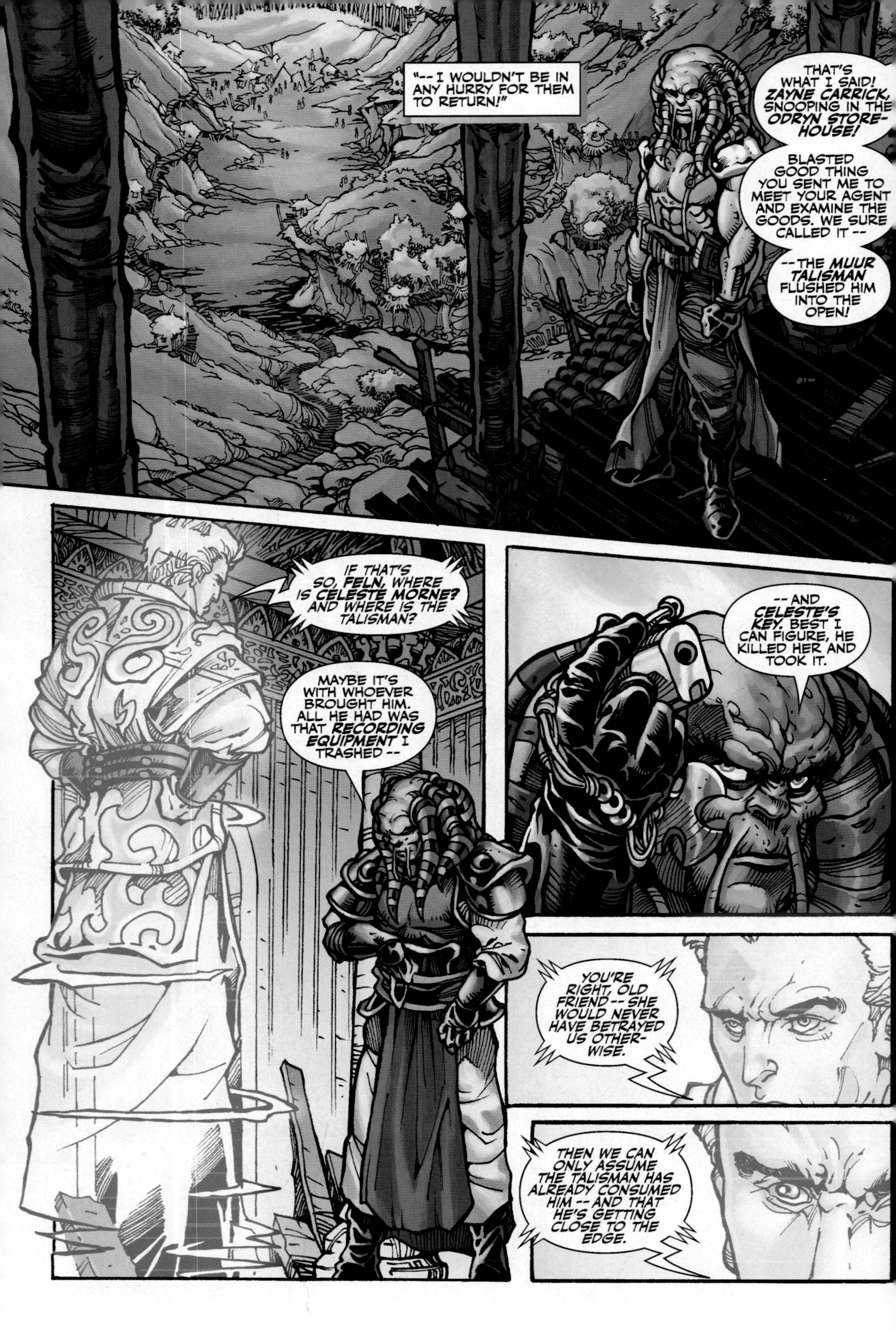
"-- I WOULDN'T BE IN ANY HURRY FOR THEM TO RETURN!"
THAT'S WHAT I SAID! ZAYNE CARRICK, SNOOPING IN THE ODRYN STORE-HOUSE!
BLASTED GOOD THING YOU SENT ME TO MEET YOUR AGENT AND EXAMINE THE GOODS. WE SURE CALLED IT --
-- THE MUUR TALISMAN FLUSHED HIM INTO THE OPEN!
IF THAT'S SO, FELN, WHERE IS CELESTE MORNE? AND WHERE IS THE TALISMAN?
MAYBE IT'S WITH WHOEVER BROUGHT HIM. ALL HE HAD WAS THAT RECORDING EQUIPMENT I TRASHED --
-- AND CELESTE'S KEY. BEST I CAN FIGURE, HE KILLED HER AND TOOK IT.
YOU'RE RIGHT, OLD FRIEND -- SHE WOULD NEVER HAVE BETRAYED US OTHER-WISE.
THEN WE CAN ONLY ASSUME THE TALISMAN HAS ALREADY CONSUMED HIM -- AND THAT HE'S GETTING CLOSE TO THE EDGE.

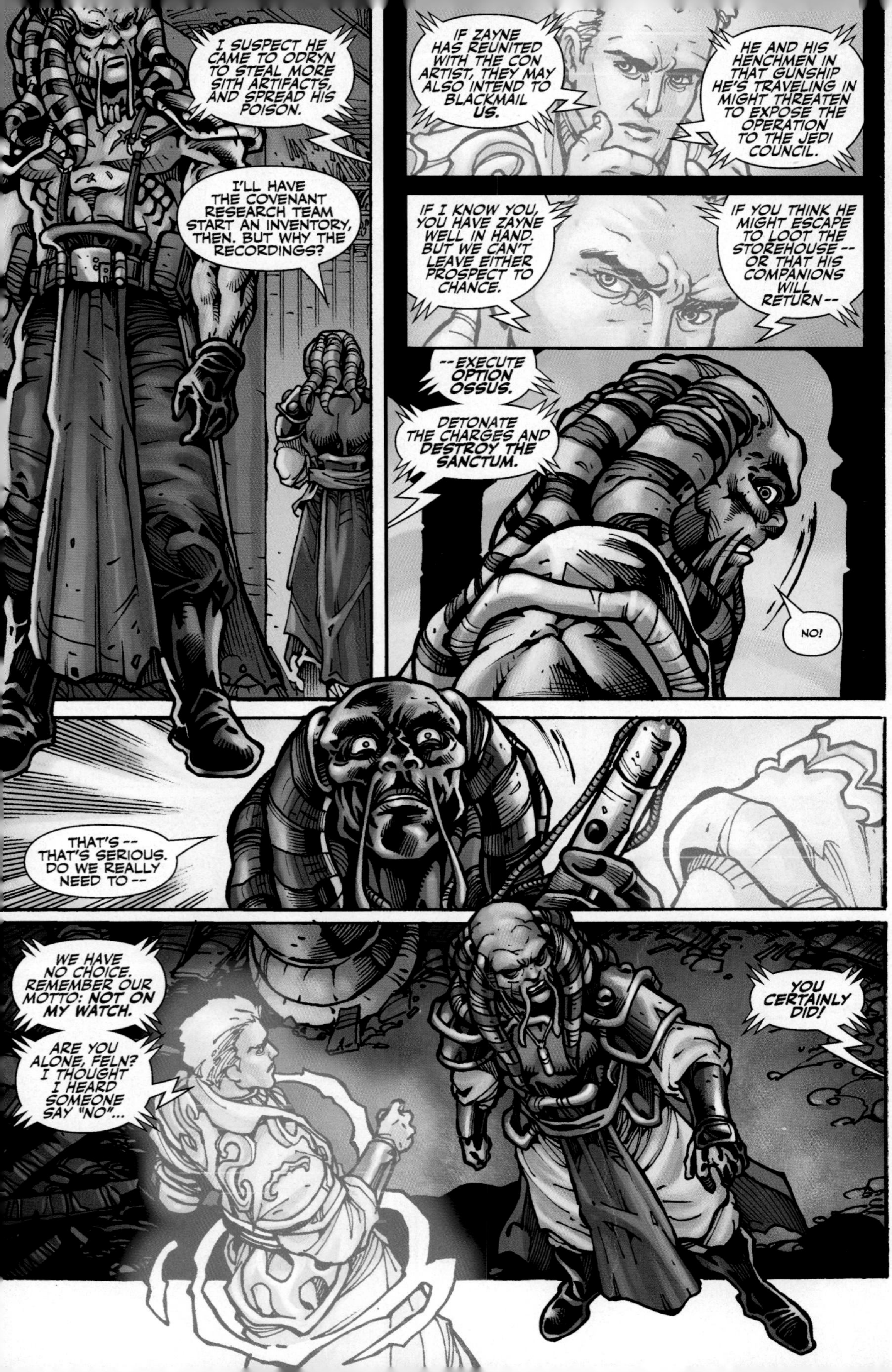
I SUSPECT HE CAME TO ODRYN TO STEAL MORE SITH ARTIFACTS, AND SPREAD HIS POISON.
I'LL HAVE THE COVENANT RESEARCH TEAM START AN INVENTORY, THEN. BUT WHY THE RECORDINGS?
IF ZAYNE HAS REUNITED WITH THE CON ARTIST, THEY MAY ALSO INTEND TO BLACKMAIL US.
HE AND HIS HENCHMEN IN THAT GUNSHIP HE'S TRAVELING IN MIGHT THREATEN TO EXPOSE THE OPERATION TO THE JEDI COUNCIL.
IF I KNOW YOU, YOU HAVE ZAYNE WELL IN HAND. BUT WE CAN'T LEAVE EITHER PROSPECT TO CHANCE.
IF YOU THINK HE MIGHT ESCAPE TO LOOT THE STOREHOUSE -- OR THAT HIS COMPANIONS WILL RETURN --
-- EXECUTE OPTION OSSUS.
DETONATE THE CHARGES AND DESTROY THE SANCTUM.
NO!
THAT'S -- THAT'S SERIOUS. DO WE REALLY NEED TO --
WE HAVE NO CHOICE. REMEMBER OUR MOTTO: NOT ON MY WATCH.
ARE YOU ALONE, FELN? I THOUGHT I HEARD SOMEONE SAY "NO"...
YOU CERTAINLY DID!

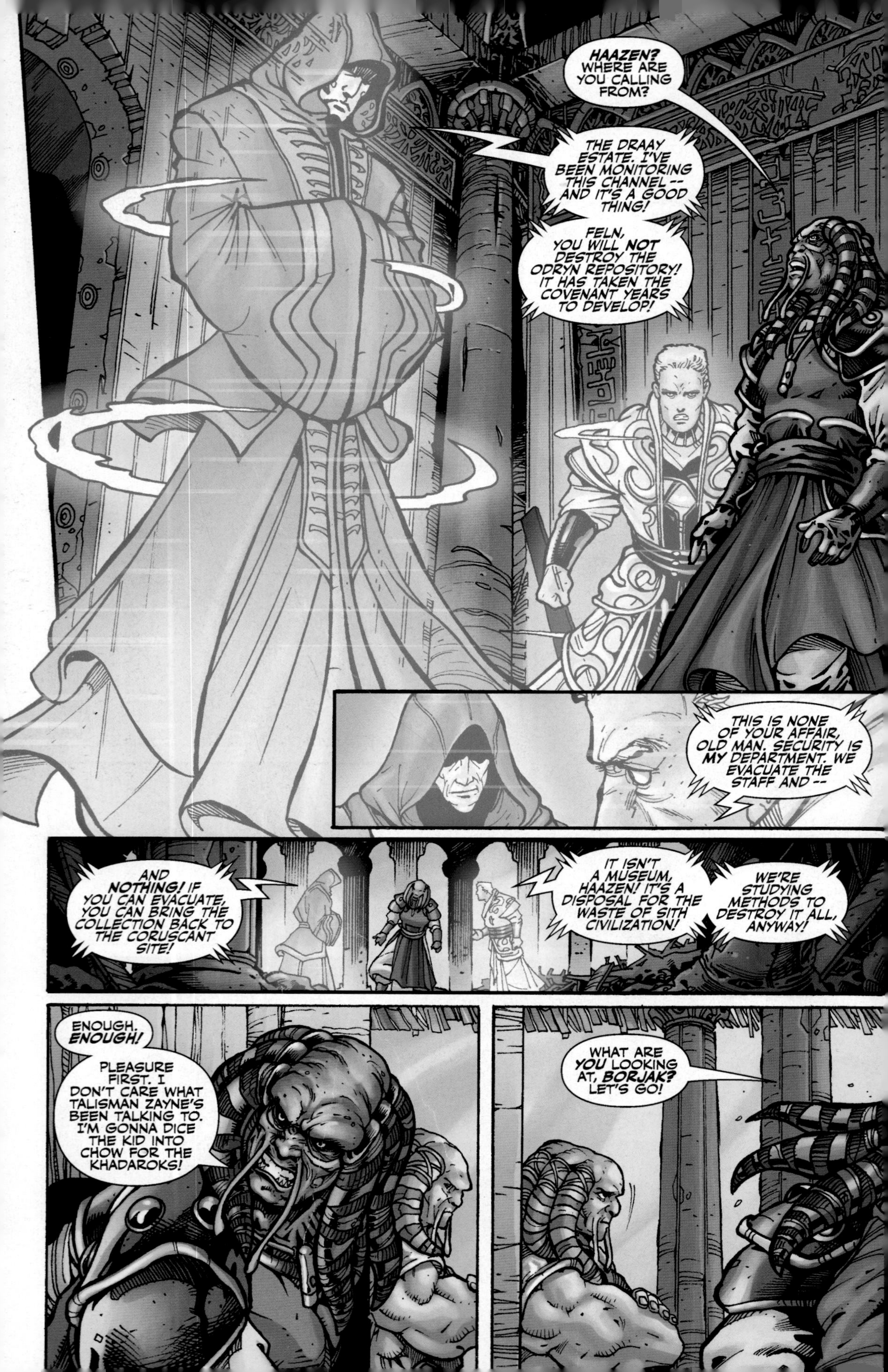
HAAZEN? WHERE ARE YOU CALLING FROM?
THE DRAAY ESTATE. I'VE BEEN MONITORING THIS CHANNEL -- AND IT'S A GOOD THING!
FELN, YOU WILL NOT DESTROY THE ODRYN REPOSITORY! IT HAS TAKEN THE COVENANT YEARS TO DEVELOP!
THIS IS NONE OF YOUR AFFAIR, OLD MAN. SECURITY IS MY DEPARTMENT. WE EVACUATE THE STAFF AND --
AND NOTHING! IF YOU CAN EVACUATE, YOU CAN BRING THE COLLECTION BACK TO THE CORUSCANT SITE!
IT ISN'T A MUSEUM, HAAZEN! IT'S A DISPOSAL FOR THE WASTE OF SITH CIVILIZATION!
WE'RE STUDYING METHODS TO DESTROY IT ALL, ANYWAY!
ENOUGH. ENOUGH!
PLEASURE FIRST. I DON'T CARE WHAT TALISMAN ZAYNE'S BEEN TALKING TO. I'M GONNA DICE THE KID INTO CHOW FOR THE KHADAROKS!
WHAT ARE YOU LOOKING AT, BORJAK? LET'S GO!

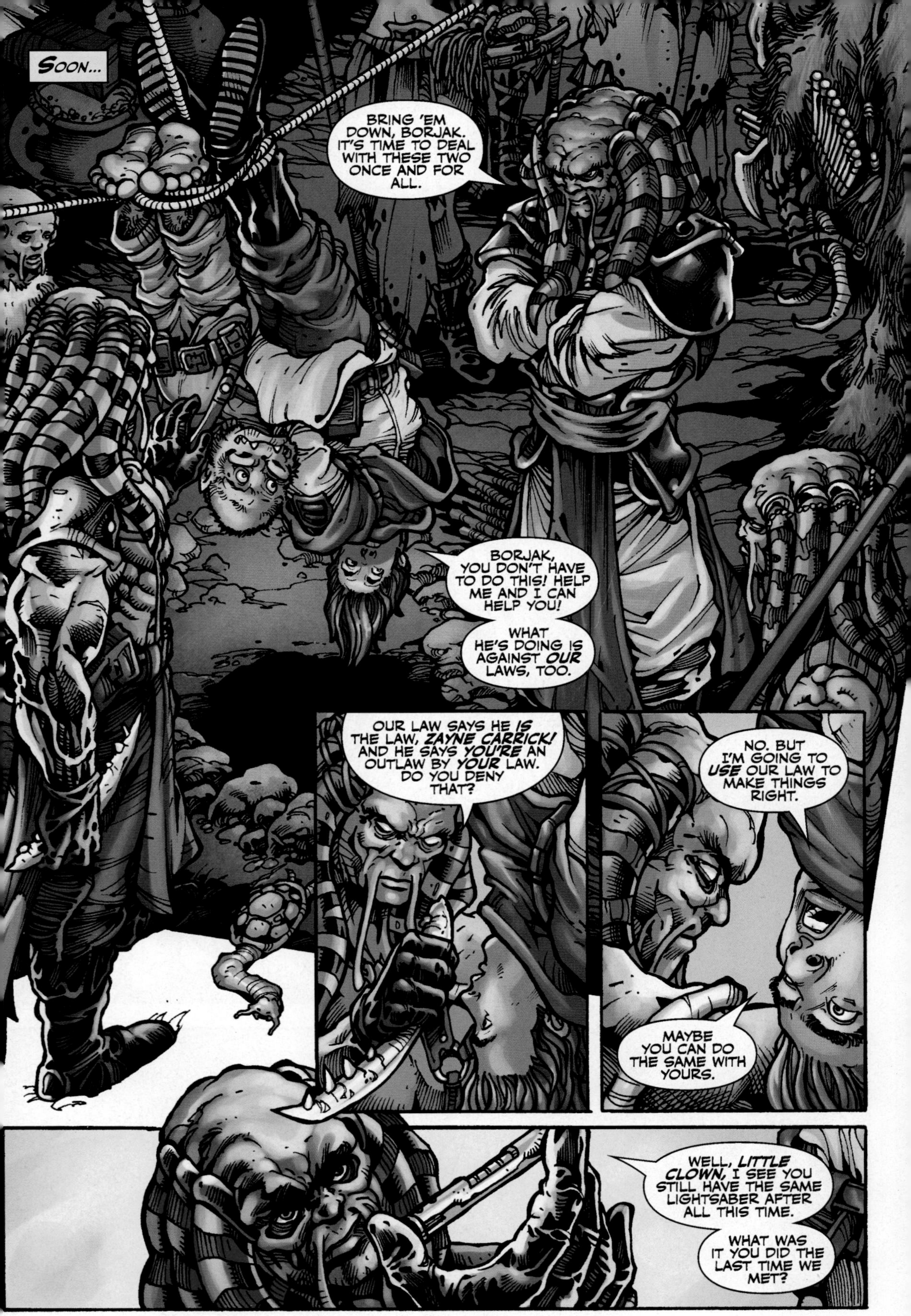

SOON...
BRING 'EM DOWN, BORJAK. IT'S TIME TO DEAL WITH THESE TWO ONCE AND FOR ALL.
BORJAK, YOU DON'T HAVE TO DO THIS! HELP ME AND I CAN HELP YOU!
WHAT HE'S DOING IS AGAINST OUR LAWS, TOO.
OUR LAW SAYS HE IS THE LAW, ZAYNE CARRICK! AND HE SAYS YOU'RE AN OUTLAW BY YOUR LAW. DO YOU DENY THAT?
NO. BUT I'M GOING TO USE OUR LAW TO MAKE THINGS RIGHT.
MAYBE YOU CAN DO THE SAME WITH YOURS.
WELL, LITTLE CLOWN, I SEE YOU STILL HAVE THE SAME LIGHTSABER AFTER ALL THIS TIME.
WHAT WAS IT YOU DID THE LAST TIME WE MET?

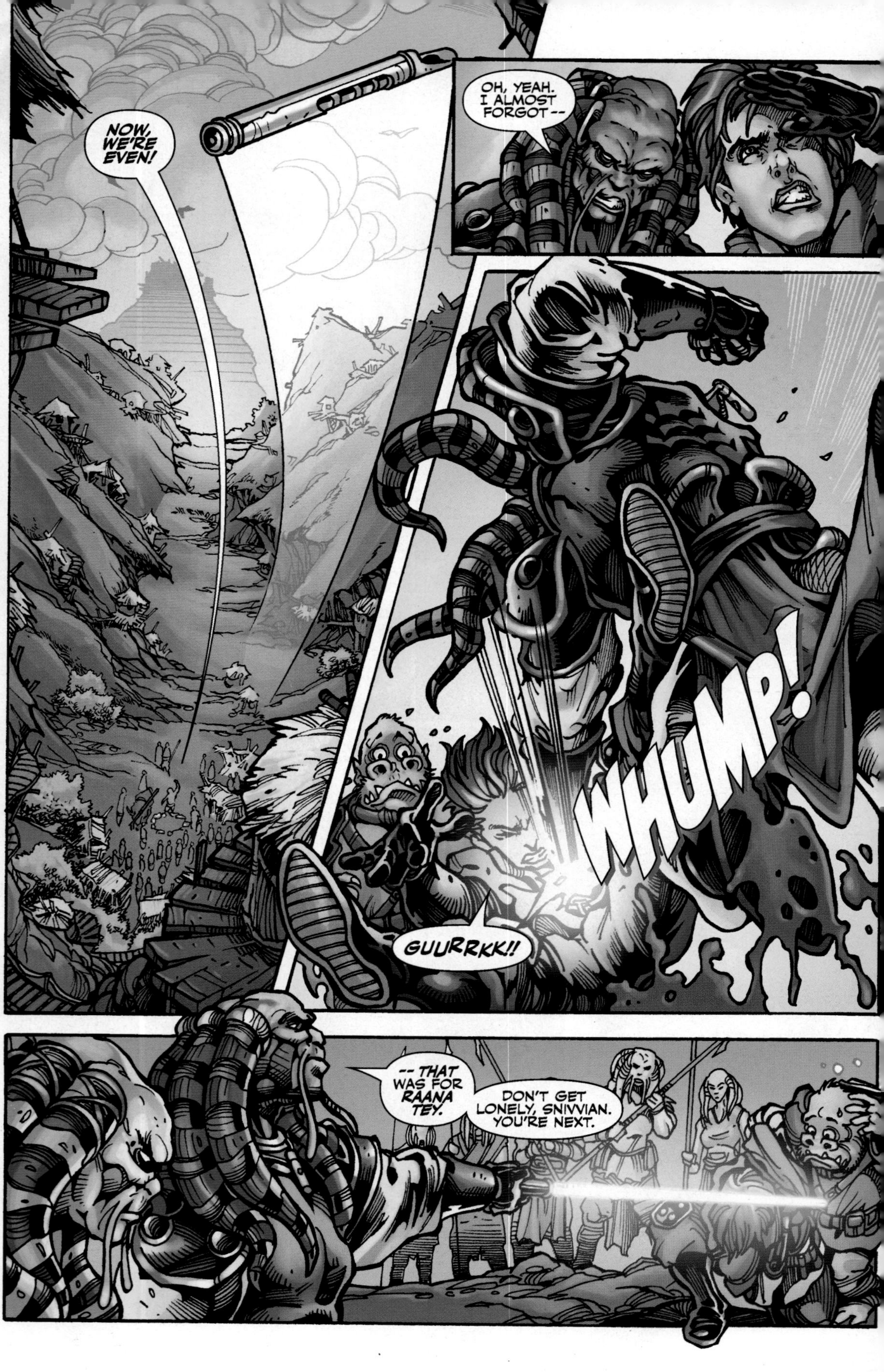

NOW, WE'RE EVEN!
OH, YEAH. I ALMOST FORGOT --
WHUMP!
GUURRKK!!
-- THAT WAS FOR RAANA TEY.
DON'T GET LONELY, SNIVVIAN. YOU'RE NEXT.

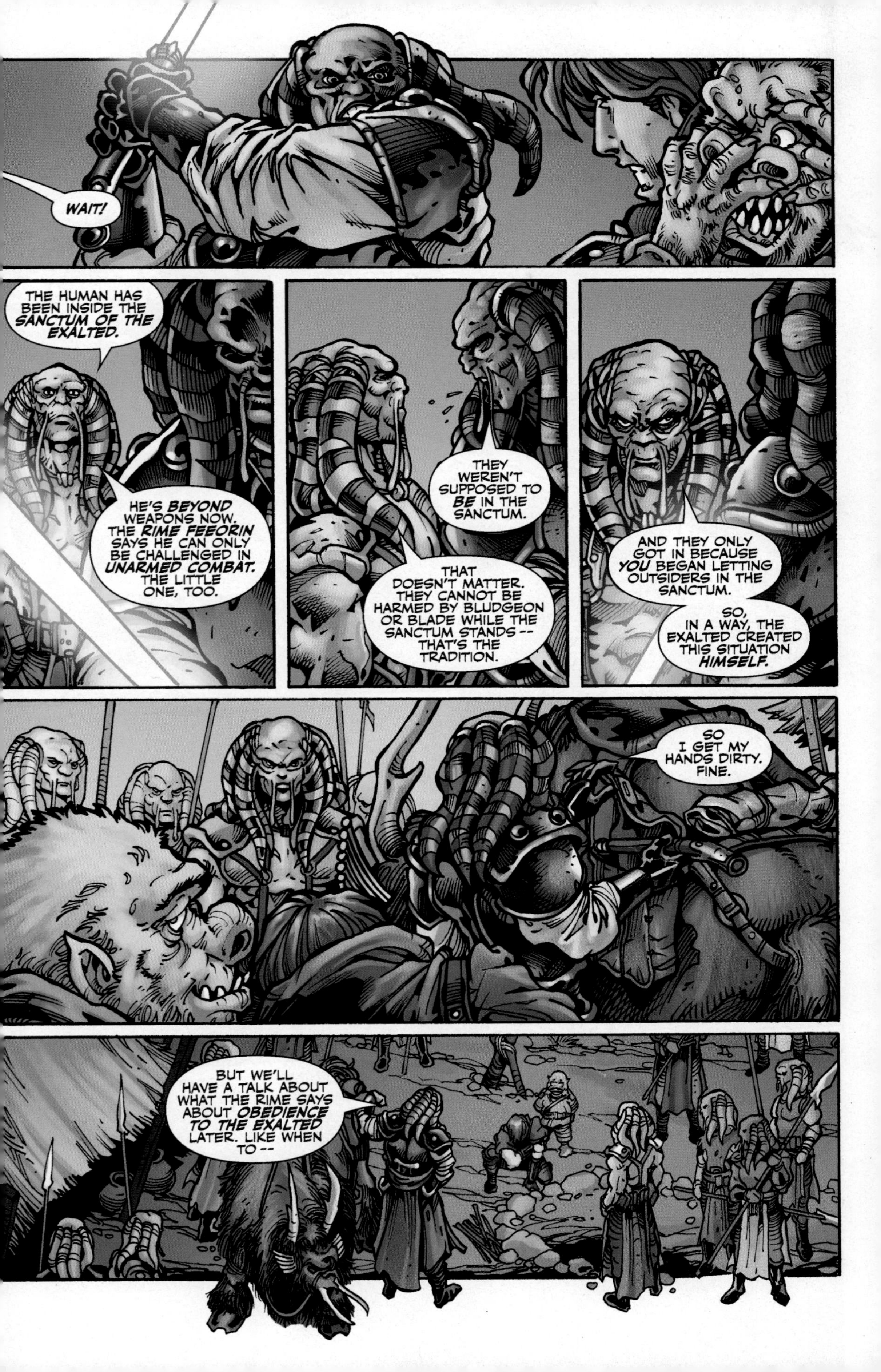
WAIT!
THE HUMAN HAS BEEN INSIDE THE SANCTUM OF THE EXALTED.
HE'S BEYOND WEAPONS NOW. THE RIME FEEORIN SAYS HE CAN ONLY BE CHALLENGED IN UNARMED COMBAT. THE LITTLE ONE, TOO.
THEY WEREN'T SUPPOSED TO BE IN THE SANCTUM.
THAT DOESN'T MATTER. THEY CANNOT BE HARMED BY BLUDGEON OR BLADE WHILE THE SANCTUM STANDS -- THAT'S THE TRADITION.
AND THEY ONLY GOT IN BECAUSE YOU BEGAN LETTING OUTSIDERS IN THE SANCTUM.
SO, IN A WAY, THE EXALTED CREATED THIS SITUATION HIMSELF.
SO I GET MY HANDS DIRTY. FINE.
BUT WE'LL HAVE A TALK ABOUT WHAT THE RIME SAYS ABOUT OBEDIENCE TO THE EXALTED LATER. LIKE WHEN TO --

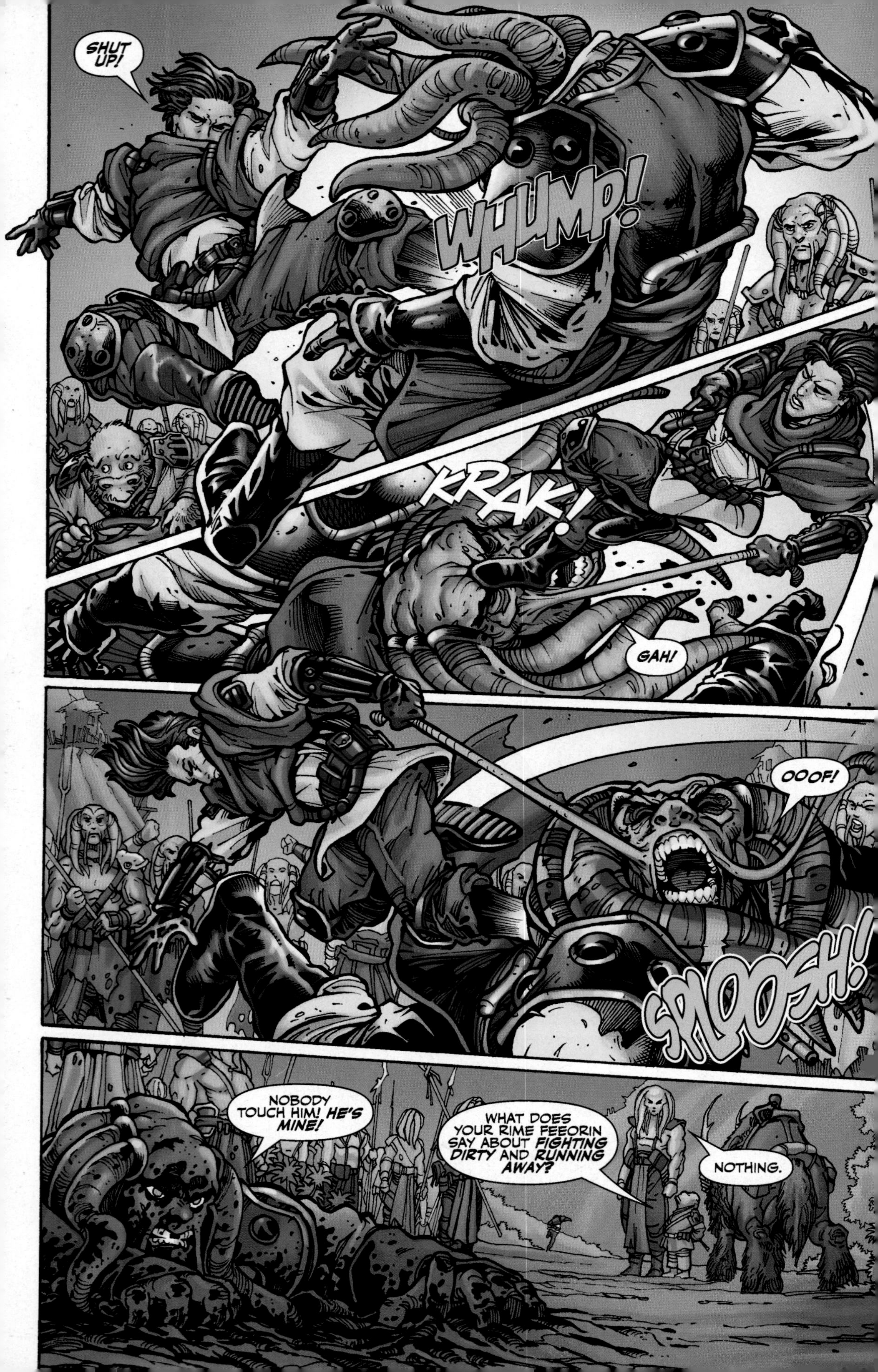
SHUT UP!
WHUMP!
KRAK!
GAH!
OOOF!
SPLOOSH!
NOBODY TOUCH HIM! HE'S MINE!
WHAT DOES YOUR RIME FEEORIN SAY ABOUT FIGHTING DIRTY AND RUNNING AWAY?
NOTHING.

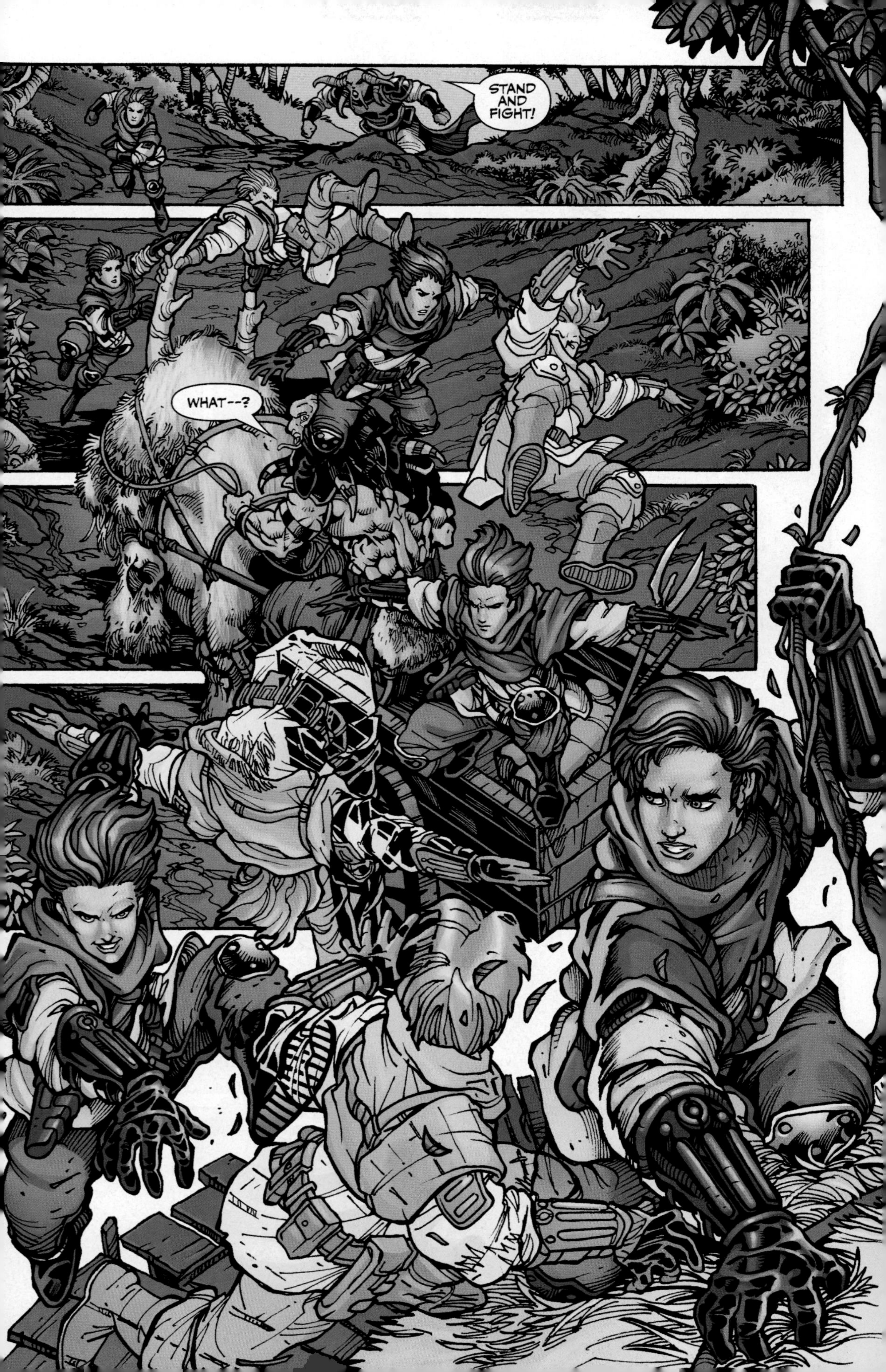
STAND AND FIGHT!
WHAT--?

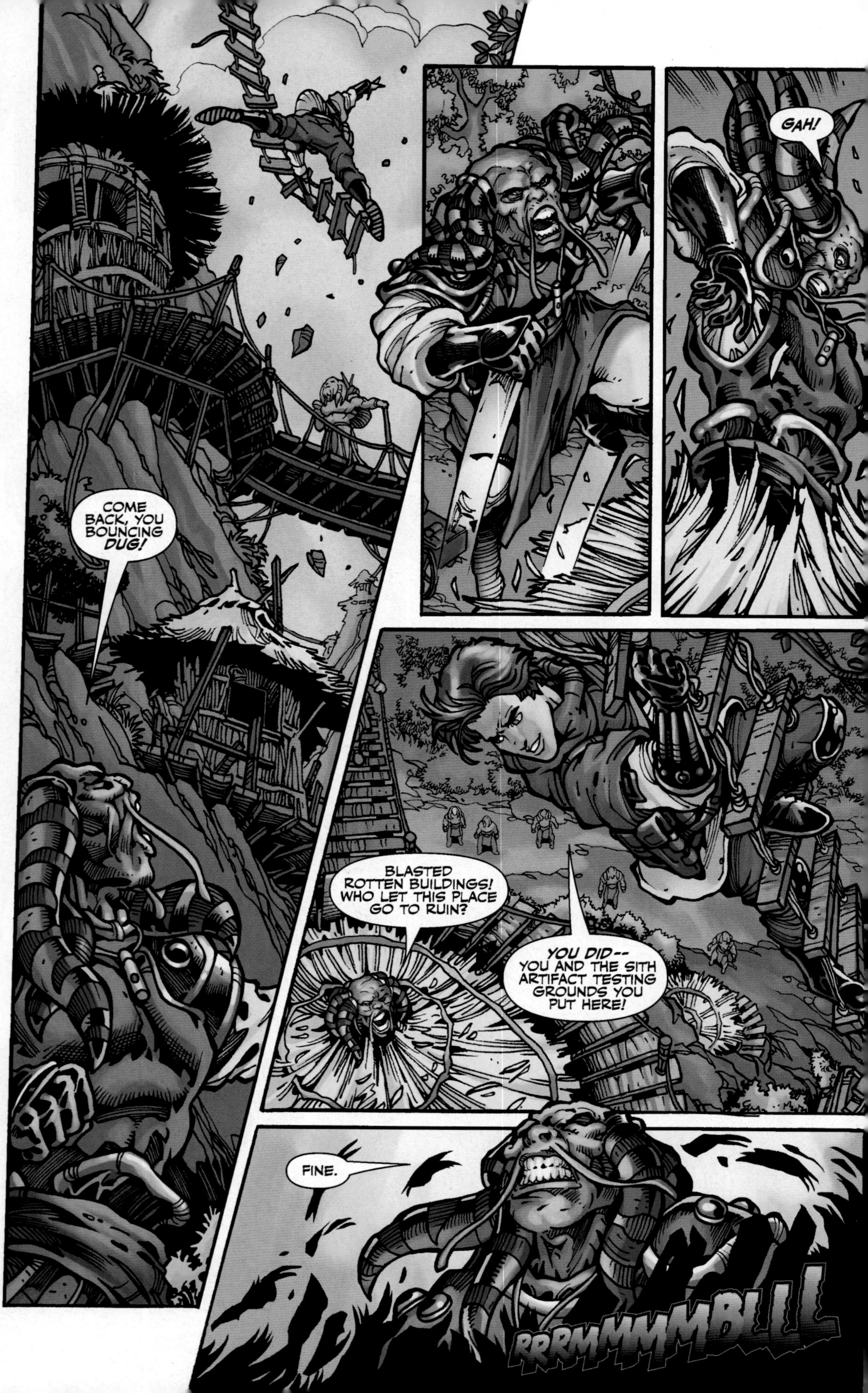

COME BACK, YOU BOUNCING DUG!
GAH!
BLASTED ROTTEN BUILDINGS! WHO LET THIS PLACE GO TO RUIN?
YOU DID-- YOU AND THE SITH ARTIFACT TESTING GROUNDS YOU PUT HERE!
FINE.
RRRMMMMBLLL

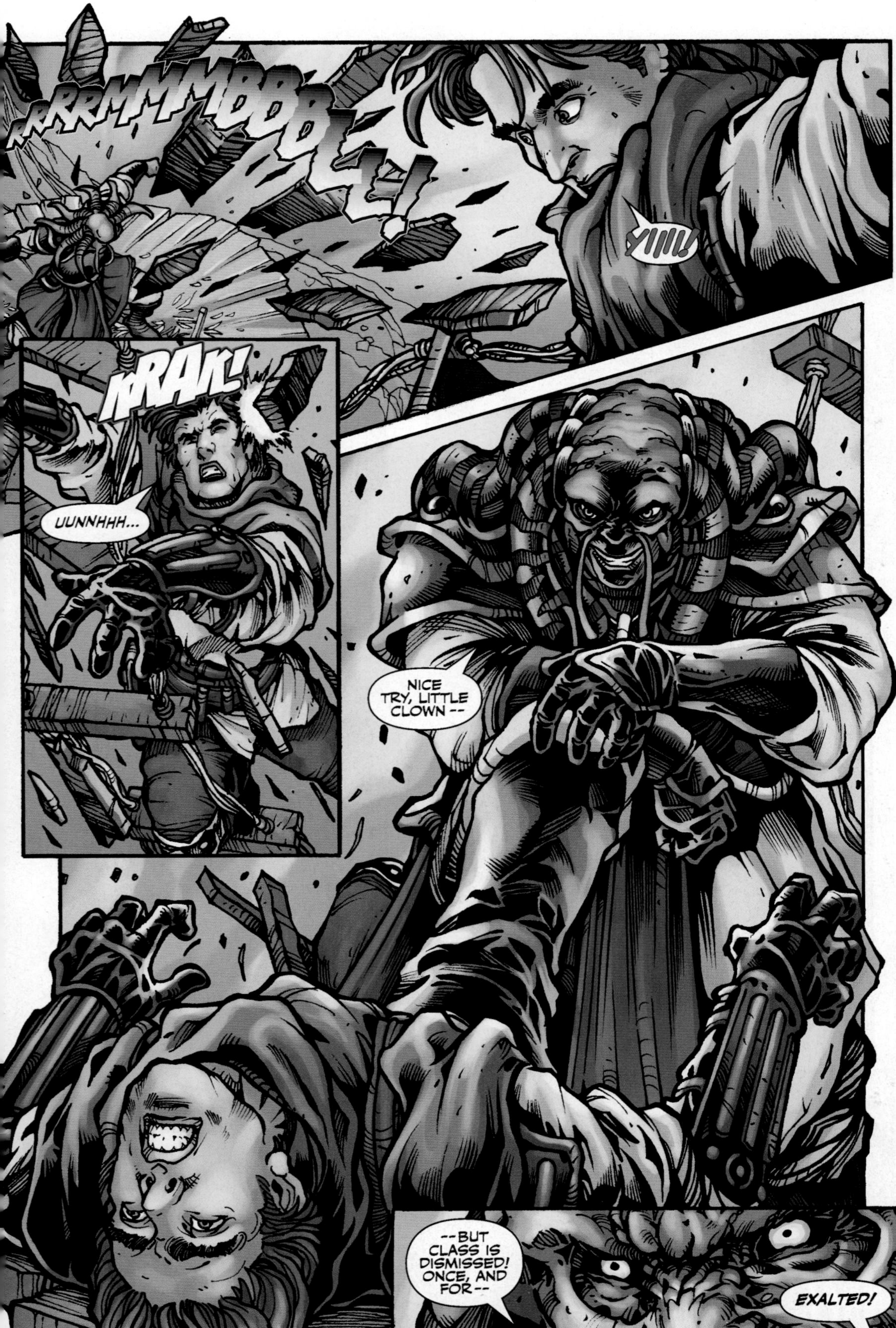

RRRMMMBBBL!
YIII!
KRAK!
UUNNHHH...
NICE TRY, LITTLE CLOWN --
--BUT CLASS IS DISMISSED! ONCE, AND FOR --
EXALTED!

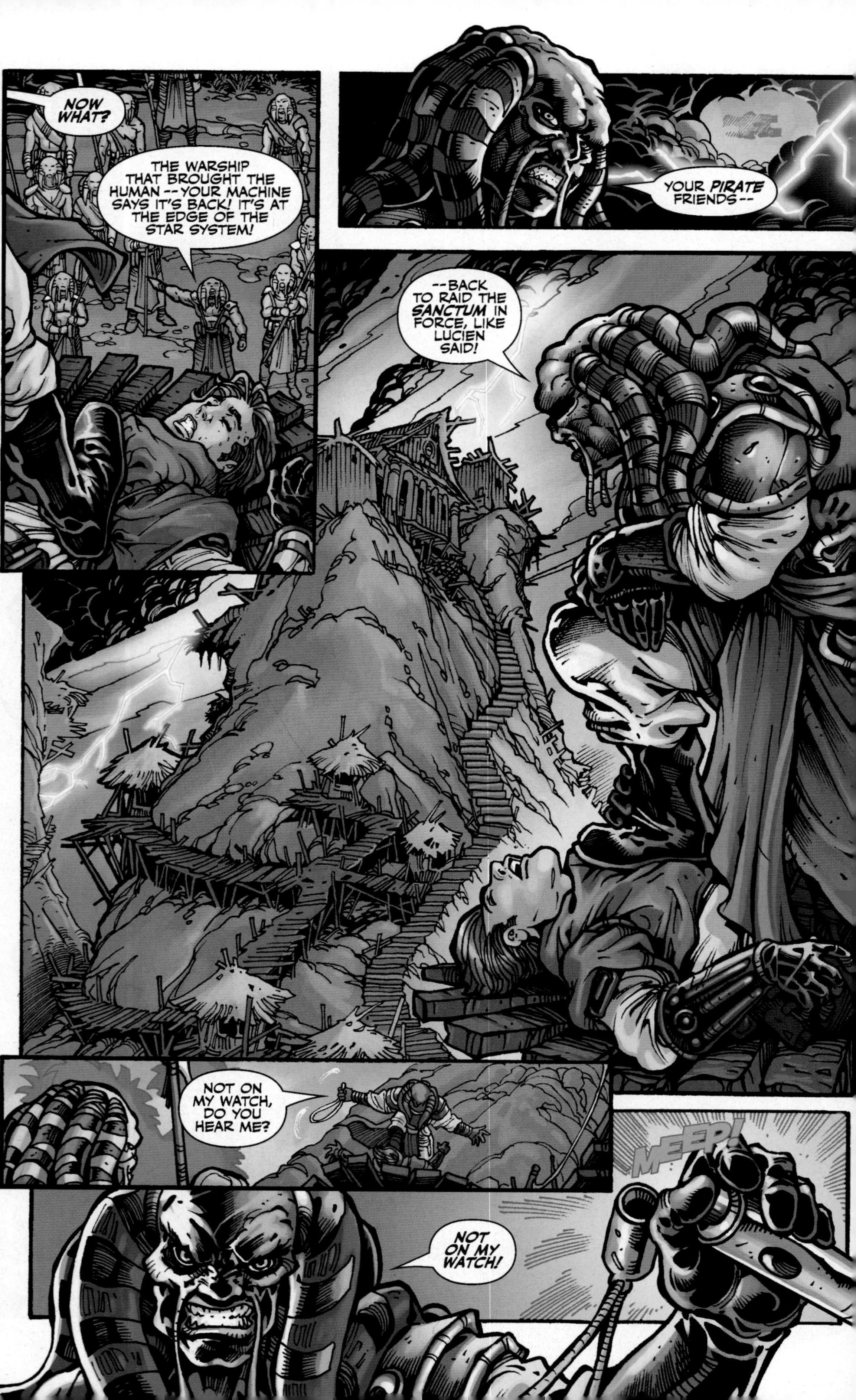
NOW WHAT?
THE WARSHIP THAT BROUGHT THE HUMAN -- YOUR MACHINE SAYS IT'S BACK! IT'S AT THE EDGE OF THE STAR SYSTEM!
YOUR PIRATE FRIENDS--
--BACK TO RAID THE SANCTUM IN FORCE, LIKE LUCIEN SAID!
NOT ON MY WATCH, DO YOU HEAR ME?
MEEP!
NOT ON MY WATCH!

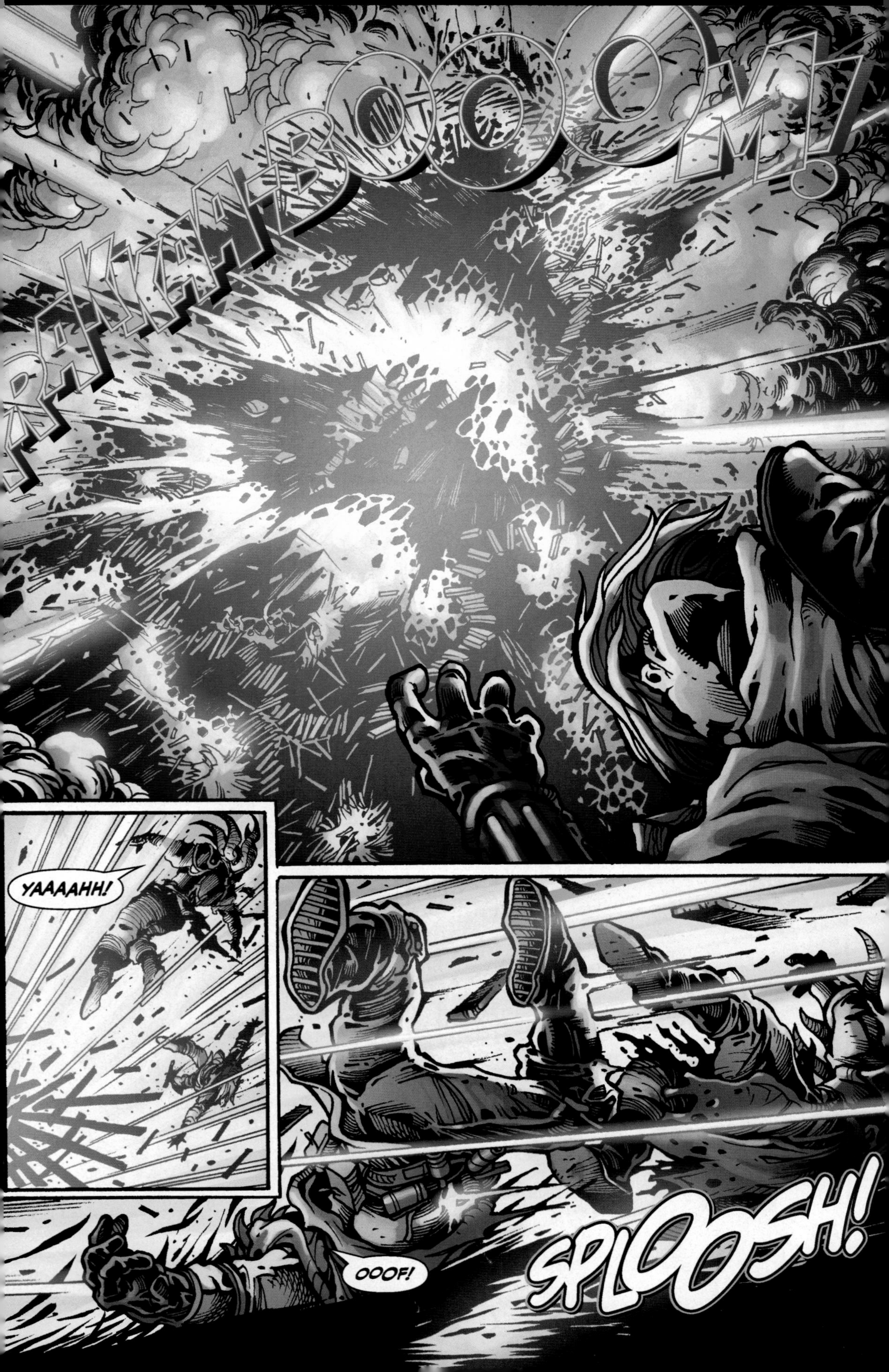
KA-BOOOM!!
YAAAAHH!
OOOF!
SPLOOSH!

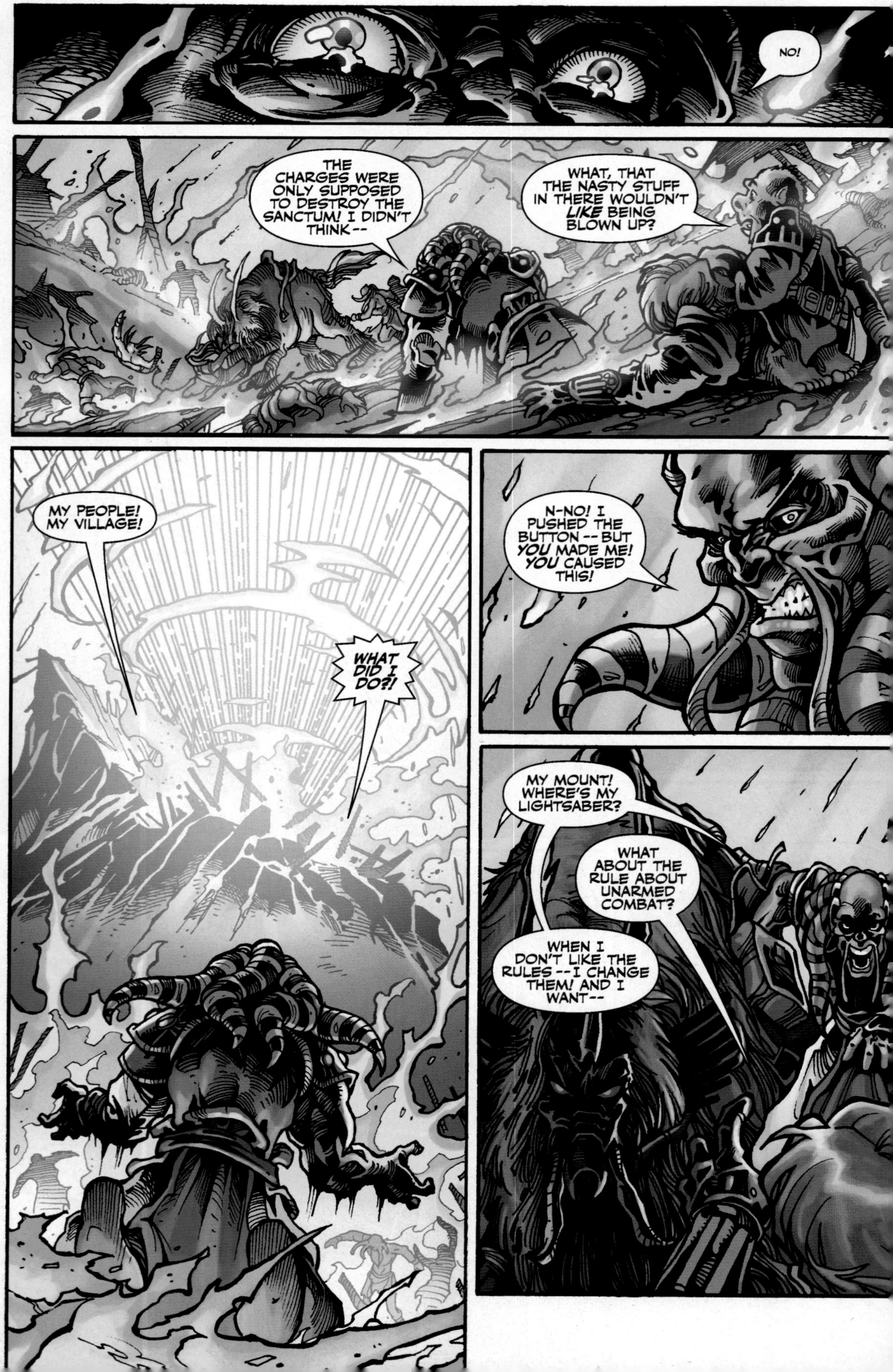
NO!
THE CHARGES WERE ONLY SUPPOSED TO DESTROY THE SANCTUM! I DIDN'T THINK--
WHAT, THAT THE NASTY STUFF IN THERE WOULDN'T LIKE BEING BLOWN UP?
MY PEOPLE! MY VILLAGE!
WHAT DID I DO?!
N-NO! I PUSHED THE BUTTON--BUT YOU MADE ME! YOU CAUSED THIS!
MY MOUNT! WHERE'S MY LIGHTSABER?
WHAT ABOUT THE RULE ABOUT UNARMED COMBAT?
WHEN I DON'T LIKE THE RULES--I CHANGE THEM! AND I WANT--

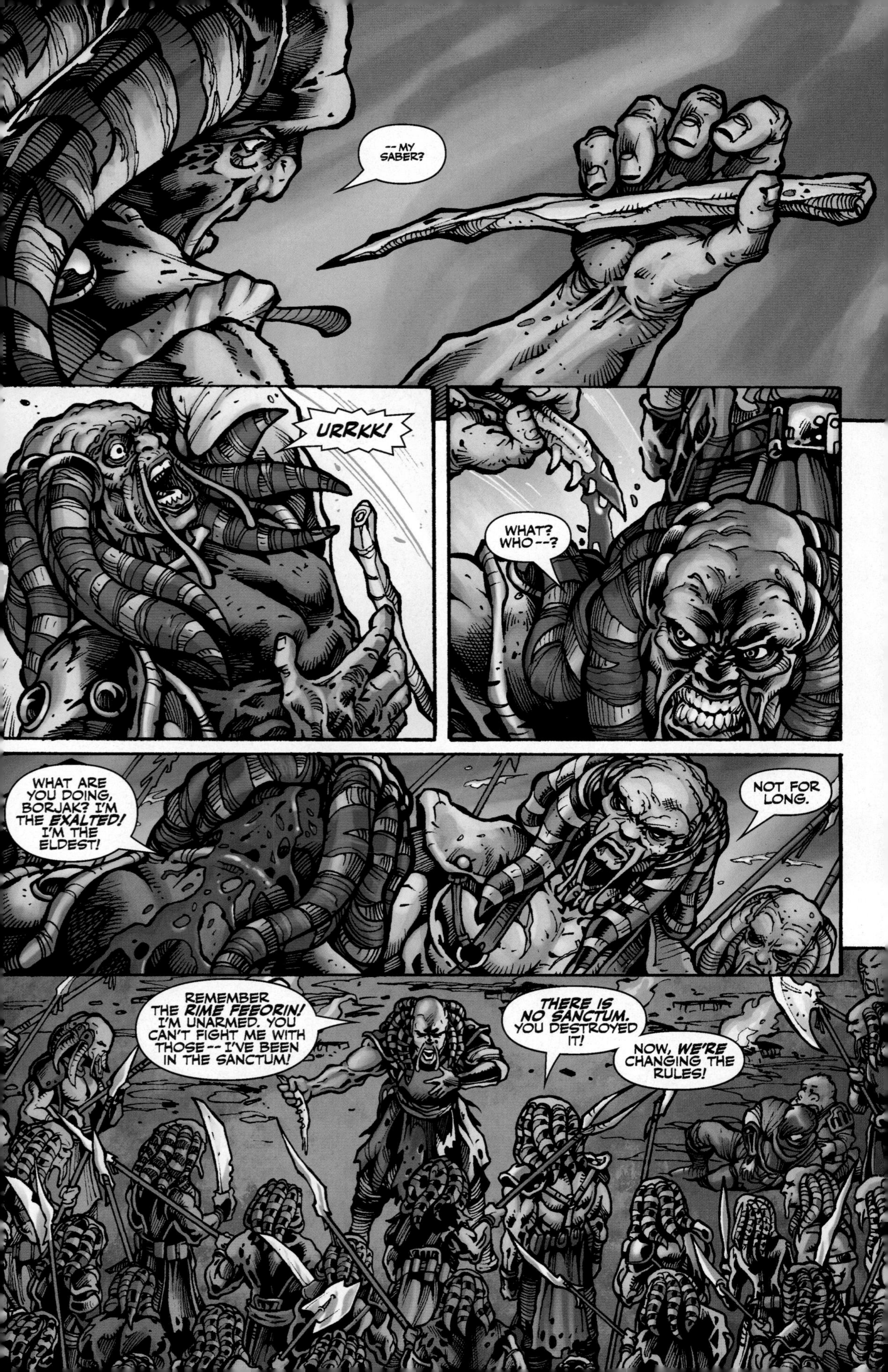

-- MY SABER?
URRKK!
WHAT? WHO--?
WHAT ARE YOU DOING, BORJAK? I'M THE EXALTED! I'M THE ELDEST!
NOT FOR LONG.
REMEMBER THE RIME FEEORIN! I'M UNARMED. YOU CAN'T FIGHT ME WITH THOSE-- I'VE BEEN IN THE SANCTUM!
THERE IS NO SANCTUM. YOU DESTROYED IT!
NOW, WE'RE CHANGING THE RULES!

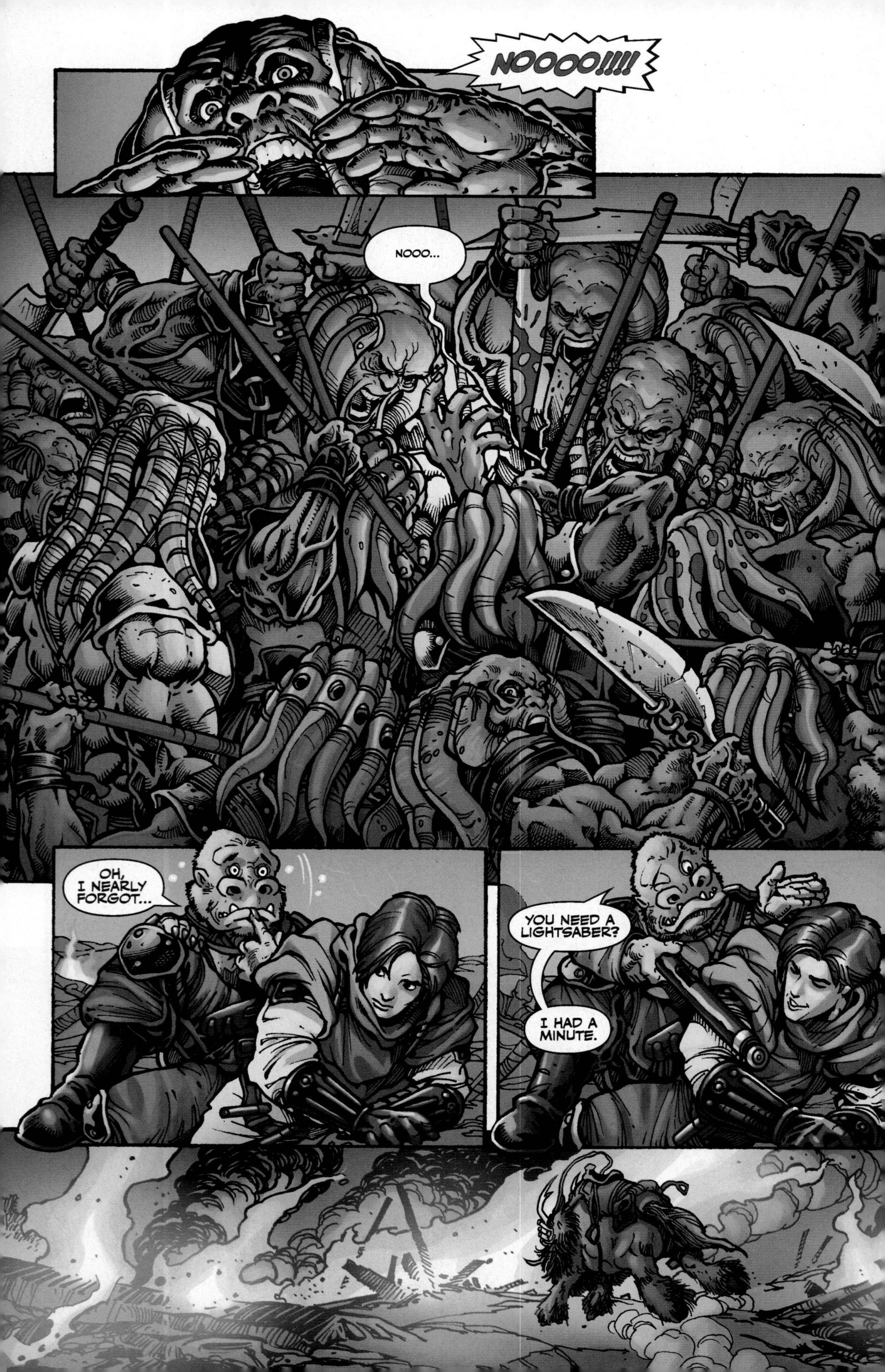
NOOOO!!!!
NOOO...
OH, I NEARLY FORGOT...
YOU NEED A LIGHTSABER?
I HAD A MINUTE.

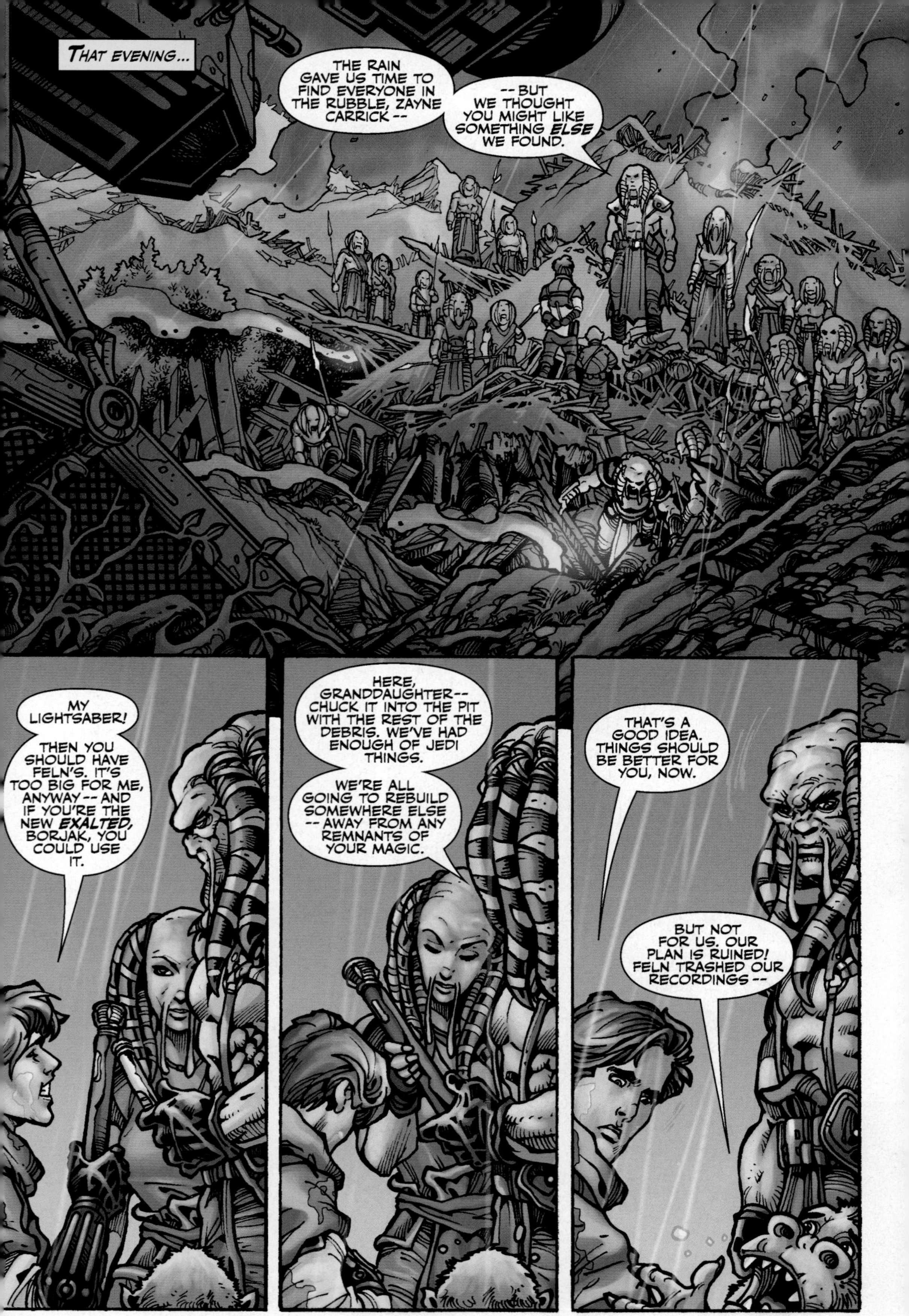
THAT EVENING...
THE RAIN GAVE US TIME TO FIND EVERYONE IN THE RUBBLE, ZAYNE CARRICK --
-- BUT WE THOUGHT YOU MIGHT LIKE SOMETHING *ELSE* WE FOUND.
MY LIGHTSABER!
THEN YOU SHOULD HAVE FELN'S. IT'S TOO BIG FOR ME, ANYWAY -- AND IF YOU'RE THE NEW *EXALTED,* BORJAK, YOU COULD USE IT.
HERE, GRANDDAUGHTER -- CHUCK IT INTO THE PIT WITH THE REST OF THE DEBRIS. WE'VE HAD ENOUGH OF JEDI THINGS.
WE'RE ALL GOING TO REBUILD SOMEWHERE ELSE -- AWAY FROM ANY REMNANTS OF YOUR MAGIC.
THAT'S A GOOD IDEA. THINGS SHOULD BE BETTER FOR YOU, NOW.
BUT NOT FOR US. OUR PLAN IS RUINED! FELN TRASHED OUR RECORDINGS --

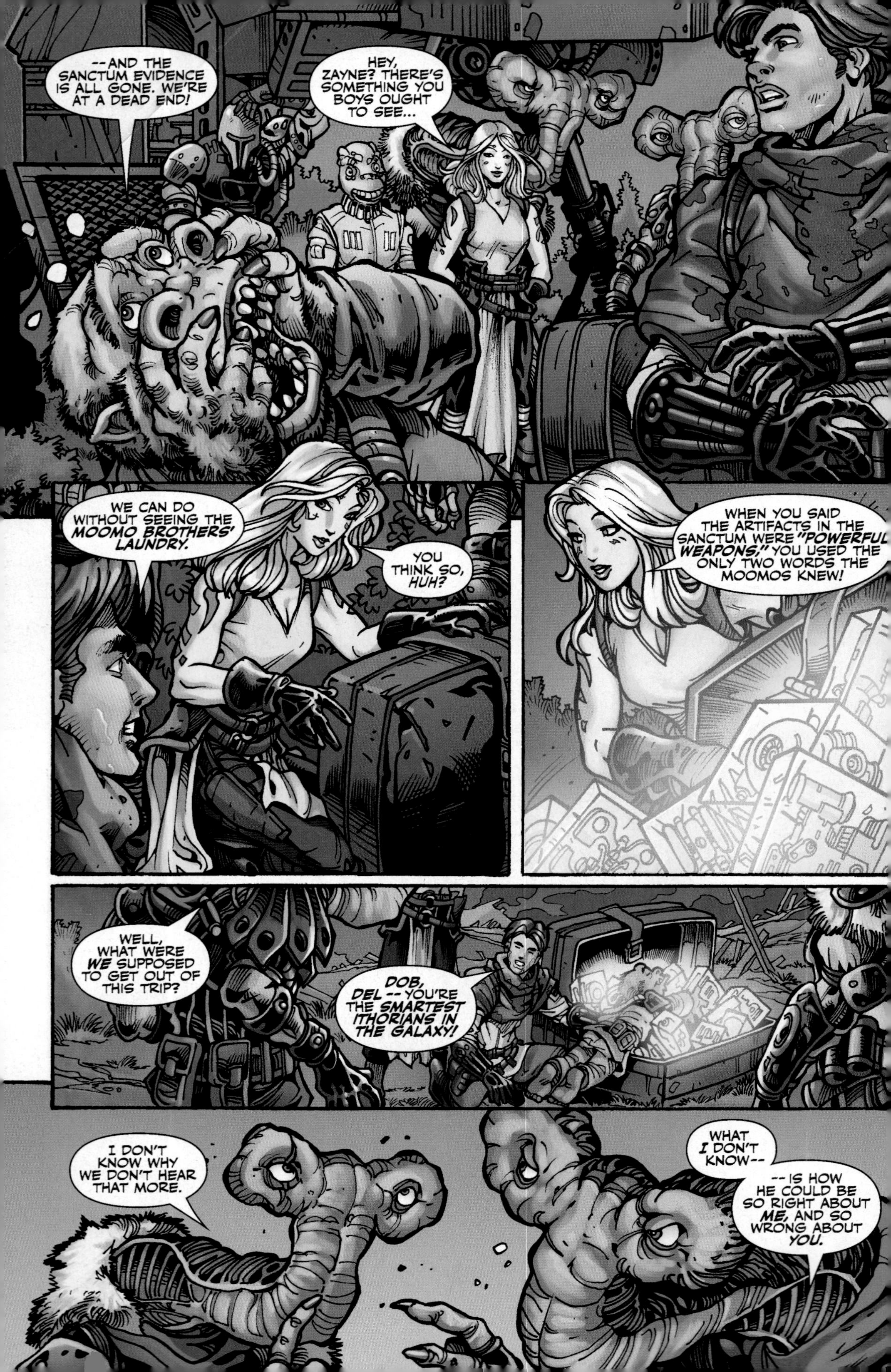
--AND THE SANCTUM EVIDENCE IS ALL GONE. WE'RE AT A DEAD END!
HEY, ZAYNE? THERE'S SOMETHING YOU BOYS OUGHT TO SEE...
WE CAN DO WITHOUT SEEING THE *MOOMO BROTHERS'* LAUNDRY.
YOU THINK SO, *HUH?*
WHEN YOU SAID THE ARTIFACTS IN THE SANCTUM WERE *"POWERFUL WEAPONS,"* YOU USED THE ONLY TWO WORDS THE MOOMOS KNEW!
WELL, WHAT WERE *WE* SUPPOSED TO GET OUT OF THIS TRIP?
DOB, DEL--YOU'RE THE *SMARTEST ITHORIANS IN THE GALAXY!*
I DON'T KNOW WHY WE DON'T HEAR THAT MORE.
WHAT *I* DON'T KNOW--
--IS HOW HE COULD BE SO RIGHT ABOUT *ME,* AND SO WRONG ABOUT *YOU.*

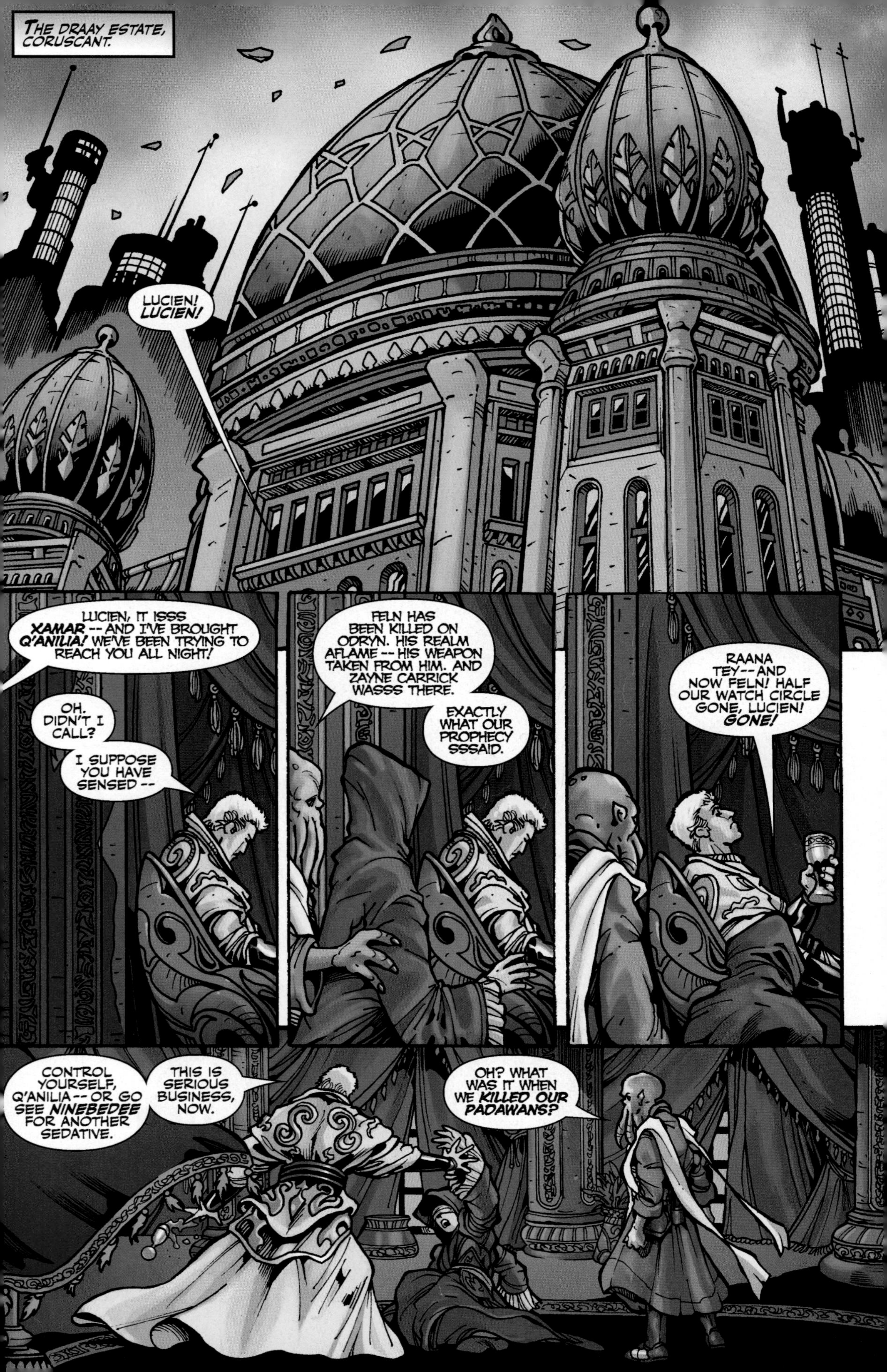
THE DRAAY ESTATE, CORUSCANT.
LUCIEN! LUCIEN!
LUCIEN, IT ISSS XAMAR -- AND I'VE BROUGHT Q'ANILIA! WE'VE BEEN TRYING TO REACH YOU ALL NIGHT!
OH. DIDN'T I CALL?
I SUPPOSE YOU HAVE SENSED --
FELN HAS BEEN KILLED ON ODRYN. HIS REALM AFLAME -- HIS WEAPON TAKEN FROM HIM. AND ZAYNE CARRICK WASSS THERE.
EXACTLY WHAT OUR PROPHECY SSSAID.
RAANA TEY -- AND NOW FELN! HALF OUR WATCH CIRCLE GONE, LUCIEN! GONE!
CONTROL YOURSELF, Q'ANILIA -- OR GO SEE NINEBEDEE FOR ANOTHER SEDATIVE.
THIS IS SERIOUS BUSINESS, NOW.
OH? WHAT WAS IT WHEN WE KILLED OUR PADAWANS?

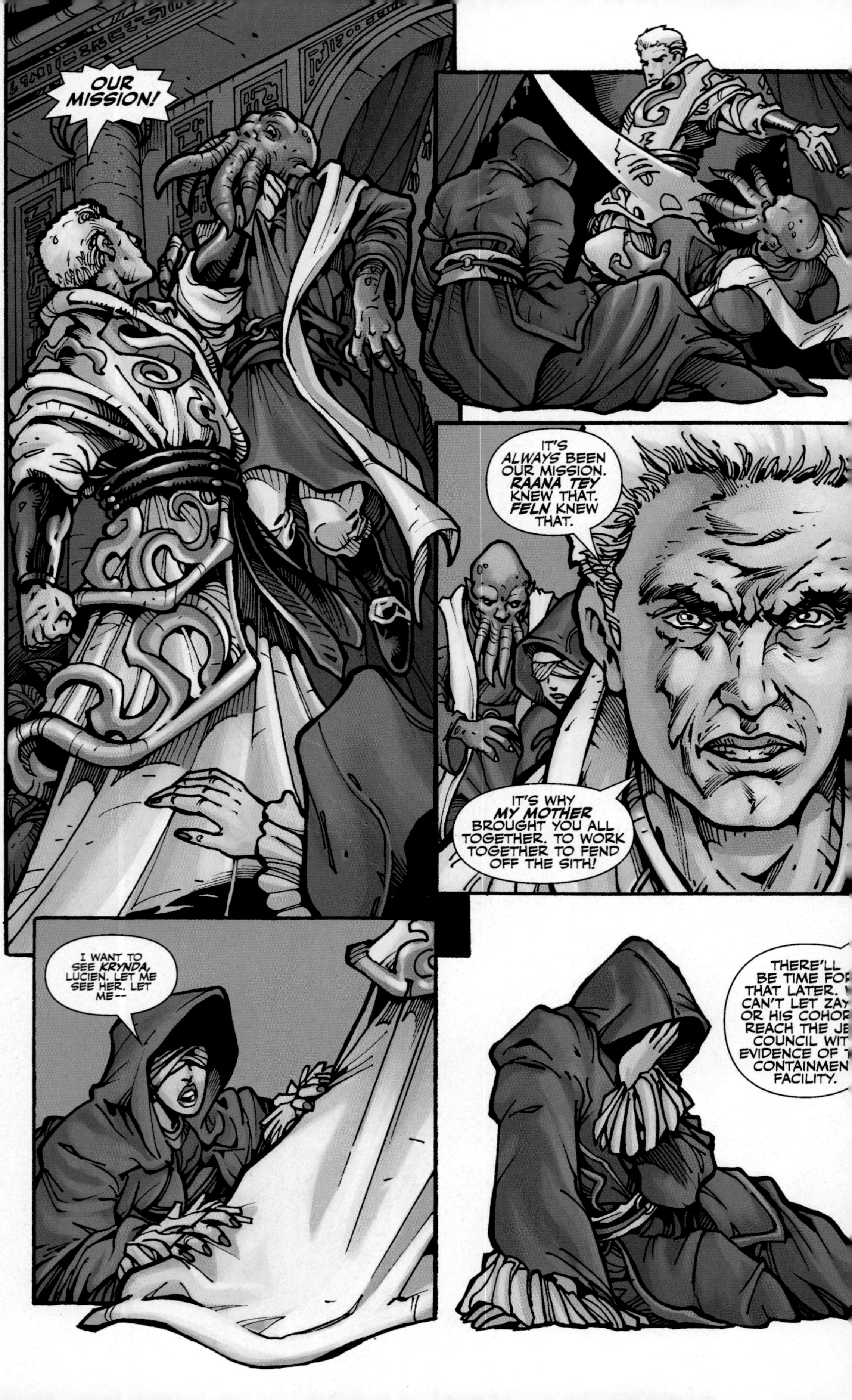
OUR MISSION!
IT'S ALWAYS BEEN OUR MISSION. RAANA TEY KNEW THAT. FELN KNEW THAT.
IT'S WHY MY MOTHER BROUGHT YOU ALL TOGETHER. TO WORK TOGETHER TO FEND OFF THE SITH!
I WANT TO SEE KRYNDA, LUCIEN. LET ME SEE HER. LET ME--
THERE'LL BE TIME FOR THAT LATER.
CAN'T LET ZAY
OR HIS COHOR
REACH THE JE
COUNCIL WIT
EVIDENCE OF
CONTAINMEN
FACILITY.

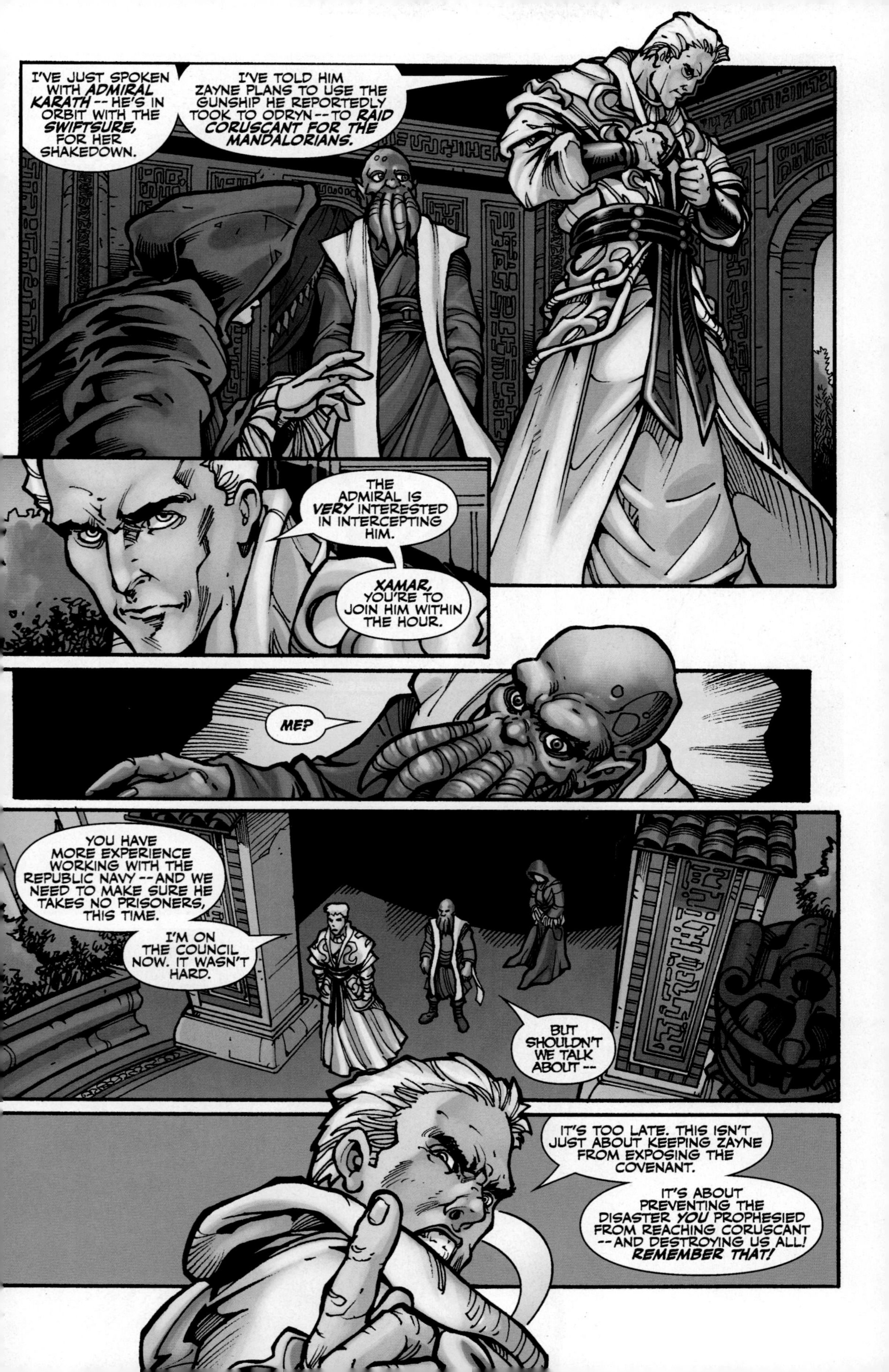
I'VE JUST SPOKEN WITH ADMIRAL KARATH -- HE'S IN ORBIT WITH THE SWIFTSURE, FOR HER SHAKEDOWN.
I'VE TOLD HIM ZAYNE PLANS TO USE THE GUNSHIP HE REPORTEDLY TOOK TO ODRYN--TO RAID CORUSCANT FOR THE MANDALORIANS.
THE ADMIRAL IS VERY INTERESTED IN INTERCEPTING HIM.
XAMAR, YOU'RE TO JOIN HIM WITHIN THE HOUR.
ME?
YOU HAVE MORE EXPERIENCE WORKING WITH THE REPUBLIC NAVY--AND WE NEED TO MAKE SURE HE TAKES NO PRISONERS, THIS TIME.
I'M ON THE COUNCIL NOW. IT WASN'T HARD.
BUT SHOULDN'T WE TALK ABOUT--
IT'S TOO LATE. THIS ISN'T JUST ABOUT KEEPING ZAYNE FROM EXPOSING THE COVENANT.
IT'S ABOUT PREVENTING THE DISASTER YOU PROPHESIED FROM REACHING CORUSCANT --AND DESTROYING US ALL! REMEMBER THAT!

DIDN'T-- DIDN'T OUR ROGUE MOON VISION SHOW--

THAT I WASSS THE NEXT TO DIE?

YESSS. IN SSSPACE, WITH THE REPUBLIC NAVY. BY FRIENDLY FIRE.

YOU CAN'T GO, XAMAR. YOU CAN'T! YOU CAN'T RUN TOWARDS IT!

NOR, IT SSSEEMS, CAN I RUN FROM IT.

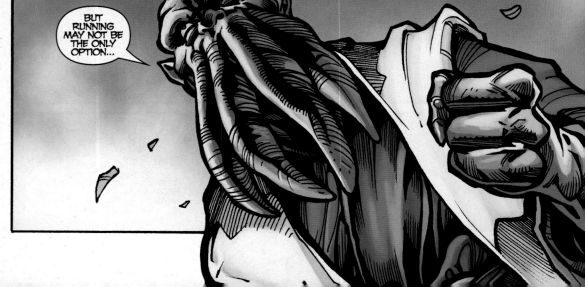

BUT RUNNING MAY NOT BE THE ONLY OPTION...

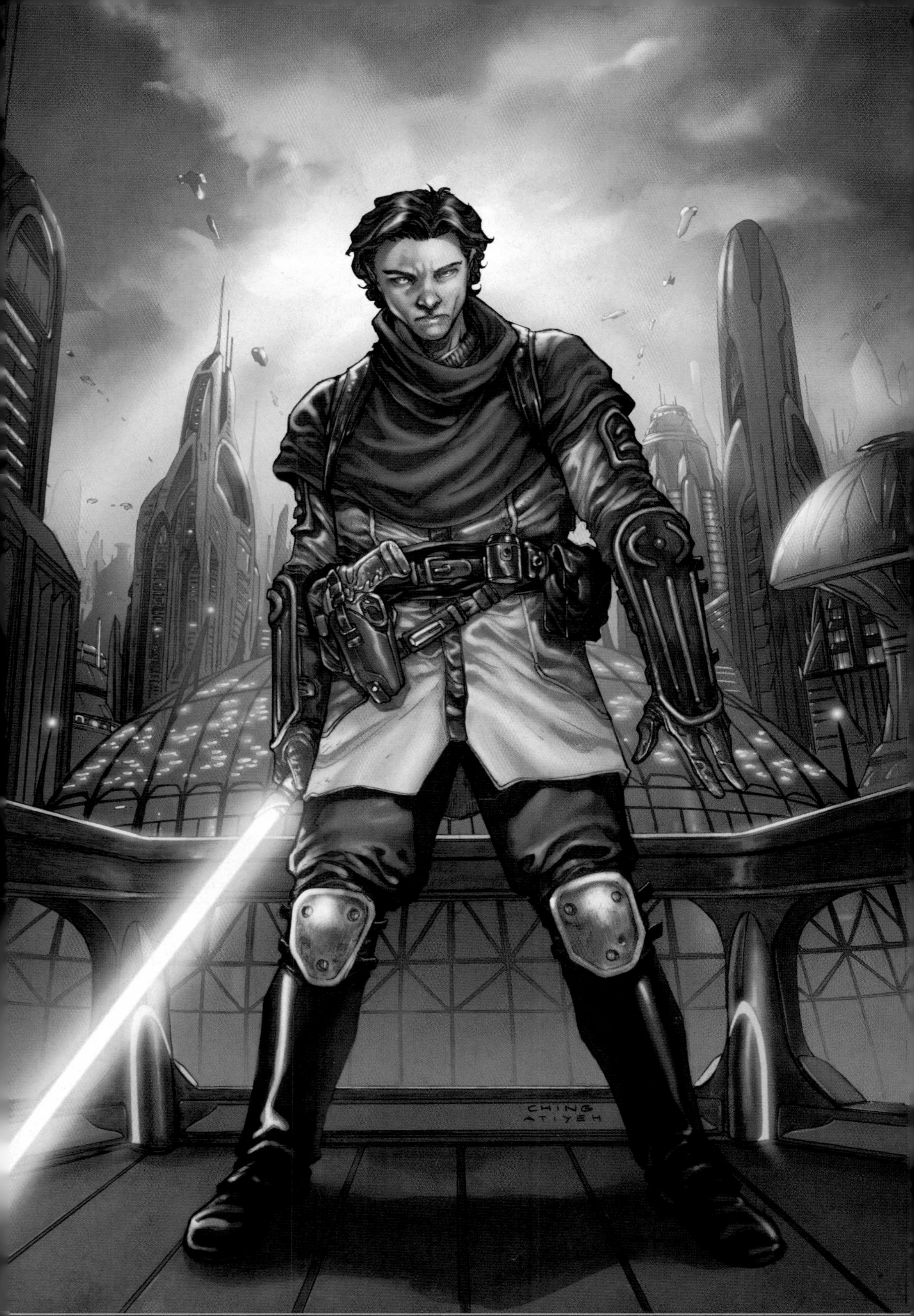
CHING
ATIYEH

STAR WARS: KNIGHTS OF THE OLD REPUBLIC #31 — "TURNABOUT"

WRITER: JOHN JACKSON MILLER • ARTIST: ALAN ROBINSON • COLORIST: MICHAEL ATIYEH • LETTERER: MICHAEL HEISLER
ASSISTANT EDITOR: FREDDYE LINS • EDITOR: DAVE MARSHALL • COVER ARTISTS: BRIAN CHING & MICHAEL ATIYEH

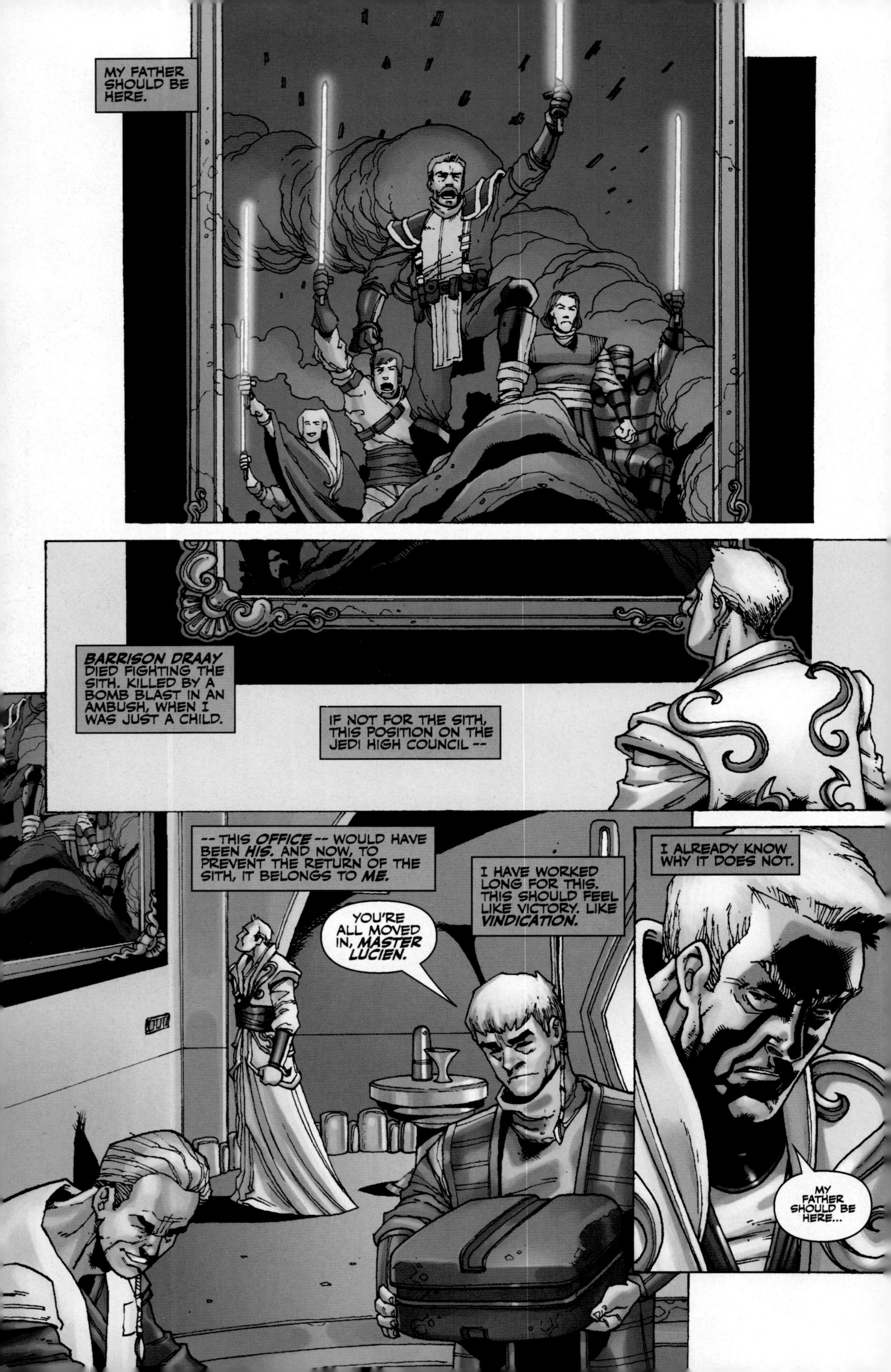
MY FATHER SHOULD BE HERE.
BARRISON DRAAY DIED FIGHTING THE SITH. KILLED BY A BOMB BLAST IN AN AMBUSH, WHEN I WAS JUST A CHILD.
IF NOT FOR THE SITH, THIS POSITION ON THE JEDI HIGH COUNCIL --
-- THIS OFFICE -- WOULD HAVE BEEN HIS. AND NOW, TO PREVENT THE RETURN OF THE SITH, IT BELONGS TO ME.
YOU'RE ALL MOVED IN, MASTER LUCIEN.
I HAVE WORKED LONG FOR THIS. THIS SHOULD FEEL LIKE VICTORY. LIKE VINDICATION.
I ALREADY KNOW WHY IT DOES NOT.
MY FATHER SHOULD BE HERE...

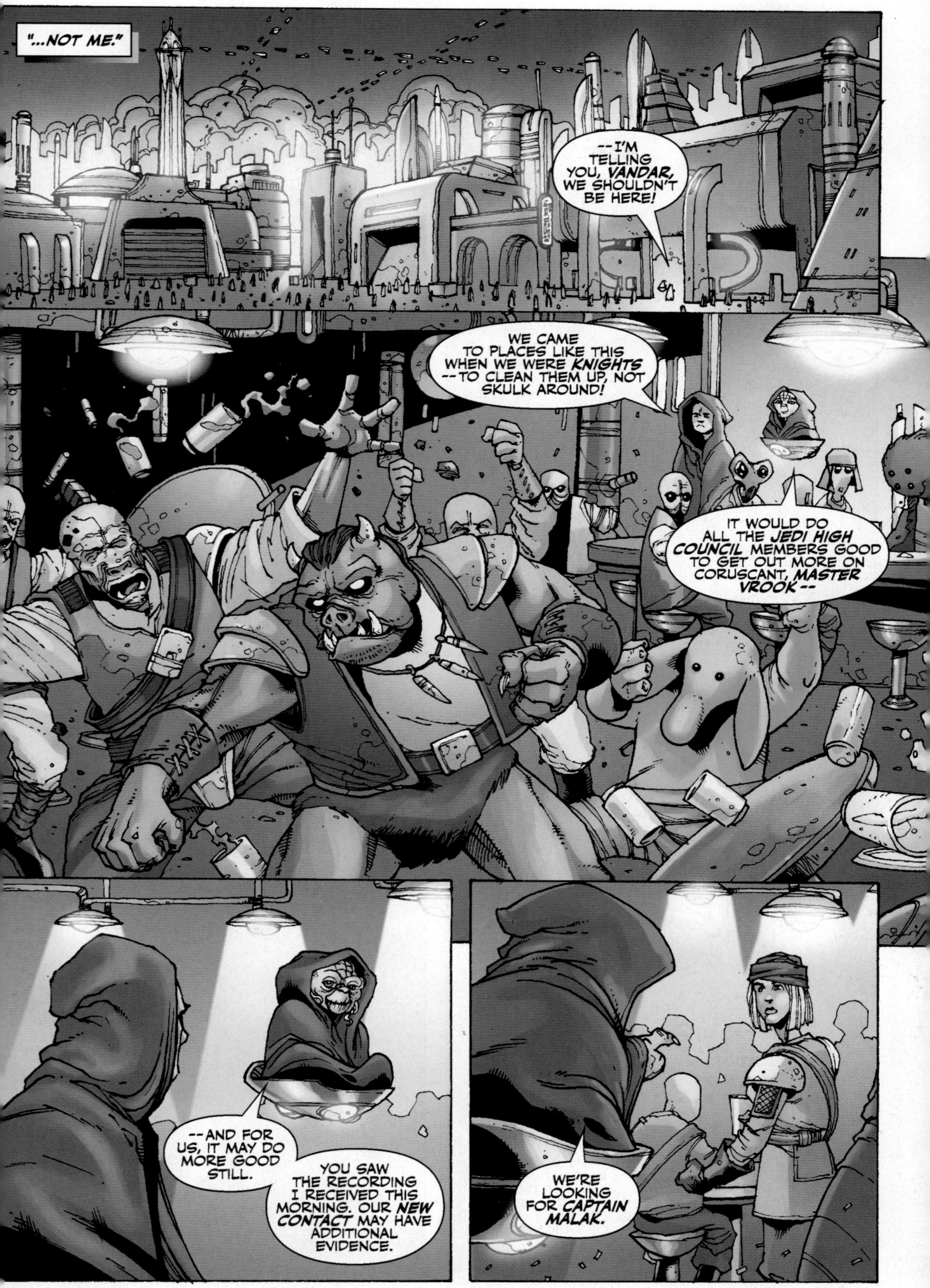
"...NOT ME."
--I'M TELLING YOU, VANDAR, WE SHOULDN'T BE HERE!
WE CAME TO PLACES LIKE THIS WHEN WE WERE KNIGHTS --TO CLEAN THEM UP, NOT SKULK AROUND!
IT WOULD DO ALL THE JEDI HIGH COUNCIL MEMBERS GOOD TO GET OUT MORE ON CORUSCANT, MASTER VROOK--
--AND FOR US, IT MAY DO MORE GOOD STILL.
YOU SAW THE RECORDING I RECEIVED THIS MORNING. OUR NEW CONTACT MAY HAVE ADDITIONAL EVIDENCE.
WE'RE LOOKING FOR CAPTAIN MALAK.

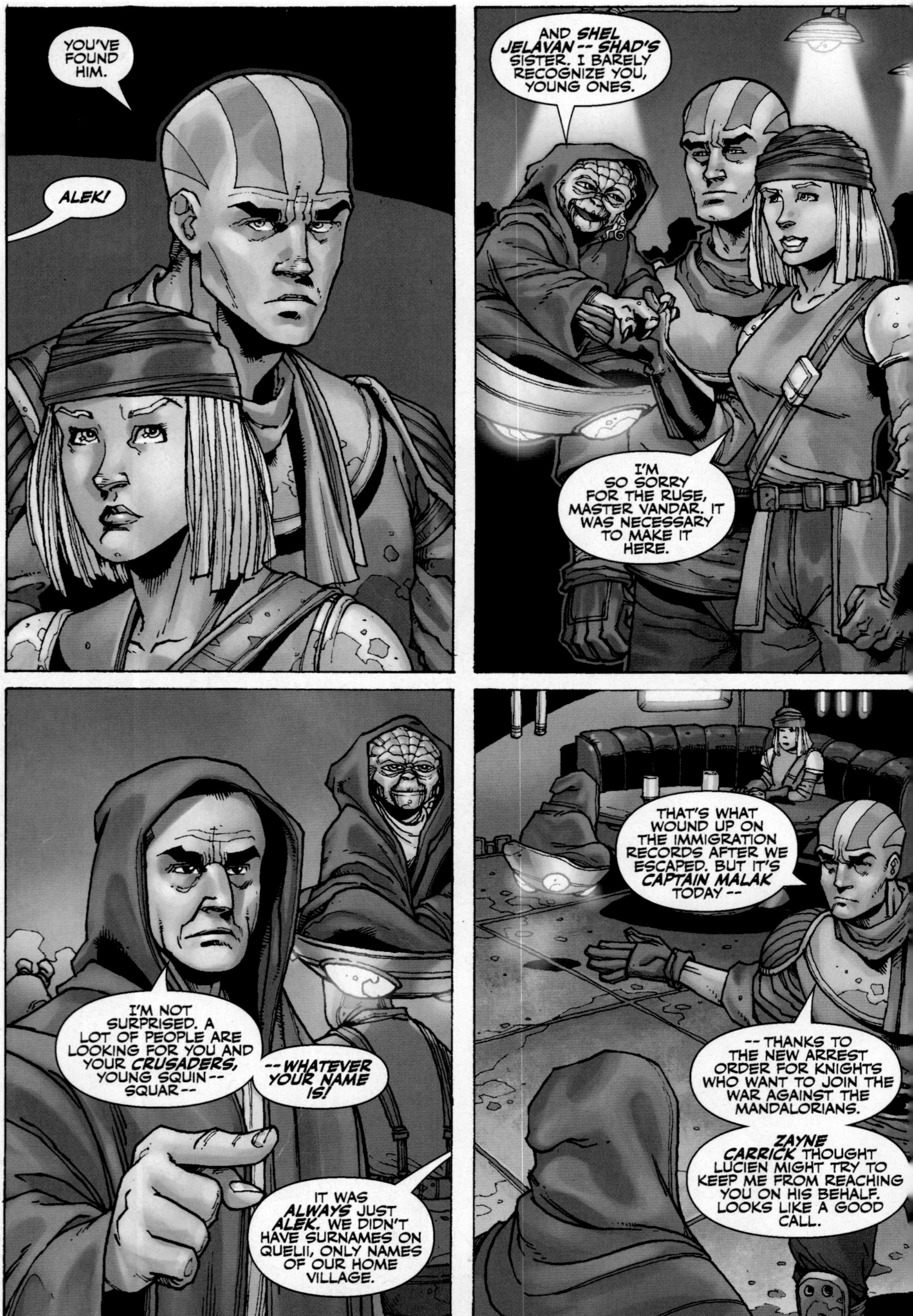
YOU'VE FOUND HIM.
ALEK!
AND SHEL JELAVAN -- SHAD'S SISTER. I BARELY RECOGNIZE YOU, YOUNG ONES.
I'M SO SORRY FOR THE RUSE, MASTER VANDAR. IT WAS NECESSARY TO MAKE IT HERE.
I'M NOT SURPRISED. A LOT OF PEOPLE ARE LOOKING FOR YOU AND YOUR CRUSADERS, YOUNG SQUIN-- SQUAR--
--WHATEVER YOUR NAME IS!
IT WAS ALWAYS JUST ALEK. WE DIDN'T HAVE SURNAMES ON QUELII, ONLY NAMES OF OUR HOME VILLAGE.
THAT'S WHAT WOUND UP ON THE IMMIGRATION RECORDS AFTER WE ESCAPED. BUT IT'S CAPTAIN MALAK TODAY --
-- THANKS TO THE NEW ARREST ORDER FOR KNIGHTS WHO WANT TO JOIN THE WAR AGAINST THE MANDALORIANS.
ZAYNE CARRICK THOUGHT LUCIEN MIGHT TRY TO KEEP ME FROM REACHING YOU ON HIS BEHALF. LOOKS LIKE A GOOD CALL.

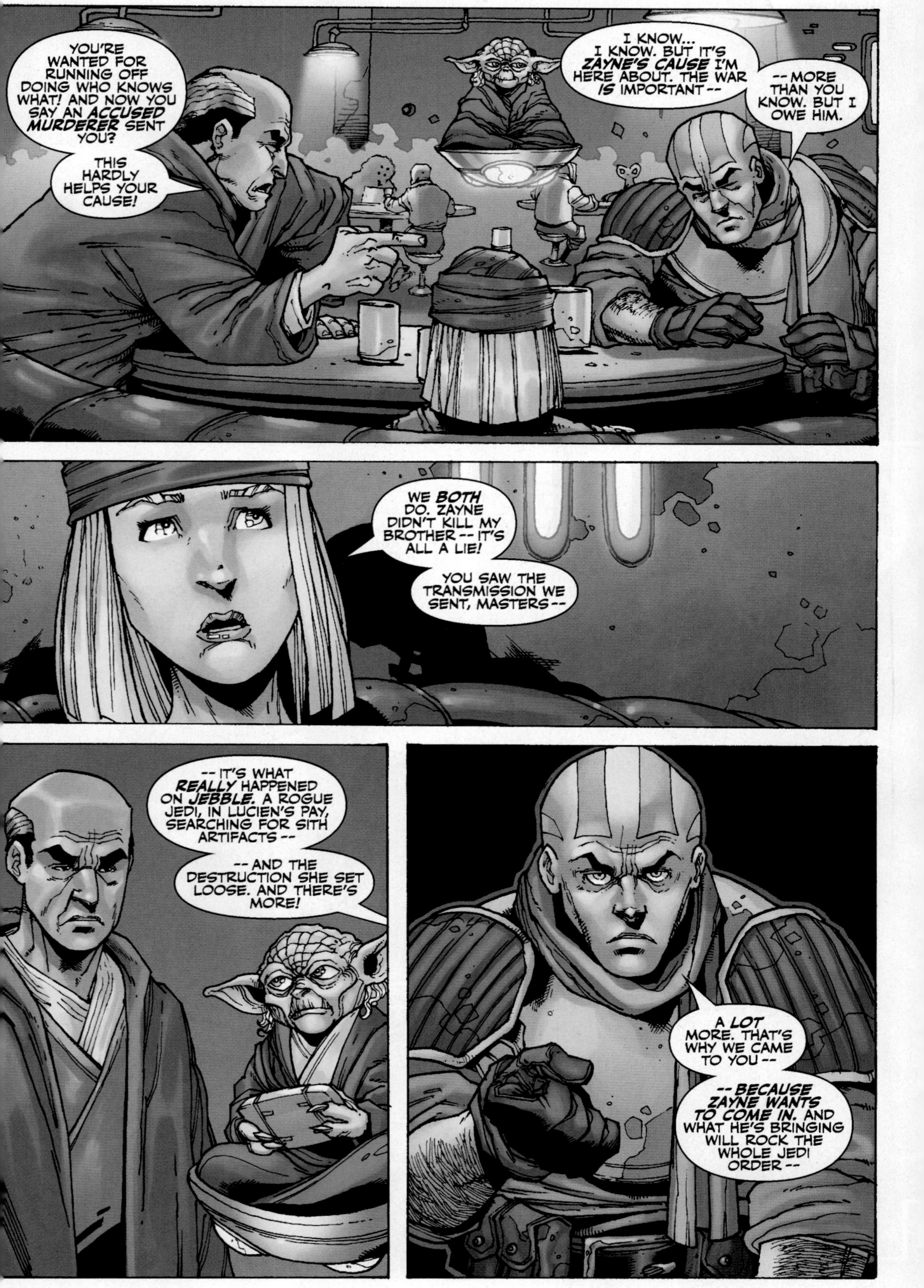
YOU'RE WANTED FOR RUNNING OFF DOING WHO KNOWS WHAT! AND NOW YOU SAY AN ACCUSED MURDERER SENT YOU?
THIS HARDLY HELPS YOUR CAUSE!
I KNOW... I KNOW. BUT IT'S ZAYNE'S CAUSE I'M HERE ABOUT. THE WAR IS IMPORTANT --
-- MORE THAN YOU KNOW. BUT I OWE HIM.
WE BOTH DO. ZAYNE DIDN'T KILL MY BROTHER -- IT'S ALL A LIE!
YOU SAW THE TRANSMISSION WE SENT, MASTERS --
-- IT'S WHAT REALLY HAPPENED ON JEBBLE. A ROGUE JEDI, IN LUCIEN'S PAY, SEARCHING FOR SITH ARTIFACTS --
-- AND THE DESTRUCTION SHE SET LOOSE. AND THERE'S MORE!
A LOT MORE. THAT'S WHY WE CAME TO YOU --
-- BECAUSE ZAYNE WANTS TO COME IN. AND WHAT HE'S BRINGING WILL ROCK THE WHOLE JEDI ORDER --

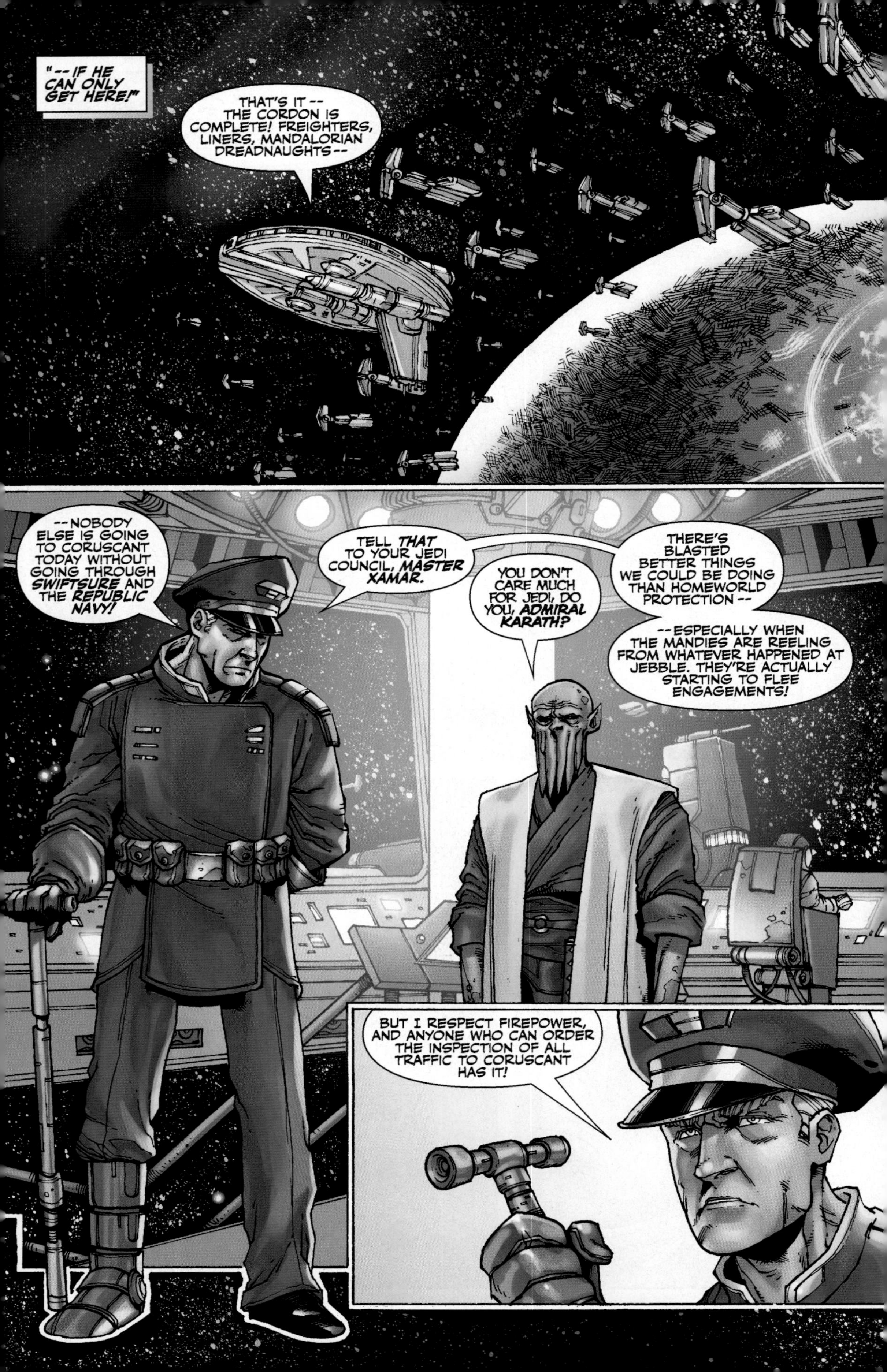
"--IF HE CAN ONLY GET HERE!"
THAT'S IT -- THE CORDON IS COMPLETE! FREIGHTERS, LINERS, MANDALORIAN DREADNAUGHTS--
--NOBODY ELSE IS GOING TO CORUSCANT TODAY WITHOUT GOING THROUGH *SWIFTSURE* AND THE *REPUBLIC NAVY!*
TELL *THAT* TO YOUR JEDI COUNCIL, *MASTER XAMAR.*
YOU DON'T CARE MUCH FOR JEDI, DO YOU, *ADMIRAL KARATH?*
THERE'S BLASTED BETTER THINGS WE COULD BE DOING THAN HOMEWORLD PROTECTION --
--ESPECIALLY WHEN THE MANDIES ARE REELING FROM WHATEVER HAPPENED AT JEBBLE. THEY'RE ACTUALLY STARTING TO FLEE ENGAGEMENTS!
BUT I RESPECT FIREPOWER, AND ANYONE WHO CAN ORDER THE INSPECTION OF ALL TRAFFIC TO CORUSCANT HAS IT!

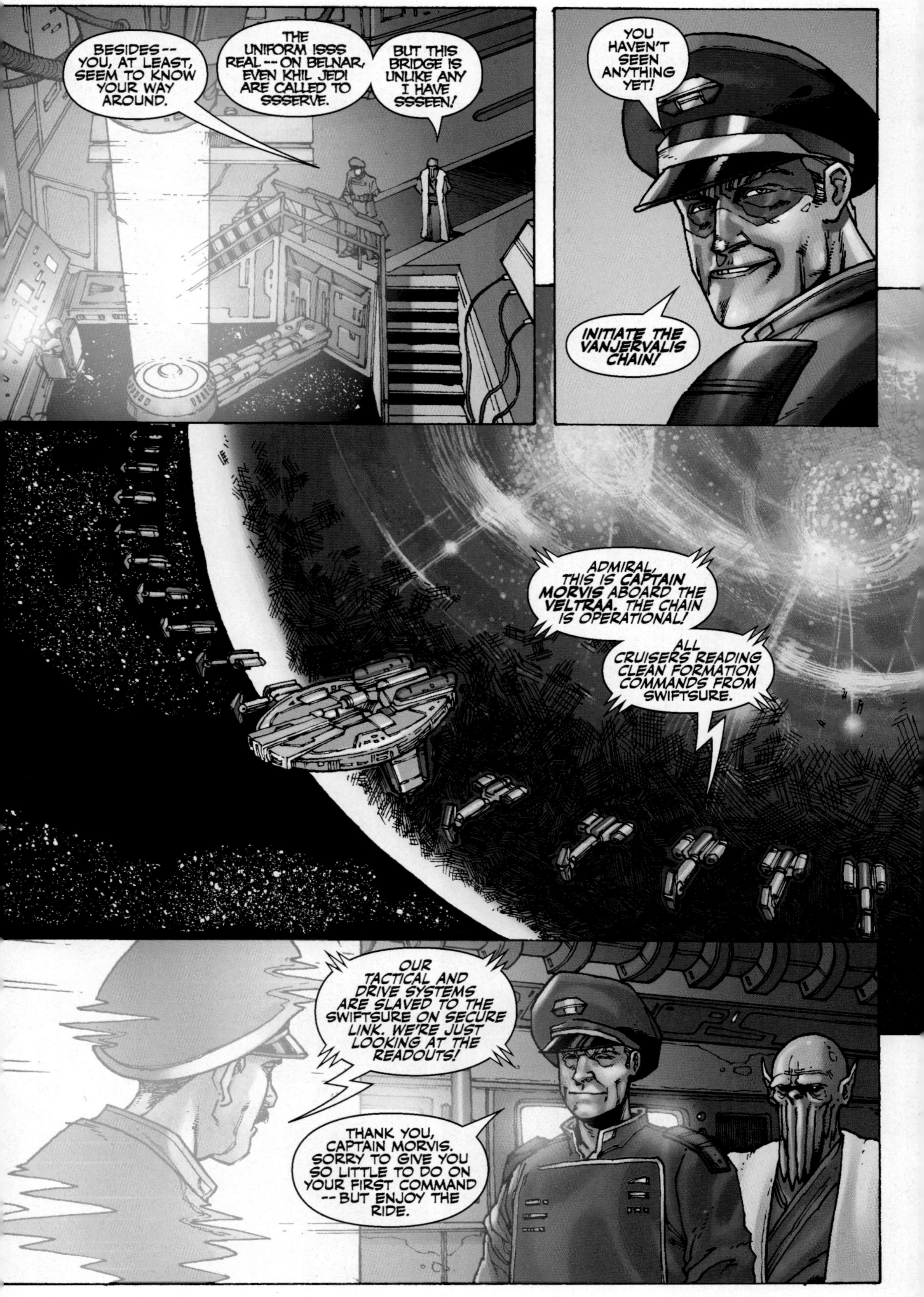
BESIDES-- YOU, AT LEAST, SEEM TO KNOW YOUR WAY AROUND.
THE UNIFORM ISSS REAL--ON BELNAR, EVEN KHIL JEDI ARE CALLED TO SSSERVE.
BUT THIS BRIDGE IS UNLIKE ANY I HAVE SSSEEN!
YOU HAVEN'T SEEN ANYTHING YET!
INITIATE THE VANJERVALIS CHAIN!
ADMIRAL, THIS IS CAPTAIN MORVIS ABOARD THE VELTRAA. THE CHAIN IS OPERATIONAL!
ALL CRUISERS READING CLEAN FORMATION COMMANDS FROM SWIFTSURE.
OUR TACTICAL AND DRIVE SYSTEMS ARE SLAVED TO THE SWIFTSURE ON SECURE LINK. WE'RE JUST LOOKING AT THE READOUTS!
THANK YOU, CAPTAIN MORVIS. SORRY TO GIVE YOU SO LITTLE TO DO ON YOUR FIRST COMMAND --BUT ENJOY THE RIDE.

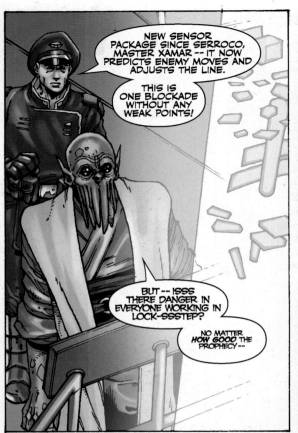

NEW SENSOR PACKAGE SINCE SERROCO, MASTER XAMAR -- IT NOW PREDICTS ENEMY MOVES AND ADJUSTS THE LINE.

THIS IS ONE BLOCKADE WITHOUT ANY WEAK POINTS!

BUT -- ISSS THERE DANGER IN EVERYONE WORKING IN LOCK-SSSTEP?

NO MATTER *HOW GOOD* THE PROPHECY --

-- I MEAN, THE *PREDICTION*, SHOULDN'T THERE BE TIME FOR CONTEMPLATION?

I TEND TO AGREE -- BUT THE NAVY CALLS THE SHOTS. AND I'D FLY A LEAKY LIFEPOD FOR ANOTHER SHOT AT ZAYNE CARRICK!

YOU MET ZAYNE, ADMIRAL -- HOW DID THE BOY SSSEEM TO YOU?

NOT ALWAYS MAKING SENSE -- AND ABSOLUTELY SURE HE'S RIGHT. *LIKE A JEDI.*

I DON'T KNOW IF HE'S A KILLER, A SPY, OR JUST CRAZY. ALL I DO KNOW --

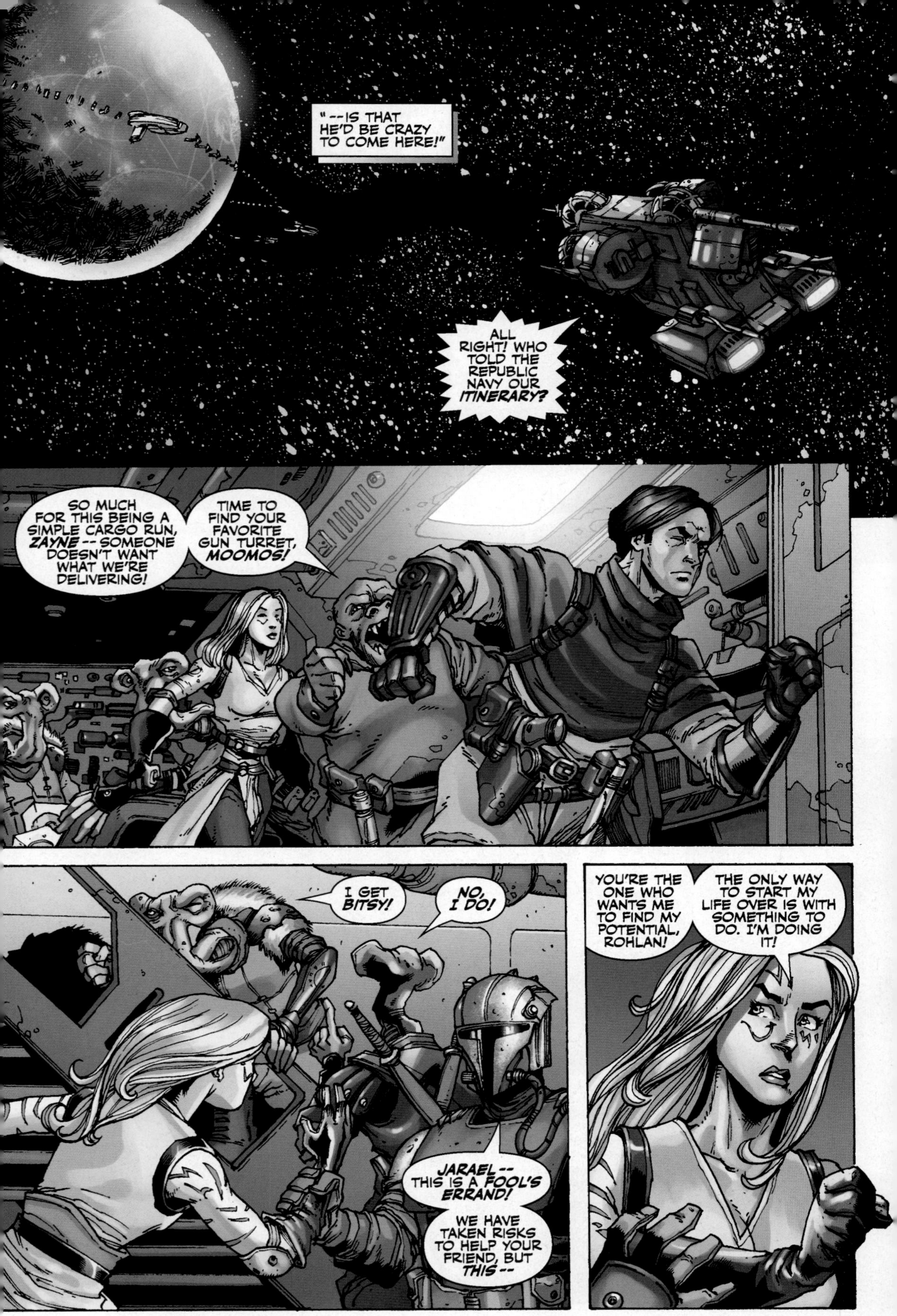
"--IS THAT HE'D BE CRAZY TO COME HERE!"
ALL RIGHT! WHO TOLD THE REPUBLIC NAVY OUR ITINERARY?
SO MUCH FOR THIS BEING A SIMPLE CARGO RUN, ZAYNE -- SOMEONE DOESN'T WANT WHAT WE'RE DELIVERING!
TIME TO FIND YOUR FAVORITE GUN TURRET, MOOMOS!
I GET BITSY!
NO, I DO!
JARAEL -- THIS IS A FOOL'S ERRAND!
WE HAVE TAKEN RISKS TO HELP YOUR FRIEND, BUT THIS --
YOU'RE THE ONE WHO WANTS ME TO FIND MY POTENTIAL, ROHLAN!
THE ONLY WAY TO START MY LIFE OVER IS WITH SOMETHING TO DO. I'M DOING IT!

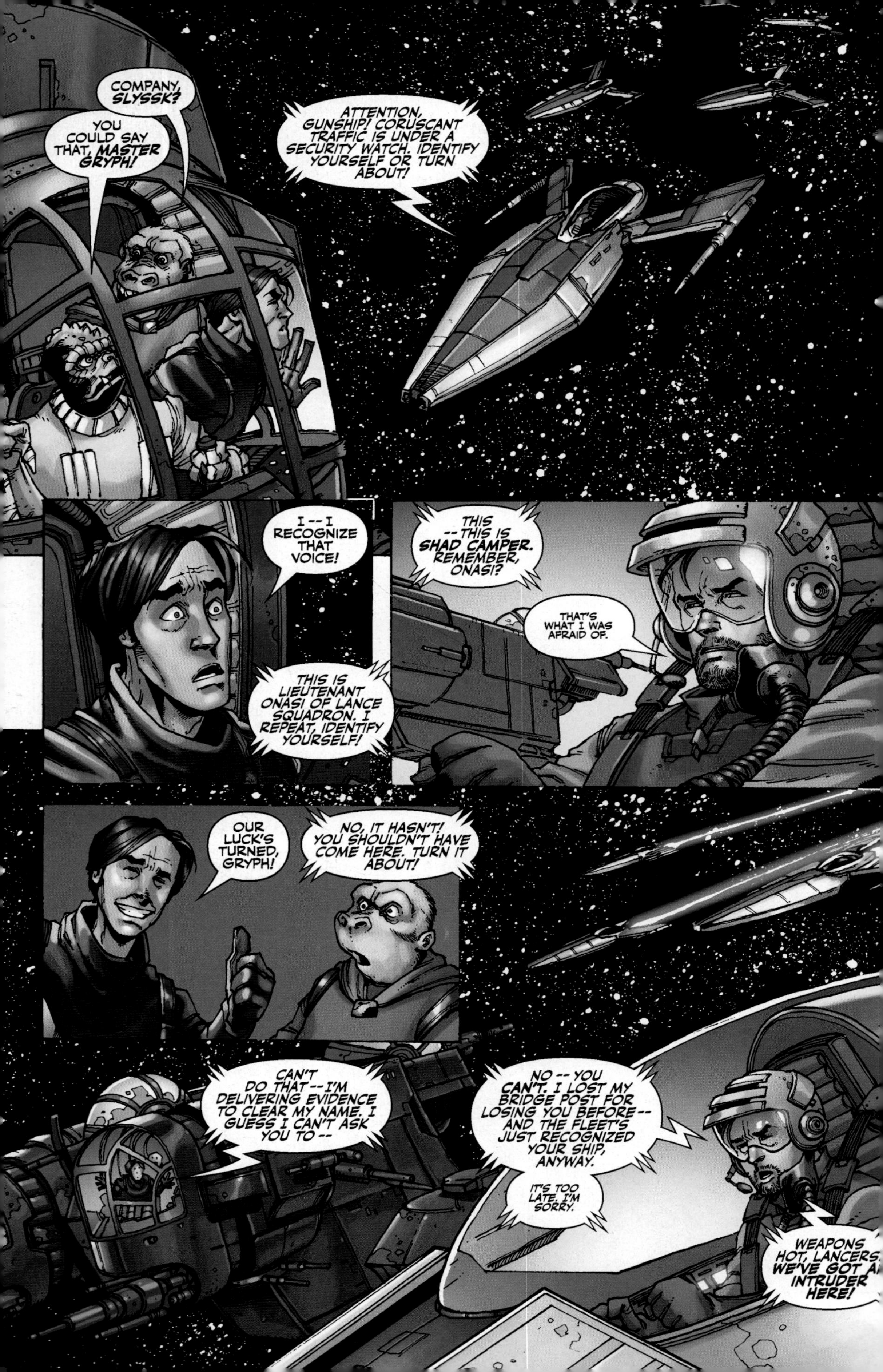
COMPANY, SLYSSK?
YOU COULD SAY THAT, MASTER GRYPH!
ATTENTION, GUNSHIP! CORUSCANT TRAFFIC IS UNDER A SECURITY WATCH. IDENTIFY YOURSELF OR TURN ABOUT!
I -- I RECOGNIZE THAT VOICE!
THIS IS LIEUTENANT ONASI OF LANCE SQUADRON. I REPEAT, IDENTIFY YOURSELF!
--THIS --THIS IS SHAD CAMPER. REMEMBER, ONASI?
THAT'S WHAT I WAS AFRAID OF.
OUR LUCK'S TURNED, GRYPH!
NO, IT HASN'T! YOU SHOULDN'T HAVE COME HERE. TURN IT ABOUT!
CAN'T DO THAT--I'M DELIVERING EVIDENCE TO CLEAR MY NAME. I GUESS I CAN'T ASK YOU TO --
NO -- YOU CAN'T. I LOST MY BRIDGE POST FOR LOSING YOU BEFORE-- AND THE FLEET'S JUST RECOGNIZED YOUR SHIP, ANYWAY.
IT'S TOO LATE. I'M SORRY.
WEAPONS HOT, LANCERS. WE'VE GOT AN INTRUDER HERE!

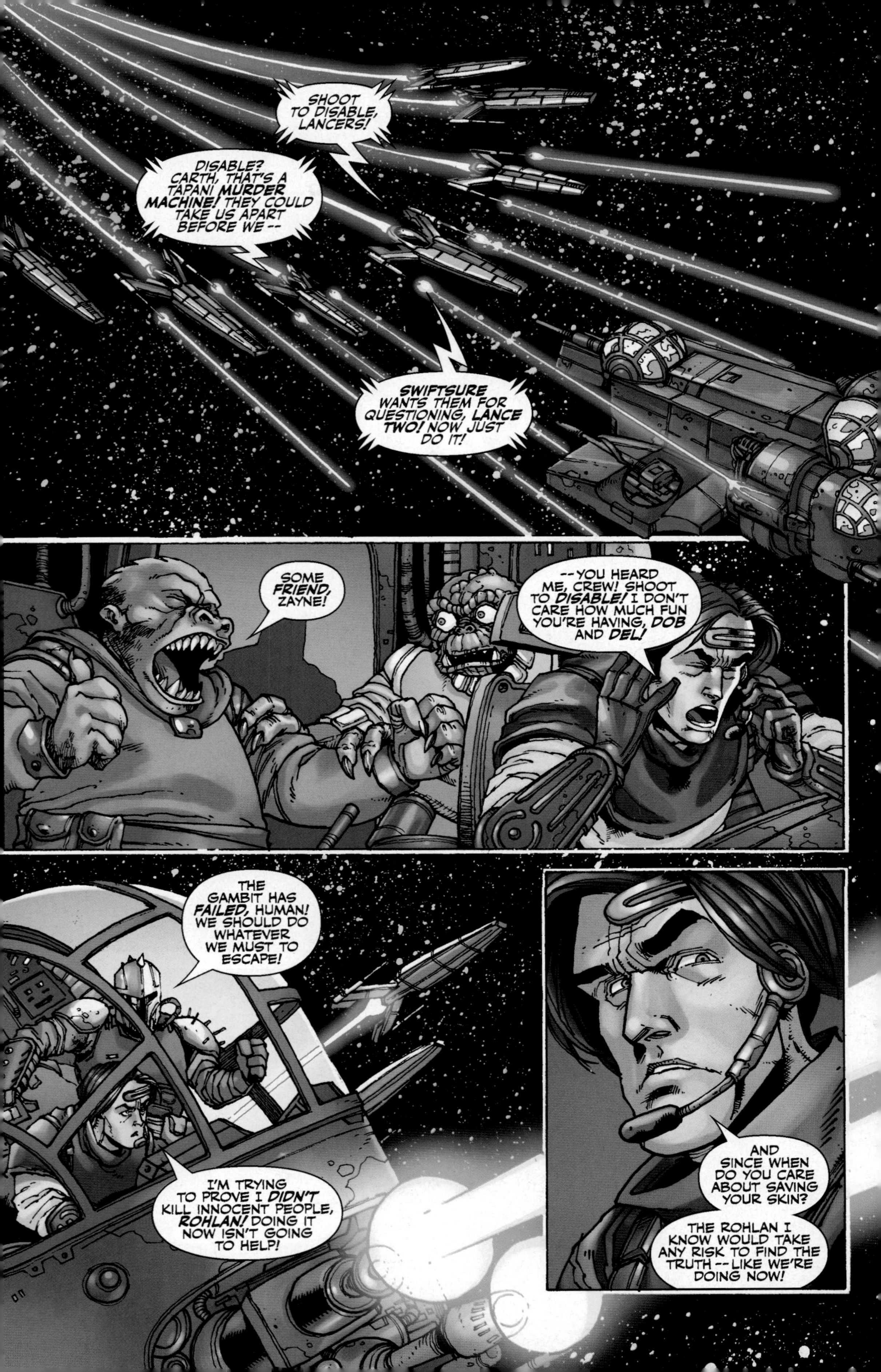
SHOOT TO DISABLE, LANCERS!
DISABLE? CARTH, THAT'S A TAPANI MURDER MACHINE! THEY COULD TAKE US APART BEFORE WE --
SWIFTSURE WANTS THEM FOR QUESTIONING, LANCE TWO! NOW JUST DO IT!
SOME FRIEND, ZAYNE!
--YOU HEARD ME, CREW! SHOOT TO DISABLE! I DON'T CARE HOW MUCH FUN YOU'RE HAVING, DOB AND DEL!
THE GAMBIT HAS FAILED, HUMAN! WE SHOULD DO WHATEVER WE MUST TO ESCAPE!
I'M TRYING TO PROVE I DIDN'T KILL INNOCENT PEOPLE, ROHLAN! DOING IT NOW ISN'T GOING TO HELP!
AND SINCE WHEN DO YOU CARE ABOUT SAVING YOUR SKIN?
THE ROHLAN I KNOW WOULD TAKE ANY RISK TO FIND THE TRUTH -- LIKE WE'RE DOING NOW!

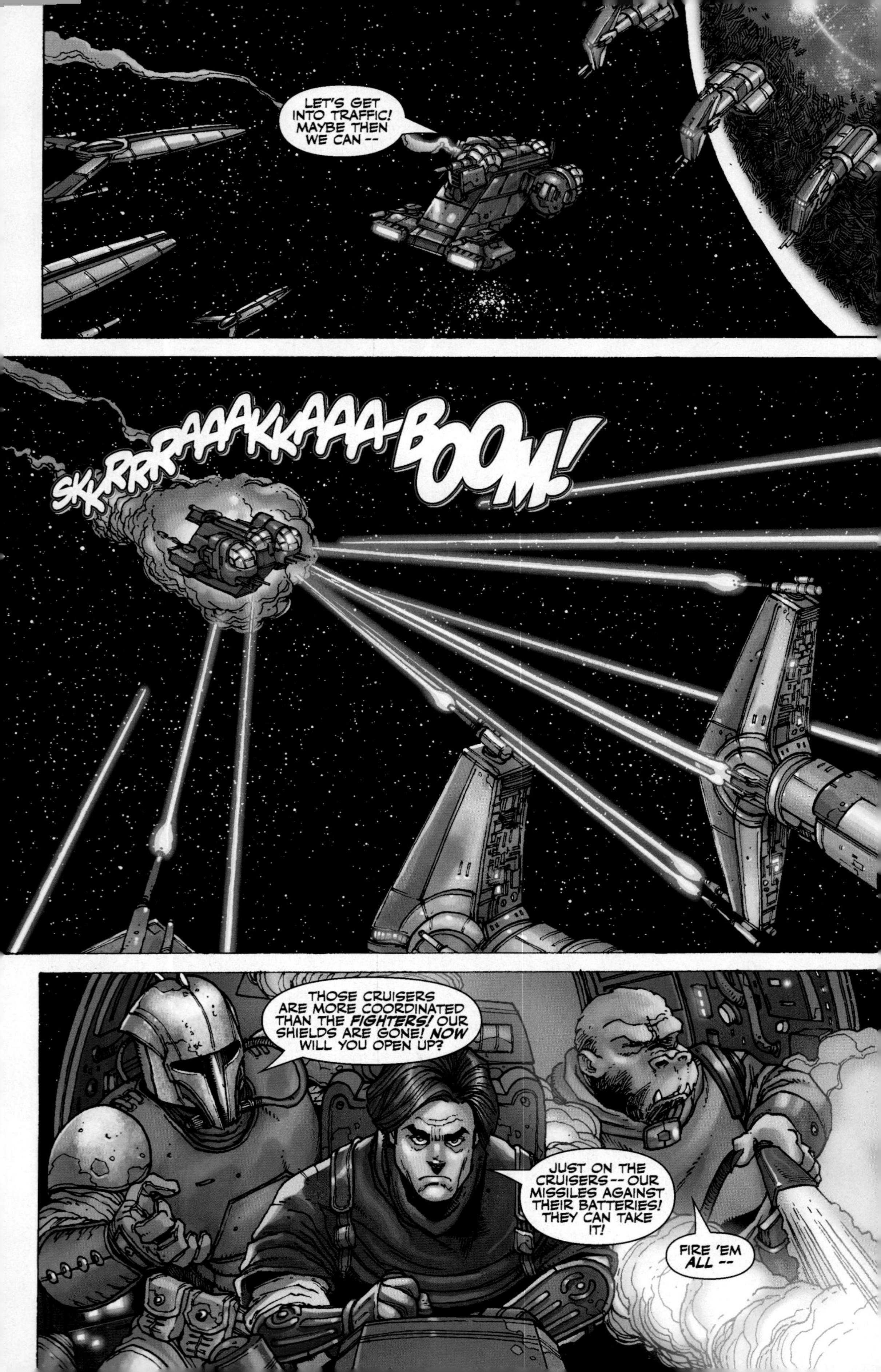
LET'S GET INTO TRAFFIC! MAYBE THEN WE CAN --
SKKRRRAAAKKAAA-BOOM!
THOSE CRUISERS ARE MORE COORDINATED THAN THE *FIGHTERS!* OUR SHIELDS ARE GONE! *NOW* WILL YOU OPEN UP?
JUST ON THE CRUISERS -- OUR MISSILES AGAINST THEIR BATTERIES! THEY CAN TAKE IT!
FIRE 'EM *ALL* --

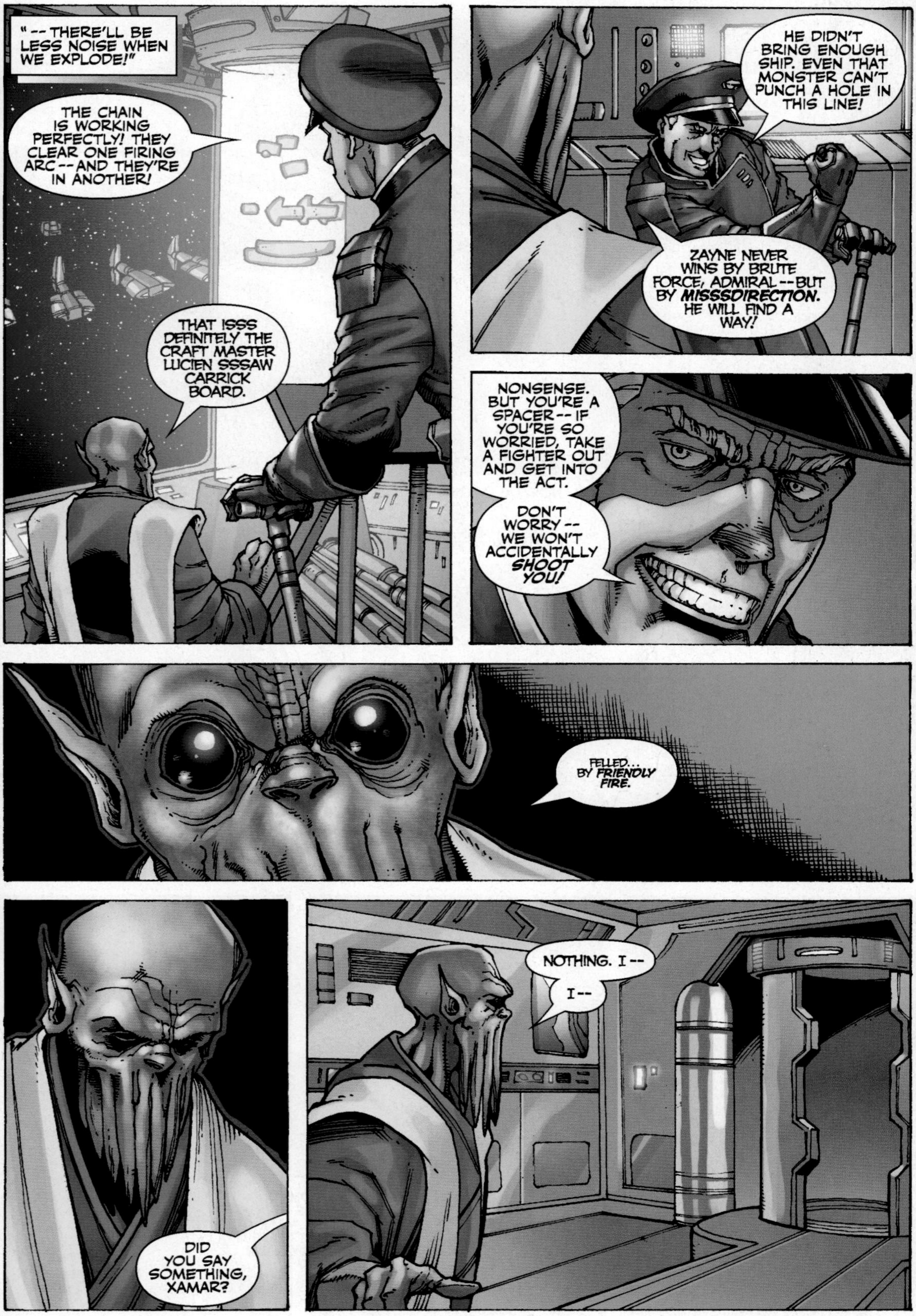

"-- THERE'LL BE LESS NOISE WHEN WE EXPLODE!"
THE CHAIN IS WORKING PERFECTLY! THEY CLEAR ONE FIRING ARC -- AND THEY'RE IN ANOTHER!
THAT ISSS DEFINITELY THE CRAFT MASTER LUCIEN SSSAW CARRICK BOARD.
HE DIDN'T BRING ENOUGH SHIP. EVEN THAT MONSTER CAN'T PUNCH A HOLE IN THIS LINE!
ZAYNE NEVER WINS BY BRUTE FORCE, ADMIRAL -- BUT BY MISSSDIRECTION. HE WILL FIND A WAY!
NONSENSE. BUT YOU'RE A SPACER -- IF YOU'RE SO WORRIED, TAKE A FIGHTER OUT AND GET INTO THE ACT.
DON'T WORRY -- WE WON'T ACCIDENTALLY SHOOT YOU!
FELLED... BY FRIENDLY FIRE.
DID YOU SAY SOMETHING, XAMAR?
NOTHING. I --
I --

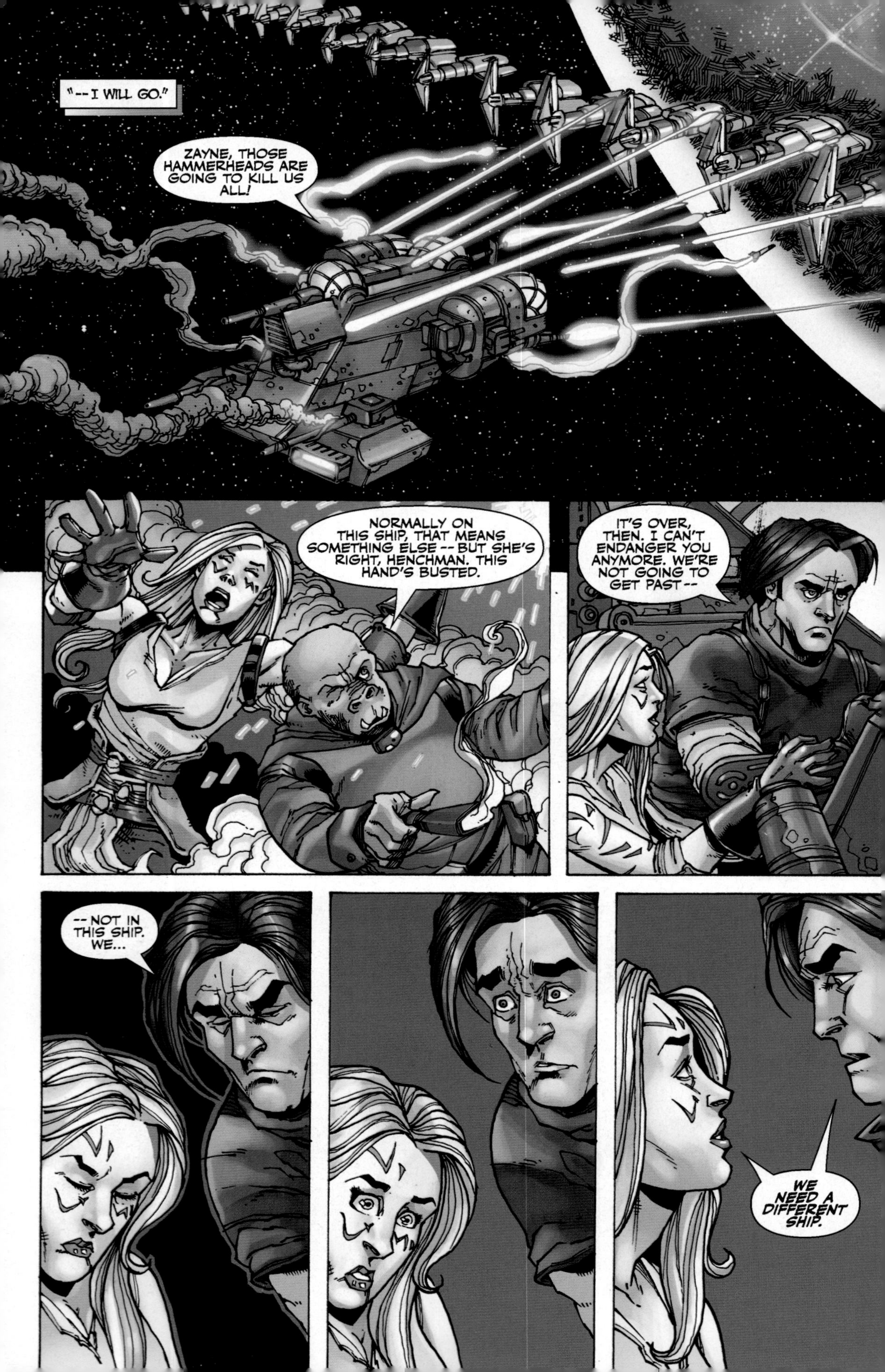
"-- I WILL GO."
ZAYNE, THOSE HAMMERHEADS ARE GOING TO KILL US ALL!
NORMALLY ON THIS SHIP, THAT MEANS SOMETHING ELSE -- BUT SHE'S RIGHT, HENCHMAN. THIS HAND'S BUSTED.
IT'S OVER, THEN. I CAN'T ENDANGER YOU ANYMORE. WE'RE NOT GOING TO GET PAST --
-- NOT IN THIS SHIP. WE...
WE NEED A DIFFERENT SHIP.

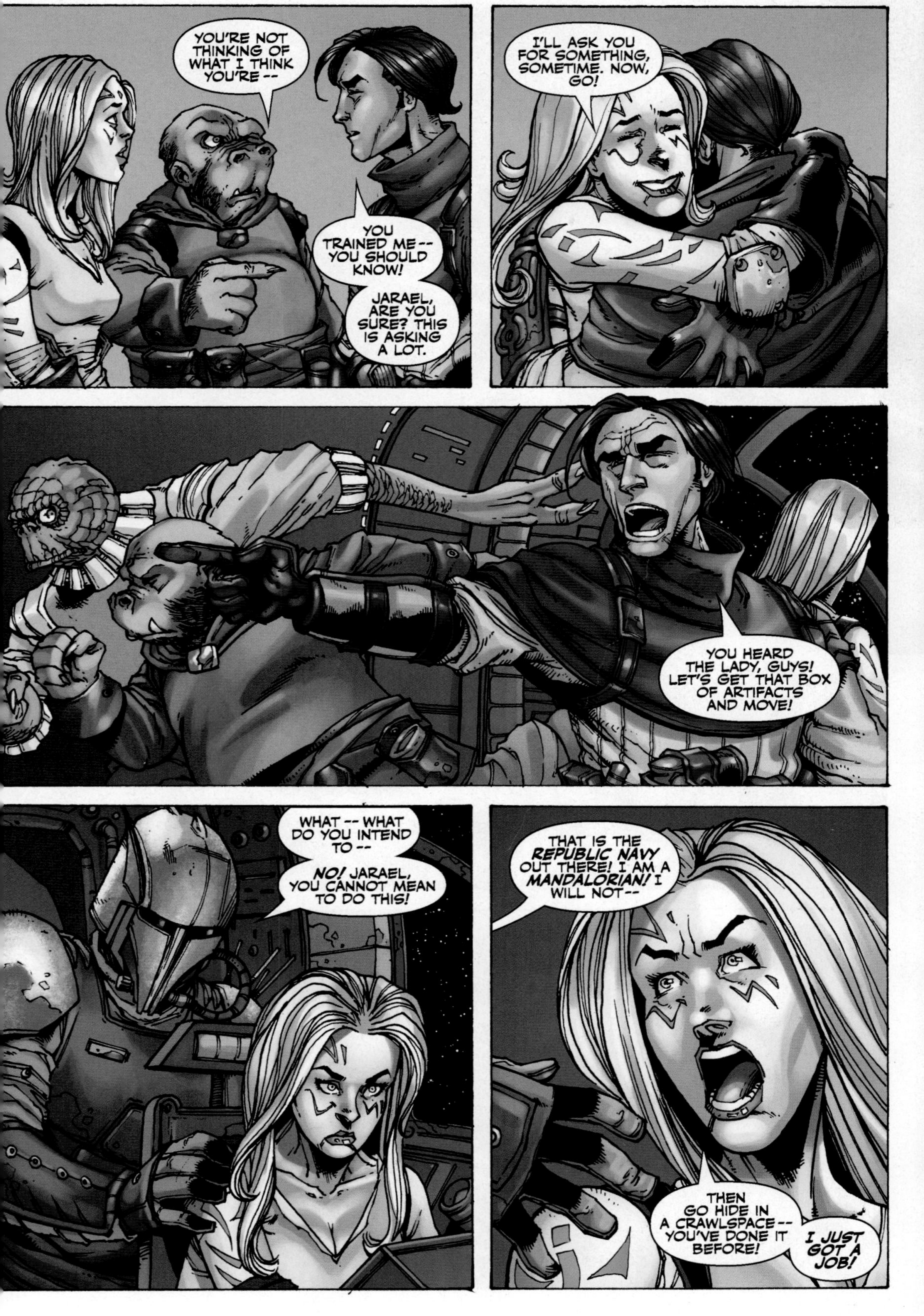
YOU'RE NOT THINKING OF WHAT I THINK YOU'RE --
YOU TRAINED ME -- YOU SHOULD KNOW!
JARAEL, ARE YOU SURE? THIS IS ASKING A LOT.
I'LL ASK YOU FOR SOMETHING, SOMETIME. NOW, GO!
YOU HEARD THE LADY, GUYS! LET'S GET THAT BOX OF ARTIFACTS AND MOVE!
WHAT -- WHAT DO YOU INTEND TO --
NO! JARAEL, YOU CANNOT MEAN TO DO THIS!
THAT IS THE REPUBLIC NAVY OUT THERE! I AM A MANDALORIAN! I WILL NOT--
THEN GO HIDE IN A CRAWLSPACE -- YOU'VE DONE IT BEFORE!
I JUST GOT A JOB!

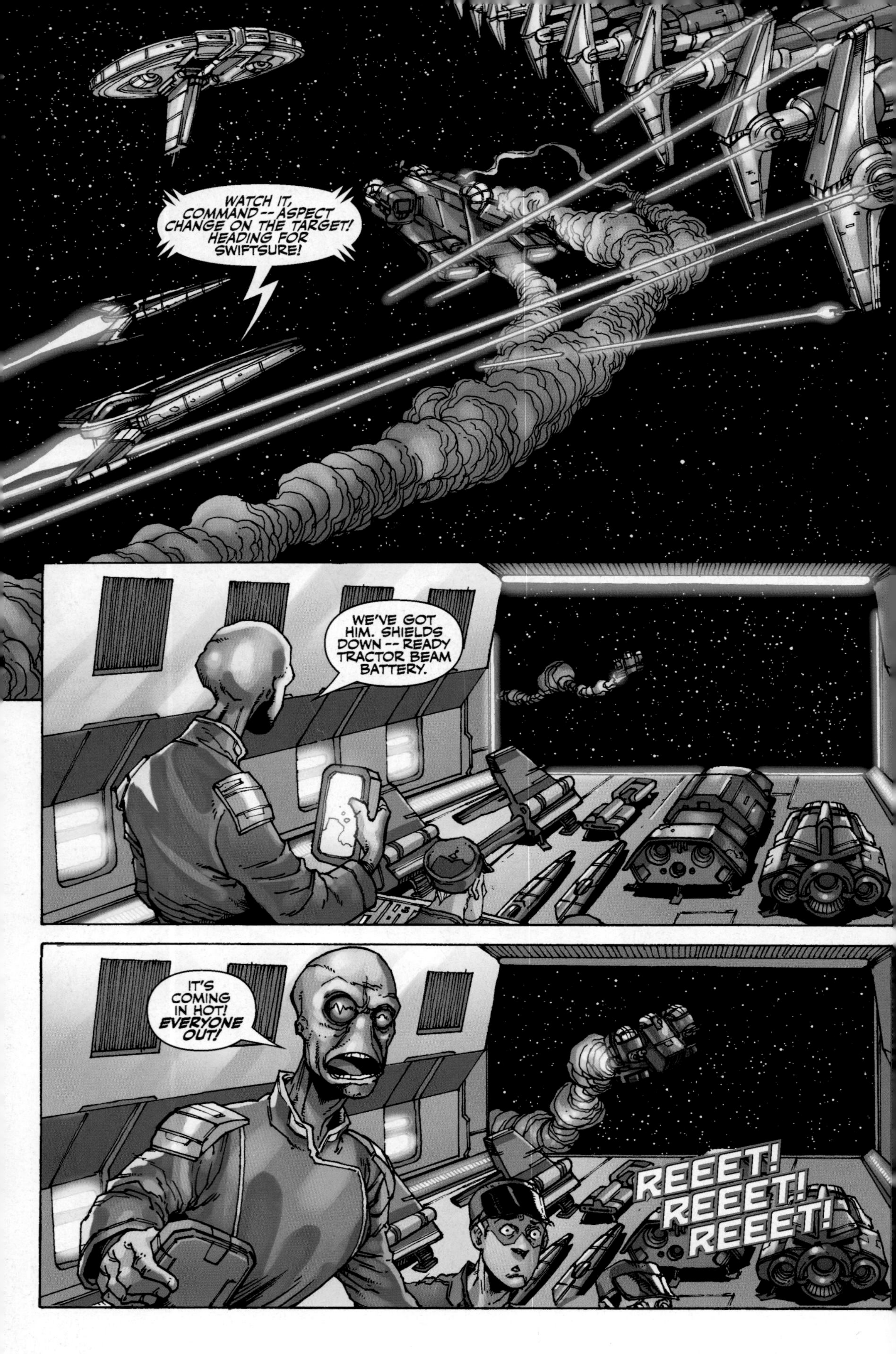
WATCH IT, COMMAND -- ASPECT CHANGE ON THE TARGET! HEADING FOR SWIFTSURE!
WE'VE GOT HIM. SHIELDS DOWN -- READY TRACTOR BEAM BATTERY.
IT'S COMING IN HOT! EVERYONE OUT!
REEEET! REEEET! REEEET!

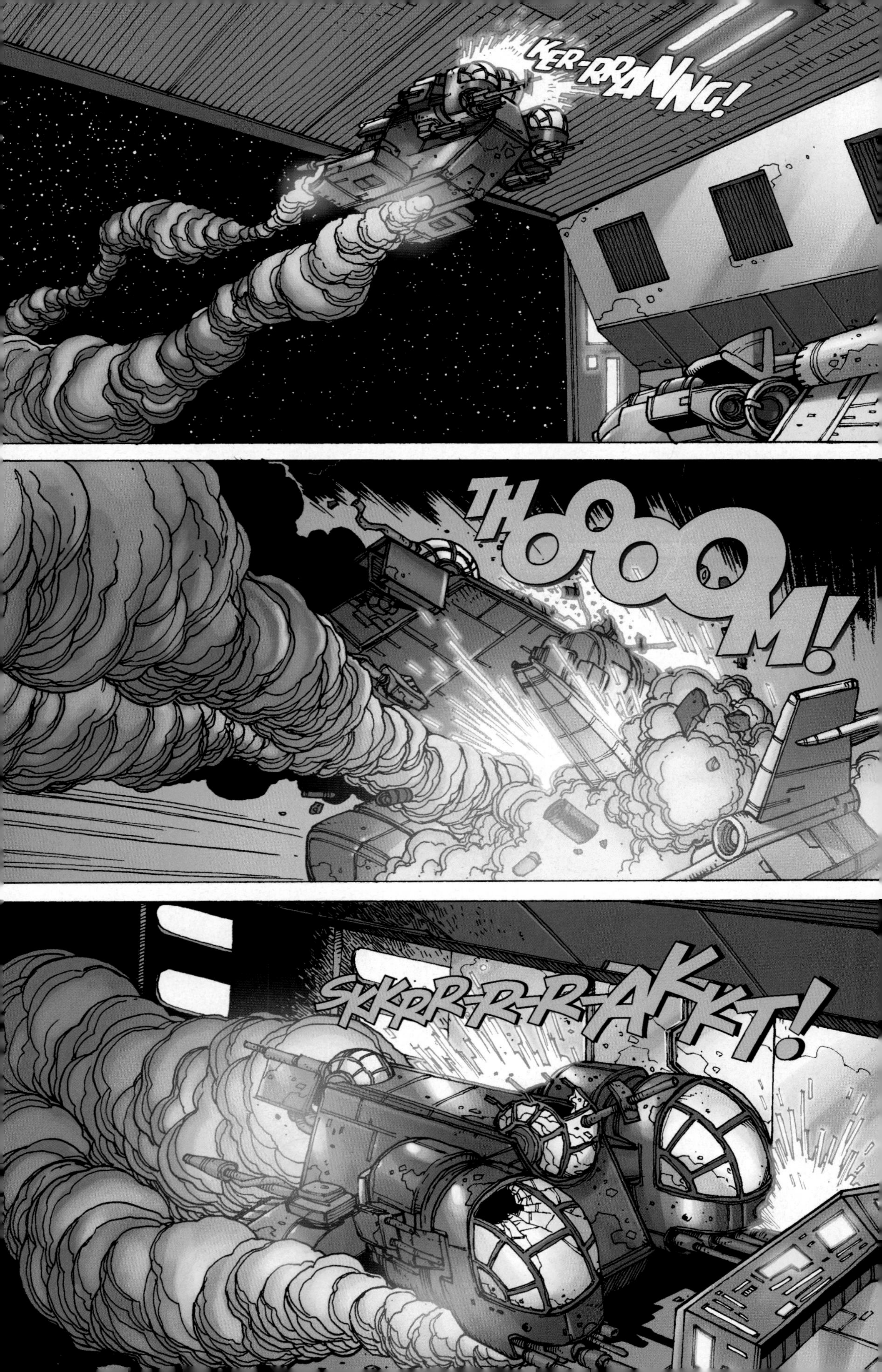

KER-RRANNG!
THOOOM!
SKRRR-R-R-AKKT!

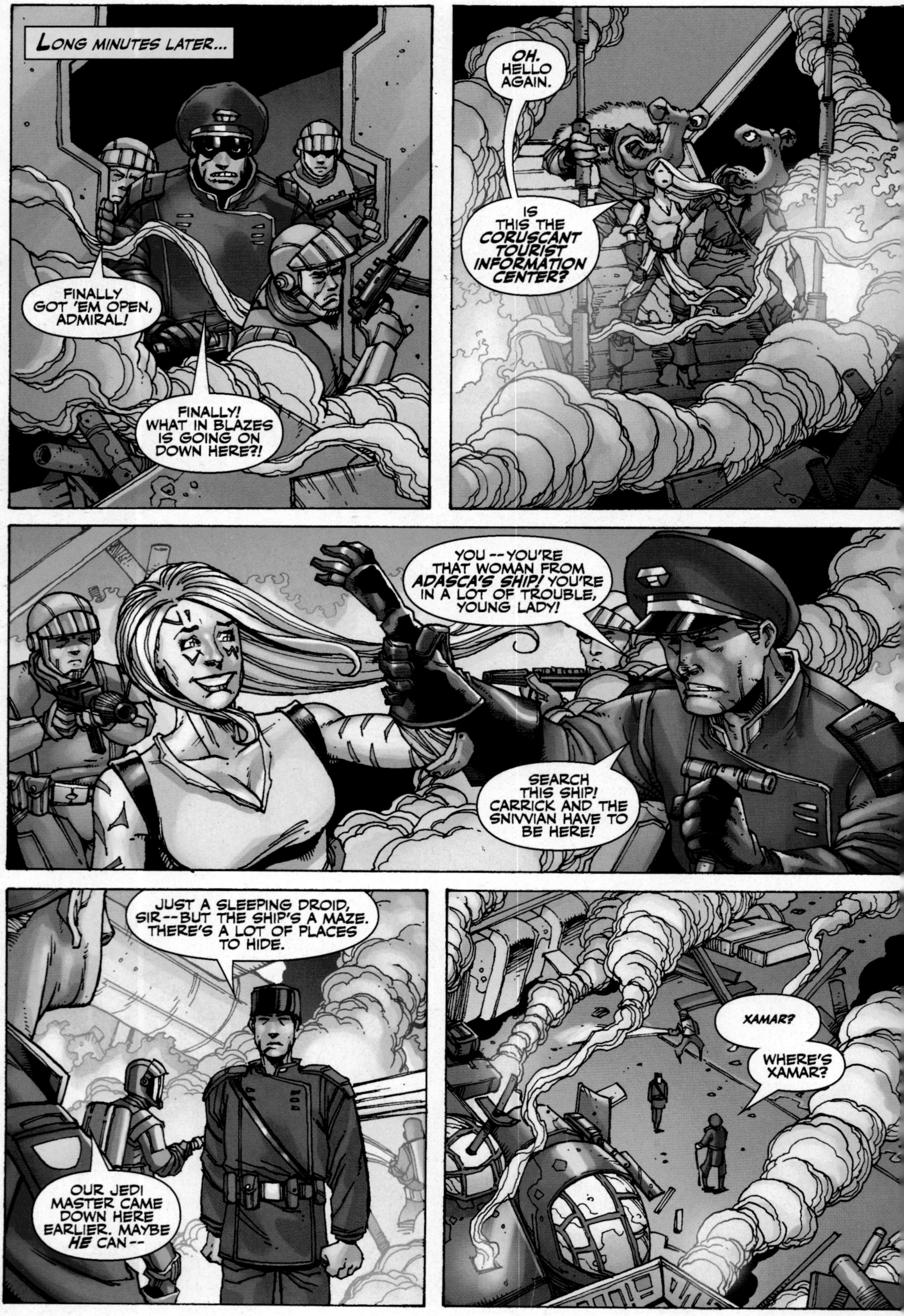
LONG MINUTES LATER...
FINALLY GOT 'EM OPEN, ADMIRAL!
FINALLY! WHAT IN BLAZES IS GOING ON DOWN HERE?!
OH. HELLO AGAIN.
IS THIS THE CORUSCANT TOURIST INFORMATION CENTER?
YOU--YOU'RE THAT WOMAN FROM ADASCA'S SHIP! YOU'RE IN A LOT OF TROUBLE, YOUNG LADY!
SEARCH THIS SHIP! CARRICK AND THE SNIVVIAN HAVE TO BE HERE!
JUST A SLEEPING DROID, SIR--BUT THE SHIP'S A MAZE. THERE'S A LOT OF PLACES TO HIDE.
OUR JEDI MASTER CAME DOWN HERE EARLIER. MAYBE HE CAN--
XAMAR?
WHERE'S XAMAR?

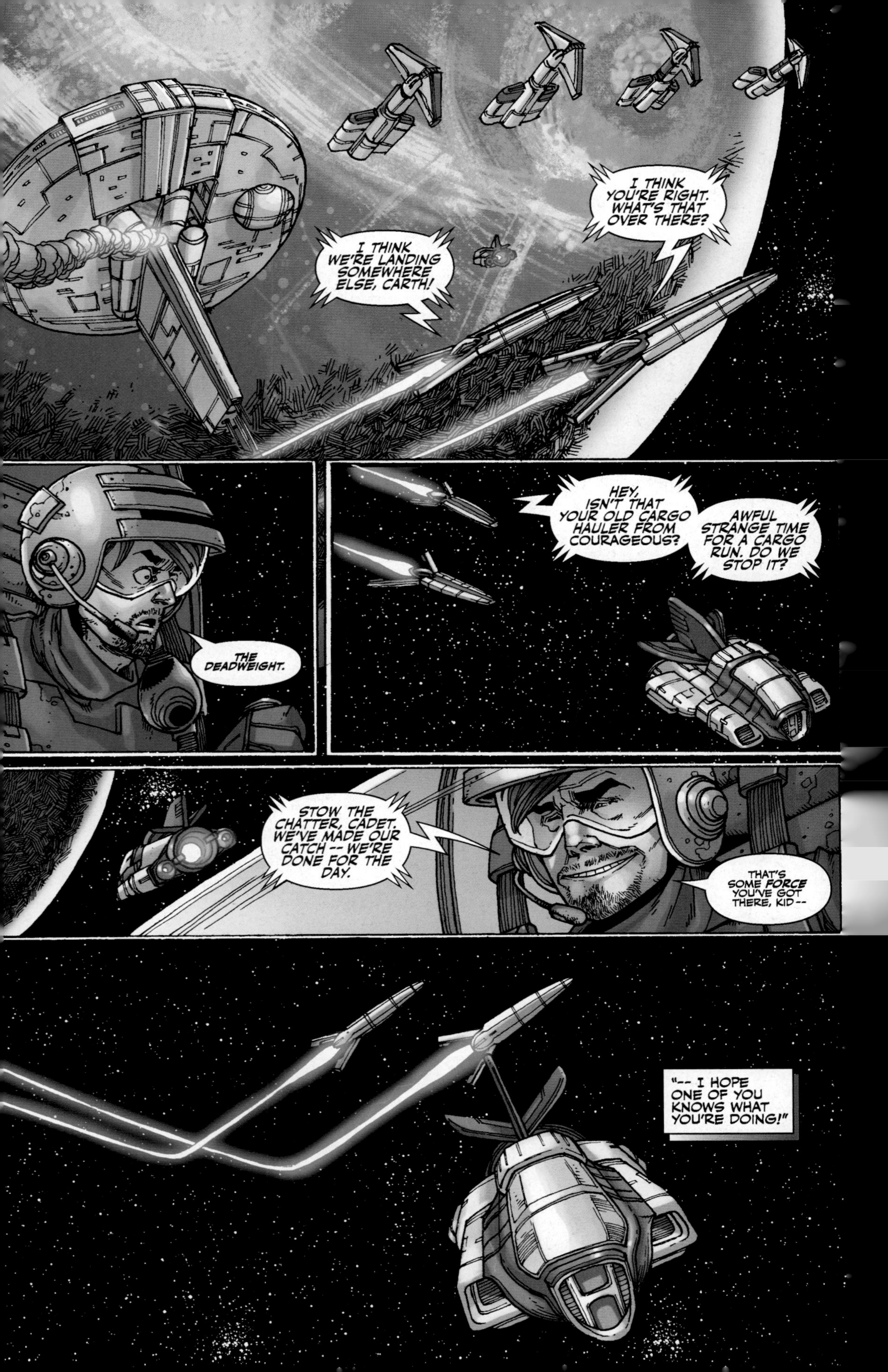
I THINK WE'RE LANDING SOMEWHERE ELSE, CARTH!
I THINK YOU'RE RIGHT. WHAT'S THAT OVER THERE?
THE DEADWEIGHT.
HEY, ISN'T THAT YOUR OLD CARGO HAULER FROM COURAGEOUS?
AWFUL STRANGE TIME FOR A CARGO RUN. DO WE STOP IT?
STOW THE CHATTER, CADET. WE'VE MADE OUR CATCH -- WE'RE DONE FOR THE DAY.
THAT'S SOME FORCE YOU'VE GOT THERE, KID --
"-- I HOPE ONE OF YOU KNOWS WHAT YOU'RE DOING!"

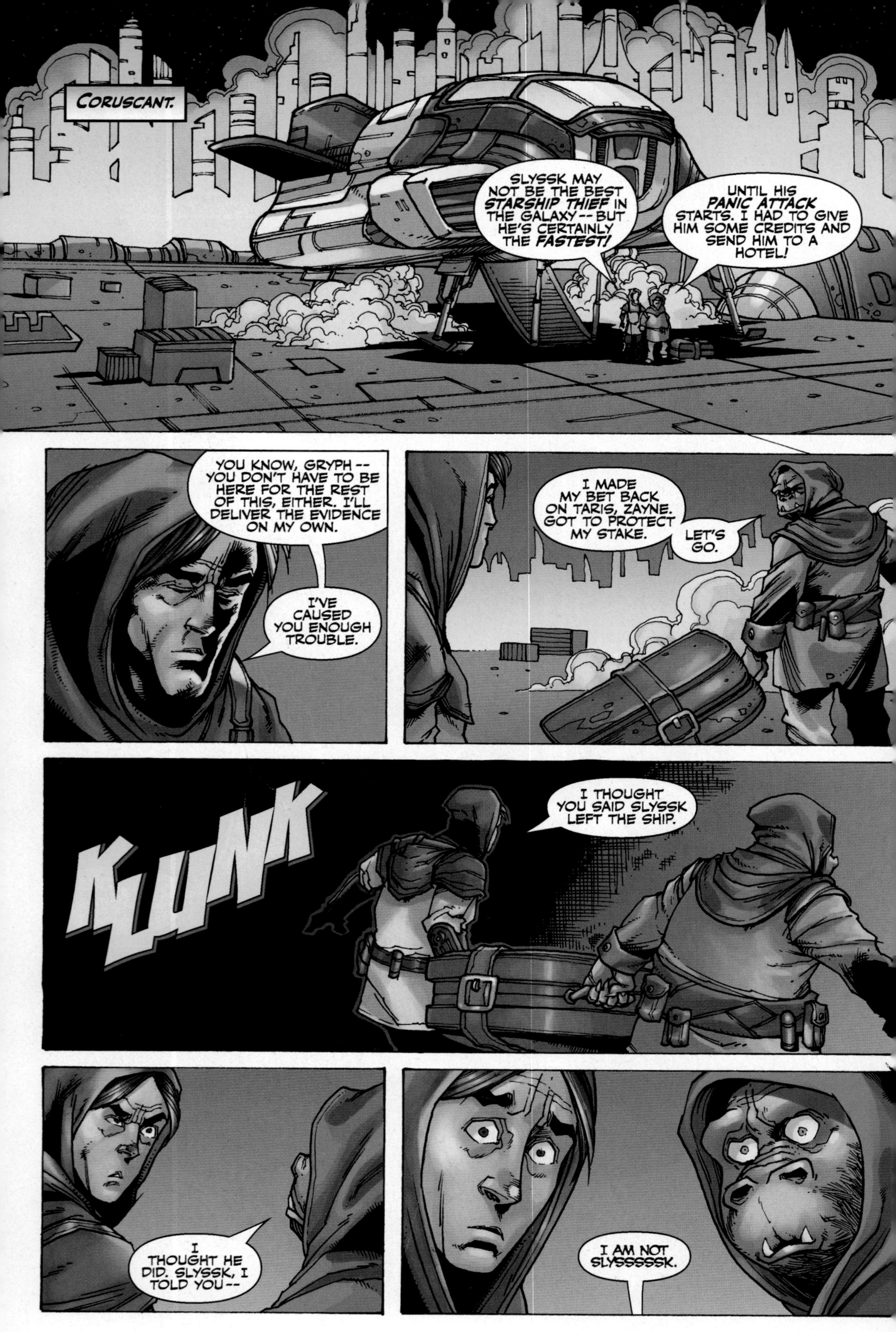
CORUSCANT.
SLYSSK MAY NOT BE THE BEST STARSHIP THIEF IN THE GALAXY -- BUT HE'S CERTAINLY THE FASTEST!
UNTIL HIS PANIC ATTACK STARTS. I HAD TO GIVE HIM SOME CREDITS AND SEND HIM TO A HOTEL!
YOU KNOW, GRYPH -- YOU DON'T HAVE TO BE HERE FOR THE REST OF THIS, EITHER. I'LL DELIVER THE EVIDENCE ON MY OWN.
I'VE CAUSED YOU ENOUGH TROUBLE.
I MADE MY BET BACK ON TARIS, ZAYNE. GOT TO PROTECT MY STAKE.
LET'S GO.
KLUNK
I THOUGHT YOU SAID SLYSSK LEFT THE SHIP.
I THOUGHT HE DID. SLYSSK, I TOLD YOU --
I AM NOT SLYSSSSSK.

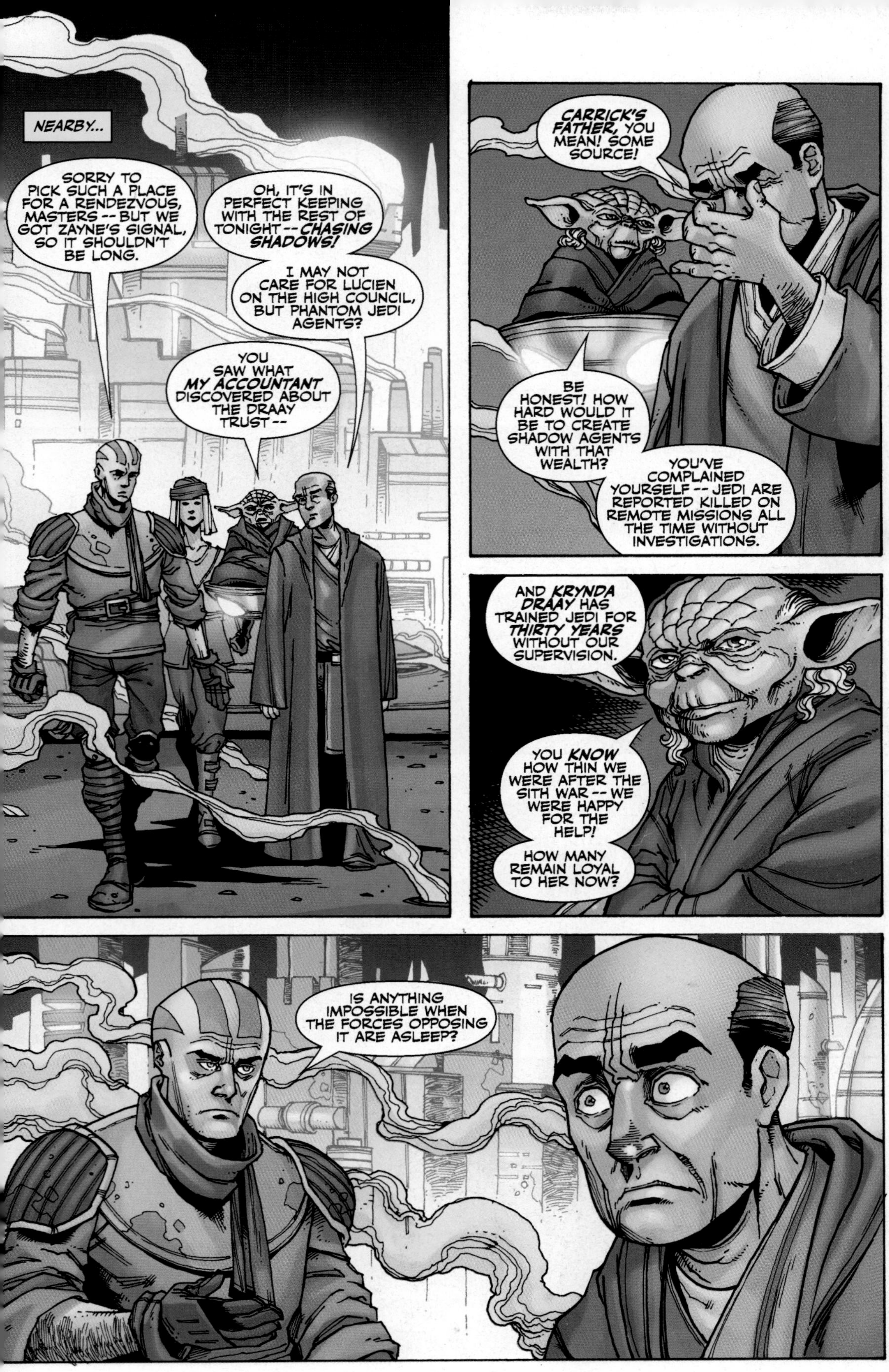

NEARBY...
SORRY TO PICK SUCH A PLACE FOR A RENDEZVOUS, MASTERS -- BUT WE GOT ZAYNE'S SIGNAL, SO IT SHOULDN'T BE LONG.
OH, IT'S IN PERFECT KEEPING WITH THE REST OF TONIGHT -- CHASING SHADOWS!
I MAY NOT CARE FOR LUCIEN ON THE HIGH COUNCIL, BUT PHANTOM JEDI AGENTS?
YOU SAW WHAT MY ACCOUNTANT DISCOVERED ABOUT THE DRAAY TRUST --
CARRICK'S FATHER, YOU MEAN! SOME SOURCE!
BE HONEST! HOW HARD WOULD IT BE TO CREATE SHADOW AGENTS WITH THAT WEALTH?
YOU'VE COMPLAINED YOURSELF -- JEDI ARE REPORTED KILLED ON REMOTE MISSIONS ALL THE TIME WITHOUT INVESTIGATIONS.
AND KRYNDA DRAAY HAS TRAINED JEDI FOR THIRTY YEARS WITHOUT OUR SUPERVISION.
YOU KNOW HOW THIN WE WERE AFTER THE SITH WAR -- WE WERE HAPPY FOR THE HELP!
HOW MANY REMAIN LOYAL TO HER NOW?
IS ANYTHING IMPOSSIBLE WHEN THE FORCES OPPOSING IT ARE ASLEEP?

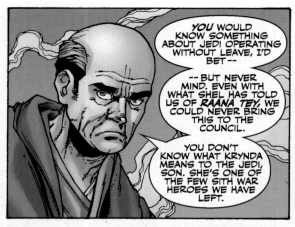

YOU WOULD KNOW SOMETHING ABOUT JEDI OPERATING WITHOUT LEAVE, I'D BET--

--BUT NEVER MIND. EVEN WITH WHAT SHEL HAS TOLD US OF *RAANA TEY*, WE COULD NEVER BRING THIS TO THE COUNCIL.

YOU DON'T KNOW WHAT KRYNDA MEANS TO THE JEDI, SON. SHE'S ONE OF THE FEW SITH WAR HEROES WE HAVE LEFT.

YOU ACCUSE HER, YOU WON'T ROCK THE ORDER. YOU'LL TEAR IT APART!

AND KARATH HAS TOLD EVERYONE ZAYNE'S A MANDIE SPY. THE BOY COULD BRING BACK A *CARTLOAD OF REAL SITH ARTIFACTS*--

--AND THE DRAAYS COULD SAY THE MANDALORIANS SUPPLIED THEM! NO, NO, IT'S NOT ENOUGH!

WHAT-- WHAT WILL IT TAKE?

ONE OF THEIR NUMBER MUST TURN, SHEL. SOMEONE WHO'S SEEN EVERYTHING FROM THE BEGINNING.

SOMEONE MUST RAISE HIS VOICE.

SSSOMEONE MIGHT.

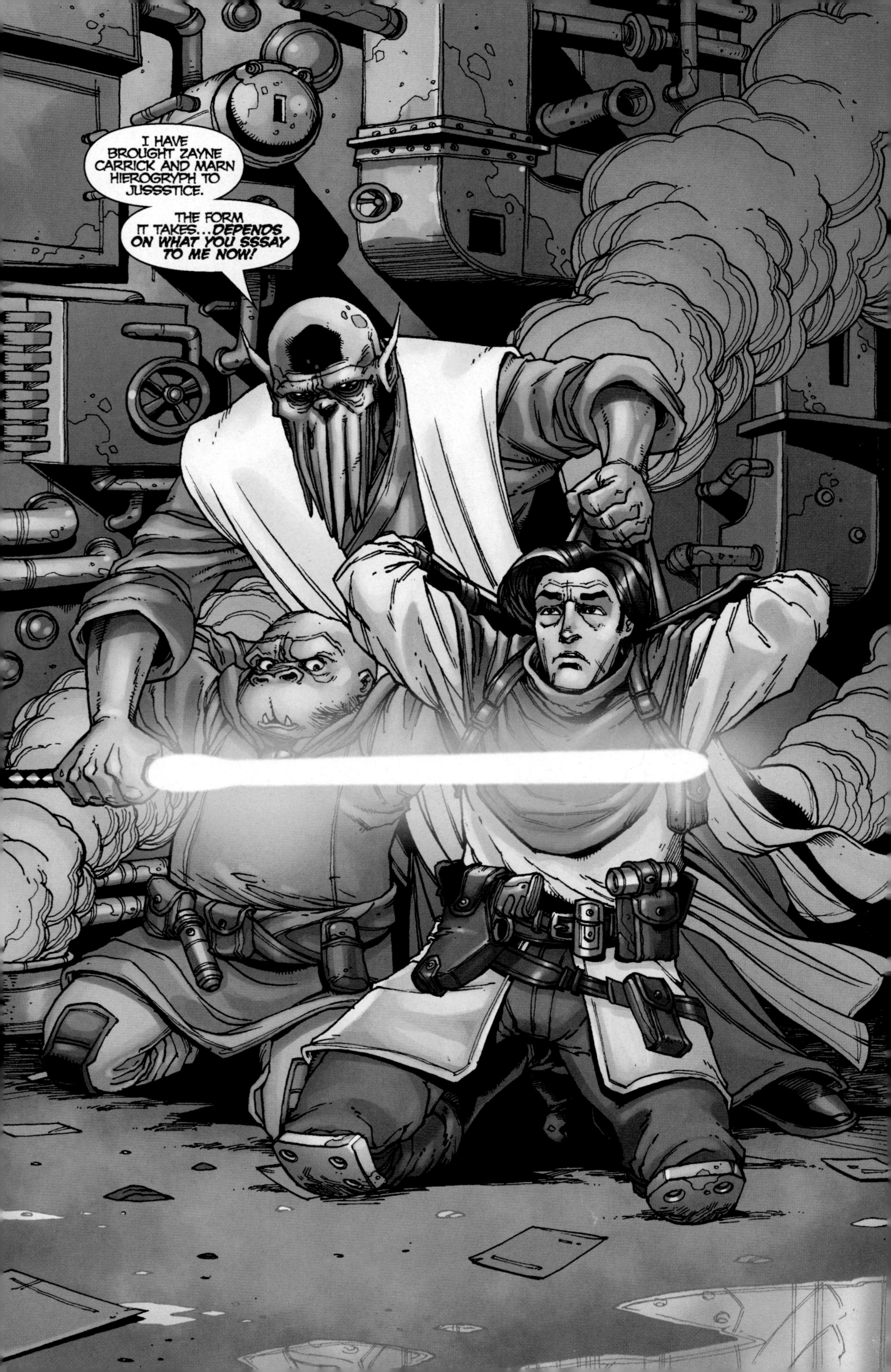
I HAVE BROUGHT ZAYNE CARRICK AND MARN HIEROGRYPH TO JUSSSTICE.
THE FORM IT TAKES... *DEPENDS ON WHAT YOU SSSAY TO ME NOW!*

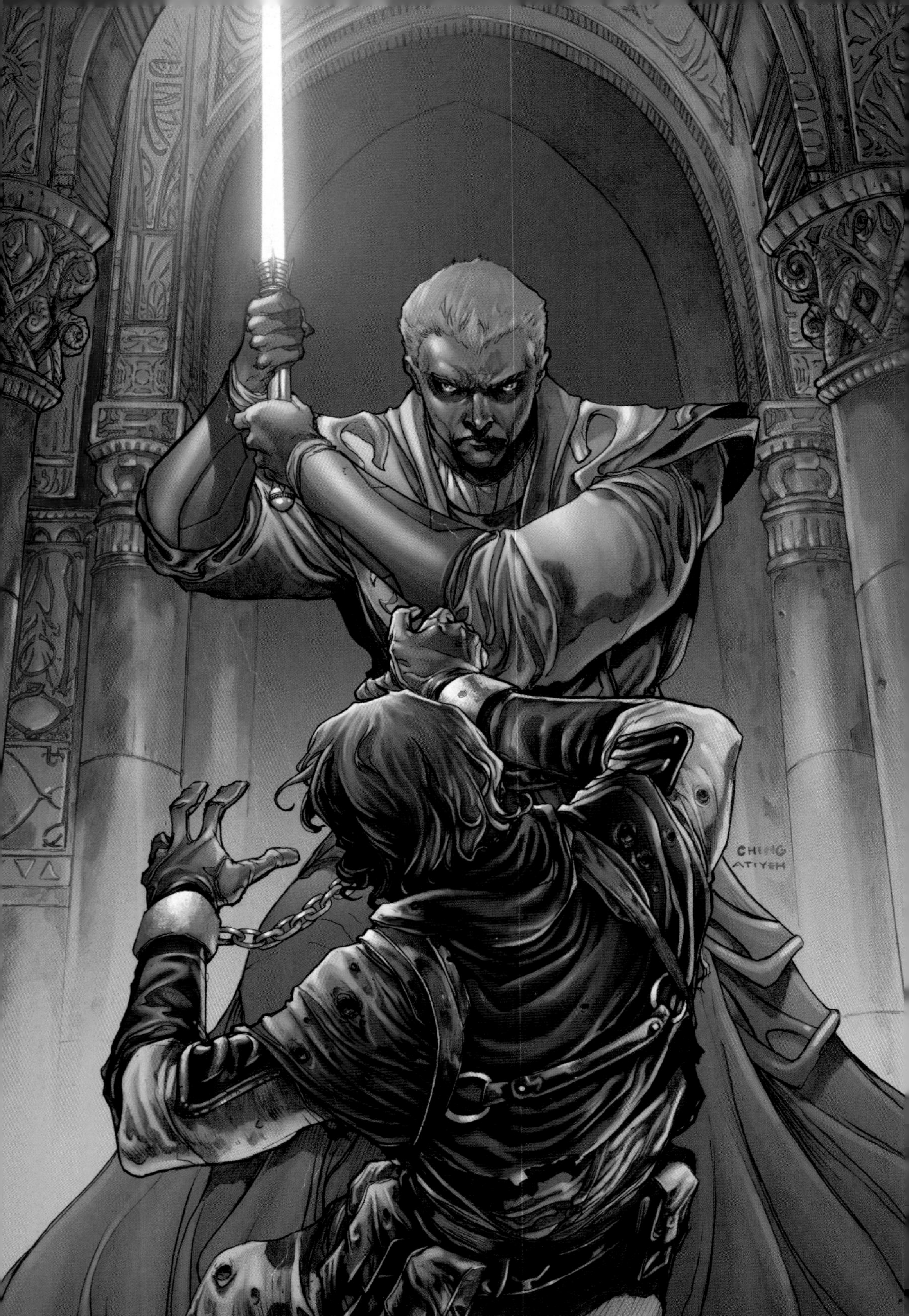
CHING
ATIYEH

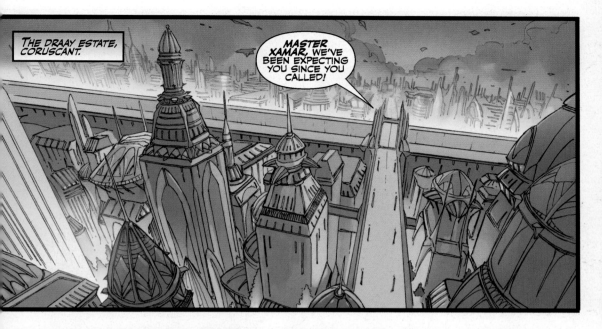

THE DRAAY ESTATE, CORUSCANT.

MASTER XAMAR, WE'VE BEEN EXPECTING YOU SINCE YOU CALLED!

THEN YOU KNOW YOU HAD BESSST OPEN THE GATE.

ABSOLUTELY. BUT YOU DON'T MIND IF WE JUST GET A LOOK AT THE GREAT--

OPEN THE GATE!

-- ZAYNE CARRICK?

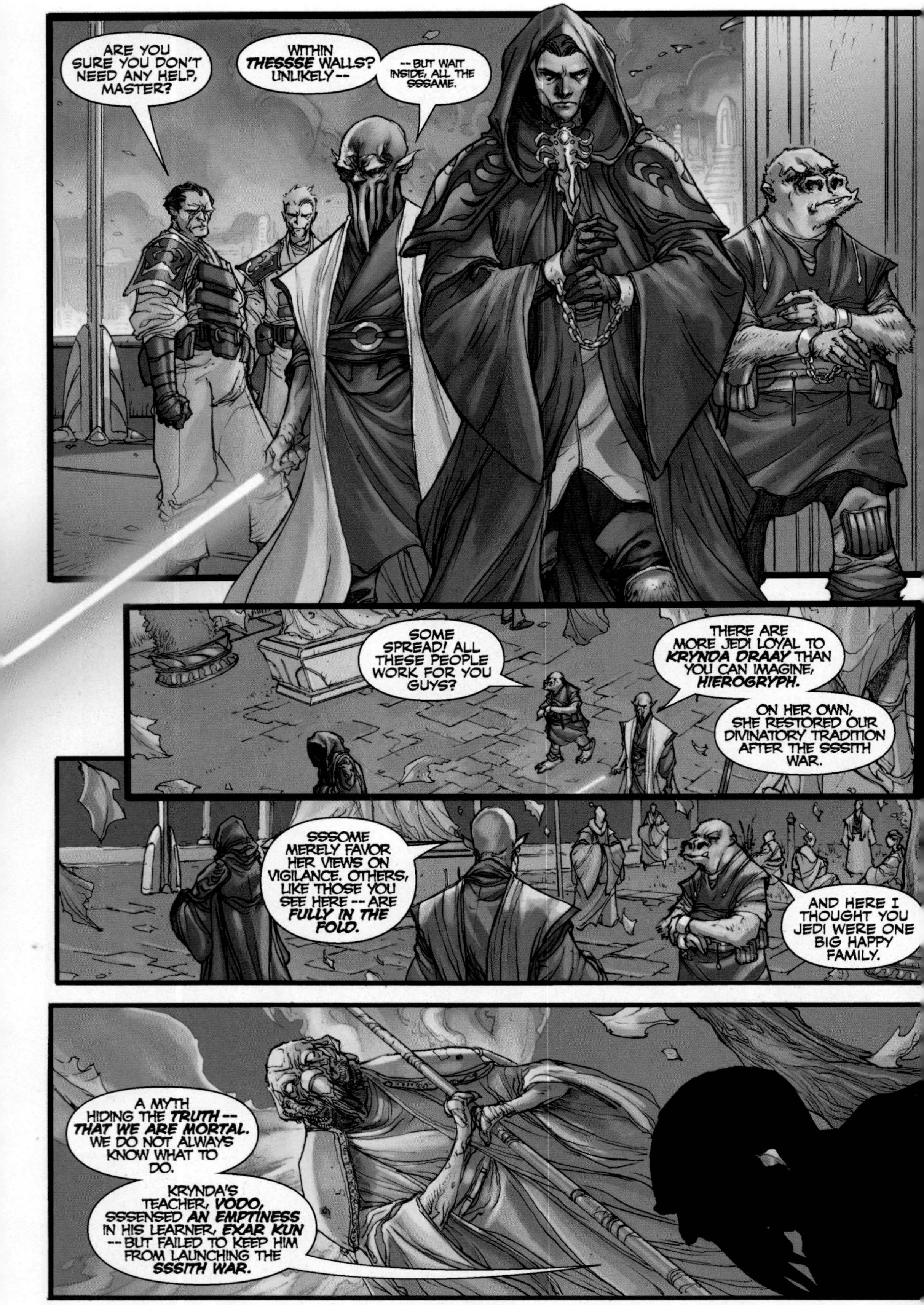
ARE YOU SURE YOU DON'T NEED ANY HELP, MASTER?
WITHIN THESSSE WALLS? UNLIKELY --
-- BUT WAIT INSIDE, ALL THE SSSAME.
SOME SPREAD! ALL THESE PEOPLE WORK FOR YOU GUYS?
THERE ARE MORE JEDI LOYAL TO KRYNDA DRAAY THAN YOU CAN IMAGINE, HIEROGRYPH.
ON HER OWN, SHE RESTORED OUR DIVINATORY TRADITION AFTER THE SSSITH WAR.
SSSOME MERELY FAVOR HER VIEWS ON VIGILANCE. OTHERS, LIKE THOSE YOU SEE HERE -- ARE FULLY IN THE FOLD.
AND HERE I THOUGHT YOU JEDI WERE ONE BIG HAPPY FAMILY.
A MYTH HIDING THE TRUTH -- THAT WE ARE MORTAL. WE DO NOT ALWAYS KNOW WHAT TO DO.
KRYNDA'S TEACHER, VODO, SSSENSED AN EMPTINESS IN HIS LEARNER, EXAR KUN -- BUT FAILED TO KEEP HIM FROM LAUNCHING THE SSSITH WAR.

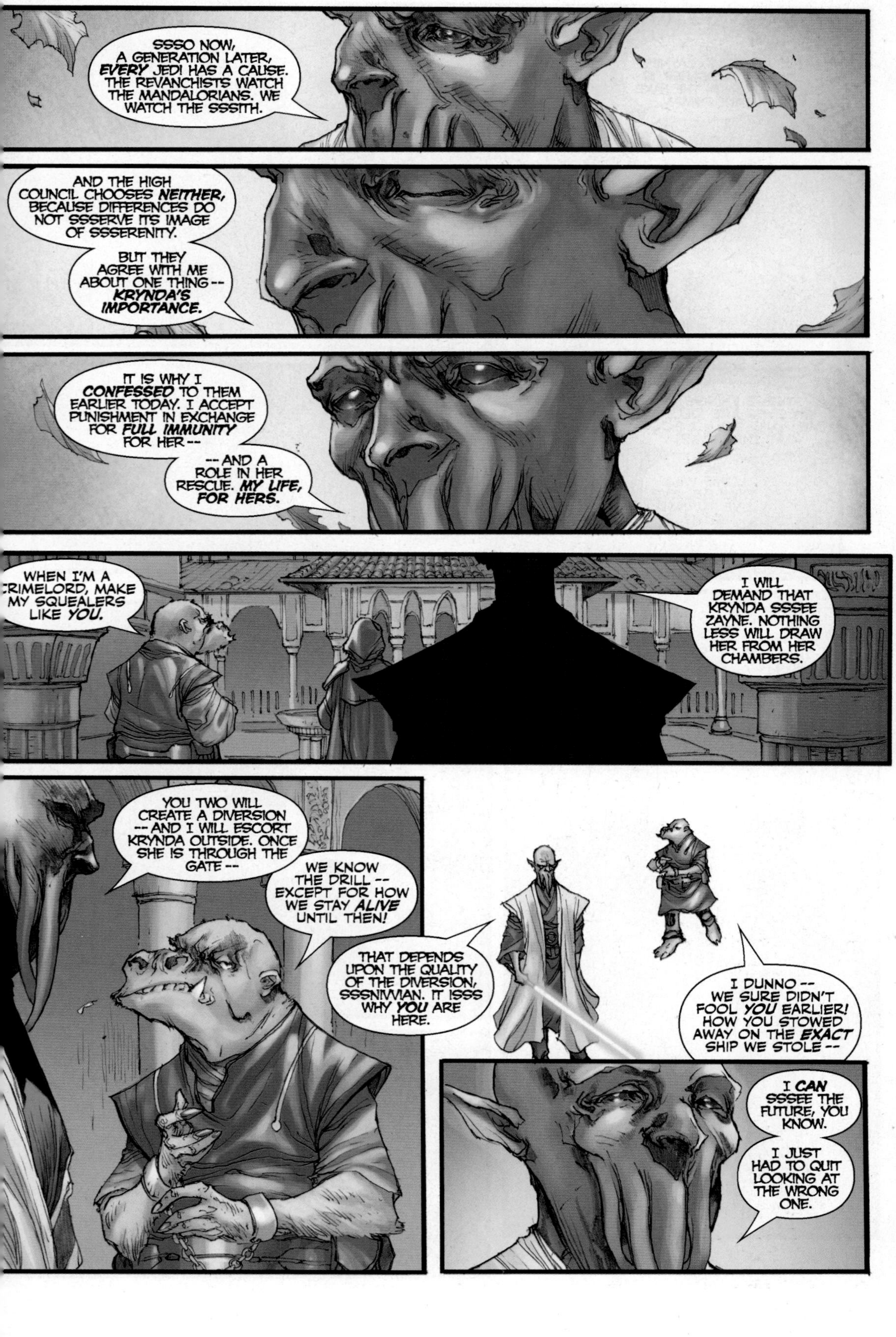
SSSO NOW, A GENERATION LATER, EVERY JEDI HAS A CAUSE. THE REVANCHISTS WATCH THE MANDALORIANS. WE WATCH THE SSSITH.
AND THE HIGH COUNCIL CHOOSES NEITHER, BECAUSE DIFFERENCES DO NOT SSSERVE ITS IMAGE OF SSSERENITY.
BUT THEY AGREE WITH ME ABOUT ONE THING -- KRYNDA'S IMPORTANCE.
IT IS WHY I CONFESSED TO THEM EARLIER TODAY. I ACCEPT PUNISHMENT IN EXCHANGE FOR FULL IMMUNITY FOR HER --
-- AND A ROLE IN HER RESCUE. MY LIFE, FOR HERS.
WHEN I'M A CRIMELORD, MAKE MY SQUEALERS LIKE YOU.
I WILL DEMAND THAT KRYNDA SSSEE ZAYNE. NOTHING LESS WILL DRAW HER FROM HER CHAMBERS.
YOU TWO WILL CREATE A DIVERSION -- AND I WILL ESCORT KRYNDA OUTSIDE. ONCE SHE IS THROUGH THE GATE --
WE KNOW THE DRILL -- EXCEPT FOR HOW WE STAY ALIVE UNTIL THEN!
THAT DEPENDS UPON THE QUALITY OF THE DIVERSION, SSSNIVVIAN. IT ISSS WHY YOU ARE HERE.
I DUNNO -- WE SURE DIDN'T FOOL YOU EARLIER! HOW YOU STOWED AWAY ON THE EXACT SHIP WE STOLE --
I CAN SSSEE THE FUTURE, YOU KNOW.
I JUST HAD TO QUIT LOOKING AT THE WRONG ONE.

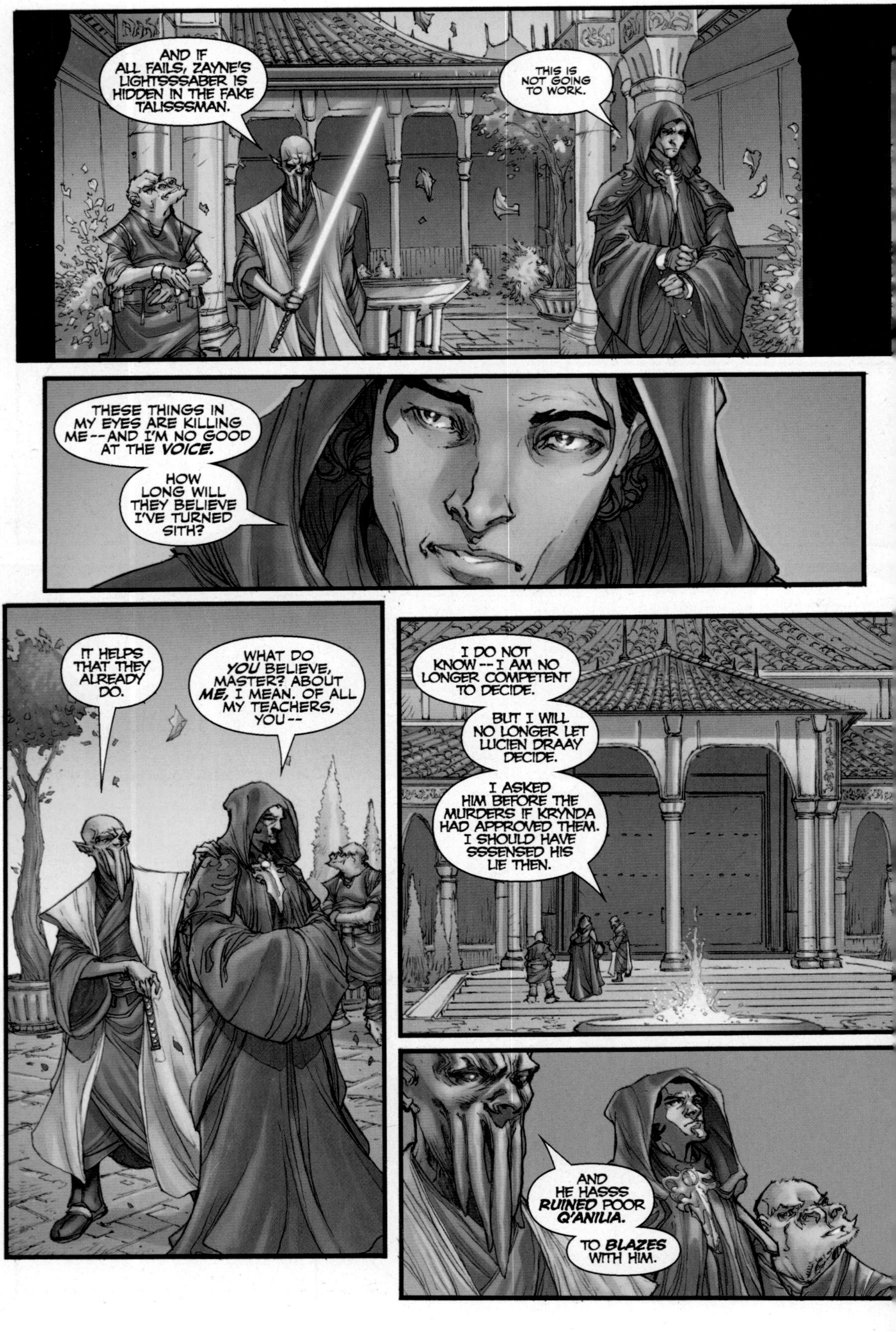
AND IF ALL FAILS, ZAYNE'S LIGHTSSSABER IS HIDDEN IN THE FAKE TALISSSMAN.
THIS IS NOT GOING TO WORK.
THESE THINGS IN MY EYES ARE KILLING ME--AND I'M NO GOOD AT THE *VOICE.*
HOW LONG WILL THEY BELIEVE I'VE TURNED SITH?
IT HELPS THAT THEY ALREADY DO.
WHAT DO *YOU* BELIEVE, MASTER? ABOUT *ME,* I MEAN. OF ALL MY TEACHERS, YOU--
I DO NOT KNOW--I AM NO LONGER COMPETENT TO DECIDE.
BUT I WILL NO LONGER LET LUCIEN DRAAY DECIDE.
I ASKED HIM BEFORE THE MURDERS IF KRYNDA HAD APPROVED THEM. I SHOULD HAVE SSSENSED HIS LIE THEN.
AND HE HASSS *RUINED* POOR *Q'ANILIA.*
TO *BLAZES* WITH HIM.

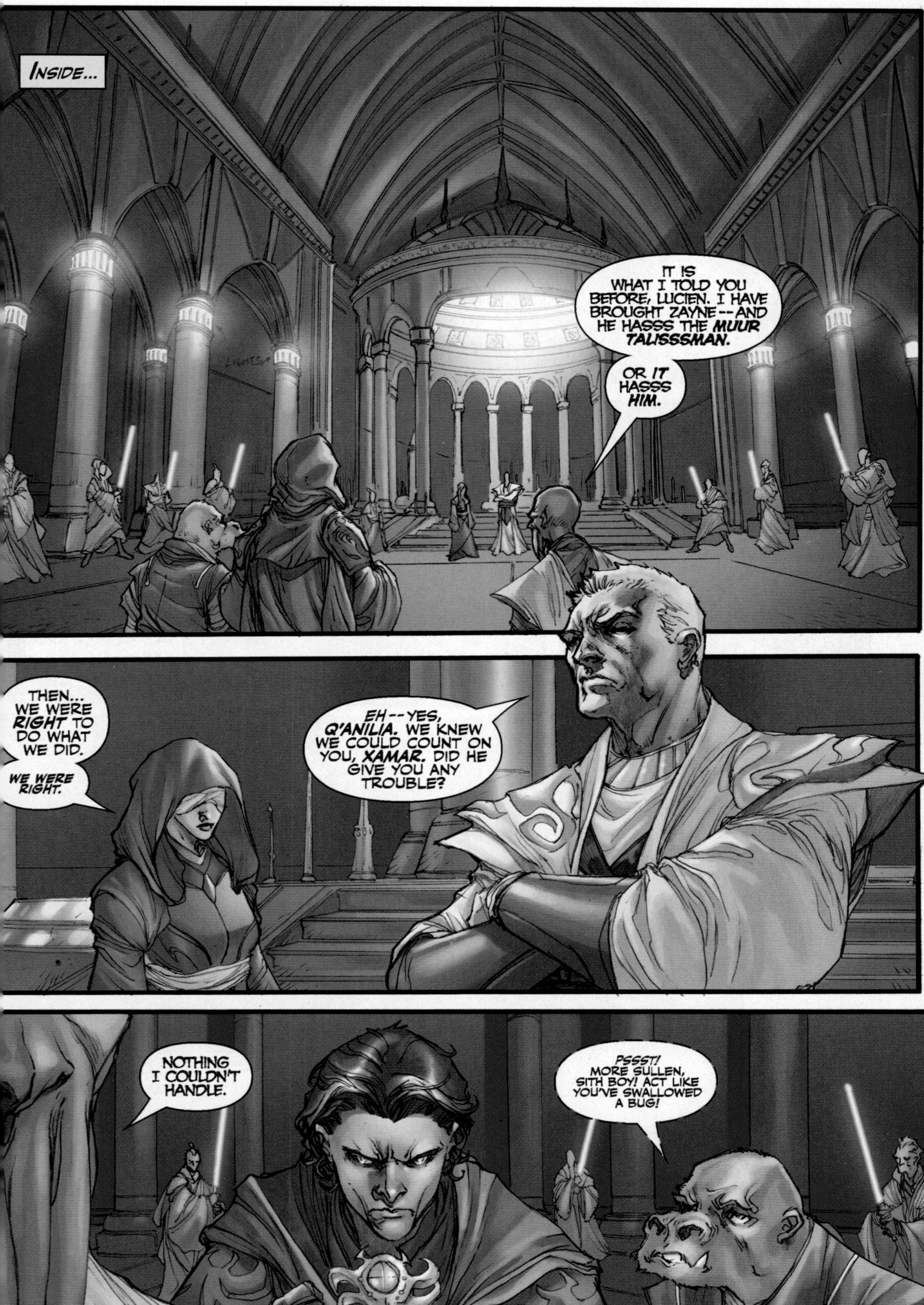
INSIDE...
IT IS WHAT I TOLD YOU BEFORE, LUCIEN. I HAVE BROUGHT ZAYNE--AND HE HASSS THE MUUR TALISSSMAN.
OR IT HASSS HIM.
THEN... WE WERE RIGHT TO DO WHAT WE DID.
WE WERE RIGHT.
EH--YES, Q'ANILIA. WE KNEW WE COULD COUNT ON YOU, XAMAR. DID HE GIVE YOU ANY TROUBLE?
NOTHING I COULDN'T HANDLE.
PSSST! MORE SULLEN, SITH BOY! ACT LIKE YOU'VE SWALLOWED A BUG!

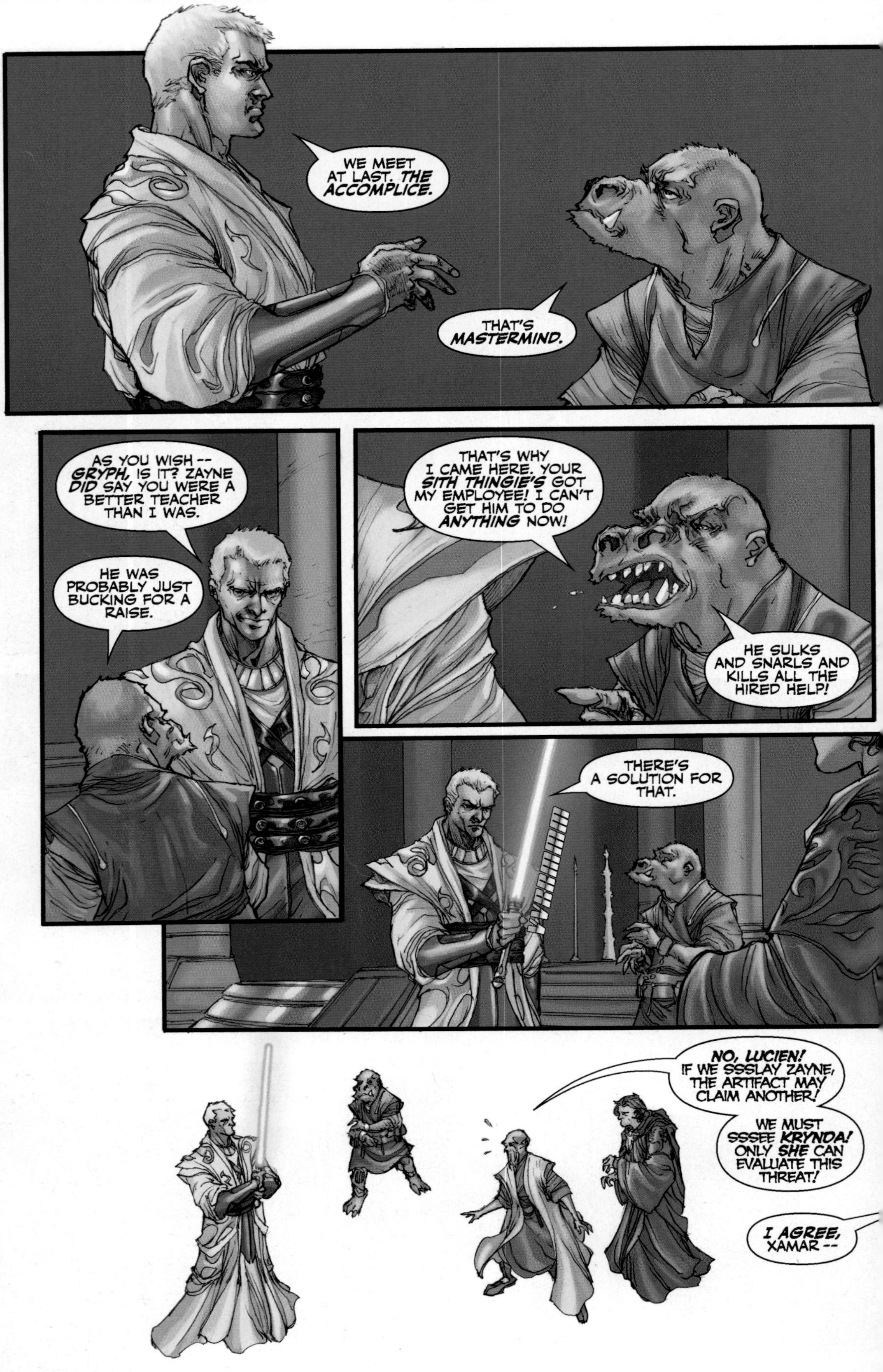

WE MEET AT LAST. *THE ACCOMPLICE.*
THAT'S *MASTERMIND.*
AS YOU WISH -- *GRYPH,* IS IT? ZAYNE *DID* SAY YOU WERE A BETTER TEACHER THAN I WAS.
HE WAS PROBABLY JUST BUCKING FOR A RAISE.
THAT'S WHY I CAME HERE. YOUR *SITH THINGIE'S* GOT MY EMPLOYEE! I CAN'T GET HIM TO DO *ANYTHING* NOW!
HE SULKS AND SNARLS AND KILLS ALL THE HIRED HELP!
THERE'S A SOLUTION FOR THAT.
NO, LUCIEN! IF WE SSSLAY ZAYNE, THE ARTIFACT MAY CLAIM ANOTHER!
WE MUST SSSEE *KRYNDA!* ONLY *SHE* CAN EVALUATE THIS THREAT!
I AGREE, XAMAR --

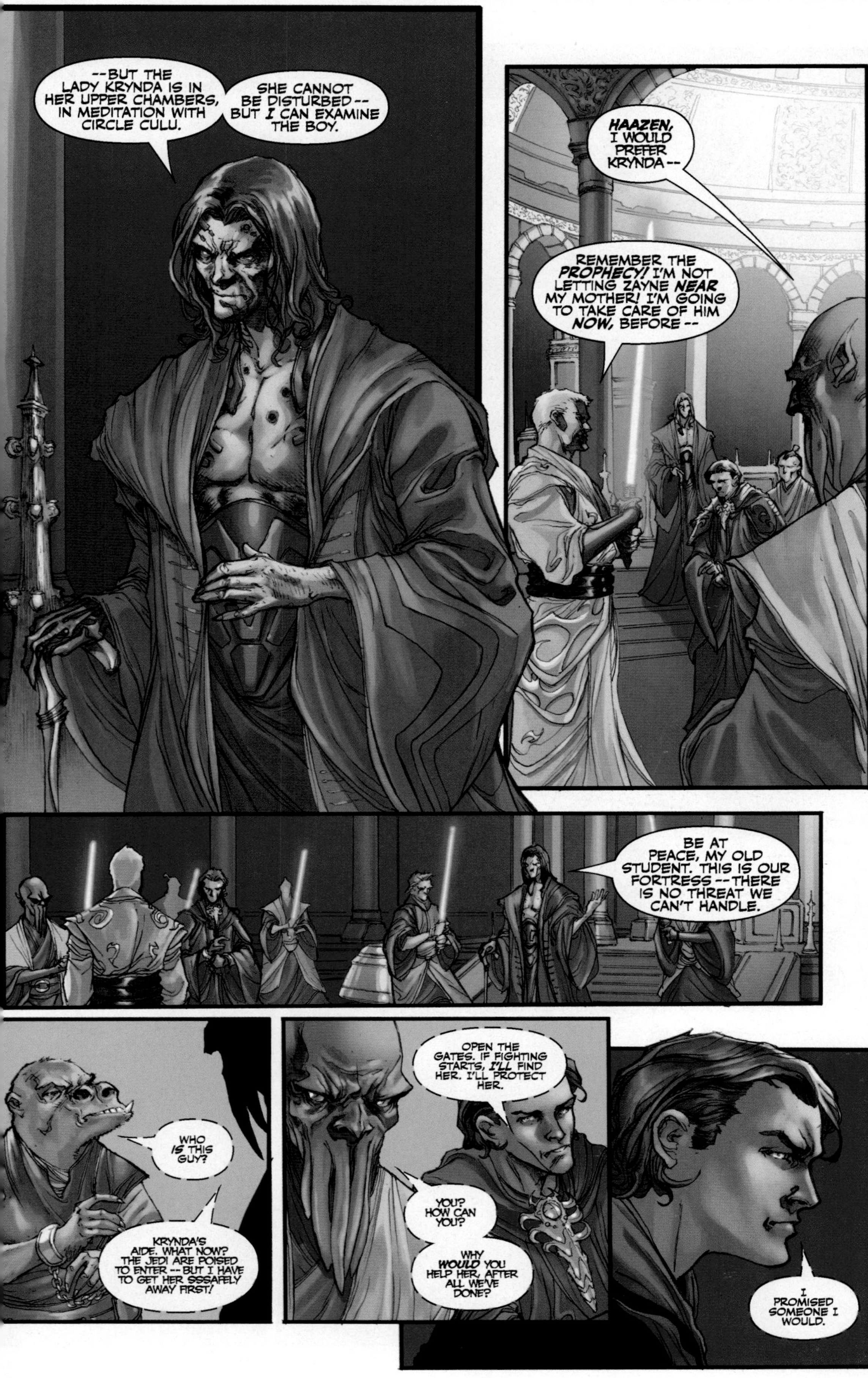
--BUT THE LADY KRYNDA IS IN HER UPPER CHAMBERS, IN MEDITATION WITH CIRCLE CULU.
SHE CANNOT BE DISTURBED-- BUT I CAN EXAMINE THE BOY.
HAAZEN, I WOULD PREFER KRYNDA--
REMEMBER THE PROPHECY! I'M NOT LETTING ZAYNE NEAR MY MOTHER! I'M GOING TO TAKE CARE OF HIM NOW, BEFORE--
BE AT PEACE, MY OLD STUDENT. THIS IS OUR FORTRESS--THERE IS NO THREAT WE CAN'T HANDLE.
WHO IS THIS GUY?
KRYNDA'S AIDE. WHAT NOW? THE JEDI ARE POISED TO ENTER--BUT I HAVE TO GET HER SSSAFELY AWAY FIRST!
OPEN THE GATES. IF FIGHTING STARTS, I'LL FIND HER. I'LL PROTECT HER.
YOU? HOW CAN YOU?
WHY WOULD YOU HELP HER, AFTER ALL WE'VE DONE?
I PROMISED SOMEONE I WOULD.

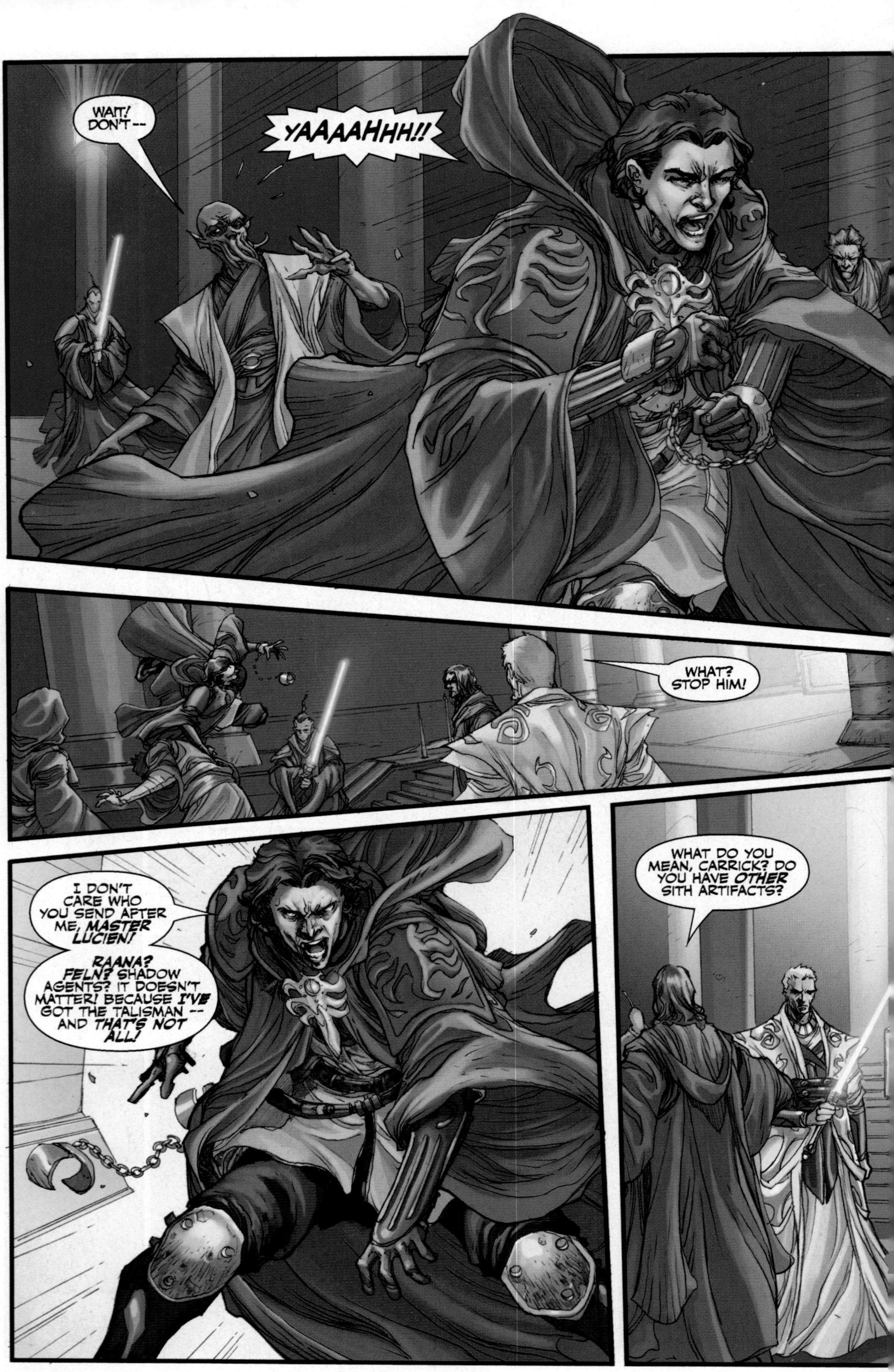
WAIT! DON'T --
YAAAAHHH!!
WHAT? STOP HIM!
I DON'T CARE WHO YOU SEND AFTER ME, MASTER LUCIEN!
RAANA? FELN? SHADOW AGENTS? IT DOESN'T MATTER! BECAUSE I'VE GOT THE TALISMAN -- AND THAT'S NOT ALL!
WHAT DO YOU MEAN, CARRICK? DO YOU HAVE OTHER SITH ARTIFACTS?

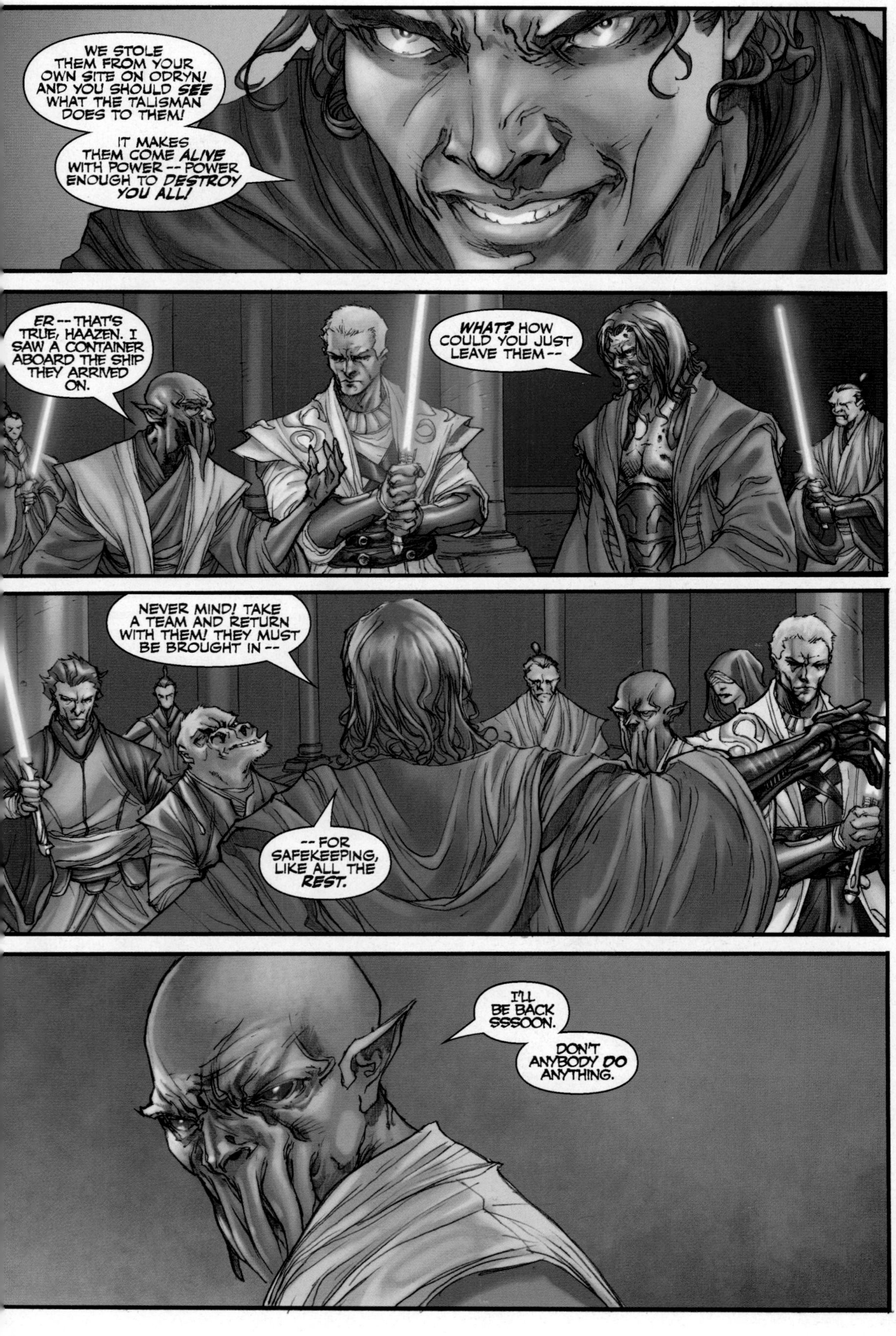

WE STOLE THEM FROM YOUR OWN SITE ON ODRYN! AND YOU SHOULD *SEE* WHAT THE TALISMAN DOES TO THEM!
IT MAKES THEM COME *ALIVE* WITH POWER -- POWER ENOUGH TO *DESTROY YOU ALL!*
ER -- THAT'S TRUE, HAAZEN. I SAW A CONTAINER ABOARD THE SHIP THEY ARRIVED ON.
WHAT? HOW COULD YOU JUST LEAVE THEM --
NEVER MIND! TAKE A TEAM AND RETURN WITH THEM! THEY MUST BE BROUGHT IN --
-- FOR SAFEKEEPING, LIKE ALL THE *REST.*
I'LL BE BACK SSSOON.
DON'T ANYBODY *DO* ANYTHING.

GARRAGOR, KLYDEKER -- FETCH THE DIAGNOSTIC EQUIPMENT FROM MY STUDY. THE *BIG* CASE.

DON'T WORRY -- WE'LL ALL BE RIGHT HERE.

YOU CAN COME DOWN, YOUNG MAN. NO ONE WILL HARM YOU.

BE CAREFUL. I AM HAVING TROUBLE SENSING HIS INTENTIONS.

NONSENSE. WE ONLY WANT TO UNDERSTAND -- AND HELP. OUR COVENANT'S MISSION REQUIRES IT.

THERE ARE MORE OF US THAN YOU CAN IMAGINE, ZAYNE. KEEPING WATCH. STUDYING THE FUTURE --

-- INSURING NO INNOCENT JEDI IS TEMPTED BY THE DETRITUS LEFT OVER FROM PAST STRUGGLES WITH THE SITH.

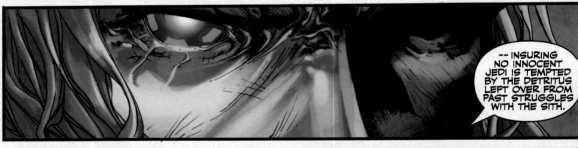

STRUGGLES THAT DAMAGED US *ALL* --

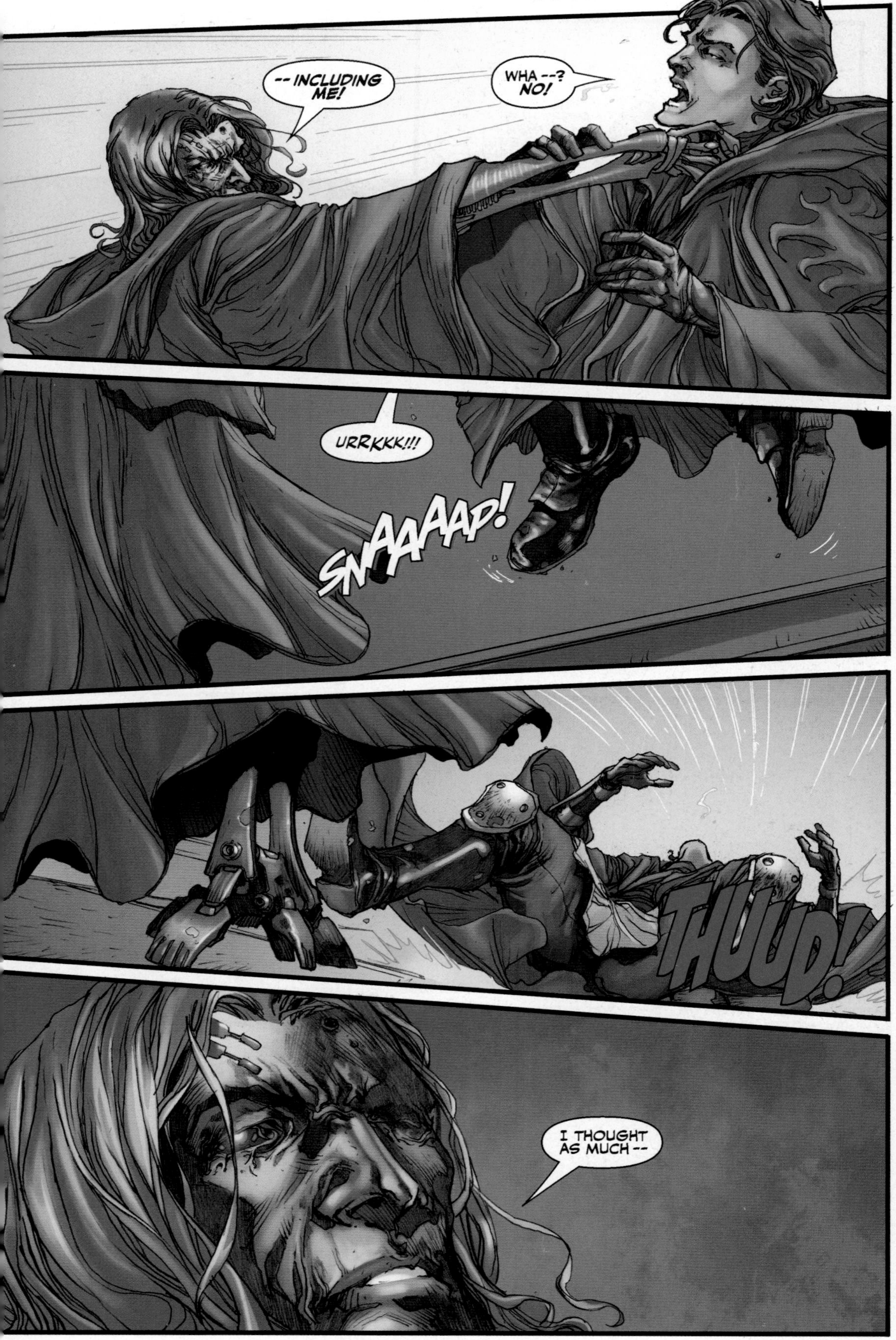
-- INCLUDING ME!
WHA --? NO!
URRKKK!!!
SNAAAAP!
THUUD!
I THOUGHT AS MUCH --

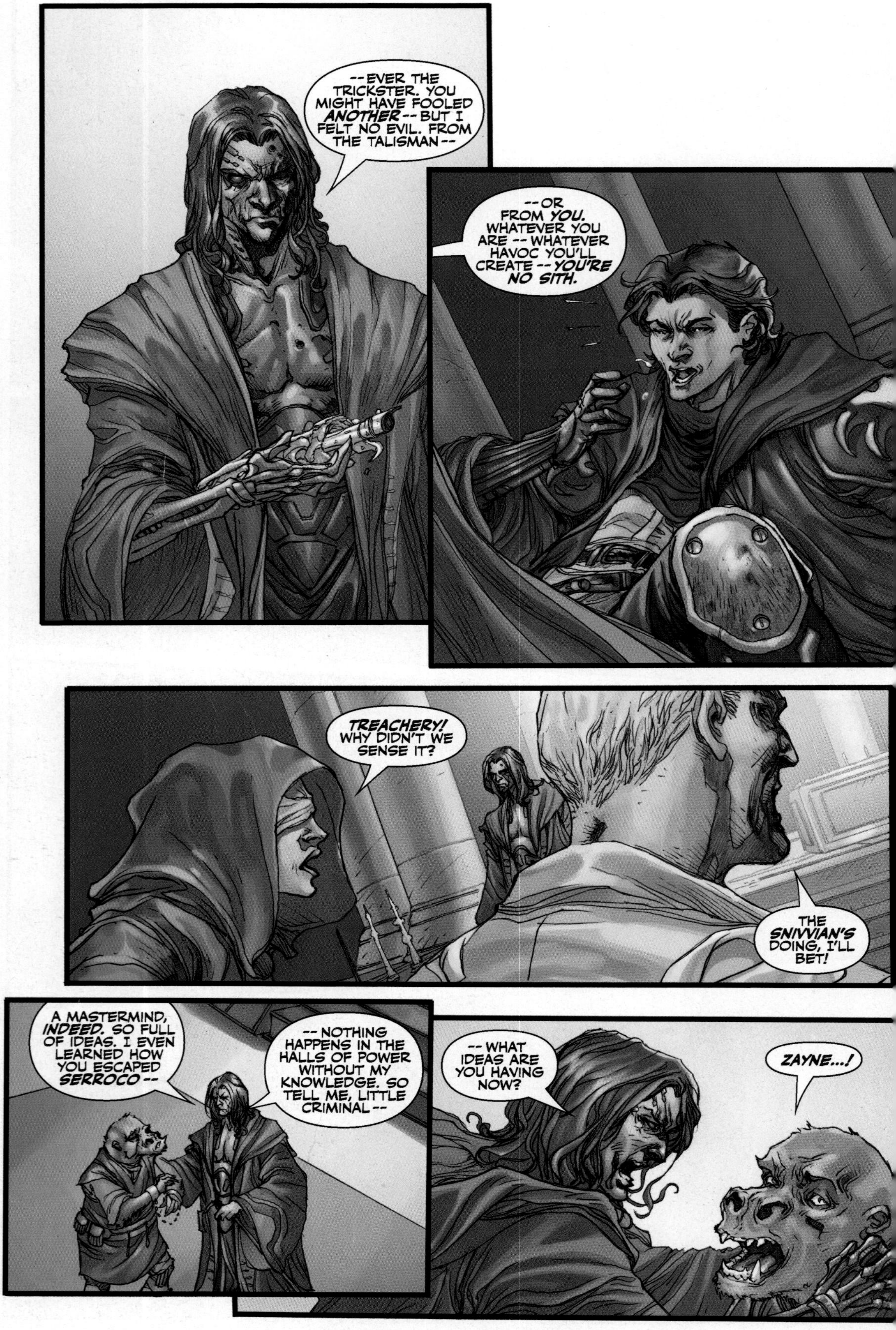
--EVER THE TRICKSTER. YOU MIGHT HAVE FOOLED ANOTHER--BUT I FELT NO EVIL. FROM THE TALISMAN--
--OR FROM YOU. WHATEVER YOU ARE--WHATEVER HAVOC YOU'LL CREATE--YOU'RE NO SITH.
TREACHERY! WHY DIDN'T WE SENSE IT?
THE SNIVVIAN'S DOING, I'LL BET!
A MASTERMIND, INDEED. SO FULL OF IDEAS. I EVEN LEARNED HOW YOU ESCAPED SERROCO--
--NOTHING HAPPENS IN THE HALLS OF POWER WITHOUT MY KNOWLEDGE. SO TELL ME, LITTLE CRIMINAL--
--WHAT IDEAS ARE YOU HAVING NOW?
ZAYNE...!

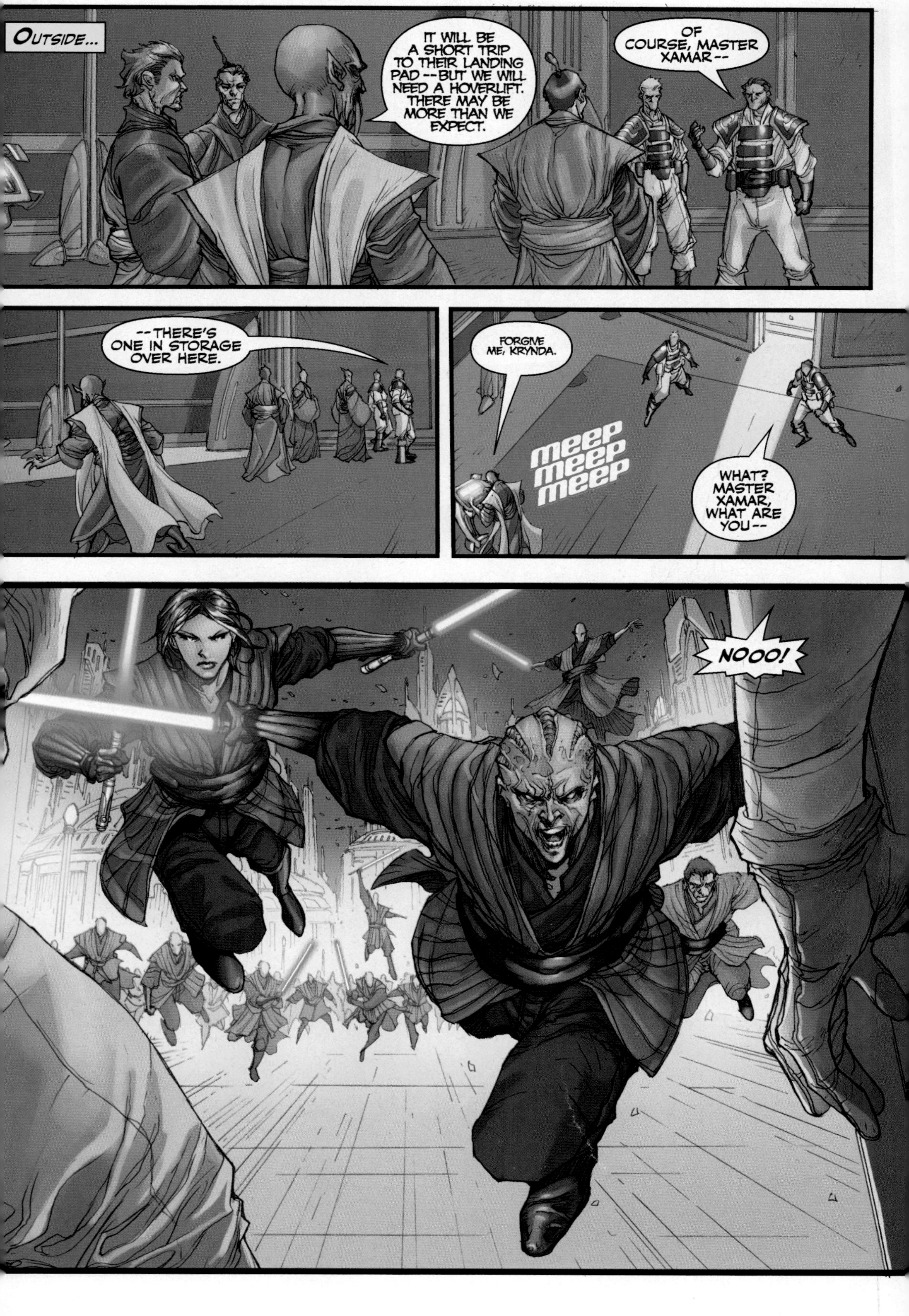
OUTSIDE...
IT WILL BE A SHORT TRIP TO THEIR LANDING PAD --BUT WE WILL NEED A HOVERLIFT. THERE MAY BE MORE THAN WE EXPECT.
OF COURSE, MASTER XAMAR--
--THERE'S ONE IN STORAGE OVER HERE.
FORGIVE ME, KRYNDA.
meep meep meep
WHAT? MASTER XAMAR, WHAT ARE YOU--
NOOO!

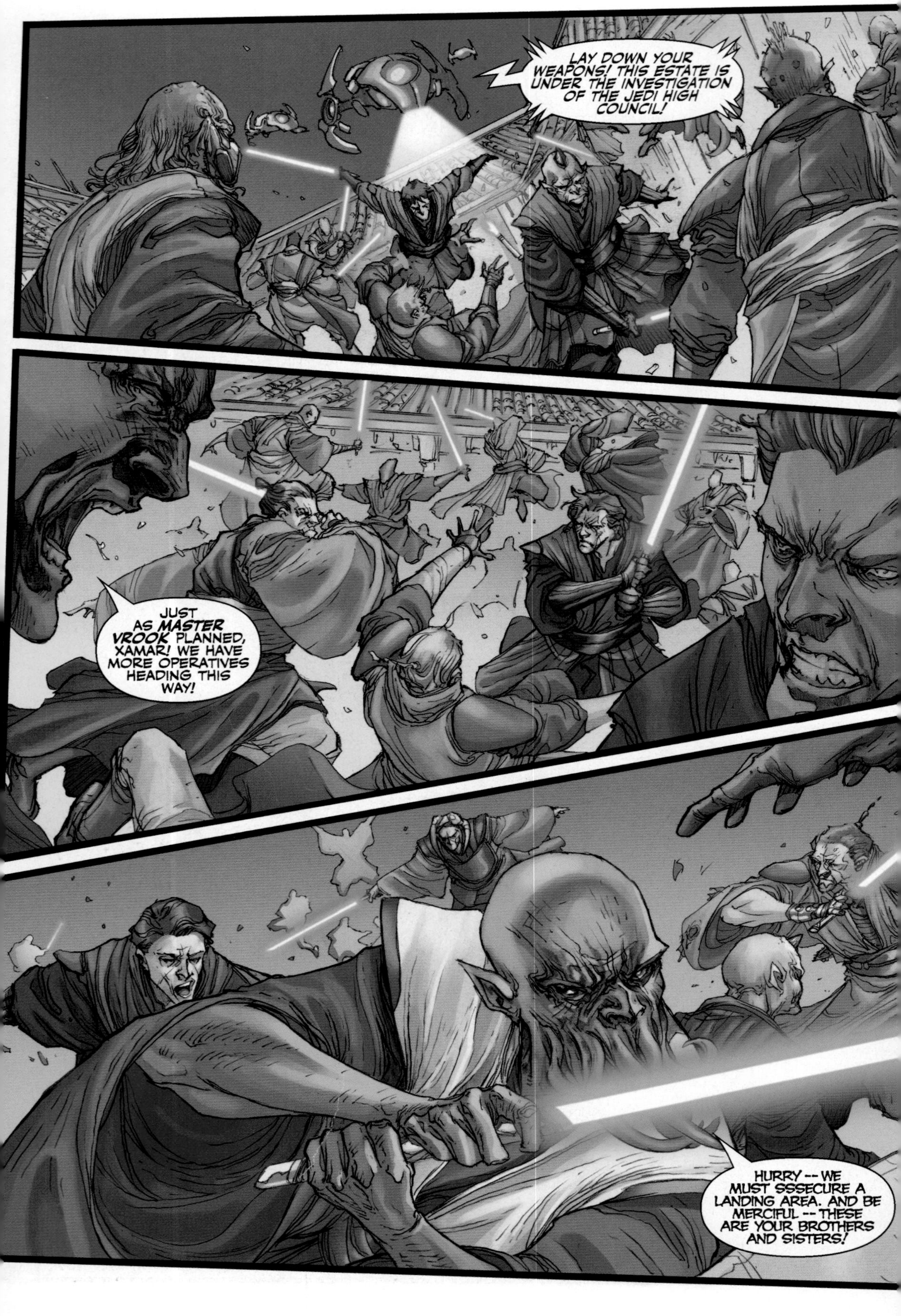
LAY DOWN YOUR WEAPONS! THIS ESTATE IS UNDER THE INVESTIGATION OF THE JEDI HIGH COUNCIL!
JUST AS MASTER VROOK PLANNED, XAMAR! WE HAVE MORE OPERATIVES HEADING THIS WAY!
HURRY -- WE MUST SSSECURE A LANDING AREA. AND BE MERCIFUL -- THESE ARE YOUR BROTHERS AND SISTERS!

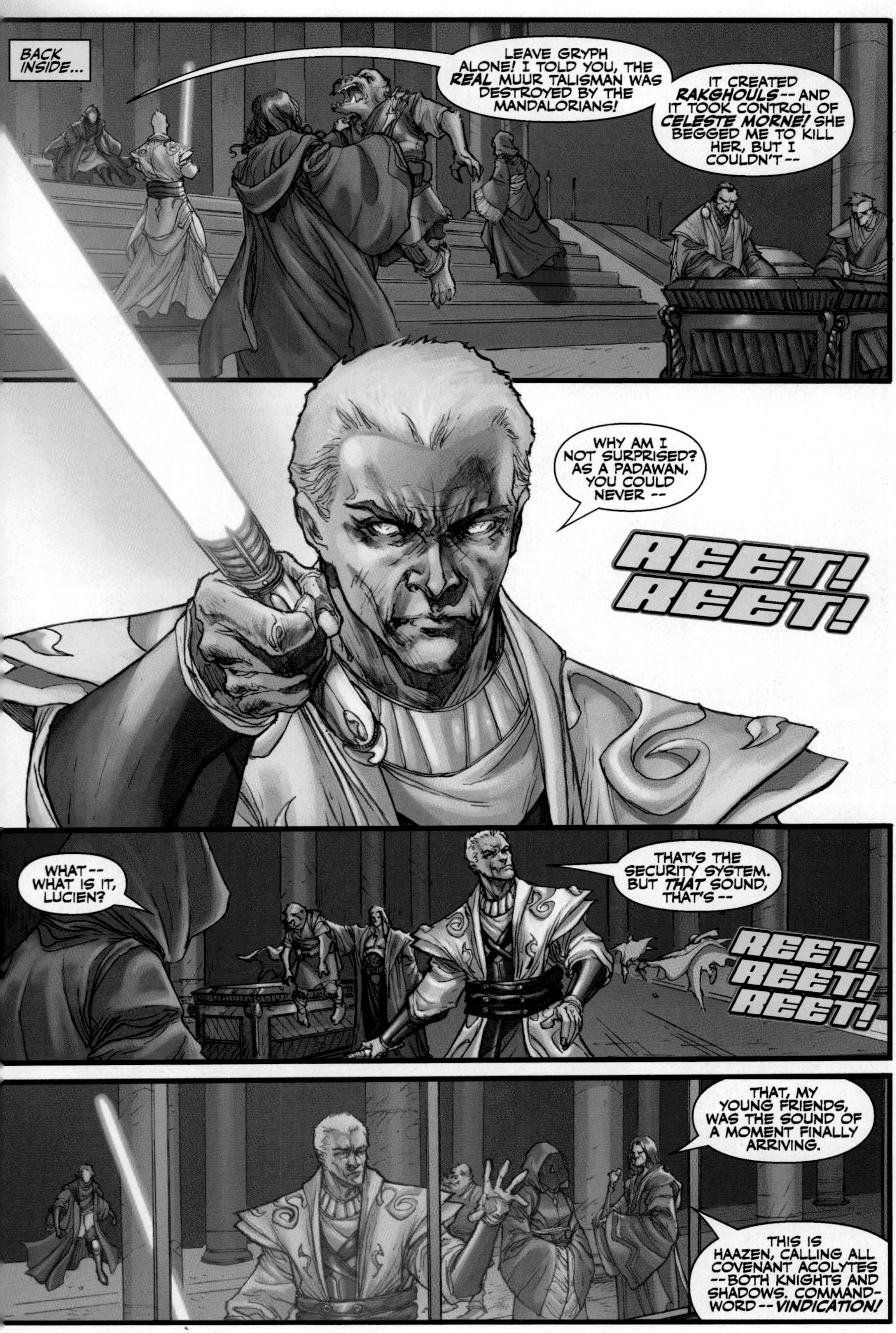
BACK INSIDE...
LEAVE GRYPH ALONE! I TOLD YOU, THE REAL MUUR TALISMAN WAS DESTROYED BY THE MANDALORIANS!
IT CREATED RAKGHOULS-- AND IT TOOK CONTROL OF CELESTE MORNE! SHE BEGGED ME TO KILL HER, BUT I COULDN'T--
WHY AM I NOT SURPRISED? AS A PADAWAN, YOU COULD NEVER --
REET! REET!
WHAT-- WHAT IS IT, LUCIEN?
THAT'S THE SECURITY SYSTEM. BUT THAT SOUND, THAT'S --
REET! REET! REET!
THAT, MY YOUNG FRIENDS, WAS THE SOUND OF A MOMENT FINALLY ARRIVING.
THIS IS HAAZEN, CALLING ALL COVENANT ACOLYTES --BOTH KNIGHTS AND SHADOWS. COMMAND-WORD--VINDICATION!

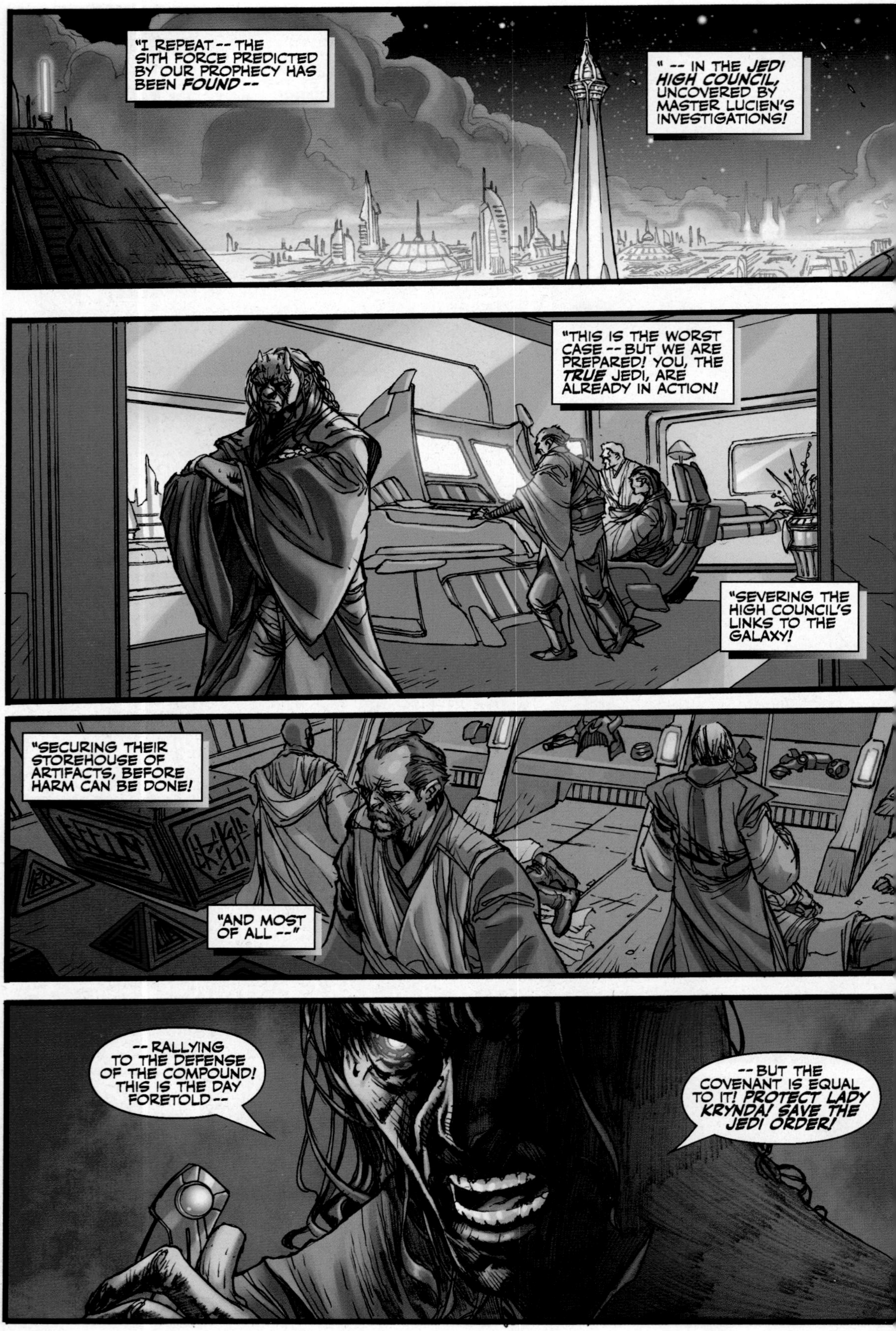
"I REPEAT -- THE SITH FORCE PREDICTED BY OUR PROPHECY HAS BEEN FOUND --
" -- IN THE JEDI HIGH COUNCIL, UNCOVERED BY MASTER LUCIEN'S INVESTIGATIONS!
"THIS IS THE WORST CASE -- BUT WE ARE PREPARED! YOU, THE TRUE JEDI, ARE ALREADY IN ACTION!
"SEVERING THE HIGH COUNCIL'S LINKS TO THE GALAXY!
"SECURING THEIR STOREHOUSE OF ARTIFACTS, BEFORE HARM CAN BE DONE!
"AND MOST OF ALL --"
-- RALLYING TO THE DEFENSE OF THE COMPOUND! THIS IS THE DAY FORETOLD --
-- BUT THE COVENANT IS EQUAL TO IT! PROTECT LADY KRYNDA! SAVE THE JEDI ORDER!

AN *INSURRECTION*.

AND LUCIEN MADE IT POSSIBLE. HIS POSITION ON THE JEDI COUNCIL GAVE US THE ACCESS WE NEEDED.

I DIDN'T WANT THIS, Q'ANILIA.

THIS WAS SOMETHING WE DISCUSSED IN CASE THE SITH INFILTRATED THE COUNCIL -- AND THREATENED TO TAKE THE ARTIFACTS THERE.

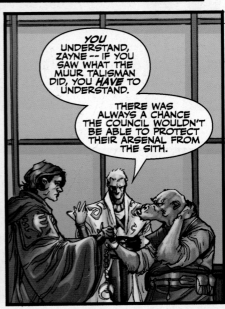

YOU UNDERSTAND, ZAYNE -- IF YOU SAW WHAT THE MUUR TALISMAN DID, YOU *HAVE* TO UNDERSTAND.

THERE WAS ALWAYS A CHANCE THE COUNCIL WOULDN'T BE ABLE TO PROTECT THEIR ARSENAL FROM THE SITH.

WE HAD TO BE ABLE TO DO IT *FOR* THEM.

I DIDN'T *WANT THIS!*

OF COURSE YOU DID. I'VE ALWAYS GIVEN YOU WHAT YOU WANTED --

-- AND WHAT YOU DIDN'T WANT, I *MADE* YOU WANT.

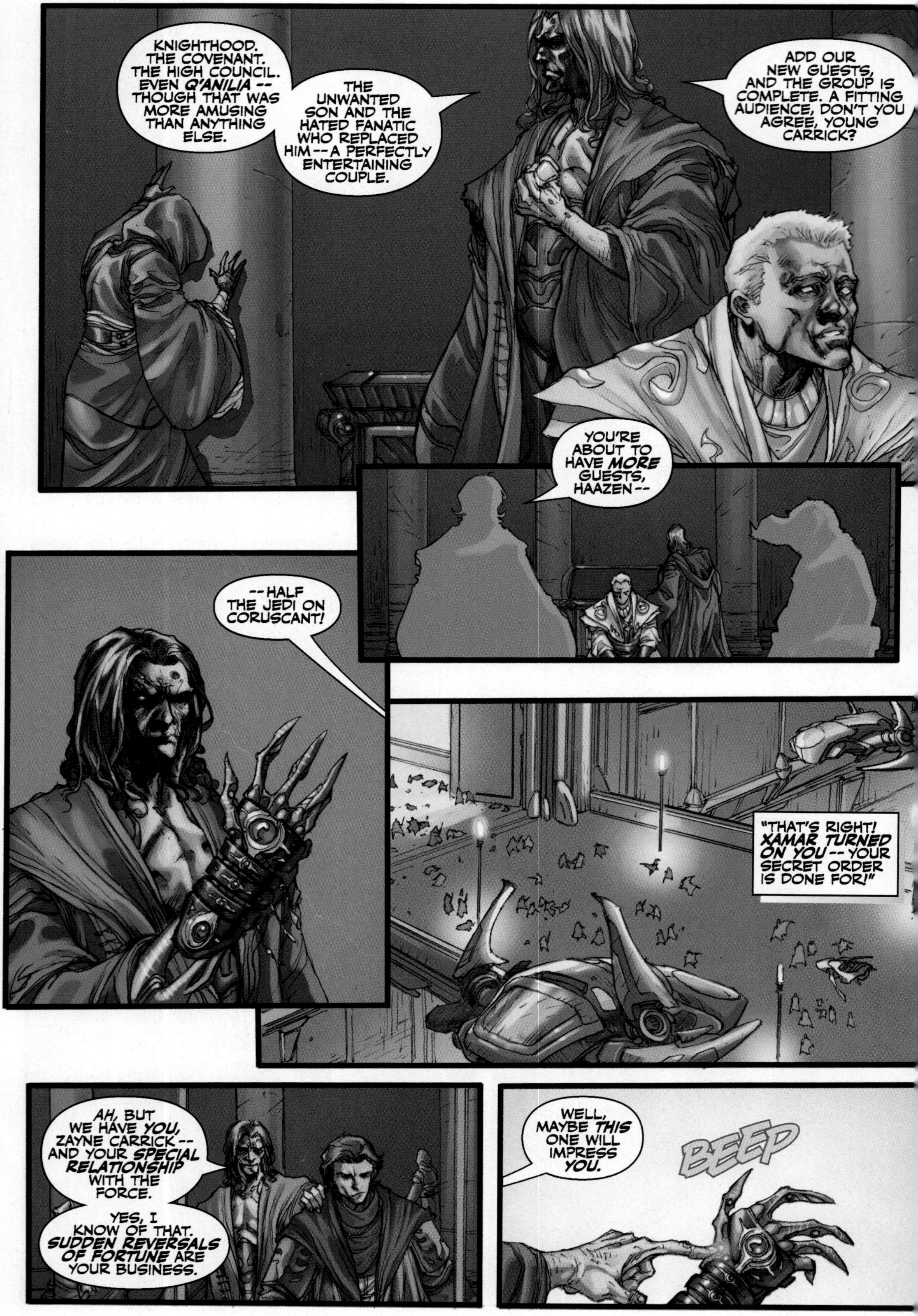
KNIGHTHOOD. THE COVENANT. THE HIGH COUNCIL. EVEN Q'ANILIA -- THOUGH THAT WAS MORE AMUSING THAN ANYTHING ELSE.
THE UNWANTED SON AND THE HATED FANATIC WHO REPLACED HIM -- A PERFECTLY ENTERTAINING COUPLE.
ADD OUR NEW GUESTS, AND THE GROUP IS COMPLETE. A FITTING AUDIENCE, DON'T YOU AGREE, YOUNG CARRICK?
YOU'RE ABOUT TO HAVE MORE GUESTS, HAAZEN --
-- HALF THE JEDI ON CORUSCANT!
"THAT'S RIGHT! XAMAR TURNED ON YOU -- YOUR SECRET ORDER IS DONE FOR!"
AH, BUT WE HAVE YOU, ZAYNE CARRICK -- AND YOUR SPECIAL RELATIONSHIP WITH THE FORCE.
YES, I KNOW OF THAT. SUDDEN REVERSALS OF FORTUNE ARE YOUR BUSINESS.
WELL, MAYBE THIS ONE WILL IMPRESS YOU.
BEEP

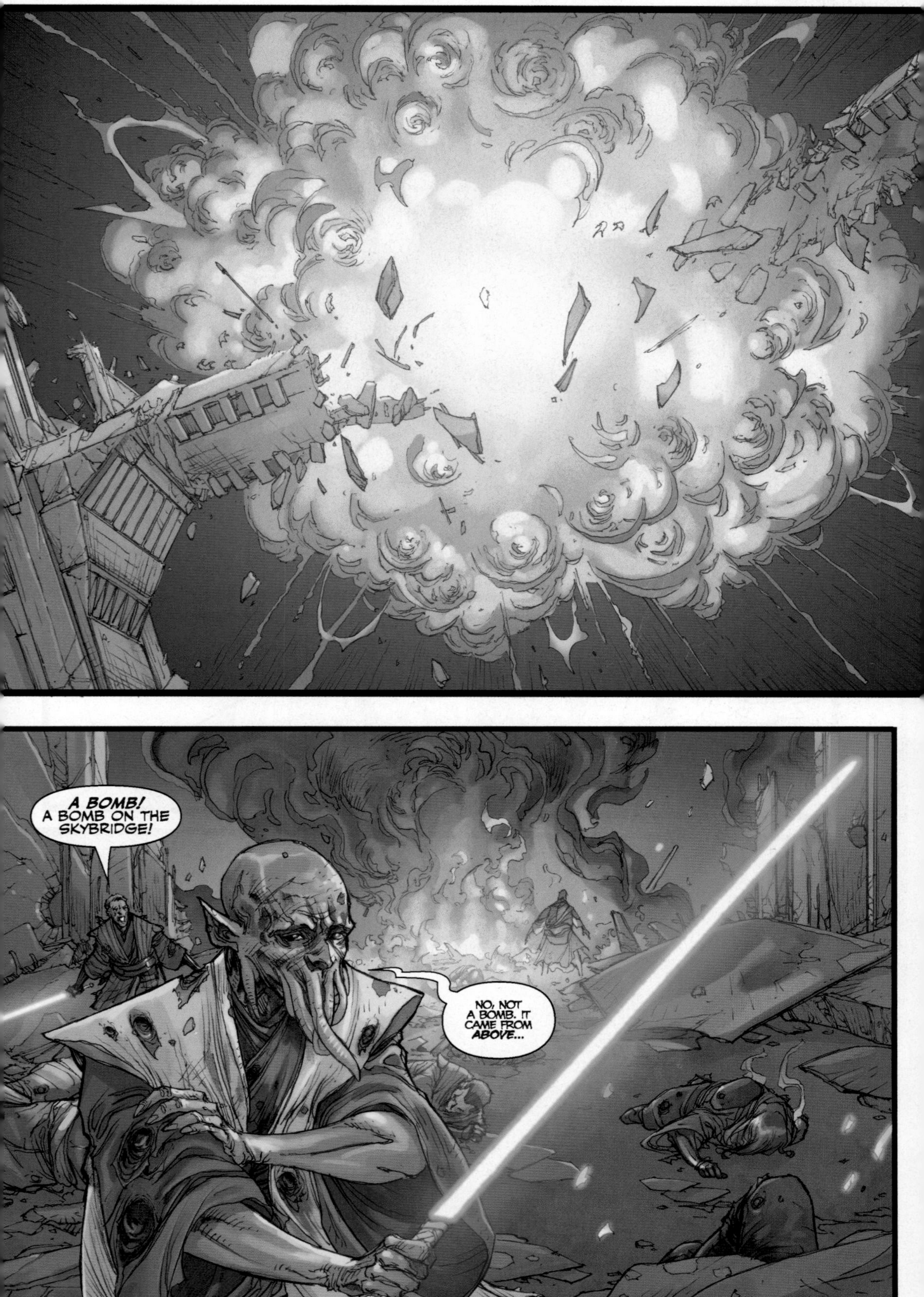
A BOMB! A BOMB ON THE SKYBRIDGE!
NO, NOT A BOMB. IT CAME FROM ABOVE...

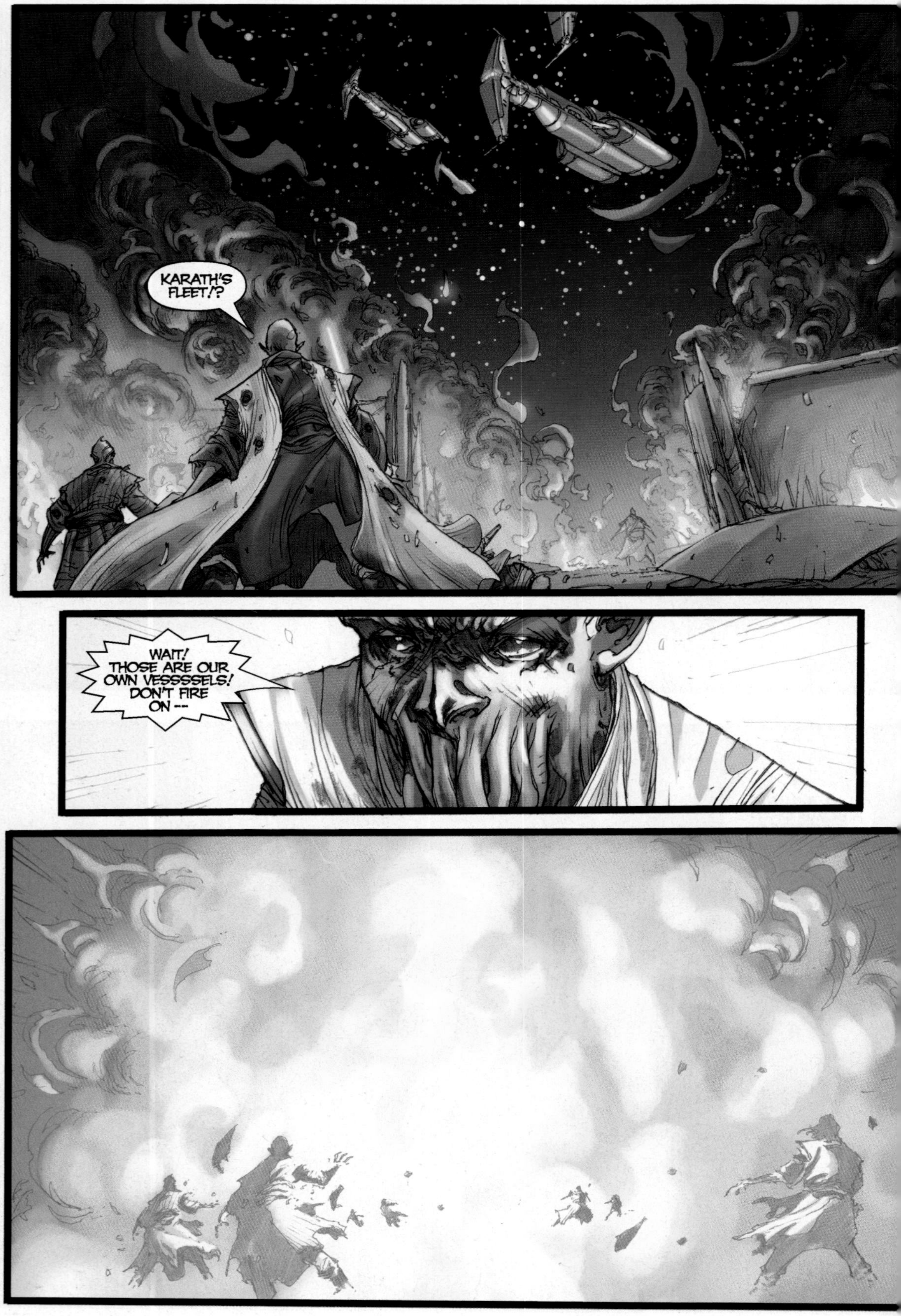
KARATH'S FLEET!?
WAIT! THOSE ARE OUR OWN VESSSSELS! DON'T FIRE ON --

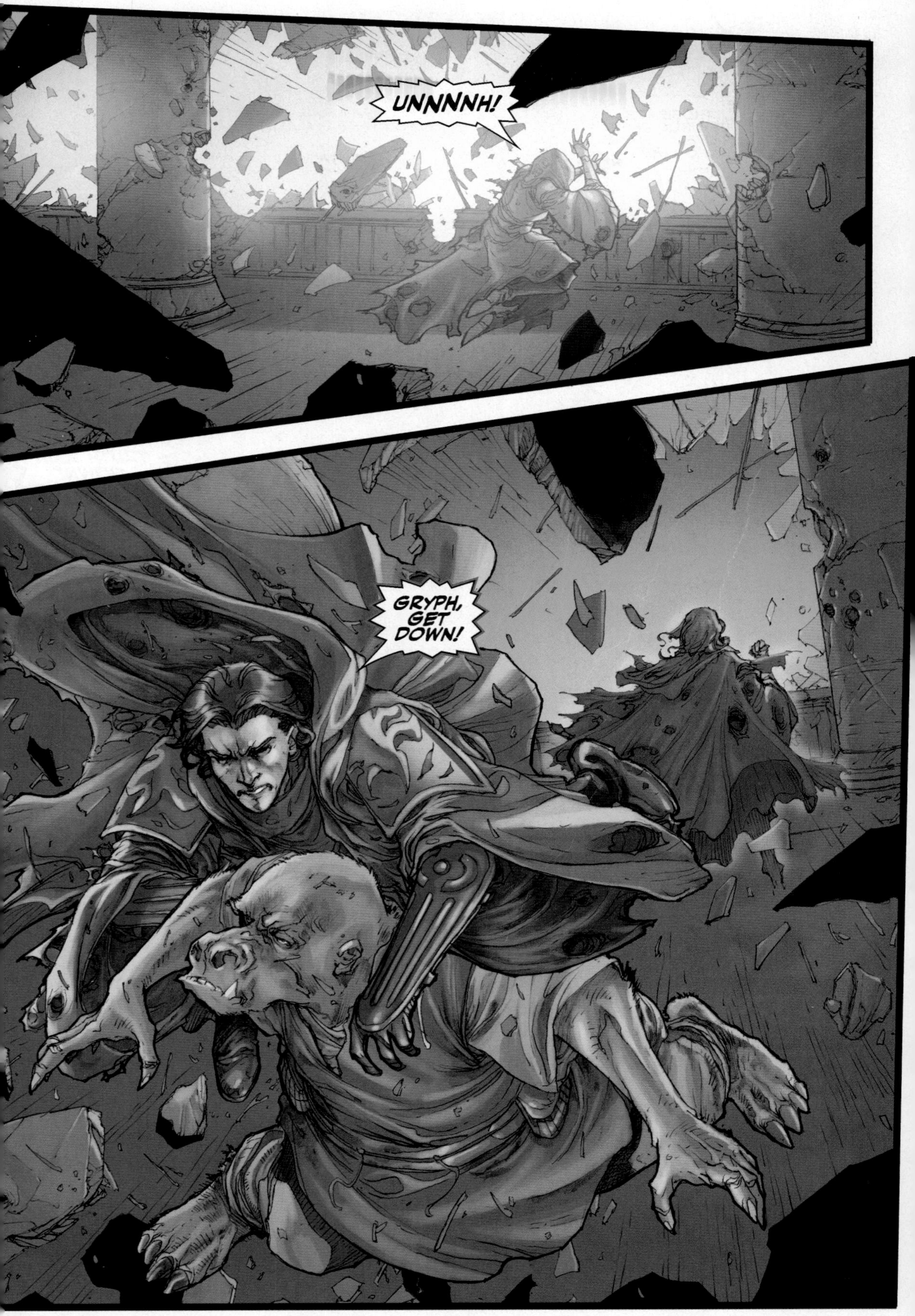
UNNNNH!
GRYPH, GET DOWN!

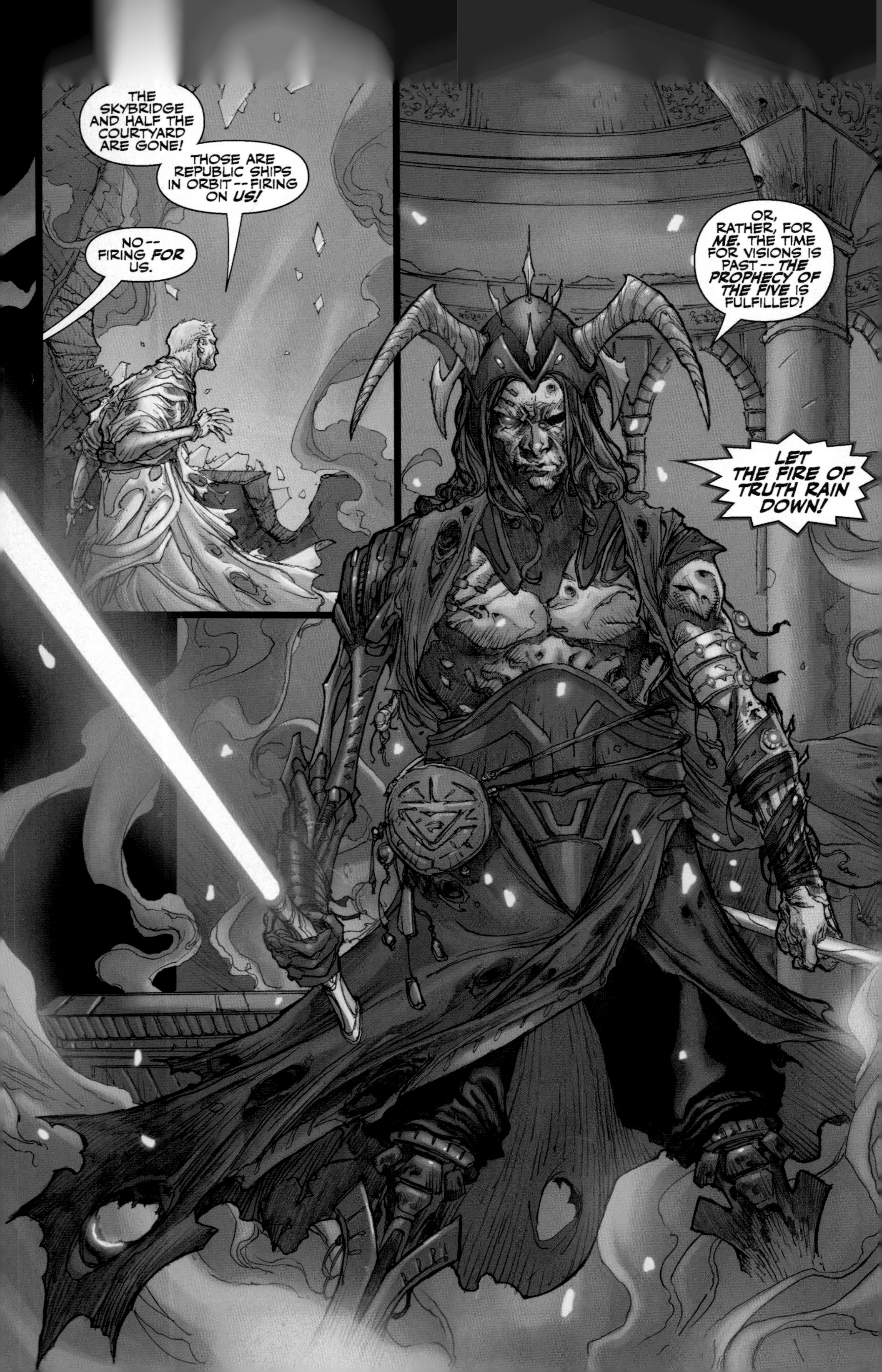
THE SKYBRIDGE AND HALF THE COURTYARD ARE GONE!
THOSE ARE REPUBLIC SHIPS IN ORBIT--FIRING ON *US!*
NO--FIRING *FOR* US.
OR, RATHER, FOR *ME.* THE TIME FOR VISIONS IS PAST--*THE PROPHECY OF THE FIVE* IS FULFILLED!
LET THE FIRE OF TRUTH RAIN DOWN!

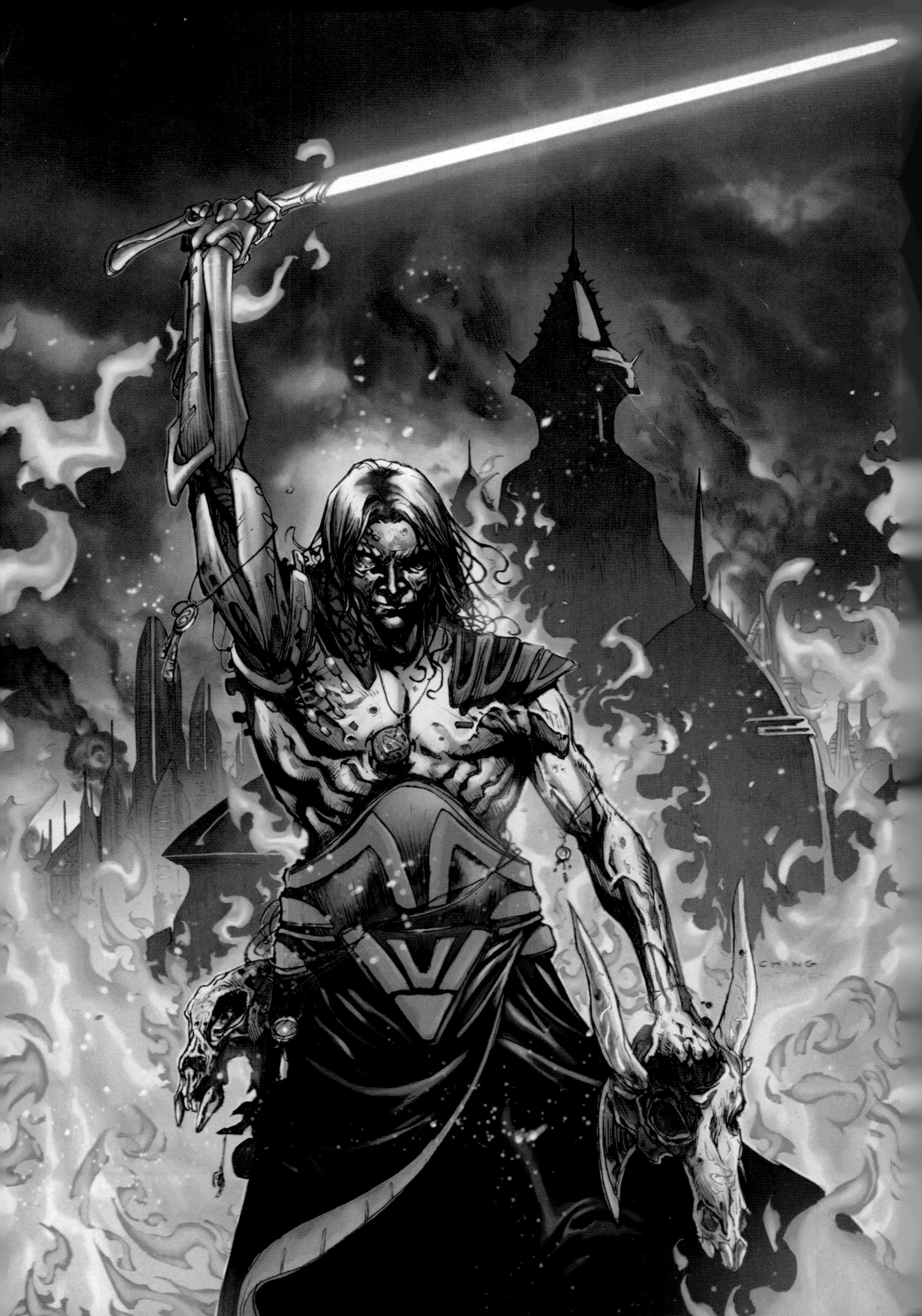

STAR WARS: KNIGHTS OF THE OLD REPUBLIC #33 **— "VINDICATION, PART 2"**

WRITER: JOHN JACKSON MILLER • PENCILER: BONG DAZO • INKER: JOE PIMENTEL • COLORIST: MICHAEL ATIYEH • LETTERER: MICHAEL HEISLER
ASSISTANT EDITOR: FREDDYE LINS • EDITOR: DAVE MARSHALL • COVER ARTISTS: BRIAN CHING & MICHAEL ATIYEH

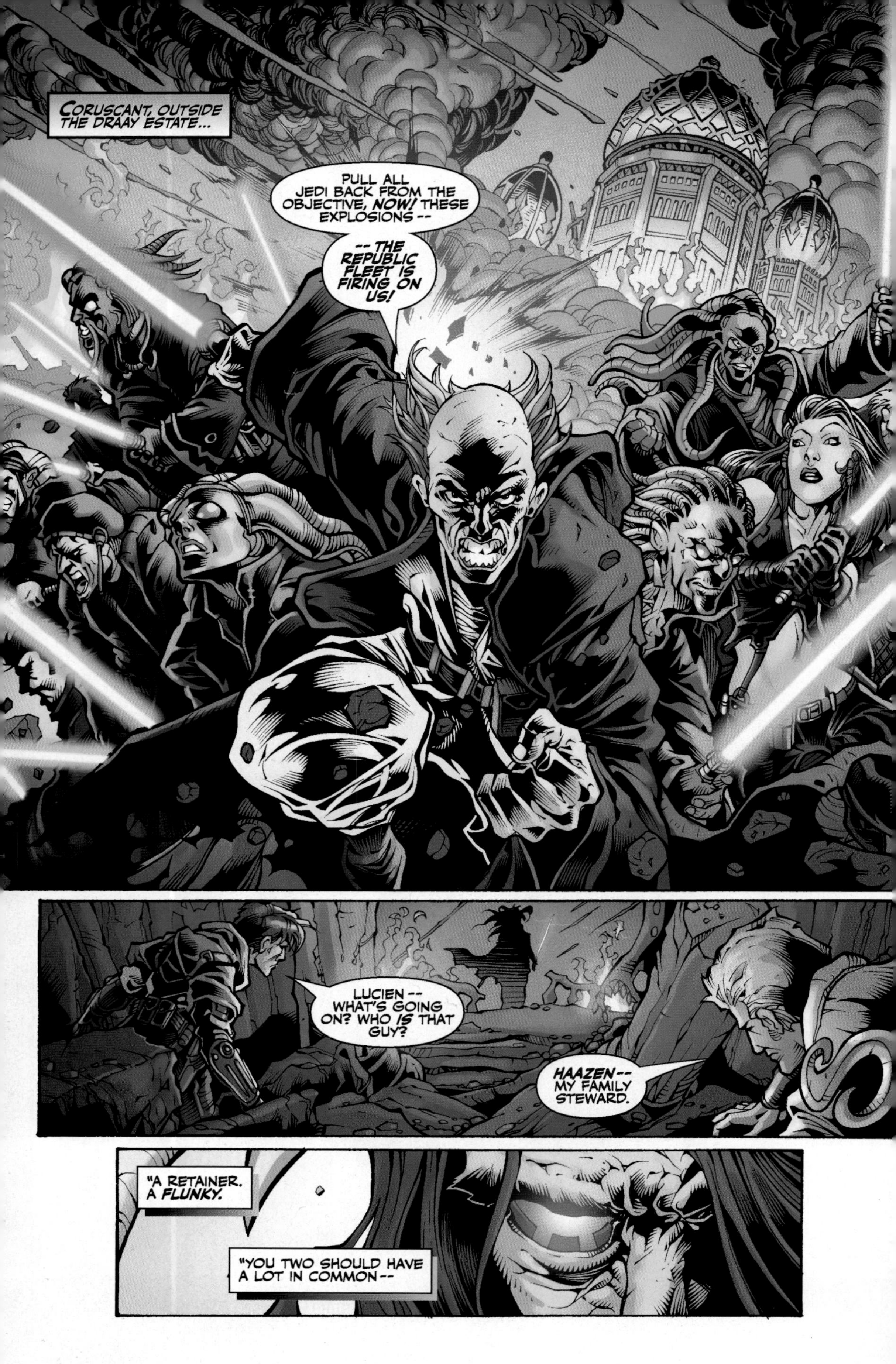
CORUSCANT, OUTSIDE THE DRAAY ESTATE...
PULL ALL JEDI BACK FROM THE OBJECTIVE, NOW! THESE EXPLOSIONS --
-- THE REPUBLIC FLEET IS FIRING ON US!
LUCIEN -- WHAT'S GOING ON? WHO IS THAT GUY?
HAAZEN -- MY FAMILY STEWARD.
"A RETAINER. A FLUNKY.
"YOU TWO SHOULD HAVE A LOT IN COMMON --

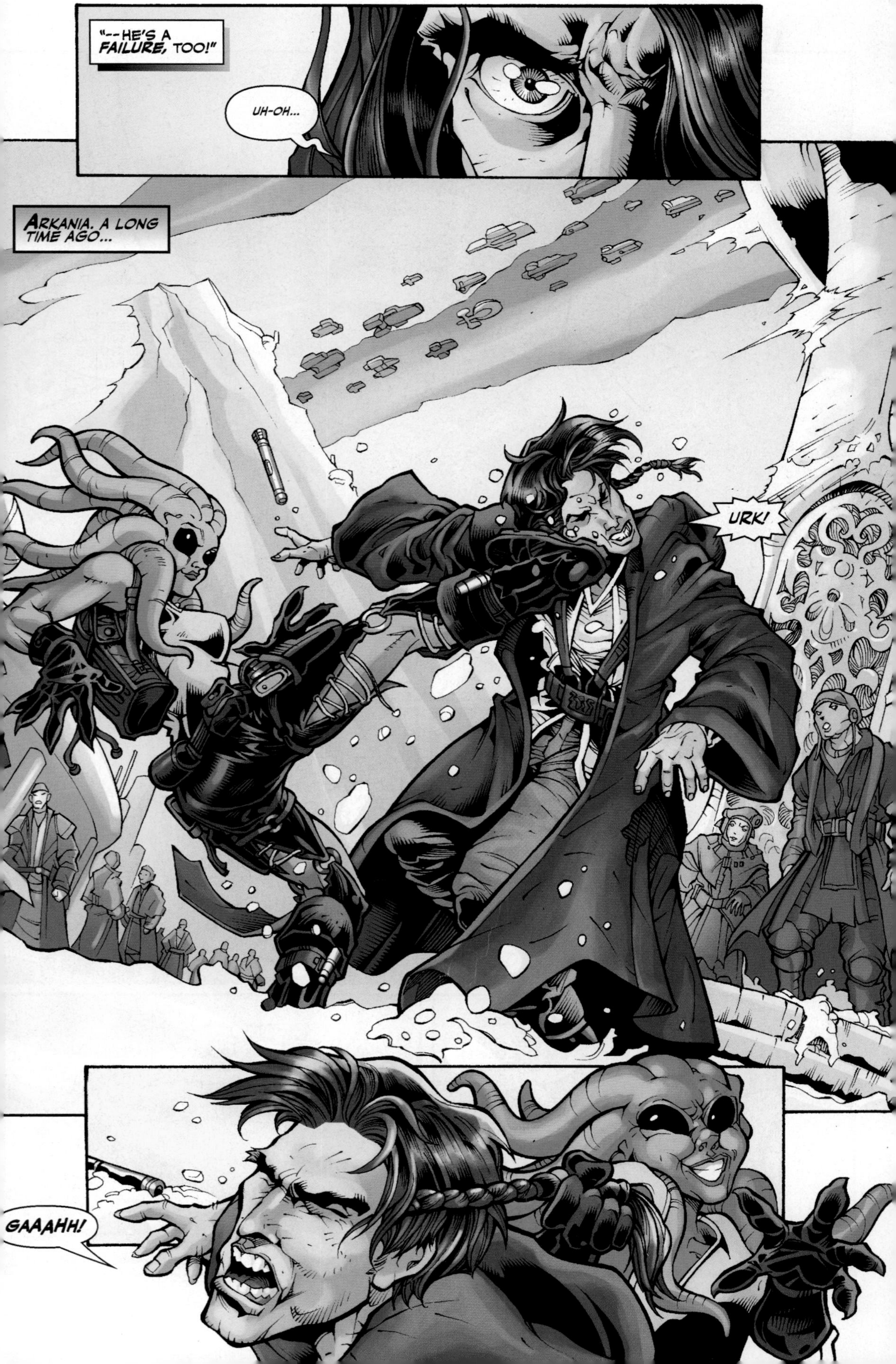
"--HE'S A FAILURE, TOO!"
UH-OH...
ARKANIA. A LONG TIME AGO...
URK!
GAAAHH!

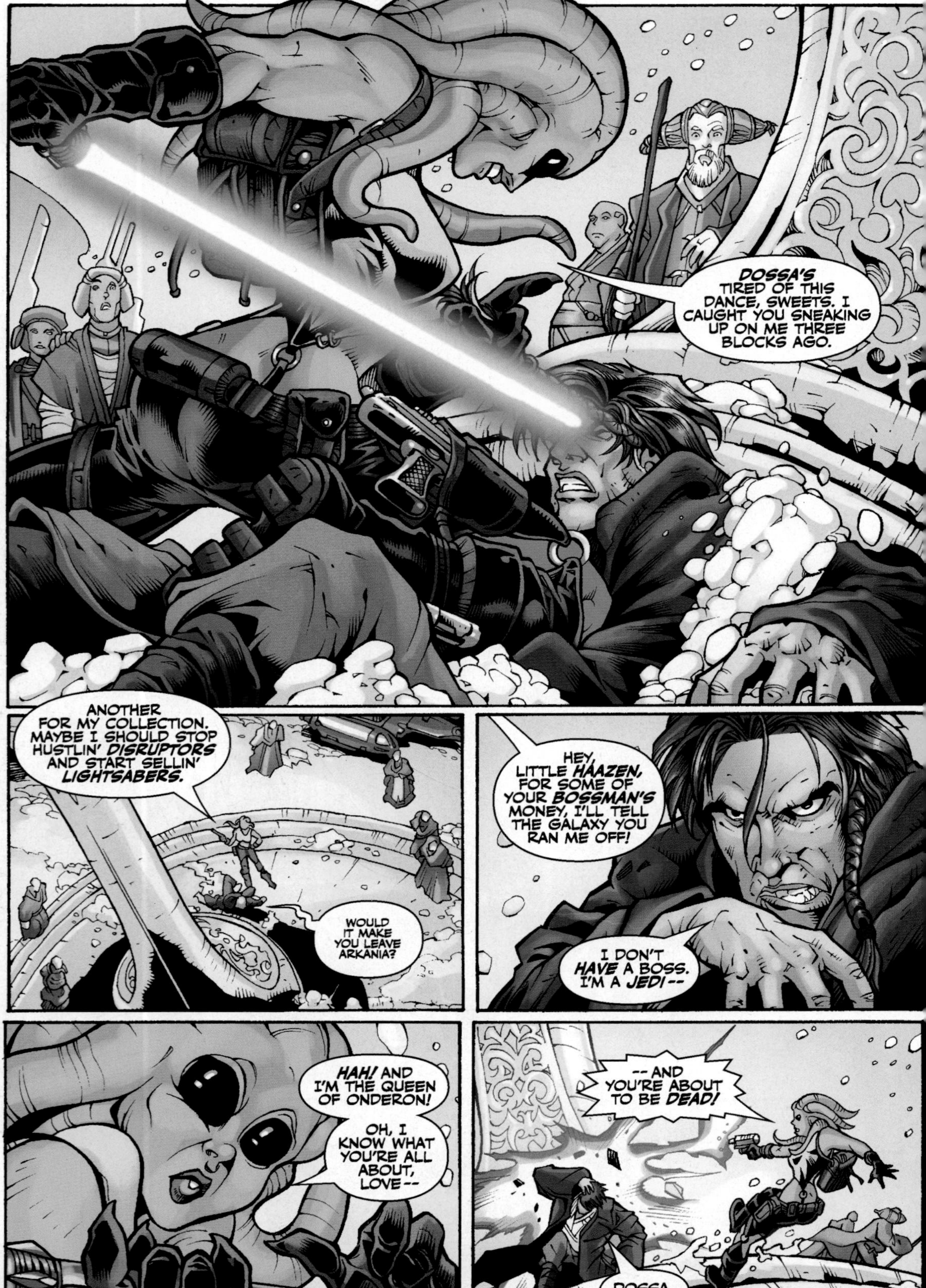
DOSSA'S TIRED OF THIS DANCE, SWEETS. I CAUGHT YOU SNEAKING UP ON ME THREE BLOCKS AGO.
ANOTHER FOR MY COLLECTION. MAYBE I SHOULD STOP HUSTLIN' DISRUPTORS AND START SELLIN' LIGHTSABERS.
WOULD IT MAKE YOU LEAVE ARKANIA?
HEY, LITTLE HAAZEN, FOR SOME OF YOUR BOSSMAN'S MONEY, I'LL TELL THE GALAXY YOU RAN ME OFF!
I DON'T HAVE A BOSS. I'M A JEDI--
HAH! AND I'M THE QUEEN OF ONDERON!
OH, I KNOW WHAT YOU'RE ALL ABOUT, LOVE--
--AND YOU'RE ABOUT TO BE DEAD!
DOSSA, DON'T!

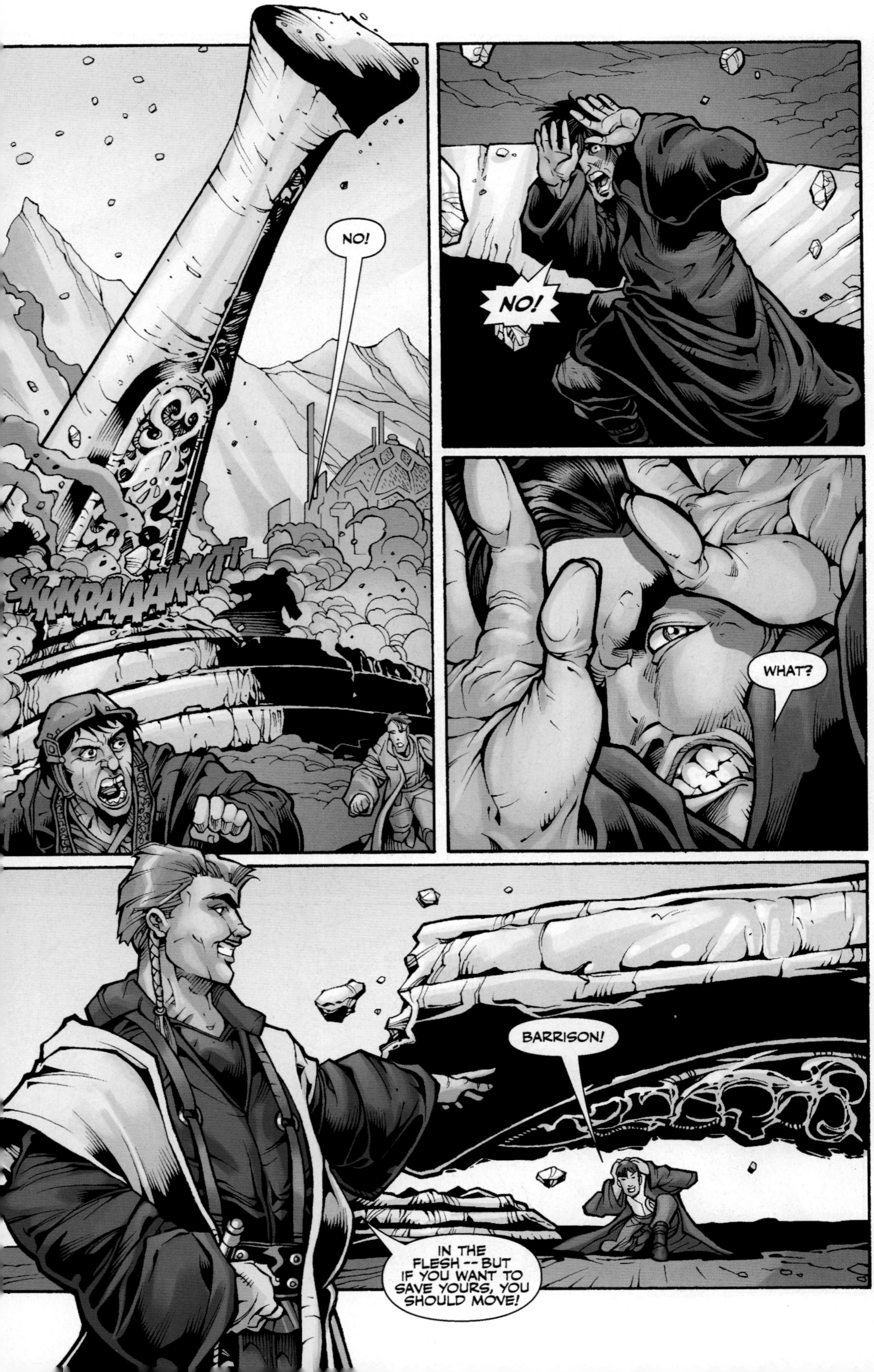

NO!
SKKRAAAAKKT
NO!
WHAT?
BARRISON!
IN THE FLESH -- BUT IF YOU WANT TO SAVE YOURS, YOU SHOULD MOVE!

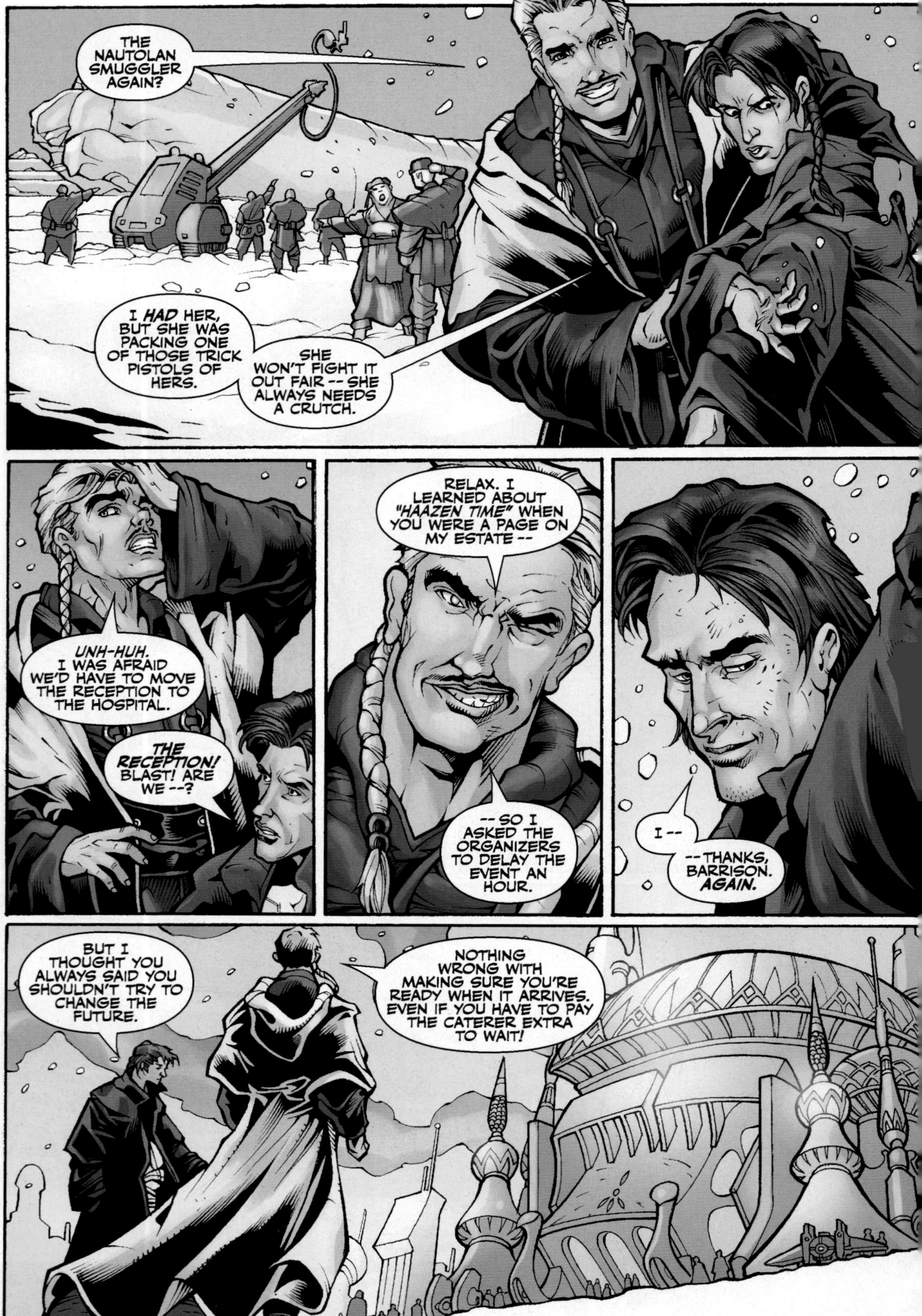
THE NAUTOLAN SMUGGLER AGAIN?
I HAD HER, BUT SHE WAS PACKING ONE OF THOSE TRICK PISTOLS OF HERS.
SHE WON'T FIGHT IT OUT FAIR -- SHE ALWAYS NEEDS A CRUTCH.
UNH-HUH. I WAS AFRAID WE'D HAVE TO MOVE THE RECEPTION TO THE HOSPITAL.
THE RECEPTION! BLAST! ARE WE --?
RELAX. I LEARNED ABOUT "HAAZEN TIME" WHEN YOU WERE A PAGE ON MY ESTATE --
-- SO I ASKED THE ORGANIZERS TO DELAY THE EVENT AN HOUR.
I --
-- THANKS, BARRISON. AGAIN.
BUT I THOUGHT YOU ALWAYS SAID YOU SHOULDN'T TRY TO CHANGE THE FUTURE.
NOTHING WRONG WITH MAKING SURE YOU'RE READY WHEN IT ARRIVES. EVEN IF YOU HAVE TO PAY THE CATERER EXTRA TO WAIT!

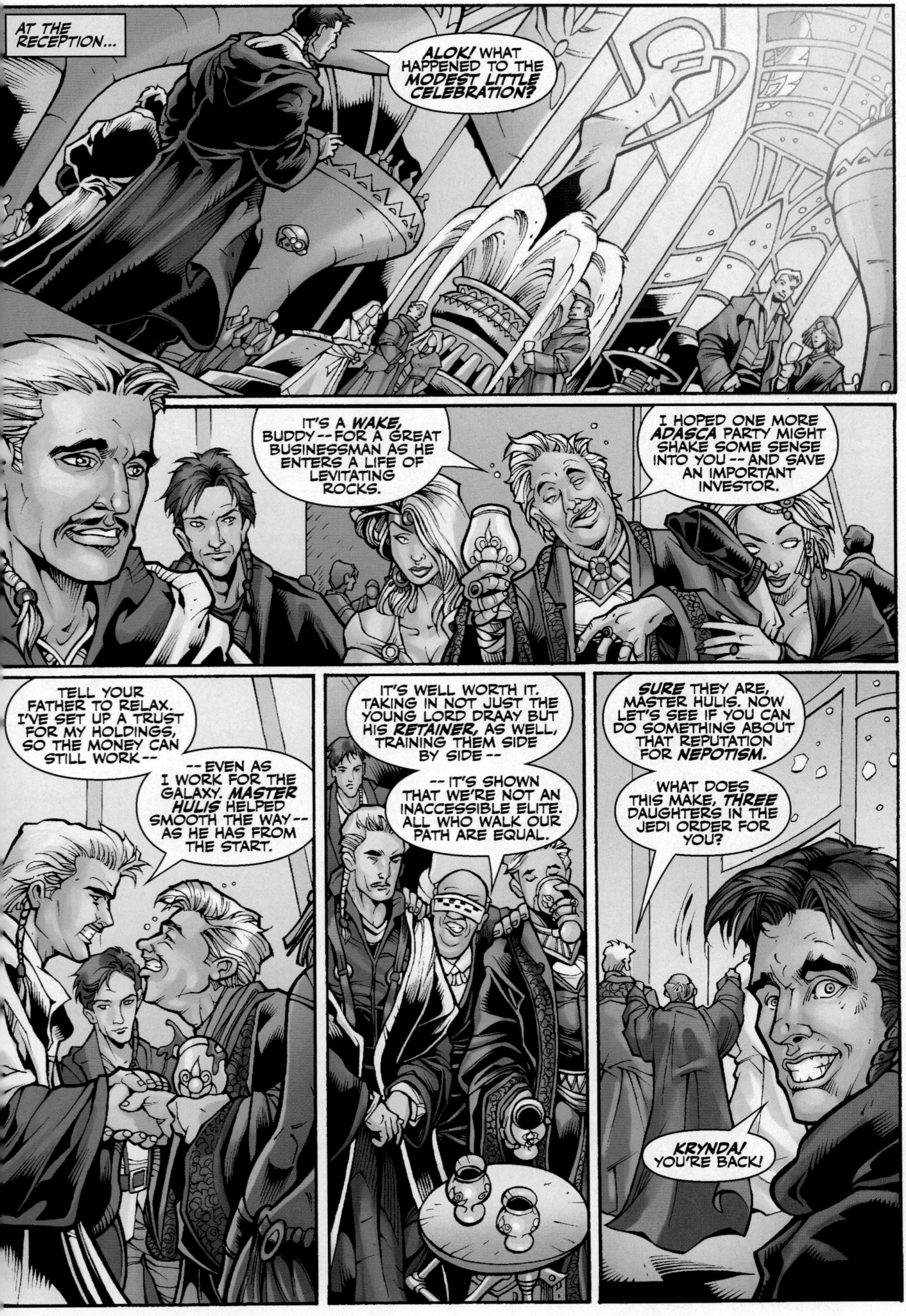
AT THE RECEPTION...
ALOK! WHAT HAPPENED TO THE MODEST LITTLE CELEBRATION?
IT'S A WAKE, BUDDY--FOR A GREAT BUSINESSMAN AS HE ENTERS A LIFE OF LEVITATING ROCKS.
I HOPED ONE MORE ADASCA PARTY MIGHT SHAKE SOME SENSE INTO YOU--AND SAVE AN IMPORTANT INVESTOR.
TELL YOUR FATHER TO RELAX. I'VE SET UP A TRUST FOR MY HOLDINGS, SO THE MONEY CAN STILL WORK--
--EVEN AS I WORK FOR THE GALAXY. MASTER HULIS HELPED SMOOTH THE WAY--AS HE HAS FROM THE START.
IT'S WELL WORTH IT. TAKING IN NOT JUST THE YOUNG LORD DRAAY BUT HIS RETAINER, AS WELL, TRAINING THEM SIDE BY SIDE--
--IT'S SHOWN THAT WE'RE NOT AN INACCESSIBLE ELITE. ALL WHO WALK OUR PATH ARE EQUAL.
SURE THEY ARE, MASTER HULIS. NOW LET'S SEE IF YOU CAN DO SOMETHING ABOUT THAT REPUTATION FOR NEPOTISM.
WHAT DOES THIS MAKE, THREE DAUGHTERS IN THE JEDI ORDER FOR YOU?
KRYNDA! YOU'RE BACK!

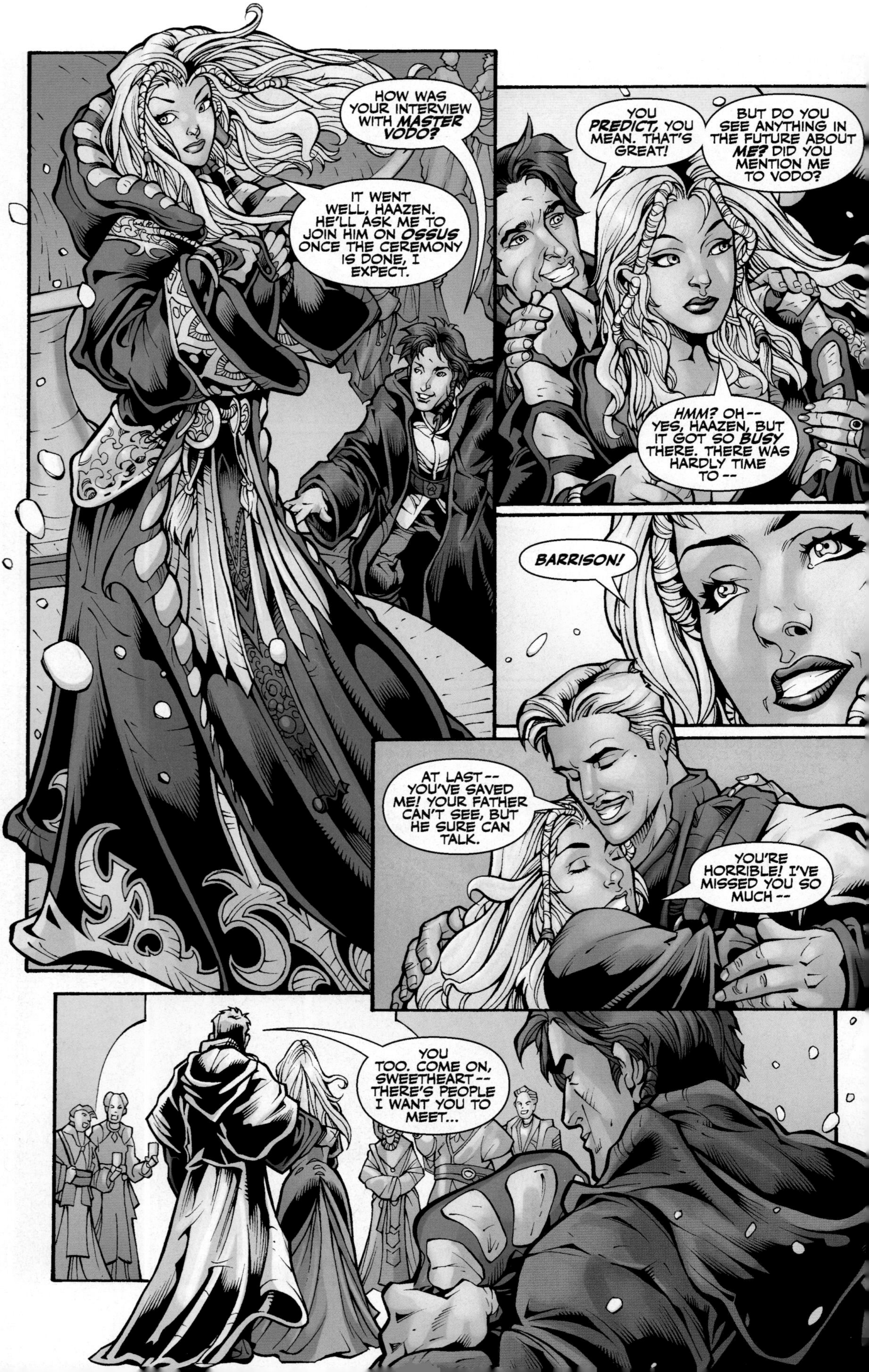
HOW WAS YOUR INTERVIEW WITH MASTER VODO?
IT WENT WELL, HAAZEN. HE'LL ASK ME TO JOIN HIM ON OSSUS ONCE THE CEREMONY IS DONE, I EXPECT.
YOU PREDICT, YOU MEAN. THAT'S GREAT!
BUT DO YOU SEE ANYTHING IN THE FUTURE ABOUT ME? DID YOU MENTION ME TO VODO?
HMM? OH -- YES, HAAZEN, BUT IT GOT SO BUSY THERE. THERE WAS HARDLY TIME TO --
BARRISON!
AT LAST -- YOU'VE SAVED ME! YOUR FATHER CAN'T SEE, BUT HE SURE CAN TALK.
YOU'RE HORRIBLE! I'VE MISSED YOU SO MUCH --
YOU TOO. COME ON, SWEETHEART -- THERE'S PEOPLE I WANT YOU TO MEET...

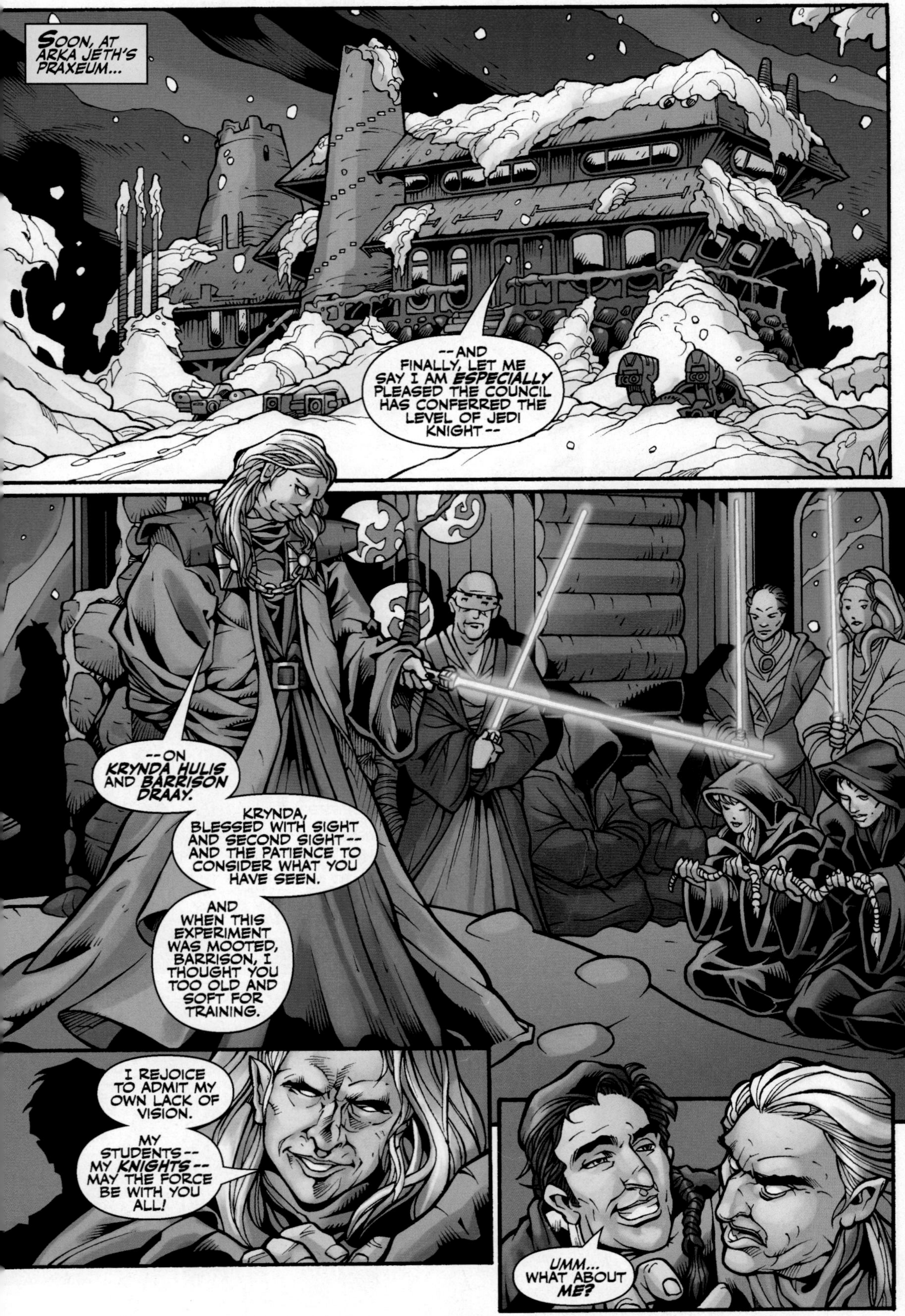
SOON, AT ARKA JETH'S PRAXEUM...
--AND FINALLY, LET ME SAY I AM ESPECIALLY PLEASED THE COUNCIL HAS CONFERRED THE LEVEL OF JEDI KNIGHT--
--ON KRYNDA HULIS AND BARRISON DRAAY.
KRYNDA, BLESSED WITH SIGHT AND SECOND SIGHT-- AND THE PATIENCE TO CONSIDER WHAT YOU HAVE SEEN.
AND WHEN THIS EXPERIMENT WAS MOOTED, BARRISON, I THOUGHT YOU TOO OLD AND SOFT FOR TRAINING.
I REJOICE TO ADMIT MY OWN LACK OF VISION.
MY STUDENTS-- MY KNIGHTS-- MAY THE FORCE BE WITH YOU ALL!
UMM... WHAT ABOUT ME?

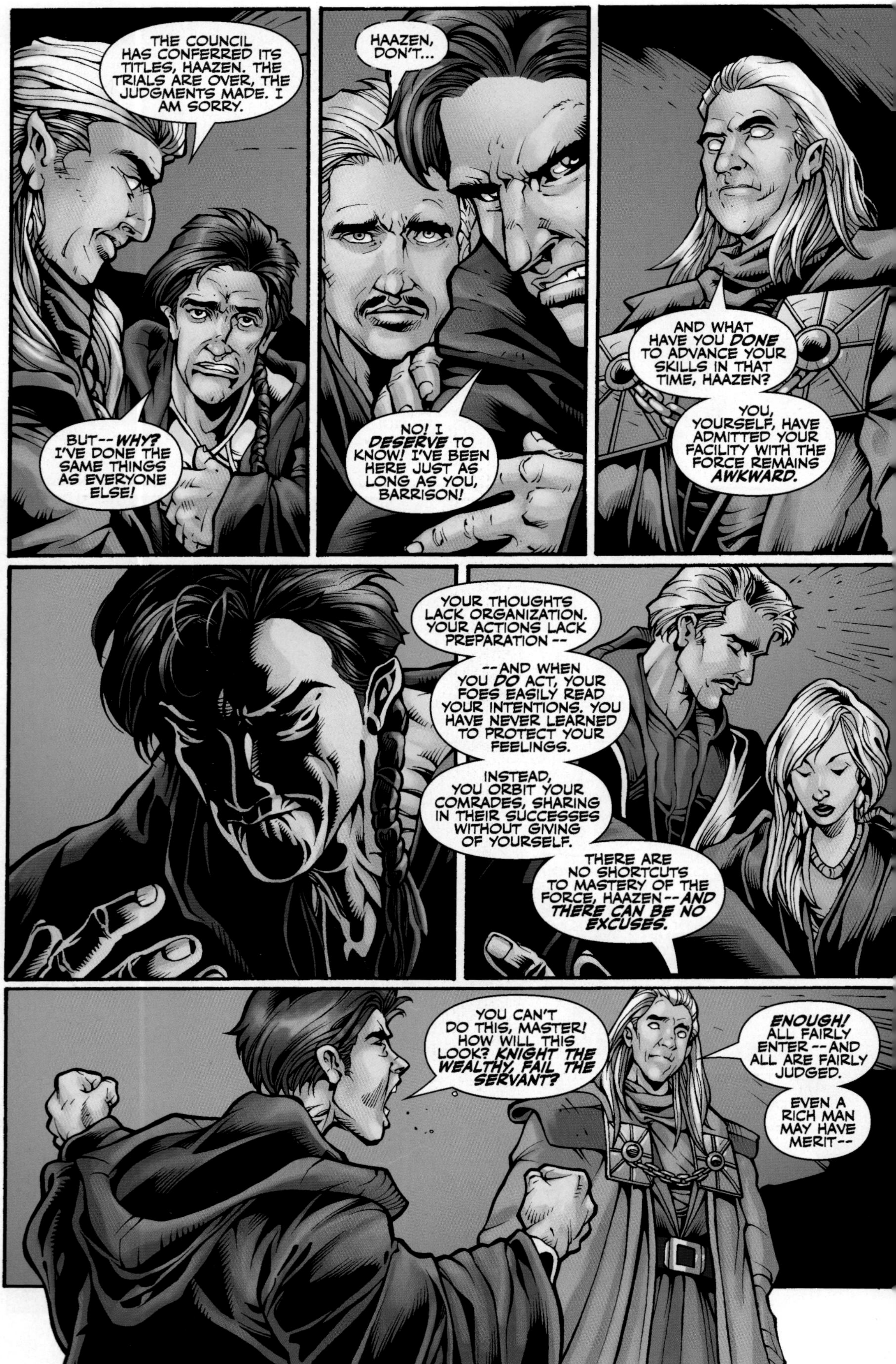
THE COUNCIL HAS CONFERRED ITS TITLES, HAAZEN. THE TRIALS ARE OVER, THE JUDGMENTS MADE. I AM SORRY.
BUT-- *WHY?* I'VE DONE THE SAME THINGS AS EVERYONE ELSE!
HAAZEN, DON'T...
NO! I *DESERVE* TO KNOW! I'VE BEEN HERE JUST AS LONG AS YOU, BARRISON!
AND WHAT HAVE YOU *DONE* TO ADVANCE YOUR SKILLS IN THAT TIME, HAAZEN?
YOU, YOURSELF, HAVE ADMITTED YOUR FACILITY WITH THE FORCE REMAINS *AWKWARD.*
YOUR THOUGHTS LACK ORGANIZATION. YOUR ACTIONS LACK PREPARATION --
--AND WHEN YOU *DO* ACT, YOUR FOES EASILY READ YOUR INTENTIONS. YOU HAVE NEVER LEARNED TO PROTECT YOUR FEELINGS.
INSTEAD, YOU ORBIT YOUR COMRADES, SHARING IN THEIR SUCCESSES WITHOUT GIVING OF YOURSELF.
THERE ARE NO SHORTCUTS TO MASTERY OF THE FORCE, HAAZEN--*AND THERE CAN BE NO EXCUSES.*
YOU CAN'T DO THIS, MASTER! HOW WILL THIS LOOK? *KNIGHT THE WEALTHY, FAIL THE SERVANT?*
ENOUGH! ALL FAIRLY ENTER--AND ALL ARE FAIRLY JUDGED.
EVEN A RICH MAN MAY HAVE MERIT--

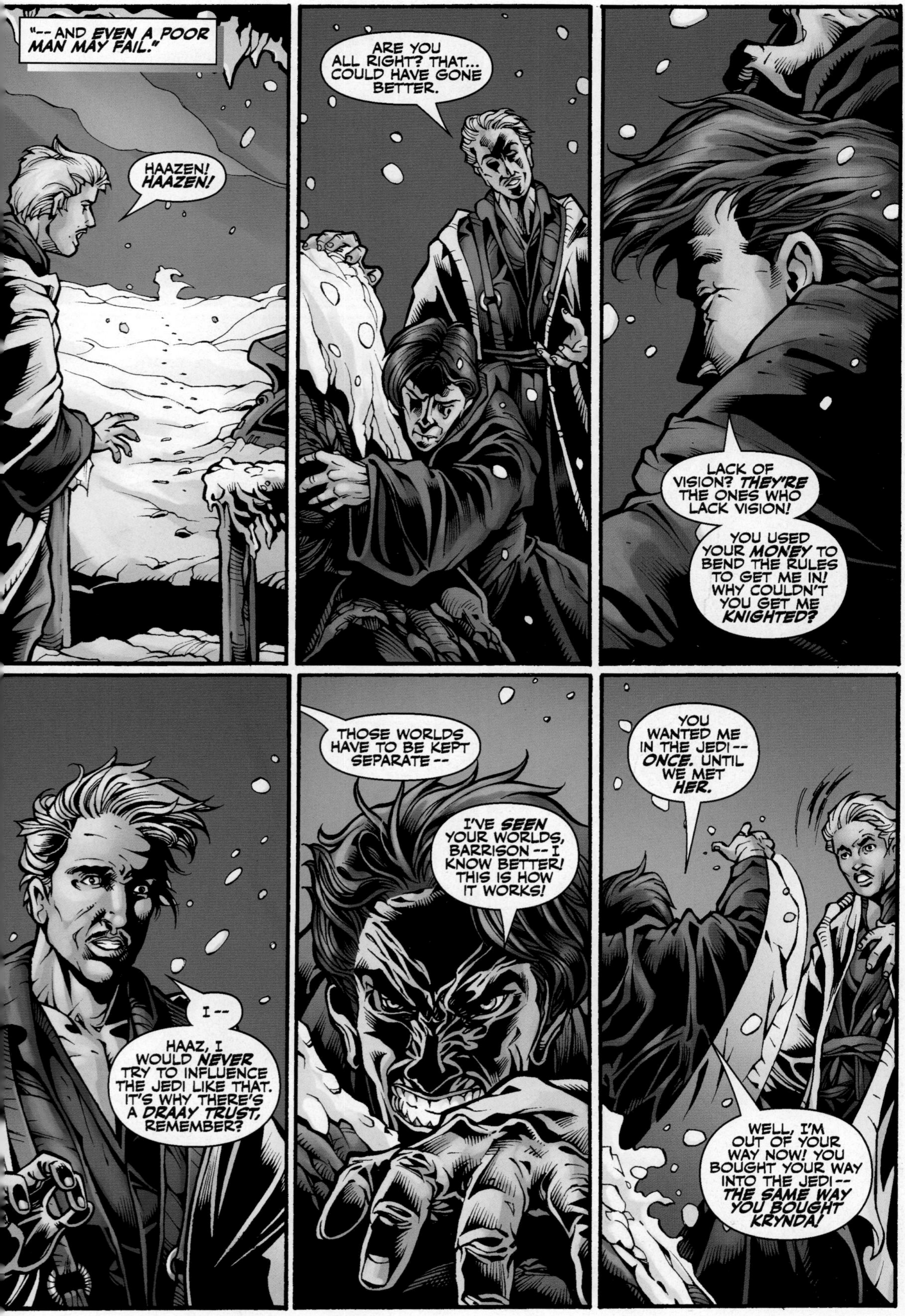
"-- AND EVEN A POOR MAN MAY FAIL."
HAAZEN! HAAZEN!
ARE YOU ALL RIGHT? THAT... COULD HAVE GONE BETTER.
LACK OF VISION? THEY'RE THE ONES WHO LACK VISION!
YOU USED YOUR MONEY TO BEND THE RULES TO GET ME IN! WHY COULDN'T YOU GET ME KNIGHTED?
I --
HAAZ, I WOULD NEVER TRY TO INFLUENCE THE JEDI LIKE THAT. IT'S WHY THERE'S A DRAAY TRUST, REMEMBER?
THOSE WORLDS HAVE TO BE KEPT SEPARATE --
I'VE SEEN YOUR WORLDS, BARRISON -- I KNOW BETTER! THIS IS HOW IT WORKS!
YOU WANTED ME IN THE JEDI -- ONCE. UNTIL WE MET HER.
WELL, I'M OUT OF YOUR WAY NOW! YOU BOUGHT YOUR WAY INTO THE JEDI -- THE SAME WAY YOU BOUGHT KRYNDA!

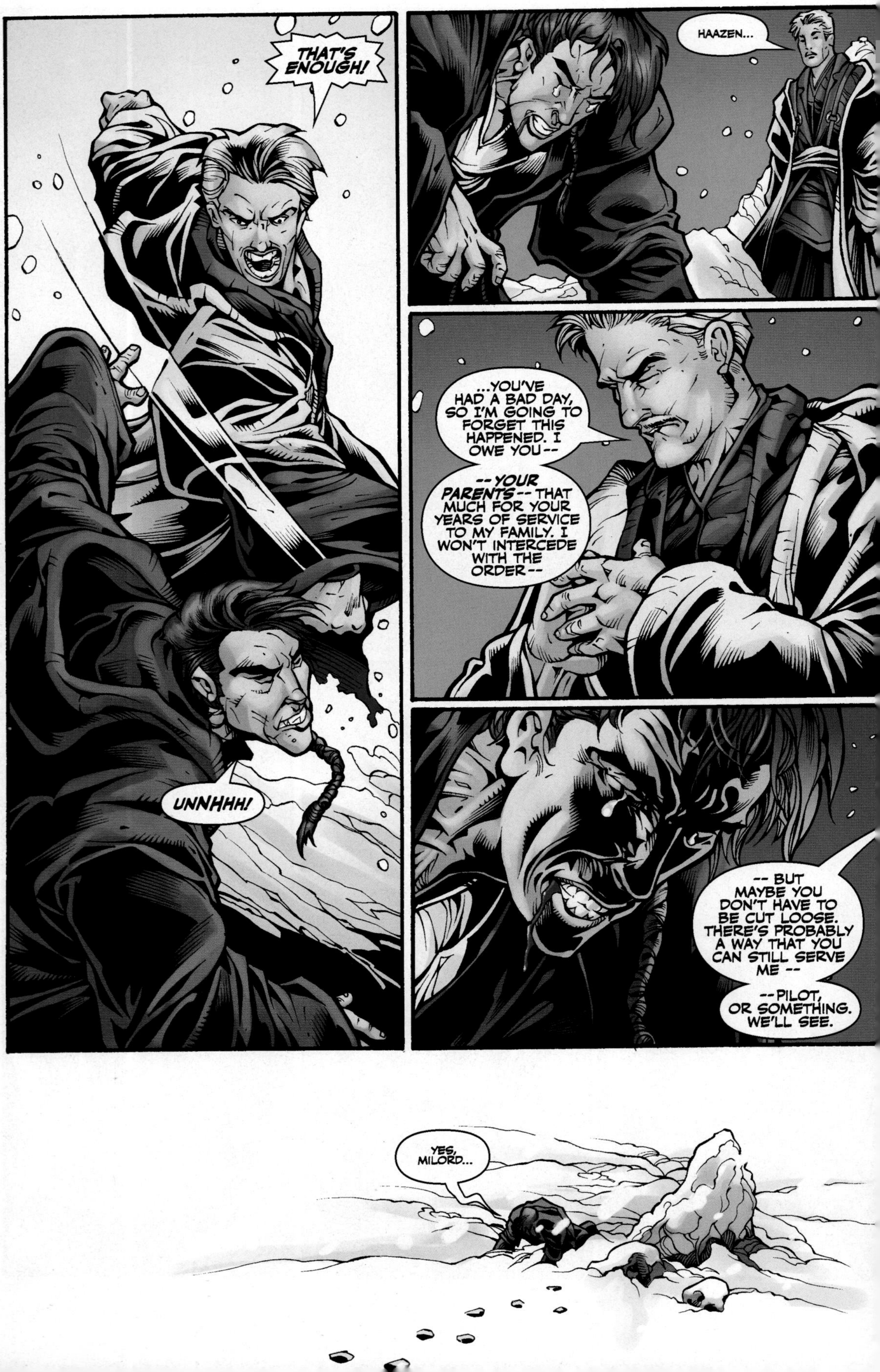
THAT'S ENOUGH!
UNNHHH!
HAAZEN...
...YOU'VE HAD A BAD DAY, SO I'M GOING TO FORGET THIS HAPPENED. I OWE YOU--
--YOUR PARENTS--THAT MUCH FOR YOUR YEARS OF SERVICE TO MY FAMILY. I WON'T INTERCEDE WITH THE ORDER--
-- BUT MAYBE YOU DON'T HAVE TO BE CUT LOOSE. THERE'S PROBABLY A WAY THAT YOU CAN STILL SERVE ME --
--PILOT, OR SOMETHING. WE'LL SEE.
YES, MILORD...

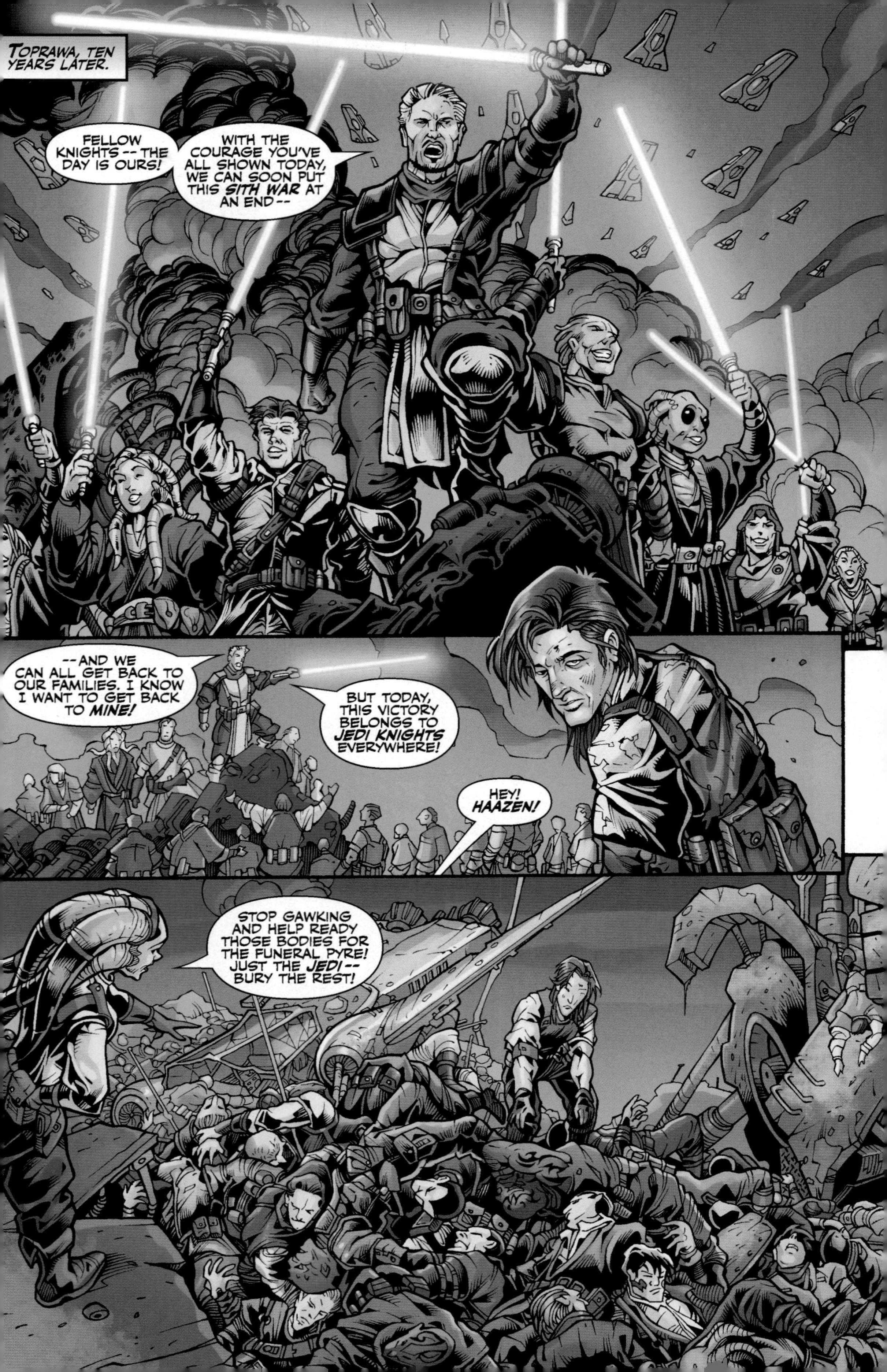
TOPRAWA, TEN YEARS LATER.
FELLOW KNIGHTS -- THE DAY IS OURS!
WITH THE COURAGE YOU'VE ALL SHOWN TODAY, WE CAN SOON PUT THIS SITH WAR AT AN END --
-- AND WE CAN ALL GET BACK TO OUR FAMILIES. I KNOW I WANT TO GET BACK TO MINE!
BUT TODAY, THIS VICTORY BELONGS TO JEDI KNIGHTS EVERYWHERE!
HEY! HAAZEN!
STOP GAWKING AND HELP READY THOSE BODIES FOR THE FUNERAL PYRE! JUST THE JEDI -- BURY THE REST!

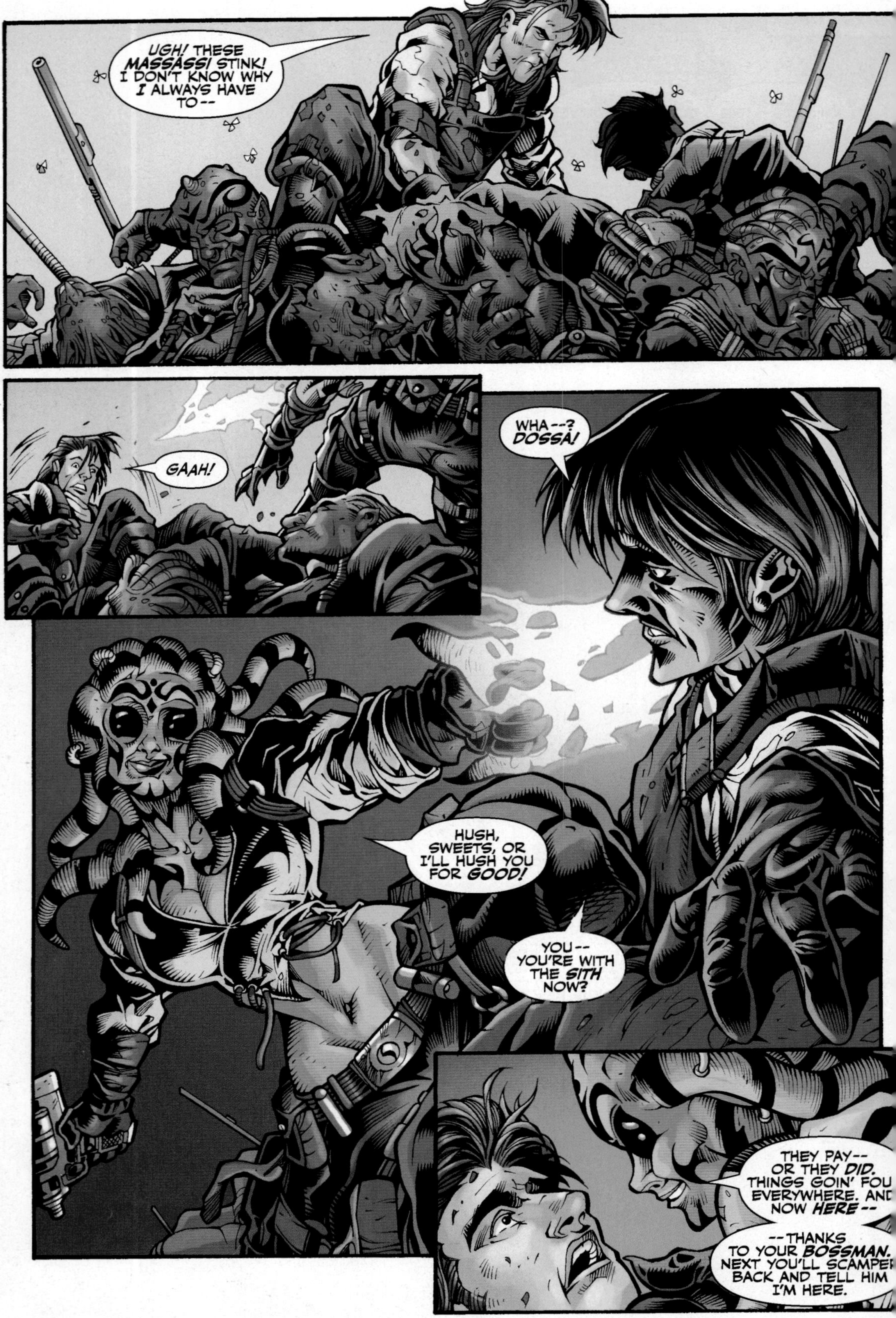
UGH! THESE MASSASSI STINK! I DON'T KNOW WHY I ALWAYS HAVE TO--
GAAH!
WHA--? DOSSA!
HUSH, SWEETS, OR I'LL HUSH YOU FOR GOOD!
YOU-- YOU'RE WITH THE SITH NOW?
THEY PAY-- OR THEY DID. THINGS GOIN' FOU EVERYWHERE. AND NOW HERE--
--THANKS TO YOUR BOSSMAN. NEXT YOU'LL SCAMPER BACK AND TELL HIM I'M HERE.

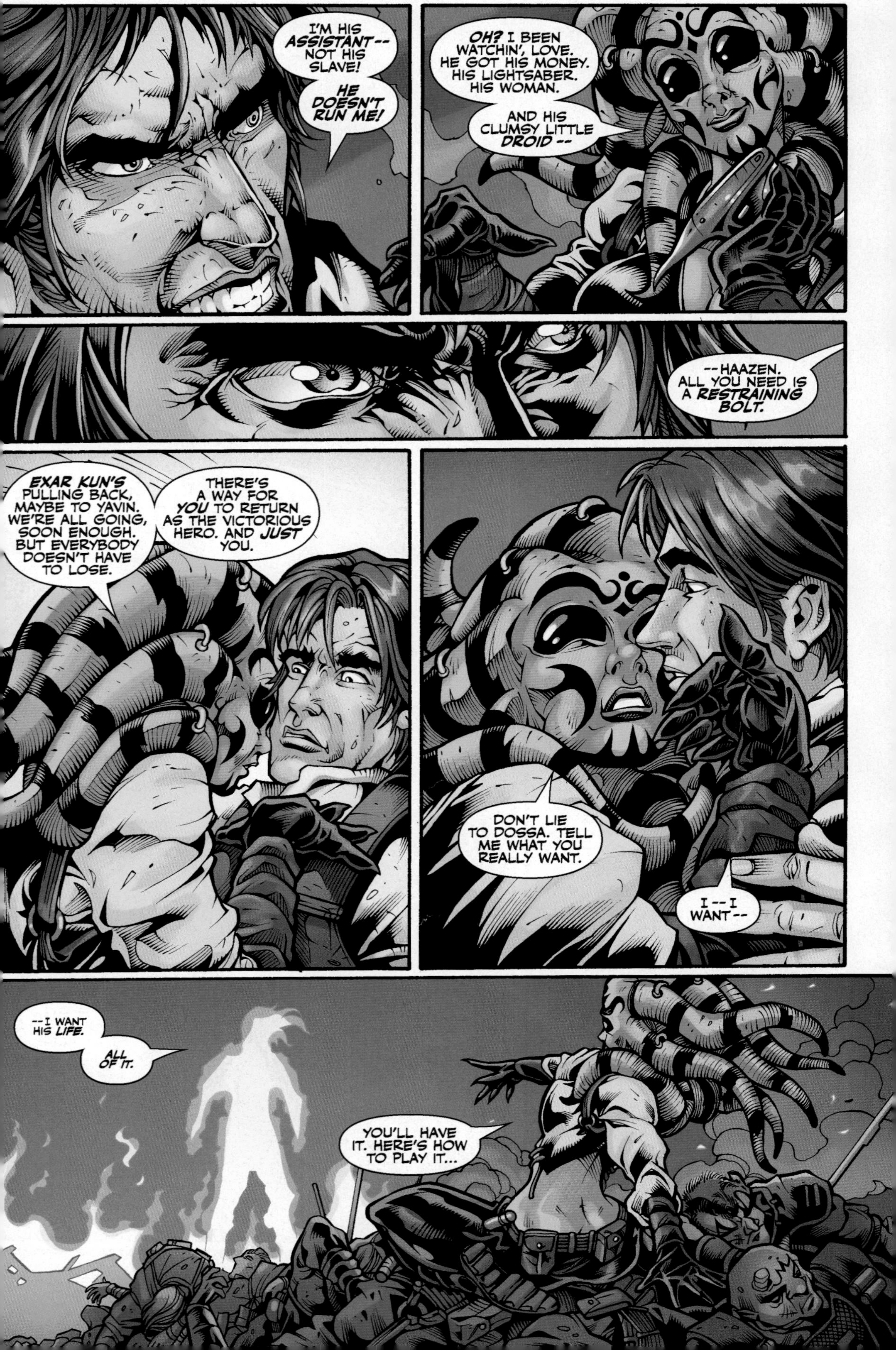
I'M HIS ASSISTANT-- NOT HIS SLAVE!
HE DOESN'T RUN ME!
OH? I BEEN WATCHIN', LOVE. HE GOT HIS MONEY. HIS LIGHTSABER. HIS WOMAN.
AND HIS CLUMSY LITTLE DROID --
--HAAZEN. ALL YOU NEED IS A RESTRAINING BOLT.
EXAR KUN'S PULLING BACK, MAYBE TO YAVIN. WE'RE ALL GOING, SOON ENOUGH. BUT EVERYBODY DOESN'T HAVE TO LOSE.
THERE'S A WAY FOR YOU TO RETURN AS THE VICTORIOUS HERO. AND JUST YOU.
DON'T LIE TO DOSSA. TELL ME WHAT YOU REALLY WANT.
I -- I WANT --
-- I WANT HIS LIFE.
ALL OF IT.
YOU'LL HAVE IT. HERE'S HOW TO PLAY IT...

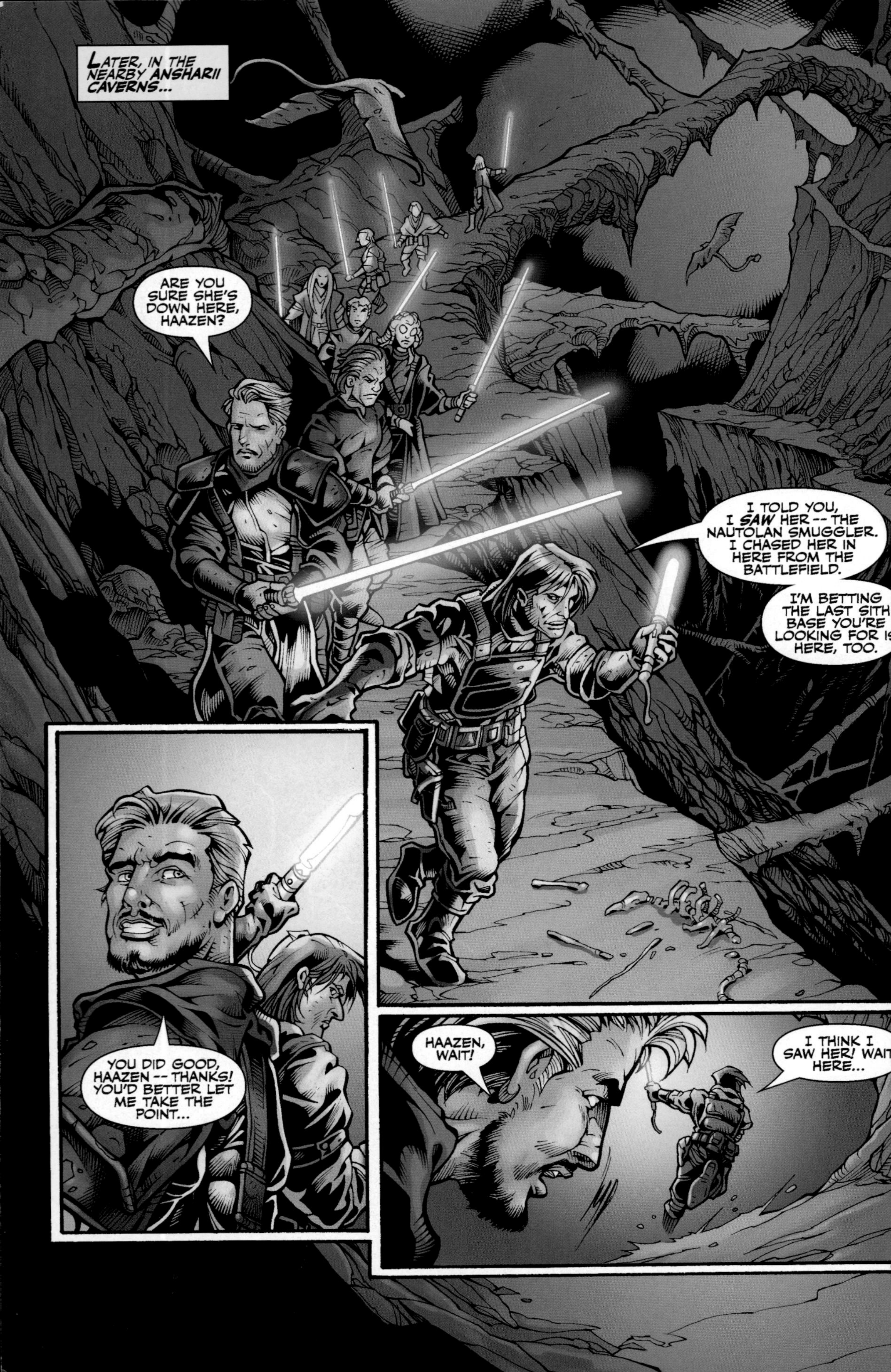
LATER, IN THE NEARBY ANSHARII CAVERNS...
ARE YOU SURE SHE'S DOWN HERE, HAAZEN?
I TOLD YOU, I *SAW* HER -- THE NAUTOLAN SMUGGLER. I CHASED HER IN HERE FROM THE BATTLEFIELD.
I'M BETTING THE LAST SITH BASE YOU'RE LOOKING FOR IS HERE, TOO.
YOU DID GOOD, HAAZEN -- THANKS! YOU'D BETTER LET ME TAKE THE POINT...
HAAZEN, WAIT!
I THINK I SAW HER! WAIT HERE...

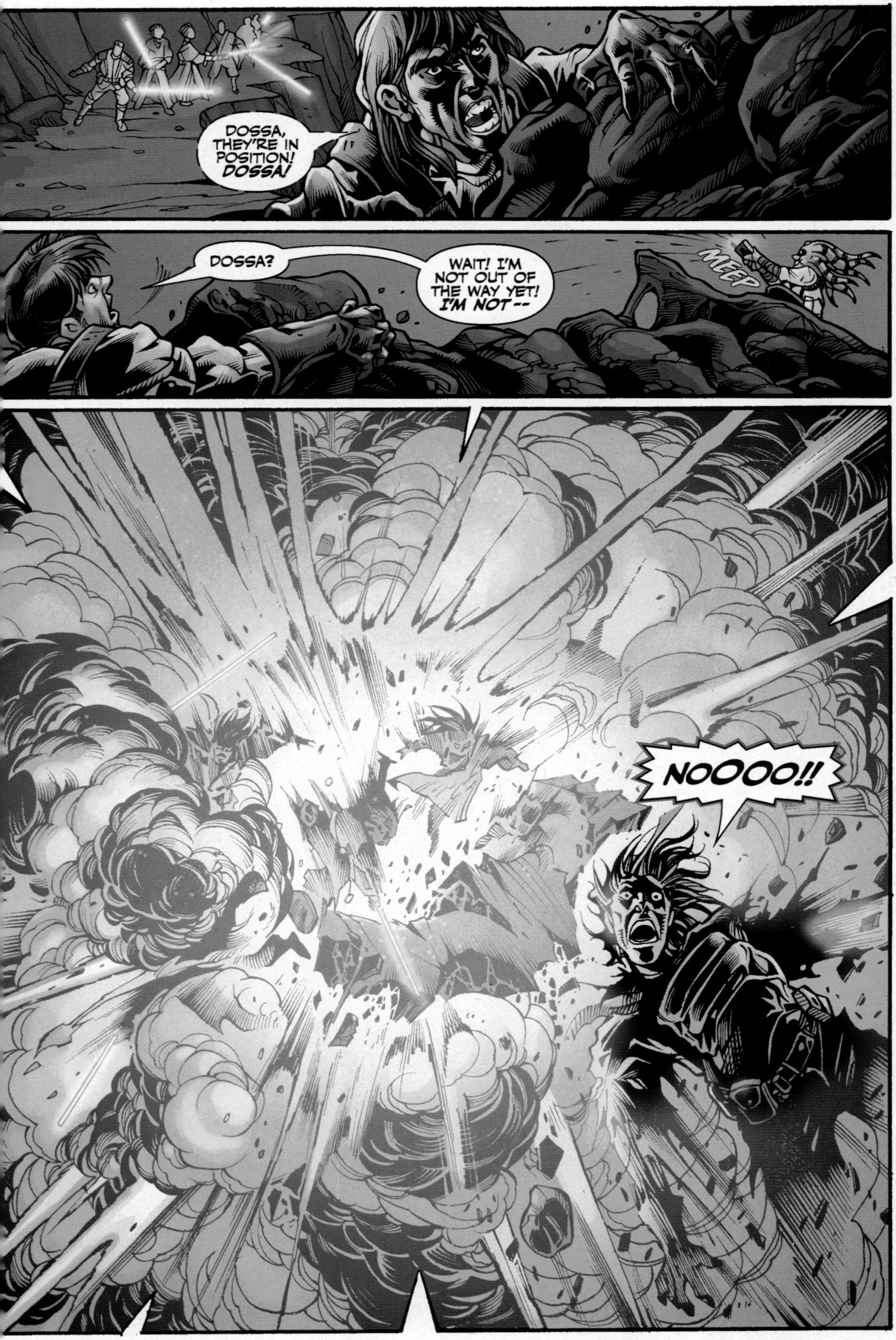
DOSSA, THEY'RE IN POSITION! DOSSA!
DOSSA?
WAIT! I'M NOT OUT OF THE WAY YET! I'M NOT --
MEEP
NOOOO!!

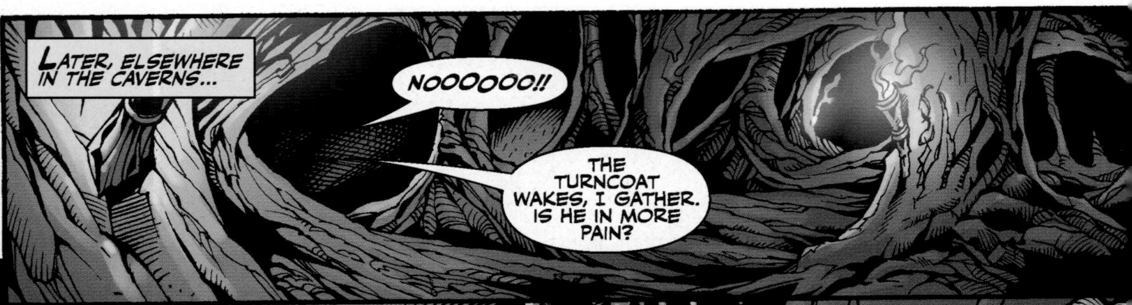
LATER, ELSEWHERE IN THE CAVERNS...
NOOOOOO!!
THE TURNCOAT WAKES, I GATHER. IS HE IN MORE PAIN?

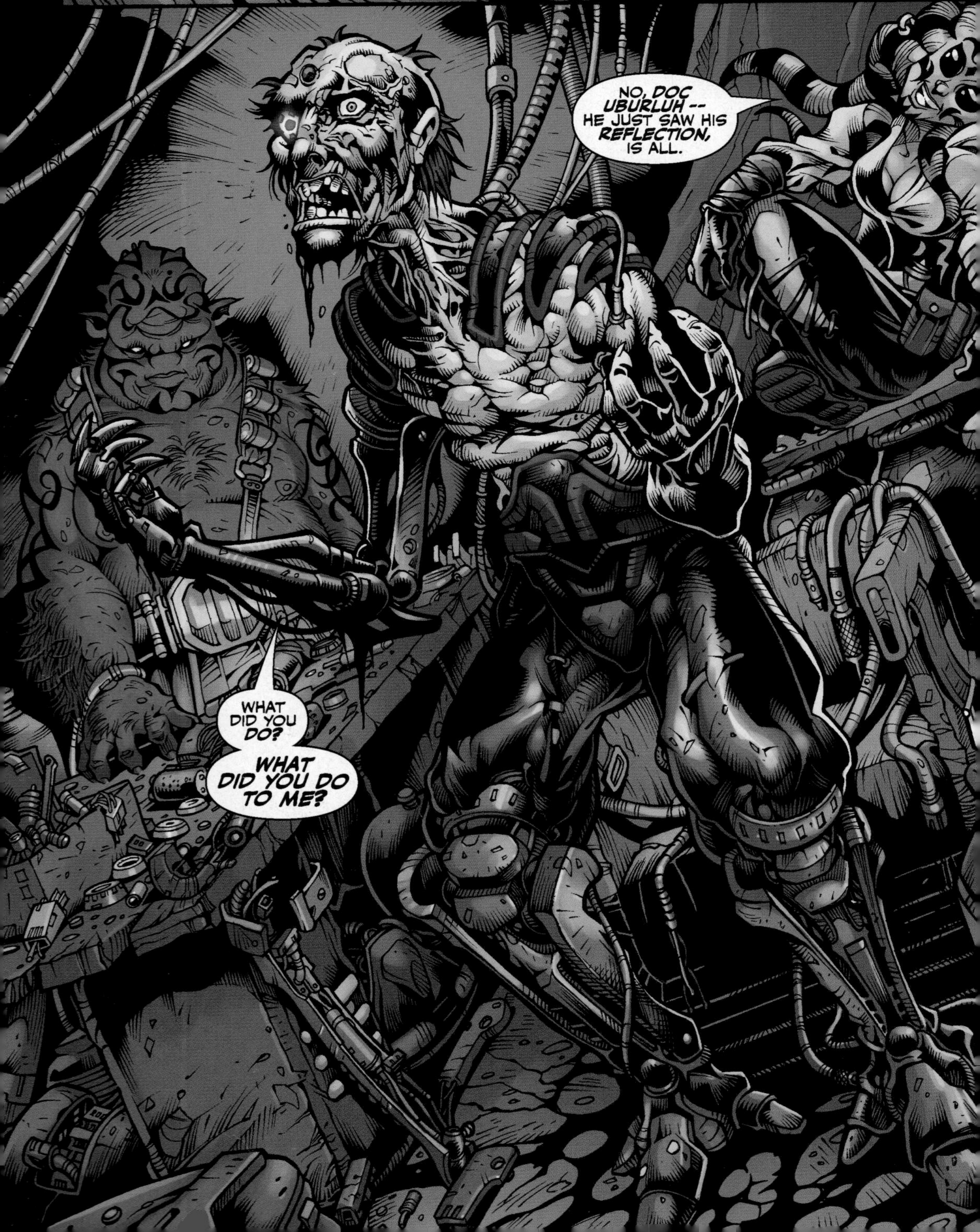
NO, DOC UBURLUH -- HE JUST SAW HIS REFLECTION, IS ALL.
WHAT DID YOU DO? WHAT DID YOU DO TO ME?

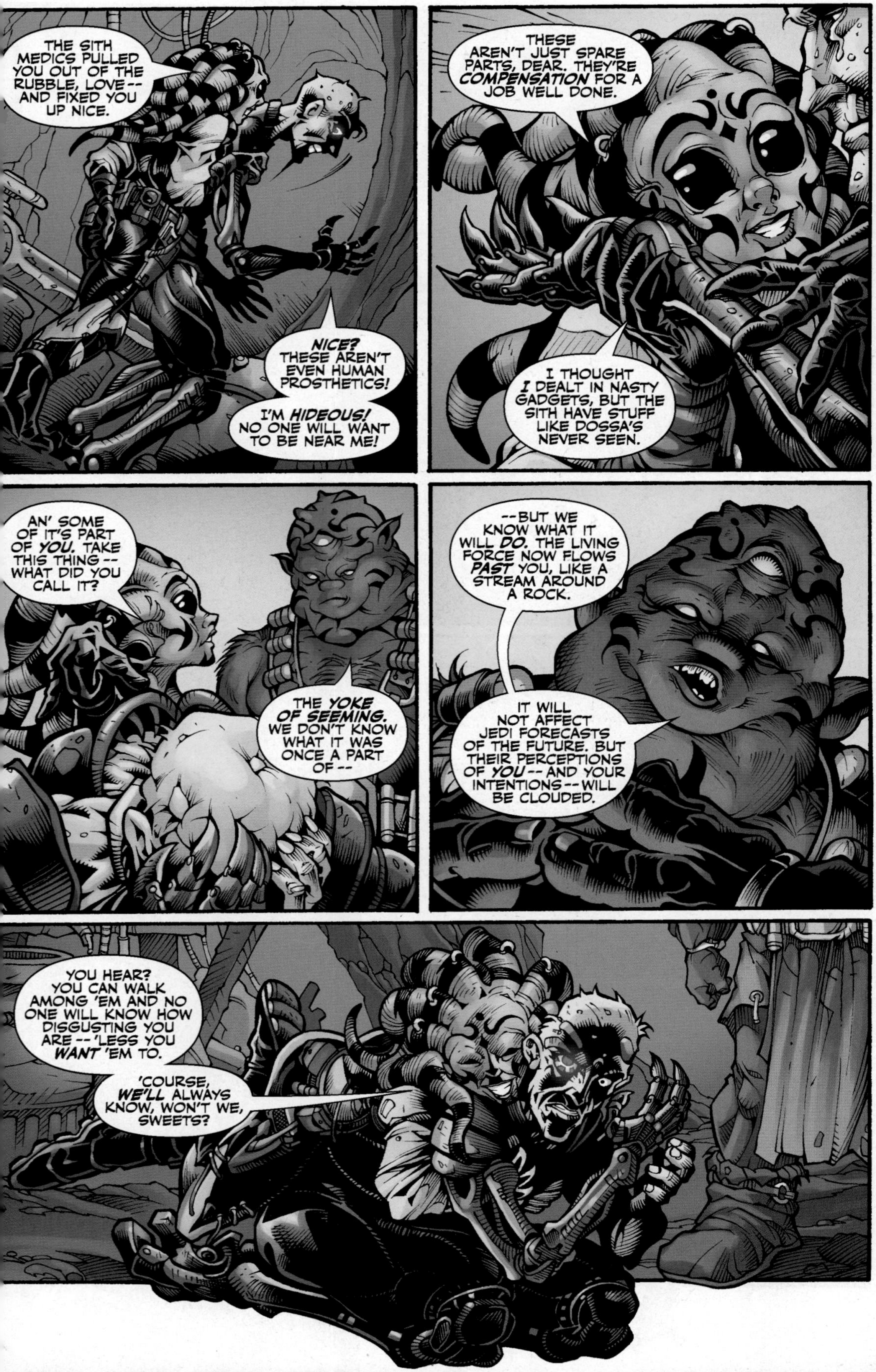

THE SITH MEDICS PULLED YOU OUT OF THE RUBBLE, LOVE-- AND FIXED YOU UP NICE.
NICE? THESE AREN'T EVEN HUMAN PROSTHETICS!
I'M *HIDEOUS!* NO ONE WILL WANT TO BE NEAR ME!
THESE AREN'T JUST SPARE PARTS, DEAR. THEY'RE *COMPENSATION* FOR A JOB WELL DONE.
I THOUGHT *I* DEALT IN NASTY GADGETS, BUT THE SITH HAVE STUFF LIKE DOSSA'S NEVER SEEN.
AN' SOME OF IT'S PART OF *YOU.* TAKE THIS THING-- WHAT DID YOU CALL IT?
THE *YOKE OF SEEMING.* WE DON'T KNOW WHAT IT WAS ONCE A PART OF--
--BUT WE KNOW WHAT IT WILL *DO.* THE LIVING FORCE NOW FLOWS *PAST* YOU, LIKE A STREAM AROUND A ROCK.
IT WILL NOT AFFECT JEDI FORECASTS OF THE FUTURE. BUT THEIR PERCEPTIONS OF *YOU*--AND YOUR INTENTIONS--WILL BE CLOUDED.
YOU HEAR? YOU CAN WALK AMONG 'EM AND NO ONE WILL KNOW HOW DISGUSTING YOU ARE--'LESS YOU *WANT* 'EM TO.
'COURSE, *WE'LL* ALWAYS KNOW, WON'T WE, SWEETS?

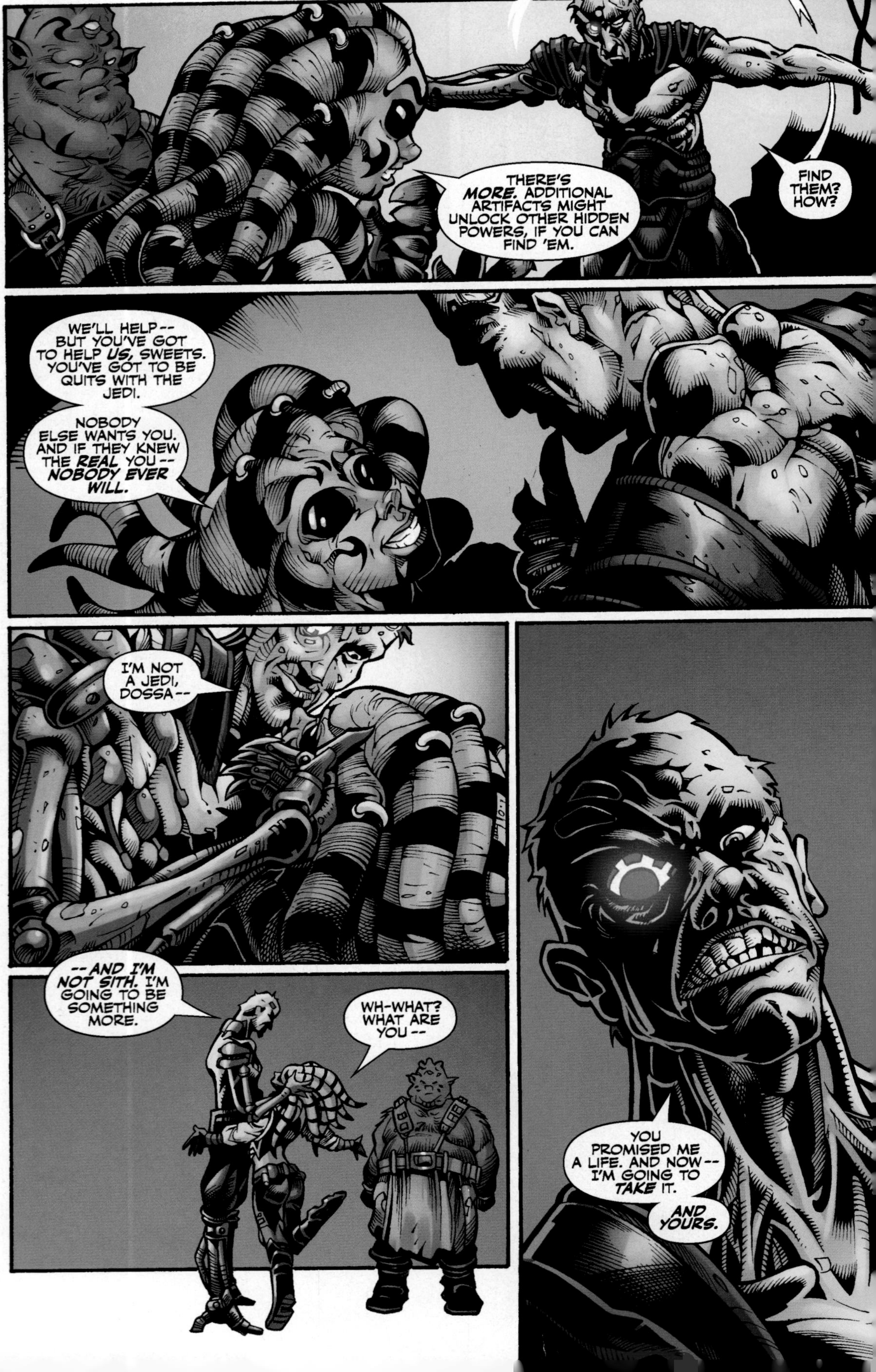
THERE'S MORE. ADDITIONAL ARTIFACTS MIGHT UNLOCK OTHER HIDDEN POWERS, IF YOU CAN FIND 'EM.
FIND THEM? HOW?
WE'LL HELP-- BUT YOU'VE GOT TO HELP US, SWEETS. YOU'VE GOT TO BE QUITS WITH THE JEDI.
NOBODY ELSE WANTS YOU. AND IF THEY KNEW THE REAL YOU-- NOBODY EVER WILL.
I'M NOT A JEDI, DOSSA--
--AND I'M NOT SITH. I'M GOING TO BE SOMETHING MORE.
WH-WHAT? WHAT ARE YOU--
YOU PROMISED ME A LIFE. AND NOW-- I'M GOING TO TAKE IT.
AND YOURS.

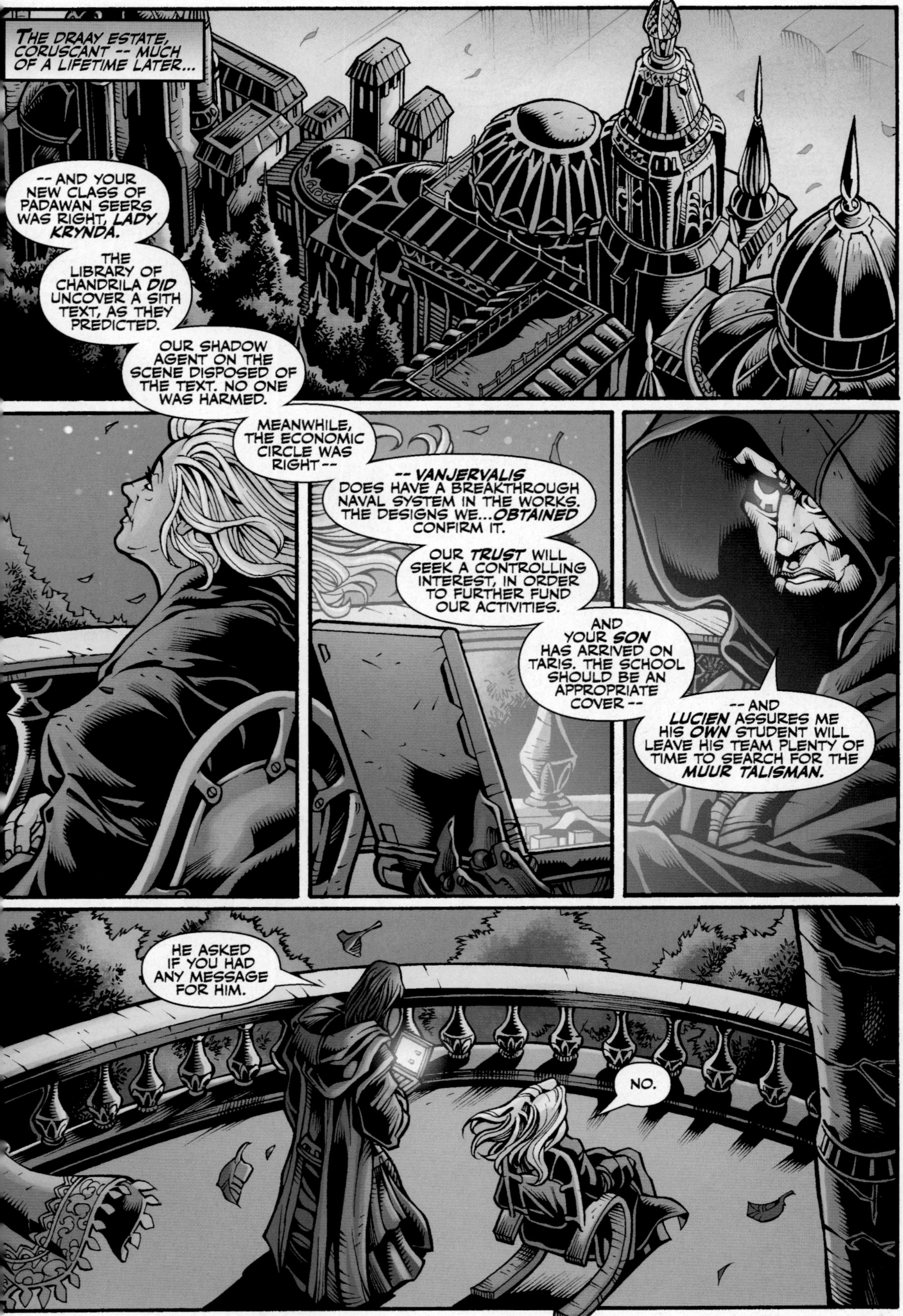

THE DRAAY ESTATE, CORUSCANT -- MUCH OF A LIFETIME LATER...
-- AND YOUR NEW CLASS OF PADAWAN SEERS WAS RIGHT, LADY KRYNDA.
THE LIBRARY OF CHANDRILA DID UNCOVER A SITH TEXT, AS THEY PREDICTED.
OUR SHADOW AGENT ON THE SCENE DISPOSED OF THE TEXT. NO ONE WAS HARMED.
MEANWHILE, THE ECONOMIC CIRCLE WAS RIGHT--
-- VANJERVALIS DOES HAVE A BREAKTHROUGH NAVAL SYSTEM IN THE WORKS. THE DESIGNS WE...OBTAINED CONFIRM IT.
OUR TRUST WILL SEEK A CONTROLLING INTEREST, IN ORDER TO FURTHER FUND OUR ACTIVITIES.
AND YOUR SON HAS ARRIVED ON TARIS. THE SCHOOL SHOULD BE AN APPROPRIATE COVER --
-- AND LUCIEN ASSURES ME HIS OWN STUDENT WILL LEAVE HIS TEAM PLENTY OF TIME TO SEARCH FOR THE MUUR TALISMAN.
HE ASKED IF YOU HAD ANY MESSAGE FOR HIM.
NO.

HAAZEN, I--

-- I APPRECIATE YOUR SERVICE.

I NEVER COULD HAVE -- I NEVER *WOULD* HAVE -- ORGANIZED THE COVENANT ON MY OWN. WE'VE ACCOMPLISHED SO MUCH.

WELL.

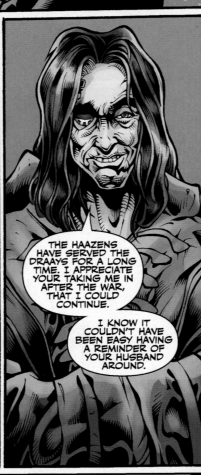

THE HAAZENS HAVE SERVED THE DRAAYS FOR A LONG TIME. I APPRECIATE YOUR TAKING ME IN AFTER THE WAR, THAT I COULD CONTINUE.

I KNOW IT COULDN'T HAVE BEEN EASY HAVING A REMINDER OF YOUR HUSBAND AROUND.

I -- I THINK ABOUT THAT TIME MORE AND MORE AS THE YEARS GO BY, MILADY. *BEFORE*, AT THE ACADEMY.

DO YOU EVER THINK ABOUT WHO I -- WHO *WE* WERE THEN?

YOU OVERSTEP YOURSELF, HAAZEN. WHO YOU WERE, WHAT YOU DID, WHAT YOU WANTED -- IS *IRRELEVANT*.

THAT PERSON IS DEAD, IF HE EVER LIVED. AND I -- I ONLY EVER THINK OF THE FUTURE.

YES, MILADY --

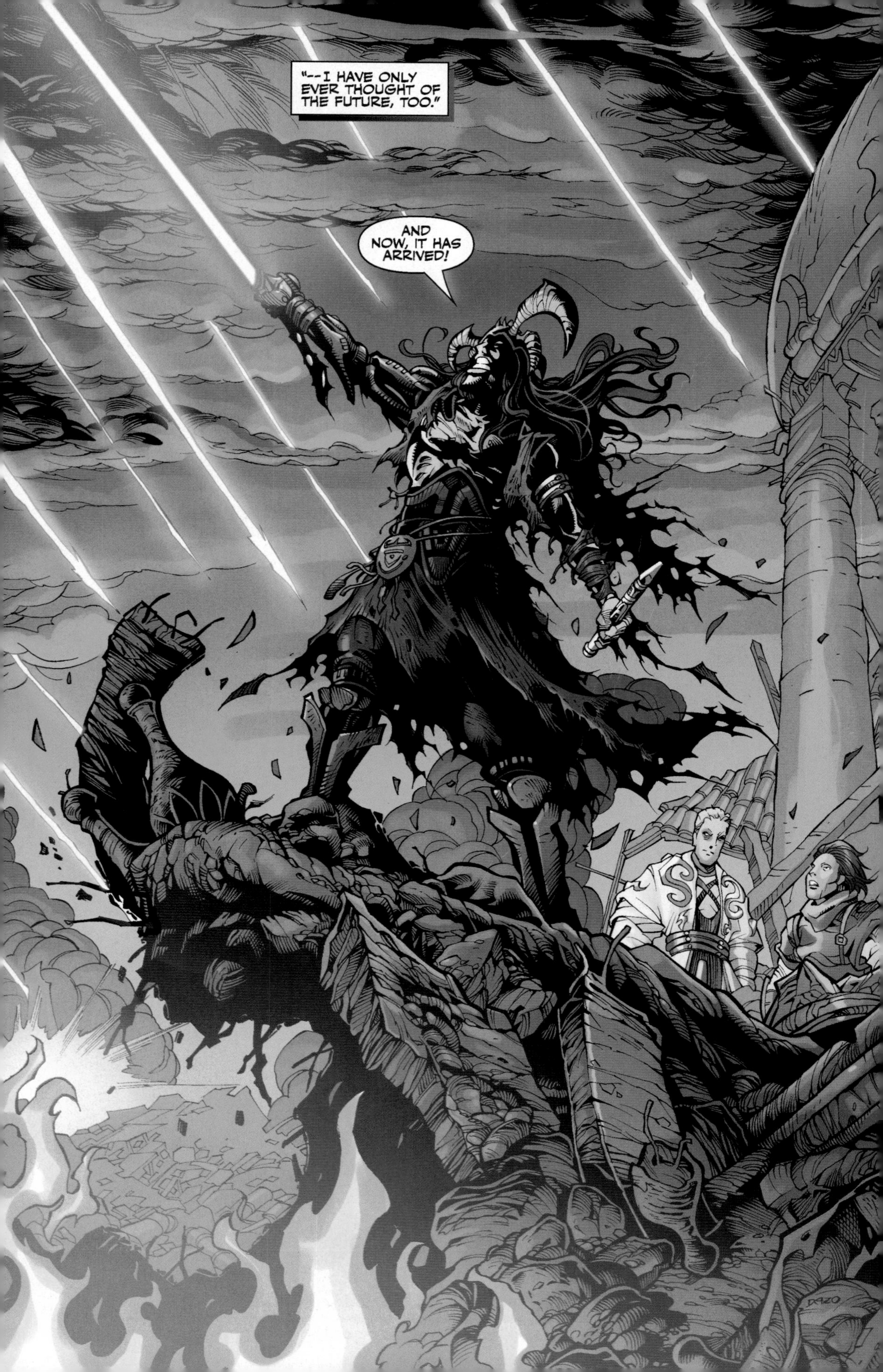
"--I HAVE ONLY EVER THOUGHT OF THE FUTURE, TOO."
AND NOW, IT HAS ARRIVED!

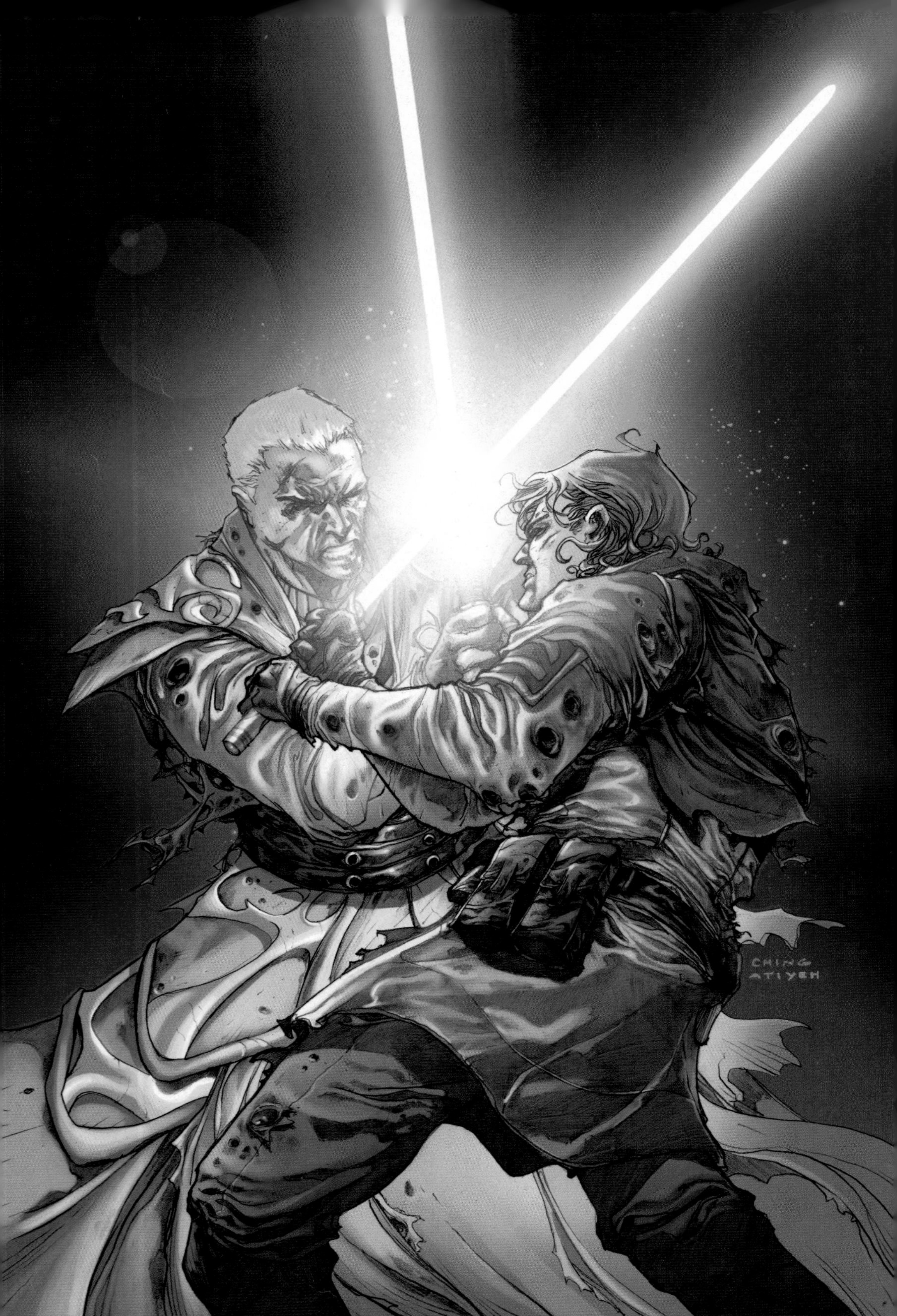
CHING
ATIYEH

***STAR WARS: KNIGHTS OF THE OLD REPUBLIC* #34 — "VINDICATION, PART 3"**

WRITER: JOHN JACKSON MILLER • ARTIST: BRIAN CHING • COLORIST: MICHAEL ATIYEH • LETTERER: MICHAEL HEISLER
ASSISTANT EDITOR: FREDDYE LINS • EDITOR: DAVE MARSHALL • COVER ARTISTS: BRIAN CHING & MICHAEL ATIYEH

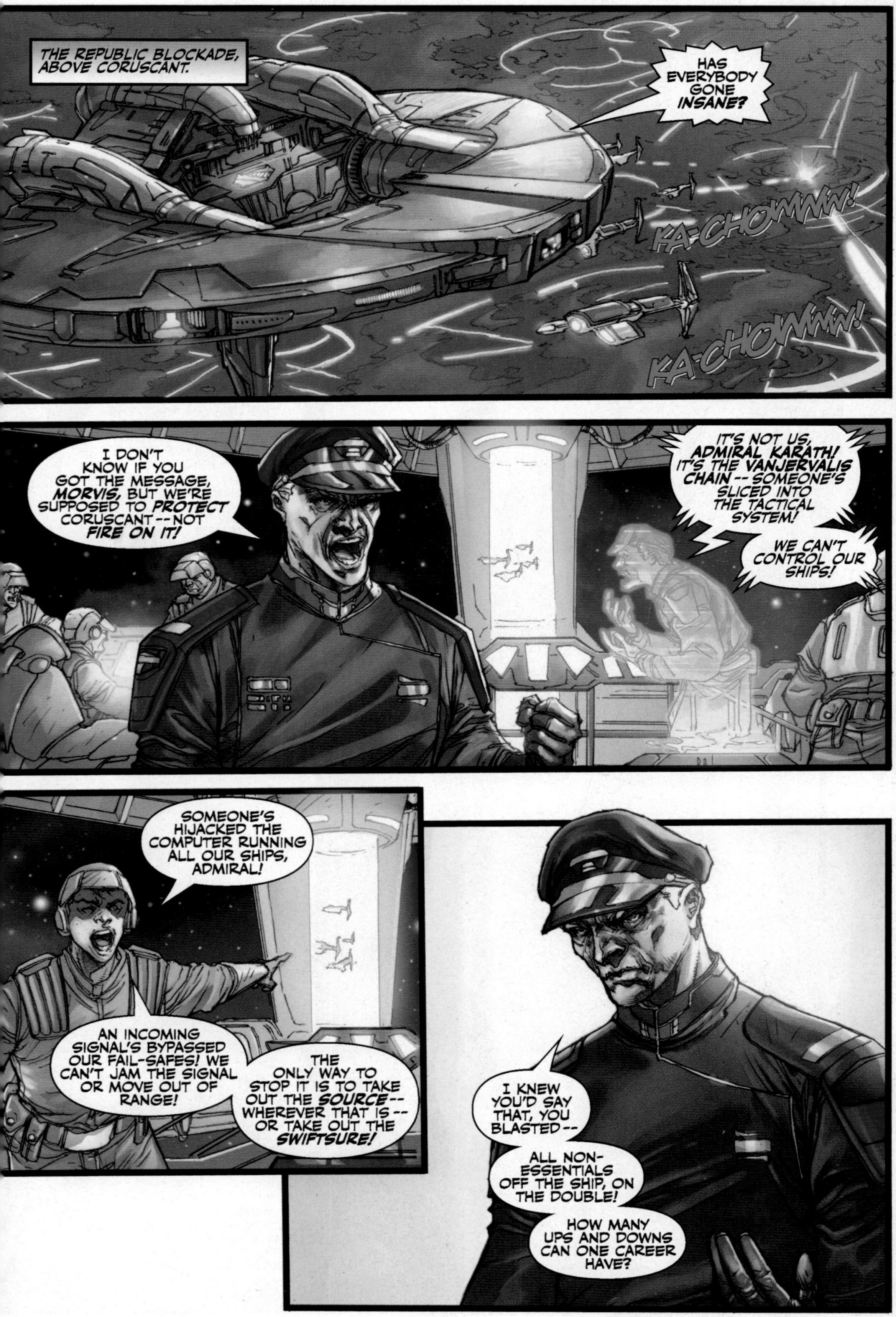
THE REPUBLIC BLOCKADE, ABOVE CORUSCANT.
HAS EVERYBODY GONE INSANE?
KA-CHOWWW!
KA-CHOWWW!
I DON'T KNOW IF YOU GOT THE MESSAGE, MORVIS, BUT WE'RE SUPPOSED TO PROTECT CORUSCANT--NOT FIRE ON IT!
IT'S NOT US, ADMIRAL KARATH! IT'S THE VANJERVALIS CHAIN--SOMEONE'S SLICED INTO THE TACTICAL SYSTEM!
WE CAN'T CONTROL OUR SHIPS!
SOMEONE'S HIJACKED THE COMPUTER RUNNING ALL OUR SHIPS, ADMIRAL!
AN INCOMING SIGNAL'S BYPASSED OUR FAIL-SAFES! WE CAN'T JAM THE SIGNAL OR MOVE OUT OF RANGE!
THE ONLY WAY TO STOP IT IS TO TAKE OUT THE SOURCE--WHEREVER THAT IS--OR TAKE OUT THE SWIFTSURE!
I KNEW YOU'D SAY THAT, YOU BLASTED--
ALL NON-ESSENTIALS OFF THE SHIP, ON THE DOUBLE!
HOW MANY UPS AND DOWNS CAN ONE CAREER HAVE?

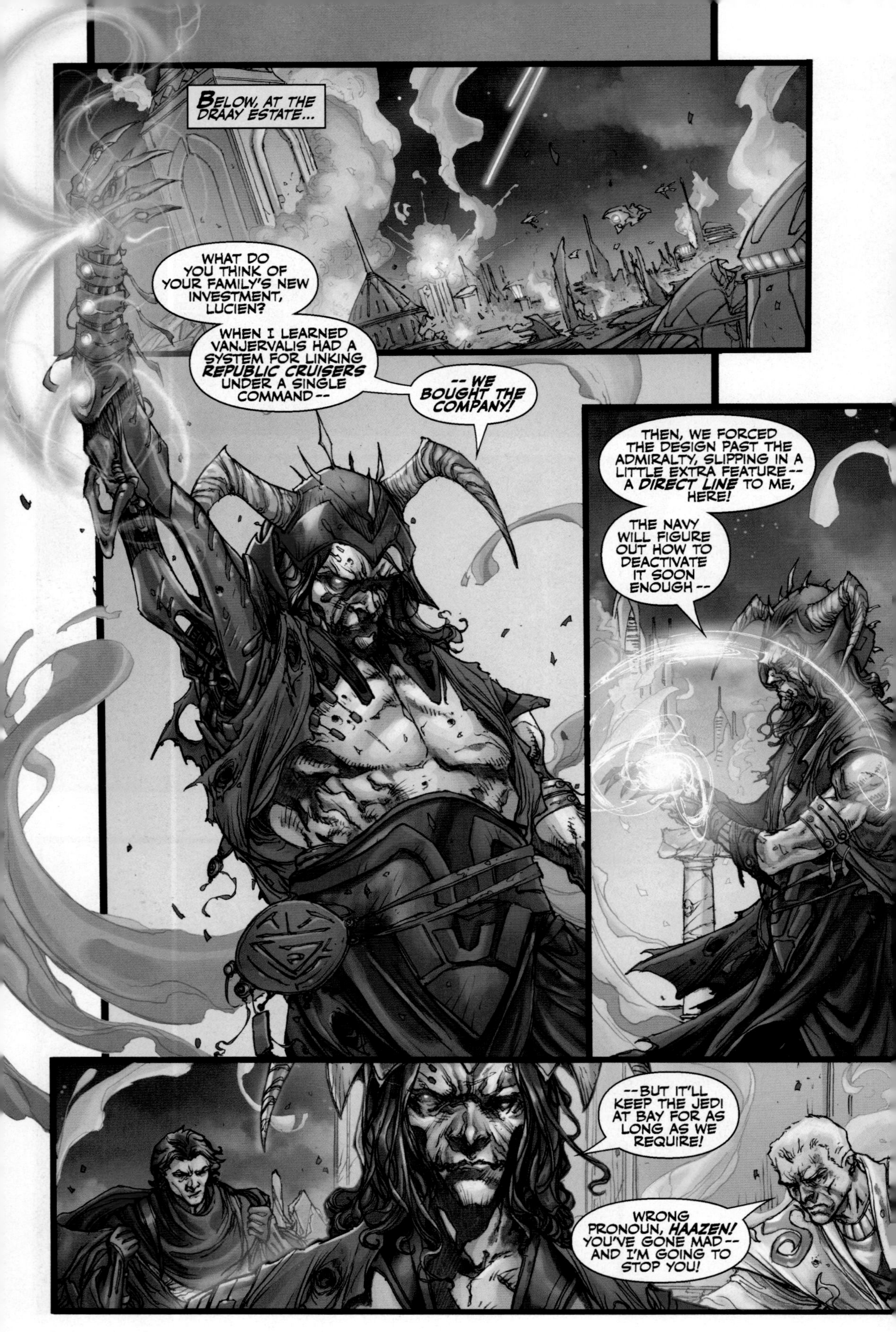
BELOW, AT THE DRAAY ESTATE...
WHAT DO YOU THINK OF YOUR FAMILY'S NEW INVESTMENT, LUCIEN?
WHEN I LEARNED VANJERVALIS HAD A SYSTEM FOR LINKING REPUBLIC CRUISERS UNDER A SINGLE COMMAND--
-- WE BOUGHT THE COMPANY!
THEN, WE FORCED THE DESIGN PAST THE ADMIRALTY, SLIPPING IN A LITTLE EXTRA FEATURE-- A DIRECT LINE TO ME, HERE!
THE NAVY WILL FIGURE OUT HOW TO DEACTIVATE IT SOON ENOUGH--
--BUT IT'LL KEEP THE JEDI AT BAY FOR AS LONG AS WE REQUIRE!
WRONG PRONOUN, HAAZEN! YOU'VE GONE MAD-- AND I'M GOING TO STOP YOU!

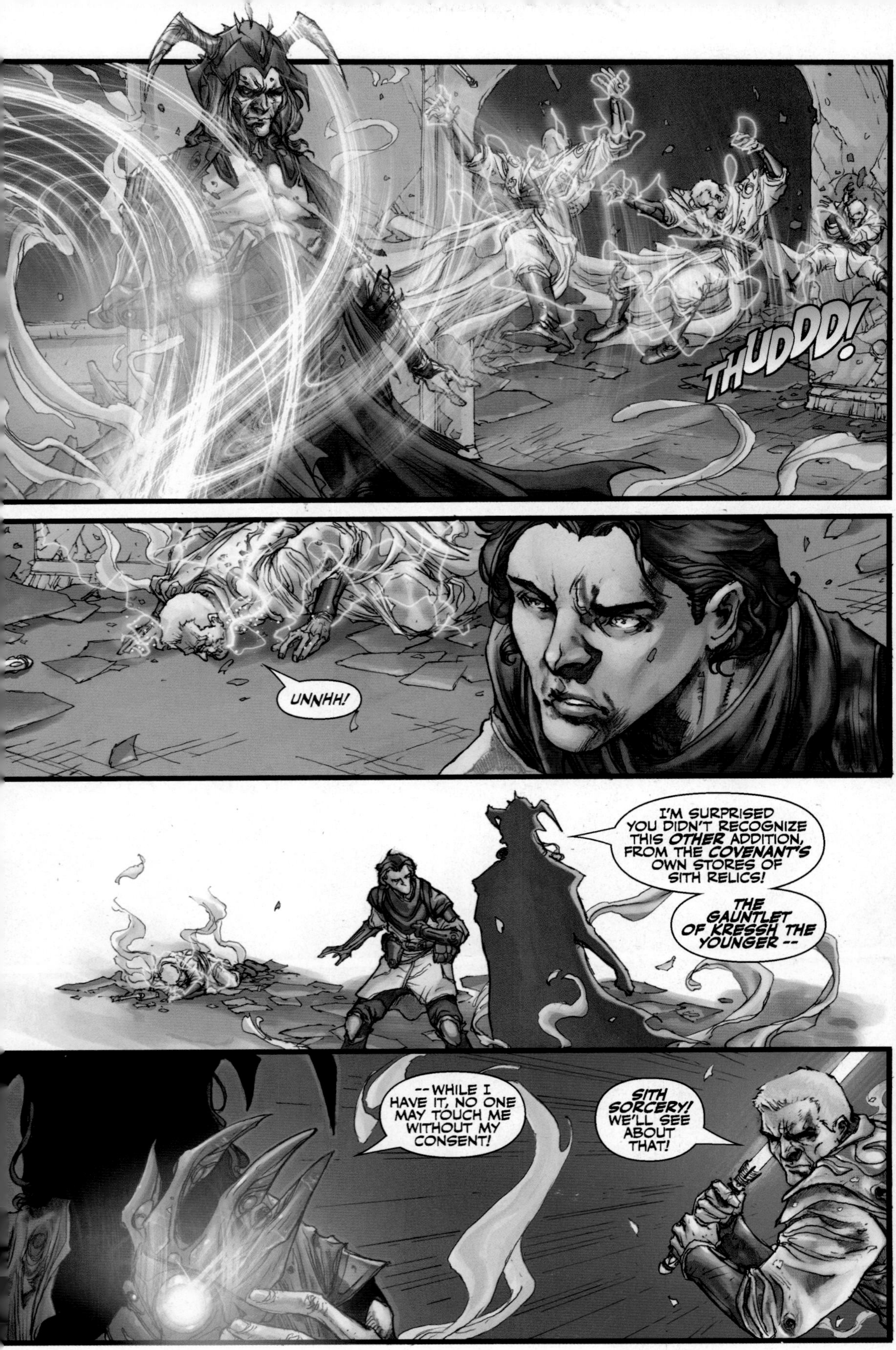
THUDDD!
UNNHH!
I'M SURPRISED YOU DIDN'T RECOGNIZE THIS OTHER ADDITION, FROM THE COVENANT'S OWN STORES OF SITH RELICS!
THE GAUNTLET OF KRESSH THE YOUNGER --
--WHILE I HAVE IT, NO ONE MAY TOUCH ME WITHOUT MY CONSENT!
SITH SORCERY! WE'LL SEE ABOUT THAT!

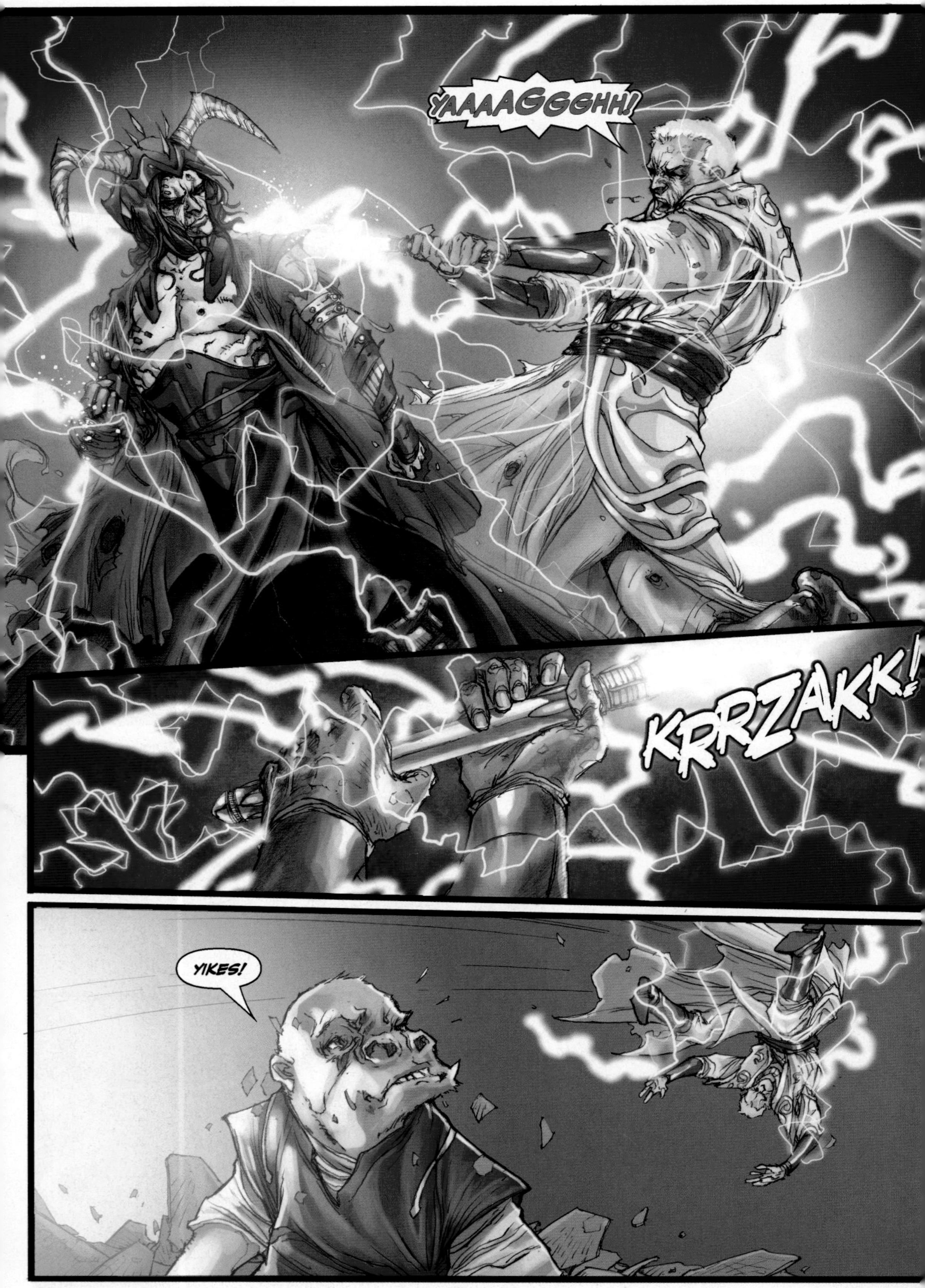
YAAAAGGGHH!
KRRZAKK!
YIKES!

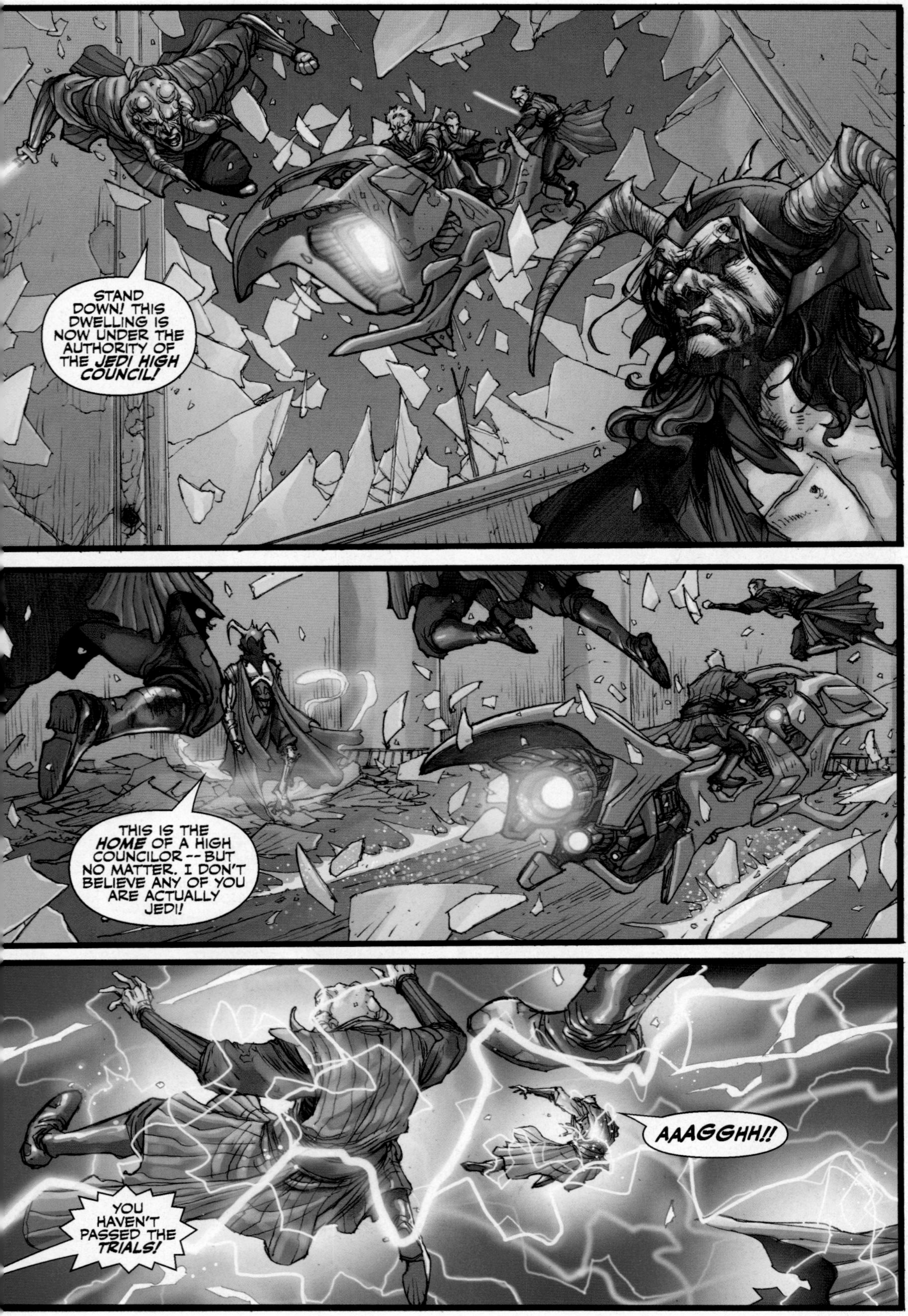
STAND DOWN! THIS DWELLING IS NOW UNDER THE AUTHORITY OF THE JEDI HIGH COUNCIL!
THIS IS THE HOME OF A HIGH COUNCILOR -- BUT NO MATTER. I DON'T BELIEVE ANY OF YOU ARE ACTUALLY JEDI!
AAAGGHH!!
YOU HAVEN'T PASSED THE TRIALS!

WHY BOTHER WAKING UP IF THE NIGHTMARE'S STILL GOING?

LUCIEN! ARE YOU--

TAKE YOUR BLASTED HANDS OFF ME, ZAYNE!

HAAZEN TOUCHED YOU EARLIER WHEN YOU HAD YOUR LIGHTSABER! WHY DIDN'T YOU KILL HIM *THEN?*

WHAT? I DIDN'T KNOW WHO HE *WAS!*

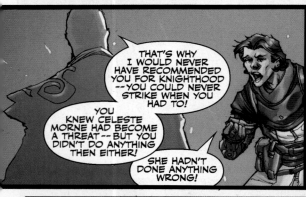

THAT'S WHY I WOULD NEVER HAVE RECOMMENDED YOU FOR KNIGHTHOOD --YOU COULD NEVER STRIKE WHEN YOU HAD TO!

YOU KNEW CELESTE MORNE HAD BECOME A THREAT -- BUT YOU DIDN'T DO ANYTHING THEN EITHER!

SHE HADN'T DONE ANYTHING WRONG!

THAT DOESN'T MATTER -- THE *POTENTIAL* DANGER WAS ENOUGH! YOU HAVE TO BE ABLE TO STRIKE EVEN AN INNOCENT --

WHAT, LIKE *YOU* DID?

LOOK HOW THAT WORKED OUT!

GENTLEMEN, RELAX. WE'RE ALL FRIENDS HERE -- PART OF THE SAME TEAM. INDEED, THE SAME *FUTURE.*

"ONE FOR THE DARKNESS, ONE FOR THE LIGHT. ONE FROM THE DARKNESS STANDS IN THE LIGHT--

--WHILE ONE FROM THE LIGHT STANDS IN THE DARKNESS. THE LAST ONE STANDS APART FROM ALL."

IT IS KRYNDA'S PROPHECY OF THE FIVE --

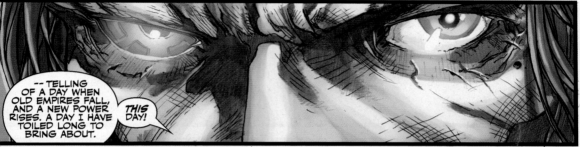

-- TELLING OF A DAY WHEN OLD EMPIRES FALL, AND A NEW POWER RISES. A DAY I HAVE TOILED LONG TO BRING ABOUT.

THIS DAY!

I ONCE THOUGHT THE FIVE MASTERS OF YOUR CIRCLE MIGHT SUIT THOSE ROLES, LUCIEN, BUT THAT CHANGED --

-- AS I PERCEIVED THE ROLE I WANTED FOR MYSELF. AND SO NOW, WE HAVE THE CAST RIGHT HERE.

Q'ANILIA OF THE LIGHT STANDS IN BLIND DARKNESS -- OUR LITTLE CRIMINAL, MASTER GRYPH, HAS CHOSEN THE LIGHT.

I HAD THOUGHT ZAYNE WOULD BE OUR ONE FOR THE DARKNESS -- BUT IT SEEMS HE IS OUR ONE FOR THE LIGHT.

NO MATTER -- THERE IS ANOTHER FOR THE DARKNESS.

YES! YOU!

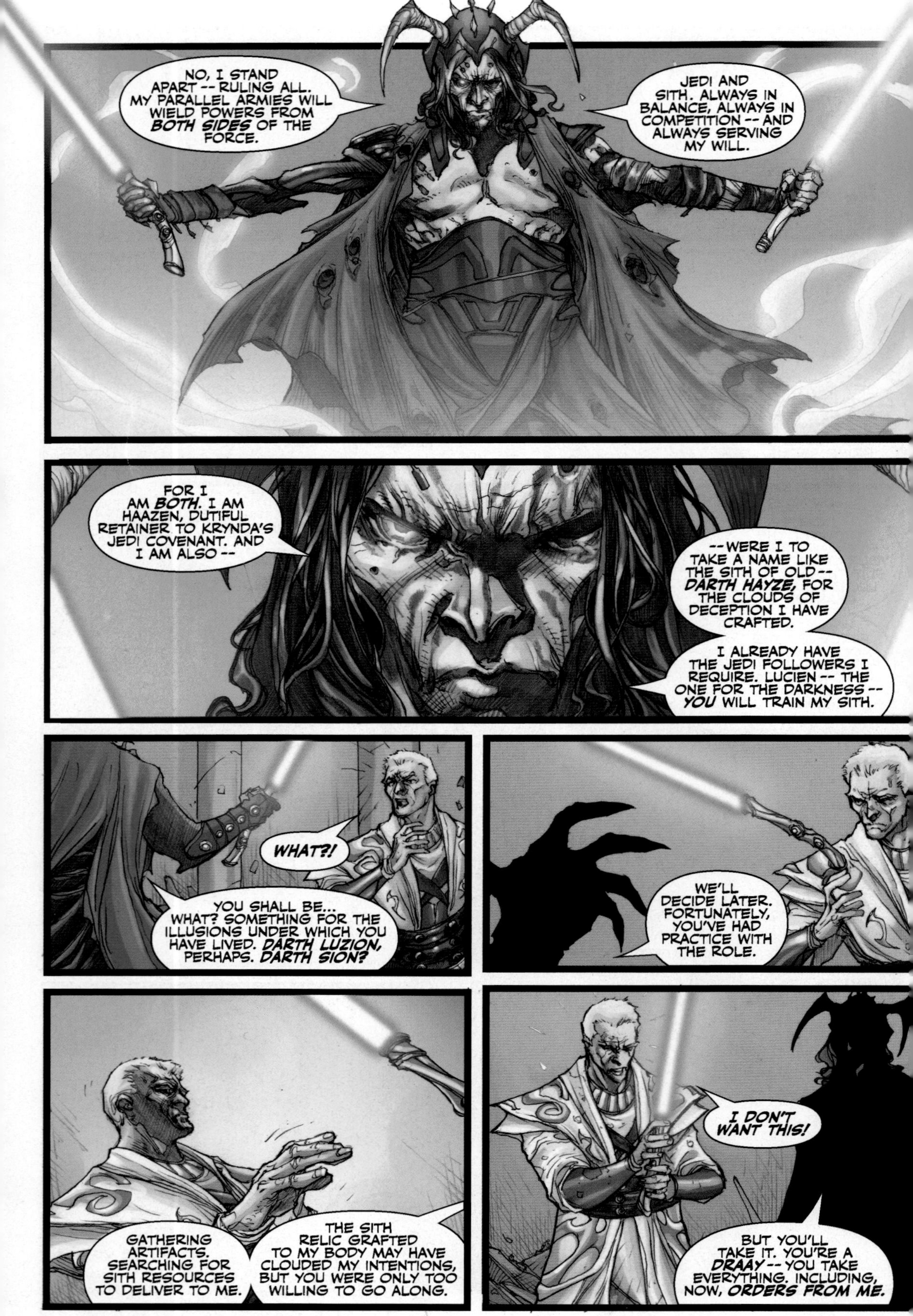
NO, I STAND APART -- RULING ALL. MY PARALLEL ARMIES WILL WIELD POWERS FROM BOTH SIDES OF THE FORCE.
JEDI AND SITH. ALWAYS IN BALANCE, ALWAYS IN COMPETITION -- AND ALWAYS SERVING MY WILL.
FOR I AM BOTH. I AM HAAZEN, DUTIFUL RETAINER TO KRYNDA'S JEDI COVENANT. AND I AM ALSO --
-- WERE I TO TAKE A NAME LIKE THE SITH OF OLD -- DARTH HAYZE, FOR THE CLOUDS OF DECEPTION I HAVE CRAFTED.
I ALREADY HAVE THE JEDI FOLLOWERS I REQUIRE. LUCIEN -- THE ONE FOR THE DARKNESS -- YOU WILL TRAIN MY SITH.
WHAT?!
YOU SHALL BE... WHAT? SOMETHING FOR THE ILLUSIONS UNDER WHICH YOU HAVE LIVED. DARTH LUZION, PERHAPS. DARTH SION?
WE'LL DECIDE LATER. FORTUNATELY, YOU'VE HAD PRACTICE WITH THE ROLE.
GATHERING ARTIFACTS. SEARCHING FOR SITH RESOURCES TO DELIVER TO ME.
THE SITH RELIC GRAFTED TO MY BODY MAY HAVE CLOUDED MY INTENTIONS, BUT YOU WERE ONLY TOO WILLING TO GO ALONG.
I DON'T WANT THIS!
BUT YOU'LL TAKE IT. YOU'RE A DRAAY -- YOU TAKE EVERYTHING. INCLUDING, NOW, ORDERS FROM ME.

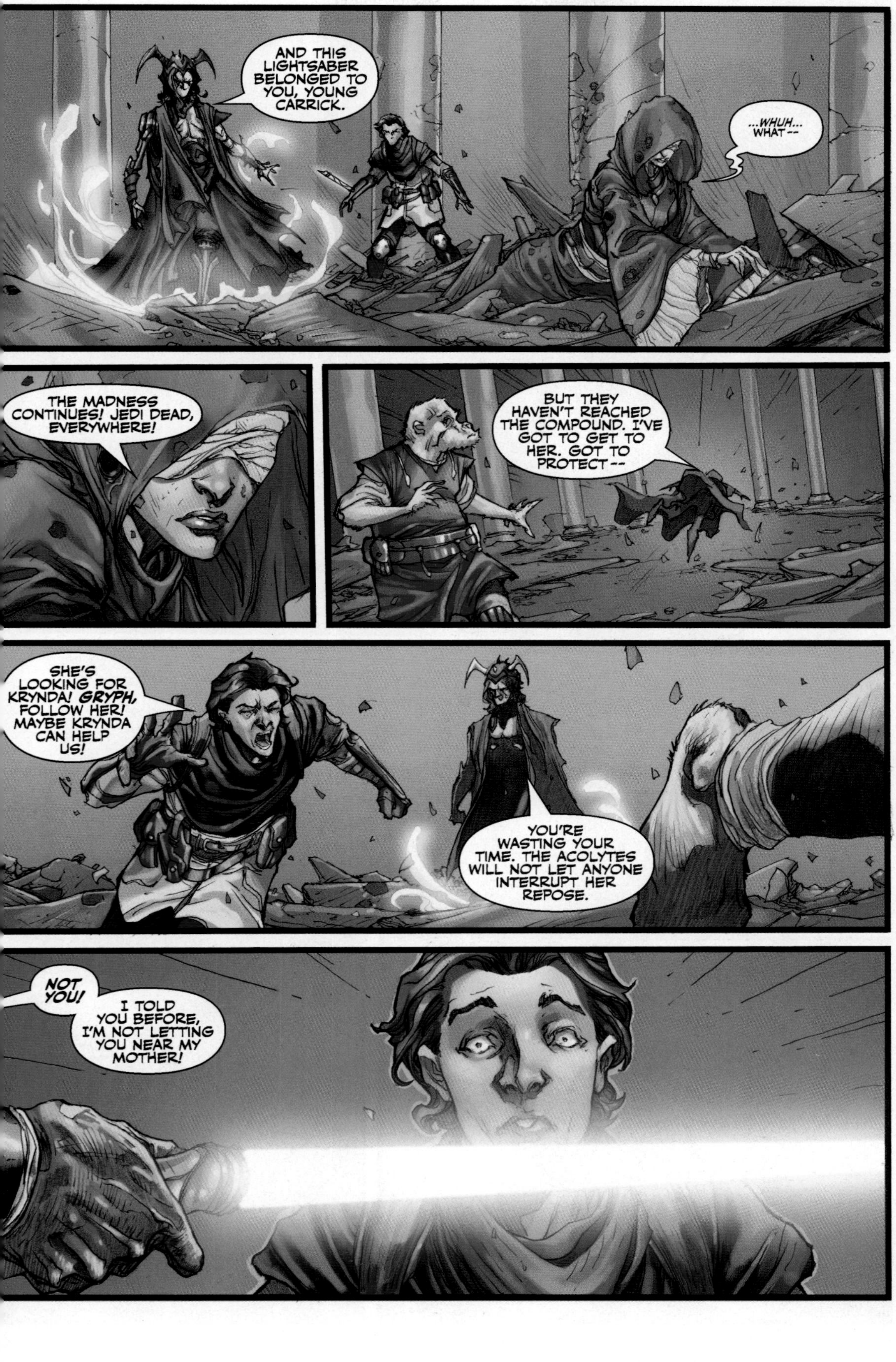
AND THIS LIGHTSABER BELONGED TO YOU, YOUNG CARRICK.
...WHUH... WHAT--
THE MADNESS CONTINUES! JEDI DEAD, EVERYWHERE!
BUT THEY HAVEN'T REACHED THE COMPOUND. I'VE GOT TO GET TO HER. GOT TO PROTECT--
SHE'S LOOKING FOR KRYNDA! GRYPH, FOLLOW HER! MAYBE KRYNDA CAN HELP US!
YOU'RE WASTING YOUR TIME. THE ACOLYTES WILL NOT LET ANYONE INTERRUPT HER REPOSE.
NOT YOU!
I TOLD YOU BEFORE, I'M NOT LETTING YOU NEAR MY MOTHER!

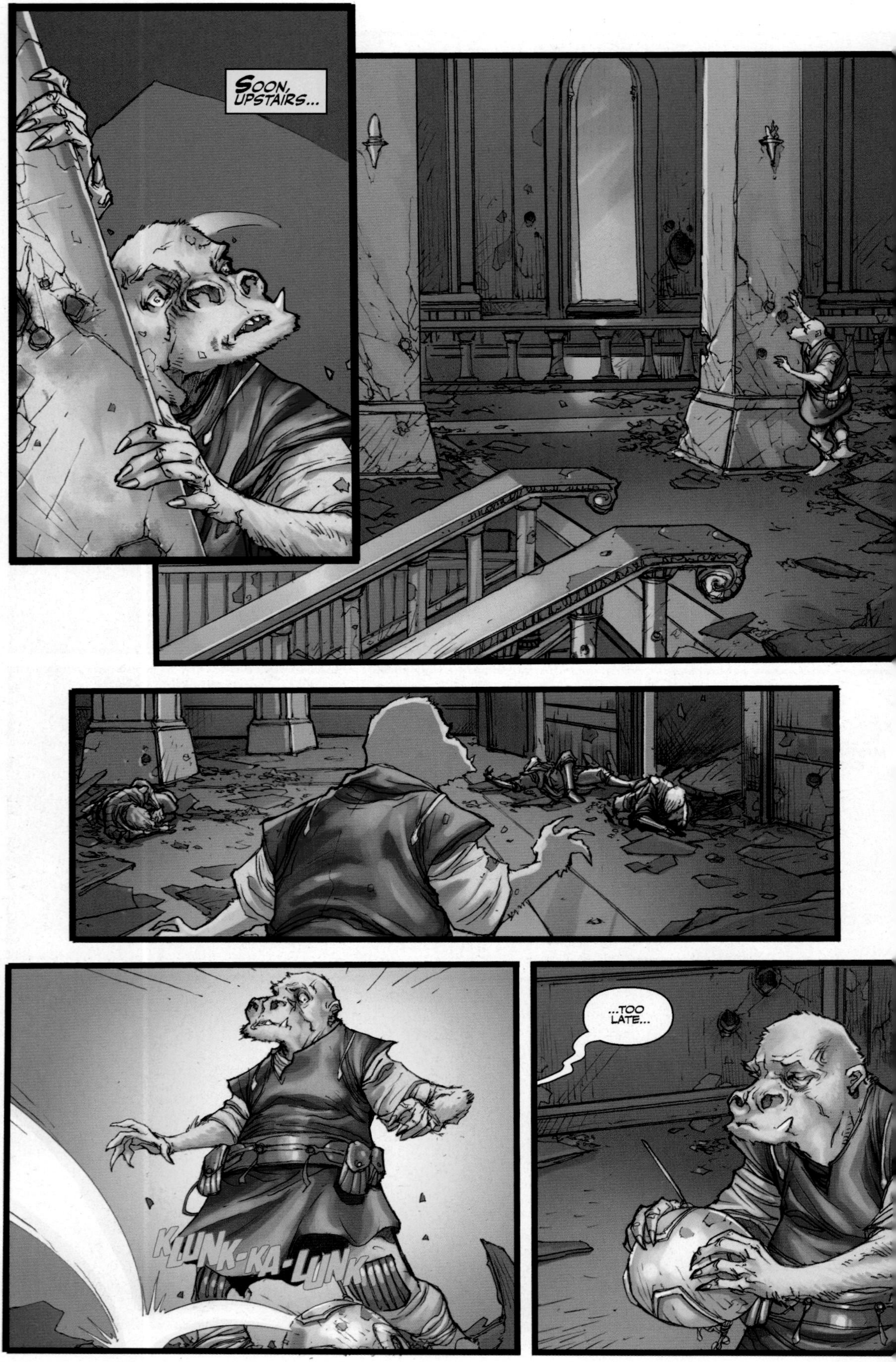
Soon, upstairs...
KLUNK-KA-LUNK
...too late...

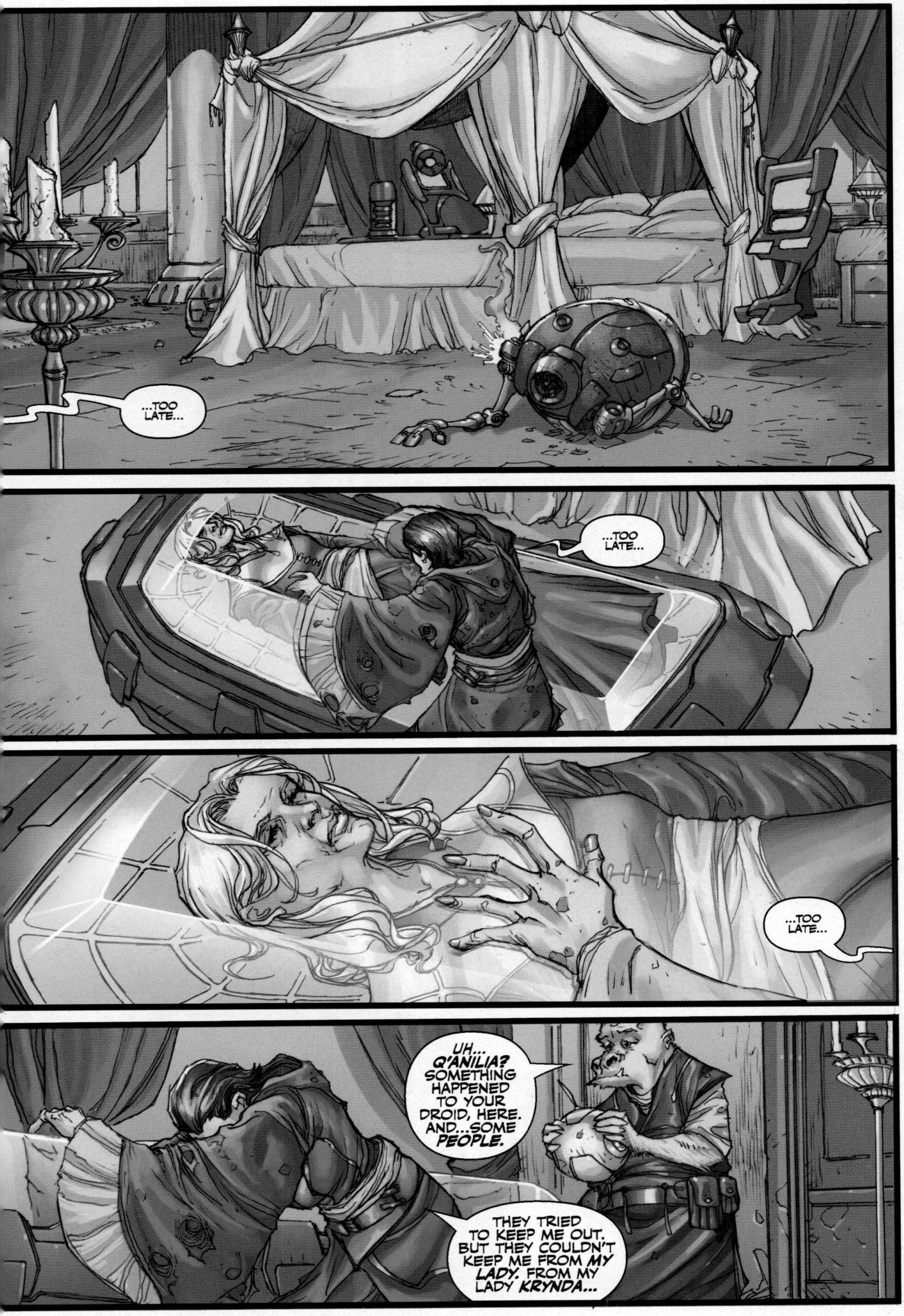
...TOO LATE...
...TOO LATE...
...TOO LATE...
UH... Q'ANILIA? SOMETHING HAPPENED TO YOUR DROID, HERE. AND...SOME PEOPLE.
THEY TRIED TO KEEP ME OUT. BUT THEY COULDN'T KEEP ME FROM MY LADY. FROM MY LADY KRYNDA...

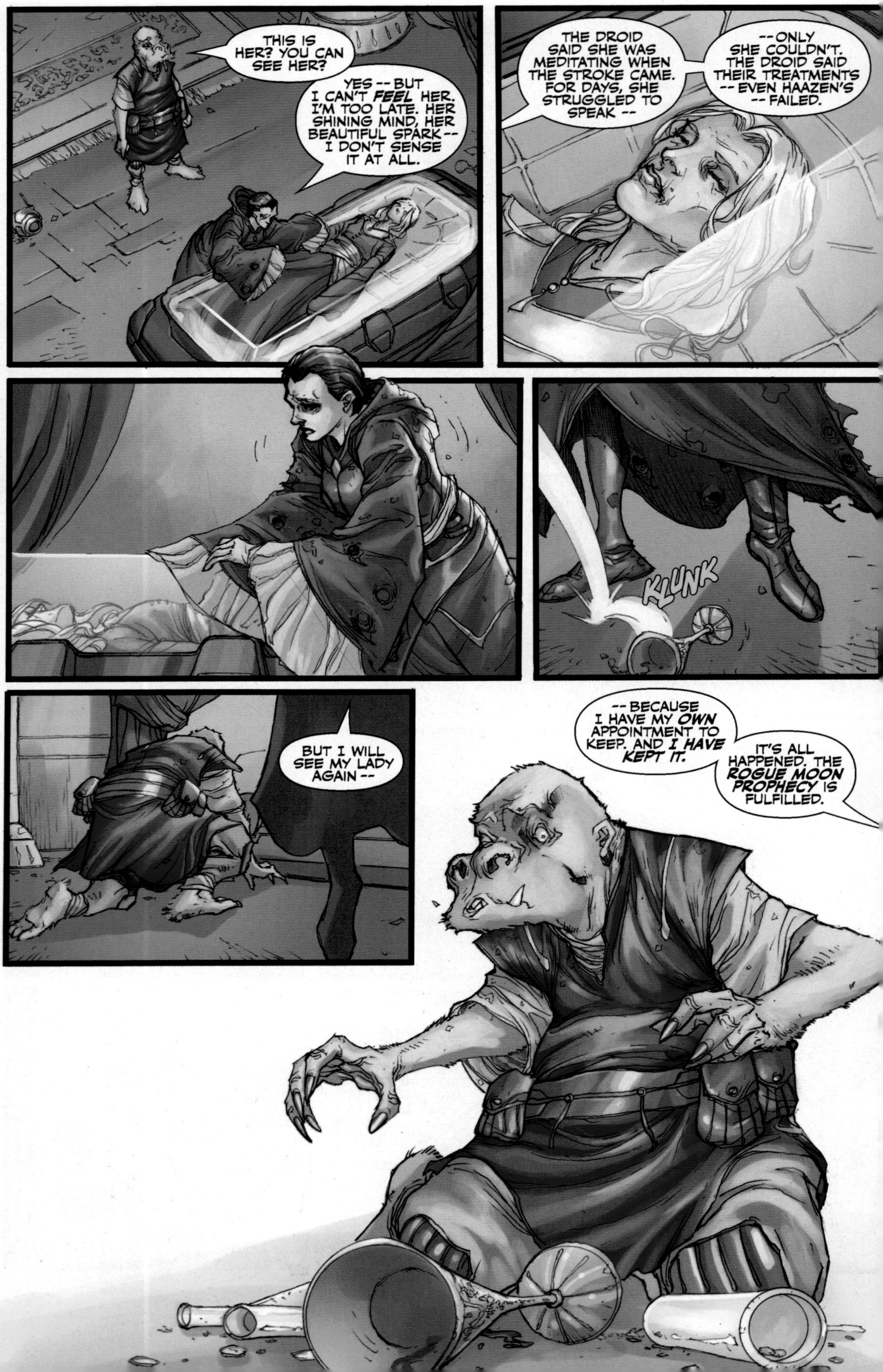
THIS IS HER? YOU CAN SEE HER?
YES -- BUT I CAN'T FEEL HER. I'M TOO LATE. HER SHINING MIND, HER BEAUTIFUL SPARK -- I DON'T SENSE IT AT ALL.
THE DROID SAID SHE WAS MEDITATING WHEN THE STROKE CAME. FOR DAYS, SHE STRUGGLED TO SPEAK --
-- ONLY SHE COULDN'T. THE DROID SAID THEIR TREATMENTS -- EVEN HAAZEN'S -- FAILED.
KLUNK
BUT I WILL SEE MY LADY AGAIN --
-- BECAUSE I HAVE MY OWN APPOINTMENT TO KEEP. AND I HAVE KEPT IT.
IT'S ALL HAPPENED. THE ROGUE MOON PROPHECY IS FULFILLED.

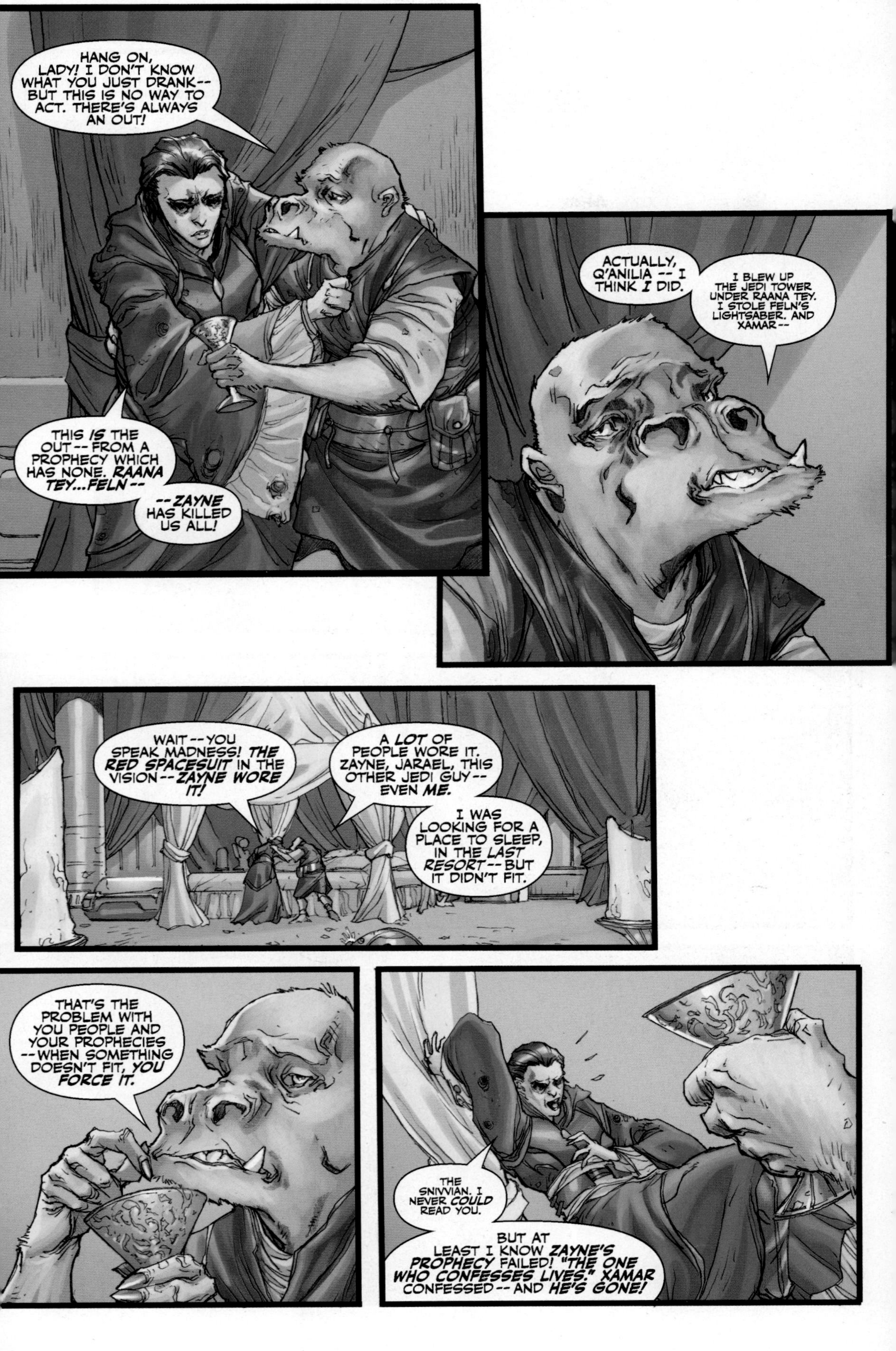
HANG ON, LADY! I DON'T KNOW WHAT YOU JUST DRANK-- BUT THIS IS NO WAY TO ACT. THERE'S ALWAYS AN OUT!
THIS *IS* THE OUT-- FROM A PROPHECY WHICH HAS NONE. *RAANA TEY...FELN--*
--*ZAYNE* HAS KILLED US ALL!
ACTUALLY, Q'ANILIA -- I THINK *I* DID.
I BLEW UP THE JEDI TOWER UNDER RAANA TEY. I STOLE FELN'S LIGHTSABER. AND XAMAR--
WAIT--YOU SPEAK MADNESS! *THE RED SPACESUIT* IN THE VISION--*ZAYNE WORE IT!*
A *LOT* OF PEOPLE WORE IT. ZAYNE, JARAEL, THIS OTHER JEDI GUY-- EVEN *ME.*
I WAS LOOKING FOR A PLACE TO SLEEP, IN THE *LAST RESORT*-- BUT IT DIDN'T FIT.
THAT'S THE PROBLEM WITH YOU PEOPLE AND YOUR PROPHECIES --WHEN SOMETHING DOESN'T FIT, *YOU FORCE IT.*
THE SNIVVIAN. I NEVER *COULD* READ YOU.
BUT AT LEAST I KNOW *ZAYNE'S PROPHECY* FAILED! *"THE ONE WHO CONFESSES LIVES."* XAMAR CONFESSED-- AND *HE'S GONE!*

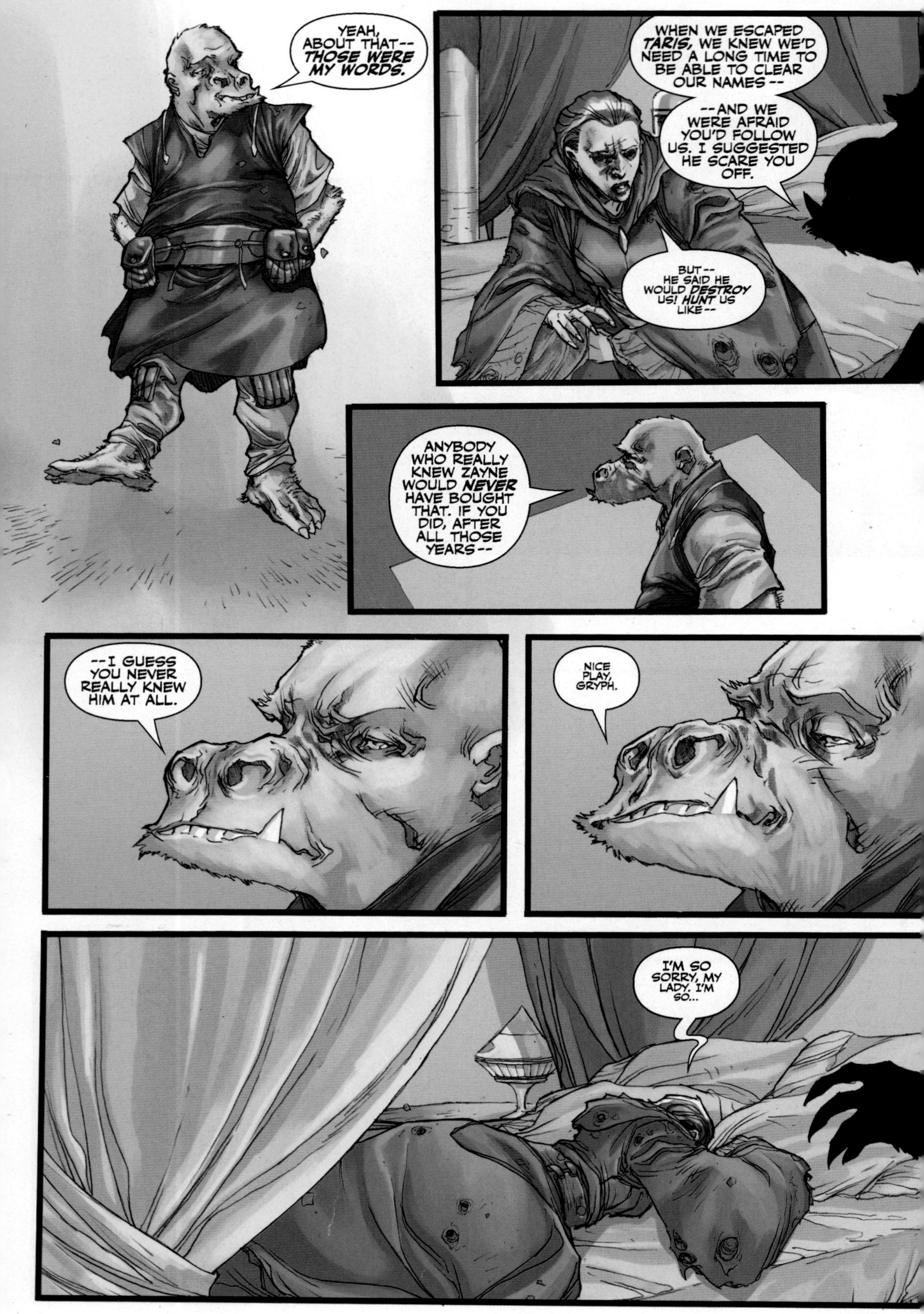
YEAH, ABOUT THAT-- THOSE WERE MY WORDS.
WHEN WE ESCAPED TARIS, WE KNEW WE'D NEED A LONG TIME TO BE ABLE TO CLEAR OUR NAMES --
--AND WE WERE AFRAID YOU'D FOLLOW US. I SUGGESTED HE SCARE YOU OFF.
BUT-- HE SAID HE WOULD DESTROY US! HUNT US LIKE--
ANYBODY WHO REALLY KNEW ZAYNE WOULD NEVER HAVE BOUGHT THAT. IF YOU DID, AFTER ALL THOSE YEARS--
--I GUESS YOU NEVER REALLY KNEW HIM AT ALL.
NICE PLAY, GRYPH.
I'M SO SORRY, MY LADY. I'M SO...

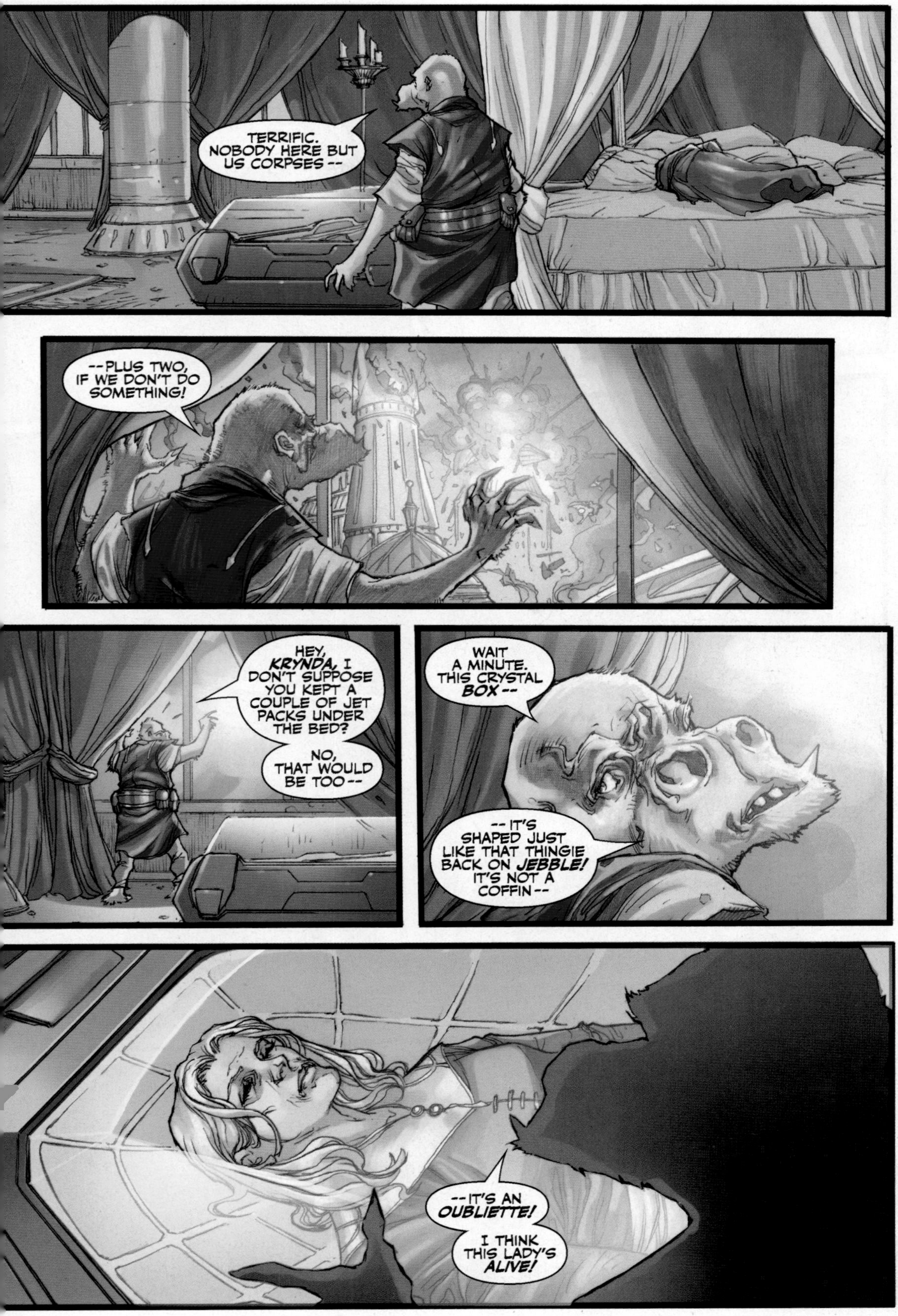
TERRIFIC. NOBODY HERE BUT US CORPSES --
--PLUS TWO, IF WE DON'T DO SOMETHING!
HEY, KRYNDA, I DON'T SUPPOSE YOU KEPT A COUPLE OF JET PACKS UNDER THE BED?
NO, THAT WOULD BE TOO --
WAIT A MINUTE. THIS CRYSTAL BOX --
-- IT'S SHAPED JUST LIKE THAT THINGIE BACK ON JEBBLE! IT'S NOT A COFFIN --
--IT'S AN OUBLIETTE!
I THINK THIS LADY'S ALIVE!

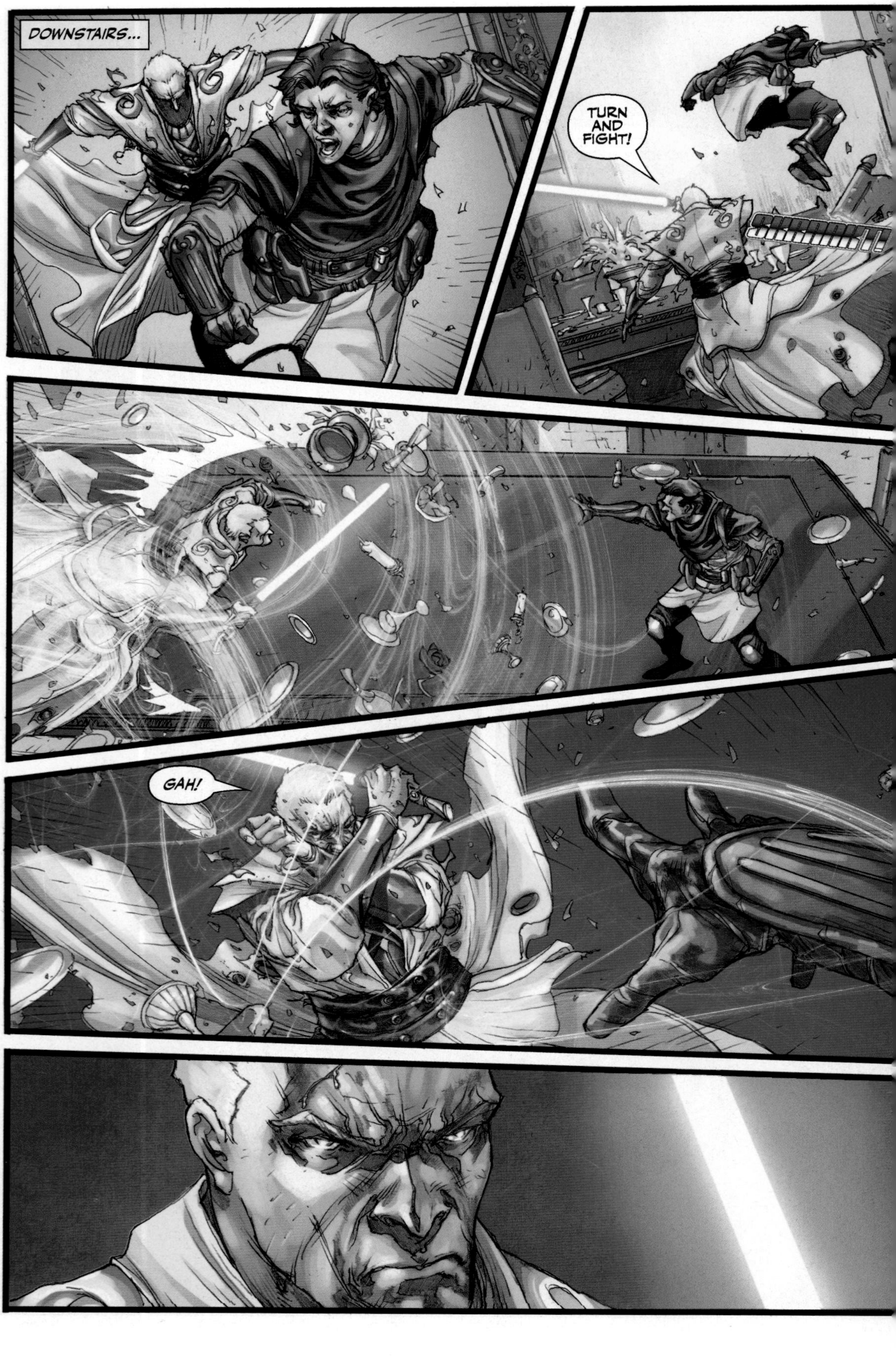
DOWNSTAIRS...
TURN AND FIGHT!
GAH!

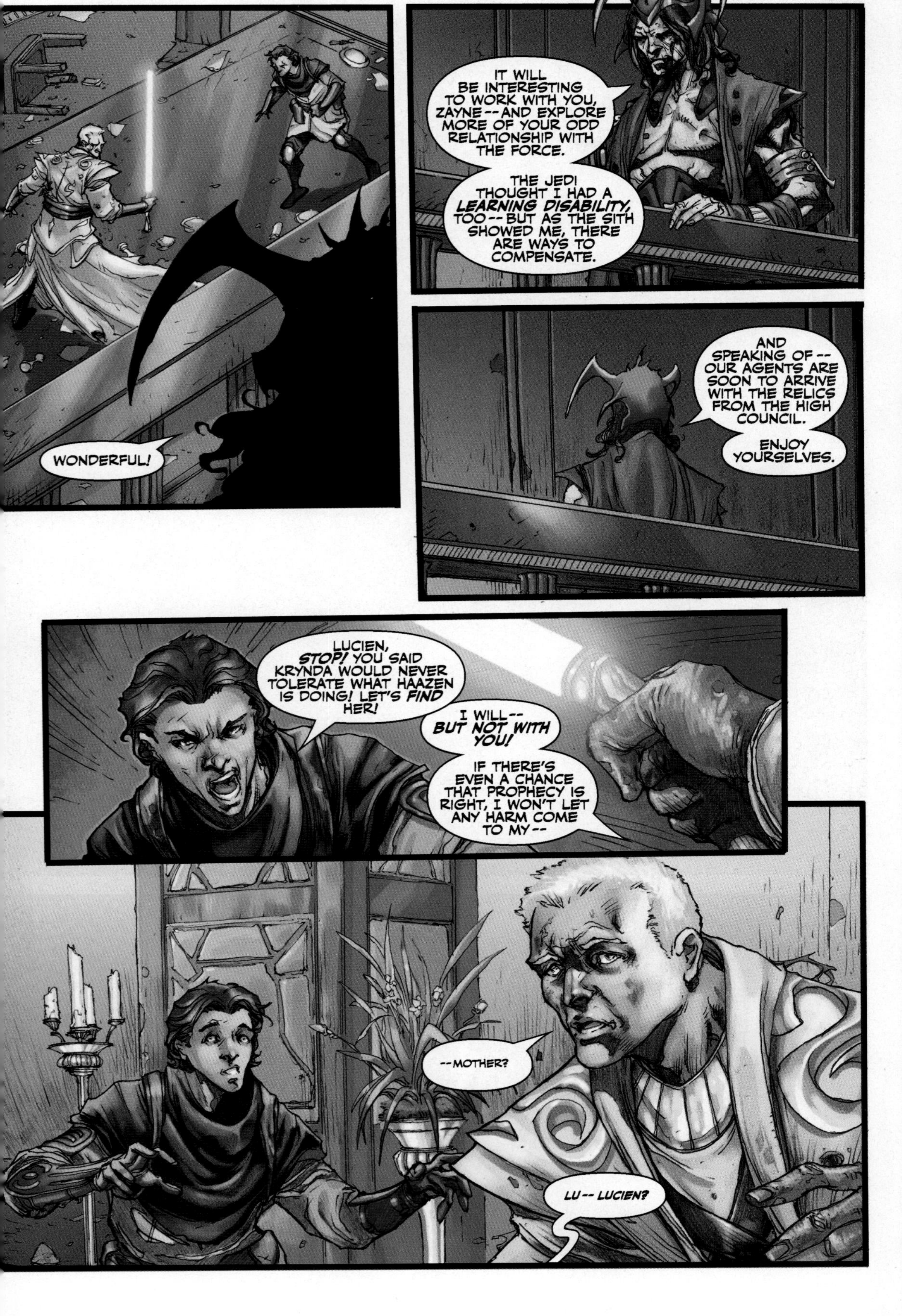
WONDERFUL!
IT WILL BE INTERESTING TO WORK WITH YOU, ZAYNE--AND EXPLORE MORE OF YOUR ODD RELATIONSHIP WITH THE FORCE.
THE JEDI THOUGHT I HAD A LEARNING DISABILITY, TOO--BUT AS THE SITH SHOWED ME, THERE ARE WAYS TO COMPENSATE.
AND SPEAKING OF--OUR AGENTS ARE SOON TO ARRIVE WITH THE RELICS FROM THE HIGH COUNCIL.
ENJOY YOURSELVES.
LUCIEN, STOP! YOU SAID KRYNDA WOULD NEVER TOLERATE WHAT HAAZEN IS DOING! LET'S FIND HER!
I WILL--BUT NOT WITH YOU!
IF THERE'S EVEN A CHANCE THAT PROPHECY IS RIGHT, I WON'T LET ANY HARM COME TO MY--
--MOTHER?
LU--LUCIEN?

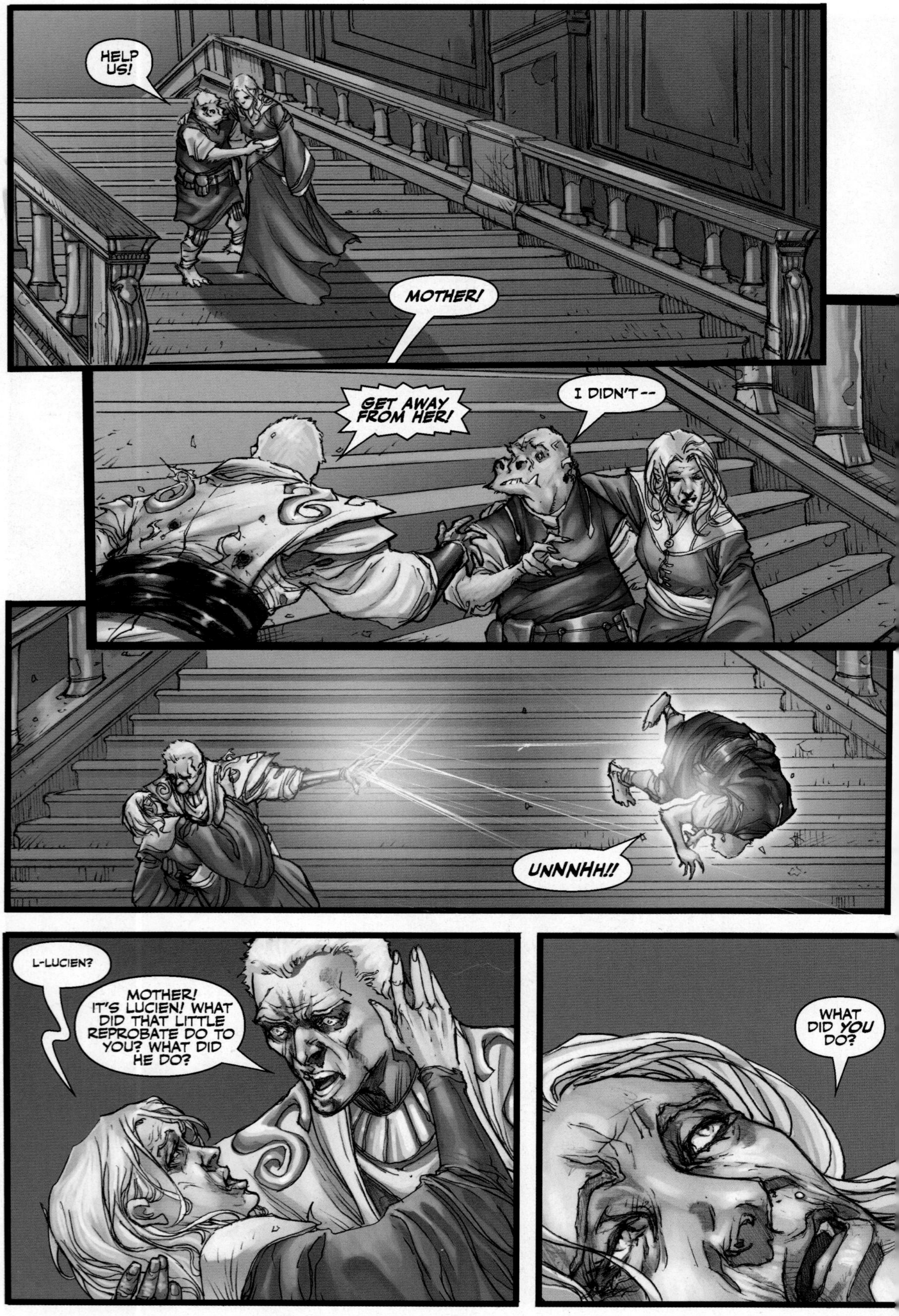
HELP US!
MOTHER!
GET AWAY FROM HER!
I DIDN'T --
UNNNHH!!
L-LUCIEN?
MOTHER! IT'S LUCIEN! WHAT DID THAT LITTLE REPROBATE DO TO YOU? WHAT DID HE DO?
WHAT DID YOU DO?

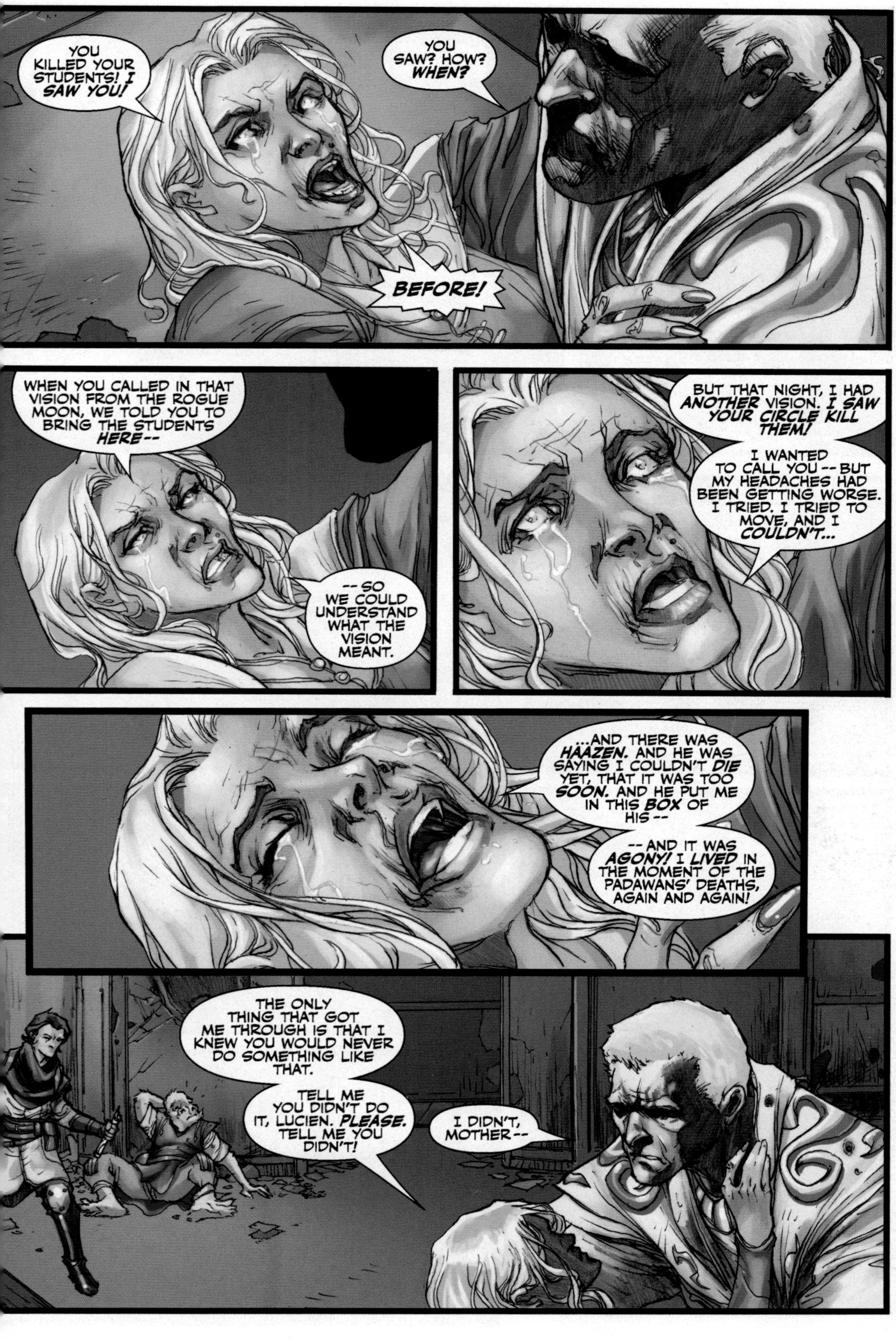
YOU KILLED YOUR STUDENTS! I SAW YOU!
YOU SAW? HOW? WHEN?
BEFORE!
WHEN YOU CALLED IN THAT VISION FROM THE ROGUE MOON, WE TOLD YOU TO BRING THE STUDENTS HERE--
--SO WE COULD UNDERSTAND WHAT THE VISION MEANT.
BUT THAT NIGHT, I HAD ANOTHER VISION. I SAW YOUR CIRCLE KILL THEM!
I WANTED TO CALL YOU -- BUT MY HEADACHES HAD BEEN GETTING WORSE. I TRIED. I TRIED TO MOVE, AND I COULDN'T...
...AND THERE WAS HAAZEN. AND HE WAS SAYING I COULDN'T DIE YET, THAT IT WAS TOO SOON. AND HE PUT ME IN THIS BOX OF HIS --
-- AND IT WAS AGONY! I LIVED IN THE MOMENT OF THE PADAWANS' DEATHS, AGAIN AND AGAIN!
THE ONLY THING THAT GOT ME THROUGH IS THAT I KNEW YOU WOULD NEVER DO SOMETHING LIKE THAT.
TELL ME YOU DIDN'T DO IT, LUCIEN. PLEASE. TELL ME YOU DIDN'T!
I DIDN'T, MOTHER--

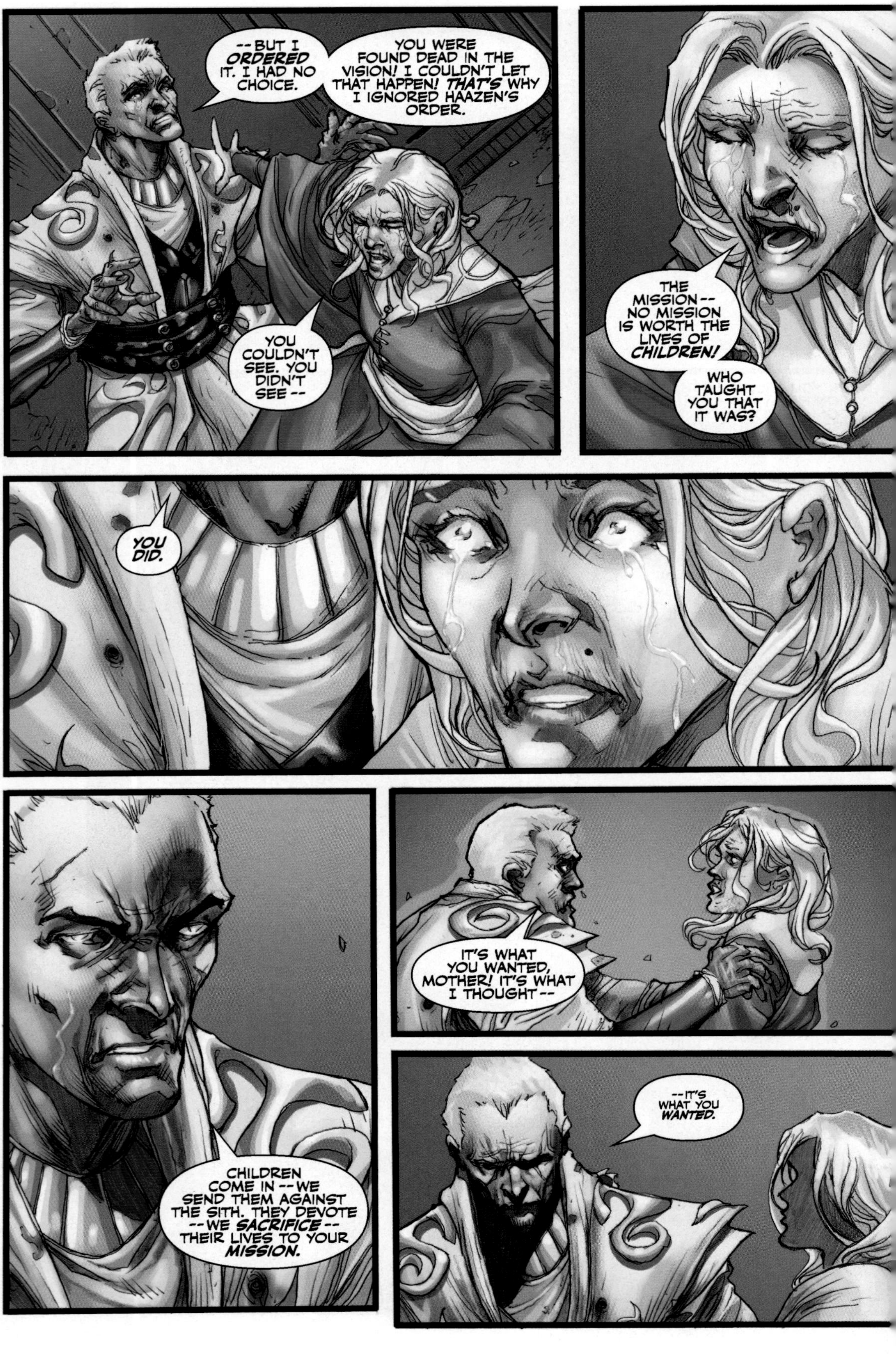
--BUT I ORDERED IT. I HAD NO CHOICE.
YOU WERE FOUND DEAD IN THE VISION! I COULDN'T LET THAT HAPPEN! THAT'S WHY I IGNORED HAAZEN'S ORDER.
YOU COULDN'T SEE. YOU DIDN'T SEE--
THE MISSION--NO MISSION IS WORTH THE LIVES OF CHILDREN!
WHO TAUGHT YOU THAT IT WAS?
YOU DID.
CHILDREN COME IN--WE SEND THEM AGAINST THE SITH. THEY DEVOTE--WE SACRIFICE--THEIR LIVES TO YOUR MISSION.
IT'S WHAT YOU WANTED, MOTHER! IT'S WHAT I THOUGHT--
--IT'S WHAT YOU WANTED.

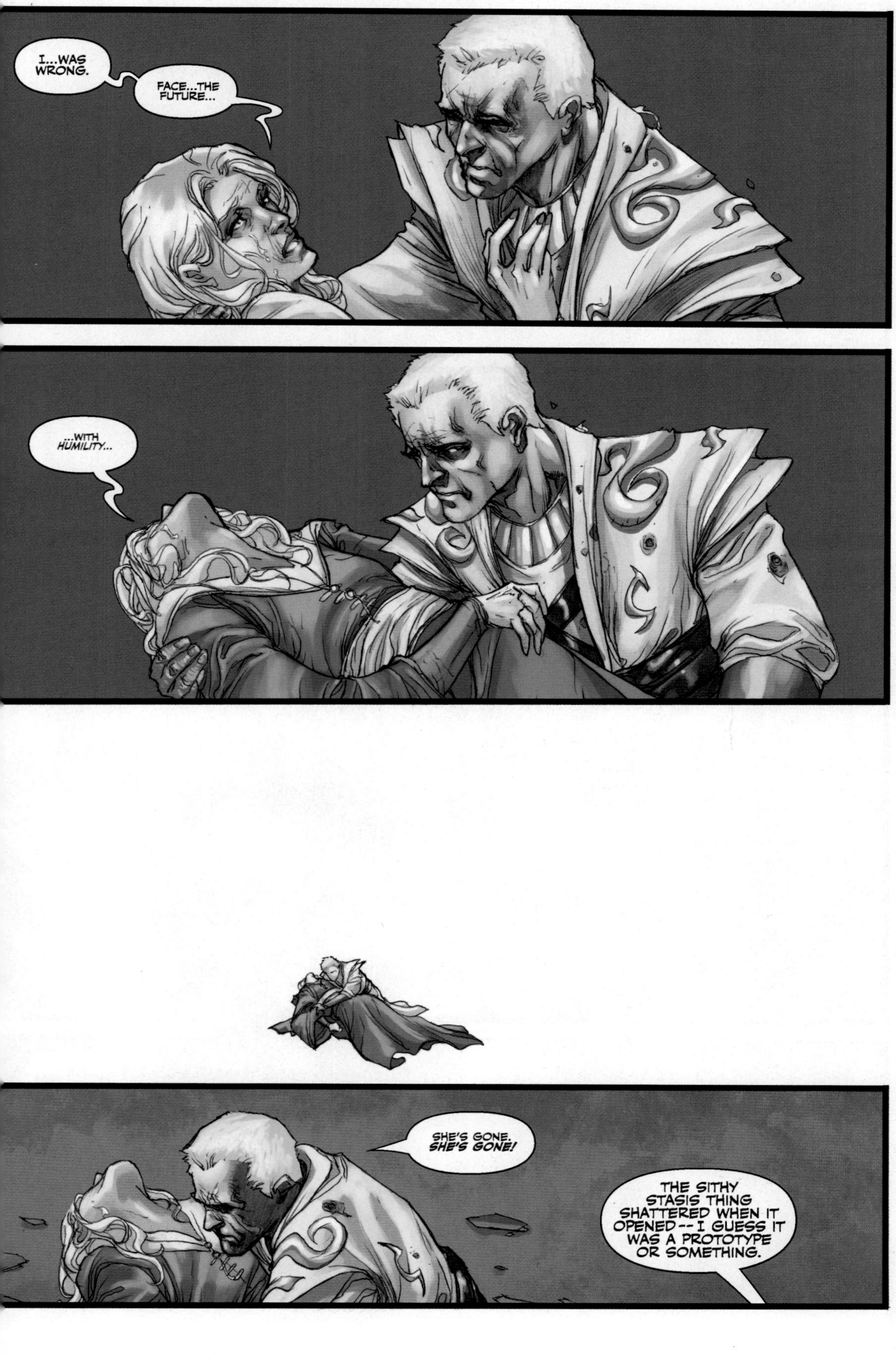
I...WAS WRONG.
FACE...THE FUTURE...
...WITH HUMILITY...
SHE'S GONE. SHE'S GONE!
THE SITHY STASIS THING SHATTERED WHEN IT OPENED -- I GUESS IT WAS A PROTOTYPE OR SOMETHING.

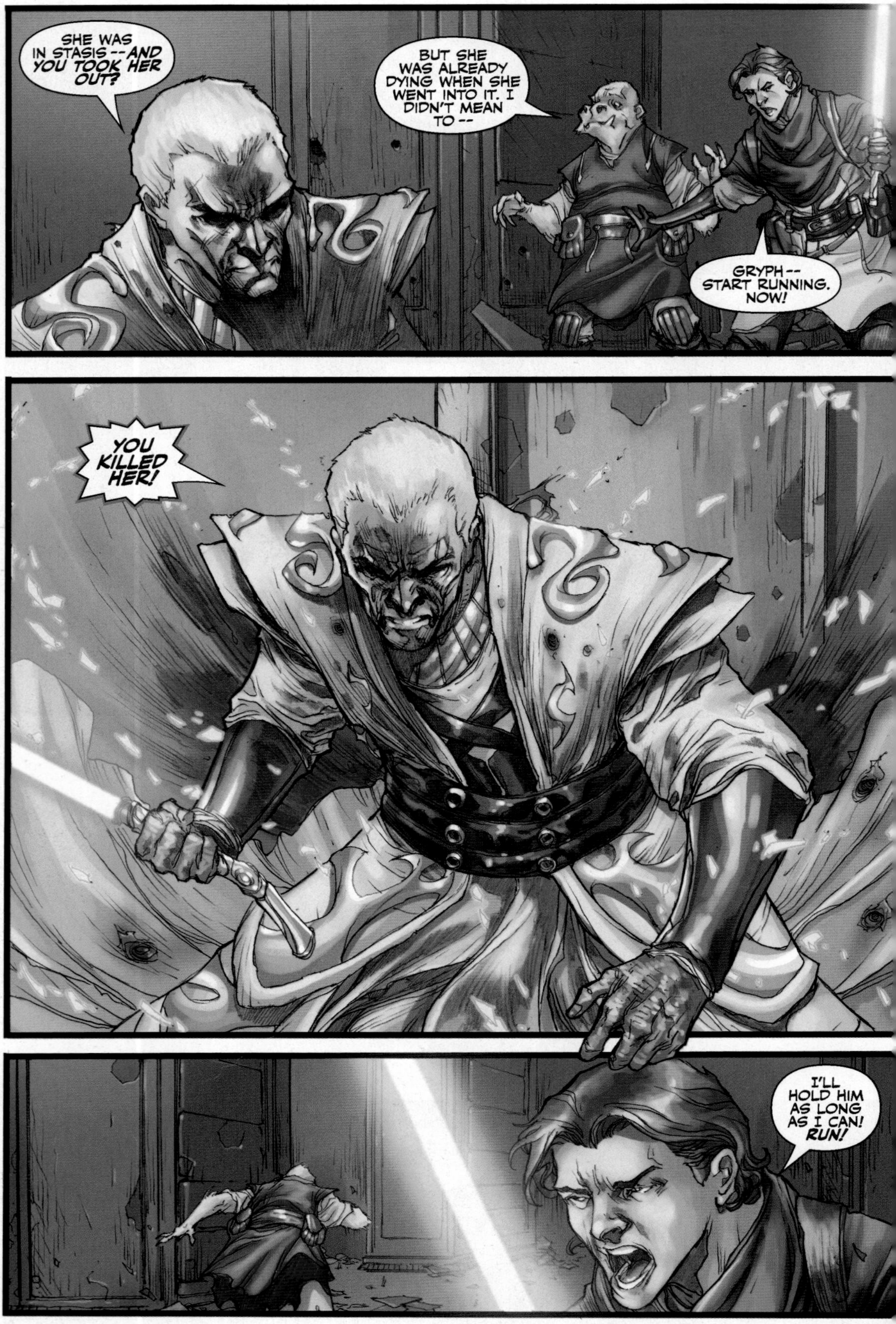
SHE WAS IN STASIS -- AND YOU TOOK HER OUT?
BUT SHE WAS ALREADY DYING WHEN SHE WENT INTO IT. I DIDN'T MEAN TO --
GRYPH -- START RUNNING. NOW!
YOU KILLED HER!
I'LL HOLD HIM AS LONG AS I CAN! RUN!

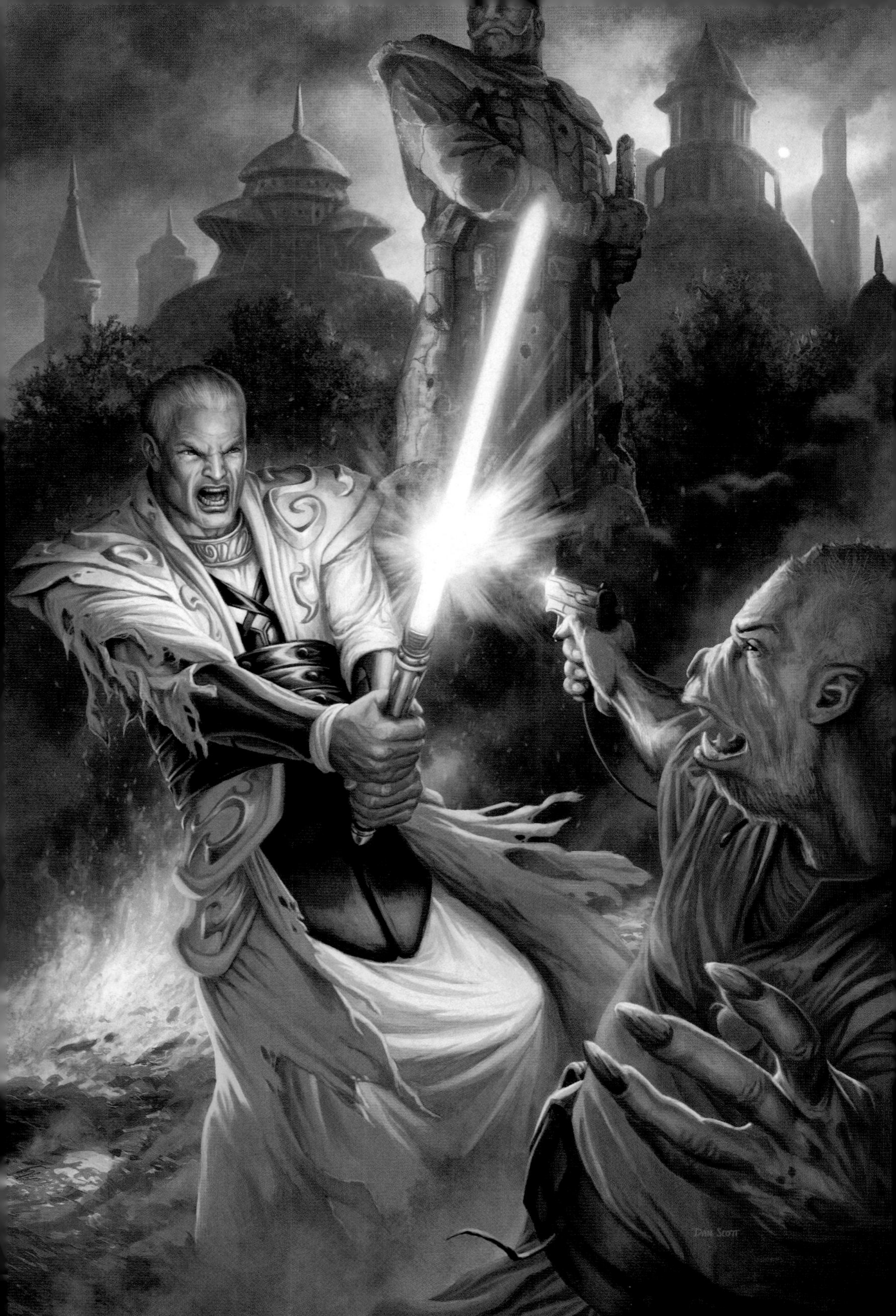

STAR WARS: KNIGHTS OF THE OLD REPUBLIC #35 — "VINDICATION, PART 4"

WRITER: JOHN JACKSON MILLER • ARTIST: BRIAN CHING • COLORIST: MICHAEL ATIYEH • LETTERER: MICHAEL HEISLER
ASSISTANT EDITOR: FREDDYE LINS • EDITOR: DAVE MARSHALL • COVER ARTIST: DAN SCOTT

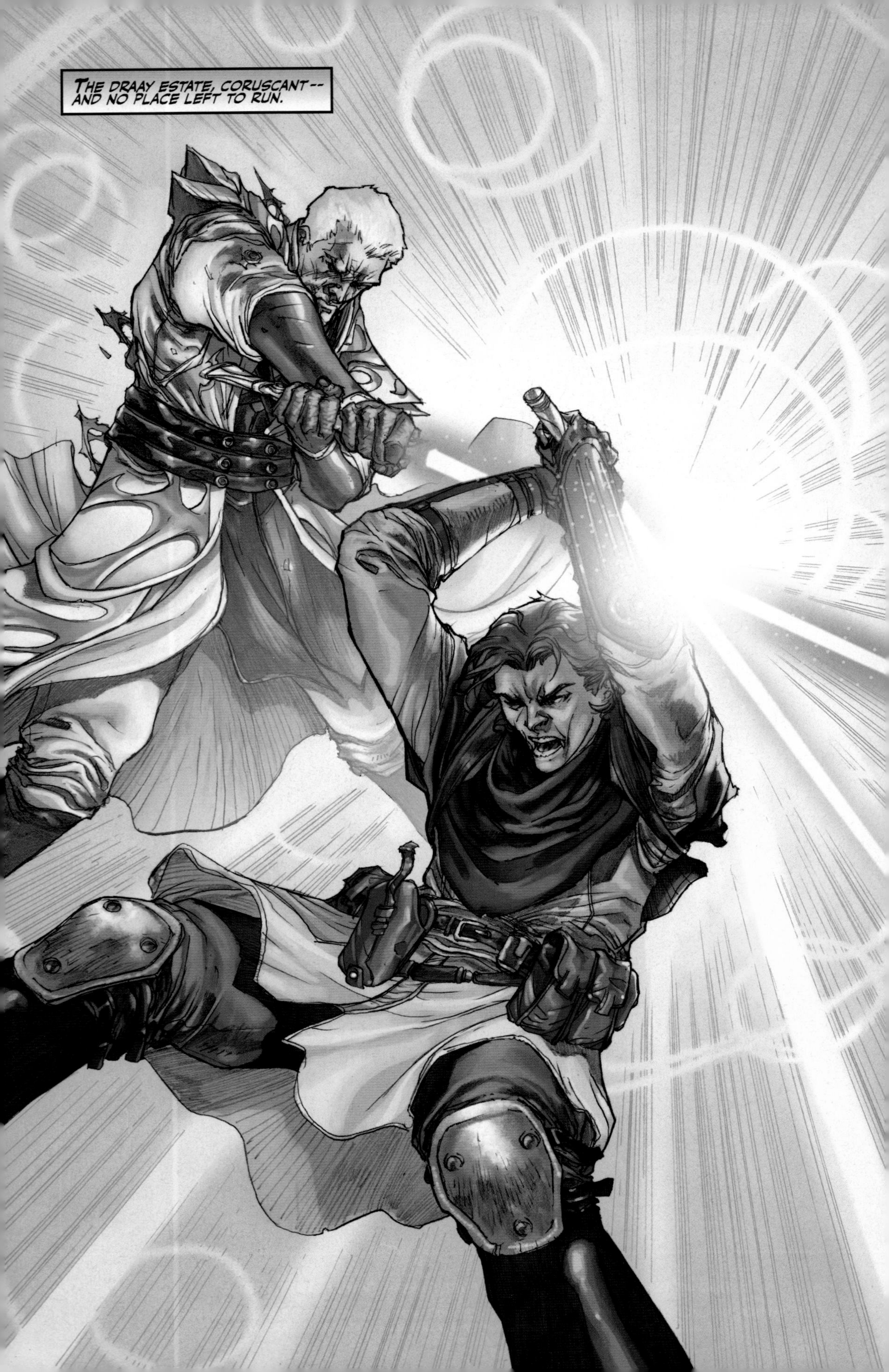
THE DRAAY ESTATE, CORUSCANT--
AND NO PLACE LEFT TO RUN.

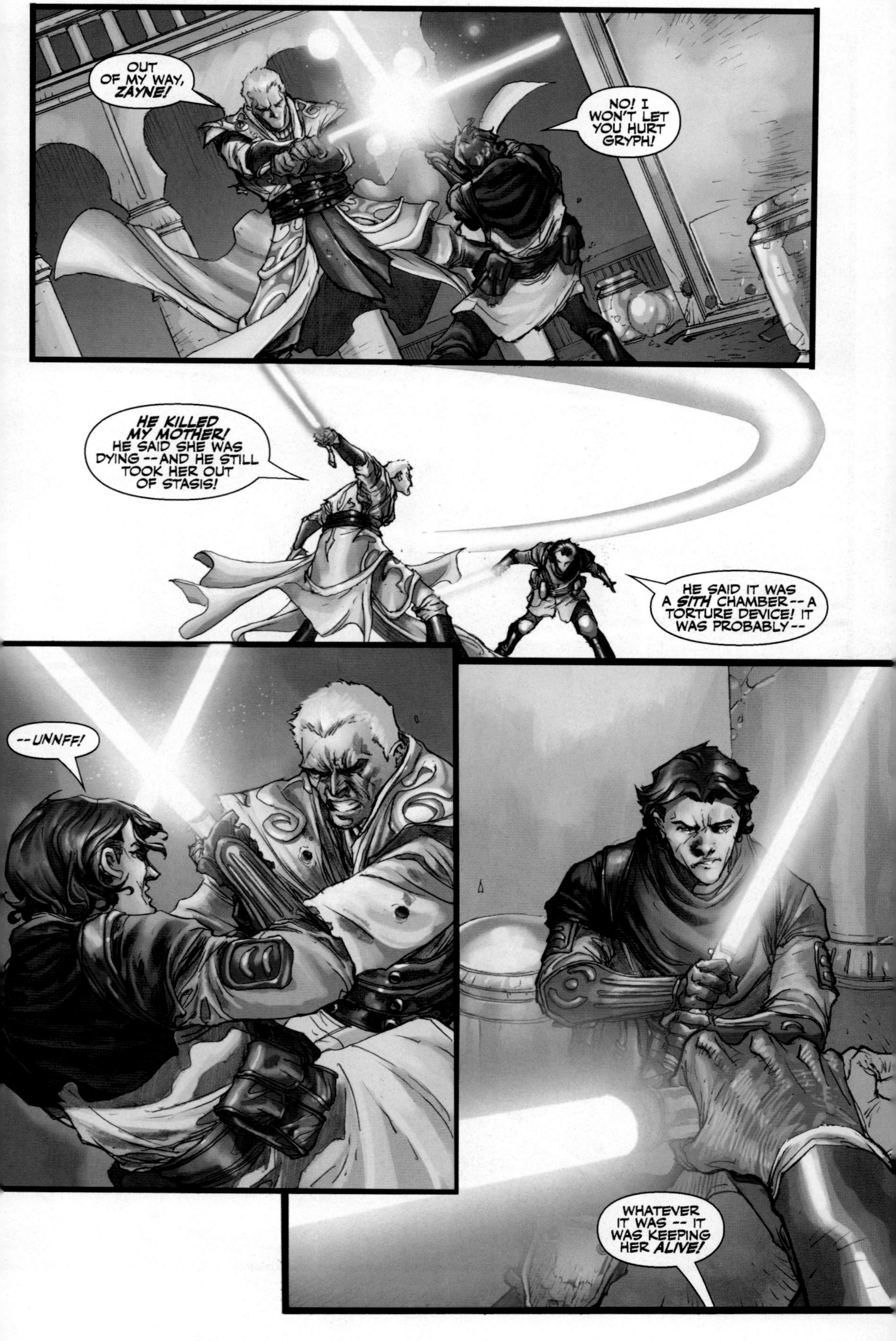
OUT OF MY WAY, ZAYNE!
NO! I WON'T LET YOU HURT GRYPH!
HE KILLED MY MOTHER! HE SAID SHE WAS DYING -- AND HE STILL TOOK HER OUT OF STASIS!
HE SAID IT WAS A SITH CHAMBER -- A TORTURE DEVICE! IT WAS PROBABLY --
-- UNNFF!
WHATEVER IT WAS -- IT WAS KEEPING HER ALIVE!

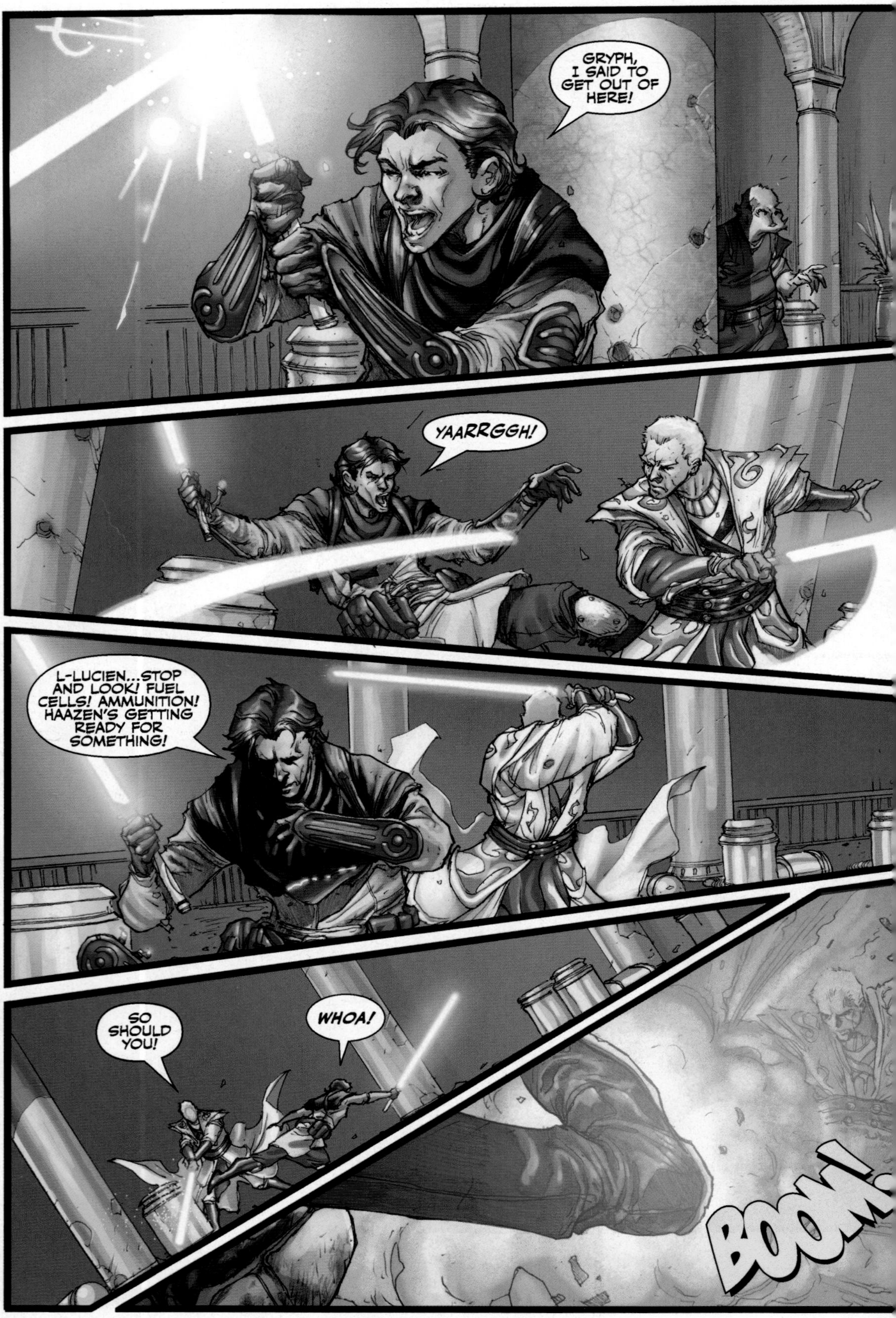
GRYPH, I SAID TO GET OUT OF HERE!
YAARRGGH!
L-LUCIEN...STOP AND LOOK! FUEL CELLS! AMMUNITION! HAAZEN'S GETTING READY FOR SOMETHING!
SO SHOULD YOU!
WHOA!
BOOM!

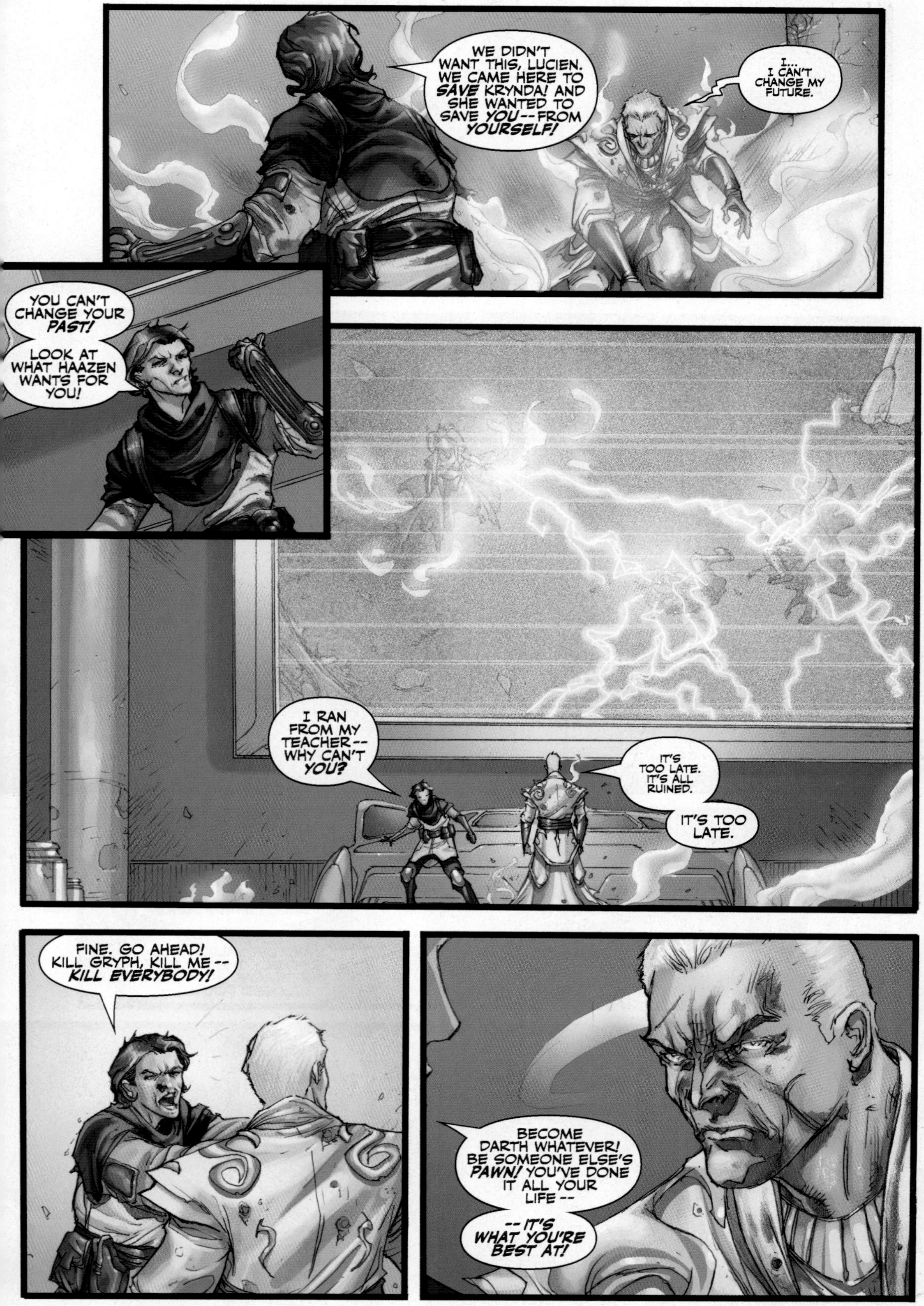

WE DIDN'T WANT THIS, LUCIEN. WE CAME HERE TO SAVE KRYNDA! AND SHE WANTED TO SAVE YOU--FROM YOURSELF!
I... I CAN'T CHANGE MY FUTURE.
YOU CAN'T CHANGE YOUR PAST!
LOOK AT WHAT HAAZEN WANTS FOR YOU!
I RAN FROM MY TEACHER-- WHY CAN'T YOU?
IT'S TOO LATE. IT'S ALL RUINED.
IT'S TOO LATE.
FINE. GO AHEAD! KILL GRYPH, KILL ME-- KILL EVERYBODY!
BECOME DARTH WHATEVER! BE SOMEONE ELSE'S PAWN! YOU'VE DONE IT ALL YOUR LIFE --
-- IT'S WHAT YOU'RE BEST AT!

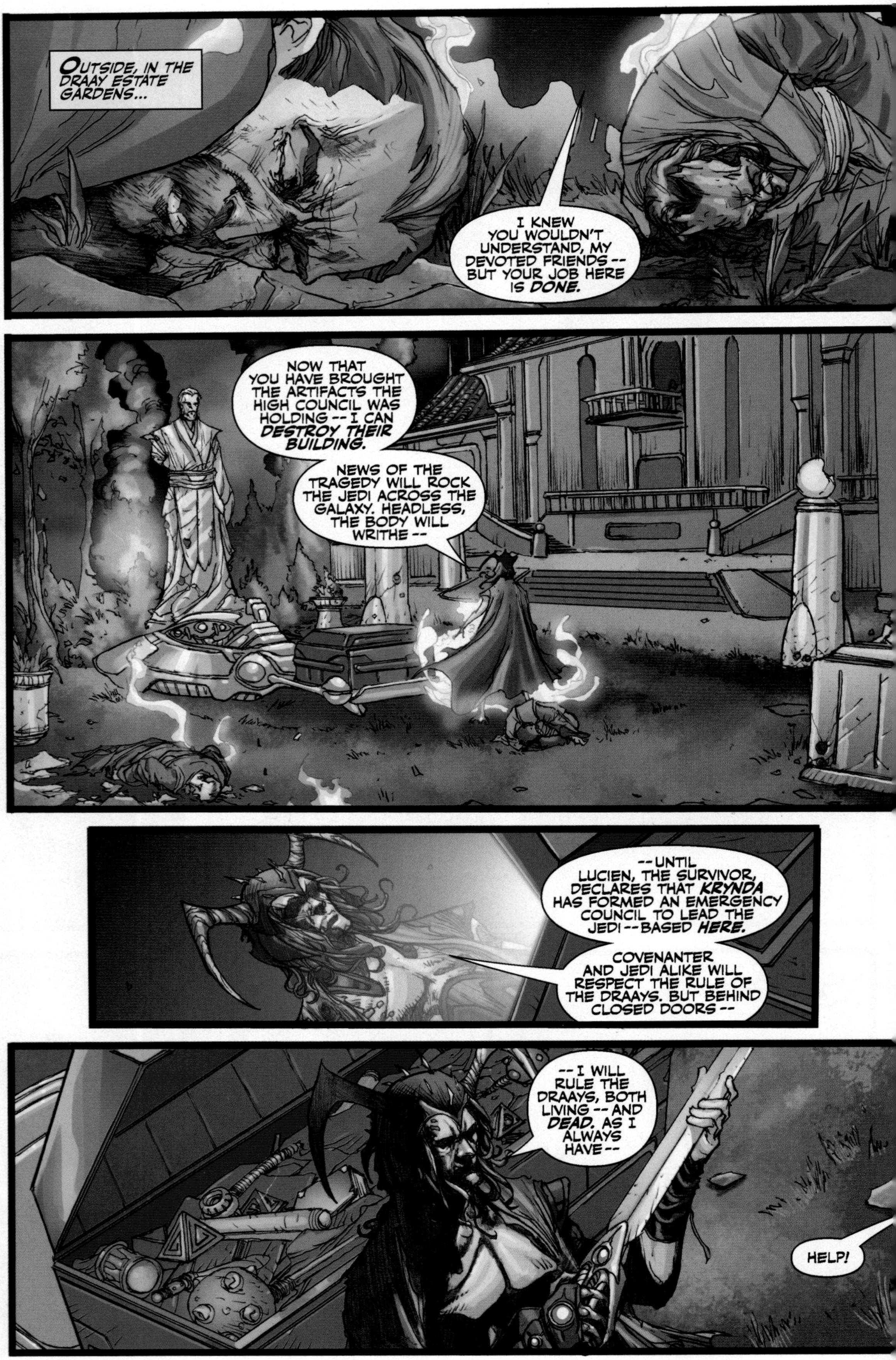
OUTSIDE, IN THE DRAAY ESTATE GARDENS...
I KNEW YOU WOULDN'T UNDERSTAND, MY DEVOTED FRIENDS -- BUT YOUR JOB HERE IS DONE.
NOW THAT YOU HAVE BROUGHT THE ARTIFACTS THE HIGH COUNCIL WAS HOLDING -- I CAN DESTROY THEIR BUILDING.
NEWS OF THE TRAGEDY WILL ROCK THE JEDI ACROSS THE GALAXY. HEADLESS, THE BODY WILL WRITHE --
--UNTIL LUCIEN, THE SURVIVOR, DECLARES THAT KRYNDA HAS FORMED AN EMERGENCY COUNCIL TO LEAD THE JEDI --BASED HERE.
COVENANTER AND JEDI ALIKE WILL RESPECT THE RULE OF THE DRAAYS. BUT BEHIND CLOSED DOORS --
-- I WILL RULE THE DRAAYS, BOTH LIVING -- AND DEAD. AS I ALWAYS HAVE --
HELP!

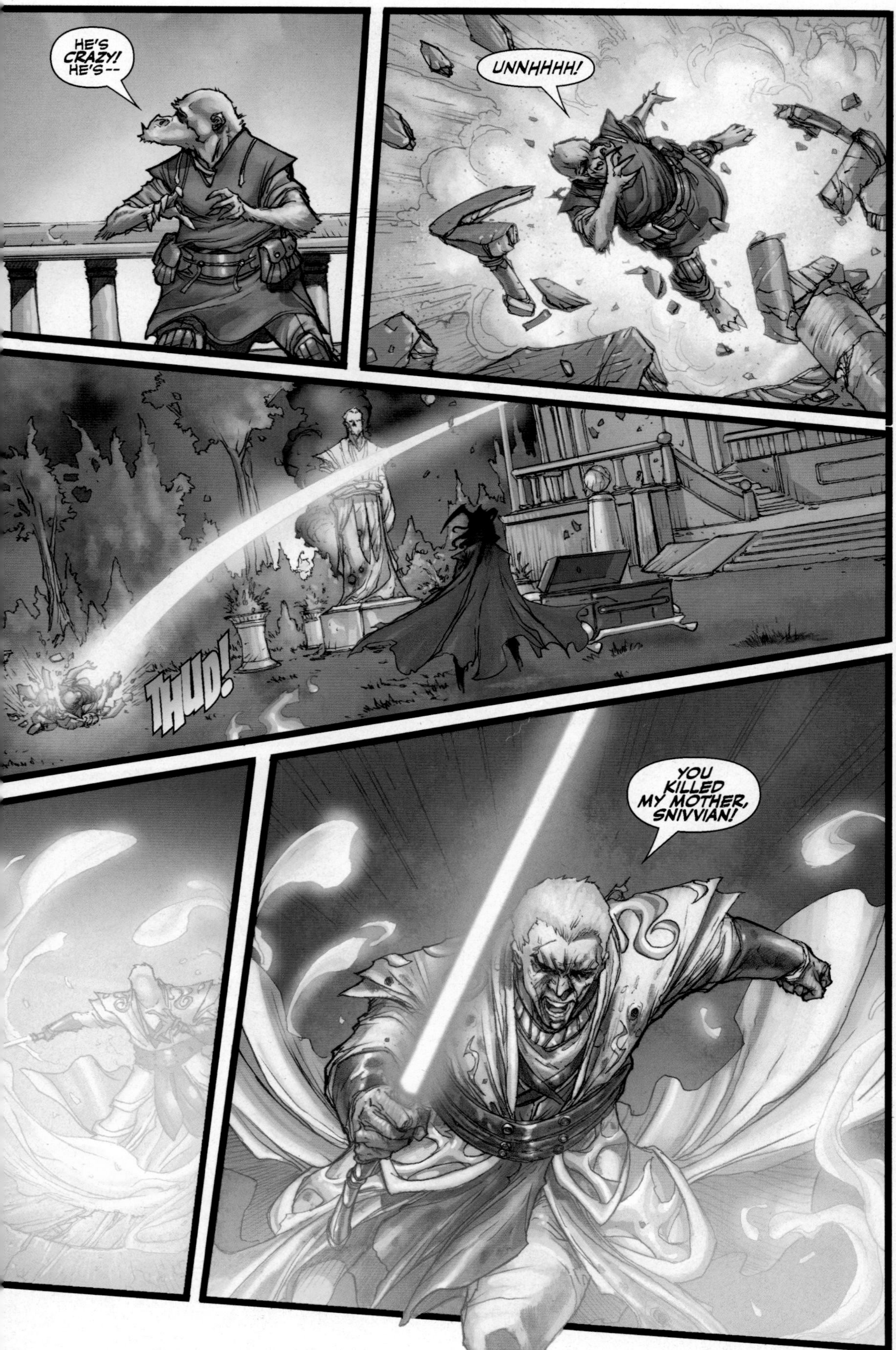
HE'S CRAZY! HE'S--
UNNHHHH!
THUD!
YOU KILLED MY MOTHER, SNIVVIAN!

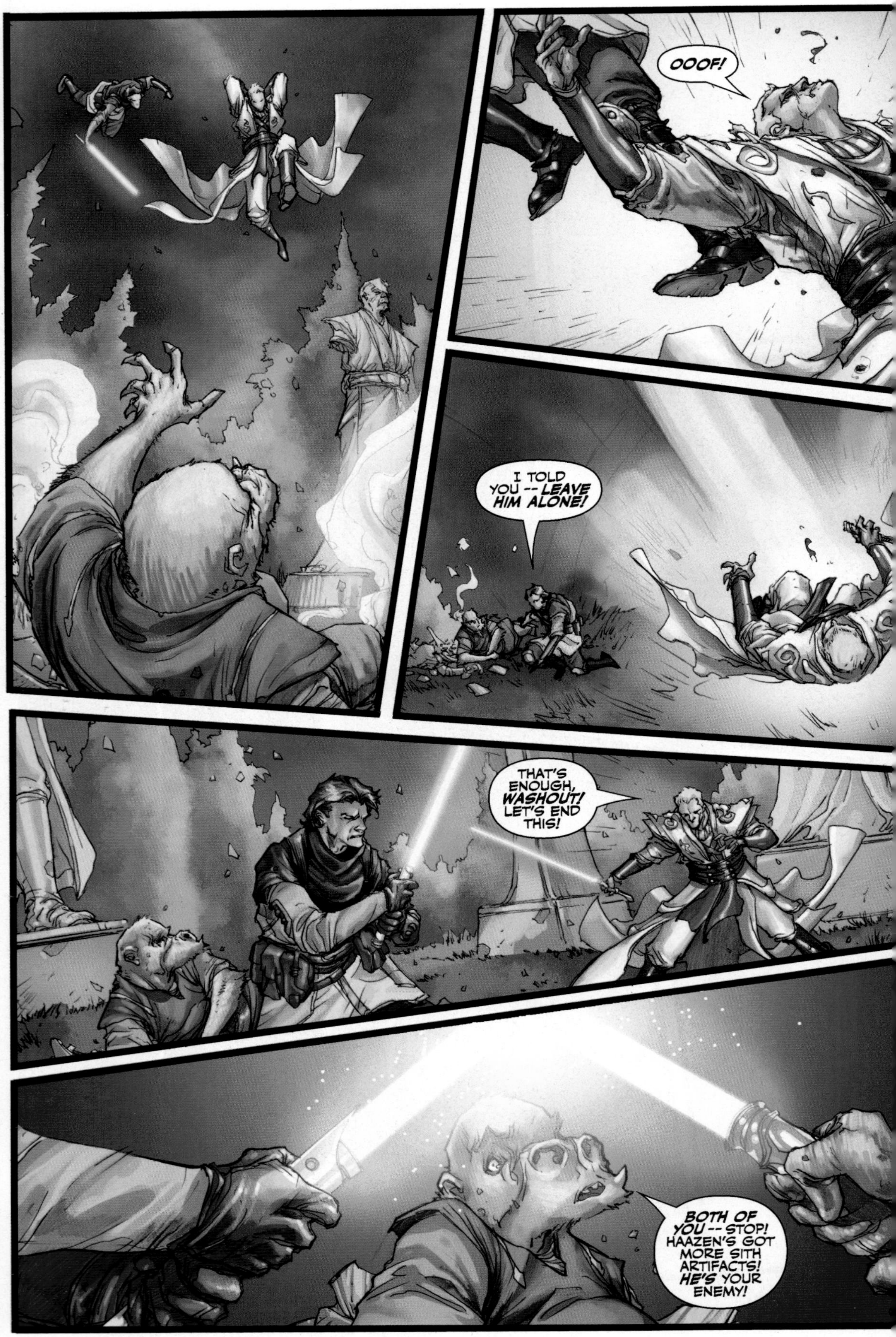
OOOF!
I TOLD YOU -- LEAVE HIM ALONE!
THAT'S ENOUGH, WASHOUT! LET'S END THIS!
BOTH OF YOU -- STOP! HAAZEN'S GOT MORE SITH ARTIFACTS! HE'S YOUR ENEMY!

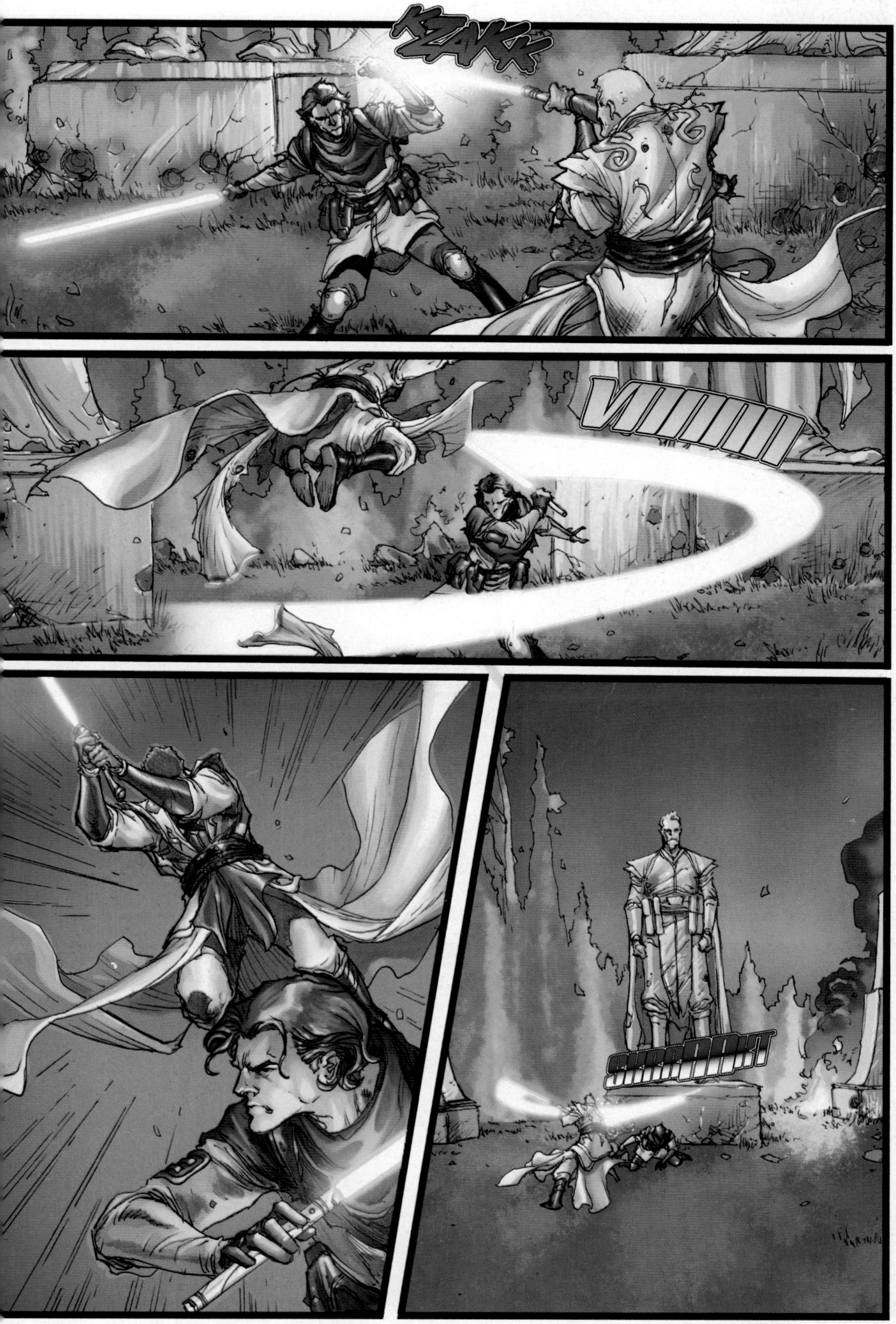
KZAKK

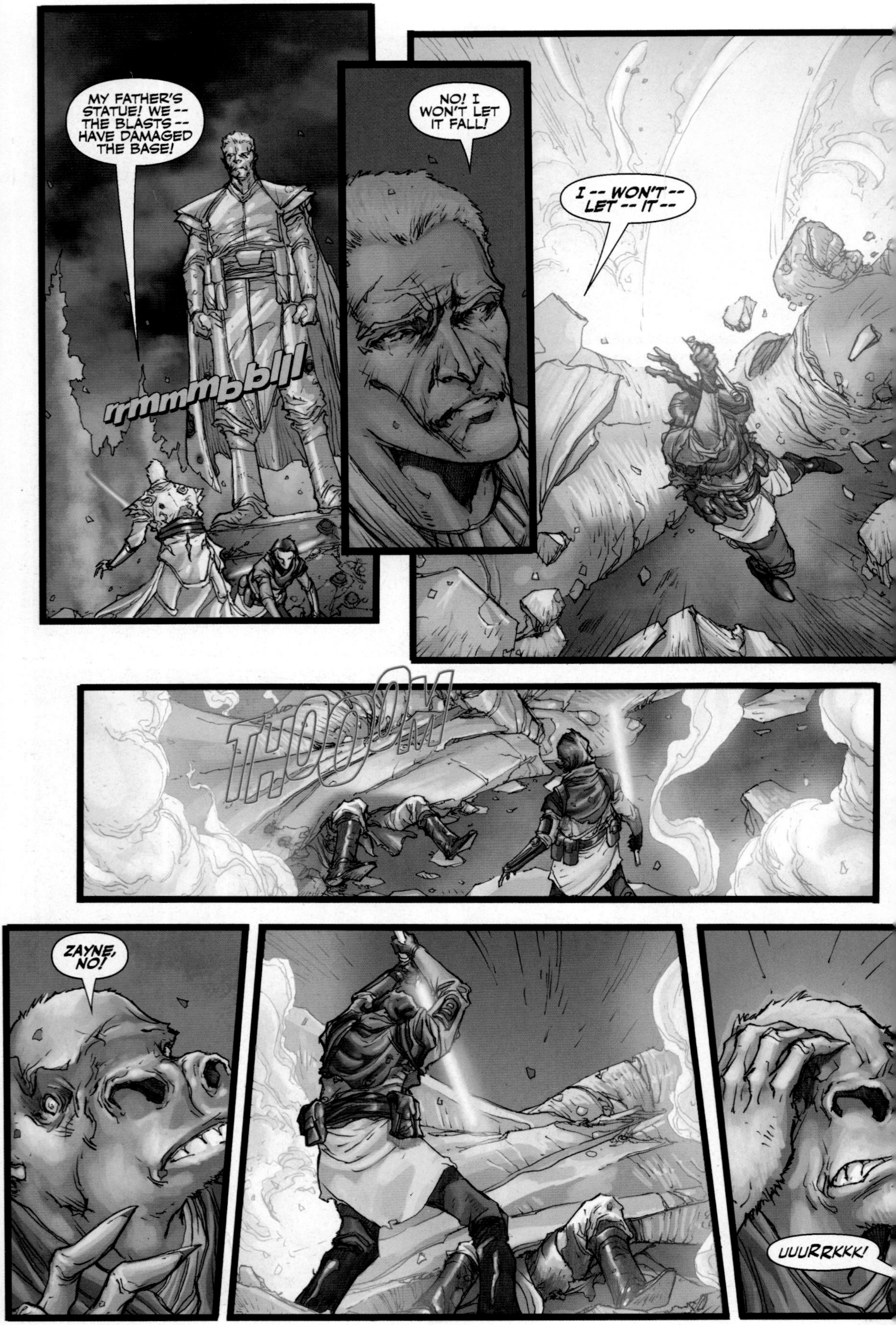
MY FATHER'S STATUE! WE -- THE BLASTS -- HAVE DAMAGED THE BASE!
rrmmmbblll
NO! I WON'T LET IT FALL!
I -- WON'T -- LET -- IT --
THOOOOM
ZAYNE, NO!
UUURRKKK!

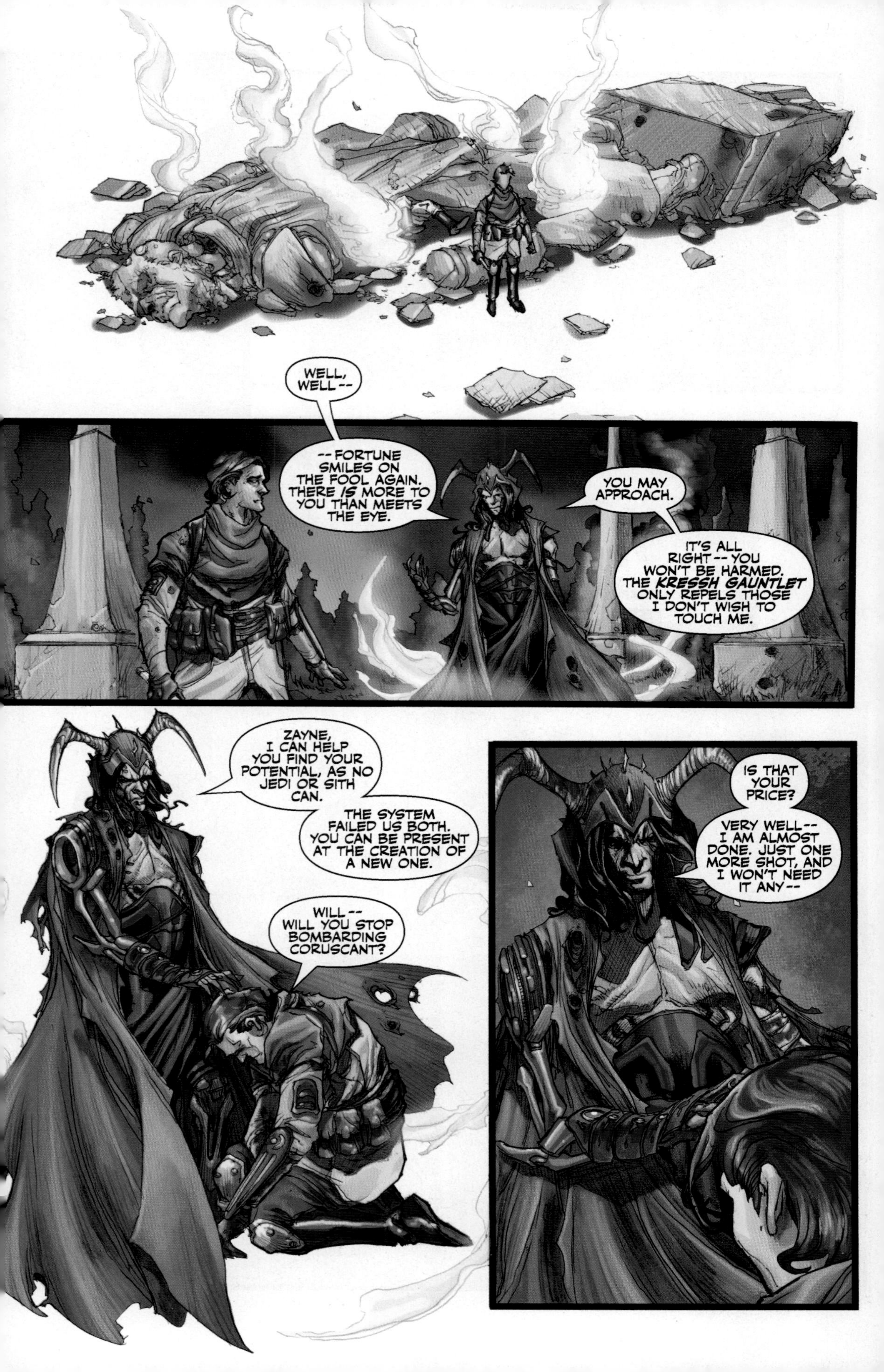
WELL, WELL --
-- FORTUNE SMILES ON THE FOOL AGAIN. THERE *IS* MORE TO YOU THAN MEETS THE EYE.
YOU MAY APPROACH.
IT'S ALL RIGHT -- YOU WON'T BE HARMED. THE ***KRESSH GAUNTLET*** ONLY REPELS THOSE I DON'T WISH TO TOUCH ME.
ZAYNE, I CAN HELP YOU FIND YOUR POTENTIAL, AS NO JEDI OR SITH CAN.
THE SYSTEM FAILED US BOTH. YOU CAN BE PRESENT AT THE CREATION OF A NEW ONE.
WILL -- WILL YOU STOP BOMBARDING CORUSCANT?
IS THAT YOUR PRICE?
VERY WELL -- I AM ALMOST DONE. JUST ONE MORE SHOT, AND I WON'T NEED IT ANY --

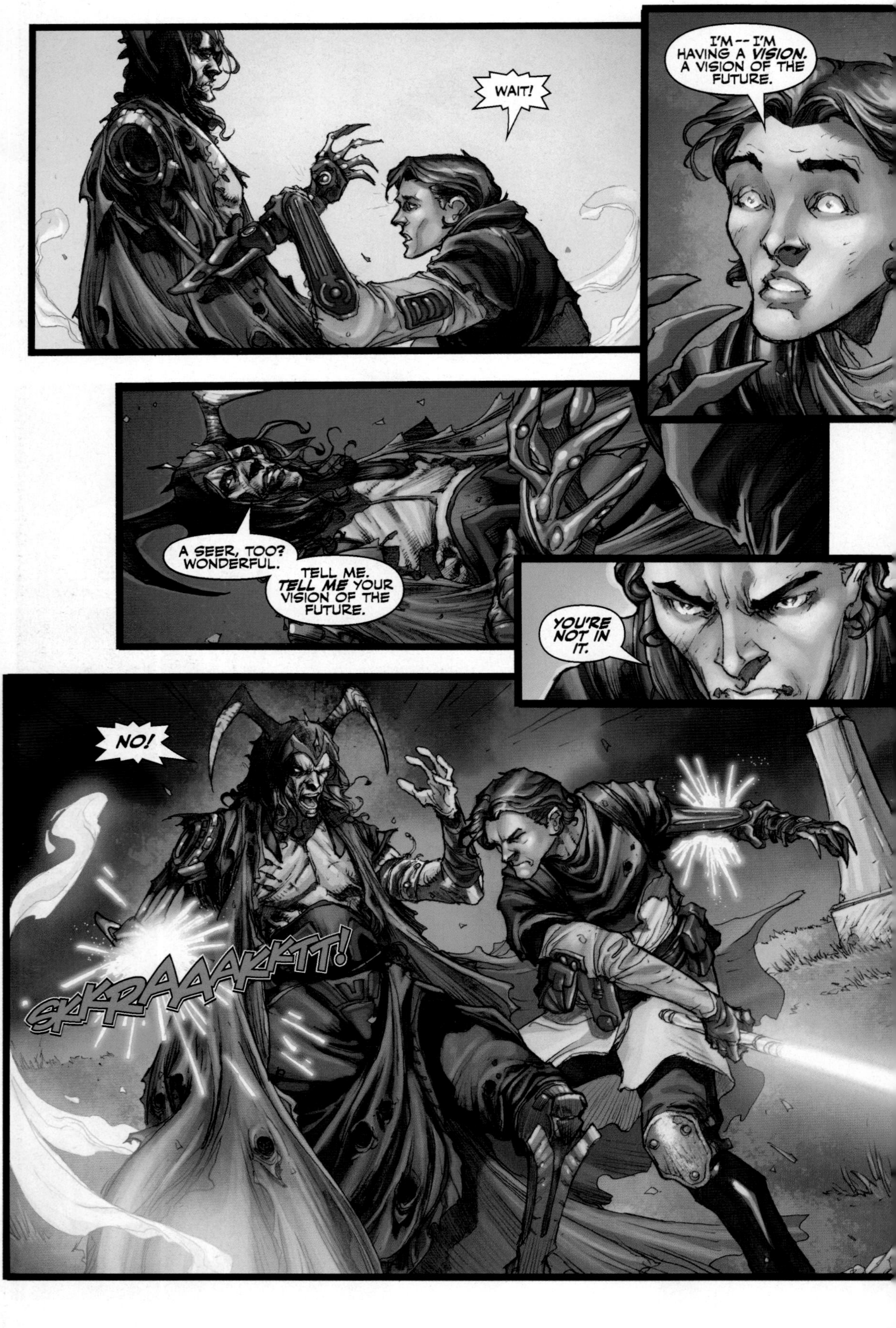
WAIT!
I'M -- I'M HAVING A VISION. A VISION OF THE FUTURE.
A SEER, TOO? WONDERFUL.
TELL ME. TELL ME YOUR VISION OF THE FUTURE.
YOU'RE NOT IN IT.
NO!
SKKRAAAAKKTT!

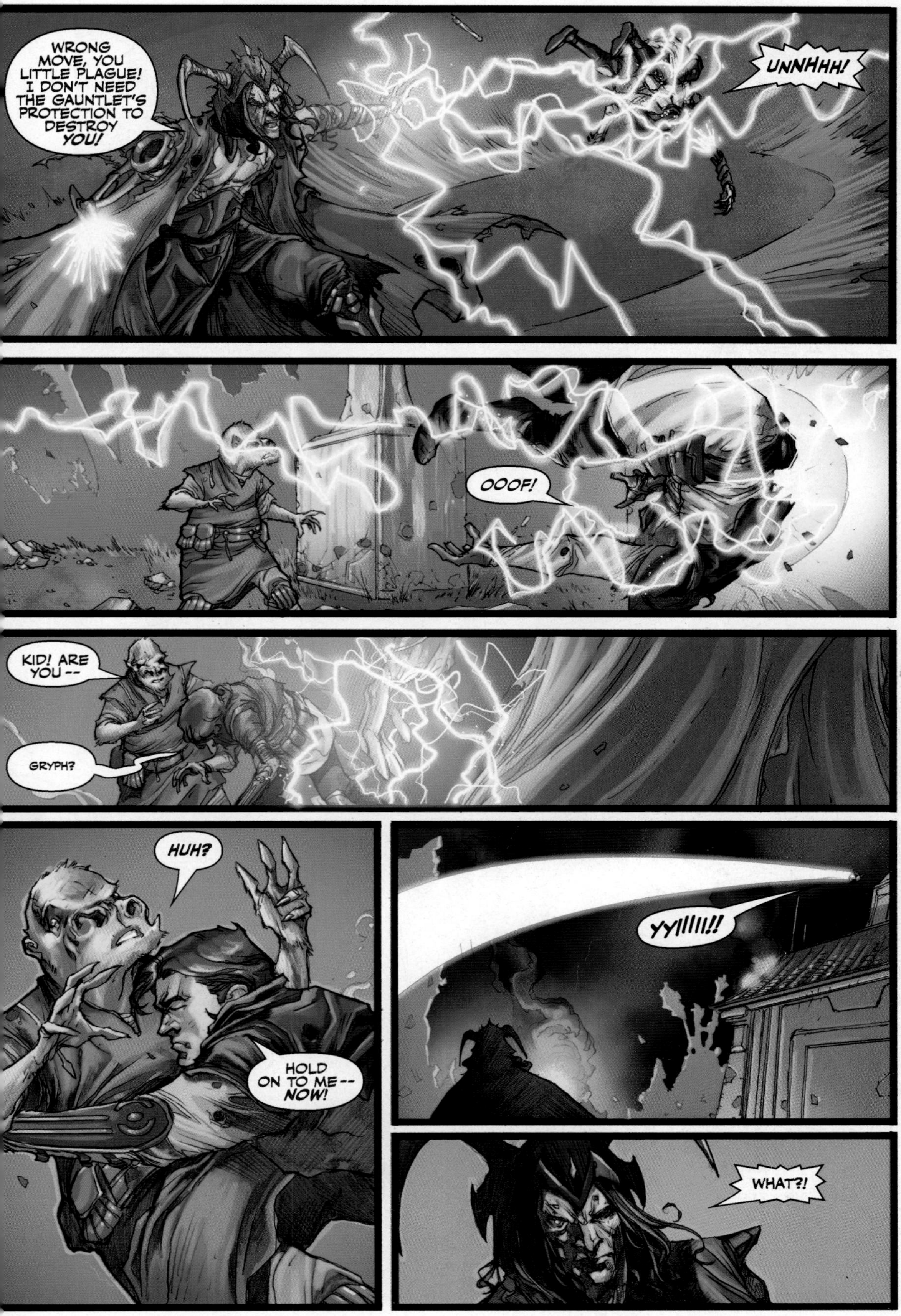
WRONG MOVE, YOU LITTLE PLAGUE! I DON'T NEED THE GAUNTLET'S PROTECTION TO DESTROY YOU!
UNNHHH!
OOOF!
KID! ARE YOU --
GRYPH?
HUH?
HOLD ON TO ME -- NOW!
YYIIIIII!!
WHAT?!

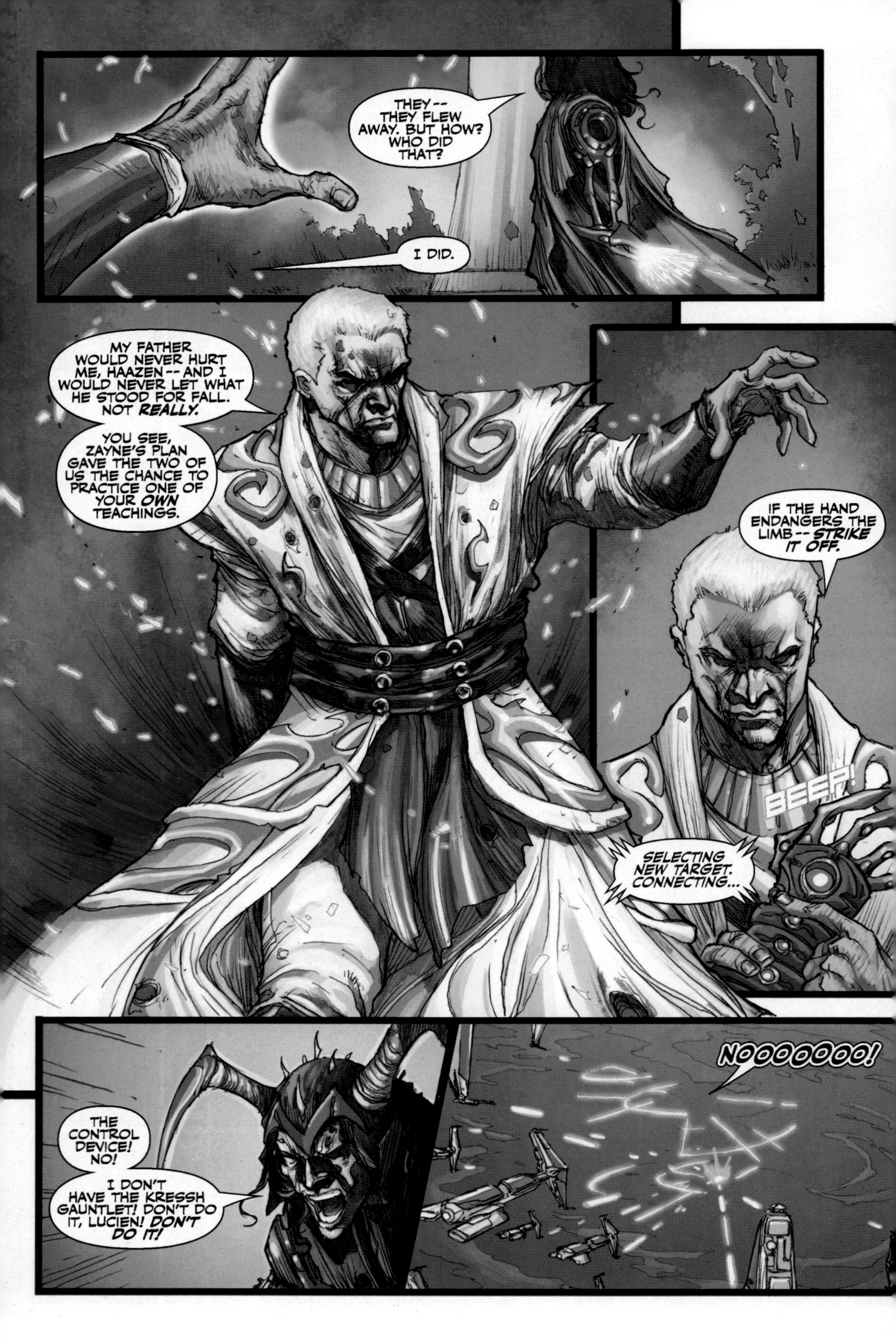

THEY-- THEY FLEW AWAY. BUT HOW? WHO DID THAT?
I DID.
MY FATHER WOULD NEVER HURT ME, HAAZEN--AND I WOULD NEVER LET WHAT HE STOOD FOR FALL. NOT *REALLY.*
YOU SEE, ZAYNE'S PLAN GAVE THE TWO OF US THE CHANCE TO PRACTICE ONE OF YOUR *OWN* TEACHINGS.
IF THE HAND ENDANGERS THE LIMB--*STRIKE IT OFF.*
BEEP!
SELECTING NEW TARGET. CONNECTING...
THE CONTROL DEVICE! NO!
I DON'T HAVE THE KRESSH GAUNTLET! DON'T DO IT, LUCIEN! *DON'T DO IT!*
NOOOOOOO!

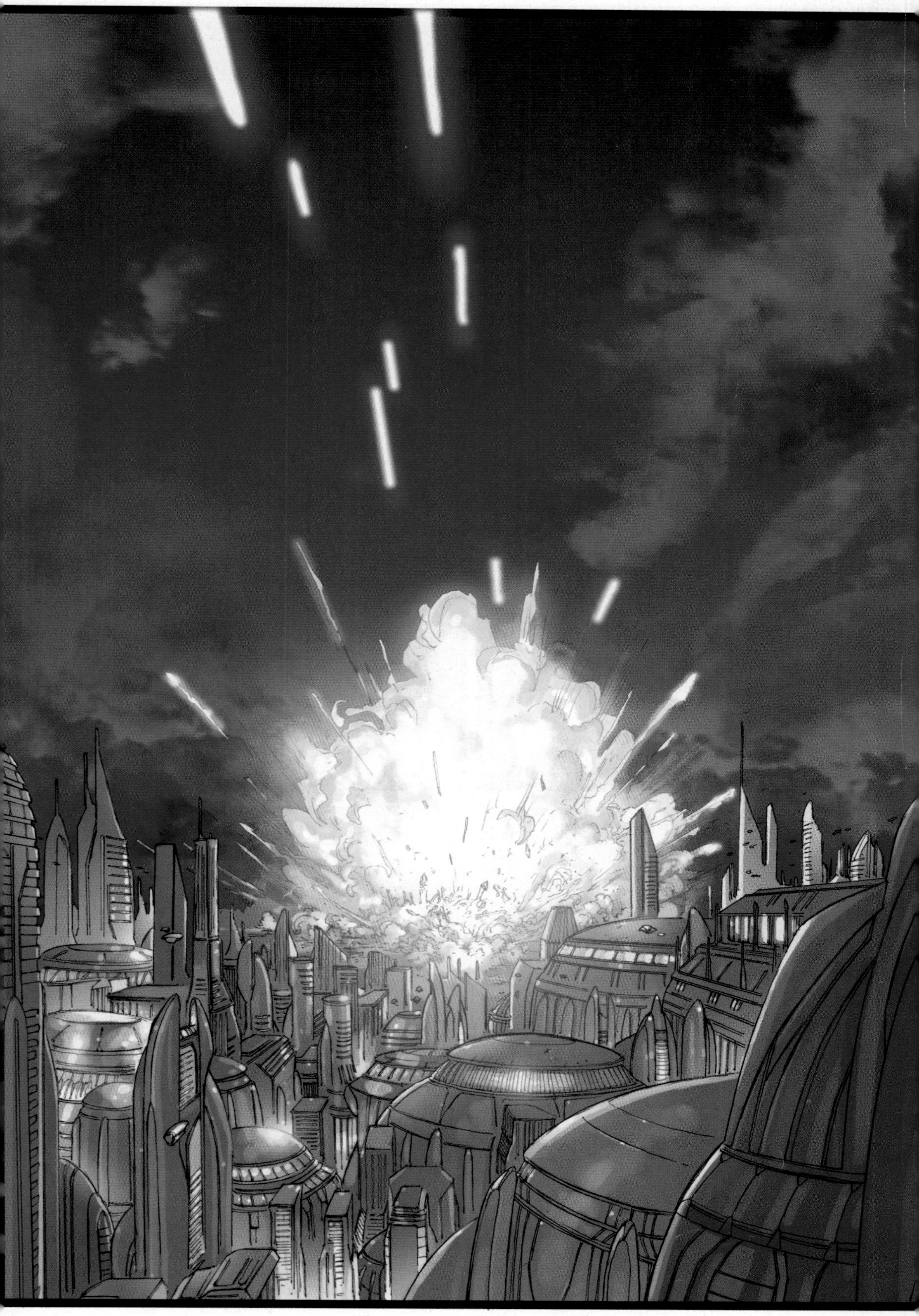

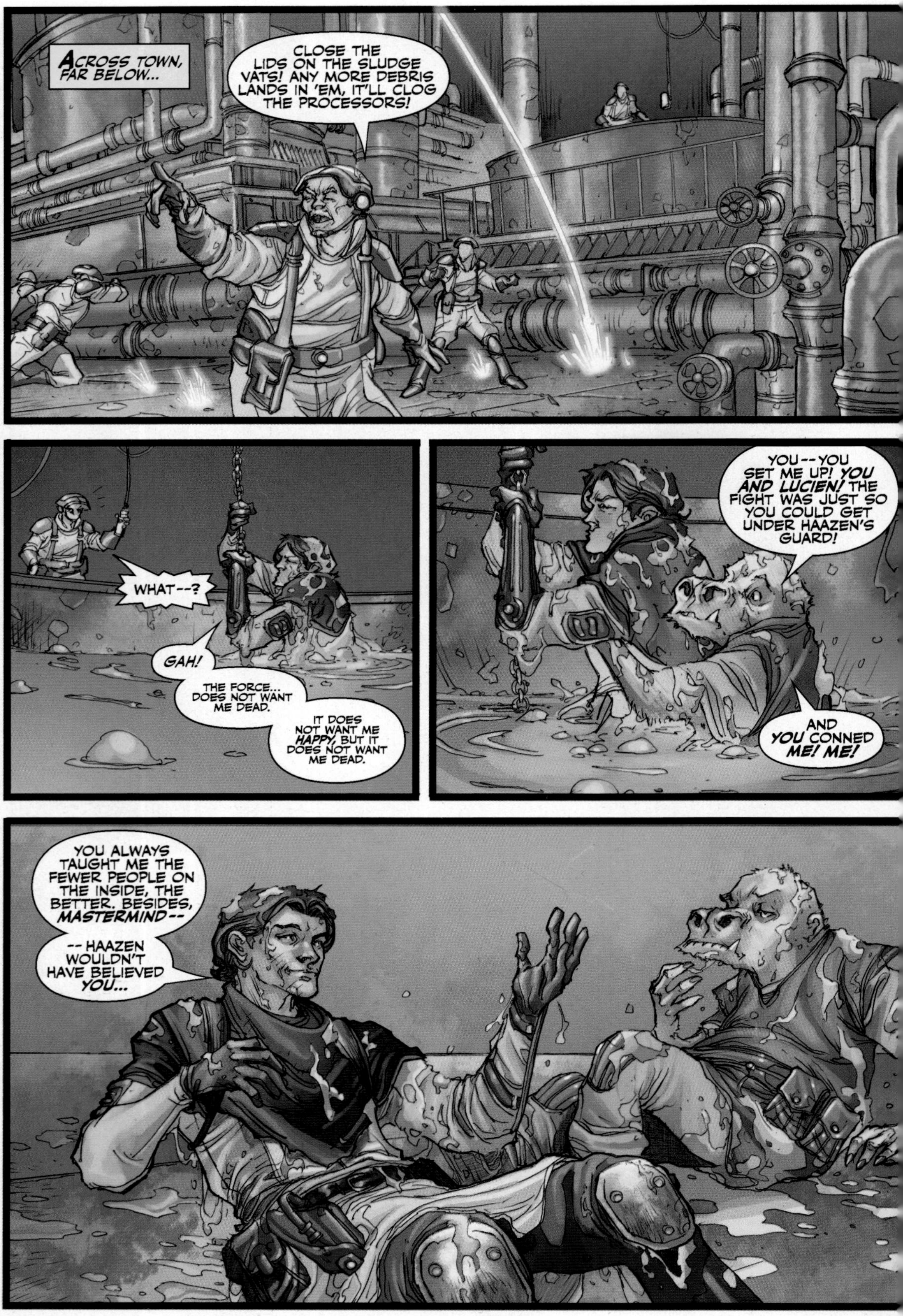
ACROSS TOWN, FAR BELOW...
CLOSE THE LIDS ON THE SLUDGE VATS! ANY MORE DEBRIS LANDS IN 'EM, IT'LL CLOG THE PROCESSORS!
WHAT--?
GAH!
THE FORCE... DOES NOT WANT ME DEAD.
IT DOES NOT WANT ME HAPPY, BUT IT DOES NOT WANT ME DEAD.
YOU--YOU SET ME UP! YOU AND LUCIEN! THE FIGHT WAS JUST SO YOU COULD GET UNDER HAAZEN'S GUARD!
AND YOU CONNED ME! ME!
YOU ALWAYS TAUGHT ME THE FEWER PEOPLE ON THE INSIDE, THE BETTER. BESIDES, MASTERMIND--
--HAAZEN WOULDN'T HAVE BELIEVED YOU...

DAYS LATER...

THANK YOU, CITIZENS! WITH JEDI HELP, YOUR NAVY WAS ABLE TO FOIL THE *TERROR PLOT* BY THE *MANDALORIANS*--

-- A FUTILE EFFORT TO BREAK OUR SPIRITS! AND WHILE THE HEROIC *DRAAY FAMILY* IS AMONG THE FALLEN --

-- OUR RESOLVE IS UNBROKEN! AND SOON, SAUL KARATH AND *SWIFTSURE* WILL TAKE THE FIGHT TO *THEM!*

AS SOON AS THEY INSTALL A *NEW COMPUTER,* THAT IS!

GRYPH, THAT--THAT'S NOT REMOTELY WHAT HAPPENED!

IT'S WHAT THEY ALL AGREED TO. REPUBLIC, JEDI -- THEY'RE *ALL* EMBARRASSED. HAAZEN RAN THE *LONG CON* LIKE A PRO.

THE COVER-UP HAS TO BE JUST AS GOOD. SO WHILE THEY'VE CLEARED US OF THE MURDERS--

--ONLY THE PADAWANS' *FAMILIES* ARE BEING TOLD WHAT REALLY HAPPENED. AND THE JEDI PAID OFF THE BOUNTIES ON US --

--EVEN PAID THE *MOOMOS,* FOR OFFICIALLY BRINGING US IN. THAT SHOULD DO WONDERS FOR THEIR REPS!

I JUST WISH THE JEDI HAD MADE PEACE WITH ALEK --

--*MALAK,* I MEAN. BUT THEY'RE MORE SET AGAINST JEDI FIGHTING IN THE WAR THAN EVER.

YEAH, THEY'VE JUST SEEN WHAT HAPPENS WHEN JEDI FORM THEIR OWN *CLUBS!*

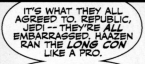

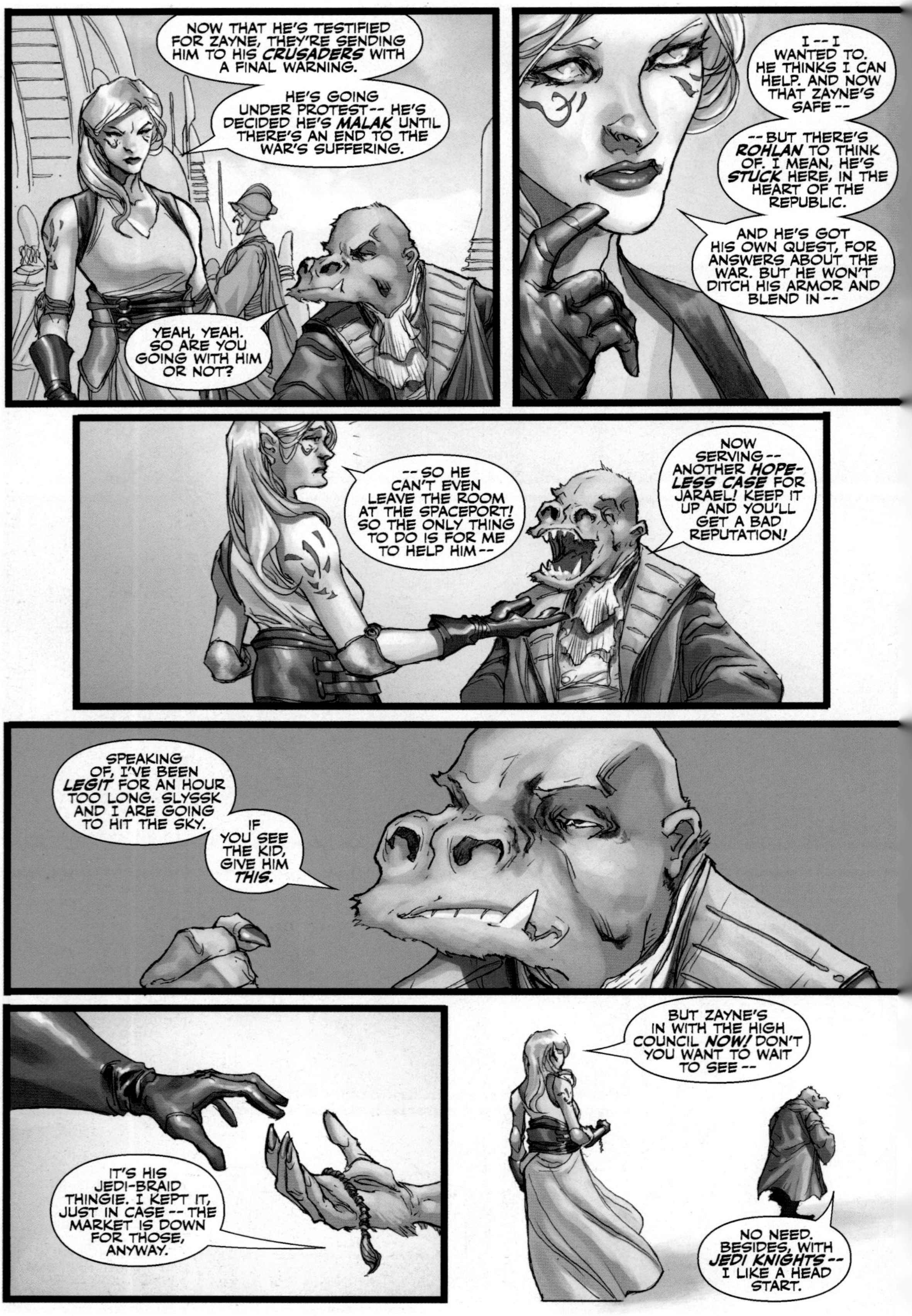
NOW THAT HE'S TESTIFIED FOR ZAYNE, THEY'RE SENDING HIM TO HIS CRUSADERS WITH A FINAL WARNING.
HE'S GOING UNDER PROTEST-- HE'S DECIDED HE'S MALAK UNTIL THERE'S AN END TO THE WAR'S SUFFERING.
YEAH, YEAH. SO ARE YOU GOING WITH HIM OR NOT?
I -- I WANTED TO. HE THINKS I CAN HELP. AND NOW THAT ZAYNE'S SAFE --
-- BUT THERE'S ROHLAN TO THINK OF. I MEAN, HE'S STUCK HERE, IN THE HEART OF THE REPUBLIC.
AND HE'S GOT HIS OWN QUEST, FOR ANSWERS ABOUT THE WAR. BUT HE WON'T DITCH HIS ARMOR AND BLEND IN --
-- SO HE CAN'T EVEN LEAVE THE ROOM AT THE SPACEPORT! SO THE ONLY THING TO DO IS FOR ME TO HELP HIM --
NOW SERVING -- ANOTHER HOPE-LESS CASE FOR JARAEL! KEEP IT UP AND YOU'LL GET A BAD REPUTATION!
SPEAKING OF, I'VE BEEN LEGIT FOR AN HOUR TOO LONG. SLYSSK AND I ARE GOING TO HIT THE SKY.
IF YOU SEE THE KID, GIVE HIM THIS.
IT'S HIS JEDI-BRAID THINGIE. I KEPT IT, JUST IN CASE -- THE MARKET IS DOWN FOR THOSE, ANYWAY.
BUT ZAYNE'S IN WITH THE HIGH COUNCIL NOW! DON'T YOU WANT TO WAIT TO SEE --
NO NEED. BESIDES, WITH JEDI KNIGHTS -- I LIKE A HEAD START.

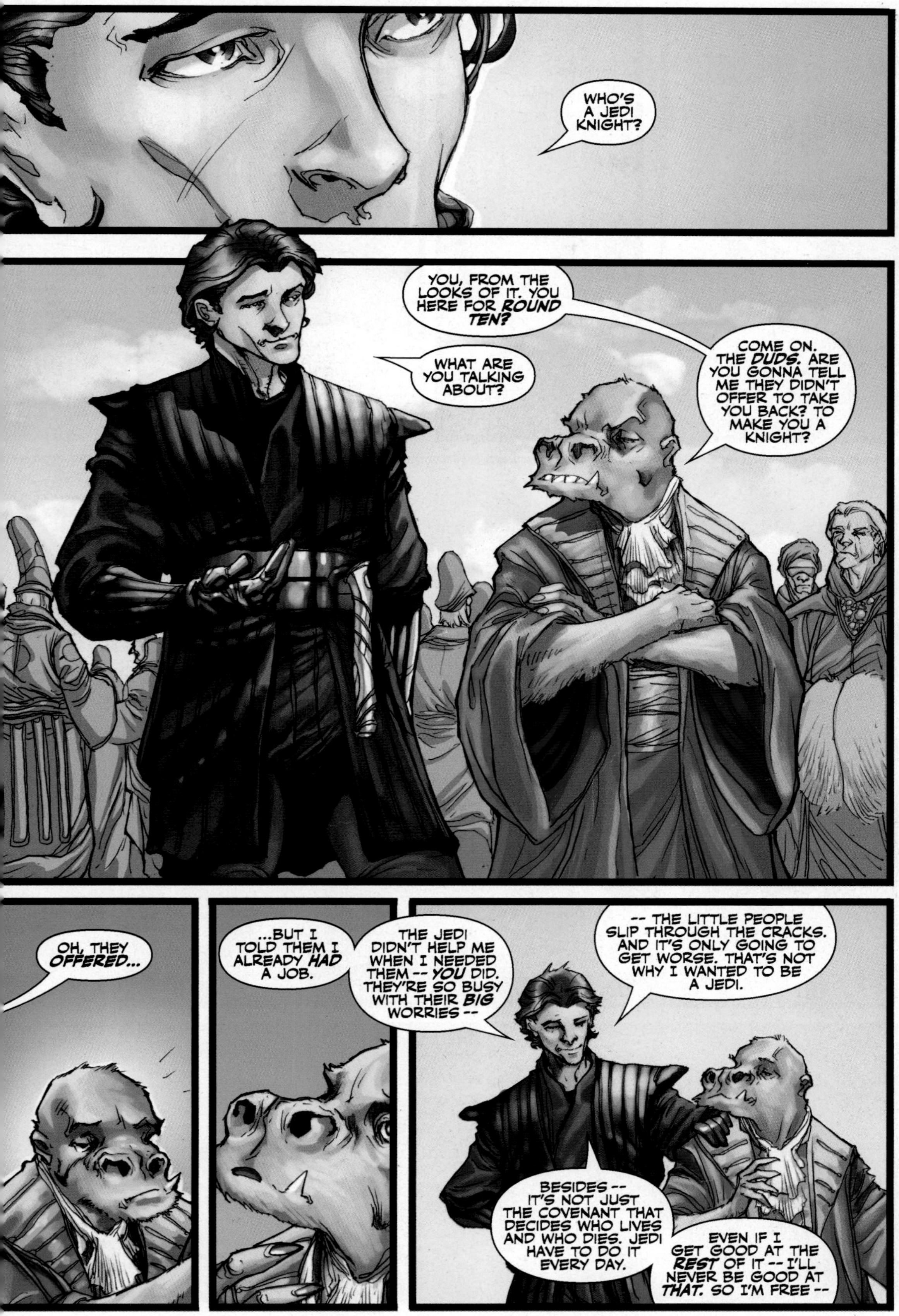
WHO'S A JEDI KNIGHT?
YOU, FROM THE LOOKS OF IT. YOU HERE FOR *ROUND TEN?*
WHAT ARE YOU TALKING ABOUT?
COME ON. THE *DUDS.* ARE YOU GONNA TELL ME THEY DIDN'T OFFER TO TAKE YOU BACK? TO MAKE YOU A KNIGHT?
OH, THEY *OFFERED...*
...BUT I TOLD THEM I ALREADY *HAD* A JOB.
THE JEDI DIDN'T HELP ME WHEN I NEEDED THEM -- *YOU* DID. THEY'RE SO BUSY WITH THEIR *BIG* WORRIES --
-- THE LITTLE PEOPLE SLIP THROUGH THE CRACKS. AND IT'S ONLY GOING TO GET WORSE. THAT'S NOT WHY I WANTED TO BE A JEDI.
BESIDES -- IT'S NOT JUST THE COVENANT THAT DECIDES WHO LIVES AND WHO DIES. JEDI HAVE TO DO IT EVERY DAY.
EVEN IF I GET GOOD AT THE *REST* OF IT -- I'LL NEVER BE GOOD AT *THAT.* SO I'M FREE --

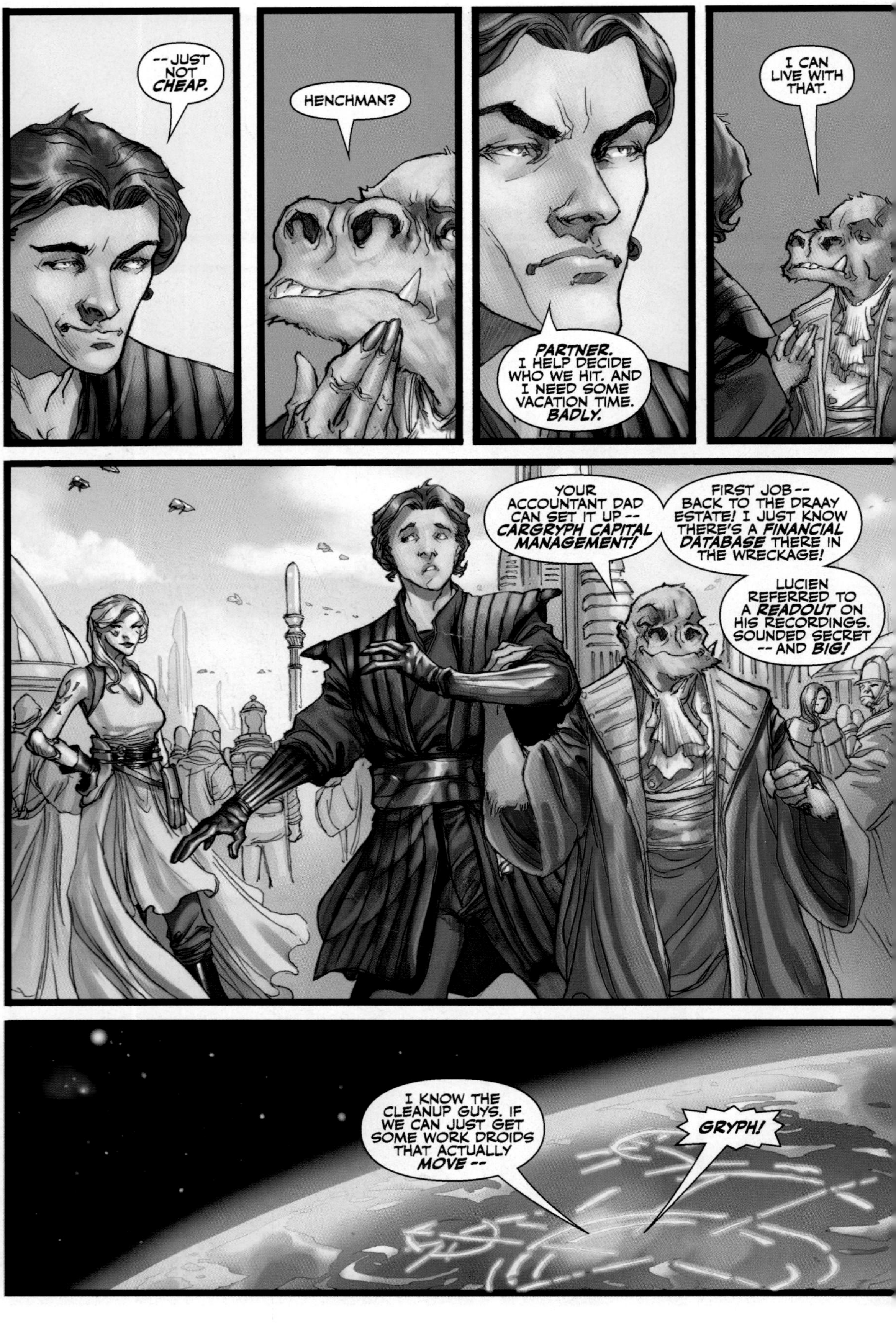
--JUST NOT *CHEAP.*
HENCHMAN?
PARTNER. I HELP DECIDE WHO WE HIT. AND I NEED SOME VACATION TIME. *BADLY.*
I CAN LIVE WITH THAT.
YOUR ACCOUNTANT DAD CAN SET IT UP-- *CARGRYPH CAPITAL MANAGEMENT!*
FIRST JOB-- BACK TO THE DRAAY ESTATE! I JUST KNOW THERE'S A *FINANCIAL DATABASE* THERE IN THE WRECKAGE!
LUCIEN REFERRED TO A *READOUT* ON HIS RECORDINGS. SOUNDED SECRET --AND *BIG!*
I KNOW THE CLEANUP GUYS. IF WE CAN JUST GET SOME WORK DROIDS THAT ACTUALLY *MOVE*--
GRYPH!

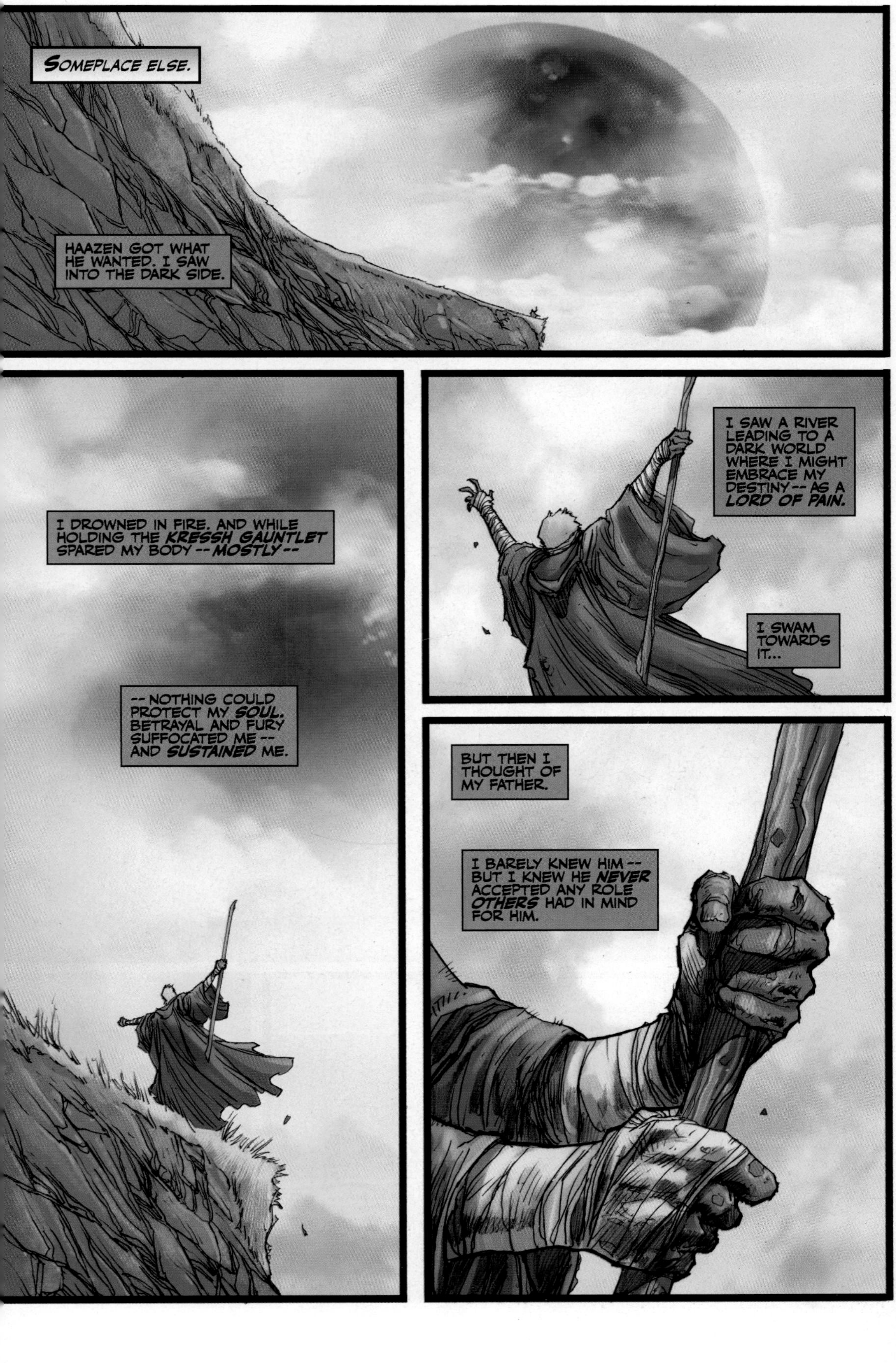
SOMEPLACE ELSE.
HAAZEN GOT WHAT HE WANTED. I SAW INTO THE DARK SIDE.
I DROWNED IN FIRE. AND WHILE HOLDING THE KRESSH GAUNTLET SPARED MY BODY -- MOSTLY --
-- NOTHING COULD PROTECT MY SOUL. BETRAYAL AND FURY SUFFOCATED ME -- AND SUSTAINED ME.
I SAW A RIVER LEADING TO A DARK WORLD WHERE I MIGHT EMBRACE MY DESTINY -- AS A LORD OF PAIN.
I SWAM TOWARDS IT...
BUT THEN I THOUGHT OF MY FATHER.
I BARELY KNEW HIM -- BUT I KNEW HE NEVER ACCEPTED ANY ROLE OTHERS HAD IN MIND FOR HIM.

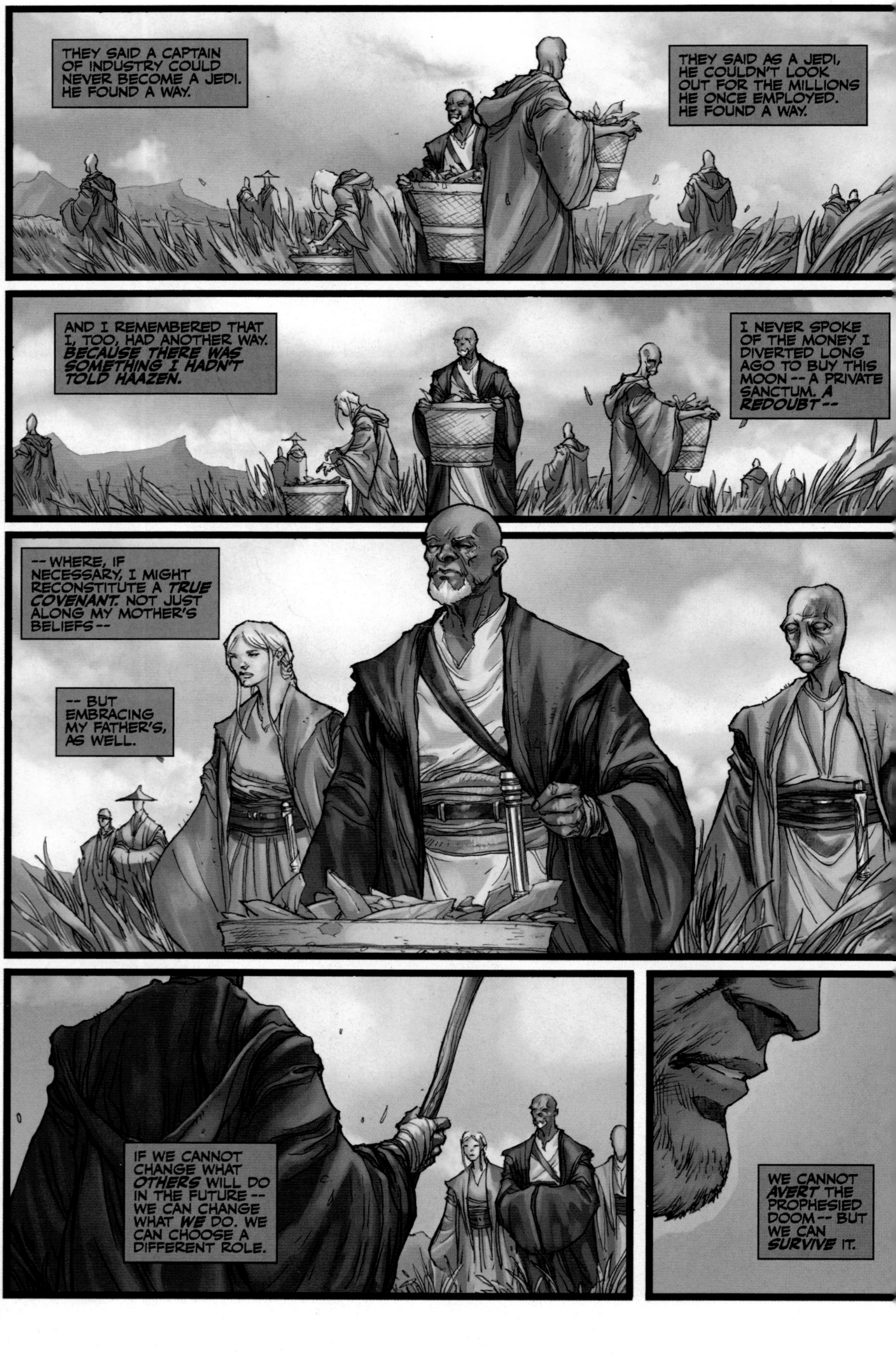
THEY SAID A CAPTAIN OF INDUSTRY COULD NEVER BECOME A JEDI. HE FOUND A WAY.
THEY SAID AS A JEDI, HE COULDN'T LOOK OUT FOR THE MILLIONS HE ONCE EMPLOYED. HE FOUND A WAY.
AND I REMEMBERED THAT I, TOO, HAD ANOTHER WAY. BECAUSE THERE WAS SOMETHING I HADN'T TOLD HAAZEN.
I NEVER SPOKE OF THE MONEY I DIVERTED LONG AGO TO BUY THIS MOON -- A PRIVATE SANCTUM. A REDOUBT--
--WHERE, IF NECESSARY, I MIGHT RECONSTITUTE A TRUE COVENANT. NOT JUST ALONG MY MOTHER'S BELIEFS--
-- BUT EMBRACING MY FATHER'S, AS WELL.
IF WE CANNOT CHANGE WHAT OTHERS WILL DO IN THE FUTURE -- WE CAN CHANGE WHAT WE DO. WE CAN CHOOSE A DIFFERENT ROLE.
WE CANNOT AVERT THE PROPHESIED DOOM -- BUT WE CAN SURVIVE IT.

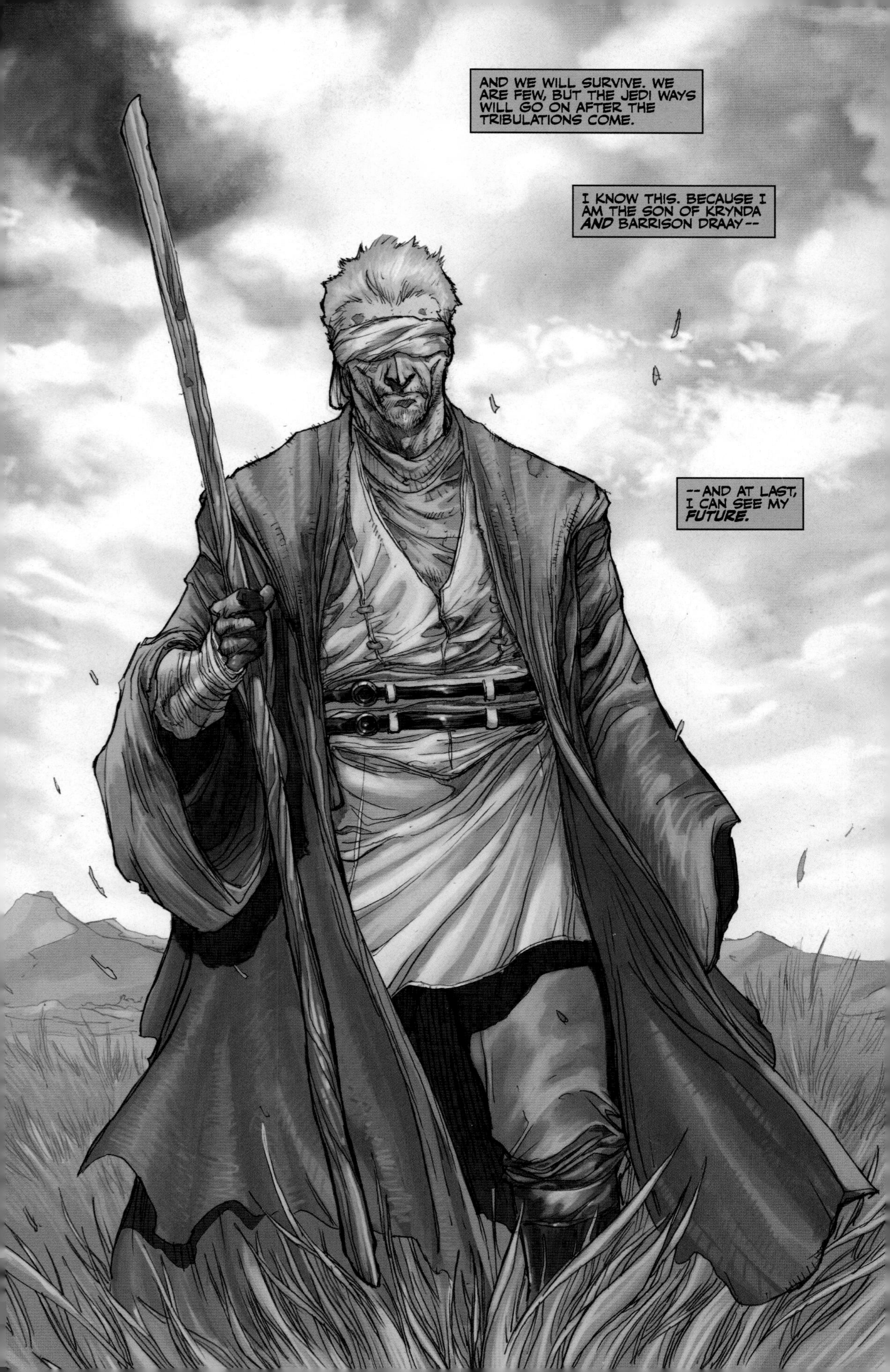
AND WE WILL SURVIVE. WE ARE FEW, BUT THE JEDI WAYS WILL GO ON AFTER THE TRIBULATIONS COME.
I KNOW THIS. BECAUSE I AM THE SON OF KRYNDA *AND* BARRISON DRAAY--
--AND AT LAST, I CAN SEE MY *FUTURE.*

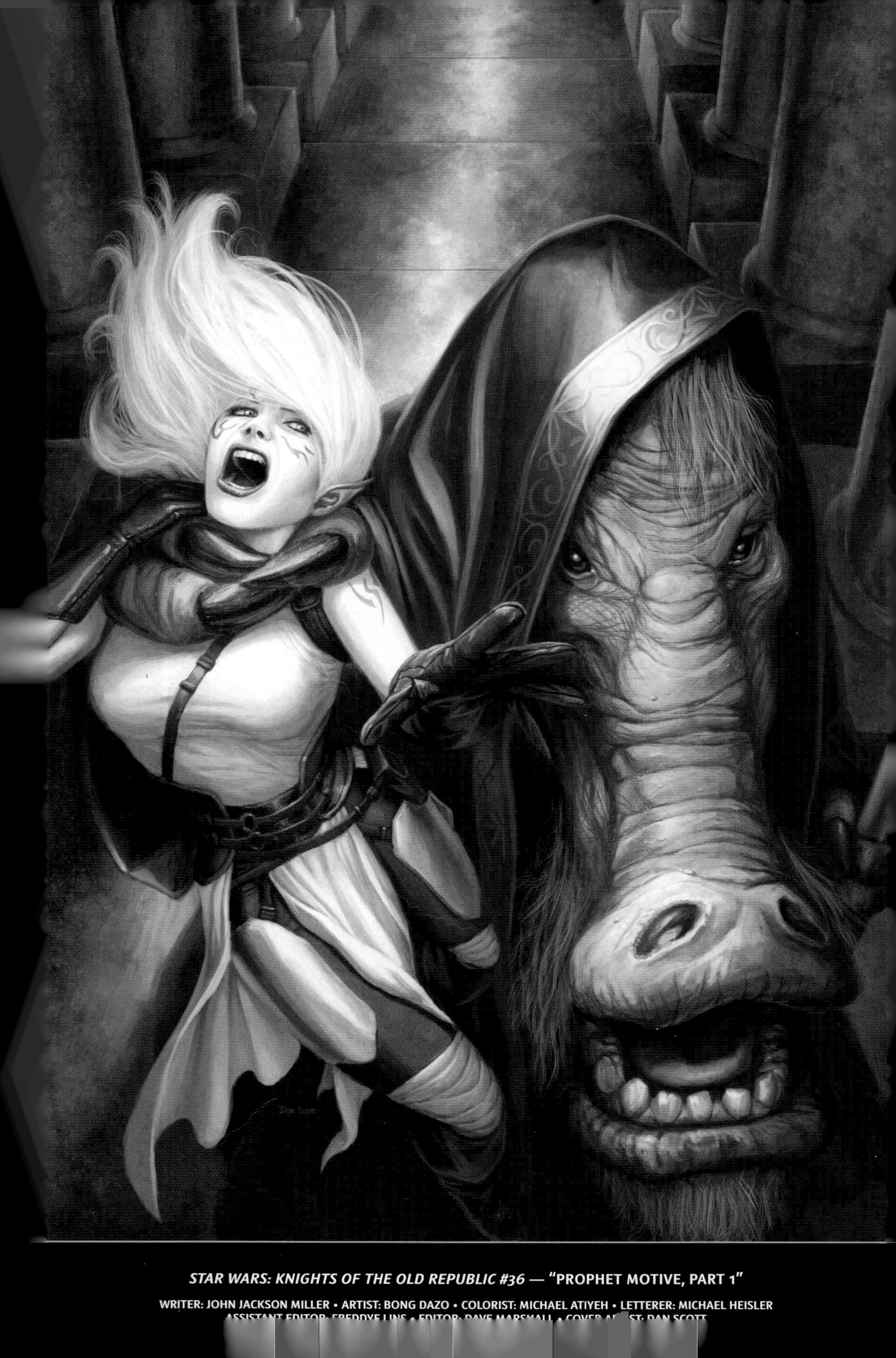

***STAR WARS: KNIGHTS OF THE OLD REPUBLIC #36* — "PROPHET MOTIVE, PART 1"**

WRITER: JOHN JACKSON MILLER • ARTIST: BONG DAZO • COLORIST: MICHAEL ATIYEH • LETTERER: MICHAEL HEISLER
ASSISTANT EDITOR: FREDDYE LINS • EDITOR: DAVE MARSHALL • COVER ARTIST: DAN SCOTT

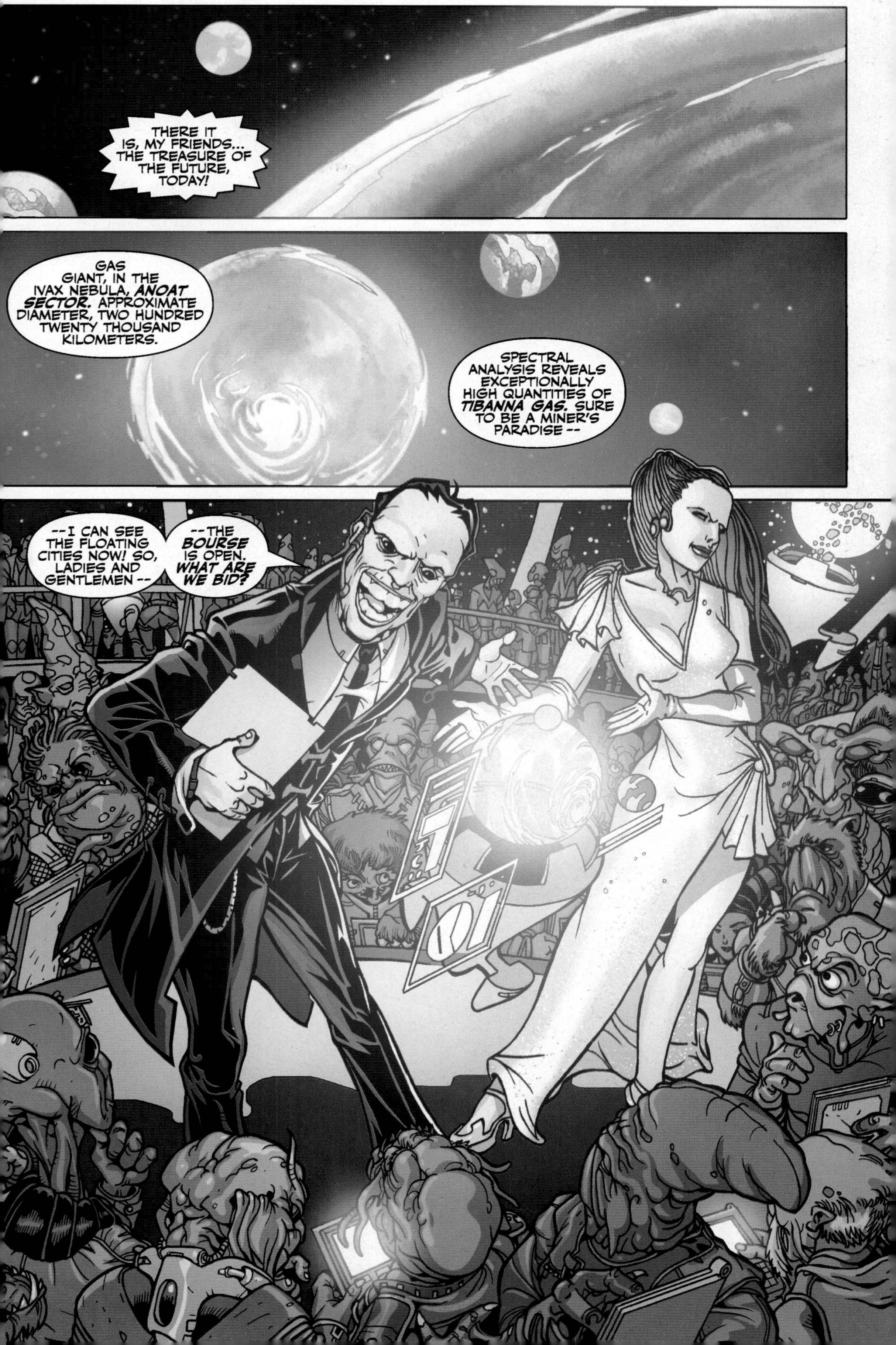
THERE IT IS, MY FRIENDS... THE TREASURE OF THE FUTURE, TODAY!
GAS GIANT, IN THE IVAX NEBULA, ANOAT SECTOR. APPROXIMATE DIAMETER, TWO HUNDRED TWENTY THOUSAND KILOMETERS.
SPECTRAL ANALYSIS REVEALS EXCEPTIONALLY HIGH QUANTITIES OF TIBANNA GAS. SURE TO BE A MINER'S PARADISE --
--I CAN SEE THE FLOATING CITIES NOW! SO, LADIES AND GENTLEMEN --
--THE BOURSE IS OPEN. WHAT ARE WE BID?

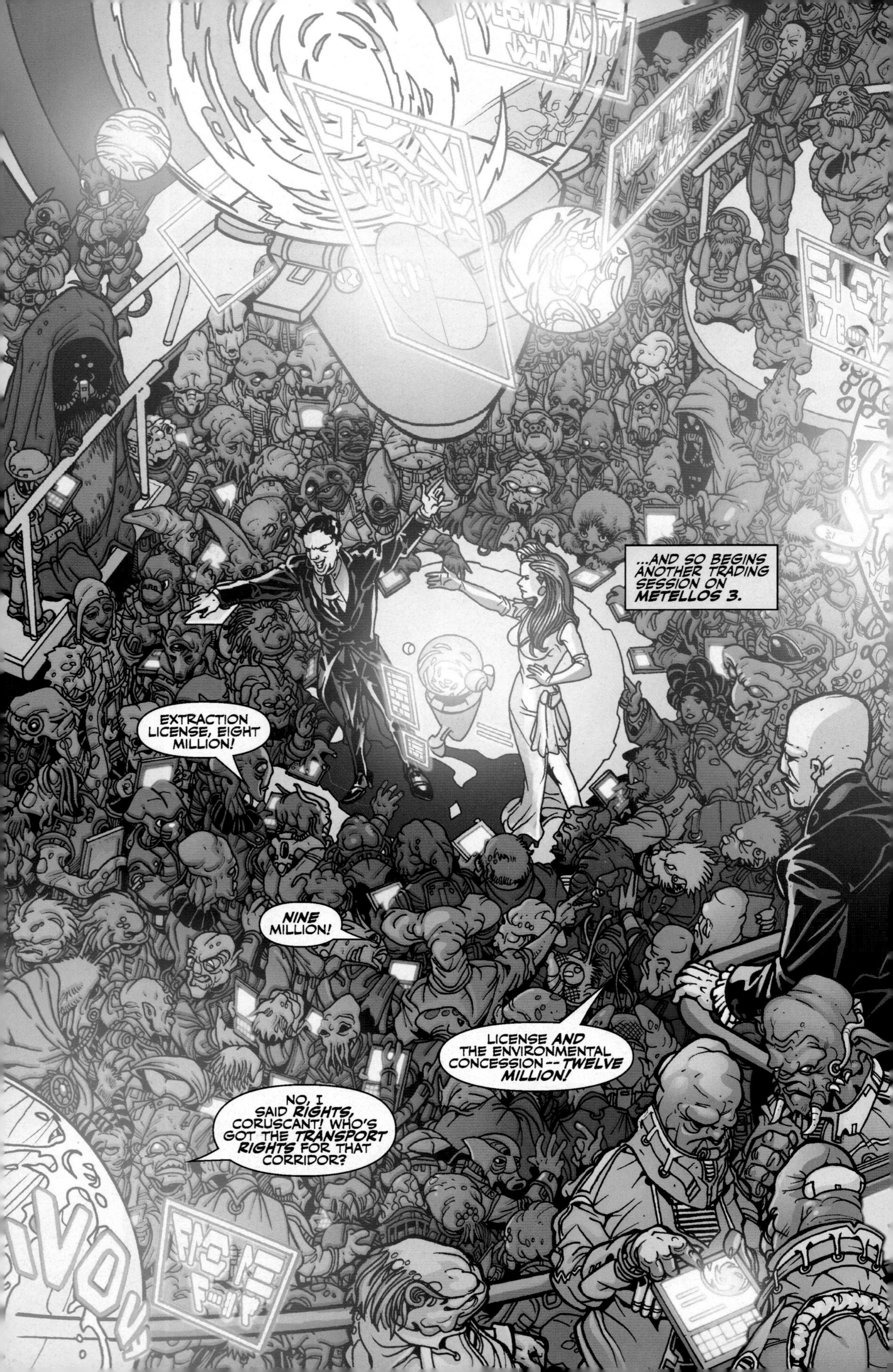
...AND SO BEGINS ANOTHER TRADING SESSION ON METELLOS 3.
EXTRACTION LICENSE, EIGHT MILLION!
NINE MILLION!
LICENSE AND THE ENVIRONMENTAL CONCESSION -- TWELVE MILLION!
NO, I SAID RIGHTS, CORUSCANT! WHO'S GOT THE TRANSPORT RIGHTS FOR THAT CORRIDOR?

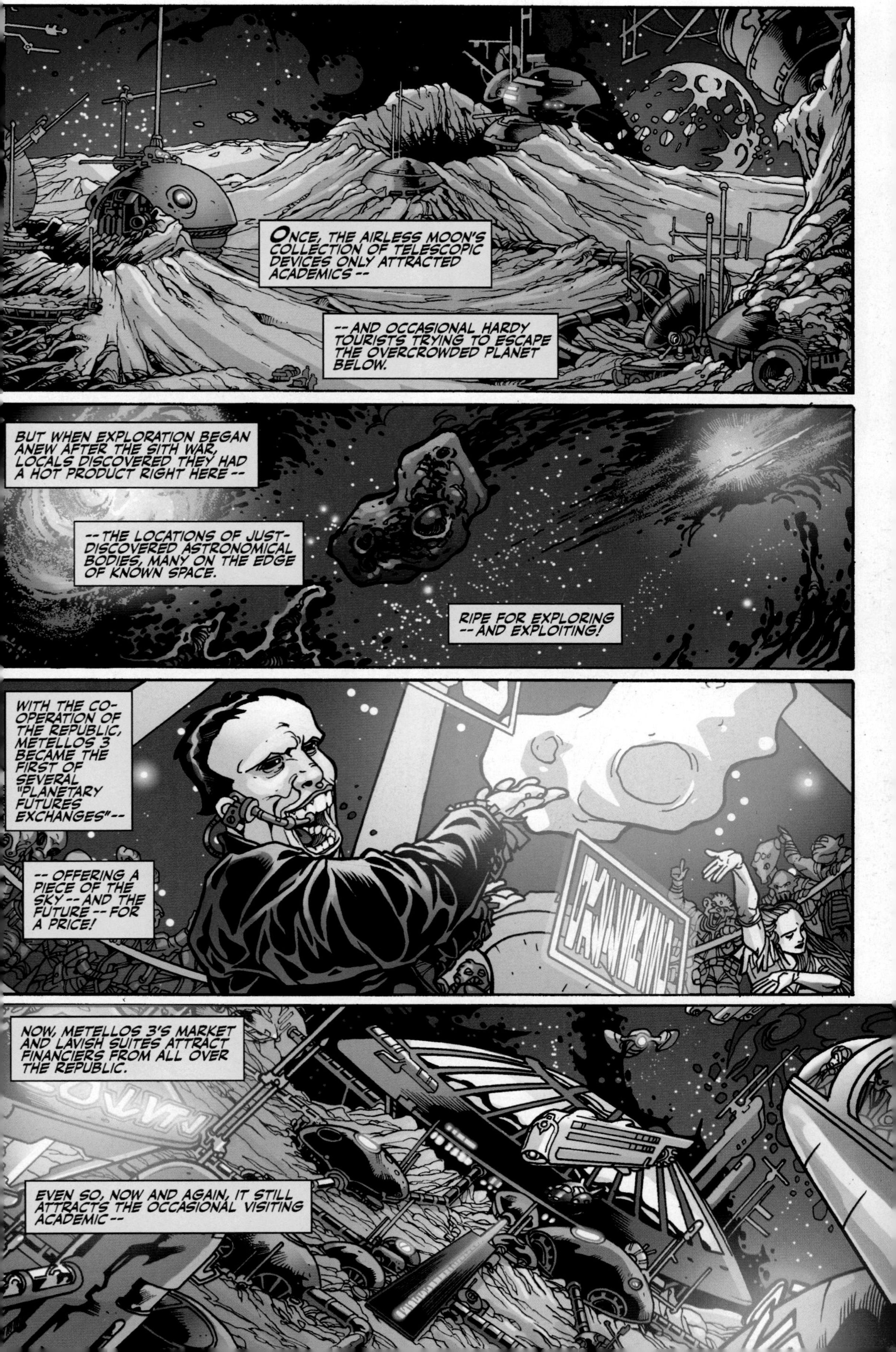
ONCE, THE AIRLESS MOON'S COLLECTION OF TELESCOPIC DEVICES ONLY ATTRACTED ACADEMICS --
-- AND OCCASIONAL HARDY TOURISTS TRYING TO ESCAPE THE OVERCROWDED PLANET BELOW.
BUT WHEN EXPLORATION BEGAN ANEW AFTER THE SITH WAR, LOCALS DISCOVERED THEY HAD A HOT PRODUCT RIGHT HERE --
-- THE LOCATIONS OF JUST-DISCOVERED ASTRONOMICAL BODIES, MANY ON THE EDGE OF KNOWN SPACE.
RIPE FOR EXPLORING -- AND EXPLOITING!
WITH THE CO-OPERATION OF THE REPUBLIC, METELLOS 3 BECAME THE FIRST OF SEVERAL "PLANETARY FUTURES EXCHANGES"--
-- OFFERING A PIECE OF THE SKY -- AND THE FUTURE -- FOR A PRICE!
NOW, METELLOS 3'S MARKET AND LAVISH SUITES ATTRACT FINANCIERS FROM ALL OVER THE REPUBLIC.
EVEN SO, NOW AND AGAIN, IT STILL ATTRACTS THE OCCASIONAL VISITING ACADEMIC --

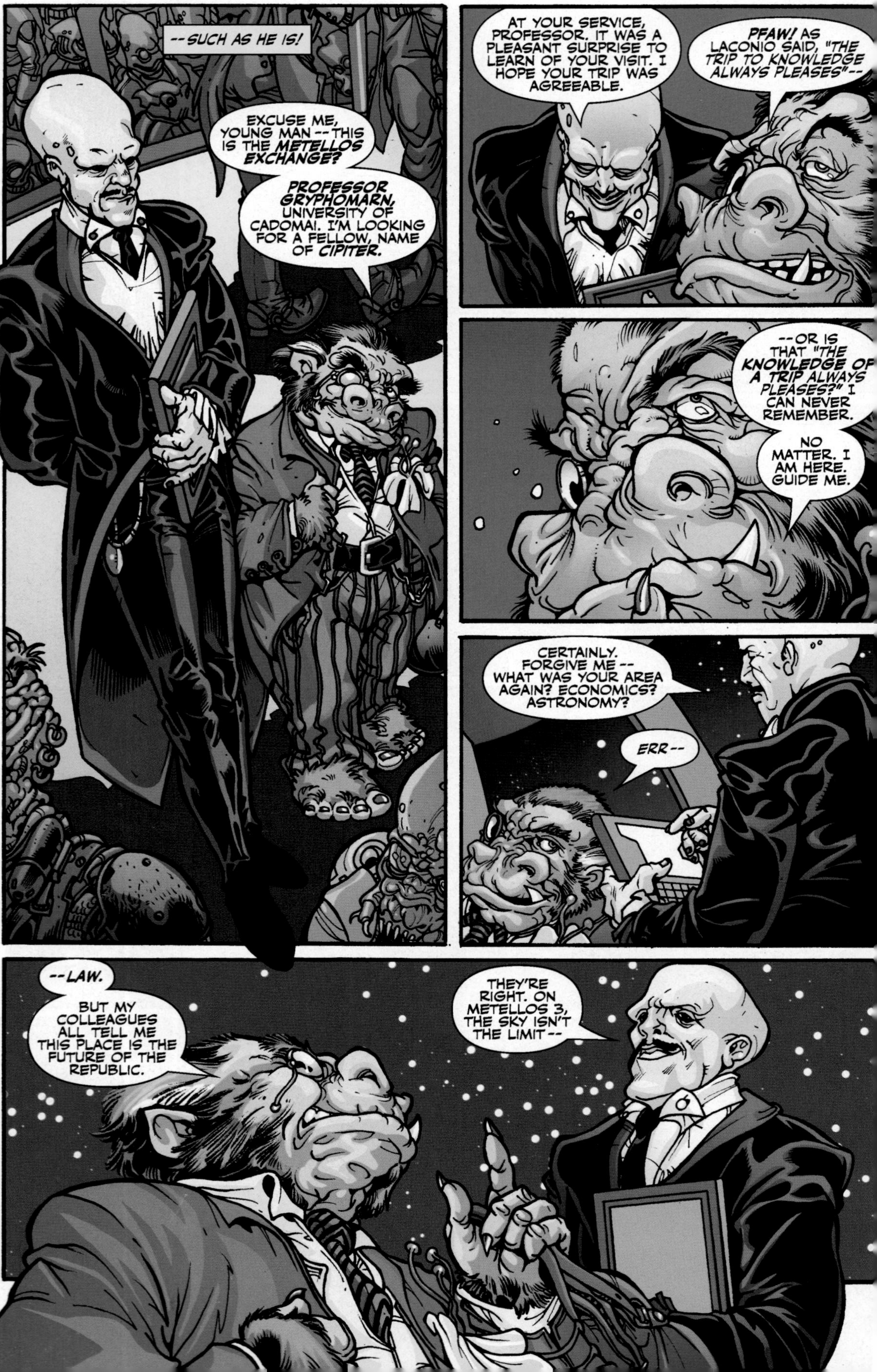
--SUCH AS HE IS!
EXCUSE ME, YOUNG MAN--THIS IS THE METELLOS EXCHANGE?
PROFESSOR GRYPHOMARN, UNIVERSITY OF CADOMAI. I'M LOOKING FOR A FELLOW, NAME OF CIPITER.
AT YOUR SERVICE, PROFESSOR. IT WAS A PLEASANT SURPRISE TO LEARN OF YOUR VISIT. I HOPE YOUR TRIP WAS AGREEABLE.
PFAW! AS LACONIO SAID, "THE TRIP TO KNOWLEDGE ALWAYS PLEASES"--
--OR IS THAT "THE KNOWLEDGE OF A TRIP ALWAYS PLEASES?" I CAN NEVER REMEMBER.
NO MATTER. I AM HERE. GUIDE ME.
CERTAINLY. FORGIVE ME--WHAT WAS YOUR AREA AGAIN? ECONOMICS? ASTRONOMY?
ERR--
--LAW.
BUT MY COLLEAGUES ALL TELL ME THIS PLACE IS THE FUTURE OF THE REPUBLIC.
THEY'RE RIGHT. ON METELLOS 3, THE SKY ISN'T THE LIMIT--

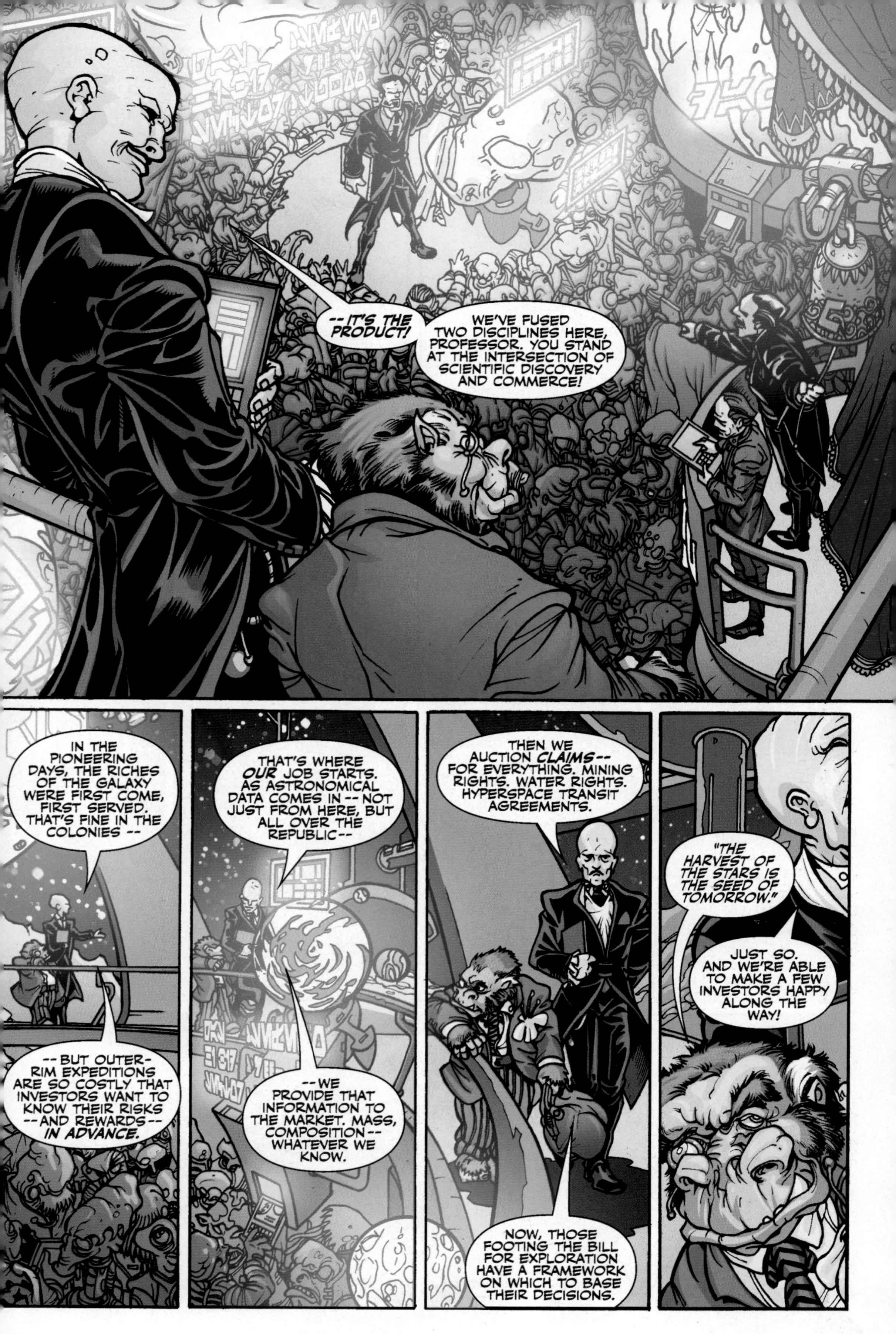
--IT'S THE PRODUCT!
WE'VE FUSED TWO DISCIPLINES HERE, PROFESSOR. YOU STAND AT THE INTERSECTION OF SCIENTIFIC DISCOVERY AND COMMERCE!
IN THE PIONEERING DAYS, THE RICHES OF THE GALAXY WERE FIRST COME, FIRST SERVED. THAT'S FINE IN THE COLONIES --
-- BUT OUTER-RIM EXPEDITIONS ARE SO COSTLY THAT INVESTORS WANT TO KNOW THEIR RISKS --AND REWARDS-- IN ADVANCE.
THAT'S WHERE OUR JOB STARTS. AS ASTRONOMICAL DATA COMES IN -- NOT JUST FROM HERE, BUT ALL OVER THE REPUBLIC--
--WE PROVIDE THAT INFORMATION TO THE MARKET. MASS, COMPOSITION-- WHATEVER WE KNOW.
THEN WE AUCTION CLAIMS-- FOR EVERYTHING. MINING RIGHTS. WATER RIGHTS. HYPERSPACE TRANSIT AGREEMENTS.
NOW, THOSE FOOTING THE BILL FOR EXPLORATION HAVE A FRAMEWORK ON WHICH TO BASE THEIR DECISIONS.
"THE HARVEST OF THE STARS IS THE SEED OF TOMORROW."
JUST SO. AND WE'RE ABLE TO MAKE A FEW INVESTORS HAPPY ALONG THE WAY!

BUT DON'T THEY ALSO CALL IT A *FINANCIAL FAD?*

SOME FAD! OURS IS A *NECESSARY* PRODUCT. YOU'RE A JURIST--

--YOU *KNOW* HOW MUCH IS WASTED WHEN CORPORATIONS ARGUE OVER A FIND. PROSPECTORS AND SQUATTERS THEY CAN BUY OFF--

"--BUT WHEN BANTHAS BATTLE, NO ONE PLOWS THE CROPS." CLEVER--

--BUT HOW CAN ANYONE CLAIM RIGHTS TO PLACES THAT MAY NOT BE VISITED FOR YEARS TO COME?

YES, WELL--

--AH, OUR CLAIMS ARE REALLY MORE LIKE *FUTURES CONTRACTS.* WE SIMPLY OFFER A PICTURE OF THE PLACE--

--A PROPHECY, SO TO SPEAK. *OUR CUSTOMERS* DECIDE ITS VALUE--AND WE TAKE A PORTION OF THE TRADE, OF COURSE.

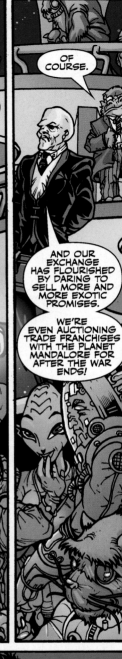

OF COURSE.

AND OUR EXCHANGE HAS FLOURISHED BY DARING TO SELL MORE AND MORE EXOTIC PROMISES.

WE'RE EVEN AUCTIONING TRADE FRANCHISES WITH THE PLANET MANDALORE FOR AFTER THE WAR ENDS!

WELL, THEN...I *HAVE* COME TO THE RIGHT PLACE.

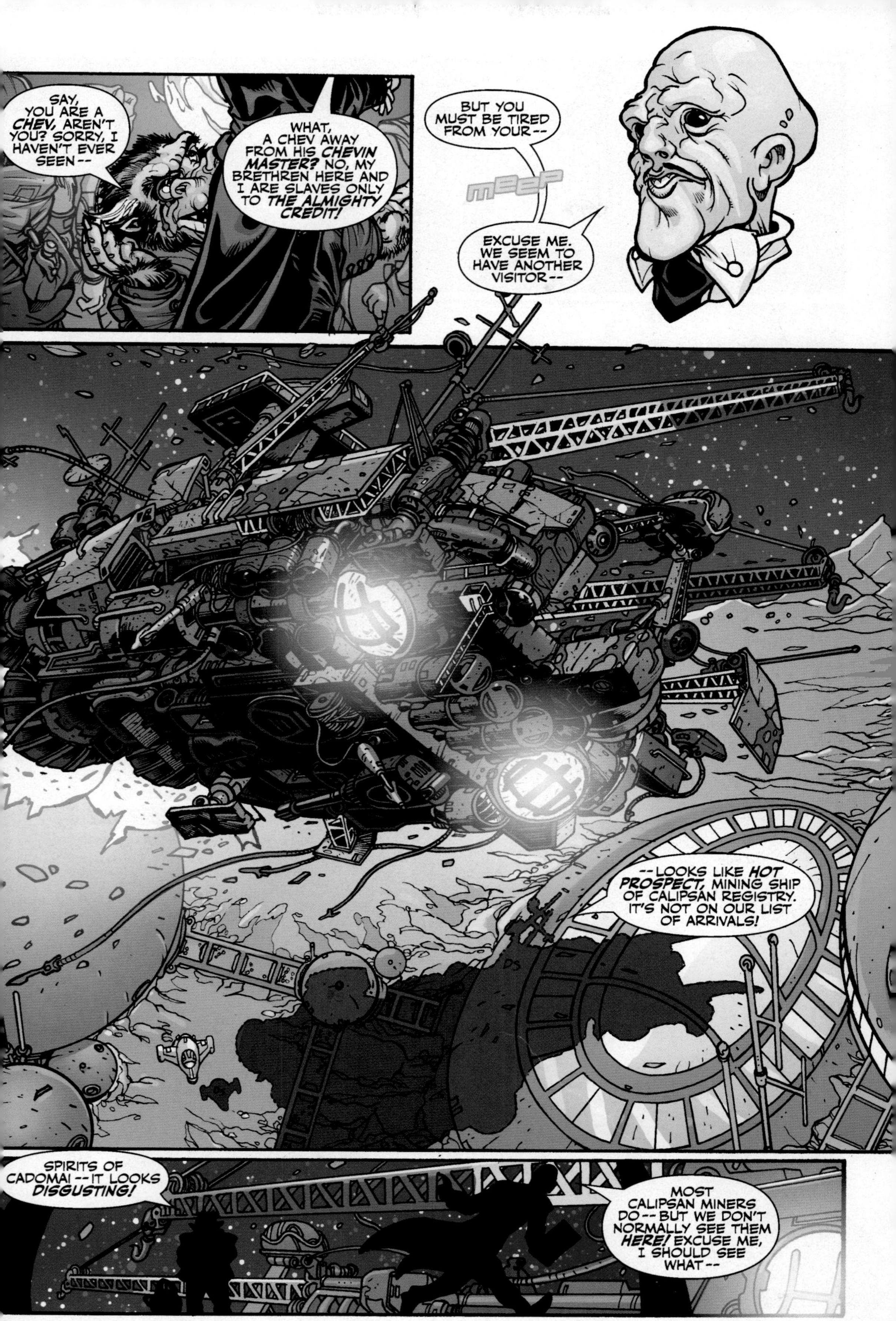
SAY, YOU ARE A *CHEV,* AREN'T YOU? SORRY, I HAVEN'T EVER SEEN--
WHAT, A CHEV AWAY FROM HIS *CHEVIN MASTER?* NO, MY BRETHREN HERE AND I ARE SLAVES ONLY TO *THE ALMIGHTY CREDIT!*
BUT YOU MUST BE TIRED FROM YOUR--
MEEP
EXCUSE ME. WE SEEM TO HAVE ANOTHER VISITOR--
--LOOKS LIKE *HOT PROSPECT,* MINING SHIP OF CALIPSAN REGISTRY. IT'S NOT ON OUR LIST OF ARRIVALS!
SPIRITS OF CADOMAI--IT LOOKS *DISGUSTING!*
MOST CALIPSAN MINERS DO--BUT WE DON'T NORMALLY SEE THEM *HERE!* EXCUSE ME, I SHOULD SEE WHAT--

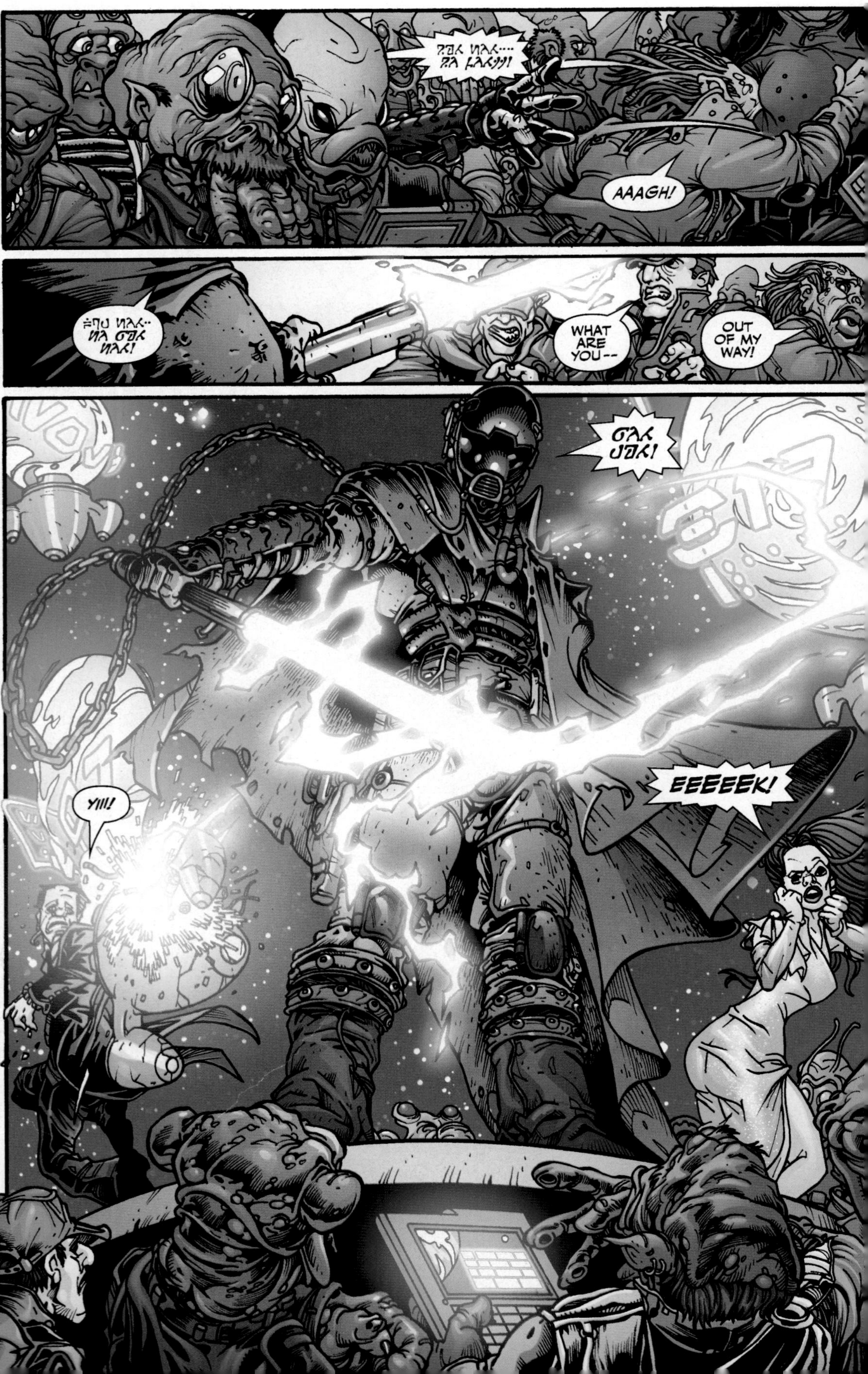
AAAGH!
WHAT ARE YOU --
OUT OF MY WAY!
EEEEEK!
YIII!

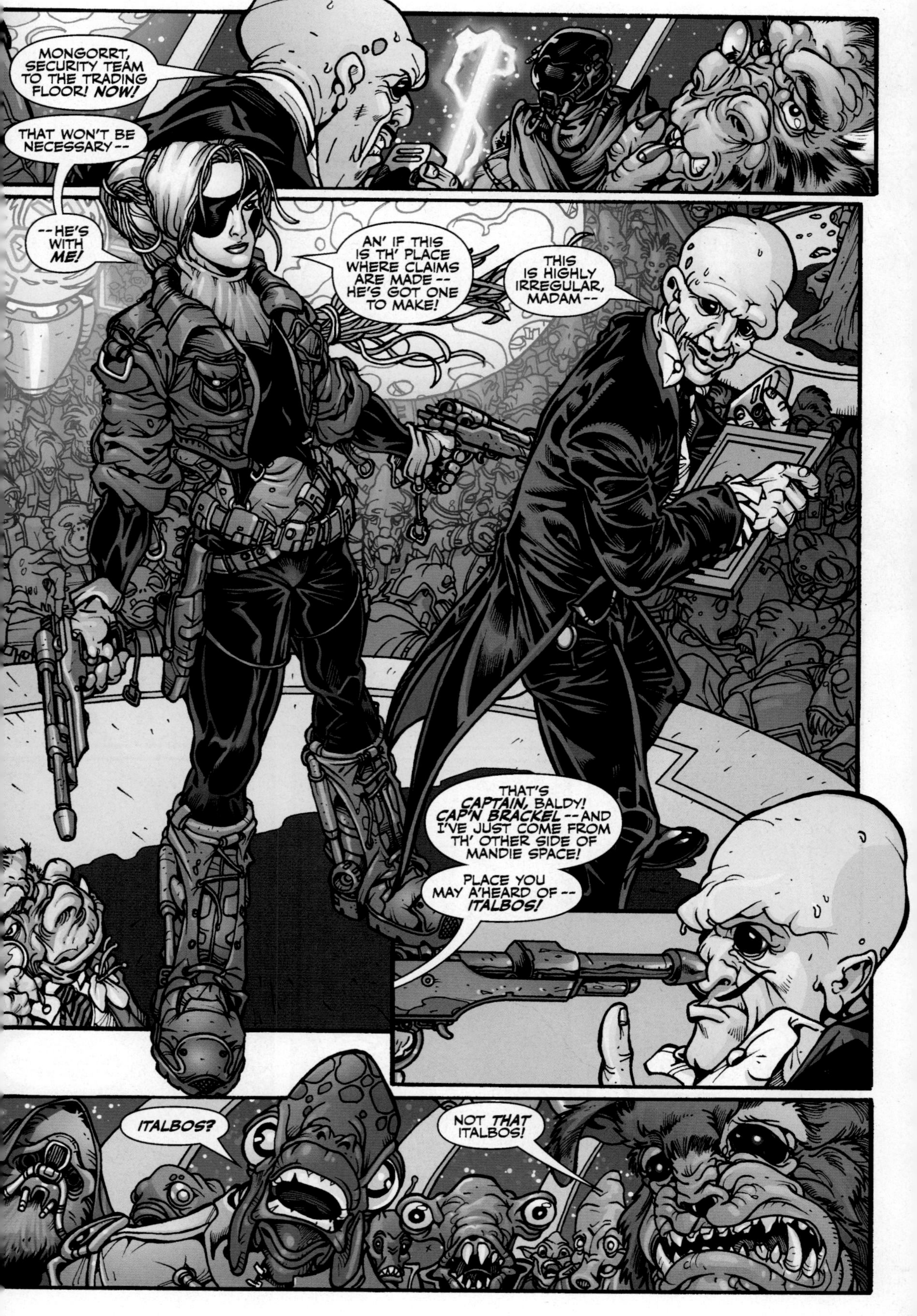
MONGORRT, SECURITY TEAM TO THE TRADING FLOOR! NOW!
THAT WON'T BE NECESSARY --
-- HE'S WITH ME!
AN' IF THIS IS TH' PLACE WHERE CLAIMS ARE MADE -- HE'S GOT ONE TO MAKE!
THIS IS HIGHLY IRREGULAR, MADAM --
THAT'S CAPTAIN, BALDY! CAP'N BRACKEL -- AND I'VE JUST COME FROM TH' OTHER SIDE OF MANDIE SPACE!
PLACE YOU MAY A'HEARD OF -- ITALBOS!
ITALBOS?
NOT THAT ITALBOS!

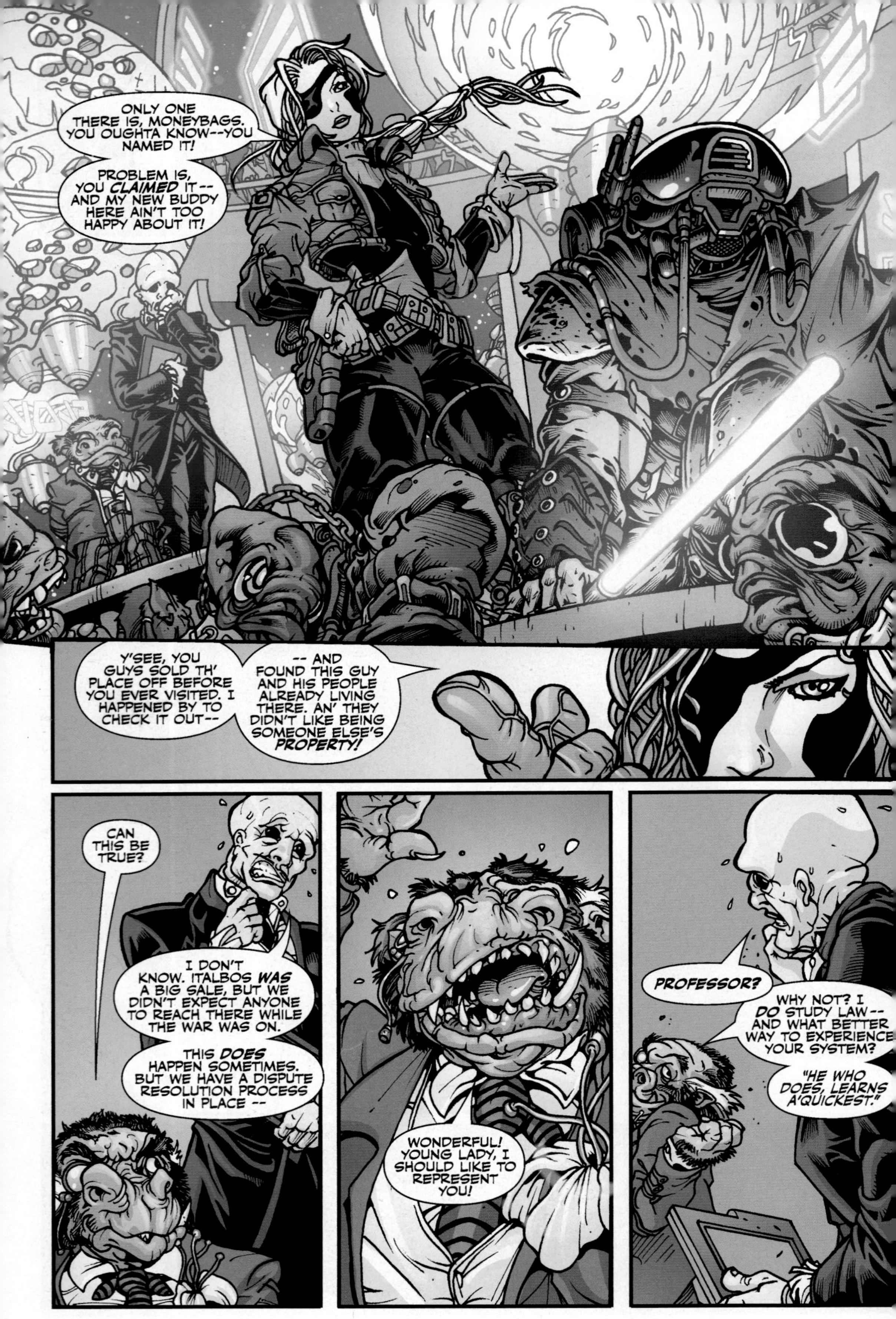

ONLY ONE THERE IS, MONEYBAGS. YOU OUGHTA KNOW--YOU NAMED IT!
PROBLEM IS, YOU CLAIMED IT -- AND MY NEW BUDDY HERE AIN'T TOO HAPPY ABOUT IT!
Y'SEE, YOU GUYS SOLD TH' PLACE OFF BEFORE YOU EVER VISITED. I HAPPENED BY TO CHECK IT OUT--
-- AND FOUND THIS GUY AND HIS PEOPLE ALREADY LIVING THERE. AN' THEY DIDN'T LIKE BEING SOMEONE ELSE'S PROPERTY!
CAN THIS BE TRUE?
I DON'T KNOW. ITALBOS WAS A BIG SALE, BUT WE DIDN'T EXPECT ANYONE TO REACH THERE WHILE THE WAR WAS ON.
THIS DOES HAPPEN SOMETIMES. BUT WE HAVE A DISPUTE RESOLUTION PROCESS IN PLACE --
WONDERFUL! YOUNG LADY, I SHOULD LIKE TO REPRESENT YOU!
PROFESSOR?
WHY NOT? I DO STUDY LAW -- AND WHAT BETTER WAY TO EXPERIENCE YOUR SYSTEM?
"HE WHO DOES, LEARNS A'QUICKEST."

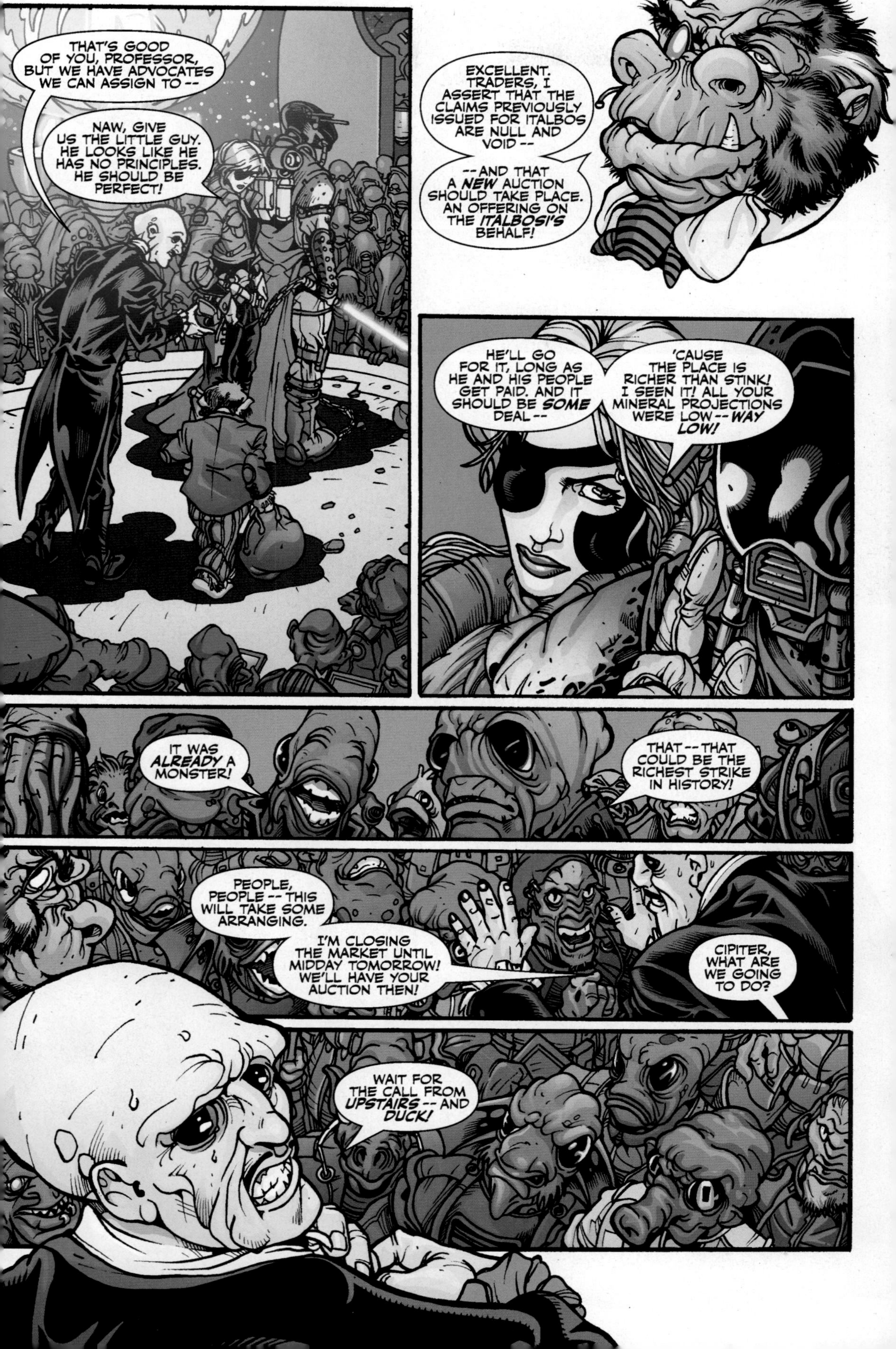
THAT'S GOOD OF YOU, PROFESSOR, BUT WE HAVE ADVOCATES WE CAN ASSIGN TO --
NAW, GIVE US THE LITTLE GUY. HE LOOKS LIKE HE HAS NO PRINCIPLES. HE SHOULD BE PERFECT!
EXCELLENT. TRADERS, I ASSERT THAT THE CLAIMS PREVIOUSLY ISSUED FOR ITALBOS ARE NULL AND VOID --
-- AND THAT A NEW AUCTION SHOULD TAKE PLACE. AN OFFERING ON THE ITALBOSI'S BEHALF!
HE'LL GO FOR IT, LONG AS HE AND HIS PEOPLE GET PAID. AND IT SHOULD BE SOME DEAL --
'CAUSE THE PLACE IS RICHER THAN STINK! I SEEN IT! ALL YOUR MINERAL PROJECTIONS WERE LOW -- WAY LOW!
IT WAS ALREADY A MONSTER!
THAT -- THAT COULD BE THE RICHEST STRIKE IN HISTORY!
PEOPLE, PEOPLE -- THIS WILL TAKE SOME ARRANGING.
I'M CLOSING THE MARKET UNTIL MIDDAY TOMORROW! WE'LL HAVE YOUR AUCTION THEN!
CIPITER, WHAT ARE WE GOING TO DO?
WAIT FOR THE CALL FROM UPSTAIRS -- AND DUCK!

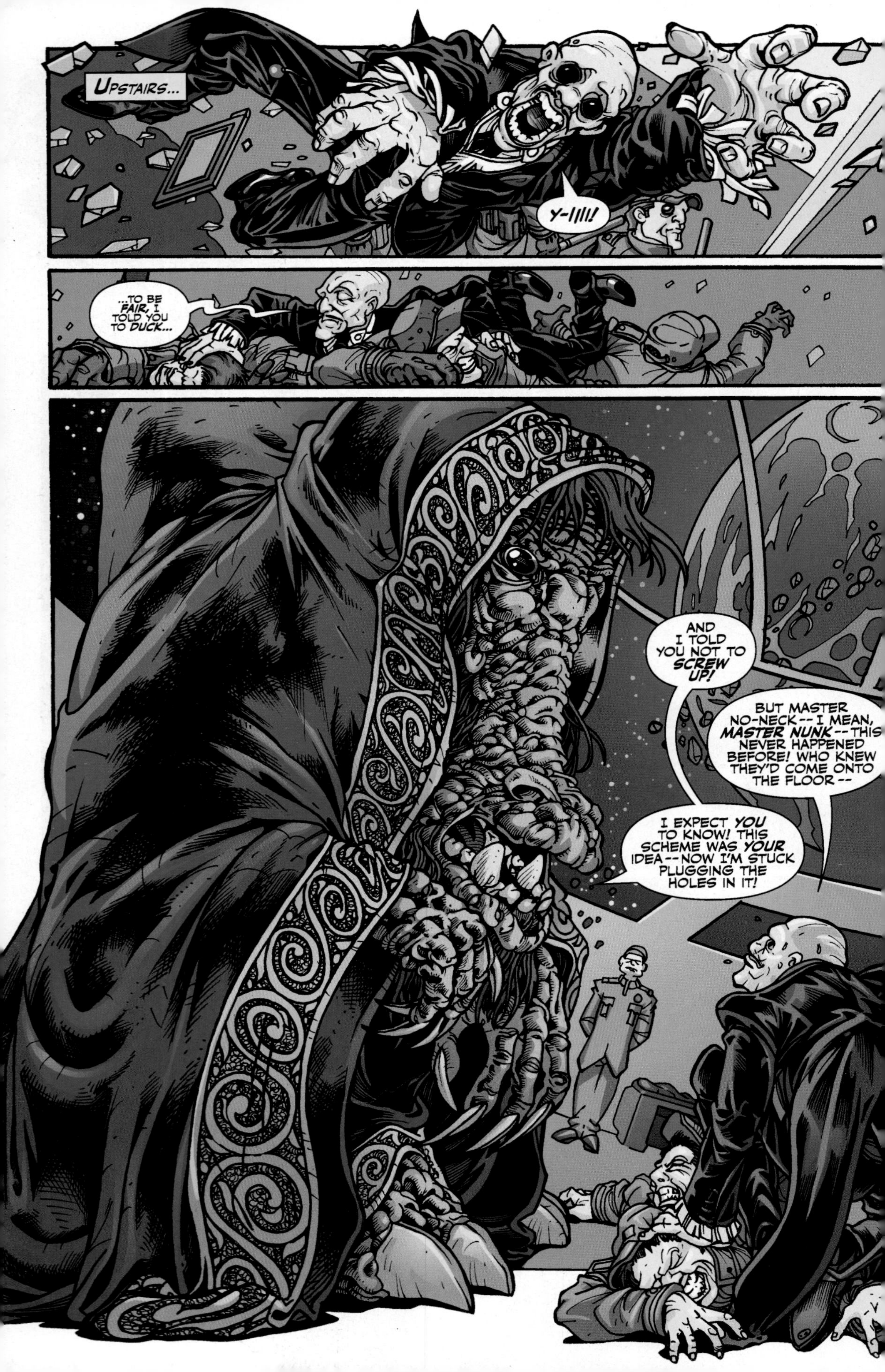
UPSTAIRS...
Y-IIII!
...TO BE FAIR, I TOLD YOU TO DUCK...
AND I TOLD YOU NOT TO SCREW UP!
BUT MASTER NO-NECK-- I MEAN, MASTER NUNK-- THIS NEVER HAPPENED BEFORE! WHO KNEW THEY'D COME ONTO THE FLOOR--
I EXPECT YOU TO KNOW! THIS SCHEME WAS YOUR IDEA--NOW I'M STUCK PLUGGING THE HOLES IN IT!

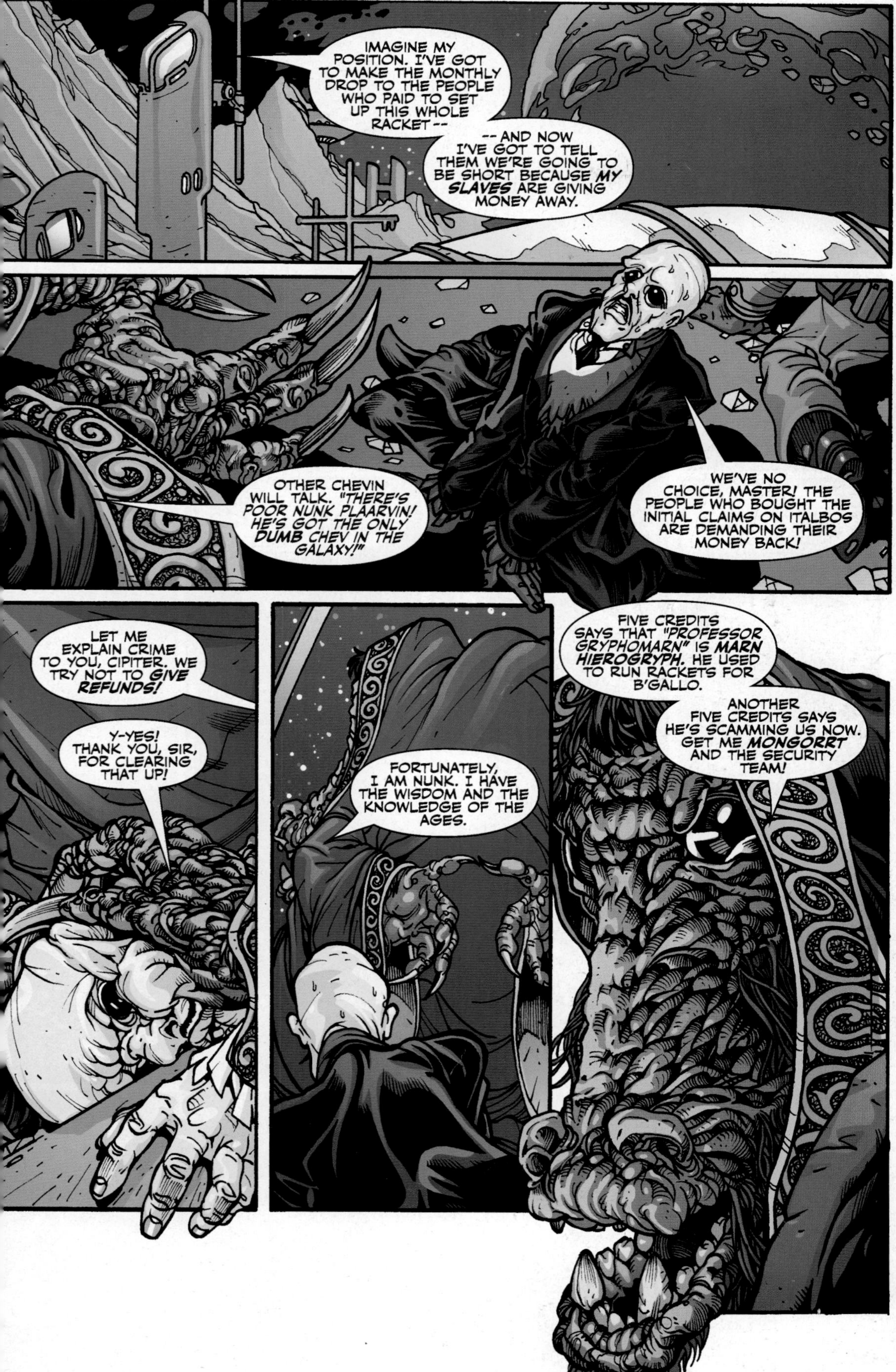
IMAGINE MY POSITION. I'VE GOT TO MAKE THE MONTHLY DROP TO THE PEOPLE WHO PAID TO SET UP THIS WHOLE RACKET--
--AND NOW I'VE GOT TO TELL THEM WE'RE GOING TO BE SHORT BECAUSE *MY SLAVES* ARE GIVING MONEY AWAY.
OTHER CHEVIN WILL TALK. *"THERE'S POOR NUNK PLAARVIN! HE'S GOT THE ONLY* **DUMB** *CHEV IN THE GALAXY!"*
WE'VE NO CHOICE, MASTER! THE PEOPLE WHO BOUGHT THE INITIAL CLAIMS ON ITALBOS ARE DEMANDING THEIR MONEY BACK!
LET ME EXPLAIN CRIME TO YOU, CIPITER. WE TRY NOT TO ***GIVE REFUNDS!***
Y-YES! THANK YOU, SIR, FOR CLEARING THAT UP!
FORTUNATELY, I AM NUNK. I HAVE THE WISDOM AND THE KNOWLEDGE OF THE AGES.
FIVE CREDITS SAYS THAT *"PROFESSOR GRYPHOMARN"* IS ***MARN HIEROGRYPH.*** HE USED TO RUN RACKETS FOR B'GALLO.
ANOTHER FIVE CREDITS SAYS HE'S SCAMMING US NOW. GET ME ***MONGORRT*** AND THE SECURITY TEAM!

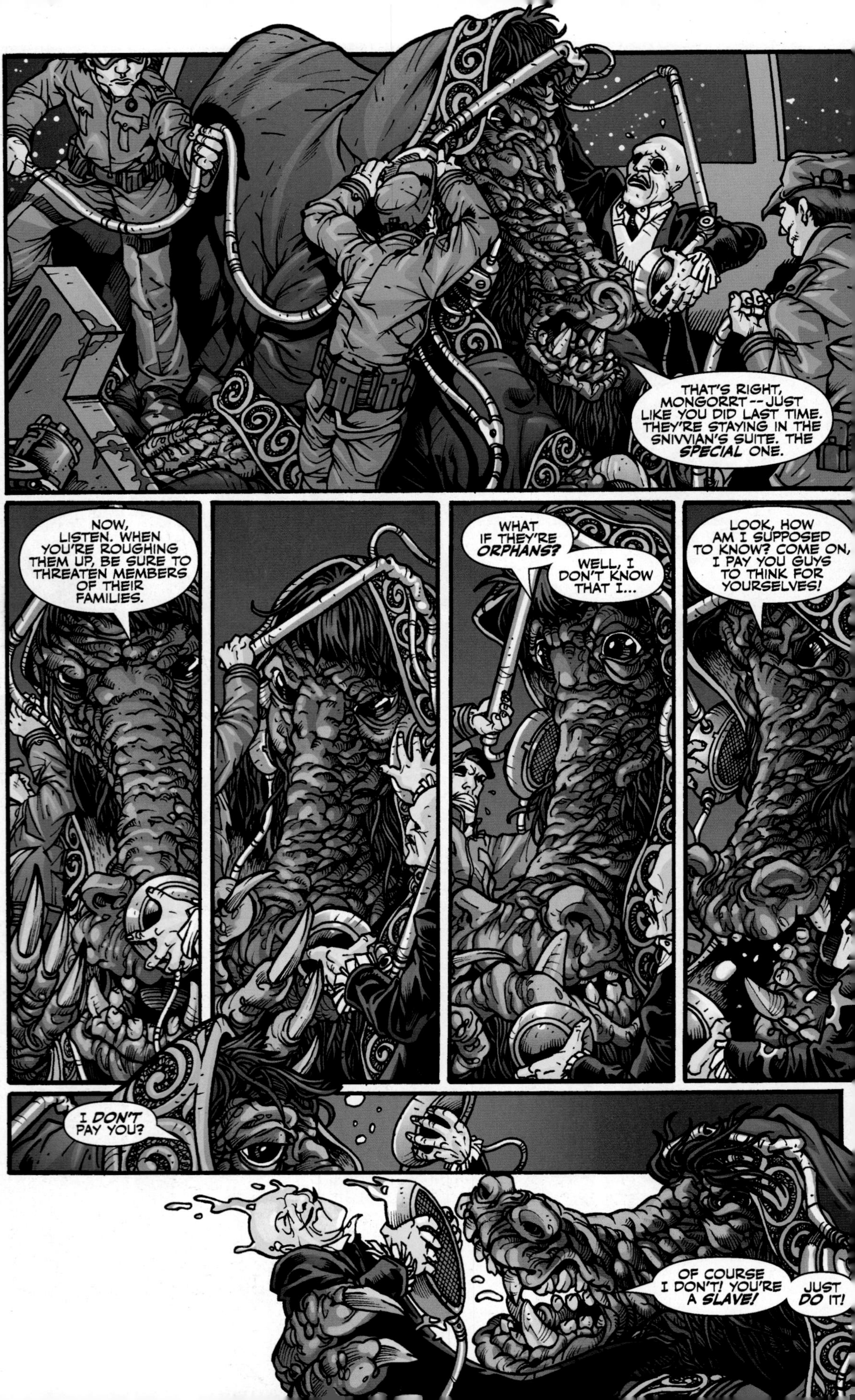
THAT'S RIGHT, MONGORRT--JUST LIKE YOU DID LAST TIME. THEY'RE STAYING IN THE SNIVVIAN'S SUITE. THE SPECIAL ONE.
NOW, LISTEN. WHEN YOU'RE ROUGHING THEM UP, BE SURE TO THREATEN MEMBERS OF THEIR FAMILIES.
WHAT IF THEY'RE ORPHANS?
WELL, I DON'T KNOW THAT I...
LOOK, HOW AM I SUPPOSED TO KNOW? COME ON, I PAY YOU GUYS TO THINK FOR YOURSELVES!
I DON'T PAY YOU?
OF COURSE I DON'T! YOU'RE A SLAVE!
JUST DO IT!

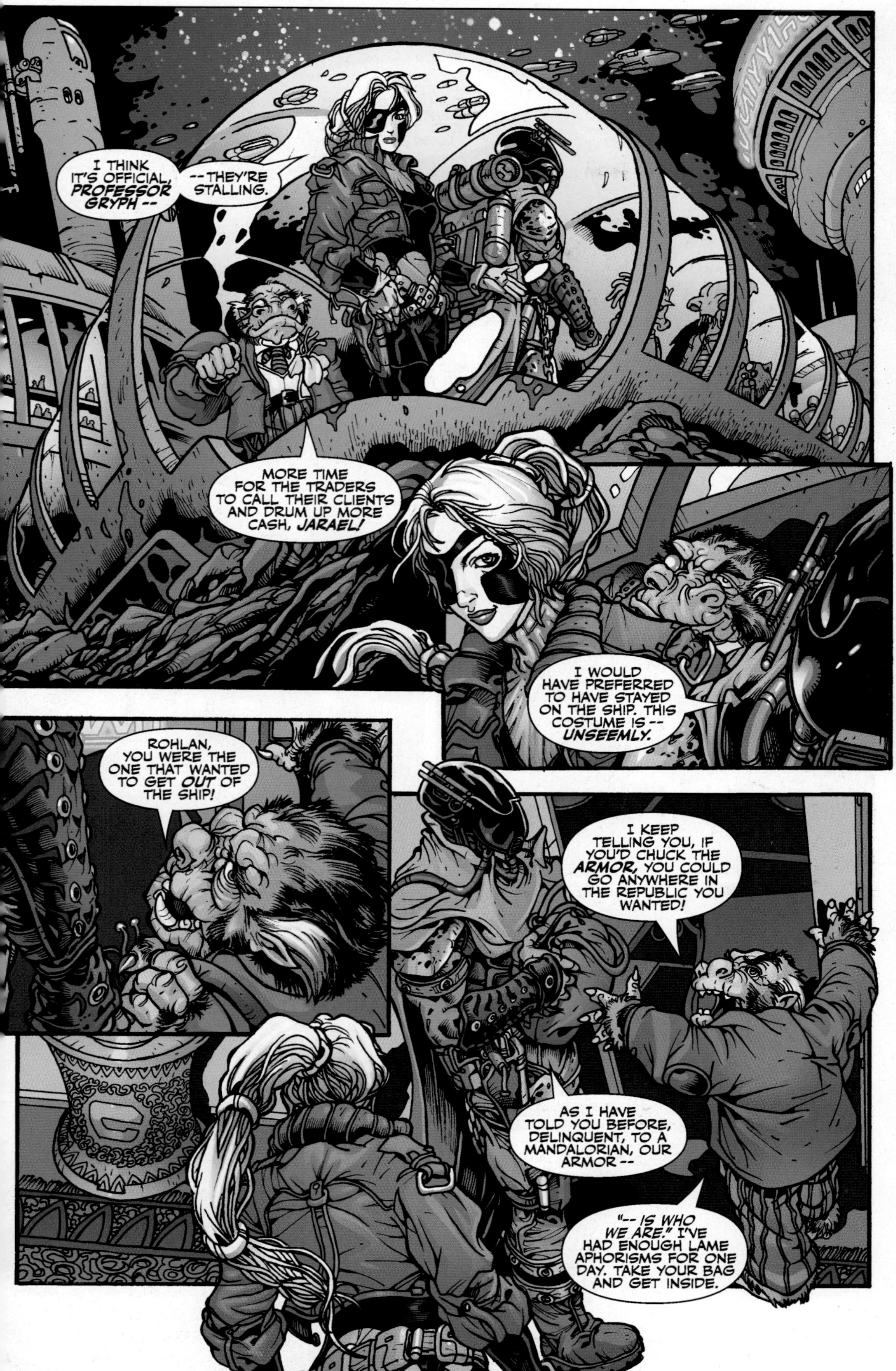

I THINK IT'S OFFICIAL, PROFESSOR GRYPH --
-- THEY'RE STALLING.
MORE TIME FOR THE TRADERS TO CALL THEIR CLIENTS AND DRUM UP MORE CASH, JARAEL!
I WOULD HAVE PREFERRED TO HAVE STAYED ON THE SHIP. THIS COSTUME IS -- UNSEEMLY.
ROHLAN, YOU WERE THE ONE THAT WANTED TO GET OUT OF THE SHIP!
I KEEP TELLING YOU, IF YOU'D CHUCK THE ARMOR, YOU COULD GO ANYWHERE IN THE REPUBLIC YOU WANTED!
AS I HAVE TOLD YOU BEFORE, DELINQUENT, TO A MANDALORIAN, OUR ARMOR --
"-- IS WHO WE ARE." I'VE HAD ENOUGH LAME APHORISMS FOR ONE DAY. TAKE YOUR BAG AND GET INSIDE.

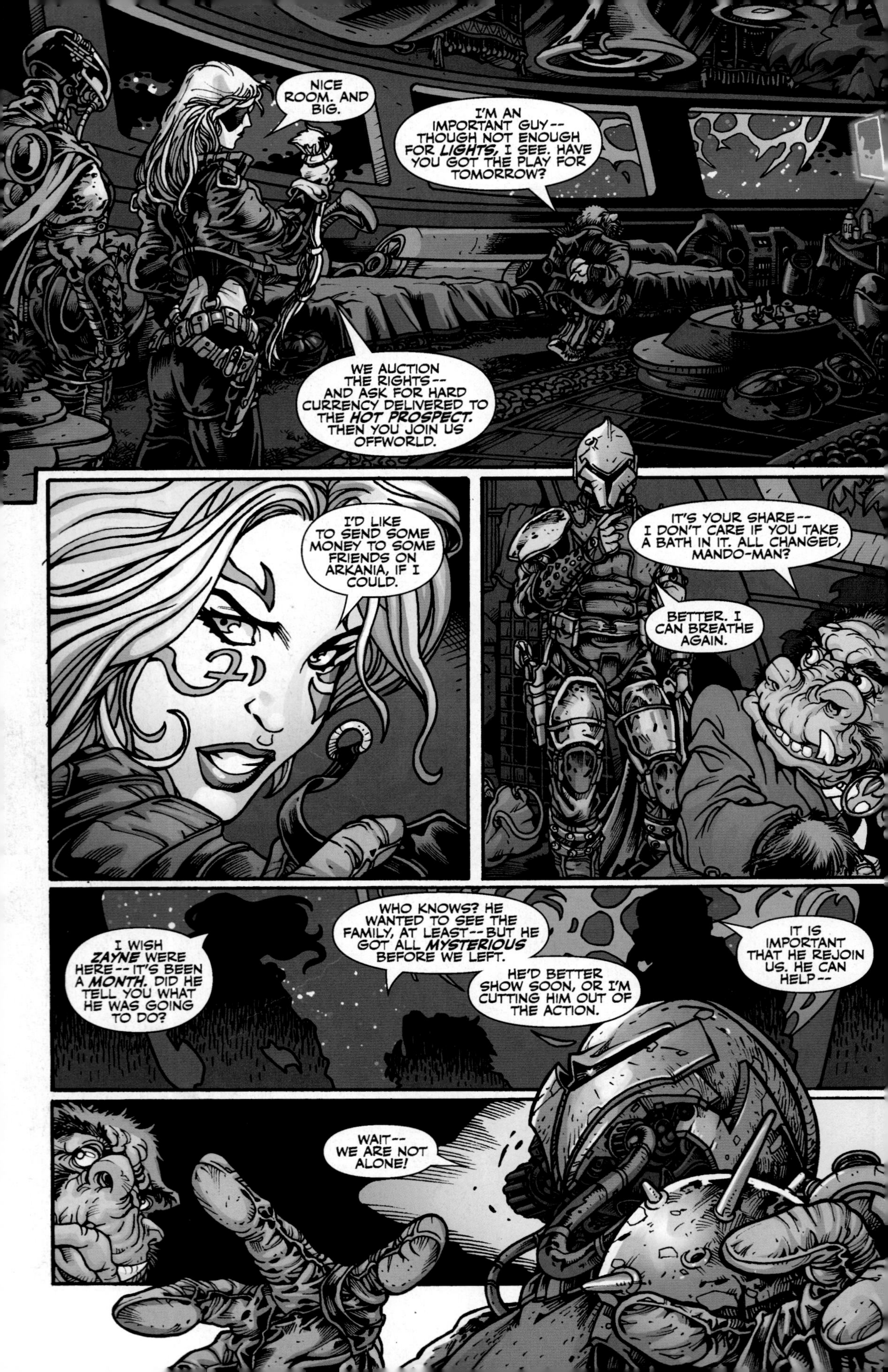
NICE ROOM. AND BIG.
I'M AN IMPORTANT GUY-- THOUGH NOT ENOUGH FOR LIGHTS, I SEE. HAVE YOU GOT THE PLAY FOR TOMORROW?
WE AUCTION THE RIGHTS-- AND ASK FOR HARD CURRENCY DELIVERED TO THE HOT PROSPECT. THEN YOU JOIN US OFFWORLD.
I'D LIKE TO SEND SOME MONEY TO SOME FRIENDS ON ARKANIA, IF I COULD.
IT'S YOUR SHARE-- I DON'T CARE IF YOU TAKE A BATH IN IT. ALL CHANGED, MANDO-MAN?
BETTER. I CAN BREATHE AGAIN.
I WISH ZAYNE WERE HERE--IT'S BEEN A MONTH. DID HE TELL YOU WHAT HE WAS GOING TO DO?
WHO KNOWS? HE WANTED TO SEE THE FAMILY, AT LEAST--BUT HE GOT ALL MYSTERIOUS BEFORE WE LEFT.
HE'D BETTER SHOW SOON, OR I'M CUTTING HIM OUT OF THE ACTION.
IT IS IMPORTANT THAT HE REJOIN US. HE CAN HELP--
WAIT-- WE ARE NOT ALONE!

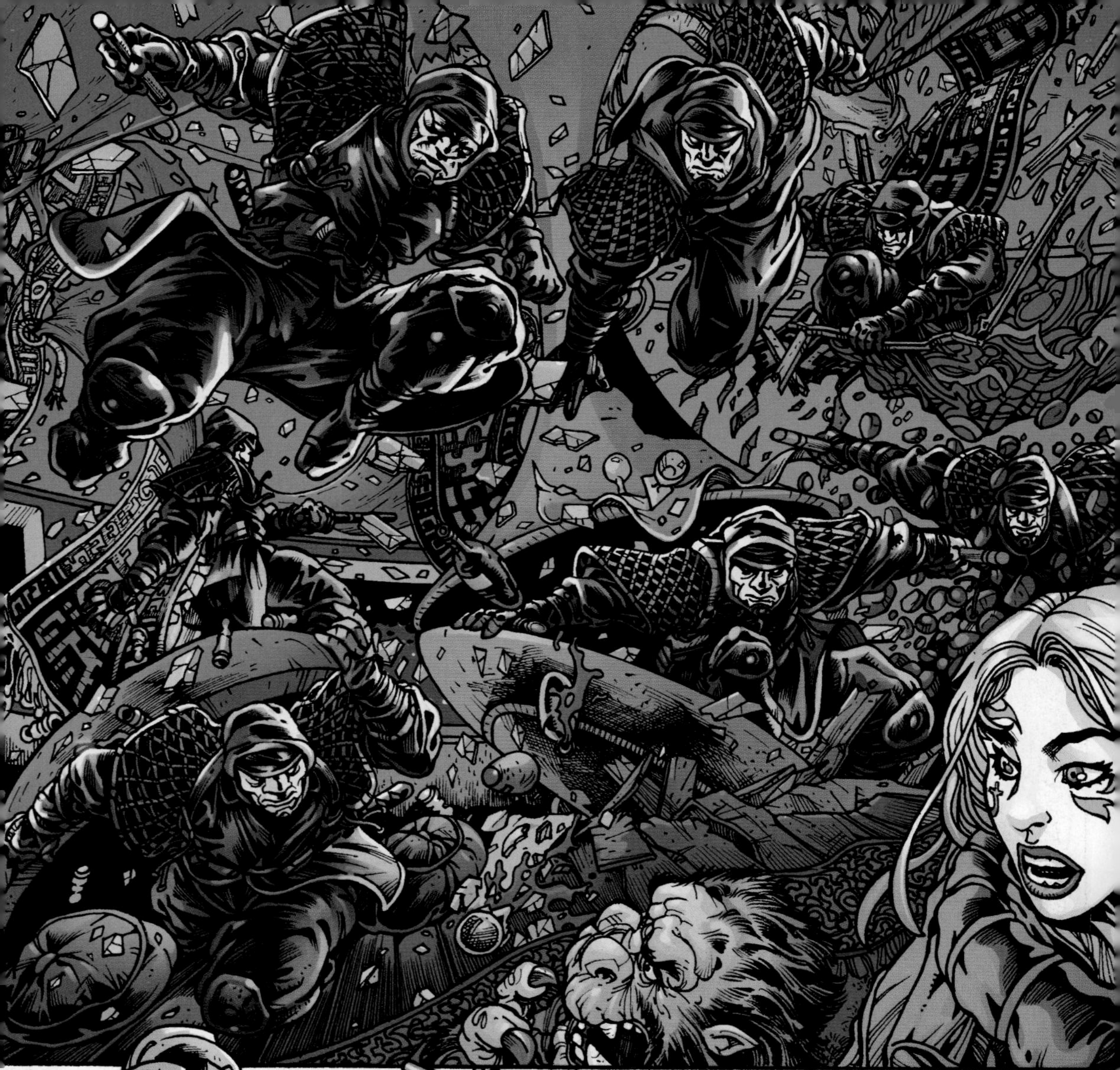

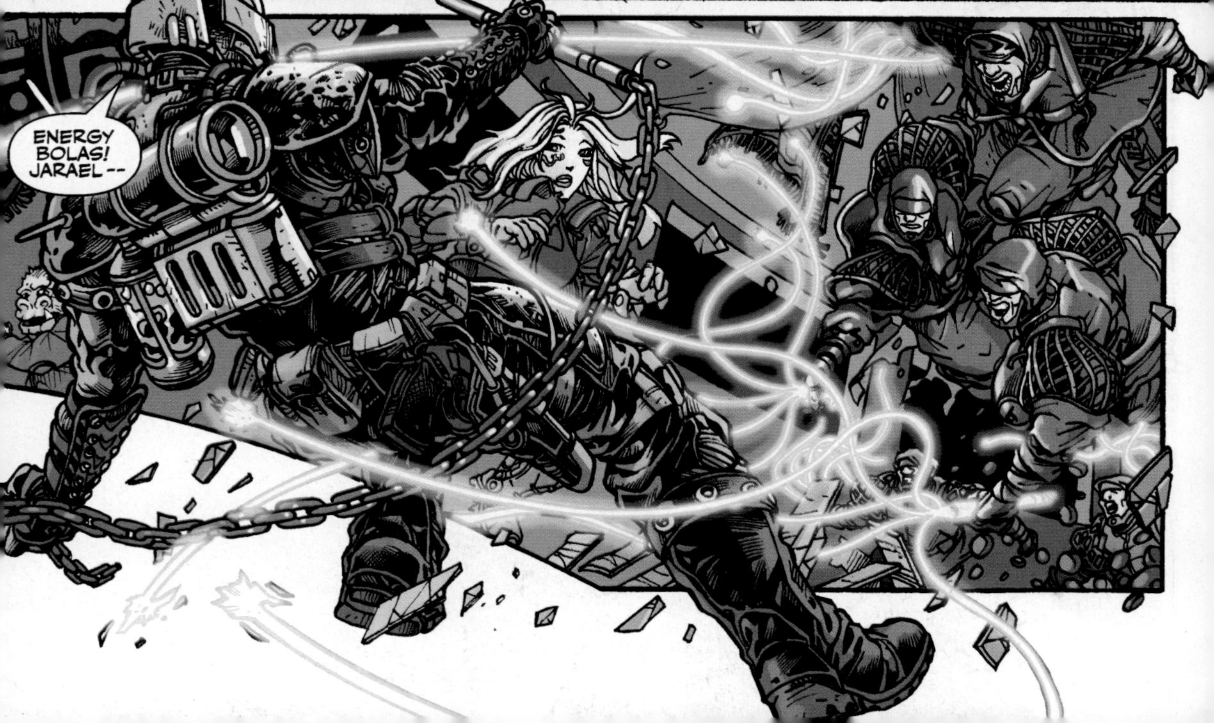
ENERGY BOLAS! JARAEL--

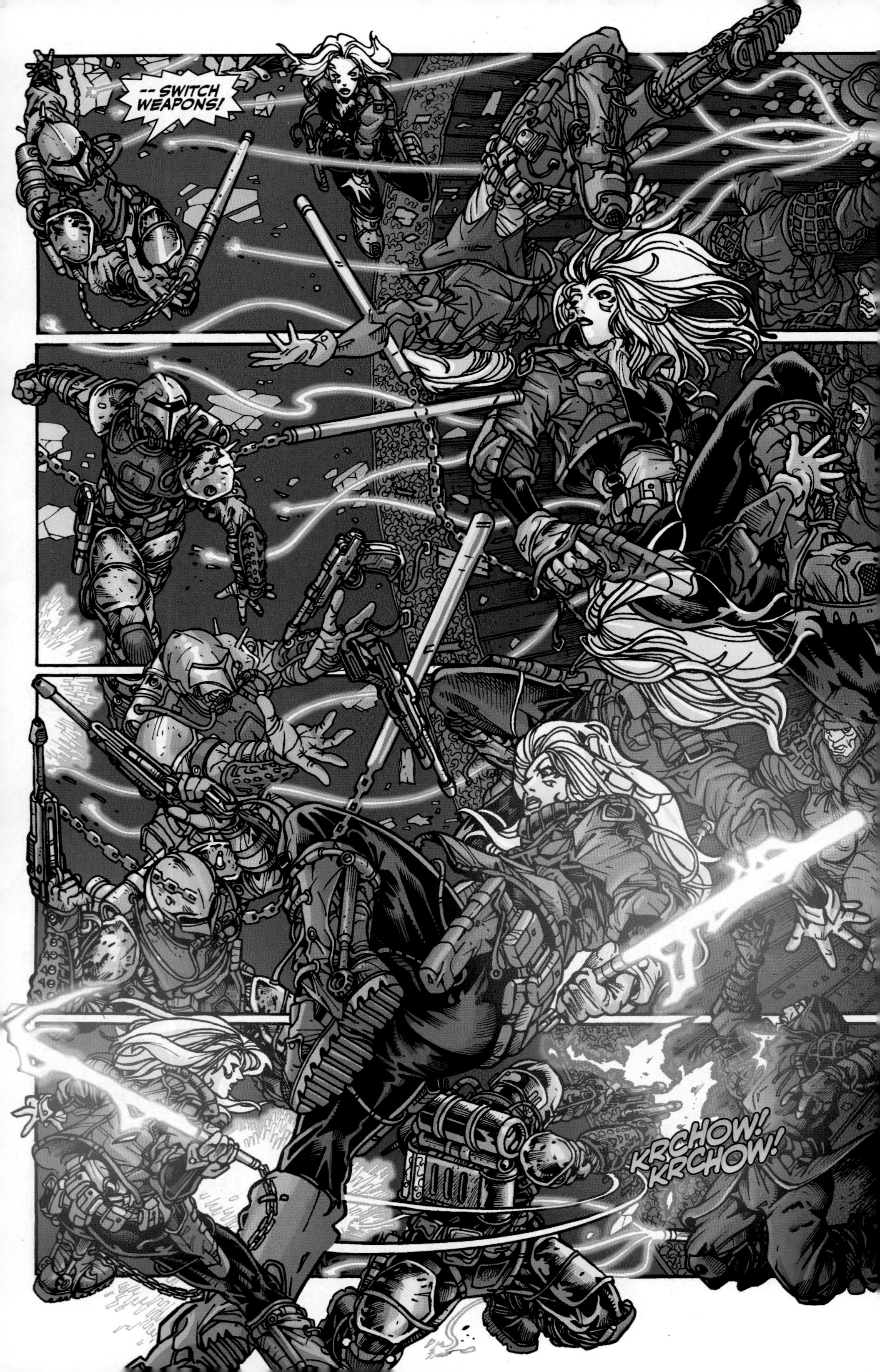
-- SWITCH WEAPONS!
KRCHOW! KRCHOW!

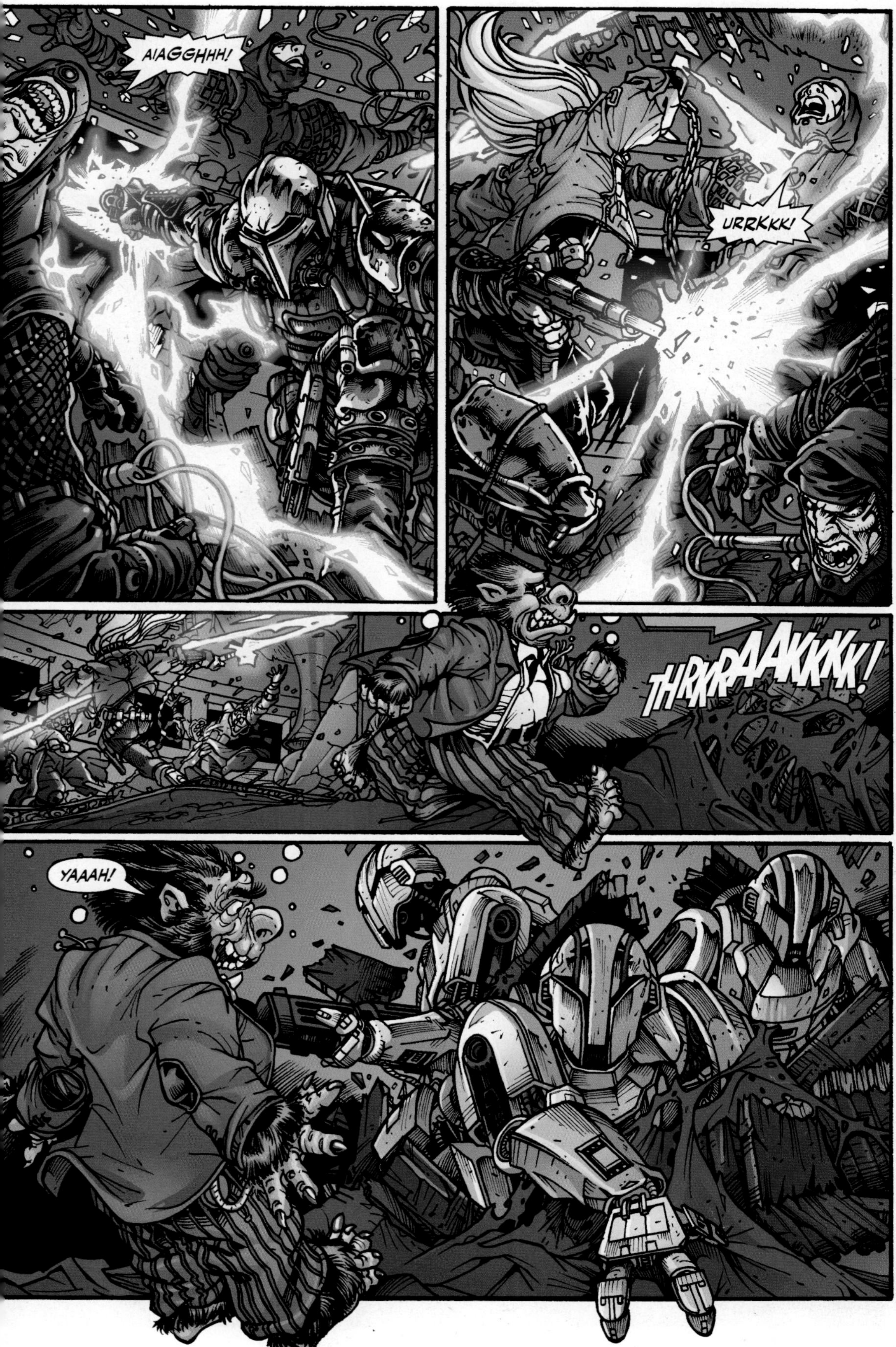
AIAGGHHH!
URRKKK!
THRKRAAKKKK!
YAAAH!

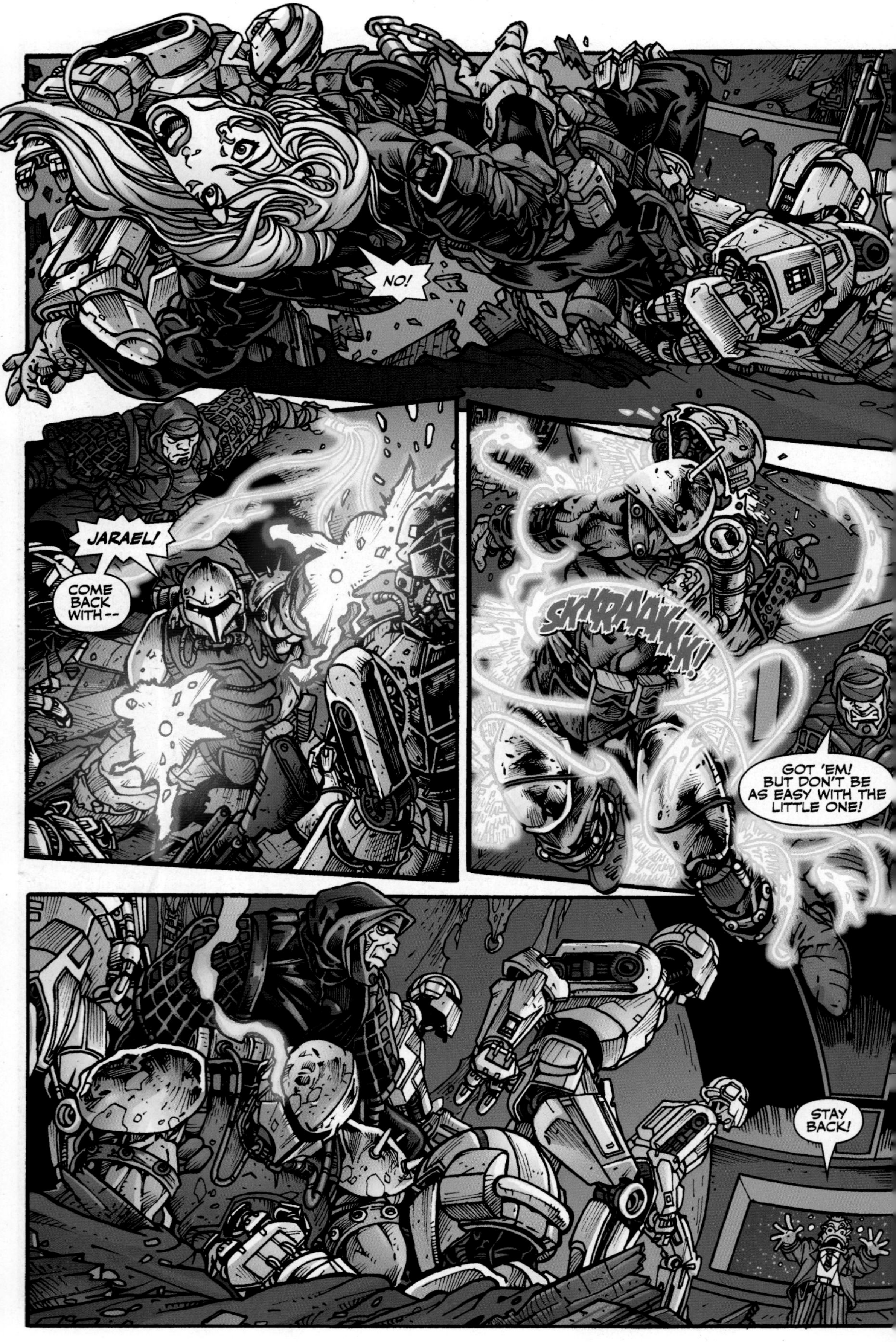
NO!
JARAEL!
COME BACK WITH--
SKKRAAAKKK!
GOT 'EM! BUT DON'T BE AS EASY WITH THE LITTLE ONE!
STAY BACK!

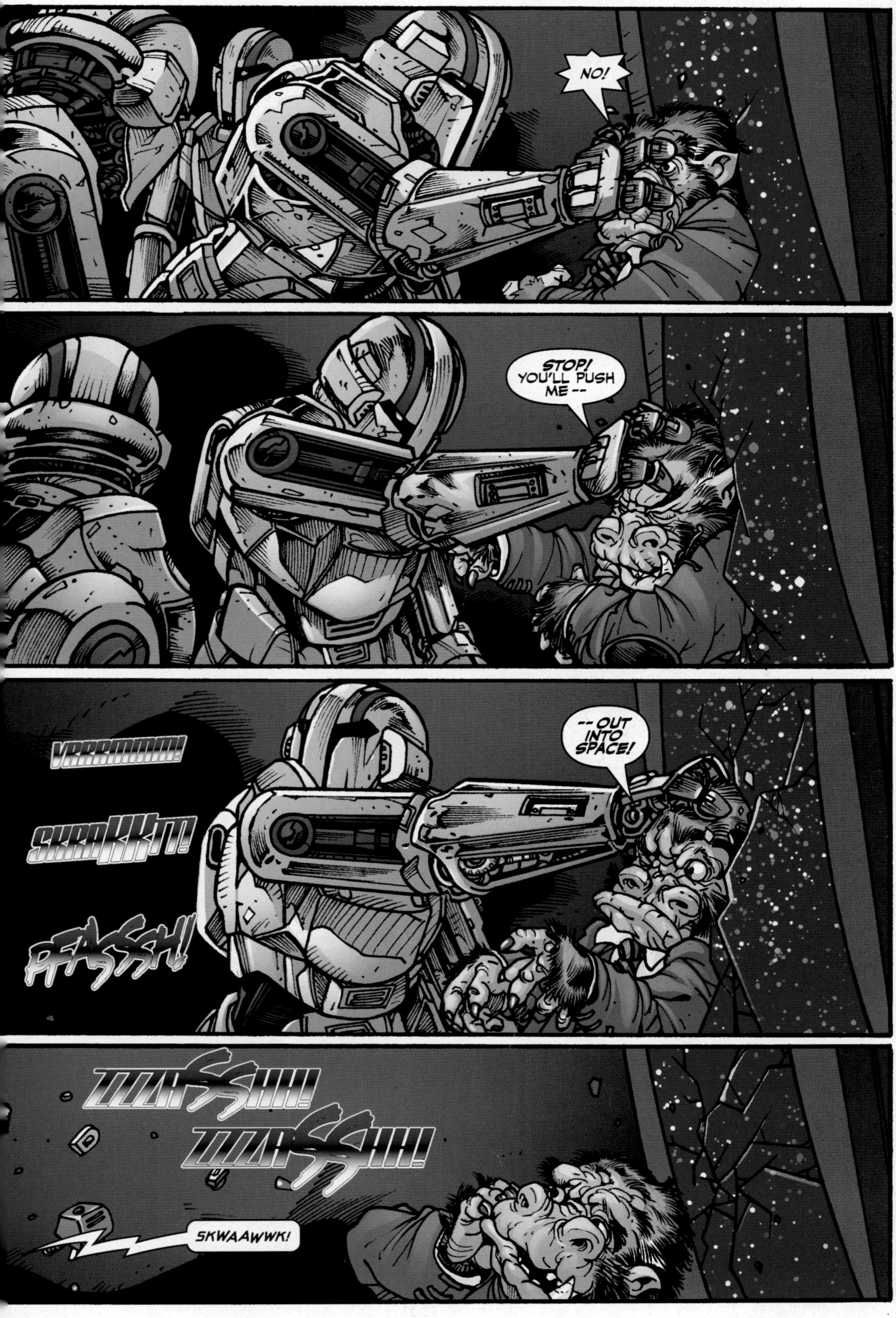
NO!
STOP! YOU'LL PUSH ME --
VRRRMMM!
SKRAKKTT!
-- OUT INTO SPACE!
ZZZAFSSHH!
ZZZAFSSHH!
SKWAAWWK!

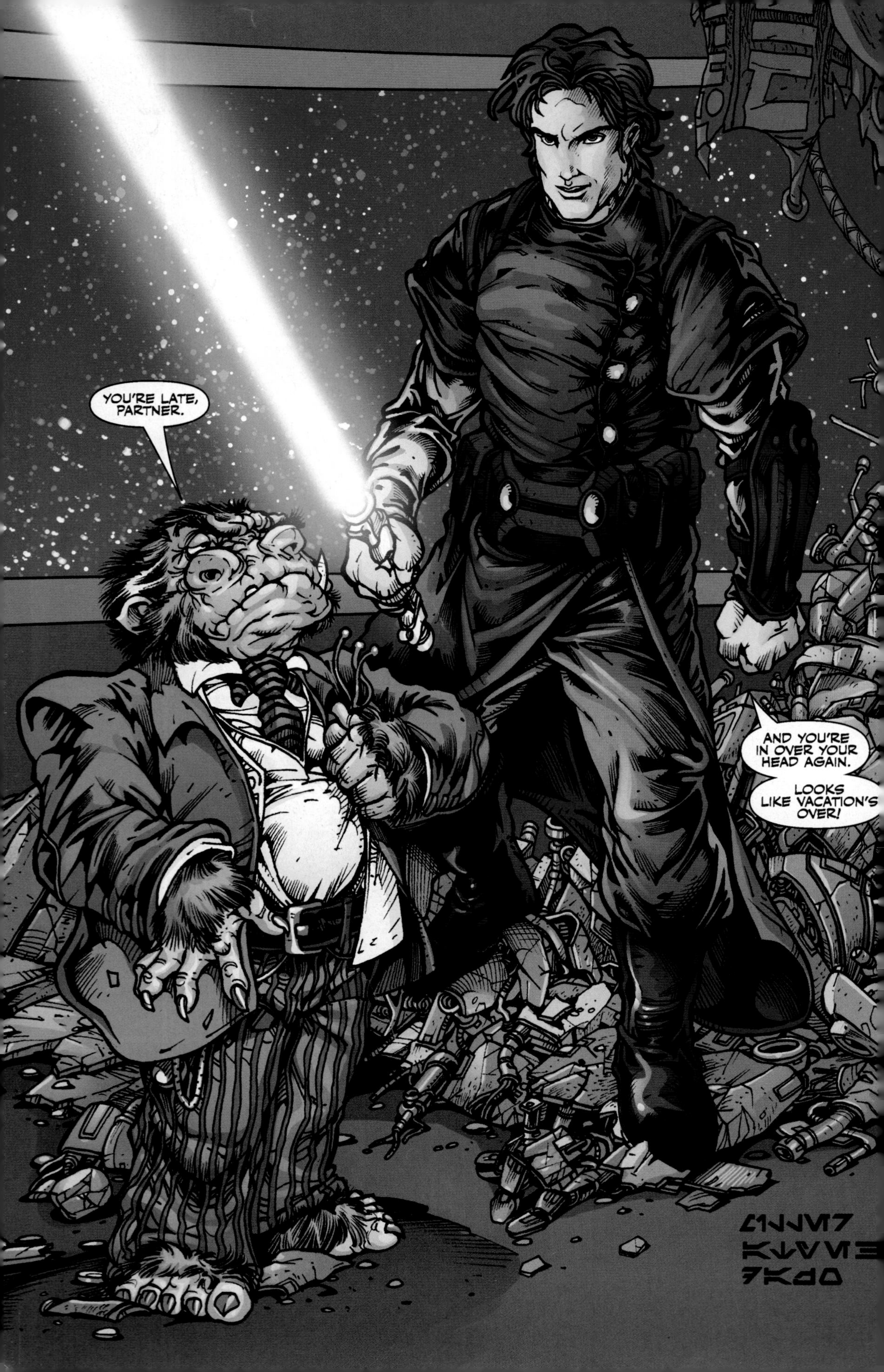
YOU'RE LATE, PARTNER.
AND YOU'RE IN OVER YOUR HEAD AGAIN.
LOOKS LIKE VACATION'S OVER!

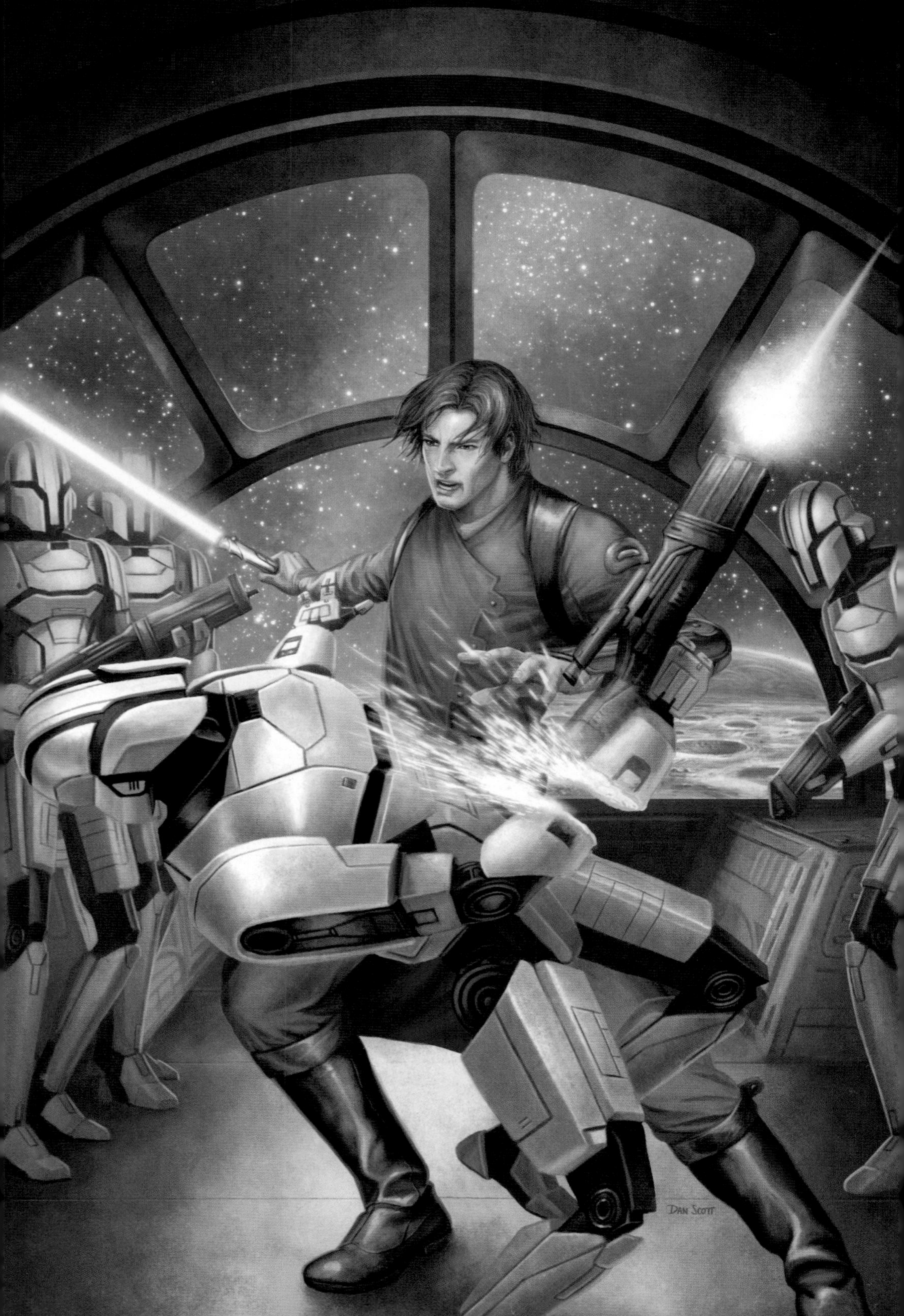
DAN SCOTT

STAR WARS: KNIGHTS OF THE OLD REPUBLIC #37 — "PROPHET MOTIVE, PART 2"

WRITER: JOHN JACKSON MILLER • ARTIST: BONG DAZO • COLORIST: MICHAEL ATIYEH • LETTERER: MICHAEL HEISLER
ASSISTANT EDITOR: FREDDYE LINS • EDITOR: DAVE MARSHALL • COVER ARTIST: DAN SCOTT

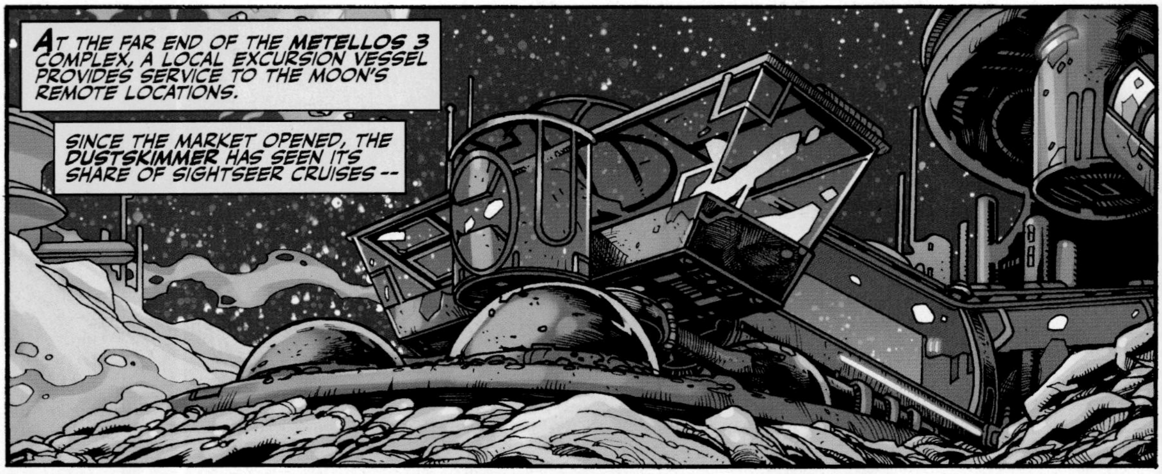
AT THE FAR END OF THE METELLOS 3 COMPLEX, A LOCAL EXCURSION VESSEL PROVIDES SERVICE TO THE MOON'S REMOTE LOCATIONS.
SINCE THE MARKET OPENED, THE DUSTSKIMMER HAS SEEN ITS SHARE OF SIGHTSEER CRUISES --

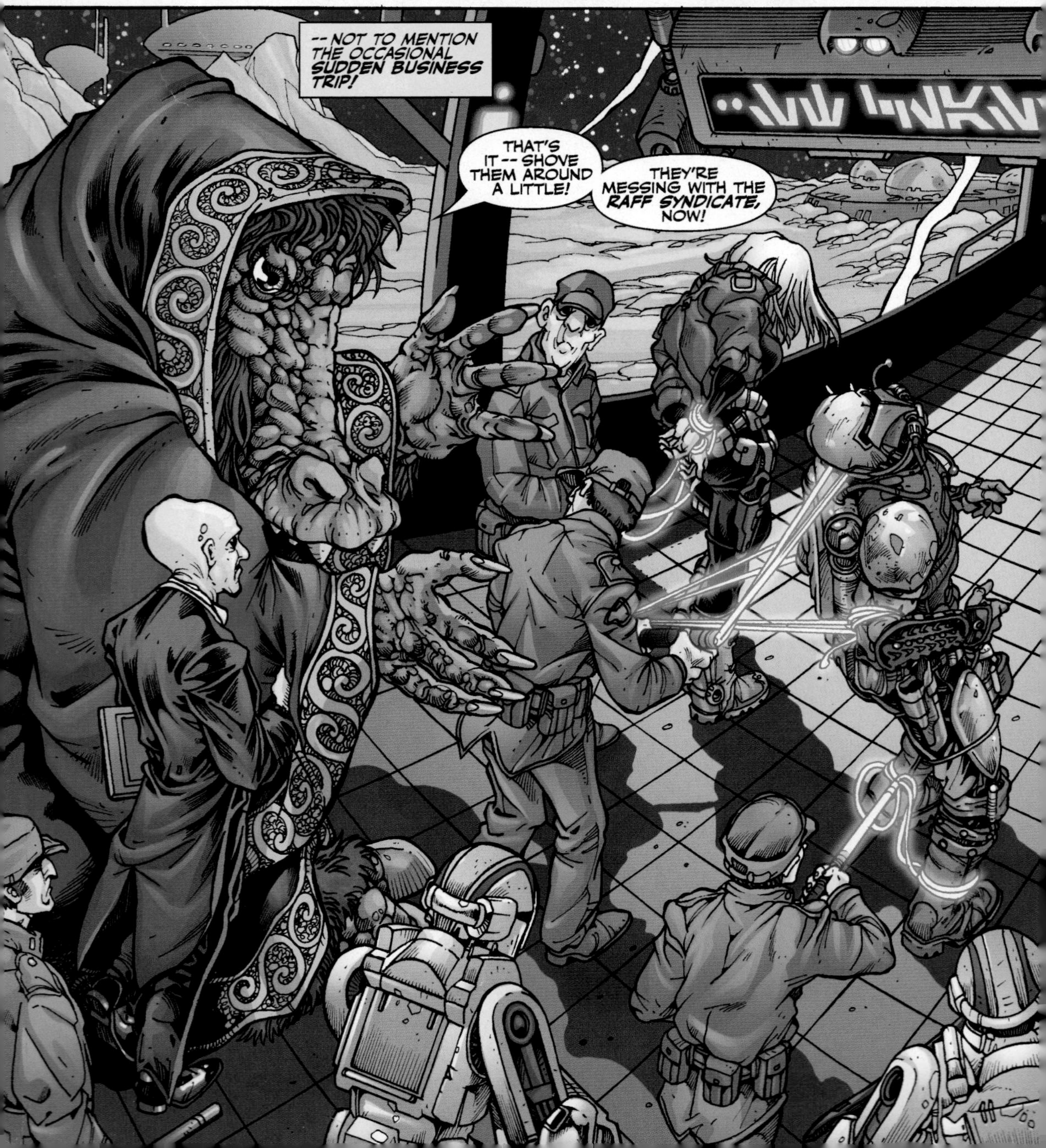
-- NOT TO MENTION THE OCCASIONAL SUDDEN BUSINESS TRIP!
THAT'S IT -- SHOVE THEM AROUND A LITTLE!
THEY'RE MESSING WITH THE RAFF SYNDICATE, NOW!

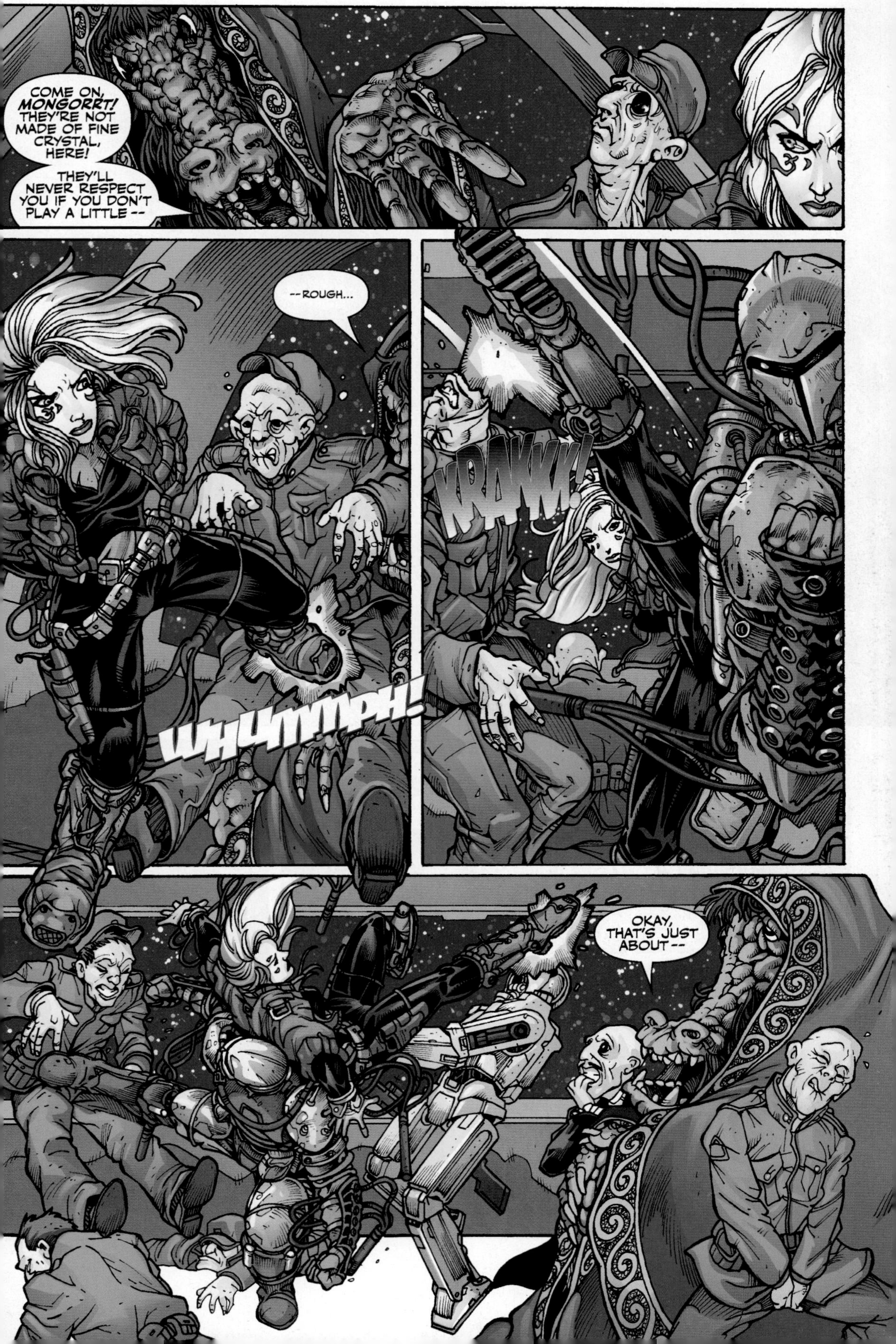
COME ON, MONGORRT! THEY'RE NOT MADE OF FINE CRYSTAL, HERE!
THEY'LL NEVER RESPECT YOU IF YOU DON'T PLAY A LITTLE --
--ROUGH...
WHUMMPH!
KRAKKK!
OKAY, THAT'S JUST ABOUT --

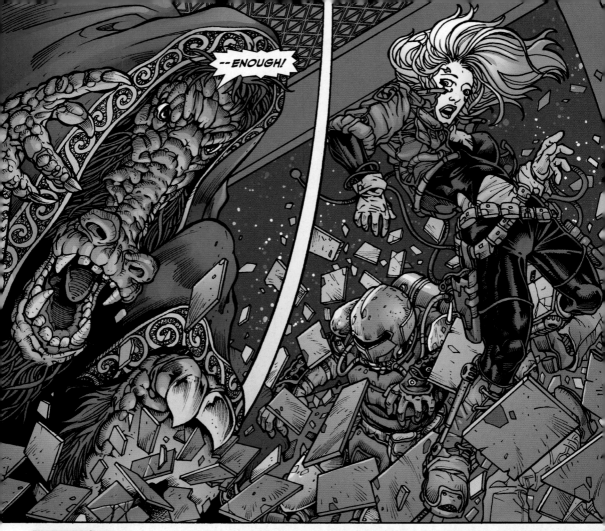

--ENOUGH!

NOW, CAN YOU KEEP CONTROL OF THEM THIS TIME-- OR DO I NEED TO DO THAT, TOO?

YES, MASTER NO-NECK-- I MEAN, *NO, MASTER NUNK!*

ELECTRIFY THE RESTRAINTS!

YOU'RE FEISTY, ARKANIAN-- BUT YOU'RE NOT WHO YOU WERE CLAIMING TO BE.

AND *A MANDALORIAN!* I'M TEMPTED TO GIVE YOU TO THE REPUBLIC. WITH THE WAR ON, THEY'D LOVE THAT!

YEAH, THEY'D LOVE THAT!

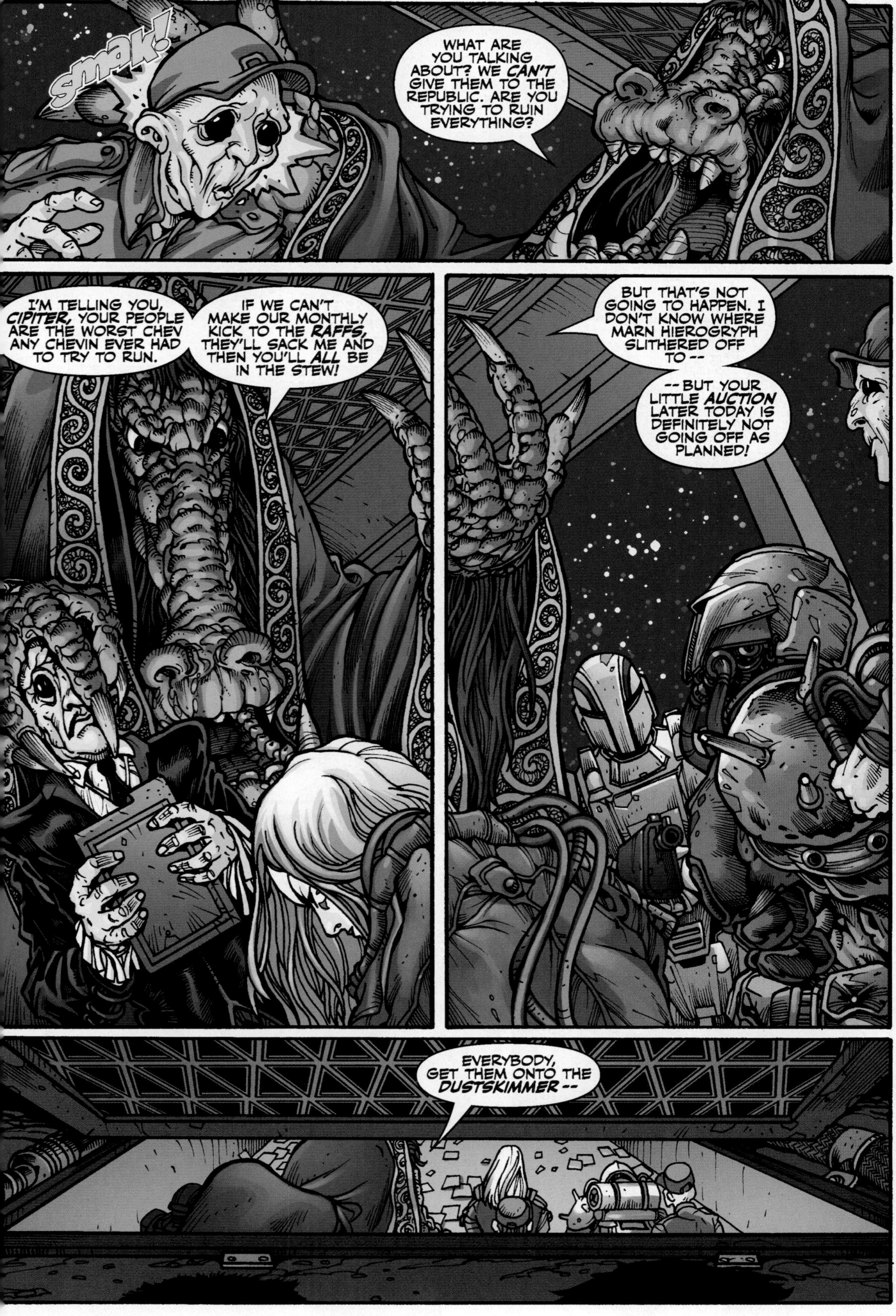
SMAK!
WHAT ARE YOU TALKING ABOUT? WE CAN'T GIVE THEM TO THE REPUBLIC. ARE YOU TRYING TO RUIN EVERYTHING?
I'M TELLING YOU, CIPITER, YOUR PEOPLE ARE THE WORST CHEV ANY CHEVIN EVER HAD TO TRY TO RUN.
IF WE CAN'T MAKE OUR MONTHLY KICK TO THE RAFFS, THEY'LL SACK ME AND THEN YOU'LL ALL BE IN THE STEW!
BUT THAT'S NOT GOING TO HAPPEN. I DON'T KNOW WHERE MARN HIEROGRYPH SLITHERED OFF TO --
-- BUT YOUR LITTLE AUCTION LATER TODAY IS DEFINITELY NOT GOING OFF AS PLANNED!
EVERYBODY, GET THEM ONTO THE DUSTSKIMMER --

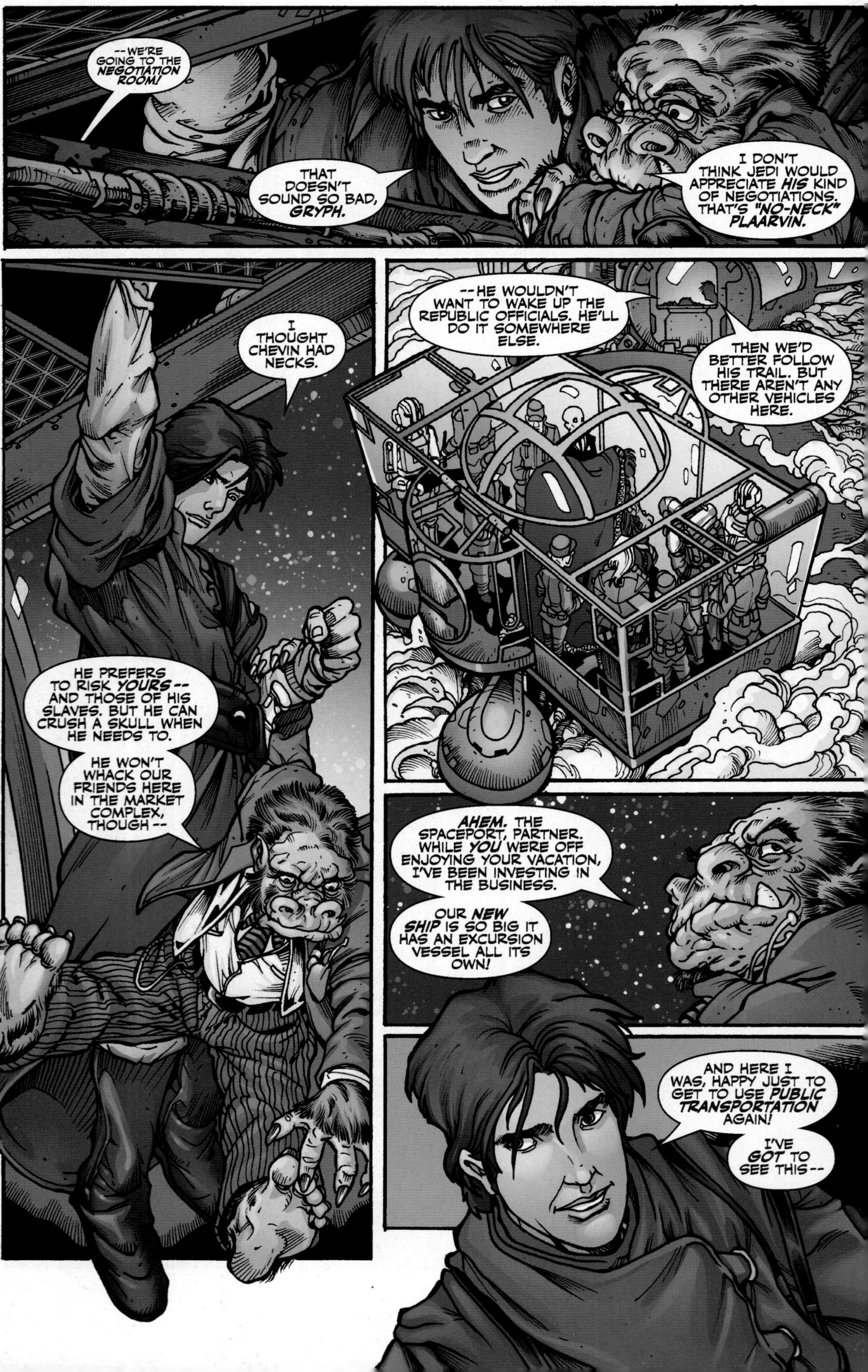
--WE'RE GOING TO THE NEGOTIATION ROOM!
THAT DOESN'T SOUND SO BAD, GRYPH.
I DON'T THINK JEDI WOULD APPRECIATE HIS KIND OF NEGOTIATIONS. THAT'S "NO-NECK" PLAARVIN.
I THOUGHT CHEVIN HAD NECKS.
HE PREFERS TO RISK YOURS-- AND THOSE OF HIS SLAVES. BUT HE CAN CRUSH A SKULL WHEN HE NEEDS TO.
HE WON'T WHACK OUR FRIENDS HERE IN THE MARKET COMPLEX, THOUGH--
--HE WOULDN'T WANT TO WAKE UP THE REPUBLIC OFFICIALS. HE'LL DO IT SOMEWHERE ELSE.
THEN WE'D BETTER FOLLOW HIS TRAIL. BUT THERE AREN'T ANY OTHER VEHICLES HERE.
AHEM. THE SPACEPORT, PARTNER. WHILE YOU WERE OFF ENJOYING YOUR VACATION, I'VE BEEN INVESTING IN THE BUSINESS.
OUR NEW SHIP IS SO BIG IT HAS AN EXCURSION VESSEL ALL ITS OWN!
AND HERE I WAS, HAPPY JUST TO GET TO USE PUBLIC TRANSPORTATION AGAIN!
I'VE GOT TO SEE THIS--

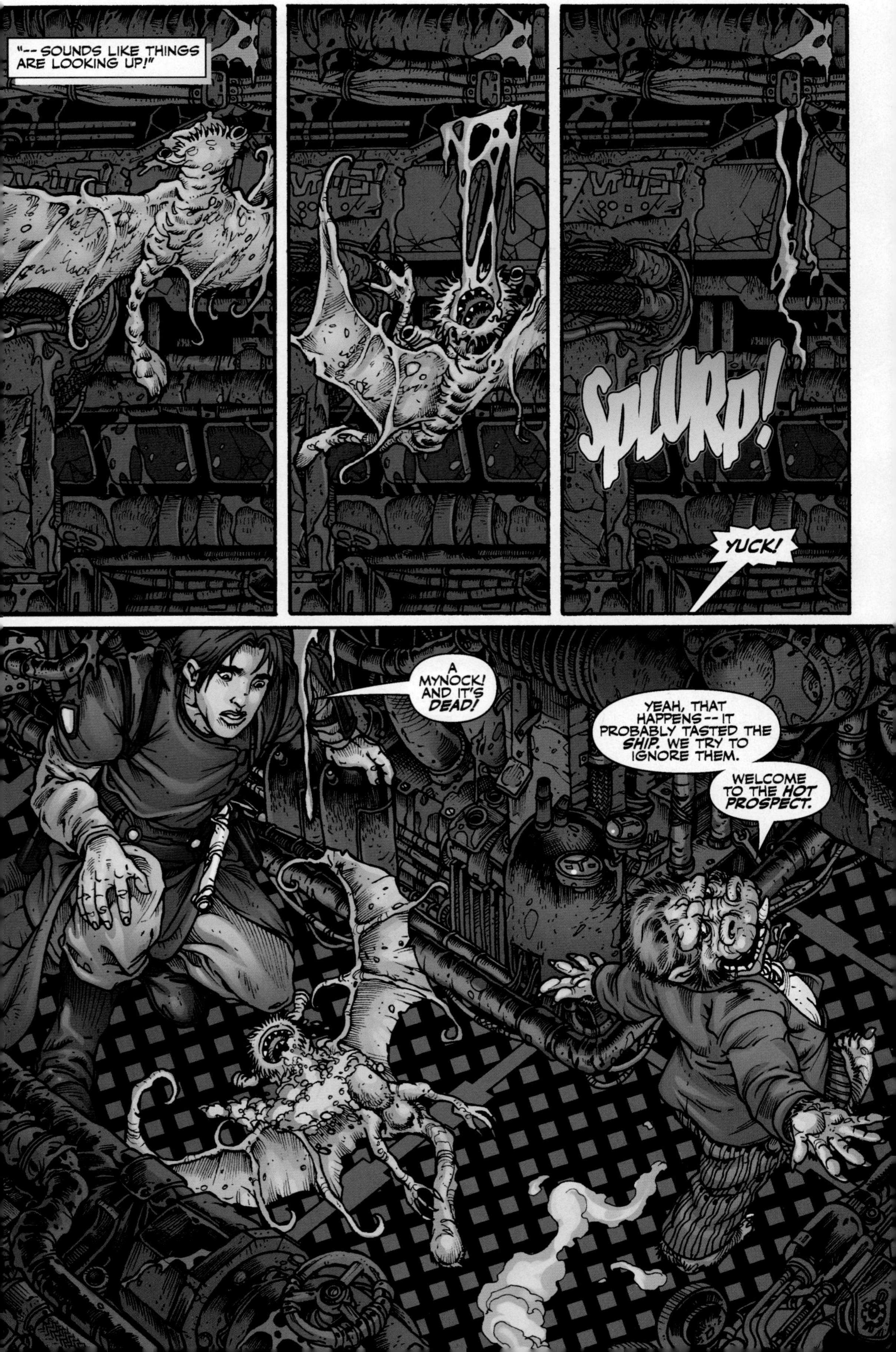
"-- SOUNDS LIKE THINGS ARE LOOKING UP!"
SPLURP!
YUCK!
A MYNOCK! AND IT'S *DEAD!*
YEAH, THAT HAPPENS -- IT PROBABLY TASTED THE *SHIP.* WE TRY TO IGNORE THEM.
WELCOME TO THE *HOT PROSPECT.*

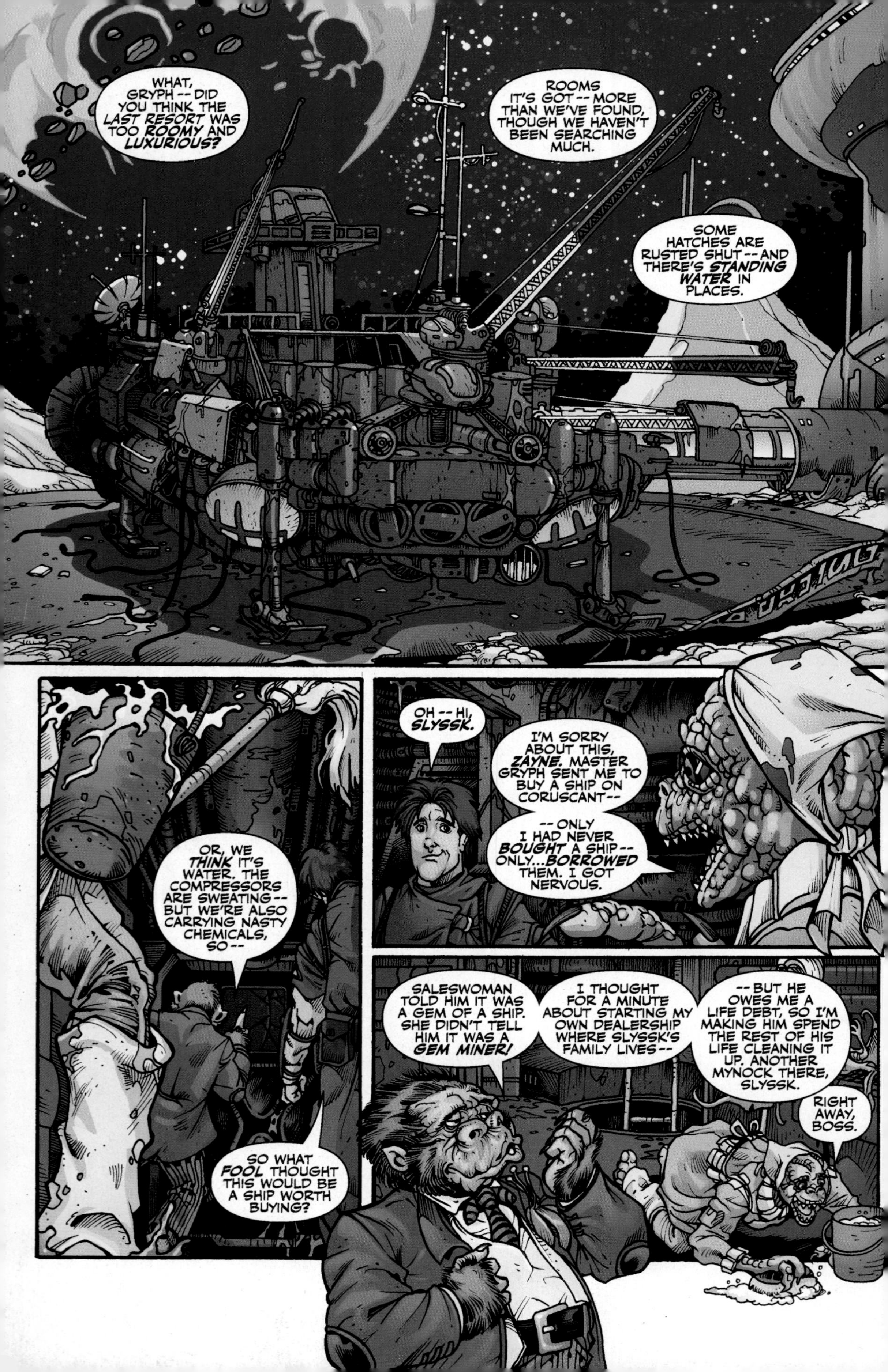
WHAT, GRYPH -- DID YOU THINK THE LAST RESORT WAS TOO ROOMY AND LUXURIOUS?
ROOMS IT'S GOT -- MORE THAN WE'VE FOUND, THOUGH WE HAVEN'T BEEN SEARCHING MUCH.
SOME HATCHES ARE RUSTED SHUT -- AND THERE'S STANDING WATER IN PLACES.
OR, WE THINK IT'S WATER. THE COMPRESSORS ARE SWEATING -- BUT WE'RE ALSO CARRYING NASTY CHEMICALS, SO --
SO WHAT FOOL THOUGHT THIS WOULD BE A SHIP WORTH BUYING?
OH -- HI, SLYSSK.
I'M SORRY ABOUT THIS, ZAYNE. MASTER GRYPH SENT ME TO BUY A SHIP ON CORUSCANT--
-- ONLY I HAD NEVER BOUGHT A SHIP -- ONLY... BORROWED THEM. I GOT NERVOUS.
SALESWOMAN TOLD HIM IT WAS A GEM OF A SHIP. SHE DIDN'T TELL HIM IT WAS A GEM MINER!
I THOUGHT FOR A MINUTE ABOUT STARTING MY OWN DEALERSHIP WHERE SLYSSK'S FAMILY LIVES --
-- BUT HE OWES ME A LIFE DEBT, SO I'M MAKING HIM SPEND THE REST OF HIS LIFE CLEANING IT UP. ANOTHER MYNOCK THERE, SLYSSK.
RIGHT AWAY, BOSS.

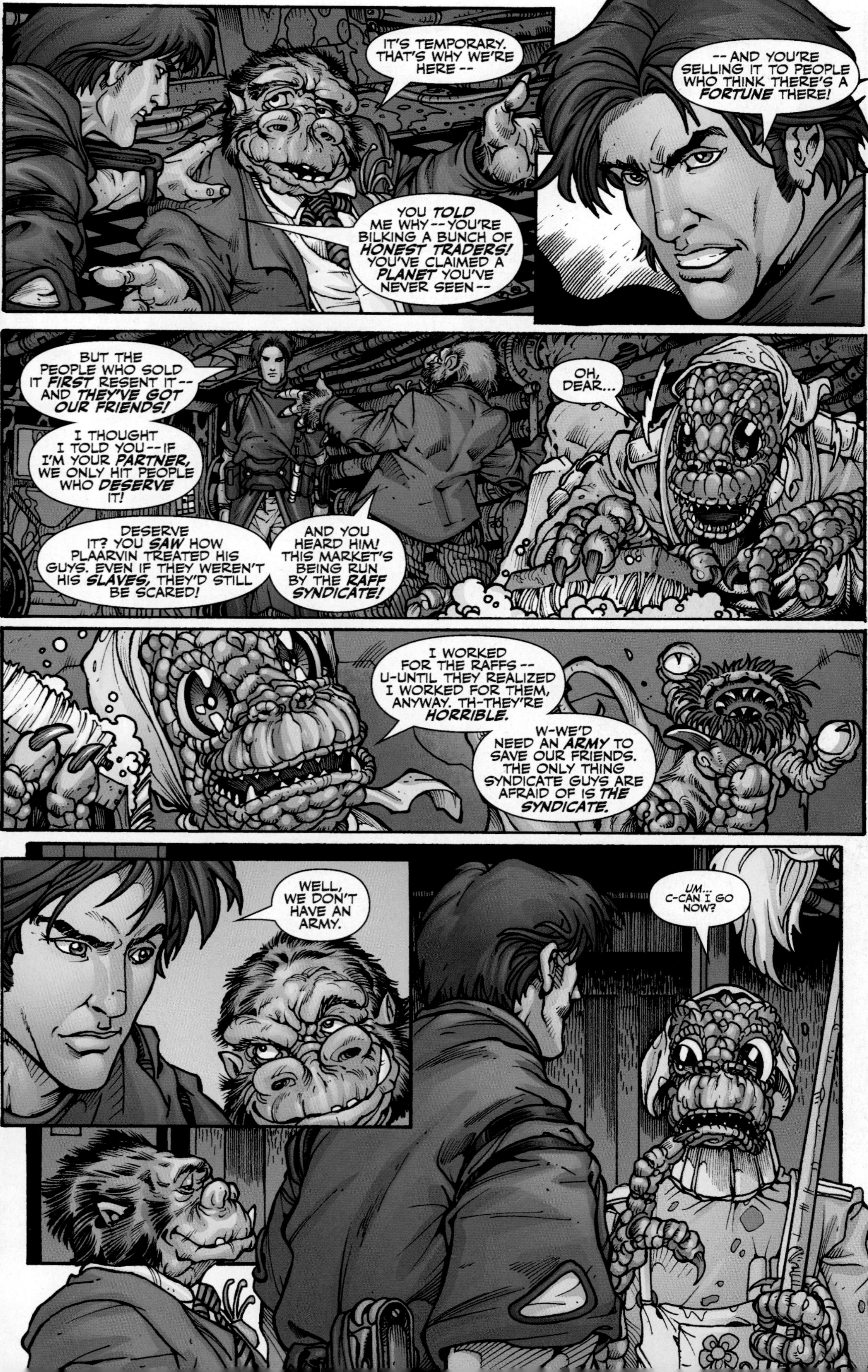

IT'S TEMPORARY. THAT'S WHY WE'RE HERE --
YOU TOLD ME WHY -- YOU'RE BILKING A BUNCH OF HONEST TRADERS! YOU'VE CLAIMED A PLANET YOU'VE NEVER SEEN --
-- AND YOU'RE SELLING IT TO PEOPLE WHO THINK THERE'S A FORTUNE THERE!
BUT THE PEOPLE WHO SOLD IT FIRST RESENT IT -- AND THEY'VE GOT OUR FRIENDS!
I THOUGHT I TOLD YOU -- IF I'M YOUR PARTNER, WE ONLY HIT PEOPLE WHO DESERVE IT!
DESERVE IT? YOU SAW HOW PLAARVIN TREATED HIS GUYS. EVEN IF THEY WEREN'T HIS SLAVES, THEY'D STILL BE SCARED!
AND YOU HEARD HIM! THIS MARKET'S BEING RUN BY THE RAFF SYNDICATE!
OH, DEAR...
I WORKED FOR THE RAFFS -- U-UNTIL THEY REALIZED I WORKED FOR THEM, ANYWAY. TH-THEY'RE HORRIBLE.
W-WE'D NEED AN ARMY TO SAVE OUR FRIENDS. THE ONLY THING SYNDICATE GUYS ARE AFRAID OF IS THE SYNDICATE.
WELL, WE DON'T HAVE AN ARMY.
UM... C-CAN I GO NOW?

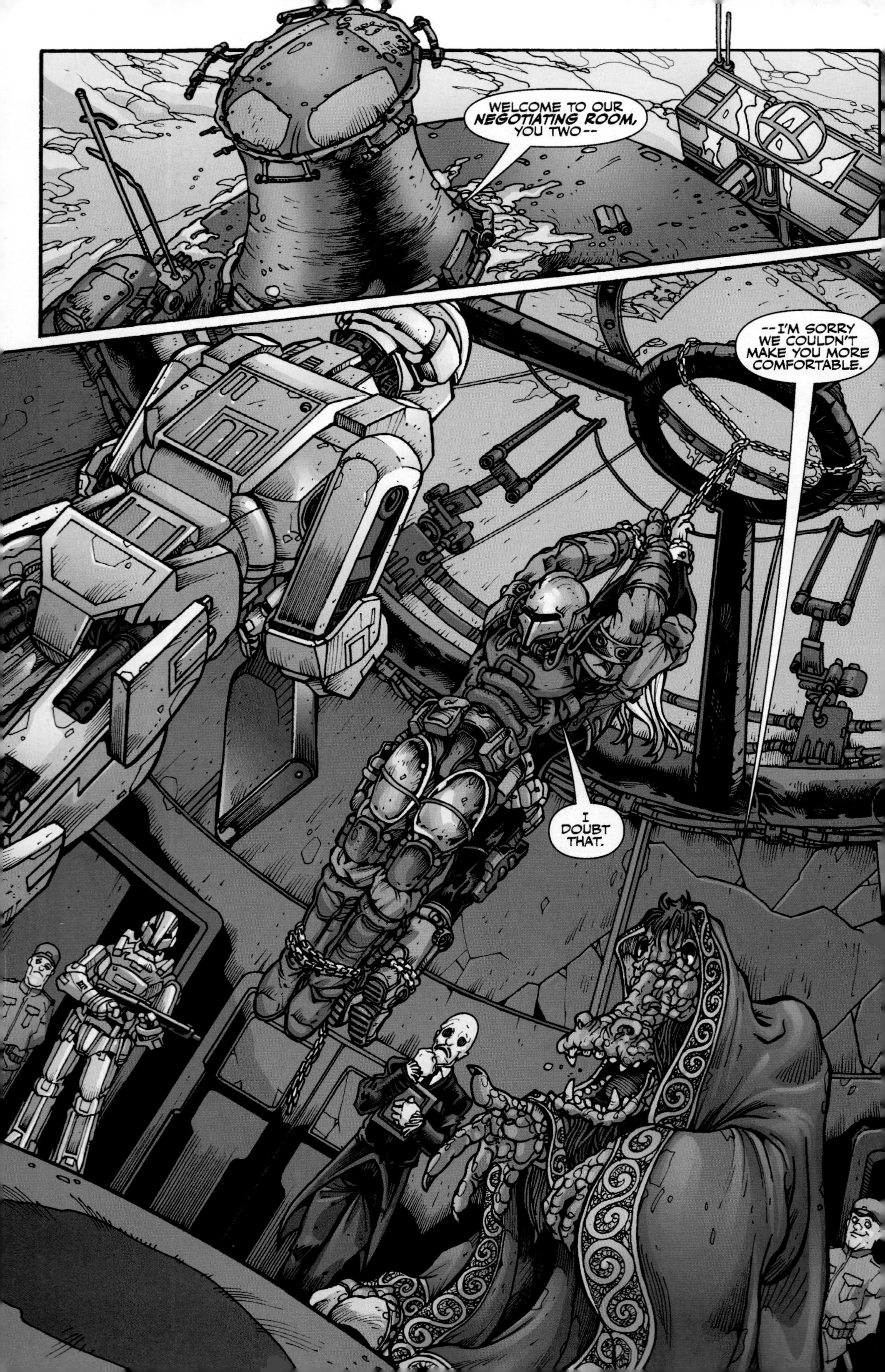
WELCOME TO OUR NEGOTIATING ROOM, YOU TWO--
--I'M SORRY WE COULDN'T MAKE YOU MORE COMFORTABLE.
I DOUBT THAT.

HEH! NO, THIS WAS ONCE A SOLAR OBSERVATORY -- 'TIL THE FUNDING WENT SOMEWHERE CALLED *FLASHPOINT.* HEARD OF IT?

IN PASSING.

WELL, IT WAS GOOD TIMING. SEE, MY PEOPLE GET A PIECE OF EVERY TRANSACTION IN THE MARKET, NICE AND LEGAL --

-- ONLY GUYS KEEP SHOWING UP WITH COUNTERCLAIMS. SO WE PRETEND TO PAY THEM TO GO AWAY --

-- ONLY WE BRING THEM *HERE.* TO GO AWAY.

ACTIVATE THE --

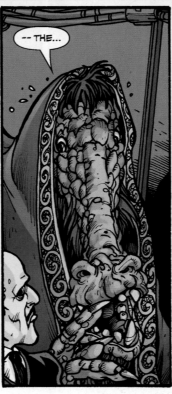

-- THE...

WELL, YOU KNOW. THE *THING.*

JUST DO IT, ALL RIGHT?

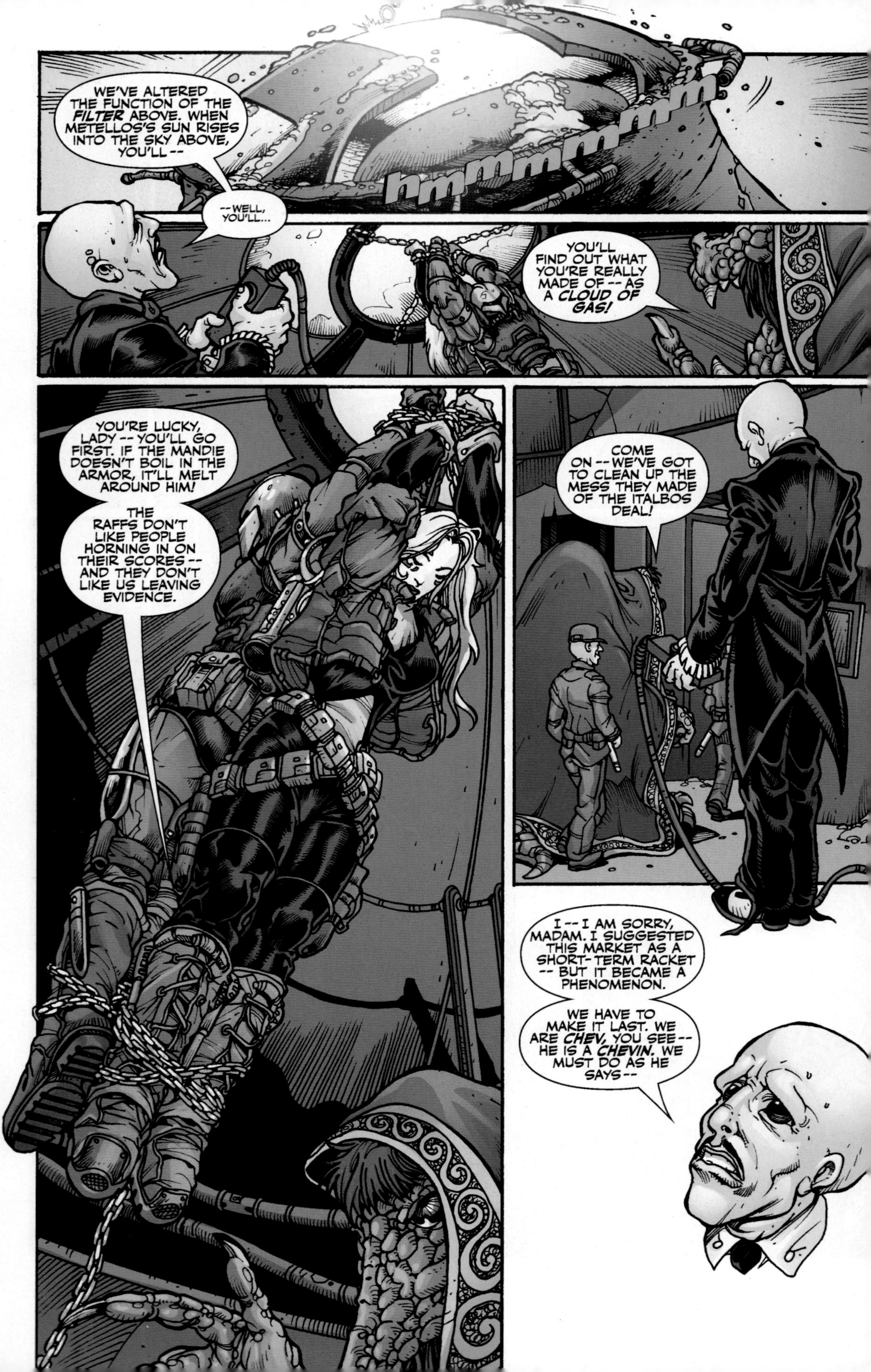
WE'VE ALTERED THE FUNCTION OF THE FILTER ABOVE. WHEN METELLOS'S SUN RISES INTO THE SKY ABOVE, YOU'LL --
hmmmmmmmm
--WELL, YOU'LL...
YOU'LL FIND OUT WHAT YOU'RE REALLY MADE OF -- AS A CLOUD OF GAS!
YOU'RE LUCKY, LADY -- YOU'LL GO FIRST. IF THE MANDIE DOESN'T BOIL IN THE ARMOR, IT'LL MELT AROUND HIM!
THE RAFFS DON'T LIKE PEOPLE HORNING IN ON THEIR SCORES -- AND THEY DON'T LIKE US LEAVING EVIDENCE.
COME ON -- WE'VE GOT TO CLEAN UP THE MESS THEY MADE OF THE ITALBOS DEAL!
I -- I AM SORRY, MADAM. I SUGGESTED THIS MARKET AS A SHORT-TERM RACKET -- BUT IT BECAME A PHENOMENON.
WE HAVE TO MAKE IT LAST. WE ARE CHEV, YOU SEE -- HE IS A CHEVIN. WE MUST DO AS HE SAYS --

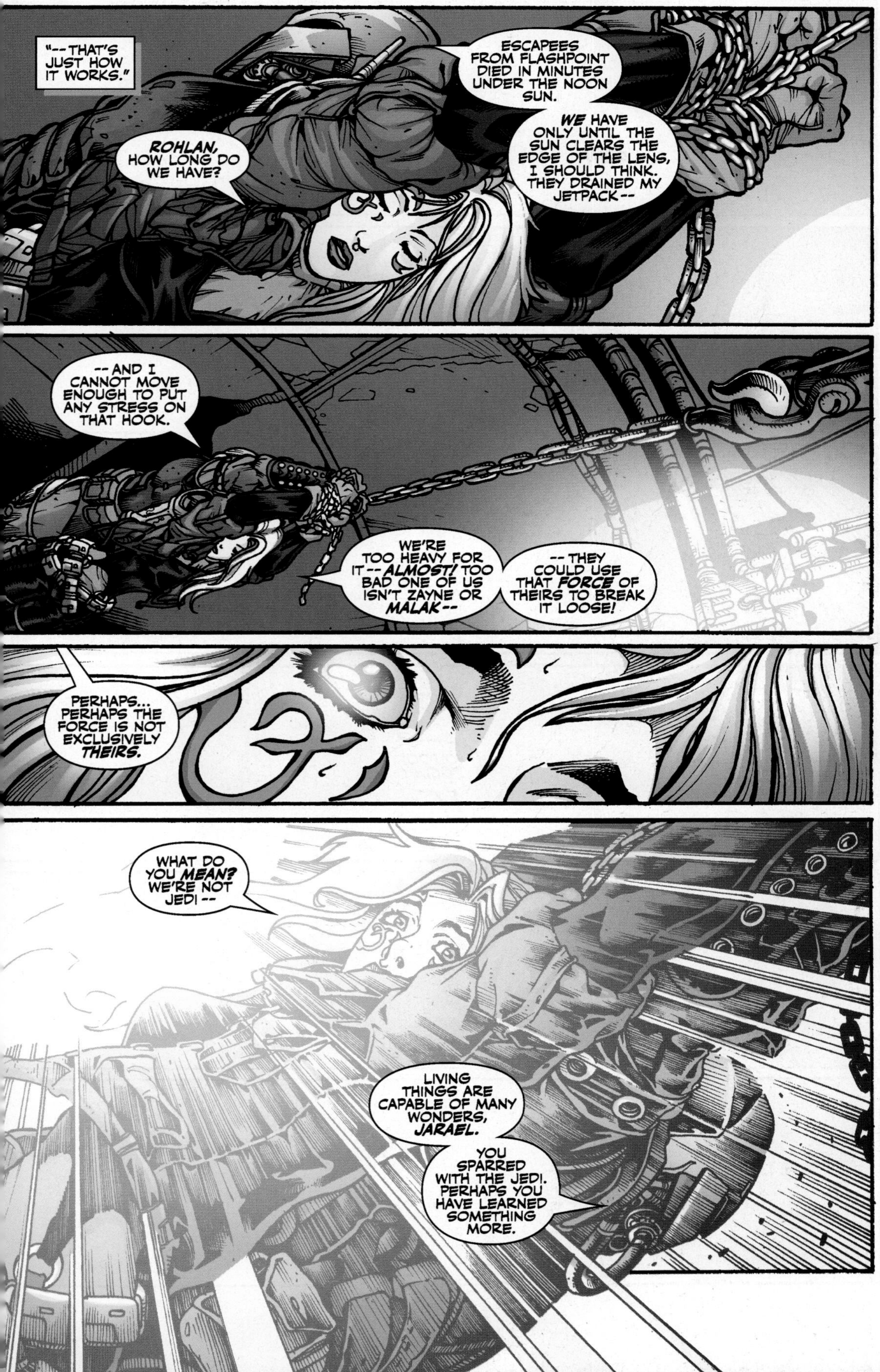
"--THAT'S JUST HOW IT WORKS."
ESCAPEES FROM FLASHPOINT DIED IN MINUTES UNDER THE NOON SUN.
WE HAVE ONLY UNTIL THE SUN CLEARS THE EDGE OF THE LENS, I SHOULD THINK. THEY DRAINED MY JETPACK--
ROHLAN, HOW LONG DO WE HAVE?
--AND I CANNOT MOVE ENOUGH TO PUT ANY STRESS ON THAT HOOK.
WE'RE TOO HEAVY FOR IT--ALMOST! TOO BAD ONE OF US ISN'T ZAYNE OR MALAK--
--THEY COULD USE THAT FORCE OF THEIRS TO BREAK IT LOOSE!
PERHAPS... PERHAPS THE FORCE IS NOT EXCLUSIVELY THEIRS.
WHAT DO YOU MEAN? WE'RE NOT JEDI --
LIVING THINGS ARE CAPABLE OF MANY WONDERS, JARAEL.
YOU SPARRED WITH THE JEDI. PERHAPS YOU HAVE LEARNED SOMETHING MORE.

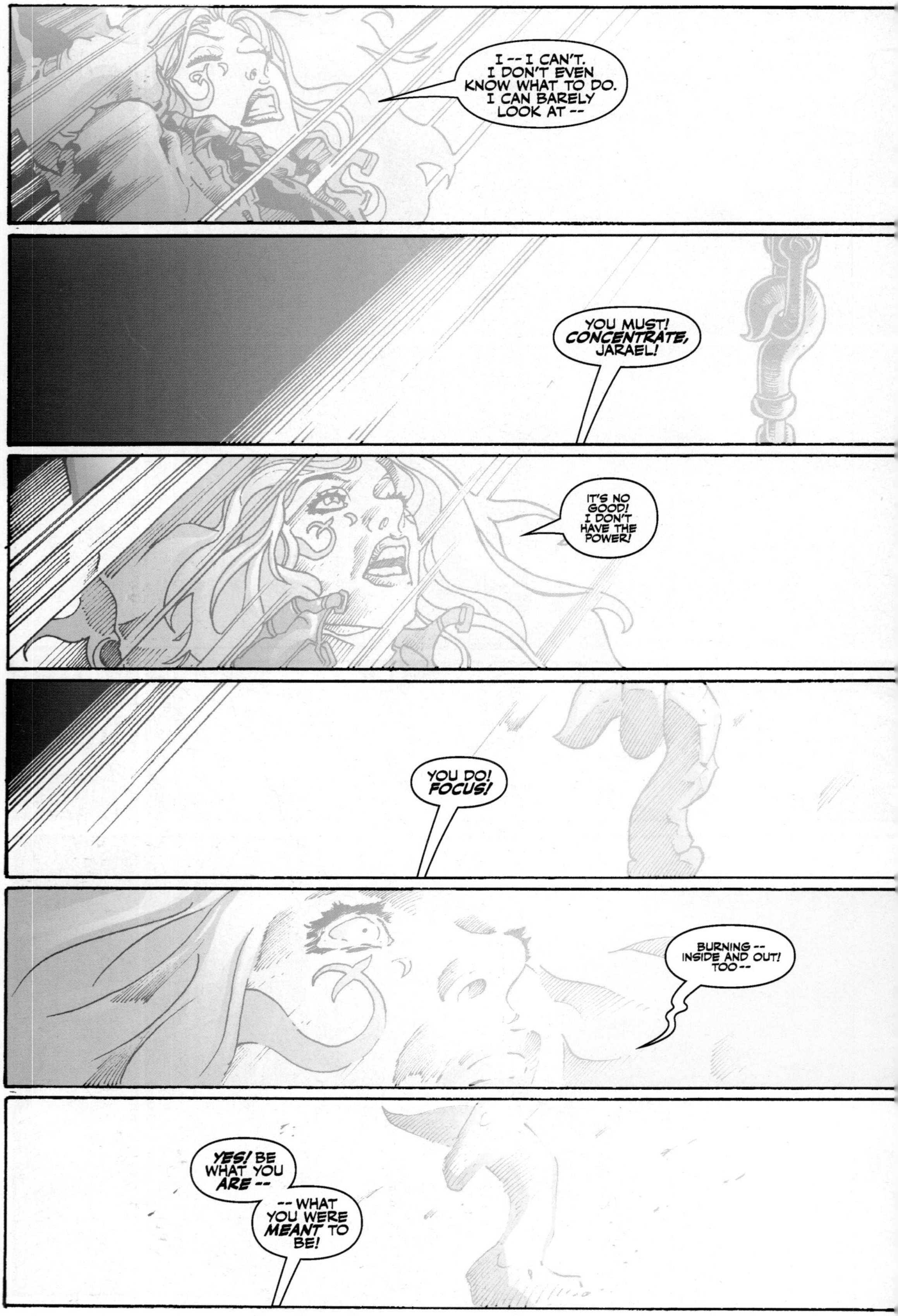

I -- I CAN'T. I DON'T EVEN KNOW WHAT TO DO. I CAN BARELY LOOK AT --
YOU MUST! CONCENTRATE, JARAEL!
IT'S NO GOOD! I DON'T HAVE THE POWER!
YOU DO! FOCUS!
BURNING -- INSIDE AND OUT! TOO --
YES! BE WHAT YOU ARE --
-- WHAT YOU WERE MEANT TO BE!

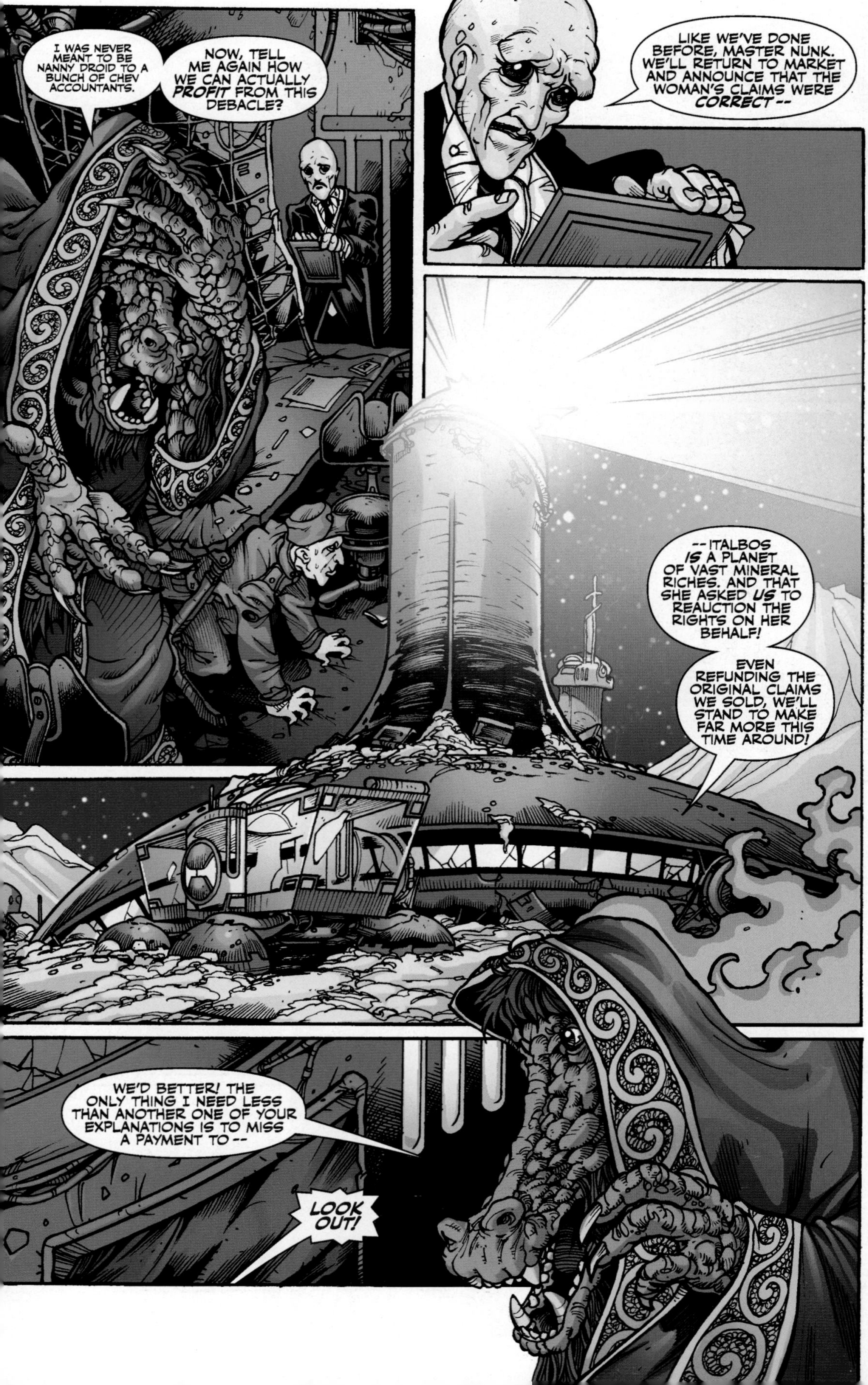
I WAS NEVER MEANT TO BE NANNY DROID TO A BUNCH OF CHEV ACCOUNTANTS.
NOW, TELL ME AGAIN HOW WE CAN ACTUALLY *PROFIT* FROM THIS DEBACLE?
LIKE WE'VE DONE BEFORE, MASTER NUNK. WE'LL RETURN TO MARKET AND ANNOUNCE THAT THE WOMAN'S CLAIMS WERE *CORRECT* --
-- ITALBOS *IS* A PLANET OF VAST MINERAL RICHES. AND THAT SHE ASKED *US* TO REAUCTION THE RIGHTS ON HER BEHALF!
EVEN REFUNDING THE ORIGINAL CLAIMS WE SOLD, WE'LL STAND TO MAKE FAR MORE THIS TIME AROUND!
WE'D BETTER! THE ONLY THING I NEED LESS THAN ANOTHER ONE OF YOUR EXPLANATIONS IS TO MISS A PAYMENT TO --
LOOK OUT!

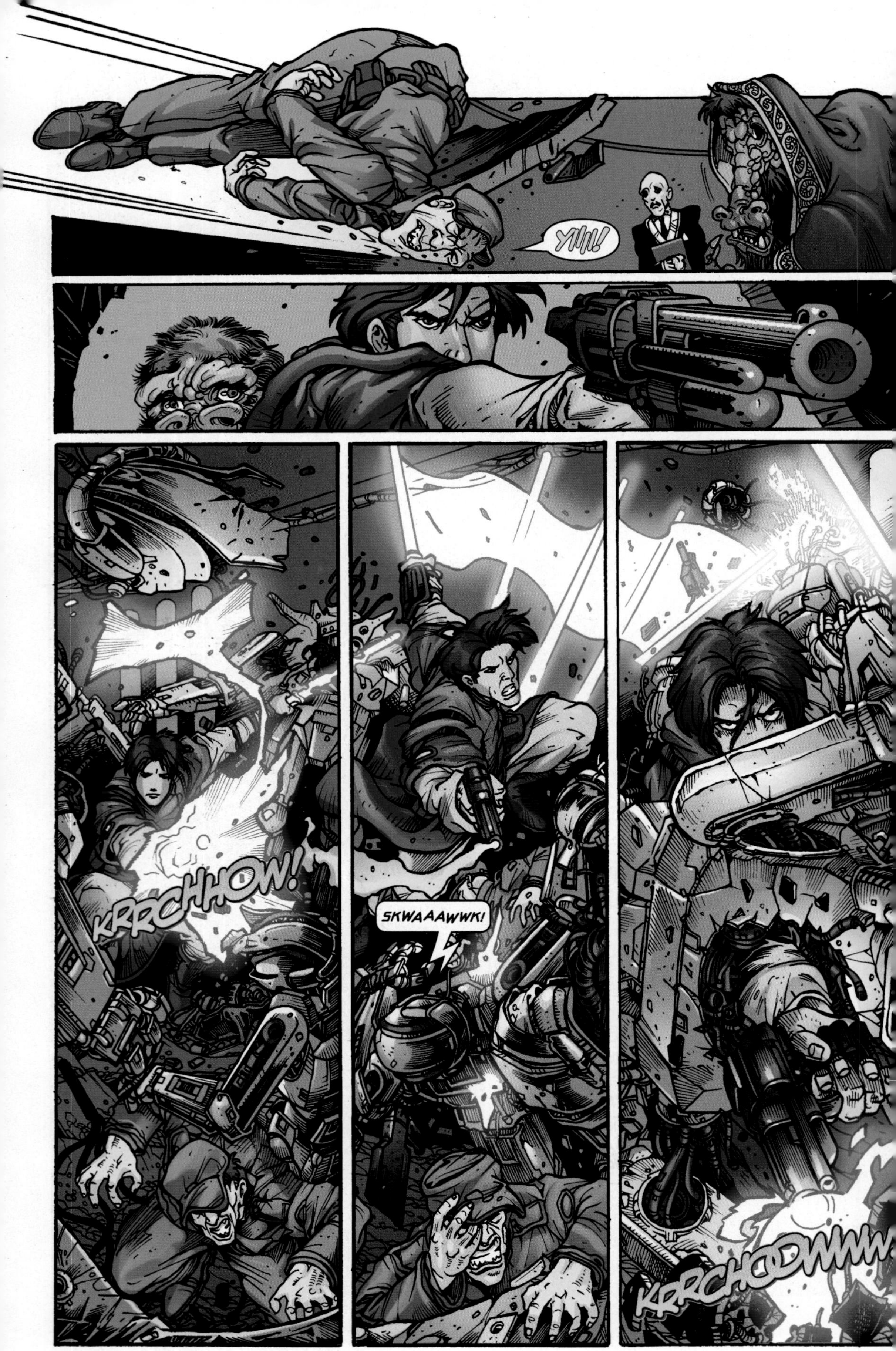
YIII!
KRRCHHOW!
SKWAAAWWK!
KRRCHOOWWW

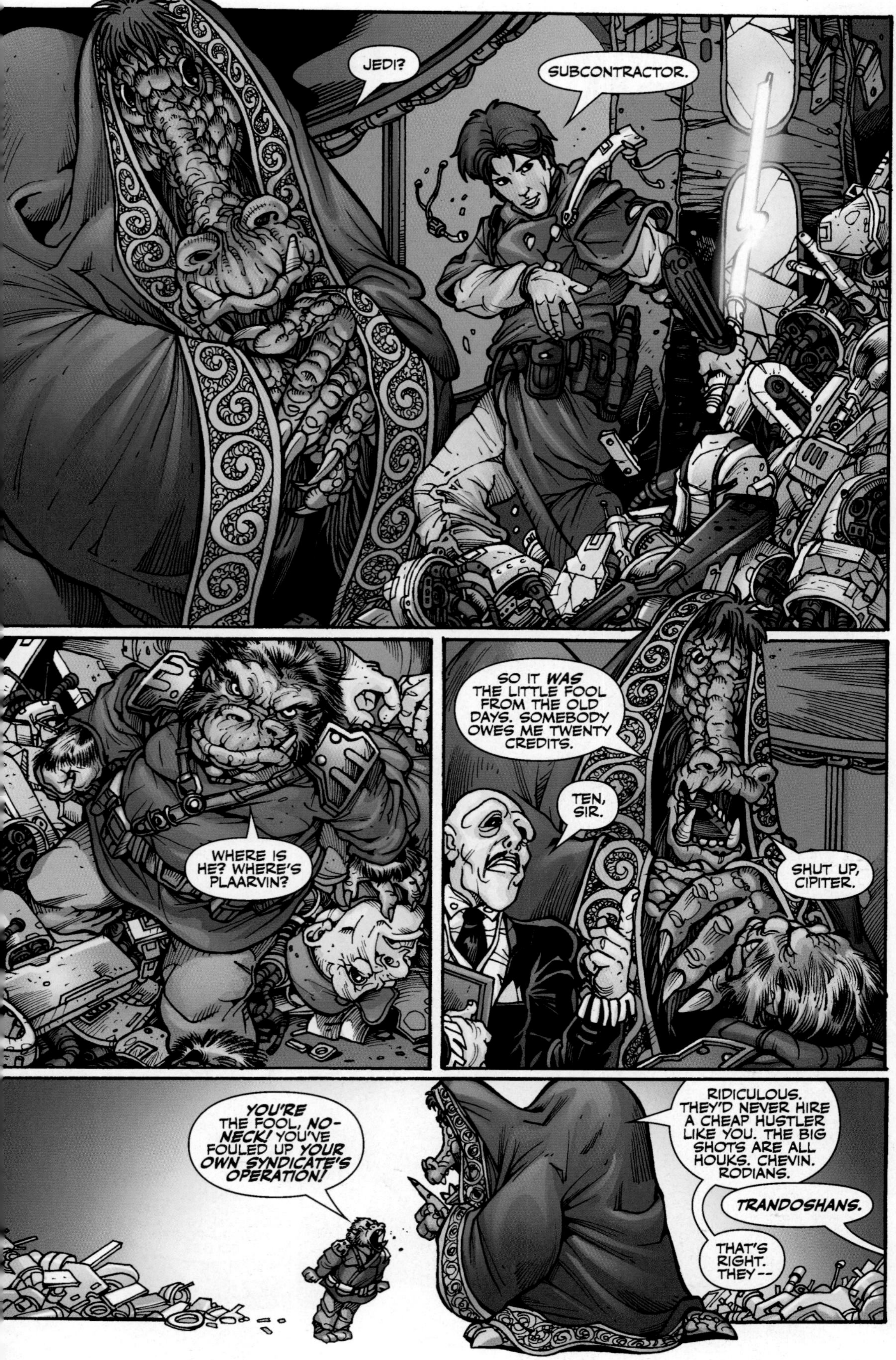
JEDI?
SUBCONTRACTOR.
WHERE IS HE? WHERE'S PLAARVIN?
SO IT WAS THE LITTLE FOOL FROM THE OLD DAYS. SOMEBODY OWES ME TWENTY CREDITS.
TEN, SIR.
SHUT UP, CIPITER.
YOU'RE THE FOOL, NO-NECK! YOU'VE FOULED UP YOUR OWN SYNDICATE'S OPERATION!
RIDICULOUS. THEY'D NEVER HIRE A CHEAP HUSTLER LIKE YOU. THE BIG SHOTS ARE ALL HOUKS. CHEVIN. RODIANS.
TRANDOSHANS.
THAT'S RIGHT. THEY--

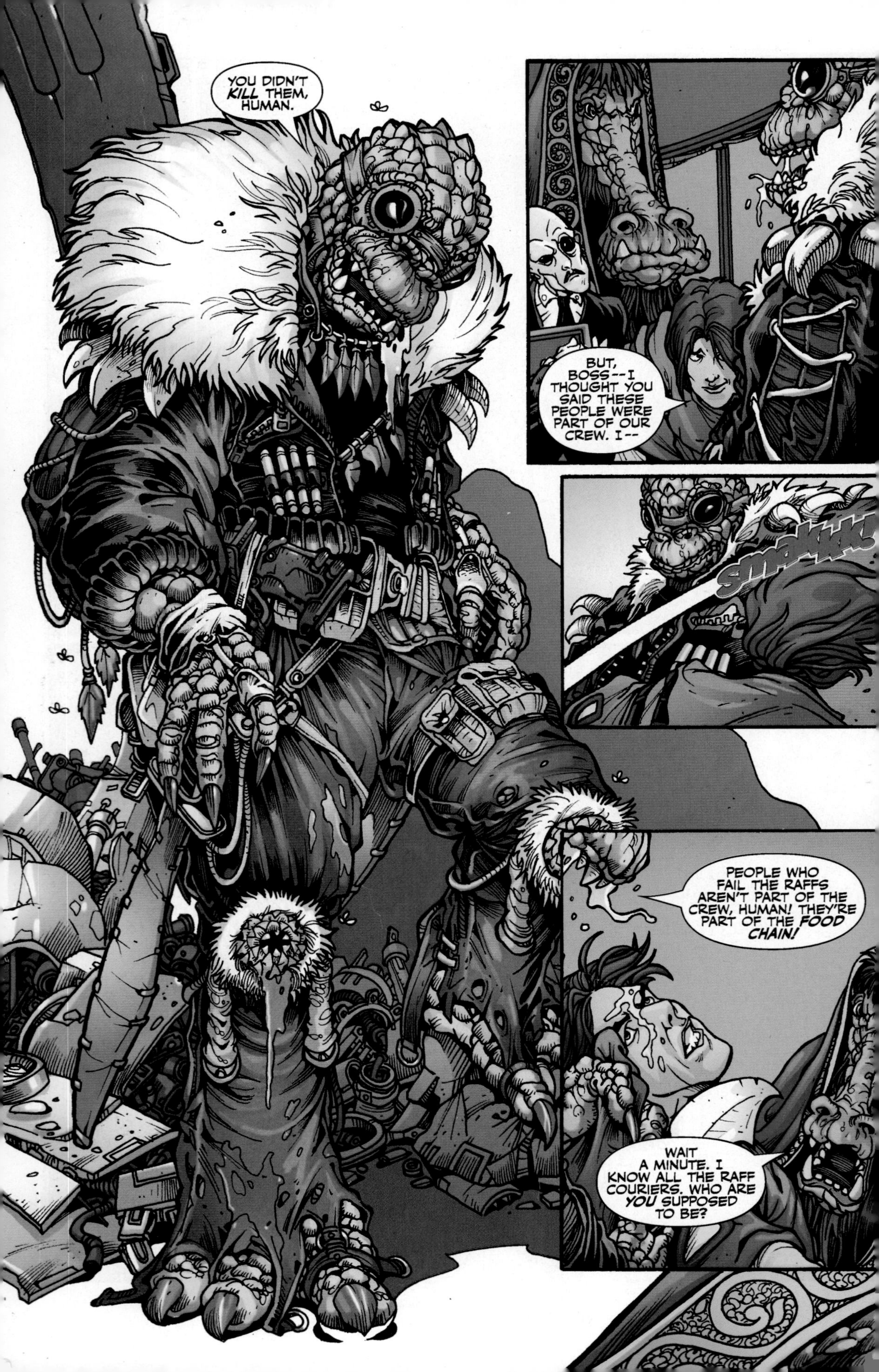
YOU DIDN'T KILL THEM, HUMAN.
BUT, BOSS--I THOUGHT YOU SAID THESE PEOPLE WERE PART OF OUR CREW. I--
SMAKKK!
PEOPLE WHO FAIL THE RAFFS AREN'T PART OF THE CREW, HUMAN! THEY'RE PART OF THE FOOD CHAIN!
WAIT A MINUTE. I KNOW ALL THE RAFF COURIERS. WHO ARE YOU SUPPOSED TO BE?

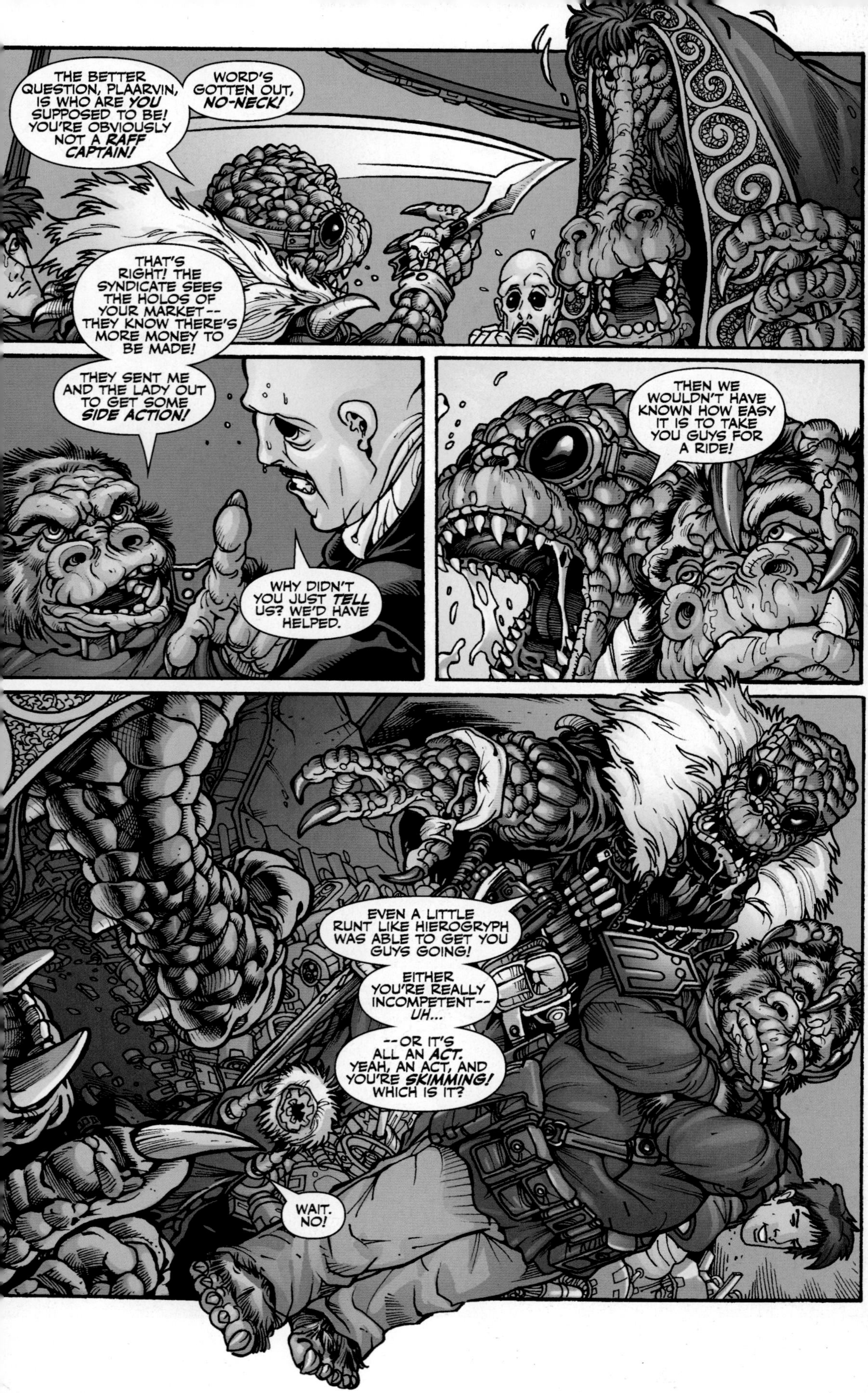
THE BETTER QUESTION, PLAARVIN, IS WHO ARE YOU SUPPOSED TO BE! YOU'RE OBVIOUSLY NOT A RAFF CAPTAIN!
WORD'S GOTTEN OUT, NO-NECK!
THAT'S RIGHT! THE SYNDICATE SEES THE HOLOS OF YOUR MARKET-- THEY KNOW THERE'S MORE MONEY TO BE MADE!
THEY SENT ME AND THE LADY OUT TO GET SOME SIDE ACTION!
WHY DIDN'T YOU JUST TELL US? WE'D HAVE HELPED.
THEN WE WOULDN'T HAVE KNOWN HOW EASY IT IS TO TAKE YOU GUYS FOR A RIDE!
EVEN A LITTLE RUNT LIKE HIEROGRYPH WAS ABLE TO GET YOU GUYS GOING!
EITHER YOU'RE REALLY INCOMPETENT-- UH...
--OR IT'S ALL AN ACT. YEAH, AN ACT, AND YOU'RE SKIMMING! WHICH IS IT?
WAIT. NO!

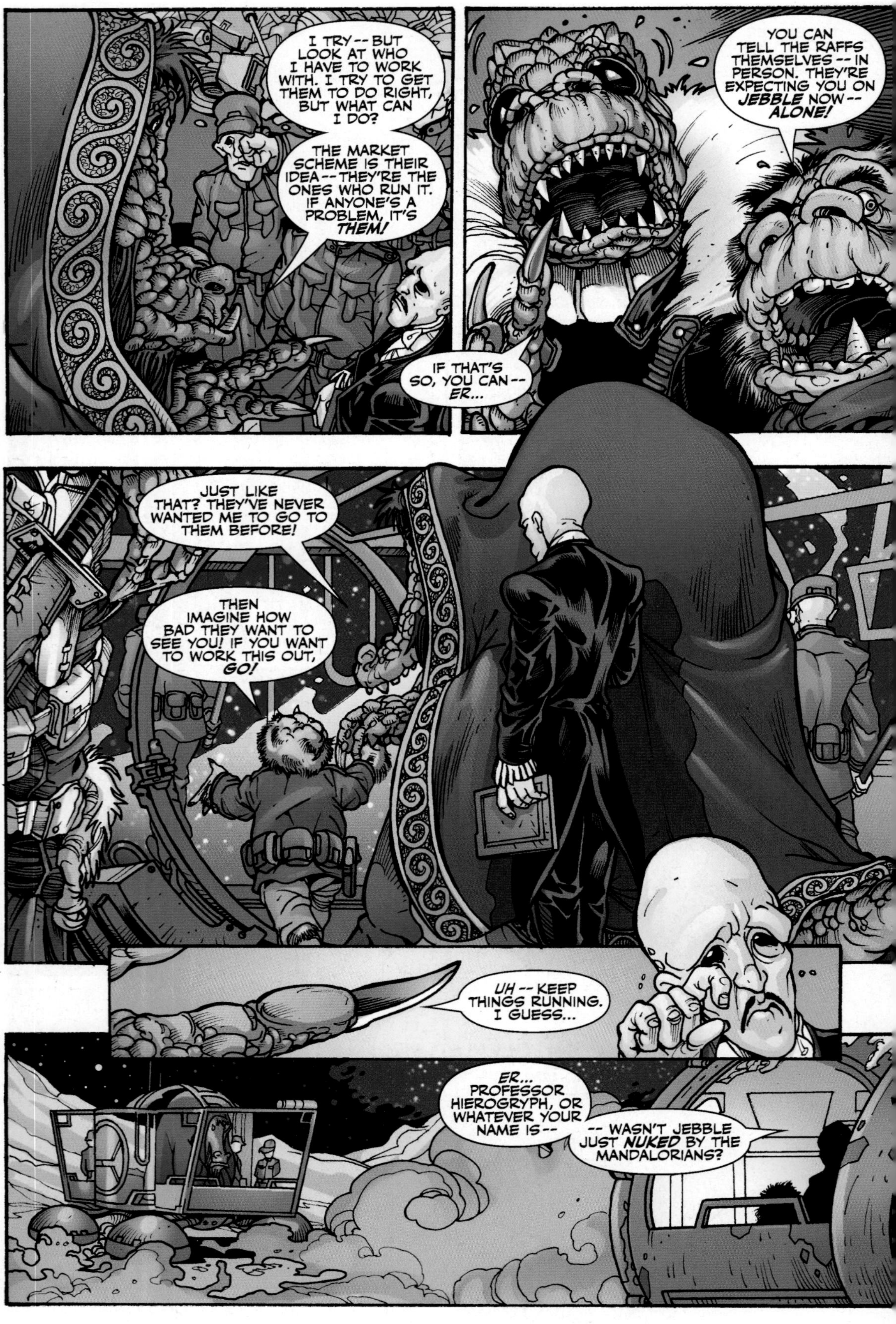
I TRY -- BUT LOOK AT WHO I HAVE TO WORK WITH. I TRY TO GET THEM TO DO RIGHT, BUT WHAT CAN I DO?
THE MARKET SCHEME IS THEIR IDEA -- THEY'RE THE ONES WHO RUN IT. IF ANYONE'S A PROBLEM, IT'S *THEM!*
IF THAT'S SO, YOU CAN -- *ER...*
YOU CAN TELL THE RAFFS THEMSELVES -- IN PERSON. THEY'RE EXPECTING YOU ON *JEBBLE* NOW -- *ALONE!*
JUST LIKE THAT? THEY'VE NEVER WANTED ME TO GO TO THEM BEFORE!
THEN IMAGINE HOW BAD THEY WANT TO SEE YOU! IF YOU WANT TO WORK THIS OUT, *GO!*
UH -- KEEP THINGS RUNNING. I GUESS...
ER... PROFESSOR HIEROGRYPH, OR WHATEVER YOUR NAME IS --
-- WASN'T JEBBLE JUST *NUKED* BY THE MANDALORIANS?

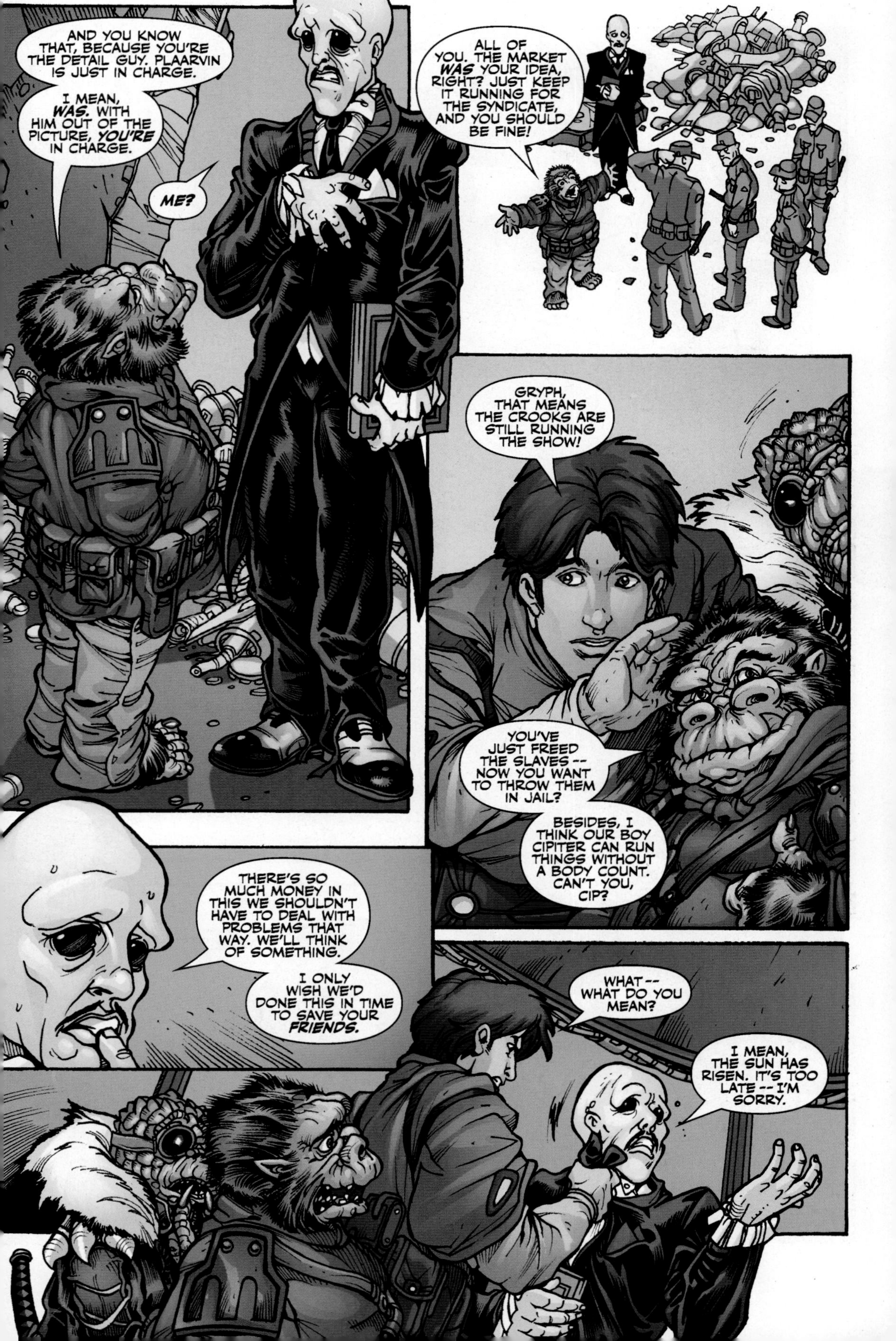
AND YOU KNOW THAT, BECAUSE YOU'RE THE DETAIL GUY. PLAARVIN IS JUST IN CHARGE.
I MEAN, WAS. WITH HIM OUT OF THE PICTURE, YOU'RE IN CHARGE.
ME?
ALL OF YOU. THE MARKET WAS YOUR IDEA, RIGHT? JUST KEEP IT RUNNING FOR THE SYNDICATE, AND YOU SHOULD BE FINE!
GRYPH, THAT MEANS THE CROOKS ARE STILL RUNNING THE SHOW!
YOU'VE JUST FREED THE SLAVES -- NOW YOU WANT TO THROW THEM IN JAIL?
BESIDES, I THINK OUR BOY CIPITER CAN RUN THINGS WITHOUT A BODY COUNT. CAN'T YOU, CIP?
THERE'S SO MUCH MONEY IN THIS WE SHOULDN'T HAVE TO DEAL WITH PROBLEMS THAT WAY. WE'LL THINK OF SOMETHING.
I ONLY WISH WE'D DONE THIS IN TIME TO SAVE YOUR FRIENDS.
WHAT -- WHAT DO YOU MEAN?
I MEAN, THE SUN HAS RISEN. IT'S TOO LATE -- I'M SORRY.

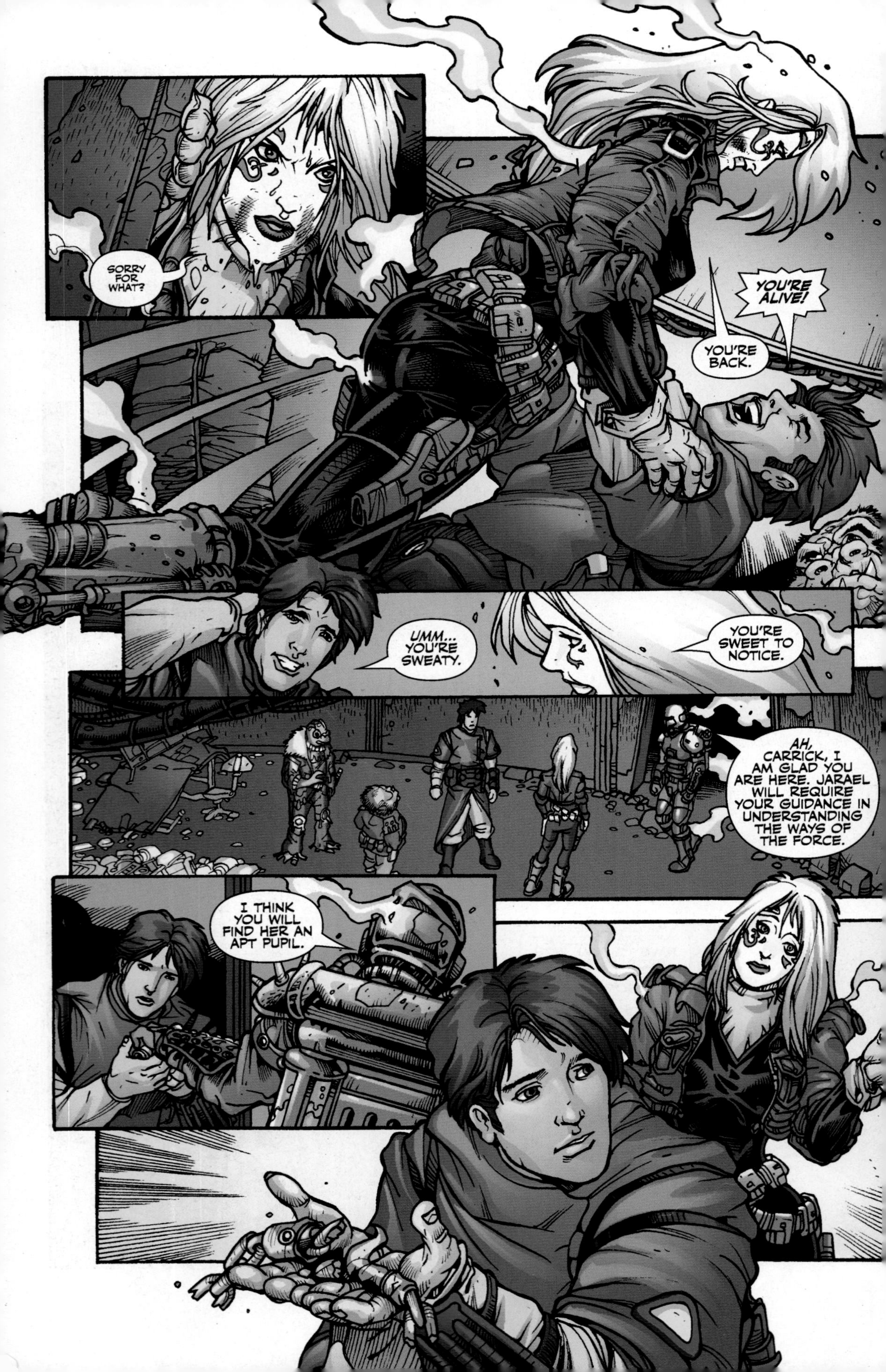
SORRY FOR WHAT?
YOU'RE ALIVE!
YOU'RE BACK.
UMM... YOU'RE SWEATY.
YOU'RE SWEET TO NOTICE.
AH, CARRICK, I AM GLAD YOU ARE HERE. JARAEL WILL REQUIRE YOUR GUIDANCE IN UNDERSTANDING THE WAYS OF THE FORCE.
I THINK YOU WILL FIND HER AN APT PUPIL.

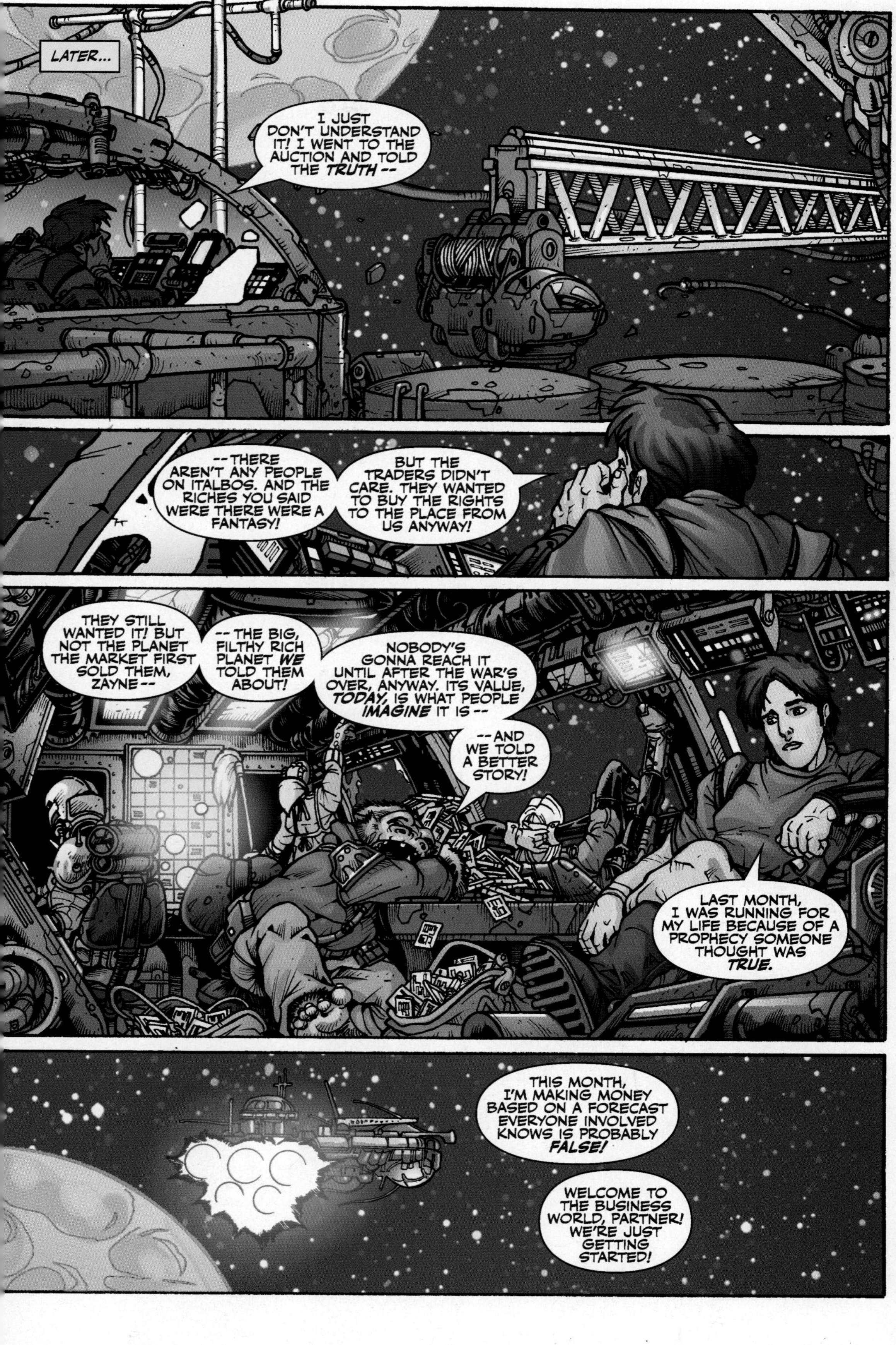
LATER...
I JUST DON'T UNDERSTAND IT! I WENT TO THE AUCTION AND TOLD THE TRUTH --
-- THERE AREN'T ANY PEOPLE ON ITALBOS. AND THE RICHES YOU SAID WERE THERE WERE A FANTASY!
BUT THE TRADERS DIDN'T CARE. THEY WANTED TO BUY THE RIGHTS TO THE PLACE FROM US ANYWAY!
THEY STILL WANTED IT! BUT NOT THE PLANET THE MARKET FIRST SOLD THEM, ZAYNE --
-- THE BIG, FILTHY RICH PLANET WE TOLD THEM ABOUT!
NOBODY'S GONNA REACH IT UNTIL AFTER THE WAR'S OVER, ANYWAY. ITS VALUE, TODAY, IS WHAT PEOPLE IMAGINE IT IS --
-- AND WE TOLD A BETTER STORY!
LAST MONTH, I WAS RUNNING FOR MY LIFE BECAUSE OF A PROPHECY SOMEONE THOUGHT WAS TRUE.
THIS MONTH, I'M MAKING MONEY BASED ON A FORECAST EVERYONE INVOLVED KNOWS IS PROBABLY FALSE!
WELCOME TO THE BUSINESS WORLD, PARTNER! WE'RE JUST GETTING STARTED!

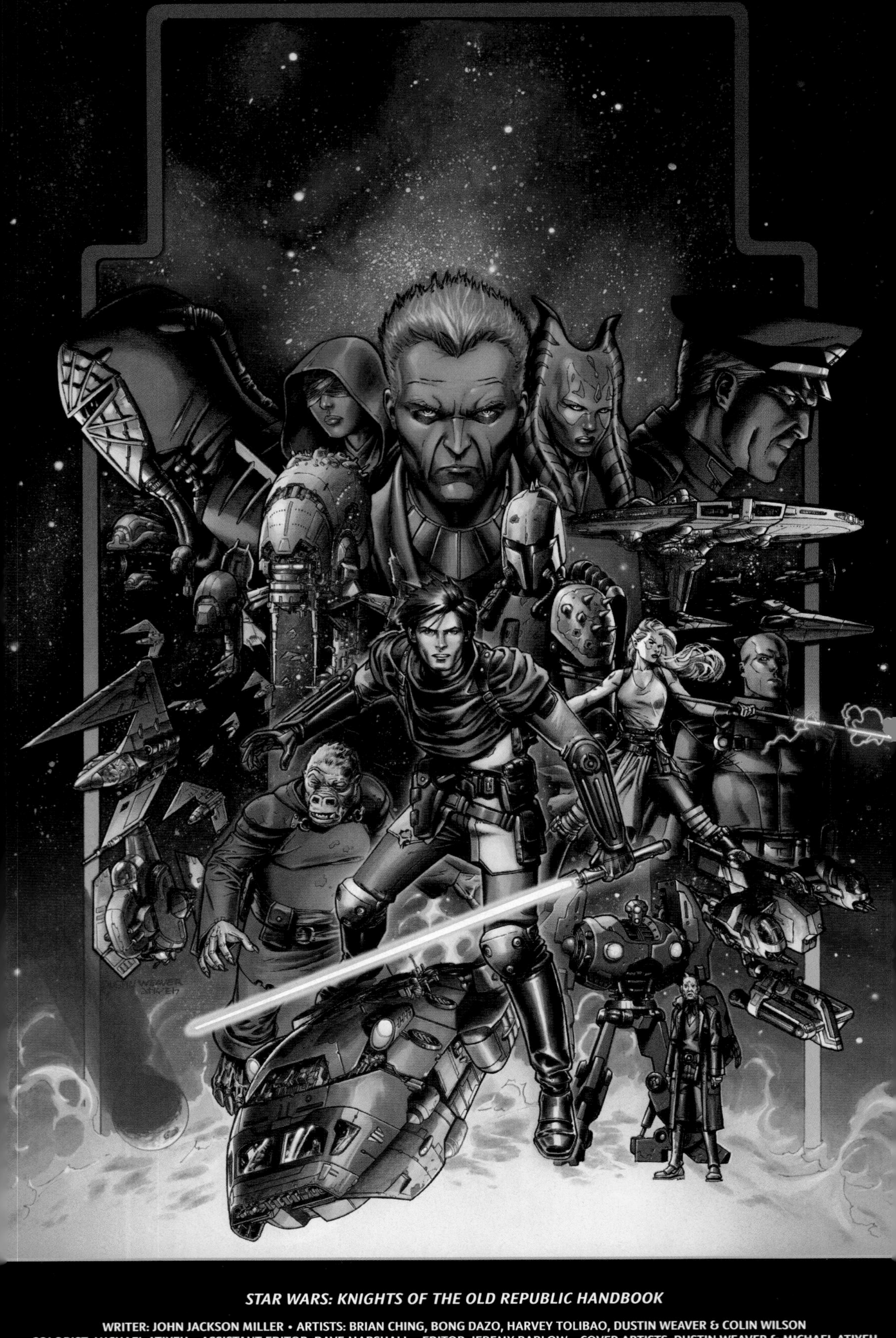

STAR WARS: KNIGHTS OF THE OLD REPUBLIC HANDBOOK

WRITER: JOHN JACKSON MILLER • ARTISTS: BRIAN CHING, BONG DAZO, HARVEY TOLIBAO, DUSTIN WEAVER & COLIN WILSON
COLORIST: MICHAEL ATIYEH • ASSISTANT EDITOR: DAVE MARSHALL • EDITOR: JEREMY BARLOW • COVER ARTISTS: DUSTIN WEAVER & MICHAEL ATIYEH

A long, long time ago . . .

Zayne Carrick thought his great adventure was over. Worst in his Padawan class, he was sure he wouldn't become a Knight.

Until the fateful evening when, late to the Knighting ceremony, he entered to find his fellow students dead at their Masters' feet! And his own Master, Lucien, threatening to finish the job—by killing him!

Zayne fled—aided and, sometimes, hindered—by a company of fugitives, all running from different things. With their help, Zayne discovered the truth: his Masters were part of a Covenant of prognosticators sworn to snuff out any return of the Sith to the galaxy— and they had foreseen one of their students bringing down the Order.

Framed for his classmates' murder and on the run, Zayne declared to the Taris Masters his intention to turn the tables—hunting them until one of them confessed. But, just as before, fate took a different turn. The Mandalorians, a rampaging horde of nomads, picked that moment to attack the Republic, catching Zayne and company in the crashing waves of history. History, in which he has already played no small part—and history which his Masters still believe he will change for the worse!

Always in motion is the future. So is a fugitive Jedi—if he wants to live!

Zayne Carrick

Arvan and Reiva Carrick's third child of five (and their only son), Zayne Carrick was brought from his frontier homeworld of Phaeda to the Jedi Academy on Dantooine just after his fifth birthday. Master Vandar Tokare recognized that the child had difficulties manipulating the Force, but was pleased enough with his personality to hope he might become a diplomatic asset one day.

But while Zayne mastered some skills, he struggled with others, leading educators to suspect a Force-learning disability they had no way to address. His four classmates since childhood promised to help him along, and it was as a group that they were assigned to the five Masters of the Jedi outpost on Taris, then still a non-aligned world.

But the Masters had other concerns besides teaching. They belonged to a secret society within the Order known as The Covenant—and had come to Taris to watch for the potential return of the Sith. No wonder, then, that Zayne found his own Master Lucien to be remote and unhelpful.

It was luck—or the Force—that made Zayne late for the ceremony where he would learn his fate as a Jedi. Capturing Gryph, the hoodlum he was assigned to apprehend, he rushed upstairs with the news—only to find his four lifelong friends dead at their Masters' feet! Not understanding why, Zayne knew immediately he would be next—and fled with Gryph. Improbably, the two escaped, only to find themselves blamed for the Padawans' deaths.

After discovering the truth—that his Masters had foreseen that one of their students would collapse the Jedi Order—he turned himself in to avoid any harm to the new friends he had made while on the lam. But the Masters intended to kill his friends anyway to cover up their crime—and those same friends helped Zayne escape.

Zayne declared, via holographic message, his intention to hunt down his hunters in his drive for justice. But order had collapsed on Taris after his escape, opening the door for the Mandalorian invasion. That, and other clues, led Admiral Karath to conclude Zayne had been

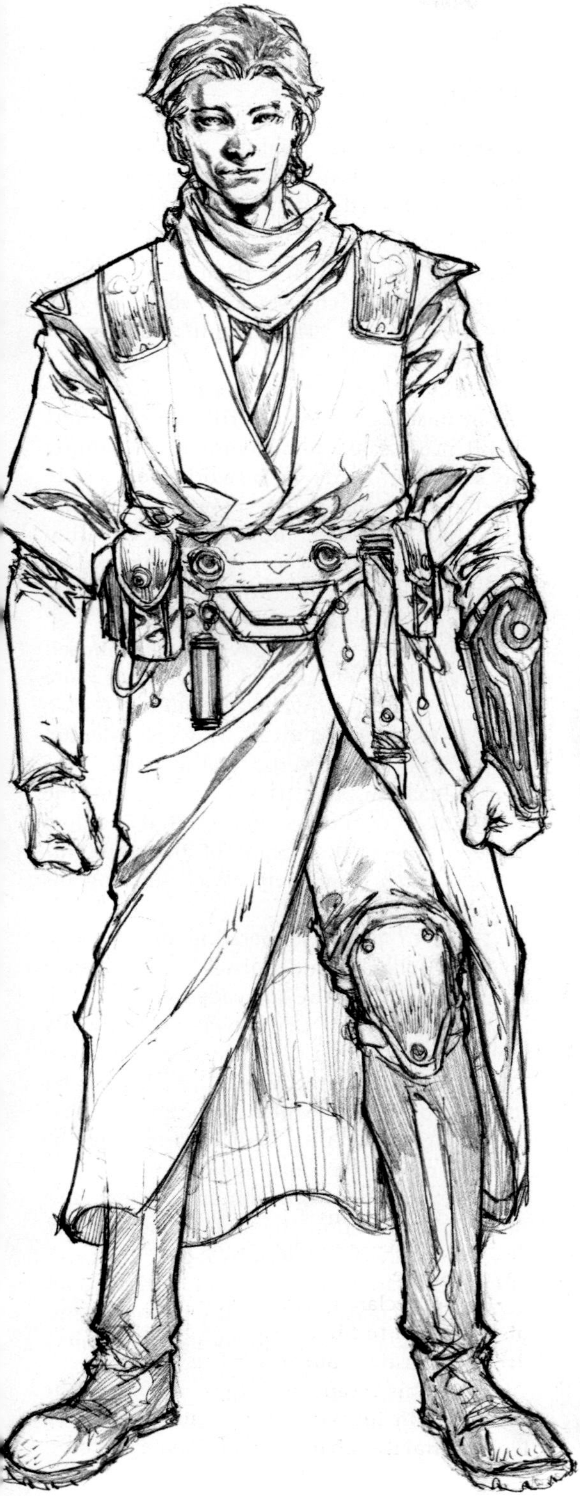

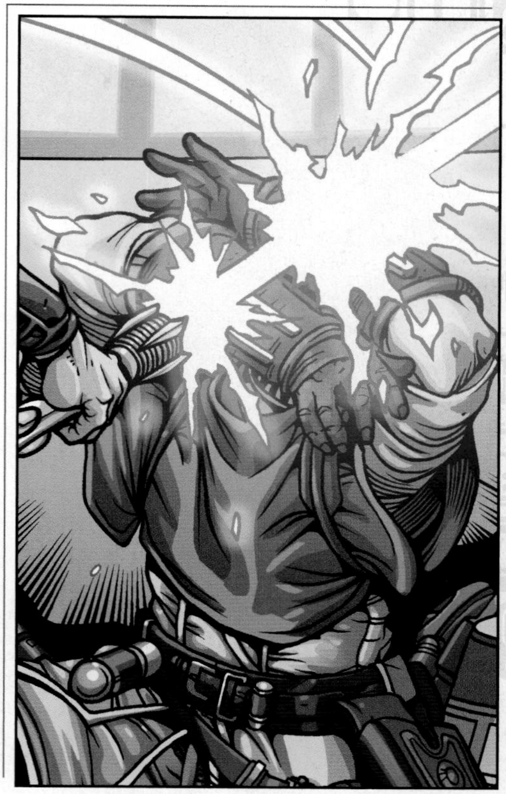

a saboteur—and to charge him with treason. So when Zayne predicted through the Force that the Mandalorians would immolate the cities of Serroco, Karath ignored the warning and jailed him instead. Zayne spent his nineteenth birthday in the brig.

But Zayne's reunion with Master Lucien found them both imprisoned—by Lord Adasca, seeking to keep them away from his bid for galactic power. Forging a temporary truce, Zayne and his Master foiled the plan—and Zayne slipped away to Taris again, where Gryph had fled. Only, now, Taris was quaking under the heels of Mandalorian invaders!

Zayne wears a pair of phrikite vambraces designed by Camper to protect his forearms from lightsaber attacks. He is also a speederbike aficionado, having spent his teen years on Taris, home of the swoopbike.

Marn "The Gryph" Hierogryph

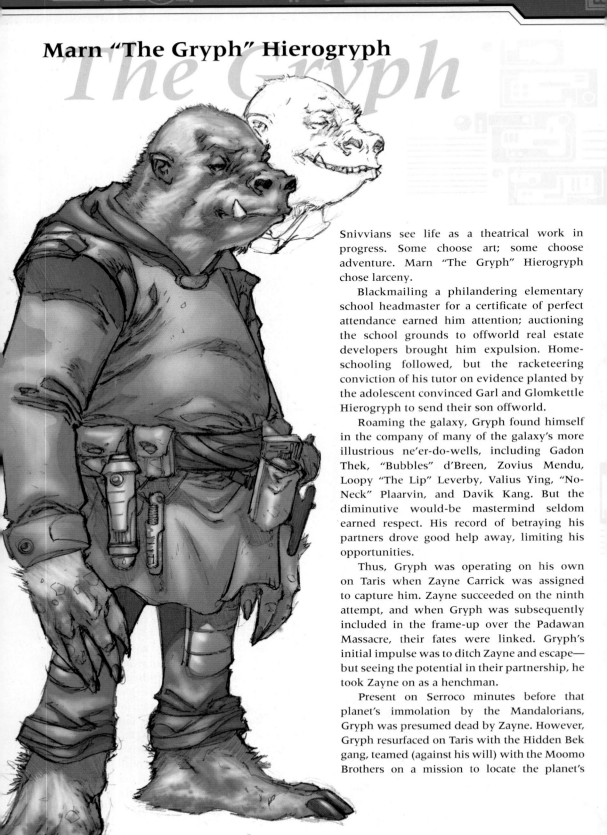

Snivvians see life as a theatrical work in progress. Some choose art; some choose adventure. Marn "The Gryph" Hierogryph chose larceny.

Blackmailing a philandering elementary school headmaster for a certificate of perfect attendance earned him attention; auctioning the school grounds to offworld real estate developers brought him expulsion. Home-schooling followed, but the racketeering conviction of his tutor on evidence planted by the adolescent convinced Garl and Glomkettle Hierogryph to send their son offworld.

Roaming the galaxy, Gryph found himself in the company of many of the galaxy's more illustrious ne'er-do-wells, including Gadon Thek, "Bubbles" d'Breen, Zovius Mendu, Loopy "The Lip" Leverby, Valius Ying, "No-Neck" Plaarvin, and Davik Kang. But the diminutive would-be mastermind seldom earned respect. His record of betraying his partners drove good help away, limiting his opportunities.

Thus, Gryph was operating on his own on Taris when Zayne Carrick was assigned to capture him. Zayne succeeded on the ninth attempt, and when Gryph was subsequently included in the frame-up over the Padawan Massacre, their fates were linked. Gryph's initial impulse was to ditch Zayne and escape—but seeing the potential in their partnership, he took Zayne on as a henchman.

Present on Serroco minutes before that planet's immolation by the Mandalorians, Gryph was presumed dead by Zayne. However, Gryph resurfaced on Taris with the Hidden Bek gang, teamed (against his will) with the Moomo Brothers on a mission to locate the planet's

missing senator. While Gryph has yet to explain his whereabouts between the Battle of Serroco and the Taris Siege, he has ominously assured Zayne that as soon as they reach Republic space, "the answer will be obvious."

As Snivvians are nearly impossible for humans to tell apart, Gryph has developed a number of aliases over the years, ranging from eel mogul Baron Hieromarn to Remulus Horne, the folk balladeer who infamously persuaded viewers to contribute 384,000 credits to his non-existent charity before his "holo-thon" was yanked from the 'feed.

Slyssk

Where other Trandoshans love to hunt, Slyssk preferred stealing their kill to prepare for dinner. Driven to find a trade that better suited his meekness and kleptomania, Slyssk learned starship piracy as an underling in a Raff Syndicate chopshop—only to be kicked out before learning how to fly the ships he stole.

After hiring him to steal a ship, Gryph made the mistake of seeming to save Slyssk's life. Slyssk immediately devoted his questionable services to Gryph, the first person to whom he had ever owed a lifedebt. Slyssk served surprisingly well as a cook for Gryph's flying restaurant, the Little Bivoli, before somehow escaping the inferno of Serroco. Gryph has sworn his hireling to secrecy, preferring to tell the story of the escape in his own time.

Jarael

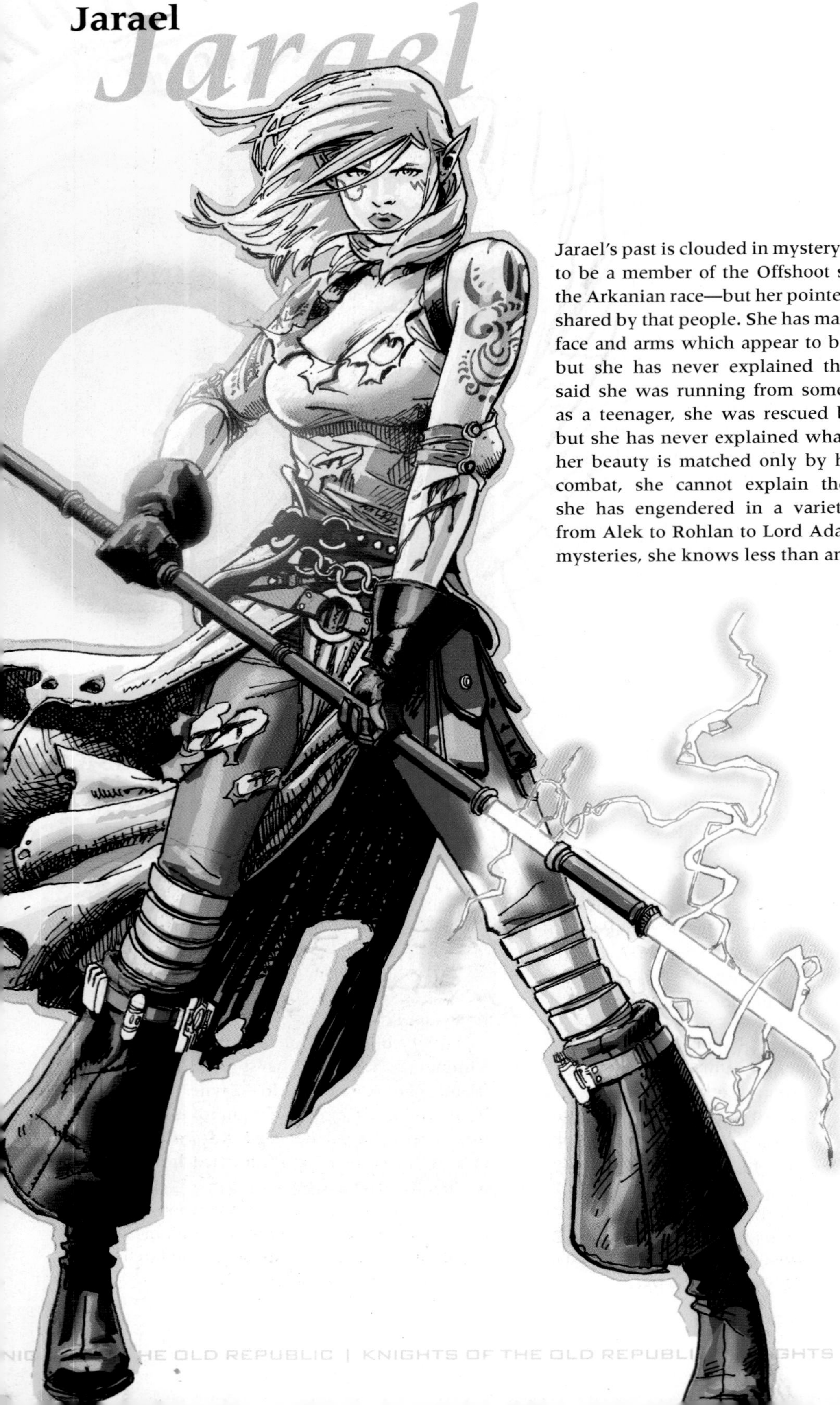
Jarael

Jarael's past is clouded in mystery. She appears to be a member of the Offshoot subspecies of the Arkanian race—but her pointed ears are not shared by that people. She has markings on her face and arms which appear to be permanent, but she has never explained them. She has said she was running from something when, as a teenager, she was rescued by Camper—but she has never explained what. And while her beauty is matched only by her talents in combat, she cannot explain the fascination she has engendered in a variety of people, from Alek to Rohlan to Lord Adasca. Of some mysteries, she knows less than anyone.

Jarael and Camper spent years on the run together on his ship, *The Last Resort*—most of it spent in the dark and forbidding Lower City of Taris. Opportunities were limited. Jarael and Camper deliberately avoided contact with the Black Vulkars and Hidden Beks, the swoop gangs that ruled the area, instead keeping to the hovels around Junk Junction. To buy food, Jarael worked as a day laborer hauling scrap metal to a Kedorzhan reclamation plant—working hard while the increasingly addled Camper tinkered with the electronic tidbits he found. The younger Jarael found some diversion in the abandoned wardrobe left in a defunct clothing factory, but fun was not for working days—and as Camper faltered, every day for Jarael became a working day.

Work was harder to come by after the plant closed, and increasingly she and Camper took to selling those items he built that actually worked. Visitors to *The Last Resort* were likely to be fugitives like themselves, and a popular item was the "Camper Special," a shipping container that enabled an organic-on-the-run a handy (if cramped) means of escape.

That's what brought Zayne Carrick and Gryph to *The Last Resort*—and while Jarael initially refused to help them, the sudden arrival of the Jedi Masters and the Constable took the decision out of her hands. Fearful of having his presence reported to Adascorp, Camper launched the ship for the first time in years.

When Jarael and Camper finally parted company with Zayne, Camper fell ill—and Jarael felt forced to turn for help to the leader of Adascorp himself, the charismatic Lord Adasca. Fascinated by her, Adasca used Jarael as leverage to make Camper work for him.

Jarael cursed herself for being taken in. Kindnesses shown to her by the first three friends she made offworld—Zayne, Alek, and Rohlan—had lowered her guard. So it was that when Camper defeated Adasca and fled to parts unknown, Jarael blamed herself for driving her friend away.

Jarael wields a shockstaff, a weapon created by Camper. It causes temporary numbness in any flesh it strikes, but can be adjusted to burn off its charge in one violent bolt.

Rohlan Dyre

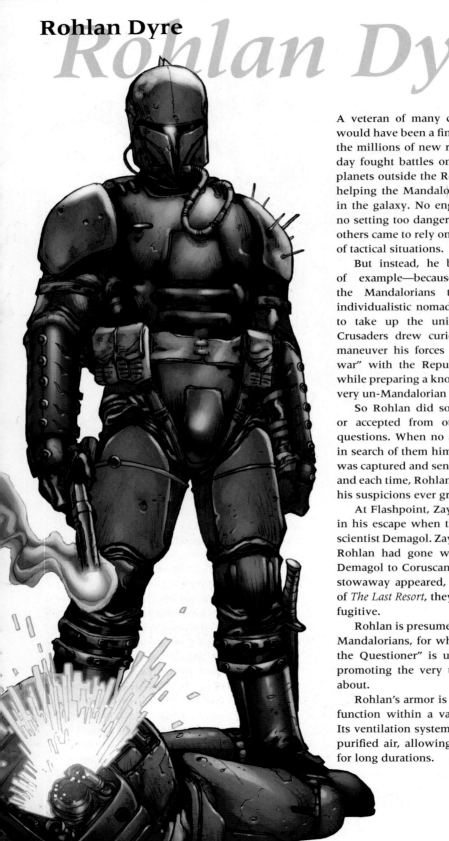

A veteran of many campaigns, Rohlan Dyre would have been a fine model Mandalorian for the millions of new recruits that joined in his day fought battles on a variety of Outer Rim planets outside the Republic's zone of control, helping the Mandalorians reclaim their place in the galaxy. No engagement was too fierce, no setting too dangerous for the warrior—and others came to rely on his quick, clear analyses of tactical situations.

But instead, he became a different kind of example—because of his analysis of the Mandalorians themselves. Seeing the individualistic nomads around him beginning to take up the uniform look of the Neo-Crusaders drew curiosity. Seeing Mandalore maneuver his forces into a deceptive "phony war" with the Republic—taking its measure while preparing a knockout blow—that seemed very un-Mandalorian to Rohlan, indeed.

So Rohlan did something he never did— or accepted from others—before: he asked questions. When no answers came, he set off in search of them himself. Repeatedly, Rohlan was captured and sent back to the front lines— and each time, Rohlan ran in search of answers, his suspicions ever growing.

At Flashpoint, Zayne Carrick aided Rohlan in his escape when the two captured the evil scientist Demagol. Zayne and company thought Rohlan had gone with the Jedi conducting Demagol to Coruscant—but when an armored stowaway appeared, emerging from the hold of *The Last Resort*, they knew they had a fellow fugitive.

Rohlan is presumed dead by the majority of Mandalorians, for whom the story of "Rohlan the Questioner" is used as a cautionary tale promoting the very uniformity he wondered about.

Rohlan's armor is airtight, allowing him to function within a vacuum for several hours. Its ventilation system provides him with cool, purified air, allowing him to stay in uniform for long durations.

Camper

As the grizzled inventor known as Camper, Gorman Vandrayk traded a harsh life for one of opportunity—and then traded back!

A member of a subspecies persecuted by Arkanians, Camper was one of the last of his people allowed to attend university. He thrived there, winning awards for his work in biology, cybernetics, and engineering. But it was his work for Adascorp, discovering a way to control the colossal Exogorths, that changed his life again. Realizing the company had military aims for his concepts, he fled, going into hiding for a third of a century.

Spending so long on the run wore on Camper, who became increasingly addled. But Zayne Carrick's arrival brought him out of hiding—and into the clutches of Adascorp, which had never forgotten him. Out from under the burden of hiding, Camper felt vigor and purpose returning—he turned his great weapon on his captors and fled into unknown space.

Elbee

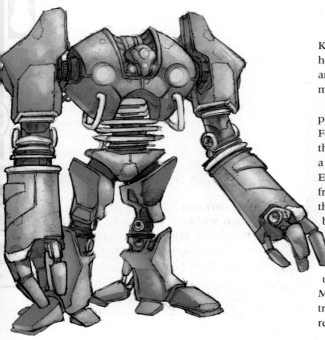

Kellenech Technologies built Elbee (T1-LB) for heavy menial tasks well before the Sith War, and like many hardy droids by that defunct maker, he continued to serve for decades.

When Elbee accidentally saw his Masters plotting against their Padawans, Lucien used the Force to hurl him off a cliff. After Zayne recovered the droid, Camper rebuilt Elbee, giving him a larger brain and the power of speech. But Elbee has taken poorly to the upgrade, and frequently refuses to move, fearing a repeat of the illogical events on the cliff. He can sometimes be motivated by reverse psychology—or by references to his would-be destroyer, Lucien. LB stands for "loader, bulk," a designation used for an entire line, given the droids' ubiquitous, anonymous natures. Duwani Mechanical Products obtained the T1-series trademark at the Kellenech liquidation, repurposing it for its own brand of utility droids.

Krynda Draay

Daughter of a Miraluka father and a human mother, Krynda Draay inherited positive traits from both species. She has both the "Force sight" of the blind Miraluka and functioning human eyes. Jedi speculate this coincidence may be the source behind Krynda's incredible powers of prognostication. Her first mentor, Vodo Siosk-Baas, referred to her as the "eyes of the Jedi."

But Krynda's attention strayed from larger events when she married a financier-turned-Jedi, the dashing Barrison Draay. The difficult birth of their child, Lucien, prevented Krynda from taking part in the Sith War that soon followed—and she lost much in that conflict. First her former Master; then her half-sister, a fellow Jedi; and, finally, her husband. Devastated, Krynda went into seclusion.

After years of solitude, Krynda was drawn back into Jedi affairs after meeting Q'Anilia, a gifted Miraluka student. Gathering more young seers around her, Krynda encouraged them to form a Covenant with the Force—watching for the return of the Sith who had taken so much from her.

Haazen

As Barrison Draay's retainer, Haazen followed his Master into the Jedi Order, where the egalitarian nature of that service made the two as equals—for a time. After Haazen failed his Jedi trials, Lord Draay used his influence to keep him on as his personal squire during the Sith War. Draay died in the War, and Haazen nearly did too—only to live on, horribly disfigured as the result of botched battlefield cybernetic work.

Krynda took Haazen as her aide, allowing him to handle the family estate, her relations with the Order, and Lucien's Jedi training. Haazen helped her organize the Covenant, and, following the deaths of the Taris Padawans, he strongly expressed her displeasure over the handling of the event to Lucien.

Haazen also acts as Lucien's go-between with his mother—though, in fact, Lucien's relationship with both of them is equally testy.

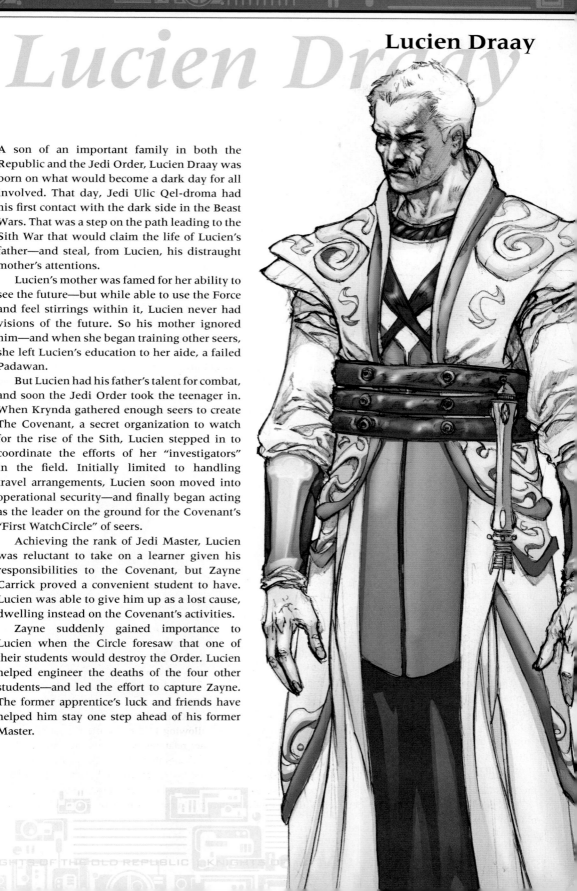

Lucien Draay

A son of an important family in both the Republic and the Jedi Order, Lucien Draay was born on what would become a dark day for all involved. That day, Jedi Ulic Qel-droma had his first contact with the dark side in the Beast Wars. That was a step on the path leading to the Sith War that would claim the life of Lucien's father—and steal, from Lucien, his distraught mother's attentions.

Lucien's mother was famed for her ability to see the future—but while able to use the Force and feel stirrings within it, Lucien never had visions of the future. So his mother ignored him—and when she began training other seers, she left Lucien's education to her aide, a failed Padawan.

But Lucien had his father's talent for combat, and soon the Jedi Order took the teenager in. When Krynda gathered enough seers to create The Covenant, a secret organization to watch for the rise of the Sith, Lucien stepped in to coordinate the efforts of her "investigators" in the field. Initially limited to handling travel arrangements, Lucien soon moved into operational security—and finally began acting as the leader on the ground for the Covenant's "First WatchCircle" of seers.

Achieving the rank of Jedi Master, Lucien was reluctant to take on a learner given his responsibilities to the Covenant, but Zayne Carrick proved a convenient student to have. Lucien was able to give him up as a lost cause, dwelling instead on the Covenant's activities.

Zayne suddenly gained importance to Lucien when the Circle foresaw that one of their students would destroy the Order. Lucien helped engineer the deaths of the four other students—and led the effort to capture Zayne. The former apprentice's luck and friends have helped him stay one step ahead of his former Master.

Q'Anilia

Covenant founder Krynda Draay has always loomed large in the life of Q'Anilia. A Miraluka orphan with both Force sight and precognitive abilities, Q'Anilia learned of her heroine early on when the newly opened Culu Memorial Center on Alpheridies recommended she be brought to Krynda on Coruscant. Krynda realized the child's potential and, ironically, became more of a mother to Q'Anilia than she was to her own son, Lucien. As a member of the Covenant's First WatchCircle, Q'Anilia made Krynda's mission her own.

Contemplative and logical, Q'Anilia is capable of making hard decisions when it comes to the Covenant's mission—including the premeditated murder of Shad, her beloved student. She frequently acts as advisor to Lucien, offering opinions she believes Krynda would support—advice Lucien does not always welcome. It is one more complication to a professional and personal relationship that has now lasted more than three decades.

Xamar

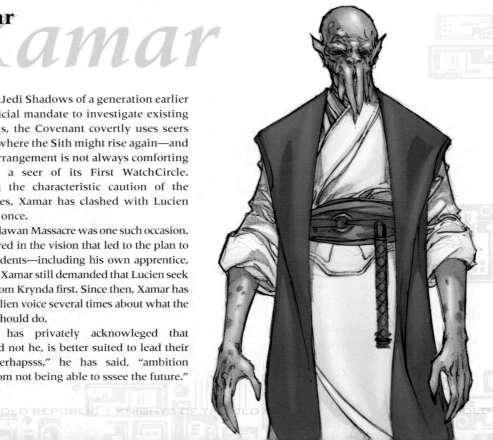

Where the Jedi Shadows of a generation earlier had an official mandate to investigate existing Sith threats, the Covenant covertly uses seers to predict where the Sith might rise again—and act. That arrangement is not always comforting to Xamar, a seer of its First WatchCircle. Exhibiting the characteristic caution of the Khil species, Xamar has clashed with Lucien more than once.

The Padawan Massacre was one such occasion. Xamar shared in the vision that led to the plan to kill the students—including his own apprentice, Gharn. But Xamar still demanded that Lucien seek approval from Krynda first. Since then, Xamar has raised his alien voice several times about what the Covenant should do.

Xamar has privately acknowledged that Lucien, and not he, is better suited to lead their efforts. "Perhapsss," he has said, "ambition comesss from not being able to sssee the future."

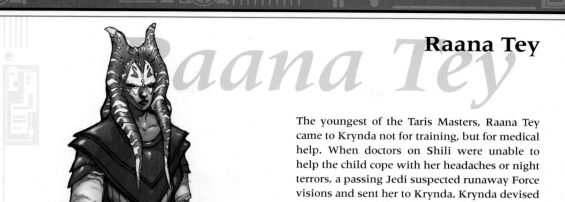

Raana Tey

The youngest of the Taris Masters, Raana Tey came to Krynda not for training, but for medical help. When doctors on Shili were unable to help the child cope with her headaches or night terrors, a passing Jedi suspected runaway Force visions and sent her to Krynda. Krynda devised therapy sessions in which the other Covenant seers would help Raana Tey regulate her thoughts and cope with day-to-day life.

The grateful Raana Tey devoted herself to the Covenant's cause, her Togruta nature propelling her to acts of wild individualism as she traveled with them. But her nightmares worsened after she murdered Kamlin, her Falleen apprentice—and the break-up of the WatchCircle by the Jedi Council removed the support system upon which she had come to rely. By the time she was ordered by the Chancellor to return to Taris—alone—her sanity was already at serious risk.

Feln

Feeorin get stronger as they get older—and while Feln is not public about his age, he is easily the oldest member of the First WatchCircle of the Covenant. Hailing from Odryn, a planet of climatic extremes, Feln was already one of the most well-traveled adults of his species when he journeyed to Coruscant to study with the Jedi.

Krynda was amazed at Feln's precognitive abilities, immediately taking him under her tutelage. While the galaxy outside knows little that happens on Odryn, Feln has suggested that those talents came in handy to him in his life there. But it was his dire vision on the Rogue Moon that led to his murder of his student, Oojoh.

If Lucien can be said to have friends, Feln is perhaps his closest. Rough and tumble in his approach to life, the wisecracking giant soldiers on in his seemingly futile quest to get Lucien to smile.

The Last Resort

The Last Resort

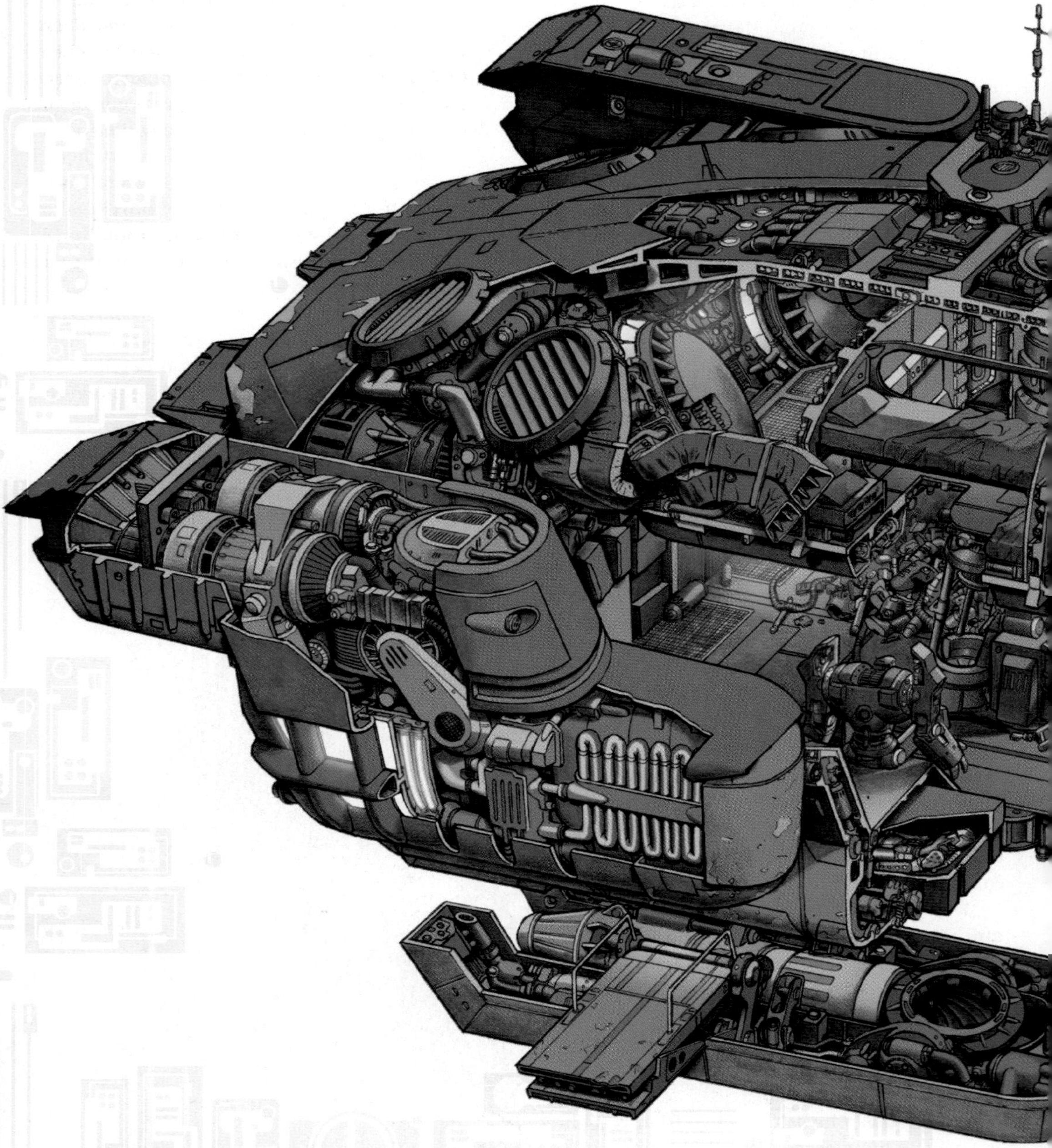

One of the last models to leave the Amalgamated Hyperdyne and Refuse Management assembly yards on Corellia before civil suits over safety recalls finally broke the company, *The Last Resort* is both home and laboratory for Gorman Vandrayk, also known as Camper. For several years before the Padawan Massacre, the ship sat idle in Junk Junction in the Lower City of Taris, accumulating such a collection of tents and awnings around it that many visitors never realized it was a spaceship!

Camper made many modifications to the ship in his time on Taris, including configuring a powerful cannon at the expense of the ship's shields and hyperdrive. But his inattention to the ship's life support system during its idle period nearly killed him, as the accumulated allergens released when the ship finally took off eventually triggered the Arkanian Offshoot equivalent of anaphylactic shock in humans.

Camper's workshop is on the cargo deck level, which has also served as home to Elbee and several "Camper Special" compartments. The upper deck, accessed by a single ladder, has an array of living compartments rearward from the cockpit.

The Last Resort has not been seen since Camper used it to lead the Exogorths into Wild Space. But Jarael hopes her friend will return—with the ship that was home to her for so many years.

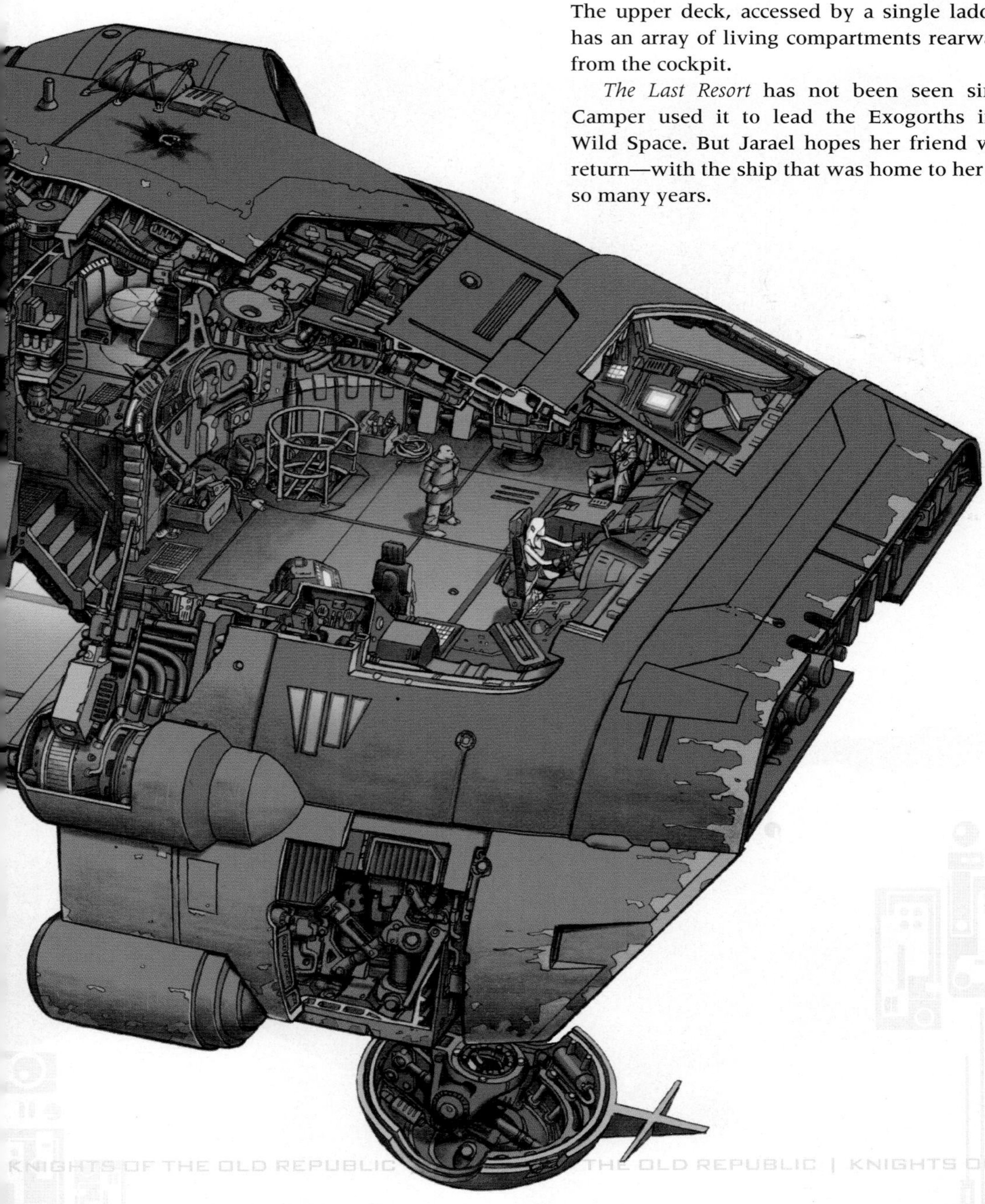

Moomo Williwaw

Orphanmaker

Known as the "Orphanmaker" by its designers, the Pelagia Duplex Command Assault Gunship was developed to protect the Tapani Sector against the chaos of the Sith War. The ships performed that feat well, winning the admiration of Baron Karoll "The Mad" Cilarnus, who sought his own private version with double the already healthy standard supply of armaments.

The result (which appears to never have had an official name apart from the pejorative nickname in the drive yards, "Overkill") never took flight for the Baron, whose company was placed in receivership after a series of unsound investments. No military would buy the craft,

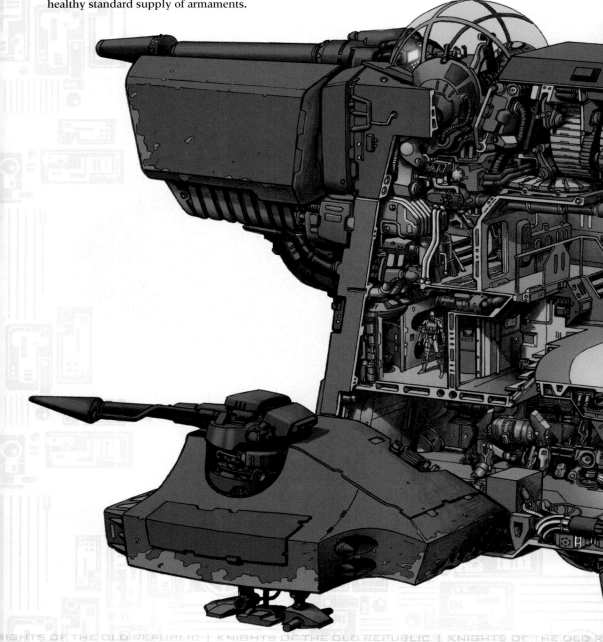

which bristled with weapons in inopportune places, including some that put the ship's gunners in each others firing arcs.

In a decision said by some to be the only moment of agreement in their lives, bounty hunters (and weapon fetishists) Dob and Del Moomo. saved the ship from the scrapyard. Naming the ship the *Moomo Williwaw*, the two immediately moved their private arsenals into the craft and set to work adding to its already ludicrous armaments—giving it "a few more sets of teeth," as Del said.

The intent of the dual cockpit design in the original line was to allow the ship's co-captains to split up command of port and starboard offensive operations. However, Dob and Del make more use of its redundant piloting controls, which they use to abruptly seize control of the ship from each other. Passing ship captains have reported seeing the *Williwaw* spinning in place for as much as an hour while these disputes are resolved.

The *Williwaw* became the temporary home to Zayne Carrick and company when the Moomos were hired to convey Marn Hierogryph to Taris.

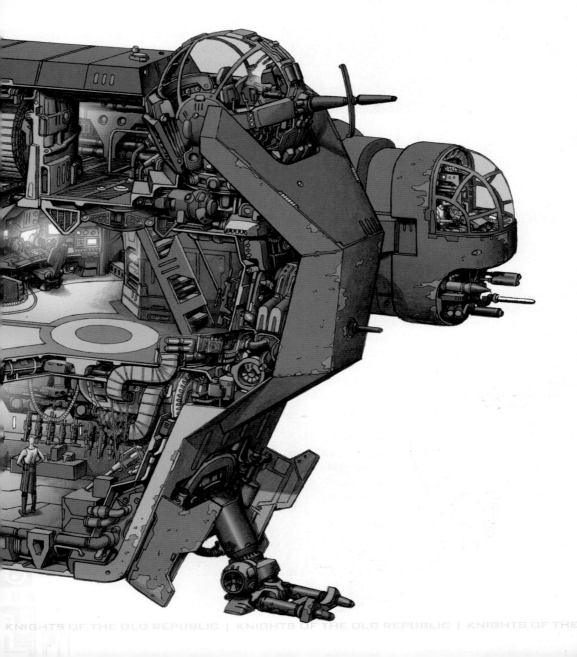

Courageous

One of six *Inexpugnable*-class tactical command ships to launch from the Rendili/Vanjervalis Drive Yards at Corellia, *Courageous* was present at several early battles in the Republic's conflict with the Mandalorians.

Like the other "Inexies," *Courageous* was designed to sell more *Hammerhead*-class cruisers. Its innovative bridge merged visual and electronic data by suspending holographic images over a transparent deck, thus uniting logistical command for as many as sixty-four cruisers. Helmsmen referred to the configuration as the "wishing well," an ironically lighthearted term coming from people seemingly suspended over the abyss. Vertigo was a frequent complaint!

Mandalorians boarded and captured *Courageous* on its escape from Serroco. At Omonoth, Mandalore boasted his war axe was constructed from the melted-down hull, but the exact disposition of the ship has not been confirmed. Remaining ships of the line include *Indefatigable*, *Swiftsure*, and *Tremendous*.

Arkanian Legacy

Launched at the ceremony at which Arkoh Adasca came into his inheritance, the *Arkanian Legacy* represents both Arkania's lofty ambitions—and its greatest folly. Built to serve as Adascorp's mobile corporate base, *Legacy* included a research hospital, an arboreum, a conservatory, and one of the greatest art museums to be found in the galaxy. It was also the staging point for Adasca's ill-fated attempt to grab power on a galactic scale.

Legacy was at its peak population of 104,079—mostly pureblooded Arkanians—when Lord Adasca captured Camper. As the ship made its multiple-stop journey to Omonoth, Adasca quietly began rotating residents unaware of his plan off the ship to other assignments.

Ravaged by the Exogorths unleashed by Camper, the derelict ship remains adrift in contested space. Republic forces have been unable to determine how many, if any, of the ship's population remain aboard, much less mount a rescue and recovery operation.

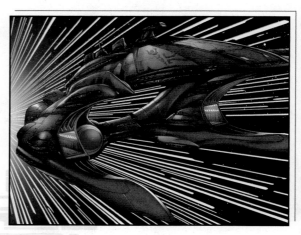

Alek "Squint" Squinquargesimus

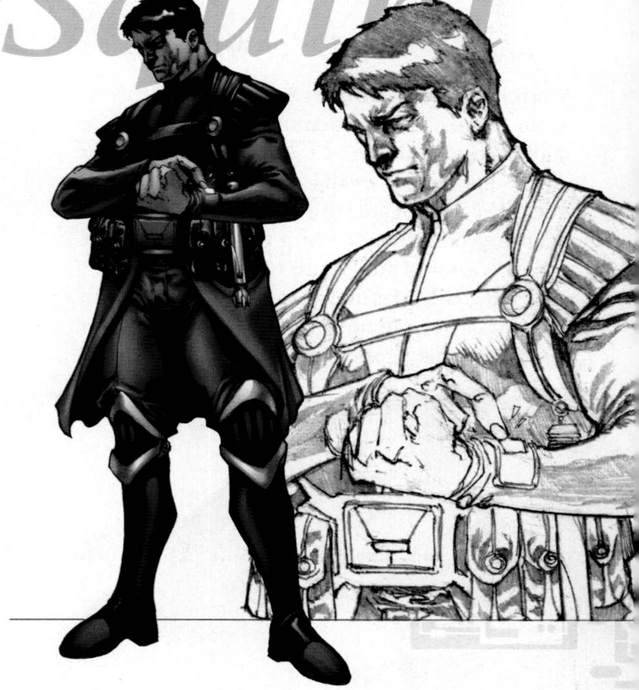

Years after Krynda formed her Covenant to watch for the Sith, other Jedi worried about another threat—the Mandalorians. When Mandalore directed his Neo-Crusaders to attack the Republic, the Order soon found it had Crusaders of its own, itching to take up the fight and reclaim lost worlds. One was Alek, a young Knight with a tongue-twister of a surname. His steely-eyed determination impressed others, as did his physical acumen—he became known as "Squint" while still a Padawan.

When a fellow Knight grew concerned about the Mandalorians, Alek was drawn to the cause. Calling his friend "Master" of this new movement, Alek helped recruit other Jedi to help scout the Mandalorian lines—only to be captured himself. Imprisoned on Flashpoint, Alek was subjected to Demagol's horrific experiments. Zayne and company rescued Alek, allowing him to rejoin his movement with both a new appreciation of the young fugitives—and a growing fondness for Jarael.

The Revanchist

The Revanchist

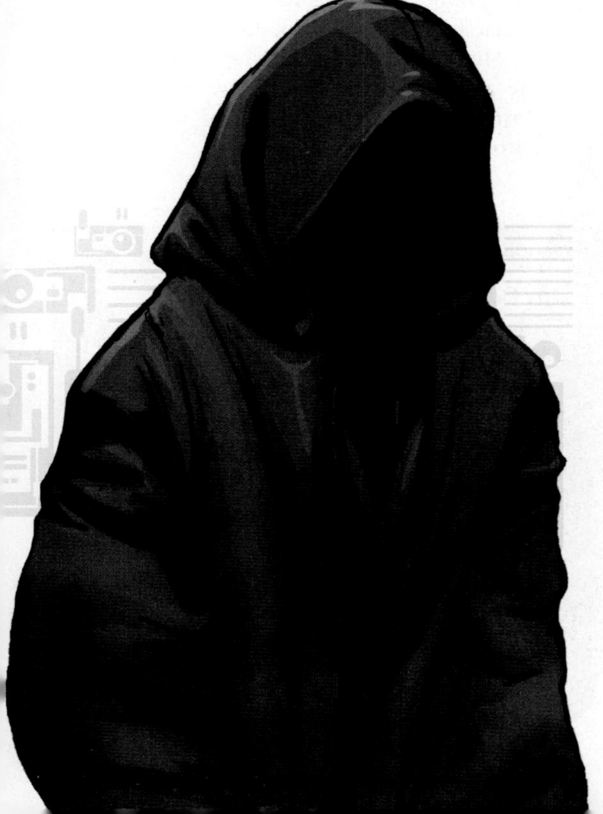

Notoriety follows Alek's friend and honorary "Master," despite the Knight's efforts to put the movement first. Already known throughout the Order, the Knight attracted attention as a lone voice warning the Jedi against the Mandalorian threat. Republic media played up the internal dispute—although the efforts of the "Jedi's own crusader" to win followers were initially treated as a curiosity.

That changed as the Mandalorian wars dawned. The push for intervention created celebrity for the Knight, whom reporters dubbed "The Revanchist Leader"—and finally, "The Revanchist." That snappy nickname, created for the anxious consumers of wartime broadcasts, only antagonized the High Council further. The Order wasn't interested in the war—and no one Knight, no matter how outspoken, was going to push them into it.

"Who I am is not important—my message is," countered The Revanchist, but as far as the media was concerned, the roles had been cast. They had their crusading savior, if only the Jedi would listen . . .

Admiral Saul Karath

Saul Karath

Correllian by birth, Saul Karath came from hardscrabble beginnings. His father, journeyman laborer Craddock Karath, was rarely home, and as the oldest son, Saul took the role of surrogate father for his four siblings, working double shifts at a munitions factory. Space wars and adventure were far away.

That changed when an outrage from the Sith War hit close to home. Though he would never speak of what propelled him, Saul responded by quitting his job and volunteering for the Navy. Too poorly connected to enter the Academy and too young to serve officially in any event—Karath won the attention of Fleet Captain Vanicus, who allowed him to serve as captain's steward, one of the non-commissioned laborers on his ship.

There began a thirty-plus-year career that followed anything but a straight line through the Republic Navy. For every success, a setback followed. But Karath never soured on the Navy, making the institution his family. His efforts were rewarded with *Reciprocity*, his first command as captain, where he found success protecting convoys against pirates and setting him up for his eventual assignment to *Courageous* and the protection of Taris against the Mandalorians.

Karath felt the Republic's forces were too few to face the Mandalorians—and was proven right in the Onslaught that followed. He was forced to abandon *Courageous* at Serroco—but, again, fate intervened to protect his career. Finding himself as the ranking Republic representative at the treasonous Lord Adasca's secret summit with Mandalore, Karath's knowledge about—and public silence about—the event became valuable assets to his superiors.

Mistrustful of Mandalorians and Jedi since the Sith War, Karath initially viewed Zayne Carrick as a possible spy and continues to harbor suspicions.

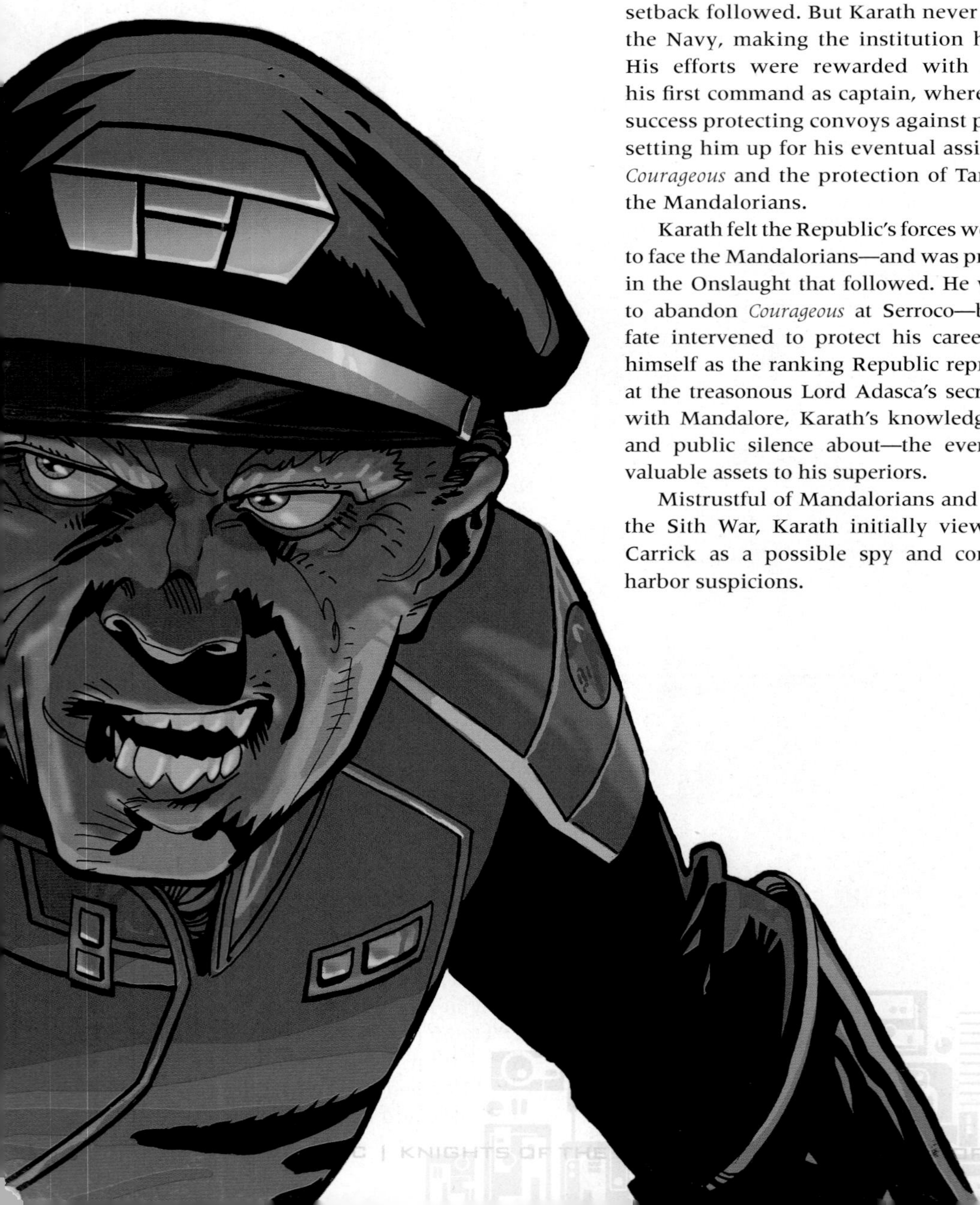

Lieutenant Carth Onasi

Carth Onasi

Carth Onasi's career path resembles that taken by his mentor, Saul Karath—which may explain the admiral's fondness for this jack-of-all-trades. Born on Telos IV, Onasi worked as both a mechanic and police officer before joining the local militia. His heroics in a piracy sting brought him to the attention of a recruiter with the Republic Navy.

But the road to the Starfighter Corps—his initial aim—was winding, as the personnel-starved Navy sent recruits wherever they were needed. Onasi got his flight hours in a fighter—but he also gained experience working security, running communication stations, and flying cargo. It was all fine with him—and with Karath, who recognized Onasi's sharp wits during an engagement on *Reciprocity* by inviting him to work his bridge on *Courageous*. Onasi jumped at the chance to serve with the legendary spacefarer.

Onasi has developed a friend in Zayne Carrick, believing him to be innocent. He also has a wife, Morgana, and a son, Dustil, that he rarely sees due to the war.

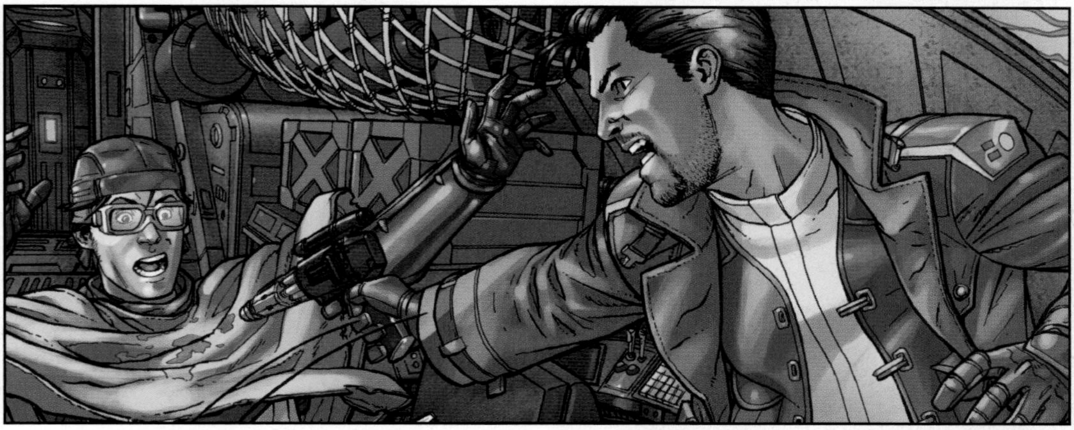

Commander Dallan Morvis

Dallan Morvis

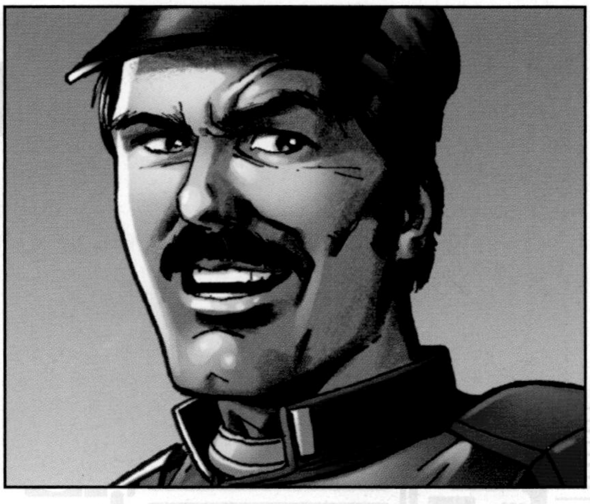

With a father serving as the director of the Coruscant Financial Exchange and a mother serving her third term as the senator from Chandrila, Dallan Morvis was groomed for big things. But unlike the typical upper-cruster thrust onto the Naval Academy at Coruscant, Morvis has become an asset to the Admiralty. Upon graduation, he took an assignment as a junior liaison between Admiral Sommos's staff and the Vanjurvalis design team.

That led to his first bridge posting as a lieutenant on then-Captain Karath's frigate, *Reciprocity*. Seeing in Karath a leader on the rise, Morvis followed him to *Courageous*—and into war with the Mandalorians. Morvis is often irritated by junior officer Carth Onasi, whom he sees as a competitor for the admiral's favor.

Demagol

Demagol

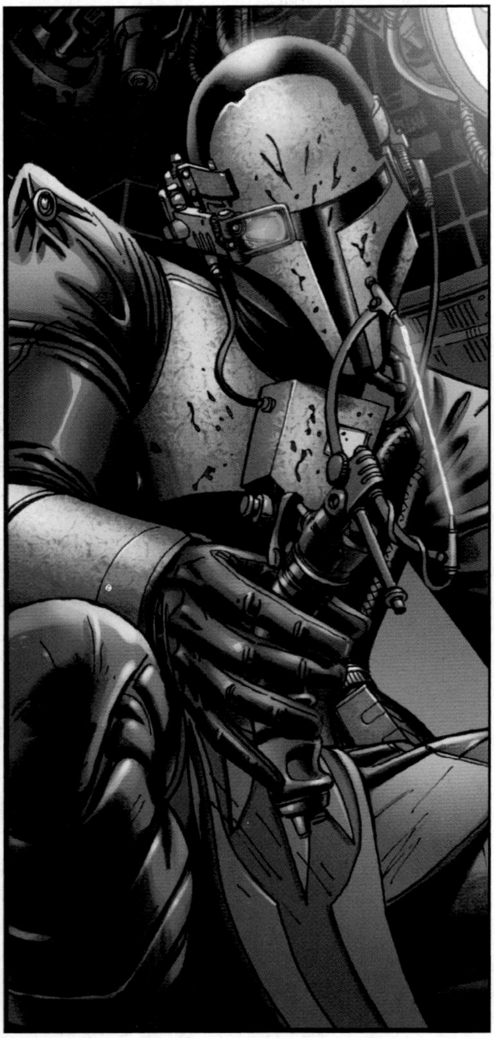

The name Demagol is a contraction of *demar agol*—literally, "to carve flesh"—and while this "doctor" considers himself a sculptor of life, even his fellow Mandalorians consider him a butcher. Yet Demagol has long served as the inquisitive mind behind the clans' muscle.

Before Flashpoint, Republic intelligence officials knew that much about Demagol—and little else. With Demagol's species, age, and even his true name a mystery, Republic Intel was forced to rely on Mandalorian oral histories for information. These stories portrayed a diabolical specter moving through the decades, using the conquered peoples of the Outer Rim as subjects for his studies. By the time of the Onslaught on Serroco, Demagol's stature was second only to Mandalore himself—yet he was less interested in battles than the opportunities they provided him to advance his grisly projects.

One such project involved the Jedi, hated by Mandalorians still smarting from the humiliations of the Sith War years before. Demagol took on the challenge of discovering the biological bases for Jedi powers. Initially, Jedi were kidnapped for the purpose—but once hostilities with the Republic opened, a stream of new Jedi "research subjects" poured into his lab on Flashpoint.

That ended when Zayne Carrick, working with the deserter Rohlan, captured Demagol and turned him over to Alek and his comrades. The Mandalorians believed their flesh-carver to have died on Flashpoint—but in fact, his former "patients" had made a date for him with interrogators on Coruscant!

That date was never kept. Soon after leaving Flashpoint, his captors discovered the doctor had been drugged to edge of death. Demagol fell into a coma before reaching Coruscant, where he continues to be held. Republic officials yet hope to thwart what they see as Demagol's self-inflicted attempt to escape their justice!

Mandalore

Mandalore

The name of the traditional leader of the galaxy's greatest nomadic army, Mandalore (spelled Mand'alor by his people), has been handed down through the ages, often with a suffix. But Mandalore the Indomitable was dominated during the Sith War. Defeated in combat by Ulic Qel-droma, he and all his clans were made to serve that Jedi's purposes.

That Mandalore fell in the conflict, and some time afterward, a new Mandalore attempted to rebuild his peoples' esteem through conquest. First, against non-aligned worlds on the Outer Rim, and later, against the Republic whose Jedi humiliated them.

While Republic officials are unsure whether the Mandalore they face now is the Taung soldier that replaced Mandalore the Indomitable years ago—or another successor who took his name and mask—this much is clear: this Mandalore's methods have seemed increasingly unorthodox to many, both within his ranks and without. Mandalore has shown a willingness to acknowledge political considerations, something seen by others as irrelevant. Mandalore's promotion of the "Neo-Crusader" movement from a fanatical fringe to a key regulative element of his forces seems, to many, surprisingly calculated for a leader of a rampaging horde.

Cassus Fett

Cassus Fett

Little is known in the Republic about Cassus Fett, reputed to be the architect of many of Mandalore's victories, including the Onslaught on Serroco. Reports suggest the warrior's influence goes far beyond field command.

Where earlier Mandalorians had been a disorganized mob, conquering systems without always assimilating them, those of Cassus's day gained structure, allowing the clans to hold what they took. Rather than adopting the rigid bureaucratic hierarchy of the Republic forces, Fett suggested using the Neo-Crusader sect as an elite, embedding them alongside new recruits to promote Mandalorian practices and norms. Fett also is rumored to have held a role in war production.

The methodical Fett's influence rose after the reported death of his sometime rival Demagol, and he was personally sent to oversee the siege of Taris.

Arkoh, Lord Adasca

Lord Adasca

The eighth member of the House of Adasca to hold the title of Lord, Arkoh Adasca learned his roles from father Alok and grandfather Argaloh. Beyond the ceremonial duties of head of one of Arkania's industrial dynasties, he inherited control of Adascorp, the galaxy's largest bioengineering firm.

From the start, the youthful Lord Adasca raised the spirits of Arkanians struggling to understand their place in the galaxy, appealing to their sense of purpose while subtly playing on strains of racial supremacy. While not officially in political control of Arkania, the charismatic Adasca nonetheless rallied many of his people to treason by completing Operation Dark Harvest, a political gambit of galactic scale. But this proved an overreach, and unlikely allies united to foil the plot.

Attacked by the very Exogorths he tried to enslave, Lord Adasca remains unaccounted for and is presumed dead by the Republic, which has sought to keep the matter secret to protect its position on Arkania. Ownership of Adascorp remains contested, with no obvious heir to Arkoh's controlling interest.

Jervo Thalien

Jervo Thalien

The first Skrilling ever to hold the post of chairman of the board of Lhosan Industries, Jervo Thalien was a pivotal figure in the political scandal that followed the Mandalorian Onslaught. Founded on Taris years before as the first major manufacturer of swoop bikes, Lhosan had not completed its plans to diversify offworld when the Mandalorians began approaching Taris's nearby resource systems.

Jervo bought time by working with Goravvus to bribe Senators to bring remote Taris into the Republic. But when the Mandalorians invaded and newly named Senator Goravvus became a champion for the Resistance, Jervo sought to locate his former go-between, for fear of the testimony he might give.

Dob & Del Moomo

"The kindest thing that may be said about the Moomo Brothers is that they stand tall as examples of why it is wrong to stereotype beings by their species." That backhanded compliment, from a member of their own Ithorian race, accompanied the expulsion of the two from their mellow, pacifistic home "for the safety of the herd." But in truth, Dob and Del have historically done as much damage to themselves as to anyone else.

Antagonism between the two began in early childhood, when they managed to cycle an airlock they were both in to rid the family of the other. Resuscitation succeeded; rehabilitation failed. As adult exiles, the two sought their fortunes as muscle-for-hire, always working together, despite their history. Del has remarked that, however dangerous their assignment, "I don't worry none 'cause I already know Dob will kill me first."

Abortive assignments followed with "Bubbles" d'Breen, Valius Ying, Jervo Thalien, and even the Jedi Covenant. Yet for reasons that remain a mystery to the fringer community, the Moomos continue to be recommended for important jobs despite their pathetic success rate. "They both think they're the smart one," Marn Hierogryph once said. "They're both wrong."

As seen by their ship, the *Moomo Williwaw*, Dob and Del share a fascination with weaponry, the only subject on which they are well-informed. Where Del's tastes run to explosives, Dob claims to have learned the word "bludgeon" in seventeen languages (though he cannot identify who speaks those languages, or where).

The only distinguishing physical difference between the two is a scar over Del's right eye, which he received as a youngling when he caught his head in an operating trash compactor. Confronted elsewhere, Dob denied responsibility, saying that he did not know where the trash compactor was and that he couldn't get the ignition switch to work, anyway.

Taris

With wealthy industrialists above and poor aliens and Outcasts below, Taris has seen many economic ups and downs. But the siege by the Mandalorians has forced its residents to cooperate to survive, waging a desperate defense from the city's lower levels.

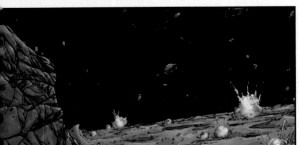

Rogue Moon

The Taris system's inner asteroid belt is home to a Rogue Moon, orbiting in the opposite direction. Its only weather is a constant rain of rocks, making it a place of interest as a Jedi training ground.

Flashpoint

Named for its incredibly short days and its proximity to its star, Flashpoint became a military flashpoint as well when Mandalorians took over its stellar research station for use as a Jedi prison.

Telerath

A gorgeous garden world, Telerath was the site of a unique experiment in face-to-face banking. But this clever merger of high finance and lush surroundings faltered when the Mandalorians threatened to invade.

Serroco

The Mandalorians made an example of muddy Serroco, home to the simple Stereb people, by bombarding its cities. But thanks to Zayne and Carth, many Stereb yet survive underground.

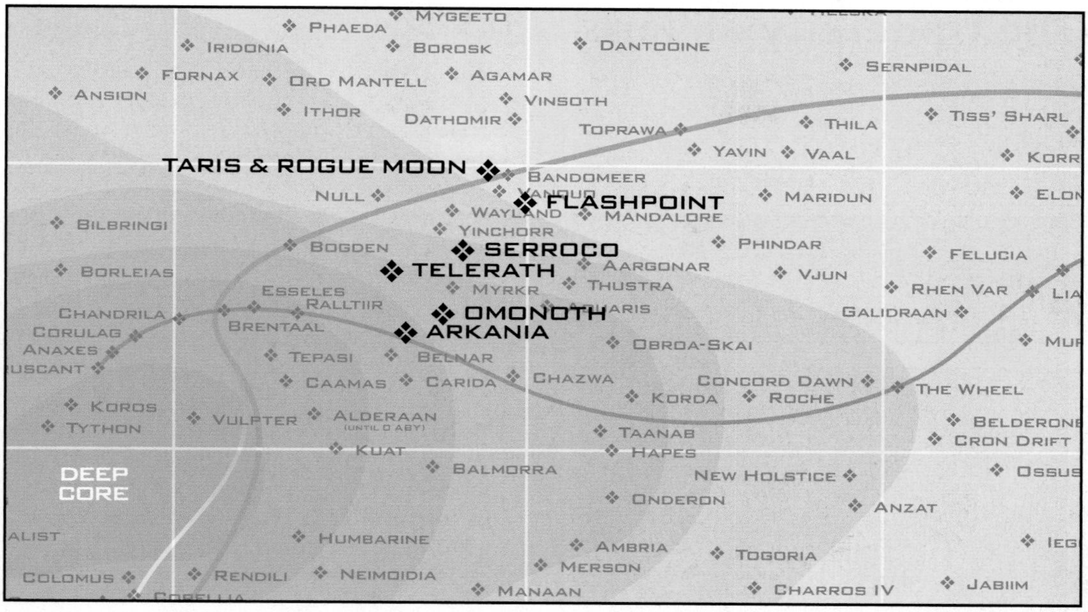
MYGEETO
PHAEDA
IRIDONIA
BOROSK
DANTOOINE
SERNPIDAL
FORNAX
ORD MANTELL
AGAMAR
ANSION
VINSOTH
ITHOR
DATHOMIR
TOPRAWA
THILA
TISS' SHARL
YAVIN
VAAL
TARIS & ROGUE MOON
BANDOMEER
NULL
FLASHPOINT
MARIDUN
WAYLAND
MANDALORE
BILBRINGI
YINCHORR
BOGDEN
SERROCO
PHINDAR
FELUCIA
BORLEIAS
TELERATH
AARGONAR
VJUN
ESSELES
MYRKR
THUSTRA
RHEN VAR
RALLTIIR
CHANDRILA
OMONOTH
GALIDRAAN
CORULAG
BRENTAAL
ARKANIA
ANAXES
OBROA-SKAI
TEPASI
BELNAR
CAAMAS
CARIDA
CHAZWA
CONCORD DAWN
THE WHEEL
KOROS
KORDA
ROCHE
TYTHON
VULPTER
ALDERAAN
(UNTIL 0 ABY)
BELDERONE
TAANAB
CRON DRIFT
KUAT
HAPES
DEEP CORE
BALMORRA
NEW HOLSTICE
ONDERON
ANZAT
HUMBARINE
AMBRIA
TOGORIA
MERSON
COLOMUS
RENDILI
NEIMOIDIA
MANAAN
CHARROS IV
JABIIM

Arkania

Like Taris, icy Arkania contrasts the lovely floating cities of the Purebloods with the wretched existence of the Offshoots far below. Living on the tundra outside the exhausted gem mines they used to work, they are allowed little access to the Pureblood areas.

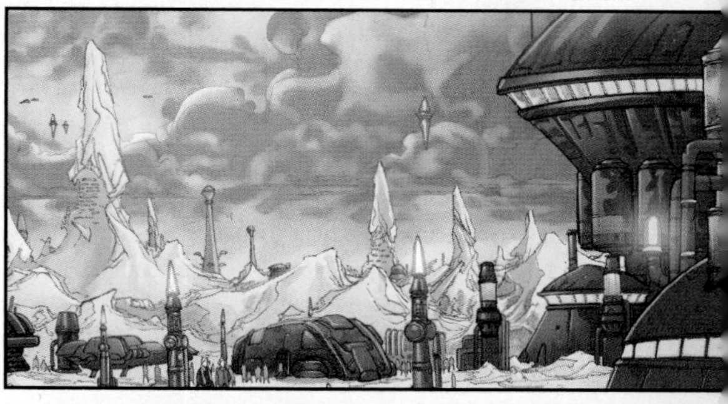

Omonoth

A dying star expelling a mess of materials, Omonoth attracted many Exogorths which were then targeted for enslavement by Adascorp. The system remains in contested territory between the Mandalorians and Republic.

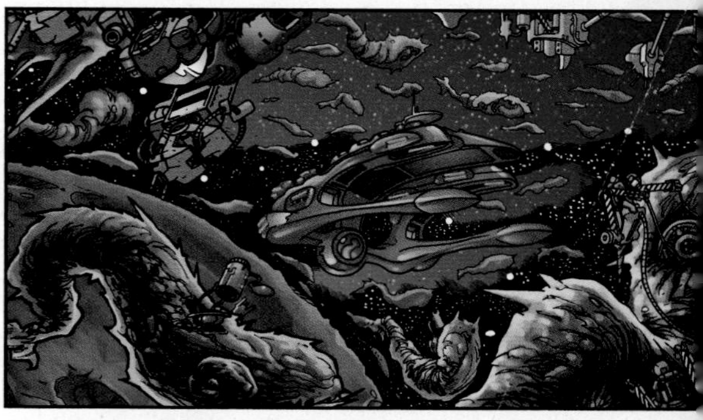

Coruscant

The capital of the Republic is also home to the Draay Estate, the nerve center of the Jedi Covenant. From here, the Covenant coordinates its own unofficial early warning system against the Sith.

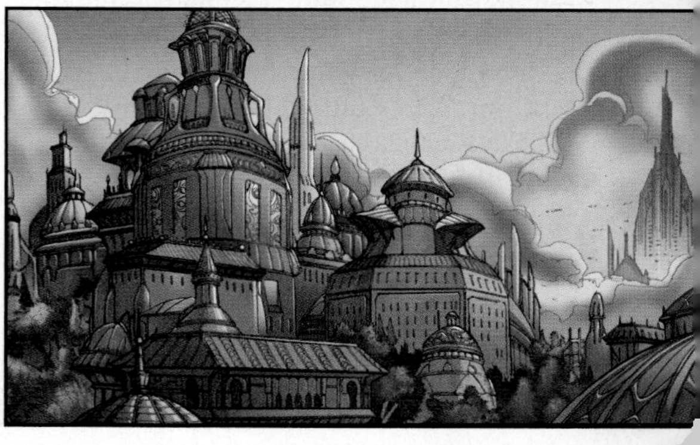

The Undercity of Taris

Undercity

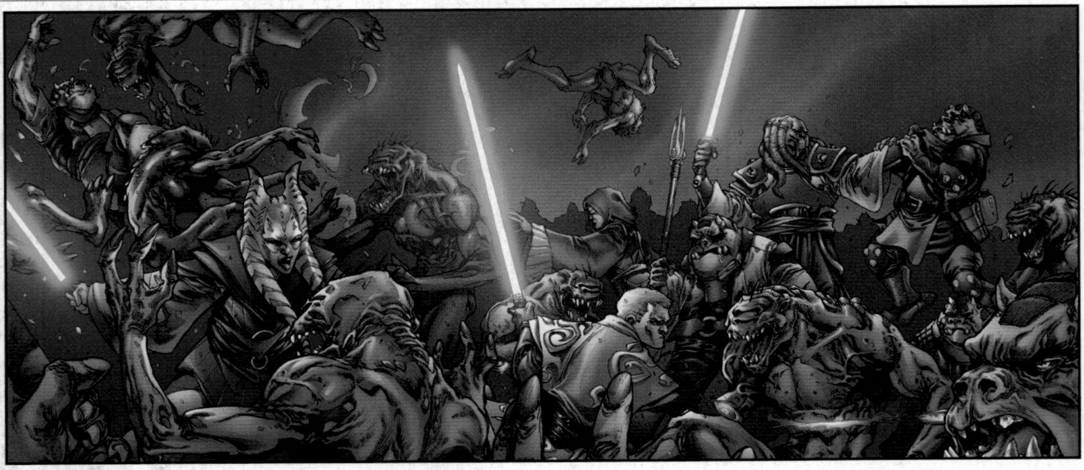

Newcomers to Taris—like the Mandalorian invaders—quickly learn that the planet's geography isn't just measured by latitude and longitude; it's vertical. Years of industrial expansion pushed the Upper City of Taris ever higher—even as prejudice forced its least fortunate ever downward.

Beneath the bleak, gang-infested Lower City lies an even more horrible world—The Undercity, a claustrophobic confusion of abandoned industrial tunnels, sewers, collapsed mine shafts, and natural caverns. Nothing should be able to live in this hostile place—but many things do, including a desperate group called the Outcasts along with those now seeking refuge from the encroaching Mandalorians.

Ironically, the Undercity's greatest threat springs not from the local Gamorrean slavers or the wretched and inhabitable conditions, but from the refugees themselves. Many have been transformed into Rakghouls—hulking, mindless brutes bent on destruction. It is unknown how or when the Rakghoul Plague broke out in this filthy place, but the method of transmission is clear—the bite of a Rakghoul eventually transforms its victim into another Rakghoul in a blinding, otherworldly flash.

The Plague has taken the bodies and sanity of uncounted millions over the years—and would have taken more, had the residents aboveground not acted to seal the entrances to the Undercity. However with the Mandalorians invading, the status of those gateway seals is unknown.

So complex, so ancient are the mazes of the Taris undercity, that many feel they hide great secrets. The Outcasts have long sought a "Promised Land," fabled to be an impregnable underground utopia.

The Jedi Covenant's contingent on Taris suspected the presence of the Muur Talisman, a powerful object obliquely described in certain Sith Holocrons and desired by many during the "Golden Age" of the Sith. The Covenant's efforts to locate and contain this curious artifact—as part of its mission to restrain and eliminate all Sith influences—came to an end when they were forced to leave Taris following Zayne Carrick's escape.

STAR WARS: VECTOR VOL. 1 TPB INTRODUCTION BY RANDY STRADLEY

HOW "VECTOR" CAME TO BE,
OR, CONFESSIONS OF A COMIC BOOK MONGER

I have a confession to make. Though it pains me to say it, I must admit that the story you're about to read has its roots (well, the very tips of them, anyway) in crass commercialism. It started with an observation made by fellow editor Chris Warner about the vast, multi-issue, multi-series crossover "events" which our competitors roll out on an almost annual basis. "That's the comics industry for you," said Chris. "We never run out of the same idea."

He was right. But the reason behind this repetition of the "same idea" is solid: the crossovers always sell. And I got to thinking, *why can't we have the same idea with* Star Wars? *Why can't* Star Wars *comics generate some of that crossover money?* The continuity in *Star Wars* runs from thousands of years prior to Luke Skywalker's birth, to over one hundred fifty years beyond it. We had four regular series of titles, each set in a different era of *Star Wars* history; why couldn't we tell an epic story which touched upon each of the points we were exploring along the *Star Wars* timeline? Why *shouldn't* we? As long as we didn't contradict established events, it could work — and we could (hopefully) attract new readers to our comics.

So much for commercial concerns. I was sure we could find a way to make the logistics work, but I knew that in order to win over readers, the story also had to mean something to the characters in each of our comics series, while at the same time affecting the *Star Wars* mythos as a whole. A story played out on a massive stage, but with only a few characters in the spotlight at any one time. A big story that remained intensely personal. And there was one final caveat: each chapter of "Vector" had to be accessible to readers who might not know anything more about *Star Wars* than what they had seen in the films. What could be easier?

Fortunately, our team—writers John Jackson Miller (*Star Wars: Knights of the Old Republic*), Mick Harrison (*Star Wars: Dark Times*), Rob Williams (*Star Wars: Rebellion*), John Ostrander and his co-plotter and artist Jan Duursema (*Star Wars: Legacy*), editor Jeremy Barlow, and then-assistant-editor Dave Marshall (well, and myself) — made the task seem, if not easy, then at least possible. Our discussions began with months of email messages and eventually ended with a summit meeting attended by most of the principals. Everybody had suggestions, everyone contributed important plot or character points, and along the way that "same idea" became something new. Together we managed, I believe, to come up with a tale that is truly epic in its scope, while being personal in its focus. I hope you'll agree.

Randy Stradley
editor

P.S. — And, yes, the comics achieved their commercial goals.

CHARACTER NAME PRONUNCIATION GLOSSARY, FROM ISSUE #36'S LETTERS PAGE

Zayne Carrick: ZAYN KAYR-rick
Hierogryph: HIY-roh-griff
Lucien: LOO-shun
Q'anilia: kah-NEEL-yah
Xamar: ZAY-mar
Raana Tey: RAH-nah TAY
Jarael: ja-RAYL
Rohlan: ROH-lun
Demagol: dem-uh-GOLL
Haazen: HAH-zen (yes, not the same as HAYZE)
Moomo: MOO-moh
Adasca: ah-DAS-kah
Haydel Goravvus: HAY-del guh-RA-vus
Pulsipher: puhl-si-FUR
Odryn: OH-dren

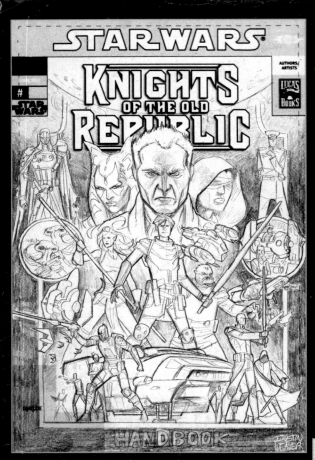

STAR WARS
KNIGHTS
OF THE OLD
REPUBLIC
AUTHORS/ARTISTS
LUCAS BOOKS
#
STAR WARS
BARCODE
HANDBOOK
DUSTIN WEAVER

STAR WARS: KNIGHTS OF THE OLD REPUBLIC HANDBOOK
COVER SKETCH BY DUSTIN WEAVER

STAR WARS
KNIGHTS
OF THE OLD
REPUBLIC
#
STAR WARS
BARCODE
DUSTIN WEAVER

UNUSED COVER SKETCH BY DUSTIN WEAVER

IMAGES COURTESY OF THE ARTIST

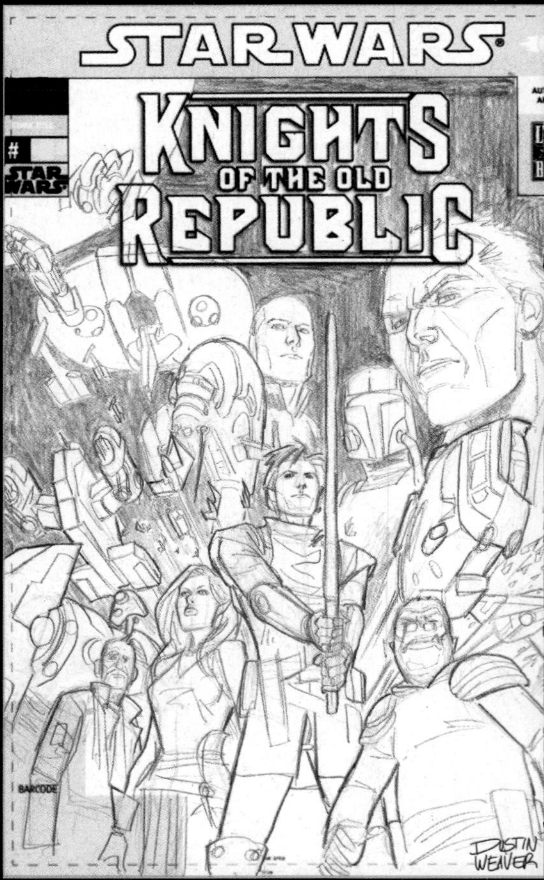